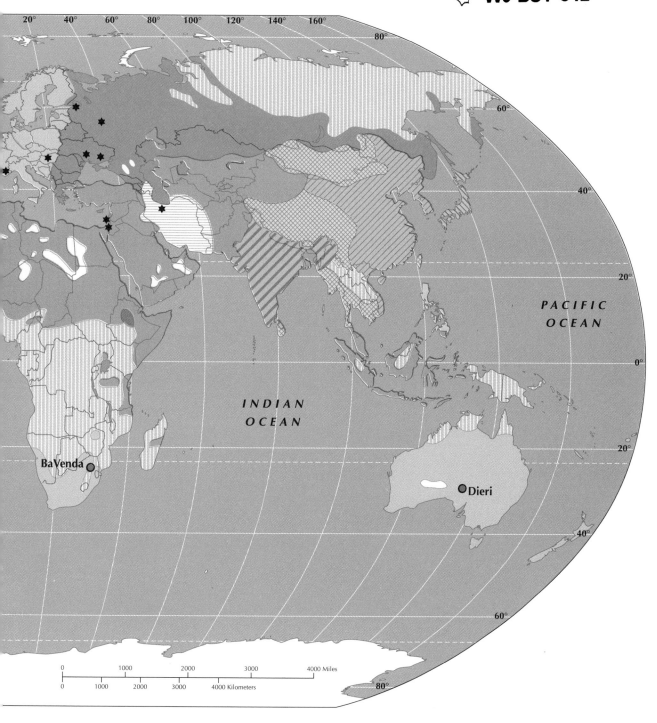

A HISTORY OF THE WORLD'S RELIGIONS

A HISTORY OF THE WORLD'S RELIGIONS

Tenth Edition

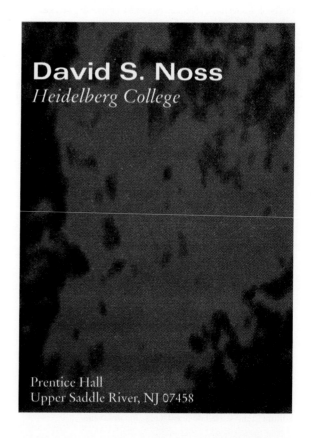

David S. Noss
Heidelberg College

Prentice Hall
Upper Saddle River, NJ 07458

Library of Congress Cataloging-in-Publication Data

Noss, David S.
A history of the world's religions /
David S. Noss.—10th ed.
p.   cm.
Includes bibliographical references and index.
ISBN 0–13–010532–5
1. Religions.   I. Title
BL80.2.N59 1999
291—dc21   98–19235
                                                     CIP

Editorial Director: Charlyce Jones Owen
Acquisitions Editor: Karita France
Assistant Editor: Emsal Hasan
Editorial Assisant: Jennifer Ackerman
Director of Production and Manufacturing: Barbara Kittle
Manufacturing Manager: Nick Sklitsis
Manufacturing Buyer: Bob Anderson
Production Editor: Jean Lapidus
Creative Design Director: Leslie Osher
Interior and Cover Designer: Maria Lange
Photo Research Supervisor: Melinda Reo
Visual Researcher: Beth Boyd
Line Art Coordinator: Guy Ruggiero
Copy Editor: Michele Lansing
Indexer: Richard Genova
Repermissions Specialist: Irene Hess
End Papers: Carto-Graphics

This book was set in 10/12 Minion by Stratford Publishing Services,
and was printed and bound by Courier Companies, Inc.
The cover was printed by Phoenix Color Corp.

Earlier editions, entitled *Man's Religions,* copyright © 1949, 1956, and 1963 by Macmillan Publishing Company;
Copyright © 1969, 1974, and 1980 by John B. Noss; copyright © 1984 and 1990 by Macmillan Publishing Company.

© 1999, 1994 by Prentice-Hall, Inc.
Simon & Schuster/A Viacom Company
Upper Saddle River, New Jersey 07458

Printed in the United States of America
10 9 8 7 6 5 4 3 2 1

ISBN: 0-13-010532-5

Prentice-Hall International (UK) Limited, *London*
Prentice-Hall of Australia Pty. Limited, *Sydney*
Prentice-Hall Canada Inc., *Toronto*
Prentice-Hall Hispanoamericana, S.A., *Mexico*
Prentice-Hall of India Private Limited, *New Delhi*
Prentice-Hall of Japan, Inc., *Tokyo*
Simon & Schuster Asia Pte. Ltd., *Singapore*
Editora Prentice-Hall do Brasil, Ltda., *Rio de Janeiro*

For Beth
with
Love, Admiration, and Gratitude

CONTENTS

Later Hinduism: Religion as the Determinant of Social Behavior 102

Jainism: A Study in Asceticism 148

Buddhism in Its First Phase: Moderation in World Renunciation 160

The Religious Development of Buddhism: Diversity in Paths to Nirvana 182

Sikhism: A Study in Syncretism   236

Part 3

The Religions of East Asia   249

Native Chinese Religion and Daoism   250

Confucius and Confucianism: A Study in Optimistic Humanism   284

The Religious Development of Judaism 408

Christianity in Its Opening Phase: The Words and Work of Jesus in Apostolic Perspective 442

The Religious Development of Christianity 472

PREFACE

This Tenth Edition is the first one to appear without the name of my elder brother, John B. Noss, on the cover. It is now almost twenty years since his death in 1980, but it is still in a profound sense *his* book. It is more than fifty years since I first "assisted" him by retyping part of the original draft.

At a time when religious studies tended to focus on the biographies of founders of religions or on comparing the diversities of contemporary practice, the preface to the first edition spoke of two special needs to be met; both were the unique concerns of historians. The first was to include "descriptive and interpretative details from the original source materials" and the second "to bridge the interval between the founding of religions and their present state."

Those who have used successive editions will recognize a continuing faithfulness to those needs as well as a special concern for an audience of teachers and students. Over the years some seven hundred institutions have adopted the book and over one hundred teachers have contributed critiques and suggestions toward the shaping of future editions.

Resisting trends toward the abbreviating and "dumbing down" of college textbooks to accommodate diminishing reading skills, this edition maintains a standard of thoroughness. Instead of abridgment it offers enhancements: additional help in the form of highlighted terms keyed to its chapter-end glossaries, reinforcement of key ideas in the form of brief, boxed quotations, and new line drawings to relieve solid columns of text.

Many teachers find a kind of liberation in putting a thorough text in the hands of students. This ensures a ready and reliable reference, relieves the pressure on the instructor to "cover" everything in lectures, and frees up class time for questions and discussions on topics of immediate interest.

The study of world religions needs to encompass the immediate and the existential as well as the rational—the empathic as well as the analytical. Serving as editor of John's book has been on the one hand a challenge to emend each inaccuracy but also a profound experience of what it is like to look out upon the world through the eyes of a wise person. Because it is John's book I dare to wish for its readers the gentle, ironic spirit of its first author.

Special thanks are due to two of my colleagues at Heidelberg College: Dr. Philip B. Harner and Dr. Leon J. Putnam for careful reviewing and suggestions and to Prof. Fritz Wenisch, University of Rhode Island and Keith Burkum of Felician College for extraordinarily thorough reading and helpful comment. The staff at Beeghly Library have been unfailingly helpful as have Karita France, acquisitions editor, Emsal Hasan, assistant editor, and Jean Lapidus, production editor, of Prentice Hall.

David S. Noss
Heidelberg College

The author will welcome contributions to the "Faculty Lounge" link on his home page www.heidelberg.edu/~dnoss/ or e-mail comments to dnoss@nike.heidelberg.edu

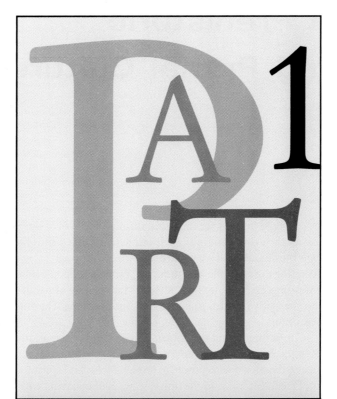

PART 1

SOME
PRIMAL AND
BYGONE
RELIGIONS

Religion in Prehistoric and Primal Cultures

None of us can hope to see the world through the eyes of our prehistoric ancestors. We pore over their cave paintings, their implements, the disposition of bodies and artifacts in their burial sites, and we make conjectures. Although there is no clear warrant for interpreting the probable intentions of prehistoric people by analogy to those of more recent primal cultures, we find ourselves taking note of parallels simply because there are no alternative models to inform our suppositions. The analogies should be viewed with caution.

Conjectures about prehistoric cultures and observations of isolated primal cultures in the recent past converge on one vital function of religion: the linking of the visible, everyday world with powerful unseen forces and spirits. Myths and rituals provide ways of feeling at home in the universe, ways of behaving with the least strain toward mysterious realities in the immediate environment—natural forces, ancestral spirits, and the powers felt to be functioning through the social institutions of communal life.

When in times past primal groups began to communicate and share their conceptions in wider, more complex relationships, they developed a longer reach of thought in which "high gods" and wide-reigning deities of the universe appeared.

In order to understand this, it is well to begin as far back in time as we can go. Therefore, we turn briefly to prehistoric times.

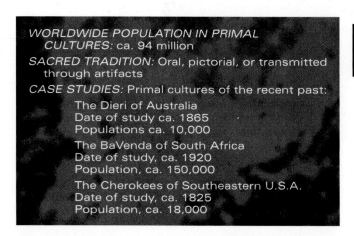

WORLDWIDE POPULATION IN PRIMAL CULTURES: ca. 94 million

SACRED TRADITION: Oral, pictorial, or transmitted through artifacts

CASE STUDIES: Primal cultures of the recent past:

The Dieri of Australia
Date of study ca. 1865
Populations ca. 10,000

The BaVenda of South Africa
Date of study, ca. 1920
Population, ca. 150,000

The Cherokees of Southeastern U.S.A.
Date of study, ca. 1825
Population, ca. 18,000

I. BEGINNINGS: RELIGION IN PREHISTORIC CULTURES

O ancient cousin,
O Neanderthaler!
What shapes beguiled, what shadows fled across
Your early mind?

Here are your bones,
And hollow crumbled skull,
And here your shapen flints—the last inert
Mute witnesses to so long vanished strength.

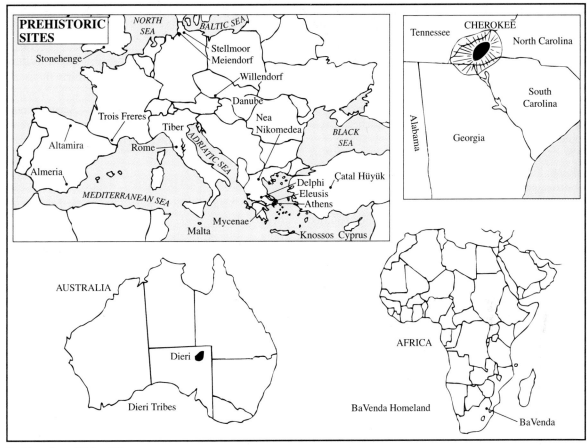

Prehistoric and Primal Sites

What loves had you,
What words to speak,
What worships,
Cousin?

———J.B. Noss

If we could find answers to these questions, they might help us determine when and how religion began. But that is not certain. Because religion is a product of the earliest attempt of the human mind to achieve a sense of security in the world, the Neanderthals may not have been the first to be religious. But who were? There is no telling. It is unlikely that such prehominids as *Homo habilis* and the related *Australopithecus* from about three million years ago were capable of religious feeling, for when we consider the remains they left—the sharp-edged flints they seem to have picked up as implements

in their difficult struggle for existence—we can tell very little about the degree of their intelligence, much less whether they were religious. Even the nearer-to-our-time Peking Sinanthropus, roughly the contemporary of the Javan Pithecanthropus and the Heidelberg races, cannot be known to have behaved religiously, although they heated their caves with fire, shaped stones into tools and weapons, hunted successfully, and collected human heads, whose brains they seem to have extracted and eaten. (Was it because they had a respect for a magical potency or simply because they found it a delicacy? We simply do not know.)

The Old Stone Age: Neanderthals

The Neanderthal people who flourished from two hundred and thirty thousand down to thirty thousand years ago over an area stretching from southern Spain across Europe to Hungary and Israel, are regarded today as probably a separate species, replaced by *Homo sapiens,* rather than blending into it. Nevertheless, their graves furnish the earliest clear evidence of religious practice in the Old Stone Age.

Some of the dead were given careful burial. Alongside the bodies, which were usually in a crouching position, food offerings (of which broken bones remain) and flint implements—hand axes, awls, and chipped scrapers were placed. It is generally assumed that such objects were left to serve the dead in an afterlife. Other grave offerings were less utilitarian and more purely expressive: a body in the Shanidar care in Iraq was covered with at least eight species of flowers! There also are signs of other forms of ritualized veneration.

The Neanderthals apparently treated the cave bear with special reverence. They hunted it at great peril to themselves and seem to have respected its spirit even after it was dead. They appear to have set aside certain cave bear skulls, without removing the brains—a great delicacy—and also certain long (or marrow) bones, and to have placed them with special care in their caves on elevated slabs of stone, on shelves, or in niches, probably in order to make them the center of some kind of ritual. Whether their bear cult, if it was such, was a propitiation of the bear spirit during a ritual feast, a form of hunting magic to ensure the success of the next hunt, or a sacrifice or votive offering to some divinity having to do with the interrelations of human and bear is a matter of conjecture.

Another subject of debate is the Neanderthal treatment of human skulls. Some of the skulls are found, singly or in series, without the accompaniment of the other bones of the body, each decapitated and opened at the base in such a way as to suggest that the brains were extracted and eaten. The evidence is inconclusive about whether the emptied skulls were placed in a ritual position for memorial rites or the Neanderthal people were headhunters who ate the brains in some sacramental way of sacrificial victims, the newly dead, or enemies to acquire the soul force in them. The fact that not all bodies were buried intact and that large bones of the human body were often split open to the marrow suggests that human cadavers were a source of food, whether or not they were sometimes consumed in a ritual fashion.

When we come to the later and higher culture levels of the Old Stone Age, beginning thirty thousand years ago—to the period of the so-called Cro-Magnon people of Europe and their African and Asian peers—we are left in less doubt about the precise nature of Old Stone Age religious conviction and practice.

The Cro-Magnons

The Cro-Magnons were, like the Neanderthals, members of the species *Homo sapiens,* but they were more fully developed in the direction of the species today and even somewhat taller and more rugged than the modern norm. They came into a milder climate than that which had made so hazardous the existence of the Neanderthal people whom they replaced. In the warmer months, like the Neanderthals before them, they lived a more or less nomadic life following their game; during the colder seasons they used caves and shelters or lean-tos under cliffs. They lived by gathering roots and wild fruits and by hunting, their larger prey being bison, aurochs, an occasional mammoth, and especially the reindeer and the wild horse. Evidence of the Neanderthals' hunting prowess has been found at their open-air camp, discovered at Solutré in south central France, where archeologists have unearthed the bones of 100,000 horses, along with reindeer, mammoths, and bison—the remains of centuries of feasting. The Cro-Magnons never tamed and domesticated the horse, but they found it good eating. The horse, bearded and small, moved in large herds, was highly vulnerable to attack, and was not dangerous.

In a somewhat similar fashion as the Neanderthals, the Cro-Magnons buried their dead, choosing the same types of burial sites, not unnaturally, at the mouths of their grottos or near their shelters; they surrounded the body, which was usually placed under a protective stone slab, with ornaments such as shell bracelets and hair circlets, and with stone tools, weapons, and food. Because some of the bones found at the grave sites were charred, it is possible—but it is conjecture—that the survivors returned to the grave to feast with the dead during a supportive communal meal. Of great interest is the fact that they practiced the custom of painting or pouring red coloring matter (red ochre) on the body at burial, or at a later time on the bones during a second burial.

Cave Painting: Magic for the Hunt

Paint played a large part in the Cro-Magnons' lives in fact. Their most remarkable cultural achievement was painting and modeling. As prime exemplars of Franco-Cantabrian art around the Mediterranean (40,000–10,000 B.C.E.), they could draw, paint murals, mold clay figures, carve in the round, or engrave on bone and antlers with a realism unsurpassed by the art of any known primeval people. Their chief subjects were animals of the hunt: the bison, horse, wild boar, reindeer, cave bears, and mammoths. Human figures were comparatively rare; when painted, they were often mere stick figures; when carved, they were in the form of statuettes that were distended, suggestive of pregnancy or an ovoid symbolization of fertility.

Many of the engravings and paintings were executed on the walls of gloomy caves by the light from torches or shallow soapstone lamps fed with fat. So far from the cave's mouth and in such nearly inaccessible places did the artists usually do their work that they could hardly have intended an everyday display of their murals. What then did they have in mind?

The answer that seems the most consistent with all the facts is that the practices of the Cro-Magnons included, to begin with, a religioaesthetic impulse, the celebration of a sense of kinship and interaction between animal and human spirits, which Rachel Levy calls "a participation in the splendour of the beasts which was of the nature of religion itself."A* But there seem to have been magico-religious purposes as well—attempts to control events. That there were specialists among them who were magicians (or even priests) seems beyond doubt. A vivid mural in the cavern of Les Trois Frères shows a masked man, with a long beard and human feet, who is arrayed in reindeer antlers, the ears of a stag, the paws of a bear, and the tail of a horse, and probably represents a well-known figure in primal communities, the *shaman*,** a person who is especially attuned to the spirit world and called upon to deal with it on behalf of others. Whether or not the shamans were the actual artists, they probably led in ceremonies that made magical use of the paintings and clay figures. Just as in primal cultures of today it is believed that an image or a picture can be a magical substitute for the object of which it is the representation, so the Cro-Magnons may have felt that creating an image of an animal subjected it to the image maker's power. The magical use made of the realistic murals and plastic works of the Paleolithic era is suggested in several clear examples. In the cavern of Montespan there is a clay figure of a bear whose body is covered with representations of dart thrusts. Similarly, in the cavern of Niaux, an engraved and painted bison is marked with rudely painted outlines of spears and darts, mutely indicating the climax of some primeval hunt; evidently the excited Cro-Magnon hunters (gathering before the hunt?) ceremonially anticipated and ensured their success by having their leaders (shamans or priests?) paint upon the body of their intended quarry, so vividly pictured on the cave's wall, representations of their hunting weapons.

The Fecund Goddess-Mother

Another motif quite different from magic for the hunt appears in Upper Paleolithic paintings and carvings. Tiny sculpted figures of the human female, usually four to six inches high, emphasized fecundity: hips, buttocks, breasts, thighs, and vulva are sculpted into an oviform fullness. In classifying goddess symbols, Marija Gimbutas has called this creviced double "the power of two": intensified fertility. Cave paintings also deal with fertility magic. One mural shows mares in foal, and another, in the rock shelter of Cogul, Spain, depicts nine women surrounding a naked male, who seems to be either the subject of a tribal initiation at puberty or the leader in a ritual connected with fertility magic.

It thus appears that Paleolithic cultures employed both fertility and hunting magic, with evident faith in their value as methods of control.

Burial Customs

Of direct religious significance are the beliefs implicit in the burial customs of the Cro-Magnons and related peoples of the Upper Paleolithic period. Because the dead, or their bones, were covered with red paint

*In this book the sources of all quotations are designated by a small capital letter, followed by a number if a book is quoted from more than once. Books quoted from are listed in the section "References for Quotations" and are there designated by capital letters. This device is adopted for the convenience of readers and to save space.

**Terms appearing in the glossary at the end of each chapter are highlighted as they first appear in the text.

The "Venus" of Willendorf

The Conventional "Venus" ascription is inappropriate. This Upper Paleolithic limestone figure is not a goddess of love in a pantheon of deities, and she is not a model of seductive beauty. The ovoid abdomen and thighs and the thin arms pressing down as though in breast-feeding signify abundant procreative and nurturing capacity. This is the fecund Goddess as Lifegiver. *(Courtesy of the American Museum of Natural History. Neg. # 326474.)*

(symbolizing, no doubt, the redness of the lifeblood), the belief cannot have been less than that the dead survived in some real sense, although there may have been no conception of the survival of a nonphysical spiritual entity; whatever survived had a ghostly corporality and actual bodily needs and desires.

Associated with such beliefs may have been both awe and fear of the dead. Memories of the dead while they yet lived could have contributed to both of these feelings, and so also dreams and visions in which the dead appeared. But the determinative factor in creating such a sense of something superhuman about the dead could have been a conception perhaps then already well developed—that of a highly potent realm of being or process operative in the forms and forces of nature.

There are indications from about 15,000 B.C.E. that some Upper Paleolithic peoples made offerings to powers of nature as well as to their dead. In Germany, at Meiendorf, and later on at Stellmoor, young does with large stones placed inside of their rib cages were evidently submerged in run-off lakes left by the retreating glaciers of the last ice age; perhaps the hunters sacrificed these animals to some nature power or supernatural "master (or mistress) of the animals" on whom their success depended. The Upper Paleolithic peoples also had a bear cult, not unlike that of the Neanderthals; they may have wished to propitiate a bear god, or to keep it in a favorable frame of mind. If so, however, they also applied coercive measures (magic), as shown by their murals and clay figures of bears, the clay images sometimes punctured with wounds and the painted figures spouting blood from mouth, nostrils, and body wounds, apparently in the death agony. Clearly, whatever religion they had was inextricably combined with procedures designed to ensure hunting success.

The Middle Stone Age

This brings us to the Mesolithic or Middle Stone Age (beginning about 10,000 B.C.E.), the transitional age that saw the vanishing of the ice sheet and a gradual shift from nomadic to village life. The nomadic hunters who stalked animals through the forests springing up behind the retreating ice caps and continued to use Old Stone Age spears and cutting tools to kill and dismember their prey were gradually outnumbered and displaced by stationary tribes who were able to supplement the meat supplied by hunters and the berries, grain, fruits, and edible plants gathered by women and children with fish caught by bone hooks and fiber nets, all of this in more or less fixed locations. The hunters, skillful in their use of bows and arrows, were now aided by domesticated dogs that joined them in the hunt. Fishermen, too, could now use dugout canoes to increase their catch.

W. H. McNeill aptly suggests the new directions taken by religion at this time.

> A critical turn must have come when collectors of wild-growing grain came to understand that allowing a portion of the seed to fall to the ground at harvest time assured an increased crop in the following year. Perhaps this idea was connected with concepts of the spirit of the grain, propitiation of that spirit, and the reward that befitted a pious harvester who left part of the precious seed behind.[B]

It may have been that the mother-goddess idea was extended to include her stimulation of the seed springing from the soil in the form of edible plants, for the earth was early conceived to be a fertile and productive mother.

The relics of this age suggest an awe of nature—numerous round symbols of the sun and moon; stones and pillars, which were probably venerated; and suggestions of star and tree worship. The mingling of old fears with a certain sophistication rising from the power obtained through the use of new inventions is shown in the fact that axes and spears were seemingly venerated as fetishes. That magic had grown into a complex system is suggested by the many painted pebbles that have been preserved, covered with crude symbols probably having magical significance, although this may not afford a correct explanation of their use, because no one can at this distance be sure what they really meant.

The Neolithic Age

The Neolithic age (7000–3000 B.C.E.) is distinguished by several revolutionary developments: early forms of agriculture, with active tilling of the soil; domestication of animals and their gathering into flocks and herds; advances in the arts of pottery, plaiting, weaving, and sewing; establishment of settled communities, accompanied by great growth in the population; the building of permanent housing; the invention of wheeled carts; and the first surgery.

Further developments occurred in religion. The mythic Mother Goddess or Great Goddess of earlier hunting cultures had been generally associated with creation and regeneration. Now agriculture directed its attention more closely to the miraculous earth. Female divine power went beyond the animal models of birthing and nurturing to watering, tending, and protecting the whole world of vegetation: there were mistresses of waters and a Vegetation Goddess of the pregnant earth. Studies of Old Europe (centered in the Balkans), conducted by Marija Gimbutas, reveal a pantheon of mostly female deities subsequently obscured, but not fully displaced, by later Indo-European patriarchal and gender-polarized views.

> In Old Europe the world of myth was not polarized into female and male as it was among the Indo-European and many other nomadic and pastoral peoples of the steppes. Both principles were manifest side by side. . . . The male god, the primeval Dionysus, is saturated with a meaning closely related to that of the Great Goddess in her aspect of the Virgin Nature Goddess and Vegetation Goddess. All are gods of Nature's life cycle, concerned with the problem of death and regeneration, and all are worshipped as symbols of exuberant life.
>
> The pantheon reflects a society dominated by the mother. The role of woman was not subject to that of a man, and much that was created between the inception of the Neolithic and the blossoming of the Minoan civilization was a result of that structure in which all resources of human nature, feminine and masculine, were utilized to the full as a creative force.[D]

We shall pick up the story of the Minoan civilization and other ancient civilizations in the next chapter. But to prepare for further study of the fundamental motifs in the early development of religions, we need to clarify some of the terminology commonly in use and then illustrate its application in case studies of primal religions of the recent past.

> "The main theme of Goddess symbolism is the mystery of birth and death and the renewal of life, not only human but all life on earth and indeed in the whole cosmos."
>
> —Marija Gimbutas[C]

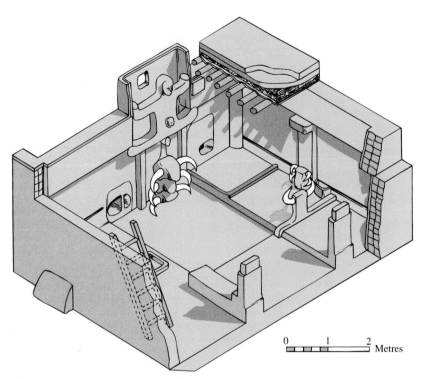

Shrine from Çatal Hüyük, Central Anatolia

On the wall of this structure from the seventh millennium B.C.E., the "Birthgiving Goddess" is shown in relief. Circles emphasize the uterus area. The bulls' heads below may have served to assert or strengthen the Birth-giver's powers. Later reliefs and engravings stylized such upraised arms and spread legs as double "M" or toad-shaped ideograms of the Great Goddess. *(Adapted from Marija Gimbutas,* The Goddesses and Gods of Old Europe, *University of California Press, 1982, p. 176, and James Mella art,* Çatal Hüyük, a Neolithic Town in Anatolia, *1967.)*

0   1   2 Metres

II. BASIC TERMINOLOGY: CHARACTERISTICS OF RELIGION IN PRIMAL CULTURES

Among primal cultures, attitudes toward the extraordinary are variegated. When we measure the beliefs and practices of any one locality against those of another, almost any particular belief or practice can be matched with its opposite or contradiction. On the surface, generalization would appear to be difficult.

But similarities exist. Primal cultures have certain general characteristics, and their religious practices have a number of common, although seldom universal, features.

1. Awe Before the Sacred

Human beings regard anything sacred or holy with ambivalent feelings of fear and attraction. Rudolph Otto, in his famous study, *The Idea of the Holy,* distinguished "the holy" from moral perfection or intellectual respect, calling it "the numinous." He characterized it as a *mysterium tremendum et fascinans.* Like a child before a great bonfire, the believer trembles with mingled dread and fascination. In most tribal communities, the sacred possesses such significance that no one deals with it carelessly or casually. It is defined, not by the kind of causation behind it (in modern terms "natural" or "supernatural"), but by *potency:* Thus a sneeze may be perceived as expelling a "spirit," but it may be a commonplace spirit, not one potent with sacred significance.

The sacred signifies extraordinary potency, both enlivening and deadly, a power for quick good or bad, and one's attitude toward it may determine whether good or bad will ensue. Anything sacred carries

> "[The numinous is] a special term to stand for 'the holy' minus its moral factor . . . and minus its 'rational' aspect."
>
> —Rudolph Otto[E]

with it the promise of a blessing; but rarely can anyone but qualified persons, such as chiefs, shamans, priests, and heads of families, deal with the sacred without harm. Impious handling of sacred objects may cause sudden death. The proper approach therefore is with a sense of holy mystery, awe, and reverence.

2. Expression of Anxiety in Ritual

In the presence of the sacred there is a certain anxiety. Will the holy power be stirred to action? Will this action be favorable? As soon as this anxiety arises, there is a need to act and speak in ways that may promise a favorable outcome. This is one of the fundamental bases of all religious ritual. Malinowski, the famous anthropologist, has put this point well as far as magical rituals are concerned.

> In a maritime community depending on the products of the sea there is never magic connected with the collecting of shellfish or with fishing by poison, weirs, and fish traps, so long as these are completely reliable. On the other hand, any dangerous, hazardous, and uncertain type of fishing is surrounded by ritual. In hunting, the simple and reliable ways of trapping or killing are controlled by knowledge and skill alone; but let there be any danger or any uncertainty connected with an important supply of game and magic immediately appears. Coastal sailing as long as it is perfectly safe and easy commands no magic. Overseas expeditions are invariably bound up with ceremonies and ritual.[F]

Many religious rituals are similarly motivated. First, there is a primary anxiety arising from crises or strains in the life of the individual or the community, and this calls forth rituals whose purpose is to provide restoration and reassurance. But once these rituals have been firmly established, with their mythical and institutional accompaniments, a secondary anxiety, lest the rituals have *not* been promptly enough nor properly performed, gives rise to further rituals of purification and expiation.

3. Ritual and Expectancy

But not all rituals are expressions of anxiety, although those that allay anxiety have a more than average intensity and urgency. Many rituals are expectant in character. They presuppose their own causal efficacy; they are performed to bring health, offspring, productivity of the soil, fertility of cattle, and other benefits desired by the community as well as the individual. Rituals also celebrate such annual events as the return of spring, sowing, and harvesting; they fit into a calendar of periodic rites. Other rituals are less regular in their recurrence because they mark spaced-out changes in the status of individuals, such as elevation to tribal leadership or kingship, which usually has a pronounced sacral character, or they may mark transition of maturing individuals from one social status to another. Among the latter rites are those recognized and named by Arnold van Gennep as "rites of passage," that is to say, they are rites in connection with birth, name giving, initiation, betrothal, marriage, death, and the like. These events change the status not only of the individuals involved but also of their parents and other relatives and associates. The rites first of all "separate" these persons from their former state or condition of life, including their community status; further, they smooth their "transition" to a new state and "reintegrate" them into the community in their new roles. An obvious example is this: Marriage changes a boy and girl into a husband and wife; when a child is born to them, they gain the status of parents, and their own parents become grandparents, whereas their brothers and sisters become uncles and aunts; if one dies, the other becomes either a widower or widow, and so on. Typical of the rites of passage are the initiation rites we shall note among the Australian aborigines (p. 22).

Rituals have a basis in myth, and vice versa.

4. Myth and Ritual

The making of myths is universal among human cultures. In fact, myths are a necessity. Primal groups find them vital for the maintenance of the patterns of group life. Among the Australian aborigines, for example, myths are invoked to explain and give the weight of a supernatural origin and authority to the customs, ceremonials, and beliefs of the tribes (p. 22). This is a major aspect of ritual development.

> "Awe is the best component of humanity."
>
> —Goethe

It frequently happens that tribes find themselves following old customs and rituals whose precise meaning now eludes them. In this situation it is natural for them to seek an explanation of their need to follow what would otherwise be meaningless rites by saying, "The Fathers taught us to do these things," and then to push back the origins beyond remembered fathers to mythical Progenitors or Culture Heroes at the beginning of the world. Or some "high god" (p. 22) may be cited as the first author of "our tribe and way of life." It will be seen at once that myths here serve the very necessary function of providing binding sanctions for tribal custom and belief. Specifically, they tell in story form of the imposition, by an original authoritative father figure, of an awesome primeval decree that is expressed in the institutions and traditions of the community: "Do thus-and-so without fail. It is for your good."

But myths have other important roles. A large place must be given to cosmogonic or "creation" myths. It is of course speculative to seek reasons for their being told in such numbers and in such variety. One reason is undoubtedly the need to have an explanation of why the earth is so suited to human habitation. Someone—perhaps the High God or a Culture Hero—dove into the waters to bring up the sand with which the habitable earth was made or forced apart the close-lying sky father and earth mother to make room for the gods, humans, animals, and vegetation they had engendered, or brought these forth from an underground cave, or fought with giants for the materials with which he put the world together.

Closely related to creation myths are those that seek an explanation for the way things are in the world, how they have come to be as they are (etiological tales). Whereas questions like "Was there a First Cause?" would be greeted with incomprehension, specific questions like "Why are humans, bears, and wolves as different as they are?" might stir imaginative individuals to compose and pass on to others a myth drawn from their memories and dreams and particularly from what they thought the elders of their youth might say, if they were alive. We shall see that many myths of the Cherokees take this form.

The quasihistorical myth is of another sort. It is the elaboration of an original happening, involving usually a hero or pioneer figure, into a tale of wonder, through all of whose episodes thrills the magic of a heroic name, until that character, looming transfigured through the magico-religious aura in which it is invested, glows with divinity. Such myths often have been expanded in later times into sagas and epics in which their presumed truth is overlaid with entertaining episodes created by the imagination.

Ralph Linton proposed what one might call a "boredom theory" to account for complex theologies and elaborate mythic systems.

> The variety of religious beliefs and practices is almost infinite, yet the system developed by each society appears to meet all of its needs. Some groups have developed elaborate creeds. It seems that man enjoys playing with both his mind and his muscles . . . the human capacity for being bored, rather than social or natural needs, lies at the root of man's cultural advance.[G]

5. Types of Magic

"Magic" may be loosely defined as an endeavor through an utterance of set words, or the performance of set acts, or both, to control or bend the powers of the world to one's will. It cannot be wholly divorced from religion, as we have heretofore noted, but it is discernibly present when an emphasis is placed on forcing things to happen rather than asking that they do.

Sir James G. Frazer has made one type of magic famous. The inclusive name he gave it is "sympathetic magic." It often takes an "imitative" form based upon analogy: the assumption that look-alikes act alike, or, more significantly, that like influences or even produces like; therefore, if one imitates the looks and actions of a person or an animal (or even of a thundercloud), one can induce a like and desired action in the imitated being or object.

The outcomes are described as productive, aversive, or "contagious."

Productive Magic. The Cro-Magnon hunting magic, we can readily see, was a form of imitative magic. In many parts of the world it is still believed that exhortation in words and action may spur the growth of sprouting grain. The person tending the crop may use words of encouragement or command or even leap again and again to induce, or perhaps compel, the sprouts to grow. To cite still another example from a countless number, natives often seek an end to drought by going to a steep hill and rolling rocks down its slope while beating drums and shouting "boom!" This is done to bring on a rainstorm.

Aversive Magic. Sympathetic magic also may serve aversive or destructive purposes. If someone, for example, makes an image (imitation) of an enemy, perhaps in wax, and stabs it with pins, the hated one will die. It is frequently quite enough just to describe in detail the terrible things that will happen to an enemy, and then either command (usually by a curse) or pray and predict that they must occur, and they may!

Contagious Magic. Frazer also found a form of sympathetic magic that he called "contagious." Things conjoined and then separated remain sympathetic with each other. Thus, severed hair or fingernails retain a magical sympathy with the person to whom they once belonged, and therefore black magic performed on them causes damage to that person. This type of magic has many ramifications.

These and other practices may be grouped under various headings. It will be helpful here to consider them as exemplifying two methods of control of spirit power.

Methods of Control

1. *Fetishism.* This much-abused term is used here to refer to any resort to the presumed power in inanimate things. This includes the veneration and use of certain objects into which useful powers do not have to be induced, because they are already there. These are the so-called natural fetishes—the curiously marked pebbles, aerolites, bones, odd-shaped sticks, and the like—which seem from the moment of finding to bring good fortune and to frustrate the evil designs of one's foes. But on its more actively magical side, fetishism involves inducing useful powers into a variety of inanimate objects, stuffed sometimes into an antelope's horn or other receptacle, and confining them there for the purpose of securing their assistance in a great variety of projects.

Both natural and manufactured fetishes are regarded as possessing a vague sort of personality, at least an active will. This idea accounts for the prevailing attitude taken toward them, especially in Africa. There a fetish is reverenced in the most obviously anthropomorphic way. It is first treated as an object of

Shaman with Crescent-Disk Device behind an Elk
Bessov-Noss, Russia

worship, addressed with prayer and presented with offerings. This done, a favorable issue is awaited with hope. But if the desired result does not follow, the attitude of the owner changes; the owner begins coaxing and cajoling, then proceeds to stern commands, scolding, and finally whipping or other chastisement. If there is still no result, the conclusion is either that the spirit has left the fetish, in which case it is useless and another must be found to take its place, or that the spirit, still in the fetish, has been rendered impotent by some more powerful fetish or spirit power in the neighborhood. In the latter case, the magician must be visited and the fetish charged with more power, or substituted with another of adequate potency.

2. *Shamanism.* In this case spirits are conjured into or out of human beings by one who is similarly spirit possessed. The shaman of Siberia has been selected to give a name to this practice because, in this communal role, a shaman is typical of all witch doctors, medicine men and women, exorcists, and sorcerers. The shaman achieves a frenzy of spirit possession and is lifted up to the spirit level, in both consciousness and power. In that state, the shaman establishes control over certain spirits, especially those of disease and death, either to drive them into people (bedevilment or sorcery), or to expel them from people (exorcism), especially in the case of illness.

When shamans seek outright control over spirits, the function is a *magical* one. But it should be noted that they may also act as *religious* specialists, skilled in persuasion. They attract the spirits, for example, in order to talk with them or to have them talk to audiences through them in many different voices; they use special techniques—drumbeating, dancing, autohypnotic concentration, chanting, drugs, and the like—to go into deep trances, while close-packed audiences watch; during trances their spirits travel to faraway places, over mountains, under the sea, or under the earth, and they find out what other spirits intend, thus divining the future, or what is happening to the dead; to the latter they sometimes offer guidance, based on other spirit journeys, especially if they are lost and cannot find their way to their final resting place. In other words, the shaman functions as a priest or magician.

6. Prayer

In the performance of rituals aimed at exerting a favorable influence on spiritual powers, solemn actions, gestures, and dance patterns are naturally involved. But so are words. Nothing could be more natural than to accompany action with speech. As we have seen, such speech might hope to be coercive and force the spirits to yield, or to utter a spell. But far more of the ritual is likely to be in the form of prayer; that is, it is petitionary.

Prayers in preliterate cultures can be (but rarely are) individual and spontaneous, and so without a set form; public rituals, on the other hand, are formal and structured, and often of a fixed kind, their words inherited perhaps from earlier times, to be repeated word for word without the slightest error. Where the gods and spirits have an anthropomorphic character, formal prayers generally contain the elements found in more literate societies, namely adoration, confession of wrongdoing and promise of atonement, thanksgiving in grateful recognition of past favors, and supplication or petitions of a more or less specific kind. After praise and thanksgiving, it is safe to petition for more favors. But prayers in general have to be made only hopefully, without any certainty of success. Magic and divination convey more certainty.

7. Divination

Divination may be said to bypass prayer, for the answer to prayer is revealed as a rule only in subsequent events; divination, on its part, aims at immediate knowledge of the intentions or dispositions of the spiritual powers. Here lies its value for those who turn to it.

There is a clear connection between shamanism and divination, that is, between rapport with spirit powers and insight into what is obscure and hidden in the present and future. Such insight is thought to occur during specific divination rites. Shamans may use their own inherent power (magic) or may establish dependent prophetic relations with the supernatural (a situation that is primarily religious). In general, the belief is that the shaman or necromancer possesses the power to make contacts in the spirit world, including communion with the spirits of the dead, and thus gains otherwise inaccessible information about things and events on, above, and under the earth. Often the shaman is believed to be the "familiar" of a single spirit or soul, and thus, "in the know." In other contexts, where priests rather than shamans are the central figures, divination has an explicit religious aspect. It relies on divine inspiration, either through direct communion with the god or through oracles like those in which the ancient Greeks believed: words whispered by the oaks of Dodona speaking for Zeus (p. 45) entranced utterances muttered by the priestess at Delphi (p. 45) when Apollo communicated through her. Another aspect of divination is the reading of omens in the flight of birds, the sound of thunder, dreams, visions, the appearance of comets, eclipses, "signs in the stars," accidents, sudden death, and like phenomena. In many parts of the world diviners have developed techniques for interpreting cracks in dried mud or in rock formations or, again, in the patterns of wind and water at specific locations (geomancy). Equally favored have been the methods for predicting events from the movements and conformations of the stars (astrology). Divination seems to have been such a necessity that it is virtually universal.

8. Belief in Mana

Mana is a Melanesian term, adopted by anthropologists as a convenient designation for the widespread, although not universal, belief in an occult force or indwelling supernatural power as such, distinct from either persons or spirits. It is not the only term of the kind in circulation among primal peoples. The same sort of reaction is reflected in various parallel terms used by some American Indians (Sioux, Iroquois,

Algonquin), some tribes of Morocco, the Pygmies of middle Africa, the Bantu of South Africa, and aboriginal people in many parts of the world. Although the role of this force differs from one area to another, all such terms refer to the experienced presence of a powerful but silent force in things or persons, especially any occult force believed to act of itself, as an addition to the forces naturally or usually present. It is a force that is thought to be transmissible from objects in nature to human beings, from one person to another, or again from persons to things. It has had special importance in the South Seas. In the last analysis, the concept of mana indicates response to the vitally significant or extraordinary in quality, as distinguished from the ordinary, the usual, or the normal in quality. The extraordinary in quality—whether in events or in the character of some forceful human being or powerful beast—by its very nature draws attention to itself.

9. Animism

There is a general acceptance among present-day primal religions of the animistic belief that all sorts of motionless objects as well as living and moving creatures possess souls or spirits, and that every human being has a soul or souls leaving the body temporarily during dreams and finally at death. This notion of souls and spirits has a meaning quite distinct from that of mana, the last being in itself impersonal, although a soul or spirit may manifest it or be its outlet in action. Souls and spirits are usually conceived of in a thoroughgoing anthropomorphic fashion. They have shape, mind, feelings, and will or purpose; they are like living people in being amenable to reason in good moods and aggressively quarrelsome when angry or upset; they like flattery, devotion, loyalty; they are often not to be trusted out of one's remembrance; eternal vigilance is the price of being on the right side of them, and one must be ever alert to continue in their good graces, once obtained. To use the language of E. B. Tyler, "all nature is possessed, pervaded, crowded with spiritual beings."[H1]

> "Animism in its full development includes the belief in souls and in a future state, these doctrines practically resulting in some kind of active worship."
>
> —E. B. Tylor[H2]

10. Veneration and Worship of Powers

It has been said truly that man has worshiped everything he could think of beneath the earth, everything between earth and heaven, and everything in the heavens above.[1] Sometimes it is the object itself that is worshiped as living and active, heavily charged with mana. Sometimes, the object is not worshiped for itself but for the spirit or soul lodged or inhering in it. In a third mode, the object is not worshiped at all; it becomes a symbol of the reality which *is* worshiped and which it visibly and tangibly represents. All three of these modes of worship may at times occur simultaneously, for, as in the case of the worship of images in India, some naive worshipers regard the image itself as alive, others suppose there is a spirit resident in it, and the cultivated or philosophically minded devotee makes use of it as a convenient thought center for symbolizing the reality behind all. At the symbolic level, worship and prayer serve the social purpose of intensifying commitment to the values represented by the object or deity worshiped. Such rites are classified as *"rites of intensification."*

Short of worship, which expresses adoration, are veneration and awe. These include respect and the acknowledgment of the presence of sacred power or quality. Sometimes it is difficult to know where veneration ends and worship begins.

The veneration of stones has been widespread and goes back to prehistoric times. The stones may be of any size, from pebble to boulder, and in any amount, single, in series, or even in heaps. Often they are remarkable in shape or composition. Sometimes they are shaped by human art or skill, as in the case of flint tools or weapons. Aerolites are often venerated, the classic instance being that of the Ka'ba stone at Mecca, which every Muslim pilgrim kisses or touches to acquire holiness from it. Veneration of shaped stones, and of any tool or implement, not only existed in prehistoric times but may also be found today in Africa, Oceania, India, Japan, and among North American Indians. Among some natives of the Philippine Islands the headman's weapons are said be charged with a vital force

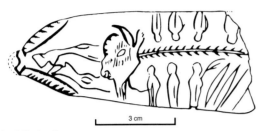

```
├────── 3 cm ──────┤
```

An Offering?
Men and Bison—Dordogne, France

that can act of itself. A passage from an account of these people says of one chieftain: "He was no ordinary mortal. . . . His companions insisted that his headaxe and spear killed at his bidding.ᴶ This sort of belief is not uncommon. The axe was long venerated in the rural districts of Germany and Scandinavia. Veneration of this kind was general in the Greco-Roman world.

The veneration of plants and trees is also widespread, not only in isolated but in more complex cultures as well. Survival of such veneration in sophisticated societies is seen in the use of the Christmas tree and maypole. It is said that in Europe, in the Upper Palatinate, woodsmen still murmur a plea for forgiveness to a large, fine tree before they cut it down. Not only do trees and plants inspire reverence, but they also represent an inexhaustible productivity. Deification of trees, and also of plants and grains, is a natural tribute to the mysterious growth forces of nature. Trees help crops grow, assist flocks and herds to multiply, and make women fertile. Barren women are sometimes married to trees so that they may become fruitful.

Animal veneration also is common. In animistic hunting cultures it sometimes reflects fear of retaliation by the spirit of the slain prey. The Cherokees believed that various animals could cause specific diseases: failure to take the proper measures (respectful apologies and aversive techniques) after killing a deer, for example, could result in rheumatism. Another impulse toward veneration springs up naturally when people believe that if they can somehow share in the magnificent powers of some animals, they will gain greatly in strength, vision, and cunning.

Again, the veneration may grow out of a more generalized sense of kinship. (See totemism, discussed in Section 16.) The relationship is often conceived to be so close that many peoples have had little difficulty believing that the soul of someone at death, and even during life, readily passes into the body of an animal, and vice versa. Myths and fairy tales abound in characters such as frog maidens, bird women, and vampires who alternately appear in human and bat shapes; weretigers and werewolves have contributed a thrill to many a tale of disaster and bloodshed. The lion in Africa, the tiger in Malaya, the eagle, the bear, and the beaver in North America, the bull in Greece and Egypt, the cow in India, Africa, and Scandinavia, the buffalo in South India, and the kangaroo in Australia are among the fierce and strong or gentle and life-sustaining creatures that people have honored with their veneration. Similarly, reverence has been paid to the goose, the dove, and the snake. The last, whether in the form of the sinuous serpent or the winged dragon, has been reverenced under a hundred forms and symbols, of which both the water connections and the phallic associations have been among the chief fascinations for the worshiper.

We may conjecture that it was later in the history of religions that reverence for the "elements" of the world, considered in the abstract—earth, air, fire, and water—appeared, although fire, the least abstract because least diffused, has been revered since the dawn of historic times, and probably in the Old Stone Age. The Parsis still honor it. The sky (or space) came at last to be worshiped as the home not only of gods and goddesses, but of the clouds, wind, sun, moon, and stars, themselves regarded as animate. Water, more difficult to conceive of abstractly, was venerated in its discrete forms—mountains, springs, rivers, lakes, and finally the sea—whose hold upon the imagination is such that its worship characterized all early civilizations and continued late into the Middle Ages, when the Doge of Venice was annually married to the Adriatic. In much the same way, humans have sometimes worshiped Earth, the universal mother and grain bearer.

11. Recognition of a Supreme Being

This is the natural place to raise the disputed question as to whether primal peoples have been widely given to religious relationships with a Supreme Being. It is common to find among many of them a recognition of the existence of a deity far up in the sky or at great remove, who has made everything—man, woman, earth, sea, and sky—and who at a distance sees all that goes on among them, and sometimes disapproves but does not often interfere. Among groups like the Pygmies of Africa, the Fuegians of South America, and the Australian bush peoples, the belief in such a high deity has been even clearer and more definite.

A dispute has arisen among anthropologists as to whether this high deity has the religious significance of the nearer spirit powers of the earth. In most tribal communities with animistic beliefs, individuals have not had to be concerned on a daily basis about the high deity. The high deity is supreme and uncreated, existing from the beginning, but other spirits are much more active as determiners of destiny down on the earth. If there have been any exceptions to this comparative evaluation, we come across them among the Australian bush peoples and the Fuegians. The former, in some localities, address prayers for food to the Supreme Being. Yet the members of one of the Fuegian tribes used to speak of this deity in the third person, as if there were no direct dealings between them. Moreover, they sometimes issued threats, which would preclude real supremacy. But this matter may be left in dispute. Probably, the idea of a great Originator who has little to do with humanity in the ordinary course of life arose very naturally when an answer was attempted to such questions as "Where did our rituals come from?" or "Who began everything?" or "Who was the First Father?" or "Who was the First Mother?" Unable to think that any of the local powers with which they had daily dealings could have originated all things, they hit upon a rather speculative monotheistic explanation. But because the being they inferred seldom entered their lives, he or she was in most instances a deistic postulate rather than an ever-present religious reality.

12. Taboo

Taboos are prohibitions or "hands-off" warnings applied to many things, persons, and actions because they are considered sacred or dangerous or socially forbidden. Specifically, there are things that may not be touched or handled, words that may not be said, persons who must be avoided or who may be approached only to a certain distance, actions that may not be performed, and places that may not be entered. If we define the term broadly enough, taboos are found in every religion and any society.

Many taboos are based on fear of mana; others reflect the dread of pollution. Some set up a hedge around the god. Still others seek to avoid the loss of power, health, or luck. This by no means exhausts the range of taboo. Many different things, acts, sacred words, names, and places are on the list of the avoided. Sharp weapons, iron, blood, head and hair (they contain spirit), cut hair and nails (even when severed from the body they retain a generous portion of spirit), spittle, certain foods, knots and rings, and much more are in this category.

In many parts of the world (Native Americans are an exception) the person of a chief is taboo. This is partly to protect the chief from harm, but even more it is to protect others from mana: to touch the body, or the clothes, or the cooking utensils, or even the carpet or floor space of one so heavily charged with power is highly dangerous; immediate steps must he taken to counteract the fatal consequences to the intruder. When entering the chief's presence the utmost precautions must be observed.

More than one instance is on record of men and women who died of fright upon learning that they had unwittingly eaten the remains of a chief's meal. Their bodies apparently could not survive so powerful a dosage of mana-imbued substance.

There are taboos upon other persons. In many parts of the world warriors have been taboo before and after battle. This is only partly because they are in an awesome state of excitement and are dangerous. More particularly, they are not to be distracted. Women especially should keep their distance and even remain hidden from sight; in some cultures they are strictly forbidden to approach a warrior for some hours before battle, for sex before battle drains his power. And he is taboo after battle because he has been polluted by bloodshed. Manslayers are in fact usually untouchable until expiation or ceremonial cleansing has taken place and removed the contagion of death and the wrath of the departed spirit. Generally, a taboo is put on all of those who have had any contact with the dead, and this extends even to the hired mourners.

13. Purification Rites

Ceremonies of purification and cleansing have been referred to more than once in the previous discussion of taboo. The reference was inescapable. The existence of taboos means to believers not only a very real element of danger in taboo breaking, because of the vindictive or retributive action of outraged powers, but also the guilt and uncleanness of the unfortunate taboo breaker. This uncleanness and contamination are such that the whole community may be put in jeopardy. The taboo breaker is ostracized, and may even come under the sentence of death until cleansed of the defilement.

But taboo breaking is not the only source of pollution. Birth, death, bloodshed, blood itself, and contact with tabooed persons are each sources of pollution. And there may be a supernatural condition, such as the presence of an unclean spirit haunting a family or a village, a condition involving as its consequence the need of removing the objectionable presence.

If an unclean spirit haunts a community or enters a man or woman, it may be expelled by introducing a more powerful spirit whose presence will be cleansing. Personal purification is effected in various ways. Common among the methods are fasting, shaving the hair and cutting the nails, crawling through cleansing smoke fumes produced during an elaborate ritual, passing between fires or jumping through fire, washing with water or blood; and cutting or gashing the body to let out the evil with the rushing blood.

But while a major motive for purification rites is getting a cleansing from pollution, there also exists the motive of purifying oneself for future ritual. The officiants may purify themselves for rites they are to perform by fasting, abstention from sex, ablutions, and the like, while those who will be present may undergo similar if less stringent purification. The Cherokee purifications before the Green Corn Festival are an example (p. 33).

14. Sacrifices and Gifts

Sacrifice has usually entailed the giving up or destroying (e.g., burning) of something, animate or inanimate, human, animal, or vegetable, to cause it to pass from human possession to that of the spirit powers or gods. The simplest form of sacrifice is always the giving of offerings, gifts of value of many sorts, in the hope of pleasing the spirits. But originally the sacrifices seem to have been more radical than this and to have involved animal and human sacrifice, because the spirits as well as humans needed the vitality and strength present in life and blood.

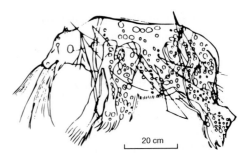

Bear Ceremonialism—Shedding Blood
Les Trois Freres

When members of certain cultures discover that particular powers behave in an unusual or uncontrollable way, they may offer sacrifices with a view to placating or conciliating the powers they cannot coerce; such sacrifices are propitiatory. When they believe they have offended the powers by their actions, they may offer sacrifices intended to expiate or atone for their misdoings. Or they may hope to open the way for the inflow of supernatural power into themselves, and then their sacrifice is of a sacramental kind. One form of such sacrifice shares something—for example, a sacred meal—with the spirit powers. All of these forms of sacrifice bear the marks of religion, but magic is also generally implicated. It is obvious that sacrifices may do something to or for the spirit powers; in particular, they may impart added or needed strength and vigor. Survivals of this belief may be found in Homer and among the early Romans. Homer implies that the gods not only lose prestige but power as well when men cease to sacrifice to them. The Romans, we shall find, felt that since their sacrifices increased the *numen* or spiritual power of the gods, the gods owed them a return of favors, which was confidently expected (pp. 57–58). In Latin, this understanding is expressed in *Do ut des* ("I give that you may give").

Insofar as the powers are dependent upon humans for the vitalizing elements in the sacrifices, the sacrifices gain a magical potency to coerce them. We shall take note in another chapter that in Vedic times in India a highly sophisticated development converted worship and sacrifice into magic: the priests promised and guaranteed that their rituals would force the gods to do as they directed (p. 88).

A somewhat different development has resemblances to aversive magic. Sacrifices are offered to dreaded powers in mingled fear and hope that they will stay away or cease to afflict the group with sickness, drought, or some other calamity. Sacrifices, because of their momentousness and cost to the givers, carry great weight even with ill-disposed powers.

15. Attitudes Toward the Dead

An important realm of ideas is found in attitudes toward the dead. The notion of the complete extinction of the personality at death is often difficult to reconcile with our daily experience. A person who has been a daily companion leaves at death a great void in our lives; our habits must be adjusted to the loss; we think of the absent one often; our visual and auditory memories are for some time so vivid that the mere remembrance gives back a living presence; in dreams, we converse with the absent person.

These experiences were as vivid, certainly, to our prehistoric ancestors as they are to us. But close upon this conviction that the dead have an afterlife comes a real uneasiness. The dead, it is realized, have a way of hanging about. This is embarrassing, because they do not play their old part in the round of daily existence.

Very early our ancient forebears developed measures of security against troublesome interference by the dead. They raised a heap of stones over the dead body, or tied it up with strong cords, or in some cases even drove a stake through the chest in order to pin the body to the earth. These practices were designed to keep the dead from "walking." At the same time, offerings were left at the burial place to keep the dead satisfied and content. Many of these customs still survive. The dead, in more than one region of the world, are still carried out feet foremost, so that they may be "pointed away." This procedure is often followed by a zigzag progress on the part of the corpse bearers, to bewilder the dead and keep them from finding their way back. Another custom involves taking the body from the house by some other than the ordinary exit, through the window or through a hole made in the wall, which is immediately closed up. Some Bantu forest dwellers along the Congo strew thorns on the grave and upon the path leading back to the village to prick the feet of the dead and prevent their return. Sometimes magical barriers are erected against the dead, such as fences around the grave, or hedges of twigs to simulate a trackless forest, or deep lines drawn across the path to represent an impassable river.

It might be concluded that such customs presuppose hostility on the part of the dead. This interpretation is, however, not accurate. It would be truer to say that until the dead have found their way to their final resting place in the hereafter and are at peace, they tend to linger; often they feel lost and in need of comfort. They have not yet become adjusted to their new state and want to be sustained by the assurance that the living still care for them. Only if this assurance is denied them do they become disturbed and perhaps inimical. It is hard for the living, however, to know how the dead feel, whether pleased or angry. It is well to be wary—and this precaution is always taken—but the dead often are friendly. This is especially true of ancestors. Ancient Chinese civilization was founded on the optimistic faith that ancestral spirits are eager to aid their descendants, and will do so if only the living pay them proper regard.

We have already seen in our discussion of shamanism (p. 11) that the dead are presumed to have knowledge that the living do not possess and that necromancers may call up the spirits of the dead to assist in divination.

Out of the double purpose of serving the dead who remain nearby and of helping those who are about to depart for the bourn of the hereafter has arisen the worldwide custom of making offerings at the grave. Food and drink are as much a need of the dead as of the living. The endeavor to placate or assist the dead begins even before burial and is especially evident when interment takes place. Weapons, clothing, furniture, every sort of precious object (including sometimes, as in historic Egypt, miniature ovens, wooden loaves, chairs, servants, and the like), are placed in the grave or tomb. In many parts of the world, living wives and servants were "sent along," being either slain upon the grave, burned on a pyre, buried alive, or sealed in tombs. Within living memory, kings' deaths in Africa have been the occasion of the "sending along" of hundreds of men and women.

16. Totemism

Our survey of the general characteristics of primal religions concludes with a brief mention of a group of practices rather hard to define. There is, however, a common characteristic present in all of the diverse forms of totemism. It is that totemism recognizes the existence of a more or less intimate relationship between certain human groups or particular individuals and classes or species of animal, plant, or inanimate object in nature. The recognition of this relationship results in special social groupings (a phenomenon known as social totemism) and also in rituals binding the human groups to their totemic counterparts (cult totemism). The cult rituals are so diverse as to defy generalization.

The rituals of the aborigines of Australia are noteworthy in being very closely tied to tribal survival, as we shall see. Their tribes are hard put to find enough food to enable them to survive, and totemism has provided what appears to them to be a solution to the problem. Each class of animal, plant, and inanimate object having a place in the food supply has become the totem of a clan within the tribe. The basic realizations here might be put in these terms: "Our food supply depends on there being a plentiful supply of animals, plants, and substances that go into the making of food. May all animals and plants increase and be abundant! Let therefore each of the tribe's clans having an animal or vegetable totem promote the abundance of the species especially sacred to it, by practicing magic, offering prayer, and providing constant care and solicitude. Although those not belonging to the clan may eat of the totem freely, let the totemic clan regard it as taboo, and eat of it sparingly even on the allowed occasion of the periodic sacramental meal when the clan partakes of it." Included among the totems are such things as rain (necessary to the existence of animal and plant alike and infrequent in central Australia) and substances like red ochre (necessary to the decoration of those practicing, among other things, the fertility rites). The aborigines have added to these practices the social provision of exogamy, prescribing marriage outside of the totemic clan.

Other varieties of totemism are found in North and South America, Africa, India (where it exists weakly), and the South Seas. In these areas the particular features of totemism vary, sometimes widely. Where the food supply is ample, the Australian devices for increasing it are replaced by other interests. In North America, for example, it has been characteristic for Indian tribes to divide into a number of groups that express their individuality by taking their name from some animal, bird, or natural object. In most cases the sense of special relationship with the totem has issued in a myth of descent that derives the members of the clan and their totem from a common ancestor. Sometimes the relationship between the members of the clan and the totem has taken the form of a "mystic affinity." In other cases the rituals seek to propitiate the totem group. Occasionally a tribe's totems are chosen exclusively from either birds or animals. In Australia and elsewhere, single clans have occasionally had two or more totems. And of course the attendant rituals vary widely in both importance and complexity.

III. CASE STUDY: THE DIERI OF SOUTHEAST AUSTRALIA

That the feel of primal religion cannot well be caught from an analysis by categories must be obvious. For a more complete understanding we need to project ourselves in our imaginations into some particular place and situation and thereby gain a sense of beliefs and practices in the milieu that produced them.

Some isolated Dieri aborigines of Australia continued at a stage of culture remaining somewhere between Paleolithic and Neolithic. Our account pictures them as they were observed by A. W. Howitt in the 1860s when they were still using stone tools exclusively and when their group beliefs and practices were relatively undisturbed. In what follows, some passages are in the present tense, but readers will be aware that the intervening century and a quarter has in fact brought new tools and that there has been considerable erosion of their traditional culture.

The Dieri inhabit the land to the east and southeast of Lake Eyre in south Australia, a region of minimum rainfall and very high temperatures, with low trees dotting the arid plains. Except in cold weather, when they put on warm kangaroo, wallaby, and opossum skins, they wear only a hip girdle, to which the men attach their weapons. They live in scattered tribes, each occupying a definite territory and speaking a common dialect. Their culture is a food-gathering one, for they are "a people which neither tills nor sows, and which does not breed and pasture animals, but only collects and kills."[K] With them, as was the case with the Tasmanians, the spear is still the most important weapon, but it is provided with a separate hardwood or flaked-stone head, often fitted with barbs; to hurl it through the air they use a throwing stick. Their knives and axes are of chipped stone. To their credit is the evolution of two kinds of boomerang, one of which is so shaped and twisted that it returns to the sender. Tribal life, though geographically set apart from that of other settlements, is not completely independent, reciprocity with neighboring tribes being at least as general as hostility. Here totemism plays a powerful role in establishing lines of relatedness crossing and crisscrossing the tribal barriers.

The Dieri were divided into two exogamous intermarrying moieties or classes, called *murdus*. The class names were Matteri and Kararu. No Matteri could marry a Matteri, no Kararu a Kararu. The Matteri were subdivided into smaller groups, each having a totem, typical examples of such being the caterpillar, cormorant, emu, eagle, hawk, and wild dog. None of these totem groups, of course, could intermarry. The Kararu had as totems such diverse entities as the carpet snake, crow, rat, frog, bat, shrew mouse, red ochre, and rain. Each individual acquired his group totem from his mother, descent being reckoned through the female line.

Executive power in each division of the tribe resided in the oldest man of the totem group, its *pinnaru* or head. The pinnarus were collectively the headmen of the tribe, and among them one was usually superior to the others. The headmen were of chief importance in the initiation ceremonies, which will be described later.

The Medicine Man

From the magico-religious standpoint, the outstanding individual in the group was the *kunki* or medicine man. He was credited with the power to communicate directly with supernatural beings, called *kutchi*, and with the *Mura-muras*, the highly regarded spirits of the legendary heroes (a superhuman race) believed to have preceded the Australians as their prototypes and to have taught them their rituals. He was thought to have obtained his power from these supernatural beings. Through them he interpreted dreams, counteracted evil spells, and drove out evil spirits. It was believed he could project into his victims substances such as quartz crystals or bones.

That meant death, of course. He also was thought to have the power of surreptitiously abstracting from individuals their body fat, which he used as a powerful magical infusion; such fat stealing was the *real* cause of the subsequent death of the robbed individuals. A special function of his was to act as a diviner when the relatives of the dead sought the identity of the person or persons who had planned the death, for death was not considered a natural event; it was always due either to magic or to the machinations of the kutchi. As to sickness this side of death, if a kutchi had caused anyone to fall ill, the medicine man could drive it out. But sickness was not always due to a kutchi; it might be the result of a "pointing of the bone." That is, some enemy had secured an accomplice, and they had performed a secret ceremony in which they had made magical use of a human shinbone, pointing it at the person they hoped to sicken and then uttering a magic spell. As soon as a person became ill, therefore, friends would consult the kunki and others to find out if anyone had "pointed the bone." If the sick one died, and suspicion of having "pointed the bone" fell on any person, the latter was summarily dealt with by a *pinya,* or party of revenge, which went out at the behest of the older men of the tribe (the tribal council) to track down and kill or severely beat the accused.

Rainmaking

Because of the oft-recurring periods of drought, the medicine man acquired great importance as a rainmaker and weather changer. The whole tribe united in the ceremony that he and his colleagues conducted. The theory was that the clouds are bodies in which rain is produced by the Mura-muras, who live on the elevated plain that is the sky. For the rainmaking ceremony, members of the tribe dug a hole two feet deep, twelve feet long, and from eight to ten feet wide, over which they erected a long hut of twigs and boughs. The hut was occupied by the old men, and during the ceremony their arms were cut by the principal medicine man with a sharp piece of flint, the blood was made to flow on the other men who were sitting

Pointing the Bone

An Australian witch doctor points a sharpened bone at a victim some distance away while "singing" an imprecation. If the victim learns of the performance, his fright and consternation are such that it is not unusual for him to sicken and die. *(Courtesy of Australian News and Information Bureau.)*

around. Then two medicine men, whose arms had previously been lanced, threw handfuls of down in the air. The blood symbolized rain, the down clouds. The ceremony ended when the men, young and old, butted down the hut with their heads. The piercing of the hut symbolized the piercing of the clouds, and the fall of the hut a downpour of rain. Meanwhile, the rain-making Mura-muras were besought to grant heavy rainfall, in view of the damage caused by the drought and the famine-stricken condition of the people. The significance of the following quotation needs no pointing out:

> Should no clouds appear as soon as expected, the explanation given is that the Mura-mura is angry with them; and should there be no rain for weeks or months, they suppose that some other tribe has stopped their power.[1.1]

Totemic Food Ritual

Another and even more important ceremony was designed to exert an influence upon a Mura-mura, called Minkani, buried deep in a sandhill. Because the

motive of the ceremony, a typically totemic ritual, was to increase the food supply of carpet snakes and lizards in the sandhills, the men who took part in it had these reptiles as their totems.

> When the actual ceremony takes place, the women are left at the camp, and the men proceed alone to the place where the Mura-mura is to be uncovered. They dig down till damp earth is reached and also what they call the excrement of the Mura-mura. The digging is then very carefully done till, as the Dieri say, the "elbow" of the Mura-mura is uncovered. Then two men stand over him, and the vein of the arm of each being opened, the blood is allowed to fall upon the Mura-mura. The Minkani song is now sung, and the men, in a state of frenzy, strike at each other with weapons, until they reach camp, distant about a mile. The women, who have come out to meet them, rush forward with loud outcries, and hold shields over their husbands to protect them, and stop the fighting. The Tidnamadukas (members of the totem-group of the Tidnama, a small frog) collect the blood dropping from their wounds, and scatter it, mixed with "excrement" from the Minkani's cave, over the sandhills.[1.2]

**Australian Aborigines
Dancing a Corroboree**

In dancing a corroboree the Australian natives imitate birds, animals, fish, and men, and also the movements of storms and floods. They accompany their dances with cries and calls, while those standing by engage in ritual chanting. *(Courtesy of Australian News and Information Bureau.)*

This was expected to make the lizards and carpet snakes more plentiful.

The Dieri had the belief that the sun sets in a hole in the earth and travels underground to the east, where it rises in the morning. They called the Milky Way the river of the sky. The sky was another country, with trees and rivers. There the spirits of the dead and the Mura-muras lived. The dead who went to the sky country found it a good place, but they could, and did, roam the earth, visiting people in sleep. If the medicine man considered a dream visit by the spirit of a dead person to be a real vision and not just a fantasy, he directed the one to whom the vision had come to leave food at the grave and to light a fire at it. This was a necessary precaution, for the dead could do harm.

Death Rituals

When a Dieri was dying, relatives separated into two groups. The members of one group, composed of the father, uncles and their children, and *noas* (could-be spouses, according to totem rules), sat down nearby and threw themselves wildly on the body as it expired.

Those of the other group, including the mother, mother's sisters, mother's brothers, younger brothers and sisters, and elder sister, remained at a distance, anxious not to look into the dead one's face. This was for protection, because the longing of the deceased might draw them in, and they might die. The men of the second group dug the grave. Those of the first group went into mourning by painting themselves with white coloring matter (gypsum); those of the second used red ochre mixed with gypsum. If the deceased was influential, food was placed at the grave for many days, and in winter a fire was lit for the ghost to warm itself by. Before the corpse was lowered into the grave, it was questioned as to who had caused its death; the corpse replied by falling from the hands of the two men holding it in the direction of the guilty person! Interpreters then tried to determine the identity of the culprit's tribe, and even the name of the individual culprit.

Then the curious regard of the Australian aborigines for the magical properties of human fat asserted itself. An old man who stood in the relation of *kami* (maternal grandfather or cousin) to the deceased stepped into the grave and cut off all of the fat adhering to the face, thighs, arms, and stomach, and passed it around to be swallowed by relatives. These relatives partook of the fat as follows: the mother ate her children, and the children their mother; a man ate his sister's husband and his brother's wife. Mother's brothers, mother's sisters, sister's children, mother's parents, or daughter's children also were eaten; but the father did not eat his children, nor the children their father. The deeper purpose of this modified cannibalism is quite evident—the desire to be at one with and to share the virtue and strength of the deceased.

When the grave was filled in, a large stack of wood was placed over it, the whole group to which the deceased belonged shifted camp, and for fear of offending the dead, no one spoke of or referred to the corpse again. Some Dieri groups feared the rising of the dead so much that they tied the toes of the corpse together, bound the thumbs behind its back, swept the ground clean around the grave at dusk, and looked for tracks in the morning. Should tracks appear, the body was reburied elsewhere, on the theory that the first grave was not satisfactory, and the dead person, not lying easy, rose and walked.

A High God?

The adult males (but not the women and the uninitiated boys) of most tribes in southeastern Australia attributed all of their customs and rituals ultimately to a high god or old man of the sky who was eternal and uncreated, having existed from the beginning of all things, and was supreme and without equal, a sort of headman of the sky country. They believed firmly that he initiated the rites and ceremonies taught to them by their ancestors and practiced so faithfully in the old days by the Australian tribes. He was called among the tribes various secret names, known only to initiated males, such as Nurrundere, Biamban, Bunjil, Mungangama, Nurelli, and the like. Often he was referred to as "Our Father." Some tribesmen felt that he was not much concerned about their doings; others, such as the Kurnai, thought he watched over them constantly. Howitt did not find clear evidence of belief in such a primeval high god among the Dieri and their neighbors of the Lake Eyre country, but that may have been

because he was not told as much as he thought he was. It begins to appear, when all of the evidence is considered, that practically all of the Australian tribes held a belief in some kind of high god, and the Dieri probably did too.

The most recent findings of anthropologists have introduced some concepts unknown to Howitt. In particular, one aspect of the evidence is given special prominence—the fact that the Australian cosmogony or account of the beginning of things generally starts with chaos, formlessness, and unconsciousness. Then comes a Dawn Period, known as the *Alcheringa* or "dream time," when certain Dawn Beings arose (they were uncreated) and, moving like figures in a dream, shaped the earth out of its preexistent materials into its present structure and established the various species and their habits and customs. The High God was the first of these Dawn Beings, and after giving instructions concerning the customs and rituals of men in after times, he ascended to the sky country, while other Dawn Beings, perhaps unable or forbidden to follow him, established totemic centers on earth.

Puberty Rites

We come finally to the fascinating subject of the initiation ceremonies so distinctive of the aborigines all over the Australian continent.

Whenever a Dieri boy or girl reached puberty, initiatory rites were planned to complete the transformation or rebirth of the boy into a man and the girl into a woman. The ceremonies for boys were especially thorough, carried out in different stages over a period of months. All of the available tribespeople from miles around gathered for the final ceremonies. It was the principal headman of the tribe who decided when the youths should be initiated. He informed the council of elders who the youths were and when the different ceremonies should take place.

The earliest ceremony had the clear significance that the boys were about to undergo a ritual death in order to rise or be reborn as men. The death symbol was a ceremony by which each boy's two lower middle-front teeth were knocked out by chisel-shaped pieces of wood. The teeth, thus dislodged, were buried twelve

Australian Rock Shelter Painting
These stylized paintings are associated either with a clan hero, the increase of natural species, or favors for the dead. This depends upon the rituals performed before them. *(Courtesy of the American Museum of Natural History. Neg. # 330835.)*

months later, eighteen inches underground. At about the same time (or as early as in the boy's ninth year), a ceremony with a similar meaning took place, that of circumcision, at which time each boy's father stooped over him and gave him a new name. Some time later there occurred, suddenly and without warning to the young men, the curious *Kulpi* rite, or ceremony of subincision, after which, and only then, the youth was considered a thorough man.

Meanwhile, there took place the rite called the *Wilyaru* ceremony, which definitely cut off a youth from childhood and from any former dependence on the womenfolk. It is described in the following way:

> A young man without previous warning is led out of the camp by some older men who are of the relation of *Neyi* (approximately cousin, in this case) to him, and not of near, but distant relationship. On the following morning, the men, old and young, except his father and elder brothers, surround him, and direct him to close his eyes. One of

the old men then binds the arm of another old man tightly with string, and with a sharp piece of flint lances the vein about an inch from the elbow, causing a stream of blood to fall over the young man, until he is covered with it, and the old man is becoming exhausted. Another man takes his place, and so on until the young man becomes quite stiff from the quantity of blood adhering to him. The reason given for this practice is that it infuses courage into the young man, and also shows him that the sight of blood is nothing, so that should he receive a wound in warfare, he may account it a matter of no moment.[13]

The deeper meaning of the rite is that the spirit and wisdom of the older men were transforming the youth into an adult by making him of one blood with them.

In the next stage of the ceremony the blood-covered youth was gashed with a sharp piece of flint on his neck and back, so that when the wounds would heal he would bear raised scars as a sign that he was a

Wilyaru. At the completion of the rite, he was given a bullroarer, a paddle-shaped slab of wood fastened to a string made of human hair from ten to twelve feet long. This was his first face-to-face encounter with the actual source of the vibrant roar that had formerly terrified him and the women of the camp when they heard it issuing from the distance of the bush. Even the men, he now learned, considered it to have supernatural effects and to speak with an authoritative voice to all living beings. It was the symbol and the voice of the Mura-muras, who had given the tribe its sacred rituals and traditions. Presented now with one that was to be returned to a secret hiding place when not used, he was taught how to whirl it and told never to show it to women or tell them about it.

After this an important psychological experience was required of him: he was sent away alone into the bush for a testing period (his "walkabout"). He was to be on his own until his wounds were healed and all of the blood with which he was covered had been worn off. He was to rehearse in his mind the lessons he had learned.

> The young man is never seen by the women, from the time he is made *Wilyaru* till the time when he returns to the camp, after perhaps many months. . . . During the time of his absence his near female relatives become very anxious about him, often asking as to his whereabouts. There is great rejoicing in the camp when the *Wilyaru* finally returns to it, and his mother and sisters make much of him.[14]

But he was now a man and did not belong to the women any more.

The Dieri and neighboring tribes united in the remaining ceremony, the *Mindari*, which was a general get-together and dancing of the initiates and the men and women and was often the occasion for amicable settlement of any disputes since the last Mindari.

Behind all of this was the running oral commentary of the older men, carefully explaining the supernatural origin and meaning of each ceremony, beginning with a retelling of the tribal myths in regard to them. The youths were admonished in their tribal duties and responsibilities. The totemic rules and relationships were defined with exactness. Plainly the laws and customs of the community were sacrosanct and

on no consideration to be departed from. The tribal morality thus came to each member of the community with the full weight of religious sanctions behind it. One might as well rebel against nature as against tribal morality!

IV. CASE STUDY: THE BAVENDA OF SOUTH AFRICA

The BaVenda (or Vhavenda) were studied by Hugh Stayt in the 1920's.* As one of many Bantu-speaking peoples of South Africa, they are known today as the Venda, and they number over half a million. They live mostly south of the Limpopo River in the Northern Transvaal, but also in Zimbabwe.

At the time of Stayt's study, the BaVenda numbered about 150,000 persons. Although many aspects of their culture have changed very little, we will use the past tense and the older name to indicate the state of magico-religious practice at the time of Stayt's study. Still showing pastoral skills, they afford an illuminating study of religion at the beginning of the agricultural stage.

The BaVenda lived in cylindrical huts, with conical grass-thatched roofs, the main structural elements being strong stakes bound together with withes. They kept large herds of cattle, by which they reckoned their wealth, though they depended for actual livelihood upon agriculture. Their crops included maize, Kaffir corn, millet, beans, pumpkins, watermelons, vegetable marrow, and sweet potatoes, the ground being worked with a hoe, mainly by women. Until the introduction of manufactured products from Europe, the native industries included such arts as weaving, skin dressing, iron smelting, hoe making, and copper refining.

The social organization was complex. Each individual was a member of a number of independent groupings. The four mentioned next are the most important. One belonged to one's own family circle and also to a large group, a patrilineal lineage, through

---

*This account, which attempts only to present the magico-religious conceptions and practices of the BaVenda, is drawn from the very inclusive book *The BaVenda*, by Hugh A. Stayt (Oxford University Press, 1928). Quotations are by permission of the publisher.

which descent, succession, and inheritance were reckoned. In addition to this, there were close affectional ties with a whole matrilineal lineage. Lastly, one belonged to a lineage group of totemic character and was called by the name of some animal, plant, or inanimate object (lion, dove, pig, elephant, goat, water buffalo, crocodile, etc.) to which one had to pay the special regard due a totem.

The attitude of the BaVenda toward the supernatural was displayed in beliefs and practices that ran the whole gamut of religious ideas, from belief in something like mana, through animism and ancestor worship, to belief in a supreme god, mysteriously presiding over his creation.

Animism and Fetishes

A fundamental concept was the belief that every object, animate or inanimate, possessed a kinetic power for good or evil. For example, when Stayt inquired about a small piece of wood worn as a charm around the neck of one of the BaVenda for protection when traveling, he discovered that

> it was taken from a bough of a tree overhanging a difficult climb on a well-frequented path. This bough was grasped by every passer-by in order to assist him over the difficult place. In this way the power of that particular bough was inordinately increased, ... and it became the obvious source from which effective charms for the timid traveller could be obtained. Conversely, the history of some powdered wood, possessing a great deal of power to do evil to the traveller, disclosed the fact that in a well-trodden path a small root caused annoyance to every passer-by, being in a spot where it almost inevitably knocked his toe. This root, unlike the friendly bough, became a source of evil power, and its wood was used for charms to bring harm to the traveller.[M1]

Shamans and Diviners

The magico-religious practices of the BaVenda were guided by specialists. The shaman (*nganga*) and the diviner (*mungoma*) were the most important persons in the BaVenda community.

The nganga had power to cure disease. His rigorous training in his craft had qualified him to be either a specialist in one family of diseases or a general practitioner treating all diseases. Through the use of such drugs, emetics, and poisons as are found in plants, he treated a variety of ailments, such as malaria, rheumatism, pneumonia, insanity, and toothache, often with success. The healing agents were supposed to contain different types of power, and by mixing them in certain ways the nganga directed their energy into the desired channels. It is important to observe, however, that the disease itself was rarely thought to be due to natural causes. It was nearly always attributed to spiritual agencies, either to the adverse influence of offended ancestral spirits or to the much more malevolent operations of the chief obsession of the BaVenda—wizards and witches.

Two Types of Witchcraft

Wizards and witches (sing. *muloi*, pl. *vhaloi*) were universally feared. Vhaloi could be of either sex, but were usually thought to be women. They were of two kinds. The first consciously and deliberately practiced the malevolent art, by themselves or with the aid of a conscienceless nganga won over by a large fee. The motive that most often moved them was hatred, an intense desire to destroy the person or persons disliked.

> A very simple way of killing an enemy is for a muloi to obtain from the nganga a death-dealing powder. Looking in the direction of the enemy he blows the powder towards him, saying at the same time, "You must die!" The closer the powder can be brought to the victim the more rapid will be his death.[M2]

The second kind of muloi was unwittingly a muloi. The circumstances surrounding cases like this were often tragic. The sense of conscious innocence was no protection from suspicion. It was believed that anyone, at any moment, could become, subconsciously or during sleep, a person possessed by some hideous spirit that had entered the body, perhaps from a hyena, crocodile, owl, or snake. During the day, such a muloi, not suspecting the possession, would be an innocuous member of the village community, but during the night would turn into a destroyer of health, property, and life! It then became an urgent matter to ferret out the evil one and exact a severe penalty. A diviner or nganga could detect a culprit by occult means, but mere appearances might have been enough to fix suspicion, as the following passage proves:

> A farmer at Lwamondo shot a crocodile, and to his extreme concern the bullet ricochetted from its hide and severely wounded a boy some distance away; this boy, when he returned to his village, after recovering from the wound, was straightway dubbed a muloi, and he and all his relatives were obliged to leave that part of the country. The people had absolutely no doubt that he was a crocodile, disguised in human form, otherwise the bullet that hit the crocodile could never have hit him as well.[M3]

The pathetic fact is that the supposed muloi was usually convinced, to his or her own great horror, that he or she was guilty as charged.

Suspected persons were brought before the diviner or mungoma, whose special function was, in distinction from that of the nganga, to determine the identity of evildoers. Because all deaths, save those of very old people, were due to witchcraft, he specialized in detecting those who had caused death. He ostensibly did all his divining by throwing a set of dice, which were read after they came to rest, or by floating seeds in a divining bowl. Woe to the person he designated guilty!

The Cult of the Dead

The cult of the dead played a primary role in the religious life of the BaVenda. To them, human souls were a combination of breath and shadow, two elements that departed from every living creature at death. The soul, after leaving the body at death, had to find a new place in which to rest. It usually lingered for a while at the grave. Soon it would search for a better abiding place. It might reveal itself to its descendants in dreams and thus make its needs known. Or it might find another body. There were isolated instances of belief among the BaVenda in reincarnation, especially of ancient chiefs, in lions, leopards, and snakes. But the most desirable state to which the souls of the dead could attain was to be held in the memory of living descendants and to be cherished and cared for by them.

When anyone died, every relative tried to be present at the deathbed; to be absent was to invite suspicion of complicity in the death. The first action after death was to cut off a portion of the garment of the deceased and preserve it for the diviner against the time when the cause of death would be determined. The relatives kept the place of burial a secret, lest an enemy might dig up the remains and practice witchcraft with them. A characteristic bit of ritual was for the eldest son to murmur over the grave of his mother, as he tossed in the first clod of earth, "You can rest in peace, my mother. So do not trouble us; I will give you all that you require."[J4]

The period of mourning, marked by shaving the heads of all of the relatives, continued until the cause of death had been discovered by the diviner and the death avenged. It was highly important thereafter to keep the ancestral spirit satisfied, for all trouble to the living was caused either by witchcraft or the dissatisfaction of the dead. So that the ancestral spirits might be focused or symbolized in something tangible, the ancestors of the father's lineage were collectively represented either by a cow and sacred black bull, regarded as the embodiments of the patrilineal spirits, or by two large, cylindrical, highly polished stones, embedded near the hut of the headman of the lineage. The spirits of the mothers were represented by a black female goat. In addition to this, the male members of the lineage were individually represented by a spear, laid up in the hut of the head of the lineage with those earlier placed there, and the female members by an iron or copper ring, or by a miniature hoe fastened to a stick and carried by a female descendant.

A Supreme Spirit

In addition to the ancestral spirits, there was a belief in a host of other powers, less defined in form and character. Some were mountain spirits, the sight of whom brought death to the traveler and spirits in streams and pools, armed with death-dealing bows and arrows. A great many spirits lived in rivers and lakes, some, or perhaps most, of whom were ancestral. But the greatest and most shadowy of all spirits was the mysterious Supreme Being, Raluvhimba. This elusive, monotheistic deity was associated with the creation of the world and was thought to live somewhere in the heavens. "The word *luvhimba*," says Stayt, "means eagle, the bird that soars aloft; the BaVenda have a very real idea of this great power travelling through the sky, using the stars and wind and rain as his instruments."[M5] Raluvhimba was seen as being remote and inscrutable, as were the similar deities of the other Bantu peoples, but the BaVenda were exceptional in the amount of respect they paid him, usually through their chiefs. They associated him with the rainmaker, Mwari, of the Bantus of Matebeleland, and sought his favors therefore especially in time of drought, the bringing on of which was credited to him. Any thunderous noise was his voice. In 1917, a meteor burst in the middle of the day at Khalavha, with a loud humming sound and a crash that sounded like thunder. The BaVenda rushed into the open in all their villages, with cries meant to express joy, clapping their hands and blowing horns, in order to give a warm welcome to the tremendous god. The same sort of demonstration followed an earthquake, the people shouting "Give us rain! Give us health!" But Raluvhimba was not approached by individuals, nor by families in private devotion; he was worshiped either by the whole people at once or by a representative of the whole people speaking in their names. Here was an unusually clear instance of a transitional practice by which an originally aloof high god became in the world religions the one true God to whom not only the group, but also individuals, could pray.

V. CASE STUDY: THE CHEROKEES OF THE SOUTHEASTERN WOODLANDS

A representative Native American religion to study is that of the Cherokees before their forced removal to Oklahoma in 1838. The Cherokee territory during the two or three centuries before their removal extended over the Appalachian highlands along the present borders of North Carolina and Tennessee and parts of South Carolina and Georgia. Although the Cherokees were quick to adopt many features of the material culture of whites, it is clear that they maintained a stable and an internally consistent conceptual system and pattern of ceremonial practice. Their Green Corn Ceremony has many parallels in the Eastern and Southeastern woodlands and, according to archaeological evidence, it has deep roots in Mississippian cultures. As a result of the efforts of Sequoyah, a Cherokee who

spoke no English, the traditions were set down in their own language, a derivative of Iroquoian. In the only case of the adoption of a writing system without immediate white prompting, Sequoyah designed and perfected an ingenious syllabary of eighty-six symbols, which became standard by 1819.*

The name Cherokee, which has fifty different spellings, seems to have been conferred by a neighboring tribe. Suggested meanings include "people of different speech," "cave people," and "fire people." But the name the Cherokees used to refer to themselves, *Ani'-yun'-wiya'*, has a satisfying clarity. It means "real people."

William Bertram, writing in 1789, commented on their physical appearance.

> The Cherokees are the largest [tallest] race of men I ever saw. They are comely as any, and their complexions are bright, being of the olive cast of the Asiatics. . . . The women are tall, slim, and of a graceful figure, and have captivating features and manners.[N1]

The Shape of the World

There is no Cherokee myth of the creation of the cosmos. The stories begin with the shaping that took place when living creatures were already in existence "beyond the arch of the sky," and the focus is upon the establishment of an orderly structure.

James Mooney's compilation on "How the Earth Was Made" starts with a domed sky of solid rock already in place. Below was a flat middle world, and below that there was a third realm. Mooney believed the original genesis myth survived only in fragments, some of them tainted by biblical ideas. In his description, we come to a time "when all was water," in the middle world, and the subsequent shaping is specific to the Cherokee habitat.

> When all was water, the animals were above in Galunl'ati, beyond the arch; but it was very much crowded, and they were wanting more room. They wondered what was below the water, and at last Dayuni'si, "Beaver's Grandchild," the little Waterbeetle, offered to go and see if it could learn. It

*The principal sources on which this account is based are William Bartram's *Observations on the Creek and Cherokee Indians* (1789), James Mooney's *Myths of the Cherokees* (1900), other early works by Mooney and Hans Olbrecht, and recent publications by John Witthoft and Charles Hudson.

darted in every direction over the surface of the water, but could find no firm place to rest. Then it dived to the bottom and came up with some soft mud, which began to grow and spread on every side until it became the island which we call the earth. It was afterward fastened to the sky with, four cords, but no one remembers who did this.[O1]

This myth goes on to describe how the Great Buzzard was sent out to make the island ready. He flew low over the soft ground, and when he reached Cherokee country he was very tired so that each downward stroke of his wings made a valley and where they turned up there was a mountain. "When the animals above saw this, they were afraid that the whole world would be mountains, so they called him back, but the Cherokee country remains full of mountains to this day.[O1]

The Sacred Ordering of Space

The two sacred numbers of the Cherokee are four and seven. The four cords suspending the island earth mark the cardinal directions that impose horizontal spatial order. The directions, in turn, are matched with colors that symbolize and govern four inevitable realities of social experience:

Beneficent: East, Red, Power (War/Success)
             South, White, Peace

Malevolent: West, Black, Death
             North, Blue, Weakness
             (War/Defeat)

According to the myth "How the World Was Made," when the animals came down to the island earth it was still dark, so they got the sun and set it to come up from below and pass from east to west just overhead. This proved to be too hot, so they adjusted it by "handbreadths" (not literal, but intervals of space) until "the seventh height" was reached. This proved to be just under the sky arch and just right. The sacred number seven often applies to a measure of intensity or a vertical hierarchy of power. As the actual number of Cherokee tribal clans, it also signifies a "just right" total.

The orderly structure of the Cherokee conceptual system establishes ideal, pure, or original states. The fiery sun cleanses the ideal upper world, while water, its opposite, cleanses the lowest realm. The diminished denizens of the compromised middle world use fire and water to improve their imperfect environment.

Categories of Living Things

In the creation myth intelligent and articulate animals and perfect plants dwelt above the sky dome in a kind of ideal preexistence. Over time they became diminished, often through failures of stamina or perseverance. "How the Earth Was Made" continues as follows:

When the animals and plants were made—we do not know by whom—they were told to watch and keep awake for seven nights, just as young men now fast and keep awake when they pray to their medicine. They tried to do this, and nearly all were awake through the first night, but the next night several dropped off to sleep, and the third night others were asleep, and then others, until, on the seventh night, of all of the animals only the owl, the panther, and one or two more were still awake. To these were given the power to see and to go about in the dark, and to make prey of the birds and animals that must sleep at night. Of the trees only the cedar, the pine, the spruce, the holly, and the laurel were awake to the end, and to them it was given to be always green and to be greatest for medicine, but to others it was said, "Because you have not endured to the end you shall lose your hair every winter."[O2]

Human beings came late, and for what might be called ecological reasons, their original powers also were diminished.

Men came after the animals and plants. At first there were only a brother and sister until he struck her with a fish and told her to multiply, and so it was. In seven days a child was born to her, and thereafter every seven days another, and they increased very fast; until there was danger that the world could not keep them. Then it was made that a woman should have only one child in a year, and it has been so ever since.[O2]

In the Cherokee conceptual system, the major categories of living things—people, animals, and plants—lived in harmony, but people increased rapidly and the animals found themselves cramped. Enmity grew between people and animals, but plants remained friendly. Animals put illnesses into people, not because they were killed to meet human needs, but rather for the indignity of being *disrespectfully* slaughtered. Plants furnished remedies for the ills put upon people.

The categories were further divided: humans into matrilineal clans; animals into four-footed, flying, and verminous groups (the latter included snakes, fish, and other denizens of the watery underworld). Preeminent in each of these categories were the deer, eagle/hawk, and rattlesnake. Plants also were divided into an elaborate system of subcategories.

Living things that do not fit neatly into the categories of a conceptual system attract attention in any culture. In literate cultures this means constant revisions and additions in the system. For a preliterate culture in which categories are not elaborately expanded, these anomalies take on dimensions of supernatural power and mythic prominence. Charles Hudson suggests that violations of the categories of order were given prominence in order to highlight the horror of chaotic admixture. "Although it may seem paradoxical, these anomalous beings in the Southeastern Indian belief system were by-products of their search for order and intellectually they helped to sustain that order."[P1]

The Cherokees attributed special powers and significance to such anomalies as the following: four-footed creatures that fly (the bat and the flying squirrel); plants that capture and eat insects (Venus's-flytrap and the pitcher plant); and water beetles that "walk" and also swim under water. Thus there is a myth explaining how the eagles and hawks fitted wings for bats and flying squirrels so they could play in their lacrosse-style ball game, and how expert they proved to be. A Cherokee ball player appropriates the magic by attaching a piece of bat's wing to his ball stick. The anomalous plants and animals offered special benefits: Venus's-flytrap roots had extraordinary medicinal powers, and the water beetle, by spinning a basket on her back, devised a way to bring fire to humankind.

Kinship with Animals

Three of the seven Cherokee clans bore animal names: Wolf, Deer, and Bird. Two clan names signify Paint and Long-hair; the meaning of the names of the remaining two are uncertain. As compared to the elaborate totemic relationships found among some other Native American groups, the ties between clans and their named ref-

Sacred Anomaly
Water Spider (fire bringer)

erents were relatively weak; however, myths of the region suggest descent from the totem or attribute the clan name to abilities or mannerisms shown by its early members. There are few taboos and special rites required of clans because of their names. But the kinship between all humankind and certain animals was important, not only in light of potential harm from the species, but also out of a kind of empathic imagination.

The bear, for example, as an anomalous creature (four footed, yet often walking upright), was in a special kinship class. His diet was similar to that of humans, and his footprints and his feces resembled those of humans—points of importance among hunters who identify animals by their spoor. Some myths spoke of bears as having been descended from a primal forest-loving boy (and later his clan) who isolated themselves from other humans by seven days of fasting and then taking to the woods and eating only what was to become the diet of the bears. In a myth concerning the origin of diseases, the bear is the only animal that does not sponsor a disease to put upon humankind. He gets no credit for this, but is deemed foolish for not invoking clan retaliation. Therefore, "the hunter does not even ask the bear's pardon when he kills one."[O3]

One touching story tells of bears trying unsuccessfully to use bows and arrows. In the myth "The Bear Man," a human meets a bear who takes him as a guest to a council of bears. (Even before they see him, the bears ask each other, "What's that stink in here?")

[After a dance] the bears noticed the hunter's bow and arrows, and one said, "This is what men use to kill us. Let us see if we can manage them, and maybe we can fight man with his own weapons." So they took the bow and arrows from the hunter to try them. They fitted the arrow and drew back the string, but when they let go it caught in their long claws and the arrows dropped to the ground. They saw that they could not use the bow and arrows and gave them back to the man.[03]

In another account, one of the bears said, "One of us has already died to furnish the bowstring, and if we now cut off our claws we must all starve together. It is better to trust to the teeth and claws that nature gave us, for it is plain that man's weapons were not intended for us."[04]

Dimensions of the Spirit World

The Cherokees took for granted the animistic premise that each creature has a soul or spirit, a double, separable from the flesh-and-blood body. Fears of reprisal for the killing of animals, partly deflected by appropriate apologies and ritual countermeasures, were further softened by a corollary view that some spirits have an allotted life span such that their "killed" bodies would reincarnate themselves from blood spots left behind. Mighty warriors were sometimes believed to be invulnerable because their spirits withdrew from their bodies.

There are myths of a variety of categories of spirit beings: Little People much like the leprechauns, and whole clans of "immortals" (*Nunne'hi*), who made appearances and behaved as though they were ordinary people but who could also vanish at will. Sometimes they arrived in the midst of battles, aided the Cherokees, and then mysteriously disappeared.

The Sun and the Moon

Supreme among the spirits was the Sun, generally considered female, addressed in some rituals as "The Apportioner" (of day and night, and perhaps of good and evil fortune, life and death). Relationship to the Sun is not described in abstractions such as all powerful or all knowing, but simply as kinship. In myths, the Sun speaks of people as her maternal grandchildren. Her consort, the Moon, calls people "my younger brothers," employing the term used by a male. The coupling that produced their offspring occurred at night.

The Sun was a young woman and lived in the East, while her brother the Moon lived in the West. The girl had a lover who used to come every month in the dark of the moon to court her. He would come at night and leave before daylight . . . and he would not tell her his name. . . . At last she hit upon a plan to find out, so the next time he came she slyly dipped her hand into the cinders and ashes of the fireplace and rubbed it over his face, saying, "Your face is cold; you must have suffered from the wind," and pretending to be very sorry for him, but he did not know that she had ashes on her hand. . . .

The next night when the Moon came up in the sky his face was covered with spots, and then his sister knew he was the one who had been coming to see her. He was so much ashamed to have her know it that he kept as far away as he could at the other end of the sky all the night. Ever since he tries to keep a long way behind the Sun, and when he does sometimes have to come near her in the west he makes himself as thin as a ribbon so that he can hardly be seen.[05]

Priests, Witches, Medicine, and Conjury

There are mythic references to a time when there was a hereditary order, a clan from which priests were elected. Tradition holds that these priests became overbearing and abused their authority, especially with regard to women. Finally, the abduction and violation of the wife of the brother of a high chief led to an uprising in which every member of the order was slain. In later times, the practice of sorcery (or conjury, as it is called in southern Appalachia), dream interpretation, and divination was distributed among a variety of persons in all of the clans.

As is often the case in the identification of shamans, the Cherokees were likely to recognize special spirit powers in individuals marked by some deviation from ordinary norms: a twin, especially the younger (the extra), or a person with a salient talent or physical abnormality. Humans or supernaturals who demonstrated extraordinary powers were called *ada'wehi*, "wonder worker."

Healings utilized herbs and medicines administered by family members or priests. Although the medicines may in fact have been adopted for their proven effectiveness, the rationale for their use was usually in terms of analogy: sympathetic magic was applied for productive or aversive effects. Yellow jaundice was treated with medicine made from yellow roots or flowers. A pregnant woman was given a decoction of slippery elm bark (for a slippery birth canal) and it would be taboo for her to eat speckled trout lest her child would be speckled with birthmarks. Persons subject to rheumatism were not to touch animals like squirrels or cats (animals that hump their backs up in rheumatic-like postures).[P2]

Anyone might incur the burden of a food taboo, often as a penalty for subjecting some creature to an indignity. One myth recounts how a man who failed to heed a *gaktun'ta* (taboo) against eating squirrel endured the horror of watching himself turn slowly into a snake.

Frequently the application of conjury combined the use of physical substances with incantations and symbolic acts rooted in the conceptual system. The cure for rheumatism (an "intrusion" sponsored by deer) might involve potions made from "bear's bed fern" (deer keep away from bears) rubbed onto the body and a ceremonial chant summoning mythic dogs (the natural enemy of deer) from the four primary directions governing the earth: the Red Dog of the East, the Blue Dog of the North, the Black Dog of the West, and the White Dog of the South. Each is hailed for having "drawn near to hearken," addressed as a great wonder worker and petitioned.

> "... O great *ada'wehi*, you never fail in anything. O, appear and draw near running, for your prey never escapes. You are now to remove the intruder. Ha! You have settled a small part of it far off there at the end of the earth."[Q1]

The ceremony would be repeated at dawn, at midmorning, and at high noon—times when the Sun (Beneficence) was in the ascendancy.

The use of conjury to win the affections of a potential lover or alienate a rival was common. The following is a formula to be recited by a man washing himself in a stream:

> "Listen! O, now instantly, you have drawn near to hearken, O *Ageyaguga* [the Moon]. You have come to put your red spittle upon my body. My name is _____. The blue has affected me. You have come

and clothed me with a red garment. She is of the _____ clan. She has become blue. You have directed her paths straight to where I have my feet, and I shall feel exultant. Listen!"[Q2]

Charles Hudson points out that the appeal is to the moon because it was thought to influence women. Saliva is rubbed over the face or other parts of the body because it is the essence of being. Red is attractive to women, and blue is an emblem of lonely longing for the opposite sex.[P3]

Hudson also points out that the line between white (beneficial) magic and black (destructive) magic was not sharply drawn in Cherokee culture. The term for a witch applied to either sex, but the distinction between a priest and a witch was important. While a priest might sometimes devise negative conjury, his grounds were fundamentally meant to be moral or legal. Witches, on the other hand, were thought to be by nature amoral; they shortened the lives of others in order to add to their own lifespans. They were imposters in human form and could change themselves into other animals to accomplish their selfish goals. In a case of outright murder, the killer's clan was obligated to execute the killer or pay a life for a life, but in the case of killing a witch, no such obligation existed, and the clan of the witch had no vengeance claim.

Quartz crystals were widely used in *divination*. Held up to the light, the crystals flashed propitious or ominous colors. Individual warriors consulted them to learn whether they should go forward or retire. Red and black beads held between the fingers of a diviner gave good or evil signals by what was believed to be the spontaneous movement of one or the other. Dream interpretations were the most specific. Bad news indicators were more common than good ones: dreams of fish and snakes foreshadowed loss of appetite, sickness, and death; dreams of eagles required the sponsoring of an elaborate and a costly eagle dance to avert death in the family.

Rites of Passage

Birth

Birthing, which took place in a menstrual hut, was followed immediately by cleansing with water and a rubdown with bear oil. The father fasted for four days, and couples were forbidden to touch each other or take food together for three months. Male children were wrapped in the skins of the cougar (predator) and females in the skins of deer or bison (food source). Infants were bound to a cradle board, the band across the forehead drawn tight enough to flatten the head shape—a custom discontinued in the colonial period.[P4]

Puberty Rites

Ranking among boys was established by competitive activities such as use of the bow, staying on watch all night, tolerating pain, running, and ball games. Later, such ranking would extend to war titles and seating in deliberative councils. Girls learned cooking, pottery, basketry, and garden tending. At the onset of menses, they were initiated into the taboos and rules connected with the menstrual hut.

Marriage

As one might expect in a matrilineal culture, the women of the lineage played the central role in marriage arrangement. William Bartram gives the following account in notes added to a manuscript:

> A man who wants a wife never applies in person; he sends his sister, his mother, or some other female relation to the female relations of the woman he names; they consult the brothers and uncles on the maternal side, and sometimes the father; but this is a compliment only, as his approbation or opposition is of no avail. If the party applied to approved the match, they reply accordingly to the woman who made the application. The bridegroom then gets together a blanket, and such other articles of clothing as he is able to do, and sends them by the women to the females of the family of the bride. If they accept them, the match is made; and the man may then go to her house as soon as he chooses. And when he has built a house, sown his crop and gathered it in, then made his hunt and brought home the meat, and put all this in the possession of his wife, the ceremony ends, and they are married.[N2]

Under the matrilineal social structure of the Cherokees, the marriage bond was not primary. One's first allegiance was to the lineage and not to the spouse, a fact that accorded the same level of dignity and freedom to males and females. As Hudson puts it,

"A Cherokee woman . . . could more or less go to bed with whomever she chose, and her husband could do little or nothing about it."[P5]

Death

Burial customs reflected both the animistic and the purity/pollution conceptual frames of the Cherokees. The spirit of a dead person lived on and needed respectful attention. Widows were expected to make their grief visible through unkempt hair and unattractive clothing. The basic fear was that, if a ghost sensed disrespect, it would linger and cause illnesses and misfortune rather than going off to *tsuginai,* the ghost country. In addition to flattering attention, specific aversive steps were sometimes taken: burning cedar twigs, making loud noises, running about and shouting to drive off the ghost. Elaborate burial mounds testify to tribal mortuary practice in Mississipian times, but, in the centuries just before removal to Oklahoma, ceremonies and burials seem to have been dispersed among clans and individuals. The member of the lineage who actually handled the corpse became polluted and needed special cleansing rituals. A Moravian diary reports the following:

> Among the Indians a body is given to a certain man for burial. He buries it in complete secrecy but must remain apart from other people for several days and may not enter any house. His food is passed to him in vessels from which no one else may afterward eat.[R]

Rites of Intensification and Renewal

Most important among Cherokee ceremonies were: (1) rites to heighten resolve and increase physical stamina for warfare (or, on a smaller scale, for group hunting), and (2) the annual Green Corn Ceremony for cleansing, disease avoidance, and renewal at the transition point in the maize-growing cycle.

Warfare

The principal purpose of war was to make a forceful reply to an offense, to terrorize enemies, and to keep them at a distance. The Cherokees did not employ warfare to extend their territories or to expand their economic (hunting) domains. In the conceptual system, warfare was a *pure* activity, a moral obligation to preserve order and balance, not an attempt to steal lands or permanently subjugate other tribes. Misunderstandings with colonists illustrate this clan logic. Charles Hudson cites the following example:

> If a British colonist killed a Cherokee, the Cherokees were likely to go to war against the British people, but if a Cherokee killed a British colonist, the British did not usually go to war against the Cherokees but demanded instead that the Cherokees hand over the man who did the killing, a demand that was as frustrating as it was incomprehensible to the Cherokees.[P6]

The British, in other words, did not play by clan retaliation rules: One should either blame all Cherokees and therefore make war, or blame the individual and demand that *the lineal clan* make recompense or execute the offender or a surrogate. The tribal chiefdom had no authority to force a clan to turn someone over to outsiders.

Under the matrilineal system, property rights were the domain of women, and senior Beloved Women held high places in tribal councils. Since war captives were potential property or adoptive family members, their fate was generally left to the senior Beloved Woman of a clan: Should the captive be killed, kept as a slave, or adopted?

Given that the aims of war were to preserve the clarity and balance of moral order, intensification rites stressed purgation and abstention. Warriors fasted briefly, abstained from sex, and took great quantities of "black drink," a tea made largely from roasted leaves and twigs of a holly (*ilex vomitoria*), which induced vomiting. The drink was rich in caffeine, a general stimulant and an intensifier for psychic preparation through tales of war and death. The purifying sacred fire of the war ceremony provided coals to be taken along on the expedition in a special clay box, and members of the war party took care not to sleep directly on the ground, lest their strength be sapped.

Myths Concerning Food Sources

The mythic rationale for the need to propitiate and celebrate food sources makes it clear that in the ideal condition of the distant past humankind had an abundance of food, but through misdeeds ease of access was forfeited. The myth "Kanati and Selu: the Origin of Game and Corn" tells us that Kanati, the Lucky Hunter, had access to a cavern in which all of the game animals were confined. All he had to do was make arrows and a bow, lift the rock door, and take what he needed. Trouble began when his at-home-dwelling son met and began to run with his "He-who-grew-up-wild" twin. By spying on their father, they learned how to make bows and arrows, discovered the cavern, and let all the game rush out. Kanati ruefully observed, ". . . after this when you want a deer to eat, you will have to hunt all over the woods for it."[O6]

Similarly, the boys spied on their mother Selu ("Corn") when she went to the storehouse. They saw her rub her body and ripe corn fell from it into a basket. "Our Mother is a witch," they concluded (because she was feeding them disguised excrement?), "We must kill her." Back at the house she knew their thoughts and said,

> ". . . when you have killed me, clear a large piece of ground in front of the house and drag my body seven times around the circle. Then drag me seven times over the ground inside the circle, and stay up all night and watch, and in the morning you will have plenty of corn."[O7]

The boys killed her but cleared only seven little patches of ground. "This is why corn grows only in a few places and not all over the world." They dragged the body of Selu and wherever her blood fell corn sprang up, but instead of dragging seven times they dragged only twice, ". . . which is the reason the Indians still work their crop but twice."[L8] The soil-enriching and protective property of Selu's blood may account for the fact that a woman from the menstrual hut should walk circuits around her cornfield at night.

The Green Corn Ceremony

The pivotal importance of the Green Corn Ceremony in the Cherokee calendar is summed up by Charles Hudson, who observes that one would have to combine Thanksgiving, New Year's, Yom Kippur, Lent, and Mardi Gras observances to approach its equal. In the ceremony one finds nearly all of the major elements of the Cherokee worldview. Those things that distinguish the human being from other animals are in the foreground:

Protecting the Cornfields

For the Cherokees, blood had both productive and aversive power. On the one hand, the sacrificial blood of the Corn Mother produced fertility. On the other hand, the menstrual blood taboo could be used to protect a crop. Here a Cherokee woman leaves the menstrual hut in the dark of night to drag her cloak in a circuit around the cornfield leaving a trail to avert blight and ward off small animals and vermin. *(Engraving by John Smallie/Drawn by Captain S. Eastman, U.S. Army. From H. R. Schoolcraft,* Indian Tribes of the U.S., *Vol. 5, Lippincott, 1855, p. 71.)*

the fire builder, the bow hunter, and the corn grower. Fire, the purifier, is repurified; the roles of the two sexes and their links to the two great food-providing activities are reaffirmed and celebrated. Motifs of penitence, forgiveness, and new beginnings are prominent.

The Green Corn Ceremony, or Busk, took place at the first ripening of the new crop, most commonly in August. It was observed throughout the eastern woodlands from the Iroquois of the north to the Seminoles of Florida. The differences between the Cherokee ceremonies and those of their neighbors, the Creeks, are difficult to reconstruct in detail, but a comprehensive study by John Witthoft has enumerated certain elements described next as common to virtually all of the Southeastern tribes.[5]

The ceremonies, which might vary from three to as many as eight days, began with the cleansing of the central ground in front of the town rotunda or temple mound, removing litter, food bits, and even surface soil for ritual disposal. Guards were posted to keep polluted persons or animals, especially dogs, out of the area.

In the ritual of fire renewal, all old fires were extinguished and hearths cleaned. According to Bar-

tram, old clothing, household items, and excess supplies were put in a common pile and burned. Then the high priest of fire making twirled a dowel in a partly drilled-out piece of poplar, willow, or white oak and ignited splinters of pitchpine at the smoking friction point. The new fire was placed in a ceremonial bowl (reminiscent of the myth of the water spider bringing fire to humans in a bowl on her back), and households were invited to take fresh fire to their hearths. On the central ground subsidiary fires were kindled along the axis of each of the four color/directions. Individuals might rub ashes of the new fire on the chin, neck, and belly. There were eloquent exhortations and warnings: the sacred fire would punish those who continued in impurity or in immoral behavior.

In the daytime, males sat in the square after cleansing themselves internally by the black drink emetic. They fasted for one or more days. At night, there were series of dances, some by men, some by women, some by both sexes in countergroups, and some "friendship dances," in which men and women alternated. Titles of the songs and dances, such as a "bear dance," "buffalo dance," "meal dance," and "small frog dance," suggest that the whole pantheon of upper beings were being honored. All-night dancing recalled the admonitions in a myth to keep watch so that corn would grow. (Similarly, cobs from the first tasting would be preserved reverently for four days commemorating the body of the Corn Goddess Selu, which lay on the ground for four days after she was killed.)

It was strictly forbidden to eat any of the new crop before reaching the proper point in the ceremonial. Before new corn was consumed, there were rituals of skin scratching (to let out bad blood) and the cleansing ritual of "going to water," formalized ceremonial dipping under the water of a river seven times. Just as failure to take aversive steps after killing a deer would bring on rheumatism, the eating of new corn without completing the proper rites would lead to proliferation of intestinal worms. In addition to ritual, special medicines were used to prevent this. Since parasites are unlikely to be acquired from corn, it is possible that these measures may have emerged out of a need for symmetry, a parallel to the negative consequences of taking animals without precautionary steps. Perhaps the mythic origin of corn as excreta from the body of Selu suggested worms as the form of retaliation.

The Green Corn Ceremonial marked an annual new beginning and was an occasion for amnesties. Wrongdoers who had fled to peace towns or refuge towns were allowed to return, and couples who wished to dissolve their marriages became free to remarry. In summary, the ceremonies repaired the ties between humans, animals, and the ideal upper world so that all the categories of existence were affirmed to be in order.

GLOSSARY

animism the attribution of a discrete indwelling spirit to every material form of reality such as plants, stones, and so on, and to natural phenomena such as storms, earthquakes, and the like

aversive magic the use of extraordinary materials, rites, and spells to ward off or destroy agents deemed harmful

contagious magic a form of sympathetic magic based on the view that things once conjoined continue to influence each other when separated; thus magic performed on a lock of hair may affect the person from whom it came

cosmogony a theory or myth regarding the origin of the universe, the earth, and living beings

divination the employment of magical practices (lottery, augury, or special psychic powers, etc.) for the purpose of gaining knowledge of future events or events unknowable by ordinary investigation

fetishism veneration and use of natural or prepared material objects (fetishes) imbued with special potency (mana) for purposes of averting evil effects or acquiring values

mana an invisible potency believed to inhabit extraordinary and awesome persons, objects, or phenomena

necromancy communication with the dead for purposes of divination or magically influencing the course of natural events

productive magic the use of extraordinary materials, rites, or spells to gain desired products, values, or effects

rites of intensification prescribed forms of ceremony, worship, or veneration used for purposes of strengthening communal values or increasing spiritual potency

rites of passage prescribed forms of ceremony used to mark and celebrate significant events in the life stages of an individual: birth, puberty, marriage, ordination to a special role, death, and so on

shamanism a mode of dealing with the spirit world through the agency of an individual set apart as spirit possessed and specially equipped to deal with superhuman forces (The term shaman is generically applied to healers, exorcists, sorcerers, magicians, fetish priests, and the like.)

sympathetic magic the effort to control events, animals, or persons by extraordinary means that are imitative or analogical in form (A doll or effigy, for example, may be stabbed or burned as a means of casting a spell upon a living being, or red ochre powder may be used to restore the glow of life to a pallid body.)

taboo a strict prohibition applied to a person, a thing, or an action (the taboo is mandated by a superhuman sacred law and the exclusions from use, approach, or mention are tacitly accepted as beyond rational explanation or challenge.)

totemism the recognition of a special relationship between a human group or an individual and a class or species of animals, plants, or inanimate objects (The ritual relationship is usually seen as mandated by superhuman forces for the mutual benefit of the humans and the totemic objects.)

Bygone Religions That Have Left Their Mark on the West

When scores of local tribes coalesce into nations, the same elements that made up their primal beliefs and practices reappear in combined and more articulated forms. Developed religions do not withdraw their roots from primal soil. And so we may be sure that there were higher beings not unlike the Mura-muras of the Dieri, Raluvhimba of the BaVenda, and the Corn Mother of the Cherokees, among the predecessor primal religions out of which Ishtar, Zeus, and Odin emerged as composite divinities. Though some of the developed religions of the ancient world have disappeared, their heritage, in turn, infuses the religions of today.

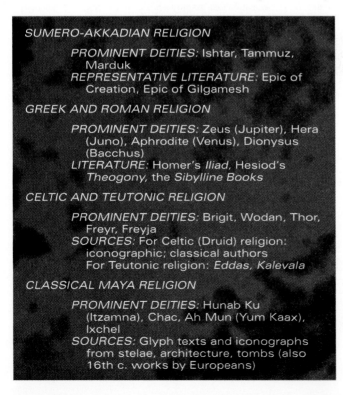

SUMERO-AKKADIAN RELIGION

    PROMINENT DEITIES: Ishtar, Tammuz, Marduk
    REPRESENTATIVE LITERATURE: Epic of Creation, Epic of Gilgamesh

GREEK AND ROMAN RELIGION

    PROMINENT DEITIES: Zeus (Jupiter), Hera (Juno), Aphrodite (Venus), Dionysus (Bacchus)
    LITERATURE: Homer's *Iliad,* Hesiod's *Theogony,* the *Sibylline Books*

CELTIC AND TEUTONIC RELIGION

    PROMINENT DEITIES: Brigit, Wodan, Thor, Freyr, Freyja
    SOURCES: For Celtic (Druid) religion: iconographic; classical authors
    For Teutonic religion: *Eddas, Kalevala*

CLASSICAL MAYA RELIGION

    PROMINENT DEITIES: Hunab Ku (Itzamna), Chac, Ah Mun (Yum Kaax), Ixchel
    SOURCES: Glyph texts and iconographs from stelae, architecture, tombs (also 16th c. works by Europeans)

I. MESOPOTAMIA

Mesopotamia, lying fertile and flat between the twin rivers that watered it, was open to invasions and attack from every quarter. The temporal and the changeful were always present. Nothing remained stable for long; the pleasures of life had to be quickly snatched.

Or let us state facts in this way: the prehistoric hunters and fishers in the swamps at the conjunction of the Tigris and Euphrates Rivers gave place to a culture of villages, each with its temple; then villages, layer on layer, gave place to, or came under the dominance of, cities—Erech, Eridu, Lagash, Ur, Nippur, and others. Cities fought each other until one dominated another, and the Sumerian kingdoms rose, to be followed and absorbed by Semitic empires, and these by the Persian. Also in the same way the gods of the fields and streams and those of the sky took to the towns, organized themselves

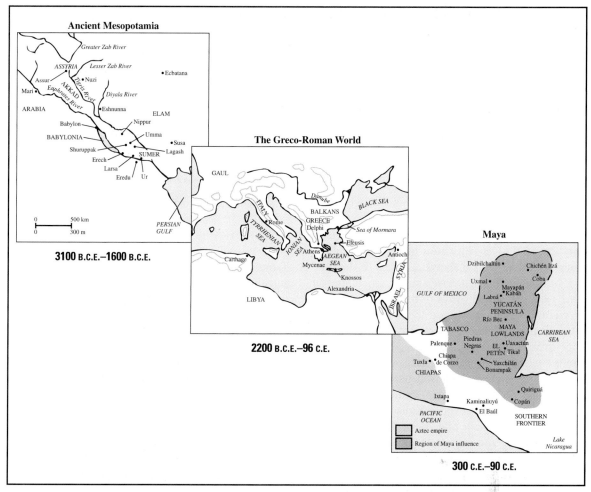

Ancient Mesopotamia, 3100 B.C.E.–1600 B.C.E.; The Greco–Roman World, 2200 B.C.E.–96 C.E.; Maya 300 C.E.–90 C.E.

into a superstate with governing power lodged in a council of the gods, fought, made love, and merged into a vast pantheon with innumerable names.

The Sumero-Akkadian Pantheon*

It has been said that there were nearly two thousand deities! Many of them, however, had only the status of stewards, servants, messengers, and warriors of the greater gods. Every part of nature was represented. Six deities eventually became important over wide areas. Each was the deity of a big city. An (Anu), the sky god, was the chief deity of Uruk and nominally still the "pristine king and ruler" of the gods, but he was over-

shadowed by Enlil (Bel), the god of wind and flood, who became the god of the lands beneath, conferring power upon kings, and a great warrior, the chief deity at Nippur. His son Nanna (Sin), the moon god, reigned at Ur. Utu, who later took the Semitic name Shamash, was the sun god at Larsa, and when Larsa

*The Sumerian pantheon, the first to be formulated in Mesopotamia, was largely adopted by the Semitic-speaking Akkadians when the latter established themselves in the northern half of the area, hence the title of the present topic. Upon first mention in the following account, the Sumerian names will be given first, with the Akkadian equivalents in parentheses. It will be noted in the parentheses that the Sumerian name is modified in some cases, but in other cases it is replaced by a new name, presumably Semitic. Only a few Sumerian myths survive intact. The rest are in fragments; we shall therefore be considering the Akkadian versions of these myths and the Akkadian names.

was destroyed, at Sippar. Enki (Ea), the water god, who also was the wisdom god, made his home in Eridu. Ninhursag (Aruru), also known as Nintu and Ninmah, the mother goddess, prevailed at Kish.

It was usual for the male deities, major or minor, to have a consort, worshiped in a separate sanctuary built on to his temple. To this rule, there were some exceptions. In the Sumerian myth the mother-goddess Ninhursag was unmarried, and An's wife had no importance, her place being taken by her daughter, the virgin love goddess and mistress of the sky, Inanna. The gods were hospitable to one another. No regnant deity excluded other cults from his or her city. Even though the chief temple always belonged to the chief god, other deities might have smaller sanctuaries in other parts of the city. (Thus in the Akkadian period Sin received worship in Harran and Shamash in Uruk, although they were not the regnant deities.) Apparently they deserved a place there, because, as the Semitic terminology had it, each was the *bel* or "owner" of a large tract of land nearby and should have a proper residence (temple) in the nearest city.

It was natural that the Akkadians should group these deities into triads and divine families. In due course Anu, Bel, and Ea were believed to divide the physical universe among them as the rulers, respectively, of heaven above, earth beneath, and the waters on and under the earth. Another (and later) triad had a more agricultural significance. It was composed of Shamash, the sun god Sin, the moon god, and Ishtar, the Semitic goddess of fertility, who, with unequaled ability to keep her name and functions dominant, was mentioned separately in the listings and not identified with the mother-goddess Ninhursag and her aliases Ninmah, Nintu, Mami, Aruru, and others. (Just as Inanna of Uruk, the Sumerian queen of the heavens [Venus] and goddess of love and fertility, was mentioned separately and not as a mother goddess.)

Ishtar, a Universal Goddess

Of all the deities who emerged in Sumer and Akkad, Ishtar was to come closest to being universally worshiped. As a virginal love goddess, a queen of fertility, and even a woman warrior, she was the focal female deity adored in cults that spread to all sectors of the fertile crescent and beyond. By her attachment to

Enlil (Bel) God of Storm and Flood

Tammuz (Sumerian *Dumuzi*), the god of the spring sun and its awakening in soil and beast, she established herself as a great lover in her own right. As the goddess of fertility, she gave children to women and life to vegetation. As the planet Venus, she was "the queen of heaven and the stars." Strangely, she also was a cruel warrior goddess, at least among the Akkadians. Her worship was destined to spread far to the west, to Palestine and to Egypt. Even the Zoroastrians were unable to resist her, and after changing her name to Anahita, "the Spotless One" (and thus purifying her!), they gave to her almost as great a prominence as to Ohrmazd himself. We shall meet her again.

Marduk of Babylon

The greatest rival of Ishtar was Marduk. His prominence may be assigned, curiously enough, to sheer political good fortune. It happened that the sixth king of the first dynasty of Babylon, Hammurabi, the same who issued the world-famous law code, made this city the capital of a powerful kingdom stretching from the Persian Gulf to the central provinces embraced between the Tigris and Euphrates. It was an achievement of permanent significance, for Babylon thus became and was to remain, through twenty centuries of change, one of the great cities of the world. And with its rise to power, Marduk, its god, rose to greatness too. Not prominent before, he practically absorbed the surrounding gods. Not only did he link to himself Ea of Eridu as his father (whereby he absorbed Ea's earlier son, Ninurta, a vegetation and war god) and make Nabu of Barsippa, the fire god, his son and the scribe of the gods, he also absorbed from them some of their functions—the wisdom of Ea's and Nabu's power over destiny. The chief attributes of Enlil of Nippur also were transferred to him (including the victory over Tiamat, described in the next section), so that he might be acknowledged as the lord of the heavens. Finally, the religious literature of Babylon was extensively revised to give him the prominent role his city demanded for him.

The Babylonian Myths and Epics

Evidence from cuneiform inscriptions shows that the Sumerians and Akkadians had fertile imaginations. They loved to tell stories about their gods and goddesses. Although it does not serve our purpose to explore the whole of this mythology, the following episodes, in part because of their intrinsic qualities but especially because of the striking parallel to the flood story of the Hebrew Scriptures, are of more than usual interest.

1. The Creation

The Sumerians, we have learned, believed that the first thing that existed was the primordial sea (associated with the goddess Nammu), from which emerged heaven (An) and earth (Ki), united as though they were a large mountain in the midst of the sea. An and Ki produced within or between them Enlil, air, and as the air began to stir in the darkness within the mountain it separated sky and earth. Then, to see better, Enlil begot the moon-god Nanna, who in turn begot the sun-god Utu, presumably to make the light brighter. By this time the world had come into being, for the sky (An) by expansion of the air below (Enlil) had reached a great height, and the earth (Ki) had made a solid floor below, with sun and moon to bring light. When air moved across earth (or when Enlil united with his mother Ki) and received the aid of water (Enki), plants and animals came into being. Finally, humankind was created by the joint efforts of Nammu, the primeval sea, Ninmah, mother earth, and Enki, the water god.[A]

But according to another legend (Akkadian or Semitic in origin?), the present world order was formed after a primeval struggle for control of the tablets of destiny between the dragons of darkness and chaos, led by the bird-god Zu (or in other accounts by Tiamat) and the gods of light and order, headed by

Ninurta, the war god. But the Babylonian priests recast whatever materials they inherited, and they made Marduk both the hero of the struggle against chaos and also the creator of the world and of humankind. Their story began with Apsu, the god of fresh water, and Tiamat, the dragon of the unbounded salt water (chaos). By their intermingling, this pair over a period of years produced the gods, but the youthful gods were so lively and eager to be creative that Apsu, who preferred tranquillity, could not rest and resolved to destroy them, against the wish of Tiamat.

> Apsu, opening his mouth,
> Said unto resplendent Tiamat:
> 'Their ways are verily loathsome unto me.
> By day I find no relief, nor repose by night.
> I will destroy, I will wreck their ways,
> That quiet may be restored. Let us have rest!'
> As soon as Tiamat heard this,
> She was wroth and called out to her husband.
> She cried out aggrieved, as she raged all alone,
> Injecting woe into her mood:
> 'What? Should we destroy that which we have built?
> Their ways indeed are most troublesome, but let us
>   attend kindly!'[B1]

But before Apsu could execute his plan, he was destroyed by Ea, who got wind of it, whereupon Tiamat resolved on avenging him. She created monsters to be her allies, and both Anu and Ea fled before her. Not until Marduk, who was assured by the gods that he would be their chief, came forth to meet her in combat was she halted.

> Then advanced Tiamat and Marduk counselor of
>   the gods;
> To the combat they marched, they drew nigh to battle.
> The lord spread out his net and caught her,
> The storm wind that was behind him, he let loose in
>   her face.
> When Tiamat opened her mouth to its widest,
> He drove in the evil wind, that she could not close
>   her lips . . .
> He made her powerless, he destroyed her life;
> He cast down her body and stood upon it.[C1]

After next subduing the monsters she had arrayed against him, Marduk turned back to Tiamat and split her open like a shellfish into two halves. With one half he made the canopy, which holds back the waters that are above the heavens; with the other half he formed the covering, which lies above the waters under the earth. He constructed stations for the gods in the heavens. With Ea's help he made humankind from the blood of the god Kingu, Tiamat's ally and second husband. Seeing what he had done, the delighted gods bestowed on him many titles as their undisputed leader and king.[B2]

2. The Flood

The original flood story was Sumerian and came out of grim experiences with the overflowing of the two rivers. Several of the later versions of the tale, mostly fragmentary, have been handed down to us. The finest of these forms part of the Gilgamesh epic, into which it was inserted as an interesting interpolation. According to this narrative, the gods decided in anger to send a flood upon the earth. Their secret decision was revealed to one man. The good god Ea felt kindly toward Utnapishtim and told him about it. The man immediately proceeded to build an ark.

> 120 cubits high were its sides,
> 140 cubits reached the edge of its roof.[C2]

As Utnapishtim later told Gilgamesh (we quote in part),

> I brought up into the ship my family and household,
> The cattle of the field, the beasts of the field, craftsmen,
>   all of them I brought in.
> A fixed time had Shamash appointed saying
> 'When the ruler of darkness sends a heavy rain,
> Then enter into the ship and close the door.'
> The appointed time came near, . . .
> There came up from the horizon a black cloud.
> Adad thundered within it . . .
> Adad's storm reached unto heaven,
> All light was turned into darkness . . .
> The water climbed over the mountains . . .
> The gods feared the deluge,
> They drew back, they climbed up to the heaven of Anu.
> The gods crouched like a dog, they cowered by the wall.
> Ishtar cried like a woman in travail,
> The queen of the gods cried with a loud voice:

Marduk Battling with Tiamat
Marduk, winged and carrying a sword and sickle, assaults Tiamat with double tridents. Tiamat, on her part, retreats, with gaping jaws and widespread lion claws, on bird feet and with wings outstretched. From a wall panel in the palace of Ashurnasiripal II, 885–860 B.C.E. *(Drawing based on an original in the British Museum, London.)*

> 'The former race is turned to clay.'
> When the seventh day drew nigh, the tempest ceased;
>   the deluge,
> Which had fought like an army, ended.
> Then rested the sea, the storm fell asleep, the flood
>   ceased . . .
> All mankind was turned to clay . . .
> I opened the window and the light fell upon my face,
> I bowed, I sat down, I wept,
> And over my face ran my tears,
> I looked upon the world, all was sea.
> After twelve days (?) the land emerged.
> To the land of Nisir the ship made its way,
> The mount of Nisir held it fast, that it moved not . . .
> I sent forth a dove and let her go.
> The dove flew to and fro,
> But there was no resting place and she returned.
> I sent forth a swallow and let her go,
> The swallow flew to and fro,
> But there was no resting place and she returned.
> I sent forth a raven and let her go,
> The raven flew away, she saw the abatement of the waters,
> She drew near, she waded, she croaked, and came
>   not back.

*Then I sent everything forth to the four quarters of
    heaven, I offered sacrifice,
I made a libation upon the mountain's peak.*[C3]

The close parallels to the Hebrew Scriptures are obvious.

3. Ishtar's Descent to the Land of the Dead

If the obscure reference to Tammuz at the end of the story of Ishtar's descent is correctly interpreted, Ishtar went down into the Nether World to recover her dead lover, the personification of the strong sun of springtime, whose vigor fades away in the autumn. When she came to the door of the Land of No Return, she called imperiously to the porter,

*O gatekeeper, open thy gate,
Open thy gate that I may enter!
If thou openest not the gate so that I cannot enter,
I will smash the door, I will shatter the bolt,
I will smash the doorpost, I will move the doors,
I will raise up the dead, eating the living.
So that the dead will outnumber the living.*[B3]

Being commanded to do so by the goddess of the dead, the porter admits the queen of heaven, but as she passes through each of the seven gates, he takes an article of clothing or jewelry from her, until she enters the inner circle of the lower world stark naked. Held there in durance, she goes through much suffering, for the pest-god Namtar afflicts her successively with sixty diseases. Meanwhile, men and animals in the upper world grow listless and dull, unable to reproduce their kind. Love and fertility have left the earth. The gods are distressed.

*Forth went Papsukkal before Sin his father, weeping,
His tears flowing before Ea, the king
'Ishtar has gone down to the nether world, she has not
    come up.'*[B4]

Ea sends a messenger to Hades, and the goddess of the dead reluctantly orders Namtar to sprinkle Ishtar with "the water of life." She, restored to bloom and health, begins her journey back to the upper world, at each gate receiving back the clothing and jewelry of which she had been divested.

**Offering to Inanna (Ishtar)
As Vegetation Goddess**

A more poetically satisfying account of the disappearance of the vegetation goddess at the approach of winter and of her return in the spring has never been conceived.

4. The Journey of Gilgamesh

The most finished and literary of the Babylonian epics, the story of Gilgamesh's journey, begins with the tale of the friendship of Gilgamesh, the ruler of the city of Uruk (Erech), with the wild man Enkidu, who dies prematurely for offending the goddess Ishtar. It then tells of his journey, through many perils, in search of immortality, to the realm of the departed beyond the western (the Mediterranean?) "waters of death," where his ancestor Utnapishtim dwells, and concludes with his disconsolate return to Uruk, after being robbed by a serpent of the herb of immortality which Utnapishtim enabled him to find at the bottom of the sea. The whole story is full of the pathos of human disappointment in the face of death. Gilgamesh, about to embark on the waters of death in the west, addresses a barmaid dwelling by the sea.

O barmaid, let me not see the death I constantly fear.

The barmaid said to him, to Gilgamesh,

*'Gilgamesh, where are you wandering to?
You will not find the life you seek.
When the gods made mankind,*

They set death as the lot of humans,
But they kept life in their own hands.
So, Gilgamesh, fill your belly;
Be happy day and night;
Take pleasure every day;
Day and night dance and play.
Wear clean clothes;
Wash your head; bathe in water;
Enjoy the child who holds your hand;
Let your wife be happy with you.
This is what man's lot is![D1]

Here breathes indeed the spirit of the people of Babylonia. They had no hopes such as the Egyptians had of pleasantness in the world beyond. All joy was in this life.

Sacrifice and Magic

To ensure to themselves the blessings of this life, the Babylonians resorted to their priests for sacrifices, incantantions, ritual prayers, and the reading of the stars. They listened in rapt attention to the songs for the flute and the songs of prostration that were offered up before the gods. The liturgies were long, but they mellowed the gods. And if the gods would not be kind, there were incantations—powerful and compelling—to which the gods must give heed perforce, and which the evil spirits could not choose but obey. The worshipers paid the priests well to supplicate Ishtar.

I have cried to thee, suffering wearied, and distressed, as
thy servant.
See me, O my lady; accept my prayers . . .
Forgive my sin, my iniquity, my shameful deeds, and
my offense.
Overlook my shameful deeds; accept my prayer . . .
Let thy great mercy be upon me.[B5]

The priests could do more than pray; they could put a spell on the evil spirits in the body of the suppliant while standing by the sickbed, or on the roof of the patient's house, in a reed hut by the river, or in the temple compound; they could speak for the patient in peremptory tones.

Out of my body away!
Out of my body far away!
Out of my body, for shame!

My body do not oppress!
By Shamash, the mighty, be ye exorcised!
By Ea, the lord of all, be ye exorcised!
By Marduk, the chief exorciser of the gods, be ye
exorcised![D2]

The priests were busy men, well organized for their task, and offering many services to their clientele. They had learned during the centuries, from before 3200 B.C.E. (!), to act through what must be called in each case the temple corporation, a legal entity often possessed of large landholdings and run according to strict business methods, with all receipts and expenditures recorded in written signs on clay tablets. The temple structures administered by the corporations were large buildings, constructed of thick courses of sun-dried brick and occupying spacious temple compounds, in the center of which often stood man-built mountains encased in brick, called *ziggurats,* with a shrine on its top. In these compounds the priests performed their lengthy rituals, especially from the second to the fifth days of the twelve-day new year's festival. Here also they conducted schools for the teaching of reading, writing, and arithmetic, and here, as well, they practiced divination, in the ambitious endeavor to read the signs of the times and to foretell the future.

Divination and Astrology

Divination was in fact one of the main functions of the priesthood. One whole order of priests specialized in the interpretation of dreams and of omens perceived in natural events. They devoted much attention to the reading of the omens in the sheep's liver, for they thought the will and intentions of the gods were revealed in the creases on the surface and the physical peculiarities inside the liver. But the most important of their divining methods, for us if not for them, was their astrology. The origins of it go back to Sumerian times. In the attempt to establish what might be called scientific method in reading the will of the gods in the disposition of the heavenly bodies, the diviners kept accurate and detailed records of the movements they observed in the heavens, and thus prepared the way for scientific astronomy in our own day. The astronomical instruments devised for space measurement and time study of the stars were amazingly precise and accurate.

The contemporary revival of astrology as a method of predicting from the movement and position of the stars and planets the course of individual and world events owes much to the study of celestial omens by the Babylonians; however, it was the later Greeks (in the Hellenistic period) who evolved astrology into a detailed theory of the influence of celestial bodies on human affairs. Western astrologers as well as Hindu and Muslim practitioners have depended on Hellenistic rather than Babylonian sources for their theories of the zodiac and horoscopes.

We turn next to Greece.

II. GREECE

The last century has seen a thorough revision of earlier ideas of classical Greek religion. Homer is no longer taken at face value. His pantheon, described with his bright and winged words and in conception poetically unsurpassed, was for many centuries accepted in the West as an accurate rendering of early Greek religion. In the light of recent scholarship, it is not that at all. We see now that the scholars who read off the characteristics of the Greek gods from the statues of the classic age and the lines of Homer should have paid more attention to what Gilbert Murray called "the crude and tangled superstitions of the peasantry of the mainland," half revealed and half concealed in the poetry of Hesiod. It is clear from a study of such folklore that much that was pre-Greek lay at the base of Greek religion. The beauty and balance of the Homeric pantheon was in truth a triumph of unification and sublimation.

In brief, we have here another case of tribal amalgamations accompanied by a mingling and reordering of the gods.

The Gathering of the Gods in Early Hellas

The determinative fact in the formation of early Greek religion is the northern invasions beginning in about the twentieth century B.C.E. The invaders were formidable horse-borne warriors of Aryan or Indo-European speech, who came down from the northern parts of Greece in their chariots to establish themselves as masters of the earlier, so-called Helladic peoples. Historians are not certain of the origins of all of the groups involved, but they basically agree that the earliest true civilizations, those of the Minoans in Crete (who flourished about 2200–1500 B.C.E.) and of the Bronze Age Aegeans of the Greek archipelago and mainland (2500–1100 B.C.E.), known to the later Greeks as "Pelasgians," were pre-Greek.

The Minoan civilization, part of what Marija Gimbutas has called Old Europe, was destroyed about 1450 B.C.E., probably first by the volcanic explosion of the nearby island of Kalliste (modern Thera) and then by invasions (by the Achaeans?) from the mainland. While Crete was by no means defenseless, archeological traces of structures and implements of warfare are relatively sparse. An agricultural rather than a nomadic herding/hunting way of life furnished complementary gender roles. Images reflecting Minoan religious practices are notable for the preeminence of female roles, depicting priestesses as well as goddesses of fertility and renewal of life. At all events, the Cretan palace of Knossos was destroyed, and subsequent social patterns reflected the more patriarchal patterns of the conquerors.

The Cretan culture, however, had earlier spread to the Greek mainland, and produced in the northeastern parts of the Peloponnesus and further north the Mycenaean civilization, of which the Homeric (or Achaean) Age was probably a late form. It is likely that the Achaeans—leaders among the long-haired, light-skinned invaders from the north—adopted the Mycenaean culture after mastering its

> "The term *Old Europe* is applied to a pre-Indo-European culture . . . matrifocal and probably matrilinear, agricultural and sedentary egalitarian and peaceful. . . . In this culture the male element . . . represented spontaneous and life stimulating—but not life generating—powers."
>
> —Marija Gimbutas[E]

Tree-cult Goddess, Crete

creators, both in Greece and Crete. Finally, during the twelfth century B.C.E., waves of northerners—the formidable Dorians and their allies—overthrew the Mycenaean civilization, thus causing a widespread displacement that resulted in Greek settlements along the coast of Asia Minor, composed of Ionians and Aeolians, and of Dorians too. When everyone had settled down again, the historic Greek city-states came into being, and the patterns of Greek religion, now so familiar to us, began to form.

The Mingled Pantheon

These new patterns in religion were combinations of many different elements. Gradually, a pantheon of deities was assembled. The Indo-European invaders contributed to the divine *sunoikismos,* or "mingling together," at least of these deities: their chief god Zeus, the *Pater,* sky father and rainmaker (a name that reappears as Dyaus Pitar among the Indo-Aryans and Jupiter among the Romans); Demeter, the earth mother; and Hestia (the Vesta of the Romans), virgin goddess of the hearth, sister of Zeus, and a goddess from the far Indo-European past, honored with libations at the beginning and end of every sacrifice. But

many of the gods had no such distant origin. Rhea seems to have been Minoan, Athena Mycenaean (at least when we first glimpse her), and Hermes and Hera Aegean or Helladic. Apollo appears to be from Ionia, Aphrodite from Cyprus or Cythera, and Dionysus and Ares from Thrace. It was as though the gods flocked together to Olympus from all points of the compass.

Interaction with the Gods

It is thus quite evident that the Greeks of classical times felt themselves surrounded by deities whose assistance they needed. They were polytheists for reasons similar to those that made polytheists of the Egyptians and Mesopotamians: the powers and forces dwelling in and under the earth (the *chthon*) and in the sky and under the sea were immediately known in daily life and were found to be diverse as well as numerous. In describing them, the Greeks were anthropomorphic, for they preferred to take their analogies and symbols from human life and personality. It is important to notice that they did not think that the deities on whom they most depended were transcendent and far removed. Rather, they were close at hand, as close as the hearth (Hestia), the *herma* or boundary stone in the street (Hermes), the shrine before the house, which was perhaps sacred to Apollo of the Roads, the large jar in the storeroom sacred to Zeus Ktesios (guardian of the family possessions), and the courtyard, watched over by Zeus Herkeios. As H. J. Rose has said, "For everyday happenings, the gods were about everyone's path and might be invoked at any moment, to confirm an oath, avert evil, heal sickness, or bless all manner of actions."F All formal occasions required the invocation of a god or gods— marriage, for instance, or the reception of a newborn baby into the family circle, or at the death and burial of members of the family. Farming and other occupations could not be successfully pursued, nor could a journey on land or sea be attempted without the approval of the gods. The address to the gods on such occasions was simple and courteous but not servile, a natural, almost unreflective gesture of cooperation and community, not dominated by fear.

If a deity was known to be far removed, its existence might be recognized, but no prayer or sacrifice was offered to it; there was no use in sacrificing to a deity unaware of the act. Thus, Hades, the god of the underworld, and Ouranos, the god of heaven, although readily believed in, were not worshiped in Greek homes. On the other hand, Zeus was often invoked because he was nearby as well as far away, and the same was true of Apollo, who, not identified with the sun until a late date, received daily honors as the patron of many human arts and skills.

This down-to-earth interaction with the deities resulted in crediting them with complex functions.

The Complex Functions of the Major Deities

Geographically, Greece is made up of small valleys and plains, each hedged in by mountains or confined between a semicircle of hills and the sea. Unlike Egypt and Mesopotamia, which threw people together, Greece separated them. Before the northern invasions, the divided inhabitants of Helladic Greece worshiped in their isolated territories many nature spirits, sought the aid of a variety of fertility powers, and engaged in diverse rites connected with magic, taboo, and the cult of the dead. The northerners who came flooding in imposed not only a new language and a certain hearty

cheerfulness but also uniformity in the names of the gods, and thenceforth the chief gods and goddesses were identified with the local powers that could in anywise be absorbed by them, taking over their functions, rites, and histories, while also adding their own qualities.

Zeus

Zeus is an instructive instance of how an invader's god takes over the duties of local divinities. Because he began as the great sky father, ruler of the upper air and the giver of rains, as he made his way through Greece he was identified with many mountaintops. Not only was he Zeus of Olympus, but Zeus Lykaios in Arcadia, Zeus Laphystios in southern Thessaly, and Zeus Kithairon in Boeotia. But he also assumed other, down-to-earth duties. He was the god of fertility in many districts, and in at least three places a deity of the underworld. As Zeus Polieus he was the guardian of several city-states. As Zeus Aphiktor he was the united cry of the suppliants, itself become deity and forcibly beating its way to heaven. At Athens he was Zeus Phratrios, and received on his altar the votes cast by the members of the phratry when a father brought his child for enrollment. At Dodona he spoke oracles through the murmuring leaves of the sanctuary oak. Generally, of course, he was the Cloud Compeller, the Rain Maker, carrying his bright thunderbolt, hurled amid earthshaking tremors, but the thunderbolt sometimes had the judicial use of punishing the wickedness of men. As the source of genius, he fathered a large progeny of heroes, kings, and founders of cities. Nor was Hera his first wife. When he first arrived in the north at Dodona, he brought with him out of the unknown past a consort called Dione, and in other places he had other wives. But Hera was destined to become his permanent spouse.

Hera

Hera is an instance from the other side—the side of the conquered. She brought to her union with Zeus a past of her own. It was at least as respectable as his. Her origins are obscure and dateless. Because the cow plays an important part in early legends about her, she may originally have been a cow goddess. In Mycenaean times she was the Argive Korê (Maiden), and sported in more than sisterly fashion on the plains of Peloponnesian

Argos with Hercules, the strong young hero of that region. But she also was connected, by myth at any rate, with Argos in Thessaly, where as a matronly friend she helped Jason, another strong young hero, to launch the ship Argo, when he set out from Pagasae in search of the Golden Fleece. She seems not to have been at that time the goddess of the earth, but a majestic maiden identified with the passage of the year. For her sake Zeus parted with Dione and became her heavy-browed consort. They had their troubles. In accounting for their early quarrels, Jane Harrison has advanced the following interesting theory:

> The marriage of Zeus and Hera reflects the subjugation of the indigenous people by incoming Northerners. Only thus can we account for the fact that the divine husband and wife are in constant unseemly conflict. Of course, a human motive is alleged; Hera is jealous, Zeus in constant exasperation. But the real reason is radical conflict.[G]

Perhaps this explanation will do, or perhaps another: she was the queen of the hinterlands and of backward mountaineers among whom the proto-Greek matrilinear tradition persisted, and Zeus, the lord of the patrilinear northerners, married her to win a footing. However this may be, their marriage was not long unhappy. It was later declared a great success and became in Greek eyes a "holy union," the very ideal of married existence. Hera became the patroness of married women, their counselor and example.

Apollo

In the person of Apollo an even greater yoking of diverse functions is seen. He was probably not Hellenic. In the *Iliad,* at least, he is on the side not of the Greeks but of the Trojans, an implacable and a feared foe of the "bronze-clad" warriors besieging Troy. Perhaps, as the myths suggest, he was originally from the island of Delos, or from the plains of Asia Minor. His origin cannot be surely traced. Very early he stood for pastoral and agricultural interests. Certainly he was not originally a sun god. He was a shepherd for Laomedon near Troy and for Admetos in Thessaly. He may once have been a wolf god, but as shepherd he protected his flocks and herds from the fangs of his lupine brethren. In agricultural areas, groves and trees were under his protection; the laurel was sacred to him. Out of pastoral love of song, he drew to him with his lively playing on the lyre devoted youths and maidens. He heartily believed in youth, and he was the sponsor of athletic contests, himself drawing a strong bow. He was Hekatebolos, "the shooter from afar."

> Behind his shoulders hung
> His bow, and ample quiver; at his back
> Rattled the fateful arrows as he mov'd.[H1]

His arrows not only drew blood but pierced men with deadly sickness. (He also was the god of healing until he was displaced by his son Aesculapius.) He slew on the slopes of Mt. Parnassus in Greece the Python, whom he then displaced at Delphi. (Like Zeus, he supplanted or absorbed many local spirits.) His exploit at Delphi was an important act, with far-reaching results in the development of Greek religion, for as a consequence of it he became the god of revelation. No other god was the source of such direct oracles except Zeus. In the center of his temple at Delphi the famous vent in the earth, from which issued from time to time an intoxicating vapor, and when the priestess, named Pythia, sat on the tripod amid the fumes, she muttered words that were universally thought to be from Apollo. It was in this belief that for centuries many famous men of Greece journeyed

> to Delphi, where
> Phoebus,* on earth's mid navel o'er the world
> Enthroned, weaveth in eternal song
> The sooth of all that is or is to be.[I]

He often was asked for an oracle before a town was founded, and afterward became its patron. Not until very late, and then perhaps as the result of an Egyptian or other foreign influence, was he identified with Helios the sun, who drives his golden car from heaven's eastern gates to the dim regions of the night.

Other Deities

The story of the other deities is similar. Artemis, the virginal deity of the wild, ranging through the mountains and forests with her nymphs in maidenly reserve

---

*One of Apollo's epithets. It means "bright" or "pure."

but thoroughly at home with the untamed animals of her domain, was also the gentle lover of children, the protectress of men and maidens, and the solicitous friend who sought to ease the pangs of childbirth. Curiously, in Ionia, where she was a favorite, she became the Artemis of Ephesus, a motherly goddess, connected with fertility, her front covered with breasts.

Hermes, who came from deep in the pre-Hellenic period, outgrew his earliest symbol, a simple cairn of stones such as peasants in the rock-strewn land raised at the edges and corners of fields and associated with their dead. Cairns served in mountain tracts and elsewhere as way markers, and Hermes was thus thought to guide travelers to their destination. After he became identified with a square stone pillar, called the *herma,* sometimes surmounted with his head, he was, as it were, pulled up out of the ground, where he had stood immovable, and given winged feet. He led the spirits of the dead down to Hades, and as the swift messenger between Zeus and the earth below he was clothed in a long belted chiton and made to wear a cap or a broad-brimmed hat and wingèd boots.

Other deities showed a similar complexity of function. Poseidon was god of the sea, but was originally a horse god guarding inland lakes and streams (was he driven into the sea by invaders?). Athena, the wise and virginal warrior maiden, was originally perhaps an owl goddess (for the owl was sacred to her, and she herself turned on occasion into a bird disappearing upward into the sky), but her most ancient image in Athens was of olive wood, and so she was in some way connected with the fertility of the important olive crop. Demeter, goddess of the fertile soil, was, as mother of slender and beauteous Persephone (the Korê, the Maiden), also connected with the underworld. Into all of these deities many local gods and spirits were absorbed and sublimated. Even Aphrodite, the goddess of love, a latecomer, perhaps the Western form of Ishtar of Babylon, was reborn from the foam of the sea, clear-skinned and delicate and beautiful, still a little amoral, yet shorn of the accompaniments of temple prostitution and self-mutilation that attended the worship of her Oriental counterparts. Only Dionysus seemed unassimilable and untamed. (Further on, we shall see why.)

The Homeric Pantheon

In Homer the gods no longer live in widely separated places. They are a family domiciled on high Olympus, more a heavenly region now than the actual mountaintop in Thessaly. There Zeus, the Cloud Compeller, is kind, and white-armed Hera is his "golden-throned" queen. The other gods may absent themselves on occasion from their cloud-girt palaces, but usually Zeus must know where they have gone and what they have done. The gods, not without back talk, submit to his discipline, for he is the father of most of them. His best-beloved daughter is grey-eyed Athena, the maiden goddess of wisdom. A favored son is Apollo, the archer god, he of the flowing golden locks, who both heals and hurts. Artemis, "delighting in wild boars and swift hinds," is the shy daughter who often absents herself in mountain hideaways. Ares, "piercer of shields," is the savagely warlike son whom Zeus at times scolds sternly.

> Come no more to me,
> *Thou wav'ring turncoat, with thy whining prayers:*
> *Of all the Gods who on Olympus dwell*
> *I hate thee most; for thou delight'st in nought*
> *But strife and war; thou hast inherited*
> *Thy mother, Hera's, proud, unbending mood,*
> *Whom I can scarce control.*[H2]

Aphrodite, the enticing goddess of love, is a daughter of Zeus by Dione and is married to her half-brother, the lame god of the forge and the fire, Hephaestus, a son of Zeus by Hera, but she is unfaithful to him and has a notorious amour with Ares. Still another son of Zeus, born of his affair with Semele, is Dionysus, but in Homer he puts in an appearance and nothing more. Of greater importance is Hermes, the Heavenly Guide, whose birth was the consequence of the love of Zeus and Maia. He is primarily the herald and messenger of the gods, but he is sharp and cunning and not above consorting with thieves on those occasions when he gets away by himself, as when he departs from Olympus to guide souls to and from Hades. Poseidon, the god of the sea, and Hades (Pluto), the god of the underworld, are full brothers of Zeus, born like him of Kronos and Rhea, and Demeter is his sister by the same parents, but Homer does not have her come to Olympus.

Model of Delphi in about 160 C.E.

Detail showing the Temple of Apollo. The temple of Apollo, Parthenon-like, dominates the scene in this suggested restoration of the famed seat of the priestesses who uttered the "Delphic oracles." Casts, Scale 1:200. Five hundred years earlier, Socrates came to Delphi when there were fewer buildings and less wealth, but perhaps more belief. *(The Metropolitan Museum of Art, Dodge Fund, 1930. 30.141.2 Neg # 85606)*

Divine Functions Rationalized

Here then is the tight-knit family group of the gods of Homer. On the whole they form a very aristocratic company. As gods they are in charge of natural forces, but more clearly characterized and set off from those forces than they had been in earlier days. Their functions have been both sublimed and simplified. They are no longer "primitive." The Minoan fetishes, the deities in animal form, the mother goddesses, are gone. The earlier Bronze Age involvements with animal and human fertility, or with vegetation, death, and the underworld, have been largely refined out of them. Their personalities are no longer portentous with vague, mysterious force; they have come into the light of day and are sharply defined, clear-cut, distinct from one another. No two are alike. Indeed they are all but earthy men and women, with thoughts, desires, moods, and passions all too human. Though immortal, they are no longer incalculable and unknown and terrible. Aesthetically, they are attractive, charming, amusing, civilized, better proportioned and more beautiful than humans—they were indeed Homer's priceless gift to the future artists of Greece. In marble and bronze, their stately, poised, and unblemished bodies were in time to rise in marketplaces and on acropolises, their wondrous heads gazing calmly down from the pediments and pedestals of temples, lordly and aloof, as from another and more perfect world. Mortals could look at them only with wonder and envy.

And yet the awesome quality, which makes gods bear in their persons a *mysterium tremendum,* had left them!

Perhaps the last sentence is a little overstated. The gods in Homer do exert supernatural effects, for when Zeus nods all Olympus shakes, and once when Poseidon hurried to Olympus in three immense strides,

> *Beneath th' immortal feet of Ocean's Lord*
> *Quak'd the huge mountain and the shadowy wood.*[H3]

Poseidon's cry—and that of every god—is thunderous:

> *As of nine thousand or ten thousand men,*
> *In deadly combat meeting in the shout.*[H4]

The gods also have great power over human lives, whether for bane or blessing. By their will cities fall, men die, and armies fail. But in this they show little concern for justice in the modern sense; rather they place first the demonstrating of the excellence (*areté*) befitting their divine status, exercising their powers over lesser beings and evoking honors and sacrifices from humankind.

In Homeric times, justice was central neither to gods nor to humankind. When a deity was described as "good" (*agathos*), this meant *successful* in protecting favored persons or causes (as when Zeus succeeded in protecting the Greeks before Troy and Apollo made good in protecting his favored ones, the Trojans). In the same sense, a human father was "good" when he was a good provider. Gods and humans had *areté* when they had the will to excellence, the virtue of vigor in pursuit of their fundamental interests. In such a scheme of things, justice, while good, was secondary to achieving one's aims.

The Primacy of *Moira* (Fate)

But yet, with all of this, the might of the gods is gravely limited. There is something more powerful than they, to which even Zeus, the Cloud Compeller himself,

submits, though he could change it by the power of his will. This is *moira* or what is allotted (fated) to each person as a share, an appointed portion in life and its happenings. Moira does not stand alone; with it operate vague forces—Blind Folly, Terror, Strife, Turmoil, Rumor, Death. Powerful though they are, the gods are contained within the total frame of Nature and History along with humans. Though they are superhuman, their powers are not boundless.

The Homeric epics helped bring about a sense of unification among the Greeks. Culturally, all Hellas was seen as one. But it may be doubted whether in local worship, prayer, and sacrifice, the aesthetically pleasing Homeric pantheon won the people even a little away from their ancient loyalties.

Hesiod's *Theogony*

Hesiod (eighth century B.C.E.) did no better. In a characteristic effort of Greek rationalism, he tried to bring the gods into some semblance of order by raising the question of their origin (theogony).

Influenced perhaps by Middle-Eastern attempts in this direction, he declared in his *Theogony* that the pristine Chaos had given place by cosmic evolution to Earth (Gaea or Ge), Tartarus (the Pit), and handsome Eros (Love). Chaos itself produced Night and Darkness, and they, in turn, by the power of Eros, mated to bring forth Day and Air. Without mating, Night gave issue to Sleep, Dream, Death, Old Age, Misery, Friendship, and Discord. Similarly, Discord of herself, without husband, gave birth to Hunger, Toil, Murder, Battle, and other forms of human strain and struggle, while Earth brought into being unaided Heaven (Ouranos or Uranus, the starry heavens), the Mountains, and the Ocean. Mating with Ocean, Earth produced creatures of the sea, and then taking as husband Ouranos, conceived the first great gods but was unable to give birth to them because Ouranos prevented his children from emerging from the mother (the depths of the earth). With her aid, however, Kronos came forth, stole upon his sleeping father, and castrated him with a sickle. The flowing blood impregnated Earth, and she brought forth the Furies (Erinyes), the Titans (Giants), and certain nymphs, while from the sea foam forming around the castrated members sprang Aphrodite, the goddess of love. The triumphant

Kronos married his sister Rhea, who had now been born, but fearing overthrow himself, he swallowed his children as they were born. Then Rhea, with the help of grandmother Earth, substituted a stone for Zeus, the last born, and Kronos swallowed it unknowingly. Zeus was hidden by his grandmother in a cave in Crete and finally emerged to subdue his father and force him to disgorge the young gods and goddesses he had swallowed. Thereafter, Zeus began his reign as king of the gods.

This was Hesiod's attempt to bring rational order out of mythological chaos, but although he satisfied the Greeks theologically, he did not much alter the day-to-day practice of religion, which still defied order.

The Everyday Religion of the Household

The day-to-day observance of religion by the common folk of Greece was mainly a matter of household pieties and attendance at a public ceremony. In the countryside, the chief concern was with Pan, the pasturer (a frisky male with horns, pointed ears, a tail, and goat's feet); Demeter, the earth mother; Hermes ("he of the stone heap"); *daimons* (various kinds of spirits full of mana, some being closer than a brother— Socrates had one, he said); *keres,* or vague powers, bringing on such harmful states as old age, death, and destructive passions like jealousy and overweening pride; *erinyes,* the "furies," punishers of lapses from the appointed path (moira), often set upon the living by the disappointed or outraged dead, bent also on correction or revenge; ghosts; "heroes," that is, the noble dead, half human, half divine, and still powerful and protective; and chthonian deities, dwelling underground, to be appeased in fear for their association with death or to be reverenced for their fertility and resurrective powers. Besides all of these, countryfolk concerned themselves with omens, taboos, magic (by which to lay ghosts and promote the fertility of the fields, the livestock, and

womankind), and the long-standing traditional rituals of the household.

Meanwhile, townsfolk, besides adhering to the religion and magic of the household, attended the city festivals that honored the greater gods of the pantheon. To these we turn next.

The Athenian Festivals

By and large the Athenians thought of their deities by seasons of the year. The official year began in summer with a great sacrifice to Apollo, called the Hecatombaia, because 100 head of cattle were supposed to be offered. Just before summer (May), the Thargelia honored him with a purification rite in which two filthy men, draped with black and yellow dried figs, were chased through the streets and driven as scapegoats from the city. In late summer and early fall, three other festivals celebrated his power to promote neighborliness, raise up "helpers," and give aid to agriculture.

Athena, the chief patroness of the city, received highest honors during the Panathenaea, held every year, but every fourth year with special pageantry, to celebrate her "birthday." Performed in midsummer, it was one of the great festivals of the city. A long procession carried a newly embroidered mantle, mounted like a sail on a ship on wheels, to her image on the Acropolis. There were accompanying sacrifices and games. Earlier in the summer each year festivals of beautification and lustration, the Kallynteria and Plynteria, purified both her temple and the city. Devotees carried an ancient image of her to the sea to be bathed.

Demeter and her daughter Persephone received honor in later summer and fall at no less than five city festivals. The first was the Eleusinia (not to be confused with the Eleusinian mysteries), held every two years and with great splendor every fourth year. In the course of its games the prize given to the winning athletes was barley from one of Demeter's holy fields, the Rarian Plain. The other festivals (the Proerosia, Thesmophoria, Haloa,

> "Greek religion was decidedly a thing of every day. The gods were not confined to their temples or to their heaven or nether realm, but were in the streets and houses of the people."
>
> —H. J. Rose[F]

and Skirophoria) included a magic ploughing, a seeding of the earth with suckling pigs and sacred cakes (a kind of fertility magic), and a magical ritual during which worthy matrons made broad jokes to encourage the fertility powers.

The greatest of the spring festivals, the Diasia, was in honor of Zeus. It included a *holocaust,* the Greek word for a whole-burnt offering. Hera was honored along with him in January during the Gamelia, which celebrated their "holy marriage," and there were two other festivals, one in November and another in July.

Artemis' connection with animals received notice at three fertility festivals in the spring, but the great god of the season was Dionysus. In April or May the Great Dionysia took six days to perform. It had, and still retains, great literary importance, because it was the occasion for the performance, under the supervision of the priest of Dionysus, of the immortal tragedies of Aeschylus, Sophocles, and Euripides and the comedies of Aristophanes. Religion and art were here memorably combined.

The Mystery Religions

Even while the Homeric pantheon was being established throughout Greece as the group standard for conceiving of the appearance and behavior of the gods, an excitingly satisfying way for the Greeks to *feel* the gods within them and thus to share in their immortal nature, made its appearance. This was the way of the mysteries—a way that offered to individuals private and personal religious satisfactions and assurances not provided by the official public sacrifices to the gods.

So ardent indeed became the devotees of these cults that they practiced their rites even when great public crises impended and average citizens were thinking only of a common danger. Herodotus, in a famous passage, tells of a rapt group that pursued the Eleusinian rites, even while Attica was being ravaged by the land army of Xerxes and the Greeks hov-

ering off the coast were debating whether to hazard their fleet at Salamis. Witnesses on the Persian side were filled with superstitious dread, Herodotus says, when they saw the procession of devotees going along the sacred way from Eleusis toward Athens, raising "a cloud of dust such as a host of thirty thousand men might raise," and singing the mystic hymn to Dionysus. One said to another,

> Demaretus, it is certain that some great calamity will fall upon the king's host. For, since Attica is deserted, manifestly it is something more than mortal, coming from Eleusis to avenge the Athenians and their allies. If it descends upon the Peloponnese, there will be peril for the king himself and his land army; but if it turns towards the ships at Salamis, the king will be in danger of losing his fleet. This feast is held by the Athenians every year for the Mother and the Maid, and any Athenian or other Greek who wishes is initiated. The sound you hear is the song of the Iacchos [Dionysus] which they sing at this festival.

And Demaretus answered,

> Hold your peace and tell no man of this matter, for if these words should come to the king's ears, you will lose your head, and neither I nor any man living will be able to save you.[K1]

The mysteries were so called because they were rites that were kept secret from all except the initiates. Under the guidance of a *hierophant* ("the revealer of holy things"), the candidates underwent (1) a preparatory purification, such as a procession to the sea and washing in it, (2) instruction in mystic knowledge, usually given behind closed doors in a mystic hall, (3) a solemn beholding of sacred objects, followed by (4) the enactment of a divine story, generally in the form of a pageant or play, in which the cult divinities were impersonated, and (5) a crowning or wreathing of each of the candidates as a full-fledged initiate. Accompanying these acts, which might spread over a number

> **"No visits delight us more than those to shrines, no occasions are more pleasant than festivals, nothing we do or see is more pleasant than our actions and sights before the gods."**
>
> —Plutarch[J]

of days, were processions and sacred revels, including night-long ceremonies, which simultaneously afforded a release of tension and a deepening of the sense of mystic participation in supernatural realities.

The Eleusinian Mysteries

The oldest and most restrained of the mysteries were the Eleusinian. The central figures in the rites were Demeter and her daughter, Persephone, the Korê or Maiden. As everyone knew, the Korê had been snatched away to the underworld by Hades (Pluto) so that she might be his bride, but her mother, through long days of searching and mourning, had refused to make the corn grow, and at last Zeus bade Hades to allow the maiden to return to earth. But the unwary maiden had eaten a pomegranate seed, cunningly given to her by Hades, and when, as the hymn that has come to us from the seventh century B.C.E. relates, her anxious mother asked,

> Child, hast thou eaten of any food in the world below?
> Tell me; for if not,
> Then mayest thou dwell beside me and Father Zeus,
> Honored among all the Immortals;
> But if thou hast,
> Thou must go back again into the secret places of
>   the earth
> And dwell there a third part of every year,
> And whensoever the earth blossoms with all sweet
>   flowers of spring,
> Then from the misty darkness thou shalt rise and come
>   again,
> A marvel to gods and men,[K2]

Alas, Persephone had to confess she had done that which required her annual return to the underworld.

The entire story of Demeter and the Maiden was elaborately reenacted, mostly by women. At some time, Dionysus, as Demeter's associate (he being the life force in vegetation, the vine, and reproductive animals, including humans), was introduced into the story; it is not clear when. The mystery itself was withheld from the public, but all of Athens could see the parade to the sea to bathe the candidates, and any citizen also could witness the procession along the sacred way from Athens to Eleusis bearing along the image of the young Dionysus (Iacchos). The participants hoped to obtain a "better lot," a more glorious immortality in the next world, this, apparently, not as a reward of virtue, but rather by assimilation of the resurrective powers of Demeter, the Korê, and Dionysus. According to the hymn quoted earlier,

> Blessed among men upon earth is he who has seen
>   these things;
> But he that is uninitiate in the rites and thus has no
>   part in them
> Has never an equal lot in the cold place of darkness.[K3]

It should be added that this nonmoral hope shocked even the Greeks. Plutarch preserves a comment attributed to Diogenes the Cynic: "Is Pataikion the thief going to have a 'better lot' after death than Epaminondas, just because he was initiated?"[K4]

The Dionysiac and Orphic Cults

The decorous Eleusinian mystery cult was far surpassed in violence and excitement by the practices of the Dionysiac cult. These had a Thraco-Phrygian origin and construed the intoxication that followed the ritual use of the wine of Dionysus as possession by the god. Added excitement was provided by sacramental communion with the god in eating the flesh and drinking the blood of a kid or bull identified with him and actually torn asunder—a rite called *omophagia*. All Greece was familiar with the Dionysiac *maenads* (or Bacchae)—women, maddened by divine possession, "rushing" or "raging" in the frenzy of tearing in pieces the sacred animal—and knew too of the sad fate of Orpheus, the inventor of the mysteries of Dionysus, who became himself the victim of the rite of omophagia and was torn to pieces by the maenads in Thrace when in grief at his second loss of Eurydice he paid them no heed.

But if the Dionysiac cult remained incurably wild, its mild Orphic offshoot, whose conventicles spread throughout the Mediterranean world—or wherever Greeks were—including southern Italy, Crete, and Cyprus, had this to commend it: by eating the raw flesh of the suffering and dying god (Zagreus-Dionysus), the

Dionysus

initiates might strengthen the divine element in themselves; by following the Orphic rules of purity, wearing white garments, abstaining from all meat (except that of the god in the mystery), avoiding the breaking of taboos against sex indulgence and pollution, and being generally ascetic, as Orphism demanded, they might refine the evil out of themselves and avoid going to the place of punishment after death. More positively, by being worthy they might hope to enjoy a better lot in the next world and at the same time increase their sense of spiritual security in this one. Ultimately, they might altogether escape the necessity of rebirth, in which the Orphics believed, and go to the Isles of the Blest.

That these ideas should have had a part in the development of one of the great schools of Greek philosophy may seem at first sight surprising. But it is true that in the philosophic brotherhood that Pythagoras founded the Orphic coloring was strong. The Pythagorean brothers believed that the major task of one's life was to purify the soul, and by following Orpheus (or perhaps Apollo) they hoped to bring their souls into a state of serenity, understanding, and godlike poise. Their studies in medicine, music, astronomy, mathematics, and pure philosophy were designed to nourish in their souls the divine elements, so that they would not hereafter have to suffer transmigration from earth body to earth body, but could regain a spiritual state of purity and insight.

This was not the only case of the search in Greek thought for higher ground.

Greek Religion and the Tragic Poets

The tragedies of Aeschylus, Sophocles, and Euripides revolve around the awful theme that disasters and doom are brought upon men and women by the gods. This is what the myths long had said, but it was not always clear whether the gods were impelled by a just purpose, by sheer willfulness, or by the decrees of an inexorable Fate to which even gods are, willy-nilly, the ministrants. The great dramatists addressed themselves to the human problems that this confusion raises, and in so doing produced passages of moral and religious reflection that have no parallel in ancient literature outside of the powerful utterances of the Hebrew prophets.

In the fifth century, Aeschylus and Sophocles more or less followed the poet Pindar in exalting Zeus to the moral height of being the administrator of a cosmic justice. The other deities continue to exist alongside Zeus, but they yield at once to his will when he overrules them in the name of the justice he is imposing. No longer is Fate blind. Aeschylus, in general, places Zeus in the superior position of either commanding Fate or being served by it. It therefore is really Zeus who dispatches the avenging Furies who punish the sins of mortals ever continuing and multiplying from generation to generation among the wrongdoers. Aeschylus' great trilogy, the *Oresteia*, indeed vigorously declares,

> *Zeus, the high god!—whate'er be dim in doubt,*
> *This can our thought track out—*
> *The blow that fells the sinner is of God,*
> *And as he wills, the rod*
> *Of vengeance smiteth sore. . . .*
>
> *For not forgetful is the high gods' doom*
> *Against the sons of carnage: all too long*
> *Seems the unjust to prosper and be strong,*
> *Till the dark Furies come,*
> *And smite with stern reversal all his home,*
> *Down into dim obstruction—he is gone,*
> *And help and hope, among the lost, is none.*[L]

Though in *Prometheus Bound* the tortured Titan, who is its central figure, defies Zeus as being unjust, it is evident that Aeschylus thought that Zeus had learned something from this encounter, and was in no doubt that the king of the gods should be approached with the utmost piety as the righteous moral governor of the world.

Sophocles, the wise, tenderhearted, and supremely poised dramatist, gave to the character of Zeus some of his own humanity of feeling. Following some hints supplied by Aeschylus, who, however, in general makes Zeus stern and fearsome in his moral fervor, Sophocles softens the great god's judgments with mercy. He makes Polynices, for instance, in *Oedipus at Colonos*, begin his final plea to his royal father by reminding him that Clemency sits by the side of Zeus, sharing his throne and entering into all of his decisions, a fact that should influence earthly potentates and make them more merciful. Yet Sophocles also is sure that the favor of Zeus is not easily gained, for one must be pure in word and deed, as Zeus indeed wills from on high, if one is to experience at all the divine clemency.

Euripides, a generation later, filled with doubts that had perhaps been raised in his mind by the Sophists or by such bold minds as Anaxagoras, lifts his voice with less conviction in behalf of obedience to the gods. Although it is a difficult thing for us to decide when Euripides is putting words into the mouths of his characters and when he is speaking his own mind, it seems certain that he had come to question the justice and integrity, if not of Zeus, at least of Apollo, Aphrodite, and others among the gods. Often he pities mortals stricken and hurled to earth by the unpitying gods. He makes the proud and pure-hearted Hippolytus cry,

> Ah, pain, pain, pain!
> O unrighteous curse! . . .
> Thou, Zeus, dost see me? Yea, it is I;
> The proud and pure, the server of God,
> The white and shining in sanctity!
> To a visible death, to an open sod,
> I walk my ways;
> And all the labor of saintly days
> Lost, lost without meaning.[M1]

Meanwhile a maiden of the chorus has already uttered the amazing reproof,

> Ye gods that did snare him,
> Lo, I cast in your faces
> My hate and my scorn.[M2]

And the men have chanted in discouragement overwhelming their uncertain faith,

> Surely the thought of the Gods hath balm in it always,
>   to win me
> Far from my griefs; and a thought, deep in the dark of
>   my mind,
> Clings to a great Understanding. Yet all the spirit
>   within me
> Faints when I watch men's deeds matched with the
>   guerdon they find.
>   For Good comes in Evil's traces;
>   And the Evil the Good replaces;
>   And Life, 'mid the changing faces,
>   Wandereth weak and blind.[M3]

But Euripides was by no means a total disbeliever, it would seem. He was really seeking a notion of God purged of the misconceptions of mythology and tradition. His true voice perhaps comes to us in the groping words:

> Thou deep Base of the world, and thou high Throne
> Above the World, whoe'er thou art, unknown
> And hard of surmise, chain of Things that be,
> Or Reason of our Reason; God, to thee
> I lift my praise, seeing the silent road
> That bringeth justice ere the end be trod
> To all that breathes and dies.[M4]

In this "strange prayer," as the poet himself calls it, the questing spirit of Euripides, like that of his philosophic contemporaries, seems to seek a new theology.

The Philosophers and the Gods

That the philosophers would go far beyond the Homeric point of view was clear from the start. Greek philosophy began as monism: everything in the universe is some form or another of one thing. Thales said this substance was water. Anaximenes that it was air, Heraclitus that it was fire, and Anaximander that it was undifferentiated and infinite. Whatever it was, it was creative or divine, they all agreed. Xenophanes was sure that the creative power was "one god greatest among gods and men, not like mortals in form, nor yet in mind. He sees all over, thinks all over, and hears all over."[K5] But human beings insist on seeing him in their likeness, and so have fallen into the anthropomorphic fallacy (the mistake of ascribing human shape and feelings to nonhumans), as J. M. Cornford put it:

Homer and Hesiod have ascribed to the gods all things that among men are a shame and a reproach—theft and adultery and deceiving one another.

Mortals think that the gods are begotten, and wear clothes like their own, and have a voice and a form.

If oxen or horses or lions had hands and could draw with them and make works of art as men do, horses would draw the shapes of gods like horses, oxen like oxen; each kind would represent their bodies just like their own forms.

The Ethiopians say their gods are black and flat-nosed; the Thracians, that theirs are blue-eyed and red-haired.[K6]

Plato

Plato had a different criticism. In the *Republic,* where he considers the education of youth, he fears the moral ill effects of teaching the Homeric myths in unexpurgated form.

> The narrative of Hephaestus binding Hera his mother, or how on another occasion Zeus sent him flying for taking her part when she was being beaten, and all the battles of the gods in Homer—these tales must not be admitted into our State, whether they are supposed to have an allegorical meaning or not. For a young person cannot judge what is allegorical and what is literal; anything that he receives into his mind at that age is likely to become indelible and unalterable; and therefore it is most important that the tales which the young hear first should be models of virtuous thoughts.[N1]

A similar moral criticism is leveled by Plato against the mystery religions. The trouble with the mysteries is that they do not recommend justice for the sake of justice; they practice virtue for the sake of the rewards it brings, the "shower of benefits which the heavens, as they say, rain upon the pious."

> They produce a host of books written by Musaeus and Orpheus, . . . according to which they perform their ritual, and persuade not only individuals, but whole cities, that expiations and atonements for sin may be made by sacrifices and amusements which fill a vacant hour; . . . the latter sort they call mysteries, and they redeem us from the pains of hell, but if we neglect them no one knows what awaits us.[N2]

Plato was far from denying the existence of the gods. But they were, he said, neither as wayward and fallible as Homer pictured them nor as easily swayed from impartial justice as the mysteries implied. They were true to, and dependent in function on, a higher power. There was above them, and behind all other beings and things, a Creator, or an Artisan, who had identified himself with the highest of all values, the Good. It was he who in the beginning beheld the realm of ideal forms, which not even he created, and was inspired by them to make a world that participated in their structure and that, in mountains, plains, and seas, gods, humans, and animals, bodied forth the good, the beautiful, and true in various degrees. As for man or woman, each is a soul in a body, and the soul needs to grow toward the highest good, that it may no longer have to suffer continued rebirth but go into that state in which it may, like God, behold and enjoy forever the hierarchy of the ideal forms, in all their truth, beauty, and goodness. The gods, on their part, desire none of the superstitious worship and magical rituals that humans have developed in their honor. They desire and expect only that each soul shall achieve the fullest development and seek the supreme good that the high god has set before it. Firm in these beliefs, Plato, in his old age, contended that atheism or any assertion that God is indifferent to humankind or can be bought off by gifts or offerings should be treated as being dangerous to society.

Aristotle

Aristotle, at least in his earlier period, found no need in his philosophy for the traditional gods of the Greeks, but yet, in considering the highest kind of being, had to posit God the Prime Mover, that is, a being causing all the movements of celestial and terrestrial bodies by attraction toward himself, while himself being actually without motion. Aristotle, the Stoics, and the Neo-Platonists were as much emancipated as Plato from the confining bonds within which their lesser countrymen were straining toward a fuller, freer life and greater wisdom.

III. ROME

What we have found to be true of the religion of Greece is even more true of the religion of Rome: the literature of the classical period is not a good guide to early religious belief. The writings of the Romans whom we know best—those who flourished during the days of the late Republic and the early Empire—must be critically analyzed so that the references to the religion of early Rome may be isolated and given their proper value. For if we wish to form a true picture of early Roman religion, we must first lift off, as it were, the accumulated upper layers, representing the borrowings from Etruscan and Greek religions and the more esoteric importations from Egypt and the Middle East, and then proceed to look at the underlying ancient customs and rituals of the Latins.

Like its Greek counterpart, the Italian peninsula was inhabited at first by a non-Indo-European population. At some time early in the second millennium B.C.E. there occurred invasions from the north by Indo-European (initially Celtic) tribes. Late in this period these tribes crossed the Apennines and settled down along the Tiber and on the hills to the east. They came to be known as the Latins, and their territory as Latium. They were not, however, to be left in undisturbed possession. They were joined in the eighth century B.C.E. by a kindred people called the Sabines, who came down from the mountains to the east. Shortly before this, the territory to the north—historic Etruria—was settled by invaders, perhaps shipborne, from the eastern Mediterranean, the energetic Etruscans, who for so long were the chief enemies of the Romans and for a while dominated them completely. Incursions of foreigners occurred also in the far south, almost too far away at first for the Romans to pay any heed. These were the Greeks of Magna Graecia, who had come to southern Italy as a result of the Dorian invasions of southern Greece. Thus the Latins found themselves in the eighth century B.C.E. between the Etruscans on the north and the Greeks on the south. Soon effects upon the development of their religious ideas and practices began to appear.

At first, Rome was one of the lesser Latin towns. Its rise to importance dates from the complete merging of its several communities on the famous seven hills and their enclosure in the sixth century B.C.E. by a long, stout encircling wall. Gradually the surrounding areas came under its control; at last Rome became the leader of all of Italy. By the close of the third century B.C.E., Carthaginian resistance to Roman dominance was broken, and the Roman imperium thereafter extended itself over the entire Mediterranean world.

The Religion of Early Rome

The religion of early Rome had, like the city itself, humble beginnings. The chief holy places were at first outside of its territory. Diana was worshiped in the grove of Aricia on Lake Nemi, her temple there being sacred for the whole Latin federation, and on the Alban hill to the east all Latium united in the festival in honor of Jupiter Latiaris.

In later times the Romans referred to the earliest strata of their religion as "the religion of Numa," as though their traditional lawgiver, who could not have invented it, had prescribed it for them. It was a religion very close to magic, precise and scrupulous in its sacerdotalism, with much attention given to charms, taboos, and the reading of omens. Its most general feature was the attention it paid to supernatural forces or potencies called numina (sing. numen). This word, derived from a verb meaning to affirm (nod) or command, came to refer generally to efficacious power, a meaning suggestive to some of a free floating power such as the mana of primal religions of the South Seas. But the terms are not equivalent: mana imbued persons and objects with power; numen flowed out from

> "Ancient Roman religion knew no mythical histories of personal gods, no genealogies, no marriages or children, no heroic legends, no worship of legendary heroes, no cosmogony, no conceptions of life in the underworld—in a word, nothing of that which Homer and Hesiod had so abundantly supplied for the Greeks."
>
> —Carl Clemen[01]

individuals exerting their will. The great gods wielded it impressively and conferred it upon mortals and upon the ritual scene, priests, altars, and sacred objects.

Deities dispensing numen were venerated by name in the earliest times, but the assignment of fully personalizing distinguishing traits came slowly. The early gods and spirits were assigned only a vague character. So little distinct personality had the spirits and powers of the fields and the farmhouse that the early Romans generally regarded them simply as forms or functional expressions of numen to which descriptive or personal names were to be assigned only to distinguish them from each other. Consequently, they made no anthropomorphic images of them, had no pictures of them in their minds that they cared to draw on a wall or paint on a vase. It was only later that they learned from the Etruscans and Greeks how to visualize and humanize their gods.

The Religion of the Home

The early Romans were mainly engaged in farming, homemaking, child raising, and war. When they desired success in farming, they turned to relevant sources of numen known to and named by them from of old: to Saturnus for sowing, to Ceres for growth of grain, to Consus for harvesting, and to Ops for safe storage of the grain. Tellus fructified the tilled soil. Flora brought blossoms to field and bough, Pomona ripening to the fruit on the bough. Faunus presided over the woods, the Lares over the sown fields, the Pales over the open pasture where the livestock fed. Terminus was the numen of the boundary stone, Fons of the springs, and Volturnus of the running river. Even more minute subdivisions of function appear in pontifical litanies invoking twelve minor deities presiding over ploughing of the fallow, second ploughing, running the furrows, sowing, ploughing under, harrowing, hoeing, weeding, reaping, carting home, storing in the granary, and bringing out for use. Regnant over all, Jupiter as great sky father brought rain and sunshine.[P1]

In homemaking and child raising there was a similar assignment of deity to locus of numen (the process seems not to have been the reverse). Janus was the numen in the door, defending the threshold, and Vesta, equally, if not more ancient and important, was on the hearth, present, as was Hestia in faraway Greece,

in the flame. It was the responsibility of the man of the house, as its priest, to be on good terms with Janus, and of the women to worship Vesta at her place on the hearth and to present her with a portion of each meal before anyone ate. The Penates were the numina who presided over the cupboard, preserving its store of food from harm. At first indefinitely conceived, they were in later days identified with whoever was the patron deity of the home—Ceres, Juno, Jupiter, or someone else. More closely concerned with the history of the family, as a source of numen that exercised watch and ward over the whole household, was the Lar Familiaris. Originally the Lares were guardians of the sown fields and of the crossroads, then more narrowly of the family estate, and finally of the household in particular, receiving from the family regular worship on the Calends, Nones, and Ides of every month. A potency hard to define exactly was the *genius,* the energy and vitality of each male, considered the essence of his manhood. It was almost a separate being, a guardian and an exterior power, resident both in the man and in his marriage bed. Each male revered and was expectant toward his genius, as was each female toward her corresponding *juno,* but special honor was paid to the Genius Paterfamilias, particularly on the birthday of the family's head. This genius was considered to be somehow symbolized by the house snake, a sort of double of the numen of the head of the house.

It should be emphasized before we go on that all of these sources of numen were honored and propitiated by a variety of ceremonies and festivals, whose essence consisted not so much in words as in acts, for in them religion was inextricably bound up in magic and taboo. Where we can recover enough of it for examination, the symbolism in these worshipful performances is usually transparently clear. The Romans wasted no time with vague sentimentality. A marked feature of all of their rituals was their severely formal character. We find no suggestion of close person-to-person relationships. Cyril Bailey characterized the typical Roman as being essentially practical.

> His natural mental attitude was that of the lawyer. And so in his relation towards the divine beings whom he worshipped, all must be regulated by clearly understood principles and carried out with formal exactness. . . . Both sides are under

obligation to fulfil their part: if the man has fulfilled "his bounden duty and service," the god must make his return: if he does not, either the cause lies in an unconscious failure on the human side to carry out the exact letter of the law, or else, if the god has really broken his contract, he has, as it were, put himself out of court and the man may seek aid elsewhere.[Q]

Here lies the reason why in Roman ceremonies the omission or displacement of a single word in the ritual or any deviation in the correct behavior of the participants was believed to make the whole performance of no effect. Hence, too, the need of priests, for they alone could preserve the ceremonies intact from olden times and perform them without error, or, if they were not the performers, they alone could coach the lay officiants in the right procedure.

The Religion of the State

The religion of the early Roman state was in essential respects the domestic cult nationalized. It was very well organized. The chief deities had priests (*flamines*) publicly assigned to them. But the state ceremonies were not always in their charge. In the time of the monarchy, the king was the chief priest and performed some important ceremonies. In all later periods magistrates frequently did the same, even though religious affairs were supposedly placed in the hands of the pontifices.

On the publicly prescribed days set down on the state calendar, which totaled 104 days of each year, the priests of the various deities performed a long list of ceremonies and sacrifices. They went about their tasks meticulously and dryly, whether or not anyone but themselves was on hand. They washed their hands, put on immaculate garments, and were in a state of moral as well as physical purity. Pliny the Elder (23–79 C.E.) wrote concerning their prayers,

[The] words differ according to whether one wishes to obtain favorable omens, to ward off ominous auguries, or to present supplications, and we see the highest magistrates using precise formulae in their prayers; to prevent any word from being omitted or inverted, someone first reads out the formula from a written text, another is responsible for careful supervision, a third must give

orders for silence, while a flute player is heard to cover all other noises.[R]

The question may well be raised, to which gods were all of these state ceremonies dedicated? In some cases no special deities seem to have been involved. We have the list, however, of the state deities who were addressed on the other occasions. This list sounds strange indeed in the ears of those accustomed to think that the Greek and Roman religions were like peas in a pod. Alphabetically listed, the deities are "Anna Perenna, Carmenta, Carna, Ceres, Consus, Diva Angerona, Falacer, Faunus, Flora, (Fons), Furrina, Janus, Jupiter, Larenta, Lares, (? Lemures), Liber, Mars, Mater Matuta, Neptunus, Ops, Pales, (Palatua), Pomona, Portunus, Quirinus, (? Robigus), Saturnus, Tellus, (? Terminus), Vejovis, Vesta, Volcanus, Volturnus."[O2]

The familiar names of Janus, Jupiter, Mars, Vesta, Neptune, and Vulcan appear, but Juno, Venus, Apollo, Minerva, and Mercury are absent. Of the names on the list, nothing is known any longer about Falacer and Furrina, although flamines were appointed to serve them. Others are hardly better known to us. Many dropped from public notice altogether in later days. Why is anybody's guess. We may note, however, a significant fact: Those that survived to enjoy later prominence were as important to the city as they had been to the country.

Jupiter

Jupiter (Diespiter of Diovis Pater = Father Jove) was of dateless origin. He is, of course, the Indo-European Dyaus Pitar, or Zeus Pater, and came over the mountains into Italy in the same manner as he entered Greece. As in Greece, he absorbed the functions of many local Italian gods. His most exalted title was Optimus Maximus. In consequence of being the god of lightning, thunder, and rain, he acquired the epithets Fulminator, Tonans, and Pluvius, and because he was the god of light, he was honored by having the days of the full moon made sacred to him. He predetermined the course of human affairs and gave men foregleams of coming events by signs in the heavens and the flight of birds, which the augurs were appointed to read; hence he was called Jove Prodigialis, the prodigy sender. His lightning was often a judgment, a catastrophic punishment for evildoing, for he was the guardian of the laws of the state and of the sanctity of oaths. In Rome, his temple was built on the Capitoline hill, whence he was called Jupiter Capitolinus. In later days, as the special protector of Rome, he shared in the imperial glories of that city and acquired such titles as Imperator, Invictus, Victor, and Praedator. He received the worship of the consuls of the Republic when they took up their offices. The celebrated "triumphs" of returning generals were spectacular processions winding to the shouts of the joyous populace through the city, carrying booty and captives to his temple.

Mars and Quirinus

Mars and Quirinus were the two war gods. Mars, identified by the Greeks with Ares, was perhaps originally the protector of the fields and herds from inimical powers of any kind, animal, human, or superhuman. He became increasingly associated with war as the Roman imperium was extended, and his original character changed. But the homely, protective nature of his early activity is seen in the description Cato has left us of the procession of a farmer and his family along his farm's boundary line three times around, accompanied by a pig, a sheep, and an ox, the victims that were afterward solemnly sacrificed. During the sacrifice, the farmer offered libations to Janus and Jupiter, and prayed thus like a lawyer,

> Father Mars, I pray and beseech thee that thou mayest be propitious and of good will to me, our house and household, for which cause I have ordered the offering of pig, sheep, and ox to be led round my field, my land, and my farm, that thou mightest prevent, ward off and avert diseases, visible and invisible, barrenness and waste, accidents and bad weather; that thou wouldest suffer the crops and fruits of the earth, the vines and shrubs to wax great and prosper, that thou wouldest preserve the shepherds and their flocks in safety, and give prosperity and health to me and our house and household; for all these causes, for the lustration and purification of my farm, land, and field, as I have said, be thou enriched by the sacrifice of this offering of suckling pig, lamb, and calf.[5]

In Rome, where a similar ceremony took place on the Campus Martius around an altar to the god that stood there, Mars's sacred symbols were the lance and shield,

his sacred animal the wolf, and his servitors the Salii and the Flamen Martialis.

Of Quirinus we know almost nothing, except that he was the war god of the community on the Quirinal, while Mars was from the Palatine. Quirinus was served by a flamen and had a festival dedicated to him that took place on February 17 (the Quirinalia). Perhaps he represented defense where Mars stood for offense, for he seems to have been the numen of assemblies or convocations.

Janus and Vesta

Janus and Vesta were ritualistically linked together as the first and last deities invoked in any ceremony. Janus, as the keeper of the door, was invoked at the opening of almost anything. He was the god of beginnings, and thus of the first hour of the day, of the Calends of every month, and, in the calendar of later days, of the first month of the year (January). His original symbol in Rome was simply a gateway standing at the northeast corner of the Forum. It was under the king's charge, and later was assigned the services of a priest called the Rex Sacrorum, highest in dignity of all the priests. Like Vesta, Janus was not originally personalized; the door, opening and closing, was his only sign, just as the pure flame, guarded by the vestal virgins in the temple of Vesta, sufficed there to show forth the goddess.

Changes Due to Etruscan Influence

Though the facts are not entirely clear, it is certain that Rome came under Etruscan dominance during the whole of the sixth century B.C.E. This brought about some significant changes. The Etruscans were energetic and commercial minded. Recognizing the strategic position of Rome, they built a wall around it that enclosed enough space for a population of 200,000. They sought to make residence in the city attractive to plebeians, and therefore favored them as against patricians. And they introduced some entirely new trends in Roman religion.

New deities were brought in, without seriously disturbing, at first, the old entrenched customs. Diana left her grove at Aricia for a temple erected to her on the Aventine. The triumvirate of Jupiter, Mars, and Quirinus was overshadowed by a well-housed triad composed of Jupiter, Juno, and Minerva, established on the Capitoline in a bright new temple of Etruscan artistry.

The association of Jupiter and Juno, here begun, later led to their being regarded as husband and wife. This was the first clear instance of marriage among the Roman gods. The earlier Roman religion had furnished some instances of the yoking of male and female names, but this had signified so much less than marriage or family connection that scholars find in it only fresh evidence that the early Romans did not unambiguously know what sex their numina had: sometimes, to be safe, they gave them names signifying both sexes. But Juno became Jupiter's consort and thus took on much more of the aspects of distinct personality than before. Originally, she had simply imparted numen to women and girls (as men had their genius, so women had their juno), and in the form of Juno Lucina she had been invoked at the moment of childbirth. Now she attained the characteristics that caused visiting Greeks to identify her with Hera.

Minerva may have been Etruscan. Her character paralleled that of Athena. She was the goddess of wisdom and the patroness of arts and trades. In due time her aid was sought in war, hence she was represented as wearing a helmet and a coat of mail, and she carried a spear and a shield in the manner of her Greek counterpart.

This visualizing of Minerva as an anthropomorphic deity points to an innovation of the Etruscans which was of the first importance. They set images of the gods in the temples they built. In the temple on the Capitoline, they erected two rows of columns down the center of the sanctuary, and at the northwestern end they placed three images—a statue of Jupiter flanked by one of Juno and another of Minerva. Here was the initial step that led to the imaging and personalizing of all the deities. Even Janus acquired a head—but with two faces, one looking forward and one backward. But these changes were not purely Etruscan.

Borrowings from the Greeks

Just as the political power of Rome under the Etruscans was extending southward through Italy, Greek cultural influence began to penetrate northward. Especially impressive to the Romans was Greek ritual.

Etruscan Minerva

It provided vital elements of warmth and poetry hitherto lacking in Roman religion. The Romans on their part proved ready to adopt many new conceptions offered by the Greeks, without meaning to abandon any of their old ways.

Of far-reaching moment was the introduction into Rome during the sixth century B.C.E. of a collection of oracles credited to the Cumaean Sibyl—the famous Sibylline Books. These books, stored in the basement of the Capitoline temple, were committed to a newly created order of patrician priests, two in number, the *duoviri sacris faciundis* ("the two charged with sacred matters"), whose number was later increased to ten and still later to fifteen. These priests were asked on many grave occasions to consult the oracles; in each case they afterward announced, without revealing the verses consulted, the course of procedure that they said was advised. Because the oracles were of Greek origin, the *viri sacris faciundis* usually prescribed as remedies for impending or present disaster, or for public perplexity, resort to deities and ceremonies not before known to the Romans, except perhaps by report. As a result, extensive adoptions into Roman religion took place.

It cannot be said that the Sibylline advisors suggested changes without precedent. Castor and Pollux had already been brought to Rome by way of the Latin town of Tusculum, and Hercules had also arrived by way of the town of Tiber. But the Sibylline Books gave impetus to a process that might otherwise have been slow. In 493 B.C.E. their verses were interpreted to advise the erection of a temple to house Ceres, Liber, and Libera (= Demeter, Dionysus, and Persephone). A temple for Apollo, as a healing god, was next prescribed. Similarly, Greek rites in honor of Poseidon were imported by identifying him with the Roman Neptune. Hermes came to Rome also, but under the name of Mercury, for he was to be the god of commerce (*mercatura*). Later, in much the same way, and with an accompanying Greek ritual, Aphrodite made her appearance as Venus (who had been a minor Italian deity, perhaps of the garden). At about the same time, a pestilence led to the advice that Aesculapius, the god of healing, be introduced at once and provided with a temple. These fully personalized deities added an entirely new dimension to Roman religion, as did the importation of astrology from Mesopotamia through the Hellenistic Greeks; it became widely popular on the grounds that heavenly bodies sent out emanations that influenced individuals and events on earth.

Sometimes the Sibylline advisors suggested a *lectisternium*. Here the Greek ritual called for the introduction of a whole group of gods, appearing as wooden figures, elegantly attired and reclining on couches around a banquet table, on which was placed a sacramental meal! Livy reports that in 399 B.C.E., during a severe pestilence, Apollo, Latona, Hercules, Diana, Mercury, and Neptune were together propitiated in this manner. Nor was this the last time this rite was performed. The gods were becoming more human every day.

And as if stirred into original creation by these importations, the Romans added (or rather, resurrected from former times) new deities of their own: Fides to personalize the quality of loyalty celebrated in the title "Fidius" assigned to Jupiter, and Victoria to do the same for his qualities as Jupiter Victor. A goddess of luck and good fortune appeared also under the name of Fortuna. Each of these was given a separate temple within the city.

Along with all of this came increased interest in the myths and epics of Greece. As a consequence, many of the Greek myths were adapted to the Italian scene and to Roman history and were reissued in new form, although most were simply taken over with slight change, to become part of the Roman heritage. The life histories of Jupiter, Juno, Minerva, and others were built

up out of the Greek elements into stories ranging over an international scene but with an Italian coloring. At the same time, inventive (if not supremely imaginative) minds fell to work on Roman traditions and elaborated Italian myths about Romulus and Remus, Aeneas, Tiberinus, and others. The way for Ovid and Vergil, the poets of the future, was thus prepared.

Cults from Eastern Mediterranean Areas

As the Romans grew away from a completely agricultural economy toward an urban and imperial point of view, increasing numbers of people lost their rootage in the soil, and with it the meaning-filled activities of pursuing their own subsistence. There was room for speculation and skepticism.

Mystic cults, promising richer emotional satisfactions, came from the Orient. The first of these was the Magna Mater, Cybele, introduced from Phrygia on the advice of the Sibylline oracles. An embassy of five prominent Roman citizens went during the protracted crisis of the Second Punic War (218–201 B.C.E.) to fetch a sacred stone, dropped from heaven, in which Cybele was thought to be resident.

But the city fathers took a rather sober view, on closer acquaintance with Cybele, of the wildness and fanaticism of her devotees. They passed a law, which was not abrogated until the Empire, forbidding Romans to enter her priesthood, because it usually meant their castration; she had to be served by priests brought in from Asia Minor. The people, however, were allowed to, and did, go to her temple to seek her aid, for this life and the next.

Upon Cybele's arrival, the mystery religion of Bacchus (Dionysus), with its secret rites, followed. There was swift response to it, not only in Rome but throughout the Italian peninsula. But the upper classes hated secrecy of any kind and were highly suspicious of it; they came to believe the worst of the Bacchanalian orgies. Accordingly, the cult was suppressed by a decree of the Senate in 186 B.C.E. But it came to life again and was allowed to continue under the strict supervision of the state.

In the years that ensued, other Eastern cults gained a footing and grew in influence. Ma of Cappadocia, Adonis of Syria, Isis and Osiris (Serapis) of

Egypt, and Mithras of Persia were all brought to Rome, and each in some measure supplied the religious experience and hope of immortality that the state religion, which had now fallen into the hands of agnostic politicians and of priests who also had lost faith, was powerless to call forth or sustain.

The Last Phases

The history of Roman religion during the last century of the Republic (150–49 B.C.E.) suggests the operation of forces moving in a direction exactly opposite to those of an earlier time. The movement was no longer centripetal, but centrifugal. The state religion had degenerated into pure formalism—the structure was there, but it was empty and void. For one thing, Rome itself was like a deity (Dea Roma) and no longer needed the help of the old gods in the old way. The educated classes, enlightened or disillusioned by Greek philosophy, pursued the atheistic way of the Epicureans, or the pantheistic way of the Stoics, or else lapsed into indifference. The attitude of Cicero was typical: he inclined toward Stoicism, but he was an eclectic and would commit himself nowhere because his skepticism prevented him from doing so. Religion was something to discuss pleasantly over the dinner table or with friends in a moment of leisure, but apart from its value as a political binding element, it was of no vital concern to thinking persons.

The attempt of Augustus Caesar to bring the world back to normal, after a generation of unnerving civil wars, by reviving the old Roman religious practices led him to repair the decaying temples of Rome, induce men to enter again the old priesthoods, and build new temples, such as that on the Palatine in honor of Apollo, the patron of his house. But this was not in itself sufficient. It affected Rome only, and even there it aroused only a mild response. He knew already how advantageous it was to him politically to be regarded outside of Italy as a god. The world needed to look to some one power, worship of which might bind it together, and perhaps none might be as useful for this purpose as the ongoing genius (*numen*) of the imperial house. To encourage this feeling, Augustus erected a temple in the Forum, furnished with specially appointed priests and dedicated to the honor of Divus Julius (Julius Caesar, his father by adoption),

who had already been declared a god by the Roman Senate in 42 B.C.E. As for himself, he permitted the erection of shrines in which his genius was worshiped (though not himself). These events set the stage for the introduction of an official imperial cult.

The Imperial Cult

In the provinces it became mandatory, as a sign of loyalty to the Roman imperium, to pay reverence to the Emperor's genius, and sometimes to the Emperor himself. Although throughout life Augustus steadfastly refused honors to himself in person, it was inevitable that after his death his name should be enrolled with those of the gods and that a temple should be erected to him, with priests in attendance. Not all of the emperors immediately after him were accorded this honor, but in due time consecration of the emperor as a god became part of every imperial funeral. At last the aura of divinity came to attach itself to emperors *before* death. Caligula and Domitian were two who demanded worship while living, and Nero, vain of his musical and poetical attainments, enjoyed being equated with Apollo.

What is significant here is this: when it was apparent that the multiplicity of religions led only to contrifugal scattering, emperor worship was conceived in an attempt to reverse the flight from the common center. But it was not enough; it just barely served. In a fundamental sense, it was not cosmic enough, not able to link together individuals, society, and the universe under one inclusive meaning or purpose.

IV. EUROPE BEYOND THE ALPS

In the early history of Greece and Rome we met with bands of southward-surging Indo-Europeans; in northern Europe we find them everywhere. (Later in our story we shall meet them also in India, Iran, and Armenia.) One of the puzzles of history is where these people originated and what sent them on their far-flung journeys, radiating outward like the spokes of a wheel, south, west, north, and southeast. But whatever moved them from their prehistoric homeland (in southern Russia and the Ukraine?), they succeeded, thanks to their mastery of the chariot, cavalry attack, and the wielding of long two-handed swords from horseback, not only in subjugating the resident tribes in their path, outnumbered though they were, but also in superimposing their language upon those current among the tribes they conquered, together with many elements of their magic and religion. The ancient Celts and Teutons developed religious practices and beliefs which, in spite of assimilation of many variant local conceptions and customs, nevertheless illustrate what the original Indo-European worldview might be expected to become when not radically altered by the infusion of foreign ways of behaving and believing.

The Celts

We have already met the Celts in northern Italy. As far as we can determine from the uncertain records, the Celts moved originally from their first homeland to northwestern Germany, where they merged with proto-Nordic and Alpine tribes to form a new amalgam of ethnic groups marked by tall, green-eyed, red-haired people. Then they broke up by migrating westward across the Channel to the British Isles, southwestward into France (Gaul) and thence into Spain, southward into Italy and Greece, and far to the southeast into Asia Minor, where they held on for centuries to the province to which they gave their name (Galatia, the place of the Gauls).

The Celts, according to the *Commentaries* of Julius Caesar, mostly worshiped a god Caesar identifies as Mercury, but he does not give us the Celtic name. (The god was possibly the Odin we shall meet later, a god of magic and the dead, and the source of the inspiration of orators and poets.) He says they also worshiped Apollo, Mars, Jupiter, and Minerva. To this list he adds Dispater, god of the netherworld, to whom he says the Gauls traced their origin. He is joined by Tacitus, the Elder Pliny, and Lucan in the statement that the Celts were led by their priests (the Druids) in sacrifices and animal and tree worship.

The Druids

It appears that there were three hereditary orders among the Celts of Gaul and of Ireland: priests (*Druides*), warrior nobility (*equites*), and artisans (*plebs*). Under Druid leadership, ceremonies were conducted in forest sanctuaries, in homes, and in sacred groves. Caesar tells us that the Druids had political as well as religious functions. They played a role in the election of kings, served as ambassadors or legates, and took part in battles. Their teachings were preserved orally only and could not be learned without a long period of training, sometimes lasting up to twenty years. These teachings, according to Caesar, concerned not only religious and magical matters but also the movements of the stars, the size of the world, and the general constitution of the universe at large.

How truly Caesar understood what he described cannot be known, but it does seem probable, although we are not at all certain, that the Druids engaged in speculations that the world would someday come to an end, that there would be a doomsday overwhelming men and gods, when fire and water would swallow up the earth, the sky would fall, and all humankind would perish, to make way for a new heaven and earth and a new race of men. In any event, the Celts laid great stress on Fate as something that could only be delayed, never prevented.

The Celts found divinity in nature all around them, for they revered it in the sky, mountains, stones, trees, lakes, rivers, springs, the sea, and every kind of animal—the boar, bear, bull, horse, hare, ram, stag, even the crow, and many female as well as male creatures—the cow, for example. (The snake also received its share of regard, so when St. Patrick came to Ireland, there grew the legend that he not only drove the ancient gods and goddesses into the hills and glens to serve a lower function as fairies, but also rid Ireland of snakes: in short, he could not tolerate veneration of them.) Some Celtic gods and goddesses were part animal and part human in shape. Others resembled Epona, the Gallic fertility goddess, who carried a cornucopia while on horseback or while seated among horses.

Fertility Rituals

Another certain fact is that the Celts were much concerned with fertility in field, flock, and womankind. There were many fertility powers, male and female, and a number of mother goddesses. It was common to revere the last in groups of three and to portray them holding in their laps children or baskets of fruit in evidence of their influence on fruitfulness. Among the recurrent ceremonies of the Celts was the May Day festival. It has survived in a token form as the Maypole dance in Europe and America. The ancient Celtic festivals bore all of the marks of fertility magic. It was a widespread practice to light bonfires on the hills about May 1 and then do the following things: drive cattle through or between them, have the people dance a sun dance around them, bring new fires from them to the home hearths, and then carry some of the burning brands around the fields like shining suns. There also was a May king and a May queen who symbolized, or were thought of as incarnations of, the vegetation spirits in and below the ground. It is likely that they were given in marriage to each other to stimulate fertility in soil and flock.

Roman sources report incidences of human sacrifice and their own steps taken to suppress the practice. They write that sacrifices were made not only to promote fertility but more generally to appease, thank, or gain the help of the gods. Though victims from the tribe were sometimes chosen—wives or children, at times—it was more common to offer up prisoners of war or thieves and other criminals. Murderers, for example, were turned over to the Druids for sacrifice to the gods. The Roman authors tell us that the victims were sometimes slain beforehand by arrows or by stakes driven through their temples, but it also was a practice to build a large effigy of wicker or wood and straw, then to fill it with human and animal victims and to have the Druids set it on fire. It may be assumed that such sacrifices were very special occasions, for example, in celebration of victory, or at the funeral of an important person, and that ordinarily only animal sacrifices were offered, men and dogs joining in the feast after the sacrifice, the dogs, as Arrian tells us of the Galatian Celts, being decked with garlands of flowers. In modified form, some of these rites have come down to our own day. Carl Clemen offers us the following instances from France:

> In the district round Grenoble to this day a goat is slaughtered at harvest-time. Its flesh, with the exception of one piece, which is kept for a year, is eaten by the reapers, and out of its skin the farmer has a coat made, which is believed to have healing virtue. In Pouilly an ox is killed, its skin being kept till the next seed-time. Undoubtedly these animals represent the spirit of vegetation. In former days in Brie on the 23rd of June, and down to the year 1743 in a certain street in Paris on the 3rd of July, a

> human effigy was burnt, the people fighting for the *debris.* . . . Finally, there are certain phrases still current in many districts of France which contain an allusion to the killing of a human being or an animal at harvest-time. When the last sheaf is being garnered or threshed the people say, "We are killing the old woman," or "the hare," "the dog," "the cat," or "the ox."[O2]

Frazer's *The Golden Bough* assembles hundreds of similar instances of the survival in Europe of ceremonies from a pre-Christian time.

The Teutons

Appearing in history later than the Celts, the Teutons began to press westward from the southern shores of the Baltic as Anglo-Saxons and Jutes, southward as Saxons, Alamanni, Lombards, Frisians, and Franks, northward as Scandinavians, and southeastward as Goths and Vandals.

Teutonic tradition comes to us chiefly through two Icelandic works, the *Poetic Edda,* an anthology of hymns to the gods and heroic poems, said to have been assembled by Saemundr the Wise (1056–1133 B.C.E.), and the *Prose Edda,* the work of Snorri Sturluson, a thirteenth-century Christian, scholar, and skeptic, who tried to provide a practical manual for young poets who would wish to draw upon the traditional myths of Iceland for their material. Also important as authentic sources are the Norse *sagas* and *scalds* (poems), of which eight or ten are especially significant.

From these sources we get a rather crowded picture of a score of gods and goddesses, some ancient, some late, whom we must suppose to have come forward or receded in importance with passing time. One of the oldest was the sky god Tiw or Tiwaz (Ziu, Tiu, or Tyr), whose name has possibly the same root as Zeus and the Dyaus Pitar of the Indo-Aryans. (The name appears again in the word of Anglo-Saxon descent *Tuesday*.) He was originally the shining sky but relinquished his high place and predominance to become a god of law, fertility, and war. In contrast to him, Donar (Thumor or Thor), the red-bearded god of thunder (*donner*) and rain, and therefore of agriculture and the oak, grew in importance with the years, becoming the center of a cult that spread throughout the Teutonic world. Carrying his famous thunder hammer, Miollnir, in iron-

Sequanian Goddess

Typical of Celtic mother figurines protecting village fountains and promoting fertility of flocks, herds, crops, and humankind, this young goddess with center-parted braided hair received homage in the territory of the Celtic Sequani tribe who inhabited the Alsatian River courses around modern Besançon in the early days of the Roman Empire. Borne along in an aquatic wildfowl vessel, she holds out her hands in a gesture of blessing. *(Giraudon/Art Resource, N.Y. S0132535.A0003405.)*

gloved hands, as Thor he rode in a sky chariot drawn by two he-goats. He became the chief god in Norway and Iceland. (We now have his name in *Thursday*.) If Thor was popular with the common folk, one-eyed Wodan or Odin (also Othin), the cunning, if not tricky, god of earth, magic, and the dead, was exalted by the ruling princes and war chiefs, because he was, for them, a god of war who protected heroes and caused his two Valkyries or war maidens to carry warriors fallen in battle to his great hall in the sky, Valhalla. When traveling through the heavens, or visiting the underworld, he gal-loped upon the eight-legged horse Sleipnir, accompanied by his wolves, Geri and Freki. In heaven, he surveyed the world from the windows of Valaskialf, his home, supporting on either shoulder two ravens, Huggin (Thought) and Munin (Memory), who whispered in his ear their reports of all that they had seen while in flight. His dreaded spear, Gungnir, made by dwarfs, never missed. Knowing and seeing all, he was the source of the wisdom of seers and poets. (We still honor him in our *Wednesday*.) Snorri of Iceland calls him the chief of the Aesir, the gods in heaven, who dominate the Vanir, the fertility gods beneath. He is called All-Father, and he, as we shall see, assisted at the creation.

Fertility, Death, and Doom

Three things seem to have concerned the Teutonic peoples greatly—fertility, death, and the end of the world. As to the first, they did not put all of their reliance on the life-quickening rain of Thor. They turned also to Freyr (Frey, Fricco), symbolized by the stallion and the boar, "lord" of fertility in humans, animals, and vegetation, and lord, too, of summer; they turned as well to his twin sister and wife Freyja (the "Lady"). Freyr and Freyja were quite possibly son and daughter of the god of fruitfulness and wealth, Njörd, or Njörth, symbolized by the prosperity-bringing ship coming to shore after a voyage, and the goddess Nerthus, of whom Tacitus had so much to say.

Freyr and Freyja were the divine May king and May queen whose magical embrace brought the revival of life in spring. But the cycle of spring, summer, and autumn was symbolized by other gods and goddesses, the most notable of whom is Balder, whose tragic death (autumn?) is recorded in the well-known myth. Balder (the blessed Light) was the kindest, most noble, and most gentle of the gods. His mother Frigg, consort of Odin and queen of the gods (for whom *Friday* is named), took oaths from all things not to hurt him, but she neglected to pledge the mistletoe. Thinking Balder invulnerable, the gods had great sport throwing every kind of object at him, always without harming him, but Loki, the malicious one and trickster among the gods, learned that the mistletoe had not been sworn and persuaded the blind but powerful Hödr (Höther) to hurl a sprig of mistletoe at Balder, and he was slain. Balder perforce descended to Hel, the world of the dead, there to await liberation at the end of the world. Sometimes in the Eddas, the underworld Hel is personified by Loki's daughter, Hel, a repulsive and dreadful creature who assigns to all who are sent to her their places in the underworld.

Death was a disturbing thought to the Teutons, for it was too often only the beginning of troubles. Until the corpse of a man decayed, it could do harm as a specter or vampire (a belief the Norse shared with the Chinese on the other side of the world), and the corpse itself was in danger of being torn to pieces by wolves out of hell, by horse-shaped demons, or by swooping eagles, such as the giant wind demon Hraesvelg. On the other hand, the spirits of the dead, if they had been good in life and were faithfully reverenced after death, could bring good fortune to their descendants.

The convictions concerning the afterlife seem confused. In later times the Teutons believed both that the dead lived on in their burial harrows and yet that they traveled nine days and nights by the Hel-way to the underworld, where they sat in the great hall of Hel on benches and drank beer (mead). But the warriors went to Valhalla—at least those whom Thor favored—and there they feasted on boar's flesh behind the 540 great doors of the shield-thatched hall, and then rose to fight each other in the courtyard for self-conditioning and sport.

The reason the warriors of Valhalla adopted a regimen of self-conditioning lay in their knowledge that Wodan would need their services in the cosmic conflict that would take place at the time of the Doom of the Gods (the Götterdämmerung). At this point, Teutonic thought reached a certain profundity—or was it no more than a dramatic view of time and history?

Snorri's Prose Epic

According to Snorri (in the *Prose Edda,* reflecting the myths not only of the Viking Age but probably of earlier Germanic peoples as well), the first state of things, the Ginnunga Gap—a yawning gulf or opening suspended between a region of mist and cold, Niflheim, and a region of glowing heat, Muspelheim—generated from its rime and slush a cosmic giant, Ymir. In a similar way, according to a parallel tradition, there also emerged a cosmic cow, Audumla, whose milk-filled udders fed Ymir and made it possible for him to generate other beings. Presently from under the hands and feet of Ymir came the frost giants; the cow Audumla also, while licking the salty ice to the north, de-iced and freed Buri, a giant who became the grandsire, through his son Bor and daughter-in-law Bestla, of Wodan, Vili, and Ve. Rising against Ymir, Wodan and his brothers slew and dismembered the primal giant, making the earth from his flesh, trees from his hair, mountains from his bones, the earth-encompassing sea from his blood, clouds from his brain, and the bowl of heaven from his hollow skull. (The Hindus and the Chinese have similar stories of the earth's origin to tell.) From the sparks out of Muspel-heim, the sun, moon, and stars were formed. The three brothers then took the eyebrows of Ymir to make a raised plain, called Midgard, to be the abode of men, and from two trees by the sea they formed the first man and woman, Askr and Embla, the parents of the human race. The three brothers also created dwarfs to live in dens under the earth and in stones and hills. In the region above the earth, they made Askgard, the abode of the gods, with its great halls and palaces, and between heaven and earth they put a rainbow bridge, guarded against the giants by the god Heimdall. So runs the story of creation in the *Prose Edda,* although other sources, such as the poem *Voluspa* in the *Poetic Edda,* tell the story somewhat differently, but it is not to our purpose to inquire further.

An uneasy world order was now established. The frost giants were exiled to the shores of Utgard, the earth-encompassing sea; the gods dwelt in Askgard and men in Midgard; the dead gathered in Hel, its gate in Niflheim guarded by the watchdog Garm. Off in the sea, all around the flat earth lay the huge submerged coil of the evil Midgard serpent. (Using an ox head as bait, Thor once fished him up in a battle so fierce that he stamped his foot through the bottom of his boat.) Outside the world in Muspelheim, the region of heat, were the ferocious Fenriswolf, bound by a magic chain of the gods, and the giant Sutr, the bold leader of the fire giants. The gods of Askgard, the rulers of this uneasy world, passed down Bifrost, the rainbow bridge, to stand under the world tree to pass judgment.

How exactly the world tree, Yggdrasil, fits into this picture is difficult to say, but the old tree was "the pillar" between the nine regions of the world. Under its three roots were the three regions where dwelt the dead, live human beings, and the exiled frost giants. The regions of the sky were sustained by its branches. (Here is a conception the Teutons shared with the Celts, Slavs, Mesopotamians, Hindus, and numerous groups in central Asia.)

But the Teutonic peoples knew that this world order would not last forever. In a hall under the world tree dwelt the three Norns or Fates, representing the past, the present, and the future, who fixed the lot or destiny of each individual at birth. This was an impor-tant conception, for the destiny or *wyrd*—from which the English word *weird* is derived—thus fixed was a

Thor Fishing for the Midgard Serpent

fate determined beyond appeal for gods and humans alike, and could not be stayed. The Norns would some-day make known the hour of doomsday. That hour would come when the old tree would groan and trem-ble; the Fenriswolf would break his chain and come raging to earth; the giant Sutr would lead the fire giants in an assault upon the gods; the frost giants would storm in from the edges of the world; the Midgard serpent, thrashing heavily in the sea, would toss great tidal waves across the earth. The watchdog of Hel would set up a howl and let Loki lead his allies past him up to earth to join in the overthrow of the world order. The invaders would storm Bifrost, only to have that frail bridge break under them. Then the final battle of the world would take place on the plains of earth, with the gods and the heroes of Valhalla going down in defeat; humankind would suffer apparent extinction, and the earth would be burned up by the victorious forces of fire and chaos.

After a while, a new earth would emerge from the sea, and the sons of Wodan and Thor, together with Balder and Hödr released from Hel, would establish a new and more promising world order. Human life would begin again from two survivors of the Götter-dämmerung and its accompanying world conflagration.

This remarkable conception of time and history links the Teutonic peoples with those of India, who also believed, and still do, in world cycles. It is obvious also that Christianity, when it came, could and did profit by the expectation of the death of the old gods and the return of gentle, cruelly slain Balder from Hel. The Viking resistance to Christianity delayed the conversion of Scandinavia until the tenth century. The kings of Denmark and Norway were baptized in that century, and Iceland adopted Christianity shortly afterward, about the year 1000.

The youngest of the Scandinavian epics, the Finnish *Kalevala,* reflects and transmutes the theme of the twilight of the old gods. A treasury of folk poetry first compiled in 1835 (but incorporating strands from at least three hundred years earlier), it accepts the inevitability of change with mingled sadness and appreciation. The hero Väinämöinen departs for lofty regions singing for the last time to the strains of his marvelous *kantele* (harp). He gives way to a virgin and her child, but he leaves behind the kantele, the heritage in song of the old ways.

V. MESOAMERICA: THE MAYA*

Six centuries (300–900 C.E.) spanned the classic flowering of Maya civilization, the most impressive of a constellation of Mesoamerican cultures. Scores of archaeological sites in the Yucatan peninsula and along the present borders of Guatemala and Honduras have revealed spectacular architectural achievements: lofty pyramid temples, ceremonial courts, and magnificent elevated highways. Most significant of all are the hundreds of monoliths (stelae) bearing hieroglyphs, many of them with specific calendric information. For reasons that may never be clear (climate change? soil exhaustion? social disintegration?), the great ceremonial complexes fell rather abruptly into disuse well before military incursions from the north brought infusions from other cultures, particularly the Aztec. Tropical vegetation and erosion relentlessly dismantled the material structures, while other Mesoamerican groups, and ultimately the Spanish invasions, imposed

whole new structures of thought. Yet some distinctive Mayan conceptual frames and values endured to leave their marks on the culture of Central America today.

In religious terms, the significant Mayan marks are not so much in the aspects of Mayan culture that fascinate scholars and impress tourists: the architecture, the art the glyphs and intricate calendric system. Rather, they are the fundamental attitudes of devotion and the feelings for the sacred, which are almost universal among *campesino* peasants today. The Maya retain a devout attitude toward the sources of sustenance: soil is sacred, especially the *milpa* maize plot; and the maize itself is so treasured that it is spoken of with a reverential prefix, much like "Your Honor." The ancient Mayans focused so sharply on the sacred significance of time that they assigned separate divine sponsorship to each day in the seasonal round. They found it natural that the fruits of the earth should be offered to the divine providers and shared with all of their human children. These views seem to foreshadow elements of liberation theology in Central America today.

The Shape of the World

For a detailed impression of Mayan cosmology (and many other elements of Mayan religion in the classic period) one must supplement meager hieroglyphic clues with accounts first written in the sixteenth century: the *Popol Vuh* (ca. 1530), Bishop Diego Landa's *Relación de la cosas de Yucatán* (ca. 1560), and the *Books of Chilam Balam.* While it is hazardous to infer too much about earlier times from these records, occasional convergence of details with hieroglyphic information in codices and stelae suggests that major concepts in the mythology were preserved.

The Maya saw the dome of the sky as seven layered: six ascending steps in the east, a cap, and six descending steps in the west—thirteen compartments in all. The sky was supported by four gods, the Bacabs. Bishop Landa's account says they were children of Hunab Ku, "single existing god," a remote creator deity. The Bacabs were correlated with compass directions and colors: the red Bacab at the east, the white at the north, the black at the west, and the yellow at the south. Apparently the world rested upon a huge crocodile-like dragon, or perhaps on four of them—many deities

---

*This account is based largely on works by David Friedel, S.G. Morley, Linda Schele, J. Eric S. Thompson, and A.M. Tozzer.

Woman Grinding Maize

appearing in four aspects, a configuration also found in the Cherokee vision of the shape of the world. In fact, J. Eric S. Thompson suggests a theory of common origin from ancient Asian migrations. The association of colors and celestial dragons with four world quarters he finds to be ideas "too complex and unnaturalistic to have been evolved independently in both Asia and America."[T1]

According to the *Popol Vuh* of the Quiche Maya, the creation required three attempts. There was only water at the beginning. The creator gods spoke the word "earth" and land appeared. Then they produced vegetation and animals of the sort who could not speak to offer praise and also produced higher creatures made of mud. The mud creatures could speak, but they were unintelligent and they dissolved in water. There was a second creation using wood, but these puppets still were unintelligent and showed no gratitude. The other animals turned against them: "Why did you give us nothing to eat?" A few of the wood puppets escaped and became the ancestors of the monkeys.

In the third attempt, the ancestors of the Quiche Maya were made from the quintessential provender, a gruel of yellow and white maize. This time, the original four were *too* gifted; so the gods, not wishing humans to be so nearly their equal, dulled their vision with a bit of mist. Wives were created for them. Then the morning star appeared, the sun arose, and the humans worshipped their makers.[T2]

Thompson points out in his account that the culminating event was not the creation of humankind, but the dawn of time and the beginning of worship.

The Shape and Feel of Time

Both the hieroglyphic and the calendric systems probably originated with the pre-classic Olmec culture but were vastly extended. There was a sacred year (*tzolkin*) of 260 days and a seasonal maize-crop year (*haab*) of 365 days. In the sacred year, a cycle of twenty named days (each with its glyph) was rotated, each having a number prefix from one to thirteen (see page 71). The numbers were repeated so that at 260 days each number had been combined with each named day. The civil year was composed of nineteen months (eighteen months of twenty days and a closing month of five days). The interfacing of the calendars can be imagined as the meshing of cog wheels as illustrated. The *tzolkin* wheel will make seventy-three revolutions and the *haab* wheel fifty-two before they return to their original positions. Once every fifty-two civil years the glyph of any given "day bearer" will fall on the first day of the year and become the "year bearer."

The foregoing suggests the mechanics of measurement, but it is the "feel" or the weight of time that is religiously significant. As Thompson puts it,

> The Maya conceived of the divisions of time as burdens carried through all eternity by relays of divine bearers. These hearers were the numbers by which the different periods were distinguished. The burdens were carried on the back, the weight supported by tumplines across the forehead.... [In a hieroglyph] the night god, who takes over when the day is done, is in the act of rising with his load. With his left hand he eases the weight on the tumpline; with his right hand on the ground he steadies himself as he starts to rise. The artist conveys in the strain reflected in the god's features the physical effort of rising from the ground with his heavy load.[T3]

Such imagery suggests the sharing of the good or evil fortune according to the aspect of the bearer god with whom the year began. Actually, only four day names could fall at the beginning of a year.

> Thus if the year began with the day Kan, one could look forward to a good crop because Kan was merely an aspect of the maize god; if the day Muluc was the year-bearer, good crops would also be expected since Muluc was the rain god. On the contrary, the influences of the day gods Ix and

Cauac were malevolent, so years which started with them would be disastrous.[T4]

Lest the year-bearer omens seem to make for a rigidly fated future, it should be emphasized that there were many means of modification claimed by priests so that rites of expiation and hedging could be employed.

Finally, the Mayans' obsession with time took them deep into the past and far into the future in their calculations: one inscription sweeps back 400 million years. Coupled with this was a conviction that history repeats itself, so that one can prepare for repetitions of good or evil eras if the calculations are accurate enough.

Priests, Royalty, and Peasant

The disparity between the grandeur of ceremonial complexes and the lifestyle of peasants dwelling in thatched huts by their slash-and-burn milpa raises many questions. Clearly there were hierarchies of a hereditary priest royalty that researched calendric detail and presided at the high temple complexes. In the classic period, these may not have been residential palaces but sites visited only for ceremonies. The stupendous expenditure of effort to build these complexes testifies to firm organization and centralized power. But how wide was the gap between priests and peasantry, and how much did relationships change over time? Thompson suggests that abuse of power may have led to a breakdown of the compact between the elite and the peasantry and contributed to the rapid decline at the end of the classic period. On the other hand, the relatively infrequent appearance of military or coercive enforcement figures in hieroglyphs and art suggests that for most of the period peasants donated labor willingly and did not feel totally excluded from the cult system. Morley estimated that a Maya peasant or *milpero* could produce enough maize for his family in forty-eight work days. "Here," he wrote, "is the surplus time—roughly nine to ten months—during which the ancient Maya ceremonial centers were built."[U1]

> "The Maya did not set the human race so far apart from the rest of created life as we do, but then the Maya had and still has a deeper sense of his unimportance in creation."[T5]
>
> —J. Eric S. Thompson

The highest office among the elite was the *halach uinic* or "true man," essentially a civil head chief but also *ex officio* a religious authority. Next there were high priestly ranks, the *ahau can mai* or "rattlesnake-tobacco" and *ah kin mai* or "priest-powdered-tobacco." Their main duties were the education and ordination of regular priests, *ah kin* "day prognosticators," who dispensed divinatory advice and presided at all but the most important ceremonies. There were also specialists, *chilam,* for trance prophesy and other functionaries for sacrifice. An order of virgins tended sacred fires in the temples.

The Deities

Mayan deities appear in four modes. Following the pattern of Ake Hultkranz, we will group the deities as (1) celestial and remote, (2) fertility and domestic, (3) death and war, and (4) calendric and ceremonial.

1. Among the celestial deities the name Itzamna is prominent but the reference is complex. Often he is identified as son to Hunab Ku, the dimly apprehended "single existing god." He is a creator, lord of day and night, the one who infuses the breath of life into humankind. But again he is a calendric deity, the patron of the day Ahau, the last and most important of the twenty Maya days. On the other hand, his name may derive from *itzam* ("lizard"), and he may be a deified culture hero from the city of Itzmal in northern Yucatan, portrayed as a bearded old man with a Roman nose. As a ceremonial deity Itzamna makes frequent appearances in the yearly calendar: at the New Year as an averter of calamities, in the month of Uo as a source of auguries; in the month of Zip as a god of medicine (along with his wife Ixchel); and in the month of Mac as a guarantor with Chac of a good crop. Itzamna in his special manifestation as Kinich Ahau, the sun god, is a spouse to the moon goddess Ixchel. Clearly a process of assimilation has interlaced deities known by a variety of names in local areas. A further process tended to favor an oversimplified dualism, assigning deities to either benevolent or

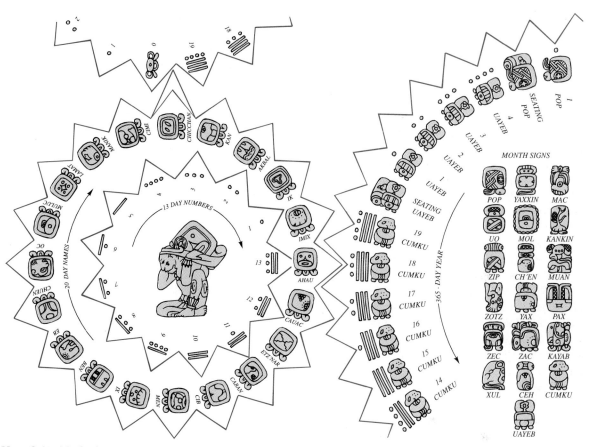

Maya Calendric Cycles

The Maya identified each day in a 260-day Sacred Round by a combination of a number and a name. Represented on the left as cog wheels, the wheel of 13-day *numbers* turns inside the wheel of 20-day *names*, producing the 20 × 13 possible combinations. The cog wheel on the right represents 18 20-day "months" (plus a 5-day interval, "UAYEB") making up a 365-day Seasonal Round to mesh with the Sacred Round. The central meshing shows how each day has two titles: a numbered name from the Sacred Round and a numbered month-name from the Seasonal Round. Only once every 52 Seasonal Years does any given year-bearer (like 13 Ahau shown center left) coincide with the beginning of a year. Such 52-year cycles constituted a Calendar Round. *(Adapted from J. Eric S. Thompson,* The Rise and Fall of Maya Civilization, *2d ed., University of Oklahoma Press, 1966, p. 176. Courtesy of the University of Oklahoma Press.)*

malevolent groups. Itzamna was clearly in the benevolent camp.

2. Fertility and domestic deities were intimately related to everyday life, for the divine origins of human beings, the nourishment of their bodies, and the maintenance of their communal life were intertwined. According to Schele's decipherment of seventh-century Chan-Bahlum texts from Palenque, there was a first Mother who shed blood causing maize—the raw material of humanity—to sprout from the waters of the Otherworld. By this act she taught people how to offer their blood to nourish life, maintain the social order, and commune with ancestors in the Otherworld.[V] In later times the functions, related to fertility and domestic life, were assigned to several different deities.

Chac, the rain god, is the most prominent fertility deity. Ah Mun, the god of corn, and Ixchel, patroness of pregnancy, childbirth, medicine, and weaving, are also prominent. In the ancient codices the glyph of Chac, the rain god, appears more frequently than those of any other deity. He is honored also in four color and directional forms along with the four sky-supporting Bacabs. His symbols are a "T" shape, suggesting that rain consists of his tears, and the snake, a water emblem. Associated with Chac is Kukulcan, "Wind," sometimes as an alternate manifestation, and sometimes as a separate god. Chac is usually a benevolent deity, but occasionally, when his glyph is accompanied by the death symbol, he is connected with cloudburst damage, floods, or rotting harvests.

Ah Mun is the god of all crops, but maize, of course, is preeminent. He is universally depicted as a youth with a corn cob as a headdress. He is not powerful in himself. Sometimes he is pictured as under the protection of the rain god, and sometimes he is in combat with the death god. In the myths of the origin of corn it is not this stripling but one of the four great Chacs whose thunderbolt finally (after the three other Chacs have failed) splits open the mountain rock with a thunderbolt and releases the maize. Occasionally he is associated with Yum Kaax, "the lord of the forest."

Ixchel, the patroness of human fertility, childbirth, medicine, and weaving, must have inherited these functions from a major preclassical mother goddess. She holds them apart from the mythic tales that first cast her as wanton wife to the Sun, and then elevated the couple to Sun God and Moon Goddess. In the myths her light as the moon is dim because the sun did not want her to match his brilliance and tore out one of her eyes. Perhaps because her sun husband was associated with the benevolent Itzamna, the dualistic sorting process saw her, on balance, as malevolent. Snake symbolism associates her with water. Perhaps she was once Mistress of the Waters, but the beneficent aspects of this role are assigned to Chac. An illustration in the Dresden codex associates her with the old woman who destroys the world in a flood. Yet Ixchel's nurturant roles as mother and midwife, weaver and healer through medicine, magic, and divination are not extinguished. For centuries her image was placed underneath the marriage bed in the hope of promoting conception. As for confusion in later days, the title of "Our Mother," together with the fact that Spanish paintings sometimes showed the Virgin Mary standing on a crescent, could not fail to reinforce identifications with this moon goddess/mother goddess. Does not the cycle of time bring round the same deities in alternate forms?

3. The gods personifying death and war probably gained most prominence near the end of the classical period. Their realm was beneath the earth. *Ah Puch,* the god of death, has a skull for a head, bare ribs, and spiny vertebral projections. If he is shown with flesh, it is bloated and covered with black circles signifying putrefaction. As chief demon Hunhau, he presided over the lowest of the nine Maya underworlds. His companions included the dog and the owl. *Ixtab,* the goddess of suicide, deserves mention chiefly because the Maya believed that suicides went directly to heaven. She is shown hanging from the sky by a loop of rope. The god of war, depicted with black around his eye and down his cheek, ruled over violent deaths and sacrifices. At such ceremonies he is often paired with the god of death. The sacrificial flint knife is one of his emblems. An ambivalent black deity *Ek Chuah* was in one role a war captain and a merchant of death, but in another as a benevolent sponsor of travelling merchants and patron of the crop cacao.

4. The calendric and ceremonial deities sponsored the thirteen segments of the upper world and the nine levels of the lower world. There was a single god for each world level, but each segment also could be conceived as having a separate sponsoring deity. There were nine glyphs for the deities of the lower world, and it may be that the glyphs for the first thirteen numerals applied also to the deities of the upper world, but they have other identifications with more prominent deities. The thirteen different katuns or twenty-year periods each had a patron as did the nineteen months of the Maya year and the twenty day names. Certainly there was plenty of material for the curriculum of the priestly seminaries!

Rites of Passage

Each stage of a person's life was dominated by calendric horoscopes interpreted by priests. Among the highland Cakchiquel Maya even the name of a child was fixed automatically as the day name of the date of his or her birth. If this was the practice in northern Yucatan during the classical age, it had been abandoned before the Spanish arrived. More commonly, children were carried to a priest for a horoscope and for the conferring of four individual names: the given name, the father's family name, the combined family names of both parents, and a nickname. As was the practice of the

Cherokee in later times, the classical Maya used boards and bindings to flatten the foreheads of infants.

At the age of three or four, boys had a white bead tied in their hair and girls began to wear a red shell (symbolic of virginity) tied to a waistband. When children reached puberty, these emblems would be removed at a family ceremony. Bishop Landa described the rite, saying that the Maya name for it was "the descent of the gods." After purificatory bathing and questioning about their habits in regard to personal purity, candidates had a white cotton cloth put over their heads. After the cloth had been tapped nine times with a sacred bone, there would be further anointing with "virgin" water (collected in caves and presumably not contaminated by seeping through soil), sharing wine, tobacco, and a neighborhood feast. Guests would be sent away with pieces of the white head cloths as talismanic gifts.[U2] Soon after puberty, boys would move into the unmarried men's house but would continue to spend their days working for their fathers. Girls remained at home and were considered marriageable after puberty.

Marriages, usually arranged by a professional matchmaker, always involved a bride price. Even the "dowry" of household necessities was furnished by the groom's family, and the groom pledged himself to work for the bride's father for a period of six or seven years. These customs have survived among the Maya of the present day.

In funerary rites and burials the contrast between peasants and the elite was extreme. At the peasant level the body of the deceased would be wrapped in cloth after putting some maize and a jade bead or two (money) in the mouth. The body was buried along with a few images and some work tools behind the hut or under its floor. Commenting on Christian burial crypts, a modern Mam Maya in Guatemala remarked that bodies should be right by the maize plot. "The earth gives us food; we should feed it."[S6]

Individual Offerings and Prayers

Maize was absolutely the essence of the *milpero*'s working life and sustenance. Even in the present with other grains available, it is 80 percent of his diet. Treasuring maize and showing honor by addressing it as "Your Grace" and making offerings to it came naturally. As Thompson writes, "The maize seems to be fighting beside him in an unending defense against every kind of enemy."[S7] With such a vivid sense of alliance it is no wonder that the Maya personified maize and placated it with offerings.

Before clearing land or sowing, the Maya fasted, practiced continence, and made offerings. Sometimes the offering was his own blood drawn by piercing the ear, the tongue, or the foreskin and drawing a straw through it. The offered blood could be smeared on the mouth of an idol or allowed to drop on the milpa. Alternatively the supplicant might make an offering of copal (an aromatic resin burned as an incense) or pour out a libation of *balche,* a fermented corn beer. The principle *"Do ut des"* (I give so that you will give) does not seem at all crass to the Maya, nor does it diminish his devout expressions of gratitude. Prayer is a sensible way of making a contract explicit. Thompson writes,

> Maya prayer is directed to material ends; I cannot imagine a Maya praying for ability to resist temptation, to love his neighbors better, or for deeper insight into the ways of God or his gods. There is no concept of goodness in his religion, which demanded a bloody, not a contrite heart.[W1]

There are reinforcing tales of retribution visited upon those who failed to make a milpa offering. One such *milpero* saw a tall man—Chacs were reputed to be tall—stripping ripening ears from his crop. "I am here gathering that which I sent." The tall one lights a cigar with a lightning bolt, disappears in a thunderclap, and promptly a hailstorm destroys the remaining crop of the peasant who did not pay up.[W2]

Public Ceremonial Sacrifices

At the ceremonial centers the priests presided over sacrifices of animals and human beings. The crucial act was cutting out the heart and thrusting it into the mouth of a hungry

> "As maize cannot seed itself without the intervention of human beings, so the cosmos required sacrificial blood to maintain life."[V2]
>
> —Linda Schele

idol. Human sacrifice was in no way as frequent among the Maya as it was to become among the war-like Aztecs of later times. Among the Maya it was clearly viewed not so much as a punishment as a test of devotion and the offering of a costly gift. To be sure, most victims were not volunteers but slaves, malefactors, war captives, or persons who had made an error in carving a sacred image or a monolith. It appears that courage and decorum on the part of the victim were expected and usually obtained on the basis of trust in the afterlife.

Offerings of all kinds to the rain gods and the water spirits took place at cenotes (natural deep cisterns) and wells. Young girls were preferred because of their purity. Each was instructed to take questions to the water deities. At midday, if they were still alive, they would be pulled out to report the answers. The chances of surviving were slim. Thompson writes that the victims may have been bound: "A victim paddling around in the water for several hours in no way enhanced the dignity of the rite."[V3] He adds that most victims were devout and cooperative but that there was a tale of "one pert hussy who roundly declared that if she were thrown in, she'd be damned if she would ask the gods for a good maize crop or anything else." Another victim was sought, presumably a more pious girl.[V3]

Standing Captive

The fact that we are startled by the spunk of the of the aforementioned "pert hussy" suggests that Mayan civilization was thoroughly unlike her in spirit. Perhaps no religion in the world was ever so obsessed as the Mayans were with calendric and horoscopic clues to fate and how to escape it. And perhaps none were so devoutly committed to the acceptance of fate.

GLOSSARY

astrology a method of predicting the course of individual lives and world events by relating them to the movements and positions of stars and planets

chthonian (tho'nĭ ăn) forces powers or deities dwelling in or under the earth

daimon a spirit full of mana, often an inward mentor, a source of inspiration and a moral guardian to an individual

Druid a member of a Celtic order of priest magicians or wizards whose rituals, centering on animal and tree worship, were said to include human sacrifice

genius a male guiding (tutelary) spirit or daimon, originally specific to the head of the clan, but later applied to an individual or a place

juno a female tutelary spirit, counterpart to a genius

moira what is allotted, fate in Greek thought

numen divine potency emanating from a deity, person, or thing; sometimes the divine part of a deified person

oracle a divine or an especially authoritative revelation (or the person who delivers it), often an ambiguous or enigmatic utterance spoken through a medium in a trance state

pantheon a set of deities, usually all of the divine beings venerated in a culture or region

theogony an account of the origin of the gods

wyrd a Teutonic term for "what happens," chance, fate, or destiny, sometimes generically personified, sometimes conceived as operating through three personifications called Norns

ziggurat a type of pyramidal structure erected by ancient Mesopotamians, a man-made mountain with stepped-back terracing encased in brick and topped by a shrine

PART 2

THE RELIGIONS OF SOUTH ASIA

Early Hinduism
The Passage
from Ritual Sacrifice
to Mystical Union

The word "India" is an umbrella encompassing a more diverse collocation of cultures and languages than, say, "Europe." If one hesitates to make a generalization about "Europe," even more caution should be exercised in regard to "India." So, also, the sub-sets of Indian faiths comprehended under the term *Hinduism* have an almost unlimited diversity. No possibility exists of bringing them under one summarizing phrase or of suggesting that they are in agreement about what should be said and done in the world. They are really not one religion, but rather a family of religions. The term *Hinduism* is of relatively recent coinage, and it was first used by outside observers looking on at what seemed to them a distinctive religious and cultural complex. Modern Hindus have become accustomed to using it themselves when speaking or writing in English, but among themselves they use the ancient word *dharma* ("way of life and thought").

This range and complexity of beliefs and practices among Hindus has led observers to make a distinction between the "broader" and "narrower" meanings of Hinduism. As a rule, the broader definition is preferred by most Hindus. To them, Hinduism is the whole complex of beliefs and institutions that have appeared from the time when their ancient (and most sacred) scriptures, the Vedas, were composed until now. Western scholars, however, are inclined to prefer the narrower definition, according to which the so-called Vedic and Brahmanistic periods are considered developments preparatory to Hinduism proper, the latter being identified with the vast social and religious system that has grown among the peoples of India since about the third century B.C.E.

COMPONENTS: Pre-Aryan
   Indus Valley Civilization, *ca.* 2500–1500 B.C.E.
     Indigenous (Dravidian) primal cultures: Hunting and gathering, agricultural
   Aryan nomadic religion

EMERGENCE OF BRAHMINISM: ca. 1500 B.C.E.
LITERATURE: Vedas 1500–800 B.C.E.

   Brahmanas, 850 B.C.E.
   Upanishads, 500 B.C.E.
   (Extended chart on p. 101)

DEITIES OF DEATH AND SKY: Rudra, Indra, Varuna, Rita, Ushas
RITUAL DEITIES: Agni, Soma, Brahmanaspati

Hinduism in the narrower sense is hardly less amazing and diverse than when it is considered in its broader meaning. Hindus have an extraordinarily wide selection of beliefs and practices from which to choose: they can be (to use Western terms) pantheists, polytheists, monotheists, agnostics, or even atheists; dualists, pluralists, or monists. They may follow different moral standards, or they may choose instead a supramoral mysticism. They may live an active life or a contemplative one; they may spend much time on domestic religious rituals, as most of them do, or dispense with these completely. They may worship regularly at a temple or not

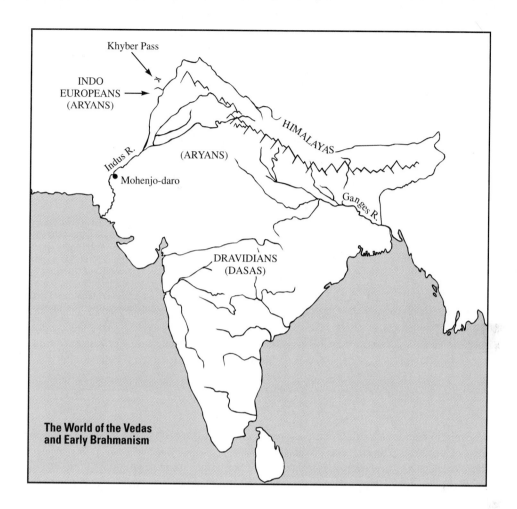

The World of the Vedas and Early Brahmanism

go at all. Their only general obligation is to abide by the rules of their caste and to trust that by doing so they will be freed from rebirth altogether or at least lifted by transmigration to a less burdensome next life.

Pre-Aryan India

India is a land whose peoples have long histories, some going back to prehistoric times. Aboriginal tribes with Stone Age cultures, identified by anthropologists as proto-Australoids, still survive in central Indian jungles. South India is dominated by millions of dark-skinned peoples, speaking Dravidian languages, who have a prehistoric origin. Elsewhere, tribes with a Mongoloid heritage have held territories in northeast India since at least the early second millennium B.C.E.

The invaders of northwest India from about 1800–1500 B.C.E. (the Indo-Aryans) found a long-established population there. They called the natives who resisted them *Dasas* or (*Dasyus*), and described them as dark-skinned, thick-lipped people who possessed cattle and spoke in a strange language. The Dasas may have been surviving representatives of an earlier fast-declining culture that had been developed before 2000 B.C.E., along the Indus River and its tributaries, by a

"Yogin" Deity

A tiny (1.4 × 1.4 in.) steatite seal from Mohenjo-Daro (2500–1500 B.C.E.) depicts an ithyphallic seated figure with horns or a horned headdress. Some see a trident symbol and a frontal face flanked by two side faces suggesting a prototype of the god Shiva. Others see a buffalo head with side dewlaps suggesting a royal counterpart to the fertility goddess, perhaps a prototype of the buffalo demon Mahisha. *(Courtesy of Central Asian Antiquities Museum, New Delhi.)*

people of mixed origin and diverse ethnic composition, who combined to produce a Bronze Age civilization with a well-developed art and architecture (brought to light by excavations of fortified cities at Harappa in the Punjab and Mohenjodaro in Sind), matched, it seems, by an equally advanced religion that contained at least in germ the ideas now embodied in the Hindu doctrines of the Law of Karma and reincarnation.

Archaeological remains include many mother-goddess figurines and small steatite seals frequently featuring the bull and the buffalo. One seal shows a seated human figure with legs in the yoga position. On the head there are horns curving away from a mitre-shaped central projection. One interpretation sees a prototype of the Hindu god Shiva: a trident headpiece over a frontal human face flanked by two side faces. Another interpretation perceives a buffalo head with side dewlaps, suggesting that the hybrid figure represents a royal counterpart to the fertility goddess. Unfortunately no extended samples of writing have been found, and the brevity of the texts upon the seals frustrates useful deciphering.

The disappearance of the Indus civilization was probably due more to increasing aridity of the climate than to the invasion of Indo-Aryan tribes.

The Coming of the Indo-Aryans

Sometime about the middle of the second millennium B.C.E. peoples who were eventually to conquer India began to make their way through the passes of the Hindu Kush Mountains. The conquerors themselves were to be profoundly remade by the Indian environment. Their tribes were typically composed of tall, light-skinned people of Indo-European stock, calling themselves Aryans. For a long time they had been moving eastward, looking for a permanent home. At last, during a period of several centuries, they issued from the mountains upon the plains of northwest India. They were of the same complex ethnic group to which belonged the powerful tribes that moved south, west, and north in Europe and with the infusion of their blood and language brought into being the historic Greeks, Latins, Celts, Germans, and Slavs. While the original migrations were still in process, the Indo-Aryans, as we call them, seemingly went south from Europe and then east toward the rising sun. After an unknown number of years spent on the steppes of Bactria and along the Oxus River, they began (perhaps because of drought?) to migrate again, this time into India. Another large branch of the same ethnic group broke into Iran (ancient Persia). They had been fellow wanderers with the Indo-Aryans, but at a parting of the ways had turned southward. Time was to see great changes in language, habits, and ideas among both the Iranians and Indo-Aryans, and a difference in religious outlook as wide as that between Hinduism and Zoroastrianism, but the original similarities in both language and religion can still be traced without difficulty.

The Indo-Aryans, whose horse-drawn chariots, unknown to India before, subdued the unwarlike native inhabitants, the Dasas, settled first on the upper branches of the Indus River. They had been a nomadic people, but now they began to live in simple village groups among their flocks and herds. As they moved southeastward along the base of the Himalaya Mountains and began to adjust themselves to the new climate, their life became less pastoral and more agricultural in character. The men seem to have been fully occupied with herding their cattle and waging warfare, while the women carried on the homemaking and gardening. The animals they brought into India with them were those of a pastoral people—cows, horses, sheep, goats, and dogs. Of elephants, monkeys, and tigers they had, as yet, no knowledge. They clung to their ancient diet of milk and meat and continued the custom, probably formed centuries before (indeed, the Iranians had an identical practice), of making a stimulating liquid they called *soma*, squeezed from a stalk whose identity is still uncertain, which they drank during lengthy rituals after it was mixed with milk. They thought their gods enjoyed this potion as much as they, therefore they offered them libations of it whenever they sacrificed.

In the vanguard of the Aryan advance the struggle with the dark-skinned Dasas was continuous, and as successive waves of invaders piled up from the rear, there were intertribal clashes that were to be immortalized later in the great Hindu epics, the *Ramayana* and the *Mahabharata*. By the time the whole region of the Five Rivers (the upper branches of the Indus) was occupied, the problem of mastering the new territory had been met by the ruling class.

Aryan Social Structure

Each tribe had over it a chieftain, called a *rajah* (same root as Latin *rex*), whose office was generally heredi-

tary. The functions of the chieftain rapidly became complex, as more and more territory came under his sway, until, toward the end of the Vedic period, he was distinguished from other citizens by a large retinue, a palace, and glittering apparel. He was expected not only to maintain a private army for the protection of his people but also to gather around him numbers of priests to aid him in securing divine blessing on his subjects and the gods' approval of his own acts. Far outnumbering the warriors who formed the rajah's private army and the priests who served both ruler and people were the farmers and herders, whose home life was still much like that of their forebears. The father or *pitar* (same root as Latin *pater*, German *vater*, English *father*, etc.) was the head of the family, the owner of its property, and, in these early days, still its family priest. The wife and mother or *matar* (Latin *mater*, German *mutter*, etc.) was a comparatively free individual, much less secluded than her descendants in the Ganges Valley had been. Her authority in the home over the children and servants was relatively free from restraints. Wives joined with their husbands in conducting domestic rites. (Women are named as authors of some of the hymns in the *Rig-Veda*.) Daughters were free to remain unmarried without censure and had a voice in selecting a husband and in shaping the marriage contract.

Having been accustomed for centuries to moving toward new horizons and hazards, the Aryans settled down slowly. Only one substitute for lost adventure remained to them, and they seized upon it: they continued their wanderings in imagination when denied them in fact, and surveyed the world about them with nimble wit. They had hardly won a place for themselves in India before they began to further develop their oral tradition. Their ritual sacrifices became more elaborate. Folktales and epic stories took shape. At the same time, the hymns and prayers of their priests gave voice to their expanding religious conceptions. Out of these last, together with ancient magic runes and spells, have come Hinduism's earliest sacred writings, the *samhitas* ("collections"), four in number: the *Rig-Veda, Sama-Veda, Yajur-Veda,* and *Atharva-Veda*. (The word *veda* means "sacred knowledge," having the same root as the English *wit* and *wisdom*, the Greek *oida*, the Latin *video*, and the German *wissen*.) Our knowledge of the gods of the Indo-

Aryans is principally drawn from the four Vedas, which constitute the inner "heard" (*shruti*) core of Aryan sacred literature. (See the chart on p. 101.) We turn first to the oldest of the four.

The *Rig-Veda*

The *Rig-Veda* (literally, "the Veda of stanzas of praise") is an anthology of religious poetry in ten books, containing over 1,000 hymns and reflecting the religious devotion of long-established family and other groups before and during the Vedic Age. At first these hymns (some by individuals) existed only in oral form. They are prayers addressed to a single or often to two or more deities, called *devas* or "shining ones," a word identical with the Latin *deus* (whence also comes, of course, the English word *deity*), whose residences were found in three regions—the earth, the heavens, and the intermediate air.

When the Aryans engaged in public worship, they had no temples, nor even sacred precincts of a permanent kind, but worshiped under the open sky, as the ancient Iranians did. They used areas of trimmed and swept grass in the center of which they prepared a cleared space or altar site, consisting of bare or shallowly scooped-out earth, and large enough to contain as many as three fires—a western one (the *garhapatya*, round in shape, representing the earth, the only one mentioned in the *Rig-Veda*), an eastern one (the *ahavaniya*, square in shape, representing the four-directional heavens), and a southern one (the *dakshina*, shaped like a half moon and representing the dome of air between earth and heaven).

It may be that in early Vedic times only one fire, the garhapatya, was used, but this is far from certain; at least it is the only one named. In later days the altar ground was raised a foot or more (instead of being hollowed out) and was often built of square bricks formed into unusual shapes to resemble, for example, two triangles, or a woman, falcon, tortoise, or something else.

Public Rites

Several orders of priests officiated at public rites inside the altar ground. A seat on strewn grass near the fires was reserved for the invisible divine guests. The offerings consisted of one or more of the following: clarified, or melted, butter (*ghee*), grain, soma, and a goat, a sheep, a cow, an ox, or a horse (the horse sacrifice being the costliest and most effectual). In time, as the sacrifices lengthened into elaborate ceremonies, priests, each with special functions, took charge. One might be the *adhvaryu* or altar builder, who also prepared the materials for sacrifice and manually administered them, reciting the appropriate words as he did so. Another was the *hotar*, the libation pourer and invoker of the gods, who would call down the gods to enjoy the sacrificial offerings and soma set out in vessels on the grass:

> Thou hast made prayers the means of thine exalting, therefore we wait on thee with hymns, O Indra. . . .
> Mark well our sacrificial cake, delighted: Indra, drink
> Soma and the milk commingled.
> Here on the sacrificer's grass be seated. . . .[A1]

Another priest might be the *agnidh* or kindler of the sacrificial fire. But as time went on, the foremost came to be the *brahmin*, the one who in his person represented the central sacred petition or *brahman* (the prayer).

Brahman and the *Brahmin's* Role

The word *brahman* was used in different senses. It had the wider meanings of "holy word," "sacred knowledge," and "incantation," with the implication in this last case of the presence of magic power. Mystic utterance was *brahman* too. The word applies not only to the words and stanzas (*mantras*) of the *Rig-Veda* but to the incantations and spells of the *Atharva-Veda*. Another word was used in the *Rig-Veda* to convey a similar meaning, *vac* or speech, with the connotation of Holy Utterance or Word, thus making it equivalent to *brahman* or an alternative to it. *Vacaspati* is one of the names of Brahmanaspati (or Brihaspati, the power of prayer deified).

It is important to understand that the brahmin was not merely one who used verbal symbols to point to sacred realities or to address gods. Rather than signifying some external deity, the sacred syllables constituted the holy power in the living moment. Or, to put it another way, the sacred reality actualized itself in the brahmin's throat.

During the sacrifice, the oblation, whether of grain, flesh, liquid, or a combination of these, was prepared on the garhapatya fire, poured or placed on the ahavaniya fire, in part placed on the ground on cushions of grass or poured there for the gods, and in part eaten or drunk by the participants in the sacrifice. The proffering of the soma libation (often the principal rite) was the final act in a long series of ritual events stretching over more than one day: the finding or purchase of the plant from which the juice was to be extracted, its reverent transportation by cart or on human heads to the location of the pressing out, the drawing of the water for the soaking of the now dried-out stems, the squeezing of the stems between "pressing-stones" after they were swollen with water, the straining of the liquid through woolen strainers (an act marked by a characteristic sound interpreted with some exaggeration as "the bellowing of a bull," and by a flash of thin "golden" color), the mixing of the liquid with milk or honey, and finally its offering to the gods and its distribution to the human participants, in whom the intoxicating or hallucinatory effect was almost immediate.

The soma may have been extracted from hemp, that is, a plant like marijuana, or it may have been something less pronounced in its effects, like the juice of rhubarb stalks. But it now seems most likely that it was the hallucinogenic plant *Amanita muscaria,* a mushroom whose juice is poisonous in full strength, but hallucinogenic and intoxicating when diluted with milk, water, and honey. This seems very much like the plant described in the *Rig-Veda, a* plant with no roots, leaves, fruit, or seeds, but with a white stem, red cap, and juice that was golden.

These sacrificial rituals both drew upon and gave rise to an ever-growing mythology. On page 9, we saw how ritual gives rise to myth as well as myth to ritual. We have cases in point here. The myths of the Indo-Aryans were already well developed when the latter entered India, but did not cease to change and grow thereafter. Because the sacrificial rituals were designed to achieve human security in both changing and settled situations, the gods were at times *reconceived* and endowed with new powers. In the process,

once-potent older gods faded into the background, and other gods, regarded as more capable of meeting altered needs, took their place. The rituals themselves required the introduction of divine powers or presences, such as Agni, Soma, and Brihaspati (p. 84).

Sacrifice and Cosmic Origins

Further, quite new cosmic gods emerged when the rituals were understood to affect not only the gods but the cosmos itself. This happened when the sacrifices became such central and compelling events in themselves that the whole world was affected by and involved in them—so much so that the cosmos became a sacramental structure throughout, and was held to have had its own origin in a cosmic sacrifice. There are passages in the Vedas and in the interpretive literature, the Brahmanas and Upanishads, that conceive of the universe as having been in its totality a cosmic cow or a horse or man that was primordially sacrificed and dismembered to produce the mountains, rivers, earth, and living creatures of everyday experience. Thus, according to *Rig-Veda* X.90, the original cosmic Man, Purusha, allowed the gods (who seem to emerge from nowhere (was it from Purusha himself or from some extra- or pre-cosmic space?) to make a sacrifice of *him.*

> When they divided Purusha how many portions did
>   they make?
> The Brahman [Brahmin]was his mouth, of both his
>   arms was the Rajanya [Kshatriya] made.
> His thighs became the Vaisya, from his feet the Sudra
>   [Shudra] was produced.
> The moon was gendered from his mind, and from his
>   eye the sun had birth; . . .
> Forth from his navel came mid-air; the sky was
>   fashioned from his head;
> Earth from his feet. . . .[A2]

The names of the four classes of castes appear in the previous passage—and we will come to a further discussion of caste later. At this point we need only observe that even in this earliest reference the four groups are pictured as separate creations in the original cosmic order.

In the *Satapatha-Brahmana* another cosmogony sees a sacrificial horse as the primal being.

Verily, the dawn is the head of the sacrificial horse, the sun its eye, the wind its breath, the fire its open mouth. The year is the body of the sacrificial horse, the sky its back, the air its belly, the earth the under part of its belly. . . .[B1]

The idea that the whole world originated from a cosmic sacrifice appears also in a hymn (*Rig-Veda* X.81) that honors Vishvakarman as the world maker, or world architect, because he performed a primordial sacrifice in which he was, paradoxically, both the sacrificial victim and the craftsman who, with arms and feet reaching everywhere, brought the world into being. A hymn (X.121) with a slightly different idea celebrates Hiranyagarbha, the Golden Egg or Germ (or, according to another reading, the womb of great waters—the primordial sea—that bore the golden egg) as that from which sprang Prajapati, the Creator, the Maker of gods, humans, and animals, who, it would seem, did his creating from the materials supplied by the egg or germ itself.

The rituals thus gave rise to startling myths describing the origin of all things.

Deities of Earth and Sky

These new elements of myth were, of course, based on conceptions drawn from an earlier mythology. Many of the deities invoked were obviously of very ancient date. Faith in three of them was shared with the Iranians, the Hittites, the Greeks, and the Romans. They were Dyaus Pitar or Father Sky (whom we have already met as Zeus Pater of the Greeks, Jupiter of the Romans), his mate Prithivi Matar or Mother Broad-Earth (Gaea Mater of the Greeks), and Mitra (the Mithra of the Iranians), a highly moralized god representing faith keeping and loyalty, but perhaps originally a sun god. In the *Rig-Veda*, however, these deities are conceived of rather vaguely and appealed to seldom, being displaced from their earlier preeminence by gods and goddesses who appeared more effectual in northwest India.

Indra

Prominent among the latter was blustering Indra, ruler of the gods of the mid-region of the sky and particularly the god of storms, especially of the rainstorms (monsoons) that end the dry season. He was the god of war as well. To his worshipers he seemed a gigantic figure, with long flowing hair and a wind-tossed beard through which he shouted and roared with a loud voice. Clasping in his hand the enemy-destroying thunderbolt, the *vajra,* he took the field as the ally and patron of the Aryans. Small wonder that their enemies fled. In the greatest of his annual feats, he smote the drought-dragon Vritra, which was holding back the waters in the mountain fastnesses. For this dangerous exploit he fortified himself well; hard-fighting, hard-drinking Aryan hero that he was, "in the three Soma-bowls he quaffed the juices." Then with his deadly thunderbolt "he slew the Serpent that rested on the mountains; and quickly flowing, swift to the ocean down sped the waters."[C1] His worshipers would chant adoringly,

In whose command are the horses, the cattle, the villages, and all the chariots; who begot the Sun and the Dawn, who is the leader of the waters—he, O men, is Indra.

Whom the two battle ranks meeting in conflict invoke, vanguard and rearguard, both the enemies; they utter various invocations—he, O men, is Indra.

Without whom men do not conquer, whom in battle they invoke for help; who is the pattern for all, who is the shaker of the unshaken—he, O men, is Indra. . . .

May we, O Indra, at all times thy friends, with goodly offspring, praise thee in the assembly.[C2]

Such laudation must not, of course, be taken as evidence of monotheism in the strict sense. The worshipers were prone to flattery that would please, and hence, unlike the ancient Greeks, whom otherwise they resembled in significant respects, they did not elevate one deity

> **"Indra's heroic deeds will I proclaim, the first ones which the wielder of the vajra [weapon] accomplished. He killed the dragon, released the waters, and split open the sides of the mountains. . . . He alone rules over the tribes as their king."**
>
> —Rig-Veda I.32[D]

to permanent Olympic supremacy, but spoke of each of their divinities as being supreme—at least during the prayers.

Henotheism

The Vedic attitude is best described as ritual or devotional henotheism (i.e., temporary flattering elevation of one of many gods to the highest rank that can be accorded, verbally or ritualistically). Franklin Edgerton says of this,

> . . . [E]ither the particular god of the moment is made to absorb all the others, who are declared to be manifestations of him; or else, he is given attributes which in strict logic could only be given to a sole monotheistic deity. Thus various Vedic gods are each at different times declared to be creator, preserver, and animator of the universe, the sole ruler of all creatures, and so on. Such hymns, considered separately, seem clearly to imply monotheism; but all that they really imply is a ritualistic henotheism. As each god comes upon the stage in the procession of rites, he is impartially granted this increasingly extravagant praise, until everything that could be said of all the gods collectively is said of each of them in turn, individually. We see that Vedic henotheism is rooted in the hieratic ritual, without which it perhaps would hardly have developed.[E]

Rudra (Shiva)

In sharp contrast with Indra was the dread mountain god Rudra not often addressed but greatly feared, the fierce author of disastrous storms sweeping down from the snows of the Himalayas, who, in his proper nature, was no ally of the Aryans at all but the destroyer of their goods and persons. Fear and awe accompanied his presence. His worshipers approached him in humility and trembling supplication, beseeching him as "an immortal one" to be "auspicious" (*shiva*) rather than malevolent, and to be merciful to their children and grandchildren. They would beseech,

> Kill not our great or our small, our growing one or our full-grown man, our father or our mother. Injure not, O Rudra, our dear selves.

> Injure us not in our cattle or horses. In thy wrath, O Rudra, slay not our heroes. We invoke thee ever with sacrifices.[C3]

But then again Rudra was found to be at times a gentle healer, presiding (in his mountain fastnesses?) over medicinal plants. He had his helpful as well as his destructive side. This is of some importance historically, for his greatest significance lies in the fact that he is the early form of later Hinduism's great god Shiva, the Destroyer (and Reviver).

Ushas, a Goddess

Except for Ushas, female deities in the Vedic literature were largely mothers, wives, sisters, and lovers. Lacking clear characterization, they were personifications: the primal waters (Apah), rivers (Saraswati, Ganga), and the ritual power of speech (Vac).

Ushas, the Dawn (the Greek Eos), is eternally young and nubile, a "maid in white robes," shining afar in her chariot drawn by red-spotted horses.[C4] Her male attendants, the Asvins, twin horsemen of the dawn, speed behind her through the sky on a chariot with golden seat, reins of gold, axle and wheels of gold, and with a flight so swift that it exceeds the twinkling of an eye.

Other nature deities were Vayu, the wind, bearer of perfumes, and the tempestuous little Maruts, or storm spirits, "swift as wind . . . robed in rain . . . the singers of heaven."[C5] There were a number of sun gods, probably representing different phases of light; for example, Surya, mounting up with fleet yellow horses and causing the constellations, flooded with the radiance of his all-beholding eye, to "pass away, like thieves, together with their beams";[A3] Savitar, the "golden-haired, bright with sunbeams," who traversed the "ancient dustless pathways well established in the air's mid-region";[A4] and Yama, the first man to die, now the God of the dead, the judge and ruler of the departed.

Then there was Vishnu, the far strider who encompassed the extent of earth, air, and sky in three swift strides and thus redeemed the world from night. Of him it may be said that, though destined along with Rudra to surpass the rest of the Vedic deities and to become a major Hindu god, he was not prominent in the *Rig-Veda* and had there lost almost all of his solar characteristics.

Varuna

Morally far above the other gods stood the awe-compelling deity Varuna, originally the god of the high-arched sky, who was later assigned the inclusive function (analogous to maintaining order among the stars) of directing the forces making everywhere for natural and moral orderliness. His sphere lay in part in the domain of natural laws, for it was he who upheld the physical order of the world against the forces making for its breakdown. In another direction, it was his concern to keep men obedient to the moral law. He was the discloser of sin, the judge of truth and falsehood. His spies were busy finding men out. When men sinned, it was to Varuna that they prayed for forgiveness, so that the acts that were reckoned as sins in those pioneer times appear in the prayers they addressed to him.

> If we have sinned against the man who loves us,
> have ever wronged a brother, friend or comrade,
>   The neighbor ever with us, or a stranger, O
> Varuna, remove from us the trespass.
>   If we, as gamesters, cheat at play, have cheated,
> done wrong unwittingly or sinned of purpose,
>   Cast all these sins away like loosened fetters,
> and, Varuna, let us be thine own beloved.[A5]

Because Varuna's interest lay in maintaining order in the universe—physically, morally, and ritualistically—it was natural that he should be associated with Mitra, the god of loyalty, honor, and promise keeping, already mentioned, and also with the mysterious abstract principle called Rita (Latin *ritus,* English *rite*). Rita was conceived to be the indwelling principle in everything in the universe that shows regularity and order of action; in accordance with Rita, the divine norm of the universe, day succeeds night, summer follows spring, the sun keeps his appointed course, and human beings go from birth to death, invisibly guided.

Liturgical Deities

There are still other gods in the *Rig-Veda* who are deified elements of ritual—beings who might be called the *liturgical deities* because they were chiefly associated with and were in part or wholly outgrowths of the act of worship itself. They are Agni, the god of fire; Soma, the divine presence in the juice of the soma plant; and, not well known to the populace but very important to the priests, Brahmanaspati (or Brihaspati), the deified power of the sacred prayer word.

No sacrifice was effectual without the presence of Agni (Latin *ignis)*, the god of fire in general, celestial or terrestrial, but especially of the altar fire. Invoked with earnest petition before his coming, which was conceived of always as a new birth (whether on altar or hearth), he was praised and adored with utmost sincerity. (Those who care for historical comparisons will here see a connecting link with the fire ceremonies of the Zoroastrians.) As fire purifies and cleanses, so Agni removed sin and guilt. He drove away the demons and protected the home whose hearth he occupied. He was light and wisdom, a seer into dark corners, a resolver of mysteries, from whom it was well to have guidance. He consecrated marriage, was a spiritual husband of maidens, a brother of men. He was priest, oblation bearer, and mediator between gods and human beings. His worshipers knew their weal depended upon his presence.

The participation of the god Soma (the Haoma of the ancient Persians) also was necessary in the sacrifice. His introduction was, we have seen, a central feature of the ritual. Both gods and humans needed him. Hence, during each ceremony, soma juice was poured into the grass where the gods invisibly sat, and as they too drank, the worshipers chanted,

> *We have drunk Soma and become immortal;*
> *We have attained the light, the gods discovered.*
> *What can hostility now do against us?*
> *And what, immortal god, the spite of mortals?*[F]

A third liturgical deity, Brahmanaspati (Brihaspati), represented a subtle blending of prayer, the prayer (chaplain), and the power of prayer personified. Although the creative power of sacred speech or utterance had been personified as a female (Vac) in the *Rig-Veda*, she is replaced in liturgical tradition by a male deity able to move the gods and compel them to grant their favors.

> *Sublime Brihaspati easy of access, granteth his friends*
> *most bountiful refreshment. . . .*

*Glorify him, O friends, who merits glory: may he give
prayer fair away and easy passage.*[A6]

It was the doctrine of the priests that Brahmanaspati had to be present along with and in the ritual, or it would be but empty sound. If he were indeed active, prayer would have an efficacy so great that it would be compulsive upon gods and humans alike; there could be no failure of fulfillment. A moment's consideration will show how much importance this faith gave to the correctly pronounced priestly utterance or prayer word, the *brahman*. It took on the force of an independently existent principle. Equal importance attached to the priest who uttered it, the holy Brahmin. The pray-er (priest), the prayer, and the deity addressed coalesce as manifestations of one Ultimate Principle.

The Other Vedas

The other Vedas are in many respects dependent upon, even appendages of, the *Rig-Veda*. The *Yajur-Veda* is mostly prose and was meant to supply dedications, prayers, and litanies to accompany the devotional use of the *Rig-Veda*. The *Sama-Veda* is a collection of rhythmic chants mainly for the use of the singing priests at the soma sacrifices, its hymns in great part borrowed from the *Rig-Veda*.

The *Atharva-Veda* is more independent. A treasury of charms, incantations, maledictions, and spells of great antiquity, many of them clearly of non-Aryan origin, it afforded expression to aspects of experience left largely inarticulate in the *Rig-Veda*—fear, passion, anger, hate, physical distress, and the human effort to amend it. It could be argued that the expensive priestly rituals we have reviewed in the previous section were for the ruling elite ("the rich"), whereas the rites of the *Atharva-Veda* were those of the common people ("the poor") in their homes and villages. This Veda abounds in magic blessings and curses. In a manner reminiscent of European magic, it presents remedial charms that were supposed to remove all

evil—or bring down the fell strokes of fate on some unlucky hated head.

> Away from us many thousand-eyed, immortal evil dwell!
> Him whom we hate may it strike, and him whom we hate do thou surely smite.[H1]

Magic and Rudimentary Science

An example of the type of magic spell common in this Veda may be cited. One who wished to promote the growth of his hair might gather the sacred root that prevented baldness and have the following words, at various points in the procedure, chanted:

> As a goddess upon the goddess earth thou wast born, O plant! We dig thee up, O nitatni, that thou mayest strengthen the growth of the hair.
> Strengthen the old hair, beget the new! That which has come forth render more luxurious.
> That hair of thine which does drop off, and that which is broken root and all, upon it do I sprinkle here the all-healing herb.[H2]

The ancient instructions direct the patient to have his head anointed with the black concoction made from the plant mentioned, and have it applied by a medicine man clothed in black who has eaten black food in the early morning before the rise of the crows (black, too, of course). One cannot fail to see in the symbolism here employed an expression of the hope for the growth of new black hair.

This sort of thing may invite a smile, but it was not altogether misguided, for it was linked to inquiries of a broader kind that were more speculative in probing the secrets of the universe than even the tenth book of the *Rig-Veda*. Still other inquiries were close to being scientific. Several of the sections of the *Atharva-Veda* (particularly II.3 and X.2) exhibit great interest in the vital organs, body secretions, and bones of the human body, which are separately distinguished and often exactly described. Apparently,

> "[For the Brahman priest] the one transcendent essence dwelt anonymously within all—within the officiating priest, the victim offered, and the divinities that accepted the sacrifice."
>
> —Heinrich Zimmer[G]

an anatomically informed medical art was being developed. Indeed, one of the verses in the *Atharva-Veda* says that there were then hundreds of medical practitioners at work and thousands of herbs in use.

The Close of the Vedic Period

Vedic literature, taken as a whole, illustrates the exuberant culture which the early Indo-Aryans developed. Very clearly, this vigorous people faced life positively and, in the main, confidently, on many fronts. In their literary self-expression they gave promise of great things to come.

One such promise has to be mentioned. Toward the close of the Vedic period, when the priests were growing in numbers and power and were making religion and the search for knowledge their whole life-work, the yearning for assurance of unity in the totality of things began to express itself. So we have in the later hymns of the *Rig-Veda* the sudden emergence of such grand figures as Vishvakarman, "He Whose Work is the Universe"; Prajapati, "Lord of Creatures," the Creator; and Purusha, already mentioned, the Cosmic Man or Person, giving life to all animated beings, and indeed bringing the whole world into existence out of himself. Most arresting is the 129th hymn of the tenth book, addressed to a great unnamed cosmic reality, referred to quite simply as *That One Thing*, a neutral principle or an activity said to have existed before there was a universe. This hymn contains an early speculation about the origin of creation, and may be rendered thus:

> *Then there was neither being (Sat) nor non-being (Asat):*
> *There was no air, nor firmament beyond it.*
> *Was there a stirring? Where? Beneath what cover?*
> *Was there a great abyss of unplumbed water?*
>
> *There was no death nor anything immortal;*
> *Nor any sign dividing day from night.*
> *That One Thing, breathing no air, was yet*
> *   self-breathing;*
> *No second thing existed whatsoever.*
>
> *Darkness was hidden in a deeper darkness;*
> *This All was as a sea without dimensions;*
> *The Void still held unformed what was potential,*
> *Until the power of Warmth (tapas) produced the*
> *   sole One.*

> *Then, in that One, Desire stirred into being,*
> *Desire that was the earliest seed of Spirit.*
> *(The sages probing in their hearts with wisdom*
> *Discovered being's kinship to non-being.*
>
> *Stretching their line across the void, they pondered;*
> *Was aught above it, or was aught below it?)*
> *Bestowers of the seed were there; and powers;*
> *Free energy below; above, swift action.*
>
> *Who truly knows, and who can here declare it?*
> *Whence It was born, and how this world was fashioned?*
> *The gods came later than the earth's creation;*
> *Who knows then out of what the world has issued?*
>
> *Whether the world was made or was self-made,*
> *He knows with full assurance, he alone;*
> *Who in the highest heaven guards and watches;*
> *He knows indeed, but then, perhaps, he knows not!*[A7]

From all points of view this is an amazing composition; the last six words are especially striking in their quizzical quality. It is clear that the priests were developing by the end of the Vedic Age considerable philosophical ability. This was their response to an urge to determine the origin of the world and of all things. Before the mountains were brought forth, before the gods came into being, before any portion of the visible universe existed, there was a nameless but all-originative being. The priests were excited at the thought. Was there any name they could give it? They wondered. Men had made many attempts heretofore, with less than complete adequacy. When hymning Vac (Holy Utterance) as an ultimate in human knowledge, they sang,

> *They call it Indra, Mitra, Varuna, Agni, and it is*
> *   heavenly noble-winged Garutman.*
> *To what is One, sages give many a title: they call it Agni,*
> *   Yama, Matarisvan. . . .*[A8]

The Brahmins were disposed to think further of the matter.

Aryan Conquest and Compromise

All this time the Aryans were still on the move. They were pressing down the Ganges Valley, pushing before them, eastward and southward, the dark-skinned natives. Although they acquired control of the Ganges River Valley, they were not all conquering. The Vedic literature contains references to hostile *Panis,* peoples of some power and wealth, who for a long time refused to patronize the Aryan priests and their rituals, and even conducted raids on Aryan herds, often with impunity, although such raids were eventually the cause of wars. More important, there were large districts along the base of the Himalayas, in the delta of the Ganges, and throughout south India, which maintained their independence for centuries and did not learn Vedic Sanskrit or practice the ceremonies conducted in it. (There are, in fact, grounds for thinking that these anti-Brahmanical areas gave rise to the religious movements we know as Jainism and Buddhism.)

However, although religious resistance continued, the lifestyles of the governing classes in all areas changed gradually; there was widespread imitation of Aryan social and political customs and procedures. In effect, then, as time went on, the whole land, one way or another, came under Aryan sway. Meanwhile, the Aryan intruders settled down—and change overtook *them.*

II. BRAHMANISM, CASTE, AND CEREMONIAL LIFE

The Rise of the Class System (*Varna*)

By about the end of the seventh century B.C.E. the Aryan occupation of the Ganges Valley had resulted in the organization of a number of distinct principalities or states, some ruled monarchically by hereditary rajahs, many still in the form of loose groupings of largely non-Aryan clans, not unlike republics, with the tribes governed by a central council of chieftains. In the areas they occupied, the Aryans formed the upper strata of a still-fluid social order; below them were the non-Aryans. And now, though the separation between the classes was not hard and fast, the Brahmins were beginning to say that there had emerged four distinct social groups: the Brahmins or priests, the ruling Kshatriyas (or Rajanyas), the Vaisyas or common people (artisans and cultivators, including Aryo-Dasas, for there was considerable mixture in the

Ganges plain before a check could be put to it), and finally the Shudras or servants, presumably the Dasas or non-Aryan natives. The first three classes, the Brahmins said, should be more and more careful to hold themselves aloof from the last. There had now arisen the distinctions of *varna* (literally, "color"), the Brahmin word for class.

Modern usage employs the term *jati* (kin group) to refer to the castes of India, the 3,000 or so endogamous kinship or guild groups making up the operative social structure of the present. (We will have more to say about *jati* later.) Although *varna* is often translated as "caste," it is less confusing to render it as "class" when referring to the ancient religious view of social rank and referring to "classes of castes" in the modern period.

Not only was marriage across the class barrier forbidden, but also friendly social intimacies like drinking from the same cup or sitting down to the same meal, on account of the frequency with which questions regarding purity of blood arose in consequence of such connections. There existed too a struggle for social prestige between the ruling nobles and the Brahmins, each group, in the name either of custom or supernatural prerogative, claiming final and supreme authority.

Brahmin Ascendancy

The Brahmins had by now developed phenomenal power. The migration down the Ganges provided them with an opportunity that they were not slow to grasp. The nobles were busy fighting and administering new territory and had to rely upon the priests more and more to carry on the necessary religious functions. Meanwhile, the supreme regard in which all held the brahman, or holy power in the sacrificial prayer, resulted in swiftly raising the prestige of those whose function it was to utter it. Indeed, the Brahmins finally came to claim a position of even more vital importance than the gods. As we have already seen, the sacred formula, once uttered, was deemed to have a compulsive and magical efficacy. Even gods had to obey it. The priests therefore declared that they occupied the central place of power; they were the pivotal beings in a vast process reaching into all parts of the universe, hell, earth, and heaven. Through the sacrifices they performed—some of which took weeks and months to complete—they changed the very course of cosmic events. By now the names of the gods possessed little more than a ritualistic significance; the sacrifice was the thing of greater moment, and especially the utterance of the sacred prayer formulas in connection with the sacrifices.

That these rituals of the priests veered away from religious supplication toward magical coercion is clearly evident in certain treatises, the *Brahmanas*, which they compiled to be appended to the four Vedas. (See page 101.)

The *Brahmanas*

Each of the four Vedas had attached to it its own *Brahmana* or *Brahmanas* that sought to direct the priests in their use of the hymns and prayers. The *Rig-Veda* has two that have survived, the *Aitareya* and the *Kaushitaki*. The White *Yajur-Veda* has the famous *Satapatha-Brahmana*, the Black the *Taittiriya-Brahmana*. The *Sama-Veda* has eight *Brahmanas* attached to it because it was heavily used in the soma rituals, but none of them is notable enough to name. The *Atharva-Veda* has one *Brahmana*, the *Gopatha*.

The *Brahmanas* are a curious and voluminous body of literature. Originally they were oral directions committed to memory by candidates for priestly office in the various priests' schools. Written down for the first time during the period around 300 B.C.E., or perhaps even later, and then frequently redacted, they were designed both to give practical directions in exhaustive detail for the conduct of all manner of sacrifices and to explain the inner meaning of these rites. The *Brahmanas* were thus the textbooks of the different schools or families of Brahmins, with a hint here and there of a philosophy of worship. No literature affords more detailed instruction for ritual performances.

When one reads them, the *Brahmanas* leave behind two striking impressions: first, that the priests were fascinated by and completely absorbed in the process of elaborating and interpreting their rituals, and second, that they regarded these rituals as having not only a compelling but even a creative power, for they caused events to occur at the demand of words and ritual acts alone.

Public Rites

The sacrifices described in the *Brahmanas* can be divided into domestic and public ones. The public rites occurred at the harvesting of rice, barley, millet, and other grains, at the full and new moon, at the beginning of spring, during the long rainy season, in the autumn, and again at the celebration of victories in war, at the "consecration" of kings, and when gods were called down to be propitiated and persuaded. Lengthy public rites also attended the building of altars, the soma sacrifices, and the installing of the three great fires on the altar ground. The lengthiest of all public rites was the *Asvamedha* or Horse Sacrifice, which took over a year to complete and involved in its beginning the gathering and proffering, if not the actual sacrifice, of 609 animals. But the priests assured the rajahs who wished to assert through the sacrifice their world power and who alone could afford the expense of it, "This is the atonement for everything. He who performs the Asvamedha redeems all sin."[B2]

Domestic Rites

Domestic rites were far simpler, usually taking place within the house and using the hearth fire fed with fresh fuel by the householder. The morning and evening offerings of rice or barley to Agni (the *Agnihotra*) are an example. More complicated was the outdoor monthly proffering of pinda (cereal cakes) to the ancestral spirits. In order to provide a sampling from the Brahmanas that might indicate what they are like, the following description of this ceremony in the *Satapatha-Brahmana* is condensed. It will be noticed that each act is carefully explained. The householder or "sacrificer" stands by with his upper garment reverently tucked up under his waistband. The officiating priest is an *adhvaryu*.

> He (the adhvaryu) presents it in the afternoon. The forenoon, doubtless, belongs to the gods; the mid-day to men; and the afternoon to the fathers [i.e., ancestors]; therefore he presents it in the afternoon.
>
> While seated behind the Garhapatya, with his face turned toward the south, he takes that material for the offering from the cart. Thereupon he rises and threshes the rice while standing north of

the Dakshina fire. Only once he cleans the rice; for it is once for all that the fathers have passed away; and therefore he cleans it only once.

He then boils it. While it stands on the Dakshina fire, he pours some clarified butter on it—for the gods they pour the offering into the fire; for men they take the food off the fire; and for the fathers they do in this very manner: hence they pour the ghee on the rice while it stands on the fire.

After removing it from the fire, he offers to the gods two libations in the fire. He offers both to Agni and Soma. To Agni he offers because Agni is allowed a share in every offering; and to Soma he offers because Soma is sacred to the fathers.

Thereupon he draws with the wooden sword one line (furrow) south of the Dakshina fire—that being in lieu of the altar: only one line he draws, because the fathers have passed away once for all.

He then lays down a firebrand at the farther (south) end of the line. For were he to present that food to the fathers, without having laid down a firebrand, the Asuras and Rakshas [malicious spirits] would certainly tamper with it.

He then takes the water-pitcher and makes the fathers wash their hands, merely saying, "N.N., wash thyself!" naming the sacrificer's father; "N.N., wash thyself!" naming his grandfather; "N.N., wash thyself!" naming his great-grandfather. As one would pour out water for a guest when he is about to take food, so in this case.

Now those stalks of sacrificial grass are severed with one stroke, and cut off near the root—the top belongs to the gods, the middle part to men, and the root-part to the fathers: therefore they are cut off near the root.

He spreads them along the line with their tops towards the south. Thereon he presents to the fathers three round cakes of rice. With "N.N., this is for thee!" he presents one cake to the sacrificer's father. [Similarly he presents a cake each to the grandfather and the great-grandfather.] He presents the food in an order directed away from the present time, because it is away from hence that the fathers have once for all departed.

He then mutters, "Here, O fathers, regale yourselves: like bulls come hither, each to his own share!"

He then turns round so as to face the opposite (north) side. "Let him remain standing with bated breath until his breath fail," say some, "for thus far extends the vital energy." However, having remained so for a moment—

He again turns round and mutters, "The fathers have regaled themselves: like bulls they have come each to his own share."

Thereupon he takes the water-pitcher and makes them wash themselves, merely saying, "N.N., wash thyself!" naming the sacrificer's father; "N.N., wash thyself!" naming his grandfather; "N.N., wash thyself!" naming his great-grandfather.

He then pulls downs the tuck of the sacrificer's garment and performs obeisance. He mutters, "Give us houses, O fathers!" for the fathers are the guardians of houses. After the cakes have been put back in the dish containing the remains of the boiled rice, he (the sacrificer) smells at the rice; this smelling being the sacrificer's share. The stalks of sacrificial grass cut with one stroke he puts on the fire; and he also throws away the firebrand.[B3]

This rite is one of the simplest; descriptions of other rites explain the logic of their procedure at greater length and with frequent citing of myths that validate and confirm them. Mingled with the directions for the sacrifices are expressions of genuine spiritual aspiration and a growing sense of a principle of unity in the universe. Progress toward the conception of such unity is made. The theories of creation suggested in the later hymns of the *Rig-Veda* are fused here into a monotheistic compromise in which Prajapati, the Lord of Creatures, becomes Brahma Svayambhu (Brahma Self-existing), the personal creator of the universe. It had occurred to the more speculative of the priests that if the holy power that worked through the prayer formula could alter the course of cosmic events, then that power, capable as it was of forcing obedience from gods and humans alike, must be an ultimate of some kind. Was it perhaps the true central power in the universe? Could the ultimate reality of the universe be called Brahman?

The authors of the *Brahmanas* here took a long stride forward, and in a direction along which Indian philosophy was destined to go far.

The Philosophy of the Upanishads

One of the greatest speculative eras in the history of religion now opened. Many alert minds in India pressed on to new and philosophically profound interpretations of existence. The oral compositions which, over a period of three or four centuries terminating about 300 B.C.E., expressed these ideas are among the appendages, "Vedanta," attached to the Vedas. They are the famous treatises known as the *Upanishads*, truly indispensable for the study of the religions of India. They conclude the first half of what later came to be a two-part classification of Hindu sacred literature: *Shruti*, "That which is heard" (Vedic), and *Smriti*, "That which is remembered" (Non-Vedic).

The Upanishads (meaning "sittings near a teacher," in the sense of "discussions on ultimate wisdom") are often in the form of dialogues, composed with memorization in view and therefore frequently too repetitive for modern ears, but they are not less profound or subtle for all that. In them, Kshatriyas, and in some instances men and women of other classes, are dramatized as taking part in the discussions, the women as readily and ably as the men. In the *Brihadaranyaka* the great Yajnavalkya's knowledge is validated only after it has been put to the test by the feisty questions of the woman Gargi (3:8.2–12), and his mother Maitreyi turns away from the wealth he offers her, preferring knowledge of Brahman (2:4.1–14).

As a matter of fact, the Upanishads were probably not composed entirely by Brahmins. There is good reason to think that non-Brahmins, especially Kshatriyas, composed some of them—particularly those that reflect the dualistic rather than the monistic point of view; for the Kshatriyas were, one concludes, more inclined than the Brahmins to the proto-Hinduism surviving from pre-Aryan times, the down-to-earth fertility rites and magical practices based on accepting the reality of the external world and its magical forces.

Ritual Interiorized

A movement toward interiorizing religious practice may be noted. This tendency took two forms.

First, there was a trend toward asceticism, that is, away from activity in the world toward inward activity of the mind and spirit. Ascetics and meditative thinkers were increasing in number and were rivaling the priests in commanding the highest respect. Even Brahmins were retiring to the forests and engaging in meditation and dialogue. This was not really a new kind of behavior. The *Rig-Veda* mentions ascetics, calling them *muni* and *vratyas*. The mood of the Aryans

was changing. More and more of them were inclined to give up the world and seek emancipation (*moksha*) from its illusion and pain.

Second, there was a trend away from ritualism. It is true that, as appendages to the Brahmanas and their supplements, the Aranyakas, the Upanishads (the earliest ones, the *Brihadaranyaka* and the *Chandogya* in particular) are far from relinquishing sacrifice as a religious practice or an ideal of life, but they in effect react against ritualism by finding equivalents, not to say substitutes, for the rites around the altar. They find these in the acts and the states of body and mind of ascetics and sages (*rishis*). The *Satapatha-Brahmana* had already suggested that each sacrifice was, on the one hand, Prajapati, the Lord of Creatures (= Purusha being offered up anew as he was at the creation), and on the other, the Sacrificer, who offers himself along with his sacrifice; so we have the equation, the sacrificer = the sacrifice = Prajapati. Another line of reasoning, which threads the devotional life of Hinduism from beginning to end, considers the heat (*tapas*) generated by the austere devotion of the ascetic in the forest equivalent to the fire on the altar, and his mental repetition of the Vedic chants equivalent to their recitation beside the altar. (See the description of the third stage in the life career of the Brahmin, p. 110.) By shifting from altar sacrifices to their equivalents, one could continue living in the spirit of the rituals of the Brahmanas, and although discarding them in practice, retain them in essence. This would be to interiorize the rituals through passage from sacrifice offered to the gods "out there" to sacrifice occurring within the self.

Accompanying this shift from outer to inner sacrifice was a new emphasis on the high worth of the spirit or the soul, one's inner self (*atman*). Compared to this inner self, the natural world (*prakriti*, matter), including the body and its sensory and mental states, is of an inferior order. To choose to ignore the inner self and be content with the natural world would be an act of ignorance that could only result in illusion and suffering. Hence, although ritual sacrifices as a means of altering the natural world would have some merit in improving one's lot, salvation is best attained by breaking away from the natural world and from one's sensory and mental experience in it, through asceticism and meditation, that is, by "abandoning the body" and "freeing the soul."

Hermitage Scene

Although this is a Rajput painting from the early nineteenth century, it describes a situation almost as old as Hinduism itself, the retirement of holy men and sages from the world into forests to discuss the meaning of life and the nature of reality. Here a white-haired ascetic seems to be teaching a younger disciple inthe manner of the sages of the Upanishads. *(Courtesy, Museum of Dine Arts, Boston. Ross-Coomaraswamy Collection.)*.

The Trend toward Monism

To take the view just outlined and to go no farther with it was to rest, as some Upanishads (e.g., the *Shvetasvatara*) did, in the minority opinion of the Upanishads, namely, in a dualism of nature (prakriti) and soul or spirit (atman). But many Upanishadic thinkers went on beyond such a point to equate and then merge these two in a unified view (monism). In their search for inner connections between things, they found equivalences and identical samenesses everywhere. For instance, in the *Chandogya Upanishad,* the fire on the altar is identified with the fire in the sun and the fire in the sun with the creative power (heat, tapas) of Being itself (Brahman).

This presence everywhere of heat as a creative power was anticipated in the Vedas. In the creation hymn (p. 86) heat ("the power of warmth") brought That One Thing itself into active being. Heat is everywhere. The Vedas noted that the heat of the sun vaporizes the moisture of land and sea and brings rain; the same heat ripens fruits and grains; the hearth and altar fires by their heat cook the food of homes and sacrifices; the energies of Indra and the other gods are a result of their inner fires, and the activities of men have a like stimulus; the heat of the stomach "cooks" its food; all events both within and outside the body require heat

to come to pass. Similar reasoning found the presence everywhere of water and food. In one brahmana (*Tait.* 2.8) Food declares, "I am the real essence of the universe. My force sets aglow the suns of heaven."

The activity of bees extracting nectar from flowers by heat (or energy) is the same as the activity of priests extracting the honey of blessing from soma juice and milk heated on the sacrificial fire, and this again is exactly what the mind does when extracting the highest good from a warm contemplation of the ritual. The light that shines above all the worlds, and on everything, is the same light that is within man and that can be experienced when we touch his body and perceive the warmth of its inner fire. This tendency to view all things as essentially equivalent was intensified when the gods and all other objects in the universe were conceived to be forms or elements derived by self-distribution from one originative source or ground of being, a cosmic Person or Cow or Horse sacrificing itself by self-dismemberment and seeking now its reconstitution or reunification by drawing its parts together again. Ultimately, all things are bound together, not only by likeness of activity but in actuality, that is to say, in *being*. Man comes to see not his separateness from the gods and his fellows but his and their identity with an eternal, all-inclusive Being or Reality, and begins to seek his deliverance (moksha) from separateness by mystical union with it.

Brahman

This all-inclusive being or reality is most commonly called Brahman. In the Upanishads, the word has moved out of its early Vedic setting: it no longer refers only to the holy power of prayer but it applies directly to the ultimate reality. Brahman is a neuter word. (In some texts it is written Brahma and easily confused with the name of a deity, Brahma. To reduce the chance of confusion, an *n* is appended in our quotations.)

The Upanishads attempt no precise definition of Brahman. Descriptions vary. Some of the treatises, for the most part the later ones, conceive Brahman as a kind of deity endowed with personality.

> *Immortal, existing as the Lord,*
> *Intelligent, omnipresent, the guardian of this world,*
> *Is He who constantly rules this world . . .*[11]

Many passages indiscriminately intermingle impersonal and personal designations for this ultimate reality. In other passages the personal designation seems to be resorted to more from habit or as a concession to the troubled imagination than anything else. The "limitless One" is described as *He* [who] awakes this world."

> Verily, in the beginning this world was Brahma[n], the limitless One—limitless to the east, limitless to the north, . . . limitless in every direction. Incomprehensible is that Soul, unlimited, unborn, not to be reasoned about, unthinkable—He whose soul is space! In the dissolution of the world He alone remains awake. From that space, He, assuredly, awakes this world, which is a mass of thought. It is thought by Him, and in Him it disappears. His is that shining form which gives heat in yonder sun and which is the brilliant light in a smokeless fire, as also the fire in the stomach which cooks the food. For thus it has been said: "He who is in the fire, and he who is here in the heart, and he who is yonder in the sun—he is one."[12]

Some treatises, the earlier ones, regularly refer to Brahman as a neuter something, without motion or feeling, the impersonal matrix from which the universe has issued and to which it will in time return. This It, this One Thing, is the substantial substratum of everything.

> Verily, this whole world is Brahma[n]. Tranquil let one worship It as that from which he came forth, as that in which he will be dissolved, as that in which he breathes.[13]

Brahman and He-She/It

The later Upanishads show an awareness of the problem posed by the alternative pronouns He-She and It. If "He-She" is Deity, then "It" is beyond, while yet inclusive of, Deity. (In the terminology of Meister Eckhart, the medieval mystic, "It" is the "God beyond God.") These Upanishads therefore make a distinction between Brahman made manifest as a person (He-She) and Brahman unmanifest (It). Thus the *Maitri Upanishad* says,

> There are, assuredly, two forms of Brahman: the formed and the formless. Now that which is formed is unreal [or not fully real]; that which is formless is real [i.e., ultimately real].[14]

In this ascription of relative unreality to the formed Brahman we have an intimation of a later more elaborated doctrine, the doctrine of *maya,* according to which the Unmanifest is the source and ground of all manifested things and beings (the world and all that is in it, including the formed or personal Brahman). But these are not wholly real. Only the hidden Brahman is utterly real and imperishable.

Some Upanishads have employed yet other terms to make this distinction explicit. Faced with the problem of how a formless, actionless being could create a world of visible and changing forms, they say that the unmanifest Brahman expressed its inherent creative power by producing Hiranyagarbha, the Golden Egg, which at the dawn of creation emerged on "the sea of Brahman" and became the active creator God, Brahmā. (Note that *Brahmā* is masculine, not neuter, and that the accent is on the final vowel.) Through Brahman's inherent "magical power" (maya) Brahmā created the world. As a personal god occupying a sovereign position, his title is *Ishvara,* "Lord," a title that is also given to Shiva the Destroyer and Vishnu the Preserver in other contexts.

Manifest and Unmanifest Brahman

In a further effort of clarification, some late Upanishads say that the personal god is *Saguna Brahman* ("Brahman with attributes"), while the unmanifest, unknowable, imperishable, and unconditioned Brahman is *Nirguna Brahman* ("Brahman without attributes"). The latter is so indescribable that references to It must be abstract and negative; one is obliged to say of It *"Neti, neti"* ("[It is] not this, nor that"). On the other hand, Saguna Brahman may be both known and described; He is the Lord God regnant in the heavens who responds to human love and prayer.

It is evident, then, that the unmanifest and formless Nirguna Brahman is the ultimate, and the personally manifest Saguna Brahman is the immediate, source of the external world; as He-She and It (Deity and the all-inclusive One) Brahman is the constitutive element and the pervasive presence in all that is objective, all that is outside of us, the whole world of nature given to us by our senses. In the conversation in the *Brihadaranyaka Upanishad* between the renowned Brahmin, Gargya Balaki, and the king of Benares, a Kshatriya who is his superior in philosophic understanding, there is a progressive definition of Brahman as the reality within and yet beyond the sun, the moon, lightning, space, wind, fire, water, mirrors, sounds that reverberate, the different quarters of the heavens, shadows, and bodies.[15] Other Upanishads have the same general tenor. All things, all creatures, are ultimately phases of That One—"the priest by the altar, the guest in the house."[16] "Stretched forth below and above, Brahma[n], indeed, is this whole world, this widest extent."[17]

Brahman and Atman

But this is only half the fact. Brahman is also all that is subjective, the whole inward world of reason, feeling, will, and self-consciousness, with which the innermost self is identified. All that goes on in the soul of man, and the soul itself, are phases of That One. The term for the inner self here employed is *atman,* a word used philosophically to denote the innermost and unseen

self of a person as distinct from the body, sense organs, and mentality; that is to say, it refers to the transcendental self, not to the empirical self (*jiva*) whose mental and psychological characteristics are developed in the body and are knowable through sense experience. Many of the Upanishads insist that, contrary to popular belief in the absolute individuality of the human soul, there is an actual identity between Brahman and atman, and that this is true of any and every atman, whether it is found in human beings, beast, insect, flower, fish, or any other living thing. "Yajnavalkya," cries an eager inquirer in the *Brihadaranyaka,* "explain to me him who is the Brahma[n] present and not beyond our ken, him who is the soul in all things." "He is your soul," comes the answer.

> He who, dwelling in the earth . . . in the waters . . . in the fire . . . the atmosphere . . . the wind . . . the sky . . . the sun . . . the quarters of heaven . . . the moon and stars . . . space . . . darkness . . . light. . . . He who, dwelling in all things, yet is other than all things, whom all things do not know, whose body all things are, who controls all things from within—He is your soul, the inner Controller, the Immortal. . . .
>
> He who, dwelling in breath . . . in speech . . . the eye . . . the ear . . . the mind . . . the skin . . . the understanding, yet is other than the understanding, . . . He is the unseen Seer, the unheard Hearer, the unthought Thinker, the ununderstood Understander. Other than He there is no seer. Other than He there is no hearer . . . no thinker . . . no understander. . . . He is your soul, the Inner Controller, the Immortal.[18]

"That Art Thou"

Such a passage sufficiently suggests the conclusion to which this sort of reasoning led. The true self of a person and the world soul (*paramatman,* the universal atman) are one, identical. This identity is expressed in the *Chandogya Upanishad* in the formula *Tat tvam asi,* which means, "That (or It) art thou!"[19] In other words, the All-Soul is the very stuff of which the human soul is formed. And the Upanishads vary in considering whether this stuff is mental stuff or material stuff. It is all being (*sat*), consciousness (*cit*), and bliss (*ananda*), and also their opposites. Nothing takes place in the individual self that does not have its source and ground in *the* Self. We may therefore equate Brahman, the objective All, and Atman, the inner self, and call the ultimate reality henceforth Brahman-Atman, recognizing thereby that the objective and subjective are one.

It may not be said that this is the unequivocal finding of all the Upanishads. Some of them do not go so far and are monotheistic rather than monistic. None of them quite reaches the later Vedantic doctrine that because Brahman-Atman alone exists, the whole universe is either outright illusion or the "sport," "play," or "art" of the creative All-Soul. There is still a recognition of a relative or derivative reality of the universe; it is something that has been breathed forth by Brahman-Atman and pervaded by his or its being. And yet, perhaps "breathed forth" and "pervaded by" do not sufficiently suggest the close-knit unity of being that subsists between the Subjective and the Objective. The *Brihadaranyaka* rather clearly insists that though things and selves may be spoken of as emanations from, creations of, or constructs pervaded by Brahman-Atman, "as a razor would be hidden in a razor case,"[110] all things ultimately *are* Brahman-Atman without any qualifications. (Brahman-Atman is both razor and razor case.)

The Chandogya Upanishad, playing upon the phrase *Tat tvam asi,* tells the following story:

Now there was Shvetaketu Aruneya. To him his father said: "That which is the finest essence—this whole world has that as its soul. That is Reality. That is Atman. That art thou, Shvetaketu."

"Do you, Sir, cause me to understand even more."

"So be it, my dear," said he . . .

"Bring hither a fig."

"Here it is, Sir."

"Divide it."

"It is divided, Sir."

"What do you see there?"

"Those rather fine seeds, Sir."

"Of these, please divide one."

"It is divided, Sir."

"What do you see there?"

"Nothing at all, Sir."

Then he said to him: "Verily, my dear, that finest essence which you do not perceive—verily, my dear, from that finest essence this great Nyagrodha (sacred fig) tree thus arises. Believe me, my dear," said he, "that which is the finest essence—this whole world has that as its soul. That is Reality. That is Atman. *That art thou,* Shvetaketu."[112]

Experiential Unity

The thinkers of the Upanishads did not stop here. Knowing that their philosophy was grounded in mysticism, and not alone in a search for knowledge, they said that when the human soul *knows* its complete identity with Brahman, it celebrates this knowledge with a feeling of unity approaching ecstasy. The experience of such assured knowledge was pronounced so beatific as to be indescribable, a blissfulness,

Wherefrom words turn back,
Together with the mind, not having attained.[113]

Undoubtedly, most of the writers of the Upanishads knew of, if they did not themselves practice, the technique of such realization of identity with or complete absorption into Brahman. In this technique the prospective Brahman knower would sit meditating in profound quiet of mind, seeking to know, verily *know,* not have an opinion or a mere belief, but be spiritually certain, that the internal knower and the external world of sense had alike the same ground of being; that he or she and the tree nearby were one, because they were both phases of the One, in short *were* Brahman-Atman and not any other. The certitude of such unity came to one when one was more in a nonconscious than a conscious state. (Strictly speaking, one would be

> "This soul of mine within the heart is smaller than a grain of rice, or a barleycorn, or a mustard-seed, or a grain of millet, or the kernel of a grain of millet; this soul of mine within the heart is greater than the earth, greater than the atmosphere, greater than the sky, greater than the worlds. . . . This soul of mine within the heart, this is Brahma[n]."[111]
>
> —The *Chandogya Upanishad*

Essence of the Ultimate
Vocalized: "Om"

neither conscious nor nonconscious. One would be as in a trance in which sense of personal identity melted away.) In seeking analogies for it, the later Upanishadic thinkers declared that there are three mental states which may be usefully compared with it: the state of waking consciousness, the state of dreaming sleep, and the state of deep, dreamless sleep. All are states of consciousness, but as modes of experience of truth and reality all three are found defective, especially the first two, because in them there is a persistence of the consciousness of a duality of subject and object, self and not-self, ego and non-ego. Deep, dreamless sleep is nearest to affording an analogy for the state of union with Brahman because it represents a sinking back into a type of nonconsciousness in which subject and object are no longer distinguished.

Pure Consciousness: *Turiya*

But a fourth state of consciousness that underlies but yet transcends the first three—Pure Consciousness—comes into full being only with the experience of union with Brahman (called *turiya* or *caturtha*). This state is considered the highest of all states of mind because it represents the purest being of soul, when the soul is sleeplessly intent and when subject and object are indistinguishable in the purity of being. A modern interpreter from India identifies it as "pure intuitional consciousness, where there is no knowledge of objects internal or external."[1] *The Mandukya Upanishad* contains an interesting definition of it.

> The fourth state is not that which is conscious of the subjective, nor that which is conscious of the objective, nor that which is conscious of both, nor

that which is simple consciousness, nor that which is an all-sentient mass, nor that which is all darkness. It is unseen, transcendent, the sole essence of the consciousness of self, the completion of the world.[2]

In the turiya state the world and the self are not obliterated as they would be in deep, dreamless sleep, but both the self and the world are held together in their pure essences, stripped of all distortion and illusion and experienced as being united with the being of Brahman-Atman, where their reality is found to subsist. To experience such a state of consciousness is to attain moksha, final liberation, release from rebirth.

Cosmic Cycles: *Kalpas*

One doctrine evolved during this period does, however, provide for a periodical dissolution or suspended being of all souls and of the entire world. This is the famous theory of the cyclic destruction and re-creation of the world. According to this theory, the world dissolves away at the end of every *kalpa* or period of created being, and all of the souls in the universe depart from their bodies into a state of suspended being. After a period of absolute nullity and repose, called a *pralaya,* the world comes again into being, and the long-quiescent souls take up a new embodiment in vegetables, animals, human beings, gods, and demons. The castes are re-formed, the Vedas recomposed, and another kalpa proceeds to its inevitable end, with history generally repeating itself again.

Such conceptions contain the germ of much future philosophizing. The six great systems of Hindu philosophy (p. 111) were to develop from these first-fruits of speculation. The Indian mind had indeed launched out into the deep.

First Appearance in Indian Thought of Reincarnation and Karma

It was in this same period that a new color was given to Indo-Aryan thought by the adoption of two doctrines that were to become permanent elements in the outlook of India. Both make their first definite appearance in Indian literature in the Upanishads, but they were very probably not inventions of the time. They may have been taken over from earlier beliefs. In any case they are not in the earlier Aryan spirit; rather, they derive their relevance from India itself, considered as the thought-evoking background of human living.

Samsara

The first of these doctrines, the belief in a birth-death-rebirth-redeath cycle of change, is not peculiar to India. It is widely held in both primal and highly developed cultures. The Sanskrit term *samsara* (sequence of change) is connected in the Upanishads with the idea of an imperishable atman (soul) to produce a doctrine of transmigration of the soul from life form to life form, the reincarnation of the atman in a succession of bodies. (In other contexts, in Buddhism for example, samsara is the scene of impermanence; lives give rise to other lives, but the notion of an imperishable transmigrating soul entity is not superimposed.)

In the Upanishads the reasoning runs like this: the soul of a person who dies does not, except in the single case of one who at death returns into indistinguishable oneness with Brahman, pass into a permanent state of being in heaven or hell or elsewhere; the soul, rather, is reborn into another existence that will terminate in due time and necessitate yet another birth. Rebirth follows rebirth, with the one exception named, in an endless chain. The successive births are not likely to be on the same plane of being. Rebirth may occur for a finite period of time in any of the series of heavens or hells, or upon earth in any of the forms of life, vegetable, animal, or human. It may thus be either higher or lower than the present or any past existence. A man of low social status now may be reborn as a rajah or a Brahmin, or, more likely, an outcaste, an animal, a beetle, a worm, a vegetable, or a soul in hell.

"Those who are of pleasant conduct here—the prospect is, indeed, that they will enter a pleasant womb, either the womb of a Brahmin, or the womb of a Kshatriya, or the womb of a Vaisya. But those who are of stinking conduct here—the prospect is, indeed, that they will enter either the womb of a dog, or the womb of a swine, or the womb of an outcast."[114]

—The *Chandogya Upanishad*

Karma

But what determines the nature of the next birth? What causes it to enter a higher or lower state of existence? The second of the new doctrines, and the one peculiar to India, provides the answer. One's future existence is determined by the Law of Karma (*karma* meaning "deeds" or "works"), the law that one's thoughts, words, and deeds have an ethical consequence fixing one's lot in future existences. Looked at retrospectively, karma is the *cause* of what is happening in one's life now.

The Law of Karma assumes that everything one does, each separate deed of one's life, weighed along with every other deed, determines destiny. Single acts have each their inevitable consequence that must be worked out to the uttermost, whether for good or for evil. This is the extreme view. Many Hindus, who construe the law as being less rigorous in its weighing of the consequences of each separate act, say it is simply the law that one reaps what one sows, or to put the fact in terms of another metaphor, that deeds shape not only character but also the soul, so that in a person's next incarnation the soul, having a definite shape, "can find reembodiment only in a form into which that shape can squeeze."[K] In any case, the law operates like a law of nature. The process is quite impersonal. "There is no judge and no judgment; no punishment, no repentance or amends, no remission of sins by divine clemency . . . just the inexorable causal nexus of the eternal universe itself."[L]

In a somewhat later time than the one we are considering here, the exact recompense of one's deeds was thus precisely estimated.

In consequence of many sinful acts committed with his body, a man becomes in the next birth something inanimate, in consequence of sins committed by speech, a bird, and in consequence of mental sins he is reborn in a low caste. . . . Those who committed mortal sins, having passed during large numbers of years through dreadful hells, obtain, after the expiration of that term of punishment, the following births. The slayer of a Brahmin enters the womb of a dog, a pig, an ass, a camel, a cow, a goat, a sheep, a deer, a bird, a Kandala, and a Pukhasa. . . . A Brahmin who steals the gold of a Brahmin shall pass a thousand times through the bodies of spiders, snakes, lizards, of aquatic animals and of destructive Pukhasas. . . . Men who delight in doing hurt become carnivorous animals; those who eat forbidden food, worms; thieves, creatures consuming their own kind. . . . For stealing grain a man becomes a rat; . . . for stealing a horse, a tiger; for stealing fruits and roots, a monkey; for stealing a woman, a bear; for stealing cattle, a he-goat.[M]

The discouragement that this kind of prospect evoked is well expressed in the *Maitri Upanishad:* "In this sort of cycle of existence (*samsara*) what is the good of enjoyment of desires, when after a man has fed on them there is seen repeatedly his return here to earth? Be pleased to deliver me. In this cycle of existence I am like a frog in a waterless well."[115] The unhappiness that characterized the emotional revulsion from the Law of Karma is clearly expressed here.

Of course, the principle of karma also could be seen as the sure means to ultimate freedom, for pure actions guarantee emancipation from samsara. This bright side of karmic consequence is infrequently celebrated in the Upanishads, but the assurance of ultimate justice and present security of position were to play a large part in the evolving system of castes.

The Place of Caste in the Religious Dogma

During the period around 500 B.C.E., the caste system, so distinctive of Hindu social life, was gradually establishing itself, although its final form took centuries to evolve. The four classes (varna) were now as follows: first, the Brahmins; then the Kshatriyas; below these, the Vaisyas or "producers"; and, last, the Shudras or servants. It is possible that the Brahmins had imposed upon a more complex configuration this fourfold classification, for they wanted to establish their supremacy—and they succeeded. Outside of the caste system altogether—"beyond the pale"—were the outcastes, including a group that was "untouchable." (The term *outcaste* should usually be read as a noun;

that is, in most cases, outcastes were not groups expelled—"cast out"—but those that were "never in.") The outcastes constituted the dregs of society, unclean and without the hope of ever rising in the social scale, unless they happened to be individuals outcasted temporarily for infraction of caste rules and awaiting reinstatement after expiation of their offenses. The stratification of society proceeded further. In succeeding centuries, hard-and-fast lines were drawn, not only between but also within each class. The main classes fissured into hundreds of subcastes, *jatis,* each forbidding intermarriage into other subcastes and otherwise restricting freedom of association.

But our interest here is not in the social extension of the caste system (for that, see pp. 141–143) but rather in its place within the religious dogma evolved by the Brahmins. When the caste system was linked with the Law of Karma, the inequalities of life had at once a simple and comprehensive explanation. The existence of caste in the social structure immediately acquired a kind of moral justification. If a man was born a Shudra, it was because he had sinned in previous existences and did not deserve a better lot. A Brahmin, on the other hand, had every right to exalt his position and prerogatives; by good deeds in previous existences he had merited his present high station. And here, too, the ranking of the castes with the Brahmins at the top, the Kshatriyas next, the Vaisyas third, and the Shudras last seemed justified by a spiritual sliding scale, as it were: the class in society with the best record of spiritual attainment should be at the top.

So, at least, the Brahmins argued, and in spite of die-hard resistance, the Kshatriyas, with no notion of contradicting the fact of transmigration and the consequences of karma in determining destiny, and thus deprived of any weighty counterargument to offer, had to be content at length with second place. They did, however, play a significant role in fostering views at variance with Brahminism, which eventually surfaced in Jainism and Buddhism.

The social consequence of the moral justification of caste was apparent in another direction. Any attempt to level the inequalities of society and lay a broader basis for social justice and reward now became either impious or morally wrongheaded. Heavy social and religious penalties could be invoked against those who questioned the Law of Karma as fixing the just retribution or reward for deeds done in former lives.

The Need of a Way of Release

The Aryans who came into India were a robust and optimistic people, but this confident frame of mind persisted only as long as the mood expressed in the Vedas did. With the rise of the caste system, the adoption of the beliefs in reincarnation and the Law of Karma, and the development among the sensitive few of a world-denying asceticism, disaffection with the world grew in ancient India. This turning inward for fulfillment had other causes too. There were undoubtedly physical and psychological conditions contributing to it. Up to the time of their descent into the Ganges Valley, the Aryans had not finally given up their nomadic habit of life. The world still appealed to them as a sphere of action and adventure. But after they had descended the Ganges River plain and ended their wanderings, their life in that hot and enervating climate became less active. Keen minds will not cease from thinking under such conditions. Thought may substitute for legs and provide the intellectualist, sensualist, or lover of romantic dreams with vicarious adventure—that of the mind and imagination. And yet, should this world be held to be the only realm of existence, such minds tend to grow heavy and come to rest more and more in negations.

Moksha

Yet for such Hindus there is a classical antidote for such discouragement, an ultimate solution for it. It is this: "You who think this life is evil and are so distressed by the prospect of ever-recurring rebirths are forgetting something. There is a realm that is eternal and changeless, not at all like this world that is so full of change and decay, of becoming and passing away. You can be liberated into it, if you try." Such Hindus are in fact saved from pessimism when they accept the faith that this world is not the only realm, that endless suffering is not their inevitable lot, that there is a realm of reality not hopelessly involved in becoming, changing, disintegrating, and perishing—namely, the realm of true being and true freedom, moksha.

There were in India, as everywhere else, of course, the worldly many who worried little about the disillusionments of the sensitive "philosophic" few. They were attached to their homes and fields, their villages and towns, their spouses and children, and they delighted in food, sex, and position in the social scene. Nirvana was not for them—not yet.

To this point the ideas we have been examining have been steadily tending. The further history of Indian religions, orthodox or heterodox, is essentially that of a search for the solution of the problem, how may one reach a state of experience or being that transcends this life's imperfections? Negatively, since rebirth is seen to supply a network of suffering extended over great stretches of time and space, how may one achieve release from the round of rebirths? More positively, how may one know and experience the truly real as against the deceptively and only partially real?

Barely four centuries passed from the time the Aryans entered the Ganges plain until this problem became both clear and urgent. The mind of India has been at work on it ever since.

GLOSSARY

agni (ŭg'-ni) the sacred fire, as *Agni*, the ritual priest god of fire and light

Aryans (Indo-Europeans) seminomadic peoples who migrated from eastern Europe and central Asia westward to become the ancestors of the Greeks, Romans, Celts, and Teutons, and eastward to Persia and India (*ca.* 1500 B.C.E.); their Sanskrit culture infuses the dominant tradition in India today.

asvamedha (äsh-vŭ-mä'-dŭ) the ancient Aryan horse sacrifice

Atharva-Veda (ŭt-hŭr'-vŭ-vä'-dŭ) Brahmanic ritual poetry dedicated to meeting practical needs: healing illness, casting spells to win a lover, averting bad luck, or expiating sins (See chart on p. 101.)

atman (ät'-mŭn) the essence of consciousness, the soul; ultimately the subjective component of *brahman*

Brahmā (brŭ-mä') (masculine) the Creator; although less popular than Shiva and Vishnu, he is a member of the supreme triad (*trimurti*) with them and a sharer of the title Ishvara ("Lord").

brahman (brä'-mŭn) (neuter) in Vedic literature a mana-like magical potency especially associated with sacred utterances (mantras) and prayer; in later philosophical works, *Brahman* is the ultimate ground of all forms and phenomena, the World Soul.

Brahmanas (brä'-mu˝n-u˝z) commentaries on the Vedas stressing the potency of Brahmanic ritual for control over gods, nature, and humankind (See chart on p. 101.)

Brahman-Atman (brä'-mŭn-ŭt-mŭn) a compound term to indicate the essential identity of individual consciousness with the eternal *Brahman,* the universal World Soul

Brahmin (conventional English spelling) a member of the *Brahmana* or priestly class of castes, the highest group in the *varna* ordering of society

Brihaspati (Brahmanaspati) a ritual deity, the power of prayer personified

Dasas (Dasyus) dark-skinned indigenous inhabitants of northwest India subdued by invading Aryans; the Dasas were probably survivors from the Indus Valley culture and kindred peoples of the Punjab.

Dravidians a major racial and linguistic family of dark-skinned non-Aryan peoples most numerous in south India; whether they are descendants of the Indus Valley culture is uncertain.

henotheism flattering ritual attribution of supreme position and a vast array of powers to one of many gods, temporarily ignoring, but not denying, the existence of the others

Indra god of storms and the monsoon, slayer of Vritra in a mythic cosmogony in the *Rig-Veda*

jiva (jē'vŭ) the principle of vitality, the empirical self, or the embodied *atman*

kalpa a world age or aeon, a unit in the cycle of periodic dissolutions and reconstitutions of all things

karma "deeds," "works," the principle of inexorable cause and effect

Kshatriyas (kshä'-trĭ-yŭz) (Rajanyas) the warrior-chieftain class of castes, the second ranking group in varna

moksha release, liberation from the cycle of *samsara*

monism the metaphysical view that ultimate reality is made up of only one substance; diversity is only apparent and can be traced to one substrate

prakriti (prŭ-krĭ'-tē) the eternal self-subsisting material world, Nature

purusha as *Purusha,* the original cosmic Person; in later philosophies, pure consciousness, the nonmaterial, coeternal counterpart to *prakriti*

Rig-Veda a collection of over 1,000 Sanskrit hymns, the liturgical handbook of early Aryan *hotar* priests, the oldest portion of Brahmanic "revealed" (*shruti*) sacred literature (See chart on p. 101.)

Rudra mountain god of the north wind, sometimes destroyer, sometimes healer, later worshiped under the name *Shiva,* "auspicious"

samsara sequence of change, impermanence, the cycle of rebirth-redeath that afflicts every living being until release (*moksha*)

shruti "that which is heard," the most sacred core of Brahmanic literature (See chart on p. 101.)

Shudra worker class of castes, fourth and lowest ranking in the *varna* social order

smriti "that which is remembered," secondary level of sacred writings that derive from revelation but are composed by human authors (See chart on p. 101.)

---

*The pronunciation of words that are not found in standard dictionaries is indicated by a system of diacritical marks that are to be sounded approximately like the italicized letters in the following words: ärtistic, ădd, bĕll, fāme, ēve, hĭt, pīne, gō, ŏdd, ôr, fŏŏt, fōōd, oıl, bŭt, menü, bûrn, ūnite, säuerkraut, chin, H like ch in German ach or Scotch loch. Where, however, pronunciation seems to present no difficulty, it is not suggested.

Many Sanskrit terms ending in *a* or *ha* are pronounced in modern Hindi with only a slight exhalation of the breath. *Jaganatha* thus becomes almost jŭgänŭtt, *ashrama* becomes äshrŭmm, *Jakata* jŭtŭkk, *ahankaru* ŭhŭnkŭrr, *marga* mŭrg, and so on. It should be added that a *v* is today usually pronounced like a *w*.

soma sacred drink; as *Soma,* the ritual priest-god of libations

tapas austerity-generated "heat"; subjectively, each impulse mastered stokes the inner fire of psychic power; universally, containment generates warmth incubating the cosmic germ/egg

Upanishads (ŏŏ-pän'-ĭ-shŭdz) "sitting near a teacher," commentary treatises expanding on the philosophical meanings found in the *Vedas* (See chart on p. 101.)

Ushas white-robed goddess of the dawn; eternally young, she rides a chariot driven by her male attendants, the twin Asvins.

Vaisyas (vī-shyŭz) the merchant, artisan, and small landholder class of castes, third in the *varna* order

Varuna (vŭ-rŏŏ'-nŭ) Vedic deity of the night sky, keeper of the natural and moral order

Veda ancient Brahmanic ritual poems and hymn (See chart on p. 101.)

Vedanta (vā-dän'-tŭ) "the end of the *Vedas,*" commentary treatises (*Upanishads*) on the *Vedas* (See chart on p. 101.) in later times, one of the six recognized systems of Hindu philosophy.

The Hindu Scripture*

The following chart applies to both early and later Hinduism (chapters 3 and 4).

Shruti ("That Which Is Heard") Vedic Sacred Literature

1. Samhita—"Collection" (of hymns)
   a. *Rig-Veda*—1028 hymns (*ca.* 1500–900 B.C.E.)
   b. *Sama-Veda*—"Chant" (Verses of *Rig-Veda* arranged for liturgical use.)
   c. *Yajur-Veda*—"Sacrifice" (200 years later)
      Sukla (white) recension—pure mantras
      Krishna (black) recension—mantras plus sacrificial formulae
   d. *Atharva-Veda*—magical spells and incantations
2. *Brahmanas* (*ca.* 850 B.C.E.—key concepts: Varna (caste)
   Latter part: Aranyakas (*ca.* 500 B.C.E.)
3. *Upanishads* "Vedanta" (*ca.* 500 B.C.E.)—philosophical works
   Key concepts: Brahman, Atman, Maya, Yoga, Nirvana

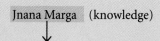

Karma Marga (works)
↓

Jnana Marga (knowledge)
↓

Smriti ("That Which Is Remembered") Non-Vedic Sacred Literature

1. Vedāngas—phonetics, grammar, etymology, prosody, medicine
2. Dharma Shastras—conduct, hygiene, administration
   Laws of Manu (*ca.* 200 B.C.E.)—a later development of the Brahmanas included
3. Nibandhas—codifications of Vedic laws
4. Purānas and Epics—popular literature
   a. Purānas: esp.
      Bhagavata Purāna, glorying Vishnu and Krishna
      Suta Samhita, glorifying Siva (Advaita philos.)
   b. Epics:
      Rāmāyana
      Mahabharata (includes the *Bhagavad Gita*)
5. Darshanas—the six schools of philosophy
   a. Sankhya
   b. Nyāya
   c. Vedānta
   d. Yoga
   e. Vaishesika
   f. Mīmāmsā
6. Agamas or Tantras (Sectarian scriptures)
   a. Shaivism
   b. Vaishnavism
   c. Shaktism
7. Writings of revered gurus
   a. Shankara *ca.* 800 C.E.
   b. Ramanuja 12th century C.E.
   c. Ramakrishna d. 1886

Bhakti Marga (devotion)
↓

*Adapted from V. Raghavan in K. W. Morgan, *The Religion of the Hindus.*

Later Hinduism
Religion as
the Determinant
of Social Behavior

The religious awakening that occurred in India in the sixth century B.C.E. manifested itself, not only in the rise of the Brahmanism, but also in Jainism and Buddhism, religions we will consider in later chapters. The urgency of the need to which the latter two were an answer had been such as to drive people to seek near-at-hand practical modes of release from their growing sense of the essential misery of existence rather than to turn for remedy or solace to philosophical speculation or to priestly sacrifices that did not immediately help individuals where they hurt most. So Brahmanism was being rejected as being ineffectual for souls inwardly pained. Such rejection did not require as much intellectual temerity then (the sixth to the third centuries B.C.E.) as in later periods of India's history, for apart from the rituals of the Brahmanas, which were not to be deviated from by so much as a hair, Brahmanism was still open-ended and tentative, and so it was far from clear what might be settled upon as the right or true point of view. This was particularly apparent in the Upanishads. In fact, Jainism and Buddhism were not altogether novel in their philosophical and moral positions, for what they advocated in these areas was already suggested in pre-Aryan religion and in the growing oral Vedic literature, the Upanishads especially. Their radicalism was in their rejection of the sacrificial system of the Brahmanas and their refusal to give the Brahmins first place or prescriptive rights in discovering the way from misery to freedom.

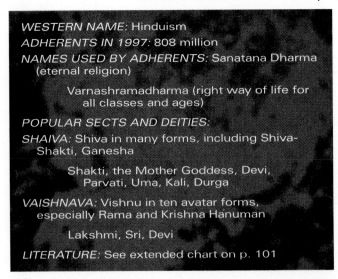

WESTERN NAME: Hinduism

ADHERENTS IN 1997: 808 million

NAMES USED BY ADHERENTS: Sanatana Dharma (eternal religion)

Varnashramadharma (right way of life for all classes and ages)

POPULAR SECTS AND DEITIES:

SHAIVA: Shiva in many forms, including Shiva-Shakti, Ganesha

Shakti, the Mother Goddess, Devi, Parvati, Uma, Kali, Durga

VAISHNAVA: Vishnu in ten avatar forms, especially Rama and Krishna Hanuman

Lakshmi, Sri, Devi

LITERATURE: See extended chart on p. 101

Reasons for Dissent

Rulers and princes (the Kshatriyas) were particularly aroused to dissent. They did not like either the social or religious implications of Brahmanism. The Kshatriyas, some of whom were of non-Aryan background, possessed among their ranks many brilliant minds, and

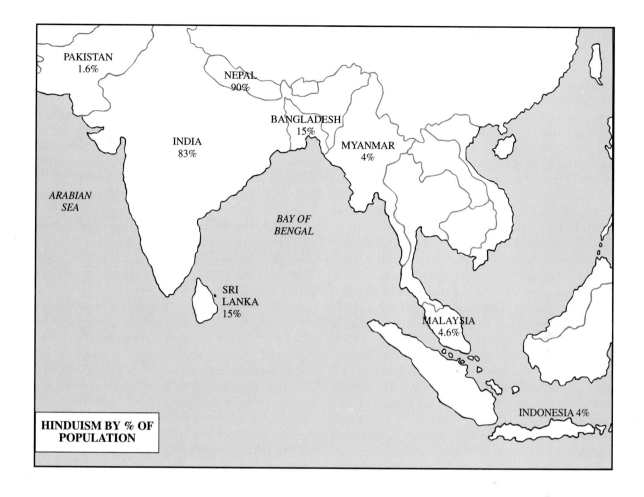

PAKISTAN
1.6%

NEPAL
90%

BANGLADESH
15%

MYANMAR
4%

INDIA
83%

*ARABIAN
SEA*

*BAY OF
BENGAL*

SRI
LANKA
15%

MALAYSIA
4.6%

INDONESIA 4%

**HINDUISM BY % OF
POPULATION**

these were not slow to detect encroachment on the ruling caste's domain. The costly sacrifices that the Brahmins prescribed might ease the anxieties of those who feared or hoped in the gods, but they did not satisfy the doubtful. Goodness had in it something more than ceremonial zeal and the offering of sacrifices. Moreover, as might be expected, the monism toward which the Upanishads and their expositors tended struck many of the realistically inclined members of the ruling class as absurd. Jainism expressed, in part, their common-sense revolt against a worldview that devalued the individual and regarded the world as an illusion. On the other hand, it seemed to the ethically minded that Brahmanism's solution to the problem of human misery by sacrifices was utterly beside the point—not only a waste of goods and time but misleading. This was particularly the position taken by early Buddhism.

In the turmoil and clash of opinion that reigned, Brahmanism perforce changed its early character.

I. CHANGES IN BRAHMANISM: THE FOUR GOALS AND THE THREE WAYS

It required a revolution in thought to make the shift from seeking the help of the gods by sacrifices on the three great open-air altars to the internalizing of these procedures by ascetics dwelling alone in the forests. The revolution had two striking aspects: first, the fire on the altar was replaced by the inner fire (*tapas*) in the ascetic's heart, and, second, the communal sacrificial rites were replaced by the solitary struggle of the individual seeking to disentangle the inner self (*atman*) from its multiform physical entrapment. In the centuries that followed, this revolution led to the development of a method mentioned in the late Upanishads and called *yoga* ("yoking") because it united theory with experience, thought with ultimate reality. It became a highly evolved technique for disciplining mind and body and making more certain the desired ultimate liberation. The final results are reflected later in this chapter.

The Brahmins who did not take the road of solitary self-emancipation ("the Way of Knowledge") were forced to adapt their sacrificial system more and more to settled communities in fixed locations. Major changes occurred during the millennium from 300 B.C.E. to 700 C.E. with the building of temples, the making of images of the gods, and the instituting of festivals at temples that became the focus of year-round pilgrimages.

Furthermore, the Brahmins who chose to continue in the performance of priestly duties found themselves also involved in what are known in the West as pastoral duties: they performed marriages, presided at births and deaths, taught as *gurus* in the homes, and substituted for the householder as ritualists in worship ceremonies or *pujas* honoring the gods of the household.

That Brahmanism, in the form of later Hinduism, rose victorious over its rivals is due to its self-adaptation to changing conditions. The Brahmins never organized under a central authority, never adopted any concerted tactics either of defense or of attack upon the heretical systems. They ultimately prevailed not by being intolerant and defiant toward these other creeds, but by being tolerant toward them. Instead of totally outlawing the distinctive Jainist and Buddhist religious and philosophical views, the Brahmins moved to accommodate them under the umbrella of evolving Hinduism, modifying and directly absorbing some views and simply making room for others.

The Unchanging Needs of Ordinary People

When the Brahmins underwent the revolution of thought that took so many of them out of the performance of ritual and into meditation and mystical union with ultimate reality, ordinary people were marginally aware of it but were not forced into any radical change. They went on for centuries with the rituals to which they were accustomed and which have largely survived, in modified forms, of course, to the present day. This is an important fact that needs stressing: the people of India have been and are deeply absorbed in the household rituals by which they hope to be attuned rightly to their supernatural environment.

The very resistance of the common people to change won the Brahmins over to meeting their needs. Temples, festivals, pilgrimages, images of the gods, music, and dance were the joint product of priests and people seeking to meet the general need.

The inclusiveness and tolerance of the Brahmins on the one hand, and the day-to-day acceptance of custom and tradition by the people on the other hand, combined to bring about a quiet development of doctrines, attitudes, and laws during the centuries that followed. Here inclusion rather than exclusion was the rule. Hence, we find ourselves now facing two inclusive sets of judgments that were generally accepted, one that endorsed four permissible goals in life, and another that recognized not just one but three ways of salvation.

The Four Permissible Goals in Life

For Brahmins, the dharma (sacred law) encompassed all permissible human pursuits, but in realistic accommodation to the terms of everyday life, four goals came to be regarded as being appropriate to the samsaric world of rebirth and redeath. The first two allow paths of desire; the last two extol duty and renunciation. Significantly, the first two are treated exclusively from a male point of view in the classic treatises—as though desire apart from duty could have no place in the life of a female. The four permissible goals are:

1. *Kama*, or pleasure, especially through love. So great a place does the desire for gratification occupy in human life that some Hindus have regarded it as the presence of the god Kama, carrying a flowery bow armed with five flower arrows that pierce the heart and fill it with desire. Not only is enjoyment a permissible human goal, but pleasure seekers need not go unguided. Those who are awkward in love or

unskilled in the pleasure bringing arts of poetry and drama may find instruction either in Vatsyayana's *Kamasutra* (if they seek knowledge of the art of love) or in the *Natyasastras* (if their interest is in the literary arts and skills). Should some persons openly choose to make pleasure their aim, they are not criticized, provided they stay within the bounds set by general social rules. They may even be commended for vitality and a sense of direction. But it is thoroughly understood, nevertheless, that in this or some future existence they will come to realize that pleasure is not enough and that they really want something more deeply satisfying.

2. *Artha*, or power and substance—immediately, things, material possessions; ultimately, high social position or success—is the second permissible goal. As envisioned for males the path of *artha* is pictured as follows: a man who is able and alert may quite naturally wish for great possessions and the power and influence that may be obtained through them. This is understood to be a legitimate aspiration, but it requires ruthlessness and toughness. "The big fish eat the little ones." Machiavelli was anticipated in more than one piece of Indian literature. In the *Arthasatras* (attributed to Kautiliya Kamandaki, and others) or in the beast fables of the *Panchatantra* one may find both sober and humorous instruction in the ruthless competition involved in this way of life. No special blame rests upon the seeker of wealth and power, for his model may well be a great and noble king, but it is recognized once again that if he is allowed to learn for himself, either in this or in some future existence, he will discover that he has not sought the highest goal. He will learn that a deeper satisfaction and a more authentic happiness come from following the path of renunciation.

3. *Dharma*. Derived from the root *dhr*, "to sustain," dharma was first conceived as the undergirding and regulating principle sustaining the universe. Considered in its stricter sense as religious and moral law, it sets the standards for a worthier and more deeply satisfying life than that offered by kama and artha.

In broad terms, one who follows the dharma is faithful in the performance of prescribed duties and is ready to surrender personal pleasure and social success for the sake of the smooth working of the divinely ordained society. Patterns of mutual obligation make up an intricately ordered grid of duties and benefits, and the particulars of dharma as duty for each individual are specific to the person's position in regard to caste, gender, and stage of life. These are spelled out in the *Code of Manu*, and other sacred law books, the *Dharmasatras*.

It should be noted that in the classical texts the attitude toward women in relation to the dharma is ambivalent. On the one hand, the faithfulness and unflagging devotion of women to their fathers, husbands, and sons is the very epitome of dharma: the popular epics are full of accounts of evil men redeemed by the unwavering devotion of their wives. On the other hand, the female principle is seen as being the most potent and dangerous of natural forces and the sexuality of women as by far the most hazardous of the snares along the path of dharma.

Whatever one's position in life, Brahminic literature avers, one should expect that obedience to ethical principles will be attended by profound joy. But that joy, however great, is not lasting. There is of course only one ultimate satisfaction.

4. *Moksha*, release or liberation, was at one time subsumed under dharma in a scheme of just three goals for human aspiration, but by the time of the great epics it was separately identified and elevated as the culmination of the first three, the one ultimately satisfying condition. Negatively, this goal means release from the round of rebirth and redeath and all of the miseries of human existence; positively, it means pure freedom, liberation from both existence and nonexistence into a realm for which no human description is adequate. Sanskrit literature sometimes refers to this liberated condition as *nirvana*, "extinction" (of ignorance and clinging to the world of rebirth and redeath). In Buddhism it is the preferred reference to the bliss of enlightenment.

The Three Ways of Salvation

The essential vigor of the older faith was demonstrated further by the fact that the three ways of release or liberation recognized by orthodox Hinduism were clearly worked out and described: a Way of Works, a Way of Knowledge, and a Way of Devotion. Each of the ways was referred to as a *marga* ("path") or a *yoga* ("discipline").

II. THE ORDERED SOCIETY: THE WAY OF WORKS

The Way of Works, *Karma Marga,* is a very old way. It could be called the way of ritual, especially domestic ritual. Followed by the overwhelming majority of the people, it has the triple advantage of being practical, understandable, and enjoying the sanctity of age-old custom. Not markedly emotional, and still less intellectual, it is a methodical and hopeful carrying out of rites, ceremonies, and duties that add to one's merit (favorable karma). Many a Hindu has believed that by sacrificing to gods and ancestors, revering the rising sun, keeping the sacred hearth fire alight, and performing meticulously the rites and ceremonies that are appropriate at a birth, a death, a marriage, or a harvest, one can acquire enough merit to pass at death into one of the heavens or be reborn as a Brahmin with a real predisposition toward achieving final union with Brahman, the Absolute.

The Way of Works is defined for the first time in the *Brahmanas,* where there occurs a list of "man's debts" in the way of good works. The list, addressed to male heads of households, is simple and severe. Each man owes to the gods sacrifices, which are good works *par excellence;* in addition, he owes to his seers and teachers the study of the Vedas, to the ancestral spirits offspring, and to his fellow men hospitality. If he discharges these debts faithfully, he has done his whole duty, and by him "all is obtained, all is won."[A] But the simplicity of the conception, with its heavy emphasis on sacrifices, was modified during the passage of the years, and gradually various codes sprang into existence, combining old and new customs into authoritative systems. Eventually the modifications were set down in new law books. Typical of these law books (the famous *Dharma Shastras*) is the *Code of Manu,* composed as a collection of rules of life by legalistically minded priests beginning about 200 B.C.E. to 200 C.E. (See p. 101.) We turn to this famous law book next.

The *Code of Manu*

All of the law books, starting with the *Code of Manu,* lay heavy stress on rites of passage, that is, rites that mark events in the life of each individual from birth to death and beyond. Not only must one observe of the rules of one's caste—never marrying outside of it and breaking none of the strict dietary laws and social regulations laid down for it—but one must also be faithful in performing for oneself and others many religious rites and ceremonies. The *Code of Manu* prescribes for each individual a long list of sacramental rites for each significant episode of life—for example, at birth, at name giving, at the first taking out to see the sun, the first feeding with boiled rice, the first hair cutting, initiation into puberty, marriage, and so on. But rites of passage are only part of the whole dharma. There are honors owing to the tutelary deities of the household. The head of the house must see to it that these are properly worshiped each day and that before each meal they are presented with portions of prepared food, fresh from the hands of the lady of the house. No one may eat until this has been done.

Among the most important of all rites are those following death and directed toward ministering to the ancestral spirits. These are called the *shraddha* rites. To most Hindus it would appear true that without these ceremonies the afterlife of the soul as ancestor would be cut short, and the soul would have at once to resume the course of rebirth in accordance with the Law of Karma.

Shraddha Rites: *Pinda*

The shraddha rites, consisting as they do of periodical offerings of memorial prayers and food substances, are thought to be necessary to the very being of the ancestral spirits; without these attentions their strength would completely fail, and they would be swept away into the unknown. The most important elements in the food offerings are the *pinda* (food balls, usually of cooked rice pressed into a firm cake); these are commonly supposed to provide the dead with a kind of corporeal substance, a "new body." According to one view,

> On the first day the dead man gains his head; on the second his ears, eyes, and nose; on the third his hands, breast, and neck; on the fourth his middle parts; on the fifth his legs and feet; on the sixth his vital organs; on the seventh his bones, marrow, veins, and arteries; on the eighth his nails, hair, and teeth; on the ninth all the remaining limbs and organs and his manly strength. The rites of the

tenth day are usually specially devoted to the task of removing the sensations of hunger and thirst which the new body then begins to experience.[B]

Pinda are offered to father and mother, to relatives on the father's and mother's side, and to those who have died away from home without rites and who are therefore especially in need of strengthening attentions. (The immature, however—girls who die unmarried and boys who have not reached the age of initiation—have no shraddha rites performed for them.) The pinda must be offered by a male descendant; hence, one must have sons or cease to exist with the same identity after death! Most spirits are considered amply provided for by the obsequy rites immediately following death, but the leading males receive further attentions, once a month for the first year, and then yearly thereafter on the anniversary of death.

The domestic rites we have been considering are customarily distinguished from public ceremonies. Two groups of sutras are devoted to the two kinds of rites: the *Grihya* sutras, which describe the domestic ceremonies and the *Shrauta* sutras, which were originally written to describe the public rites surviving from the sacrifices of Vedic days.

The Duties of Women

There is a Way of Works for women. It is easily stated: Women's duty is to serve meekly their men. In line with her dependent status, a woman should occupy herself with household duties, yielding unquestioning obedience to the senior woman at the head of the female side of the family and worshiping her men. As a faithful wife aspiring to dwell with her husband in the next existence, she should honor and obey him in this, and never displease him, even though he be destitute of virtue, unfaithful, or devoid of good qualities. "A husband must be constantly worshiped as a god by a faithful wife."[C2]

In certain ultraorthodox quarters, but even there with decreasing frequency, the wife is taught to show honor to her husband by prostrating herself and touching her head to his feet; or, again, she may adore the big toe of his right foot when he is about to rise in the morning, bathing it as one would an idol, and even offering incense to it and waving lights before it, as though it belonged to a great god.

In the *Padmapurana,* the wife's rule of life is put in the following uncompromising terms:

> There is no other god on earth for a woman than her husband. The most excellent of all good works that she can do is to seek to please him by manifesting perfect obedience to him. Therein should lie her sole rule of life.
>
> Be her husband deformed, aged, infirm, offensive in his manner; let him be choleric, debauched, immoral, a drunkard, a gambler; let him frequent places of ill-repute, live in open sin with other women, have no affection for his home; let him rave like a lunatic; let him live without honor; let him be blind, deaf, dumb, or crippled; in a word, let his defects be what they may, a wife must always look upon him as her god, should lavish him with all her affection and care, paying no heed whatsoever to his character and giving him no cause whatsoever for disapproval.
>
> A wife must eat only after her husband has had his fill. If the latter fasts, she shall fast, too; if he touch not food, she also shall not touch it; if he be in affliction, she shall be so, too; if he be cheerful, she shall share his joy. She must on the death of her husband allow herself to be burnt alive on the same funeral pyre; then everybody will praise her virtue.[D]

The last part of this quotation refers to the practice of becoming a *sati* (or *suttee*): a woman who sacrifices herself in fire as an act of devotion. The practice is honored in upper-caste literature, and in one region it was even urged in *advance* of a husband's death if he was deemed likely to fall in battle—a precaution against a wife's falling into the hands of the enemy. Becoming a sati has been forbidden by law since 1829, but isolated episodes of voluntary or induced immolation of widows (and of some unwanted wives) still occur. (See p. 144.)

> "In childhood a female must be subject to her father, in youth to her husband, when her lord is dead to her sons; a woman must never be independent."[C1]
>
> —The *Code of Manu*

After a husband's death a wife may not marry again; she may "never even mention the name of another man," but must keep watch over herself lest she entice one to evil, and until death remain quiet, patient, and chaste, striving to fulfill "that most excellent duty which is prescribed for wives who have one husband only."[C3] The widow "who, from a desire to have offspring, violates her duty to her deceased husband, brings on herself disgrace in this world," and instead of joining her husband in the next existence will "enter the womb of a jackal."[C4]

From their superior position, men are required, however, to honor women. Their own welfare and happiness, as well as the blessing of offspring, depend thereon. Special gifts of ornaments, clothes, and dainty foods are enjoined on holidays and festivals. But this is the honor bestowed by superiors upon those who serve them well. Male superiority must not be lost sight of. A Brahmin, therefore, may not eat in the company of his wife, nor look at her while she eats, and he is prohibited from watching her while she dresses herself and applies collyrium to her eyes.

The preceding paragraphs summarize the stipulations of the *Code of Mana* in regard to women. We shall see in subsequent sections of this chapter that in practice much has changed, even though in theory much remains the same.

To its devotees the Way of Works was an action-filled and satisfying path to salvation. To later students of the Veda, however, exclusive reliance upon ritual observance appeared inferior to another, more philosophic mode of salvation, the *Jnana Marga*, "Way (or Path) of Knowledge," also called the *Jnana Yoga*, "The Discipline of Knowledge."

III. THE REFLECTIVE MODE: THE WAY OF KNOWLEDGE, THE UPANISHADS

The solution to the problem of life through the Way of Knowledge (or Insight) is based on the thinking in the Upanishads. Only those who shared the philosophic passion of the Upanishads could follow it.

The premise of the Way of Knowledge is the belief that the cause of human misery and evil is Ignorance (*Avidya*, Unwisdom or Non-seeing). Human beings are so darkly ignorant about their own nature that all of their actions have the wrong orientation. Mental error, not moral transgression, is the root of human misery and evil.

All of the Hindu philosophical systems agree in this presupposition. It is distinctive of the Hindu point of view.

And yet these same philosophical systems do not agree on the propositions to be erected on its basis. By Western rules of logic, the Upanishads present mutually incompatible versions of the Knowledge that lead to liberation. On the one hand, a dualistic view (later elaborated as the Sankhya school) finds matter and spirit coeternal and separate realities. (Ignorance is the failure to comprehend the distinction.) On the other hand, a monistic view denies the eternal objective reality of matter. (Ignorance is the mistaken notion that matter is real.) Later orthodoxy recognized six separate philosophies, which we will examine in Section IV of this chapter.

At this point a sketch of the best-known viewpoint, monism, will suffice as an example of a Way of Knowledge.

Knowledge in Monistic Term

According to the monistic view, the evil of the human situation lies in this: We persist in thinking of ourselves as real and separate selves, when this is not the fact, for since Brahman-Atman is the sole real being, in whose unity there exists no duality, each self is in reality Brahman-Atman and not another. It is hard to realize such a truth, the monistic philosophers admit; too often, "in this Brahma-wheel the soul flutters about thinking that itself and the Actuator are different."[E1] But persistence in the ignorance-fostered illusion that the individual self and the world it knows exist apart from and are other than the All-Soul is the cause of the world-entangled life of human kind and of their incessant births into one existence after another. As long as a self continues ignorant and lives on in the illusion of separate selfhood, then that selfhood is bound to the ever-turning wheel.

To clarify and illustrate this idea the monists, from the time of the Upanishads, have often resorted to analogies. They say that the relation between the individual and Brahman-Atman is similar to that between rivers and the ocean within which they disappear. The individual is also said to be like a wave rising from and sinking again in the sea, or like a drop of spray that momentarily flies above the sea. A brief amplification of this last analogy will further bring out the meaning. A drop of brine beheld apart from the ocean, flying, let us say, across the face of the sea, may be viewed under two aspects. Under the first, it appears to be an individual drop of a certain size and consistency, with a particular location in time and space differentiating it from any other drop or any other entity whatever. Under the second view, however, this is a misleading description of the case, for the drop is in reality only the ocean in the air, only *apparently* a thing by itself, a pure individual. This second view of the nature of the drop is that supported by Hindu monism. By analogies such as this the belief is driven home that all created things, all the "appearances" that commonsense realism accepts as being exactly as they seem, are in reality Brahma-Atman and are not what they seem. They all have reality, but it is the reality of being Brahman-Atman.

For humankind, then, salvation comes with right understanding, and then

> *The knot of the heart is loosened,*
> *All doubts are cut off,*
> *And one's deeds (karma) cease.*[E3]

Intuitive Certitude

There remains this point to make clear: How does one *know* "the knot of the heart is loosened." When does faith in union become knowledge of union?

Here, all of the intellectual systems agree that knowledge of union is not merely a matter of accepting good doctrine. There are varieties of acceptable doctrine, and the adoption of any one variety comes short of salvation itself. Salvation itself—the saving knowledge that one has reached a state of consciousness that admits one into the realm of reality where karma ceases to exert its effects and rebirth reaches an end—comes by an ecstatic flash of certitude in the midst of deep meditation.

This flash of certitude is the ultimate goal of the Way of Knowledge. To reach it requires long preparation and self-discipline.

The classical conception of the life preparation required to reach this last step in the Way of Knowledge is given in the *Code of Manu*. The ideal career of the Brahmin is there outlined for all India to admire and for Brahmins to emulate. The code includes many rules for females, but the focus is upon the male career. There are four stages or *ashramas* in the ideal life plan. Under one exacting program, the Way of Works and the Way of Knowledge are interfused. The stages are (1) that of student of religion, (2) that of married man and householder, (3) that of forest hermit, and (4) that of *sannyasin* or mendicant "holy wanderer." The stages apply only to members of the upper three (the "twice born") classes of castes, and detailed rules are spelled out as male duties, but the broad principles apply to females as well.

The Four Stages (*Ashramas*)

1. *The Student.* It was proposed that when the young Brahmin had passed through the sacramental rites surrounding early childhood (at birth, name giving, the first taking out to see the sun, the first feeding with boiled rice, the first hair cutting, and so on), he should enter upon the initial stage of his conscious journey to salvation, that of student of religion. This was to begin with ceremonial investiture with the mark of caste, the sacred cord, during which solemnity, while tending the sacred fire and going through holy rites of purification, he would experience his second or spiritual birth. His initiation into manhood thus effected, he was conducted to the home of a teacher to study the Vedas, the purificatory and sacrificial rites, and the duties of his caste. His residence at the house of his

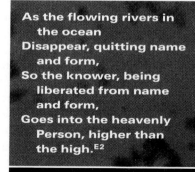

As the flowing rivers in the ocean
Disappear, quitting name and form,
So the knower, being liberated from name and form,
Goes into the heavenly Person, higher than the high.[E2]

—The *Mundaka Upanishad*

teacher was to last for an indefinite period, perhaps until his twenty-fifth year, depending on the number of Vedic treatises he wished to study. His teacher meanwhile was not expected to supply him with food; that was to be obtained by the student himself, by going from house to house, begging bowl in hand.

Girls in the learning stage of life remained at home. Their teachers were the senior women of the household, and the subject matter was domestic duties.

2. *The Householder.* When a young man reached the end of his period of study, he was to leave his teacher and enter upon the second stage of his life. He was now to rejoin his family, marry, and take up the duties of householder. This was thought to be obligatory. No Brahmin, however deep his religious preoccupation, was considered worthy or wise unless he left a son to carry out the periodical rites owed to his ancestors and to propagate another generation. The stage of householder was to be closely regulated by ancient religious rules and filled with ceremonies, all of which he was to perform with utmost diligence. He was to be well aware that every householder of necessity injures living things, especially in cooking.

> A householder has five slaughter-houses as it were, viz., the hearth, the grinding-stone, the broom, the pestle and mortar, and the water-vessel, by using which he is bound with the fetters of sin. In order successively to expiate the offenses committed by means of all these five, the great sages have prescribed for householders the daily performance of the five great sacrifices. Teaching and studying is the sacrifice offered to Brahma, the offerings of water and food called Tarpana the sacrifice to the ancestors, the burnt oblation the sacrifice offered to the gods, the Bali offering that offered to the Bhutas [good and evil spirits of many sorts], and the hospitable reception of guests the offering to men.[C5]

He was to be extremely careful in his diet. He was never to break any caste rules. At length, sometimes after many years, when he saw his "skin wrinkled and his hair white, and the sons of his sons,"[C6] he was to enter upon the third stage of his career.

3. *The Hermit.* In retirement "to the forest" a man unburdened himself of the responsibilities of maintaining a household; leaving the pursuit of mate-

rial security to the next generation, he concentrated on the dharma and religious rites. He was not absolutely required to separate himself physically from the homestead, but the ideal was to retire to the forest as a commitment to spiritual goals.

As a hermit he was not expected to live an easy life. His whole thought was to be concentrated on developing a complete indifference toward everything in the world to which he had been previously attached.

> Abandoning all food raised by cultivation, and all his belongings, he may depart into the forest, either committing his wife to his sons, or accompanied by her. Taking with him the sacred fire and the implements required for domestic sacrifices, he may reside there. Let him offer those five great sacrifices according to the rule. Let him wear a [deer-] skin or a tattered garment . . . be always industrious in privately reciting the Veda . . . never a receiver of gifts . . . compassionate toward all living creatures. . . . Let him not eat anything grown on ploughed land or in a village. . . . In order to obtain complete union with the supreme Soul, he must study the various sacred texts contained in the Upanishads . . . abandoning all attachments to worldly objects.[C7]

When he had become wholly and purely spiritual, he was released from any further offering of sacrifices to gods and ancestors, and free therefore to let his sacred fire die out, for it was now "reposited in his mind." He needed no longer to read the sacred texts; they, too, were reposited in his mind. If she were still with him, his wife would see that he had reached liberation from all earthly ties and would depart, leaving him alone in the forest. Thus would be ushered in the fourth and last stage of his existence.

The observance of this stage is virtually obsolete in modern India, surviving only in an individual's inclination to stay aloof from the day-to-day operation of a family business or to spend some hours in seclusion for study or contemplation.

4. *The Sannyasin.* The final stage, that of the homeless wanderer, required renunciation of every earthly tie. The initiatory ritual included cremation of an effigy symbolizing death to the world, and giving up all claim to possessions, name, and status. (Contemporary Indian law recognizes such statutory death

for both men and women and permits no return to former status after the ritual.) In modern India, only a tiny minority of men "take sannyas."

A woman's participation in the sannyasa stage would be through her husband, her consent being either taken for granted or forced upon her. The *Code of Manu* implies that when a man becomes a *sannyasin* and leaves his wife she loses part of her status as a spouse and becomes no longer "his," but a widow by holy abandonment. He, however, is still somehow "hers" as an earthly manifestation of the divine and a pathway to moksha. Alternatively, a man may permit his wife to become a *sannyasini,* continuing to serve him in celibate cohabitation. Theoretically she will continue to be "his" for up to seven more lives. Instances in which a woman becomes a *sannyasini* in her own right are rare, tending to occur in modernized bhakti sects such as the Lingayats (Virasaivas), among whom widow remarriage is also permitted.

The *Code of Manu* pictured the final stage as a means of completing the Way of Knowledge: the achievement of spiritual union with the Infinite. Death might overtake a person before the realization of absorption into the eternal Brahman, but the ideal was to reach the experience through meditation. "All depends on meditation," states the *Code of Manu,* "for he who is not proficient in the knowledge of that which refers to the supreme Soul reaps not the full reward."[C8] The *Code* gives us a vivid description of the final situation.

> Let him always wander alone, without any companion. . . . He shall possess neither a fire nor a dwelling. . . . Let him go to beg once a day. . . . When no smoke ascends from the kitchen, when the pestle lies motionless, when the embers have been extinguished, when the people have finished their meal, when the remnants in the dishes have been removed, let the ascetic beg. . . . The roots of trees for a dwelling, coarse worn-out garments, life in solitude and indifference towards everything, are the marks of one who has obtained liberation. Let him not desire to die, let him not desire to live, let him wait for his appointed time, as a servant waits for the payment of his wages. . . . By deep meditation let him recognize the subtle nature of the supreme Soul, and its presence in all organisms. . . . He who has in this manner gradually given up all attachments reposes in Brahman alone. . . . He attains the eternal Brahman. . . .[C9]

Sannyasin
Posture of Penance

To the present day this final state of absorption in the Ultimate (*samadhi*) is the goal toward which all who take the Way of Knowledge aspire. But it is not easy to attain it by purely intellectual processes. From the very first it was felt that the body had to assist the mind in suspending, at least in part, its normal functions. The Upanishads contain the first hints about a method, called *Yoga,* beginning with "restraint of the breath, withdrawal of the senses from objects," and ending with "contemplation" and "absorption."[E4]

Of Yoga and yogins (those who practice Yoga) we shall hear later (see p. 113). But we may note now that the followers of the Yoga disciplines gave great support to the Way of Knowledge as a primarily important method of release from the burdens of life and the ignorance of a mind seduced by the senses. While Yoga is concerned primarily with techniques of meditation, it is considered part of the Way of Knowledge.

IV. THE REFLECTIVE MODELS: THE SIX ACCEPTABLE SYSTEMS

The Hindu word for "view of the nature of things" is *darshana,* and perhaps it should not be translated "system of philosophy," for a darshana does not aim, as Western systems do, to arrive, as nearly as possible, at a strictly objective, disengaged, and purely cognitive view of things; rather, it seeks by an intuitive searching to dispel the ignorance that prevents liberation from *maya* through "seeing the Real." "In India," says Mircea Eliade, "metaphysical knowledge always has a soteriological purpose,"[F1] that is, it seeks salvation, by liberation of soul or spirit. But if we remember that in the present context the term *philosophy* is to mean what it originally did, "love of wisdom" (rather than "scientific objectivity"), we can safely use it.

During the millennium, from 500 B.C.E. to 500 C.E., the acceptable systems of Hindu philosophy took shape. In another thousand years they were refined into final fixed form. Their number is far greater than six, but Hindus themselves have singled out these six as being the most significant, because among them they cover the whole ground gone over by all of the acceptable philosophical views. The acceptable systems are: Sankhya, Yoga, Nyaya, Vaisheshika, Vedanta, and Mimansa. These six have in common the one assumption that is considered necessary by Hindus to meet the conditions of orthodoxy, namely that the Vedas are the inspired and final rule of faith. It is usually understood that in this case the Vedas include the early commentaries and interpretations (the Brahmanas and Upanishads) that are appended to the original four books.

We shall not follow the Hindu savants in considering each of the six philosophies in order; we are chiefly interested in those that have had the greatest effect on religion: Sankhya, Yoga, and Vedanta.

The Sankhya System

This important darshana, the Sankhya philosophy, stands in sharp contrast with the monism expressed in the Upanishads. Indian tradition considers it the oldest darshana of all. In a preliminary form—an early, unsystematized dualism perhaps older than the earliest Upanishads—it may have been the common source of much that is in Jainism, the Upanishads, early Buddhism, and the *Bhagavad Gita*. Its mythical (or semimythical) founder is said to have been one Kapila, born at Kapilavastu a century before Gautama Buddha. He is said to have made his views known to Asuri, who transmitted them to Panchashikha, who became known in turn to Ishvarakrishna, but this

gives us a timescale that is certainly foreshortened, for the last named is the author of the oldest systematic statement of the Sankhya philosophy, the *Sankhyakarika*, which probably was not written before 200 C.E.

The Sankhya philosophy is in its original form staunchly atheistic and dualistic, maintaining that there are two eternal (and only two) categories of being: (1) matter (*prakriti*), which when structured becomes the natural world, and (2) souls or spirits (*purusha*, selves). Neither are *maya*, that is, illusory; both are real. The mere presence of souls or spirits activates prakriti, as dancers at a command performance are activated by the presence of a king, and the characteristic features (*gunas*) of the natural world become manifest. The three modes of activity that constitute the natural world (*gunas* means strands, bonding agencies) are: (1) a luminous, good, wise, and pure one called *sattva* (clarity and goodness, matched with insight), (2) an active, driving, "dust-raising" one named *rajas* (energy, "red" with passion), and (3) a stolid, dark, and moody one known as *tamas* (darkness, inertia, stubborn conservatism). Physical objects (bodies, inanimate or animate) result from the clusterings of dense elements under the impulsion of tamas; psychological phenomena in multisensed creatures (sense experience, emotions) rise from the stimulus of rajas; mental and psychic activities spring from a predominance of sattva. The world of nature is composed of twenty-four elements or principles (*tattvas*, thatnesses), including the five gross elements (*sthulabhutani*: ether, air, fire, water, earth), higher intellect (*buddhi*), mind (*manas*), and ego consciousness (*ahankara*), each with a different combination of the gunas. It should be emphasized that these last three, translated "intellect," "mind," and "ego consciousness," are manifestations of physical (material) reality. They may mirror or counterfeit *purusha* (pure consciousness or spirit), but they remain entirely on the side of *prakriti* (matter) in the cosmic duality.

The special physical characteristics of an individual at any one moment are due to the degree to which any one of the gunas predominates. If a person is intelligent, pure, and happy, sattva prevails; if emotional or energetic, rajas; if dull or crude, tamas. (This threefold analysis has had an influence in India far beyond the bounds of the Sankhya school, and in fact has affected many aspects of Indian thought and life—including, unfortunately, a tendency to associate the light-bright to dark-stupid continuum with the hierarchy of castes.) Primal prakriti evolves into a wide range of phenomena from the grossest matter to the highest manifestations of intelligence, but they are all aspects of Nature and are not to be identified with or derived from souls or spirits.

As for the realm of souls or spirits (purusha), it is not constituted of a single All-Soul, for Brahman-Atman is nonexistent, but of an infinite number of individual souls, each independent and eternal. These souls or spirits are "pure," "eternal," "passive," and "without qualities" (without gunas) such as human experience discerns. Detached as they are from the realm of "nature," they are basically indifferent to what goes on in it. Each spirit, declared Ishvarakrishna, "is that which sees [witnesses]; [but] it is isolated, indifferent, a mere inactive spectator."[F2] Why it should be associated as it is with a body and mind in life after life is an insoluble mystery; but it is. In the higher reaches of human thought, the intellect (buddhi) comes to see that the soul or spirit needs to be liberated from its association with bodies and minds (lively matter, prakriti), but it is unable to free itself; the freeing comes from the natural, not the spiritual side. What has to happen in the realm of nature is that the higher intelligence of humankind, in its moments of insight or "awakening," should become aware of its own illusionary character; free itself from the suffering brought on by its lack of understanding (avidya, ignorance); and rid itself of the false identification of its own physical and mental processes with the purusha, an identification that is entirely erroneous and a source of suffering that beclouds the purusha's true detachment and eternal freedom. When the human intellect destroys its illusions and in the process destroys (unstructures) itself as well, it will enable the soul or spirit to actualize its freedom by final passage into a state of eternal but unearthly existence in the purity of the spirit. Here, too, salvation is sought by the Way of Knowledge.

In summary, the Sankhya philosophy emphasizes the conviction that the spirits are forever aliens in the natural world and that their liberation consists in remaining uninvolved with it. In their true being they are free and detached, but their presence attracts prakriti elements (tattvas), and these must be led by insight (buddhi) to relinquish their attachment and allow each spirit a final freedom.

The Yoga System

The Yoga system of mental discipline has been greatly developed since it was first mentioned in the Upanishads, and it has won an important place in the practice of the Way of Knowledge. It became a highly refined technique in the hands of Patanjali (second century C.E.), a yogin who derived most of his ideas from the Sankhya system, though he differed from it in accepting as part of his worldview a modified theism (reliance on Ishvara, an eternally pure spirit who helps yogins). The philosophical basis of Yoga is, however, not as important historically as the practical measures, the technique of meditation and concentration developed in connection with it. These practical measures are a psychologically sophisticated modification of the purely metaphysical way to "release and liberation."

Yoga's greatest appeal lies in its physiological and psychological measures to assist the mind in the effort to concentrate. It consists largely of special postures, methods of breathing, and rhythmical repetition of the proper thought formulas. The typical procedure, that of the classic Raja Yoga of Patanjali, has the following eight steps:

1. Performing the five desire-killing vows, or Yama, a step by which the yoga-aspirant abstains from harming living things (that is, practicing ahimsa), from deceit, stealing, unchastity (taking the brahmacharya vow), and from acquisitiveness.

2. Observance, or Niyama, of self-disciplinary rules—cleanliness, calm, mortification, study, and prayer.

3. Sitting in the proper posture, or Asana; for example, with the right foot upon the left thigh, the left foot upon the right thigh, the hands crossed, and the eyes focused on the tip of the nose.

4. Regulation of the breath, or Pranayama, where the aim is to reduce the whole of being alive to one or two simple and rhythmic processes, all of the muscles, voluntary and involuntary, and the nerve currents being brought under control. The aspirant is advised to sit upright, with head, neck, and back in a straight line, and to breathe in and out rhythmically,

while, perhaps, inwardly repeating the sacred word *AUM*. (Later refinements of this step suggested breathing up the left nostril, then out of the right, holding the breath between times, in order to allow nerve currents to descend the spinal column and strike forcefully the reserves of nervous energy at the base of the spine and release them.)

5. Withdrawal of the senses from all sense objects, or Pratyahara, much as a tortoise retreats under its shell by drawing in its head and limbs. This step shuts out the outside world.

6. Concentration, or Dharana, during which the mind is held steadily to the contemplation of a single idea or an object until it is emptied of all else.

7. Meditation, or Dhyana, a half-unconscious condition affording a transition to the last step.

8. Samadhi, a trance in which the mind, now emptied of all content and no longer aware of either object or subject, is absorbed into the Ultimate and is one with the One.

The central feature of Yoga practice, whether in this or its other forms, is the use of the mind to suppress its own conscious movements, the whole body being so disciplined as to aid in the gradual suspension of consciousness and the bringing on of a state of pure ecstasy that is without thought and without sensation. The result is felt to be a complete freeing of the true self from the external world and natural causation.

A later and more esoteric form of Yoga, and one often advised by yogic teachers, is a tantric form of Hatha Yoga or "the Yoga of power." It conceives of the body as interconnected by many "conduits" or *nadis* (veins, arteries, nerves), three of which are the most important. Two of these run along the two sides of the spinal column and connect the loins and throat. The third, known as the *susumna*, runs within the spinal column from the *cakra*, or power center behind the genitals (where sleeps the *kundalini*, named from an attribute of the Hindu goddess Kali, in itself a latent source of energy, "coiled like a serpent") and moves upward through other power centers in the belly, the heart, the throat, and between the eyebrows to the *sahasrara*, the power center at the top of the head. The aim of Hatha Yoga is to arouse "the serpent power" of the *kundalini* and cause it to rise with mounting energy through the other *cakras* or "wheels" of power and produce illumination of the consciousness in the head (samadhi).

Extraordinary claims of psychic power are made by those who accept the intuitions that accompany or follow mastery of Yoga: for example, that the yogin actually achieves levitation, can transcend the limits of space and time and be in several places or times at once, or can acquire the powers and qualities of anything upon which he or she chooses to concentrate. But, of course, the chief aim of Yoga is none of these things; it is, rather, the experience of utter and complete freedom of the self from earthly bonds.

The Vedanta System: Three Versions

The name of the Vedanta system is derived from the source of its leading doctrines, the Upanishads, which were commonly called the Vedanta—that is, "the concluding portions of the Vedas." An exciting basis for future speculation was contained in the Upanishads, and eventually three quite different versions evolved: a monist (nondualist) view, a qualified nondualist view, and a dualist view.

Those who were sure that intuition superseded and transcended common sense proceeded with speculative enthusiasm to propound the monistic doctrine that the external world and human consciousness are alike maya or aspects of the world illusion arising from primal creative energy, and claimed the authority of the Upanishads for it. Advanced Indian thought has usually sided with them.

The first attempt to set forth the monistic teachings of the Upanishads in a consistent philosophic system is contained in the difficult aphorisms of the *Vedanta Sutra*. These are said to have been prepared by Badarayana, a noted teacher who lived, it seems probable, during the first century before the Christian era. His aphorisms were meant to be committed to memory and were so pithy as to be ambiguous and confusing in effect. Even during his lifetime his own oral commentary was necessary to render them intelligible. During the centuries that followed, such oral interpretation, often rather dubiously supported by the original text,

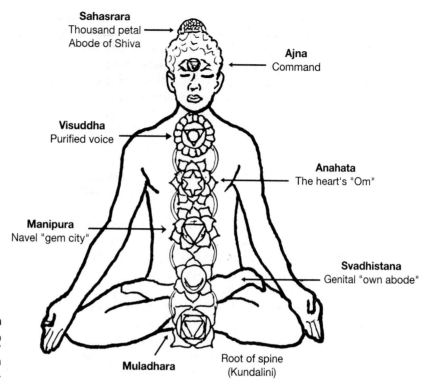

Sahasrara
Thousand petal
Abode of Shiva

Ajna
Command

Visuddha
Purified voice

Anahata
The heart's "Om"

Manipura
Navel "gem city"

Svadhistana
Genital "own abode"

Tantric Hatha Yoga
In meditation, Kundalini is induced to
rise through the seven "lotus centers"
(*cakras*) toward climactic union with
Shiva in the realm of nonduality.

Muladhara

Root of spine
(Kundalini)

was continued and resulted finally in the rise of three different systems of Vedanta philosophy—those founded by Shankara (788–820 C.E.), Ramanuja (1040?–1137), and Madhva (1199–?).

1. Shankara's "Nondualism" (*Advaita*)

For Shankara, the world (*prakriti*), the individual ego (*jiva*), and Brahman, while not absolutely one, do not really exist separately but are in reality "not different," (*advaita*), "not-two" (nor three or more). The impersonal and indescribable Brahman is wholly beyond the reach of human experience (absolutely nonempirical). Besides It, the eternal, the undecaying, the full-of-being, all else is "transient, impure, unsubstantial, like a flowing river or a burning lamp, lacking in fibre like a banana, comparable to foam appearance, a mirage, a dream"; in short, a product of maya. The empirical world is thus phenomenal, neither existent nor nonexistent and truly unexplainable; it "rests on" Brahman as its basis, but Brahman is in no way directly involved

in it causally, for the universe has actually been developed, through maya, by Ishvara, the creative and personal manifestation of the unmanifest Brahman.

The source of this view is traced back to the later Upanishads, in which, as for example in the *Shvetasvatara Upanishad*, it declared,

> Sacred poetry, the sacrifices, the ceremonies, the
>   ordinances,
> The past, the future, and what the Vedas declare—
> This whole world the illusion-maker [mayin] projects
>   out of this Brahman,
> And in it by illusion the individual soul [jiva] is confined.
> Now, one should know that Nature [Prakriti] is
>   illusion,
> And that Mighty Lord [Ishvara] is the illusion-maker![E5]

But the illusion conjured up by the Mighty Lord is not said to be absolute. Shankara was true to the spirit of Indian philosophy in treating this point with great subtlety. He started with an initial advantage. By denying the ultimacy of the phenomenal world and regarding it as maya, he avoided both the difficulty encountered by the Sankhya philosophy of maintaining that the universe and the soul, both equally real, are in association but not in junction, and the problem in Buddhism arising from its doing away with the soul while at the same time affirming the fact of ever-recurring rebirth.

Human beings, according to Shankara, are dealing with something real when they look about them, but they are merely relying on their sense perceptions for knowledge. The everyday world in which their experiences take place is the subjective spatiotemporal frame of reference through which their ignorance (avidya, nonknowledge) misperceives the Real. The notion that the objects of sense experience are "realities" is the work of this ignorance. Ignorance is, indeed, the sort of reaction that constructs the everyday world by a process, just as the piece of rope lying by the roadside is seen in the twilight as a snake, or the distant post as a man. To believe that one has seen a snake or a man in such circumstances is to submit uncritically to the illusion-making power that produces the phenomenal world.

Furthermore, to believe in the independent reality of the individual soul, as is the common experience, is to move in the world of maya and to have only the lower kind of knowledge, but to know that our selves and Brahman-Atman are not two is to apprehend reality and have the higher knowledge. Similarly, to credit the world of sense-experienced objects in space and time, if one accepts their reality, to the work of the Creator, Ishvara, the living god principle, worshiped and sacrificed to by the people under such names as Vishnu, Shiva, and Rama, is to apprehend the absolute truth through the appearances created by ignorance. In reality, there is only Brahman-Atman, solely existent, spaceless, timeless, and eternal. The Upanishads have rightly said: *Tat tvam asi!* ("That art thou!"). Emancipation from the long-drawn-out recurring dream of the cycle of rebirth comes only with the lifting of the veil of ignorance that prevents one from knowing that the soul is and always has been identical with Brahman.

This, it may be seen, is the logical culmination of the monistic speculations of the Upanishads.

But Shankara ignored the devotional life of the masses in framing his philosophy. His whole concern was to go back to the Vedas and Upanishads and interpret them as offering final release through the advaita philosophy only. Long before his time the sects inspired by devotion to gods had appeared. (We shall meet them under the next topic.) Shankara regarded their theism as basically erroneous; at best, the devotional life of the people had only relative merit.

But the advocates of *bhakti* (devotion), were to find a powerful champion when Ramanuja came to the defense of the way of devotion in general and of Vaishnavism (worship of Vishnu) in particular, seeking to prove that they were truly Vedic and orthodox, and what is more, that bhakti as a way of salvation had truth to back it up.

2. Ramanuja's "Qualified NonDualism" (*Vishisht-Advaita*)

Ramanuja was a monist insofar as he based himself on such passages in the Upanishads as *Brihadaranyaka* III.vii.3, where Brahman is declared he who is the Inner Controller of the whole universe in its every part. (See p. 93.) But he qualified his monism (whence one of its names, "qualified monism") by finding in the Upanishads, and certainly in the *Bhagavad Gita,* not only a stress on the unity of all things and beings in Brahman, but also an affirmation of differentiation. He concluded that the physical world, individual souls, and the ultimate Reality or Supreme Being are each real, although nondivisible, for the first two make up the "body" of the last; they are the forms through which God manifests himself. The ultimate Reality is a personal not an impersonal being. His name is Vishnu. In short, Vishnu is Brahman. The ultimate Reality is, therefore, not as Shankara said, abstract, without qualities, and unknowable, but a concrete person endowed with every desirable quality, possessing omniscience, all pervading, all powerful, all loving, and merciful. He reveals himself as God in five ways. First, he shows himself to the liberated souls in a heavenly city, where under a jeweled canopy he sits on Shesha, the world serpent, and is attended by Lakshmi and other consorts (p. 130). Second, he manifests himself in accumulation of knowledge, and in the universe at large in creation, preservation, persistence, ruling might, and ability to overcome opposition.

Third, he appears in the ten *avataras* (to be described later on p. 130). Fourth, he dwells within the human heart, accompanies his devotees wherever they go, and sometimes appears in visions. And fifth, he presents himself in the images people make of him. The best goal of humankind—and the happy lot of those who render Vishnu proper devotion (bhakti)—is not absorption in an impersonal Absolute (although this can be achieved) but going to heaven to enjoy Vishnu's presence in full consciousness.

3. Madhva's "Dualism" (*Dvaita*)

Madhva maintained that the individual soul is not one with nor to be identified with an Absolute or Supreme Soul, here or hereafter. In his dualist (*dvaita*) view, there is a difference in kind between God (Vishnu) and individual souls (jivas). Souls are real and so is the physical world. His view is monotheistic, for he believed that the souls that are saved will enjoy bliss in the presence of the Supreme Soul (Vishnu); others are doomed to spend eternity either in the hells or in endless transmigration. How does salvation come? It comes, Madhva said, through Vayu, the wind god, the son of Vishnu. He is the vehicle of the grace of God, and a sort of holy spirit who breathes his life-giving power into those he saves. This version of the Vedanta contains more than an echo of Islam and Christianity, which were by Madhva's time known in India. It has had, like Ramanuja's version, an immense influence not only on the followers of Vishnu but on all India. Many modern liberal thought movements credit their general attitude, if not the substance of their beliefs, to Ramanuja or Madhva or both.

V. THE DEVOTIONAL MODE: THE WAY OF DEVOTION, THE *BHAGAVAD GITA*

Perhaps the greatest single element in the successful resistance of Hinduism to absorption by Buddhism was the attitude of the common people of India. Through the long years of the crisis and slow recovery of Hinduism, ordinary people, not greatly affected by the intellectual excitement of the upper classes, simply went on being religious in their own way. Their way was the way of devotion (*bhakti*). Monism and ascetic self-discipline were bypassed and Brahmanism given less importance because a prized relationship, charged with emotion, sprang up between a devotee and some god or goddess who could be reached by *bhakti* and *puja* (worship). This relationship was not only heart warming, it satisfied a deep religious yearning. So some four centuries into the Christian era there came into being a powerful *bhakti* movement that was to dominate Indian religious life for well over 1,000 years (as we shall later see in Sections VI and VII of this chapter).

The Brahmins, perceiving all of this, worked out a justification for it. Whereas the more sophisticated minds were encouraged to seek the Way of Knowledge, the people were to get help from gods and goddesses. The *Code of Manu*, in fact, contains more than one intimation of the presence of a new factor in the religious outlook, and with it the rise of a third way of salvation or release, rivaling the Way of Works and the Way of Knowledge. It mentions temples and temple priests for the first time in Hindu literature. *Bhakti Marga*, "The Way (or Path) of Devotion," also called *Bhakti Yoga*, "The Discipline of Devotion," had come into being.

Bhakti may be defined as ardent and hopeful devotion to a particular deity in grateful recognition of aid received or promised. It often assumes the form of a passionate love of the deity, whether god or goddess. Its marks are surrender of self to the divine being and acts of devotion in temple worship and in private life and thought.

The Instincts of Ordinary People

Bhakti thus emerged prominently at a comparatively late period, but it brought with it the savor of ancient faith. That it did emerge prompts the reflection that the needs of ordinary people can never long be denied. From primitive times they have sought the favor of gods and goddesses, and they cannot be made to believe that devotion to deities does not bring salvation. Their experience has been that the world is filled with powers greater than themselves from whom saving help may come. The common people never could follow the philosophers and meditative intellects down the Way of Knowledge; they were not capable of long and close introspection into the obscure movements of their own soul. Not that they held the findings of the intellectual classes to be untrue. On the contrary, they regarded them with respect, much as the layperson today applauds, without understanding, the incomprehensible theories of an Einstein. But such acknowledgment of the rightfulness in their own sphere of the reasoning of pundits does not now, and never did in India, affect the daily course of life. The average person thinks: "The Brahmin's way may be all right for the Brahmin, but I must follow my prescribed way as best I can in this life. In some future existence I may be a Brahmin."

In popular Hinduism the far-reaching effect of bhakti on the external forms of religion has been incalculable. Many different sects seek salvation through devotion. No denial of the efficacy of the Way of Knowledge and of the Way of Works is implied. It is even admitted that these may have a superior efficacy. But the positive claim is made that devotion to deity is a true way of salvation in itself.

Literary Expression in the *Bhagavad Gita*

The most influential literary recognition of Bhakti Marga as a true way of salvation was made in the famed *Bhagavad Gita* or *Song of the Blessed Lord,* one of the great classics of religious literature. To it we must devote special attention, for it has very greatly influenced Hinduism for nearly 2,000 years.

Although the poem is often printed and esteemed as a separate work, it is a segment fitted into the enormous epic, the *Mahabharata,* which was composed over a period of eight hundred years, 400 B.C.E. to 400 C.E. (Estimates of the time of interpolation range from the third century B.C.E. to the second century C.E.) The epic contains 100,000 couplets, and deals mainly with the exploits of Aryan clans, specifically with the fall of the Kuru (Kaurava) princes at the hands of their relatives the Pandavas (sons of Pandu), directed by the hero-god Krishna, an *avatar* (alternate form) of Vishnu. In every respect a remarkable poem, it has been increasingly admired and used for devotional and intellectual needs than any other Hindu work—this in spite of its eclectic character, philosophically and otherwise. Its verve and emotional power have won many converts to its doctrines.

Although it makes the attempt to synthesize or interweave into one way of life all three ways of release—knowledge, works, and devotion—the Gita's greatest historical significance lies in its endorsement of bhakti as a true way of salvation or liberation. It grants that knowledge leads to unconditioned release. The doing of good works, too, is not to be underrated. But it protests against the performance of the prescribed works merely out of desire for the rewards that accrue, and says that such working for rewards secures only certain transient blessings in the next existence. It goes on, next, to take a position far in advance of the common Brahmin opinion when it declares that the performance of works, if carried out without any desire for reward, but only for the god, or for righteousness' sake, can win release on the basis of such works alone. But religious devotion is best of all.

The Epic Setting

The Gita's endorsement of bhakti comes in the course of a story dramatically conceived and told. Arjuna, the great warrior of the family of Pandavas, hesitates suddenly when on the point of leading his brothers and their allies into battle against the Kuru princes, sons of his uncle, the blind Dhritirashtra, and thus his close relatives. The hero-god Krishna is his charioteer and stands at his side poised for instant action. But it is not Arjuna who acts; it is the Kuru leader, his uncle, who orders the conch shell to be blown as the signal for battle.

> Then at the signal of the aged king,
> With blare to wake the blood, rolling around
> Like to a lion 's roar, the trumpeter
> Blew the great Conch; and, at the noise of it,
> Trumpets and drums, cymbals and gongs and horns,
> Burst into sudden clamor; as the blasts
> Of loosened tempest, such the tumult seemed!
>   Then 'twas—
> Beholding Dhritirashtra's battle set,
> Weapons unsheathing, bows drawn forth, the war
> Instant to break—Arjuna spake this thing
> To Krishna the Divine, his charioteer:
> "Drive, Dauntless One! to yonder open ground
> Betwixt the armies; I would see more nigh
> Those who will fight with us, those we must slay
> Today!"[G1]

But when Krishna drives the chariot, with its milk-white steeds, between the lines, Arjuna marks on each hand

> the kinsmen of his house
> Grandsires and sires, uncles and brothers and sons,
> Cousins and sons-in-law and nephews, mixed
> With friends and honored elders; some this side,
> Some that side ranged.[G2]

At this sight his heart melts with sudden compunction. He addresses his charioteer in tones of anguish:

> "Krishna! as I behold, come here to shed
> Their common blood, yon concourse of our kin,
> My members fail, my tongue dries in my mouth,
> A shudder thrills my body, and my hair
> Bristles with horror; hardly may I stand.
>
>   . . . What rich spoils
> Could profit; what rule recompense; what span
> Of life seem sweet, bought with such blood?
> Seeing that these stand here, ready to die,
> For whose sake life was fair, and pleasure pleased,
> And power grew precious—grandsires, sires, and sons,
> Brothers, and fathers-in-law, and sons-in-law,
> Elders and friends!"
>
> So speaking, in the face of those two hosts,
> Arjuna sank upon his chariot-seat,
> And let fall bow and arrows, sick at heart.[G3]

When Krishna tries to stir the reluctant warrior with the charge: "Cast off the coward-fit! Wake! Be thyself! Arise, Scourge of thy foes!" Arjuna's only reply is to reiterate his doubts and ask Krishna's counsel.

Krishna's Advice

Krishna's answer is made in the course of a long dialogue whose design, in the first instance, is to exalt caste duty above every other consideration, no matter what is entailed, and without thought of reward. Arjuna is told that his duty as a Kshatriya is to fight, when war is joined, whether in doing so he kills his relatives or not. The Gita plainly says that it is far more beneficial to the ultimate good to perform one's own birth-determined duties (*sva-dharma*), even ineptly, than to perform the duties of another, however well. Forsaking one's sva-dharma is sin; its result is social chaos. (Over the centuries the ordered society of India was firmly undergirded by this view—but in recent history profound difficulties in redeploying human resources have resulted from it.)

As for Arjuna's personal destiny, if he fights and is killed, he will enter the Swarga-heaven; if he is victorious, he will mount a king's throne. As to those he may slay, grief for them would be lacking in reflection. The soul (*atman*) cannot be slain.

> Thou grievest where no grief should be! thou speak'st
> Words lacking wisdom! for the wise in heart
> Mourn not for those that live, nor those that die.
> Nor I, nor thou, nor any one of these,
> Ever was not, nor ever will not be.
> All, that doth live, lives always! . . .
>   . . . Indestructible.
> Learn thou! the Life is, spreading life through all . . .
> But for these fleeting frames which it informs
> With spirit deathless, endless, infinite,
> They perish. Let them perish, Prince! and fight!
> He who shall say, 'Lo! I have slain a man!'
> He who shall think, 'Lo! I am slain!' those both
> Know naught! Life cannot slay. Life is not slain![G4]

Action and Knowledge Reoriented

Having thus looked philosophically at the immediate difficulties, Krishna proceeds to tell the still emotionally disturbed warrior that there are two ways of reaching the goal of salvation. One is the discipline of knowledge (Jnana Yoga), and the other is the discipline of action (Karma Yoga). Both lead to final peace.

But these paths, as it were, cross and even coalesce. For no one can ever rest in thought even for a moment without action, while properly disciplined action requires, and ends in, knowledge. As a hero god counseling a warrior, Krishna seems at one point to say that retirement

> "Better is one's own duty [*svadharma*, obligation by caste and life stage] though imperfectly carried out than the law of another carried out perfectly."
>
> —Bhagavad Gita 3:35[H]

from action to engage in meditation is inferior to disciplined action undergirded by the truth found in
Krishna himself, but he says even more emphatically
that both meditation and action are ways to final self-
identification with Ultimate Reality.

However, both action and thought must be
rightly oriented. To begin with, action must be disinterested action—performed from duty alone, without
thought of fruits (rewards).

> Let right deeds be
> Thy motive, not the fruit which comes from them.
> And live in action! Labor! Make thine acts
> Thy piety, casting all self aside.
> Contemning gain and merit. . . .
>   Therefore, thy task prescribed
> With spirit unattached gladly perform,
> Since in performance of plain duty man
> Mounts to his highest bliss. . . .
>   For My sake, then,
> With meditation centered inwardly,
> Seeking no profit, satisfied, serene,
> Heedless of issue—fight![G5]

Meditation as Devotion (Bhakti)

As for meditation, it should be disciplined by the
knowledge that all things—all actions—proceed from
and are infused by the eternal World Spirit, Brahman.
Here, the term *Brahman* is not to be understood as
having a strictly impersonal connotation. *Brahman is
Vishnu and Vishnu is Krishna.* Those who attach themselves to Vishnu through Krishna, as Arjuna is invited
to do, may therefore experience the reality of union
with Brahman by *bhakti* (devotion). The yogin whose
greatest desire is to enjoy the ecstasy of perfect release
by absorption into the Ultimate may find such release
through meditative absorption in a Person—either
Vishnu, a deity on high, or Krishna, if the incarnation
in the gallant charioteer proves more attractive.

> Sequestered should he sit,
> Steadfastly meditating solitary,
> His thoughts controlled, his passions laid away,
> Quit of belongings. In a fair, still spot
> Having his fixed abode—not too much raised,
> Nor yet too low—let him abide, his goods

> A cloth, a deerskin, and the Kusa-grass.
> There, setting hard his mind upon The One,
> Restraining heart and senses, silent, calm,
> Let him accomplish Yoga, and achieve
> Pureness of soul, holding immovable
> Body and neck and head, his gaze absorbed
> Upon his nose-end, rapt from all around,
> Tranquil in spirit, free of fear, intent
> Upon his Brahmacharya vow, devout,
> Musing on Me, lost in the thought of Me.
> That Yojin, so devoted, so controlled,
> Comes to the space beyond—My peace, the peace
> Of high Nirvana! . . .
>   He who thus vows
> His soul to the Supreme Soul, quitting sin,
> Passes unhindered to the endless bliss
> Of unity with Brahma[n]. He so vowed,
> So blended, sees the Life-Soul resident
> In all things living and all living things
> In that Life-Soul contained. And whoso thus
> Discerneth Me in all, and all in Me,
> I never let him go; nor looseneth he
> Hold upon Me; but dwell he where he may,
> Whate'er his life, in Me he dwells and lives![G6]

In this remarkable passage, the Gita seeks to
assimilate the doctrines of the Upanishads to its partial theism. (The theism is only partial, because it has
so pronounced a pantheistic side.)

Ritual as Devotion

With similar purpose, Krishna's "I am" poetry absorbs
the Way of Works. Ritual and sacrifice are mere aspects
of Himself: "I Brahma[n] am! the one eternal God!"
Hence,

> I am the Sacrifice! I am the Prayer!
> I am the Funeral-cake set for the dead!
> I am—of all this boundless Universe—
> The Father, Mother, Ancestor and Guard!
> The end of Learning! That which purifies
> In lustral water! I am OM! I am
> Rig-Veda, Sama-Veda, Yajur-Ved;
> The Way, the Fosterer, the Lord, the Judge,
> The Witness; the Abode, the Refuge-House,

The Friend, the Fountain and the Sea of Life
Which sends and swallows up! Seed and Seed-sower,
Whence endless harvests spring! . . .
Death am I, and Immortal Life I am,
Arjuna! SAT and ASAT, Visible Life
And Life Invisible![G7]

The Ultimate Vision: Brahman in God Form

And then, as Arjuna looks on with wonder, Krishna is transfigured before him into Vishnu, the eternal Brahman in god form, displaying to the astounded warrior his true reality, endowed with numberless mouths, countless eyes, "all-regarding" faces turned in every direction, and clothed in ornaments, wreaths, and divine apparel scented with heavenly fragrance.

If there should rise
Suddenly within the skies
Sunburst of a thousand suns
Flooding earth with rays undeemed-of,
Then might be that Holy One's
Majesty and glory dreamed of![G8]

At this sight, which makes his every hair bristle with awe, Arjuna gives voice to his adoration, and then prays that the too-sublime vision be removed and the god return to the kindly disguise of Krishna, the charioteer. The god accedes to this request and then proceeds to deliver the heart of the Gita's message; he demands an utter surrender, that of perfect faith in himself—unconditional bhakti—as the way to full and final release.

Cling thou to Me!
Clasp Me with heart and mind! so shalt thou dwell
Surely with Me on high. But if thy thought
Droops from such height; if thou be'st weak to set
Body and soul upon Me constantly,
Despair not! give Me lower service! seek
To read Me, worshipping with steadfast will;
And, if thou canst not worship steadfastly,
Work for Me, toil in works pleasing to Me!
For he that laboreth right for love of Me
Shall finally attain! But, if in this
Thy faint heart fails, bring Me thy failure! find

Refuge in Me! let fruits of labor go,
Renouncing all for Me, with lowliest heart,
So shalt thou come; for, though to know is more
Than diligence, yet worship better is
Than knowing, and renouncing better still.
Near to renunciation—very near—
Dwelleth eternal Peace! . . .[G9]

Take my last word, my utmost meaning have!
Give Me thy heart! adore Me! serve Me! cling
In faith and love and reverence to Me!
So shalt thou come to Me! I promise true.
Make Me thy single refuge! I will free
Thy soul from all its sins! Be of good cheer![G10]

The Ideal Devotee

The first of the two aforementioned passages is followed by a complementary counsel concerning the conduct toward one's fellows that would be the most exemplary, advice that strongly commended itself to Mahatma Gandhi in a later time. Krishna declares that he loves the selfless, nonviolent man,

Who hateth nought
Of all that lives, living himself benign,
Compassionate, from arrogance exempt,
Exempt from love of self, unchangeable
By good or ill; . . . who troubleth not his kind,
And is not troubled by them; clear of wrath,
Living above all gladness, grief or fear,
That man I love! . . . Who, unto friend or foe
Keeping an equal heart, with equal mind
Bears shame and glory, with an equal peace
Takes heat and cold, pleasure and pain; abides
Quit of desires, hears praise or calumny
In passionless restraint, unmoved by each, . . .
That man I love![G11]

These passages have had historic importance, not only because of their beauty, but also because of their influence on the intimate life of thousands of Hindu leaders and holy men, down to Mahatma Gandhi, as we have noted. Though philosophically the *Bhagavad Gita*'s whole conception of reality and the meaning of life is shot through with unresolved inconsistencies, its practical effect has been to stimulate and deepen Hinduism on its religious side and to make the Bhakti Marga of popular Hinduism intellectually respectable. It must be quite evident at this point that neither the Way of Knowledge, which is so highly intellectual and self-discipliniary, nor the Way of Works, which is so largely moral and practical, can satisfy the religious need of the average person as the Way of Devotion can. The *Bhagavad Gita*, therefore, has won for itself a unique place in the esteem of all Hindus, and though the followers of Vishnu lay first claim to it as their most blessed scripture, educated Hindus of all sects honor it as a worthy expression of the emotional factor in religion.

There is yet another reason why the *Bhagavad Gita* is so appreciated in India. In it, Krishna throws wide open the gate of the Way of Devotion and invites all wayfarers, whatever their sex or caste, to enter.

> Be certain none can perish, trusting Me!
> O Pritha's Son! whoso will turn to me,
> Though they be born from the very womb of Sin,
> Woman or man; sprung of the Vaisya caste
> Or lowly disregarded Sudra—all
> Plant foot upon the highest path.[G12]

Nothing could be more suited to meet the profound and unspoken need of millions in India for a ray of hope in their troubled bondage to social and religious restrictions.

VI. THE DEVOTIONAL MODELS: EPICS, *PURANAS*, AND DEITIES

The bhakti, devotional spirit epitomized in the *Bhagavad Gita*, was destined to grow and grow. During the Gupta period (300–500 C.E.), when Indian culture entered a golden age, and particularly under the Gupta emperors themselves (320–570 C.E.), teachers of the masses appeared, seeking to meet the popular need for rituals, symbols, and images that would provide the people with a clearer conception of personal gods (ishvaras), who, besides having cosmic powers, were near enough to be approached through bhakti and *puja* (worship).

This was the era when bhakti came into its own, a development that strongly attracted the masses and enlisted the support of poets and singers of deep religious feeling. It was a time of religious awakening expressed in songs and hymns that won a warm response among the people and established trends in Indian religion that have persisted to the present time. There also were important carryovers into architecture. During a period of 1,000 years, beginning with the Guptas, rulers and people joined in the erection of monumental shrines and temples that survive to this day as rich and ornate affirmations of religious faith.

The human developments that accompanied this outward manifestation of inward feelings were equally noteworthy. The songs and hymns expressing rapturous delight in the gracious love of deity for devotee were accompanied both by individual displays of bhakti and also by the appearance of sects devoted to such deities as Shiva and Vishnu and their divine spouses. A further, more esoteric development was the practice of secret rites that celebrated (and sought) the psychophysical union of devotee and god or goddess. (These rites will be described later in this chapter under Shaktism, and under Buddhist Tantrism in chapter 7.)

The Sects and Their Literature

In all parts of India, sects thus arose that have widely dominated the religious scene until the present. *Sectarian* is undoubtedly too strong and partisan a word to characterize most Hindus, because they preserve their freedom to worship different deities as the need arises, but many Hindus nevertheless find greater satisfaction by becoming part of a distinctive religious group with its own literature, leaders, and rituals. The spectrum of sectarian Hinduism is enormously broad, and one cannot begin to enumerate the regional variations within the larger families of sects. The largest sects have been the Shaiva (Shivaite) and the Vaishnava (Vishnuite). The former, in their several varieties, seem to have been dominant over other groups during the thousand years after 100 C.E. It was the Shaiva who, during the seventh to twelfth centuries, developed the extraordinary connections between eroticism and religion so manifest in their rites (Shaktism), architecture,

The Brihadisvara Temple at Tanjore in South India
The tower or pyramid shown here rises on a square base, the shrine proper, to a height of 215 feet. It was completed in the eleventh century by Rajaraja Deva Chola in honor of Shiva. It is in the Southern or Dravidian style, marked by horizontal lines, and it is surmounted by a dome on a hexagonal base. *(Courtesy of the Government of India Tourist Office.)*

sculpture, and literature. Then the scene shifted. From 1100 C.E. to the present, it was Vaishnavism's turn to win the greater part of popular support.

An expansion of the roles of women in religious practice correlates with the growth of devotionalism. Unlike the Western assignment of courting songs to male troubadors, the articulation of romantic love is traditionally a female role in India. Thus devotees who composed love songs to a god found it natural to play the part of a female in the process. (For examples of the spiritualization of eroticism, see pp. 132–133.)

Epics and Puranas

A new and abundant literature was both cause and effect of all of this. By the time the sects arose, the Vedas, the Upanishads, and the Dharmasastras had become the special province of the Brahmins and those who pursued Brahmanical learning. The epics the *Mahabharata* and the *Ramayana*, with their underlining of the value of bhakti, especially in such interpolations as the *Bhagavad Gita,* struck a more popular chord and gave rise to the literature of the sects. As special loyalties were developed, literature sprang up to extend speculation and mythology in one direction or another. These writings are the numerous *Puranas* ("Ancient Lore") and *Tantras* ("Threads," "Basic Teachings") (see p. 101). Although it was widely taught that Shiva and Vishnu were of equal importance and complementary to each other, rivalries and antagonisms sprang up at certain points between the followers of one or the other. Differing beliefs were expressed in the Puranas, eighteen of which are generally held to be authoritative. Neatly divided into three groups of six each, they exalt, as the case may be, Brahma, Vishnu, or Shiva above the rest. Taken

Temple at Khajuraho

A famous temple at Khajuraho, in central India, erected in honor of Shiva, between 950 and 1000 C.E. by the kings Dhanga and Ganda. Nearby are temples honoring Vishnu and Brahma. This temple in Northern or Nagara style displays in its thousands of sculptures and reliefs an explicit eroticism symbolic of the union of the soul and Brahman-Atman. *(Courtesy of the Government of India Tourist Office.)*

together, the Puranas are an inexhaustible treasury of folklore and myth, some extraordinarily rich in symbols. When the female counterparts or shaktis of Shiva occupy the center of attention, we have the numerous Tantras, the manuals or textbooks that are the expression of Tantrism.

Devotional Poetry

To this extensive literature should be added the collections of devotional poetry so precious to the Tamils of south India (and so respected elsewhere); there a highly emotional bhakti was expressed by religious poets, chanters, and storytellers, some of whom attained the status of prophets and saints in their own lifetime. Among the devotees of Shiva, these inspired

individuals came to be known as Nayanars ("leaders"), while the devotees of Vishnu called their poets Alvars ("deep ones," "divers into the depths"). Typical collections of hymns of the Nayanars appear in *The Twelve Tirumarai* and of the Alvars in the *Divyaprabandham.*

Words from a sixth-century Tamil poet assure us that deities, seemingly fearsome and remote, will respond to devotion with disarmingly human simplicity.

> *When you see his face, praise him with joy,*
> *Worship him with joined palms, bow before him,*
> *So that his feet touch your head . . .*
> *Holy and mighty will be his form, rising to heaven, but*
> *his sterner face will be hidden, and he will show you*
> *the form of a young man, fragrant and beautiful;*

and his words will be loving and gracious—
'Don't be afraid—I knew you were coming!'[11]

Here the quest of the Way of Knowledge seeking to merge the self with Brahman-Atman, the impersonal being beyond the personal god, is bypassed, because an "aspect" of the Ultimate Source of all things is found experientially to be more real than It is.

Another Tamil prayer-poem takes the form of an intimate and a loving expression of gratitude.

Into my vile body of flesh,
*   you came, as though it were a temple of gold,*
and soothed me wholly and saved me,
O Lord of Grace, O Gem Most Pure.
Sorrow and birth and death and illusion you took from
*   me and set me free.*
O Bliss! O Light! I have taken refuge in you,
*   and never can I be parted from you."*[12]

In the *Bhagavata Purana,* Krishna as a god confesses that he is more moved by a devoted heart than by Yoga, brilliant logic, moral perfection, Vedic chanting, or dedicated renunciation.

Yoga does not subdue me, nor Sankhya, nor *dharma,* nor recitation of the Veda to oneself, nor religious austerity, nor abandonment, as does strong devotion to me.

I am overcome by *bhakti* alone.[J]

As a whole, this bhakti-oriented literature supplied the common people with the stories and symbols they needed to sustain their devotional life; in fact, it supplanted the classical Vedic literature in giving substance and satisfaction to ordinary folk.

The Triad of Gods: Trimurti

The Brahmins were of course aware of the bhakti movement even before it gathered momentum, and early on tried to save what they could of the older, more intellectual, more cosmic ideas of the Ultimate. Bhakti literature, as it proliferated regionally, elevated many local gods and goddesses. Rather than disparage the local deities, the Brahmins furnished a schema of what has come to be called the Great Tradition. The

mythic process gradually assimilated locally favored deities as alternate forms (avatars) of the older Sanskrit pantheon. At the pinnacle of the framework, the Brahmins advanced the concept of the *Trimurti* or Triad of Gods. In early Gupta times they were saying that three great deities—Brahma, Vishnu, and Shiva—have among them achieved a significant cosmic manifestation of Brahman-Atman; they perform between them the functions of creation, preservation, and destruction. This was an intellectually satisfying and comprehensive synthesis. However, the common people of India have never, at least in practice, been completely won over to such a schematic view; they prefer to focus on one great God at a time—usually Shiva or Vishnu—and gain his favor or that of his consort(s).

Brahmā

Of the three great gods, Brahmā, the Creator, is the least widely worshiped. (The masculine accented terminal *a* in his name distinguishes it from the unaccented neuter term *Brahman* in the name for the Absolute, Brahman-Atman.) Scarcely a half dozen temples are now dedicated to him. He may be compared to the "high god of primitive peoples," no longer active on earth after having finished the work of creation. In art he is depicted as a kingly personage with four heads, severely reading the Vedas, and he is shown riding a white wild goose, symbolic of his aloofness.

Shiva

Shiva is one of the great gods of Asia. His followers have given him the title Mahadeva, "the great god," and he measures up to the name. His character is most complex and has some fascinating aspects. As the later form of the dread god Rudra of Vedic days, he still is (in an important aspect) the Destroyer. In the words of the *Yajur Veda,* he is "the threatener, the slayer, the vexer, and the afflicter." His presence is felt "in the fall of the leaf," and he is the bringer of disease and death, and, hence, a "man-slayer." His presence is felt at the funeral pyre, and he should be honored there. But he is not purely evil. His name shows that he is, or can be made, "auspicious" (*shiva*). It is of some interest to

Shiva as Nataraja

This bronze from the Madras Museum (one of many like it) shows Shiva dancing within a ring of fire. His upper right hand holds a small drum for beating out his rhythm, his upper left a devouring flame. His lower right hand is raised in the "fear not" gesture, although the arm carries a cobra, while his left points to a foot lifted to symbolize "release." The other foot is planted on the squirming body of the demon of ignorance and heedlessness. The whole figure dramatizes the vital processes of the universe, bringing both death and new life. *(Courtesy of the Government of India Tourist Office.)*

speculate about the origin of this name. At the end of the Vedic Age, Rudra seems to have been so feared that his name was never mentioned. This was all in the spirit of the European proverb, "Speak of the devil, and he is sure to appear." Like the peasants of Europe in similar circumstances, the Indo-Aryans spoke of him preferably through descriptive titles. At length the word *shiva,* at first applied to other deities also, came to stand for him alone. Not only *could* he be auspicious, if he would, but perhaps a flattering reference to him as such would *make* him so?

Moreover, there were reasons for believing he had a constructive and helpful aspect. Originally, he was a mountain god given to destructive and punitive raids on the plains, but those who penetrated to his mountain fastnesses discovered that under his kindly care grew medicinal herbs for the healing of men and women. Could it be that his sole interest was destruction? Was not his coming often "a blessing in disguise?" After all, pure destructiveness achieves no lasting results in tropical countries; the death and decay of vegetation is but the prelude to the rise of new forms of life, all the more vigorous for having humus to feed on. Besides, in a land where reincarnation is an accepted belief, death means almost instantaneous release into new life. By suggestions flowing from realizations such as this, the functions of Shiva received a meaningful enlargement.

He became identified with the processes of reproduction in every realm of life—vegetable, animal, and human. He seemed to have taken over the phallic emblems and characteristics of the fertility gods of pre-Aryan India. The sex energy that was identified with him was represented to the eyes of his worshipers by the *lingam* and *yoni,* conventional emblems of the male and female reproductive organs. With a reverent sense of the mystery of divine and human creative force, Shiva's worshipers, in their homes as well as in their temples, approach these symbols in devout worship. In the same reverent spirit, the Shiva-worshiping sect founded in the twelfth century C.E., called the Lingayats numbering some eight million today, carry with them, usually in a capsule hung around the neck, a soapstone lingam without which they would never think of appearing in public.

By a further development of this association of ideas, Shiva stands for Life itself, as pure energy or force. He is often shown dancing on the squirming body of the demon of delusion, with his four arms gracefully waving in the air, one hand holding a small drum, another a flame or fire pot. Poised on one leg, his whole figure shows a tremendous vitality, and it is felt that the dance is speeding the cycles of birth and death. Vitality is suggested by endowing Shiva with a third eye placed vertically in the middle of the forehead and picturing him as having a blue body and a dark throat encircled by a necklace of serpents. Some images display him with five or six faces varying in expression, all of which, taken together, suggest his multiple attributes and energies.

At first view it may come as a surprise that Shiva also is the patron of ascetics and holy men. He often is represented as being himself deep in meditation, his naked body smeared with ashes and his hair braided after the fashion of an ascetic. The rationale of the ascription to him of ascetic interests seems to be something like this: The ascetic "destroys" his lower self to allow his higher or spiritual self to come to expression; the body must be curbed to free the soul; all worldly affections and lusts must be rooted out. The result will be a great access of power. But such regeneration is just what Shiva most desires to further. He is therefore on the side of the ascetics.

Although the name "Shiva" generally points to a male divinity, his dual attributes are assigned gender labels: the ascetic, contemplative (*purusha*) side is conceived as male; the active energy or shakti (*prakriti*) side is conceived as female. Hence, lingam and yoni appear together, and Shiva Ardhanarishvara images show a vertically divided androgyne.

Also associated with Shiva are Ganesha, the elephant-headed god, and Nandi, the white bull.

Ganesha is Shiva's son by Parvati, his mountaineer consort. The elephant head, found everywhere in Shiva's temples, symbolizes Ganesha's cunning and his elephantlike ability to remove obstacles by great strength. Nandi, whose milk-white or black bull-image reclines in Shiva's temples, and whose representative, the live white bull, wanders in the temple courts and down the streets in freedom, is Shiva's temple chamberlain and the guardian of quadrupeds.

Goddess Power: Devi/Durga/Kali

Independently, the goddess Devi may appear as untamed energy. She is Durga "the unapproachable," Chandi "the wild," or Kali "the black." As such, she is destructive to demons but protective of devotees. More conventionally, Devi appears as a gracious, nurturing spouse: the lovely Parvati or the motherly Uma.

Durga was apparently an indigenous goddess worshiped with blood offerings among pre-Aryan meat-eating and blood-drinking tribal groups. In her fierce independence she was the antithesis of the Brahmanic feminine ideal. To this day, her village devotees, in what is often considered a separate Shakta religion, find in her both a punishing and a fiercely protective Mother. Loyalty to her is decidedly this worldly: she is not so much a path to moksha through a spouse as an independent judge and champion. Eventually she was also assimilated into the Aryan pantheon through a variety of myths. One suggested that the gods brought her into being to overcome the buffalo demon Mahisha, whose austerities had earned him invincibility to all male opponents. Mahisha, seeing her unprotected by any male and enamored by her seductive appearance, brushed aside her combative warnings as mere love play. She tore him to pieces. Later attributions show Durga as associated not only with *shakti* (cosmic energy) but also with *prakriti* (primal nature) and *maya* (creative illusion making) and the fertility of vegetable and animal life.

Kali wears around her dark neck a necklace of skulls and uses her four strong arms as flails to demolish her victims before she fills her mouth with their flesh. But she is infinitely generous and kind to those whom she loves and who love her in return. In Bengal she is adored as the great Mother; mystics and seers like Ramakrishna and Vivekananda have devoted

Durga Killing the Buffalo Demon

Mahisha, the chief of the *asuras* (demons in the Hindu pantheon, took on the form of a buffalo, but when Durga on her lion mount cut off his head, he reverted to human form, brandishing sword and shield. He was no match for the multiarmed goddess, about to skewer him with her trident, pierce him with an arrow, and cut him to pieces. *(Courtesy of the Victoria and Albert Museum. CT No. 11099)*

themselves to her with the most intense kind of passionate attachment (bhakti).

Tantric Shaktism

While worship of the goddess serves many purposes m villages all over India, some northeastern (Bengali) varieties are clearly pointed toward the attainment of moksha through practices based on a specific ideological system. Because there is also a Buddhist Tantrism, this worship is more precisely called Tantric Shaktism. As practiced, it has what have been called its "right-hand" and "left-hand" forms. Right-hand Shaktism has a refined and philosophic aspect; it centers attention on the white or benignant side of shakti, that is, the benevolent phases of the energy of nature, considered under the symbol of a mother goddess, "combining in one shape life and death." Recent Bengali poets and swamis, like Tagore and Ramakrishna, have made much of this aspect of the mystery and reality of the universe. They identify shakti with maya, the illusion-creating power that has produced the beautiful and terrible phenomenal world. Thus Ramakrishna, in adoring the black goddess Kali as the fitting symbol of Reality, truly and justly understood, could exclaim,

> When I think of the Supreme Being as inactive, neither creating, nor preserving, nor destroying, I call him *Brahman* or *Purusha,* the impersonal God. When I think of him as active, creating, preserving, destroying, I call him *Shakti* or *Maya . . .* the personal god. But the distinction between them does not mean a difference. The personal and the impersonal are the same Being, in the same way as are milk and its whiteness, or the diamond and its lustre, or the serpent and its undulations. It is impossible to conceive of the one without the other. The Divine Mother (Kali) and *Brahman* are one.[L1]

> Kali is none other than He whom you call *Brahman.* Kali is Primitive Energy (Shakti). . . . To accept Kali is to accept Brahman. . . . Brahman and his Power are identical.[K2]

Left-hand Shaktism is both primitive and highly sophisticated. Its rites are essentially magical and esoteric. Durga and Kali, as representatives of the violent side of shakti, are the favorite manifestations of divine energy. Being identified with them means being swept into conventionally forbidden expressions of natural impulse. In secret rites, the details of which are not fully known, the carefully screened adherents meet in "circle worship" marked by dancing, drinking of wine and blood, and ritualistic sex acts. The five M's ordinarily forbidden, are indulged in, namely, wine (*madya*), meat (*mansa*), fish (*matsya*), parched grain (*mudra*), and sexual union (*maithuna*). It is understood to be highly dangerous to the participant's welfare (karmic position) if pleasure is sought. Rightly, the aim is to have such tight control of the senses

Ganesha, the Elephant-headed Son of Shiva
The good-natured Ganesha's potbelly attests to his huge appetite for food. He has the elephant's ability to remove obstacles and is besought by his devotees before any undertaking to overcome possible difficulties. He is learned in the scriptures and is wise. Among the symbols he carries, the most prominent is a goad such as elephant drivers use. *(The Asia Society, New York: Mr. and Mrs. John D. Rockefeller 3rd Collection.)*

as to rise entirely above pleasure to a complete self-identification ("nondualistic union") with holy natural force, ultimately with the purpose of riding the back of this "tiger" into Nirvana.

Vishnu and Lakshmi

As Shiva has his Parvati (or Devi), so Vishnu has his faithful and loving Lakshmi, who takes form as his consort in every one of his avatars (as Radha, Sita, etc.). This stone panel from the temple at Khajuraho (*ca.* 1000 C.E.) shows the mutual devotion of the pair. She shares in Vishnu's activities as Preserver. *(Courtesy of the Government of India Tourist Office.)*

Vishnu

The third member of the great Hindu triad is called Vishnu, the Preserver. He is always benevolent, primarily the conservator of values and an active agent in their realization. Unlike the complex Shiva, he is the perfect and patient exemplar of winsome divine Love. He watches from the skies, and whenever he sees values threatened or the good in peril, he exerts all of his preservative influence in their behalf. He therefore rivals Shiva in popularity among the masses. The stories of his divine activity attract a growing following. He is usually represented with four arms, in two hands holding the symbols of his royal power, the mace and

the discus, and in two others the emblems of his magic power and stainless purity, the conch and the lotus, respectively. His head is surmounted by a high crown and diadem, his feet are blue, his vesture yellow, and he has the lotus eyes so admired by Hindus. When reclining, he is shown resting on the world serpent, Shesha or Ananta; his vehicle is the bird Garuda, and a fish is his symbol. His shakti or spouse is the lovely goddess of fortune and beauty, Lakshmi.

Vishnu's rise to high popular favor is in part due to Vedic mythology. In the Vedas, as we have seen, he is a solar deity. Taking their cue from the fact that the sun redeems the earth from darkness in his passage between earth and sky, the Vedic people developed the myth relating how, when the demon-king Bali seized control of the earth, Vishnu appeared in the form of a dwarf and meekly asked and obtained from the amused giant the promise of as much ground as he could traverse in three steps. The bargain concluded, Vishnu at once returned to his own shape and restored heaven and earth to gods and men by encompassing them in two swift strides. By not taking a third stride across hell, he left it in the demon's possession. This myth provided the intimation concerning the character of Vishnu's interests and activity that has led to his rise in popular esteem. It was seen that he "comes to earth" in *avataras* or "descents" when needed. He has not come down once only, his devotees have urged. Besides descending as a dwarf, he was incarnate in Rama, the ideal king of the *Ramayana*, and in Krishna, the warrior-hero and pastoral lover of the *Mahabharata* and folklore. Indeed, a fast-developing mythology went on to relate that he had had animal as well as human avatars.

Other Avatars of Vishnu

The avatars of Vishnu have been traditionally set at ten, though popular belief has much enlarged the number. Of the traditional list, nine avatars are said to have already occurred, while the tenth is yet to come. We have already mentioned three of them. In the other avatars, Vishnu became in turn a fish, which rescued the first man, Manu, from being swept away in a world flood; a tortoise, which swam under Mt. Mandara and assisted the gods in using it to churn the nectar of immortality and other valuable products from the ocean of milk; a boar, which, with its tusks, lifted the sunken earth above the depths of the sea into which it had been plunged; a man-lion, who tore to pieces a demon father attempting to kill his son because he prayed to Vishnu; a Brahmin warrior hero, who twenty-one times utterly defeated the Kshatriya caste and finally established Brahmin supremacy; and Gautama, the founder of Buddhism. The tenth avatar is to be that of Kalki, a messiah with a sword of flame, riding on a white horse, who shall come to save the righteous and destroy the wicked at the end of the fourth and depraved world period. (To some, the horse is so prominent that they name this avatar the Ashvatara, "the Horse Avatar.")

It is significant that the Buddha is on the list. One suspects that the name of the great founder of Buddhism was added to Vishnu's avatars as a tactical maneuver, designed, and successfully too, to reconcile Buddhism and Hinduism. How well it served to facilitate Indian Buddhism's return to the motherfold of Hinduism will be seen in the chapter on the religious development of Buddhism.

Rama

Incomparably the most popular of the avatars are those of Rama and Krishna. Rama is the ideal man of the Hindu epics, and his wife is the ideal woman. As the *Ramayana* relates, Rama's happy marriage to Sita, a beauteous princess of the royal house of Mithila, was followed by great trouble. The demon king of Ceylon, Ravana, treacherously seized Sita and carried her off to his island home. In great distress, Rama enlisted the aid of Hanuman, the monkey general (the earliest detective in world literature, by the way, and now a Hindu god in his own right). The monkey general was able to conduct an extensive search from the vantage point of the treetops, and Sita was finally found. Rama fought and slew Ravana, and Sita, after successfully passing through an ordeal of fire to prove her chastity, rejoined her mate. Throughout Indian Asia the influence of the Ramayana in various versions can hardly be overstated. Personal names, political analogies, spousal commitments, and theological doctrines spring from it. In northern India, most people learn of

Rama not from the Sanskrit epic but from the Hindi sixteenth-century *Ramcaritmanas* of Tulsidas, a pious "mental reservoir" of Rama truth, recasting the story to emphasize his divine character. Even hostile demons are seen as devotees in the making. Rama's romantic love affair with Sita is exalted, and his double abandonments of her go unmentioned. She and Hanuman are the models for human bhakti.

Millions make Rama the object of their devotion, and his image is often worshiped in a manner to suggest that he is no mere savior hero but the all-God. There are, in fact, two phases of Rama worship: (1) reverential respect for Rama as a hero who was an avatar of Vishnu, and (2) theistic worship of Rama, which gives him exclusive devotion as the supreme deity. (His name was Mohandas, Gandhi's favorite name for God. Gandhi died sighing "Ram, Ram.")

It would be interesting to explore, as we cannot here, the theological doctrines that evolved as a result of the theistic attitude to Rama. Yet one doctrinal issue calls for mention. It has to do with the famous controversy about whether Rama saves by the "monkey-hold" or by the "cat-hold"—that is, with an individual's cooperation or without it. One group of Rama devotees contends that Rama saves only through the free cooperation of the believer with him; the believer must cling to the god as a baby monkey clings to its mother when the latter is swinging off to safety through the trees. The other group believes that salvation is of God only, and that Rama saves his chosen ones by carrying them off as a cat carries a kitten by the scruff of the neck.

Krishna

Highly regarded though Rama is, Krishna is even more popular, both as an avatar and as a god. His character is more complex than Rama's, presenting two distinct aspects not easy to reconcile. The *Mahabharata* shows him in one phase, pastoral poetry and folklore in another. In the *Mahabharata,* he is serious and severe, a resourceful war hero. Throughout the strenuous episodes of the epic he seems primarily anxious to direct the attention of all humanity to Vishnu, the god form of the Absolute, of whom he is the incarnation. In this connection (as we have already noted in our summary of the portion of the *Mahabharata,* known as the *Bhagavad Gita*), he asks for the unconditioned devotion of true bhakti toward himself as the earthly form of Vishnu, the supreme Lord of the World. The other Krishna is a mischievous and amorous wonder worker, the pivotal figure in a vast folklore. In the *Bhagavata Purana,* Hindu imagination has dwelt lovingly on his childhood as a pantry-haunting "butter-thief" and fat little playfellow. Thousands of Hindu women worship him daily in this phase, gazing upon his chubby infant images with much devotion. But this Krishna is more representatively portrayed as an enchanting pastoral figure. In most of the folktales, he is a sprightly and an amorous cowherd, with a melodious flute at his lips, piping as he moves among the cattle the ravishing airs that win him the love of the *gopis* or milkmaids, with whom he dallies in dark-eyed passion. He unites himself with hundreds of these adoring ones (one Purana says 16,000 adoring ones!), but values above all the beautiful Radha, his favorite mistress. The erotic literature that has sprung up to describe this phase of the god's activity bears some resemblance in general tone to the literature of Shaktism, though it prefers expression in story to the latter's philosophy and Tantrism.

The sects that give Krishna a more or less exclusive devotion (bhakti) rank him as high as the Rama worshipers do their paragon. In Bengal, one sect sets Radha beside Krishna as his eternal consort and directs worshipers to seek the favor of both diligently, in the hope of being transported at death to the pleasure groves of the Brindaban heaven, where Krishna and Radha make love forever, in ever-young delight. It is not unexpected that the extremes of left-hand Shaktism occur in some Krishna cults, yet virtually all of the devotees of Krishna stress love of the god as a spiritual rather than a carnal passion. The infatuation of the gopis for the divinely adorable cowherd is given a symbolic meaning; even their transports of love, the thrilling sensation at the roots of the hair, the choking emotion, and the swooning are said to give a true picture in sensuous imagery of the exaltation produced in the worshipper who is looking upon the image of Krishna and thinking of his love. In modern song-fest devotional gatherings (*bhajanas*) devotees, male and female, imagine themselves as gopis as they dance around a picture of Krishna, singing love songs to him.

VII. THE DEVOTIONAL LIFE

Village Observances

The common people of India are not monotheistic. Even though experience or family habit leads a person to adopt one god or goddess as a patron or tutelary deity to be enshrined in the home and honored with name repetitions and special devotions at dawn and dusk, nevertheless all supernatural beings are honored. The number of these deities is uncountable. Hindus are accustomed to saying that there are thirty-three crores, some 330 million. With this understanding, villagers go from shrine to shrine as the need arises. If they wish to have obstacles to some undertaking removed, they worship Ganesha, the elephant-headed son of Shiva; if they need greater bodily strength for some heavy work, they pray to Hanuman, the monkey god; if a father is dying, they pray to Rama. Their hopes for immunity from cholera, safety on a journey, the enjoyment of good fortune, or the health of their cattle take the villagers to still other deities. Their reverence is expressed not only at the shrines or before images; they may worship anywhere, recognizing symbols of Shiva in round stones lifted from the river, or venerating suggestions of Yama, the god of the dead, in trees decorated with vermilion paint.

In this life of devotion, common people feel not only a personal need to express religious consciousness but also the necessity of worship all the time. Worship in one locality takes three different forms simultaneously. First, each person worships as the need arises, either at home or in a temple or elsewhere through individual devotional acts. Second, a priest or someone in the family, usually one of the parents, conducts the simple domestic rites in behalf of the whole family before an image or a symbol of the household god. Third, local priests conduct a ceremony of homage, a puja, at the local temple on behalf of the whole community.

Pilgrimage

But the needs of ordinary people are not fully met, even by all of the routines of the household ceremonies just described. They crave to go to holy places of pilgrimage where they may receive special blessings.

Krishna Steals the Clothes of Bathing Gopis

The *Bhagavata Purana* assigns religious meaning to this erotic prank: Krishna, the Beloved One, teasingly demands that each herdgirl come to him pressing her palms together to plead for her clothing. Her humble nakedness is said to represent the way in which any believer comes into the presence of the divine. God knows all secrets and pays no heed to finery or other material possessions. *(Courtesy of the National Museum of India, Delhi.)*

It would not be wide of the mark to say that millions of Hindus derive their chief religious satisfaction from the pilgrimages they make and the temple festivals they attend. By these activities, not only do they give testimony and expression to their faith through puja (the ritual of worship), but they enjoy themselves hugely at the associated commercial fair (*mela*).

Given the Hindu understanding of deity, it is to be expected that sacred places should multiply during the years. Indeed, from the Hindu point of view, India may be said to be growing in sanctity all of the time, owing to the slowly increasing number of sacred places to be found in it. Sacred places are of two general types: (1) sacred places as such, whose holiness made inevitable the rise of temples and shrines there, and (2) places that have become sacred *after* temples or shrines were erected on them. It is sometimes difficult, however, to know in which group to put the oldest sacred places.

Sacred places of the first type may come into being at almost any spot on mountain or plain where a cavern, strangely formed rock, fissure in the ground, hot spring, or natural wonder has given rise to a tale of spirit visitation or of a miracle, but in most cases they are along the great rivers. Hindus have long regarded their mightiest streams as being holy from source to mouth. The Puranas have glorified almost every bend and tributary with stories of some theophany—a visit of Shiva or one of his shaktis, an exploit of Rama, Krishna, or some other divine being who came to the spot to consecrate it by a significant conversation or wondrous deed. Consequently, it is a work of great merit to follow the course of a holy river from its source to its mouth and back along the other bank to the source again, stopping always at every sacred spot to read or hear again the sacred legends, visit the holy shrines, and engage in pious devotions there. But pilgrims do not often take this long and arduous journey. It is enough for them if they can go to one or more of the many temples that line the holy stream's banks, throw flowers on the river's sacred surface, bathe in the purifying flood, and carry its water home in small containers for last rites to the dying and other ministrations.

The holiest river of all—the Ganges—is known throughout India as "Mother Ganga." Its sacredness is explained by the myth that it issues from the feet of Vishnu in heaven and falls far below on Shiva's head and flows out of his hair. One of the most sacred spots along

Bathing Ghats at Benares
For many miles along the Ganges, steps or *ghats* lead down into the holy waters in which the pilgrims bathe. Special platforms offer places for rest and meditation. At nearby *ghats* cremation of the dead takes place, and the ashes are strewn on the waters. *(Photograph by Ava Hamilton. Courtesy of Simon & Schuster/PH College, F 0307.)*

its entire course is the place where it issues, strong and clear, from the Himalayas. That is the site of the famous pilgrim center Hardwar, with its long lines of steps going down into the river and its crowds of bathers seeking purification in the icy water. Equally sacred is the juncture of the Jumna River with the Ganges, at which spot a third river, the holy Saraswati, is supposed to rise to the surface. Here lies Allahabad, the city that attracts millions of pilgrims to its *melas* or religious fairs. The mouths of the Ganges, emptying through a great delta into the Bay of Bengal, are also holy, particularly Saugor Island, which lies within the delta and is the site of a sacred bathing festival at the beginning of the year.

But it is to Benares that most pilgrims go to wash away their sins. The pilgrims who enter on its hallowed territory are often so overcome with joy at the sight of its temple towers in the distance that they prostrate themselves and pour the dust of the ground on their heads as a sign of their spiritual submission.

They proceed joyfully to the bathing *ghats* (steps) along the river and are purified by immersion in the cleansing waters of sacred Mother Ganga. And when they finally turn homeward, it is with the joyous conviction that all past sins have been atoned for and the future made secure. Had any pilgrim been seized by a mortal illness within the sacred territory, all would still have been well, for whoever dies upon that sacred soil—especially if the feet are immersed in the sacred river and body is cremated with due ritual on a burning ghat—goes to Shiva's heaven of unending delight.

Astrology

Since Gupta times there has been much horoscope casting and use of astrology in India. Although Vedic India had already begun the study of the stars (with enough exactitude to warrant our calling the study astronomy), the preferred methods of foretelling the

Privileged Animals, These Cattle
To the Hindus they are sacred animals. Human beings have to walk around them. Molest one and you may find yourself in the hoosegow for cruelty to animals. *(Courtesy of Ewing Galloway, 193484)*

future were interpretation of omens and dreams and also readings taken from the size and shape of face and limbs and from such special features as birthmarks and lines appearing on the palms of the hands and soles of the feet. (The Buddha, for example, was examined, legend says, by soothsayers shortly after his birth, and the marks on his body and the soles of his feet— "the thirty-two marks of the superman"—told them he was destined for greatness.) But in Gupta and medieval times, astrology, partly because it could be resorted to without delay as needed, came into daily use and is relied upon constantly throughout India today. The family priest may be the family astrologer who aids in setting dates for weddings and journeys. It also is thought that there is more luck in the name given to a child if its first letter is taken from the stars under which the child was born. When a go-between finds a suitable girl for a boy to marry, the betrothal does not take place until the horoscopes of the couple are found favorable. Even educated Hindus who no longer believe in the practice themselves nevertheless consult astrologers before important family events to make certain that all the participants are comfortable in their minds about what is to occur.

Cow Protection

Scholars who readily appreciate the importance of the idea of reincarnation have sometimes failed to give like recognition to an equally widespread feature of Hindu religious life—the veneration of the cow. Perhaps there is less disposition to overlook this unique feature of Hindu religious practice since Katherine Mayo's *Mother India* made it a factor in an acrimonious controversy spreading over three continents. Hindus, said Mayo, hold the cow in *such* honor that they let her wander in inviolate loneliness, suffering and starving along the parched roads of India! There was an immediate reaction from India, all of it indignant. No less an advocate than Mahatma Gandhi led in the defense of "cow protection," as he liked to call it. He even named it "the central fact of Hinduism, the one concrete belief common to all Hindus," and justified it in the following memorable words:

> Cow protection is to me one of the most wonderful phenomena in human evolution. It takes the human being beyond his species. The cow to me means the entire subhuman world. Man through the cow is enjoined to realize his identity with all

that lives. . . . She is the mother to millions of Indian mankind. The cow is a poem of pity. Protection of the cow means protection of the whole dumb creation of God.[L]

Hindus are not without a case in saying that the exaltation of the cow is morally far above that of the eagle or the lion. But the Hindu attitude is rather more unreserved than the words of Gandhi would indicate.

In many parts of India cows receive at certain seasons of the year the honor given to deities. Garlands are placed around their necks, oil is poured on their foreheads and water at their feet, while tears of affection and gratitude start into the eyes of bystanders.

Cow dung is today used in most of the villages of Hindu India in many ways: as a fuel, a disinfectant element dissolved in the water used to wash floors, thresholds, and walls, an ingredient in clay mortar and mud plaster, and a medicine. In some rural regions, a dying person who wishes to guarantee a safe passage from this life into the next may grasp the tail of a cow backed up to the bedside, or, should the room be inaccessible to the animal, the invalid may hold a rope fastened to the tail of a cow outside of the room.

One observer, after a year's residence in a remote northern village, says with evident justice,

> The charge that India is consciously cruel or indifferent to cattle is certainly not substantiated by anything I saw in my village. As a rule, out of self-interest, if for no higher reason, the villagers give the cattle the best care they can provide. If they go half-starved, so do their owners.[M]

The killing of cows has in times past been visited with capital punishment; people are still outcast for it. It has been a major source of conflict between Muslims and Hindus that, on the day annually commemorating Abraham's offering up of Isaac, the Muslims sacrifice calves. From a Hindu point of view, this is an outrage against a gentle creature that spends its life in the selfless giving of its nourishment to others. (A sense of outrage centering upon taboo animal products became the triggering cause in a struggle to throw off British rule in 1857, when both Hindu and Muslim recruits refused any longer to bite percussion caps onto cartridges greased with fat from cows and pigs.)

The merit of the cow has in some degree been passed on to the ox and the bull. To free oxen dedicated to Shiva so that they may wander through the streets is a work of high merit, and when done in the name of one recently deceased is of great benefit to that person in the next life.

The Holiness of Brahmins

Holiness as a potent element in human personality has fascinated India in the past, and still does. Although men of other castes may be recognized as holy (witness Gandhi and the title given him), Brahmins have had sanctity above all others. The *Code of Manu* long since made this clear. It placed the Brahmin in the position of "the lord of this whole creation," whose birth is "an eternal incarnation of the sacred law."[C10] As priest, or as guru (teacher), or in any occupation, the Brahmin is "the highest on earth," and "whatever exists in the world is his property"; on account of the excellence of his origin, he is entitled to all.

> A Brahmin, be he ignorant or learned, is a great divinity, just as the fire is a great divinity. The brilliant fire is not contaminated even in burial places, and, when presented with oblations of butter at sacrifices, it again increases mightily. Thus, though Brahmins employ themselves in all sorts of mean occupations, they must be honored in every way; for each of them is a very great deity.[C11]

Today the mysterious quality of his person can only be preserved with difficulty, but it is being preserved. No matter what his manner of life, to kill or maltreat him is always a heinous sin. Yet it would be erroneous to conclude that each individual Brahmin is necessarily revered. He is indeed theoretically a great lord among men, whatever his occupation, but then one may regard the person of a king as sacred and still despise his spirit or mock his acts. Today, when Brahmins engage in all sorts of occupations, it is perhaps natural that in some cases they should be ridiculed, as were the monks of medieval Europe for their petty vices, especially if they adopt an air of ultrarespectability. But even those who laugh at a Brahmin may wish themselves in his place and hope after death to become a Brahmin in the next life.

Gurus

Among the most highly honored Brahmins in India are those who are *gurus*. Gurus exhibit Hinduism's conscious effort in the direction of religious education. Their function is to teach Hindus those tenets of their religion most directly bearing on home life and household ceremony.

Although this was traditionally a male role, a significant minority of female gurus have won widespread respect, especially among bhakti sects, since the nineteenth century. Ramakrishna underwent tantric initiation from a female guru, and his "spiritual wife" Sharadadevi gave leadership to his ashram, as did Mirra Alfassa to Aurobindo's ashram. The guru Janananda was the "only woman ever allowed to take *sannyasa*," by the present head of the Shankara monastery at Kanchipuram.

Those who can afford it often permanently retain a guru in their homes as a family tutor, but in most cases a guru serves a number of families and goes the rounds among them. The foremost function is to train young people in religious knowledge and to initiate them into adult responsibility by ceremonially investing them with the sacred cord. Not all gurus are Brahmins, but those who are not Brahmins are expected to have credentials of demonstrated religious training and authority.

Other "Holy Ones"

We must not overlook the "holy ones," the *sadhus, sannyasins,* and *yogins,* who are distinctive of India. Some slight differences distinguish them. The yogins are, as their name implies, those who hope that their practice of Yoga will someday give them the insight and status of sannyasins and sadhus. Sannyasins are today usually ash-smeared followers of Shiva imitating the great god's ascetic ardors, but in the classical Hindu conception they win their status by reaching the fourth stage of the ideal life career. The more inclusive term *sadhu* applies to any person of great sanctity, but especially to one who has "attained" or "arrived" at spiritual unity with ultimate reality, and thus, having enjoyed more than one experience of samadhi or trance, is now truly "holy." Most go about fully clothed—but easily identifiable by facial markings, staff, or begging bowl. As visible reminders of the final goal of liberation from samsara, they exercise a constant influence on ordinary people. A few, in the zeal of concentrated effort, go half clothed or naked, smeared with ashes, or frozen in unbroken silence. The sacred places of India are like a lodestone to the more fanatical among them. During festivals, eccentric sadhus—a special sect—march along naked, hundreds strong, and after they have passed, the people run to scoop up the dust made sacred by their footprints, so that they may rub it on themselves or carry it away.

Displays of Self-Control

The West is familiar with pictures of Hindu holy men displaying control over their bodies by reclining on beds of spikes, sitting between fires, or hanging with their heads down in the smoke, wearing feathered barbs set in their flesh, holding one or both arms (or legs) in the same position until atrophy renders them useless, looking at the sun with undeviating gaze until their eyes go blind, wearing heavy clanking chains wrapped around their legs and bodies, and so on. In these positions, or cumbered with these hampering weights, they remain together for hours, days, weeks, or years. The Western observer is filled with amazement at the mere thought of such self-imposed suffering and indomitable patience and endurance. But it would be too much to expect equal sincerity and devotion in every instance. The more philosophic holy man bears self-inflicted torment in the silence and solitude of a forest or mountain retreat, perfecting himself in the quietude of his own thought. Others crave the presence of the multitudes and live by the offerings of the pious. All of this is not without its logic. It may seem a strange sort of reasoning that leads to such maltreatment of the body, but the earnest basic purpose is there—to control the flesh for the sake of freedom of the spirit.

VIII. ISSUES AND PROBLEMS OF THE PRESENT

No generalizations can encompass the diversity of the changes (or the stable areas) across the Hindu world, but some sampling has taken place. Anthropologists have been revisiting villages studied a decade or more earlier (see, for example, K. Ishwaran, ed., *Change and Continuity in India's Villages*). Samples of trends in some areas are: (1) More deities: Gandhi and Nehru have joined the pantheon and regional deities become more widely known—Ayyapan, Vaishno Devi, and Santoshi Ma. (2) Fewer restrictions on interdining. (3) Relaxation of pollution taboos: leather, for example: as the Chamars, a scavenger caste, leave their villages (and their *jajman* "bartered labor" duties) to work for cash in factories, farmers are left to deal with dead animals by themselves. (4) Scaling down of ritual requirements especially in regard to festivals. Old restrictions yield to village-wide participation.

Our approach will be to trace historical developments in regard to selected ideological and sociopolitical issues.

A. Reactions to Western Religion and Science

Hinduism is paradoxically both one of the most liberal and one of the most conservative religions. Its liberalism flows from the intellectual freedom granted to its adherents, a freedom whereby they may even deny the inspiration of the Vedas, the holiness of Brahmins, or the orthodox conceptions of the caste system, and yet remain Hindu—*provided* that they do not break completely with the accepted moral practices of their localities or the code of social regulations to which they have been bred, especially the dietary restrictions, marriage laws, and cow veneration; in short, provided that they seek to reform Hinduism from within and are not complete rebels.

In the course of the centuries a large number of Hindu sects was allowed to adopt with little change the leading doctrines of heretical or foreign religions. The Brahmins complained and objected at times, but there was no marked disturbance of the religious peace, unless some sect broke completely with caste law, or, as occasionally happened under Muslim influence, ate the flesh of the cow.

During the nineteenth century a new type of liberalism made its appearance. It was the direct result of the favorable impressions created by the teaching of Christian missionaries and by education in Western history and science in schools established under European auspices. When this liberal movement got under-

way, other movements followed, some reactionary, some radical, some latitudinarian. They may be briefly described under the following five headings.

1. The Brahmo Samaj

We begin with the first liberal movement of rapprochement with the West. The Brahmo Samaj (Brahmanist Society) is an important movement within modern Hinduism, not so much because of the number of its members as because of its influence. It was founded in Calcutta in 1828 by Ram Mohan Roy, a Brahmin of brilliant mind, whose religious heritage contained strong Vaishnavite and Shaivite influences, from which he was partially weaned away by an education that brought him in touch with Buddhism, Zoroastrianism, Islam, and Christianity. He found in all the religions a similar spiritual core and was therefore led to organize a religious society devoted to the essence that seemed central in every religious faith. His own creed grew out of the conviction that the truth underlying all religions is the unity, personality, and spirituality of God, "the Eternal, Unsearchable, and Immutable Being who is the Author and Preserver of the Universe." Accordingly, he denounced all forms of polytheism and idolatry and advocated purging Hindu ceremonies of these elements. He welcomed any witness to the unity and personality of God. The precepts of Jesus were from his point of view, he said, "the Guide to Peace and Happiness." In seeking to formulate a universal religion he gave up many of the general beliefs of Hinduism, such as the doctrine of transmigration of souls and the theory that the soul is destined to be eventually absorbed into the World Soul.

From the beginning, no pictures or images and no animal sacrifices were permitted in the religious services of the Brahmo Samaj. The worship was conducted (for the first time by Hindus) congregationally, as in European Protestantism, with hymns, sermons, and scripture readings. Social reforms, such as abolition of suttee (to whose official outlawing Ram Mohan Roy contributed not a little) and prohibition of child marriage and polygamy, were urged but not actively sought. Agitation rather than action was the objective. The reason for this moderation lay in part in the fact that Ram Mohan Roy remained true to the social restrictions of his own caste and never ceased to wear the sacred cord of the Brahmin. He did not wish to break off communion with his fellow Hindus. He was thus able to win gifted aristocrats to his movement. The grandfather, and later the father, of the famous Bengali poet Rabindranath Tagore, became leaders in the Brahmo Samaj.

The Brahmo Samaj split in two in the 1860s when the socially minded Keshab Chandra Sen, who was brought up in an English school and had learned to love the figure of Christ as a divine social reformer, began to attack the caste system root and branch and pled for a radical sweeping away of caste restrictions, including those placed on intercaste marriages. A rupture between the radicals and conservatives followed. Keshab's adherents followed him in organizing a new society, the Brahmo Samaj of India, to distinguish it from the Adi (or Original) Brahmo Samaj, which was the name given to the old society. Later, most of his followers left him to form the Sadharan (or General) Brahmo Samaj. Keshab renamed his diminished society the Nava Bidhana Samaj or Church of the New Dispensation. During the few years of life that remained to him he came to feel more and more that he was continuing the work of Christ on earth. After his death, this startling phase of his thought was played down as much as possible by his followers.

Today, the Adi Brahmo Samaj and the Nava Bidhana Samaj are less influential than the Sadharan Brahmo Samaj, but all three groups continue to stand for a universal religion based on the unity of the human family under a caring Deity.

2. The Arya Samaj

The Arya Samaj (Aryan Society) is a movement "back to the Vedas," an effort to establish a universal religion that has had some success in India. It was founded in Bengal in 1875 by Swami ("teacher") Dayananda, a Brahmin who had had the interesting religious experience of revolting in boyhood from the worship of Shiva and then of passing as an ascetic through a period of belief in the monism of the Upanishads into a period of belief in the dualism of the Sankhya philosophy. He finally arrived at the conviction that the religion of the Vedas is the oldest and purest of all religions. He found it untainted by superstition, idolatry, or erroneous conceptions like the doctrine of avatars, and free from the objectionable features of the caste system. Finding that the term *jati* (literally "birth," the name for hereditary castes) did not appear in the Vedas, he concluded that the four *varna* classes were meant to be aptitude groupings to which any Aryan should belong by ability rather than by birth.

The Vedas, he taught, were a direct revelation from the one God and, properly understood, do not teach either polytheism or pantheism. Not only do they furnish the one true key to the past, they anticipate all future developments of thought. They have forecast such discoveries of science as steam engines, railways, buses, ocean liners, and electric lights. In them are set forth the basic principles of such sciences as physics and chemistry. The Vedas are therefore the ideal charts or blueprints of nature; there is an exact correspondence between them and the structure of the world.

Dayananda's studies, published as *The Light of Truth* in 1874, set loose the ideological headwaters for a later, much broader torrent of Hindu nationalism than he could have foreseen. The immediate outcome was the formation of the Arya Samaj, a society vehement in its criticism of foreign influences—Muslim as well as Christian and secular—but moderate enough in its activities to attract middle-class Hindus.

Two branches of the Arya Samaj now exist. One is liberal, the other conservative. Both engage in educational and philanthropic work throughout north India. In their schools, modern science, "based on the Vedas," is taught. Their adherents number perhaps half a million.

3. Theosophy

A related but unclassifiable modern religious movement is *Theosophy*. Though this movement was founded in New York City, its headquarters since 1878 have been in India, where its real inspiration lies. The realization of its aim—the establishment of unity, which they termed "Brotherhood," among all peoples—is held to be dependent on an esoteric, ancient wisdom, expressed in the Vedanta and transmitted through "masters" or "Mahatmas" who appear from age to age. These "great souls" have occult powers that give them unique control over their own bodies and over natural forces. Under their guidance, humanity, bound to the ever-turning wheel of reincarnation by the Law of Karma, will someday gain happiness—in a world that will drink as one from the one wonderful Fountain of Wisdom from which all religions have drawn their hitherto partial truths. Two women were outstanding in the leadership of the Theosophical Society, Madame Helena Petrovna Blavatsky, its co-founder (along with Colonel Henry Steel Olcott), and its English president, Mrs. Annie Besant. The Theosophists have defended prophecy, second sight, Hindu idol worship, and caste. The Society has done some useful educational work in India, Mrs. Besant being the founder of Benares Hindu University. Today it lends its support to Indian nationalism. This is natural enough, for Theosophy is, in spite of its professed hospitality to all religions, Hindu at heart.

4. The Ramakrishna Movement

The Ramakrishna movement is a response of tolerance and syncretism. The broad-minded acceptance of the essence of the Western religious tradition and its inclusion in the teachings of Hinduism may be seen very clearly in the life and opinions of perhaps the outstanding Hindu saint and seer of the nineteenth century, Ramakrishna. Born a Brahmin in Bengal, he followed the family tradition in becoming one of the priests of a Kali temple near Calcutta. With a spiritual hunger that was not appeased by the performance of his priestly functions, he longed for an immediate experience of the divine. He concentrated on the image of Kali, the Divine Mother. In gazing at her image, he experienced trance (samadhi) not once but many times and with increasing intensity, often seeing her move and come to him. He understood from the first that this was but one way of knowing God. He set out to try all the other ways. In a twelve-year period he meditated like a yogin, worshiped like a bhakta, practiced Jainism, Buddhism, and Shaktism, and experienced the reality both of Brahman without attributes (i.e., the impersonal God) and of Brahman with attributes (i.e., the personal God). Dressed like a Muslim, he prayed until he knew God as Allah. He turned to Christianity and found God in Christ. God also became real to him as Rama, as Krishna, and as Sita. All religions were to him different ways to God, and all creatures were God in so many different forms. He made friends with the members of the Brahmo Samaj; Keshab Chandra Sen particularly befriended him. He once told the latter, in a typical expression of convictions,

Everything is in the mind. Bondage and freedom are in the mind. You can dye the mind with any color you wish. It is like a piece of clean white linen: dip it in red and it will be red, in blue it will be blue, in green it will be green, or any other color. Do you not see that if you study English, English words will come readily to you? Again, if a pandit studies Sanskrit, he will readily quote verse from Sacred Books. If you keep your mind in evil company, your thoughts, ideas, and words will be colored with evil; but keep in the company of Bhaktas, then your thoughts, ideas and words will be of God. The mind is everything.[N1]

A revealing bit of reminiscence is contained in the following:

Another day I went to the parade ground to see the ascension of a balloon. Suddenly my eyes fell upon a young English boy leaning against a tree. The very posture of his body brought before me the vision of the form of Krishna and I went into samadhi.

Again I saw a woman wearing a blue garment under a tree. She was a harlot. As I looked at her, instantly the ideal of Sita appeared before me! . . . For a long time I remained motionless. I worshiped all women as representatives of the Divine Mother.[N2]

An organized group of disciples gathered around Ramakrishna during the last six years of his life, led by a young student of law who became his successor, under the name of Swami Vivekananda. A brilliant speaker and ardent apologist for the Vedanta, Vivekananda, after Ramakrishna's death, founded the Ramakrishna movement and spread it all over the world. He was the spokesman for Hinduism at the Parliament of Religions in Chicago in 1893, where he made a great impression that electrified India. He was instrumental in founding Vedanta societies in New York and other American cities. He also founded Ramakrishna centers in Europe, on the Ganges, and in the Himalayas. A marked result of his success in interpreting Hinduism to the world was a revival of interest in the Vedanta in India itself, an interest that has continued to the present time.

5. Secularism

Two senses of "secularism" need to be distinguished: (1) soft secularism, or the acceptance of a common nonreligious basis for personal and social identity, and (2) hard secularism, or the rejection of religion.

1. Soft secularism has made some headway in Indian culture. It involves a subtle shift in the perception of self and society, an acknowledgment that there is a realm of reality external to one's religious perspective, a common ground upon which human beings may interact without regard to their religious identity. In the post-Renaissance West, this acknowledgment is taken for granted. Any person nurtured in the Western world has little difficulty with the idea that individuals and social structures (and, therefore, individual rights) might be perceived entirely apart from religion: "I am first of all a human being sharing citizenship in X country with other human beings and, beyond this, I have come to identify myself as such and such in regard to the matter of religion."

This soft-secular presupposition does not come easily in India. Most Hindus find it difficult to separate their personal identity as human beings from the religious context of karmic rebirth and redeath. One's religion is one's identity. Many an individual thinks, "I am born a Hindu under karmic reality. As such I am willing (or not willing) to concede space in this karmic reality for others who inexplicably deny or reject it."

The soft-secular presupposition was in the minds of those who founded the present nominally pluralistic Indian state. The resurgence of Hindu nationalism through the powerful Bharatiya Janata Party implicitly challenges it. It is difficult to assess subtle shifts in the perception of self and society, but it seems likely that at present most Hindus are ambivalent toward the soft-secular assumption if they conceive it at all. The masses do not appear to be aware of the profound importance of a secular base for the functioning of the pluralistic society envisioned in their national constitution.

2. Hard secularism goes beyond the neutral assumption of a base beyond which one may or may not embrace religion. Asserting that religions are at best irrelevant and most often impediments to progress, this kind of secularism is easy to discern, and there is no doubt that it has had considerable growth. Though most Indians exult in the "spirituality" of India, there has been in the last century a pronounced drift toward forms of scientific materialism that are negative to traditional religious values. Some intellectuals are showing less and less interest in organized religion. They view it coldly as a mass of superstition built around an antiquated view of life and the world. They condemn its pessimistic tone, its world-denying attitude. Observing religion and religious men with more detachment and critical judgment than has ever before been possible in India, thousands have ceased to believe in the old Hindu Dharma and its ceremonies. And yet in many cases, even though religious convictions have been given up, belief has been maintained for family and social reasons.

Western humanism and departures in ideology like Marxism also have increased the process of religious dissolution. In some circles, especially where communism has survived, defiant atheism is still voiced. Recent census reports show less than 1 percent self-characterized atheists; 9 percent give no religious affiliation. Young Hindus have written for publication: "The conflict between theism and atheism is the conflict between man's slave mind and his free will."[P]

B. Social Reforms

Not only have there been changes in intellectual outlook, the past century also has seen, as our sketch of the Brahmo Samaj must have indicated, vigorous advocacy of far-reaching social changes. This has been especially true of proposed changes in caste and marriage laws, regulations that from their beginnings have constituted major sources of social and religious difficulty.

1. Caste Problems

In ancient India the rigidity of the caste system was predicated on the presumed finality of the economic structure, then relatively simple. But

> "The vegetables in the cooking pot move and leap till the children think they are living beings. But the grown-ups explain that they are not moving of themselves; if the fire be taken away, they will soon cease to stir. So it is ignorance that thinks, 'I am the doer.' All our strength is the strength of God."
>
> —Ramakrishna[O]

the social order could not be kept simple; it became more and more complex. Accordingly, the castes of ancient times virtually broke up, and the many so-called functional castes (the *jatis*) in reality superseded them. *Jati*, which means sociologically an endogamous kinship or a guild group, has functioned in Hindu minds as connoting caste; it has indicated one's position in society more closely than the term *varna*, which denotes a much broader classification. At any rate, jati has come to signify regional groups following similar occupations, marrying only within their own circles, and restricting their intimate social contacts (e.g., eating and sleeping) to members of their own special group. As early as the time of the Emperor Asoka (third century B.C.E.), the ancient Greek historian Megasthenes tells us there were in India seven castes: herdsmen, farmers, craftsmen, soldiers, magistrates, philosophers (i.e., Brahmins), and councillors, all of them endogamous and hereditary. True or not, such groups multiplied through the years into several thousand functionally distinct groups. The resultant confusion has led many reform-minded Hindus to advocate the reabsorption of the multitudinous jatis into the four classical varnas as a measure of simplification.

As can well be imagined, industrialization, to the degree that it has been introduced, has produced still further variations in caste structure.

Besides these functional castes there are race castes (tribal and national groups taken into the Hindu fold), sectarian castes (originating from sects which, ironically enough, rejected the caste system and withdrew from it, only to become yet another caste), and castes formed by invasion, migration, or crossing.

The lowest castes have been separated into the "clean" and "unclean." The clean may be generally grouped under the ancient name of Shudra. They do not follow degrading occupations, are in some sense orthodox in their social and religious practices, and are able, at least on occasion, to engage reputable Brahmins as their priests. The unclean are in general those engaged in a degrading occupation, one involving, say, defiling contacts with dead bodies, human or animal, or entailing sweeping up the dirt and refuse of the streets. The unclean castes include the leather cutters and shoemakers, the sweepers or scavengers, the cane chair makers, and the Kulis (coolies) or unskilled day laborers.

The members of these unclean and degraded castes have long been regarded by the higher castes as "outcastes" and "untouchables." Mahatma Gandhi gave currency to "Harijan" (children of God) as a way of referring to them. More recently their preferred term of self-reference, Dalits (oppressed ones), has gained wide usage. Although officially of no caste or "outside the pale" (not "cast out" but simply "never in"), Dalits themselves are organized into a complicated subcaste system.

In the past, the plight of the untouchable was pitiable. Like the despised Chandala of the *Code of Manu*, who was ranked with the village pig and homeless dog, the untouchable was an object of contempt, despised by all. Not just the touch but even the shadow of the untouchable could defile a person of high caste. In some parts of India, therefore, untouchables were required to announce their presence loudly as they came down the street, so that those who might be defiled by them could draw their skirts away or move out of reach. Passage through certain public roads and bazaars was forbidden. They were not permitted to come within so many feet of certain temples, nor could they draw water from the public well, but had to go to a well used only by their own group. If a Brahmin neared, the untouchables had to get off the road into a field. Should they approach the Brahmin too closely, the latter bathed, renewed his sacred cord, and underwent other purification. In some places outcastes could not take purchases out of the hand of the merchant, but waited until the latter deposited them on the ground and walked away, or tossed them to them. It would seem to have been the object of the higher castes to reduce the untouchables to such beaten, abject creatures that they would never so much as attempt to better their lot. (It will be remembered that the higher castes invoked the Law of Karma to justify this morally; the untouchables were suffering retribution for the past sins.)

It is easy to see why Hinduism has witnessed one attempt after another, by persons who have gained fresh insight, to get around untouchability and other restrictions imposed by the caste system, or to get rid of the caste system altogether. These attempts have been mainly of two sorts.

Opposition by Withdrawal   The earliest attempts to deal with caste restrictions were made by strong-willed, independent thinkers who invited their converts to retire from the world and enter into a casteless monastic life. Jainism and Buddhism are examples of this kind of withdrawal. For the vast majority in India, the results were not lasting. Lay members who did not enter the circle of monks continued to pattern their lives by the rules they had known under the caste system. They married and gave in marriage along caste lines, and fell back into the social roles assigned to them by other castes.

More pronounced but still temporary social effects were produced by the Shiva-worshiping Lingayats of Bombay and southern India and the Baishtams of Bengal. Inspired by a revelation, they declared that all converts were equals, free to eat, visit, and intermarry. But because they usually did not marry outside of the sect, either because they did not desire to do so or could not arrange it, members of the new sect in time became another caste. In many instances, the case of converts to Christianity was little different. Because withdrawing from Brahmin-dominated rules and rituals most often meant settling in separate villages, Christians often found themselves perceived as simply members of yet another caste, and Christians of Dalit background often suffered discrimination from other Christians.

Reform from Within   A second type of assault on the caste system sought its reform from within. This is a comparatively recent type of reform, and is usually motivated by a high social idealism, directly or indirectly influenced by Christianity and studies of Western social organization. Idealistic political reform was abetted by the erosion of old rules in a climate of technological modernization.

The unavoidable mixing of high- and low-caste people using public transportation has made it a modern convention that people of high caste may relax their observance of the old rules while on a journey, provided they are unbendingly strict when in their own villages. While traveling, they may sit beside persons whose nearness would defile them at home. In a big hotel, it is not required to be as particular as they once had to be about the food and drink served to them, for they cannot demand that every dish be prepared only by ritualistically clean hands.

In the later years of the British control of India, groups formerly known only as outcastes or untouchables organized themselves into castes and, beginning in 1935, four hundred such castes were placed on a list or "schedule." Quota percentages of places in education and employment were set aside for such "scheduled castes" as a compensatory redress for past injustices.

In 1948, Mahatma Gandhi's lifelong campaign against untouchability finally became law when India's Constituent Assembly forbade its practice "in any form." In the real world, however, discrimination has continued.

Recent policy debates have utilized broader categorizations such as "backward classes" and "peasant castes" to refer to many of the nearly destitute groups not officially recognized as "scheduled castes." These groups along with the scheduled castes make up about 52 percent of India's population—a formidable constituency. In 1990, a decision, ardently supported by the Hindu nationalist Bharatiya Janata Party, reserved 27 percent of all central government jobs for "backward castes"—in addition to the 22.5 percent for "scheduled castes." This brought on a violent backlash and acts of intimidation, but also instances of self-immolation as protest from members of higher castes in urban areas. The effect of such legislation to remedy past discrimination has sometimes strengthened caste loyalties as the advantage of collective political action has become obvious. (See Section D, Political Change.)

2. Child Marriage and Widowhood

Child marriage has existed in India for many centuries. It usually is traced to a family law, going back to the fifth century B.C.E., which required the marriage of all girls before puberty. This law (only imperfectly observed until eight or nine hundred years ago) may have originated out of a desire to forestall romantic attachments between young people of different castes, but there were other factors in the situation. For one thing, the old caste law prohibiting marriages outside of one's caste made it urgent that fathers search out eligible girls for their sons as soon as possible, lest there be none left; so parents took to betrothing their children when they were but a few months old, and marriage was frequently celebrated when the bride and groom were only seven or eight years old. Another factor—ultimately important—was the great practical usefulness of child marriage to the family system, insofar as it helped keep the family group united.

Mature daughters-in-law were comparatively hard to assimilate to a family's fixed habits; but a young bride could easily be molded and fit the family routine.

Until the early twentieth century, child marriage was shrugged off as being inevitable and unavoidable, but, largely through Western criticism, the protests of Hindu reformers, and the adverse reports of medical authorities, an acute consciousness of the problem was aroused among Hindus. Under British rule, the government, after an experimental trial with laws progressively lifting the age of consent, passed in 1930 the Child Marriage Restraint Bill, which made marriage of girls under age fourteen and boys under age eighteen illegal. Current law under a nominally secular national government sets the minimum age for the marriage of females at eighteen. As we have seen, religiously rooted marital customs erode very slowly. In the fifty years since 1941, the median age for females marrying has increased only from about 17.5 to about 18.7.

Recognizing that high dowries can lead to female feticide and infanticide and even to the extortion and murder of young brides, reformers finally succeeded in passing the Dowry Prohibition Act in 1961. Lacking enforcement, it has had only minimal effect. A 1997 estimate of the total cost of a dowry wedding, even for the poorest of families, came to about ten times the family's annual income.

One consequence of early marriage has been early widowhood. The young widow forbidden to remarry becomes an extra mouth for her in-laws to feed and may find herself somehow blamed for her husband's death and only grudgingly tolerated as a domestic helper. Estimates in 1981 showed 214,000 females widowed, divorced, or abandoned by age nineteen.

Widowers are not so unfortunate; they may remarry, if they can find a suitable bride. But this has often led to unequal marriages between middle-aged men and young wives. Ancient codes reinforce any reluctance to contract themselves to widows, and it is truly difficult to find unmarried women of their own age. Feminist groups in India assert that the freedom of males to remarry, coupled with greed for second dowries, has resulted in instances of murder, termed "accidental" deaths, of young brides from such causes as kitchen fires. Highly suspicious dowry deaths have risen by 170 percent over a ten-year period, reaching 6,200 in the year 1996.

On the other hand, demographic and economic factors are likely to accelerate change. Among urban upper classes today, religious rules against divorce are increasingly evaded, and urbanization has swollen the numbers of the very poor among whom marital regulation scarcely exists.

C. Population Problem

On less than 2.5 percent of the earth's land surface, India must provide for more than 15 percent of the global population. At a growth rate of 2 percent, the 1998 estimated population of some 990 million will be adding over 15 million more persons annually to be fed, clothed, housed, and cared for medically. It is difficult to curb population growth when religious scruples stand in the way. Hindus hesitate to interfere with life processes fixed by the Law of Karma, and having many sons has always been interpreted as a karmic blessing.

Despite the fact that opposition to birth control was a contributing factor in the ousting of Indira Gandhi from power in 1977 and in subsequent difficulties for her branch of the Congress party, the promotion of family planning continued. Indian governments, however, have stopped short of the economic penalties applied in the People's Republic of China.

In the face of high mortality of children, numerous sons are a kind of insurance, not only for securing the future for parents, but also for assuring the perpetual continuation of proper family rites in behalf of ancestors. Documented abortions in which the gender of the fetus was determined in advance have run at about 98 percent female. Suspicions of infanticide or of "systematic neglect" of young females are raised by the fact that the mortality rates for juvenile girls run higher than for boys. The rates are highest in areas where dowries are highest. Sterilization, the most common means of birth control, is generally accepted only after the birth of two sons ("One son is no sons"), and the resulting family average is 4.2 children.

D. Political Change

To pursue the topic of political change in detail would take us far beyond the scope of this volume; yet not to pursue it at all would, on the other hand, narrow our study unduly, for it is not possible to divorce Indian politics from religion.

In the generation-long, organized struggle of the peoples of India for self-determination, three factors were of supreme importance. The first was the well-founded feeling of the leading minds of India that in the intellectual sphere they had established their competence to engage in the life of reason at least equally with the world's greatest. Why then should they be kept in the role of a subject people?

The second factor was the personality and leadership of Mahatma Gandhi. With great patience, and a moral imagination not matched by any other individual in our time, he planned and led the political struggle for national self-determination. He fought with Hindu weapons—nonviolent resistance, soul force, a baffling use of tolerance and inclusive goodwill when confronted with strong opposition, but firm insistence on *swadeshi* (loyalty to one's own inherited religion and way of life). With astonishing practicality as to means but unyielding idealism in matters of principle, he morally guided the often divergent elements in the Congress Party up to and beyond the agreement with the British Raj, which established national self-determination for Hindu India.

The third factor was—and continues to be—the deep difference between Hindus and Muslims. At first, the Hindus refused to believe that such a difference existed, but the highly organized Pakistan movement proved at last convincing, and the Hindus consented to the formation of the separate Muslim state. It is hardly necessary to add that there was tragedy in this, not only for Gandhi and Nehru, the leaders of the Nationalist cause in India, but also for millions of Muslims, Sikhs, and Hindus who suffered death and displacement when partition came in 1947. Gandhi himself was assassinated in the aftermath.

The next great leader, Jawaharlal Nehru, idolized by millions as the natural successor to Mahatma Gandhi (although privately he was more of a secularist than they knew), died in office (1964), worn out by his efforts to build India into a viable modern democracy playing its full part, in a neutralist role, among the divided nations of the world. His daughter, Indira Gandhi, became prime minister in 1966, and after six years of struggle with conservative Hindu leaders found herself obliged to use dictatorial methods to achieve her somewhat radical social goals; in 1977 she

was expelled from office by disaffected Indians who feared for the survival of the Hindu Dharma in changing times, but in the elections of 1980 she made a dramatic return to power. She was assassinated by her Sikh bodyguards on October 31, 1984, in retaliation for her sending an army onto the grounds of the Sikh Golden Temple at Amritsar. One thousand separatist militants were killed. Later, 2,700 more Sikhs were killed in revenge for the assassination. After her assassination, her son Rajiv Gandhi was elected prime minister and continued most of her policies, albeit with a more conciliatory style. Even so, he too was felled by the bullet of a separatist assassin in 1991. Interlacing forces of continuity and change continue to mark the political scene. In 1998, Rajiv's Italian wife Sonia and her daughter entered the political arena. Though the Congress Party did not achieve a plurality, it made significant gains, holding out the possibility of an eventual continuation of the Gandhi/Nehru dynasty.

In an era of resurgent nationalisms in the former Soviet Union and in eastern Europe, the prospects of a factionally divided central government being able to continue to hold India together remain precarious. We shall have more to say about religious backlash in the next section and about separatism in a later chapter on Sikhism.

E. Religious Liberalism and Reaction

In recent decades, two Hindus have earnestly sought an integration of *Eastern Religions and Western Thought* (the title of a book by one of them). One, the late Aurobindo Ghose, a Bengali Brahmin, abandoned Nationalistic politics for philosophy in order to urge the possibility that "integral yoga," as he called it, may enable man to become a superman. In the eternal shakti he saw the downward movement of Reality (i.e., of the infinite, all-inclusive Brahman) in "descents, eruptions, messages or revelations." After this has had its spiritual effect on the human mind, there can be an "ascent" from the ordinary human to the superman level of being.

The other, Dr. Sarvepalli Radhakrishnan, late president of India, was an internationally known scholar and lecturer, whose cordiality to Western religion and philosophy was accompanied by consistent stress on mysticism as the very heart of religion. Consequently,

Hinduism emerges in his numerous writings as the greatest of the religions. He defended Hinduism against the criticism that it is "nonethical" (a criticism made by Albert Schweitzer) by emphasizing the moral growth that is the necessary preparation for mystic union with the ultimately real, and by pointing to the duty of applying the spiritual lessons of religion in social and political activity.

Opposing this cordiality to the West are such groups supporting orthodox Hinduism as the Mahasabha and the Rashtriya Swayamesevak Sangh (R.S.S.), the "National Purity Service Organization," which advocates making India a Hindu religious state. It was a member of the R.S.S. who assassinated Mahatma Gandhi.

Traditionally, Hindus have been tolerant of other faiths, but although this is still the case, paradoxically, the prevailing view throughout India now is that conversion from one religion to another should be discouraged. Conversion is viewed either as an effect of proselytization or as a "migration," which as its social consequence leaves the convert culturally alien and displaced, breaks up homes, separates kinsfolk, and unsettles the social and national order. Memories of Muslim pressures toward conversion and of British favor toward missionaries, who, as an extreme view puts it, "invaded" India and other Asiatic countries as "an integral part of the domination of the white races over Asia," have reinforced the Nationalist desire to preserve Indian unity and prevent "religious nationalism" from developing among minority groups, for example, the Sikhs and some aboriginal peoples under the influence of Lutheran and Roman Catholic missions.

Backlash campaigns against reform and against religious minorities are not uncommon. Since 1991, the Hindu Bharatiya Janata Party (BJP) used the existence of a mosque on the alleged site of the birthplace of Rama in the ancient city of Ayodhya as a focal issue for rallying Hindu "patriotism." On December 6, 1992, some 200,000 militant Hindus under the direction of RSS marshals descended on Ayodhya razing the sixteenth-century Babri Masjid mosque to the ground. Reprisals and communal violence ensued in both India and Pakistan.

As it gained ground in parliamentary elections, the BJP had to tone down some of its "India for Hindus only" rhetoric in order to make the needed alliances for forming a government. The election in 1997 of K. R. Narayan, an untouchable, as India's tenth president signaled that Hindu nationalism would be in no way elitist. The BJP achieved a plurality in the elections of March 1998 and succeeded in putting together a parliamentary majority, albeit a shaky one, for the Congress Party had gained renewed strength.

But one may be permitted to reflect, in conclusion, that as far as Hinduism is concerned, incalculable consequences were bound to flow from so startling a circumstance as this: a great religion of world renunciation has produced modern leaders who have not sought Nirvana in the solitude of the forest, but rather have come forth into the world to engage realistically and practically in the task of human betterment by social action.

GLOSSARY*

advaita (ŭd-vī-tŭ) nondualism; in Vedanta philosophy it is the denial of the duality of the self and the world

artha (ärt'-hŭ) power or material gain, the second of the four permissible goals in life

Arya Samaj (är'-yŭ-sō-mäj') a "back-to-the-Vedas" (but monotheistic) reform movement founded by Dayananda in 1875

ashramas (ä'-shrŭ-mŭz) the four stages of life: the student, the householder, the hermit, and the homeless wanderer

avatar (ŭv-ŭ-tŭr') alternate forms or incarnations assumed by a god

avidya (ŭ-vēd'-yŭ) ignorance; in Vedanta, mistaking *maya* for reality; in Sankhya, confusing *purusha* with *prakriti*

Bhagavad Gita (bäg'-ŭ-väd gē'-tä) the "Song of the Blessed Lord," about ways of salvation emphasizing the way of *bhakti*

Bhagavata Purana (bäg'-ŭ-vä'-tŭ pōō -rä'-nŭ) a popular epic about the exploits of Krishna as child wonder worker, lover, and king

bhakti (bŭk'-tē) devotion; as Bhakti Yoga (or Bhakti Marga), one of three ways to *moksha,* more popular than the Way of Works or the Way of Knowledge

*For a guide to pronunciation, refer to page 99.

Brahmo Samaj (brä'-mö sü-mäj) an eclectic religious reform movement founded by Ram Mohan Roy in 1828, blending Hindu monotheism with ethics tinged by Christian thought

dharma (dŭr'-mŭ) duty or moral law, sometimes a generic term for religious thought and practice

Durga (Kali) a fearsome yet benevolent goddess, personifying *shakti*, cosmic energy; a consort of Shiva

dvaita (dvī'-tŭ) duality; among Vedanta philosophies a characteristic of Madhva's viewpoint

gopis (gō'-pees) milkmaids and young wives; their love trysts with Krishna in the *Bhagavata Purana* are paradigms of a believer's *bhakti* relationship to God

guna a strand, quality, or attribute, of sense-experienced matter; see *sattva, rajas,* or *tamas*

guru (gôo'-rôo) a spiritual guide or teacher

Harijans "Children of God," Gandhi's term for outcastes or untouchables

jati birth, family; a specific term for caste

jnana (jŭ-nyä'-nŭ) knowledge or understanding, a way to *moksha*

Kali (Durga) "the dark one," a form of *shakti*, fierce as a scourge of demons but also the Divine Mother of all

kama pleasure, one of the four goals, especially appropriate to the householder stage of life. As *Kama,* the love god, he shoots flower arrows

Krishna the dark avatar of Vishnu, mischievous child, lover of *gopis,* and ideal warrior king

Lakshmi goddess of good fortune and prosperity, the favorite wife of Vishnu

lingam phallic symbol, representing Shiva as the male principle, usually ringed by the female *yoni*

Madhva thirteenth-century philosopher who further modified Ramanuja's qualified nondualism into a fully dualistic (*dvaita*) system

Mahabharata (mŭ-hä'-bä-rŭ-tŭ) the great Indian epic about the five Pandava brothers, progenitors of Bharata (India); its many interpolations include the *Bhagavad Gita*

Manu name of a mythic father of the human race; the *Code of Manu* (*ca.* 200 B.C.E.–200 C.E.) set out Brahmanic law

marga a path or way as in *Karma Marga* (the Way of Works), *Jnana Marga,* and *Bhakti Marga*

maya the creative art of the cosmic mind, conscious illusion-making power

Panchatantra (pŭn-chŭ-tŭn'-trŭ) animal fables set in a narrative frame depicting them as lessons in practical wisdom (*niti*), a contrast to academic Brahmanic learning

Patanjali (pŭ-tŭn'-jä-lē) author of the *Yogasutras,* the key work in the Yoga school of philosophy

prakriti (prŭ-krĭ'-tē) the material world, nature; in Sankhya dualism the coeternal counterpart to *purusha,* pure consciousness; in *advaita* Vedanta a product of *maya*

puja worship, cultic rites in temples or in homes

puranas (pōō-rä'-nŭz) popular epics, collections of stories and poems about favorite sectarian gods and sages

rajas one of the three *gunas,* red, restless, impetuous, and feverish

Ramakrishna nineteenth-century saint and seer who proclaimed the oneness of all religions; his disciple, Vivekenanda, founded the Vedanta-oriented syncretistic Ramakrishna movement in his honor

Ramanuja (rä-mŭn'-oo-jŭ) twelfth-century author of a qualified-nondual (*vishisht-advaita*) theistic Vedanta school

Ramayana (rä-mä'-yŭ-nŭ) epic of the struggles of Rama and his allies in rescuing Sita from the demon Ravana

samadhi (sŭ-mä'-dĭ) the final trance state in yogic practice, a foretaste of *moksha* in which distinctions of subject and object are transcended

Sankhya (säng'-kyŭ) the dualist philosophical view affirming the eternally separate reality of matter (*prakriti*) and spirit (*purusha*)

sannyasin (sŭn-nyä-sēn) one who renounces all earthly ties, seeking *moksha* as a mendicant; the fourth *ashrama*

sati a virtuous widow cremated to join her dead husband; later, the performance of self-immolation

sattva the most refined of *gunas,* white, light, intelligent, and revealing

shakti cosmic energy; in *Shaktism,* personified as the consort of gods and yogins, especially Shiva

Shankara (shŭn'-kŭ-rŭ) ninth-century advocate of the nondualist or *advaita* interpretation in Vedanta

Shiva a major god; asceticism generates his *lingam*-symbolized potency as destroyer/creator

tamas the dark *guna,* inert, dull, and heavy

tapas psychic "heat" energy generated by asceticism, often a general reference to austerities

Vishisht-advaita (vĭsh-ĭsht'-ŭd-vī'-tŭ) qualified nondualism, a theistic branch of Vedanta associated with Ramanuja

Vishnu a major god hailed as the "Preserver"; among his ten official avatars are Rama and Krishna

yoga techniques of discipline for overcoming bondage; as Patanjali's *Yogasutras,* the foundation for one of the six acceptable philosophical systems

yoni a ring, the vaginal emblem encircling the phallic *lingam* in Shiva/Shakti symbolism

Jainism
A Study
in Asceticism

Out of the complex matrix of early Hindu civilization, in which ideas held over from pre-Aryan religion vied for attention with ideas drawn from the Vedas and elaborated in the Upanishads, two religions endured to vex the course of Hinduism with alternative answers to the central problem of Indian life: how to find release from karma and the continual round of rebirths entailed by it. One of them, Jainism, was destined to win adherents in India only. The other, Buddhism, spread rapidly over the whole of India and overflowed its boundaries, attaining new forms and a permanent footing to the south and east in Sri Lanka, Burma, Thailand, Cambodia, Laos, and Vietnam, and to the north in China, Korea, Japan, Tibet, and Mongolia. It supplied these regions with some profoundly satisfying answers to universal human needs. But it was destined at length to all but die out in India itself, except upon the fringes of that amazing land. For one thousand years, Hinduism grew quietly, reaching for assent, and its eventual return to dominance over the field of religion is something of a marvel.

When we turn to see what Jainism had to offer, our Occidental minds are apt to receive an initial shock. To anyone bred in the prevailing and hedonistic attitudes of the West, Jainism may at first glance seem an adjustment to life, as rigorously world denying as any the history of religions affords.

Like Buddhism, which arose about the same time, Jainism was a reaction to some tendencies set in motion by the Brahmins. At that time (the sixth century B.C.E.), the Brahmanic sacrificial system had reached its peak in the valley of the Ganges, and then encountered a stout and outspoken opposition. In the regions to the north of the Ganges and farther east, resistance to the language, customs, and religion of the Aryans lingered. The caste system

WESTERN NAME: Jainism

FOUNDER: Nataputta Vardhamana, 599–527 B.C.E. (traditional)

ADHERENTS IN 1997: 4.9 million

TITLES: Mahavira, "Great Hero," Jina, "Conqueror," The Twenty-fourth Tirthankara

NAMES USED BY ADHERENTS: Jaina Marga, Jaina Yoga

PREVIOUS TIRTHANKARAS, "CROSSING FINDERS":

    The First, Rishabha, five *kalpas* (21,000-year world cycles, in the past
    The Twenty-third, Parshva, 8th c. B.C.E.

SECTS: Digambaras, "sky clad," mostly Dravidian and southern, successors to Nirgranthas, "unbound," 6th c. B.C.E.

    Shvetambaras, "white clad," northern and urban
    Sthanakvasis, renouncing temples and images

SACRED LITERATURE: Jaina Sutras

    Shvetambara canon in Prakrit 6th c. C.E. (portions may go back 900 years)
    Digambara canon includes material from first c. C.E.
    Later literature in Sanskrit

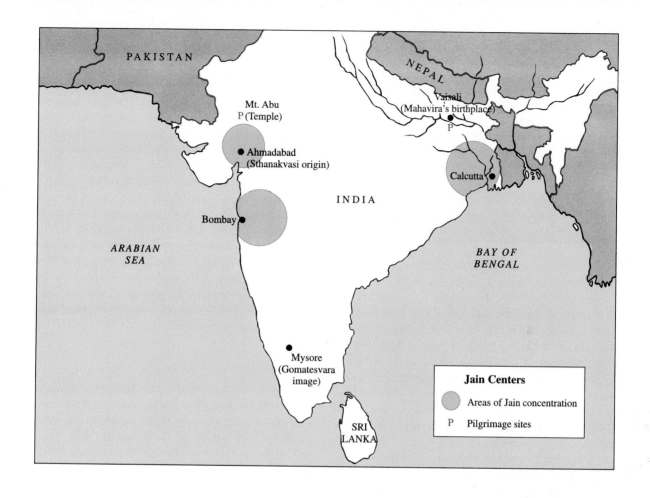

Map showing Jain Centers in India. Labeled locations include: Mt. Abu P (Temple), Ahmadabad (Sthanakvasi origin), Bombay, Mysore (Gomatesvara image), Vaisali (Mahavira's birthplace) P, and Calcutta. Surrounding regions labeled PAKISTAN, NEPAL, INDIA, SRI LANKA, ARABIAN SEA, and BAY OF BENGAL.

Jain Centers

○ Areas of Jain concentration

P Pilgrimage sites

of later days was still in the making, and when the priestly class put forward their broad claims to spiritual and social ascendancy, many, although certainly not all, in the ranks of the nobility—of whose caste Mahavira, the historical founder of Jainism, was a member—resisted these claims. The ruling classes were at that time active and able in philosophic discussion. Critical minds among them found unacceptable the monistic idealism that resolved the substantial world of everyday into a single, unknowable entity. To their commonsense eyes, each living thing and all manner of other entities were as real as they appeared to be. Humans and human souls, stones, trees, and hills, footed and flying creatures, and the fish of the sea all entered experience as realities that were independently and in their own right existent. The struggle against the monistic idealism of the Brahmins fre-

quently took the form of denying the reality of all hypothetical world souls and maintaining a position that was ultimately atheistic. Many Western authorities, therefore, think that because this view appears in the Upanishads, there must have existed a pre-Aryan dualistic worldview to which many anti-monists may have adhered—a worldview that affirmed on the one hand the reality of the physical world and on the other hand the existence of an infinite number of living souls. This position we have already identified as the minority view in the Upanishads (p. 91); it is now known as the Sankhya philosophy. It seems to have been systematized shortly before the founding of Jainism, and it is listed by the Hindus to this day as one of the six acceptable systems of philosophy (p. 111).

Mahavira belonged to the group that rejected Brahmanism and took a position like that of the

Sankhya philosophy. But he had a special commitment that led him to modify whatever convictions he had that coincided with the Sankhya point of view; he based his life on the teaching and ascetic practices of Parshva, who lived some 250 years earlier.

I. MAHAVIRA'S MANNER OF LIFE

Anyone familiar with Latin and allied tongues will see at once that Mahavira is an honorific title meaning "Great Man" or "Hero." It has quite superseded Nataputta Vardhamana, the name by which he was originally known. He is said to have been born near Vaisali (in modern Bihar) in 599 B.C.E. and to have died in 527. (These are the traditional dates set by the Shvetambara sect. However, some modern authorities think these dates are sixty years too early.) His father, it is claimed, was a rajah. Mahavira was not the oldest son—a circumstance that made it easier for him to renounce the princely life later on.

It is hard to recover the truth, of course, because of the uncertain state of the records, but the following is the story of Mahavira's life as it is told in the Shvetambara scripture, probably the older of the two main Jaina canons of sacred literature (though the chronology is debatable). The compilers of the Shvetambara canon concede that they are writing 980 years after the date of Mahavira! In any case, their story is representative of a broad range of Indian asceticism.

That Mahavira was reared in the luxury of the ancient courts of India may be gathered from the assertion that he was attended by five nurses: "a wetnurse, a nurse to bathe him, one to dress him, one to play with him, and one to carry him," and that, "transferred from the lap of one nurse to that of another, he grew up," living "in the enjoyment of the allowed, noble, fivefold joys and pleasures consisting in sound, touch, taste, color, and smell,"[A1]—the pleasures of sense he was later to renounce. He married and had a daughter. But he was not content with a prince's life. In a park outside the town dwelt a body of monks who followed the rule of the ascetic Parshva. Mahavira was much attracted to their mode of life. However, out of respect for his parents, he decided, "It will not behoove me, during the life of my parents, to enter the state of houselessness."[A2] As soon as his parents died (the legend has it that they died by careful prearrangement, in accordance with the rite of *sallakhana,* or voluntary self-starvation: "On a bed of kusa-grass they rejected all food, and their bodies dried up by the last mortification of the flesh"[A3]), Mahavira prepared to give up the princely life. He was now thirty years old, but he had to ask his brother's consent, and on the condition that he would remain in the palace one more year (thinking it over?), that consent was obtained. But he used the time to give up "his gold and silver, his troops and chariots"; he "distributed, portioned out and gave away his valuable treasures."[A4]

Joining an Ascetic Order

Then in the first month of winter, he "retired from the world." He joined the body of monks in their cells outside of the town. As part of his initiation into their order, he took off all of his ornaments and finery and retained only one garment, a robe with "a flamingo pattern." Next, he "plucked out with his right and left hands on the right and left sides of his head his hair in five handfuls." He took the required pledge, "I shall neglect my body and abandon the care of it; I shall with equanimity bear, undergo, and suffer all calamities arising from divine powers, men, or animals."[A5]

Some months after joining the order of Parshva, Mahavira went off on his own. Throwing off his robe, and thenceforth going completely naked, he began a long wandering through the villages and plains of central India in quest of release from the cycle of birth, death, and rebirth. His two convictions were (1) that saving one's soul from evil (that is, purging contaminating matter from the soul) is impossible without practicing the severest asceticism, and (2) that maintaining the purity and integrity of one's own soul involves practicing *ahimsa,* or noninjury, to any and all living beings. Neither of convictions was new, for Mahavira took them from his predecessors, but the faithfulness and sincerity with which he lived by them were remarkable.

Traveling with Goshala

Tradition says that for some years he wandered about with another naked man, Goshala Makkhali (Maskari-putra), "Goshala of the mendicant staff." Goshala was later head of the sect of Ajivakas, an ascetic group holding the strictly deterministic view that all living beings must pass without abatement or remission through rebirths lasting through 8,400,000 kalpas, unable in all of this time to alter their fate, being "bent" this way and that by an inexorable and implacable destiny, until at the end of a long, predestined ascent to a higher state, release comes automatically. There is no possibility, Goshala said, of bringing unripe karma to fruition (nor of exhausting karma already ripened) by virtuous conduct, by penance, or by chastity; there is only destiny (*niyati*). Goshala was not only fatalistic but also atheistic. There was, he said, no cause for depravity or virtue, either in one's own choices or ultimately. If he practiced nakedness and asceticism, it was because he was fated to do so; and if he fell into immorality while being an ascetic, that was fated, too.

We shall see later that this fatalistic doctrine of Goshala's aroused the determined opposition of the Buddha, when he learned of it, for he believed the opposite: that moral behavior and chastity can totally change one's karmic lot and enable one to enter Nirvana immediately after death.

The Ajivaka order, which Goshala joined and later dominated, had sufficient following to last two thousand years as a viable alternative to other faiths—Hinduism, Jainism, and Buddhism—before finally vanishing from the scene of Indian thought.

We cannot know what Goshala and Mahavira talked about; all we know is that the two naked wanderers quarreled—perhaps it was on the issue of changing one's lot by choosing to be virtuous; perhaps (who knows?) the quarrel was about Goshala's view that asceticism and sexual intercourse might be fated for the same person at the same time. Whatever the case, Mahavira went his own way, thereafter avoiding involvement with any other individual.

In moving about, Mahavira never stayed more than one night in a village or more than five in a town. He was determined to form no attachments to any

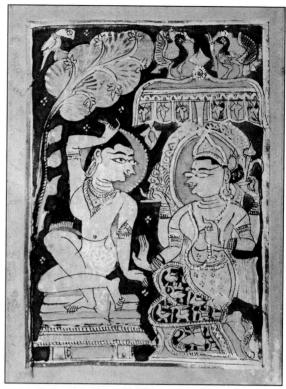

Mahavira Renouncing the World

Detail of manuscript of the *Kalpa Sutra* shows Mahavira seated beneath a tree and pulling out his hair "in five handfuls." He is attended by the god Indra, whose divinity is attested by his four arms and the canopy over his head. The unknown artist probably lived in the seventeenth century. *(Courtesy of the Museum of Fine Arts, Boston. Ross-Coomaraswamy Collection. Neg. # 17.2278.)*

place or person that might bind him to the world and its pleasures. Only during the four months of the rainy season did he remain in the same place, because then the roads and paths were teeming with life, and the principle of ahimsa required his remaining quiet.

The following passages from the Jaina documents are worthy of close study. Every phrase counts. They constitute a unique record of consistency to principle.

Meticulous Practice of *Ahimsa*

The following passage from the *Kalpa Sutra* illustrates with great vividness the unusual precautions

Mahavira took not to injure any living thing, directly or indirectly.

> Thoroughly knowing the earth-bodies and water-bodies and fire-bodies and wind-bodies, the lichens, seeds, and sprouts, he comprehended that they are, if narrowly inspected, imbued with life, and avoided to injure them.
>
> Walking, he meditated with his eyes fixed on a square space before him of the length of a man. . . . Looking a little sideward, looking a little behind, attentively looking on his path, [he walked so as not to step on any living thing].
>
> Many sorts of living beings gathered on his body, crawled about it and caused pain there. [But he exercised self-control so as not to scratch himself.]
>
> Without ceasing in his reflections, the Venerable One slowly wandered about, and, killing no creatures, he begged for his food.[A6]

Other passages condense into this picture: Mahavira apparently made it his practice, when walking, to carry a soft broom for sweeping the path wherever it might be covered with insects. Out of doors he cleared the ground before lying down to rest or sleep; inside he examined his bed to make sure it was free from eggs and living beings. He refused all raw food of any kind and took into his begging bowl only food prepared originally for someone else and left over, for if he allowed anyone to take the life out of something expressly for him, he must hold himself accountable for being the cause of the killing of a living being. He carried a cloth for straining water before drinking it, and always went carefully through a bowl of food to see if any of it was affected by eggs, sprouts, worms, mildew, cobwebs, or any living thing; if it was so affected, he removed the portions containing them before "circumspectly" eating the rest.

Rigorous Asceticism

As to the strictness with which he practiced asceticism, the next group of passages is a sufficient testimony.

> This is the rule followed by the Venerable One: When the cold season has halfway advanced, the houseless one, leaving off his robe and stretching out his arms, should wander about, not leaning against a treetrunk.

> When a cold wind blows in which some feel pain, then some houseless monks in the cold rain seek a place sheltered from the wind. "We shall put on more clothes; kindling wood, or well covered, we shall be able to bear the very painful influence of the cold." But the Venerable One desired nothing of the kind; strong in control, he suffered, despising all shelter.
>
> Sometimes in the cold season the Venerable One was meditating in the shade. In summer he [exposed] himself to the heat, he [sat] squatting in the sun.
>
> The Venerable One did not seek sleep for the sake of pleasure; he waked up himself, and slept only a little.
>
> Purgatives and emetics, anointing of the body and bathing, shampooing, and cleansing of the teeth do not behoove him.[A7]

Indifference to Abuse

Fearful of forming agreeable personal attachments, he refrained from speaking to or greeting anyone. This procured him a good deal of ill will from inquisitive villagers, but he bore all affronts with determined indifference.

> For some it is not easy to do what he did, not to answer those who salute: he was beaten with sticks, and struck by sinful people.
>
> Giving up the company of all householders whomsoever, he meditated. Asked, he gave no answer.
>
> Disregarding slights difficult to bear, the Sage wandered about, not attracted by story-tellers, pantomimes, songs, fights at the quarter-staff, and boxing matches.
>
> The dogs bit him, ran at him. Few people kept off the attacking, biting dogs. Striking the monk, they cried "Khukkhu," and made the dogs bite him.
>
> When he once sat without moving his body, they cut his flesh, tore his hair, covered him with dust. Throwing him up, they let him fall, or disturbed him in his religious postures; abandoning the care of his body, the Venerable One humbled himself.[A8]

Keeping steadfastly to this invincible self-discipline, Mahavira wandered about for twelve years, hopeful of moksha, deliverance.

Becoming a Jina (Conqueror)

The crowning experience that he sought was not withheld; it came at last. The Jaina record tells of the event with great particularity.

> During the thirteenth year, in the second month of summer, in the fourth fortnight... when the shadow had turned toward the east, ... outside the town Grimbhikagrama, on the northern bank of the river Rigupalika, in the field of the householder Samaga, in a northeastern direction from an old temple, not far from a sal tree, in a squatting position, with knees high and head low, in deep meditation, in the midst of abstract meditation, he reached Nirvana, the complete and full.[A9]

He thus became the Jina (the Conqueror), and all of his followers Jains, for he had achieved a complete "victory" over his body and the desires that bind one to this world of matter and sin.

Having attained the experience he had been twelve years in winning, Mahavira began to seek people out and teach them. Conversions to his way of life followed. And after thirty years of successful teaching and organizing, at the age of seventy-two, apparently by the rite of voluntary self-starvation (sallakhana), he "cut asunder the ties of birth, old age, and death" and was "finally liberated, freed from all pains."[A10] He is now, according to all of the Jaina sects, enjoying supreme bliss at the top of the universe to which the perfect ones go, in a state no longer subject to rebirth.

II. PHILOSOPHY AND ETHICS OF JAINISM

The story of Mahavira has been told in the previous section in the simplest way, with the smallest use of Jaina technical terms. But the followers of Mahavira thought of his course of life as operating within a philosophical and ethical context requiring for its description Jaina technical distinctions. Karma, soul, matter, salvation—all had meanings reflecting a worldview distinct from Brahmanism or Buddhism.

The Jains interpret the doctrine of karma strictly, in accordance with their idea that the consequences of one's deeds are *literally* deposited in and on the soul. Various kinds of karmas (material substances) are accumulated during this and previous births, like layers or incrustations of foreign matter that may form as many as five sheaths around the soul and must be worn off by the process of living. Or, as taught by the predecessors of Mahavira, going back to the ascetic Parshva, it is as if a rarefied material, poisonous and alien, has penetrated the soul and must be thrown off by the soul's activity.

Souls Permeated by Matter

This Jaina idea is based on a very interesting view of the relation between souls and the physical world. The latter, constituted of gross matter, space, time, the active agents of motion and rest, is the realm of non-living substance (ajivadravya), and ranges in density from solidity to the thinnest sort of substance beyond the reach of the senses; in the former case it is heavy and gross, in the latter light and volatile. Matter is eternal and consists of atoms that may cluster together into any shape or quality: earth, water, wind, sounds, colors, and sentient bodies of all sorts, including in the latter case their senses and sensations. The subtlest mode of matter is karma matter. It forms on and in the soul; whenever the latter is moved by bad desire or passion, it becomes, as it were, sticky, and gets itself covered with matter or permeated by it. Such adhesions and infiltrations of matter affect the course of transmigration, for the soul at the end of each period of existence carries the matter that vitiates its purity along with it. If it is full of matter, it sinks lower in the scale of existence, perhaps into hell; if it has only a little matter in it, it will be light enough to rise, perhaps into the heavens, and find its embodiment there in the body of some god, or rise higher still and become an eternally "liberated" being.

The soul's chief problem, that of managing to rid itself of its karma matter (which is differentiated into at least eight kinds), is in part automatically taken care of simply by the karmas exerting their effects and passing off. But the ethical activity of the soul annihilates the old karmas more swiftly, and at the same time (because any action creates a new karma) produces only those new karmas that have the briefest effects and are quickly dissipated or neutralized.

Two-Tiered Pluralism

The major fact of life that emerges from all of this is the inherent opposition of soul and flesh, mind and matter. Mahavira and his followers were pluralists, but they grouped all things into two distinct categories: (1) the ajiva, or lifeless things in the universe, especially the realm of thick, dead matter, and (2) the jiva, or living beings in the universe, to be defined more precisely as the infinite multitude of individual souls composing the realm of spirit (or living substance). The ajiva is eternal yet evil, but the jiva, also eternal, is of an infinite value, and contains all good, for souls are indestructible and infinitely precious.

Souls are classified according to the number of senses they have. Those having five senses—gods, humans, animals, and hell beings—are in the highest group. Next are the four-sensed beings, the larger insects, such as bees, flies, and butterflies. Without sight and hearing, the third group includes moths and the smaller insects. The group of two-sensed beings, possessing touch and taste, includes worms, shellfish, leeches, and minute creatures. A final group with only the sense of touch is often referred to in Jaina writings; it includes vegetables, trees, seeds, lichens, earth bodies, wind bodies, water bodies, and fire bodies.

The Liberated Soul (*Siddha*)

In their pure state, when entirely liberated from matter, all souls are perfect, possessing infinite perception, infinite knowledge, infinite power, and infinite bliss. When liberated, they rise through the universe (which is held to be shaped like a human body), and come to dwell in an umbrella-like place (the top of the skull?), known structurally as Isatpragbhara ("slightly convex") or spiritually as the Siddha-sila ("the home of the perfect ones").

The Siddhas that have entered this eternal home are not reduced to nothingness, for though they may be described as being without qualities or relations of any sort, there is no cessation of consciousness in them. "The liberated," so runs a Jaina text, "is not long nor small . . . neither heavy nor light; he is without body, without resurrection, without contact with matter; he is not feminine, nor masculine, nor neuter; he perceives, he knows, but there is no analogy (whereby to know the

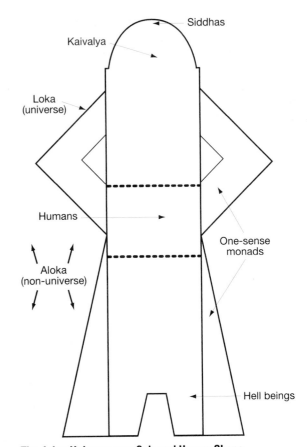

The Jaina Universe as a Colossal Human Shape
Jiva life monads float lower or higher as they accumulate or shed heavy karmic matter.

nature of the liberated soul)."[A11] And there, without further ado, the text lets the matter rest, as well it might!

No Transcendent Aid

Being indestructible and absolutely independent, souls are not phases of nor emanations thrown out by something else. The Jains from the beginning have held that there is no Brahman-Atman such as the Brahmins describe. Even if Substance, in a vast flow, holds the universe together, there is no Supreme Ruler of the world, such as the devout look to. There are numerous higher beings who might be called "gods" and who exist on the various levels of the celestial regions, but they are finite beings, subject like human beings to rebirth. No help, Mahavira taught, could be expected from such beings, themselves in need of redemption. Therefore human souls caught in the predicament of existence in the physical world and needing to find a way of escape from karma through moksha, or release, must realize that salvation is self-attained. Praying to the gods is of no avail.

> A monk or nun should not say, "The god of the sky! The god of the thunderstorm! The god of lightning! The god who begins to rain! . . . May rain fall, or may it not fall! May the crops grow! May the sun rise!" They should not use such speech. But, knowing the nature of things, he should say, "The air; a cloud has gathered, or come down; the cloud has rained."[A12]

It is no use to turn to other people, or to the words of others, for salvation. The priests are of no special authority. The Vedas are not especially sacred and cannot be used as miraculous agencies of release from rebirth. Rather than trust to these external aids, let each person realize that salvation lies within one's self. "Man," runs one of Mahavira's most emphatic utterances, "thou art thine own friend. Why wishest thou for a friend beyond thyself?"[A13]

The surest and swiftest way to reach liberation or moksha is through the power accumulated from the practice of asceticism or austerities (*tapas*). What Mahavira meant by asceticism may be seen from his own practice of it. His followers have added fasting according to certain rules and types of meditation leading to a trance state marked by complete dissociation from the outer world and transcendence of one's own physical states. This trance state is supposed to be like the one Mahavira entered in the thirteenth year of his seeking, which assured him of his final deliverance. One cannot reach such a state, the Jains hold, without complete control of the mind and passions, for acts cannot be controlled and karmas be prevented thereby from accumulating unless the mind is so controlled as to be purified of all desire for or dependence upon the world and its objects, animate and inanimate.

The Five Great Vows

Mahavira's ascetic practice was summed up (probably not by himself) in the "Five Great Vows" for monks.

These vows were later written out in very full form. In these fuller statements,[A14] there are some interesting definitions of what Mahavira meant by ahimsa and the breaking off of every attachment to the world and its objects. Ahimsa is the subject of the first vow.

> 1. The first great vow, Sir, runs thus: I renounce all killing of living beings, whether movable or immovable. Nor shall I myself kill living beings nor cause others to do it, nor consent to it. As long as I live I confess, and blame, and exempt myself of these sins, in mind, speech, and body.

There are five clauses:

> A **Nirgrantha** [ascetic; literally, naked one] is careful in his walk, not careless.
>
> A Nirgrantha searches into his mind. If his mind is sinful, acting on impulse, produces quarrels, pains, he should not employ such a mind.
>
> A Nirgrantha searches into his speech. If his speech is sinful, produces quarrels, pains, he should not utter such speech.
>
> A Nirgrantha is careful in laying down his utensils of begging.
>
> A Nirgrantha eats and drinks after inspecting his food and drink. If a Nirgrantha would eat and drink without inspecting his food and drink, he might hurt and displace or injure or kill all sorts of living beings.

The second vow concerns truth speaking.

> 2. I renounce all vices of lying speech arising from anger or greed or fear or mirth. I shall neither myself speak lies, nor cause others to speak lies, nor consent to the speaking of lies by others.

There are five clauses subjoined to this vow also, and they provide that a Nirgrantha should speak only after deliberation, so as to be sure the words are true; should never be angry, greedy, nor fearful, lest these emotions betray one into falsehood; and should not be given to mirth making, or, as we would say, "joking" or "kidding," because these forms of diversion are based on departures from fact.

> 3. The third great vow runs thus: I renounce all taking of anything not given, either in a village or a town or a wood, either of little or much, of great

or small, of living or lifeless things. I shall neither take myself what is not given, nor cause others to take it, nor consent to their taking it.

Again there are five clauses, enjoining severe self-restraint upon every form of greed.

4. The fourth great vow runs thus: I renounce all sexual pleasure. I shall not give way to sensuality, nor cause others to do so, nor consent to it in others.

The five clauses under this vow explain how a Nirgrantha refuses, even in the remotest way, to feel the allure of sex.

5. The fifth vow runs thus: I renounce all attachments, whether to little or much, small or great, living or lifeless things; neither shall I myself form such attachments, nor cause others to do so, nor consent to their doing so.

The clauses of this startlingly comprehensive vow may be condensed as follows:

If a creature with ears hears agreeable and disagreeable sounds, it should not be attached to, nor delighted with, nor disturbed by the sounds. If it is impossible not to hear sounds which reach the ear, the mendicant should avoid love or hate originated by them.

If a creature with eyes sees forms, if a creature with an organ of smell smells smells, if a creature with a tongue tastes tastes, if a creature with an organ of feeling feels agreeable or disagreeable touches, it should not be attached to them, (and) should avoid love or hate originated by them.

Of these vows the most radically ascetic is the last. The vows concerning ahimsa and the renunciation of all sexual pleasures are important, too. The renunciation of sexuality was stressed by Mahavira, who is quoted as saying, "The greatest temptation [sic] in the world are women. . . . Men forsooth say, 'These are the vessels of happiness.' But this leads them to pain, to delusion, to death, to hell, to birth as hellbeings or brute beasts."[A15] The language is sufficiently strong. Nevertheless, the fifth vow is more inclusive, and by implication contains all the rest. It does in fact make sure that, though as a monk one may be in the world, one is emphatically not of it.

Rules for Layfolk

It was obvious from the beginning that the Five Great Vows could be only for Jaina ascetics. For the layfolk, to whom the way of life prescribed in the severer code is impossible, the Jaina leaders have laid down a much modified rule of life. The lay adherents are to make twelve vows: (1) never to take the life of a sentient creature knowingly (hence, never to till the soil, nor engage in butchering, fishing, brewing, or any occupation involving the taking of life); (2) never to lie; (3) never to steal, or take what is not given; (4) never to be unchaste (or, to put it positively, always to be faithful to husband, or wife, and be pure in thought and word); (5) to check greed, by placing a limit upon one's wealth and giving away any excess; (6) to avoid temptation to sin by, for example, refraining from unnecessary travel; (7) to limit the number of things in daily use; (8) to be on guard against evils that can be avoided; (9) to keep stated periods for meditation; (10) to observe special periods of self-denial; (11) to spend occasional days as a monk; and (12) to give alms, especially in support of ascetics. Of these vows the first is undoubtedly the most important in its social effect. It constituted a limitation that must have seemed serious to the early followers of Mahavira, but at long last it actually proved to have economic as well as religious worth, for the Jains found they could make higher profits when they turned from occupations involving direct harm to living creatures to careers in business (in modern terms, as bankers, lawyers, merchants, and proprietors of land). The other moral restrictions of their creed—which prohibited gambling, eating meat, drinking wine, adultery, hunting, thieving, and debauchery—earned them social respect and thus contributed to their survival in the social scene.

III. MAHAVIRA'S FOLLOWERS

So great was the impression that Mahavira made upon his followers that legend grew rapidly about him. His birth was regarded as supernatural. He was declared to be the last of a long series of savior beings called Tirthankaras. He descended from heaven to enter the womb of a woman. When the gods discovered that this woman was a Brahmin, and therefore unworthy to bear the future "corrector" of Brahmanism, they transferred the embryo to the womb of a woman of the Kshatriya caste. He grew up sinless ("whatever is sinful, the Venerable One left that undone"[A16]) and was omniscient ("he knew and saw all conditions of all living beings in the world"[A17]).

Yet as time passed, the eminence of Mahavira was a little obscured by the veneration accorded to the twenty-three Tirthankaras who were thought to have preceded him. Parshva, his immediate predecessor, and hence the twenty-third "ford-finder" (which is what the term *Tirthankara* means), had a great temple erected in his honor on Mt. Parasnath, bearing his name, two hundred miles northwest of Calcutta. Nemi, the twenty-second, had another erected to him upon the cliff under Mt. Girnar, far in western India on the peninsula of Kathiawar. Two very holy shrines, one on Mt. Satrunjaya near Palitana, in Kathiawar, and another on the plateau of Mt. Abu in the Aravalli Hills, have been built to honor Rishabha, the first of the Tirthankaras. Although the only cultus that accords with Jainist theory is "a kind of memorial service in honor of the teacher of the way of salvation,"[B] these temples are of elaborate and distinguished design. Jainism has come, in fact, to hold a prominent place in the architectural history of India. Other temples besides those mentioned—like the ones at Ahmedabad and Ajmer in western India and a monolithic shrine of exquisite beauty at Kaligamalai in south India—have become showplaces of Indian architecture.

Three Sects

Early in the history of the faith, the Jains were divided on the question of wearing clothes. The Shvetambaras, or "the white-clad," were the liberals who took their stand on wearing at least one garment, whereas the stricter and more conservative Digambaras got their name from their insistence on going about, whenever religious duty demanded it, "clad in atmosphere." (Specifically, the occasions requiring nudity are the following: while being a monk, when on pilgrimage, or during religious fasts and rituals. The Digambaras say that any monk who owns property or wears clothes cannot reach Isatpragbhara.) The Shvetambaras were

in the north and yielded a bit both to the cold winds and to the social and cultural influences of the Ganges River plain. The Digambaras, not looked at askance by the Dravidian residents of their southland, have more easily maintained the earlier, sterner attitudes down the years. Another difference exists in the fact that whereas the Shvetambaras admit women to their monastic order and assume that they have a chance to experience moksha, the Digambaras cling to Mahavira's reputed verdict that women are "the greatest temptation in the world" and "the cause of all sinful acts." They are therefore not to be admitted to temples or to monastic life. Women, in this latter view, cannot win salvation until they have been reborn as men. That is their only hope.

Still another Jaina sect, the Sthanakvasis, tolerate no idols and have no temples. They worship "everywhere," mainly through meditation and introspection.

Monks and Laity Not Widely Separated

In general, on the Jainist principle of the equal value of all souls, human or animal, Jaina monks and laypersons are not sharply set off from each other. It is still the custom for laypersons to fast as monks at least once a year, and monks are simply laypersons who have adopted a severer self-discipline. The laity also participates with monks in the recurring events of the Jaina calendar. On the last day of their year (about the end of August) monks and laity, for example, together abstain from all food and drink and take time to review and repent of the wrongdoing and misspent hours of the past year, asking forgiveness from those wronged and paying debts. This communal act of repentance (the Paryushana) is the next day followed by a time of general rejoicing—the New Year's Day of the Jains. Other celebrations recur at longer intervals. In Mysore, for instance, where the Digambaras are largely located, every twelve years the fifty-seven-foot monolithic statue of Gomatesvara, one of the Tirthankaras, has his head anointed from the top of a scaffolding behind him by the contents of over one thousand pots of milk, curds, and sandal paste, amid the shouted acclaim of Jaina bystanders, who hope for an increase of their merit from this expression of gratitude.

Jaina Temple in Calcutta

The decorative details of this sumptuous temple in Calcutta, with its architectural elements adopted from all over the world (witness the Corinthian columns), reflect the wealth of the Jains of the great eastern city of India. Note the naked elephant-borne monks in the pavilion, who symbolize renunciation of wealth. *(Courtesy of Trans World Airlines.)*

It is generally held by Jains that the universe is eternal and that it does not periodically appear, run its course, and then disappear into a period of nullity, a pralaya (see p. 95). But they believe it does go through long periods of improvement and decline. They say that the golden age of humanity lies far in the past and that we are now in the fifth and next-to-last twenty-one-thousand-year period of steady decline; we are shorter of stature than we once were, nastier, more immoral, more than ever in need of the restraints of governmental power, and we will continue to degenerate until the sixth period of decline is past. Only then will we begin slowly to improve, period by period, until after over one hundred thousand years the golden age will return once more.

Distinctive Jaina Logic

Meanwhile, Jaina philosophy has had some effect on the thought of India at large, especially in the realm of logic. The effect has been that of curbing any tendency to over-statement. Jainist logic considers all knowledge relative and transient. To every question one may answer with both yes and no. No proposition is either absolutely true or false. The Jains are fond of their ancient illustration of the logical fallacy inherent in all human thought—the story of the six blind men who put their hands on different parts of an elephant and concluded, each to his own satisfaction, that the elephant was exactly "like a fan," "like a wall," "like a snake," "like a rope," and so on. It is only the free and purified soul, gone to the Jainist heaven, that possesses perfect knowledge.

Today the Jains number approximately 4.9 million, most residing in the Bombay area, where in early life Mahatma Gandhi felt their influence on his own outlook. The paradox of their present status is, as already indicated, that their essentially world-renouncing religion has, in the course of events, secured their economic advantage among the struggling masses of India. By the extension of the *ahimsa* principle, the Jains also find themselves taking the lead in the promotion of anti-nuclear and environmental preservationist causes.

GLOSSARY*

ahimsa (ŭ-hĭm′-zŭ) noninjury; abstention from violence and killing

ajiva (ŭ-jēv′-ŭ) nonliving, insentient matter

Ajivakas (ŭ-jĭv′-ŭ-kŭz) a determinist and an atheist order of ascetics

Digambaras (dĭg-äm′-bŭ-rŭz) literally, "clothed in air," a sect of Jainism in southern India

Goshala Makkhali (gō-shŭl′-ŭ mŭk-kŭl-ĭ) fatalist and atheist one-time companion of Mahavira; later dominated the Ajivaka order

Jina (jē′-nŭ) Victor, title of one who conquers the desires, binding souls to the world of matter

jiva (jē′-vŭ) in Jainism, the life monad, finite and permanent, recipient of karmic effects; the soul

kalpa a cosmic era; in Jainism, a "spoke" on the wheel of cyclical enhancement and deterioration

Kalpa Sutra a segment of the Shvetambara canon of scripture recounting the lives of the *Jinas*

karma action-consequence; in Jainism, a subtle mode of matter deposited in or on the soul

Mahavira 6th c. B.C.E. founder of Jainism, the twenty-fourth *Tirthankara* (personal name: Nataputta Vardhamana)

Nirgrantha (nēr-grän′-tŭ) literally, "unclothed one"; an ascetic

niyati mechanistically determined fate or destiny

Parshva 9th c. B.C.E. ascetic, predecessor of Mahavira; the twenty-third *Thirtankara* of Jainism

pralaya (prŭ′-lŭ-yŭ) a time of nullity or rest for the universe at the end of a period of dissolution

sallakhana (sūl-läk′-hŭ-nŭ) Jaina ritual suicide

Shvetambaras (shvāt-ŭm′-bŭ-rŭz) literally, "white-clad"; northern Jaina sect

Siddha a perfected one, a being who has obtained moksha

Siddha-sila Jaina "home of the perfected ones" under the dome at the apex of the universe

Sthanakvasis (stän′-ŭk-vŭ′-sēz) Jaina sect that worships without images or temples

Tirthankaras (tērt-hän′-kŭr-rŭz) literally, "ford-finders," the twenty-four Jaina hero Siddhas who showed the way to moksha

* For a guide to pronunciation, refer to page 99.

Buddhism
in Its First Phase
Moderation
in World Renunciation

The single term *Buddhism* refers to a diverse array of beliefs and practices and implies a degree of uniformity that does not exist. Like the Hindus, the Buddhists, when referring to what the West calls "Buddhism" or the "Buddhist religion," use the term Dharma (*Pali Dhamma*)—literally, "the norm, that which is true." Their only difference from the Hindus in this respect lies in their linking of this term with the teaching and moral injunctions of one man, Gautama Buddha. An alternative term is *Sasana,* which means the whole body of beliefs and practices of the Buddhist faith, broadly the Buddhist "dispensation" or "system."

Though it arose a generation later than Jainism, in the lengthening perspective of time Buddhism seems contemporaneous. Moreover, it shares with Jainism some of its deepest motives. Like Jainism it was a movement looking toward liberation of the self from the suffering entailed in living in the world. It also was a step toward independence of thought and action, springing from the Kshatriya caste and appealing to all classes and conditions of men. Like Mahavira, the monk Gautama found the philosophy of the Brahmins unacceptable and their claims unsubstantiated. He, too, came to deny the doctrine of the saving efficacy of the Vedas and of the ritual observances based upon them, and he challenged the claim of the Brahmin priesthood to prescriptive rights in showing the way to salvation.

But though Buddhism's similarities with Jainism are in some respects close, the differences in other respects are wide. Where one faith fixed its whole hope on an uncompromising and extreme asceticism, the other found deliverance in a moderate and commonsense "middle way." To the Buddha, extreme asceticism was not common sense, any more than sensuality was. Coolly and objectively, he tested every way of salvation offered by the teachers and spiritual leaders of his time, and he refused to be swept away into any vagary of religious behavior, however logically self-consistent.

WESTERN NAME: *Buddhism*
FOUNDER: *Siddhartha Gautama, ca. 563–483 B.C.E.*
LANGUAGE: *Pali*
NAMES USED BY THE FOUNDING COMMUNITY:
  The *Dhamma,* "teaching"

    The *Sasana,* "system"
    Later, *Tri-Ratna,* "The Three Jewels"
    The *Buddha,* "enlightened one"
    The *Dhamma,* "teaching"
    The *Sangha,* "order of monks/nuns"

EARLY SACRED LITERATURE: The *Tripitaka* (written canon complete *ca.* first c. C.E.)
PRINCIPAL SUBDIVISIONS:

    THERAVADA (Pali) "The Way of the Elders"; also Sthaviravada (Sanskrit)
    Later: HINAYANA, "Small Vehicle"
    MAHAYANA, "Great Vehicle," from *ca.* second c. B.C.E. from a forerunner, the *Mahasanghika,* the "Great Order"

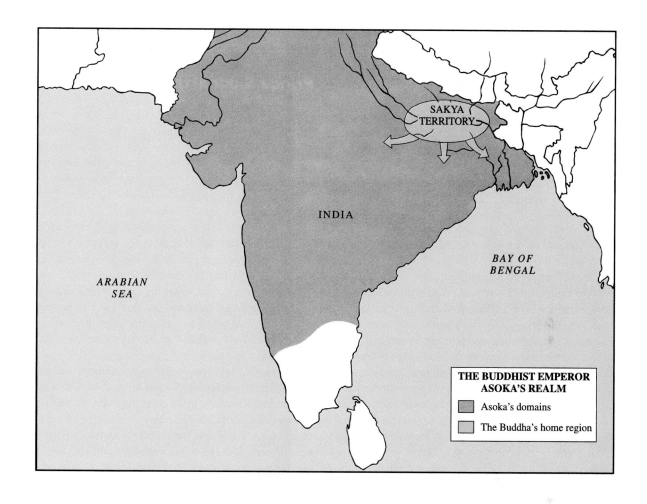

THE BUDDHIST EMPEROR ASOKA'S REALM
▨ Asoka's domains
▨ The Buddha's home region

I. LIFE OF THE FOUNDER

A Note About Sources

As in the case of Mahavira (and we shall find the same precaution advisable in other cases that will come before us), the reader must be on guard not to accept the traditional biographies uncritically. The historical personages who founded the great religions have been lovingly and reverently recalled by their followers, who have had a very human need to visualize them clearly, and have therefore unconsciously added to the accounts handed down to them the details that did this for them. It will be well if the reader says, "Here is the story that millions have taken for truth *and have lived by.*"

It should be emphasized that historical assessment of South Asian religious texts has only recently begun, and until there is something like completion of the critical analysis of the records of these religions, it will be necessary to remain in a state of skeptical suspense.

As to India, the probability is that this suspense will always have to continue, for since the peoples of India have been more idea centered than history minded, the difficulty of distilling historical truth from tradition is increased. This difficulty is, moreover, made much greater by the fact that oral transmission was the principal means of preserving literature and learning for many centuries. Even when sacred texts were put in writing (*ca.* third century B.C.E.?), they were considered somehow inferior to orally

161

transmitted materials, because the voice of an under-standing person reciting sacred texts could impart meanings and nuances not apprehended through the eye alone. The relative lateness of written transmission obviously magnifies the uncertainties of textual criticism also.

Parallel Accounts

There is a kind of parallel between the lives of Mahavira and the Buddha that led some early scholars to regard the two men as identical. Both were, for instance (*if* we are to accept the traditional accounts), born to a high station as members of prominent Kshatriya families; both experienced dissatisfaction with their lot, and though married and having one child, abandoned their homes and became wandering mendicant monks; both rejected the monistic idealism of the Brahmins; both founded monastic orders that ruled out caste distinctions; both were nonconformists from the Hindu point of view because they denied the special sacredness of the Vedic literature. Some of the parallels might be due to the fact that they both came from districts north of the Ganges where Aryan dominance was still being resisted and where Brahmanism was questioned. But it is now evident that they differed more pronouncedly than they agreed, that insofar as they were alike in careers and in beliefs, it was due partly to the similarity imposed upon them by their times and environment, and partly to sheer coincidence.

It is significant that in each case their followers set down their doctrines initially not in classical Sanskrit, the language of the Aryans, but in local dialects mixed with Sanskrit, Ardhamagadhi in the case of Jainism, Pali in the case of Buddhism.

However, in the following pages, the names of places and persons and most terms appearing in Buddhist discourse will usually be given in Sanskrit, with Pali spelling indicated when deemed advisable. Because the Sanskrit spellings have generally been used throughout all East Asia as well as in the later Buddhist literature of India, resorting to them is less confusing in an introduction than using spellings that reflect local pronunciation.

Prince Siddhartha

Siddhartha (Pali, Siddhartta) was the given name and Gautama (Pali, Gotama) the family name of the founder of Buddhism. He was perhaps born in 563 B.C.E. in northern India, some one hundred miles from Benares, in a fertile tract of country among the foothills of the Himalayas. One of the titles of the prince was to be Shakyamuni, "sage of the Shakyas," for his father was a chieftain of the Shakya clan—a tradition that gains credibility from the fact that a more distinguished pedigree could have been invented. The various Shakya families held their territory in joint control, their practice being to make political decisions in "full and frequent" assemblies. His mother reportedly died when he was a few days old, and an aunt became his stepmother through marriage with his father.

Legend has been prolifically at work on the scanty facts concerning the childhood of Gautama Siddhartha. Tradition insists that the father hoped his son would become "a universal monarch," the emperor of all India. But if this was in actual fact his expectation, it was doomed to disappointment. The young Gautama was possessed of a clear, analytic mind and sensitive spirit. He was destined to become more and more a stranger in the house of his father. The traditions undoubtedly exaggerate the luxury that surrounded him, but there is probably some truth in the stock phrases with which Gautama was afterward credited: "I wore garments of silk and my attendants held a white umbrella over me."[A1] It is hardly true, as later tradition asserts, that his father was a "king" who built "three palaces" for his son. It may well be that a chieftain's residence would not be located at a remote site but right by the market square.[A2] At sixteen, or as some accounts say, at nineteen, he married a cousin, a neighboring "princess." Legend declares that she was "majestic as a queen of heaven, constant ever, cheerful night and day, full of dignity and exceeding grace,"[B1] a paragon of wifely devotion. But inwardly Gautama became increasingly uneasy. Sometime during his twenties he seems secretly to have made up his mind to "go out from the household life into the homeless state" of the religious mendicant, and when, in his late twenties, his wife bore him a son, he must have felt free to follow his secret inclination.

The Four Passing Sights

This determination to renounce the household life has presented an interesting problem to Buddhist believers. Why, they have asked, did the fortunate prince, with so devoted a wife and father and so young a son, resolve nevertheless to renounce life under the same roof with them? With true psychological insight, they have looked for the cause not only in the spiritual reaction of the young prince to his immediate surroundings, which were of the most pleasant, but to life itself as every man must live it, whether prince or pauper. They have developed the famous legend of "the Four Passing Sights."

There are many variants of this story; the best known appears in the Jataka tales and runs something like this: Gautama's father was forewarned by soothsayers at the time of the prince's birth that his son might give up the household life and become a houseless monk, but that, on the other hand, should he be kept from taking such a step, he might become the emperor of all India ("a universal monarch"). So the father saw to it that the young prince should never experience the severities and sorrows of life, nor know the sad fact that turns so many to religion, the fact, namely, that human life is cut short by old age, disease, and death. Gautama was surrounded by young attendants. His father built him three palaces, "and in the enjoyment of great magnificence he lived, as the seasons changed, in each of these palaces."[C1] So successful was the father in keeping out of sight the aged and the sick, so thoroughly did he clear from the highways all but youths and maidens when the prince went riding, that the latter grew up in ignorance of the common fate of mortals, the constant imminence of old age, disease, and death.

The gods, looking down from the heavens and knowing that they must take a hand in the affair, sent one of their number down to earth to assume the shapes that should awaken the young prince to his true destiny. The god appeared suddenly by the wayside one day in the form of a very feeble and decrepit old man.

The prince ordered the charioteer to tell him what it was they saw, and learned for the first time of the miserable close of every person's life. On another day the prince saw the second apparition, that of a loathsomely diseased man, and knew for the first time how physical illness and misery may attend mortals all the days of their lives. The third sight was that of a dead man being carried along to a funeral pyre, and the prince came to know of the dreadful fact of death. These three awful sights robbed him of all peace of mind. (It is a fact, and perhaps the legend is based upon it, that in one of the oldest passages in the Buddhist writings he is reported as saying, "I also am subject to decay and am not free from the power of old age, sickness and death. Is it right that I should feel horror, repulsion and disgust when I see another in such plight? And when I reflected thus, my disciples, all the joy of life which there is in life died within me.")[D1]

Alarmed at the depression of spirit under which the prince labored, his father sought to cheer him with elaborate entertainment, but without success. The prince remained distraught until he beheld the fourth sight, that of a calm ascetic in a yellow robe, walking toward him as he sat under a tree by the roadside. From this person, who had gained true peace of soul, he learned how freedom from the miseries of old age, disease, and death may be won. Then, it is said, the prince made the resolve to go out from the household life into the homeless state.

The Great Renunciation

"In all the beauty of my early prime," an early passage runs, "with a wealth of coal-black hair untouched by grey—despite the wishes of my parents, who wept and lamented—I cut off my hair and beard, donned the yellow robe and went forth from home to homelessness."[E1] The Buddhist legends tell in loving detail of the struggle by which the decision to renounce his high place in the world was reached: how his father ordered dancing girls to entertain the brooding prince, but all in vain, for the prince sat silently on the couch until all the dancing girls had fallen exhausted to the floor and passed into deep slumber; how the prince then rose and stepped with inward disgust over the

Scenes from the Life of the Buddha
Asian. Sculpture, Relief. Indian, Nagarjuna konda, Andhra. 3rd century. The Great Departure, and Budda's Temptation by Mara and His Daughters. Marble. H. 56¾ inches, W. 36¼ inches. Amaranati School. *(The Metropolitan Museum of Art, Fletcher Fund, 1928.)*

sprawling forms of the sleepers, and made his way to his wife's apartment. There, gazing silently down on the sleeping mother with the infant Rahula at her side, he bade an unspoken farewell. Then, in what is called "the Great Going Forth," he went out to leap on his great white horse and ride away, with his charioteer pacing at his side, to a far place, beyond a river. Having shaved off his hair and beard and exchanged his rich garments for the coarse yellow robe, he sent back his charioteer and plunged into the forest, one of the great

anonymous group of mendicants vowed to seek deliverance from the cares of mortal existence.

Thus began a six-year period of intensive struggle for the realization of salvation.

The Six Years of Quest

The legends imply he was anxious not to reject the Brahmin philosophy until he had tested it. He went first to Rajagaha, the royal city of the province of

Magadha, and became the disciple in turn of two ascetic teachers living in hillside caves. With them he evidently practiced various Yoga disciplines. The first teacher, the ascetic Alara Kalama, taught him of "the realm of nothingness" to which a man might attain if he followed "the stages of meditation." But Gautama was disappointed; the temper of his mind was too objective and practical. So he went on to the second teacher, the ascetic Uddaka Ramaputta, who discoursed of "the state of neither-ideation-nor-non-ideation," with no better results.[E2] In the end, convinced that these teachers would not conduct him to the true way of enlightenment, he withdrew and resolved to test the extreme bodily asceticism which Jainism, among other sects, was then advocating.

After a short period of wandering, he entered a grove at Uruvela, past which flowed a clear river with, "hard by, a village for sustenance."[E3] There, sitting under the trees, he undertook for five years such rigorous self-discipline that life itself almost left him, and he became mere skin and bones. His theory, according to the earliest accounts, was that the mind becomes clearer as the body becomes more disciplined, for, thought he, "It is just as if there were a green sappy stick in the water, and a man came along with his drill-stick, set on lighting a fire and making a blaze. Do you think he could succeed by rubbing with his drill-stick that green sappy stick from the water? Toil and moil as he may, he couldn't. It is just the same with all recluses or brahmins whose lives are not lived aloof from pleasures of sense in the matter of their bodies."[E4] On the other hand, he reasoned, recluses whose lives are lived aloof from pleasures of sense find that the dry light of understanding may flame up in them at last.

Undoubtedly, ample allowance must be made for historical exaggeration, but it is said Gautama now sat with set teeth and tongue pressed against his palate seeking "by sheer force of mind" to "restrain, coerce, and dominate" his heart, until "the sweat streamed" from his armpits.[E5] He practiced restraint of breath until he heard a roaring in his head and felt as if a sword were boring into his skull; violent pain almost drove him senseless, and still no insight came. He lived for periods on all sorts of nauseous foods, dressed in chafing and irritating garments, stood for days in one posture, or, having squatted, moved asquat. He sat on

a couch of thorns, lay in a cemetery on charred bones among rotting bodies, let dirt and filth accumulate on his body till it dropped off of itself, and even ate his own excrement in the extremity of self-discipline. He reduced his diet to "only one hemp grain" or "a single grain of rice" or "one jujube fruit" a day. He became excessively thin. The *Majjhima Nikaya* credits him with the following vivid words of self-description: "When I was living on a single fruit a day, my body grew emaciated in the extreme; [my limbs became] like the knotted joints of withered creepers; like a buffalo's hoof were my shrunken buttocks; like the twists in a rope were my spinal vertebrae; like the rafters of a tumble-down roof were my gaunt ribs; like the starry gleams on water deep down in the depths of a well, so shone my gleaming eyes deep down in the depths of their sockets; and as the rind of a cut gourd shrinks and shrivels in the heat, so shrank and shrivelled the scalp of my head. . . . If I sought to feel my belly, it was my backbone which I found in my grasp."[E6]

Abandoning Ascetic Extremes

Such extraordinary self-mortification should have produced results, if the psychological theory we found him adopting was sound, namely, that meditation pursued diligently in a rigorously disciplined body brought one to the goal, but to Gautama's great distress of mind he was as far from enlightenment as ever. According to the Majjhima Nikaya, he thought to himself, "With all these severe austerities, I fail to transcend ordinary human limits and to rise to the heights of noblest understanding and vision. Could there be another path to Enlightenment"?[E7] Meanwhile, five other ascetics had joined him, hoping that he would share his knowledge with them. While they watched, he rose one day from his seat to go down to the stream, and fainted dead away. The five ascetics gathered round his motionless body and thought, "He will die. The ascetic Gautama will die." They wondered if he had now entered Nirvana. But he came to, and after lying in the shallow water near the bank of the stream, he was sufficiently refreshed in mind and body to begin life anew. With the objectivity of view that marked him all his life, he now concluded that the way of self-mortification had failed, that his body could not support his intellect, and that he would eat and drink and strengthen it.[B2] So he took his begging bowl in hand and resumed the life of a *paribbajaka* (wandering mendicant). While sitting under a banyan tree, exhausted and emaciated, he aroused the compassion of a young village girl, Sujata by name, who gave him a bowl of rice cooked in milk that she had prepared as an offering. He accepted it. Meanwhile the five ascetics had been outraged at his self-indulgence. With indignant words they departed for Benares, saying that luxuriousness had reclaimed him and that, in abandoning the struggle, he had become a backslider.

But though he had returned to common sense, Gautama could not rejoice. Six years of search along the two most widely recognized roads to salvation known to India, philosophic meditation and bodily asceticism, had yielded no results. But he did not give up the struggle. His thinking now became much more profound and meaningful.

The Great Enlightenment

He turned aside at a place now called Bodh-gaya, into a grove, and sat down at the foot of a fig tree (a tree that came to be known as the Knowledge- or Bodhi-tree, or more simply the Bo-tree), and there he entered upon a process of meditation that was to affect the thinking of millions of people after him. The Buddhist books insist that he set his teeth and said to himself determinedly, "Though skin, nerves, and bone shall waste away, and life-blood itself be dried up, here sit I till I attain Enlightenment."[A2]

On the other hand, a psychobiographer might suggest that up to this point Gautama had tried too hard altogether, so that his very determination stood between him and the state of consciousness he desired, but now, in the face of self-defeat, his will relaxed, he let his mind wander back over his previous experience. Some such questions as these might have arisen in his mind: What was he to think of his life and his search for salvation until now? Why had he failed?

And suddenly, the answer came. His inability to experience release from his suffering was due to desire (*trishna*, Pali *tanha*, "thirst," "craving"), constantly and painfully thwarted. But to eliminate misery-producing desire he must determine its causes and prevent them from issuing in the characteristic craving or thirst. A desire might have many causes, but they would be determinable. In fact, he could see that the whole context of life and thought in which he had lived abounded in causes of desire and suffering.

Gautama's focusing upon desire was anticipated in the Upanishads. Yajnavalkya says in the *Brihadaranyaka* that one's actions (karma) are motivated by one's desires. If one's desires attach one to this world, one will return repeatedly after death in other forms, until one has eliminated earthly desires by desiring *only* Brahman-Atman; then one will go forever to Nirvana. But the Buddha's emphasis was on the psychological rather than the metaphysical aspects of desiring; he connected desire with frustration and pain, and focused on this fact.

A Cosmic Interpretation

The Buddhist traditions seek to illustrate this fact by setting the future Buddha symbolically in a predicament of cosmic scope. It supposes Gautama to have been approached by the Evil One in the person of Mara, the god of Desire and Death, tempting him (i.e., seeking to cause him) to give up his quest and succumb to pleasure. The tempter brought his three voluptuous daughters accompanied by a sensuous retinue of dancers, and when they failed to beguile Gautama, he assumed his most terrible aspect and summoned a host of demons to assist him in terrifying the future Buddha and arousing at least his desire to cling to life. They assailed him with wind and rain and hurled at him such deadly missiles as uprooted trees, boiling mud, fiery rocks, live coals, and glowing ashes that turned the pitch-black darkness incandescent. But the future Buddha was sitting on an "immovable" spot under the great fig tree and remained himself unmoved. The deadly missiles entered his consciousness as sprays of flowers. In the end it was the Evil One who was affrighted, for when the unmoved one touched the fingers of his right hand to the ground ("calling the earth to witness"), a sound as of a hundred thousand roars thundered up from the sympathetic earth, and the Evil One fled.[F] Shortly thereafter, full enlightenment (*Bodhi*) came to him who sat so serenely under the Bo-Tree, for he realized that desire arises in the context twelve-linked chain of causation but that he had escaped from it into a new life, a higher form of consciousness, freed of desire and its attendant suffering.

Ecstatic Experiences

Whatever the process of his thought, he was now without desire. He felt no sensual yearnings, was purged of "wrong states of mind." The Buddhist books say he then passed into a state of "awareness" or "wakefulness" suffused by an ecstasy having four phases and culminating in "the state that, knowing neither satisfaction nor dissatisfaction, is the consummate purity of poised equanimity and mindfulness."[E8] t seemed to him "ignorance was destroyed, knowledge had arisen, darkness was destroyed, light had arisen" as he sat there "earnest, strenuous, resolute."[D2] Also, he was convinced that "rebirth is no more; I have lived the highest life; my task is done; and now for me there is no more of what I have been."[E9] He thus experienced the earthly foretaste of Nirvana (Pali *Nibbana*). From now on, he was the Buddha, the Enlightened One.

A Doctrine to Be Shared

After the ecstasy had passed, he was immediately confronted with a problem, a temptation. This is one of the best-attested facts in the Buddhist books. He had attained to a Doctrine that was "profound, recondite, hard to comprehend."[E10] Were he to preach this Doctrine or *Dharma* (Pali *Dhamma*), and were others not to understand it, that would be labor and annoyance to him. After some struggle with himself, whether he should remain "one enlightened by himself" and after "exhaustion" of his karma enter Nirvana at his death, or, postponing his final entrance into Nirvana, become a Buddha for all, a teaching Buddha, he rose and went back into the world to communicate to others his saving truth.

He sought out the five ascetics who had deserted him at Uruvela. He found them in the Deer Park at Benares, and there experienced a great personal triumph. At first, when they saw him coming toward them among the trees, they said bitterly, "Here comes the ascetic Gautama, he who eats rich food and lives in self-indulgence. Let us show him no respect, nor rise to meet him. Yet let us put out an extra seat and growl, 'If you want to sit, sit!'" But the Buddha displayed such serenity and radiance that they could not look away, nor refrain from receiving him. They rose; one came forward to relieve him of his bowl and robe; another indicated his seat; another brought water to wash his feet.

The Deer Park Discourse: A Middle Path

A prolonged and amiable discussion began. To their accusation that he had forfeited the possibility of enlightenment by abandoning asceticism and reverting to self-indulgence, he replied in the words of what is known as the Sermon in the Deer Park at Benares: "There are two extremes, O Almsmen, which he who has given up the world ought to avoid. What are those two extremes?—A life given to pleasures, devoted to pleasures and lusts; this is degrading, sensual, vulgar, ignoble and profitless. And a life given to mortifications; this is painful, ignoble, and profitless. By avoiding these two extremes the Truth-finder [the Tathagata: the Buddha's designation for himself—literally, "one who has truly arrived or has reached *Tatha*, Suchness—the indescribable Ultimate"] has gained the knowledge of the Path which leads to insight, which leads to wisdom, which conduces to calm, to knowledge, to Enlightenment, to Nirvana."[G1] He opened to them his own experience and challenged them to believe his testimony, to admit that he was an *arahat* (a monk who had experienced enlightenment), and to try the "middle way" he now advocated. The five ascetics were converted, and thus the Sangha (the Buddhist monastic order) came into being. In the Buddhist metaphor, this event "started a wheel turning"—the Wheel of the Doctrine (Dharma), and so this discourse is commonly called "The Setting in Motion of the Wheel of the Dharma."

The Buddha then energetically entered upon his itinerant ministry in north India.

The Establishment of the Buddhist Order

As the Buddha wandered about preaching, other conversions followed, some being from his own caste, the Kshatriya, until the number of his disciples rose to sixty. Then the monks multiplied rapidly. Not only Kshatriyas and members of the lower castes, but many Brahmins too joined the group of inquirers and disciples. Among these was one who became a leader among his disciples, the Brahmin Sariputta. Others came from his own class, like his cousin Ananda. Caste distinctions then were not so sharply defined in society at large as later, and in any case caste ceased to apply to individuals who joined the Buddhist order. At first, all candidates for ordination into the order were brought by disciples to the Buddha, but when in the course of time converts came from a distance and in increasing numbers, he authorized ordained monks (Pali *bhikkhus*) to confer ordination themselves, following certain simple rules. In fact, as the converts grew in number, it became expedient to inaugurate a program and draw up rules for behavior. During the dry season the Buddha annually sent his disciples out to preach, himself setting the example. During the three months of the rainy season, he and the monks gathered together, some here, some there, and lived a monastic life of self-discipline, instruction, and mutual service.

Three Refuges, Precepts for Monks and Laity

So in a very natural way rose a great order, the Sangha, governed by definite rules and schedules. The essential rules, perhaps developed after the Buddha's own time, were simple: the wearing of the yellow robe, the adoption of the shaven head, the carrying of the begging bowl, the habit of daily meditation, and subscription to the initiate's confession: "I take refuge in the Buddha, I take refuge in the Dharma (the Law or Truth), I take refuge in the Sangha (the Order)." Monks undertook to obey the Ten Precepts, and the laity to obey the first five. They may be simplified in the following way:

1. Refrain from destroying life (the principle of ahimsa).

2. Do not take what is not given.

3. Abstain from unchastity.

4. Do not lie or deceive.

5. Abstain from intoxicants.

6. Eat moderately and not after noon.

7. Do not look on at dancing, singing, or dramatic spectacles.

8. Do not affect the use of garlands, scents, unguents, or ornaments.

9. Do not use high or broad beds.

10. Do not accept gold or silver.[H]

The first four of these Precepts are the same as the first four vows undertaken by the Jaina monks, but instead of the extremely comprehensive fifth vow (renouncing all attachments) of the Jains there appears the precept against the use intoxicants. It may be said that the Precepts illustrate the Middle Way between asceticism and self-indulgence in a specially concrete way; on the one hand, self-indulgence in the pleasures of life is explicitly disavowed, and on the other hand, the more extreme ascetic practices are not enjoined. Faithfulness in carrying out the Precepts was expected. If any monk broke any of them, he made public confession of his sin before the assembly of his chapter on the bimonthly fast days.

The first five of these injunctions (known as the Five Precepts) were prescribed for all lay associates of the order. The priority given to the Sangha in effect desacralized marriage and nullified the obligations of spouses; however, the Buddha recognized that there were those who for one reason or another could not "give up the household life" but who were so sympathetic with the ideals of the order that they should be brought into active association with it. He therefore made provision for the attachment of thousands of lay associates to the order, on the condition that they undertook to obey the Five Precepts and evinced the spirit of helpfulness in promoting the growth and progress of the order. It was largely through the lay membership that the order acquired its extensive property holdings. High-born laymen of the Kshatriya caste enthusiastically donated groves, parks, and monasteries to the order.

The Parinirvana of the Buddha
Reclining figures of the Buddha always represent his final moments before departure from the world of *samsara* (rebirth-redeath). This giant figure at Anuradhapura, Sri Lanka, translates into stone some of the conventional literary descriptions of the ideal human form: "shoulders like the forehead of the elephant," "arms as supple and tapering as its trunk," and "transcending male and female form." *(Photo by Jack van Horn.)*

Women Accepted as Nuns

The Buddha's aunt and foster mother Mahaprajapati is regarded as the founder of the order of nuns (Pali *bhikkhunis*). Rebuffed when she first asked the Buddha to enter the order, she is said to have made a second effort, walking from Kapilavastu to Vesali. Ananda, seeing her swollen feet and her distress, was moved to intercede with the Buddha. After being put off several times he finally asked, "Are women capable of arahatship (reaching enlightenment)?" The Buddha conceded, "They are capable." Ananda pressed further, "How does the Blessed One deny the highest benefit to one who has suckled him?" The Buddha yielded. Yet he is said to have made the dry remark in private, "If, Ananda, women had not received permission to enter the Order, the pure religion would have lasted long, the good law would have stood fast a thousand years.

But since they have received permission, it will now stand fast for only five hundred years."[D3]

It seems well attested that a fairly large group of relatives became monks and nuns. Tradition says that the Buddha inducted his own son, Rahula, into the order and that his wife as well as his stepmother were nuns. His cousin, Ananda, stands out among all of his followers as the perfect type of devoted disciple, ministering with untiring love to his teacher's personal needs and in constant attendance upon him. Another cousin, Devadatta, so personally identified himself with the order that he became guilty of an attempted schism in the interest, ostensibly, of greater strictness. (Buddhist tradition says he was moved by jealousy.)

Rules for the order of nuns were similar to those for monks with additional restrictions designed to ensure that nuns would always be subordinate to monks. We shall have more to say about orders of nuns in the next chapter.

The Last Hours: Parinirvana

Forty-five years passed in the work of preaching, teaching, and constructive planning. At last, on a journey to an obscure town by the name of Kusinara, northeast of Benares, at the age of eighty (in about 483 B.C.E.), he came to his end. He took his midday meal in the house of Chunda, a goldsmith. Most likely the pork he ate (or, as some would have it, the dish of truffles) brought on an attack of mortal illness. He had not gone the full distance toward Kusinara when death claimed him as he lay down between two sal trees. This was the *parinirvana*, the moment of his physical death and acceptance of Nirvana.

These last hours were remembered afterward in great detail. The legend says that he spoke kindly to Ananda, who had gone aside to weep: "Enough, Ananda, do not grieve, nor weep. Have I not already told you, Ananda, that it is in the very nature of all things near and dear unto us that we must divide ourselves from them? How is it possible, Ananda, that whatever has been born should not perish? For a long time, Ananda, have you waited on the Tathagata with a kind, devoted, cheerful, single-hearted, unstinted service. You have acquired much merit, Ananda; exert yourself, and you will soon be free from all defect." He said he left a legacy for his followers: "The Doctrine (Dhamma) and Discipline (Vinaya) which I have taught and enjoined upon you is to be your teacher when I am gone." His last words were: "And now, O priests, I take my leave of you; all the constituents of being are transitory; work out your salvation with diligence."[1]

II. THE TEACHINGS OF THE BUDDHA

Rejection of Speculative Philosophy

Paradoxically enough, one must begin study of the Buddha's philosophical conceptions with the observation that he rejected philosophical speculation as the way of salvation. Purely metaphysical issues were to him of little moment. He had an intensely practical outlook, and issues unrelated to the human situation offended his common sense. The Buddhist records list a number of then-current problems in philosophy that Gautama chose not to comment on or "elucidate":

> Bear always in mind what it is that I have not elucidated, and what it is that I have elucidated. And what have I not elucidated? I have not elucidated that the world is eternal; I have not elucidated that the world is not eternal; I have not elucidated that the world is finite; I have not elucidated that the world is infinite; I have not elucidated that the soul and the body are identical; I have not elucidated that the monk who has attained (the arahat) exists after death; I have not elucidated that the arahat does not exist after death; I have not elucidated that the arahat both exists and does not exist after death; I have not elucidated that the arahat neither exists nor does not exist after death. And why have I not elucidated this? Because this profits not, nor has to do with the fundamentals of religion; therefore I have not elucidated this.[C2]

The Buddha's psychological interest is expressed in the next sentences attributed to him:

> And what have I elucidated? Misery have I elucidated; the origin of misery have I elucidated; the cessation of misery have I elucidated; and the path leading to the cessation of misery have I elucidated. And why have I elucidated this? Because this does profit, has to do with the fundamentals of religion, and tends to absence of passion, to knowledge, supreme wisdom, and Nirvana.[C2]

In other words, our basic difficulty as human beings is not so much in the way we philosophize as in the way we feel. We should devote our thinking to understanding our feelings and desires and controlling them through the power of will; in them, the chief danger lurks.

Rejection of Religious Devotion

The Buddha also rejected religious devotion as a way of salvation. His position was the sort of atheism we have already noted in Mahavira. He believed that the universe abounded in gods, goddesses, demons, and other nonhuman powers and agencies, but all without exception were finite, subject to death and rebirth. In the absence, then, of some transcendent, eternal Being, who could direct human destinies and hear and grant human wishes, prayer, to the Buddha, was of no avail; he at least did not resort to it. For similar reasons, he did not put any reliance on the Vedas nor on worship of their many gods through the performance of sacrificial rituals as a way of redemption, nor would he countenance going to the Brahmins as priests. (These are among the chief reasons why Buddhism is unacceptable to the devout Hindu.) Like Mahavira, the Buddha showed his disciples how to rely for salvation on themselves, on their own powers, focused on redemption by spiritual self-discipline.

Here was the strictest sort of humanism in religion.

Old Karma and New Karma

Though the Buddha uprooted from his worldview most of what is commonly regarded as distinctive of religion as such, he held to two major Hindu doctrines that ordinarily appear in a religious context. He believed in the Law of Karma and in rebirth. He modified both of these doctrines, however.

He gave the Law of Karma more flexibility than most later philosophers were wont to do. In his view, a person of any caste or class could experience such a complete change of heart or disposition as to escape the full consequence of sins committed in previous existences. The Law of Karma operated remorselessly and without remission of one iota of the full recompense upon all who went on in the old way—the way of unchecked desire—but it could not lay hold upon a person completely changed, who had achieved arahatship, "the state of him that is worthy." The arahats "who by steadfast mind have become exempt from evil desire" may feel assured that "their old karma is exhausted; no new karma is being produced; their hearts are free from the longing after a future life; the cause of their existence being destroyed, and no new longing springing up within them, they, the wise, are extinguished at death like a lamp."[J] There will be no rebirth for them.

It is those who are not emancipated from "the will-to-live-and-have" (tanha or trishna) who will be reborn.

Rebirth without Transmigration

The Buddha held firmly to the doctrine of rebirth, but the form he gave to that doctrine has puzzled commentators ever since. It seems he held that rebirth takes place without any actual soul substance passing over from one existence to another. Later expositors of this doctrine declared that the Buddha, after analysis of the human person, concluded, "There is no ego [atman] here to be found."[C3] This is one of the most obscure and most profound points in the Buddha's system of thought.

Instead of the age-old faith that an imperishable and a substantial soul goes over from one existence to another, its direction and status absolutely determined from stage to stage by the inexorable causal nexus of the Law of Karma, the Buddha seems to have maintained a doctrine that is surprisingly objective and modern. His reflection on his own personality led him to deny that any of its elements had any permanence. What has been called the continuing entity of the immortal soul is really to be resolved back into an impermanent aggregation or a composite of constantly changing states of being or skandhas (Pali, khandhas). These skandhas are five in number: (1) the body (rupa), (2 perception (jamjna), (3) feelings (vedana), (4) samskaras (hard to translate; literally, "configurations," "innate tendencies," or "predispositions," generated by past habits in this and previous existences; roughly, in the nearest modern equivalent, a lumping together of the "instincts" and the "subconscious"), and (5) ideation or reasoning (vijnana). It is the union of these that constitutes the individual. As long as they are held together, the individual functions as a single being, lives, and has a history. But each component is in perpetual flux. The body changes from day to day, only a little less obviously than the other states. At death, the union is dissolved, and the skandhas disperse.

What is known to us as the ego is therefore but an appearance, merely the name we give to the functional unity that subsists when the five changing skandhas set up the complex interplay that constitutes the personal life of the individual. Only the ceaseless flow of Being itself, of which these changing states are signs, has reality or permanence.

Buddhist lore abounds in similes for the mysterious death-rebirth event. The pressing of a signet ring into sealing wax is used to illustrate effective causation without the transfer of any substance. No portion of the ring is transferred to the wax, only the shape of the characters engraved on the seal. So in rebirth no soul is transferred, only the karma-laden character structure of the previous life. At the end of one existence an individual will possess definite characteristics hardened into a kind of rigidity, but at the moment of dissolution these characteristics are passed over to the soft wax of a new existence in another womb. Nothing substantial passes over, yet there is a definite connection between one complex of elements and the next.

Some interpreters say that the Buddha never denied that an entity of some sort goes from one life to the next. He refused to discuss what this entity might be, except to imply that it was impelled by karma. Although he rejected the Hindu doctrine, as found in the Upanishads, that there is an imperishable soul or self (atman) residing in the perishable body apart from the mind and the other "psychic organs" of an individual person, it would seem that he must have thought that a real, if only momentary, something— that is, an impermanent but death-transcending pulse of being, marked with certain causative characteristics (e.g., "clinging," karmic determinations, habits of doing, predispositions)—goes over to another life. If this is granted, it is clear that he was more ready to say what this transmigrating bit of being was *not* than what it was.

A further pair of examples from the *Milinda-panha* (Questions of King Milinda) put it the following way:

> Said the king [King Milinda]: "Bhante Nagasena, does rebirth take place without anything transmigrating?"
>
> "Yes, your majesty, rebirth takes place without anything transmigrating."
>
> "How, bhante Nagasena, does rebirth take place without anything transmigrating? Give an illustration."

> "Suppose, your majesty, a man were to light a light from another light; pray, would the one light have passed over to the other light?"
>
> "Nay, verily, bhante."
>
> "In exactly the same way, your majesty, does rebirth take place without anything transmigrating."
>
> "Give another illustration."
>
> "Do you remember, your majesty, having learnt, when you were a boy, some verse or other from your professor of poetry?"
>
> "Yes, bhante."
>
> "Pray, your majesty, did the verse pass over (transmigrate) to you from your teacher?"
>
> "Nay, verily, bhante."
>
> "In exactly the same way, your majesty, does rebirth take place without anything transmigrating."
>
> "You are an able man, bhante Nagasena."[C4]

It is noteworthy that in the previous example Gautama's view of the physics of lighting one candle from another is more accurate than the Hindu view of a flame as an analogy for the atman passing from body to body or modern ceremonial uses such as "passing the flame" of a Christmas or wedding candle. (The second wick is causally brought to ignition by heat from the first, but its flame is from its own hydrocarbons.)

Causal Continuity

In other words, as one process leads to another, from cause to effect, so human personality in one existence is the direct cause of the type of individuality that appears in the next. One text explains it the following way:

> This consciousness, being in its series inclined toward the object by desire, and impelled toward it by karma, like a man who swings himself over a ditch by means of a rope hanging from a tree on the hither bank, quits its first resting place and continues (in the next existence) to subsist in dependence on objects of sense and other things. . . . Here the former consciousness, from its passing out of existence, is called passing away, and the latter, from its being reborn into a new existence, is called rebirth. But it is understood that

this latter consciousness did not come to the present existence from the previous one, and also that it is only to causes contained in the old existence,—namely to karma called the predispositions, to inclination, an object, etc.—that its present appearance is due.... As illustrations of how consciousness does not come over from the last existence into the present, and how it springs up by means of causes belonging to the former existence, here may serve echoes, light, the impressions of a seal, and reflections in a mirror. For as echoes, light, the impressions of a seal, and shadows have sound, etc., for their causes, and exist without having come from elsewhere, just so it is with this mind.[C5]

This does not mean, the Buddha said, that one who is born is different from the preceding person who has passed his or her karma on at death, nor does it mean that one is the same. Such an issue is as meaningless as to say that the body is different from the self or that the self and body are the same. Since there is no permanent ego-entity accompanying the skandhas, discussions as to whether the successive personalities in a continuous series of rebirths are the same or different lack point. It is better simply to know that a kind of inner necessity (karma) leads to the origination of one life as the total result of the having-been-ness of another, and that the connection is as close as that of cause and effect, or as the ignition of a new flame from the heat of another. It is difficult to construe, but the fundamental fact remains—that what one does and thinks now carries over into tomorrow and tomorrow and tomorrow.

Interesting as this astute discrimination of distinctions is, the implications for the Buddha's larger conceptions of life and destiny are more important. The conclusions involved seem to be these: Wherever we observe it, the living world, whether about us or within ourselves, is constantly in flux, in a state of endless becoming. There is no central, planning world self, no sovereign Person in the heavens holding all together in unity. There is only the ultimate impersonal unity of Being itself, whose peace enfolds the individual self when it ceases to call itself "I" and enters the featureless purity of Nirvana.

Dependent Origination

The Buddha spoke of the experience of all this as "a mass of suffering," and this suffering comes out of a twelve-linked chain of causes and effects, the first two links arising from the previous life, the middle eight from the present, and the last two tending toward the future existence. The Buddhist books call this Dependent Origination or the Chain of Causation.

The reasoning goes like this: the first and most fundamental of the causes of the painful coming-into-being of every individual is ignorance, especially taking at face value the reality of the self and the permanence of the world. This basic fault, which is carried over from the previous life, is built into the original set or bent of the personality from birth, the predispositions (samskaras). Thus predisposed, the personality becomes conscious of or cognizes the world and itself. This in turn determines the distinctive traits one has ("name and form"; the individuality one is known by). Individuality expresses itself causally in a particular exercise of the five senses and the mind. These in turn make contact with other selves and with things. Thence arises sensation. The sensations cause desire (trishna or craving). From craving comes clinging to existence. Clinging to existence entails the process of becoming. Becoming brings on a new state of being not like the one preceding it. Finally, such a new birth inevitably entails its own "old age and death, grief, lamentation, suffering, dejection, and despair. Such is the origination of this whole mass of human suffering."[G2]

One can begin at the end and work back to the beginning, as the Buddha is said to have done, thus, in any particular case, old age and death would not have occurred if there had been no birth; birth depends for its arising on the factors making for its becoming; becoming depends on a previous clinging to existence; clinging to existence depends on desire (trishna, thirst for life); desire depends on one's sensations or feelings, and these depend on one's contacts with persons and things; contacts depend on exercise of the senses and the mind; how one exercises the senses and the mind depends on one's individual makeup (name and form); individuality depends on consciousness, and consciousness on

The Chain of Causation or Dependent Origination

thought process moves through obscure feeling states. It is *painful*, the Buddha felt, to experience continuance in a stream of consciousness made up mostly of states of incompletion.

> Now pleasant sensations, unpleasant sensations, indifferent sensations, Ananda, are transitory, are due to causes, originate by dependence, and are subject to decay, disappearance, effacement, and cessation. While this person is experiencing a pleasant sensation, he thinks, "This is my Ego [self, atman]." And after the cessation of this same pleasant sensation, he thinks, "My Ego has passed away." While he is experiencing an unpleasant sensation, he thinks, "This is my Ego." And after the cessation of this same unpleasant sensation, he thinks, "My Ego has passed away." And while he is experiencing an indifferent sensation, he thinks, "This is my Ego." And after the cessation of this same indifferent sensation, he thinks, "My Ego has passed away."[C6]

the predispositions carried over from previous existences; finally, these are grounded in the ignorance that accepts self and the self-experienced "world" as real. So at one end we have grief and lamentation, and at the other end ignorance.

Anicca, Anatta, and Dukkha (Pali terms)

These convictions were not encouraging. The Buddha discerned in them his basic reasons for withdrawal from the world. As he seems to have taught, all "composite beings" able to reason suffer from three great flaws vexing their existence: impermanence (*anicca*), the ultimate unreality of the self or atman (*anatta*), and sorrow or suffering (*dukkha*). The third aspect seemed to follow remorselessly upon the other two. The impermanence in everything that appears to exist, the ceaseless change, the endless becoming that is never quite being, filled him with weariness, a real misery; he longed for peace, the cessation of desire, for some state of consciousness with enough permanence to guarantee deliverance from the wheel of perpetual and painful becoming. This, of course, is the immemorial desire of India. Here, however, the

So the Buddha seems to have felt that it was human, no doubt, but it was foolish, it was stupid and ignorant, to cling with longing, as most people do, to sentient life and its pitifully few pleasures, when all through life the pain of change is so predominant. This will-to-live-and-have, this "thirst," this "clinging" to the world and its objects, was, it seemed, far and away the most striking of the characteristics that pass from one existence to the next, and if it could be made to die away, the chief cause of rebirth would be removed. If it could be made to die away, it should be made to do so!

To this conclusion the Buddha's profound psychological analysis of life and personality conducted him. In his ethical teaching, he sought to show all people how to answer the questions raised by it.

The *Dharma (Dhamma)* as Ethics

In Buddhism, *dharma* is a word with a whole complex of meanings. In various contexts it means: (a) observable objects (phenomena), facts, events, (b) the teaching or doctrine, that is, the Truth concerning the nature and causes of observable facts and events; and (c) as here, the conduct called for in view of the Truth revealed in facts or events.

The fundamental ethical problem to which the Buddha addressed himself was: In what way should one live to obtain surcease of pain and suffering, bring to an end the unwise will to live and have, and finally attain the fullness of the joy of liberation?

The answer to this problem he compressed into the Four Noble Truths. It is noteworthy that the word conventionally translated as "noble" (in the Four Noble Truths) is "Aryan," also the name of an ethnically defined nobility. Gautama answers the question "Who is an Aryan?" in terms of behavior rather than heredity. The true nobles are those who understand and follow the Four Truths. In the official report of his first sermon—in the Deer Park at Benares to the five ascetics—they are given thus:

> This, O Bhikkus, is the Noble Truth of Suffering: Birth is suffering; decay is suffering; illness is suffering; death is suffering. Presence of objects we hate is suffering; separation from objects we love is suffering; not to obtain what we desire is suffering. Briefly, the fivefold clinging to existence [by means of the five skandhas] is suffering.
>
> This, O Bhikkhus, is the Noble Truth of the Cause of Suffering: Thirst, that leads to rebirth, accompanied by pleasure and lust, finding its delight here and there. (This thirst is threefold) namely, thirst for pleasure, thirst for existence, thirst for prosperity.
>
> This, O Bhikkhus, is the Noble Truth of the Cessation of Suffering: (it ceases with) the complete cessation of this thirst—a cessation which consists in the absence of every passion,—with the abandoning of this thirst, with the doing away with it, with the deliverance from it, with the destruction of desire.
>
> This, O Bhikkhus, is the Noble Truth of the Path which leads to the cessation of suffering: that holy eightfold Path, that is to say, Right Belief, Right Aspiration, Right Speech, Right Conduct, Right Means of Livelihood, Right Endeavor, Right Mindfulness, Right Meditation.[K]

The eightfold path indicates that the Buddha's ethical system is not entirely negative or pessimistic. Provisionally during the ordeal of human existence, as one proceeds along the path to total detachment, some behavioral choices are desirable in the sense of being preferable to others. Ultimately, of course, all desire, all attachment, must be overcome if one is to realize Nirvana.

1. The Negative: Avoid Attachment

The first, and negative, principle in the Buddha's ethics requires strict nonindulgence of the desires known to cause suffering. But how will one know they are desires of this sort? The first three of the Four Noble Truths furnish the criteria. Reduced to the simplest form, they produce this formula: Where life becomes miserable, the misery is always found to spring from indulgence of some form of desire; hence *such* desire is to be abandoned, done away with, uprooted. Or, in one sentence, any form of desire whose indulgence entails misery is to be overcome.

So stated, the ethical thought of the Buddha strikes a note of clear common sense. It is not from this *principle* that Western minds can intelligently dissent; it is from the *application* of this principle in the further reaches of Buddhist ethics. For in such application the Buddha goes far in a negative direction. Some of his ethical judgments are common enough in most ethical systems. There is widespread agreement among the ethical philosophers, for example, that pursuit of the sensuously pleasant as an end in itself produces misery. But though the Buddha agrees with this common enough observation, he advises far more than the abandonment of sensuous desires.

Family Attachments   Ownership of houses and land, love of parents, spouses, children, or friends—these also ultimately bring woe, he taught. There is constant worry and unsatisfied desire in each case. If one clings to a spouse, then death, separation, the life of poverty, sickness, hundreds of situations are painful; the very intensity of love itself is painful. So it is with children, aged parents, and even with friends. "Let therefore no man love anything; loss of the beloved is evil. Those who love nothing and hate nothing have no fetters."[L1]

The Buddha's attitude is best presented through illustration. The legend runs that one day a grandmother appeared before him in tears. She had just lost a very dear grandchild. The Buddha looked at her gravely. "How many people are there in this city of Savatthi?" he asked, with apparent irrevelance. Upon receiving her reply, he came to the point: "Would you like to have as many children and grandchildren as there are people in Savatthi?" The old lady, still weeping, cried out yes, yes. "But," the Buddha gently remonstrated, "if you had as many children and grandchildren as there are people in Savatthi, you would have to weep every day, for people die daily there." The old lady thought a moment; he was right! As she went away comforted, she carried with her the Buddha's saying: "Those who have a hundred dear ones have a hundred woes; those who have ninety dear ones have ninety woes; . . . those who have one dear one have one woe; those who hold nothing dear have no woe."M1

If this story is true, then the Buddha would have approved, had he been alive to hear the story, of the young monk who, after being gone from home a long while, returned to his birthplace to occupy a cell built by his father for passing monks and to beg food daily at his mother's door. His mother did not recognize him in his monk's garb and emaciated condition. For three months he took food from her hands without announcing himself, and then quietly departed. When his mother heard afterward who he was, she worshiped, saying, "Methinks, the Blessed One must have had in mind a body of priests like my son. . . . This man ate for three months in the house of the mother who bore him, and never said, 'I am thy son, and thou art my mother.' O the wonderful man!" And the Buddhist account concludes, "For such a one, mother and father are no hindrances."C7

In some quarters this renunciation of family ties met with anger. "The people were annoyed, murmured, and became angry, saying, 'The ascetic Gotama causes fathers to beget no sons . . . wives to become widows . . . families to become extinct.'"G3 If his success with young men were to increase, it would threaten the existence of the human race!

Attachments to the Buddha or to the Self   The consistent Buddhist will exercise restraint even over attachment to the Blessed One, the Buddha himself.

The venerable Sariputta said this: "As I was meditating in seclusion there arose the consideration: Is there now anything in the whole world wherein a change would give rise in me to grief, lamenting, despair? And methought, No, there is no such thing." Then the venerable Ananda said to the venerable Sariputta: "But the Master—would not the loss of him give rise in you to grief, lamenting, despair?" "Not even the loss of him, Friend Ananda. Nevertheless, I should feel thus: O may not the mighty one, O may not the Master so gifted, so wonderful, be taken from us!"M2

In addition, all self-regard, all emotional bias in behalf of the empirical self, must be entirely overcome. The self-defensive and self-assertive attitudes are especially ruinous to peace. The truth of the anatta doctrine must be realized in experience. Among the qualities of the true monk are those that Kassapa exhibited when, making his rounds for alms of food, he met a leper, and in order to let the leper acquire merit by almsgiving, gave him the opportunity to cast a morsel into his own out-stretched bowl. Though in the process "a finger, mortifying, broke and fell," Kassapa felt no qualms but, back in the monastery, ate with undisturbed equanimity the food that lay beside the leprous finger in the bowl.N Equally the master of his emotions, Sariputta experienced complete release from ego-concern. "Serene, pure, radiant is your person, Sariputta," a monk exclaimed. "Where have you been today?" "I have been alone, in first *dhyana* [Pali, *jhana* or deep meditation], brother, and to me never came the thought: *I am attaining it; I have emerged from it.* And thus individualizing and egotistical tendencies have been well ejected for a long while from Sariputta."O

Like the Jains, the Buddhists determined to renounce all attachments disturbing to absolute peace of mind and soul. To them salvation, here and hereafter, meant just this, a state of perfectly painless peace and joy, a self-achieved freedom from misery of any kind. This explains why Buddhist literature makes so many lists of things to be avoided, desires to be given up, bonds to be broken: "the Three Intoxications" (greed [*lobha*], hatred [*dosa*], and ignorance [*moha*]); "the Five Hindrances" (desire for the pleasures of the senses, ill will, sloth or torpor, restlessness, and doubt); "the Ten Fetters, by which beings are bound to the wheel of existence," a listing which, it can be seen, covers much ground: (1) belief in the existence of the self, (2) doubt, (3) trust in rituals and ceremonies as efficacious for salvation, (4) lust, (5) anger or ill will, (6) desire for rebirth in worlds of form, (7) desire for rebirth in formless worlds, (8) pride, (9) self-righteousness, and (10) ignorance.

Theravada Buddhists of today commonly suppose that when a monk "conquers" the first three of the Ten Fetters, he enters the mainstream of Buddhist self-salvation and cannot be reborn more than seven additional times before entering Nirvana; when he makes considerable progress in conquering the next two Fetters, he will be reborn only once more on the human level; when he entirely conquers the first five Fetters, he cannot be reborn in any of the "worlds of form" or again have the handicap of a material body; and when he conquers all of the Fetters, he will attain the earthly experience of Nirvana and be an arahat.

2. The Positive: Living Toward Transcendent Bliss

Freedom from "fetters" obviously cannot be achieved by negative means only. It is by living toward the attainment of the right or truly liberating and joy-bringing desires that one attains the supraconsciousness, the bliss, that completely transcends and erases from everyday consciousness the kinds of desire that produce suffering.

Consider in this connection the fourth of the Four Noble Truths. The principle expressed is this: Desires whose indulgence will not result in increase of misery but rather in a decrease of it (or in entire doing away of misery) are desires that conduct steadily to salvation, the ultimate state in which all desires are swallowed up, even the desire for no desire.

It was in applying this principle that the Buddha formulated the Noble Eightfold Path, "the path that leads to no desire."

The Eightfold Path (1) The first step in the Eightfold Path is right belief; that is, belief in the Four Noble Truths and the view of life implied in them. (2) The next step, right aspiration or purpose, is reached by resolving to overcome sensuality, to have the right love of others, to harm no living being, and to suppress all misery-producing desires generally. The (3, 4) third and fourth steps right speech and right conduct, are defined as nonindulgence in loose or hurtful talk or in ill will; one must love all creatures with the right sort of love in word and deed. (5) Right means of

livelihood, the fifth step, means choosing the proper occupation of one's time and energies, obtaining one's livelihood in ways consistent with Buddhist principles. (6) The sixth step, right effort, implies untiring and unremitting intellectual alertness in discriminating between wise and unwise desires and attachments. (7) Right mindfulness, the seventh step, is made possible by well-disciplined thought habits during long hours spent in attention to helpful topics. (8) Right meditation or absorption, the eighth step, refers to the climax of all the other processes—the final attainment of the trance states that are the advanced stages on the road to arahatship (sainthood) and the assurance of passage at death into Nirvana, the state of quiescence, all karma consumed, and rebirth at an end forever.

Two things should be noted about the steps in the Eightfold Path: (1) that they fall under three headings—(a) understanding, (b) morals, and (c) concentration; (2) that they are so planned as to lead progressively to arahatship and thus finally to Nirvana. Of the three groups into which the steps of the Path fall, the first two groups are natural enough. Understanding of the *theory* and *practice* of the ethic of Buddhism is certainly necessary if the Buddhist believer is to justify having faith at all. But the third group (concentration) leads onto a different level. Here Buddhism is most akin to Hindu mysticism. The final goal here is the pure ecstasy, the supraconsciousness that follows on meditative exercises. By them one turns away in aversion from the unhappy world to spiritual realities beyond sense.

In early Buddhism part of this mental discipline consisted in certain processes of thought the Buddha himself recommended. These included, for example, deepening one's aversion to life by thinking concentratedly of the perishableness of the body and of the body's loathsome features, or by analyzing the disgusting changes wrought by death in the most beautiful human body, and then in grateful relief turning to the thought of the permanent and the eternal.

When this kind of thinking failed, some of the early Buddhists turned to Yoga methods in the hope of psychologically bringing on ecstasy. They breathed in certain ways, stared at bright objects, repeated certain formulas, and so on. The Buddha condemned giving too high a value to such technical means to ecstasy. Arahatship, he held, could be reached without resorting to any special practices of the more technical sort.

It was heretical, in fact, to seek entrance into Nirvana by the cultivation of ecstasy alone. The way to "bliss" was not the way of merely formalistic procedure; it was the way of meditating until one could see with a "sense-transcending eye" and gain an insight surpassing all normal awareness, something akin to an "awakening," as if all of life heretofore had been a dreaming sleep until one had finally awakened to reality.

The Arahat and Nirvana

The steps of the Path, we have said, lead to arahatship. This is the state of one "who has awakened," of one "who has reached the end of the Eightfold Path." The arahat is the Buddhist saint, a person who has attained wisdom and the rest of the "six perfections," namely morality, charity, forbearance, striving, and meditation. Also, the arahat has conquered "the three intoxications"—sensuality, ignorance, and the "thirst" leading to rebirth—and enjoys the "higher vision" (sambodhi) with joy, pleasure, calm, benevolence, and concentration.

The joy of the arahats is deep, for they have already had a taste of Nirvana in the trance of their enlightenment, and for the balance of their days they will know the bliss of liberation from misery-bringing desires. No longer feeling suffering and taking no pleasure in earthly joys, the arahat is able to say, "I do not wish for death, I do not wish for life." In this state one awaits with calm contentment and without apprehension the "putting out of his lamp of life"—the entrance into the final Nirvana at death. Just what this final state will be no one, being in this world, can say. It is enough to be no longer unhappy. As previously noted, the Buddha refused to give any decision as to whether an arahat does or does not exist after death. Nirvana seems at first view a completely negative conception. It means the end, "the blowing out," of the candle of craving and thus of suffering existence, so that there will be no more transmigration, and because the skandhas of the last earthly existence are dispersed and there is no ego remaining over, it would seem that Nirvana is "annihilation." But the Buddha did not say that. He did not think this was true. All he knew, or all he cared to say, was that Nirvana was the end of painful becoming; it was the final peace—it was an eternal state of neither being nor nonbeing, because it was the end of all finite states and dualities. Human knowledge and human speech could not compass it.

The Problem of Describing Nirvana

The Udana quotes the Buddha as speaking thus of Nirvana,

> There is, monks, that plane [of realization] where there is neither extension nor . . . motion nor the plane of infinite ether . . . nor that of neither-ideation-nor-non-ideation, neither this world nor another, neither the moon nor the sun. Here, monks, I say there is no coming or going or remaining or deceasing or uprising, for this is itself without support, without continuance, without mental object.[P]

In his study of contemporary Burmese Buddhism, Melford E. Spiro says, "Contemporary Burmese Buddhists exhibit three points of view concerning the meaning of nirvana. . . . A small group says that short of experiencing nirvana, nothing can be said about it (other than that it entails the absence of suffering). . . . A second group says that although we cannot say what nirvana is, it is not extinction or annihilation. Some members of this group argue that although nirvana means complete extinction of the physical aspect of life, its spiritual aspect or mind remains. Others insist that although mind, too, is destroyed, there remains a special kind of awareness. . . . The third group—those who believe that nirvana means total extinction—is the largest." He quotes a Burmese as saying that in nirvana "nothing exists"—there is no mind, no soul, no body, no feeling of any kind. "If there is some feeling, there is no neikban (nirvana). Still it is not true to say that neikban is nothing—there is something. That is, there is peacefulness."[Q]

One thing is certain: the arahat is no longer tormented by self, that is to say, by individualizing and egotistical considerations and concerns. The suggestion is made in the Pali texts—but it may be a later addition to the Buddha's teaching—that although the skandhas are not truly a self, when a human mind transcends its normal consciousness through dhyana (meditation at the plane of supraconsciousness), a true or spiritual self is actualized and begins to function. But even this spiritual self that then becomes manifest is annulled in Nirvana. Nirvana divests the self of self in any sense of the word.

The Arahat's Benevolence   The selfless arahat is nevertheless described as benevolent. As the Buddhist ideal of what one may become, the arahat is magnanimous, overflowing with good will. To grasp this is very important for our understanding of the later history of Buddhism. Although fundamentally Buddhist seekers are bent on their own self-cultivation, their own blessedness, each individual is often encouraged, in the words of the Buddha himself, to "wander alone like a rhinoceros,"[R1] forsaking such hindrances as houses and lands and kindred, nevertheless each seeker is charged to love all human beings without exception. That the Buddha himself possessed the quality of compassion for all humankind is evident in a life devoted to preaching and teaching. Though he strove to sunder every tie to particular individuals based on emotion, on the ground, as we have seen, that any such tie is misery producing, he charged his disciples to love all humanity with a mother's love.

> As a mother, even at the risk of her own life, protects her son, her only son, so let him cultivate love without measure toward all beings. Let him cultivate toward the whole world—above, below, around—a heart of love unstinted, unmixed with the sense of differing or opposing interests.[R2]

It became a part of the Buddhist self-schooling to sit quietly in a concentrated effort to call forth from the depths of the heart a love so comprehensive that it embraced every living being in the universe and at the same time so intense that it was unlimited. It was by such loving thought that the Buddhist monk prepared himself for his task of pointing the way to Nirvana.

Love without Attachment?   But here we are brought to a pause. Is this warmth of benevolent love consistent with the cloister-seeking motive that is so primary in the life of the monk yearning for Nirvana? How can love issue from anyone so engrossed in self-liberation as to seek emotional detachment in every relationship? The question is a serious one. That there is at least a practical inconsistency here was recognized

early in the history of Buddhism. In fact, it led eventually, as we shall see, to the fundamental division within Buddhism between the Mahayana and the Theravada (the Hinayana). But benevolence had a place in the full theory of the Buddha. What he evidently meant was that the love his disciples should cultivate for all humankind should be general or universal in character. This love of humanity (one may put it, the love of everyone, but not the love of any one) can be the source only of high and disinterested joy. It is not like the love of one individual for another, which is a relation of dependence and passionate attachment and therefore fraught with the miseries attendant upon unhappy chance and change.

Some Buddhists have cited a surgeon's focus (a surgeon *without* a "bedside manner") as an ideal: impersonal skill cuts away a malignancy to benefit a faceless specimen of humankind who is neither near and dear nor an enemy. (It is precisely the conflict between such detached love and the anguished love of personal attachment to patients that is exploited in virtually every TV hospital drama ever produced.)

An arahat's benevolence is not affected by the response it meets; through every rebuff, it remains inalienable. Patiently, it returns good for evil.

The secret of this patience and good will is thus explained in some of the opening sentences of the *Dhammapada*.

> If a man speaks or acts with a pure thought, happiness follows him, like a shadow that never leaves him. 'He abused me, he beat me, he defeated me, he robbed me'—in those who harbor such thoughts hatred will never cease,—in those who do not harbor such thoughts hatred will cease. For hatred does not cease by hatred at any time; hatred ceases by love—this is an old rule.[L2]

And in the *Majjhima Nikaya* occur these words, expressive of the same lofty and inalterable good will,

> If some one curses you, you must repress all resentment, and make the firm determination, 'My mind shall not be disturbed, no angry word shall escape my lips, I shall remain kind and friendly, with loving thoughts and no secret spite.' If then you are attacked with fists, with stones,

with sticks, with swords, you must still repress all resentment and preserve a loving mind with no secret spite.[M3]

The right kind of love as the Buddha himself conceived of it is best illustrated in a story. One of his most promising disciples wished to preach, it is said, among a certain wild jungle folk. The Buddha, seeking to test him, held with him the following conversation:

But, O Punna, the men of that country are violent, cruel and savage. When they become angry at you and do you harm, what will you think then?"

"I shall think them truly good and kind folk, for whilst they speak angry and insolent words, they refrain from striking or stoning me."

"They are very violent folk, Punna. What if they strike or stone you?"

"I shall think them kind and good not to smite me with staff and sword." . . .

"And what if they kill you?"

"I shall think them kind and good indeed who free me from this vile body with so little pain."

"Well said, Punna, well said! With your great gift of patience, you may indeed essay this task. Go, Punna, yourself saved, save others."[A4]

Though one must grant a fine ethical quality to this inalienable magnanimity, the difficulty for Westerners, and for the Buddhists themselves from the first, has been this: Such love is the product of an almost infinite withdrawal from everyday life. It is not a love whose chief mark is selfless self-identification with others. This was to come in a later stage of Buddhism.

GLOSSARY*

Ananda (ä'-nŭn-dŭ) Gautama Buddha's cousin; ananda literally means bliss

anatta (ŭn-ŭt'-tŭ) the unreality of the self: no atman. Sanskrit: anatman

anicca (ŭn-ich'-chŭ) impermanence, the transitoriness of all things. Sanskrit: anitya

arahat an enlightened Buddhist monk

Buddha (boō-dŭ) "awakened," title applied to Gautama after his enlightenment and later to others deemed to have achieved perfect illumination

dharma (dŭr'-mŭ) "foundation," Truth, the order of nature and causality, duty; as one of the three "jewels" Buddha, Dharma, and Sangha, it is doctrine. In the plural, dharmas are irreducible object-events, the phenomena apprehended by the mind as a sense organ. Pali: dhamma

dhyana (dyä'-nŭ) meditation at levels transcending ordinary consciousness; Pali: jhana

dukkha "sorrow," the suffering inherent in the impermanence (anicca) of the rebirth-redeath cycle

Gautama (gäu'-tŭ-mŭ) the gotra or clan name (surname) of Prince Siddhartha, the founder of Buddhism; Pali: Gotama

Hinayana "Lesser Vehicle" (less-inclusive-way), the name applied by Mahayanists to the older schools of Buddhism (who today refer to themselves as Theravadins)

Jataka (jŭ'-tŭ-kŭ) "birth story," folk versions of the exemplary lives of animals, demons, and humans, each represented as a previous life as the Buddha or some other prominent figure in Buddhism

karma in Buddhism the actions of body or mind that produce a fixed consequence for the present life or the future life. (Some freedom remains in the responses made to karma-ordained situations.) Pali: kamma

Mahayana (mŭ-hä-yä'-nŭ) "Great Vehicle," generic name assumed by sects arising in India since the second century after the Buddha's parinirvana; extant today in China, Korea, Japan, and Vietnam

Nirvana (nēr-vän'-nŭ) "cooled" or "quenched," the unconditioned state of liberation, release from the cycle of rebirth-redeath; Pali: Nibbana

Pali (bä-lē) an ancient Indic language used in early Theravada scripture

parinirvana (pä-rē-nēr-vän'-nŭ) "final" or "complete" Nirvana, for example, the Buddha in the last hours of his final departure from the world of phenomena

Sangha "assembly," the order of monks and nuns (in Mahayana usage the laity also may be included); third of the three "jewels" or "refuges" of Buddhism

* For a guide to pronunciation, refer to page 99.

Shakyamuni (shäk'yŭ-mŭ'-nĭ) "sage of the Shakyas," one of the titles applied to Gautama Siddhartha as an historical personage

Siddhartha (sid-där'-tŭ) "goal attainer," personal name given to the prince of the Shakyas who became the Buddha Gautama

skandhas (skŭn'-dŭz) "heaps," "clusters," the five impermanent aggregates (form, feeling, conception, karmic dispositions, and consciousness); by their collocation, they give rise to the mistaken sense of "self"

tanha "thirst," desire or craving, the impetus to clinging and becoming—and thus the cause of rebirth; Sanskrit: trishna

Tathagata (tŭt-hŭg'-ŭ-tŭ) "the thus-come (or gone) one," (or "such-come . . ."), a deliberately nondescriptive self-reference used by the Buddha: "the one who did that" (demonstrable but indescribable)

Theravada (tä-rŭ-vä'-dŭ) "the way of the elders," one of the Hinayana schools of Sri Lanka; adherents today use the name to refer generally to the tradition of Pali Buddhism extant in Sri Lanka, Burma, Thailand, Laos, and Cambodia

CHAPTER 7

The Religious Development of Buddhism
Diversity in Paths to Nirvana

The followers of the Buddha had what he of course could not have: they had a keen-minded, great-hearted founder to believe in and follow. It was natural that they should magnify his religious meaning for them, as indeed they did. They endowed him with a supernatural origin and intention that made him one of the world's grandest religious figures, and they surrounded him with a great company of supporting supernatural beings equally concerned as he was for human redemption from suffering.

Whether the Buddha's own outlook was religious in the strict sense is certainly debatable. His chief concern, some commentators say, was with measures to solve the problems of the self rather than with measures to secure favorable conditions in the world below or heaven above. Religion in the sense of a hopeful appeal to the gods to alter one's circumstances seemed to him misguided. Heinrich Hackmann has pointed out that in original Buddhism the gods are virtually dethroned; their heavenly seats become merely transitory places of reward, no deity in the complete sense of the word exists, worship seems an absurdity, prayer has no place, to know or not to know becomes the only primary concern, and true knowledge can be found only in the narrow circle of monks. "The great world outside is excluded. It must be left behind. The path to salvation leads not into the world and through the world, but away from it. In a life of seclusion each individual must take upon himself the heavy task of working out his own salvation by self-discipline, self-purification, study, thought, meditation, and concentration." And though the philosophical and abstract character of original Buddhism commended it to superior minds far beyond the bounds of India, "it would seem as if a special temperament were necessary to appreciate its profound appeal. Buddhism, in its original form, found no response among the masses."[A]

WESTERN NAME: Buddhism

FOUNDER: Siddhartha Gautama, ca. 563–483
   B.C.E.

ADHERENTS IN 1997: 330 million

NAMES USED BY ADHERENTS: The Dharma Path
   The Five Vows
   The Dharma,
   The Three "Jewels" or "Refuges":
   The Buddha, the Dharma, the Sangha

SUBDIVISIONS AND SACRED LITERATURE:

   THERAVADA 38% (Hinayana or Southern)
   The *Tripitaka* (The canon in Pali)
   The *Milindapanha* (Nagasena)
   The *Visuddhimaga* (Buddhaghosa)
   MAHAYANA 56% (Northern)
   Perfection of Wisdom lit. *Prajnaparamita*
      (Sanskrit)
   Madhyamika lit.
   The Lotus Sutra, *Saddharmapundarika*
   VAJRAYANA 6% (Lamaism or Tantric
      Buddhism)
   Tantras (Sanskrit and Tibetan)

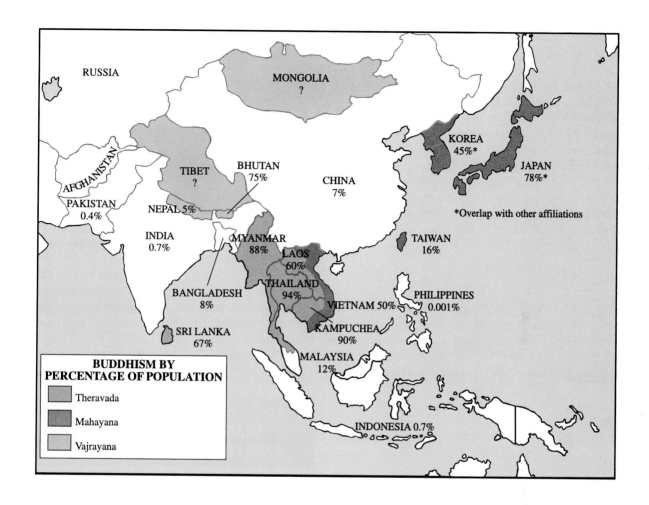

MAP LABELS:

RUSSIA

MONGOLIA
?

AFGHANISTAN

TIBET
?

BHUTAN
75%

CHINA
7%

KOREA
45%*

JAPAN
78%*

PAKISTAN
0.4%

NEPAL 5%

*Overlap with other affiliations

INDIA
0.7%

MYANMAR
88%

LAOS
60%

TAIWAN
16%

BANGLADESH
8%

THAILAND
94%

VIETNAM 50%

PHILIPPINES
0.001%

SRI LANKA
67%

KAMPUCHEA
90%

MALAYSIA
12%

INDONESIA 0.7%

**BUDDHISM BY
PERCENTAGE OF POPULATION**

Theravada

Mahayana

Vajrayana

The Founder as a Refuge

But ordinary people became interested, primarily in *the man.* Original Buddhism would not have had so great an effect on the history of religion in the Orient if the coolly rational philosophy of the sage of the Shakyas had not been mediated through a warm and friendly personality that could be adored. Fortunately for the future of Buddhism, its founder balanced the arahat ideal of self-salvation with the ideal of compassionate good will toward all living beings and practiced that compassion himself. Thus there grew up after him a cult that took refuge in *him,* the compassionate as well as enlightened one, even more than it did in his teaching, so difficult to understand and practice.

When the masses became interested, they would not be denied. By a process such as we have seen in Jainism, and will see at work in other great religions, the believers laid hold of the man behind the teaching, saw divinity in him, felt a redemptive intention in his coming among them, and adoringly surrendered themselves to him. Theirs was an early expression of the bhakti (devotional) movement that affected the whole of later Indian religion, both Buddhist and Hindu. To them he was *magical* man, with all the marks and powers of a superman. His human body was a physical housing inside which moved a heavenly being who came to earth in a "glorious body" that permeated the physical, earthly one and gave it the thirty-two marks of a superman. In India and beyond India, the common people, led by the monks who espoused

Buddhism, let those with unusual mental gifts go on constructing profound and abstruse theories (and admired them for their gifts), but they themselves engaged in something much more to their liking and much more satisfying to their deepest needs—a magical Buddhism, rich in myth and ritual.

This is a simplification of the matter, of course. The process was historically complex and required a time period of perhaps a thousand years. It was aided throughout, very much, by the monks who shared the feeling of the masses.

Lay Interests Asserted

The ordinary followers added something else. When they joined the Buddhist movement, they brought with them the long-established customs and interests of the lay world. They not only adhered to what the historians of religion call "the great tradition" (in this case the Buddha's teaching about suffering and Nirvana), they also clung to their "little (or lesser) traditions," their precautionary placation of local spirits and magical rites. As to Nirvana, it seemed to them a long way off; it was something to be sought actively only after many further existences. Meanwhile, the Law of Karma had made them laypeople, male and female; and being in and of this world, they were obliged to make their way in it. It was expected of them that they would provide not only for themselves but also for the monks, for whom they were to provide food and a respectful hearing. (Incidentally, they could accumulate much merit by doing this.) The profound distress the monks apparently felt was all but impossible for them. There were times of joy and pleasure in their lives. It was at least comforting to sit before an image of the Buddha and join others in chanting the sutras. Besides, there was joy and laughter in their homes and pleasure in the daily activities to which karma destined them. A careful observer of contemporary Buddhism remarks of some well-instructed Burmese laymen, "If their behavior is an index of their conviction, it may be said of them that, instead of rejecting the world, they are very much of it. They are attached to wives and children; they aspire to better homes and more expensive clothes; they seek the pleasures of food and sex. When

challenged, they resolve this inconsistency by saying that although the Buddhist doctrine of suffering is unassailable, they have not yet reached that state of spiritual perfection which will allow them to act upon it."[B]

Buddhism has developed in the course of time, as we shall see, still other modifications.

Indeed, there ultimately developed within Buddhism so many forms of religious organization, cultus, and belief, such great changes even in the fundamentals of the faith, that one must say that Buddhism as a whole is really, like Hinduism, a family of religions rather than a single religion. But families have a likeness, and if anything can be called the family likeness in these later developments, it is optimism restored, in one sense or another, to the heart of what was originally a way of liberation dominated by a sense of radical human misery.

I. THE SPREAD OF BUDDHISM IN INDIA AND SOUTHEAST ASIA

The First Two Centuries in India

During the first two centuries after the Buddha's death, his doctrines found wide acceptance within the basin of the Ganges. Not only did the body of monks grow, but the lay adherents increased even more rapidly and included in their number many members of the ruling classes.

The tradition has it that immediately after the Buddha's death, five hundred arahats, under the leadership of Kassapa, gathered to spend the rainy season at Rajagaha, and there recited and chanted together the contents of the *Tripitaka*. We gather that the teachings of the Buddha were early fixed in the repetitious forms of oral tradition.

When were they reduced to writing? The tradition is certainly untrue in maintaining that the monks of the so-called First Council recited the present contents of the *Tripitaka* (for example, that Ananda, the Buddha's cousin and loving attendant, recited the whole of the *Sutta Pitaka*, and Upali, another prominent disciple, the *Vinaya Pitaka*). Probably several centuries passed before the oral tradition took form as the books of the Pali canon. The choice of the Pali dialect emphasized the Buddhists' rejection of Brahminism and its Sanskrit scripture. The writings were divided into "three baskets" (which is what the word *Tripitaka* means), namely, the *Vinaya Pitaka,* or Monastic Rules, the *Sutta* (Sanskrit, *Sutra*) *Pitaka* or Discourses, and, last to be composed, the *Abhidhamma* (Sanskrit, *Abhidharma*) *Pitaka* or Supplement to the Doctrines, composed of seven works added to the Pali canon. The *Sutta Pitaka* is the most important, because the principal voice heard in the discourses is that of the Buddha himself. It is subdivided into the *Digha Nikaya* (the Longer Discourses), the *Majjhima Nikaya* (the Shorter Discourses), the *Samyutta Nikaya* (or the Connected Teachings), the *Anguttara Nikaya* (the Graduated Teachings), and the *Khuddaka Nikaya* (the Small Book Collection). The *Khuddaka Nikaya* is a miscellany of fifteen works, all of them composed some time after the Buddha. It includes the very important moral treatise, the *Dhammapada* (Verses on the Law), the *Buddha Vamsa,* giving the life of Gautama and his twenty-four predecessors, the *Theragatha* and the *Therigatha* (Hymns of the Elder Monks and Nuns), and the *Jataka,* a collection of some five hundred story-poems, which are said to be recollections by the Buddha of his former lives while he was still a bodhisattva or future Buddha.

These books were soon made the basis of commentary. In the fifth century C.E., the learned Buddhaghosa of Sri Lanka compiled (or is said to have compiled) them into the *Visuddhimagga* (the Way of Purification); he added a prose commentary on the poems of the *Jataka,* giving their complete setting in story form. An important independent treatise in supplementation of the *Tripitaka* is the *Milindapanha* (Questions of King Menander), quoted from in the last chapter. The importance of the *Digha Nikaya* and *Majjhima Nikaya* is indicated by the number of times we have quoted them heretofore, for nowhere else do we get so clear an indication of the interests and character of the historical Buddha.

About a century after the First, the Second Council met at Vaisali, and, according to tradition, fought over points of doctrine and the question of moderating the severity of the early Buddhist discipline. The result, it is said, was a schism, those who wanted the Doctrine and the Discipline interpreted more liberally seceding to form a new order of their own, calling itself the Mahasanghika, "Members of the Great Sangha," perhaps because they outnumbered those who were opposed to them, or because they included laypeople in their number, or perhaps simply because they wanted a high-sounding title. The tradition seems to be correct about the date and place of the Second Council, but there is some evidence that it is wrong about the Council being the occasion of a schism, since the Council may in fact have emphasized Buddhist unity. The schism did occur, but perhaps a few years later. The more orthodox monks were called the Sthaviravadins (Pali, Theravadins), "Adherents of the Teaching of the Elders." The Pali name survived as a designation for all of older Buddhism, the Theravada (or Hinayana) Buddhism.

The process of inner division, once in motion, produced no less than sixteen more sects during the next three centuries, and might have brought disaster to the cause had not a major accession to the Buddhist faith given it India-wide prominence.

Asoka

In 273 B.C.E. there came to the throne of Magadha, which then dominated the whole of India, one of the greatest emperors in Indian history. His name was Asoka. He was the grandson of the famous Chandragupta, founder of the Mauryan Empire (India's first), who, after forcing back and coming to terms with the Macedonian garrisons left in India in 325 B.C.E. by Alexander the Great, went on to conquer most of the rest of India for himself. Asoka on his own part added to the great domain that he inherited a fiercely resistant kingdom along the Bay of Bengal, but the bloodshed and suffering he brought on the conquered people pricked his conscience already quickened by Buddhist teachers. He publicly embraced Buddhism as his faith and became intensely interested in its propagation.

To express his "profound sorrow and regret" for the suffering he had caused by his warfare, he issued an edict, engraved upon enduring rock, for all to see, declaring that His Sacred Majesty felt remorse for the death and dislocation of so many hundreds of thousands of folk and that henceforth "if the hundredth part or the thousandth part" of all the people who were then slain, done to death, or carried away captive "were now to suffer the same fate, it would be a matter of regret to His Sacred Majesty."[C1] His Sacred Majesty would henceforth practice gentleness and bear all wrongs done to himself with all possible meekness and patience.

Realizing that the slaughter of animals for the imperial table was inconsistent with his Buddhism, Asoka cut down the palace consumption to two peacocks and one antelope daily and then forbade even this amount. He had already abolished the royal hunt. In 259 B.C.E., he issued decrees regulating throughout the empire the slaughter of animals and prohibited entirely the killing of many classes of living creatures.

The Rock Edicts

Even more important were Asoka's royal exhortations to his people to live peaceably, without violence, and to practice all of the Buddhist pieties. In 256 B.C.E., he issued a series of edicts, incised on rocks in seven widely scattered places (the "Fourteen Rock Edicts"), so that they could be read and reread by his people. These were followed by the "Seven Pillar Inscriptions," the two "Kalinga Edicts," the three "Cave Inscriptions," the four "Minor Pillar Edicts," and others. Totaling thirty-five in all, these edicts told how he wished his people to live.

> Thus saith His Sacred Majesty:—"Father and mother must be hearkened to; similarly, respect for living creatures must be firmly established; truth must be spoken. These are the virtues of the Law which must be practiced. Similarly, the teacher must be reverenced by the pupil, and fitting courtesy must be shown to relations." This is the ancient nature of things—this leads to length of days and according to this men must act.
>
> People perform various ceremonies. In sickness, at the weddings of sons, the weddings of daughters, the birth of children, departure on journeys—on those and other similar occasions people perform many ceremonies, . . . although that kind bears little fruit. . . . On the other hand, the Ceremonial of Piety bears great fruit. In it are included proper treatment of slaves and servants, honor to teachers, gentleness toward living creatures, and liberality toward ascetics and Brahmins. . . . Even if this Ceremonial of Piety fails to attain the desired end in this world, it certainly produces endless merit in the world beyond.[C2]

This is a layman's idealistic but practical creed. It is to be noted that he recommended tolerance toward ascetics (Jains?) and Brahmins. Perhaps he was not a complete convert to Buddhism. He had little interest in Buddhist ideology. There is no reference here to the Four Noble Truths, the practice of meditation, or Nirvana, the goal of the arahat. What Asoka was interested in was that his people, now that he was politically supreme over them all, should be united, and should practice piety and a common law; let them store up merit toward rebirth in a paradise hereafter. With this prospect he was more than satisfied, for he was no monk and could not reach Nirvana without becoming one.

Nirvana was for the arahats. The great mass of people had to rest content with the prospect of accumulating enough merit to enter Swarga, heaven. In some far-off rebirth they might be monks and attain Nirvana; meanwhile the bliss of paradise awaited and invited. It was enough. Still, unsubstantiated tradition says Asoka may have prepared himself for monkhood by accepting ordination into the Sangha and retiring to a monastery after forty years of rule.

Systematic Moral Education

In order to give effect to the moral exhortations contained in his inscriptions, Asoka required that the officials of the government, from the least to the greatest, give oral expositions of the Dharma to the people, and appointed Censors of the Law of Piety to supervise the populace in general and Censors of Women to supervise female morals in particular. These special officers were sent out to every part of the empire, even to the most backward and remote districts.

Asoka was much interested in Buddhism as an organized religion. To show his devotion to the memory of the Buddha, he made pious pilgrimages to spots sacred to the Blessed One. Realizing, too, that a divided

Buddhism would be weakened in its home territory, he issued edicts discouraging schism, recommending interBuddhist (and also interfaith) harmony, and called together, so a doubtful and no longer verifiable tradition relates, the Third Council, which presumably reorganized and reformed the order (the Sangha).

Most important, he seems to have conceived of Buddhism as a world religion, for he sent missionaries and ambassadors of Buddhism to lands far and near. His emissaries reached Syria, Egypt, Cyrene, and Greece. His own younger brother (or son?) headed a missionary band, as we shall next see, to Sri Lanka. All of this was the beginning of an extraordinary expansion, the full extent of which Asoka could not himself have foreseen.

Sri Lanka (formerly Ceylon)

In an exchange of gifts and compliments, Asoka first broached the subject of sending teachers of the Buddhist doctrine to Sri Lanka. Subsequently, he sent Mahinda, said by some to be his son, by others his brother, to head a band of missionaries. The civilization of Sri Lanka may be dated from that time. Buddhist shrines and monasteries rose to perpetuate the wondrous doctrine. For that perpetuation the rest of the Buddhist world came to be very grateful. Because Sri Lanka was for centuries unaffected by the sometimes catastrophic changes that went on in India itself, the Buddhist doctrine remained through the years true to the tenets of early Buddhism, with little or no change. It was, therefore, the historic destiny of the Buddhist monks of Sri Lanka to conserve for posterity the oldest Buddhist texts. The story that has come down to us is this. Mahinda brought no written records with him to Sri Lanka, but he and his associates held in memory the whole of what constitutes today the older Pali texts. The legend goes on to say that the original scriptures were rendered into the Sinhalese or island dialect, and for a time were the only complete collection of ancient texts in the whole Buddhist world. In the fifth century C.E., the great Buddhist scholar Buddhaghosa went to Sri Lanka, it is said, learned the Sinhalese tongue, and began the task of retranslating the old texts back into Pali. This interesting tale, alas, conflicts with other evidence that the Pali texts were written down *in India* about 80 B.C.E. It

was these texts that Buddhaghosa may have checked against the Sinhalese ones.

The Nuns of Sri Lanka

The women of Sri Lanka played a role in preserving and transmitting orders of nuns. It is said that at their request, Samghamitta, Mahinda's sister, came to Sri Lanka and founded a community of nuns. Their successors in later times transmitted the women's ordination lineage to China, where it survived, even though it eventually died out in Sri Lanka.

The devotional zeal of the Buddhists of Sri Lanka has been nourished through the years by the relics brought over from India. These include what the devout believe are the begging bowl, the left canine tooth, and a collarbone of the Buddha. Impressive shrines—now of great age—house these treasures.

The people of Sri Lanka are to this day predominantly of the older (Theravada) Buddhist school, sometimes called the Hinayana.

Burma and Southeast Asia

Burma and the countries of Southeast Asia also are predominantly Theravadin. All at one time or another came under the influence of Hinduism, and each, at least in the northern parts and wherever the Chinese have settled, has come under Mahayana (later) Buddhist influences, but in the main since the thirteenth and fourteenth centuries the more conservative Theravadin tendencies have prevailed. What has this meant? We shall pause to see.

The General Character of the Theravada

In the Theravadin areas, the monk is, as he always has been, the central figure. His scriptures are the ancient Pali texts and commentaries. He professes that there is no atman (self), the world is transient and the scene of sorrow, and so Nirvana is the goal. If one asks whether the Buddha exists somewhere and can help others reach Nirvana, the correct answer is always that the Buddha entered Nirvana and is therefore no longer exercising an active personal influence as a living self. The Buddha is at peace and knows nothing any more of becoming and ceasing to be. When it comes to reaching Nirvana, therefore, the monk must achieve for himself, by his own solitary meditation.

In Southeast Asia, monks take up residence in local monasteries. In villages the monasteries are small structures presided over by a single authoritative monk, assisted perhaps by several lesser monks or a few novices, and systematic meditation is not as often a part of the regimen as it is in larger monasteries.

In the larger centers the monks go forth in the morning to beg, clad in yellow robes and with shaven heads, just as in Gautama's day, and they follow the same daily schedule as of old.

A Monk's Daily Routine

It is typical for each monk to rise at the sound of a bell at daybreak, wash himself, sweep out his cell, fetch and filter a supply of water, light a candle before the Buddha image in his cell, chant a salutation, and then meditate on some aspect of the Dharma and its challenge to him. After this he takes his begging bowl, and, selecting a street, quietly goes straight down it, with eyes cast downward and not looking about; he stops at every dwelling, whether it is of high or low estate, standing in silence for the door to be opened. If there is no response, he unobtrusively goes on to the next house. (This is the theoretical ideal. In practice the streets and doorways visited are allotted by custom and pre-arrangement. Monks go to the homes of laypeople who have let it be known that they wish to contribute. Participating households usually know through the neighborhood grapevine how many monks to expect.)

Back in the monastery, the monk eats his breakfast. Then, at the sound of a bell, he joins the other monks in the assembly hall for group reverences to the Buddha, chants, and instruction by the head of the monastery. From 11:00 to 11:30 he joins the other monks in eating his main (and last) meal of the day, washes and puts aside his bowl, and back in his cell devotes the afternoon to studying and copying scriptures and to meditation, choosing perhaps one of the standard themes for meditation. T.W. Rhys Davids explained the five principal kinds of meditation in the following way:

There are five principal kinds of meditation, which in Buddhism takes the place of prayer. The first is called "Metta-bhavana," or meditation on *Love*, in which the monk thinks of all beings and longs for happiness for each. . . . The second meditation is "Karuna-bhavana" or meditation on *Pity*, in which the mendicant is to think of all beings in distress, to realize as far as he can their unhappy state, and thus awaken the sentiment of pity, or sorrow for the sorrows of others. The third meditation is "Mudita-bhavana," or the meditation on *Joy*, the converse of the last, in which he is to think of the gladness and prosperity of others, and to rejoice in their joy. The fourth is "Asubha-bhavana," the meditation on *Impurity*, in which the mendicant thinks of the vileness of the body, and the horrors of disease and corruption; how the body passes away like the foam of the sea, and how by the continued repetition of birth and death mortals become subject to continual sorrow. The fifth is "Upekka-bhavana," meditation on *Serenity*, wherein the mendicant thinks of all things that worldly men hold good or bad; power and oppression, love and hate, riches and want, fame and contempt, youth and beauty, decrepitude and disease, and regards them all with fixed indifference, with utter calmness and serenity of mind.[D]

At sundown, the monk again sweeps his cell and lights a lamp. At the sound of the evening bell he goes to another joint assembly like the morning one. After this, if he needs counsel, he goes to his superior for instruction or to confess his shortcomings and his difficulties in understanding. Finally, he retires for the night with an earnest resolve for the morrow, to struggle against desiring, against craving with renewed diligence.

Nuns and the Religious Life

The *Therigatha*, a collection of gathas (songs) attributed to elder (*theri*) nuns, throws light on the motivations of women choosing a monastic life. Seventy-one *bhikkhunis* (nuns) are characterized in the commentaries connected with the songs. They represent varied walks of life: princesses, housewives, widows, and courtesans. The legends of their lives include some who came to the order of nuns from unfavorable

Shwesandaw Pagoda, Prome, Burma
This resplendent structure is essentially a stupa. It is in the form of a spirelike cone rising from a square base of receding terraces. Each terrace is provided with smaller stupas at the corners. Other stupas surround the structure at the ground level. Since there are worship and relic chambers under the terraces, the pagoda as a whole constitutes a temple. The whole is covered with gold leaf.
(Courtesy of the Archaeological Department, Government of Burma.)

domestic situations: deprivation, a demanding husband, drudgery, or widowhood. But at least half of the commentaries tell of women in comfortable circumstances coming to their decisions on the basis of the positive attractions of Buddhist doctrine and life. Princess Sumedha, for example, turns down the marriage proposal of a Rajah and eventually makes believers of her parents and "the Rajah's people."[E]

Many of the songs develop the theme of the transience of beauty and "happiness." Ambapali, once a wealthy and beautiful courtesan of Vaisali, authored stanzas contrasting her former charms and attributes with the decay of each, always with the refrain "Not otherwise is the word of the truthful." The stanzas conclude

Such was my body once. Now it is weary and tottering, the home of many ills, an old house with flaking plaster. Not otherwise is the word of the truthful.[F]

Other poems speak of the nirvanic peace that is beyond sorrow and beyond happiness: . . . *I want no heaven of gods—Heart's pining have I trained away.*

Monks and nuns alike believed that everything in the universe, including gods, humans, and beasts, is in a state of constant flux. To abide in flux means suffering. To experience liberation from "the scene of sorrow" requires *dhyana* (Pali *jhana*), and this in turn leads to *prajna,* the highest wisdom, that is, transcendental insight penetrating beyond phenomena to final truth; in short, enlightenment (*bodhi*).

The Stages of *Dhyana*

To monks or nuns who seriously attempt to reach the highest wisdom, the question arises, What stages of *dhyana* will lead to *prajna*? The Theravada scriptures in answering this question prescribe four initial stages. In the first stage, the meditators succeed in suppressing sensual desires and other impure mental states such as ill will, sloth, and doubt (three of the Ten Fetters) and experience in such "detachment" a liberating satisfaction. In the second stage, they reach a state of mental concentration called "one-pointedness," that is, an ability to direct their thoughts to one object only, free of all distractions, a state marked by a feeling of confidence and serenity. In the third stage, the newfound confidence and serenity are transcended by a growing alienation from and indifference to everything, excepting only the meditators' own profound sense of well-being. In the fourth stage, even the sense of well-being is no longer felt, because the meditators have erased the last vestiges of self-awareness, and having thus, so to say, unselfed themselves completely, are ready to go on to Nirvana. This they reach by experiencing four further *dhyanas* admitting them to four "formless" worlds: (1) infinite space beyond all perception of formed objects, physical or mental; (2) unlimited consciousness transcending awareness of the existence of anything whatsoever; (3) emptiness or an ultimate void; and finally (4) a trance of neither ideation nor nonideation.

Although all of this is in general conformity with the Buddha's original teaching, he appears not to have advocated so structured a preparation for entrance into Nirvana; but he might have approved of the moral measures taken.

Revering the Buddha's Perfection

In another direction, the Theravadins have certainly gone against the Buddha's often-stated conviction that religious devotion is of little avail, for they have developed practices moving in the direction of devotional religion. Besides taking a reverent attitude toward the relics of the Buddha, making images of him of every size, from the minute to the colossal, and erecting giant stupas in his name, they have developed a cosmology and a view of his place in it that can only be called devotional.

The Pali texts declare (what the Buddha himself *may* have said, though it is doubtful) that the Sage of the Shakyas was not the only Buddha to appear in the world; he had predecessors in other ages—to the number of six, say some early texts, or of twenty-four, says a later text. They also affirm that the Buddha was a perfect being, omniscient and sinless, and that through countless incarnations he lived so meritoriously that he became through sheer merit a divine being who lived in the Tushita heaven. From thence he came to earth, entered his mother's womb, and was born a man. His divine nature became manifest in his enlightenment and life of pure example and teaching. His way of life is the true one for all; there is no other way out of misery into peace. He himself is at peace—perfect peace. The *next* Buddha—now a bodhisattva (Pali, bodhisatta), that is, a Buddha in the making—is Maitreya. He is waiting for the proper time to come to earth, where he will reach enlightenment and do for those in that age what Gautama has done for those in this age.

Devotional Life at a *Wat*

The religion implicit in this view of things becomes evident to any observer of the typical Theravadin religious establishment of today. In Thailand, where conditions are typical, such an establishment is called a *wat,* a cluster of buildings within a walled enclosure. The entrance is from the east and is guarded by large, grim-visaged animal or human figures in a protective stance, a carryover from the traditions of pre-Buddhist days when tutelary demons were thought essential to a well-guarded gateway. The main building in the enclosure is known as the *bot.* It usually has a curious threefold, red-tiled roof, one roof close upon another, with gilded finials of a horn-shape curving upward and said to represent snake heads. Inside, the building is designed as a hall for worship and preaching. Near the middle of the floor there may be a low dais for the leader of the preaching services, and on the floor around, mats for the congregation—laity and monks. At the end of the hall, farthest from the door, is a golden Buddha image, resplendent on a seat above the altar, with perhaps smaller standing or seated images of the same great being arranged about it, and on either side images of the two famous disciples of the Buddha, Moggalana and Sariputta, looking up worshipfully. The altar is covered with offerings of the devout, incense burners, expensive candlesticks with their candles in place, flowers in costly vases, solid gold or plated images, dishes, and bowls. These are all precious gifts to the founder of the faith and increase the merit of the givers.

During periods of instruction and prayer, a congregation sits on the polished floor before the altar and engages in group chanting.

In addition to the bot, there may be several other halls, one perhaps to house gilded Buddha images in serried rows and another to cover perhaps a reputed footprint of the Buddha in the solid rock. Also, distributed picturesquely through the compound there may be a number of stupas (*dagobas* or *phras* to the Thais), gilded towerlike structures of tapering design, usually ending in a sharp-pointed pinnacle. These are built by the laity as an act of special merit. (Indeed, the highest ambition of the devout layman is to build one during his lifetime.)

The compound as a whole also serves the public as a city park might: parents stroll with their children; a fortune teller may set up shop on a porch; and an artisan may display handicrafts under a shady tree.

The Roles of Monks and Laity

When we look at the Theravadin areas as a whole, we find an important element of the religious situation: the monks have through the centuries responded to the traditions and needs of laypeople, not only by adapting to lay customs during weddings, funerals, and periods of festival, but, what is even more important, by meeting the need to express faith in private and public activities that give laypersons something to do as well as to believe. Much of the need of Buddhist lay believers is satisfied by visits to temples to engage in private devotions and periods of instruction and meditation. But beyond this they relish group activities, such as group chanting in a Buddha-dominated sanctuary, processions through the streets, celebrations of anniversaries, and participation in public festivals originating from a Buddhist temple. The monks have faithfully cooperated in these activities.

It is standard in Theravadin areas for devout laypeople as well as monks to observe four holy days each month, these being based on the *uposathas,* or the bimonthly meetings, of the monks, going back to the beginnings of Buddhism. They are generally held at the new and full moon and two times in between.

More public than these observances are the anniversaries, especially those commemorating the Buddha's birth, enlightenment, and final entrance into Nirvana at death. In Theravadin countries these events are often commemorated together on a holy day in April. (In Mahayana lands they are observed separately along with other anniversaries honoring other Buddhas and bodhisattvas.)

In Theravadin countries special stress is laid on a time of retreat from the world, called *Vassa,* which occurs during the rainy season (July to September) when the monks stay in their monasteries and laymen, especially in Thailand and Burma, take monastic vows, live in the monasteries for three months, and return to lay life at the end of the period. (It is the general custom in Thailand and Burma for every male by the age of twenty to live in a monastery for not less than three months—less time would not be respectable: he would not be considered fit for marriage.) Each community usually celebrates the end of Vassa by presenting during a period of feast days collective gifts to the monasteries, such as yellow robes and other gifts, including a "great robe" requiring the joint stitches of many volunteers.

This is only a sampling of the full range of activities into which Theravadin Buddhists enter. It should be understood that although these pious activities are felt to increase the merits of the participants, on the whole this is often a minor consideration; the activities are devout expressions of faith in response to an impulse of self-dedication to religious goals.

One final question may be raised. What is the attitude of the devout Theravadin toward the golden image of the Buddha on its throne above the flower-laden attar in the central hall of the temple? The answer is that the attitude of the less-instructed believer is undoubtedly one of worship. In the image is seen a representation of a supernatural person who is able to hear and answer prayers. It is only the more learned monk or layperson who knows better what the truth is—that prayer increases merit, especially if it consists of the repetition of sacred words and verses, but no *answer* is expected.

II. THE RISE OF THE MAHAYANA IN INDIA

The Name

When the Mahayanists took their name (*Mahayana* means "the Great Vehicle"), the conservative, older Buddhism unwillingly accepted the name *Hinayana* ("the Lesser Vehicle"). *Yana*, "a means or method," might be visualized as a means of transportation, such as a raft or cart. If the crossing of the river analogy is used for Buddhist salvation, then Mahayana is the Great Ferry or Raft and Hinayana the Lesser Ferry or Raft. Besides the rather derogatory juxtaposition of Great and Lesser, which the Theravadins dislike, there is an implication, sometimes pointed out, of Big and Little, the Mahayana being the Big Raft transporting whole groups of believers, with a pilot in charge, and the Hinayana the Little Raft for one-at-a-time or individual transportation.

The Locus: Northwest India

After Asoka, Buddhism enjoyed great prestige throughout India for eight hundred years. And yet, forty years after his death, when Asoka's dynasty fell from power, influences hostile to Buddhism—like those of the empire of the Shungas—rose to ascendancy in central India.

But then Buddhism simply transferred its center of gravity westward. In northwestern India it began to flourish and take on new forms. In the second and first centuries B.C.E. Syrians, Greeks, and Scythians poured into the Punjab, and having made themselves its masters, became the leading spirits in a buoyant Greco-Bactrian culture. The conversion of King Menander (or King Milinda upon native tongues) brought the new kingdom within the reach of Buddhist influence. Then, in the first century C.E., the Kushans, a tribe of central Asian nomads akin to the Turks, overran Afghanistan and northwestern India and absorbed the arts and culture of the Greco-Bactrians. Their greatest king, Kanishka, had his capital in Peshawar and inquired into many religions, Zoroastrianism among them, before he adopted Buddhism. The Buddhist world had subsequent cause to be thankful that he gave his royal approval and patronage to the new and beautiful Greco-Buddhist sculpture and architecture, art forms that resulted when Greek artists were hired to lend their talents to the adornment of Buddhist themes. The curly-headed Buddhas, which they created, were destined to dominate the aesthetic consciousness of all later Buddhism, as far away as Japan.

Sometime between the third century B.C.E.—the age of Asoka, whose inscriptions give us no reason to think the religious development of Buddhism had proceeded very far—and the first or second century C.E., when Kanishka ruled northwest India, the doctrines later embodied in the Mahayana, the most elaborately developed form of Buddhism, began to take shape, especially among the Mahasanghikas, described earlier (p. 185). It was a momentous new development—more effective in making Buddhism a world religion than even Asoka's well-laid plans, for it turned the monastic way of early Buddhism into a religion that offered eternal rewards to the faithful.

The First Step: The Glorification of Gautama

This religious transformation of the original deposit of Buddhist tradition began to develop rapidly after Kanishka's conversion (whether with his encouragement or not is a matter of debate), and became public property. It is impossible now to determine precisely in just what order the various ideas arose, but the process expanded and developed certain already emerging themes in the Theravada, and seems to have pursued some such course as follows.

First, Gautama Buddha, now the object of *bhakti* (devotion), was adored and worshipped as a divine being who came to earth out of compassion for suffering humanity. A complete mythology, recorded in the *Jataka* (*ca.* second century B.C.E.), explains how through many existences the great being who became the Buddha lived according to all of "the perfections" and finally reached a place in the Tushita heaven from which he came to earth. These assertions about him were a logical consequence of certain primary assumptions: (1) that the Buddha was a person of extraordinary qualities, and (2) that when we inquire about his previous incarnation, we must believe, according to the principle of the fitness of things that marks the operations of the Law of Karma, that he could not have come from hell nor from the animal and human levels, but must have come from heaven, and without doubt from the Tushita heaven, for it is a place specifically meant for highly meritorious contemplatives. The logic here run as follows: what should or logically must have happened did, in the absence of evidence to the contrary, actually happen. Much else that the *Jataka* relates—how, as human minds apprehend, the gods went to the Tushita heaven to ask the great being to go to earth; how he assented after making five observations as to the rightness of the time and as to where and to whom he should be born; how he took the form of a white elephant and descended from heaven; how he entered the womb of his mother while she lay dreaming of this very event in a Himalayan palace of gold to which swift angels bore her; how, finally, she gave birth to him in a sacred grove with angels in attendance—all of this can be understood as being logically what must have happened and therefore did happen. To the question concerning his name before his descent to earth, the answer was, "He was a *bodhisattva*." This word, in its Pali form *bodhisatta*, occurs in rather early texts, but it is purely descriptive there; it merely recites a fact that was perfectly obvious, namely, that before Gautama was enlightened he was a person destined to be enlightened. But in the growth of the Mahayana doctrine, this word was to make religious history; it became a term of great importance.

The Next Step: Discovering Other Buddhas and Bodhisattvas

Possibly the next step followed as the result of the indirect influence of Brahmanism, which insists on a reality behind all phenomena displaying itself over and over in recurring events. Probably for more intrinsic reasons, the Mahayanists heavily emphasized a belief that the more conservative (the Theravadins) also, with less prominence, set forth, that Gautama was not the only Buddha, that there had been many Buddhas before him. Some had come to earth, and some had remained in the heavens, and some were in the making, the Buddhas of the future, the bodhisattvas.

The myth-making process was rounded out to some sort of completion when, in a manner far surpassing the modest earlier achievements in this respect, the Mahayanists recovered the names and histories of these other Buddhas and of the Buddhas to be! (The reader is doubtless puzzled. How could the names and histories of these beings be recovered without the proper documents and other historical traces? In Oriental lands, those who give full credence to intuitions, revelations, and insight into the past and future through trance visions would regard such a question as barrenly skeptical.) The literature of the Mahayana, in Sanskrit manuscript after manuscript, thus added immense stores of knowledge to the devout. Before their eyes immeasurable vistas opened up. The universe became radiant to its outer limits with compassionate beings who could and wanted to aid them. Their imaginations now had much to feed on. Furthermore, prayers were now again possible. A rich and luxuriant cultus sprang into being. The devout were furnished with wall paintings and sculptures as aids to devotion. Salvation was no longer something to be achieved only by self-effort. Divine beings with vast stores of merit were eager to share with the faithful.

Much was to flow from this. Not only was the whole aspect of Buddhism changed for the believer, but its fortunes abroad improved at once. Countries that responded slowly to the appeal of the Theravada doctrines now took up the Mahayana with eagerness.

And because the Mahayana was by nature expansive, it changed as it moved; the peoples among whom it made its way contributed to its development.

For this reason, we will trace the spread of the Mahayana before we summarize its full tenets at the height of its development.

III. THE SPREAD OF BUDDHISM IN NORTHERN LANDS

China: The Tentative Early Contacts

The story of Chinese Buddhism is very difficult to compress into a few paragraphs. Only its broadest outlines can be touched on here.

At a very early period—perhaps as early as the third century B.C.E.—China and India were in contact. Military and commercial activity found both a way over the sea and a route through central Asia, but the length and difficulty of the journey tended to make the contacts few and brief. Just how much more than the name of the Buddha, in travelers' accounts of him and his teachings, was known in China before the time of the Emperor Ming Di (58–75 C.E.), of the Later Han dynasty, is difficult to determine. Perhaps the knowledge was considerable. Chinese historians of the past have related that some half-dozen years after Ming Di began to reign he became actively interested in Buddhism, because he had seen in a dream the golden image of the Buddha flying into his room, with head glowing like the sun. According to the ancient tale, which is very likely pure legend, he sent twelve special envoys to India to bring back more exact knowledge of the teachings of the Blessed One. The envoys brought with them on their return a library of holy books, statues of the Buddha, and what was of more importance, two Buddhist monks, full of gentle missionary zeal. The monks, it was said, unloaded their holy books from the back of their horse, entered the monastery that the emperor had erected for them, and began the work of translating their sacred literature into Chinese. Incidents *like* this occurred, but perhaps not at this time nor at an emperor's

insistence. We are on sounder ground in believing that Ming Di, in 65 C.E., permitted a statue of the Buddha to be erected and the Buddhist cult to spread, without himself being an adherent of the Blessed One.

But Buddhism initially made little progress in China. It seemed in its Theravada version to be alien to the Chinese temperament and tradition. Monasticism could not easily be reconciled either with the Chinese ideal of devotion to family life or with their optimistic pursuit of material well-being. The speculative and mystical temper of Buddhism had to prove its kinship to native Chinese mysticism (Daoism) before it held any lure for them. The Chinese had first to be shown the life value of the doctrines of the transitory nature of the world, the unreality of worldly activity, the nonexistence of the self, and the need of salvation from the misery of existence. It is a well-founded tradition that during the two Han dynasties (206 B.C.E.–8 C.E. and 23–220 C.E.) family opposition to monkhood was such that a public ban lay upon the entrance of Chinese boys into monasteries.

But this attitude of coolness to Buddhism broke down, and for a number of reasons. During the period of the Hans, China was united and could devote itself to building upon earth an ideal feudal or a Confucian society, but the Later Han dynasty dissolved in the turmoil that produced the Three Kingdoms (220–280 C.E.). During the three centuries that followed, the nomad tribes of central Asia entered China in great numbers, causing disunity and misery. The scholars and intellectuals looked in vain for signs of public return to the old Chinese will to make this world a happy dwelling place for an orderly and a harmonious human family. In their great discouragement, many of them turned from the optimistic humanism of the Confucians to the mystic consolations and back-to-nature quietude of Daoism (see chapters 9 and 10). An un-Chinese contempt for the world possessed them. They became ripe for Buddhism. Indeed, there is evidence that even in the time of the Hans the Daoists had already shown an interest in Buddhism because it seemed to them to have resemblances to their own outlook. And many others felt the same interest, because the world as they knew it reduced them to hopelessness, if not actual despair.

The Appeal of Mahayana Teaching

This rather negative reason for the eventual success of Buddhism in China was more than matched by a positive one: the sheer brilliance of the advanced form of thinking discovered in the Buddhist texts, an intellectual subtlety, logical thoroughness, and profundity unparalleled in Chinese thought to that time. Intellectuals were powerfully drawn to it.

But ordinary people also were being readied for Buddhism. Among the infiltrating nomads from beyond the Great Wall were Mahayanists, who brought a gospel for the masses. From the south, too, the Mahayanist missionaries filtered in directly from India. Their flexible creed enabled them to recognize the validity of Chinese needs and modes of thought. The emphasis on filial piety that is to be found within Buddhism itself enabled them to rank this virtue alongside maintaining the sanctity of animal life, abstaining from intoxicants, and the rest of the Five Precepts of the Buddhist order. Indeed, they began to say that to fulfill the duty of filial piety, sons should supplement traditional Confucian funeral rites with Buddhist ceremonies for the dead, as a means of making the lot of their ancestors happier. Here the vivid imagery of the Buddhist monks, who drew freely from Indian conceptions of the afterlife, began to tell. China had lacked a really satisfying conception of the afterlife. Confucianism had had little to offer in the way of comfort, except the bare faith that one would join one's ancestors at death and be dependent forever thereafter on the filial piety and remembrance of one's descendants. It was in part just because Mahayana Buddhism, as it came to flower, far surpassed either Daoism or Confucianism in presenting attractive pictures of the afterlife that it began by the fourth century to exercise a wider popular appeal. This is not to say that Confucianism and Daoism were entirely displaced, but only that Buddhism won a place alongside them. (One could, indeed, be at one and the same time a Confucian seeking the internal welfare and harmony of the family, a Daoist coming to terms with external natural processes, and a Buddhist aiming at security after death. The three religions seemed to complement each other.)

North China, where the racial stock was now largely intermixed with the blood of "barbarian" invaders, and where the ancient Chinese culture was most disturbed and shaken, was the first to respond generally. South China was slower to yield. Here Confucianism still had staying power, and even the Daoists were inhospitable. Nationalistic pride was stronger there. But eventually, all over the land, monasteries sprang up, huge temples full of images of the various Buddhas of the Mahayana faith multiplied, and the intellectuals divided into many schools of Buddhist thought.

Cycles of Growth and Repression

The number of adherents to the various Buddhist groups was large, and remained large, while dynasties rose and fell. Sometimes a sternly Confucian or vigorously Daoist emperor would institute widespread persecution. But tolerant emperors often undid the work of anti-Buddhist ones, and at least the physical damage was repaired. It is difficult to compare census reports from era to era because there were varying ways of classifying the faithful. In general, governments sought to control ordinations to keep down the number of persons exempt from military service and corvee (forced labor). In some periods the privately or illegally ordained outnumbered the officially ordained by as many as six to one. It was said that the Emperor Wu Zong in 845 C.E. destroyed forty-five thousand Buddhist buildings, melted down tens of thousands of Buddhist images, and sent some four hundred thousand monks, nuns, and temple servitors back into the world. Other census figures seem less extreme. In the interval 713–741 C.E., near the middle of the Tang dynasty, a census showed 75,524 monks and 50,576 nuns. In 1077 C.E. in the Sung dynasty the figures were 202,872 monks and 29,692 nuns, a great increase in monks, but a decline in the proportion of nuns from two-thirds to about one-seventh. The census in 1677 C.E. in the Qing period showed 110,292 monks and 8,615 nuns, half as many monks as before and only about one in thirteen for the proportion of nuns.[G1]

When temples and monasteries flourished, monks and lay adherents had much to believe and do.

a.

b.

c.

d.

e.

f.

Evolution of the Buddha Image
South Asian: a. Gandharan Greco-Roman (Apollo-like) from the northwest; b. Mathuran Native Indian (full lips, flat nose) from the Ganges Valley; c. Later Indian consensus or "export" version
East Asian: d. Chinese and Southeast Asian (thin lipped, light framed), derived from Mathura; e. Chinese derivative of the Gandharan style; f. Chinese-Japanese derivative of the Indian consensus style. *(From William Willets,* Foundations of Chinese Art *[Fig. 37]. New York: McGraw Hill, 1965. p. 185.)*

In such Chinese tales as the famous medieval novel *Shui Hu Zhuan,* which Pearl S. Buck translated under the title *All Men Are Brothers,* the rambunctious warrior Li Ji Shen finds this to be the case. When he seeks refuge in the temple of Siang Guo, he is assigned by its abbot to one of its monasteries to serve as manager of a vegetable garden, and he vigorously protests. But the monk who receives guests says,

> "Listen to me. In our midst each working priest has his duty and his place. I, who am the receiving monk, do receive guests and such things. Such places where there is little to do are not easily achieved. Master of the temple, chief priest, keeper of the courts, these all care for the expenditures of the temple. You have only just come here and how can you suddenly desire to become one of these higher ones? Keeper of the accounts and of the treasure and of the stores, keeper of the particular halls, keeper of the upstairs gods, keeper of the flower gardens, keeper of the baths—all these are officiating positions, and are for the priests of the middle position. Then there are those who care for the pagoda, the one who sees to the food and to the kitchens, the one who cares for the tea, the caretaker of the latrines—these are all places for the priests of a little lower degree. You, for instance, Brother Priest, if you manage the vegetable gardens well one year, will rise to keeper of the pagoda, and after a year's good service there you will be keeper of the bath house, and only after another good year you may be master of the temple."
>
> Lu Chi Shen said, "If it is thus and there is a way to rise, I will go tomorrow."[H]

There will be more to say about Buddhism in China in Section VI of this chapter.

The Arrival of Buddhism in Korea

The introduction of Buddhism into Korea followed from its spread in China. Korea was at that time divided into three independent states, none of which had a highly advanced culture. Koguryo in the north received the monk Sundo from northern China in 372 C.E. Twelve years later, Paekche in the southwest was host to an Indian monk, Marnananta. Some fifty years later, Buddhism came to Silla in the southeast, but this was the kingdom that was to conquer its neighbors and make Buddhism the state religion in a unified Korea. A long golden age stretched through the Koryo dynasty (935–1392 C.E.). When Mongol invasions came in the thirteenth century, the close association of the Buddhist hierarchy with an ineffectual court touched off a period of decline. One of the remarkable products of this period of stress was an immense pious project of sutra printing. The complete *Tripitaka* was cut into wooden printing blocks—81,258 panels!

The Arrival of Buddhism in Japan

It was in 552 C.E. that Buddhism arrived in Japan as a gift from a beleaguered kingdom in Korea. Menaced by the power of Silla and hoping for Japanese help, the King of Paekche sent tribute and gifts to the Emperor Kimmei of Japan: a gold-plated image of the Buddha, some sacred writings, and a letter concerning the excellent but difficult Buddhist doctrine. This doctrine, the letter said, could produce immeasurable good fortune or painful retribution. This claim probably did not impress the emperor as much as the further statement that from farthest India and through all of China the doctrine had found reverent acceptance. An emperor eager to emulate whatever had made China great must have been impressed by that. He took the matter up with his councilors. Some were as receptive but as cautious as himself; others were in outright opposition to the new religion in the devout belief that the *Kami* (the native gods of Japan) would be angered. The prime minister, chief of the Soga clan, suggested favorable action. He was impressed by the magical protection offered by the Buddhas (and he

was in need of a countervailing religious sanction to use against hostile Shinto factions in the government). The emperor took the part of prudence and passed the golden Buddha image on to the head of the Soga clan to try it out on his family, to see if the Kami would object. When a pestilence broke out among the people it was thought the Kami did object, so the golden image was thrown into a canal, and Buddhism fell irretrievably out of the emperor's favor.

In due course the emperor died, and the Korean monarch sent another embassy, which included, besides the priests and two hundred sacred texts, a nun, an image maker, and a temple architect. In the spirit of courtesy, the embassy was allowed to construct a temple for its own use, and once more the Soga clan supported the view that the new religion should be given a fair trial. Again, however, a pestilence broke out, and, if we are to believe the ancient tale, again the Buddha images found a resting place at the bottom of a canal.

All looked dark for Buddhism. But presently a perplexity arose. The pestilence continued! So the head of the Soga clan advanced the thought-provoking argument that it was not the Kami who were angered—else the pestilence would have ended—but the Buddhas, who resented the coldness of their reception. The cautious authorities decided to let matters drift.

The Attractions of Buddhism in Japan

The impression left by this tale requires some correction and supplementation. To the clan leaders and the aristocracy of the court, Buddhism was attractive on many grounds. It had an abundance of scriptures, written in the Chinese characters then being adopted wholesale by the Japanese. These scriptures (which needed interpretation but no translation, once the Japanese had learned to pronounce each Chinese character with the sound of the equivalent Japanese word) greatly stimulated the imagination by their universal range, their richly symbolic imagery, their mind-stretching ideas, and their exciting applications in ritual, magic, and art. Private human needs also were met by emotionally satisfying Buddhist consolations:

scriptures for the comfort of the sick with the explicit understanding that they had magical curative effects, solemn and beautiful funeral rites, memorial services for the dead, cremation and preservation of the ashes, and scriptures and prayers for the repose of the departed spirit recited by a priest at the *butsu-dan* ("Buddha-altar") in the home (or palace), graced by a wooden memorial tablet inscribed with the name of the dead (usually the "heavenly name" made known by the priest).

By the time the next emperor reached the throne, Buddhism had made actual progress. In fact, the emperor, in spite of provincial military and priestly opposition, viewed it with favor. With new Buddhist missionaries ever arriving, the tide began to turn. In 588 C.E., when the empress Suiko ascended the throne, her nephew Shotoku Taishi, an ardent Buddhist, became regent. He sent groups of scholars to China to bring back as complete knowledge as possible both of Buddhism and of the Chinese system of government. He built the first public Buddhist temple in Japan and organized the first monastic school. To exemplify the humanitarianism of the Mahayana, he erected a hospital, a dispensary, and a house of refuge. Other Buddhist leaders donated almshouses, irrigation canals, orchards, harbors, ferries, reservoirs, and good roads. The new religion was demonstrated to be good not only for the individual, but also for society as a whole.

Having won the adherence of the court, Buddhism began slowly to reach down to ordinary people. There will be more to say about schools of Buddhism in Japan in Section VI of this chapter.

Buddhism in Tibet and Mongolia

Buddhism was late in coming to Tibet and Mongolia. It established itself in a form so different from the Theravada and even the Mahayana, as these are usually understood, that it is called by other names. Although the Tibetans prefer that their religion be called simply Tibetan Buddhism, it is sometimes given the name Lamaism because of the prominence of the *lamas* (monks), but this is misleading. Other names refer to its practices or doctrines. Thus it may be called the Mantrayana ("the Vehicle of Mantras," or "Holy Words," which emphasizes its magical character), or the Tantrayana (which points out its relation to

Tantric Hinduism, p. 128), or, better still, the Vajrayana ("the Vehicle of the Thunderbolt," which reflects its bold theology). Because of its belated coming, strange history, and stranger doctrines, it will be described separately in Section VII of this chapter.

The Decline of Buddhism in India

Oddly enough, the up curve of the Mahayana in China and Japan is matched by a swift down curve in India. This is perhaps as good a place as any to note a startling fact: Buddhism steadily declined in India after the seventh century C.E. The Chinese pilgrim Fa Xian (Fa-hsien), who visited India from 405 to 411 C.E., noted with joy the flourishing condition of both the Hinayana and Mahayana monasteries, but when his countryman Xuan Zhuang (Hsüan Chuang) came two centuries later (629–645 C.E.), decline had set in apace. Part of the decline may be assigned to the ferocious invasions of the White Huns in northern India during the sixth century, incursions that resulted in the raiding and destruction of the Buddhist monasteries and the disorganization of the Buddhist leadership. But this externally induced weakness was more than matched by an internal weakness of long standing. Buddhism expected the laity to feed and assist the monks but offered them in return few of the life-enveloping ceremonies the Brahmins were so ready to perform—ceremonies for birth and death and, in between, ceremonies for all of the promising or threatening events that favored or deeply perturbed villages, homes, and individuals. Then, too, it had been a constant threat to Buddhism as a separate movement that the followers of Vishnu, as early perhaps as the fourth century C.E., adopted the Buddha as the ninth incarnation of Vishnu. Most serious of all was the decline of creative intellectual energy within Buddhism itself. A final blow came in 1197 when the Muslims, who had entered India four centuries before, invaded the last of the Buddhist strongholds. What was left of the dispirited Buddhism in Magadha was roughly stamped out. Only a few followers of the Blessed One obscurely hung on to the faith, mostly in scattered communities in the foothills of the Himalayas.

In 1951, B. R. Ambedkar, a leader among untouchables, founded the Buddhist Society of India. His own induction to the order was witnessed by over a half million persons, and in the movement that followed, some four hundred thousand, mostly members of depressed classes in Maharashtra, declared themselves Buddhists. In 1997, there were an estimated seven million Buddhists in India, about eight-tenths of 1 percent of the population.

IV. THE HELP-OF-OTHERS MESSAGE OF THE MAHAYANA

What was the secret of the success of the Mahayana outside of India? The answer is not hard to find: most Mahayanists claimed that the Buddha *privately* taught that one does not have to save oneself but can get help.

The Divine Authors of Salvation

To the common people, the Mahayana offered the good news of the existence of multitudes of saviors, real and potential, whose chief desire was the cure or amelioration of the sufferings of men. The pure benevolence of these saviors was the best of all assurances. With their help, one could at least hope to gain heaven after death, if not what could only be self-won—Nirvana.

In the Mahayana the authors of salvation are of three kinds, falling naturally into order. They are the Manushi Buddhas, the bodhisattvas, and the Dhyani Buddhas. To believers, these Buddhas were manifest realities. Edward Conze writes,

> To the Christian and agnostic historian, only the human Buddha is real, and the spiritual and magical Buddhas are to him nothing but fictions. The perspective of the believer is quite different. The Buddha-nature and the Buddha's "glorious body" [his bodhisattva body] stand out most clearly, and the Buddha's human body and historical existence appear like a few rags thrown over his spiritual glory.[1]

1. Manushi Buddhas

Manushi Buddhas are saviors who, like Gautama, have appeared on earth in the past as human beings,

attained enlightenment, instructed men in the true way of life, and then, their duty done, realized Nirvana. They are primarily teachers. Prayers cannot now reach them.

2. Bodhisattvas

Bodhisattvas would never have become vital concepts if it had not been for the historical Buddhas, like Gautama, but in the Mahayana, if anything, they are more important and have a greater religious reality. The Theravada scriptures recognize only two beings of the kind, Gautama before his enlightenment and Maitreya. But in the full form of the Mahayana the bodhisattvas are a great, even an innumerable, company of supernatural beings who hear prayers and come actively to people's aid. The prevalent popular view of bodhisattvas, especially in China and Japan, has been that they are beings who have made a vow many existences ago to become Buddhas and have lived ever since in such a way as to acquire almost inexhaustible stores of merit. This merit is so great that they could readily achieve the full status of Buddhas and pass into Nirvana, but they are compassionate beings; out of love and pity for suffering humanity, they postpone their entrance into Nirvana and transfer their merit, as the need arises, to those who call upon them in prayer or give devotional thought to them. They sit enthroned in the heavens, looking down on the needy world, and sometimes, in redemptive pity, they descend in the guise of ministering angels to perform deeds of mercy. We have space here only for brief mention of the most widely popular among them.

Maitreya   Maitreya, the next Buddha (known in China as Milo-fo), has already been mentioned. He was honored first in India and then all over the Mahayana world. Numerous images of him show the high respect in which he has always been held, but, strange to say, worship of Maitreya never has been so ardent as in the case of some other bodhisattvas. Perhaps the faith that he is going to be the next Buddha has made for a feeling that he is, or should be, saving his merit for his earthly career and cannot give it away. Then people turned to others, like Manjusri (Chinese, Wen-shu) and Avalokitesvara (Guan-yin). The former is one of the earliest of the Mahayana creations. He is the bodhisattva who assists those who wish to know and follow the Buddhist Law (the Dharma). So he is represented as a princely figure, carrying in addition to his sword (to cut down ignorance) a book (describing the ten perfections of wisdom). Near his image there often appears that of another bodhisattva, Samantabhadra (Pu-hien), who brings happiness to his following and fosters in them his own universal kindness.

Avalokita (Guan-yin)   But the most popular bodhisattva by far, in himself and in his metamorphoses, is Avalokitesvara, or Lord Avalokita. As his Indian name seems to imply (it probably means "the Lord Who Looks Down on This Age from Above"), he has a special interest in the people of the current time. The personification of divine compassion, he watches over all who inhabit the world and is said to have come to earth over three hundred times in human form, once as a miraculous horse, to save those in peril who have called upon him. He averts not only moral catastrophes, such as rage, folly, and lust, but physical pains and disaster as well, such as shipwreck, robbery, or violent death. He grants to women the children they implore. His image usually represents him in the garb of a great prince, with high headdress, carrying in his left hand a red lotus (one of his aliases is Padmapani, the Lotus-Handed), and extending his right hand with a gracious gesture. Frequently he is shown seated on a large lotus and is called, with poetic devotion, "the Jewel in the Lotus." Sometimes he is given four, six, or many more arms—all laden with gifts to men and women. Sometimes he kneels; his postures are many.

We shall see (p. 223) that in Tibet Avalokita is paired with a consort, Tara, who is his female aspect; but in China, by a metamorphosis whose history is obscure, a gender change takes place, and the enormously popular Guan-yin, Goddess of Mercy, emerges. (In the Chinese and Japanese contexts, the gender designations are deemed unimportant, for all bodhisattvas are perceived as having transcended sexuality.) Guan-yin's attitudes are those of Avalokita in India, with the addition of the warmth of maternal feeling. Her images, upon which sculptors have lavished their highest art, show her in every variety of gracious and winsome posture. They are to be found all over China, Korea (where she is called Koan-Eum), and Japan

(where the name has been further modified to Kannon and male or neutral forms are common in artistic representation). Like her Indian alter ego, she often is shown sitting or standing on a lotus, riding on a cloud, or gliding on a wave of the sea. In her arms she often bears a child, for it is such she gives to her women adorers, and on her head she may wear a crown set with an image in miniature of Amitabha Buddha, the Lord of the Western Paradise, to whom she takes those faithful to her. Again, she may be shown without ornament.

Kshitigarbha   One other important bodhisattva is Kshitigarbha. In China, under the name of Di Zang, and in Japan, as Jizo, he ranks high in popular regard, chiefly because, at the instance of grieving relatives and friends, he descends into the hells, delivers its sufferers, and transports them to heaven. In previous incarnations he was twice a woman, which explains his untiring kindness and tender mercy and his interest in helping women in the pangs of childbirth. As if to credit him with the endeavor to be in many places at once and thus multiply his power to aid, the Chinese declared there were six of him, one for each of the six life levels of the universe. In Japan, in the character of a single being, Jizo was identified with the Shinto war god, Hachiman; represented as riding on horseback, wearing a war helmet, he became the favorite of the Japanese soldiery. But he also was the beloved friend of little children, in which relation he appeared to them in the guise of a simple, honest monk.

3. Dhyani Buddhas (Tathagatas)

The third class of savior beings is composed of Dhyani Buddhas. Their name comes from a late Nepalese tradition and has gained currency because it is terminologically convenient. The usual name in the Sanskrit texts is Tathagatas (in the sense of "those who have traveled the road to Suchness") or Jinas ("victorious ones"). These "contemplative Buddhas" differ from bodhisattvas in having fully achieved their Buddhahood, but they stand in a different category also from the Manushi Buddhas in not having achieved their Buddhahood in human form. They dwell in the heavens, and in the indefinite interval between the present time and their compassionately postponed final entrance into Nirvana they actively minister to human needs, as did Gautama between his enlightenment and death. Their name implies that they are Buddhas of contemplation (dhyana), and their images convey the impression of deep meditation and calm. Whereas the bodhisattvas are usually princely in aspect and wear rich clothes, studded with gold and jewels, to symbolize their active, world-serving role, the Dhyani Buddhas sit or stand in the simple garments of the monk, their hands held in front of them or folded in their laps in the five established *mudras* or positions, their eyes turned downward, and a quiet smile lighting up their otherwise grave and composed countenances.

Taking the whole of the Mahayanist world into account, we find the three most appealed-to Dhyani Buddhas to be Vairocana, Bhaisajyaguru, and Amitabha. They are but a few among many. The first is a solar Buddha, whose functions link him with the Persian Mithra, the Vedic Savitar, and the Mediterranean Apollo. He is a Buddha of first importance in Java, and in Japan the sun goddess Amaterasu has been called his manifestation. The second is the Buddha of Healing and has a great following in Tibet, China, and Japan (see diagram on p. 207).

Amitabha (Amida)   The third Dhyani Buddha, Amitabha (known to the Chinese as O-mi-tuo and to the Koreans and Japanese as Amida), is one of the great gods of Asia. Once he was a monk, took the vow an incalculable number of aeons ago to become a bodhisattva, rose to his present rank, and now presides over the Western Paradise, a Buddha field or domain he has called into existence, named Sukhavati, or the Land of Bliss, generally known as "the Pure Land." Because he is the kindly lord of this happy heaven of the Western quarter and freely admits all who beseech him in faith, he has surpassed even Shakyamuni, the deified Gautama, in the estimation of the masses in China and Japan. The core of the matter is this: Whereas the bodhisattvas serve present need, Amitabha assures future bliss. The hopeful devotee, unable to emulate Shakyamuni in helpfulness or to acquire the merit stored up by arahats and bodhisattvas, turns to Amitabha and has merit transferred to him from the great being's store. Some sects among the Chinese and Japanese believe that the grace of O-mi-tuo is granted in fullness to anyone who merely repeats with devotion his sacred name. A Mahayana

treatise widely read in China and Japan, *A Description of the Land of Bliss* (the *Lesser Sukhavativyuha*), says distinctly that faith in Amitabha (and his active principle, Amitayus, "immeasurable life"), quite apart from meritorious works and deeds, is alone sufficient for salvation. It declares,

> Beings are not born in that Buddha country as a reward and result of good works performed in this present life. No, all men or women who hear and bear in mind for one, two, three, four, five, six, or seven nights the name of Amitayus, when they come to die, Amitayus will stand before them in the hour of death, they will depart this life with quiet minds, and after death they will be born in Paradise [i.e., the Pure Land].[11]

In this conception, original Buddhism is completely transcended.

But this is no less true of the whole of the Mahayana scheme of salvation. No one will deny that Gautama taught and practiced good will and compassion for all, but these expressions of love were to a certain degree impersonalized, as his philosophy of life demanded. So far as possible, as we have observed before (p. 179), love was made a love for everyone, not of any *one,* and at no time was the acquiring of merit forgotten—at least in theory. But in its conception of the character of the bodhisattvas and Dhyani Buddhas, Mahayana Buddhism exalts pure altruism to supremacy in the moral sphere, and by insisting on its expression in supernatural beings who answer prayers, has moved counter to Gautama's teaching that one should not pray but should devote one's energies to something really effective—saving oneself.

The Mahayanists frankly recognize this departure from early Buddhist teaching, but they have the belief that Gautama taught several kinds of doctrine, depending on the nature of the hearers: to the weak and selfish he outlined the eightfold arahat path; to those of greater understanding and strength of character he imparted the ideal of the compassionate and altruistic bodhisattva. This version of Gautama's teaching has enabled the Mahayanists to vigorously attack the selfishness of the "Hinayanists," who are accused of abandoning the world to its fate while they seek their own salvation individually, each "wandering alone like a rhinoceros."

The Vow of the Bodhisattva

The scheme of altruism just outlined led, in actual fact, to perhaps the most inspiring of all Buddhist teachings. It may be rather awkwardly stated thus: Just as the bod-hisattvas, who are now divine but once were human, vowed in a distant past to become Buddhas and then from pure altruism postponed their entrance into Nir-vana by transferring their merit to others, so any human being of the present, man or woman, can, if he or she wishes, make a similar vow with regard to the future.

Although the bodhisattva is essentially asexual, Mahayana literature exhibits ambivalence on the ques-tion of whether females must first be reborn as males before finally achieving the bodhisattva state. In earlier tradition, one of the "thirty-two marks" of the Bud-dha's body was a penis, but the *Diamond Sutra* coun-ters that all marks are illusory. The *Lotus Sutra* described the moment when the daughter of the Dragon King became a bodhisattva thus: "At the same instant . . . the female sex of the daughter of Sagara, the Naga-king disappeared; the male sex appeared and she manifested herself as a bodhisattva."[K] In any case many of the sex-transcending bodhisattvas were rep-resented as feminine—in sculpture as early as Bharhut (second century B.C.E.) and in the celebrated forms of Guan-yin (p. 200) and the Tantric Taras (p. 224).

Everyone is potentially a Buddha and should now take the vow to be a bodhisattva. The length of time necessary to fulfill the destiny thus undertaken may be almost beyond reckoning, but true benevo-lence needs no urging and waits for nothing. The time to begin is now.

As the Mahayana doctrines developed into their fuller forms, this ideal was more clearly articulated and was linked, as will shortly appear, with a vast meta-physical background. Various stages in the career of a bodhisattva were distinguished, and a body of litera-ture emerged to convey instructions on how to enter the initiatory stages. According to a seventh-century manual, the *Bodhicaryavatara*, the initial stages can be entered upon by those who feel joy in the good actions of all living beings and who wish to spend themselves in the increase of such good. Persons of this tempera-ment may then pray to the Buddhas to aid them in acquiring enlightenment—not that they may pass into Nirvana, but rather that they may secure the good of all living beings. To this end they make their solemn vows to postpone their entrance into Nirvana until they have aided all living beings within range or until the last blade of grass shall have been set free!

In East Asia, the Buddhist monks ascend through successive degrees of ordination that culminate in that of a bodhisattva. The degree that immediately precedes the last is, significantly, that of an arahat, and this order of the degrees clearly shows how the Mahayana feels it has gone beyond the ethical ideals of the Theravada. For Mahayanists, consider that the Buddha rated com-passion above self-salvation.

V. THE MAHAYANA PHILOSOPHIES OF RELIGION

What to the people was a message of salvation was to the intellectuals and mystics a philosophy, profound and subtle. It was so all explanatory that it intrigued the minds that believed it no less than it rejoiced them.

The Background: Theravadin Schools

Most of the Buddhist philosophizing was done in India. The Theravadin (Hinayana) philosophers came first and provided the terms and issues with which the later Mahayana philosophers began. As we have seen (p. 185), after the split of the Buddhist movement into the *Sthaviravadins* and the *Mahasanghikas* further subdivisions developed. They evolved into the Ther-avada and Mahayana schools.

1. *The Sthaviravadins.* Generally, the early followers of the Buddha, led by the *Sthaviravadins,* found their philosophical point of departure in the Buddha's teaching that the commonly-believed-in self or ego is but a loose grouping of impermanent, ever-changing skandhas. They reasoned that this analysis of the human personality holds good for all objects or aggre-gates whatsoever: anything at all is a loose collection of pulsating, transitory elements, which they called *dhar-mas* (Pali *dhammas*). They tended to think of these dharmas as for a time objectively "existing"; that is, the physical and mental components into which the

so-called "selves" and "perceived objects" of the world were to be resolved were "real." They said the dharmas were, like the atoms of the Jains, "ultimates," even though they came into being, functioned, and then disappeared. The purpose of the Sthaviravadins, however, was not so much to assert a philosophical realism as to point out that everything is transient and one should not become "attached" to selves and other objects, since they are really composed of impersonal elements that are not to be clung to; one should break the bonds that tie one to such objects. How could anyone be attached to collections of dharmas linked together impermanently in chains of causes and effects that themselves appear and disappear?

2. *Sammatiya.* Some early Theravadin schools allowed their realism to carry them further. In the third century B.C.E., a school bearing the name of Sammatiya (but nicknamed the *Pudgalavadins* or Personalists) contended that there exists in each living individual a semipermanent if ultimately perishable person (*pudgala*), neither identical with nor separate from the skandhas, and that it has consciousness ("knows") and transmigrates unhappily from body to body until reaching dissolution in Nirvana.

3. *The Sarvastivadins.* Another group, the *Sarvastivadins,* contended, as their name indicates, that "everything exists." Not only present but past and future happenings (which are all aggregates of dharmas) exist simultaneously, combining momentarily according to one's karma to bring about one's present consciousness, all of this without any self or ego existing. In the list of existing aggregates of dharmas were such unconditioned realities as space and Nirvana and as yet unapprehended realities. Such things must exist, otherwise they would not appear in consciousness. Opposing groups vigorously denied this on the grounds that some of these notions are subjective and not objective, and that the argument as a whole adopted an "eternalism" that was heretical.

Two Mahayana Schools

When the Mahayana came into being in the first century B.C.E., a new era of philosophizing began that in the course of five centuries saw Hindu and Jaina philosophers engaging along with the Buddhists in what was in fact the great systematizing era in Indian thought.

In the second or third century C.E., Nagarjuna gave notable expression to the *Madhyamika* (or Intermediate) school, founded on the earlier speculations that we have just reviewed. He took a middle or an "intermediate" position between the realism that granted existence to dharmas and the idealism soon to be described as characterizing the *Yogacara* school.

1. Nagarjuna's *Madhyamika*

From his "intermediate" position, Nagarjuna was able to challenge either extreme and to say both yes and no, or neither yes nor no, to any dogmatic view. He took the step of saying outright what some of the Buddhists who preceded him refused to say, that the elements constituting perceived objects (the dharmas), when examined, are in fact no more than mental phenomena or phantasms. They are "void" or "empty" and do not really exist as experienced; they are but the figments of ignorance-clouded minds. If one sees an object, say a man, or even the Buddha, walking down the street, one really experiences seeing such an object; the experience means something in one's mental history; but the object is nevertheless not the solid, material object one initially senses it to be. One cannot say there is *nothing* "there"; but the substantiality of the external world is denied. "Everything is empty (*sunya*)." Things are not what they seem. In reality, they are empty of the characteristics assigned to them.

However, certain important qualifications must be made. What has just been argued is the transcendental truth (*paramartha-satya*). Only minds that have shed "ignorance" can apprehend it. As long as minds continue to function in the ordinary or usual way, they experience everyday or relative truth (*Samvriti-satya*). In the light of everyday truth, things seem not to be void but to have qualifications that give them existence and reality for experience. This is the realm of the relative and impure, in which people are born and reborn (the realm of samsara, the world order).

Obviously such a view of reality made for skepticism about all human knowledge. Indeed, much of Nagarjuna's extant writings deal with the relativity of human knowledge, including his own. In the two treatises that seem to be his, the *Madhyamika Karika* and the *Vigrahavyavartani,* he demolishes all positions based on samvriti-satya as self-contradictory or else antithetical to some other position similarly based; and without taking a position of his own, because any opinion that springs from human consciousness is relative only, he inclines toward a not-yet-arrived-at synthesis of the numerous antitheses he has pointed out. The truth in fact always remains out of the reach of any human formulation.

The Paradox of Sunyata (Emptiness)   The only certainty is that to a mind heretofore struggling with relative truths the thing that happens when enlightenment comes is a realization that the *ultimate* Reality that must be behind or beyond the appearances known to human consciousness as the Buddha, the world of bondage (samsara), karma, and reincarnation is ineffable: human minds and tongues can never encompass it. One must say, as Bhikshu Sangharakshita puts it, that things that are truly real subsist in a "purely spiritual world which transcends thought and speech."[L1] In this Reality, there is "neither production, nor destruction, nor annihilation, nor persistence, nor unity, nor plurality, nor coming in, nor going out."[J2] Furthermore, not only are the things of this world void, but entrance into Nirvana is equivalent to *sunyata* (emptiness), or entering a void, because it means stripping the attributes from everything and passing into what appears from "here" to be vacuity and silence, where there is no perception, no name, no concepts, no knowledge; no eye, ear, body, or mind; no taste, touch, objects; no ignorance, no decay, no death, no Four Noble Truths, and no obtaining of Nirvana.[M]

A further paradox, which Nagarjuna much delighted in, follows: samsara (the world order) and Nirvana are *identical* in the sense that they are both humanly apprehended and therefore empty suggestions of the undifferentiated Reality to which all concepts point. Since, then, the world of everyday experience—with all of its world-attached, desire-motivated selves—and Nirvana are two ways of looking at the same reality, and since both of them are, in the light of transcendental truth, empty, then neither of them is in fact a reasonable object of desire, for how can one reasonably desire the empty? The sensible Buddhist will therefore desire nothing, and in the calm of no desire find himself in Nirvana without even trying!

The Madhyamika suggestion that both samsara and Nirvana are conceptual constructions (i.e., subjective) led to the query, why and whence do ideas arise? Even illusions must have a source or ground. What this source or ground might be was made the chief concern of the *Yogacara* school, also called Vijnanavada.

2. *Yogacara* (Mind Only)
Founded in the third century C.E. by Maitreyanatha and made famous in the fourth or fifth century by the brothers Asanga and Vasubandhu, the *Yogacara* (Idealist or Mind-Only) school began where the Madhyamika left off. Under this view the source of all ideas is *vijnana* (consciousness), which is seen as the fundamental basis of experience. The mentalism or idealism at first sight seems complete. The human mind or consciousness is "the imagination of unreality" (*abhutaparikalpa*), and the objects of its thought are ideas only. How then does the mind perceive what other minds do and not just what it pleases to perceive; that is, how does it share the everyday world with other minds? How does it learn about the Buddha and seek Nirvana? The immediate answer is that there is a reservoir or store of perceptions, a cosmic receptacle of ideas gathered from previous impressions (a kind of collective consciousness) on which all minds draw. Nothing else can be said to exist; it is "the consciousness that holds all" (the *alaya-vijnana*). Since this is so, the universe is "mind only." It is in flux like an ocean, from whose tossing waves the individual mind, determined by karma, draws together the phenomenal world apprehended by the seven illusion-making levels of consciousness—sight, hearing, smell, taste, touch, discrimination between the various phenomena of the universe, and distinguishing between subject and object. The "receptacle consciousness" is the source of the illusory phenomena "perceived" by the seven other types of consciousness. (It is itself the eighth type of consciousness.) But the alayavijnana is not the ultimate reality; it operates within the Void (*sunyata*), which is the ultimate reality, and is so named because human minds (the "imagination of unreality") cannot apprehend it. To identify with the ultimate reality is, then, to abandon, through Yoga, all ideas (ideation), including awareness derived from the alaya-vijnana, and realize Nirvana, that is, be lost in or rather liberated into the Void.

In the famous treatise *The Awakening of Faith,* a Chinese Yogacara work falsely ascribed to Ashvaghosa, the ultimate ground of consciousness was named the Absolute Suchness (the Bhutatathata, "that which is such as it is"), and it was said that when a mind hampered by ignorance attempts to comprehend it, the illusion that constitutes the seeming multiplicity of the phenomenal world is produced, but in itself the Absolute Suchness is pure and at rest, the "oneness of the totality of things."

Buddhist Tantrism

One further Buddhist school needs to be considered— the *Tantric.* Although incantations and other magical formulas, together with their accompanying practices, played a minor role in the Pali scriptures, they came into greater and greater prominence in Buddhism after 200 C.E., and their vogue reached a culmination in northern India by the eighth century. They were then carried over into Tibet, where they became prominent in the Vajrayana (see Section VII of this chapter).

The central point made by Tantrism, whether Hindu or Buddhist, is that the reasoned knowledge of the schools, distilled into books, is not the most effective means of awakening one to the true faith. The *best* method is to gain live experiences under a guru able to conduct magically potent secret exercises bringing one into direct contact with reality. One can know reality best by experiencing it oneself, and the highest form of human experience is to experience the identical sameness of samsara and Nirvana (the world of physical and mental experience and the realm of eternal bliss) by experiencing through one's own body and mind the state of Voidness.

As in Hindu Tantrism (see pp. 128–129), the Buddhist rites were boldly taboo breaking; but there was as little concession to orgiastic impulses as there was in Hindu rites, the hope still being to achieve a spiritual victory. The fundamental aim was to secure "illumination" through control of the body and its psychic powers, using a modified form of the methods of Hatha Yoga. (See the paragraph on Hatha Yoga on p. 114.) There also was the aim to come face to face with the elemental forces in the world and to transcend the desires aroused by them. These rites were secret, and

only carefully selected initiates were allowed by the guru to engage in them. The rites included the forming of circles (*mandalas*), the reciting of sacred *mantras* (stanzas), the casting of hypnotic spells, the performing of magic gestures, chanting, dancing, the eating and drinking of forbidden foods and liquids (wines), and sexual union, the males as deities and the females (usually sixteen-year-old girls of low caste) in the role of goddesses or divine consorts representing prajna or holy insight. Earthly names and identities were replaced by divine ones. The approved practice in the sexual rites was to inhibit ejaculation at the moment of its occurrence by breath control and force of will, in order to cause the semen to be withdrawn into the body of the male to heighten his spiritual energy. The *tantras* ("manuals describing the rites") concealed their meaning by using a coded language called "twilight speech." "Semen was called 'camphor,' 'the thought of bodhi,' and 'elixir'; the male and female genitals were called 'thunderbolt' and 'lotus.'"[N] All the acts with which these words were cryptically associated were to be undertaken without sensual appetite or egoity, with the realization that they were "empty" and merely the means of realizing the Void.

A high role was given to sacred syllables, circles (mandalas), and sacred stanzas (mantras). "Om!" and "hum!" were constantly repeated. (We shall see instances of this in Tibet.) Mandalas were either acted out by persons in the rites, drawn and colored on the ground, traced on paper, woven into fabrics, or painted on various surfaces, with Buddhas, bodhisattvas, humans, and animals vividly rendered in color and made the object of prolonged meditation, in the hope of union with deity and liberation from samsara.

The Wisdom That Has Gone Beyond (*Prajna-paramita*)

By now the language of Buddhist scholarship was no longer Pali but a variant of Sanskrit, the classical language of India. From the beginning of the Christian Era and through the next five hundred years, a vast literature in Sanskrit began to appear. Early examples of this literature were the *Mahavastu* and the *Lalita-Vistara,* versions of the life of the Buddha filled with miracles and wonders. Next came the *Buddha-Carita* of Ashvaghosa (*ca.* 100 C.E., a famous biography of the

Buddha in the noblest verse form. There followed the *Lotus of the Good Law* (the *Saddharma-Pundarika*), which is the most beloved of Mahayanist scriptures, filled, as it is, with supposed discourses of the Buddha on Vulture Peak near Bodh-gaya; the *Sukhavati-Vyuha*, a prized description of Amitabha's Pure Land and how to get there; and a large group of sutras, one hundred or more in number, dealing with problems of the philosophy of religion. Of these last, the *Lankavatara* and *Surangama* sutras have been the most influential.

A special category of this literature, of which the popular *Diamond-Cutter* (the *Vajracchedika*, commonly called the *Diamond Sutra*) is typical, goes by the name of the *Prajna-paramita Sutras*, so called because they are "Discourses on the Wisdom That Has Gone Beyond" (a close translation), that is to say, teachings concerning transcendental wisdom (prajna). Perhaps the earliest of these was the *Astasahasrika Prajna-paramira*; it was one of the first to air the *sunyata* or emptiness doctrine we have seen emerge from early Buddhism. Most certainly this sutra was known to and was valued by the Madhyamika and Yogacara schools.

It is in this last group of treatises that we come upon a metaphor that perfectly suggests what prajna-paramita means. It is the early Buddhist metaphor of crossing a river by raft or ferry to get to the farther shore (Nirvana). In the light of this metaphor, prajna-paramita may be translated as "the Wisdom Gone to the Other Shore." The nearer bank of the river is this world, known to the senses since childhood. From it one cannot imagine at all what the Other Shore, far away, is like. But the ferry arrives, piloted by the Buddha, and when one boards it (i.e., adopts Buddhism as one's faith) and begins the crossing, the receding nearer bank gradually loses reality and the far shore begins to take shape. At length only the far shore seems real, and when one arrives there and leaves behind the river and the ferry, they too lose all reality, because one has now gained final release in the Great Beyond, which alone is utterly real. Thus, the river and both of its banks, as well as the ferry, the Buddha, and even the human goal which had been all along the ultimate bounty of Nirvana, are equally and completely void. As *concepts*, they had once been the useful means of attaining prajna or transcendental wisdom, but they are empty now and useless forever.

The reasoning, we find, is based on a famous passage in the Pali *Majjhima Nikaya*, where the Buddha asks his monks,

> What would be your opinion of this man; would he be a clever man if, out of gratitude for the raft that had carried him across the stream to safety, he, having reached the other shore, should cling to it, take it on his back, and walk about with the weight of it? . . . Would not the clever man be the one who left the raft (of no use to him any longer) to the current of the stream, and walked ahead without turning back to look at it? Is it not simply a tool to be cast away and forsaken once it has served the purpose for which it was made? . . . In the same way the vehicle of the doctrine is to be cast away and forsaken, once the other shore of Enlightenment (Nirvana) has been attained.[01]

One more point needs to be added. Not only is every human concept of reality discarded in Nirvana, but the empirical self, as one thinks of it in life, is discarded too. The *Astasahasrika Prajna-paramita* says this with great subtlety.

> The Enlightened One sets forth in the Great Ferryboat; but there is nothing from which he sets forth. He starts from the universe; but in truth he starts from nowhere. His boat is manned with all the perfections; and is manned by no one. It will . . . find its support on the state of all-knowing, which will serve it as a non-support. Moreover, no one has ever set forth in the Great Ferryboat; no one will ever set forth in it, and no one is setting forth in it now. And why is this? Because neither the one setting forth nor the goal for which he sets forth is to be found.[02]

The *Trikaya* or Triple Body

In the process of magnifying Gautama Buddha's role in human history, his followers, as we have earlier seen, saw in the historical Gautama the coming to earth of a heavenly bodhisattva. What we are now to see is the next step: considering Gautama's earthly appearance to be an "apparitional body" of a bodhisattva who remained in his heavenly place. The idea next arose that the heavenly bodhisattva (occupying a "body of

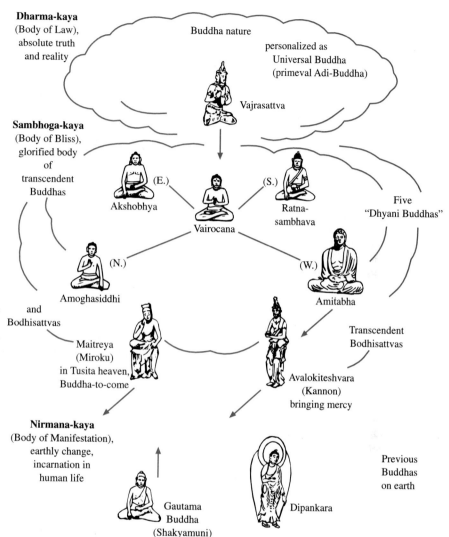

Dharma-kaya
(Body of Law),
absolute truth
and reality

Buddha nature

personalized as
Universal Buddha
(primeval Adi-Buddha)

Vajrasattva

Sambhoga-kaya
(Body of Bliss),
glorified body
of
transcendent
Buddhas

(E.)
Akshobhya

(S.)
Ratna-
sambhava

Five
"Dhyani Buddhas"

Vairocana

(N.)
Amoghasiddhi

(W.)
Amitabha

and
Bodhisattvas

Maitreya
(Miroku)
in Tusita heaven,
Buddha-to-come

Transcendent
Bodhisattvas

Avalokiteshvara
(Kannon)
bringing mercy

Nirmana-kaya
(Body of Manifestation),
earthly change,
incarnation in
human life

Gautama
Buddha
(Shakyamuni)

Dipankara

Previous
Buddhas
on earth

The Mahayana Cosmos

The conceptualization follows the three levels of the Triple Body (*Trikaya*), from the pure essence of Buddha Nature—which is also equivalent to Nirvana or Sunyata (Emptiness)—it ranges through the vast realms of the celestial meditative forms of the Bliss Body and reaches down to the manifest, transformed-to-human Gautama and to Dipankara, a legendary earthly Buddha of the remote past. *(Reprinted by permission from ICONOGRAPHY OF RELIGIONS by Albert Moore, Copyright © 1977 Fortress Press. Used by permission of Augsburg Fortress.)*

bliss") was himself a manifestation or form of Reality itself ("the dharma body," the ultimate Buddha reality, originative, unknowable, "void"). So the historical Buddha was the passing manifestation on earth of a "triple body" (the *Trikaya*). (See diagram, p. 207.)

Accordingly, we have this formulation of the Buddhist schools to consider: First is "the Body of the Cosmical or Absolute Buddha" (the *Dharmakaya*); second is "the Enjoyment Body of the Buddha," or "the Body of Spiritual Bliss" (the *Sambhogakaya*); and third is "the Body of Earthly Forms or Manifestations of the Buddha" (the *Nirmanakaya*). The first indicates the eternal Buddha reality that is the ground and source of the world known by and present to an enlightened Buddhist consciousness; it is identical to the Absolute Suchness, the Void, within which function or subsist the alaya-vijnana, prajna, and Nirvana. The Body of Spiritual Bliss is the heavenly manifestation of the

Dharmakaya, particularly in the celestial Buddhas and bodhisattvas, and capable of taking name and form and of offering help along the path to Nirvana to earthly beings. The Body of Earthly forms is a manifestation of the Body of Spiritual Bliss in earthly appearances, the prime example being the historical Buddha, Gautama.

In summary, the Dharma Body is undifferentiated and impersonal. The Bliss Body is differentiated and personal. The Earthly Body is differentiated and personal and a this-worldly manifestation of the Bliss Body in time and space limitations.

Derived originally from an analysis of the significance of Gautama Buddha, this doctrine, when applied to him, became a faith concerning him: the Absolute Suchness or Void is the ground of being from which emanates the Body of Spiritual Bliss manifested in such heavenly powers as Amitabha, Avalokitesvara, and the Bodhisattva who once dwelt in the Tushita heaven and who compassionately came down to earth to be the historical Gautama Buddha. (A still-later formulation, apparently Tibetan, considered Amitabha the celestial Buddha whose spiritual son Avalokitesvara brought into being the historical Gautama Buddha. However, there is a definite Tibetan tradition that Mahavairocana, the central figure among the five celestial Buddhas, gave rise to Gautama Buddha. In any case, the principle seems to be that Gautama Buddha's sambhogakaya is ultimately to be identified with one of the celestial Buddhas.)

When Gautama Buddha's earthly mission was accomplished, he returned to the source of all being, the Dharmakaya (= Nirvana).

Comparison with Vedanta Monism

In these doctrines the reader will find no difficulty in seeing a similarity with Hindu Vedantic speculation. They point to an Absolute (the Void) that resembles in many respects the Brahman-Atman of Hindu monism. But there is a difference that must ultimately be ascribed to the influence of the career and personality of Gautama Buddha upon Mahayana speculation. Whereas in Vedantic thought Brahman-Atman remains the unpicturable, inconceivable Absolute of strictly neutral being, in Mahayana Buddhism the

Absolute Essence or Suchness is identified with a sort of love behind things that produces Buddhas—a Buddha essence at the heart of the universe. The importance of this conclusion for religion is surely evident. For here the Buddhas, as expressions or projections of Being Itself, are not merely indifferent or unfeeling expressions of It, but rather a manifestation of compassionate love (*karuna*), drawing ignorance-clouded minds along the bodhisattva way of love back to Itself.

Applied to common people, these philosophical positions of the Mahayana led to the view that, because the Absolute Suchness or Buddha essence (the Dharmakaya) is manifest in all things, there is a Buddha nature or potentiality in every person. Anyone may take up the career of a Buddha-to-be without having to be reborn. The stimulus of this great hope penetrated throughout East Asia, and its optimistic implications thrilled the aspiring natures of the devout with a new zeal.

VI. MAHAYANA SCHOOLS OF THOUGHT IN CHINA AND JAPAN

Our study of the religious development of Buddhism would be far from complete in either scope or interest if we did not, briefly at least, consider the leading Mahayana schools and sects in China and Japan. In general, the picture is this: what the Buddhist speculative theologians of India put forward through suggestion and outreach, the Chinese took up and developed as the logical basis of their differentiations, and the Japanese, eager to learn, came forward to put the finishing touches on the Chinese developments, always adding something of their own in the process.

The formation of differing schools of thought was in some instances due to Indian teachers coming to China, but for the most part the Chinese were influenced toward variation in point of view chiefly by the Mahayana literature they read and discussed. This literature came to them in the form of translations from the Sanskrit originals or as literary works produced by the Chinese themselves. Among the earliest translations were those of the *Astasahasrika Prajna-paramita* and *Sukhavati-vyuha* sutras. Of first importance was the translation of the influential Mahayana text, the *Diamond-Cutter* (or *Diamond*) *Sutra,* translated in the fourth century C.E. Next came translations of the *Lotus of the Good Law,* and the *Awakening of Faith.* Other important influences streamed from the lengthy Sanskrit works known as the *Avatamsaka Sutra,* the *Lankavatara Sutra* and Asanga's *Compendium of the Mahayana,* which were in whole or in part translated into Chinese. The Chinese themselves seem to have composed the *Sutra of Brahma's Net,* the most widely used manual on the monastic life. Different schools of thought also justified their positions by issuing treatises like the *Practice of Dhyana for Beginners,* the *Sutra of the Sixth Patriarch,* and others.

It would be tedious for the ordinary reader were we to attempt to trace out individually the manifold differences among the schools and sects of China and Japan. Such a study would be as detailed and difficult to follow as an inquiry, say, into the differences between Protestant sects in Europe and America. Fortunately, we may pursue another course. The main trends among the Buddhist schools are clearly distinguishable and may be comprehensively considered under five headings.

1. Pure Land Schools: Jing-tu and Jōdo

In the Pure Land schools, the motive is one that appeals to common people, that of reaching a blissful haven in the very next life. The chief interest and proximate goal of the Pure Land Buddhists is the Western Paradise of Amitabha Buddha. By concentration of attention solely on this aspect of Buddhist belief an extraordinary simplification is achieved. In the later forms that this faith has taken, the strenuous life of "works" is rendered unnecessary. An unquestioning faith in Amitabha, and the devout repetition of his name, especially by the use of the formula "Namu O-mituo Fo" ("Hail, Amitabha Buddha!"), are all sufficient. The whole emphasis is on faith, and faith, together with humility, is believed to be sufficient for such a next life; in fact, the practical-minded Chinese have called the Pure Land way the "easy path," and such it appears to be.

In the early years of the Pure Land schools, other paths were not repudiated. All of the paths—study, learning, meditation, good works, strict self-discipline, monastic seclusion—were good. But this is an age of decay, and the true faith is not easy to learn, the Pure Land sects have said, citing a venerable Buddhist doctrine, most clearly expounded by the *Lotus Sutra* (and a long-held doctrine as well of Hindus and Jains). As the sutra explains it, during the first centuries after the Buddha came, the *pure* dharma or doctrine was known and really practiced; then came centuries of *compromised* dharma, when modifications of the truth appeared; since then, to meet the needs of a sinful and degenerate age, the *latter day* dharma has been evolved. The Pure Land preachers have therefore urged that the masses take the path open to all, the path to the Pure Land, where they can pursue the pure dharma as they cannot pursue it on earth.

In China the Jing-tu (Pure Land) school represents this point of view. Its most influential early leader, a converted Daoist, appeared in the sixth century C.E. He based his position on the shorter version of the Sanskrit *Sukhavati-vyuha* (see again p. 201), a second-century scripture that gave the prehistory of Amitabha Buddha, beginning millions of years (and many lives) ago; then he was a monk called Dharmakara and vowed to become a Buddha who would establish in the Western sky the Pure Land, Sukhavati, where people would be happy at last, meditate, and seek Nirvana, as they could not on earth. To help people in a degenerate age, Dharmakara drew up a list of vows by which they might reach the Pure Land, the eighteenth of which promised that by merely calling out or thinking his name at the moment of death they would bring about their rebirth in his Western paradise. This was the text adopted by the Jing-tu schools of China as their chief scripture.

The Jōdo Sect in Japan

In Japan this way of practicing Buddhism, generally called Amidism, became extremely popular. There the chief representatives of Amidism have been the Jōdo shū (Pure Land sect) and Jōdo-Shinshū (True Pure Land sect). The Jōdo sect was founded in the twelfth century by a Japanese scholar, trained at the Tendai monasteries at Mt. Hiei, whose name was Genku (later known as Hōnen Shonin or "Saint Hōnen"). As a young man he had sought vainly for peace by means of the three Buddhist disciplines ("precepts, meditation, and wisdom"), and had then found enlightenment in a library when he read in a Chinese Amidist commentary the comforting words, "Only repeat the name of Amitabha with all your heart, whether walking or standing, whether sitting or lying: never cease the practice for a moment. This is the very work which unfailingly issues in salvation."[P] He claimed, in old age, it is said, that after reading the Amidist commentary he began to repeat "Namu Amida Butsu!" ("Hail, Amida Buddha!") sixty thousand times a day, and increased this later to seventy thousand times! This was the chief expression of his faith, although he also reverenced Gautama Buddha and performed good works out of gratitude to him and as a religious duty, knowing that he could not *earn* salvation: it was Amida's gift.

The Jōdo Shinshū

The Jōdo-Shin (True Pure Land) sect, established by Genku's disciple Shinran Shonin, has introduced some radical Japanese innovations, hardly paralleled in Buddhism elsewhere, and is now the most widespread of the Japanese sects, having the greatest number of temples, monks, and teachers. It has taken the confident position that humility (the sense of human powerlessness to effect redemption) and faith in Amida's love are in themselves true signs that the redeeming grace of that Buddha has already been bestowed, and that therefore the repetition of the Amidist formula (telescoped in Japan to "Nembutsu") should not be regarded as a prerequisite to salvation but should be motivated by gratitude; for Amida seeks and saves without first requiring faith and good works. In fact, faith is solely his doing; it springs up spontaneously from Amida's spiritual presence in the heart.

Freed from celibacy, Shin priests are allowed to marry, eat meat, and live in the world like laypersons. As in the case of Christian churches, Shin institutions depend on voluntary contributions. Because the priests can marry, an innovation similar to that in Tibet has occurred: the abbots are hereditary. In the past, by acquiring political and even military power, these abbots "were even more like barons than the celibate prelates"[J3]

of the older, semimilitarized sects of the feudal era. The cheerful, world-accepting nature of the Shin sect has had a natural result: many persons have found it a highly attractive faith.

2. Meditative Schools: Chan and Zen

The goal of the meditative schools is immediate insight, enlightenment such as Gautama achieved under the Bo-tree. The method of salvation is nominally dhyana, or meditation, but salvation is actually obtained not by meditation but by insight or awakening (prajna) following on meditation. To some who are of this way of thinking, scholarly research, the reading of books, listening to lectures, doing good works, the performance of rituals, and so on are not only of little merit in themselves but often are a hindrance to true insight into the Buddha reality. One must find salvation by an inward look into one's own nature; in short, salvation is a private, personal experience.

Generally, Chan and Zen sects have accepted as normative the following four conditions:

1. A special oral transmission from master to disciple outside of the scriptures
2. No dependence upon the authority of words and letters
3. Direct pointing to the soul of man
4. Seeing into one's own nature and attaining Buddhahood

In attempting to pronounce the Sanskrit word *dhyana*, the Chinese elicited their name for this way of faith, namely, the Chan school. The founder was said to have been an Indian scholar and teacher by the name of Bodhidharma. Now no more than a dim legendary figure, he may have come to south China at the end of the fifth century at the time when the growing influence of Buddhism had claimed an imperial convert, the Emperor Wu Di of the Southern Liang dynasty. The interesting old tale, which must be viewed with

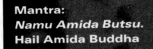

Mantra:
Namu Amida Butsu.
Hail Amida Buddha

historical skepticism because the dates do not jibe, states that the emperor sent for him. In the course of the interview, the renowned teacher was asked how much merit flowed from making imperial donations to the Buddhist order and continuing the translations of sacred books. "No merit at all!" the gruff monk replied, and went on to say to his shocked hearer that knowledge gleaned from reading is worthless; no merit flows from good works; only meditation that admits one to direct insight into the Great Emptiness of the Buddha reality, only truth revealed to one's thought when one turns inward to actualize the Buddha in one's heart, is of any value. Rejected by the emperor, Bodhidharma is said next to have gone to Mt. Su in north China and to have sat meditating with his face to a wall for nine years.

Whatever the circumstances of its origin, the Chan school began at first with just simple living and stern self-discipline as the preparation for meditation and the inward vision. It found suggestive the meditative techniques already developed by native Chinese Daoism, in both its philosophical and religious forms. (See the Daoism section, chapter 9.) At first, it disdained all scriptures and was rigorously individualistic, iconoclastic, and averse to regarding the ultimate Buddha principle ("Nothingness," "the Void") as in any sense definable. Gradually, however, the old aids to the religious life were reinstated and in a moderate way made use of. Nevertheless, it was realized that such aids cannot substitute for meditation, even though differences developed as to the nature of the meditation itself. There are different kinds of meditation. The question arose, should one "sit still" in meditation, carefully eliminating false views, without any specific aims or problems in mind, waiting and hoping for bodhi (by a gradual enlightenment), or should one focus on a tough problem with intensity, hoping to wear down the intellect to the point where it gives up and "sudden enlightenment" (realization) takes place? Ultimately, of the seven Chan sects, two survived, the Lin-Ji and the Cao-dung (Ts'ao-tung), the first devoted to abrupt procedures and stiff problems leading to sudden enlightenment, the second to a broad development of the understanding through book learning and instruction leading to gradual enlightenment. In either case, the ability to meditate properly was required, and one did not need to be learned in

Raigo: Amida Descending from the Western Paradise
Amida (Amitabha) descending from the Western Paradise, accompanied by 25 protective Bodhisattvas. Amida is embarked on a journey to assist the souls of devotees. A Muromachi period scroll, Seattle Art Museum. *(The Seattle Art Museum, Eugene Fuller Memorial Collection, 34.117.)*

history or philosophy or an expert in the traditional rites and ceremonies to attain it. Profundity of insight into one's own "heart" was all that was required. By way of illustration, the following "autobiographical" passage from a Chan text is worth quoting, for it shows how an illiterate country boy became, on account of his intuitive qualities, the renowned Sixth Patriarch, Hui-neng:

> I was selling firewood in the market (of Canton) one day when one of my customers ordered some to be sent to his shop. Upon delivery and payment

for the same as I went outside I found a man reciting a Sutra. No sooner had I heard the text of this Sutra than my mind became at once enlightened. I asked the man the name of the book he was reciting and was told it was the Diamond Sutra. I asked where he came from and why he recited this particular Sutra. He replied that he came from the Tung-tsan Monastery in Wongmui; that the Abbot in charge was Hwang-yan who was the Fifth Patriarch and had about a thousand disciples under him. . . .

It must be due to my good karma accumulated from past lives that I heard about this and that later on I was given ten taels for the maintenance of my mother by a man who advised me to go to Wongmui to interview the Fifth Patriarch. After arrangements had been made for my mother's support, I left for Wongmui, which it took me about thirty days to reach.

I paid homage to the Patriarch and was asked where I came from and what I expected to get from him. I replied that I was a commoner from Sun-chow in Kwang-tung and said, "I ask for nothing but Buddhahood."

The Patriarch replied: "So you are a native of Kwang-tung, are you? You evidently belong to the aborigines; how can you expect to become a Buddha?"

I replied: "Although there are Northern men and Southern men, North or South makes no difference in their Buddha-nature. An aborigine is different from your Eminence physically but there is no difference in our Buddha-nature."[Q]

According to the same source, this reply of the untrained country lad revealed his high capacity for understanding and insight to the Fifth Patriarch. The patriarch subsequently expounded the Diamond Sutra to him, and though the younger man originally could neither read nor write, he was so thoroughly enlightened that he became the Sixth Patriarch.

Such individuals, however, are rare, and it was recognized that most beginners need careful guidance. Hence, reading of the basic sutras or texts, assigned problems for concentrated reflection, and practical suggestions about posture and breathing during meditation have been a feature of Chan sects almost from the beginning.

In Japan, the Chan school goes by the name of Zen (for thus the Chinese word was pronounced

there). Three branches of Zen were established in the twelfth, thirteenth, and seventeenth centuries and have had a far-reaching, if quiet, influence on the whole of Japanese culture. The two Zen sects that are now most active are named from the two most durable Chinese sects: the Rinzai (so named from the Japanese pronunciation of Lin-Ji) and the Sōtō (from the Chinese Caodo). Although the Sōtō sect is numerically the larger, the distinctive features of the Zen outlook are most dramatically represented in Rinzai Zen, and what follows is for the most part according to that point of view.

In the chapter on Shinto, the native Japanese religion, we shall have the occasion to mention the attraction Zen has had for the grim, taciturn army men of Japan, resolved as they have traditionally been upon self-sacrificial and single-minded devotion to emperor and country. Beyond this circle, the stress laid by both branches of Zen upon the inward search for the essential in life has had a determinative effect on Japanese art, household furnishings, architecture, and the forms of social etiquette, especially in introducing reticence and restraint as the marks of good taste. Even the unexcelled Japanese art of flower arrangement is, it seems, a Zen by-product.

Let us see how this could be so.

Actualizing Nonduality

Zen is primarily an attempt to experience ("actualize") the unitary character of reality. "I" and "not-I" are one ("not-two"); both are aspects of Buddha reality. This becomes clear when one "sees into one's own nature," in a moment of "awakening."

Deliberative reason will not suffice here. One cannot *think* oneself into the realization that there is no duality of oneself and the world, and that "I" and "not-I" are, in the last analysis, nondual. Such a realization must come suddenly by a flash of insight, an "awakening," something the Japanese call *satori*. There are two ways of dealing with Nature. One is to distinguish, describe, analyze, and, in pursuit of practical ends, manipulate objects from the outside; this is to deal in concepts and acts that are disjunctive (dualistic) and misleading. The other way is to contemplate Nature, much as the Daoist of China does (p. 266f), from the position of one who is indistinguishably at one with it; this is to pass into the True, the Void (sunyata), the Dharmakaya, concerning which "one must be silent," for to say anything about it is to apply misleading concepts to it. A favorite Zen way of saying the same thing is to assert the converse: that one does not, properly speaking, "pass into the True (Tatha), the Void, the Dharmakaya," because Nature is "nothing but one's own true mind," and therefore the Void is also within.

Within oneself, however, there is an illusion-making ability that is exercised to the full by all of those who dwell in and cling to the world of the senses as if it were the whole of reality. But this is to submit to ignorance; truth is to be found instead "in the heart." Deep within everyone there is a Buddha nature (a nature capable of bodhi). By actualizing this Buddha nature, one ceases to reason ignorantly and acquires prajna-paramita, the wisdom that has gone beyond— to the beyond that is also within.

But even this language is not wholly satisfactory to Chan and Zen adherents. There is danger, they say in speaking of one's Buddha nature or the Beyond within as if they could be viewed as objects or as having bounds and limits. They are, in truth, Buddha reality, and as such neither external nor internal, objective nor subjective, things nor nothings; indeed such dualisms as these must be transcended by the realization (through satori) that the Buddha reality is not outside Me but is I-Myself and that I-Myself do not stand in contrast to Not-I-Myself, because the Buddha reality includes both in a nondualism that is at once, at least to the finite mind, all and yet nothing, full of life and yet void, mind itself and yet mind like empty space, I-Myself and yet free from self-limitation, formless and unconditioned.

Methods for Halting Duality-Reasoning

Zen masters in Japan follow their Chan predecessors in adopting various ways of waking novices from their illusionary slumbers, especially their clinging to objects and consequently reasoning in a dualistic strain. For the Truth cannot be known as long as they think disjunctively of myself *and* the world, the Buddha *and* I, the essence of Buddhism *for* me, the basic challenge of the Buddha *to* me, and so on, because all *are* the Buddha being (the Dharmakaya). To be able to realize their Buddha nature, learners should stop distinguishing, separating, defining, analyzing, and

Yuan Dynasty, Bodhidharma Crossing the Yangtze River on a Reed

Hanging scroll, ink on paper, 89.2 x 31.1 cm. China, Yuan Dynasty, 1279–1368. The formidable reputed founder of Chan (Zen) Buddhism, with a characteristic scowl on his face, seems to be glaring toward the approaching shore but is actually so uninvolved in the process of this world that, for all of his bulk, he floats across the river on a fragile reed. *(The Cleveland Museum of Art, John L. Severance Fund, 64.44.)*

describing; they should stop asking questions, for these are essentially dualistic and to such questions there are no answers. The trouble is that questions separate the questioner from the object one is asking questions about. A learner who persists in trying to reason things out and keeps asking questions may be slapped by the master, kicked, or thrown out into the hall. Perhaps this will break loose the hold upon objects and shock the learner out of the tendency to ask silly disjunctive questions; it may even suddenly fuse everything into nonduality and thus bring enlightenment then and there. Another tactic of the master may be to answer a question more or less non-sensically and then ask the learner to make sense of it, knowing that in bafflement the learner will have to "go beyond intellect to insight." (In Japanese terminology, this is to give the learner a *koan* to deal with.) Again, the master may recount a puzzling dialogue (which the Japanese call a *mondo*). The point is that one must realize that discursive reason misleads; that the bafflement of reason is an indication of its limited nature; that one must go beyond rational concepts to a blinding realization, like a flash of lightning, an insight transcending all rational limits.

Consider the following famous koans (most of them of Chan derivation) as saying in effect, "Stop clinging to objects, the self included; cease asking dualistic questions; instead, know in yourself the undifferentiated Void that is at the same time the ground of all discrete being."

> A monk asked Tung-shan, "Who is the Buddha?" and received the reply: "Three measures of flax."
>
> When asked by a monk, "Is there a Buddha-nature in a dog?" Chao-chou barked, "Wu" ("No!"). [Semantically "negative," but existentially *dog-sound*.]
>
> A monk asked Hui-neng to reveal the secret of Zen and was asked in turn: "What did your face look like before your parents begot you?"
>
> The great Japanese monk Hakuin replied to an inquirer by clapping both hands and then asking, "What sound does one hand make?"

The following is a mondo:

> A monk who saw Yao-shan meditating asked: "In this motionless position what are you thinking?"

> "Thinking that which is beyond thinking."
> "How do you go about thinking that which is beyond thinking."
> "By an act of not-thinking."

There are several paradoxical corollaries to this position. The time-continuum and the present moment may be experienced in contrast, but they also collapse into each other. A *haiku* (seventeen-syllable poem) by the Zen monk Bashō points toward this.

> *An ancient pond: (pause)*
> *A frog plunges in.*
> *Water sound! (plop!)*

A person meditating on this may realize oneness (nonduality) first with the silent, static continuum of "a pond" (essence), then oneness with the sudden, noisy plunge event (existential moment), and finally awaken in the *satori* of pure "plop" experiencing.

Nonduality and Gender

Nonduality applies in a practical way to gender. If there is ultimately no significant distinction between self and other, or even between oneself and one's body, then there is no place for sexuality in Buddha mind and no reason for excluding any person from a monastery on the basis of gender. Monastic rules do indeed forbid contact with persons of the opposite sex, but those who live in full awareness of nonduality (and of common sense) do not hesitate to ignore the rules on appropriate occasions.

There is a story of a senior monk and a novice who pass through a cloudburst on a walking trip. After it has cleared they come upon a young woman hesitating at the edge of a muddy flow of water across her path. With a gruff "Come on, girl," the senior monk picks her up, carries her over the water, and sets her down on the other side. The two monks travel on in silence for the rest of the day and take a silent supper at an inn. At bedtime, the novice bursts out, "How could you *do* that! You know that our rules forbid touching a female!" The elder replies, "I put her down on the other side. Are you still carrying her?"

The following *koan* from the *Mumonkan* suggests that even the great Buddha/bodhisattva Manjusri suffered a hang-up when it came to dealing with a woman.

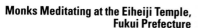

Monks Meditating at the Eiheiji Temple, Fukui Prefecture

Monks in sitting meditation (*zazen*) upon a low platform sometimes face inward toward the center of the hall and sometimes, as in this picture, face the wall. A blow across the shoulder from the monitor's stick is not a reprimand but an aid, a shock to assist in breaking away from rational thought. Sometimes the initiative for the blow comes from the monitor; sometimes the meditating monk requests the "refreshment" by bowing. *(Courtesy of Japanese National Tourist Organization, 40.)*

Once long long ago, the World-Honored One came to the place where many Buddhas were assembled. When Manjusri arrived there, the Buddhas all returned to their original places. Only a woman remained, close to the Buddha seat in deep meditation. Manjusri spoke to the Buddha, "Why can a woman be close to the Buddha seat, and I cannot?" The Buddha told Manjusri, "You awaken this woman from her meditation and ask her yourself." Manjusri walked around the woman three times, snapped his fingers once, then took her up to the Brahma Heaven and tried all his supernatural powers, but he was unable to bring her out of meditation. The World-Honored One said, "Even hundreds of thousands of Manjusris would be unable to bring her out of meditation. Down below, past one billion, two hundred million countries, as innumerable as the sands of the Ganges, there is a Bodhisattva called Momyo. He will be able to awaken her from meditation." In an instant Momyo emerged from the earth and worshiped the World-Honored One. The World-Honored One gave him the order. Momyo then walked to the woman and snapped his fingers only once. At this the woman came out of her meditation.[R]

The junior bodhisattva Momyo presumably did not think of himself as dealing with a "woman," and never

doubted his ability to do what the Buddha asked. Of course, these surface features do not exhaust the meaning of the koan, but give it an amusing piquancy.

Zen Influence upon the Arts

It is one of the talents of the Zen-trained Japanese that they can contemplate beautiful things—cherry blossoms, pine trees, field flowers, mountains—in a meditative way that allows the object and its perceiver to coexist in a unified field, through an aesthetic trance in which object and perceiver are, as it were, relocated in a timeless continuum, where they take their place side by side, as if in a landscape not of this world, present only to the Buddha mind. To take an example from such an art as archery, one does not "master" the handsome bow and shoot the arrow; the archer and bow are nondual, and in the total effort the arrow shoots itself from the bow. In the tea ceremony one surrenders self to the beautiful, restrained ritual as in an aesthetic dream having the dimensions of eternity. Paradoxically, Zen imparts both a sense of cosmic nonduality and an immediate aesthetic response to sensory reality.

The way this comes about is as follows: Although reality is one and all particulars are ultimately indistinguishable, these particulars are to be welcomed and appreciated in one's immediate experience as rightful

The "Golden Temple" of Kyoto, Japan

This architecturally exquisite structure was originally a pavilion built for the fourth shogun of the Ashikaga era in the fifteenth century. It was recently rebuilt after being destroyed by fire. Painted delicate gold, it is more an object of Zen-like meditation than a place for Buddha worship. *(Courtesy of Pan American Airways.)*

elements in the mental furniture of existence. The harmonious and the beautiful may properly delight the eye and mind of the painter or poet, while at the same time the ugly, the saddening, and the absurd also have a significant and proper place in the structure of the world. Because all things, including oneself, are transient expressions of the Buddha reality, they are to be immediately enjoyed in all of their variety and enchantment, even to the point of aesthetic intimacy and tenderness, without one's having to give up a basic nonattachment. In Zen, the Japanese say, the old Chan saying comes true: To begin with, everyone sees mountains as mountains and trees as trees; then when one seeks to come to terms with them (for example, as sensory aspects of an ultimate reality), mountains no longer appear as mountains, nor trees as trees; but finally when enlightenment is attained, mountains again are seen as mountains and trees as trees; the enlightened mind, accepting all aspects of the Buddha reality, looks once more with openhearted gladness at Nature, as directly and with as much childlike candor as the poets of the following haiku accepted the *is-ness* of their objects:

As I come along the mountain path,
What a heart-warming surprise,
This cluster of dainty violets!

Bashō

Do I see a fallen flower
Fluttering back to its branch?
Ah! A butterfly!

Moritake

Full moon, and under the trees
Patterned shadows—how beautiful
Alongside mine!

Baishitsu

Finally, the Zen sects have worked out a technique of meditation that is highly disciplined and demanding. It is called *zazen*, in which the Sōtō sect specializes; it calls for stated periods of meditation. In Rinzai Zen, in a hall designed for the purpose, the monks sit on long platforms facing each other for as long as eighteen hours day after day. Their meditations are tied in with *sanzen,* or consultation, with a "master," to whom the monk regularly reports. This plan for mental and spiritual self-discipline appeals strongly to many serious-minded Japanese, not to speak of influential soul-searchers from the West, who turn to it hopefully as a means of insight.

3. Rationalist Schools: Tian-tai in China

The intuitionist's thorough purging of the mind in the hope of enlightenment is so obviously antiintellectualist, and moreover so fundamentally grounded in feeling states rather than in reason that one can easily understand the rise of the Rationalist sects. In China, where they have been known as the Tian-tai sects, they gradually grew away from the Chan or Meditation school. The basic issue that led to their rise was the one between some hoped-for "sudden enlightenment" after the mind is emptied of all empirical content, and "gradual attainment" through study of the scriptures and a philosophically mature practice of contemplation. In the sixth century, a monk in one of the Chan monasteries in eastern China, whose name was Zhi-Yi (Chih-I or, erroneously, Chih-K'ai), was convinced by another monk called Huisi (Hui-ssu) that meditation should be balanced by a prolonged and serious study of such texts as the *Lotus Sutra.* Consequently, he took a stand for an inclusive point of view that gave equal weight to meditation and study. The Buddhist faith was, he said, greater than any of its schools, and one should open one's mind to insight from a variety of sources. Meditation (dhyana) was necessary but not all-sufficient for insight. He believed that the gathering of knowledge from teachers and scriptures, the performance of ceremonials and rituals, including chanting of phrases and sacred texts, and the regular discipline of the monastery were all very valuable in the preparation for the ecstatic vision. Because he wished to find room for every major point of view expressed by Buddhism up to his time, Zhi-Yi evolved the doctrine that the Buddha (Gautama) taught differently at the different stages of his life, according to the understanding of his hearers. At first he taught the doctrines of the Hinayana sutras, and at later periods he revealed, in progressively profounder versions, the Mahayana doctrines. The fullest revelation of

the eternal truth was made near the end of the Buddha's life and embodied in the *Lotus of the Good Law,* the favorite text of the Tian-tai school. The Buddha there reveals that he is a manifestation of a cosmic principle that pervades the whole universe and is present even in its smallest objects. All beings whatsoever can, Tian-tai has concluded, actualize their Buddha nature eventually and become Buddhas.

In accordance with the teaching of its founder, the Tian-tai school (which took its name from the mountain to which Zhi-Yi withdrew) has tried to reconcile the Hinayana and the Mahayana by subsuming both under the modified realism of the Madhyamika school of India (Nagarjuna). Three levels of truth were discerned in the Buddhist scriptures, whose teachings were reduced to three propositions; (1) all things (dharmas) are "void" because they lack substantiality; (2) all things nevertheless have temporary existence; and (3) all things are in existence and void at the same time. These three truths, when considered in all of their aspects, include one another and are in harmony. Hence, all of the Buddhist scriptures are in harmony.

Corresponding to these three truths are different levels of hearers. In the *Lotus Sutra* Gautama Buddha is portrayed as a heavenly being surrounded by a great host of disciples, arahats, gods, and bodhisattvas, to whom he expounds a complex message on the Mahayana level; it is aimed at three levels of hearers; those who are as yet unenlightened disciples hoping to become arahats; those who are near to enlightenment but seek it only for themselves and not others (pratyekabuddhas); and compassionate ones, the worthiest of all, who have postponed their entrance into Nirvana to help save all beings who might need their aid (bodhisattvas). On a more mundane level (the Hinayana plane), there are less sophisticated levels of truth, one for the naive who believe in the reality and value of the material world, another for those who confusedly seek a spiritual life in the material world, and a third for the better-oriented seekers who devote themselves to meditation.

The recognition and consideration of all of these levels have made for tolerance and breadth among Tian-tai scholars.

Tendai in Japan

The genetic relation between Chan and Tian-tai in China was reversed in Japan. There, under the name of

Tendai, the rationalist school of thought came first to Japan (as early as the eighth century), and Zen followed later as its intuitionist outgrowth.

Tendai is important historically because its founder, Saicho, who became known posthumously as Dengyo Daishi ("the Master Who Brought the Message") helped the Emperor Kwammu establish a new capital at Kyoto (Heian) and break away from the powerful Buddhist priests at Nara who had diminished his sovereignty. Saicho left Nara in dissatisfaction with the worldly ambitions and un-Japanese attitudes he found there. He meditated in seclusion on Mt. Hiei overlooking the site where the new capital was to be built. He became a trusted friend of the emperor, who sent him to China in 804 to study Tian-tai and to gain recognition for the establishment on Mt. Hiei. He returned from China an ardent advocate of the *Lotus Sutra* as the one perfect record of the words uttered by the Buddha himself when revealing his highest teaching. He criticized the Nara sects for relying on commentators rather than on the Buddha's own words. More important, he saw in Tian-tai an interpretation of Buddhism that brought out the fundamental oneness of all beings and the promise of universal salvation. Buddhism was for all the Japanese, not for monks only. He therefore gave Buddhism a nationalist turn by placing his movement at the service of court and country as "a center for the protection of the Land of Great Japan" (*Dai Nippon Koku*). He succeeded in spreading Buddhism among the common people by making it a Japanese religion, open to all. Furthermore, he and his followers were persuaded (and the common people came to accept the idea in large numbers) that the gods of the native Japanese religion (Shinto) were forms taken by the one Buddha reality. Consequently, they advocated that Shinto be called *Ichi-jitsu Shinto* ("One Reality Shinto"). Buddhism and Shinto thus appeared to be two aspects of one Truth.

His Mt. Hiei retreat near Kyoto became the most influential center of education in Japan, with some thirty thousand monks in training in the three thousand temples and study halls clustered there. Monks were required to remain in seclusion on Mt. Hiei for twelve years before departing to their posts as priests, teachers, or servants of the state.

It was at Mt. Hiei that the founders of the new sects of the twelfth and thirteenth centuries (Pure Land, Zen, and Nichiren) received their initial training and ordination.

Many important monasteries, with their attendant temples, have flourished under the knowledge-fostering Tendai sect. Their influence in Japan is pervasive and powerful still, though their lay membership is not as great as is that of some of the other Buddhist sects.

4. Esoteric or Mystery Schools: Zhen-yan and Shingon

In every religion the power of the saving name or mystic rite has at some time been stressed. The beneficial effects are sought by a kind of holy magic, performed against a background of rational belief—a pantheon or a cosmology of impressive character. The tendency to make use of wonder-working formulas and gestures issued in China during the eighth century in the rise of the Zhen-yan (Chen Yen) or "True Word" school. The chief features of this school were derived from right-hand Indian Tantrism by way of Tibet. Its general position was strongly mystical. It placed its chief reliance on a large pantheon of Buddhist savior beings, both male and female, with whom identification was sought on the higher religious levels, and whose good offices, on lower levels, were solicited through "efficacious" formulas, the use of picture charts or mandalas, gestures, invocations, and liturgies, which were believed to bring infallibly good results. By this time Prajna-paramita had become prominent among the deities, personified now as a goddess, the prajna source of all the Buddhas and even their mother, according to a popular view, which made her the female consort of the Adi-Buddha (the originative Buddha). The devotees performed their mystery rites to the accompaniment of music and bursting firecrackers, in the confident expectation of thereby obtaining the help of Buddhas in curing sickness, rescuing the dead from hell, controlling the weather, ensuring health and good fortune, and the like.

The Zhen-yan school was imported into Japan, where the name was pronounced Shingon. The Japanese adherents widened its outlook and subdued its magical features by assimilating to it the rational and eclectic interests of the Tendai sect. (The Tendai sect returned the compliment.) The Shingon has thus turned out to be as comprehensive and many sided as the Tendai. Its popular appeal has been great. It was founded in the ninth century by one of Japan's great men, Kukai (renamed Kōbō Daishi, "the Master Teacher of the Dharma"), who in China came under the tutelage of Zhen-yan masters.

The Influence of Kukai (Kōbō Daishi)

This eager and forceful person returned to Japan to teach the "true word" that all the phenomena of the universe, including human beings, are manifestations of the "body, voice, and mind"—according to the Tantras the "three secrets" known only to the fully enlightened—of a single all-inclusive, and ultimate Buddha being, manifested in the form of Mahavairocana, the Great Sun (known in Japan as Dainichi). The other Buddhas and the bodhisattvas are his emanations, phases of his "indestructible" energy at work in the universe. Gautama Buddha was his historical earthly manifestation. Mahavairocana (or Dainichi) is thus identical with the Dharmakaya of the philosophers, but he is more personal than impersonal, for he possesses body, mind, and speech, differentiated into Buddhas, bodhisattvas, gods, demons, men, animals, and plants, not to mention inanimate things and substances. Kōbō taught that by meditation, repetition of magic formulas, and the performance of gestures with hands and fingers (the esoteric use of mind, speech, and body, respectively) one can identify oneself with powerful Buddhas and bodhisattvas. The implications are elitist. The ordinary person can grasp something, but only something, of this, for it is but partially conveyed in the allegory and symbol of ritual and ceremony. For such esoteric knowledge, one must be tutored by a Shingon master. Any person should, however, be encouraged (as Gautama is supposed to have taught) in the love of temples and worship, for one can begin an ascent from any level on a ladder of ten spiritual rungs or degrees.

The Spiritual Ladder

1. ignorant, "goatish" absorption in food and sex
2. conformity to social and moral rules
3. deliverance through the hope of heaven from the childlike fear of hell or of being either a ghost or an animal after death
4. realization of the truth of the anatta doctrine that the aggregates that function as self are without a permanent soul or ego and are in flux
5. attainment of the level of the Theravada (Hinayana) monk who subdues his desires by determining their causes and overcoming them
6. rising to the Mahayana level of sharing the secret of liberation with all others in "the ocean of pain"
7. meditation on the negative aspects of this world's so-called realities, their emptiness and nothingness
8. seeing before one the true way of salvation
9. grasping and being grasped by the ultimate truth concerning the universe, its Buddha nature
10. enlightenment through realization of the mystery of the world as seen from inside, that is, the Buddha in the heart

Mandalas

In schematically presenting this synthesis of Buddhist theology, the Shingon sects have drawn up two picture charts or mandalas, each in the form of two or more concentric circles. On one (called the Diamond Mandala), Mahavairocana is shown seated on a white lotus in profound meditation, while widening rings of Buddhas and bodhisattvas wheel around him. On the other (the Womb Mandala), the six material elements of the world appear in the form of a central ring of deities, with Mahavairocana seated in the middle on a red lotus, and Hindu and Shinto gods on the outer rim. Kōbō held that prior to the advent of Buddhism the Japanese people dimly understood the true scheme of things and embodied their insight in the gods of Shinto mythology (especially the sun goddess Amaterasu), who are therefore to be equated with the more precisely and truly conceived Buddhist savior beings. This was Shingon's contribution to the formation of the Ryobu or mixed Shinto described in the chapter on Shinto. Largely through the efforts of Shingon (and Tendai), the two religions, Buddhism and Shinto, were practiced as a single faith in Japan for a thousand years.

Because it presented a doctrinal and ritual synthesis, Shingon appealed strongly both to the aristocracy and to the masses. The latter had great faith in the performances of the proficient Shingon priests, whose solemn rites for the dead and elaborate temple ceremonies fascinated and consoled them with hopes of supernatural aid. The nobility was no less delighted, for they liked especially the teaching that just as the eternal Buddhas do not rest forever in spiritual contemplation but manifest themselves in the realm of material appearances, so a person may emerge from monastic training and show the usefulness of spirituality in the secular sphere. This made it possible for numbers of young nobles to retire to Shingon monasteries for their education and then reenter the world to pursue active careers in military or political service.

In the interaction of governments with religious sects the granting of the right to ordain monks or priests is often the means by which civil authorities exert their influence. Each sect maneuvers to establish its prestige vis-à-vis other sects in the seeking of permits to establish "ordination platforms." Through their control of esoteric lore and their connections with the nobility, Shingon monasteries had a distinct advantage.

5. A Japanese National School: Nichiren

The Nichiren school is a solely Japanese phenomenon, a unique form of Buddhism in its emphasis upon nationalism and sociopolitical activism. It was founded during the Kamakura period (1192–1333) in the tumultuous thirteenth century, when the emperor was vainly struggling with the lords (daimyos) of the provinces for control of the nation and needed more religious support than he was receiving. Help came from an unexpected quarter. An intense young monk, Nichiren, the son of a fisherman, after studying the doctrines taught in a Tendai monastery, found himself deeply impressed by the comparative simplicity and truth of the scripture that was the Tendai favorite, the Lotus Sutra. He felt that the Tendai school had gone astray in giving credence to other scriptures and to voices other than that of the Gautama Buddha of the Lotus Sutra, whom he took to be the historical Buddha uttering his most advanced

> Mantra: *Namu myoho*
> Hail [to the] holy law
> *renge kyo.*
> [of the] Lotus Sutra

teachings. Tradition says that on a mountaintop, while watching the rising sun, he experienced a sense of the identity between the Buddha reality in the sun (Mahavairocana) and the Buddha reality revealed in the Lotus Sutra. To be sure he was right, he went from one Buddhist study center to another—Amidist, Zen, Shingon, and Tendai—and emerged from his search with the firm conviction that all the prevalent schools confused the basic Buddhist truths by following false paths. So he made it his aim to restore original Buddhism by launching a crusade to call the nation back to the Lotus Sutra.

He found the monasteries closed to him, so he spoke in the villages and on city streets, with increasing stridency and boldness. He charged that the degeneration of the times was due to departure from the truths of the Lotus Sutra, and that all other scriptures, and the schools using them, should be suppressed as misleading and inauthentic. He railed against the corruption of the times, which seemed to intensify with the overthrow of the emperor's power by the provincial daimyos. When he saw the people turning from addressing the evils of the present to hoping for redress in heaven, he made the Amidists and their Western Paradise objects of special attack, saying was a mark of a degenerate age when people neglected the concerns of this world for the happiness of the next. Needless to say, this provoked retaliation from public authorities. Twice he was banished to a remote region for disturbing the peace and twice he was recalled. His second banishment came when he predicted that the nation's moral weakness would invite invasion by a foreign power, but he was recalled when a nearly successful Mongol descent upon the south coast seemed a verification of his prophecy, even though the Mongol fleet was destroyed by a "divine wind" (kamikaze) typhoon. He was allowed to live in a village and to continue his attempts at religious reforms.

His message was not all negative. He advocated for his followers adoption of "three great secret truths." The first was the veneration of a *mandala* within whose frame appeared, according to his own design, symbols of the Trikaya, together with Buddhas and bodhisattvas exemplifying the Buddha nature in all creatures; second, the constant repetition of the *daimoku,* the phrase "Hail to the holy law of the Lotus Sutra (*Namu myōhō renge kyō*)" as a means of salvation; and third, the establishment of a sacred place, a *kaidan* (literally, an ordination platform), a building or location dedicated to the training of believers.

In his retirement, Nichiren became increasingly confident that he personally embodied the true legacy of Buddhism. He wrote that

> in my bosom, in Nichiren's fleshly body, is secretly deposited the great mystery which the Lord Shakyamuni [Gautama Buddha] revealed on Vulture Peak, and has entrusted to me. Therefore I know that my breast is the place where all Buddhas are immersed in contemplation; that they turn the wheel of truth upon my tongue; that my throat is giving birth to them; and that they are attaining the Supreme Enlightenment in my mouth.[5]

Nichiren's followers to this day have inherited his fervent assertiveness. For them, too, the chant *Namu myōhō renge kyō* is a mystical reification of the Dharma. It is "read by the body": each believer's throat becomes a *kaidan* where the sacred truth is ordained.

Of the three leading contemporary Nichiren sects the most striking is the ultramodern *Sōka Gakkai* (Value-Creating Society). It maintains a temple complex and headquarters at the foot of sacred Mt. Fuji, equipped with large buildings (one being the largest temple in the world), a place to which thousands of pilgrims flock each day to chant the traditional invocation to the *Lotus Sutra* and gaze at the magically powerful mandala designed by Nichiren. It also maintains an active social and political program that includes the fostering of a political party (the *Kōmeitō,* or Clean Government Society) that has run candidates for both houses of the Diet in the national elections, so far with considerable success in some urban areas.

VII. BUDDHISM IN TIBET

Although the Buddhists of Tibet are not numerous— especially when compared to the communities of believers in Burma and Southeast Asia—they receive special attention, not only because their Tantric (Vajrayana) Buddhism is unique, but also because the relative inaccessibility of their culture and its subjection to extraordinary pressure under Chinese occupation have attracted worldwide curiosity and sympathetic attention.

Buddhism was late in coming to Tibet. Long after the countries to the south and east of that high plateau had yielded to the persuasion of the Buddhist missionaries, Tibet remained unaffected. At last, about 630 C.E., a Tibetan prince, Srong Tsan Garm Po, who established a well-organized state centered in Lhasa, his capital, sent emissaries to northern India, in part with the purpose of securing the introduction of Buddhism into his realm. This sudden interest may have been due, as tradition relates, to the fact that his two wives, princesses from China and Nepal, respectively, acquainted him with their own faith and desired to practice it.

Yet Srong Tsan Gam Po's introduction of Buddhism into Tibet was not very successful. The native demonophobia was too strong for it, and besides, the Tibetans found it hard to understand. A century passed before anything effective was accomplished, and then two men came from Bengal to turn the tide. One was Padma-Sambhava, a wonder-working teacher of the esoteric Buddhism of northern India. The other, with whom Padma-Sambhava seems to have conferred, was a more conservative scholar, a teacher called Shantarakshita, who urged the building of monasteries. The former resembled a "houseless," free-wandering yogin and had the greater impact. He excited the Tibetans by his yogic skills and shamanistic powers. Through his influence the Buddhism of Bengal, with its tantric infusion of sex symbolism, took root, and ultimately, after various vicissitudes and "reforms," became the religion of Tibet, and subsequently also of Mongolia, to which it spread in the thirteenth and fourteenth centuries.

The Early "Red Hat" Sect

The history of this earlier "Red" Buddhism, so called because its adherents wore red instead of yellow gowns and hats, is complicated and hard to compress. In brief, it survived a determined royal persecution in the ninth century that wiped out Buddhism in central

Tibet. That it survived was in great part due to the fact that a preceding king, besides extending his patronage to the translation of Sanskrit texts and the publication of a Sanskrit-Tibetan dictionary, greatly increased the power of the struggling monasteries by granting them lands and the right to collect tithes from them. By giving them so much temporal power, the king unwittingly disintegrated his kingdom. Several centuries of civil turmoil followed. Kings disappeared from Tibet. In the disturbances of the tenth century, a Bengali scholar called Atissa was invited to Tibet and revived doctrinal studies. An enduring organization was set up, which produced a Tibetan saint, Milarepa ("the Cotton-clad Mila"). Then sects and subsects began to multiply, some of them becoming lax and corrupt.

One monastery, the Sakya in western Tibet, became renowned for its scholarship. (In the thirteenth and fourteenth centuries, a scholar named Bu-ston was to render a great service to world scholarship by revising and editing previously translated texts, purging them of spurious elements, and restoring them to authenticity.) In 1261, the great Mongol emperor of China, Kublai Khan, sent for the abbot of the Sakya monastery, and after a period of indoctrination was himself initiated as a believer. Kublai Khan had an open and inquiring mind. He seems to have made some attempt to hear good expositions, not only of Daoism, Confucianism, and Chinese Buddhism but also of the Muslim and Christian faiths. Of the last-named faith, Marco Polo and the Nestorian Christians in western China gave him some information. But for himself and his Mongols, he chose Tibetan Buddhism. Perhaps he felt that it was the religion best suited to his followers. He accordingly bestowed on the Tibetan abbot the title of Guo-shi ("Instructor of the Nation") and put him at the head of a newly created hierarchy designed to control all varieties of Buddhism in his empire.

Tibetan Tantric Doctrine

What was the Tibetan version of Tantric Buddhism that had emerged? It was a form of devotion to Buddhist deities, male and female, representing external and internal natural energies. It was based on manuals (tantras) having a distinctly magical and spell-making character and inculcating a psychological doctrine—the practice of which, its adherents admit, is "as difficult as walking on the edge of a sword or holding a tiger,"[14]—namely, the doctrine that passion can be exhausted by passion (the craving for food, drink, or sexual indulgence can best be overcome by rising above it while it is being satisfied). But this is not all. Contemplation of Nature, Tantrists say, reveals that all of the great natural forces, when closely inspected, are a union of male and female elements. This is true of deity as well. In India, Tantrists have held that each god has a complement in the form of an active spouse and that the god's highest power is attained from union with her, for she rouses and draws it forth. Still another belief is entwined with this: in sexual union, nonduality and, still more profoundly, the Void itself are momentarily experienced; there is an erasure of the distinction between male and female. The kind of Buddhism that finally took root in Tibet transformed original Buddhism by assimilating these Tantric doctrines to it.

Cosmic Spousal Pairs: Upaya and Prajna

The new and strange faith that resulted has some striking features. In the first place, the various Buddhas and bodhisattvas were provided with spouses or consorts. But the relationship between the pairs seems at first glance to be the reverse of that in Hinduism, where the male gods are regarded as quiescent (i.e., profound) and aloof, and their female consorts (shaktis) arouse and excite them. In Tibet, the male Buddhas and bodhisattvas represent upaya (the best course of action or means) and are active and creative, while their consorts are observant and contemplative (i.e., intuitive and wise), their generic name, significant of their function, being prajna (Tibetan shesh rab, "higher insight"), a term that supersedes their Hindu name shakti. The male principle seeks to arouse each prajna to an activity likened to fire, setting the male principle aflame in turn. Moreover, a new genealogy of the gods was now made possible. It was generally said that there were five celestial Dhyani Buddhas, namely, Amitabha in the west, Akshobhya in the east, Amoghasiddhi in the north, Ratnasambhava in the south, and Vairocana at the center, all of whom, according to one Tibetan

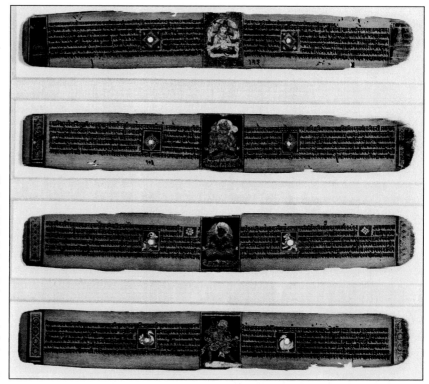

Palm Leaf Manuscript
The text of this twelfth-century Nepalese manuscript of the *Astasahasrika Prajnaparamita* (Book of Transcendental Wisdom) is interspersed with miniature paintings. Sometimes the palm leaves were strung together upon cords (like a Venetian blind) to keep them from becoming disarranged. Because they were compact and portable, such manuscripts survived Muslim depredations that destroyed many wall paintings and other monastery treasures. *(The Asia Society, New York: Mr. and Mrs. John D. Rockefeller 3rd Collection.)*

account, were fathered by the Adi-Buddha, the originative Buddha essence, mythologically pictured as a kind of far-off god wielding a magic thunderbolt (the *vajra*). (See figure, p. 207).

The accounts vary, depending on where one is. It is widely held (Tibet to Java) that the five Dhyani Buddhas are "self-born" and have existed from the beginning of time. This view is elsewhere countered by elevating one of the five, typically Vairocana, to supremacy as the Adi-Buddha. Or a sixth Buddha is added to the five (as in the aforementioned account) and given such names as Vajradhara (Tibet) or Vajrasattva (Nepal).

In Tibet, the five Dhyani Buddhas are paired off, Amitabha with Pandara, Akshobhya with Mamaki, Amoghasiddhi with Arya-Tara, Ratnasambhava with Locana, and Vairocana with Vajradhatvisvari. They were said to give rise to the five great bodhisattvas, who,

on their part, in union with their own prajnas, produced and sent down males and females to earth. Thus Avalokita, an offspring of Amitabha, was thought by some to be male and to be paired with Tara, a consort with whom (i.e., by embracing prajna or insight) he brought into existence Gautama Buddha in India. Others said Vairocana was the heavenly being that caused Gautama to appear.

In the foregoing, we note the appearance of savior beings under feminine names. These may be described either as separate deities or as a multifaceted female bodhisattva. Tara has been a widely used name and has almost a generic significance. In Buddhism she has been the feminine aspect (considered as a consort) of Avalokitesvara Avalokita when he was not himself appearing in a feminine form. As the White Tara she incarnated herself in Tibet in King Srong Tsan Gam Po's Chinese wife, and as the Green Tara in his

Bodhisattva Tara
As the feminine aspect (or consort) of the Bodhisattva Avalokita, this Tara personifies the feminine principle of wisdom or higher insight (*prajna*) to be conjoined to masculine effective means (*upaya*). Some hold that the pairing of Avalokita–Tara brought the Buddha Gautama into existence. In Tantric Buddhism, Tara in many forms is the ultimate compassionate protectress. *(The Asia Society, New York: Mr. and Mrs. John D. Rockefeller 3rd Collection.)*

Nepalese wife. In her blue form she is Ugra-Tara, the ferocious; when yellow, she is angry; in her red form she both brings wealth and promotes love. She has taken many other forms. Generally, she is regarded as compassionate, a protectress; some Buddhists believe she is incarnate in every truly pure and pious woman.

Human devotees were meanwhile believed able to identify themselves with any of the celestial Buddhas or their consorts by a period of fasting and prayer, climaxed by the utterance of powerful mystic syllables, full of magic, and the visual evocation of the divine personage, followed by a merging of identities. This was a Tibetan version of entering Nirvana. Some further doctrines were involved: that the human being is the universe in microcosm; that just as nature is pervaded by hidden energy, so the human being has secret stores of energy coiled up in the body (at the base of the spine, it was said); that the body, as the Hatha Yoga suggests, provides channels for rising spiritual powers flowing through its arteries and nerves in the regions of the spinal cord, the navel, the heart, and the neck to the head; that certain sounds and the display of groups of magic letters and images, accompanied by movements of the body and hands, can arouse as if by a thunderclap the forces of the body and put the devotee on a level with the divine power being approached.

One may now see why this system of religion has been named the Vajrayana ("the Vehicle of the Thunderbolt") to distinguish it from the Hinayana and Mahayana. Another translation of this name is "Vehicle of the Diamond." The diamond is hard and unbreakable; it cuts into everything else with the irresistibility of the thunderbolt; it flashes miniature lightning. Both are associated with bodhi or enlightenment, which comes like a lightning flash.

Public Ceremonies

The public ceremonies that were gradually evolved appealed most strongly to the common people of Tibet. Four ritual components came to be characteristic of a complete ceremony: the *mandala,* or frame, in picture form or described in the air and imagined, in which the gods were placed; the *mantras* or verses uttered; the *puja,* or offering, of one or more of the following: prayers, confessions of sin, sacrifices of flowers, lights, incense, perfumes, and ointments; and the *mudras,* or hand positions, which were believed to establish "actual contact with the gods."[T] These mudras were directed to thirty-five or more Tantric deities, great and minor, and ran in sequences that often required thirty to fifty hand patterns in each sequence. They not only attracted the presence of the benevolent powers but also drove off the evil ones. By describing with the hands certain cabalistic patterns on the air and uttering at the same time the proper Sanskrit formulas, it was believed that goblins and demons (those of the mountains, desert plateaus, cemeteries, roads, air, courtyards, dwellings, hearths, wells, and fields) could be exorcised, and by the same means ferocious animals, robbers, mad persons, souls of the unburied or of enemies, demons of the storm, spirits of bad dreams, or devils of disease and nervous ailments could be kept away.

The geographic features of Tibet predisposed its inhabitants to seek protection in religion. Their hard life on windy plateaus ten thousand feet above sea level, surrounded by mountains down whose slopes windy blasts of icy air would at any moment rush with cracking and howling sounds, made them fear at every turn the demonic in nature. Emblems of death were all around them, for terrain with insufficient topsoil to permit burials made exposed skeletal remains a familiar sight. Long before the arrival of Buddhism, Tibetans had sought comfort in an indigenous religion called Bon, a shamanistic faith that dealt in demonology, animal sacrifice, devil dancing, skullcaps, skull drums, and thighbone trumpets. It was never completely suppressed. Much of it in fact crept into Buddhist ceremonies, for example, devil dancing. On the other hand, it absorbed so much of Buddhism that only its magical practices kept it going.

Benevolence in Ferocious Forms

The demonic in nature colored even the Tibetans' conception of benevolent divine beings. Not only had they pictured in imagination numerous evil powers with distorted and hideous faces, they portrayed even the mild and beneficent Buddhas and bodhisattvas as though they were in a towering rage. The Buddha images seemed designed to frighten the wits out of the devout who approached them. But the fearsome visage had after all this a good effect: it scared off the evil demons, while it merely chastened the worshiper.

The quest for protection led in more than one direction. The prayer wheel (or mill) is an instance of the union of magic and religion. Whether the Tibetans invented it or not is a moot question, but they made

Tibetan with Prayer Wheel
Clothed in sheepskin, with a carrying frame on his back and his arms full of twigs, this Tibetan is twirling his prayer wheel, which revolves by a weight attached to it by a strap. He is protected not only against the weather but also against evil spirits. *(Courtesy of Harrison Forman World Photos.)*

universal use of it. Not strictly wheellike, it is to be described as a barrel revolving on an axis and containing within written prayers and pages of sacred writing. Tibetans used to carry miniature prayer wheels with them wherever they went. The temples had big ones, in a long line, which were whirled about one after another upon entering. To turn the crank of the portable prayer wheel and rotate the prayers was an act of devotion that assured the Buddhas that one's heart was in the right place. Some prayer wheels had paddles attached to them so that the blades could be dipped into a running stream and the prayers revolved automatically from year to year to the great merit of the owner.

Prayer wheels are less frequently seen in Tibet since the Chinese suppression of Buddhism (see p. 213f), but are very much in evidence in Vajrayana Buddhism in Nepal.

Mantras

Another protective device was the repeated utterance of the sacred Sanskrit phrase, *Om mani padme hum* ("Om! the jewel is in the lotus, hum!"). This phrase was both an expression of religious faith and a powerful spell. Repeated up the mountain and down the valley, inscribed on walls and rocks, churned about endlessly in prayer wheels, and displayed on banners and streamers, it stood for a central element in the national consciousness. Few who repeated it knew its significance; for that matter, even Western scholars are divided on whether it refers to Avalokita, as Tibetan monks have said, or to the prajnas or consorts. (In the latter case, it would have a sexual meaning.) The formula was all but a Tibetan obsession.

The priests also had, among other things, a protective function. The people looked to them for the performance of rites and the utterance of prayers to the Buddhas that would secure long life and protection against the power of death. After death, the priests performed rituals facilitating the departure of the soul from the body, conducted funerary rites, and saw to the disposal of the body—by cremation for wealthy persons or high-ranking clergy (fuel being scarce) but most often by exposing the corpse at a remote site where birds and animals would consume the flesh. And when the great monasteries held their festivals, pilgrims came from all parts, supplied with quantities of butter and cloth for the monks, their priestly protectors. For days they looked on at exciting processions, masked dances, and pageants of the monks, as if their lives depended on it. In the intervals they turned aside to honor the mythological and historical

personages depicted in sculptured showpieces wrought in butter and put on display; there was not only art but magic in them. Finally, they went home comforted by the blessing of the head lama and the assurance of the continued favor of the Buddhas.

The Clergy (*Lamas*) in History

The clergy of Tibet have had an interesting history. They and such laymen that had acquired yogic powers early on acquired the name *lamas*, a term of respect, meaning "one who is superior." For one thousand years they lived in thick-walled monasteries. These were originally of the unmilitary Indian model, but finally developed into fortresses of a distinctively Tibetan style, with massive walls rising firmly from the foundation rocks to overhanging roofs far above. The climate, with its extreme cold and long winters, made necessary the building of walled structures with plenty of room in them for winter stores. In the early days, the life that went on there was more like that of princely magicians than of monks. The Tantric Buddhism that was practiced encouraged the lamas to take spouses. Celibacy, at least among the higher clergy, became a rarity. The monasteries therefore often had hereditary heads, the abbots passing their offices on to their sons.

With the fall of the Mongol empire in China, in the second half of the fourteenth century, the conditions were created for the attempted "reform" of a now badly fissured and confused Tibetan Buddhism by the great Tibetan monk Tsong-kha-pa. He laid the foundations of the Dge-lugs-pa (pronounced Gelukpa) order, the so-called Yellow Church, whose executive head has been the Dalai Lama. Its monks are popularly known as Yellow Hats, for their hats and girdles are yellow—evidence of Tsong-kha-pa's attempt to purify Tibetan Buddhism and take it back in theory and practice toward early Buddhism. (The monasteries that resisted reform continued the use of red.) Tsong-kha-pa did not eliminate all Tantric doctrines. He reemphasized the concept of the Adi-Buddha

Mantra: *Om mani* [sacred sound] jewel [in] *padme hum.* lotus [sacred sound]

and saw in Chenregi (Avalokita) his supreme manifestation. The reform was in part the imposition of stricter monastic discipline: no meat, less alcohol, more praying. But what counted most and had the greatest future consequences was the reintroduction of celibacy.

The Reincarnation of Head Lamas

The practice of celibacy had the obvious and immediate effect of ending hereditary rule in the Yellow Hat monasteries; the abbots had no sons. But another result ultimately followed (about a century later) that gave the Yellow Church its world-famous theory of the reincarnation of the head lamas in their successors. The principle of unbroken succession has been very strong in the Orient (witness the familial organization in China and emperor worship in Japan). But the unique thing about Yellow Hat Buddhism is that it applied this principle not to the family (as in China) nor to the state (as in Japan), but to the ecclesiastical organization (here paralleling Roman Catholicism). When celibacy broke up the old type of succession, the Yellow Hats drew out of their strong Tibetan sense of continuity the theory that the grand lamas are the incarnations of the souls of their predecessors, who in turn were Buddhas incarnate. Thus the grand lama at Lhasa was considered an incarnation of Avalokita, and the abbot of Tashilunpo, the Panchen Lama, was thought to be an incarnation of Amitabha. This idea was extended to the other Yellow Hat monasteries and spread later to the branch establishments in Mongolia and Beijing.

The search for the new living Buddha when a head lama died was often prolonged and has been known to take years. The object of the search was some child, born forty-nine days after the head lama died, who showed familiarity with his predecessor's belongings, met the test of prodigies at his birth and of esoteric markings on his body, and was attended otherwise by signs such as the ghostly appearance of the symbols of the deceased lama on the walls of his home. An elaborate series of divination ceremonies was carried through. Among other sources a sacred lake furnished omens.

The grand lama at Lhasa acquired the name Dalai Lama in the sixteenth century when, in response to an invitation from a powerful Mongol chieftain, the lama journeyed to Mongolia in the guise of Avalokita incarnate and revived Buddhism there by setting up a revised pantheon, a corrected system of festivals, and a new hierarchy. The grateful Mongol chieftain bestowed upon him the title "Dalai," which means "the sea" (i.e., the measureless and profound). This visit extended the operating range and power of the Yellow Church, for it resulted in the spread of Tibetan Buddhism throughout Mongolia and the establishment of a line of prelates at Urga, who were believed to be incarnations of the soul of the famous Indian historian Taranatha. He had traveled in Mongolia and was considered by the Mongols a very great man. The success of the Yellow Church in Mongolia furnished the basis for its further spread to China, Siberia, Russia, and along the borders of India.

That Buddhism was vital in the lives of the people of the Snow Land until the Communists came is evident in the fact that one-fifth of the total population resided in the lamaseries. It was a popular ambition to have at least one son out of every family enter the priesthood. The lamaseries were not only religious establishments of venerable age, but centers of political influence and seats of learning as well. In the Yellow Church the Dalai Lama, now in exile in India, had supreme political significance, while the Panchen Lama, of the Tashilunpo monastery, had commanding spiritual prestige.

VIII. BUDDHISM TODAY

During the twentieth century a strong Buddhist revival developed in southern Asia and in Japan due to mixed causes. One cause was the arrival from the West of a religion—Christianity—whose purpose it was to supplant the native religions, but whose missionaries in the very course of seeking more conversions provided the stimulus instead for Buddhism's revival. In seeking to find points of contact with non-Christians through a more thorough understanding of the local religions, the missionary scholars—and also Westerners who became independently interested—translated and supplied commentaries to hundreds of Asian classics, Hindu, Buddhist, Daoist, and Confucian. Thus, in the very attempt to inform themselves more fully, they opened the eyes of educated Asians to the riches of their own cultures.

Another and more widespread cause of revival has been the rise of Asian nationalisms, whose early phases combined anticolonialism with disillusionment concerning the culture and religions of the West that have proved so prone to wars. Furthermore, the social revolution that has accompanied the growing industrialization of Asia, with its inevitable adoption of many techniques and attitudes of the West, has brought new aims into view—social equality, economic justice, and political self-determination. Concrete measures toward social progress through human action have replaced resignation to fate (karma). Humanism and secularism have appeared as rivals of the old religions. But the old religions have risen to these challenges and shown new strength.

The editors of a recent volume, *Engaged Buddhism: Buddhist Liberation Movements in Asia* found strong male and female leadership and plentiful resource material in India, Sri Lanka, Southeast Asia, and Japan.

In spite of the broad historical differences between Mahayana and Theravada Buddhism, theoretical and practical efforts are being made to bring about unity. Scholars of the Buddhist world now stress the complementary nature of the two divisions of Buddhism and say that the doctrinal divergences are natural and logical and presuppose a common deposit of faith. When this realization was in its initial stages, practical measures were taken toward bringing Buddhists into closer association with each other, such as the Maha Bodhi Society for Theravada Buddhism (1891), the Young East Association for Mahayana Buddhism, and the Y.M.B.A. (the Young Men's Buddhist Association, 1906). These have had a pronounced lay and missionary character. The first has long issued publications for world distribution. But the World Fellowship of Buddhists for World Buddhism, founded in 1950, has projected an even wider outreach. Its aim, to bring all branches of Buddhism together, was shown when it held Buddhist World Congresses in different Asian lands.

The whole Buddhist world was stirred by the Sixth Buddhist Council held near Rangoon from May 1954 to May 1956 in the newly built World Peace Pagoda to celebrate the twenty-five hundredth anniversary of Gautama Buddha's birth. The delegates went carefully through the world message of early Buddhism and laid plans for the conversion of the world.

Myanmar (Burma)

The former British colony of Burma became independent in 1948 and struggled through four decades of religio-political experimentation, taking a new name, the Union of Myanmar, in 1989, but the role of Buddhism in its emerging new identity is still evolving.

Unlike many of the coolly aloof Theravadins elsewhere in Asia, Burma's monks have a long history of political activism, agitating against colonialism in the decades before independence and often making common cause with Marxists in the forty years following independence.

Reaction against colonial experience took the form of rejection of external influence. For example, when an earthquake in 1975 destroyed 90 percent of the 2,217 temples and temple ruins at Pagan, most offers of international aid received no reply. The Burmese populace (then 34 million) by itself contributed some six million dollars toward restoration—this out of annual incomes averaging $174 per capita! The achievement was in part an outpouring of piety, but it also was a characteristically Burmese admixture of national pride and shrewd this-worldly promotion. One traveler reported seeing the fallen finial tip of the Shwezigon pagoda used as a collection device for donations. It was mounted on a rotating platform, and donors pitched coins into containers marked in English, "May you meet with lover," "May you pass your examination," or "May you win in lottery."

Burma's present population was estimated to be about forty-eight million, approximately 85 percent Buddhist. About 5 percent could be described as animist, 4 percent Hindu, 4 percent Muslim, and 2 percent Christian. The influence of religious minorities on the Burmese worldview has been minimal. Taking for granted innumerable rebirths, it is assumed that all Burmese are really Buddhist—though a few may be on temporary leave. The Burmese reason that the non-Buddhist Burmese in their midst have either deviated from Buddhism through predispositions entailed in their karma or are foreigners who have turned up in Burma because they have been Burmese in a former existence and have made an incomplete return.

Burma declared itself a socialist republic in 1974, but by 1988 oppressive practices and failed economic programs led to massive social uprisings in which many of Burma's 100,000 monks played active roles. The outcomes included some opening toward a free market economy along with the seizure of power by a military regime under the name State Law and Order Restoration Committee (SLORC). Some influential Buddhist groups were recruited to the SLORC, but many were drawn to an emerging National League for Democracy, a coalition which by 1991 had won as much support as 80 percent in a national poll. The SLORC clung to its power, prolonging discussion of a new constitution and bidding for Nationalist-Buddhist support. In 1992, Aung San Suu Ki and other leaders of the National League for Democracy (NLD) were released from six years of house arrest. In a further bid for Buddhist loyalty, the SLORC government arranged for an exhibition of a tooth of the Buddha (on loan from China). Meanwhile, United Nations pressure and image-burnishing brushups for tourism—"Visit Myanmar Year 1996"—resulted in repatriation of virtually all of the some 160,000 Muslim citizens of Bengali descent who had been driven into Bangladesh in 1992 by Buddhist Nationalists. Government inducements brought about a split in the Karen Christian/Buddhist insurgency organization, bringing the Buddhists into the government camp and isolating the Christian segment. Some non-Buddhists charge that they have been forced to contribute to Buddhist projects.

One development is clear: Buddhist religious orders and institutions find themselves more deeply involved in political struggles than ever before.

Sri Lanka

Once a Buddhist kingdom throughout, Sri Lanka has since the thirteenth century experienced the inflow of foreigners. The first to settle among the Sinhalese natives were Hindu-oriented Tamils from south India, who reside in the north and now account for 16 percent of the island's population. This has led to a virtual division of the island between the dry northern part, which is predominantly Hindu, and the well watered and larger southern and southwestern parts, which have been prevailingly Buddhist for two thousand years. In the sixteenth and seventeenth centuries, the Portuguese attempted to take of the island (and convert it to Catholicism), but they were ousted by the Dutch, who were in turn expelled by the British.

Early on in the British period, Buddhists began to contest the rise of Western capitalism, an unwelcome accompaniment of colonialism. They found Marxism more in harmony with Gautama Buddha's teaching of compassion, the equality of creatures, and a monk's renunciation of private property. When the British withdrew in 1947, the newly independent government declared Theravada Buddhism the state religion and set a leftist course that lasted some thirty years.

Since 1978, Sri Lanka has moved toward a market economy prospering in economic terms but suffering all the while from an agonizing civil war over ethnic and religious differences between the Sinhalese (largely Buddhist) 70 percent majority and the Tamil (South Indian Hindu) 15.5 percent minority. The repercussions have been international and disastrous. At first, the state of Tamil Nadu in India openly assisted the two secessionist parties (now essentially coalesced under the name Tamil Tigers). In 1987, the Indian government, under Rajiv Gandhi, sent military forces to keep the Tamil rebels in check until a peace arrangement could be reached. The effort failed and led to two assassinations in reprisal: Rajiv Gandhi himself in 1991 and President Premadasa of Sri Lanka in 1993.

The conflict ground on: the Tamil stronghold Jaffna fell in 1995, the government's Mullaitiva base in 1996. Whether from desperation to raise funds for war or from outlaw opportunism, the Tamil Tigers have become an international force in drug trafficking and extortion, preying especially upon overseas Tamil refugees in France, Germany, and Canada for "protection" money. The end of twenty years of bloodshed does not seem to be in sight.

Thailand

Theravada Buddhism is the state religion of Thailand, claiming 94 percent of a population of 60 million.

Thai Buddhist Teaching Pictures

Designed for the religious education of young people, such poster sets are sold at sacred sites in Thailand. At the lower level on the left, one sees the ultimate character of the world of *samsara* (rebirth). It is suffering, for birth leads to sickness, old age, and death. Such scenes set Siddhartha Gautama on the path to enlightenment. The main caption, "All bodies are transient," applies even to the deity by the Buddha's shoulder. (The gods have long life spans, but they are finite.) On the right, a modish couple flout traditional values in dress and behavior, but they cannot escape transience. Picturing them in samsaric "reality" (as embracing skeletons) points out the impossibility of finding lasting happiness through the satisfaction of desires. The legend below the couples repeats a question: "Is this happiness?" "Is this happiness?" *(Courtesy of Bhatia and Co.)*

About 200,000 monks and 100,000 novices serve in 30,000 monasteries. Recent kings (and governments acting in their names) have promoted centralized control through a patriarch and a Sangha Council representing the two major sects: the royal-sponsored Thammayut and the less-disciplined but popular Mahanikay.

Divergent tendencies have appeared in recent decades, especially in urban areas. The central establishment represented on the Council leans toward a linking of socioeconomic status with karma, meaning the elite are where they are because of previous merit, and merit-making gifts will keep them on course. This establishment is challenged by three disparate movements: (1) the Sante Asoke, a small but respected purification sect, critical of moral laxity in the mainstream and set up as a free order of monks and nuns (their leader, Phra Bhodirak, and seventy-nine of his monks and nuns were arrested and fined for violating Council and government rules regulating ordination and monkhood); (2) a materialist middle-class Buddhism, mostly Mahanikay, enjoying pastoral and magical services provided by a monk clergy that makes few moral demands on them and in turn is sometimes supportive of monks who challenge celibacy rules; and (3) a small but growing number of "modernization" or "development" monks who promote social betterment and democratic political reform.

The collapse of the Thai economy along with other Southeast Asian economies in early 1997 had the effect of strengthening the position of Buddhist institutions as they were perceived as stabilizing a traditional value system as a counter influence to reckless materialism.

Cambodia, Laos, and Vietnam

The great majority of Cambodians (Kampucheans) are ethnically Khmers. A Khmer empire flourished in Indo-China from the ninth to the fifteenth centuries, at first borrowing culturally from India and then in the twelfth century producing a stupendous twenty-five-square-mile complex of seventy major temples, including Angkor Wat, the world's largest religious monument. All of this evidenced the adoption of Theravada Buddhism as a national religion—though strong influences from Hinduism and animism remained.

When the Communist Khmer Rouge regime of Pol Pot seized power in 1976 and banned Buddhism, there were an estimated 20,000 monks and 2,500 monasteries remaining. Most of the citizenry, who had surged into Phnom Pen during the Vietnam War, were forced back into the countryside. This led to the death (often by execution) of hundreds of thousands. In 1978, Vietnam initiated a war and an invasion, and their forces replaced the Pol Pot regime. By 1989, Buddhism was reinstated as the national religion, but no more than 6,000 monks are said to have survived. Early in 1992, the United Nations authorized a peace-keeping force with authority to disarm the adherents of the four warring factions and to supervise an election in April 1993.

Elections resulted in a sharing of power between a royalist majority and a minority led by Hun Sen, representing former Khmer Rouge Leftists. In a 1997 coup, Hun Sen ousted his co-prime minister and achieved decisive control of the country.

The Kingdom of Laos became the Lao People's Democratic Republic in 1976 when the Communist Pathet Lao forces forced the monarch to abdicate and set about reeducating monks and other leaders of the traditional society. Before the change, Theravada Buddhism had been the official religion of the land, placidly coexisting with Mahayana infusions from China and the spirit (*phi*) cult animism of the hill-country tribes who made up about one-fourth of the population. By 1990, extreme Leftist economic policy had moderated. Family farms and private business and religious practices reappeared, but Prime Minister Kaysone, using the slogan "Democracy under Party leadership," made it clear that authoritarian controls would continue.

The conquest of South Vietnam by North Vietnam, which achieved the reunification of the divided country after twenty-one years and put Communists (the Vietcong) in control, was followed by stern but basically conciliatory measures designed to consolidate all elements in the population and put the nation, now called the Socialist Republic of Vietnam (the S.R.V.N.), on its feet. Since 1975, over one million refugees have emigrated to the United States, China, and other countries. Although the new regime was opposed to religion in theory, freedom of religion was declared, provided outside connections were severed. (In the 1990s, the pressing need for external development helped soften even that last proviso.) The nation remains divided religiously between Buddhists, Confucians, animists, Christians (principally Catholics), Hoa Haos (members of a neo-Buddhist, highly nationalistic secret society opposed to all foreign religious influences), and the Cao Dais (a syncretic faith drawing upon Buddhist, Confucian, Daoist, Christian, and even secular elements to form an amalgam). Although their political influence has waned, the Buddhists outnumber their rivals. They are divided broadly between Theravadins (south) and Mahayanists (north).

China and Tibet

The 1951 incorporation of Tibet into the People's Republic of China and the suppression of the Tibetan uprising of 1959 brought about the withdrawal of the Dalai Lama and many other Tibetans to India and other parts of the world. The People's Republic of China took the position that Tibet had *always* been a part of China.

In the course of "liberating" serfs and herdsmen from service to the ecclesiastical estates, the Chinese intervention destroyed the traditional structure of Tibetan society: confiscating private property; closing down the Buddhist monasteries and temples or turning them into museums; imprisoning, "reeducating," or turning back to lay life countless monks and nuns;

destroying religious artifacts such as prayer wheels, prayer flags, images, and collections of scriptures; and forcing the populace into peasant associations and communes.

Since 1979, antireligious pressures have been relaxed—the excesses being dismissed as "the work of the Gang of Four"—but talk of independence is not tolerated. Nationally there are said to be several thousand monks left out of the some 110,000 before 1959. Large numbers of former monks have come back to serve as caretakers. (Having married in the interim, they can no longer be classed as monks.)

Smoke from yak-butter votive lamps, formerly banned "to conserve energy," is rising again. Some frescoes are being restored with aid from the Chinese government. Tantric images depicting postures of sexual union are again in evidence, but are now partially clothed in silks. Beijing has let it be known that the Dalai Lama is welcome to return, but the conditions are unstated. In the rioting against Chinese occupation in the spring of 1989, many monks and former monks were arrested on the charge of instigating anti-Chinese activity. The present Dalai Lama, Tenzin Gyatso (believed to be the thirteenth reincarnation of Tsong-kha-pa), established a residence in exile at Dharmasala in India in 1959. His patient but firm resistance to Chinese domination earned him the Nobel Peace Prize in 1989. He hints that it "may not be necessary" for him to be reincarnated as a Dalai Lama, and he professes a willingness to return to Tibet on the condition of being convinced that his people are happy.

Meanwhile, a generation of expatriate future leaders are growing up in isolation from the culture of their homeland; more and more Chinese words are making their way into Tibetan speech, and in northeastern Tibet, Chinese residents outnumber Tibetans by three to one.

The tenth Panchen Lama, who had been counted as a puppet of the Chinese by many Tibetans, made a statement on January 24, 1988, to the effect that development under the Chinese had been more costly than its achievements. Four days later he was reported dead of a heart attack. Suspicions escalated the politicization of the process of identifying a successor. Dissatisfied with Gudhun Chockyi Nyima, the successor Eleventh Panchen Lama selected by the home monastery and the Dalai Lama, the Chinese government put forward its own candidate, Gyantsen Norbu. In May 1995, the Dalai Lama's candidate was abducted and put under house arrest in China. At the end of the year, the Chinese government enthroned Gyantsen Norbu as Eleventh Panchen Lama.

In March 1996, there were worldwide demonstrations in support of the right of Tibetans to self-determination. But the world powers seem unlikely to find enough at stake in Tibet to justify challenging China. Years of sporadic unrest appear to lie ahead as the struggle for autonomy is weighed against the desire to promote tourism and external investment.

In the People's Republic of China itself Buddhism has made some small recoveries, especially at famous temples and historic sites likely to appeal to tourists. But the restoration of scholarship and engagement in public life has been limited.

Women in Buddhism

Generally speaking, the roles presently open to women in Buddhism are still auxiliary. We have already noted the ancient tradition of the Buddha's reluctance in accepting orders of nuns (p. 169). Countless sutra passages reflect the idea that female seduction is a principal hazard to male monkhood.

Nuns as a proportion of the total number of monastics were quite high in the Mahayana world of Tang China. A census from 739 C.E. reported that convents made up 40 percent of all Buddhist monastic institutions. (But the units may have been much smaller than the monasteries.) In 1077, a census of individuals showed nuns comprised about 30 percent of all monastics, and by 1677 about 8 percent.[G2] A major survey (*ca.* 1935) showed nuns were about 0.12 percent of the female population and monks about 0.23 percent of the male population. It must be remembered that the level of literacy and training available to women was low and that many of those counted would have been classified as lay nuns by strict standards.[U]

As to the motivations for becoming a nun, one can only speculate. In addition to the attractions that apply also to men, women also weigh the disadvantages of their position in the society at large. In pre-Communist China, for example, there was "near-purdah" confinement to home and beyond that the

Buddhist Nuns Washing Clothes
The steep slopes of Lion Mountain are dotted with Buddhist monastic structures, many of them leading directly into caves. Nunneries are not easily distinguished from monasteries for one finds shaved heads, grey tunics, and high-pitched chanting everywhere. The blending conveys a message, for the monastics believe that truly quenching all desire causes secondary sexual characteristics to atrophy. This nunnery in Taiwan supplements meager donation support with income from furnishing lodging to pilgrims and providing elaborate vegetarian meals cleverly simulating meat and seafood dishes.
(Photo by David Noss.)

prospect of destitute widowhood in later years. Very poor women found that a nun's habit permitted begging with dignity. Wealthy women frequently endowed their own small convents as places of retreat. Among the Mahayana sects, Zen monasteries in Japan have provided the most nearly gender-free acceptance for women, and several sects in Taiwan have flourishing orders of nuns, some in an ordination lineage transmitted from Sri Lanka to China in the fifth century C.E.

In Theravada countries, women earn merit for themselves and their families by feeding mendicant monks and making frequent devotional visits to temples. In Burma, a nun is known as a *thila-shin* (one who observes the precepts), and she is ranked higher than laywomen, but below the *bhikkus* (monks). The government ranks her a "religious person" (and therefore without the right to vote), but monks count her below the *bhikkunis* of ancient times, declaring that that ordination lineage became extinct. In Thailand, white-robed lay nuns are to be found at many wats. A recent survey of fifteen institutions in Ayutthaya showed five had lay nuns on the premises. The ratio of lay nuns to male residents was about one to eight.[V] Opportunities for full-fledged ordination under the Theravada Sangha hardly exist. Determined individuals

in Thailand and Sri Lanka have obtained Mahayana ordinations in Taiwan. Recognition may be slow in coming, but the seeds of revival are present.

In Tibet, there were an estimated 25,000 nuns at the turn of the century, about 2.5 percent of the total population and about one-fifth of the number of monks. Under the Chinese Communist onslaught, some nuns fled to Nepal, India, Sikkim, and Ladakh, and about 1,000 remain in those countries. Since 1988, nunneries in Tibet are gradually reopening. Typically nuns have severely limited opportunities for education. They live in annexes under the authority of monks and are usually supported by their families rather than by the general monastery budget.

Finally, the missionary efforts of Buddhism now encircle the globe. The Jōdo Shin sects of Japanese Buddhism alone list over one hundred missionaries at work in the United States and Canada.

It is significant that Buddhist missionaries have returned to India. In 1953, the Indian government formally handed over to Buddhist care Bodh-gaya, the site of the Bo-tree under which Gautama experienced enlightenment. There is an aspiration in the hearts of many Buddhists that the whole world will someday comprehend the compassion of the Enlightened One.

GLOSSARY*

Adi-Buddha in Tantric Buddhism, the primordial "Buddha with-out beginning" (Svayambhu), "self-existent," the unitary source of the five celestial Buddhas of the North, South, East, West, and Center

Amitabha (ä-mē-täb'-hŭ) "immeasurable life," celestial (Dhyani) Buddha presiding over the Western Paradise (Sukhavati), a Bud-dha field of bliss, the Pure Land (Amida in Japan, O-mi-tuo in China)

Asoka (ä-shō-kŭ) first of the Mauryan emperors of India, a spon-sor of Buddhist teaching as evidenced in rock, pillar, and cave inscriptions

Avalokita (ä'-vŭ-lō-kē'-tŭ) "Lord of This Age," Indian deity of compassion revered in Buddhism as a bodhisattva (full sanskrit title: Avalokiteshvara)

Bashō 17th c. Japanese Zen monk, best known for his haiku poetry

Bodhidharma (bōd'-hē-dŭr'-mŭ) 5th c. C.E. founder and first patriarch of the meditative Chan (Zen) tradition

bodhisattva (bōd'-hē-sŭt'-tvŭ) "enlightened essence," a future Bud-dha, one who merits Nirvana but lingers to help others

Dalai Lama "ocean-measureless superior one," head of the Gelukpa (Yellow) sect of Tibetan Buddhism; the fourteenth incumbent now lives in exile in India

Dhyani Buddhas "contemplative" celestial Buddhas, presiding over a Buddha field of heavenly bliss and ministering to human needs: Amitabha, Vairocana, et al.

Guan-yin or Kwan-yin Chinese goddess-bodhisattva of mercy, derived from the Indian Avalokita (kannon in Japan)

Hui-neng Sixth (and last) patriarch of the meditative Chan (Zen) tradition in China, 7th–8th c.

Jōdo or Jing-tu (ching-t'u) in Japan and in China, respectively, the Pure Land school of Buddhism offering rebirth into the "West-ern Paradise" of Amitabha (Amida or O-mi-tuo Fo)

karuna (kä-rŭn-ŭ) pity, compassionate love

koan (kō-än) "case," a verbal puzzle used especially in Rinzai Zen to tempt and frustrate rational thought and force learners into nondual apprehension of reality

lama "superior one," a monk, a spiritual preceptor in Tibetan Buddhism

Madhyamika (mŭd-yŭm'-ē-kŭ) the "middle" (between being and nonbeing) doctrine of Nagarjuna, allowing a conditional dis-tinction between samsara and Nirvana, but asserting that in perfected wisdom all dharmas are empty

mandala (män-dŭ-lŭ) a "sacred circle" picture chart used for medi-tation in Tantric Buddhism

mantras (män'-trŭz) incantations, mystic truth verbally reified—most common in Tantric Buddhism

Manushi Buddhas Buddhas who, like Gautama, have taken form as human beings, taught the liberating Dharma, and gone on to Nirvana

Milarepa popular "cotton clad" Tibetan poet-saint, second patri-arch of the Kargyupa sect, 11th–12th c.

mondo "question-answer," Zen training material in dialogue format

mudra (mōō'-drŭ) a hand position, sign, token, or symbolic posture

Nagarjuna (nä'-gär-jōō'-nŭ) ca. 150–250 C.E. author of the *Madhyamika-karikas,* best-known text of the Madhyamika or "middle doctrine" school

nembutsu contraction of "Namu Amida Butsu" (Hail, Amida Bud-dha), mantra of the Japanese Jōdo sect

Nichiren "Sun Lotus," the name taken by the 14th c. founder of an aggressive and a nationalistic Japanese sect centered on the *Lotus Sutra*

prajna (prŭj-nyŭ) wisdom, a quiescent complement of *upaya* (skill in benevolent action)

Prajan-paramita (prŭj'-nyŭ pŭr'-ŭm-mētŭ) "Wisdom gone to the other shore" or "Perfection of Wisdom," a female personifica-tion in Mahyana and Tantric Buddhism

pudgala a semipermanent but ultimately perishable "personhood" neither identical with nor separate from the five *skandhas* (see glossary on p. 181)

satori Zen term for awakening or enlightenment, consciousness of the Buddha mind, of *sunyata* (Chinese: *wu*)

Shingon (Chinese: Zhen-yan) "true word," an esoteric or a mystical sect introduced in Japan by Kukai (Kōbō Daishi) in the 9th c.

Shōtōku imperial prince who fostered the introduction of Bud-dhism into Japan during the early seventh century

Sōka Gakkai a modernizing lay Buddhist movement in Japan, an outgrowth of the Nichiren sect, politically activist through the *Kōmeitō* party

stupa (stōō'-pŭ) a hemispherical or bell-shaped reliquary mound or circular tower, usually topped by an umbrella spire, a focal point for devotion and circumambulation

sunyata (shōōn-yŭ-tŭ) "emptiness," the Void, an equivalent to Nir-vana, reality stripped of all attributes experienced in *samsara* (see glossary on p. 180)

tantra "extension," commentaries and ritual manuals that took Buddhism (especially in Tibet) and Hinduism (especially in Nepal) in the direction of personified concepts (Prajna-paramita, etc.) and magical rituals: mandalas and mantras

Tara female protective divinity, consort of Dhyani Buddhas and rulers of Tantric Buddhism

Tendai (Chinese: Tian-tai or T'ien-T'ai) rationalist and eclectic schools, favoring the *Lotus Sutra,* but accepting and harmonizing many levels of Buddhism as manifestations of the Trikaya

Trikaya the "Triple Body" of Buddha reality: the Absolute (Dharma) Body, the Bliss or Enjoyment Body, and the Transformed-to-human or Condescension Body

Tripitaka (trē-pǐ′-tŭ-kŭ) "three baskets," early Buddhist scripture in the Pali language; the *Vinaya* (monastic rules), *Sutta* (discourses), and the *Abhidhamma* (supplementary doctrines)

Tushita heaven a celestial dwelling place of "satisfied ones" (bodhisattvas) during their next-to-last existence—a part of this world as distinguished from remote, timeless, Buddha fields

upaya (ōō-pä′-yŭ) "skill-in-means," compassion in action, the complement of *prajna*; in Tantric Buddhism, the male consort in symbolic coupling

Vairocana (vī-rō′-cŭ-nŭ) "shining out," celestial Dhyani Buddha of Effulgent Light (the sun), the center in the Tantric set of five; as *Dainichi* "Great Sun" in Japan, his body, speech, and mind pervade the universe

Vajrayana (vŭj-rŭ′-yä-nŭ) "thunderbolt (or diamond) vehicle," a name for Tantric (especially Tibetan) Buddhism alluding to lightning-sudden insight and jewel-in-the-lotus pairing of *upaya* and *prajna*

vijnana (vǐj-nyŭ-nŭ) "consciousness"; in Yogacara doctrine it draws upon the cosmic *alaya-vijnana* "store- or foundation-consciousness," equated with the place where the Enlightened Being is nourished: the "womb of the Tathagata"

Yogacara (yō-gǔ-chär-ŭ) the "mind only" or "consciousness only" school in Mahayana Buddhism; also called the *Vijnanavada*; taught by the brothers Asanga and Vasubandhu

Zen (Chinese: Chan) the meditative schools of China and Japan tracing their founding to Bodhidharma

Sikhism
A Study in Syncretism

Sikhism* is a comparatively young religion; its founding dates only from the fifteenth century. It emerged in northwest India, where for four centuries Hindus and Muslims had lived side by side, sometimes in open conflict, always in uneasy tension. The two traditions strongly influenced each other; unconscious borrowing had taken place despite fervent assertions of distinctness. Sikhism openly drew upon the resources of both communities and managed to develop a character of its own.

Sikhism is not in any absolute sense new. Its basic tenet—monotheism—coincides with Muslim conviction, while the pronounced bhaktic character of its devotional literature and many of the doctrines it professes are in agreement with Hinduism. Indeed, Sikhism is an outstanding example of a successful interweaving of religious traditions (syncretism) and one that has proven stable.

On the other hand, Sikhism is not simply two old religions made one. It is, rather, a genuinely fresh start. Its followers believe it to have been authenticated by a new divine revelation to the founder, Nanak. It is therefore felt by its adherents to be the opposite of an intellectual reconstruction of faith arrived at after an academic examination of the articles of older religions. God—"the True Name"—appeared to Nanak and charged him with a redemptive mission to a divided world. It is thus evident that the religion of the Sikhs is not to be confused with the rationalistic syncretisms whose adherents have been engaged in a reworking of philosophy rather than in a revival of religion in its emotional and ethical completeness.

FOUNDER: Nanak, 1469–1538, the first Guru

ADHERENTS IN 1997: 20 million

PREDECESSOR MOVEMENT: Kabirpanthis (Kabir, 1440–1518)

DEITY: The Name, identified with Allah, Vishnu (theistic), God

NOTABLE SUCCESSOR GURUS: Fifth, Arjan, compiler of the *Adi Granth*

Tenth, Govind, founder of the Khalsa (Singhs, Kaurs)

ADHERENTS: (by degree of separatist zeal)

Akali Dal, revolutionary separatist
Khalsa Dal, separatist
Nanak-panthis (Sahajdhari), Khalsa turbans, beards, and so on not required

SACRED LITERATURE: Adi Granth
Granth of the Tenth Guru

---

* This chapter on Sikhism is placed in this part of the book because it is a South Asian religion. Readers following a chronological approach may wish to read it after reading about Islam in Part 4.

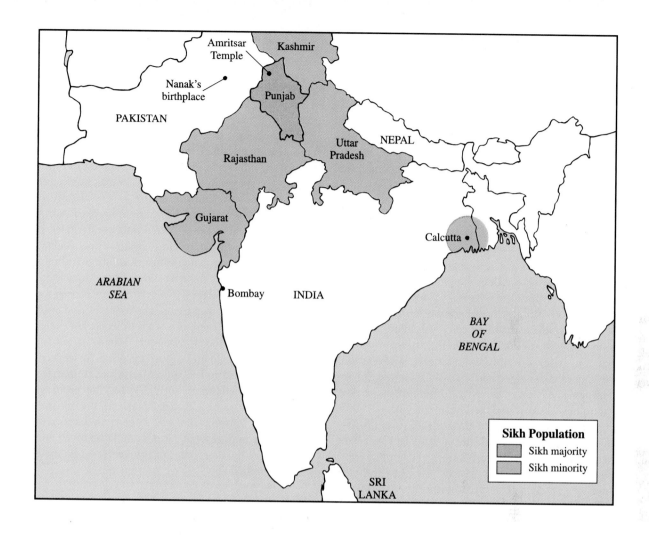

The map shows India and surrounding regions with the following labels: Amritsar Temple, Kashmir, Nanak's birthplace, Punjab, PAKISTAN, Uttar Pradesh, NEPAL, Rajasthan, Gujarat, Calcutta, ARABIAN SEA, Bombay, INDIA, BAY OF BENGAL, SRI LANKA. Legend — Sikh Population: Sikh majority, Sikh minority.

I. THE LIFE AND WORK OF NANAK

The Historical Antecedents of Nanak

Before Nanak appeared on the historical scene, the ground was prepared for him by men who had no thought of founding a new religion but who saw a need for cleansing and purifying what seemed to them a decadent Hinduism. Their recurrent efforts at reform were the indirect effects of two developments: (1) the resurgence of the thousand-year-old Bhakti movement in Hinduism, partly as a response to the stimulus of Muslim Sūfism, and (2) the severe and militant monotheism of the Muslims.

The Muslims (known in India as Musulmans) had reached India in the eighth century C.E. and in time wielded an enormous power. By the eleventh century, they firmly dominated the whole of northwest India, and then, with remorseless pressure, extended their suzerainty over most of India. As early as the twelfth century, a Hindu reformer-poet called Jaidev used the phrase that was to be a key word of Sikhism at a later date. He taught that the practice of religious ceremonials and austerities was of little value compared with "the pious repetition of God's name." This is an Islamic teaching adapted to Hindu use.

Two centuries later, another reformer named Ramananda established a Vaishnavite bhakti sect that sought to purge itself of certain Hindu beliefs and practices. He excited great discussion by "liberating" himself and his disciples both from accepted Hindu restrictions on social contacts between castes and from prohibitions against meat-eating. But his chief claim to fame today rests upon the fact that he had a follower greater than himself, who in turn won the admiration of the founder of Sikhism.

This disciple—Kabir (1440–1518)—has given his name to sects still existing in India, the *Kabir-panthis* (those who follow the path of Kabir). Kabir, reared by Muslims, had a hatred of idols, and, like the Hindu poet Namdev a generation before him, he scorned to believe that God can dwell in an image of stone. He took no satisfaction in the external forms of religion—rituals, scriptures, pilgrimages, asceticism, bathing in the Ganges, and such—if these were unaccompanied by inward sincerity or morality of life. As a monotheist, he declared that the love of God was sufficient to free anyone of any class or race from the Law of Karma. In other words, the all-sufficient means of bringing an end to reincarnation is the simple, complete love of God that absorbs the soul into the Absolute. He denied the special authority of the Hindu Vedas, wrote in the vernacular rather than in Sanskrit, attacked both Brahmin and Muslim ceremonialists for their barren ritualism, and set up in place of their standards of belief the person of the inspired spiritual leader and teacher (the guru), apart from whom, he held, the right life attitudes cannot be gained. Clearly, a combination of Hindu and Muslim elements appears in Kabir's teaching.

Upon a similar foundation of ethical monotheism Nanak was to rear his own doctrinal position.

Nanak's Youth

As nearly as the facts can be ascertained, Nanak was born in 1469 C.E. at the village of Talwandi, about thirty miles from Lahore, in present-day Pakistan. His parents were Hindus belonging to a mercantile caste locally called Khatri (probably an offshoot of the ancient Kshatriya caste), but they were comparatively low in the economic scale, his father being a village accountant and farmer. His mother, a pious woman,

was very devoted to her husband and son. The town of Talwandi, at the time of the birth of Nanak, was governed by a petty noble named Rai Bular, who was of Hindu stock but had been converted to the Muslim faith. He maintained, however, a tolerant attitude toward the adherents of the old faith and encouraged attempts to reconcile the two creeds. Nanak was in due time to excite his friendly interest.

The stories of Nanak's youth are typical examples of historical fact transmuted into wonder tales. It is said that he was a precocious youth, a poet (bakta) by nature, and so much given to meditation and religious speculation as to be worthless in the capacity of herdsman or storekeeper, two occupations chosen for him by his solicitous parents. His father agreed with some relief to his acceptance of a brother-in-law's offer of a government job in Sultanpur. Nanak set out for the district capital. During business hours he worked, it is claimed, hard and capably. Meanwhile, he married and had two children, but he spent the evenings singing hymns to his Creator. His friend, the minstrel Mardana, a Muslim who was to have an important part to play in his career, came from Talwandi to join him. Gradually they became the center of a small group of seekers.

Religious Awakening

Eventually the inward religious excitement of Nanak approached a crisis. There came a decisive experience, which was described over one hundred years later in terms of a vision of God.

> One day after bathing in the river Nanak disappeared in the forest, and was taken in a vision to God's presence. He was offered a cup of nectar, which he gratefully accepted. God said to him, "I am with thee. I have made thee happy, and also those who shall take thy name. Go and repeat Mine, and cause others to do likewise. Abide uncontaminated by the world. Practice the repetition of My name, charity, ablutions, worship, and meditation. I have given thee this cup of nectar, a pledge of My regard."[A1]

Modern Sikh scholars are convinced that this story is a reconstruction of the original experience by use of symbols of spiritual events, that the cup of nectar was

The Poet Kabir

Brought up near Benares as the son of a poor Muslim weaver, Kabir (1440–1518) is revered as a saint by Hindus, Muslims, and Sikhs, as well as by his own devotees, the Kabir-panthis. His songs in vernacular Hindi reject dogma, caste, asceticism, pilgrimages, and ritual requirements generally, calling for interior devotion free from pride and egoism. *(Courtesy of the Bodleian Library, Oxford. MS Douce Or.a.2, fol. 14. VAT reg. no. 19S 2753 34.)*

in fact the thrilling revelation of God as True Name, and that the words attributed to God perceptively interpret a profound experience of being called to prophecy. They find in Nanak's own hymns a better account.

> *I was a minstrel out of work;*
> *The Lord gave me employment.*
> *The Mighty One instructed me:*
> *"Night and day, sing my praise!"*
> *The Lord did summon this minstrel*
> *To his High Court;*
> *On me He bestowed the robe of honor*
> *Of those who exalt Him.*
>
> *On me He bestowed the Nectar in a Cup,*
> *The Nectar of His True and Holy Name.*[B1]

Under the stress of his feelings (a true expression of bhakti) Nanak is said to have then uttered the preamble of the Japji, a composition that is silently repeated as a morning devotional rite by every devout Sikh to this day.

> There is but one God whose name is True, the Creator, devoid of fear and enmity, immortal, unborn, self-existent, great and bountiful.
>   The True One was in the beginning, the True One was in the primal age.
>   The True one is, was, O Nanak, and the True One also shall be.[A2]

After three days, Nanak emerged from the forest.

> He remained silent for one day, and the next he uttered the pregnant announcement, "There is no Hindu and no Musalman."[A3]

This was the opening statement of what was to become a wide-ranging campaign of teaching that had as its object the purification and reconciliation of religious faiths.

Itinerant Campaigning

Setting out on an extended tour of north and west India, which lengthened into years of wandering, he took as his sole companion his friend, the minstrel Mardana, who, while Nanak was singing his evangelistic hymns, played an accompaniment upon a small stringed instrument called a *rebeck*. The far-traveling pair visited the chief places of Hindu pilgrimage, including Hardwar, Delhi, Benares, the Temple of Jaganatha, and holy places in the Himalaya Mountains. Undaunted by the rebuffs and hostility of religious authorities, Nanak sang and preached in marketplaces, open squares, and on street corners, pausing only to make a few converts before proceeding on his way, apparently in faith that God, the True Name, would cause the seed he broadcast to spring up and bear fruit of itself. He devised for his own wear a motley garb that at sight proclaimed his attempt to combine the two great faiths. In addition to the Hindu lower garment (*dhoti*) and sandals

> he put on a mango-colored jacket, over which he threw a white safa or sheet. On his head he carried the hat of a Musalman Qalander [mendicant], while he wore a necklace [rosary] of bones, and imprinted a saffron mark on his forehead in the style of the Hindus.[A4]

But it was not until they reached the Punjab that they had any marked success. There groups of Sikhs (literally, disciples) began to form.

According to an interesting but now discredited legend, Nanak took Mardana with him late in life into the heart of the Arab world. In the blue dress of Muslim pilgrims, staff in hand, and carrying cups for their ablutions and carpets for prayer, they are said eventually to have reached Mecca after many months. We are asked to believe

> when the Guru arrived, weary and footsore, he went and sat in the great mosque where pilgrims were engaged in their devotions. His disregard of Moslem customs soon involved him in difficulties. When he lay down to sleep at night he turned his

feet toward the Kaaba. An Arab priest kicked him and said, "Who is this sleeping infidel? Why hast thou, O sinner, turned thy feet towards God?" The Guru replied, "Turn my feet in the direction in which God is not." Upon this the priest seized the Guru's feet and dragged them in the opposite direction.[A5]

To return to more reliable data, at Kartarpur, Mardana fell ill and died. He had grown old and was wearied out with wandering. Nanak, now sixty-nine years old, did not long survive him. Knowing his end was drawing near, and with his eye on the future growth of his following of Sikhs, he made a decision that was to have far-reaching consequences. He appointed a disciple, Angad, to be his successor.

In October 1538, he lay down to die. The tradition says that Sikhs, Hindus, and Muslims gathered round him, mourning together. The Muslims, so runs the tale (which also is told of Kabir), said they would bury him after his death; the Sikhs of Hindu extraction said they would cremate him. When they referred the matter to the Guru, he said, "Let the Hindus place flowers on my right, and the Musalmans on my left. They whose flowers are found fresh in the morning may have the disposal of my body." So saying, he drew the sheet over his head and became still. When the sheet was removed the next morning, "there was nothing found beneath it. The flowers on both sides were in bloom."[A6]

Thus, even in death, Nanak reconciled Hindu and Muslim, so says the pious tale.

II. NANAK'S TEACHING

Basic Concepts

The doctrinal position of Nanak has a surprisingly simple form, in spite of its blending of the insights of two widely differing faiths. The consistency is due to adherence to a single central concept—the sovereignty of the one God, the Creator.

Nanak called his god the *True Name* because he meant to avoid any delimiting term for him, like Allah, Rama, Shiva, or Ganesha. He taught that the True Name is manifest in manifold ways and in manifold places and is known by manifold names, but he is eternally one, the sovereign and omnipotent God, at once transcendent and immanent, creator and destroyer. If any name is to be used, let it be one like *Hari* (the Kindly), which is a good description of his character; for his mercy is inexhaustible, his love greater than his undeviating justice. At the same time, God inscrutably predestines all creatures and ordains that the highest of the creatures, the human being, be served by the lower creations. (This removed the Hindu taboo against meat eating.) In these articles of Nanak's creed a Muslim element is evident.

On the other hand, Nanak subscribed to the Hindu doctrine of maya, but he did not give maya the connotation of pure illusion. By it he intended to say that material objects, even though they have reality as expressions of the Creator's eternal Truth, may build—around those who live wholly, and with desire, in the mundane world—a "wall of falsehood" that prevents them from seeing the truly Real. God, he held, created matter as a veil about himself that only spiritual minds, free of desire, can penetrate. By its mystic power, maya "maketh Truth dark and increaseth worldly attachment."[B2]

> *Maya, the mythical Goddess,*
> *Sprang from the One, and her womb brought forth*
> *Three acceptable disciples of the One:*
> *Brahma, Vishnu and Shiva.*
> *Brahma, it is said, bodies forth the world,*
> *Vishnu it is who sustains it;*
> *Shiva the destroyer who absorbs,*
> *He controls death and judgment.*
> *God makes them to work as He wills,*
> *He sees them ever, they see Him not:*
> *That of all is the greatest wonder.*[B3]

God, ultimately, not maya, is the true creator, by an emission of a Primal Utterance (Word, *Logos*).

> *God Himself created the world and Himself gave names*
> *to things.*
> *He made Maya by His power.*[A7]

The world is, then, immediately real, in the sense of made manifest by maya to the senses, but ultimately unreal, because only God is ultimately real. (Here we have a conviction resembling the advaita of Shankara but without the latter's impersonal monism, for to Nanak God is as personal as he was to Ramanuja. See again pp. 116–117.) "The world is very transient, like a flash of lightning,"[A8] Nanak sang, and he did not shrink from the parallel thought that humanity is also transient. Retaining the Hindu doctrine of the transmigration of souls, together with its usual corollary the Law of Karma, Nanak warned his hearers not to prolong the round of their births by living apart from God; that is, by choosing through egoism (haumai) and sensuous desire life in the world (maya) in preference to ego-abandoning absorption in God. An egocentric life accumulates karma. Let them think only of God, endlessly repeat his name, and be absorbed into Him; in such absorption alone lies the bliss known to Hindus as Nirvana. For salvation is not going to Paradise after a last judgment, but absorption—an individuality-extinguishing absorption—in God, the True Name.

Like the Sūfī Muslims, Nanak emphasized that God dwells within the world and is in the human heart.

> Search not for the True One afar off; He is in every
> heart, and is known by the Guru's instruction.[A9]

Sikhs call their path Nam- (Name-) Marg to distinguish it from the Hindu Karma Marga. To act always in the name and for the sake of God is better, they say, than Karma Marga, which some Hindus tend to follow for self-seeking motives instead of in the spirit of the *Bhagavad Gita*, that is, without thinking of rewards.

Distrust of Ritual

With deep distrust of ritual and ceremonial, Nanak denounced Hindus and Muslims for going through the forms of worship without really thinking about God. In fact, he felt that ritual was a positive distraction; it turned the current of people's thoughts away from God to mere forms and motions of worship. On every hand he found illustrations of his thesis. In the first Muslim religious service he attended after his call to be the Guru of God, he is said to have laughed aloud at something he noticed in the demeanor of the judge (Qazi) leading a prayer. The Muslims could scarcely wait till the service was over before pouncing on him for an explanation.

The Guru replied that immediately before prayer the Qazi had unloosed a new-born filly. While he ostensibly performed divine service, he remembered there was a well in the enclosure, and his mind was filled with apprehension lest the filly should fall into it.[A10]

Because Qazi's mind had wandered, his ritual prayer was not accepted of God, Nanak said.

He felt a similar distrust of Hindu rites, going on pilgrimages, asceticism of the extreme type, and idolatry of any sort. In the last case, he thought not only did idols distract one's thoughts from God's reality, but, as he declared with all but Muslim fervor, God could not be contained in an image of wood or stone. As for pilgrimages, merely repeating the True Name is equal to bathing at the sixty-eight places of pilgrimage. In regard to the ascetic retreat from the world, "Why go searching for God in the forest? I have found Him at home," Nanak cried.[C1]

Social Mission

Nanak believed that religion has a social mission to perform, a mission to improve the lot of people of all classes and societies. He criticized yogins, sadhus, sannyasins, and other Hindus like them for running away from the problems of life in a self-centered escape from social responsibility. The Muslim mullahs (clerics) also ignored the social principles of the Qur'an, he charged, confining themselves to the duties and rites of the mosques, and treating non-Muslims with unkindly intolerance.

The Sikhs do not despise, nor despair of improving, this world. Nor do they despise the body; the mystery of creation and of life is within it; it has nobility, and they do not have to be ashamed of it. However, Nanak warned,

> This God-built house of
> the body,

> Of which the soul is a tenant, has many doors.
> The five temptations that flesh is the heir to
> Make daily raids upon it.[B5]

The good person and the good Sikh is pure in motive and in act, prefers the virtuous, accepts others without regard to caste, craves the Guru's word and all divine knowledge as a creature craves food, loves one spouse and renounces all others, avoids quarrelsome topics, is not arrogant, does not trample on others, and forsakes evil company, associating instead only with the holy.

Nanak's creed and practice were distinctly conciliatory and peaceful, and yet it was the singular fate of the religion he established to be obliged by persecution to change with the years into a vigorously self-defensive faith, its adherents resorting to the arbitrament of the sword. This is a fascinating story, to which we now turn.

III. THE POLITICAL HISTORY OF SIKHISM

Nine gurus, as official heads of the Sikh religion, succeeded Nanak, and the body of believers grew.

Of the first four, Guru Amar Das (1552–1574) is typical. He was noted for his humility and freedom from pride of class, saying, "Let no one be proud of his caste. . . . The world is all made out of one clay."[A12] The nonviolence of early Sikh religion was evident in all he did. The Sikhs of his time lived by the rule: "If anyone ill-treat you, bear it three times, and God Himself will fight for you the fourth time."[D]

Several novel features of Sikh communal life were originated by Nanak and were continued through the years because they cemented high and low together. Congregations (sangats) were set up, primarily for worship, but also with the function of town meetings. In time,

> **Nanak to Hindus:**
> "Religion consisteth not in a patched coat, or in a Yogin's staff, or in ashes smeared over the body;
> Religion consisteth not in earrings worn, or a shaven head, or in the blowing of horns. . . .
> Religion consisteth not in wanderings to tombs or places of cremation, or sitting in attitudes of contemplation.
> Religion consisteth not in wandering in foreign countries, or in bathing at places of pilgrimage."[A11]

buildings for worship (*gurdwaras*) were built. These often served as hostels for transients and included community kitchens (*langars*) with free common meals. Social service, democracy, and harmony were thus promoted.

But because the Sikhs were increasing rapidly and were being viewed by outsiders with suspicion, if not hostility, the Fifth Guru, Guru Arjan (1581–1606), began a transition to something more self-defensively militant. This was due to a changed attitude on the part of the Muslim authorities, and within Sikhism itself to the vigor and leadership of the handsome Arjan. In addition to completing the ambitious project of his predecessors—the artificial lake of Amritsar and the Har Mandir (Temple of God) on its island—Arjan did two things of lasting significance.

The *Adi Granth* Compiled

First, Arjan compiled the *Adi Granth*, the Sikh Bible. Realizing that the devotional hymns used by the Sikhs in their worship were in danger of being lost, he brought them together into one collection. He was himself a talented poet, and half of the collection consisted of hymns of his own composition. The rest were mostly by Nanak, with a number by the second, third, and fourth gurus, and by Jaidev, Namdev, Kabir, and others. This compilation was at once recognized as notable by persons both within and outside the ranks of the Sikh following. The Muslim Emperor Akbar, of the Mughal dynasty, was told of it by his advisors, who considered it a dangerous infidel work, but Akbar was a tolerant monarch, and after hearing some readings from the Granth declared he discovered no dangerous ideas in it. He even paid Arjan a respectful visit and thus indicated his general approval. But the liberal-minded Akbar was succeeded by his more strictly Islamic son

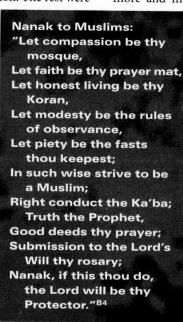

Nanak to Muslims:
"Let compassion be thy mosque,
Let faith be thy prayer mat,
Let honest living be thy Koran,
Let modesty be the rules of observance,
Let piety be the fasts thou keepest;
In such wise strive to be a Muslim;
Right conduct the Ka'ba; Truth the Prophet,
Good deeds thy prayer;
Submission to the Lord's Will thy rosary;
Nanak, if this thou do, the Lord will be thy Protector."[B4]

Jahangir, who, on the charge of political conspiracy, had Guru Arjan seized and tortured to death.

A Militant Succession

Before he died, however, Arjan accomplished his second deed of lasting significance: he left the injunction to his son, Har Govind or Hargobind, to "sit fully armed on his throne, and maintain an army to the best of his ability."[C2]

Guru Har Govind (1606–1645) obeyed the last injunction of his father. At his installation he refused to wear, as being too suggestive of pacifism, the ordinary turban and necklace that had been passed down from his predecessors. His intention was clearly expressed: "My *seli* [necklace] shall be a swordbelt, and my turban shall be adorned with a royal aigrette."[A13] He lost no time in suiting his actions to his words. He surrounded himself with an armed bodyguard, built the first Sikh strong-hold, and in due time drew thousands of Sikhs eager for military service. He was able to provide rations and clothing, as well as weapons, out of the monies in the treasury of the temple.

The Muslim world around him had been getting more and more hostile as the Sikhs, provided now with a capital city and a rich and beautiful temple, began to develop a national feeling. The Sikhs were no longer, from the Muslim point of view, an inconveniently close-knit yet otherwise harmless sect; they were a political and social reality that menaced the balance of power in northwest India. So the Muslims began to bestir themselves. And the Sikhs on their part found in themselves the qualities of fighting men. Things did not go too well at first, however. Guru Har Govind fought and was imprisoned by the same Jahangir who had put his father to death, but when, soon after that, Jahangir died, the payment of a fine released him— to fight again. Peaceful but wary consolidation of Sikh strength marked

The Golden Temple at Amritsar
On the tiny island in the lake at Amritsar the temple housing the holy *Granth,* or Sikh scriptures, receives pilgrims who come to behold the sacred book under its jeweled canopy and to join in the worship of God, the True Name. *(Courtesy of the United Nations.)*

the rule of the next three gurus, the last of whom was imprisoned and executed by the Emperor Aurangzeb.

Govind Singh, "The Lion"

The unequal struggle broke out in renewed military conflict in the time of the Tenth Guru, Govind Singh (1675–1708). On his accession this guru was called Govind Rai, but he is better known as Govind Singh, Govind the Lion. He found the Sikhs aroused for a major struggle. They were, he declared, not animated by enmity to any person but only fearlessly resolved to declare and defend the Truth. Only if they had to would they seek a separate Sikh state. He hoped the Muslims would not force the issue. Meanwhile, he exhorted the Sikhs to stand firm in their faith. While he awaited a possible clash of arms, he fortified the spirits of his followers by writing hymns, after the manner of the first gurus, but at times in a very martial style. God was reinterpreted to bring out his character of a militant Lord of Hosts in time of peril. For example,

> *I bow to Him who holdeth the arrow in His hand; I*
> *   bow to*
> *the Fearless One;*
> *I bow to the God of gods who is in the present and the*
> *future.*
>
> *I bow to the Scimitar, the two-edged Sword, the*
> *   Falchion,*
> *and the Dagger. . . .*
> *I bow to the Holder of the Mace. . . .*
> *I bow to the Arrow and the Cannon. . . .*[C3]

These words are prefaced with the startling invocation,

> *Hail, hail to the Creator of the world, the Savior of*
> *   creation,*
> *my Cherisher, hail to Thee, O Sword!*

Divine ascriptions from the language of wea-
ponry are explained as follows by a contemporary Sikh:

> The Guru regarded weapons as objects of great
> sanctity and inculcated the idea of their worship.
> He even deified them and identified them with
> God himself. Hence the use of such names of God
> as *Sarbloh* (All Steel), *Kharagket* (Emblem of the
> Sword), and *Bhagauti* (Sword.)[E]

These and his other less militant hymns were
later compiled into the *Dasam Granth*, also known as
The Granth of the Tenth Guru, and made an authoritative supplement to the First (or Adi) Granth. Among
them is the following moving proclamation of human
brotherhood:

> *One man by shaving his head*
> *Hopes to become a holy monk.*
> *Another sets up as a Yogi[n]*
> *Or some other kind of ascetic.*
> *Some call themselves Hindus;*
> *Others call themselves Musulmans . . .*
> *And yet man is of one race in all the world . . . .*
> *Worship the One God,*
> *For all men the One Divine Teacher.*
> *All men have the same form,*
> *All men have the same soul.*[B6]

Of himself and his mission he sang,

> *For this mission God sent me into the world,*
> *And on the earth I was born as a mortal*
> *As he spoke to me, I must speak unto men:*
> *Fearlessly I will declare His Truth,*
> *But without enmity to any man.*
> *Those who call me God*
> *Shall fall into the depths of Hell.*
> *Greet me as God's servant only.*[B7]

Khalsa, the Order of Singhs

There can be no question about the fact that Govind
Singh was thoroughly convinced of his divine author-
ity. When, after months of brooding, the inspiration
came to him to institute his greatest innovation, the
Khalsa ("the Pure"), through the Khanda di-Pahul or
Baptism of the Sword, he felt it was of God.

**A Sikh Preacher Addressing an Audience in the Golden
Temple at Amritsar**

The preacher probably is answering questions about the meaning
of the words of the holy *Granth* that his audience has just heard
recited in the most sacred of Sikh shrines. *(Courtesy of the United
Nations.)*

One day, after testing the sincerity of five followers, three of whom were from the so-called lower
castes, by giving them an opportunity to prove they
were willing to die for the faith, he poured water into
an iron basin and stirred it with a double-edged
sword, meanwhile mixing in Indian sweets to produce
nectar (*amrit*). He then bade each to drink five palm-
fuls of the sweetened water (important as a sign of the
extinction of caste) and then sprinkled the water five
times on each man's hair and into his eyes. Thus baptized into a new order of life, they were made to repeat
what became the war cry of the Sikhs, *Waheguru ji ka
Khalsa, Waheguru ji ki Fateh*—"The Pure are of God,
and the victory is to God."

They were charged to wear ever after the five *K's*:
(1) the *Kesh*, or long uncut hair on head and chin, (2)
the *Kangha*, or comb, (3) the *Kachh*, or short drawers,
(4) the *Kara*, or steel bracelet, and (5) the *Kirpan*, or
sword. Beyond this, they pledged themselves to worship the one invisible God, to revere the one visible
holy object, the Granth, to honor the gurus, to rise

before dawn to bathe in cold water, and then to meditate and pray. They gave up all stimulants, especially alcoholic liquors, and eschewed tobacco. They were encouraged to begin the eating of meat, provided it was from an animal slain in the prescribed manner, that is, by a single stroke of the sword. All who were thus initiated and committed to the Khalsa could bear the name Singh or Lion. (Today, girls as well as boys are initiated into the ceremonies of the five *K's* at puberty; the corresponding name for girls is *Kaur*, or "princess.")

Guru Govind himself became a Singh, by obliging the first five neophytes, after he had initiated them, to baptize him in turn. Then he threw the new cult open to men of every class, regardless of caste. To the open distress of the higher castes, many individuals from the lower classes, and even pariahs, flocked to join the guru's organization; thrilled by the baptism of the sword, they were transformed from shrinking untouchables and timid low-caste men into free and fearless soldiers, equal to the best. Clean living and an all-round diet gave them strong physiques; the enthusiasm of a confident faith gave them courage in battle; dedicated and independent leaders gave them direction.

Transition: The *Granth* as Guru

Not all Sikhs became Singhs. Some remained Nanak-panthis ("Followers of Nanak"), displaying varying shades of pacifism and remaining dubious of war making.

Although Govind Singh was successful in fighting off nearby hostile hill chieftains, his struggles with the resourceful Muslim ruler Aurangzeb were without advantage to the Sikhs. The guru lost his four sons on whom his hopes of succession depended, two in battle and two by execution, and the Sikh army was routed. After the doughty Mughal emperor died, Govind Singh was on friendly terms with his successor, Bahadur Shah, only to be himself the next to fall—by the knife of a Muslim assassin in 1708. He had provided, however, for such an event, and told his Sikhs, disappointed as he was in his hopes of succession, that after his death they were to regard the Granth as their guru; there was no need of other leadership than the teaching of the holy book.

The Sikhs were obedient. Except for a dissident few, they have had no human guru since then; instead, they have reverenced the Granth as their one divine authority. At the Golden Temple in Amritsar, it daily receives the honors of royalty. "Every morning it is dressed out in costly brocade, and reverently placed on a low throne under a jewelled canopy. Every evening it is made to repose for the night in a golden bed within a sacred chamber, railed off and protected from all profane intrusion by bolts and bars."[F] But though its words, as read from a duplicate copy, resound daily in the temple, it is written in so many languages and archaic dialects that, except for their scholars, the people must learn the meaning from popular expositions and translations into the vernacular.

The political history of Sikhism since Govind Singh's day has been one of great military renown. The Sikhs won many battles, and in due time dominated the whole Punjab. When the British came to subdue them in 1845 and 1848, they put up an exciting struggle. In 1849, the last Sikh ruler, Maharajah Dhulip Singh, surrendered to the victorious British army, and as a pledge of loyalty gave over to Queen Victoria the world-renowned Koh-i-noor diamond. After that, the Sikhs responded to the respect their conquerors felt for them, and never went back on their word to them. When the so-called Indian Mutiny broke out, the Singhs of the Khalsa, remembering the oppressions of the Muslims, rushed to the British colors and helped save India for the British crown. The crown rewarded them with trust. All over the East they were the favorite soldiery and constabulary of the British colonial power. They could be seen in Hong Kong and Shanghai as well as in the nearer areas of Singapore and Burma.

Continuing Political Unrest

Political unrest was destined to continue within the Sikh community and also between their community and succeeding central governments. Above all, they mourned the fact that their "slavery" under the British Raj had brought to an end all hope of developing in independence the form of democracy instituted by their gurus, in which the whole people, as represented in the *Panth*, or General Assembly, were the real sovereign in temporal matters, each Sikh being the equal of any other. (Women also had been granted considerable freedom. Sikh religious convocations were thrown open to them, and they were allowed to engage freely in most religious and social observances.) The Granth (and not any one official, however high in authority) was the ultimate and absolute spiritual ruler.

But when the British left the Indian subcontinent, its division into India and Pakistan in 1947 brought tragedy to the Sikhs. Half of them found themselves in Pakistan, and violent riots broke out between them and the Muslim majority. Some Sikhs, indeed, reverted to the role of Lions of the Punjab. It is estimated that 2,500,000 Sikhs had to leave Pakistan for India in exchange for the Muslims who left India. In place of the farms they left in Pakistan, the rural Sikhs had to accept much smaller homesteads in India. The economic consequences were often severe, as were the emotional consequences. The displaced Sikhs had to reconcile themselves to the loss of the holy places left behind in Pakistan, including the birthplace of Nanak.

All Sikhs are now within the boundaries of India. An ample majority are political moderates, and one of their number, Zail Singh, was elected president of India in 1982 and served until 1987. But their political status is not what they wish it to be. Some Sikhs demand complete political independence; a Khalsa Dal ("Society of the Pure") organization campaigns hard for a separate Sikh state. Others oppose this,

believing that Sikhism has a role to play in the development of Indian democracy. But even moderate Sikhs, who control the government of the state of Punjab, are stirred to vigorous protests over such sensitive questions as the diversion of Ganges water from the Punjab to neighboring, predominantly Hindu, states.

For more than a decade, terrorist activity by militant Khalsa Dal separatists has continued, bombings and shootings occurring almost weekly. The Indian government responded in 1982 by arresting 300 separatist leaders and in 1984 by raiding the Khalsa Dal base in the shore portion of the premises of the Golden Temple at Amritsar. Sikh militants retaliated, assassinating Prime Minister Indira Gandhi in 1984 and the leader of Rajiv Gandhi's Congress I Party in 1987. It is noteworthy that in sentencing the three assassins of Indira Gandhi the Delhi High Court took the unusual step of recognizing that the crime had been motivated by "the highest and noblest impulses—loyalty to one's religion."

Khalsa Dal violence escalated in 1991, resulting in nearly five thousand deaths and forcing the cancellation of elections in the Punjab. Rescheduled balloting in 1992 showed a majority for the moderate Congress Party, but the turnout of voters was the lowest in history because of Sikh extremist intimidation. Sporadic terrorist attacks continued into 1997. One assassination in particular, that of Punjab Minister Beant Singh in 1995, shook the government's confidence that violence would diminish.

GLOSSARY*

Adi Granth primary collection of Sikh scripture (mostly hymns) assembled by the Fifth Guru: Guru Arjan (1581–1606)

Dasam Granth or *The Granth of the Tenth Guru,* Govind Singh's compilation of his own writings (1698 C.E.), lost and later reassembled in several versions

Govind Singh (1675–1708) Tenth (and last) Guru in the Sikh succession, compiler of the *Dasam Granth* and founder of the Khalsa order

gurdwara a building for worship and hospitality, usually including a room for the Granth, hostel accommodations, and a community kitchen (*langar*)

guru (gŭ'-rōō) "heavy," in general usage a venerated teacher; in Sikhism one of a line of ten designated spiritual leaders, ending with Govind Singh

haumai egoism, self-centeredness, which (along with *maya*) threatens to ensnare human beings, separating them from the True Name

Japji a prayer attributed to Nanak, used in daily devotional rites

Kabir (1440–1518) poet follower of the Hindu reformer Ramananda, a monotheist precursor of Nanak in elevating inward sincerity over rituals, ascetic practices, pilgrimages, and so on

Khalsa "the Pure," core concept behind the pledges and lifestyle commitments of the militant Singh order, the "Order of the Lion," first established by Govind Singh

* For a guide to pronunciation, refer to page 99.

maya in Sikhism, not pure illusion (as in Hinduism) but the limited reality of this world, apt through *haumai* (self-centeredness) to be a snare to those who do not perceive it as a revelation of the True Name, the ultimate Reality

Nam-marg "the Path of the Name," Silk self-reference to distinguish it from Hindu paths: "Bhakti Marga," and so on

Nanak (1469–1538) founder of the religious community known as the Sikhs ("disciples")

Nanak-panthis followers of Nanak who prefer not to commit themselves to the militant rules of the Khalsa

sangat a congregation for worship and for setting Sikh community policy

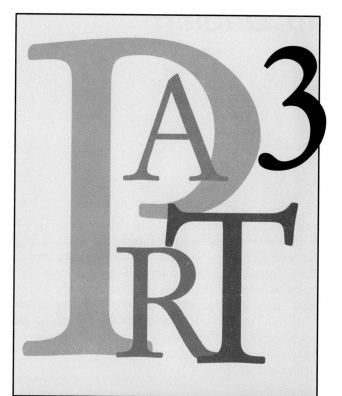

PART 3

THE RELIGIONS OF EAST ASIA

Native Chinese Religion and Daoism

The ancient Chinese scholars living in the times of Lao-zi (Lao Tzu) and Kong Fu-zi (Confucius)* believed they were enjoying the ripe results of a nearly two-thousand-year-old culture. Their backward look, if they were right, traversed a stretch of time so long that to experience anything comparable we should have to think of the landing of the Pilgrims as having taken place not in 1620, but at the time of Augustus Caesar. They were reconstructing the past with the aid of legend and myth and were undoubtedly not in possession of the true historical facts. Recent historical and archaeological investigations do throw considerable doubt on the traditional dates—but the Chinese scholars were not wrong, in the main, in assuming that their culture was both old and thoroughly Chinese.

I. THE BASIC ELEMENTS OF CHINESE RELIGION

The religions of China are a blend of many elements, native and foreign, sophisticated and naive, rational and superstitious. Because we have already glanced at Buddhism in China and are about to consider separately Daoism and Confucianism, our present topic is limited to those elements of popular religion that serve as a background and foil to more highly developed systems of thought and faith. But even this limited topic is hard to discuss within a brief compass; so many of the old and superseded beliefs and practices of China must be considered along with the beliefs and practices that have supplanted them.

WESTERN NAMES: Daoism, Folk Religion
ADHERENTS IN 1997: 220 million
NAMES USED BY ADHERENTS: Dao-jia, Dao-jiao
PHILOSOPHICAL CLASSICS: The *Dao De Jing* (*Tao Te Ching*),
 The *Zhuang-Zi* (*Chuang Tzu*),
 The *Lie-Zi* (*Lieh Tzu*)

TEXTS FOR MAGIC, DIVINATION, AND HYGIENE:
 Book of the Yellow Court
 Book of Changes (Yi Jing)

SAGES, HEROES, AND DEITIES: The Eight Immortals, the Jade Emperor, the Maiden Immortal, city gods, kitchen gods, gate gods, and innumerable spirits, dragons, and phoenixes

*In this and following chapters, the *pinyin* system of Romanization is used in spelling Chinese words (except for the Latinized names of Confucius and Mencius). In the case of a few words that appear to be well entrenched in their older Wade-Giles Romanization, that spelling will appear in parentheses after the first appearance of the word in *pinyin*. Words considered important enough for inclusion in the glossary at the end of a chapter will appear there with pronunciation help and both styles of Romanization.

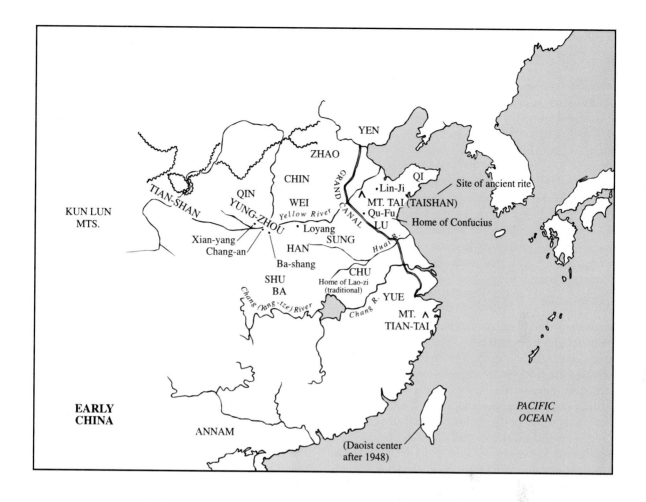

We begin by examining some of the ancient Chinese myths concerning their origins.

Mythic Ancestors

The Chinese have embodied their recognition of this fact in their popular traditions. In many myths concerning the beginnings of their history, they have told of the serpent-bodied Fu-xi (Fu Hsi), emperor and originator extraordinaire, who taught the early inhabitants of China how to domesticate animals, use iron in making hunting and fishing implements, fish with nets, write with pictograms, forecast with the Eight Trigrams, and play the musical instruments that he invented; of Shen Nung, the ox-headed Divine Farmer, who while emperor invented ox-drawn carts and instructed the people in the arts of agriculture and medicine; and of the Yellow Emperor, Huang Di (Huang Ti), most famous of all in aftertimes, who invented bricks, vessels of wood and clay, the calendar, and money, and whose principal wife introduced the people to silkworm culture. These great personages, the myths relate, were by no means the first to appear in China. Long ages lay behind them. In the distant past, but badly jumbled together by the confusing accounts, there reigned through ten great epochs, totaling two million years (!), groups of human, half-human, and animal-like sovereigns, who often occupied the throne for periods lasting up to eighteen thousand years.

Cosmogonies

Yet even these sovereigns did not go back to the absolute beginnings, for, according to an old myth whose details changed with time and location, the square earth supported at its corners the bowllike heavens on four pillars, one of which was knocked out of position by the villainous god Gong Gong (Kung Kung) so that the bowl of the heavens tipped toward one side. A goddess called Nü Gua (Nü Kua) came to the rescue, fashioned four pillars out of the legs of a tortoise (or out of multicolored rock), and lifted the heavens back to where they belonged. In another story she took mud and created human beings, molding some with care and others haphazardly by dragging a string through soft mud. According to a later myth (perhaps owing something to Indian sources), a cosmic man called Pan Gu (P'an Ku), who grew ten feet a day, appeared when the world was still in chaos, and during a period of eighteen thousand years, when the Yang or lighter elements of the chaos separated themselves and rose above the Yin or heavier elements, rehewed out places in the heavens for the sun, moon, and stars, dug out the valleys on the surface of the earth, piled high the mountains, and finally enriched the scene of his labors by his own self-distribution. "When he died his remains fell apart and formed the Five Sacred Mountains of China. His head became Tai (T'ai) Mountain in the East; his body Song (Sung) Mountain in the Center; his right arm Heng Mountain in the North and his left Heng Mountain in the South; his two feet Hua Mountain in the West."[A] His breath became "winds and clouds, his voice thunder, his flesh the fields; his beard was turned into stars, his bones into metals; his dropping sweat increased to rain, and lastly the insects [flies] which stuck to his body were transformed into people."[B]

These stories accent the Chinese belief in the great age of their native culture. But, of course, no great culture anywhere is entirely indigenous. The Chinese undoubtedly learned much from others. Certain production techniques, like the baking of pottery and the making and casting of bronze, seem to have come in from central Asia. It is uncertain now whether these borrowings were the results of contacts made through trade or whether they followed the immigration or invasion of moving peoples. The latter seems likely in view of the appearance within China, about 1300 B.C.E., of bronze arms and armor, together with horses, chariots, and the compound bow (one strengthened with bone and sinew, probably a central Asian invention).

But the West also has had its myths about China. Its historians have in the past tended to take the Chinese traditions as evidence of a changeless civilization fostered by a unified empire with a history stretching back beyond recorded time; but this is clearly incorrect, for the earlier empires were, like that of the Zhou (Chou) dynasty (1000 B.C.E.), of limited area and, as Confucius and the *Dao De Jing* (*Tao Te Ching*) bear witness, enjoyed only a temporary unity. It was not until the third century B.C.E. that Shi Huang Di (Shih Huang Ti), "the First Emperor," brought unity to a large part of present-day China and set the stage for later and more lasting efforts, during the period of the Hans, to stabilize the social order.

The Shape of Earth and Sky

About the time the monistic idealism of the Upanishads was being formulated in India, there arose in China an attempt to order the spirits—that is, to see in all of the processes of heaven and earth a display of fundamental regularity and harmony of operation.

As have many other peoples, the ancient Chinese believed that the earth was flat and motionless, with bowed heavens above. To their mind, China occupied the central place on the earth's surface. It was "the Middle Kingdom." The farther one went from the heart of China, which was where the emperor's palace and the imperial altars to heaven and earth stood, the less cultured and respectable one found the people.

When they looked up into the heavens, with the "natural piety" with which agricultural peoples view the dome of heaven by day and night, they were impressed by the order and harmony of the celestial movements. Each heavenly body followed its appointed order and course, from year to year the same. If heaven in anger summoned meteors and thunderbolts to crash to earth, that would be because it had been disturbed out of its wonted equilibrium by some occurrence on earth, perhaps some human crime.

Earth also showed a like, if less apparent, obedience to law. There was order in the unvarying succession of the seasons, the growth of plants, the upward leap of flame, the down-flowing of water, and in thousands of instances of natural process. Here, too, demonic powers, or heaven's punishing will, caused disturbance, delay, or miscarriage. Floods, tornadoes, earthquakes, drought, and unseasonable cold were not uncommon. And yet, where the earth was left to work out its processes without molestation, there was order and harmonious functioning everywhere.

The *Yang* and the *Yin*

As they pondered this matter, some early and now unknown Chinese, several centuries before Confucius, perhaps even as early as 1000 B.C.E., distinguished within every natural object two interacting energy modes, the *yang* and the *yin*. Everything that is in existence, they and their successors amplifying upon them said, is constituted by the interplay of these two modes of energy, and therefore has characteristics of each. (A whole school of Chinese philosophers devoted themselves to yin-yang interaction (400–200 B.C.E.). Their major representative was Zou Yan (Tsou Yen), fourth century B.C.E., who concentrated on the interaction of yin and yang in the five elements: earth, wood, metal, fire, and water.)

The yang is described as active, warm, dry, bright, procreative, expansive—characteristics likely to be dominant in males. It is seen in the sun, in anything with heat in it, the south side of a hill, the north side of a river, male properties of all kinds, fire. The yin is an energy mode in a lower and slower key; it is fertile and breeding, dark cold, wet, mysterious, secret, the recessive principle—likely to be dominant in females. It is seen in shadows, quiescent things, the north side of a hill, the shadowed south bank of a river. A single object may at one moment show yin characteristics and at another become a yang object aflame with energy. Thus, a dried-out log is to all appearance wholly yin in character, but if put in the fire it will prove to have yang qualities in abundance. This is not because its substance has altered, but because its inner activity has changed from one mode to another. The like is true of anything else, although there may be things in which either the yin or the yang remains a deeply dormant mode of being. Examples of objects in which one or the other mode is dominant are the ever-fiery sun, earth as a whole (predominantly yin in character), and heaven (which is full of yang energy modes). That this way of regarding the compound objects of nature is not unlike the theories of modern physical science is an inference one might draw from the following description:

> The Chinese physical world is a world of action. . . . Things are differentiated, not by the stuff of which they are composed, but by the way they act. Stuffs pass from a state of having one sort of properties to a state of having another; in the latter state they have a different name, but the only difference is one of activity. . . . To say the same thing otherwise, the Chinese seem to have lacked a conception of substance, matter, as such, since this can only exist over against that which is not material. To the ancient Chinese thinker, the differences between things consist in degree of density (itself a kind of activity) and nature of activity.[c]

Men and women are, not less than inanimate things, the product of the interaction in varying degrees of the yang and yin. They show differing proportions of the qualities of each activity mode, men being heavenly (that is, predominantly yang) and of great worth, whereas women are earthly (predominantly yin) and of less account.

Looking in another direction, one sees that the *shen*, or heavenly spirits, are yang in character and the *gui* (kuei) or earthly spirits, are yin.

Again, when a person dies, the spiritual soul, the *hun* or shen-soul, which is the seat of the mind and conscience and is yang in nature, joins the ancestral spirits as one of them; but the animating soul, the *po* (p'o), which has warmed and quickened the body (heart, stomach, liver, etc.), being a gui soul, yin in nature, is destined to sink into the ground when the body disintegrates after death.

In still another direction, the "five elements"—metal, wood, water, fire, and earth—are the result of the interaction in the cosmic sphere of yang and yin, earth being a kind of sedimentary deposit, whereas the others are more volatile.

Finally, events reveal yin and yang influences in the alternation of success and failure, rise and fall, florescence and decay in all things.

The *Dao* (Tao)

But the ancient Chinese were not content with framing a theory to account for the becoming, being and passing away of single objects. They wished also to account for the evident harmony and order in nature as a whole. To what was *this* due?

The concept at which they arrived by way of answer was the Dao. The harmony and orderliness displayed in heaven and earth were, they said, the result of the cosmic presence of the Dao. Literally, the term *Dao* means "a way" or "a road." Sometimes it denotes the "channel" of a river. In general, it means "the way to go." It refers to the standard procedure of things, the correct method of their operation or behavior.

This Dao of the universe is conceived as eternal. It would seem that the ancient Chinese distinguished between the mechanism of the universe and the powerful way in which, as if by inner necessity, it runs. To their minds it seemed that the way in which the universe runs must have existed before the universe itself did. First, the preordained Plan, the proper Way-to-Go; then the physical universe going that way.

The next step was to see that this way of nature's functioning was a way of perfection, a preestablished pattern into which all things ought to fall if they were to be in their proper place to do their proper work. The Dao is emphatically a way of harmony, integration, and cooperation. Its natural tendency is toward peace, prosperity, and health. If it were not for the perverse individuals and demonic beings who refuse to adjust themselves to it, this would quickly become evident. In fact, if the Dao were ever to be followed everywhere, heaven, humankind, and earth would form a single, harmonious unit, in every part cooperating toward universal well-being.

This state of complete harmony, the Chinese dreamed, did obtain in the Golden Age, when the legendary perfect Emperors Yao and Shun ruled their subjects by knowing and following the Dao. That was a time of universal felicity; people then lived in an earthly paradise. Such a state of perfection could return to earth if the conditions for its restoration were met. The possibility appeared to lie largely with the emperor. If he lived according to the Dao, he became the earthly instrument of a cosmic power making for peace and harmony among people, animals, and natural forces, and so prosperity existed throughout his realm.

The Ancient Chinese Theory of History

The casual reader of Chinese history and folklore might too easily conclude that imperial authority in times past was absolute and uncontrolled, and that the emperor had no wishes to consult, save his own. But this impression, however well supported by tales of imperial extravagance and arbitrary rule, would be wide of the mark. Chinese emperors schooled in the old imperial tradition carried a heavy load of responsibility, such as few monarchs in other parts of the world have had to bear. In ancient times it was believed that both crops in the fields and law and order among people were dependent on the sacrifices he performed. In his exalted position, he excelled all others in *De* (*Te*), or inherent power and virtue, and hence was the only one who could give the sacrifice its greatest efficacy.

When an emperor regularly worshiped the spirits and lived in conscientious regard for the welfare of his people, he was highly revered for fulfilling the duty of a Son of Heaven, who had been set upon the throne by its holy decree. But he was never entirely comfortable; he lived in the uneasy knowledge that his people held him strictly accountable for any failure to live by the celestial mandate, for if he did less he endangered the prosperity of the realm. If he failed to carry out the divine mandate and became licentious, lazy, and careless, calamity befell the nation as a sign of celestial displeasure, and the people had the right to revolt and depose their ruler. In such case Heaven guided some rebel to the throne who was more amenable to its will.

Among the most pathetic scenes in history are those in which we see Chinese emperors going before Heaven to plead for mercy for their people—and some light on what they themselves had wrought amiss! What had they done? They wished they knew! Let Heaven inform them, they prayed. One of the emperors of the Zhou dynasty is pictured in the *Book of Poetry* as having been in this predicament.

> Grand shone the Milky Way on high,
> With brilliant sun athwart the sky,
>   Nor promise gave of rain.
> King Seuen long gazed; then from him broke,
> In anguished tones, the words he spoke . . .
> "The drought consumes us. Nor do I
> To fix the blame on others try . . .
> Why upon me has come this drought?
> Vainly I try to search it out,
>   Vainly, with quest severe.
> God in great heaven, be just, be kind!

My cry, ye wisest spirits, hear!
Why do I this endure?"[D]

By the second century B.C.E. this idea had reached so formidable an elaboration as the following:

> If the king and his ministers do not practice the ritual courtesies; if there be no majesty (on the one hand) and no reverence (on the other), then the trees will not grow (as they should), and in summer there will be an excess of high winds. . . .
>
> If the king's mind fail to be penetrating, then the sowing and reaping will not be completed, so that in autumn there will be an excess of rumbling thunder.[E1]

Earth Worship

The religion of ancient China faithfully mirrored the agricultural character of early Chinese civilization. It made much of a mound of earth symbolizing the fertility of the soil, called the *she*, which was raised in every village, surmounted sometimes by a tree or placed in a sacred grove. This mound was the center of an agricultural cult, whose rites in honor of the local gods of the soil sought to ensure an increase in the fertility of the ground and the grow of crops. In the spring, a festival celebrated before the she included dancing and ceremonial songs, in general character resembling the European maypole festival. The she also provided in the early autumn the scene of a Chinese harvest home. When China became a feudal empire, the land was dotted with larger mounds, one in each provincial or state capital, symbolizing the territory of the feudal lord, while one at the imperial capital, composed of earth of five different colors, represented the earth principle (or soil spirit) of the whole realm. At the last mound the emperor himself, at the time of the summer solstice, ploughed a furrow and conducted a ceremony of earth worship in behalf of the empire as a whole, a practice that was continued down to modern times.

Worship of Heaven

With the passage of time, the worship of Earth lessened, while the worship of Heaven steadily increased. In the time of the Shangs (1500–1100 B.C.E.), a deity by the name of *Di* (Ti) *Shang Di* (Shang Ti) was worshiped.

Shang means "upper," and Di means basically "ruler." This Ruler on High, however, was a sort of ancestral figure, a vaguely conceived being located in the upper regions of the sky; he was far from being the Almighty God of Western religions, it seems, for he had no clearly defined character and sent down no messages preserved in scriptures. Rather, it took divination to know what he wanted or would tolerate. In time of drought the Shangs asked diviners to find out if rain was coming and before battle whether Shang Di approved.

When the Zhous began their rule, another name appeared and alternated with Shang Di. It was the word *Tian* (T'ien)—Heaven. This was in general use an impersonal designation. Originally it meant "the abode of the Great Spirits," that is, the heavens or the sky, where the higher spirits dwelt.

The Zhou and subsequent emperors, because of their reputed close relation to Heaven, bore the title "Tian Zi" (T'ien Tzu) or "Son of Heaven." They worshiped Heaven in the people's behalf at regular annual ceremonies. In later centuries at Beijing (Peking), the Chinese emperors used to perform during the winter solstice a solemn sacrifice to Imperial Heaven on the beautiful marble terraces of the Altar of Heaven south of the city (across the city from the Altar of Earth). After the Spirit of Heaven had been invited to come down and take up its abode in a large tablet inscribed "Imperial Heaven, Supreme Ruler," the emperor offered during the various stages of the ceremony incense, jade, silk, broth, and rice wine, and pressed his forehead nine times to the pavement while statutory prayers were recited by an official in a loud voice. Without this ceremony and its attendant appeals to the imperial ancestors, it was felt that the harmony between Earth and Heaven would be disrupted.

Heaven, as the regnant power among the supernatural forces of the world, and as the ultimate determiner of human affairs, dominated the entire course of Chinese religion down to the twentieth century, and the head of government (in classical times the emperor) has had a central role, especially ritually, in maintaining favorable relations between Heaven and Earth.

Divination

Among the persistent elements in native Chinese religion have been various types of divination. In the time of the Shangs, a favorite method of divination was to scrape thin some spot on a tortoise shell or a piece of bone, position it above a flame, and have diviners read the cracks that appeared. By the time of the Zhou dynasty (after 1100 B.C.E.), these cracks were seen to conform to yin and yang lines found in the *Bagua* (Pa Kua) or Eight Trigrams, the latter being all of the possible combinations of broken and unbroken lines arranged in sets of threes. The unbroken line (———) was called the *yang-yao,* because it was held to represent the male or positive principle, while the broken line (— —) was called the *yin-yao* and represented the female or negative principle. The Eight Trigrams were arranged according to later tradition within an octagon, with the yin-yang symbol in the center to represent creation.

Combined in all possible pairs, these trigrams compose sixty-four hexagrams, each representing further aspects of the universe (all of its aspects, it was held).

It was discovered that broken and unbroken stalks of the milfoil or yarrow plant, when dropped to the ground, yielded designs that could be seen to conform to one or another of the Eight Trigrams (or sixty-four hexagrams). The diviners could then read them, divine the present state of things, and predict the future. These interpretations became standard and found their way into the famous classic, the *Yi Jing* (*I Ching*) or *Book of Changes,* whose main text and three appendices have been thought to provide clues to the waxing and waning of yin and yang, not only in the processes of the universe but also in the history of man, collectively and individually. (The *Yi Jing* can be read in two ways: as a naturalistic attempt to discern the forces operating in the universe or as a supernaturalistic book of divination; we view it as the latter here.)

In the third and second centuries B.C.E., a less complicated method of reading the signs of the times (fate) was evolved from the interactions of yin and yang in the five elements: water, fire, wood, metal, and earth. Water, for example, was seen to have special connections with such things as rain, the north, kidneys, salt, and anything black, while fire was connected with warm air, the south, the lungs, eyesight, and the color red. Wood, metal, and earth also had their special connections. When omens appeared, these special connections were reviewed for clues to coming good or ill.

The Bagua or Eight Trigrams

Beginning at the top and proceeding clockwise, the trigrams represent (1) Moving Water (as rains or streams) and Moon, Kan (K'an); (2) Thunder, Zhen (Chen); (3) Earth, Kun (K'un); (4) Mountain, Gen (Ken); (5) Fire, Sun, Lightning, Li; (6) Wind and Wood, Sun; (7) Heaven or Sky, Quian (Ch'ien); (8) Collected Water (as in a marsh or lake), Dui (Tui).

In subsequent centuries and down to modern times, other methods of divination were resorted to: for example, having a geomancer (diviner of earth signs) read the indications in the flow of air and water (*feng-shui*) at a certain spot to see if it would be propitious to put a house or grave there; to have a medium sit with a tray of sand and a suspended stick so that in a trance, he or she could write characters in the sand; to shake a bamboo tube with a bundle of numbered lot sticks in it until one fell out for the temple priest to match with a printed list of prophecies, and so on (see p. 279). Palmistry, astrology, and farmer's almanacs also were popular. Not only were the common people engrossed in these forms of divination, but so were Daoist and Buddhist priests and Confucian scholars.

The Worship of Localized Spirits

The Chinese believed that all nature is alive with spirits of many different kinds. Heaven throngs with spirits, and so does earth. On the second terrace of the Altar of Heaven stood tablets for the spirits of the sun, moon, the five planets, the seven stars of the Great Bear, the twenty-eight principal constellations, the stars considered collectively, the wind, the clouds, rain, and thunder. The spirits were, of course, not all in the sky. They were in hills and streams and even in roads and cultivated fields. The Yellow River and the principal mountains of China were from time immemorial the objects of special official worship.

Not all spirits were considered beneficent. From the earliest times it was a prevailing belief that devils and demons of many sorts and kinds thronged about every human dwelling, haunted lonely spots, and infested all roads, especially when at nightfall travelers thinned out along the way and were few and far between. They lurked, too, in the shadows of forests and mountains. The different species of demons make a long list, for there were demons in water, soil, and air, all varieties of animal demons (weretigers, werewolves, werefoxes, weredogs, and domestic animals that were demons in disguise), bird demons, fish demons, and snake demons. So extensive is the list that it includes plant demons and demons in inanimate things. Also terrible were the man-eating specters, the vampires, ghouls, and gigantic devils with horned foreheads, long fangs, and a complete covering of fuzzy red hair.

Some nature spirits had a high potency for destructiveness but were inclined toward benevolence if encouraged by human respect and veneration. Among these was the fearsome-looking dragon.

It was perhaps not until the Early Han dynasty (206 B.C.E.–8 C.E.) that these spirits came to be regarded as falling into two classes: the *shen*, which are yang in character, and the *gui,* which are yin. Both kinds of spirits were considered almost infinite in number, crowding the universe in all of its parts. The shen were believed to animate heaven, the arable earth, the sun, the moon, the stars, the wind, the clouds, rain, thunder, fire, mountains, rivers, seas, trees, springs, stones, and plants. Ancestors, too, were shen.

The gui or unpredictable yin powers of the universe were ubiquitous, affecting human fate in manifold ways and making night and darkness everywhere terrorsome—unless one had a lantern.

Perhaps no people have gone to such lengths to keep the good spirits on their side as the Chinese, because no people have been more afraid of demons. The sun was supposed to be the chief dispeller of ill-disposed gui, and because the cock by his crowing announces the sunrise, he too was held to have power over the gui. Earthenware cocks were thought to have special power to ward off demons and were placed on housetops and over gateways. The triumphant march of the season of spring (so full of shen potencies) was seen in peach blossoms. Therefore, from the oldest times, branches of peach trees, peach boards with mottoes drawn from the sayings of the sages inscribed on them, sheets of red paper in imitation of peach blossoms, and similar objects were nailed to doors and gates on New Year's Day. Bonfires, torches, candies, lanterns, and firecrackers scared off the gui effectually and were used during popular festivals, especially on New Year's Day, when a general housecleaning of dangerous spirits was effected by their means.

Ancestor Veneration

We have already seen in our study of the attitudes to the dead in contemporary primal religions how natural it is for the living to be vividly aware of the continued being of persons who have recently died, especially if such persons have filled a large place in the lives of the survivors. Just the thought of them is enough to evoke their presence. One feels it not unnatural to want to talk to them, but if one should do so, they would not speak; they would merely be vaguely approving or disapproving. It is clear that faith may build upon such experiences and subsequently convince itself of the reasonableness and truth of its assumptions.

The Chinese always have tied their belief in survival after death to their once great sense of family solidarity. In the past, when they spoke of "the family," they did not mean merely father, mother, and children. They meant all that would be comprehended in an American family reunion, *and more.* For included in the family group were the ancestors, conceived as living and powerful spirits, all vitally concerned about the welfare of their living descendants but capable of punitive anger if displeased. The relationship of the living and dead was markedly one of interdependence.

On the one hand, the dead were dependent on the living for the maintenance of the strong bond tying them to the living; this bond was renewed every time prayers or sacrifices were offered to them. Prayers kept their memory alive, and sacrifices provided them with the food they needed. Not that they actually ate the meat and drink proffered them, for when the sacrifice was placed before them, it did not disappear. What they

Offering to Ancestors

6) recounted the events of the sacrifice that took place by the grave of the noble lord, including the touching and natural reaction of one of the doomed men.

Though human sacrifice continued late into Zhou times, it was gradually discontinued as it was considered barbarous. First pottery and then later on straw or paper substitutes, not only for the human but also the animal victims, evolved.

An important part of ancestor veneration was the family pilgrimage in spring and autumn to the graves of ancestors to make sacrifices and leave offerings there. The spring visit usually included the sweeping and rebuilding of the grave mounds. In autumn, sheets of paper with pictures of warm blankets and clothing were burned at the grave in order to provide the dead with protection against the coming cold.

Observances in the Home

If any single place in the home could be selected as the center of family life, it was the ancestral shrine. Even in the homes of the poor this shrine occupied an alcove built especially for it and contained wooden tablets inscribed with the names of the ancestors. Local clan organizations maintained family temples, often elaborately furnished. In front of the domestic shrine or inside of the ancestral temple, food sacrifices were offered and other ceremonies took place. Here in the presence of the ancestors proposals of marriage were received by a girl's father. Here the bridegroom's father asked approval of the marriage plans. Here the bride, by joining in the family ceremonies, became a full member of the new family. Here announcements were made to the ancestors when a journey or an important business venture was undertaken. Here all sorts of decisions were referred to the ancestors for endorsement.

In G. E. Simon's *La Cité Chinoise*, there is an interesting and a vivid description of the ancestor veneration of a few generations ago as he observed it being performed by Chinese families of wealth and standing. A part of it is here quoted.

availed themselves of, obviously, was its essence, which they inhaled, not its substance, the latter remaining for the priests and sacrificers to eat after a proper interval.

In the present, many believers aver that after the spirits have consumed the essence of offered food it is noticeably less palatable. In addition to food, all kinds of items are provided for the dead in the form of paper replicas to be burned. Money, houses, furniture, and even automobiles are transmitted to the spirit world in the form of smoke.

On the other hand, the living were just as dependent on the dead. Ancestors, if themselves properly provided for, actively promoted the prosperity of the family. Any favor done to the family was one done to them, any injury, their injury, a fact of which the friends or the enemies of a powerful family were well aware.

Funerary Customs

In the past, burials were momentous and expensive occasions. In ancient China, ancestors of wealthy families were buried with bronze vessels and hunting weapons, and sometimes also with dogs, horses, and human attendants. Some Shang kings, according to surviving bone inscriptions, were buried with one hundred to three hundred human victims, who were to be their attendants in the next world. (In ancient Egypt, Africa, Japan, and other places, similar sacrifices were made.)

In 621 B.C.E., Duke Mu of the state of Qin (Ch'in) died with the request that three of his ablest subjects be sent after him. An ode in the *Book of Poetry* (Bk. XI, Ode

At the back of the room, standing against the wall and taking up almost the whole length of it, a long table of varnished wood forms the altar. On the altar are stands holding small lacquered tablets, chronologically arranged, on which the names of the ancestors are inscribed. Hanging at the very top of the wall is the sign of deity [Tian]; and in front of the tablets are lights and incense burners. Lastly, at some distance from the altar, there is a common square table with chairs round it, and in the middle of the table a register with books on each side of it.

Everybody has put on his best clothes and is waiting. The father and mother, who in preparation for the ceremony have been abstinent from the evening before last, enter, followed by two acolytes, and take their places in front of the altar. They address a short invocation to Heaven, and those present chant the ancestral hymn. . . . A variety of things are offered: . . . a pigeon or a chicken, fruits, wine and grain, either rice or wheat, whichever is grown in the district. Or wine alone, with rice or wheat, may be offered. The two acolytes go to fetch these offerings, the wife takes them from their hands and gives them to her husband, who lifts them above his head, his wife standing beside him, and places them on the altar in sign of thanksgiving. The father then reads the names of the ancestors inscribed on the tablets, and recalling them more particularly to the memory of the family, he speaks in their name and makes them as it were arise from the grave. The corn and wine that he has just consecrated to them, which are a symbol of the efforts made and the progress realized, he now returns, on behalf of the ancestors to those present, in token of their indissoluble union. Lastly, the officiator exhorts the family to meditate on the meaning of this true communion, on the engagements that it implies, which all present swear to carry out and then, after a last prayer, a meal is served which the consecrated offerings are included.[G]

Here we have ancestor veneration at its best. But this was only the first part of the ceremony Simon saw. In the next or second part (the third part was a solemn family council) the father read from the family register the record of recent events, that the whole family, and the ancestors, too, might be fully informed, and then he read the biography of one of the ancestors.

He makes comments on it, emphasizing the claims of the said ancestor to be remembered by his descendants, and exhorts everyone to follow the example he gave. A new biography is read in this way at every meeting [twice a month] till the whole series is finished, after which they go back to the first, the second, and so on until everyone knows them all by heart, and none at least of the worthier ancestors remains unknown.[G]

It cannot be surprising that in the past anyone who was believed to have abandoned or betrayed his or her family was regarded as an outcast, despised by the populace and pursued by the vengeance of ancestral spirits. At death such persons became luckless ever, hungry ghosts, unhonored and unsung, without any family to sustain their lonely spirits with sacrifices and affection.

Family and State

Though Confucius made it his life mission to restore the rightful authority of the state over its citizens, he is thought not to have approved of the implications in the following statement of the Duke of She: "Among us there are those who may be styled upright in their conduct; if their father has stolen a sheep, they will bear witness to the fact"; for he countered with the reply, "Amongst us, in our part of the country, those who are upright are different from this. The father conceals the misconduct of the son, and the son conceals the misconduct of the father. Uprightness is to be found in this."[H] Significantly, China accepted the principle formulated by Confucius, although since 1912 the sense of duty to the nation has grown stronger. Communist leaders naturally found the family-above-government idea abhorrent—the worst of all possible ways of construing Confucianism. Education in schools pictured ancestor veneration as superstitious, and the observance of traditional rites was discouraged. On the other hand, in the period since the Cultural Revolution, there has been some

> A candidate for sacrifice:
> "Who followed Duke Mu
>   to the grave?
> Tzu-ch'e Chen-hu.
> And this Chen-hu
> Could withstand
>   a hundred men.
> But when he came to
>   the grave
> He looked terrified and
>   trembled."[F]
>
> —The Book of Poetry

increased appreciation of the family as a transmitter of fundamental moral values. But as sages decreed in ancient times, the responsibility for domestic harmony falls upon the wife.

The Grading of Social and Religious Functions in the Ancient Feudal Era

It is an interesting fact that the feudal system of ancient China, which Confucius was so anxious to conserve, was a graded hierarchy of an exceedingly thoroughgoing sort. In the heyday of the Zhou dynasty, China was divided into several hundred fiefs or vassal states. Each was small, and their total area did not much exceed the region lying north and south of the Yellow River. The ruling princes were relatives or lieges of the emperor and directly responsible to him. These states were again divided into prefectures or districts, ruled by governors and other officers. By the time of Mencius (Meng-zi) of the fourth century B.C.E., it was possible for him to dream of an ideal feudal system, ruled by a sage-king presiding over a kingdom divided into an immense number of approximately square areas, which were again subdivided into nine fields (a central field surrounded by eight others, the well-field system), the outer ones cultivated by single families for their own use, and the central one cultivated in common by all eight families for the overlord. (Tradition says that Confucius in his late teens was employed by the Duke of Lu to supervise such central fields.) It may be that Mencius was recalling an earlier period in China when its villages were surrounded by neatly divided areas, so parceled out that groups of families cultivated a public field whose produce and cattle were destined for the overlord.

More certain is the fact that the population was stratified. The emperor, as liege lord, had under him vassal lords, who held their offices in hereditary perpetuity, in five descending ranks (dukes, marquises, earls, viscounts, and barons). The vassal lords had under them the governors of the prefectures. The governors of the prefectures had under them officers, the officers subalterns, the subalterns petty officers, the petty officers assistants, the assistants employees, the employees menials, the menials helpers! (Under another system of nomenclature, the officials were chief ministers, great officers, upper scholars, middle scholars, and low scholars.) Emperors, nobles, officials, and common people were subject to detailed rules of conduct governing all their interrelations and duties.

Nor was this by any means the whole story. Long before the time of Confucius there was a general recognition of the impropriety of ordinary people or even lesser officials sacrificing to the major cosmic or earth spirits. No prince was allowed to perform any of the sacrifices that were the emperor's function, and no ordinary person could take over a prince's religious duties. The mountains and rivers were not to be addressed by unauthorized individuals, lest their spirit forces be offended or else induced to act in a way not consonant with the general welfare. In later China, therefore, from about the second century B.C.E. on, it became the settled practice for ordinary people to venerate only their ancestors and such household and personal spirits as the guardians of the door and of the stove and the gods of health and luck. They let the feudal lords or their officers venerate the hills and streams of the province for them as well as certain roads and cultivated fields, for the lords could do this acceptably, and they could not. The emperor, on his part, made a tour of the empire every seven years to perform sacrifices near or on the chief rivers and mountains of the land. And, of course, the emperor alone addressed Shang Di, or sublime Tian, in the ceremonies at the Altar of Heaven outside the capital of the empire.

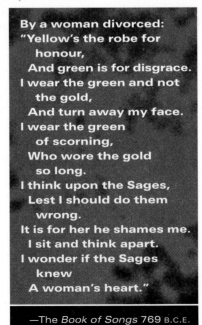

By a woman divorced:
"Yellow's the robe for honour,
  And green is for disgrace.
I wear the green and not the gold,
  And turn away my face.
I wear the green
  of scorning,
Who wore the gold
  so long.
I think upon the Sages,
  Lest I should do them wrong.
It is for her he shames me.
I sit and think apart.
I wonder if the Sages knew
A woman's heart."

—The *Book of Songs* 769 B.C.E.

The Peoples of the South

Although it was part of the theory of history of the Zhou dynasty that an emperor who ruled by the Mandate of Heaven was a universal king and that all people should defer to him as the "Son of Heaven," in actual fact the Zhou empire during its first two centuries did not reach to the Chang (Yangtze) River. When during the later Zhou period the warlords who took power into their own hands pushed Chinese authority to the south somewhat beyond the Chang (Yangtze), the two states involved, Qu (Ch'u) and Wu, found themselves dealing with, and to some extent accommodating themselves to, the Lao people (*lao* meaning "old"). The latter were known to the Chinese as "aborigines," even through Han and later times. Among these less highly organized peoples social stratification was in its beginnings and their religion was concerned with old gods, spirits of rivers, hills, and stars, and spirits of the dead. It was still a religion of rural people, and its human leaders were the *wu* (shamans), who, like their counterparts in central Asia, attracted or exorcised the spirits or visited them in trance states induced by dancing, drugs, and incantations. Daoism, next to be encountered among the religions, may have drawn some of its perspective and motivation from this native, rural faith. Lao-zi, its reputed founder, is said to have come from Qu. At any rate, some authorities say that "there is a close parallel between the images of the flight of the soul in trance used by the shamans of the south and the descriptions of the trance state in the Daoists' philosophical classic *Zhuang-zi* (*Chuang-Tzu*)."[1]

The Decay of the Feudal System and the Rise of the Schools

The period from 722 to 221 B.C.E.—a period of five hundred years—saw the gradual decay of the feudal system that we have just outlined and its replacement by a less rigid organization of society, which allowed men of lowly rank—farmers and merchants—to climb to positions of political importance and thus to break up the aristocracy of hereditary vassal lords. On the one hand, many of the old noble families were impoverished by conflicts with upstart usurpers within their realms. On the other hand, the inability of the Zhou emperors to protect their domain from

invasion by central Asian hordes, pushing in from the northwest, led to the rise of powerful nobles, each fortified for his own protection with private armies and virtually supreme in his own territory. In due time these great lords thrust the emperor to one side and sprang at each other. At the same time, the agricultural serfs began to shake themselves free from the land system that denied them possession of property and confined them to small areas. They became the owners of their own fields, and some of them by joining field to field rose to power as landed proprietors. With the rise of a money economy, merchants appeared in the villages and attained wealth. Some aristocratic families now found themselves so stripped of power and brought down to the level of common people that they were obliged to take positions and earn their livelihood by their own labor. (Confucius came, it would seem, of a noble family, and found himself so obliged.)

The decay of the feudal system finally culminated in a two-hundred-year period of violent civil disorders, called the Warring States Period. The smaller states disappeared, and the seven larger states that remained fought savagely for supremacy. The emperor by this time was an impotent figurehead, the puppet of the strongest feudal prince. Finally, in 221 B.C.E. Duke Zheng (Cheng) of the state of Qin conquered all of his rivals and, as the great Emperor Shi Huang Di, completely unified China under his arbitrary rule. The royal families of all of the states were brought tumbling down into the ranks of the common people, and the ancient feudal system was dealt a blow from which it never recovered.

In the period of the dissolution of the old order, and while the new was struggling to establish itself, a number of differing schools of thought arose to lay claim to the assent of thinking people—as always happens during a period of transition and change. Some of these schools attacked the feudal system and wished it done away with; these were the Legalists. Others wanted the feudal system to be restored in a rationalized and idealized form; among these were the Confucians. Still others would have nothing to do with any political system requiring a high degree of centralization; the Daoists took this point of view. A few, like the Mohists, whom we shall meet in the next chapter, advocated, from the standpoint of utility and common sense, a return to the old-time religion and the cultivation of a universal benevolence that would seek the welfare of all people together.

It shall now be our task to examine some of these proposals for social change or restoration and to see what religious consequences they had during the long history of Chinese religion to the present day.

Two Great Traditions

Among the ways of seeing and doing things that we have just reviewed, two great traditions outlasted all the rest. Both attempted to include the lesser (or "little") traditions under one all-explanatory set of principles. But their principles, in spite of sharing one word (Dao) as a fundamental point of departure, had different orientations. One was Confucianism, the other Daoism. The former found the key to the meaning of things in human relations, the latter in the workings of Nature, as we shall now see.

The term *Daoism* has been coined by scholars, yet it turns out to be ambiguous. It has been used to signify either (1) the type of thought found in the *Dao De Jing* and known since Han times by Chinese scholars as *Dao-jia* (*Tao-chia*), or Daoist philosophy or (2) a mixture of magic and religion with deep roots in the past known as *Dao-jiao* (*Tao-chiao*), or Daoist religion. Under either aspect, it has been a powerful influence both in China and in neighboring countries.

II. DAOISM AS A PHILOSOPHY (DAO-JIA)

Although anything like a systematic formulation of Daoist philosophy cannot be dated before the fourth century B.C.E., its beginnings occurred long before then.

The Legendary Lao-zi

Traditionally, Daoists have believed that their distinctive type of thought began with Lao-zi ("The Old Master"?), a legendary scholar or seer of whom so little can be learned, even on the hypothesis that he lived, that it has been common for some authorities to be skeptical about his having lived at all. He was born, the old

Unity with Nature
Lao-zi and Ox

tradition relates, in the state of Qu in 604 B.C.E. and obtained the important post of curator of the imperial archives at Lo-yang, the capital city. But he began to question the wisdom of having any sort of government; he thought the search for knowledge itself was vain, for it led only to a perversion of the simplicity in which people are meant to live. So, having found his position as an official a false one, he resigned from it and returned to "his own house." The rest of the story is even more questionable. Driven, it is said, by an unceasing desire for escape into the unknown, fed by his aversion to curious visitors, Confucius among them, the aged philosopher decided upon flight into the west. In a two-wheeled carriage drawn by black oxen, he set out, prepared to leave the world of deluded, society-corrupted people behind him. But the keeper of the gate at the western pass persuaded him to write down his philosophy. Lao-zi thereupon lingered in the gate-house long enough to compose the treatise that has come to be called the *Dao De Jing* or *Treatise of the Dao and Its Power*. In short, crisp sentences, some of them obscure and cryptic, he expounded his views, and then he departed over the pass, to be heard of no more.

That even in the Warring States Period this romantic story was not firmly established in tradition is all too apparent from the fact that the fourth-century-scholar Zhuang-zi makes the old master die in his bed!

The legendary Lao-zi may have lived—and there is a strong Confucian tradition that he did—but authoritative scholarship is convinced that even if such a person actually fathered the Daoist philosophy in the period prior to Confucius, he did not write the *Dao De Jing*. That great classic had a later origin. Of its dating, this must be said: the *Dao De Jing* expresses an attitude toward life and nature that presupposes a rather advanced disintegration of the feudal order; moreover, its conceptions had the freshness of a new idea for a number of brilliant minds in the Warring States Period. It may be supposed that it was they who gave to Daoism the permanently significant form of the *Dao De Jing*. And this was a great achievement. Their thinking was in part an aroused and a determined effort, in sorry times, to come to grips with unchanging reality, and in part an expression of temperamental revulsion from the ritual-minded Confucian school that came into being at about the same time.

The Pre-Daoists

Some contributory developments came first. There were forerunners (let us say that Lao-zi, an obscure originative figure, could have been among them) who prepared the way. Already in the sixth century, Confucius seems to have met some nameless representatives of a pre-Daoist school. They were anarchists who rejected "civilization." After his time, other forerunners, more clearly seen by us now, appeared. Some of them were critics of human ways and institutions, resembling the Sophists and Cynics, even then stirring up the Greeks. Few more interesting and engagingly impudent persons have ever pressed their opinions on their fellows. They spoke with wit and pungency, and a certain unconventionality in their point of view made their sayings all the more intriguing.

Yang Zhu

This unconventionality is well illustrated by Yang Zhu (Yang Chu), who lived at the end of the fifth and beginning of the fourth century. His problem seems to have been how to preserve his life whole undamaged—the general personal problem of the early Daoists. Seeing that China was in a chaotic state beyond all help that he could devise, he concluded that following nature, turning his back on society, and cultivating his own personal life was the only true good. Unabashed by the consequences of this reasoning, he said quite smartly, "Each one for himself!" and shocked the Confucians by asserting that even if all he had to do to be given the whole world would be to pluck a single hair from his shank, he would not do so. This was because he valued

his own life above even the sum of all external things. "Not allowing outside things to entangle one's person"[1] was his cardinal principle.

Shen Dao

Even more unconventional were Peng Meng and his followers, Tian Pian and the inimitable Shen Dao (Shen Tao). They resolved to discard knowledge, to be impartial and nonpartisan, to adopt an easygoing unobtrusive manner, to have no anxiety for the morrow, and to let events just take their course without interfering. Perhaps the later Daoist Zhuang-zi (Chuang-Tzu) was thinking of them when he attributed to Ziyu (Tzuyü), a Confucian (!), the following ultimate expression of a go-with-the-flow attitude:

> If my left arm should be transformed into a cock, I would mark with it the time of night. If my right arm should be transformed into a crossbow, I would look for a bird to bring down and roast. If my rumpbone should be transformed into a wheel, and my spirit into a horse, I would mount and would have no need of any other steed.[2]

It was their opinion that the wise man who has acquired the secret of the good life "follows the inevitable" and "simply moves with things." Of one of them we read,

> Shen Two discarded knowledge, abandoned self, followed the inevitable, and was indifferent to things. . . . He said: "Knowledge is not to know." He was one who despised knowledge and would destroy it. Stupid and irresponsible, he ridiculed the World's way of preferring the virtuous; careless and impractical, he condemned the world's great Sages; shifting and slippery, he changed about with circumstances; disregarding right and wrong, he was only concerned with avoiding trouble; learning nothing with knowledge and thinking, paying no attention to past or future, he stood loftily indifferent to everything.
>
> He went where he was pushed and followed where he was led, like a whirling gale, like a feather tossed in the wind, like a turning mill-stone. He was complete without defects; in action or at rest he was free from mistakes and never offended others. How could this be? Because creatures without knowledge are freed from the trouble of self-assertion and the entanglements of knowledge; in motion or at rest

they do not depart from the principles of nature. . . . Therefore, he said: "Let us be like creatures without knowledge. That will be sufficient. . . . For a clod of earth does not miss the Way [Dao]"[J3]

While Yang Zhu and Shen Dao were thus venturing their own persons, so to speak, in an attempt to find the course (Dao) that nature prescribes for those who wish to be right, superior, and happy, other and more profound, discriminating minds were assembling the *Dao De Jing* and the essays of Zhuang-zi.

The Philosophy of the *Dao De Jing*

As it stands, the *Dao De Jing* is hardly the product of one mind, although basically it may be so. Interpolations and repeated editing have altered its original form. But doubtless most of the present version comes from the fourth century B.C.E.

The *Dao De Jing* accepts unquestioningly the theory that when things are allowed to take their natural course, they move with a wonderful perfection and harmony. This is because, in such a case, the Dao (the eternal way of the universe) is not hindered in its smooth operation.

What is the Dao? Its definition is acknowledged to be difficult. The opening sentences of the *Dao De Jing* say it is impossible. The Dao that can be expressed in words is not the eternal Dao; the name that can be named is not the real, the absolute name. The Dao is wrapped in cosmic mystery, and reaching for it is groping through mystery into deeper mystery. Yet the whole world, all that has being, has emerged from the Dao's unactualized essence, its unrealized potentiality (nonbeing), and it is the sole source of the active power (De) in all existent things.

> The mightiest manifestations of active force flow solely from the Tao.
>   The Tao in itself is vague, impalpable—how impalpable, how vague! Yet within it there is Form. How vague, how impalpable! Yet within it there is Substance. How profound, how obscure! Yet within it there is a Vital Principle.[K1]

Just as the Dao encompasses both yang and yin values, holding them in balance, so the wise human being of either sex will internalize both. The *Dao De Jing*, however, sees human society as being overly dominated by *yang* (Confucian) traits, and so it emphasizes counterbalancing, *yin* values, speaking of them in the conventional feminine gender. Thus such categories as nonbeing, quietness, low position, reversion, oneness with nature, and spontaneity are extolled, and the conventional gender attributions are not meant to imply that they are appropriate only for persons of one sex or the other.

Nonbeing

Inquiry concerning the Dao takes us into the realm of preexistence and nonbeing (potentiality), yet who can prevent the question from arising: How does the Dao operate in the realm of actuality or being? Perhaps awareness of the pure potentiality of the unmanifest Dao enables spontaneous coming into being much as a floating leaf effortlessly moves with the current of a river. This is for the *Dao De Jing* the central question, really, for it considers that the chief aim of human existence must be to attain fullness of life by present harmony with the Dao.

Just as heaven and earth attain complete harmony and order only by letting the Dao take its course, so a person can attain the highest well-being only by arriving at conformity with it. Individuals have the power to choose their own ways and to build up social habits after their own plans rather than after the eternal plan of the great Dao. But thence have sprung all the ills and pains of our humankind, in the midst of the strange, queer "civilization" we have formed. We have chosen to move contrariwise to the eternal Dao, and it has been like swimming against the current. Nature is fighting us by flowing the other way. Perhaps we think we are big enough to overcome nature. But we are not. People have the power to think and feel and act as they like, and the Dao allows, or rather does not disallow, them. But not to the extent of ceasing to be itself!

> Nature is not benevolent; with ruthless indifference she makes all things serve their purposes, like the straw dogs we use at sacrifices.[K2]
>
> What is contrary to the Tao soon perishes.[K3]
>
> He who is self-approving does not shine. He who exalts himself does not rise high. Judged according to the Tao, he is like remnants of food [garbage] or a tumour on the body—an object of universal disgust.[K4]

Quietness

The Dao is quiet, so quiet that its presence goes easily undetected, save by intuition.

> The Way of Heaven is not to contend and yet to be able
>   to conquer.
> Not to declare its will and yet to get a response,
> Not to summon but have things come
>   spontaneously.[E2]

> Tao produces all things; . . .
> It produces them without holding possession of them.
> It acts without depending upon them, and raises
>   without lording it over them.[L1]

Therefore, heaven and earth—and people, too, if only they would—may safely resign themselves to it and experience complete fulfillment of being.

> The Tao is ever inactive,
> And yet there is nothing that it does not do.[L2]

Low Position

Such quietness is like that of the female, whose ascendancy in human affairs may be accounted for by the fact that she is never aggressive and yet accomplishes all things; she takes the lowest place and may be compared with a deep valley toward which all streams flow. Valleys are fertile and full of the spirit attributed in ancient times to mother goddesses. (In fact, some Chinese scholars think the Dao is a concept not unconnected with the archaic belief in mother goddesses.) The *Dao De Jing* says,

> The Spirit of the Valley never dies.
> It is called the Mystic Female.
>   The Door of the Mystic Female
>   Is the root of Heaven and Earth.
>   Continuously, continuously,
>   It seems to remain.
>   Draw upon it
>   And it serves you with ease.[M1]

The people of the world depend on aggression to achieve their aims, but let them beware!

> The man of violence does not die a natural death: I
> take this to be my basic doctrine.[N1]

Reversion

This brings us to a very important point in the *Dao De Jing*. People who do not follow the Dao way may meet with temporary success, but there is an invariable law in things, that if any movement goes to its extreme of development, it necessarily has to execute a "return" or "reversion."

> Stretch a bow to the full.
> And you will wish you had stopped in time;
> Temper a sword-edge to its very sharpest,
> And you will find it soon grows dull.
> When bronze and jade fill your hall
> It can no longer be guarded.
> Wealth and place breed insolence
> That brings ruin in its train.
> When your work is done, then withdraw![N2]

> All things come into existence,
> And thence we see them return.
> Look at the things that have been flourishing;
> Each goes back to its origin.[L3]

> Returning is the motion of the Tao.[L4]

So universal and constant in all things is the process of reversion and return that all natural process is marked by the sameness of coming into being, reaching maturity, and reverting to nonbeing (death). All things go back to their common origin; ultimately they all blend into one. The Dao at work in each of the "ten thousand things under heaven" is the same Dao, obscure but originative, hidden but all encompassing.

> Because the eye gazes but can catch no glimpse of it,
> It is called elusive.
> Because the ear listens but cannot hear it,
> It is called the rarefied.
> Because the hand feels for it but cannot find it,
> It is called the infinitesimal.
> These three, because they cannot be further scrutinized,
> Blend into one.[N3]

> Tao begets One: one begets two; two begets three; three
>   begets all things.[L5]

> Therefore the Sage embraces the One.[M2]

Oneness with Nature

As a sage, one comes to an awareness of the identity of oneself with the One Dao. The sage and all of the distinguishable phenomena of nature, the events in space and time that make their appearance to the senses, are at heart indistinguishable. They are the same in their rise and fall, their growth and decay, but above all in the derivation of their being from original nonbeing and their return to nonbeing. All of this the way of nature and is the destiny of all things.

As a sage, one therefore yields oneself to Nature (the Dao) and does not struggle to assert oneself aggressively nor strive for a sharply distinguishable identity. One humbly seeks union with the All Encompassing as the first condition of well-being.

> The ancient saying "Be humble and you shall remain
>   entire"—
> Can this be regarded as mere empty words?[L6]

This is far from having the prevailing Western attitude toward nature, that of seeking mastery of it, so as to make it submit to the will and service of human beings, which attitude, combined with scientific controls, has now at last led to defacement and pollution of the natural environment.

Spontaneity

Above all, a sage behaves naturally, responding spontaneously to the present moment. There will be no calculation, no insistence on one's own plans.

> Nature does not have to insist,
> Can blow for only half a morning,
> Rain for only half a day,
> And what are these winds and these rains but natural?
> If nature does not have to insist,
> Why should man?[O]

> Leave all things to take their natural course, and do not
>   interfere.[K5]

It may be argued that there is little of religion here. For one thing, it may be urged, the Dao is impersonal, and although persons are among its expressions, it is itself without form and void. Therefore, one meditates on the Dao but does not engage in formal worship of it. The Dao is not aware of nor does it make a compassionate response to persons; it is but the cosmic mode of action by which nonbeing becomes being. Yet religion may breathe in this rare air—a one-sidedly philosophical and intuitional type of religion no doubt, but something more than bare philosophy. For the Dao determines destiny, may even be said to be a ruling force (*De*), and conformity to it is a species of religious mysticism. The study of the Dao begins in philosophy: What is the ultimate reality? It concludes as religion: How may I be in complete accord with this reality?

The Ethics of the *Dao De Jing*

We turn now to the *Dao De Jing*'s ethics. What we have said has already suggested it. The central consideration may be expressed in two sentences—one positive, the other negative. Positively stated, the principle is that one must exhibit within oneself the procedure of the Dao and be characterized by its quietude of power, its production without possession, action without self-assertion, development without domination.

Wu-wei in Negative Terms

Negatively, the principle runs: Do not meddle with the smooth course of nature going on its blessed way. As the *Dao De Jing* puts it, it is wise to practice *wu-wei* (nonaggression, nonmeddlesome action). It is possible to achieve without doing.

> Therefore, the sage carries on his business without
> action, and gives his teaching without words.[L7]

The sage exhibits a retiring, not to say a stay-at-home disposition.

> Without going out of the door
> One can know the whole world;
> Without peeping out of the window
> One can see the Tao of heaven.
> The further one travels
> The less one knows.
> Therefore the sage knows everything without traveling,
> He names everything without seeing it;
> He accomplishes everything without doing it.[L8]

The sage has no ambitions, no desire for fame. As a sage, one is egoless and knows that the admiration of others, which most persons seek, tends to bind one to a false image of oneself that would prevent one from acting freely and spontaneously. One must quietly be oneself. One prefers in oneself—and in others—"what belongs to original nature," before any changes occurred; one seeks in oneself what is pure and undistorted; a sage therefore wants to be like a newborn child, raw silk (not yet made cloth), or an uncarved block, pu (p'u) unshaped by any person and without a name to mark its differentiation from its original state.

Such a one will appear "stupid" or "out of this world." Other people are wide awake, knowing; the sage alone appears dull, confused, even uncomprehending, like a baby who is not yet able to smile. But this is the only way to guard from prying eyes and interfering wills the precious De or natural ability that is the Dao's power at work in oneself.

The Affirmative Powers of *Wu-wei*

This seems negative at first glance, but not so, says the *Dao De Jing*. There is affirmative power in the restraint of wu wei; its attendant virtues in human life are kindness, sincerity, and humility. If one does not meddle with others, human relations will fall as the Dao brings them to pass, naturally and simply. There will be a spontaneous birth of true love, real kindness, simplicity, and contentment in the lives and relationships of people. Just the restraint of self from anger, ambition, and meddlesome action is never merely negative in its consequences; power (De) is in it, power for good.

> To those who are good to me I am good; and to those who are not good to me, I am also good—and thus all get to be good. To those who are sincere with me, I am sincere; and to those who are not sincere with me, I am also sincere—and thus all get to be sincere.[P]

The obverse of this is given in another section of the *Dao De Jing:* "It is by not believing in people that you turn them into liars."[N4] Often repeated is the conviction that in the presence of natural kindness the strong become harmless, and by its means the weak become irresistible.

> There is nothing in the world more soft and weak than water, yet for attacking things that are hard and strong there is nothing that surpasses it. . . .

> The soft over comes the hard; the weak overcomes the strong.[K6]

> The highest goodness is like water. . . . It stays in places which others despise. Therefore it is near to Tao.[L9]

Mystical Invulnerability

In developing the implications of this doctrine, the *Dao De Jing* went so far as to suggest that the Daoist sage possessed, through being in accord with the Dao, a magical power, more passive than active, which provided invulnerability to the attack of fierce beasts or violent people and immunity to the assaults of death itself. It seems to be implied that when one is possessed of the Dao one lives long, and during life is exempt from decay. In one passage this idea is put forward with a modest "I have heard," indicating that it is according to an old tradition.

> I have heard that he who possesses the secret of life, when traveling abroad, will not flee from rhinoceros or tiger; when entering a hostile camp, he will not equip himself with sword or buckler. The rhinoceros finds in him no place to insert its horn; the tiger has nowhere to fasten its claw; the soldier has nowhere to thrust his blade. And why? Because he has no spot where death can enter.[K7]

Elsewhere it is said,

> He who is endowed with ample virtue may be compared
>   to an infant.
> No venomous insects sting him;
> Nor fierce beasts seize;
> Nor birds of prey strike him.[L10]

> He who attains Tao is everlasting.
> Though his body may decay he never perishes.[L11]

We shall see presently where pursuit of this conviction led the later Daoists.

Theory of Government

Meanwhile, a word on the *Dao De Jing's* distinctive theory of government, which pervades the whole work. (Scholars incline to the view that the treatise was written initially as a manual for rulers, that is, for princes and the governing elite.)

It will readily be seen that the only political principle consistent with the *Dao De Jing's* philosophy of life is laissez-faire. Noninterference by government in the lives of citizens is the one way to peace and freedom.

> Tao is eternally inactive, and yet it leaves nothing undone. If kings and princes could but hold fast to this principle, all things would work out their own reformation.[K8]

> Now this is how I know what I lay down:
> As restrictions and prohibitions are multiplied in the Empire, the people grow poorer and poorer. When the people are subjected to overmuch government, the land is thrown into confusion. . . . The greater the number of laws and enactments, the more thieves and robbers there will be. Therefore the Sage says: "So long as I do nothing, the people will work out their own reformation. So long as I love calm, the people will right themselves. If only I keep from meddling, the people will grow rich. If only I am free from desire, the people will come naturally back to simplicity."[K9]

An interesting passage gives us the *Dao De Jing's* picture of the ideal community—a small village-state, quiet, self-contained, and always keeping at home within its tiny boundaries.

> Take a small country with a small population. It might well be that there were machines which saved labor ten times or a hundred times, and yet the people would not use them. . . . They would not emigrate to distant countries. Although there might be carriages and boats, no one would ride in them. Although there might be weapons of war, no one would issue them. It might well be that people would go back to use knotted cords [for record keeping].[E3]

The point being made here is that people should live in their natural state, avoiding sophistication and enjoying existence while eating and drinking, making love, and tilling the soil, all without aggression. The next part of the quotation is obviously addressed to a ruler who is as nonaggressive as his people.

> Make the people's food sweet, their clothes beautiful, their houses comfortable, their daily life a source of pleasure. Then the people will look at the country over the border, will hear the cocks crowing and the dogs barking there, but right down to old age and the day of their death, they will not trouble to go there [and see what it is like].[E3]

Of course, there was no room in this scheme of things for war, and we find the *Dao De Jing* firm on the point that "weapons, however beautiful, are instruments of ill omen, hateful to all creatures. Therefore he who has Tao will have nothing to do with them"[K10] unless driven to use force in self-defense. But we are hardly prepared for the following breathtaking insight:

> Therefore, if a great kingdom humbles itself before a small kingdom, it shall make that small kingdom its prize. And if a small kingdom humbles itself before a great kingdom, it shall win over the great kingdom. Thus the one humbles itself in order to attain, the other attains because it is humble. If the great kingdom has no further desire than to bring men together and to nourish them, the small kingdom will have no further desire than to enter the service of the other. But in order that both may have their desire, the great one must learn humility.[K11]

We may not, perhaps, be in sympathy with the *Dao De Jing's* political and social primitivism, but this is an amazing vision of international altruism that is still too high for us.

The Essays of Zhuang-zi (Chuang-Tzu)

Zhuang-zi (whose personal name was Zhuang Zhou) is, except for the legendary Lao-zi himself, the most famous of the philosophical Daoists. He lived during the fourth century B.C.E. and skillfully popularized the teachings of his presumed master, performing for him in this respect the same service that Mencius, Zhuan-zi's contemporary, performed for Confucius. Thirty-three essays, which may contain considerable amounts of material from his own hand, have come down to us. In their present form, they were probably compiled some centuries later from fragments of his own and his followers' writings. They are brilliantly written, with many a witty anecdote, entertaining allegory, and imaginary conversation to enhance their literary charm. He especially enjoyed tilting at the ideas expressed by contemporary Confucianism. He seems to have used the ironic propaganda device of making Confucius repudiate his love of learning and duty to society, to talk like a Daoist, but not quite be one! This will appear in some of our quotations later on.

Zhuang-zi was true to Daoist teaching in giving the Dao centrality. But he went beyond the *Dao De Jing* in elaborating a doctrine of "transformations of the Dao." Objects originate in a whirl of being and becoming, out of preceding states of existence. Times succeed each other circularly; the seasons mutually produce and destroy each other without end. The yin and yang, springing from the Dao, produce each other, influence each other, and destroy each other in a never-ceasing process quite beyond human control. In the moral realm, he said, we have attractions and repulsions, loves and hates, distinctions of the sexes and their union for reproduction, but no lasting state either of peace or its opposite. Adversity and prosperity, security and danger succeed each other according to a law of reciprocal causality.

> For there is (the process of) reverse evolution (uniting opposites).... The succession of growth and decay, of increase and diminution, goes in a cycle, each end becoming a new beginning. In this sense only may we discuss the ways of truth and the principles of the universe. The life of things passes by like a rushing, galloping horse, changing at every turn, at every hour. What should one do, or what should one not do? Let the (cycle of) changes go on by themselves![M3]

Zhuang-zi's Relativism

What seemed to Zhuang-zi to justify the Daoist restraint from action was the fact that in such a world of perfectly natural change absolute truth and absolute good are unknowable. All things are equal in their right to be and act. Whatever nature (Dao) brings to pass is at least as good and necessary as anything else it brings to pass. This is another way of saying that every creature has its own dao and de, and these are right for it. There is no standard or uniform way of doing things, no truth or right to which all creatures must

conform. Each creature should be true to its own dao and de, not to another's. As for a human being, one may well ask: When is anything just right, or not just right? There is no means of knowing.

> If a man sleeps in a damp place, he gets lumbago and dies. But how about an eel? And living up a tree is precarious and trying to the nerves—but how about monkeys? Of the man, the eel and the monkey, whose habitat is the right one, absolutely? Human beings feed on flesh, deer on grass, centipedes on little snakes, owls and crows on mice. Of these four, whose is the right taste, absolutely?[Q1]

> In regard to man's desires or interests, if we say that anything is either good or bad according to our individual (subjective) standards, then there is nothing which is not good, nothing which is not bad.[M4]

This point of view led Zhuang-zi to make the following unconventional statement about the Three Dynasties:

> Those who came at the wrong time and went against the tide are called usurpers. Those who came at the right time and fitted in with their age are called defenders of Right.... How can you know the distinctions of high and low and of the houses of the great small?[M5]

Zhuang-zi likened the confusions of human beings to the puzzlement that surely would reign in the nonhuman world if the creatures could make comparisons of excellencies and defects.

> The walrus envies the centipede; the centipede envies the snake; the snake envies the wind; the wind envies the eye; the eye envies the mind.
> The walrus said to the centipede, "I hop about on one leg, but not very successfully. How do you manage all the legs you have?"
> "I don't manage them," replied the centipede. "Have you never seen saliva? When it is ejected, the big drops are the size of pearls, the small ones like mist. They fall promiscuously on the ground and cannot be counted. And so it is that my mechanism works naturally, without my being conscious of the fact."
> The centipede said to the snake, "With all my legs I do not move as fast as you with none. How is that?"

"One's natural mechanism," replied the snake, "is not a thing to be changed. What need have I for legs?"

The snake said to the wind, "I can manage to wriggle along, but I have a form. Now you come blustering down from the north sea to bluster away to the south sea, and you seem to be without form. How is that?"

"'Tis true," replied the wind, "that I bluster as you say; but any one who can kick at me, excels me. On the other hand, I can break huge trees and destroy large buildings. That is my strong point."[Q2]

The wind was wise. It did not weaken itself by false value judgments issuing in envy. It realized that though, on an intellectual analysis of its differences from other things, it was relatively weak ("any one who can kick at me, excels me"), whenever it let itself go as nature intended it should, it was mighty and strong. Using similar logic, Zhuang-zi contends that a person should not argue about large and small, high and low, right and wrong, but let happen what will according to the transformations of the Dao. In so doing, one will join the wind, the snake, and the centipede in the economy of nature.

Take no heed of time, nor of right or wrong. But passing into the realm of the Infinite, take your final rest therein.[Q3]

Zhuang-zi's Image of a Sage

A sage, a truly natural person, can take a seat by the sun and moon and grasp the universe, because

he blends everything into one harmonious whole, rejecting the confusion of this and that. Rank and precedence, which the vulgar prize, the sage stolidly ignores. The revolutions of ten thousand years leave his unity unscathed.[Q4]

Wise persons do not wear out their senses trying to know individually and in detail the changing objects and beings of the material world. They dwell in the generality of a comprehensive view of all things. They make their spiritual home in the Dao, in which all things lose their distinctions and merge into one.

The experience here referred to is not attainable by the searchings of reason, for the reason is too actively concerned with the discrimination of particulars. Real knowing is passive, receptive.

Hear not with your ears, but with your mind; not with your mind, but with your spirit. Let your hearing stop with the ears, and let your mind stop with its images. Let your spirit, however, be like a blank, passively responsive to externals. In such open receptivity only can Tao abide.[M6]

The final goal is the ecstasy of absorption into the sustaining, omnipresent Dao, this by a Chinese kind of yoga. One cannot push one's way into this ecstasy; it must come of itself, in utter spontaneity. But when it comes, it changes the one who has experienced it. The "artificial and illusory self" has now been eliminated, and the "heavenly" has taken "full possession."[R]

Thereafter one who is sage cultivates an air of stupidity to keep people from disrupting one's aloofness from the "ten thousand things" of which the world is composed. One's mind is cool and tranquil under the realization that thoughts and dreams have little importance, for they are subjective phenomena. In a world of rapidly shifting and changing appearances, one knows it is best to be calm and not active, to accept life and not take it seriously. One is like Mr. Mengsun.

Mr. Mengsun knows not whence we come in life nor whither we go in death. He knows not which to put first and which to put last. He is ready to be transformed into other things without caring into what he may the transformed.[M7]

The Serene Philosopher

True to this conviction, Zhuang-zi, if we are to trust the anecdotes supplied by his followers, lived without worry or fret. He would not let his emotions upset his tranquility. It is said that when his wife died, his friend Hui-zi, the logician, went to condole with him, according to custom, and found him seated on the ground singing and beating time on a metal bowl, which he held between his legs. Shocked at this sight, Hui-zi said to him,

"To live with your wife, and see your eldest son grow up to be a man, and then not to shed a tear over her corpse—this would be bad enough. But to drum on a bowl, and sing; surely this is going too far."

"Not at all," replied Chuang Tzu. "When she first died, how could I help being affected? But then on examining the matter, I saw that in the Beginning she had originally been lifeless. And not only lifeless, but she had originally been formless. And not only formless, but she had originally lacked all substance. During this first state of confused chaos, there came a change which resulted in substance. This substance changed to assume form. The form changed and became alive. And now it has changed again to reach death. In this it has been like the passing of the four seasons, spring, autumn, winter, and summer. And while she is thus lying asleep in the Great House [i.e., the Universe], for me to go about weeping and wailing, would be to show myself ignorant of Fate. Therefore I refrain."[J4]

Another tale illustrates Zhuang-zi's philosophic pride. While he was walking along the road in a coarse, patched robe, with shoes fastened to his feet with strings, he met the Marquis of Wei. "Master," said the marquis, "what distress is this that I see you in?" "Pardon," replied Zhuang-zi, "poverty, not distress. The scholar who possesses knowledge of the Principle [Dao] and its action is never in distress!"[S1]

But the most famous story about Zhuang-zi is the one concerning the offer made to him while he was fishing with line and float on the bank of the river Pu. The Marquis of Chu sent two of his officials to offer Zhuang-zi the post of minister. Zhuang-zi went on fishing without turning his head and said, "I have heard that in Chu there is a sacred tortoise which has been dead now some three thousand years. And that the prince keeps this tortoise carefully enclosed in a chest on the altar of his ancestral temple. Now would this tortoise rather be dead and have its remains venerated, or be alive and wagging its tail in the mud?" "It would rather be alive," replied the two officials together. "Then," cried Zhuang-zi, "begone! I too will wag my tail in the mud."[Q5]

Primitivism

The indictment Zhuang-zi brought against his age was powerful. He idealized the past, as his Daoist predecessors and the Confucians had done. The Confucians, however, saw the past in a different way. They idealized it as a time when moral distinctions were clearly discerned and when correct behavior was easy to teach. Zhuang-zi's primitives needed no teaching.

In the days when natural instincts prevailed, men moved quietly and gazed steadily. At that time, there were no roads over mountains, nor boats, nor bridges over water. All things were produced, each for its own proper sphere. Birds and beasts multiplied; trees and shrubs grew up. The former might be led by the hand; you could climb up and peep into the raven's nest. For then men dwelt with birds and beasts, and all creation was one. There were no distinctions of good and bad men. Being all equally without knowledge, their virtue could not go astray. Being all equally without evil desires, they were in a state of natural integrity, the perfection of human existence.

But when sages appeared, tripping people over charity and fettering with duty to one's neighbor, doubt found its way into the world. And then with their gushing over music and fussing over ceremony, empire became divided against itself.[Q6]

In this primitivism of his, Zhuang-zi went much further than the *Dao De Jing*. His thesis plainly is that none of the forms and institutions of social life under the Zhou culture did anything but confuse people about their natural equality and thus corrupt their native integrity. With social institutions, he said vehemently, "gangsters appeared. Overthrow the Sages and set the gangsters free, and then the empire will be in order."[M8]

His animus against all social institutions died away when he turned his admiring eye toward nature. He taught Chinese artists in which direction to look for truth in their art. Since his time nature has been their first love, and, we are told, "he still is today the main fountain of [their] inspiration and imagination."[T]

And yet Zhuang-zi must not be supposed to have led artists to look merely at the outward forms of nature, for how much reality is there in forms taken by themselves? His inspiration for them has been in enabling them to look at the eternal Way *within* nature; that is, at the reality of which every form the poet or painter beholds is an expression, just as the poet or painter himself is. In one piquant illustration he posed for artists—and for philosophers—one of

Scholar Walking by a River

(Chen Hongshou, Chinese, 1598–1652, Ming Dynasty, 1368–1644.) In this leaf from an Album of Paintings After Ancient Masters, the scholar is faceless because his feelings are to be inferred from his surroundings, which present opposing themes. The trees, stripped by autumn, convey a sense of frailty and the brevity of life, but the crane symbolizes longevity and the land masses in the background have solidity and strength that defy the mist creeping over them. He broods on both themes, much as Zhuang-zi did. Pairs of ten-leaf albums, ink and color on silk, typical size: 24.2 x 24.7 cm. *(Courtesy of Wan-go Weng Collection, Cleveland Museum of Art. John L. Severance Fund, 1979. 27.)*

the knottiest problems of human knowledge—how to assess the reality of forms within the mind.

> Once upon a time, I, Chuang Tzu, dreamt I was a butterfly, fluttering hither and thither, to all intents and purposes a butterfly . . . suddenly, I awaked. . . . Now I do not know whether I was then a man dreaming I was a butterfly, or whether I am now a butterfly dreaming I am a man.[Q7]

But Daoism, to give the philosophical point of view this name, was not going to continue long in so intriguing a vein, philosophically defining the nature of things and the meaning of life. It also was to be a species of magical theory and practice, and Zhuang-zi, as we shall see, was to share the responsibility for giving it an impetus in this direction.

III. DAOISM AS MAGIC AND RELIGION (*DAO-JIAO*)

Although this type of Daoism assumed clear historical definition for the first time in Han times (the third century B.C.E. to the third century C.E.), its roots extended far into the Chinese past. The popular interest in the effects of yin and yang on health, happiness, and long life cannot be assigned a dated beginning. The problem of how to prolong life by mastering one's body and preventing the processes of natural decay from setting in has always interested the Chinese. No people have looked forward more than they to old age—the period of patriarchal ease and leisure.

But there also has been a strong interest in "eternal life" as an endless prolongation of earthly existence.

A somewhat ambiguous support for this interest is to be found in both the *Dao De Jing* and the *Zhuang-zi*. Some distinguished scholars discount this support, because they see in philosophical Daoism an indifference to immortality as of no consequence in comparison with present harmony with the Dao, and find therefore a sharp contrast between this indifference and the interests of the kind of Daoism aiming to produce *xian* (*hsien*) or persons who have sought and attain immortality. Other scholars disagree, because they do not see a sharp contrast but, rather, the natural emergence of two kinds of Daoism from a common rootage in ancient Chinese religion.

Pending further research, this divergence of view is bound to continue. Meanwhile, the basic difference between the two kinds of Daoism may be summarized as follows. The philosophical Daoists sought to come to terms *in this life* with the processes of the universe; they accepted, and identified themselves with, the alternations of yin and yang, life and death, being and nonbeing, differentiation and unity, thus attaining present harmony with the underlying Way of things. The immortality-seeking Daoists, on the other hand, sought in addition to health and long life personal and individual immortality by taking advantage of the processes of the universe (the Dao) to produce within themselves an immortal self ("a spiritual embryo") that would survive the death of the body—all of this by one or more of the methods we are about to review: alchemy, breathing exercises, hygiene, diet, communal religious rites, and the help of the gods.

Longevity and Immortality in the Classic Texts

Actually, the *Dao De Jing* and *Zhuang-zi*, whatever their basic preferences, gave aid and comfort by what they, or their editors, said to the seekers of long life and immortality.

The *Dao De Jing*, we have seen, suggested that anyone who possesses the secret of the Dao becomes immune to the attack of armed men and wild animals. One who is endowed with the ample virtue that the Dao engenders may be compared to an infant whom no venomous reptiles sting, no birds of prey strike.

Furthermore, "He who attains Tao is everlasting." It may well have been that the complete Daoist sage enjoyed a comparatively high degree of personal safety in town and field. But such immunity from death and harm could easily be misconstrued as evidence of superhuman or magical potencies.

Zhuang-zi (along with others, probably), further elaborated the idea by introducing some mythological references. The mythological Emperor Fu-xi, he said, obtained Dao, "and was able to steal the secrets of eternal principles." "The Yellow Emperor obtained it, and soared upon the clouds of heaven.... The Western (Fairy) Queen Mother obtained it, an settled at Shao Guang, since when and until when, no one knows."[M9]

It is of course possible that Zhuang-zi was not entirely in earnest about all of this and was speaking in hyperbole; yet consider the following passage, accepted as authentic, in which he illustrates his thesis that the Dao produces life and death as natural states and gives rulers and other men the spiritual powers that admit them to the experience of ultimate oneness:

> Nanpo Tzek'uei said to Nü Yü (or female Yü), "You are of a high age, and yet you have a child's complexion. How is this?"
>
> Nü Yü replied, "I have learnt Tao."
>
> "Could I get Tao by studying it?" asked the other.
>
> "No! How can you?" said Nü Yü. "You are not the type of person. There was Puliang I. He had all the mental talents of a sage, but not Tao of the sage. Now I had Tao, though not those talents.... I had to wait patiently to reveal it to him. In three days, he could transcend this mundane world. Again I waited for seven days more, then he could transcend all material existence. After he could transcend all material existence, I waited for another nine days, after which he could transcend all life. After he could transcend all life, then he had the clear vision of the morning, and after that, was able to see the Solitary (One). After seeing the Solitary, he could abolish the distinctions of past and present. After abolishing the past and present, he was able o enter there where life and death are no more."[M10]

The last sentence is one reason why Zhuang-zi was quoted later on by *xian* Daoists, whether mistakenly or not, as favoring the turn of Daoism toward magic and esoteric physical exercises aiming at eternal life.

Blessed Isles and Elixir Alchemy

As to prolonging life, as early as the third century B.C.E. it became an open interest of the imperial court for Shi Huang Di, "the First Emperor," is said to have been persuaded by "magicians" ("experts" in immortality) to outfit several expeditions to find Peng-lai, the Blessed Isle, where a mushroom that conferred immortality was to be found, and where mortals who imbibed its drug became immune to death. But these and all later expeditions were either lost in storms or returned without success.

Meanwhile, a search for an elixir of immortality distilled from the five elements began. There was a turn to alchemy as a way of finding a potion to prolong life. In the second century B.C.E., the Emperor Wu Di (Wu Ti) of the Han dynasty was, in spite of his patronage of Confucianism, attracted to Daoism by the empress dowager and her associates. Si-ma Qian (Ssu-ma Ch'ien), the famous Chinese historian of the first century B.C.E., records the tradition, whether true or not, that the geomancer Li Shao-jun urged the emperor to apply himself to the alchemy furnace, for thus he would gain the good graces of the spirits and learn from them the formula for converting cinnabar, a crystalized mercuric sulphide, into gold, after which he could have eating and drinking vessels made of the gold produced from the cinnabar and acquire *longevity* from the food and drink served in them. (Later, the Chinese came to connect "eatable gold" with *immortality*—if such gold could be had.) The geomancer further advised the emperor that if he performed on the sacred mountain Tai Shan (T'ai Shan) the ceremony known as *feng-shan* (in honor of Heaven or the Sovereign on High), he would not die anymore. It was thus, said the geomancer, that the Yellow Emperor Huang Di had obtained immortality. From that time on, we are told, Wu Di surrounded himself with Daoists and at their suggestion introduced many innovations into the practice of Chinese religion, against the wishes of the Confucians, who also advised him.

Hygiene and Five-Element Coordination

But the search for immortality was not confined to the aristocracy; it also was pursued by many of the common people, who found it within their capacity to follow dietary and hygienic means to spiritualization, the goal being to prevent the body's decay and to obtain longevity, if not immortality. In line with very old Chinese interests and practices (and with mounting energy and enthusiasm), the common people turned, as members of the ruling classes did, to the magical practices known and followed in the eastern coastal regions. There in the first century B.C.E. a cult arose that yoked Huang Di and Lao-zi under the term *Huang-Lao*, and hoped by this blending of powers to succeed in realizing the life-prolonging effects of Lao-zi's wu-wei and Huang Di's medicinal arts.

A central consideration here, common to all Chinese eras and philosophical schools, and not only to Daoist circles, was the belief that the sympathetic harmony of humans and Nature was based on a similarity of elements, every part having the same structure or basic nature as the whole. In short, a person is a microcosm (a miniature universe) that duplicates the universe as a whole (the macrocosm). In the dao of every part of a human being the great Dao of Heaven is reproduced. The correspondences were sought out in detail: the five physical organs of human beings and the "fives" in their psychological makeup correspond to the universe's five elements, five directions, five human relationships, five colors, and so on. No wonder then that the Chinese generally (and the Daoists in particular) have felt that the universe and humankind are mutually sensitive to each other, and that when people understand the universe, they understand themselves in their essential being; and consequently when one aligns oneself with universal processes, one experiences health, keenness of mind, and longevity, or even immortality.

Breath Control

The purpose of Daoist hygiene was to become aligned with the rhythms of the universe. From Han times onward it took a variety of forms, principally gymnastics and breath control. The aim of the gymnastics was

Daoist Elixir Rite

Detail of a long scroll in the manner of the Ming dynasty painter Jiu Ying. Most of the scroll depicts Daoist sage-adepts (xian or immortals) strolling through a tranquil landscape, perhaps in the Blessed Isles. Mountain fastnesses also were appropriate sites for the practice of alchemy. In the central scene the sages gather in a "cavern heaven" to watch a master alchemist prepare an elixir. The sages at the lower right hold emblems of immortality: the peach and the magic mushroom (*ling chi*). The stork also is a symbol of longevity. *(Courtesy of Heidelberg College Collection.)*

to keep the body, in accordance with its dao, in its natural state of health and vigor. Breath control had a more complex role; by it one quieted the body's turmoil and reached a state as pure and free from tension as an embryo in the womb, a state of "embryonic respiration." It could achieve even more remarkable feats. An adept's controlled breath was believed to descend to the soles of the feet and follow intricate channels through the body to the head; moreover, an experienced adept could breathe not only through the nose, it was said, but through the pores of the body and thus inhale moonbeams, subtle spiritual presences and exhalations of heavenly bodies, like the moon and the stars.

Holmes Welch describes "embryonic respiration" as follows:

Embryonic Respiration means a breathing like a child in the womb. Shortly before dawn the adept retires to a square chamber, and stretches out on a soft bed with a pillow two and one-half inches thick. He folds his hands and closes his eyes. Then he commences to hold his breath. Holding it for 12 heart beats is a 'little tour.' Holding it for 120 heart beats is a 'big tour.' If he can get up to 1,000, he is approaching Immortality. . . . The adept knows how to conduct his breath beyond the liver and kidneys up the spine to again to the brain, down to the chest, and up again to the throat. He guides it by the same 'interior vision' that enables him to see the gods inside his body.[U]

In a footnote, Welch adds,

This 'interior vision' was probably facilitated by CO_2 intoxication that must have resulted from holding his breath so long. CO_2 intoxication, which resembles the effect of some hallucinogenic drugs, would account for the vividness of what the adept saw inside his body, such as the God of the Spinal Column three and a half inches tall, dressed in white.[U]

Dietary and Sexual Restraints

In addition to breath control, there also was a great reliance on diet. Somehow, it came to be believed that eating meat and the five cereals (rice, millet, wheat, barley, and soybeans) clogged up and poisoned the body; they must therefore be given up, along with all wines, and one must live henceforth on fruits, berries, and roots or tubers.

Paralleling these dietary controls were sexual techniques that had evolved to enhance the body's natural vitality, prolong life, and help develop within oneself an immortal spiritual self or "embryo." These techniques resembled the sexual rites of Indian tantrism to such a degree as to suggest some borrowing (see p. 205). Called "the Way (dao) of Yin (femaleness)," they aimed to return the semen at the moment of ejaculation back to the body, where, mixed with breath, it could ascend to the brain and "repair" it.

For some time, especially during Han and later times, it was felt that in assisting this process hundreds if not thousands of deities operated both from outside the body and within its organs and were active in governing its inner condition.

Daoist Societies: Wu Dou Mi Dao

Since it proved difficult to follow individually and solitarily the techniques we have described, it became common by the second century C.E. to join, on a voluntary basis, groups of persons engaged in the same quest. In this way there arose organized Daoist societies to guide and pool the efforts of individuals. Such groups soon transcended the traditional community patterns and spread over wide areas, like churches in the Western world, a new phenomenon in China.

One such group was organized by a certain Zhang-ling, better known as Zhang Daoling (Chang Tao-ling) (34?–156 C.E.), who migrated from eastern to western China and founded a secret society aiming through faith healing to attain health and longevity; it also devoted itself to alchemy and the cultivation of the Daoist meditative trance. Because all who joined the groups of adepts that he organized had to pay a fee of five pecks of rice annually, his sect was tauntingly called the Wu Dou Mi Dao (Wou Tou Mi Tao), "the Five Pecks of Rice Way." On the foundation thus laid, his son and grandson built an organization that attracted the adherence of many followers. A unique feature of the movement was the acceptance of women in the ranks of parish leadership. "Libationers" of both sexes were trained to exorcise illness by prescribing confession of sin (conceived as the cause of illness) along with prayer and extended rituals using consecrated water and written talismans burned to ashes and swallowed. Dozens of parishes, presided over by the priestlike "libationers," grew in clusters and provided the basis for great political, and eventually military, power. In the course of time, Zhang Daoling was elevated to the heavenly rank of "Celestial Master," for he was said to have been personally ordained by Lao-zi, who appeared to him out of the spirit world. In addition, he was said to have discovered the formula for the potion of immortality, a powerful elixir of life, and to have ascended alive to heaven from the top of Dragon-Tiger Mountain, Mt. Long-hu in Jiangxi (Kiangsi), on the back of a tiger, after having prolonged his life by the use of his elixir to the ripe age of 122 years.

His influence proved to be lasting, for in the course of centuries his successors became a line of high ecclesiastics ("Celestial Masters"). Each successor of Zhang Daoling was thought to be his reincarnation, and received the support of adepts willing in times of political turmoil to revolt against the government and to seek independent power. This fact led to the official recognition of Daoism as a major religious faith. At intervals, the Way of the Celestial Masters received imperial sanction, as when the Emperor Tai Wu Di (T'ai Wu Ti) of the Northern Wei dynasty pronounced Daoism the official religion of his (limited) empire, this apparently in return for political submission of the Daoist societies. The line of Celestial Masters has continued unbroken for seventeen centuries to the present time. We shall see them on the island of Taiwan.

The Yellow Turbans

Another of the Daoist sects, the Yellow Turbans, headed by Zhang Jue (Chang Chüeh) and his two brothers, numbered hundreds of thousands of adepts, and in an attempted rising in the second century C.E. held for a time the whole of the Yellow River. In spite of the subsequent decline and failure of this and similar movements, the Daoists always hoped someday to make a serious bid for power.

Sacred Texts

Accompanying the development of magic, breath control, religious societies, and organized political forces came a proliferation of literary works (manuals, "revelations," medical instructions, compilations of tales about "saints" and "immortals," etc.) that grew into something like a canon of new sacred texts for all Daoists. The total number of these widely accepted texts (e.g., the *Book of the Great Peace*, the *Book of the Yellow Court*, the *Transcendent Jewels Scriptures*, etc.) was estimated by later Daoists to be over one thousand, many of which have survived and are used in Taiwan and other places where Daoists still practice their distinctive rites.

Daoist Magic: Ge Hong

Meanwhile, Daoist magic continued to develop. The scholar Ge Hong (Ko Hung) exerted a lasting influence through his book the *Bao Pu-zi (Pao P'u-tzu)* on magical matters, but much of his popular fame came from the story that when he was eighty-one years old a

An Immortal
He Xian-gu

friend whom he had invited to visit him found only his empty clothes—proof enough that he had disappeared among the Immortals! But he was not the only one thus to achieve immortality. Ge Hong himself told the story that the author of another book on occult matters succeeded in preparing pills of immortality and gave one to a dog, only to see it drop dead, but he had so much faith in his pill that he took one himself and fell to the ground. His elder brother, faith unshaken, took the pill with the same result. A younger brother was about to bury them, when they came back to life. They were Xian! They were Immortals!

Ge Hong's book describes the breathing exercises, sexual techniques, dietetics, alchemy, and magic of the time, so that a dip into his storehouse of fact and supposition affords us concrete examples and a review of what we have been discussing. He explains that the object of the breathing exercises was to increase the spiritual powers of the body and mind, and of the dietetics to prolong life and particularly to enable one to live exclusively on air and dew, in a state immune to illness, though death from old age could not be prevented by this method alone.

The alchemy had as its object the discovery of liquid or eatable gold, a commodity that should confer immortality on those who would swallow it. Salt, says Ge Hong, preserves dead meat; it must be possible to find some preservative for live flesh! This amalgam had to be other than one based on pure mercury, which is a yin substance and produces death. Cinnabar, a mercuric ore, was thought to be the proper substance, but the alchemists never quite succeeded in attaining the results they desired, in spite of instances cited by Ge Hong of individuals who passed on into the immortal state, but who alas took the secret of their formulas with them.

As to the magic, it could do all sorts of things in establishing control over natural processes. Ge Hong describes certain charms which, if swallowed or worn on the person, rendered one invulnerable to warlike weapons, though immunity could be gained only from the weapons specifically named in the charms. Care should therefore be taken to name every weapon by which one might ever conceivably be injured, otherwise one might be caught like the magician "who being proof against every pointed or edged weapon, was killed by a blow from a cudgel, a common weapon he had not foreseen." Other charms are mentioned for making oneself invisible, for changing one's shape at will, for freeing oneself from all bonds, and for raising and transporting oneself through space. And then there was the little pill that allowed one to walk on water. It was only necessary to take "seven, three times a day, for three years, without forgetting a single time." In another place Ge Hong describes a magical seal, which, "impressed on the dust or mud, prevents ferocious beasts or malignant goblins from passing. The same, placed on the doors of storages and stables, protects the provisions and the animals."S2

In these last sentences, of which many parallels could be cited, there is to be seen the reason for the power of the Daoist priests among the common people of China down to this century. They were notable geomancers, and doctors of miraculous effects (thaumaturgists). But to attain this power over the common people, these wonder workers had to have all of the sanctions of religion, and they obtained them, for Daoism must be regarded not only as magic and philosophy but also as a religion, a fact which we have not yet clearly seen. Our survey of the clearly religious developments in Daoism must be delayed, however, until we look into an interlude of Daoist philosophizing.

A Philosophical Revival: Neo-Daoism

During, the years of the breakup of the Later Han dynasty and the following Three Kingdoms and Six Dynasties (200–300 C.E.), there occurred the renascence of philosophical Daoism usually called Neo-Daoism. One result of this revival was the reissue of the Daoist writings of the legendary Lie-zi (Lieh Tzu), an older contemporary of Zhuang-zi about whom we know very little. The reissue took such liberties with the original text that the present *Book of Lie-zi* is only partially authentic. Its amplification of the views of Yang Zhu (Yang Chu), whom we met earlier on p. 263 is an example. The individualism of Yang Zhu is interpreted as having been based on a combination of fatalism and hedonism. If one is to let all things take their natural course, he is made to say, and not introduce any element of artificial control, then it would be well to obey one's impulses and enjoy them happily. Any restriction placed on the senses cramps nature and is a tyranny. Therefore, seek rich food, fine clothing, music, and beauty. Enjoy life and pay no attention to death. "Allow the ear to hear what it likes, the eye to see what it likes, the nose to smell what it likes, the mouth to speak what it likes, the body to enjoy what it likes, the mind to do what it likes."V

In contrast to this carefree hedonism was the seriousness of some of the philosophers of the third century who analyzed with care the *Dao De Jing*, the *Zhuang-zi*, and the *Book of Changes*: He Yan, Wang Bi, Guo Xiang, and others. They formed against a background of widespread restless speculation, called "Dark Hearing," a calming "School of Pure Conversation," dedicated to philosophy uncontaminated by worldly corruption. They had a strong sense of their public responsibility; some even maintained that Confucius, with his humanism and concern for social relations, was nearer to the Dao than Lao-zi and Zhuang-zi, who wanted people to be recluses.

Differing from them was another "school" more inclined to agree with the updated Yang Zhu, perhaps in discouragement at the breakdown of unity and order in the empire, for they professed a hedonistic indifference to the course of public events. They were called "the Seven Sages of the Bamboo Grove," and were dedicated to love of nature, natural impulse, wine, wit, and poetry. They ridiculed Confucianists and officials unmercifully, while they themselves sought solace in the wine cup and their own verse. They scorned Confucius and public-spirited sages as having "had not during their lives a single day of contentment. After

Grove had a minimal effect outside of the company of the poets, but the more serious commentators on the classics, both Daoist and Confucian, had a lasting influence in helping Daoist philosophy permeate much of later Chinese thought. We shall see shortly that Daoism was itself much affected in its religious development by Buddhism in its Chinese forms; but we have already seen, and can now more clearly understand, the reverse, that philosophical Daoism greatly affected Chan (Ch'an), or Zen, Buddhism. Nor was Daoism without effect on Confucianism and the Confucian-trained officials of later China. The quip was common in later centuries: "In office a Confucian, in retirement (or on leave) a Daoist."

Religious Daoism in Its Later Forms

In the prolonged period during which eternal life was sought through magico-religious means, what deities were addressed? There were many gods, both outside and inside human bodies, with the emphasis on them constantly shifting. Religious Daoism, however, seems always to have paid highest honors to various trinities of beings, such as Tai Yi, the Ultimate Oneness; Tian Yi, Heaven; and Di Yi, Earth. There also were exterior gods approached singly, like the God of the Stove or Kitchen (spoken of by Confucius), who was addressed by the alchemists when they went to the alchemy furnace. There also was the God of the Southwestern Corner of the House, also known to Confucius. Many others must have been locally honored; the lists shift with time and locality.

Official recognition of the religious aspects of Daoism was not long in coming. This occurred implicitly in 165 C.E. through the act of the Emperor Huan of the Second Han dynasty in ordering for the first time official offerings to Lao-zi and the building of a temple in his honor. However, what was anticipated did not get fully underway until the fifth century, when Emperor Tai Wu Di gave Daoism imperial recognition in the Northern Wei empire. But the greatest epoch of Daoism came when the Tang (T'ang) dynasty reunited China and the Emperor Li Shi-min (Li Shih-min), who reigned from 627 to 649, gave Daoism such a favored position that candidates for the civil service were examined in the Daoist religious texts.

Divination Blocks

After framing a question—and proper wording is crucial—the petitioner drops two pieces of bamboo root cut to fit together like the halves of a cashew. After bouncing about on the floor, each block will eventually settle with its convex (yang) or concave (yin) side up. The three possible combinations are not flat "yes" or "no" indications but represent the deity's response to the questioner's phrasing. The balanced yang-yin combination is favorable, "Your phrasing shows piety." Yang-yang means, "Your phrasing angers the deity." Yin-yin suggests absurdity in the question, "The deity is laughing." The blocks may be used in combination with sortilege: drawing a numbered bamboo stick from a container and then consulting a correspondingly numbered oracle passage (usually ambiguous or obscure) furnished by the temple attendant. *(Photo by David Noss.)*

their death, their reputation increased age by age; but is such empty posthumous renown a compensation for the pleasures of which they deprived themselves during their lives? Now they are praised, and offerings are made to them, without them knowing anything about it, no more than a joist of wood or a clod of earth."[53]

As we take leave of these Neo-Daoists, it should be said that the somewhat frivolous Sages of the Bamboo

Monastic Taoism flourished in the Tang period. A survey in 739 C.E. showed over one thousand monasteries and about half as many convents. A census in 1077 found eighteen thousand monks and some seven hundred nuns—both categories described as persons who had "left their families."[W] (But this did not imply celibacy in the strictest sense; monks and nuns might live in the same community. Contacts driven by lust were forbidden, but not ritualized sexual congress so controlled as to "nourish the essences.")

Response to Buddhism: Deified Sage Emperors

When Buddhism swept across China and into Korea, the Daoists, struck with amazement and yet sure that China had her own resources, so to speak, in the way of gods and spirits, began to look into their own heritage, and finding much of value, they began to imitate the powerful faith brought in from India. One cannot be sure that the effort was a sustained and self-conscious process, but what actually happened was that Chinese history was searched for personages that might compare in popular appeal with the Buddhas. Lao-zi was formally apotheosized, with the title "Emperor of Mysterious Origin," and he was provided with heavenly associates in imitation of Buddha and the Lohans (Chinese for Arahats). Daoist temples were erected, and groups of ascetics were called together in close copying of the Buddhist models. The motivation may well have been as sincere as it was nationalistic: why resort to foreign gods when the Chinese had long had their own beings who were near at hand and able to help them with a proven sympathetic response to their immediate needs?

The process ran the risk of outright fabrication. One of the most amazing incidents in all religion making seems to have taken place, if the story is to be believed, when the Emperor Zhen Zong (Chen Tsung), of the Song dynasty, effected by fraud the final step in the transformation of Daoism into a complete theism. His ulterior purpose was the recovery of his own prestige, which needed bolstering badly. At the turn of the year 1005 C.E., the emperor "lost face" because, being unable to reconquer the territories in the north previously occupied by nomad invaders from the northwest, the dreaded Kitan Tatars, who had poured into China across the Great Wall, he had been forced to make a disgraceful peace by which he ceded away large portions of north China. He consulted the Daoist soothsayers and geomancers for advice. How could he reinstate himself in the favor of his people?

The tradition has it that his minister, the wily Wang Qin-ruo, surprised the emperor by advising a fabricated revelation from Heaven, and when the emperor protested, said brazenly, "Bah! the Ancients had no such scruples. Each time the need was felt the Sages caused Heaven and the spirits to intervene in order to bring their policy into popular favor. It is precisely in this that their wisdom consisted."[S4] The emperor, much impressed, visited the imperial library and consulted the scholars there. In 1008 C.E., he called his ministers together and told them he had been informed in a dream that Heaven was about to send him a letter, and that the governor of the capital had just reported seeing a yellow scarf hanging from one of the cornices of the Gate of Heaven. The emperor then went on foot to watch the scarf being lowered. It proved to contain a letter, ostensibly from a celestial being writing in the style of Lao-zi. Officers were dispatched throughout the empire to make known the news. Another revelation followed in six months. And then, in 1012 C.E., it was disclosed that the celestial being thus communicating with the emperor was Yu Huang (Yü Huang). This being had not been heard of in China before the ninth century, but he was now raised to supremacy, and by succeeding emperors declared to be the Jade Emperor, the Pure and Great One, Author of the Visible Heaven and of the physical laws, the Controller of Time and of the processes making divination valid, and the Embodiment of Good and the Way (Dao). It was said finally that the celestial sovereign whom the ancients had called Shang Di (Imperial Ruler on High) was and always had been none other then Yu Huang, the Jade Emperor!

There was a widespread popular response, for the people were ready to make these identifications themselves. They were pleased to have so many of their favorite folklore gods given imperial recognition, and they soon became accustomed to thinking of Shang Di and the Jade Emperor as being one and the same being. The stories that began to circulate, given the latter's history, entered the body of popular tradition without difficulty.

Poets Gathering in the Orchard Pavilion

Dated 1607 (Ming dynasty), this ink wash on silk brocade recalls the general setting utilized by the blithe poets who in the third century were called the Seven Sages of the Bamboo Grove. Undoubtedly, later poets imitated earlier ones. Chinese Paintings. Ming dynsaty (1368–1644). Ch'ien Kung: Poets Gathering in the Orchard Pavilion, handscroll: ink wash on silk brocade. H. 13½" L. 14¼". *(Courtesy of the Metropolitan Museum of Art, Gift of Harry Shupak, 1953, 53. 150.)*

The popular satisfaction was increased when heaven and hell were added to the Daoist scene. Paradise was found in various places, but most delightfully in the Three Isles of the Blessed, the San Xian Shan, long held in Chinese folklore to be located somewhere in the Eastern Sea (between the Chinese and Japanese mainlands; we have already come across them in Huang Di's quest for Peng-Lai on p. 274). Hell had every appurtenance of torture and punishment, becoming a place full of ogres and goblins of every malevolent and horrifying kind. It became a major concern of the living to procure the release of relatives from this terrifying place.

Mythology Institutionalized

Whether the final product of Daoist religion making should be called Daoist in any proper sense of that word is questionable, but the Daoist priests had no hesitations, assured that because the common people shared in the decision as to which of the deities and spirits, old and new, should be the most important to them, there was no need to hold back. Although as a matter of course the Jade Emperor was granted the highest place and was commonly associated with Lao-zi and a third being, Ling Bao (Ling Pao), marshal of the supernatural beings, the three together forming the official Daoist trinity (the Three Purities), more interest and affection were shown toward adoptions from popular, originally non-Daoist, religion: the Eight Immortals, the God of the Stove, the Guardians of the Door, and the City God. To these therefore we turn for a brief description.

The Eight Immortals have long been beloved figures of folklore, being wholly and delightfully Chinese. They were xian. Their abode usually has been thought to be either somewhere in the mountains or on the Three Isles of the Blessed. They were supposed to have been (and most of them probably originally were) human beings, but they were also thought to have been ascetics to such good purpose that they achieved immortality and lived on in ageless bodies with minds and spirits ever young. Four of them have often been represented together seated under a pine tree, two of them sipping the wine heated for them by a third, while a fourth piped upon a flute in entertainment. The others were usually portrayed singly. The "Maiden Immortal," He Xian Gu (Ho Hsien Ku), was long ago a mortal, of course, but while at home with her shopkeeping parents, she lived on a diet of powdered mother-of-pearl and moonbeams and thus became immortal. She often has appeared to people floating on the clouds, carrying in her hand a lotus blossom or, at times, the peach of immortality. (Fig. 9.7 p. 277). The Eight Immortals belong to a larger group whose presiding spirits have been, for the females, the popular Fairy Queen Mother, the subject of countless tales, and, for the males, Dong Wang Gong, a less well-known being.

The God of the Stove, Zao Shan (Tsao Shen), not exclusively Daoist, has long been honored throughout China as the kitchen spirit who sits in the chimney corner, invisible, but watches all that the family does. His presence used to be constantly recalled to the remembrance of naughty children. On the twenty-fourth day of the twelfth moon, food and wine offerings were presented to his paper image, and when this image and the paper money, horses, and chariots accompanying it were burned together below the chimney, he ascended up the flue to heaven to make his annual report on the behavior of the family.

At the New Year, invocations used to be offered to two Guardians of the Door, the Men Shen, both spirits of great antiquity, and their paper images, in military garb and carrying swords or spears, were attached to the two halves of the front door to ward off evil spirits during the coming year.

The City God, Zheng Huang (Cheng Huang), was worshiped in almost every Chinese city, for five centuries officially. He was first adopted by the religion makers of the Tang dynasty, but it was not until the fourteenth century that his worship was made an official requirement. Today he belongs to the past.

Of all the other spirits honored by the Daoists there is no space here to tell. They were many. One could linger, not only with the river, soil, mountain, and star spirits and with the patron deities of all the trades and occupations, but also with the apotheosized national heroes, the gods of health and luck, and the many animal and vegetable spirits, the dragons and phoenixes and unicorns. But these must be described in some other place.

Daoism Today

For three decades after coming to power in 1949, the communist government of the People's Republic of China derided Taoism as superstition and drafted many practitioners—priests, exorcists, diviners—into military service and labor battalions. But Taoism in its broadest sense was so bound up with everyday life that it could not be eradicated. In rural areas, especially, the traditional rites of passage—birth celebrations, weddings, and funerary observances—continued much as they had before. In some communities, priests were allowed to reside in their temples, and traditional seasonal observances, such as New Year celebrations and the springtime tending of graves, went on without much change. Herbal medicine and even exorcism continued alongside newer health services.

In the 1980s restraints on Taoist institutional life were relaxed, and, in some instances, government resources were made available for restoring showcase temples. The White Cloud Abbey of Beijing was made the seat of an officially recognized National Taoist Association, and novices from other parts of the country were brought to Beijing for training.

Institutional Daoism remains alive among the expatriate Chinese communities in Malaysia, Thailand, and Singapore, but it is only in Taiwan that it can be said to be flourishing. The sixty-third Celestial Master of the Daoist "Church" fled from China to Taiwan when the Communists took over on the mainland. His presence in Taiwan led to a revitalization of religious Daoism among both the recent and long-established Chinese inhabitants. Temples have been enthusiastically restored or newly built—an estimated 7,000 by 1997. In the presence of Daoist deities and with the use of thousand-year-old liturgies, "black-heads" (priests with black headgear) and "red-heads" (exorcists trained in noisy ecstatic rites) conduct temple worship and traditional festivals. But the most important objects in the temples are not the images of the gods but the incense burners, the divination blocks, and the drums upon which the priests in festival times beat rhythmically while they chant the sacred texts and while dancers perform their acrobatic gyrations. Religion and magic are here combined, and together survive.

GLOSSARY*

Terms shown in color are pinyin forms; Wade-Giles forms are in *italics* to the right of parenthetical pronunciations.

Bagua (bä-gōōä) *Pa Kua*, the eight-trigram schema of proportional combinations of yang and yin

Dao (däu) *Tao*, the Way, the eternal principle, immanent in all things

Dao De Jing (däu dā jǐng) *Tao Te Ching*, the classical text of early philosophical Daoism

De (dā) *Te*, inherent power, the authority of authentic character and virtue

feng-shui (fŭng shōō-ĭ) *feng-shui*, geomancy, "wind and water" divination

Fu-xi (fōō shē) *Fu Hsi*, mythical emperor, teacher, and inventor, described as having a serpent's body

Ge Hong (ga-hong) *Ko Hung*, author of an influential book on Daoist magic, the *Bao Pu-zi* (*Pao P'u-tzu*)

gui (gwā) *kuei*, earthly yin spirits, ill-disposed and unpredictable

Huang Di (hwäng' dē) *Huang Ti*, mythical sage ancestor, the "Yellow Emperor," innovator (silk worm culture, etc.)

hun (hün) *hun*, the shen soul, seat of the mind; in afterlife, joining the ancestral spirits

Kong Fu-zi (koong-foo' dzŭ) *K'ung Fu-tzu*, founder of Confucianism (literally "Master Kong"—Latinized as Confucius)

Lao-zi (läu' dzŭ) *Lao Tzu*, legendary author of the earliest Daoist classic, the *Dao De Jing*

Li Shi-min (lē-shĭr-mĭn) *Li Shih-min*, 7th c. C.E. Tang emperor, instituted civil service examinations on Daoist texts

Lie-zi (lē-ā-dzŭ) *Lieh Tzu*, legendary Daoist of Zhuang-zi's time, known by the 3rd c. C.E. book of *Lie-zi*

Meng-zi (mŭng-dzŭ) *Meng-tzu*, Mencius, 4th c. B.C.E. champion of the "orthodox" school of Confucian followers

Peng-lai (pŭng-lī) *P'eng-lai*, mythic blessed isle(s), where magic mushrooms confer immortality upon the xian

po (pō) *p'o*, the gui soul, animating bodily organs; in afterlife, dwelling in the earth

pu (pōō) *p'u*, the uncarved block, Daoist symbol of the perfection of the natural state of things

Shang Di (shäng dē) *Shang Ti*, literally the "upper ruler," Heaven as a deity

shen (shĕn) *shen*, heavenly yang spirits, usually kindly

Shen Dao (shŭn däu) *Shen Tao*, Legalist and Daoist, emphasized natural tendencies and rank, over talent and wisdom: "Let us be like creatures."

Shi Huang Di (shĭ hwäng'-dē) *Shih Huang-ti*, Qin dynasty, "First Emperor," who unified China under severe totalitarian rule, 221 B.C.E.

Tai Wu Di (tī-wōō-dē) *T'ai Wu Ti*, 5th c. Northern Wei emperor, made Daoism the official religion of his realm

Tian (tī-ĕn) *T'ien*, heaven or sky

Wu Di (wōō dē) *Wu Ti*, 2nd c. B.C.E. Han emperor, patron of Confucianism as well as of Daoist alchemy and geomancy

xian (shē-än) *hsien*, Daoist sage immortals

yang (yäng) *yang*, active, warm, dry, bright, male principle in nature; complements yin

Yang Zhu (yäng jōō) *Yang Chu*, 5th–4th c. B.C.E. individualist, precursor of Daoism: "Each one for himself."

Yi Jing (ē jĭng) *I Ching*, the *Book of Changes* [in nature]; sixty-four hexagrams and text used in divination by lot

yin (yĭn) *yin*, passive, cool, moist, dark, female principle in nature; complements yang

Yu Huang (yĕ-hwäng) *Yü Huang*, the Jade Emperor, celestial Daoist "discovered" in the 10th c. to be identical with Shang Di

Zhang Daoling (jäng-däu-lĭng) *Chang Tao-ling*, 2nd c. C.E. founder of the Daoist Wu Dou Mi Dao, "Five Pecks of Rice Way"

Zhang Jue (jäng-jē-ŭ) *Chang Chüeh*, 2nd c. C.E. founder of the Daoist sect the Yellow Turbans

Zhen Zong (jän-dzoong) *Chan Tsung*, Song emperor; his fabricated "messages from Heaven" equated the Jade Emperor with Shang Di

Zhuang-zi (jwäng-dzŭ) *Chaung Tzu*, 4th c. B.C.E. Daoist; his name is the title of the classic the *Zhuang-zi*

* For a guide to pronunciation, refer to page 99.

Confucius and Confucianism
A Study in Optimistic Humanism

We are fortunate in the case of Confucius in having fairly reliable information about his attitudes and opinions. His disciples made attempts to preserve his teachings from the first, and the descriptions they left of his personal habits are detailed and probably accurate. We cannot say as much for the accuracy of the later, traditional biographies, for they present us with questionable history, containing many obviously legendary incidents. But even these doubtful accounts have value: they incorporate authentic material left by Confucius' disciples, and thus manage to present us with what seems, on the whole, a dependable portrait of an individual.

Historically, that has been the important thing. The personality of Confucius was of major importance. That the Chinese have eagerly studied and followed his teachings in the past, and have founded not only their educational procedure, but much of their governmental practice, until very recently, on the principles he was understood to have laid down is due in large part to the fact that they have had such confidence in his character, shining nobly through the traditions of his life and permeating his teachings. He was not only a wise man or a clever one, they have said; he was an incorruptible person, a human-hearted man. He was a model gentleman.

But there is something more. The character of Confucius has seemed to exemplify the principles of order and harmony for which he stood in his teachings. During most of their history the Chinese have felt that their land would be well off indeed if the application of his principles could produce more individuals with his character. Not only would there then be better order in people's personal lives, but a superior order as well in the family and in the state and harmony between earth and heaven. The moral influence of truly Confucian individuals would make this a certainty.

It is not strange that Confucius rather than the Daoists should have laid the foundation for traditional Chinese education. The Daoists turned for the secret of life to nature and its laws, but Confucius was a humanist; he found the secret of life in persons and their better relationships. No less than the Daoists, he linked his teachings with the Dao, to which he referred as the way to do things. But his emphasis differed from that of the Daoists. They sought the

WESTERN NAME: Confucianism
ADHERENTS IN 1997: 6 million
NAMES USED BY ADHERENTS: Ru-jia, Ru-jiao
    Kong-zi-jia
LITERATURE: The Analects (Lun Yu), the Great
    Learning (Ta Xue), the Doctrine of the Mean
    (Zhong Yong), the Book of Mencius, the Xun-zi,
    and the works of Han Fei, Ju Xi, and Wang
    Yang-ming
REFERENCES TO (DEIFIED?) SUPREME
    PRINCIPLE:
        The Mandate of Heaven (Tian Ming)
        The Great Ultimate (Tai Ji)

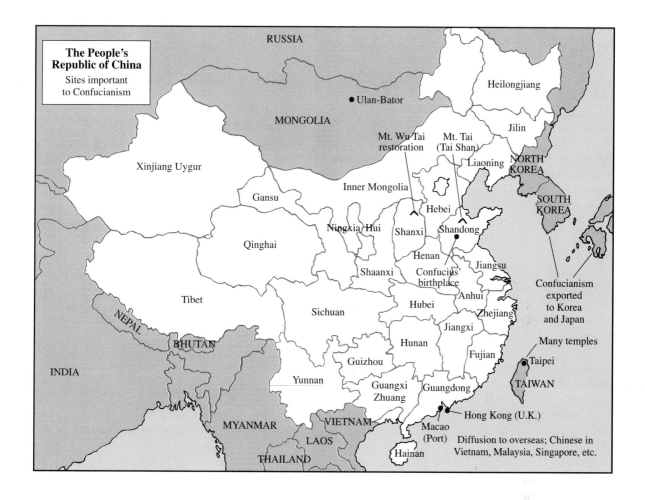

The People's Republic of China
Sites important to Confucianism

harmony of individuals with the Dao, while he desired harmony between the cosmic order and the social order, so that justice and happiness would prevail among all people in their larger groupings.

We begin by characterizing a man of the Kong (K'ung) family whose personal name was Zhong-ni. He was remembered as "Teacher Kong," Kong Fu-zi (K'ung Fu-tzu) or simply as Kong-zi (and when this name was Latinized, it became Confucius).

I. THE MAN CONFUCIUS

The best source of information on Confucius is the *Analects,* the famous collection of his sayings by his disciples, but the biographical matter in it is scant.

Later Confucian tradition therefore busied itself with supplying an abundance of biographical detail, from birth to old age. As we have already observed, much of this later material is of doubtful historical value. Is one then to credit none of it, and to stand firm on the *Analects* alone? Or is it better to go part of the way with Si-ma Qian (China's famous ancient historian, who died about 80 B.C.E.) and consider the body of tradition sound where it is not actually incredible? Neither course is satisfactory. The former does not sufficiently account for the clear-cut political aims of the Confucian school; the latter is apt to go too far in its acceptance of tradition.

If we pursue the moderate course of accepting just as much of the tradition as is needed to account for the eagerness of Confucius' disciples to take office and to set up a school of thought devoted to the training of officials and teachers, something like this brief biography results.

Confucius came from a poor but respected family in the ancient duchy of Lu, at the base of the Shandong (Shantung) peninsula. His ancestors were reputed to have been aristocratic refugees who fled from the state of Song to Lu when a revolution overthrew the ducal house. Shortly after his birth (probably in 551 B.C.E.) his father died, and he and his young mother were left in straitened circumstances. According to the *Analects* (IX. 6), Confucius said later that he was a poor man's son and could therefore do many menial things that are done by the ordinary person—things that the noble (or superior) person does not have to do. Perhaps reflection on these early struggles led him to observe in later days, "It is hard not to chafe at poverty."[A1]

In spite of their straitened circumstances, Confucius was provided by his self-sacrificing mother with the proper intellectual training to be a gentleman. It has been suggested that he studied under a village tutor, but there is no record that he did so. It may be that he had no regular teacher but learned from anyone and everyone he met and from everything he read. In any event, he became a lifelong student of the poetry and historical tradition of ancient China. He also developed a consuming interest in the several varieties of Chinese classical music (now lost to us), which he performed on the lute, often singing the old songs to this accompaniment. According to the famous autobiographical summary in the *Analects,* at age fifteen he became seriously interested in these studies; that is, he was determined to become a scholar.

But the same source of information indicates that he did not spend all of his time with his books. He did a good deal of hunting and fishing, but always with an aristocratic sense of sportsmanship, for his disciples noted, "The Master angled, but did not fish with a net; he shot, but not at birds sitting."[A2] He enjoyed chariot and carriage driving, and was well aware of the high sportsmanship demanded in archery: "A gentleman has no rivalries—except perhaps in archery; and then, as, bowing, he joins the winners or steps down to see the loser drink, throughout the struggle he is still a gentleman."[A3]

The Bureaucrat/Scholar

In his late teens, he accepted a minor government post as a collector of grain and livestock due as taxes to the Duke of Lu, and also contracted a not-too-successful marriage, which, however, realized one major objective—the bringing of a son into the world to carry on the family line. In his mid twenties, his mother died. To Confucius, this was a great personal tragedy. He at once retired from public life for twenty-seven months—a period reckoned in Chinese funerary tradition to be equivalent to three full years. Tradition insists that he more than fulfilled the conventions; at the end of the mourning period he took up his lute, but he played haltingly and was unable to sing to the notes for another five days, thus furnishing China with a classic instance of filial piety.

He now undertook the role of a teacher, offering instruction in history, poetry, government, moral conduct, and music, encouraging his students to find moral and metaphysical meanings in the *Yi Jing,* the *Book of Changes,* something he himself intended to continue. In his *Analects* he was later heard to say, "Give me a few more years to take up the study of the *Book of Changes* at the age of fifty, then I hope I shall be free from making serious mistakes."[B1]

Disciples joined him, some remaining with him for years. But though his reputation was great, and the scions of the best families in Lu were sent to him, he kept saying that his principles could be made effective in improving the now decadent social system only if he and his disciples took office in the higher echelons of government.

Tradition, not verifiable on the evidence of the *Analects,* insists that he took office in the cabinet of the Duke of Lu when he was fifty years of age, and that he ascended through the offices of minister of public works and minister of justice to the position of prime minister, but that, through intrigue occasioned by his highly successful and upright administration, he was placed in a position where he "lost face" and resigned.

Whether this is true or not, at the age of fifty-five he left Lu, accompanied by some of his disciples, and he wandered in vain for thirteen years from state to state, seeking a post under some government. The great feudal lords entertained him courteously, tongue in cheek. Some thought him a very wise and great man, yet even in this event his idea of governing by sheer force of moral example aroused no response. But if the feudal lords listened to him with respect, the officials intrigued to get rid of him. In some districts he was met with open suspicion, at the town of Kuang mobbed and imprisoned, at Pu surrounded and forced to accept armed protection, and in Song, the state whence (perhaps) his ancestors had come, obliged to escape on foot into Zheng. In this last instance his disciples, knowing a certain military officer called Huan Tuei was close on their heels, kept urging him to hurry, but he replied, "Heaven begat the power [De] that is in me. What have I to fear from such a one as Huan T'uei?"[C] Although he was fundamentally a serious man, he was not above regarding his plight humorously. As he was passing through Daxiang, a man taunted him, "Great indeed is Confucius! He knows about everything and has made no name in anything!" Confucius turned to his disciples in mock dismay. "Now what shall I take up? Shall I take up charioteering? Shall I take up archery?"[A4]

According to Si-ma Qian, his lightheartedness offended the members of his party on one occasion, when between Chen and Cai they were surrounded by a guard of hostile soldiers, who were instructed not to let them escape into the state of Chu. Food supplies ran short, some of the party fell sick and were confined to bed, but Confucius kept on reading and singing, accompanying himself with his lute. Only Yan Huei, his favorite disciple, understood his mood. He said to Confucius, "What do you care if [your ideas] are not accepted? The very fact that they are not accepted shows that you are a true gentleman [with ideas too great to be accepted by the people]." And Confucius was pleased with this flattery. "Is that so? Oh, son of Yen, if you were a rich man, I would be your butler!"[D1]

Through the good offices of one of his disciples who held a high official appointment in Lu, a cordial invitation to return was extended to Confucius by Duke Ai in 484 B.C.E., and Confucius, now sixty-seven years old, came home. Sometimes called into consultation by the duke, he otherwise passed his last years in retirement. Late Confucian tradition gave rise to the belief that he spent his time compiling the materials he used in his teaching into the famous Confucian Classics— the *Shu Jing* (*Shu Ching*) or *Book of History*, the

Portrait of Confucius

Confucius, speaking animatedly, looks the six-footer he was. His hands are joined under his voluminous sleeves. The girdle lying high on his stomach shows he is no ascetic. The rubbing from stone is dated 1748, which places it early in the Qing dynasty. Confucius wears the ceremonial hat of a high official, replete with a hat pin. He looks very much the Superior Man. *(Courtesy of the Philadelphia Museum of Art. Given by Horace H. F. Jayne, '24-36-4.)*

Shi Jing (*Shih Ching*) or *Book of Poetry*, the *Li Ji* (*Li Chi*) or *Book of Rites*, the *Yi Jing* (*I Ching*) or *Book of Changes*, and the *Chun Qiu* (*Ch'un Ch'iu*) or *Annals of Spring and Autumn*—the first four being anthologies of older source material, the last his own composition. He is also said to have compiled a sixth book, the *Yue* (*Yüeh*), or *Book of Music*, of which only a portion has survived (in Chapter X of the *Li Ji*). But all this is, as we shall see in a moment, highly doubtful. Just before his death in 479 B.C.E., he expressed discouragement about his own career, yet left his disciples more determined than ever to carry out his political and social aims.

II. THE TEACHINGS OF CONFUCIUS

Present Estimate of the Sources

A discussion of our sources of the teaching of Confucius is important, first of all, because it is generally agreed upon today that the Five Classics are not directly from Confucius' hands—if they have come from his hands at all. For one thing, his disciples edited, altered, and amplified the materials they inherited. Thus, Si-ma Qian says that Mencius, over one hundred years after Confucius, "put the *Shih* and *Shu* in order."[E1] It is especially true of the *Li Ji* that it cannot possibly be called, as it now stands, the product of Confucius' editorial work, but seems rather to date from the early years of the Han dynasty (second century B.C.E.). Apparently, Confucius' materials often were reissued in revised editions.

But there is a more fundamental point to make: A careful scholarship must recognize it as a possibility that Confucius used, rather than first assembled, the materials of the earlier editions of the Classics, and that these collections were already in existence and may have been in use by teachers before his time.

If we assume Confucius adopted the Classics as already-known and valued anthologies, then his chief purpose was to point out the lessons contained in them. As a matter of fact, the *Analects* is full of evidence of this, and in this we may see his originality. It is possible that he may have done some editing while he was about it, editing that had decisive effects. But even when we assume such editing, we cannot know where or on what materials he did it. The probability is that he did no editing at all. The editing was done by later hands.

Another fact should be made clear. The possibility that Confucius made changes in the Five Classics cannot be ruled out, but if he did so, he behaved as an editor should. He did not intrude his private convictions into these collections; he conceived his function to be merely that of a "transmitter," and that is actually what he said he was. The *Analects* records two sayings of his that testify to his great respect for the learning of the "ancients": "I am a transmitter and not a creator. I believe in and have a passion for the Ancients,"[F1] and

"I'm not born a wise man, I'm merely one in love with ancient studies and work very hard to learn them."[B2] The Classics, then, are not a source of Confucius' original ideas. His private views and interpretations can be judged uncertainly, or at best to a limited degree only, from his textbook materials.

This might seem at first glance a serious difficulty, but we have other sources of his teaching that are far more revealing. When he was using or studying the Classics, he offered his comments and interpretations to bystanders freely and in ample detail. He went further and developed his own conception of what men must do to preserve, and live by, the best insights contained in the literature he so highly valued. These comments and discussions seemed so important to those who heard them that they wrote them down on slips of bamboo, at first fragmentarily, then more fully through interpretation and paraphrase. The details of Confucius' own teaching have thus come to us through his disciples and owe much to their phrasing. Their recollections and interpretations are found in the *Four Books,* which are:

1. The *Analects, Lun Yu* (*Lun Yü*), a collection of the sayings of Confucius and some of his disciples, it might be called the salient points of his and their conversations removed from the context and condensed. Although it is of very composite origin, and though "not much more than half [of it] can be really trusted even as good second-hand evidence," as one estimate puts it,[G1] nevertheless, in spite of its inaccuracies, Confucius vividly and in his own person speaks to us through it. It is our most important source of material about him.

2. The *Great Learning, Da Xue* (*Ta Hsüeh*), originally Chapter 39 of the *Li Ji*, but since Zhu-xi's (Chu Hsi's) time removed for separate use. We cannot consider that it was from Confucius. Rather, it seems to be dependent for its point of view on Xun-zi (Hsün-tzu). Obviously a treatise in itself, it was initially designed to serve as the basis of the education of gentlemen in general, princes in particular. In classical Chinese education, his was the first text studied by schoolboys.

3. The *Doctrine of the Mean, Zhong Yong* (*Chung Yung*), also originally a part of the *Li Ji* (as Chapter 28), it is an excellent exposition of the philosophical

presuppositions of Confucian thought, dealing partic-ularly with the relation of human nature to the under-lying moral order of the universe. Its contents have been traditionally attributed to Confucius' grandson, Zi Si (Tzu Ssu), but this is now regarded as subject to serious qualification. For one thing, it is apparently composed of two parts, one later than the other. The earlier, central part *may* have come from Zi Si, but the later portion appears to have been written after the time of Mencius, perhaps in the second century B.C.E.

4. The *Book of Mencius,* dating from the third century B.C.E., a collection of the writing and sayings of the most original of the earlier Confucian thinkers, constituting the first attempt to reach a rounded sys-tematic exposition of Confucian philosophy.

It would be foolish to say that the Four Books have removed all of our difficulties. Though perhaps hardly anyone ever lived who succeeded as well as Confucius in reshaping the minds of his disciples into accurate reflections of his own, it has to be recognized that the Four Books changed with the passage of time through the editing of later hands, as must be evident from the descriptions of them just given, and therefore any competent exposition of Confucius' teachings must take these changes into account wherever they can be detected.

Book Burning and Textual Problems

One final difficulty remains. It can be said to have arisen historically and been settled for us historically. The long history of the Five Classics and the Four Books is punctuated at one point with a great threat to their survival. The first real emperor of all China, and perhaps its greatest, was Duke Zheng (Cheng) of Qin, the founder of the short-lived Qin dynasty, who con-quered and in 221 B.C.E. forcibly unified the provinces of China as that had never been done before, and who accordingly took the proud title "Shi Huang Di" or the First Emperor. We have referred to him before (p. 261). An administrative and military genius, he established a new imperial capital and abolished the old feudal land tenure system. He substituted a system in which any person could buy land and cultivate it;

but this led during Han times to the rise of a landlord-tenant system that was to last two thousand years and resulted in inequities as great as those of the feudal system.

Shi Huang Di concentrated authority in himself, redivided the empire into thirty-six new administra-tive districts, completed the fourteen-hundred-mile-long Great Wall (sections of which, especially at mountain passes, seem to have been built before his time), conceived and introduced a new currency, insti-tuted reforms among the officials (many of whom lost their jobs), substituted silk painted with a soft hair-brush for the old bamboo records incised with a metal stylus, and encouraged the resultant simplification of the writing of Chinese characters from which a new script derived. He found amidst all of these changes that his attempts to establish a new order were obstructed by traditionalists and conservatives, chief among whom were the Confucian-trained schoolmas-ters and officials who clung to the old feudal traditions and openly resisted his innovations as being destruc-tive of public order and morality.

On the advice of his prime minister, Li Si (Li Ssu), who was an advocate of the doctrines of the anti-Confucian Legalist School (see p. 303), the emperor in 213 B.C.E. ordered the famous "Burning of Books" for which Chinese scholarship has since so execrated him. His purpose was to standardize the thinking of the common people, and therefore he wished to destroy every privately owned copy of the writings that preserved the knowledge of past ways of conduct-ing public affairs, except such books as the *Yi Jing* (use-ful in divination) and manuals on agriculture and medicine. Special wrath was vented on the *Book of Poetry* and the *Book of History.* He decreed that any persons who failed to deliver up to the prefects their copies of the proscribed books should be branded with hot iron and compelled to work for four years at hard labor on the Great Wall. Some 460 scholars, many of whom were Confucian, were buried alive for trea-son, it is said, in the years that followed.

But three years after he issued his decree, Shi Huang Di died, and all of his animus against the past came at last to nothing. To do him justice, he had "merely burned the books which existed among the people, but did not burn those in the official archives."[E2] During the Han dynasty that succeeded his within five years after his death, the Confucian Classics were restored to public use, with, if anything, a heightened renown.

Were they the worse for their misadventure? Curiously enough, not as the result of their suppression, but as the result of their recopying, for they were recopied in a new script! The scholars now wrote rapidly on long pieces of silk instead of slowly on short pieces of bamboo, and they began to fill out the bare bones of the Old Texts with the interpretative glosses they had learned in the schools. Without any conscious wish to make grave alterations, they practically rewrote the *Li Ji* and added to the *Shu Jing,* the *Yi Jing,* and the *Zhong Yong.* Included in these additions were certain ascriptions of divinity to Confucius, the tradition that he was the first to compile the Five Classics, and stories of his miraculous birth. Then gradually there was a recovery of some writings, composed in the old script, which contradicted the new script writings in matters of fact, and at once the Old Text school was born. The battle between the Old Text and the New Text schools was to continue intermittently for nearly two thousand years, but it had this good result: As a consequence of the enormous amount of textual criticism that was done down the centuries, and especially by the Qing scholars of the seventeenth to nineteenth centuries, forgeries (largely Old Text) have been located, variant readings reduced, and conflicting passages clearly defined.

And now, after this long excursus, let us proceed to the most careful statement of Confucius' own teaching that we can achieve in the light of present knowledge.

The Ethical Principles of Confucius

The ethical thought of Confucius sprang from a double realization: first, that the China of his day was disturbingly corrupt, but second, that the moral condition of the country was not beyond redemption. The situation was bad, but not hopeless. Social practices had grown corrupt, but individuals had not yet become corrupt; they were still as apt to good as to evil. But why had social practices grown corrupt? Confucius answered this question quite simply: People had failed from moral causes to live by *ren* (*jen*), or the will

to seek the good of others, as those of their ancestors who were devoted to the common good had lived by it.

The common good was to be secured by the attainment of five cardinal virtues: *ren* (the root); *yi,* or righteousness by justice (the trunk); *li,* or the religious and moral ways of acting (the branches); *chi* (*chih*), or wisdom (the flower); and *xin* (*hsin*), or faithfulness (the fruit). "These five," Confucius might have said, "but the greatest of these is *jen* [ren]."[H] We shall consider two of these at some length: (a) li and its underlying principles and (b) ren (jen) or the motivating force in the moral life.

Li: Propriety

The term *li* is one of the most important words used by Confucius to formulate his program for the recovery of China. It is difficult to translate, for it means different things in different contexts. In one connection or another, means "propriety" (the usual translation, but not always adequate), "courtesy," "reverence," "rites and ceremonies," "the correct forms of social ceremony," "ritual," "ritual and music," "the due order of public ceremony," "the ideal standard of social and religious conduct," and "the religious and moral way of life." Put into its historical perspective, it means in the words of Lin Yutang, "an ideal social order with everything in its place, and particularly a rationalized feudal order, [like that] which was breaking down in Confucius' days."[D2] (Readers of Confucian texts in English need to be alert to the fact that there is an entirely different Chinese ideogram also transliterated "*li.*" It is common in Neo-Confucian texts. See the glossary.)

In the *Li Ji* (the Confucian Classic on the subject), comprehensive and illuminating discussions of the meaning of li are attempted. Although the following passages show some influence from later Confucian thought, particularly that of Xun-zi (Hsün Tzu), they may give us some glimpse into the mind of Confucius himself.

> Duke Ai asked Confucius, "What is this great *li*? Why is it that you talk about *li* as though it were such an important thing?"
>
> Confucius replied, "Your humble servant is really not worthy to understand *li.*"
>
> "But you do constantly speak about it," said Duke Ai.

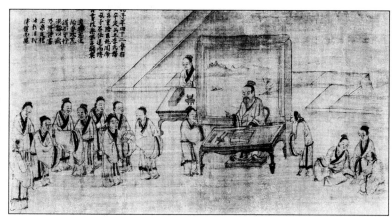

Scene from the Life of Confucius

In this drawing from the Ming dynasty (1368–1644), Confucius lectures out of doors to a large band of disciples who have gathered around him. He is forty-two years old and is the headmaster of his own private school in the duchy of Lu. Like his disciples, he keeps his hair in place with a comb. *(Courtesy of the Philadelphia Museum of Art. Purchased: Museum Funds, '29-40-212d.)*

Confucius: "What I have learned is this, that of all the things that people live by, *li* is the greatest. Without *li* we do not know how to conduct a proper worship of the spirits of the universe; or how to establish the proper status of the king and the ministers, the ruler and the ruled, and the elders and the juniors; or how to establish the moral relationships between the sexes; between parents and children, and between brothers; or how to distinguish the different degrees of relationships in the family. That is why a gentleman holds *li* in such high regard."[D3]

Confucius said [in conversation with Zuyou (Tsuyu)], "The principles of *li* and righteousness serve as the principles of social discipline. By means of these principles, people try to maintain the official status of rulers and subjects, to teach the parents and children and elder brothers and younger brothers and husbands and wives to live in harmony, to establish social institutions, and to live in groups of hamlets. . . ."

"Is *li* so very important as all that?" asked Tsuyu again.

"This *li*," replied Confucius, "is the principle by which the ancient kings embodied the laws of heaven and regulated the expressions of human nature. Therefore he who has attained *li* lives, and he who has lost it, dies. . . . *Li* is based on heaven, patterned on earth, deals with the worship of the spirits and is extended to the rites and ceremonies of funerals, sacrifices to ancestors, archery, carriage driving, "capping," [the ceremony of putting a cap on a boy when he is considered to have entered manhood], marriage, and court audience, or exchange of diplomatic visits. Therefore the Sage shows the people this principle of a rationalized social order (*li*) and through it everything becomes right in the family, the state, and the world."[D4]

Assumptions Underlying *Li*

1. Li is of vital importance in ordering and regulating the principal human relationships. These relationships are five in number. They are the relationships between ruler and subject, father and son, husband and wife, the eldest son and his younger brothers, and elders and juniors (or friends). Besides these five relationships, others are incidentally mentioned, such as the relationship between men and the spirits of the universe, between rulers and their ministers, and between diplomats, but the five aforementioned relationships are the "great" ones, because they are judged fundamental to the social order.

2. By the practice of li the principal relationships in society can be so regulated and set straight that complete harmony may reign in every home, in every village, and throughout the empire. Ultimately—and here Confucius and his school proved themselves to be true to the deepest feelings of the Chinese people about the ultimate nature of the universe—the goal is to obtain a cosmic harmony between humankind, earth, and heaven, and thus put into actual operation among humankind the Dao or the will of Heaven.

3. The forms of social ceremony that best exemplify the practice of li are observable in the manners of those ancients who sought the common welfare and exhibited a humane spirit of mutual respect and courtesy.

The last of these principles deserves more than passing notice. The ancients lived harmoniously and courteously together in a social order that was profoundly just, Confucius believed. Superiors and inferiors knew their places and behaved politely according to their several stations. So he reverently studied and tried to embody in his own conduct the ceremonial procedures of the olden time. He wished to be instrumental in getting all of China to do the same. This won him the mocking criticism of the Daoists, who raged at his formalism as being unnatural and futile. But Confucius believed he stood for "the crystallization of what is right"[D5] (one of the definitions of li in the *Li Ji*) in terms of formal behavior. For the sake of giving his conduct the force of a moral example, he acted out his principles with obvious symbolism. This accounts for his supposed meticulous behavior in the ducal court of Lu, described in Book X of the *Analects*. Consider the following description. (It may not be an authentic description of Confucius himself, but it certainly represents behavior of which he would have approved.)

> When the duke bade him receive guests, his face seemed to change, his knees to bend. He bowed left and right to those beside him, straightened his robes in front and behind, and sped forward, his elbows spread like wings. When the guest had left, he always reported: "The guest has ceased to look back."
>
> Entering the palace gate he stooped, as though it were too low for him. He did not stand in the middle of the gate, nor step on the threshold.
>
> Passing the throne, his face seemed to change, his knees to bend, he spake with bated breath.
>
> Mounting the dais, he lifted his robes, bowed his back and masked his breathing, till it seemed to stop.
>
> Coming down, his face relaxed below the first step, and bore a pleased look. From the foot of the steps he sped forward, his elbows spread like wings; and when again in his seat he looked intent and solemn as before.
>
> When bearing the sceptre, his back bent, as under too heavy a burden. He held his hands not higher than in bowing, nor lower than in giving a

> present. He wore an awed look and dragged his feet, as though they were fettered.
>
> On the duke coming to see him in sickness, he turned his face to the east and had his court dress spread across him, with the girdle over it.
>
> When summoned by the duke, he walked, without waiting for his carriage.
>
> In mounting his chariot he stood straight and grasped the cord. When in his chariot he did not look round, speak fast, or point.[A5]

This description, whether it describes Confucius himself or merely an imagined ideal Confucian official, raises the question, was Confucius just a narrow formalist, or was he a social philosopher to be taken seriously? The answer would seem to depend on whether he lived by purely formal rules or by a deeper principle.

That Confucius found in the practices of the ancients a profound principle that provided him with a key to ideal relationships among people is more than once indicated in the *Analects* and elsewhere.

Li as *Shu*: Reciprocity

> Zi-gong (Tzu-kung) asked, saying, "Is there one word which may serve as a rule of practice for all one's life?" The Master said, "Is not Reciprocity (*shu*) such a word? What you do not want done to yourself, do not do to others."[11]

In these words, Confucius formulated a law of human relationships similar to the Golden Rule of the New Testament. He happened to define reciprocity, (shu) negatively (and hence won from some Western scholars the grudging judgment that he had given China the "Silver Rule"), but the word means "fellow feeling" or "mutual consideration," and its definition need not have been put negatively. (Readers of Confucian texts in English need to be alert to the fact that there is an entirely different Chinese ideogram meaning "statecraft" but also transliterated "shu." It is common in texts of the Legalist school.) In the *Doctrine of the Mean*, Confucius is in fact quoted as having explained this central ethical principle in positive terms, making it quite comparable with Jesus' Golden Rule. He is there found saying,

> There are four things in the moral life of man, not one of which I have been able to carry out in my

life. To serve my father as I would expect my son to serve me: that I have not been able to do. To serve my sovereign as I would expect a minister under me to serve me: that I have not been able to do. To act towards my elder brother as I would expect my younger brother to act towards me: that I have not been able to do. To be the first to behave towards friends as I would expect them to behave towards me: that I have not been able to do.[11]

However, it is true that Confucius did not go as far as Jesus (or, for that matter, the Daoists of his own land) in defining the scope of the application of this ideal of ethical conduct. He made a significant reservation when confronted with the Daoist rule of returning good for evil. Someone asked him, "What do you think of repaying evil with kindness?" He replied, "Then what are you going to repay kindness with? . . . Repay kindness with kindness, but repay evil with justice."[B3] It would seem that Confucius limited the operation of the law of reciprocity, in its complete sense, to the circle of the good, because evil persons were judged unworthy of the mutual consideration prompted by fellow feeling.

Humane Character: *Ren (Jen)*

It cannot be emphasized too strongly, however, that Confucius' primary purpose was to persuade all people to cooperate in securing the general good. True virtue, he taught, lay in the expression of *ren* or the will to seek the good of others. (The Chinese character for *ren* is a composite of two characters, one for *man* (extendable to *person*) and the other for *two*. It therefore stands for the inclusion of a second person in one's plans.) It consisted in the recognition of the worth of any human being of any rank or station, and kindly behavior toward one's fellows as a consequence of this recognition. Many instances could be cited of Confucius' insistence that government should be directed toward the welfare of the whole people, that families must safeguard the good of each of their members and bring harmony into the interrelationships of old and young, and that in society at large men, knowing that all who live within the four seas are brothers, should display to each other in action their real humane and kindly character (their *ren*).

Confucius wanted government to be by ren. He was not aware (he did not live in a culture that permitted him to know) that government may be based on the democratic process of election to office by ballot, but he did demand that government be for, if not by, the people and that feudal lords be responsive to the needs of the people at large.

The Five Great Relationships

The *Li Ji* presents the following scheme as growing out of Confucius' study of *shu* as applied to the Five Relationships. (It is very doubtful whether Confucius developed so schematic a treatment of this matter, but it follows logically from his teaching.)

> Kindness in the father, filial piety in the son
> Gentility in the eldest brother, humility and respect in the younger
> Righteous behavior in the husband, obedience in the wife
> Humane consideration in elders, deference in juniors
> Benevolence in rulers, loyalty in ministers and subjects

If these ten attitudes (known as the ten *Yi* or appropriate attitudes) are generally present in society, then the highest priority (li) will be actualized, and perfect harmony will reign between all individuals. Then people will show their real humane character (ren). No quarrels, no disturbances, no injustices will exist. There will be happiness among friends, harmony in the home, peace in the state. The *Doctrine of the Mean* quotes approvingly from the *Book of Poetry*.

> When wives and children and their sires are one,
> 'Tis like the harp and lute in unison.
> When brothers live in concord and at peace
> The strain of harmony shall never cease.
> The lamp of happy union lights the home,
> And bright days follow when the children come.[12]

And the *Great Learning* (Chapter VII) quotes, from the same source, lines that may be translated in the following way:

> A prince by courteous carriage may create
> Concord at court and order in the state.

To see that Confucius was a practical sort of philosopher and did not lose himself in vague contemplation of an ideal that was conceived only in general terms, let us turn now to the subjects concerning that which he most often spoke of when amplifying on what he meant by practicing li: the relationship of fathers and sons, the relationship of rulers and subjects, and the nature of the superior man.

Filial Piety: *Xiao (Hsiao)*

Confucius did not, of course, bring into being the fact that the whole of Chinese culture has rested on the basis of the family. Yet his praise of filial piety (Xiao) made the interests of the family the first consideration of the Chinese. In the past, nothing has stood higher. In China, loyalty to the family has been one's first loyalty. No lad in China ever comes of age, in the Western sense. It is still true that his whole service is expected to be devoted to his family until death, and he is expected to obey his father and, when his father dies, his eldest brother, with a perfect compliance. This has meant in the past that every father has a great and grave responsibility to fulfill toward his family. He must seek to produce virtue in his sons by being himself the best example of it, the fact that the present communist government speaks of making itself "father and elder brother" and claims for itself the first loyalty of every citizen has not totally invalidated the personal virtue of filial piety in the context of family life.

Confucius considered this so self-evident a proposition that he laid far heavier stress on the filial piety without which the father's goodness would the remain ineffective. Here he touched a chord that has had the most resounding response in the Chinese consciousness since his time. It struck home. Consider a few of the many important utterances of Confucius on the subject (and thereby glimpse an essential aspect of the folk mind of China).

The Master said, "Whilst thy father lives look for his purpose; when he is gone, look how he

walked. To change nothing in thy father's way for three years may be called pious."[K1]

Meng Wu asked the duty of a son.
The Master said, "He shall not grieve his father mother by anything but illness."[K2]

The Master said, "Whilst thy father and mother are living, do not wander afar. If thou must travel, hold a set course."[K4]

The *Doctrine of the Mean* lays down the following influential precepts:

Confucius remarked: "The Emperor Wu and his brother, Duke Chou, were indeed eminently pious men. . . .

"In spring and autumn they repaired and put in order the ancestral temple, arranged the sacrificial vessels, exhibited the regalia and heirlooms of the family, and presented the appropriate offerings of the season. . . .

"To gather in the same places where our fathers before us have gathered; to perform the same ceremonies which they before us have performed; to play the same music which they before us have played; to pay respect to those whom they have honored; to love those who were dear to them—in fact, to serve those now dead as if they were living, and now departed as if they were still with us: this is the highest achievement of true filial piety."[J3]

Confucius may not have been as firm about it, but the majority of his followers concluded that the duty of a son is to obey his father in all things while he lives and to honor and still obey him in all things after he is dead. Indeed, the filial relationship has been made since Confucius' time the type and symbol of all life-enriching and wisdom-conserving subordination to the leadership of the old and wise. "By the principle of filial piety the whole world can be made happy and all calamities and dangers can be averted"[L] is one of the claims made for treating not only one's father as a father should be treated, but also such superior spirits as one's ancestors, elders, noted scholars, and the head of state

> "Tsu-yu asked the duty of a son.
> The Master said, 'He that can feed his parents is now called a good son. But both dogs and horses are fed, and unless we honor our parents, what is the difference?'"[K3]
>
> —Confucius

as they should be treated. The attitude of filial piety can thus be almost indefinitely extended.

Political Philosophy

Confucius was equally emphatic about the importance of the relationship between rulers and their subjects. Here he merged ethics and politics. He told everyone who would listen to him that if rulers adopt and act upon the highest moral principles, then the spiritual climate of a whole state may be changed, and all of the people from the higher officials down to the poorest and least citizens may be led to live more virtuously in their several stations. The reform of society begins at the top, among the rulers, and thence reaches down to the lower orders of society.

On one occasion the head of the Ji clan in Lu, Baron Ji Kang Zu, a person of importance, asked Confucius how to rule. The sage replied, "To govern is to keep straight. If you, Sir, lead the people straight, which of your subjects will venture to fall out of line?"[M1] The same baron in another conversation asked, "Ought not I to cut off the lawless in order to establish law and order? What do you think?" To this crucial question Confucius made the sort of reply that won him profound respect as the enunciator of ultimate ethical principles, but that made the legalists smile in derision: "Sir, what need is there of the death penalty in your system of government? If you showed a sincere desire to be good, your people would likewise be good. The virtue of the prince is like unto wind; that of the people like unto grass. For it is the nature of grass to bend when the wind blows upon it."[M2]

For an understanding of his point of view, too much stress can hardly be laid upon this fundamental conviction of Confucius. People, he held, being at heart good, are responsive to good in those to whom they look for leadership. "If a country," he insisted, "had none but good rulers for a hundred years, crime might be stamped out and the death penalty abolished." He added for good measure, "How true this saying is!"[M3]

Good Character Makes Good Governance

One of the main conclusions that Confucius' followers, thinking in his spirit, drew from his study of history is contained in the following curious piece of close-linked logic that is to be found in the *Great Learning:*

> The ancients [i.e., the ancient kings] who wished to cause their virtue to shine forth first ordered well their own states. Wishing to order well their states, they first regulated their families. Wishing to regulate their families, they first cultivated their persons. Wishing to cultivate their persons, they first rectified their hearts. Wishing to rectify their hearts, they first sought to be sincere in their thoughts. Wishing to be sincere in their thoughts, they first extended to the utmost their knowledge. Such extension of knowledge lay in the investigation of things. Things being investigated, their knowledge became complete. Their knowledge being complete, their thoughts were sincere. Their thoughts being sincere, their hearts were then rectified. Their hearts being rectified, their persons were cultivated. Their persons being cultivated, their families were regulated. Their families being regulated, their states were rightly governed. Their states being rightly governed, the whole kingdom was made tranquil and happy.[12]

In this, perhaps the most famous of all Confucian paragraphs, and in the previous quotations, it is apparent that, according to Confucian teaching, the good life is a spiritual rather than a legal attainment. A good example may prevent crime, but statutory law breeds it. A well-ordered state cannot be legislated into existence; it grows out of a contagious spirit of good will and earnestness in well-doing. Love or cooperative good will makes law unnecessary. (Daoists could agree!)

The *Doctrine of the Mean* quotes Confucius as saying to the Duke of Lu, "When the men are there, good government will flourish, when the men are gone, good government decays and becomes extinct. . . . The conduct of government, therefore, depends upon the men. The right men are obtained by the ruler's personal character. To cultivate his personal character, the ruler must use the moral law (Dao). To cultivate the moral law, the ruler must use the moral sense [ren, or the principles of true manhood]."[J4] In the words of the *Book of Poetry* concerning the good Emperor Shun,

That great and noble Prince displayed
The sense of right in all he wrought;
The spirit of his wisdom swayed
Peasant and peer; the crowd, the court.[J5]

Because Confucius believed in government by moral example, he took no interest in written laws. In fact, he is quoted as saying, "Guide the people by the law, keep them in line by punishment, and they may shun crime, but they will be shameless. Guide them by mind, keep them in line by courtesy, and they will learn shame and grow good."[K5] A high hope!

He used to admit the truth of the old saying, "To be a good king is difficult." But he went on to say, "He who realizes the difficulty of being a good king—has he not almost succeeded in making his country prosper?"[M4] What he meant was, obviously, that when a king pauses to think long enough about being a good king, he will feel within him the strong native tendencies toward virtue, and the result will be a virtuous and prosperous people. No one has defined more clearly the best hopes of a paternalistic state.

The Rectification of Names: *Zheng-ming (Cheng-ming)*

In the Confucian ideal state, a place was made for logic—or a sort of semantics. Moral and political reorganization had a side that was to be called "the rectification of names." This zheng-ming principle called for defining ideal social roles carefully and then shaping people to fit them. We must consider this concept, if Confucius discussed it (and he may not have done so), as his chief contribution to straight thinking in politics and morals. The crucial passage is in the *Analects*.

> Tsu-lu said: "The prince of Wei is awaiting you, Sir, to take control of his administration. What will you undertake first, Sir?" The Master replied: "The one thing needed is the rectification of names."[E3]

The disciple then says in bewilderment, "That is far-fetched, Sir! Why rectify them?" Confucius rebukes him for showing a lack of logical acuteness and proceeds to explain that if names are incorrect, words will be misused, and when words are misused, nothing can be on a sound footing. Li and music will languish, law and punishments will not be just, and people will not know where to place hand or foot. This is why one cannot be too careful about words and names.

In another conversation, Confucius declared that only when the ruler is ruler, the minister is minister, the father is father, and the son is son can there be good government. He meant to say that only when people know what names stand for and then act as the definitions indicate can there be true social order. Morality cannot exist apart from precision of thought and speech. To quote one eminent modern Chinese scholar, Hu Shi (Hu Shih), "Confucius considered [there was] an inseparable connection between intellectual disorder and moral perversity." Hu Shi explains Confucius' point of view further, thus,

> The rectification of names consists in making real relationships and duties and institutions conform as far as possible to their *ideal* meanings. . . . When this intellectual reorganization is at last effected, the ideal social order will come as night follows day—a social order where, just as a circle is a circle and a square a square, so every prince is princely, every official is faithful, every father is fatherly, and every child is filially pious.[N]

The principle, then, is that one must act in life in accordance with the highest, that is, the socially agreed-upon, ideal of one's true place and function in society.

The Superior Man: *Jun-zi (Chün-tzu)*

When Confucius came to describe his highest principles as embodied in a person, he used the term *jun-zi,* which in his day meant simply a man of high birth, a nobleman. But Confucius used it to describe a set of behaviors. Like other great ethical thinkers (Gautama Buddha, for example, transmuting the word Aryan, "noble," to refer to *anyone* who followed his eightfold path), Confucius thus based being a noble person upon merit rather than birth. We use the masculine word Superior "Man" because that is the way Confucius thought and spoke, but in most respects his conception would lend itself to reinterpretation in language that is not gender specific.

The kind of person Confucius most firmly believed in was the one whose mind was perfectly clear about names and duties, and who moreover acted with an altruistic uprightness (ren) and good taste (li). One must take seriously Confucius' description of this true gentleman, who as a son is always filial, as a father just and kind, as an official loyal and faithful, as a husband righteous and judicious, and as a friend sincere and tactful. It is this ideal that constitutes Confucius' greatest claim to distinction as a moral philosopher.

The Superior Man, he said, displays the Five Constant Virtues. "Moral virtue simply consists," he asserted, "in being able, anywhere and everywhere, to exercise five particular qualities: self-respect, magnanimity, sincerity, earnestness, and benevolence."[M5] This list of virtues suggests that though Confucius loved the order that punctilious observance of rules and ceremonies brings, he saw the fallacy of a merely legalistic formalism. The harmony he sought could issue only from inward uprightness, a sincere and basic feeling of mutuality with others. He had no use for the insincere politeness that comes from mere etiquette. He emphatically rejected "the glib talker," "the good-goody." Mencius quotes him as saying, "I hate things that resemble the real things but are not the real things. . . . I hate the ingratiating fellows, because they get mixed up with the good men. I hate the glib talkers because they confuse us about honest people. . . . I hate goody-goodys because they confuse us about virtuous people."[B4] In the *Analects,* we hear him saying, "Your goody-goody people are the thieves of virtue."[M6] In another connection, he remarked, "If a man is not a true man, what is the use of rituals? If a man is not a true man, what is the use of music?"[B5] This touches on the very heart of Confucius' philosophy of life, which demands integrity in one's good will.

The Superior Man *feels* like practicing li, because he is realizing his own magnanimity (ren) through it. This is an important moral point, as Y. L. Fung suggests.

The li are imposed on man from outside. But besides this outer mould, we each still have within us something which we may take as a model for our conduct. If we "can find in ourselves a rule for the similar treatment of others"; if we do to others what we wish for ourselves and "do not do to others what we do not like ourselves," then the outpourings of our nature will of themselves be in accord with what is proper. Hence while there are still occasions on which one's own natural uprightness (chih) can-

not be followed, there is none upon which *jen* (which is one's own uprightness conforming to what is proper) may not be acted upon. This is why *jen* is the "all pervading" principle of Confucius' teaching, and the center of his philosophy.[E4]

Because of the perfect adjustment he has achieved between his manners and motives, the Superior Man embodies in his conduct a Golden Mean among men. To the Superior Man decorum is as natural as breathing. He has a compelling sense of duty, but no difficulty in carrying it out. "In his progress through the world he has neither narrow predilections nor obstinate antipathies."[M7] His uprightness never takes the form of rudeness, because he controls its expression by the rules of good taste. He is modest. He is universal in his outlook. He is simple, honest, and a lover of justice. "He weighs men's words and observes the expression on their faces."[M8] Then his response is tactful but conscientious and truthful. In trying to establish his own character, he also tries to establish the character of others. "The higher type of man makes a sense of duty the groundwork of his character, blends with it in action a sense of harmonious proportion, manifests it in a spirit of unselfishness, and perfects it by the addition of sincerity and truth."[M9] Surely a noble ideal of manhood—whether attainable or not on the basis of Confucius' ethics! And this noble man never forgets himself. He obeys the inner law of self-control. He keeps his head, and with it his equilibrium and his virtue. "Not even whilst he eats his meal will the superior man forget what he owes to his fellowmen. Even in his hurried leave-takings, even in moments of frantic confusion, he keeps true to his virtue."[F2] He is a real gentleman because he lives by a superior law—a law of proportion and equilibrium in acting on his inner motives, and of mutuality and fellow feeling in regard to others.

The Golden Mean: *Zhongyong (Chungyung)*

It was left to the Confucian school to develop the doctrine of the Golden Mean. Confucius spoke of it, apparently, only suggestively and in passing.

Since I cannot find people who follow the Golden Mean to teach, I suppose I will have to work with those who are brilliant or erratic, *kuang* (*k'uang*), and those who are a little dull but careful, *zhuan* (*chuan*). The brilliant but erratic persons are always ready to go forward (or are too active), and the dull but careful persons always hold themselves back (or are not active enough).[B6]

One of his sayings had the ambiguous but profoundly suggestive character that always excites speculation and leads to further development of thought. It has been both narrowly and broadly translated, as the following two English versions show. The succinct, less explanatory rendering is:

> That virtue is perfect which adheres to a constant mean.[M10]

In the more philosophically phrased translation, this becomes:

> The use of the moral sentiment, well balanced and kept in perfect equilibrium—that is the true state of human perfection.[O]

Perhaps Confucius (if he used the word at all) meant by *Zhongyong* the word in dispute) something like the Middle Way of early Buddhism, even then being worked out in India. And, if we sense his meaning aright, he was as well touching upon a theme that the Greeks, in the person of Aristotle, far away "across the roof of the world," were soon to place at the center of their ethics.

There is no doubt, whatever suggestions he may have made along this line, that Confucius himself was a good example of one who walks the middle way and does nothing in excess. He had true decorum. He himself was modest about his achievements. "In three ways I fall short of a gentleman. Love is never vexed; wisdom has no doubts; courage is without fear."[A6] But he knew he possessed one qualification of the superior type; he had a compelling sense of duty. "To divine wisdom and perfect virtue," he said, "I can lay no claim. All that can be said of me is that I never falter in the course which I pursue and am unwearying in my instruction of others—this and nothing more."[M11] "There are men, I daresay, who act rightly without knowing the reason why, but I am not one of them. Having heard much, I sift out the good and practice it;

having seen much I retain it in my memory. This is the second order of wisdom."[M12] "I am a transmitter and not an originator, and as one who believes in and loves the ancients, venture to compare myself with our old Peng"[F3]—the Chinese Methuselah, an ancient sage of the eleventh (?) century B.C.E., who was said to have disappeared, as Lao-zi was said to have done years later, into the west. There is little boasting here, and yet in his old age he is quoted as saying calmly,

> At fifteen I had my mind bent on learning. At thirty I stood firm. At forty I had no doubts. At fifty I knew the decrees of Heaven. At sixty my ear was an obedient organ for the reception of truth. At seventy I could do what my heart desired without transgressing what was right [the *ju* (*chü*) or law of the Tao].[13]

Religious Teaching

It may be granted that Confucius was primarily a teacher of ethics. Some would say that little more need be added; he was no more than that. But this is a contention that cannot be maintained. In private belief and in public practice, he exhibited faith in religious reality. So carefully, moreover, did he adhere to the established religious ceremonies of his time that he set an example that was, until this century, officially considered the Chinese ideal.

However, his attitude in religion was critical and discriminating, even marked by an evident restraint, for he was rationalistic and decidedly humanistic in his outlook. Only in the milder sense of the word can he be called mystical or supernaturalistic. His position in matters of faith was this: Whatever seemed contrary to common sense in popular tradition, and whatever did not serve any discoverable social purpose, he regarded coldly. In his teaching, he avoided discussing such subjects as prodigies, feats of strength, crime, and the supernatural, apparently because he did not wish to spend time discussing perturbing exceptions to human and natural law. "Absorption in the study of the supernatural is most harmful," he said,[M13] not that he disbelieved in the supernatural, but that it would not do to let the pressing concerns of human welfare suffer neglect. It is from this point of view that we should weigh two sayings of his that have perhaps received too much attention. His disciple Zu-yu asked him about one's duty to the spirits of the dead. He replied, "Before we are able to do our duty by the living, how can we do it by the spirits of the dead?"[M14] He defined what he believed was the proper attitude with great exactness, thus, "To devote oneself earnestly to one's duty to humanity, and, while respecting the spirits, to keep aloof from them, may be called wisdom."[E5]

Yet the effect of his desire to support whatever made for unity in the state and harmony in the home was that he went as far as he could in observing the rites and ceremonies of his time. One might even hazard the opinion, with Lin Yutang, that "Confucius would undoubtedly have been a High Churchman," could he have been a Christian.[D6] Perhaps his interest in the stabilizing moral effect of the old inherited rituals was strengthened by his own aesthetic satisfaction in them. At any rate, at the village exorcisms he put on court dress and stood on the east steps. He took seriously the ceremonial bath before religious worship. When one of his disciples suggested doing away with the sheep offering at the new moon, he disagreed, saying, "Tzu, you love the sheep; I love the ceremony!"[14] On going into the Great Temple he asked about everything. This once brought from a bystander the criticism that he knew shockingly little about the rites, but when he heard this, he said that asking about everything was part of the rite. In offering sacrifices to ancestors, he behaved as though they were physically present, and this was also his attitude toward the other spirits to whom sacrifices were made. He felt it his duty to participate in the sacrifice actively, saying, "For me, to take no part in the sacrifice is the same as not sacrificing."[K6] Asked the meaning of the Grand Sacrifice to the Imperial Ancestors, he said, "I do not know. He who knew its meaning would find it as easy to govern the Empire as to look upon this"—pointing to his palm.[M15]

His endorsement of ancestor worship seems to have been unreserved. In a quotation from the Doctrine of the Mean, given on an earlier page, we were assured that he judged the Emperor Wu and his brother, the Duke of Zhou, to be eminently pious men, because they repaired and put in order the ancestral temple each spring and autumn, carefully arranging the sacrificial vessels, the regalia, and the heirlooms of the family and presenting appropriate sacrifices at the same time. He is said to have thought that the great

emperors of the past were fortunate indeed; after their deaths, their descendants continued to sacrifice to them for many generations.

What, in view of all this, was Confucius' own philosophy of religion? Was he teasing his disciples when, while he was seriously ill and Zu-yu asked to be allowed to say prayers for him, he parried with, "Are such available?" "Yes," said Zu-yu; and the Manual of Prayers says, 'Pray to the spirits above and to those here below!'" Thereupon, Confucius said, "My praying has been going on a long while."[F4] The exact meaning of this remark is difficult to determine, of course, and so we must turn elsewhere for further evidence.

Doing the Will of Heaven

The clue to his own belief is contained in the conviction that when one practices the moral law one does the will of Heaven. The writer of the Doctrine of the Mean (reputed, but probably apocryphally, to be Confucius' grandson) says that Confucius made it evident that the truths handed down from the ancient Emperors Yao and Shun "harmonize with the divine order which governs the revolutions of the seasons in the Heaven above and . . . fit in with the moral design which is to be seen in physical nature upon the Earth below."[J6] This seems to be a pretty accurate statement of Confucius' real, though perhaps never expressed, intent. One can hardly call such an attitude supernaturalistic or monotheistic. It is vaguely mystical, and at the same time aloof from the concerns of popular religion. An inquirer once asked, "Why do people say it is better to be on good terms with the kitchen god than with the god of the southwestern corner of the house?" Whereupon Confucius replied sharply, "Nonsense; if you have committed sins against Heaven, you haven't got a god to pray to."[B7]

The basic fact is that, for himself, he felt that he had the backing of Heaven. He must indeed be ranged with the other religious leaders whom we have studied. He had a prophetic consciousness all his own. Once, in the city of Kuang, he was surrounded by a threatening crowd, and his disciples feared for his life; but he said, "Since King Wen [the founder of the Zhou feudal order] died, is not the tradition of King Wen in my keeping or possession? If it be the will of Heaven that this moral tradition should be lost, posterity shall never again share in the knowledge of this tradition. But if it be the will of Heaven that this tradition shall not be lost, what can the people of K'uang do to me?"B8 (There is a play on words here which may be suggested by a similar pun in English: "The Great One (*Wen*) is dead, but is not the One (*Wen*) Way in my keeping?") We have heard him on another occasion exclaiming "Heaven begat the power [De] that is in me. What have I to fear from such a one as Huan T'uei?" There were thus moments when he felt clearly that his message to his times was one that carried eternal significance, because it had its origin in the moral order of the world. His teaching seemed to him to be firmly grounded in the ultimate nature of things. It was a conviction to which we cannot justly deny the adjective "religious."

III. THE CONFUCIAN SCHOOL— ITS RIVALS AND CHAMPIONS

The Formation of the Confucian School

In the following famous passage, Mencius gives the tradition concerning the mourning of Confucius' disciples:

> When Confucius died, after three years had elapsed, his disciples collected their baggage, and prepared to return to their several homes. But on entering to take their leave of Tzu Kung, as they looked toward one another, they wailed, till they all lost their voices. After this they returned to their homes, but Tzu Kung went back, and built a house for himself on the altar-ground, where he lived alone three years, before he returned home.P

This was, presumably, the beginning of the Confucian school. Most of its members—said to have numbered seventy in all—scattered and offered their services to the feudal lords. "The important ones," says Si-ma Qian, "became teachers and ministers (of the feudal lords). The lesser ones became friends and teachers of the officials or went into retirement and were no longer seen."E6 Some started schools devoted to spreading the teachings of the master. Many helped during the next generation to gather the material that

was ultimately fashioned into the *Analects*. Gradually, during a period of three or four centuries, the Confucian school produced the *Great Learning*, the *Doctrine of the Mean*, the *Book of Filial Piety* (the *Xiao Jing*, destined to become a great favorite but not to be listed in the canon of the Four Books), the present *Book of Rites*, and the commentaries on the *Book of Changes* and the *Annals of Spring and Autumn*. Some other writings which have not survived, came from their hands. Among the leaders of the school in the second generation was Zi-si, the scholarly grandson of Confucius, who, like his grandfather, devoted himself to teaching.

The spread of Confucian thought was impeded, however, by two factors: the final decay of the Zhou feudal system during the Warring States Period (403–221 B.C.E.), and the rise in this period of the many different schools of thought that proposed moral and political solutions for the perplexities of the times. Only the princes descended from the old feudal families and the usurpers who wished to keep their positions by a prolongation of the feudal order listened readily to the Confucian scholars. But though many of the feudal princes would have liked to see Confucianism make headway, they thought it had no chance. The world was changing. And furthermore, in the community at large there was widespread scorn of the highbrow *ru jiao* (*ju chiao*), the "scholar—or literatus—school," and its advocates.

We can understand this better if we look briefly now at some of the rival schools of thought.

Rival Views: (1) The Daoists

The compilers of the *Dao De Jing* were not gentle toward the Confucians. The scorn they felt toward all advocates of social discipline or managed economy was directed especially at the Confucians (although Mohists and Legalists were just as abhorrent to them). Consider the implications of the following verses:

> *The man of superior virtue never acts,*
> *Nor ever (does so) with an ulterior motive.*
> *The man of inferior virtue acts,*
> *And (does so) with an ulterior motive . . .*
> *(When) the man of superior li acts and finds no*
> *response,*
> *He rolls up his sleeves to force it on others.*

Therefore:
After Tao is lost, then (arises the doctrine of) kindness,
After kindness is lost, then (arises the doctrine of)
*   justice.*
After justice is lost, then (arises the doctrine of) li.
Now li is the thinning out of loyalty and honesty
*   of heart.*
And the beginning of chaos.[B9]

Or of these, which seem directly aimed at Confucians:

On the decline of the great Tao,
*   The doctrines of "love" and "justice" arose.*
When knowledge and cleverness appeared,
*   Great hypocrisy followed in its wake.*

When the six relationships no longer lived at peace,
*   There was (praise of) "kind parents" and "filial sons."*
When the country fell into chaos and misrule,
*   There was (praise of) "loyal ministers."*[B10]

Though Zhuang-zi writes at greater length, and with equal scorn, he does not achieve a more rapierlike thrust than this, even when he says,

Of old the Yellow Emperor first interfered with the natural goodness of the heart of man, by means of charity and duty. In consequence, Yao and Shun . . . tortured the people's internal economy in order to conform to charity and duty. They exhausted the people's energies to live in accordance with the laws and statutes. Even then they did not succeed. . . . By and by, the Confucianists and the Motseanists [Mohists] arose; and then came confusion between joy and anger, fraud between the simple and the cunning, recrimination between the virtuous and the evil minded, slander between the honest and the liars, and the world order collapsed. . . .

Then, when dead men lay about pillowed on each other's corpses, when . . . criminals were seen everywhere, then the Confucianists and the Motseanists bustled about and rolled up their sleeves in the midst of gyves and fetters! Alas, they know not shame, nor what it is to blush![B11]

But sometimes Zhuang-zi preferred to laugh at Confucius by making him say Daoist things, as in this delicious bit of mockery:

Yen Huei spoke to Chungni (Confucius), "I am getting on."

"How so?" asked the latter.

"I have got rid of charity and duty," replied the former.

"Very good," replied Chungni, "but not quite perfect."

Another day, Yen Huei met Chungni and said, "I am getting on."

"How so?"

"I can forget myself while sitting," replied Yen Huei.

"What do you mean by that?" said Chungni, changing his countenance.

"I have freed myself from my body," answered Yen Huei. "I have discarded my reasoning powers. And by thus getting rid of my body and mind, I have become One with the Infinite. This is what I mean by forgetting myself while sitting."

"If you have become One," said Chungni, "there can be no room for bias. If you have lost yourself, there can be no more hindrance. Perhaps you are really a wise one. I trust to be allowed to follow in your steps."[B12]

Rival Views: (2) The Mohists

Another sort of rivalry was expressed by the philosopher Mo-zi (Mo Tzu) or Mo Di (Mo Ti), *ca.* 468–390 B.C.E. He was an earnest, humane sort of man who thought that the government should operate strictly under religious sanctions, always insist on simplicity and thrift everywhere, and do away with all Zhou institutions, in order to build up a community of workers generally alike in station and filled with homely good will and kindness toward each other and all humankind.

Even though his school of thought died out and his name was for two thousand years known only to Chinese scholars, Mo-zi was an important figure in his time and remains so in any history of Chinese philosophy and religion. He lived at the height of the dislocations of the Warring States Period, for he was born not long after the death of Confucius, probably in Lu. He seems to have spent his early life under Confucian influence and for a short time became an official in Song and then an envoy from Song to Wei. He broke away from Confucianism and adopted a less formal, more broadly democratic attitude, perhaps as a result of living in Song, where the Zhou culture was apparently regarded by the inhabitants as an oppressive system.

Mo-zi was motivated by two major aims. The first was to unite all of his fellow human beings in a working community altruistically devoted to the common good, and the second was to have all persons do the will of Heaven and the spirits, Heaven being conceived as the Sovereign on High (Shang Di), from whom a universal love or benevolence is flowing out to all creatures.

In pursuing the first aim, Mo-zi argued for universal love on grounds of hardheaded self-interest.

> Mutual attacks among states, mutual usurpation among houses, mutual injuries among individuals; the lack of grace and loyalty between ruler and ruled, the lack of affection and filial piety between father and son, the lack of harmony between elder and younger brothers—these are the major calamities in the world.
>
> But whence did these calamities arise? . . .
>
> They arise out of want of mutual love. At present feudal lords have learned only to love their own states and not those of others. Therefore they do not scruple about attacking other states. The heads of houses have learned only to love their own houses and not those of others. Therefore they do not scruple about usurping other houses. And individuals have learned only to love themselves and not others. Therefore they do not scruple about injuring others. . . . Therefore all the calamities, strifes, complaints, and hatred in the world have arisen out of want of mutual love. . . .
>
> How can we have the condition altered?
>
> It is to be altered by the way of universal love and mutual aid.
>
> But what is the way of universal love and mutual aid?
>
> It is to regard the states of others as one's own, the houses of others as one's own, the persons of others as one's self. When feudal lords love one another there will be no more war; when heads of houses love one another there will be no more mutual usurpation; when individuals love one another there will be no more mutual injury. When ruler and ruled love each other they will be gracious and loyal; when father and son love each other they will be affectionate and filial; when elder and younger brothers love each other they will be harmonious. When all the people in the world love one another, then the strong will not overpower the weak, the many will not oppress the few, the wealthy will not mock the poor, the honored will not disdain the humble, and the cunning will not deceive the simple. And it is all due to mutual love that calamities, strifes, complaints, and hatred are prevented from arising. Therefore the benevolent exalt it.[Q1]

Lest anyone should think that this is all impractical idealism, Mo-zi asserts, "If it were not useful then even I would disapprove of it. But how can there be anything that is good but not useful?"[Q2]

The essence of his thesis is that the principle of universal love and mutual aid "pays off," as we say today. "Whoever loves others is loved by others; whoever benefits others is benefited by others; whoever hates others is hated by others; whoever injures others is injured by others."[Q3] Love pays all around, but hate never works. Unfortunately, "the gentlemen of the world" fail to see that this is so.

Within the state there should be no waste of wealth nor of the time of the laborers that is equivalent to wealth. Time-consuming and expensive rituals, ceremonies with long passages of music, and the like were to be pared down to a minimum. It was not that they were evil in themselves, but they took too much time and were useless in promoting the increase of wealth and population. He condemned for like reasons the economic waste of the funerals so beloved of the Confucians. Funerals and mourning periods should be simplified and shortened, he insisted. All pious and cultural embroideries on life should be minimized until the common welfare was better served. Even recreation was out of the question.

This reasoning brought down on Mo-zi the wrath of Confucians and Daoists alike. The latter found him too interfering; the former said he sacrificed culture and the amenities that make life pleasant for bare economic benefit. In words of condemnation that were to carry great weight in the future and help keep the tide running against Mo-zi, the Confucian scholar Mencius said,

> The words of Yang Chu and Mo Ti [Mo-zi] fill the empire. If you listen to people's discourses throughout it, you will find that they have adopted the views of the one or the other. Now, Yang's

principle is—"Each for himself"—which does not acknowledge the claims of the sovereign. Mo's principle is—"To love all equally"—which does not acknowledge the peculiar affection due to a father. To acknowledge neither king nor father is to be in the state of a beast.[Q4]

But Mo-zi, who never lived to hear but actually anticipated these criticisms, found justification for his way of life in the sanctions of Heaven. He was sure of two things; first, that Heaven *wanted* all people to love each other equally, and second, that this belief had a high utility. It is a great incentive to universal love if people just believe that Heaven is the source and sanction of it. He severely condemned his contemporaries for skepticism with regard to the spirit worship that the ancient sage kings of the Xia dynasty practiced, and he taught with religious fervor that heaven above and earth below are spheres in which a universal love is operating.

> I know Heaven loves men dearly.... Heaven ordered the sun, the moon, and the stars ... the four seasons ... sent down snow, frost, rain, and dew ... established the hills and rivers, ravines and valleys ... appointed dukes and lords to reward the virtuous and punish the wicked.... This has been taking place from antiquity to the present.... Heaven loves the whole world universally. Everything is prepared for the good of man.[Q5]

> Now, what does Heaven desire and what does it abominate? Heaven desires righteousness and abominates unrighteousness.... For, with righteousness the world lives and without it the world dies; with it the world becomes rich and without it the world becomes poor; with it the world becomes orderly and without it the world becomes chaotic. And Heaven likes to have the world live and dislikes to have it die, likes to have it rich and dislikes to have it poor, and likes to have it orderly and dislikes to have it disorderly. Therefore we know Heaven desires righteousness and abominates unrighteousness.[Q6]

Mo-zi was very well aware, it seems, that "the gentlemen of the world" would reject his proposals as impractical and revolutionary. Hence it is touching to hear him say,

> The gentlemen of the world would say: "So far so good. It is of course very excellent when love becomes universal. But it is only a difficult and distant ideal." ... This is simply because the gentlemen of the world do not recognize what is to the benefit of the world, or understand what is its calamity.[Q7]

Rival Views: (3) The Legalists (*Fa-jia*)

Of greater force at the time than Mo-zi's attack upon the Confucians was the opposition of the so-called School of Law (*fa-jia*). This loosely associated group was composed of thinkers of a wide variety of views who agreed on one thing—that the disjointed and easy-going feudal system must give place to a social order held together by a tough, all-embracing law in all the states. The Confucian ideal of government by moral example and polite ideal behavior seemed impracticable to these hardheaded realists. Many of them laid down rules that startlingly anticipate present-day fascist totalitarianism. Others took a position closely resembling Machiavelli's; the ruler should, they said, make and unmake laws and alliances according to expediency and immediate advantage, or according to the changing drift of the Dao! Above all, because human beings are creatures to be ruled for their own good by playing upon their desire for material rewards and their fear of suffering and punishment, the laws must be made clear and strong, so that people will know what will bring rewards and what will bring punishment. From the standpoint of the ruler, humans taken in the mass are like a flock of geese or a herd of deer—they need the discipline of strong laws to make them into one homogeneous whole, obedient to the ruler in peace and war.

The Legalists were powerful in the councils of the various states during the Warring States Period (from 403 to 221 B.C.E.) and left a permanent impression on Chinese political and ethical theory. One of their earliest representatives was the ultrarealistic Shang Yang (Lord Shang), who served for some time as minister in the far western state of Qin, but finally became involved in a bloody intrigue that led to his falling in battle and his body being crushed by chariots (338 B.C.E.). He advised rulers to confine their people to two activities—farming and fighting.

That through which the country is important and that through which the ruler is honored is force. . . . Bring about a condition where people find it bitter not to till and where they find it dangerous not to fight.[G2]

Among the Legalists he was held to be the leader of those who emphasized strict administration of the law (*fa*). Another group, headed by Shen Dao, a contemporary of Mencius, emphasized princely authority, or *shi* (*shih*), alleging, "The reason why . . . subjects do not dare to deceive their ruler, is not because they love him, but because they fear his awe-inspiring power (*shi*)."[E7] A third group emphasized *shu*, or statecraft, in the handling of people and affairs. Their leader was Han Fei.

Han Fei (d. 233 B.C.E.), like Shang Yang, left his native state and went to the state of Qin. Tradition says that he did this to persuade the duke of Qin not to invade Han, his native state. He had already written his book, the *Han-fei-zi* (*Han-fei-tzu*), and the duke found it to his liking. This same duke, as the totalitarian Emperor Shi Huang Di, would later conquer the various states, including Han, and unify China. We see in Han Fei's essays that along the way he had acquired a deep admiration for the *Dao De Jing*. He studied, too, under the Confucian scholar Xun-zi. These influences appear in his writings and give them a richness and depth not found in other Legalist treatises. Unfortunately, Han Fei fell a victim to intrigue, and while in prison he was either poisoned or, as one story has it, committed suicide on the secret advice of his jealous former friend Li Si.

Han Fei believed that everyone is naturally selfish and materialistic. One's religion, obedience to the ruler, relations to parents, spouse, and children, and dealings with others are all permeated by a desire for advantage. That people love each other Han Fei did not deny, but such love, he maintained, was secondary to the desire for advantage.

There is nothing like the warm feelings between sons and fathers; and anyone who wants to act on the basis of public morality and issue prohibitions to those under his jurisdiction must needs take into account the intimacy of the flesh-and-blood relation. But there is something more [than love] in the relationship of fathers and mothers with their sons. If a son is born, then they congratulate each other. If a daughter is born they (may) kill it. Both these have come out of the mother's womb, and when it is a boy, congratulations, when it is a girl, death! The parents are thinking of convenience later on. They calculate on long-term profit. Thus it is that even fathers and mothers in their relation to their children have calculating minds and treat them accordingly.[G3]

He makes a better case of his thesis when he turns to the farm.

When a man sells his services as a farm hand, the master will give him good food at the expense of his own family, and pay him money and cloth. This is not because he loves the farm hand, but he says: "In this way, his ploughing of the ground will go deeper and his sowing of seeds be more active." The farm hand, on the other hand, exerts his strength and works busily at tilling and weeding. He exerts all his skill cultivating the fields. This is not because he loves his master, but he says: "In this way I shall have good soup, and money and cloth will come easily." Thus he expends his strength as if between them there were a bond of love such as that of father and son. Yet their hearts are centered on utility, and they both harbor the idea of serving themselves.[E8]

Han Fei was impressed by certain lessons he had learned from a study of the *Dao De Jing*. People are as they are because of the Dao. The ruler should emulate the Dao and not be too active nor too deeply involved in arranging every matter himself.

Be too great to be measured, too profound to be surveyed. . . . Hence the saying, "The ruler must not reveal his wants, for if he reveals his

"An appeal to humaneness (ren) alone does not enable a father to control unruly children; still less can it enable a ruler to govern a mass of people to whom he is bound by no ties of kinship. Force can always secure obedience; an appeal to morality, very seldom."

—Han Fei Tzu, Ch. 49

wants, the ministers will polish their manners accordingly. . . . If the likes and dislikes of the ruler be concealed, the true hearts of the ministers will be revealed." . . . Accordingly the ruler, wise though he may be, should not bother but let everything find its proper place.[G4]

Han Fei warns his prince that statecraft and wu-wei have a close connection. He draws a clear and deadly picture of the perils that surround a prince if he fails to be properly aloof in accordance with the Dao.

> Ministers, in relation to the ruler, have no tie of kinship, but serve him solely because constrained by the force of circumstances. Therefore those who minister to a ruler always watch the mental condition of their master without stopping even for a moment; whereas the lord of men remains idle and arrogant over them. . . .
>
> If the lord of men has much confidence in his son, then wicked ministers will utilize his son to accomplish their selfish purposes. . . . If the lord of men has much confidence in his wife, then wicked ministers will utilize her. . . .
>
> The physician sucks patients' cuts and holds their blood in his mouth, not because he is intimate with them like a blood relation, but because he expects profit from them. Likewise, when the cartwright finishes making carriages, he wants people to be rich and noble; when the carpenter finishes making coffins, he wants people to die early. Not that the cartwright is benevolent and the carpenter is cruel, but that unless people are noble, the carriages will not sell, and unless people die, the coffins will not be bought. Thus the carpenter's motive is not hatred for anybody, but his profits which are due to people's death. For the same reason, when the clique of the queen, the princess, the concubine, or the crown prince is formed, they want the ruler to die early; for, unless the ruler die, their positions will not be powerful. Their motive is not hatred for the ruler, but their profits are dependent on the ruler's death.

The hard, realist conclusion is then drawn,

> Therefore the lord of men must specially mind those who will profit by his death.[G5]

It was these thinkers of the School of Law who, as we have previously noted, prepared the ground for the ruthless and autocratic Shi Huang Di, "the First Emperor." But we have run a little ahead of our story. Han Fei and his associates (but not Lord Shang) came after Mencius and Xun-zi, the great Confucian champions, for they came at the end of the two-century movement that culminated in the political triumph of their conceptions. Meanwhile, the Confucians had been struggling without much success for influence and power. Fortunately, for their long-term prospects, a series of brilliant variations on the Confucian theme appeared from the pens of Mencius and Xun-zi, and Confucianism took on added significance.

Mencius: The "Orthodox" Champion

We turn first to the celebrated scholar whom Confucians many centuries later (in the time of Zhu Xi) regarded as having come closest to Confucius' true meaning (see p. 313). Born about one hundred years after the death of Confucius, Mencius (whose Latinized name was derived from *Meng-zi*, "Scholar Meng") was the greatest writer of the Confucian school. He magnified and gave studied emphasis to the master's belief in the innate goodness of individual persons and the adequacy of the feudal system to develop and maintain that goodness. Mencius, whose personal name was Meng Ke (Meng K'o), was a native of Cou (Ts'ou), a small state near Lu, and early came under Confucian influence. The way in which his love of learning was aroused is told in a delightful tradition that caused later Chinese to regard his mother as an ideal parent. According to this apocryphal tale, his father died young, and his mother lived alone with her small son near a cemetery. After a while she began to worry, because she noticed that he was playing constantly at the etiquette of attending funerals, so she moved with him to a house near a marketplace, whereupon the boy, influenced again by his environment, began to play at buying and selling. She liked this so little that she made haste to take a house near a school, in the expectation—which was fulfilled—that he would pattern his behavior after the pupils and teachers whom he observed. (This story, incidentally, neatly illustrates Mencius' teaching that surroundings so greatly influence human beings that all they need is the right kind.)

In time, Mencius became a scholar in his own right, in a school that was, it is likely, conducted by disciples of Zu Si (Tsu Ssu), Confucius' grandson. Later, he sought office under the Duke of Qi, but the duke proving beyond "reform" (in the Confucian sense, of course), he departed, and like his master, wandered from state to state, exhorting rulers to follow the Confucian way, but always in vain. So he found it expedient to retire to Cou, his native place, to spend the rest of his days—until his death in 289 B.C.E. at the age of eighty-one—teaching and writing in the graceful if somewhat academic style that won favor for the doctrines of Confucius among the intelligentsia of the time.

The mellow flavor and genial atmosphere of Mencius' writings are evident in almost any quotation from him. He believed wholeheartedly in the innate goodness of human nature.

> If men become evil, that is not the fault of their original endowment. The sense of mercy is found in all men; the sense of shame is found in all men; the sense of respect is found in all men; the sense of right and wrong is found in all men. The sense of mercy is what we call benevolence or charity. The sense of shame is what we call righteousness. The sense of respect is what we call propriety. The sense of right and wrong is what we call wisdom, or moral consciousness. Charity, righteousness, propriety and moral consciousness are not something that is drilled into us; we have got them originally with us.[D7]

All human beings possess these fundamental qualities as "tender shoots" or "seeds"[G6] within them, ready to grow. Sometimes they ripen into the fullness of the virtue that is seen in the moral nature of a sage. No person is born without them. Often quoted by the Chinese themselves is the following argument:

> All men have the sense of compassion for others.... What I mean by all men having a sense of compassion is that if, for instance, a child is suddenly seen to be on the point of falling into a well, everybody without exception will have a sense of distress. It is not by reason of any close intimacy with the parents of the child, nor by reason of a desire for the praise of neighbors and friends, nor by reason of disliking to be known as the kind of man (who is not moved by compassion). From this point of view we observe that it is inhuman to have no sense of modesty and the need for yielding place to a better man, inhuman not to distinguish right and wrong.[G7]

And yet, all individuals, though morally equal in the sense that they are all alike essentially good, or good at heart, are not equal in moral achievement. Some use their minds; others do not. This creates distinctions among them that alter their status in a properly constituted society.

> There is a saying, "Some labor with their minds, and some labor with their strength. Those who labor with their minds govern others; those who labor with their strength are governed by others. Those who are governed by others support them; those who govern others are supported by others." This is a principle universally recognized.[16]

This fact is so puzzling to one of Mencius' disciples that he asks, "All are equally men, but some are great men, and some are little men—how is this?" Mencius replies, "Those who follow that part of themselves which is great are great men; those who follow that part which is little are little men."[17]

But why are not more great individuals in evidence? Mencius would seem to suggest that environment and circumstances have a great deal to do with the extent to which different individuals fulfill their natural powers.

> In good years the children of the people are most of them good, while in bad years the most of them abandon themselves to evil. It is not owing to their natural powers conferred by heaven that they are thus different. The abandonment is owing to the circumstances through which they allow their minds to be ensnared and drowned in evil.[18]

> **"The tendency of man's nature to good is like the tendency of water to flow downwards. There are none but have this tendency to good, just as all water flows downwards."[15]**
>
> —Mencius

The best environment and the most encouraging circumstances for the flowering out of essential human goodness are found under a paternalistic feudal system, provided the latter is administered for the benefit not of the aristocrats, but of the people. It is recorded that when Mencius went to see King Xuan (Hsüan) of Chi (Ch'i), the king, who had ambitions to become the emperor of China, asked what virtues a man must display to gain imperial sway. Mencius answered, "The love and protection of the people."

> The king asked again, "Is such a one as I competent to love and protect the people?" Mencius said, "Yes. . . .
>
> "Treat with the reverence due to age the elders in your own family, so that the elders in the families of others shall be similarly treated; treat with the kindness due to youth the young in your family, so that the young in the families of others shall be similarly treated—do this, and the empire may be made to go round in your palm. . . .
>
> "Now, if your Majesty will institute a government whose action shall be all benevolent, this will cause all the officers in the empire to wish to stand in your Majesty's court, and the farmers all to wish to plough in your Majesty's fields, and the merchants, both travelling and stationary, all to wish to store their goods in your Majesty's marketplace."[19]

It may thus be seen that though Mencius is conservative as far as the form of his ideal society is concerned—it is the old feudal system—yet he makes a strong point of it that

> the people are the most important element in the state. . . . Therefore to gain the peasantry is the way to become Emperor.[E9]

He hit hard at the greedy and power-hungry councilors who made common cause with Shang Yang and later Legalists.

> Those who nowadays serve their sovereigns say, "We can for our sovereign enlarge the limits of the cultivated ground, and fill his treasuries and arsenals." Such persons are nowadays called "Good ministers," but anciently they were called "Robbers of the people."[110]

Mencius realized full well from studying his times that war destroyed the possibility of attaining his ideals of government, so he constantly inveighed against it. War makers also are "robbers of the people." Furthermore, war not only harms the state but signifies Heaven's punishment for offenses against its dispensations. When a kingdom is badly governed, Heaven lets the strong triumph over the weak, until corruption is unbounded. Then the righteous, thoroughly aroused, unite in rebellion and, with Heaven's sanction, drive the hopelessly corrupt ruler from his throne.

This brings us to Mencius' religious views, a type of mysticism. He believed, as did Confucius, in a guiding will or appointment of Heaven. Heaven sees and hears, and "there is an appointment for everything."[111] Those who exercise their minds to the utmost and study their own natures know Heaven and Heaven's will. It is Heaven that creates the inner disposition.

> What belongs by his nature to the superior man cannot be increased by the largeness of his sphere of action, nor diminished by his dwelling in poverty and retirement—for this reason, that it is determinately apportioned to him by Heaven.[112]

To look with sincerity into this inner disposition is to know Heaven through it. In contradistinction to the Daoists, Mencius believed that the predispositions toward moral order are complete within us. So, as Chan Wing-tsit puts it, "instead of looking to nature in order to know ourselves, we look within ourselves in order to know nature."[R1] It is thus that we may fulfill our destiny as Heaven prepares it for us.

At this point Mencius made a suggestion that was to have great influence, over a thousand years later, on the Neo-Confucians. He believed that within each person there is a "vast-flowing vital energy"[G8]; he called it qi (ch'i), a sort of élan vital. Anyone who lives rightly removes the inner obstructions to the free flow of this force. It will not do to try to help its growth, he said. Qi is already present and charged with a great potential of force, and all it needs is to have the channels cleared for it by uprightness, and then it will flow. The spiritual person thus gains a power that projects influence far and wide.

> Such is the nature of this energy that it is immensely great and immensely strong, and if it

be nourished by uprightness and so sustain no injury, then it pervades the whole space between the heavens and the earth.[G9]

Later generations were to play down Mencius' confidence in the goodness of human nature, but his optimism, gentleness, love of wisdom, and pacifism were eventually to increase his influence among the literati, so that he ultimately took rank next to Confucius in Confucian eyes.

Xun-zi (Hsün Tzu): The "Heterodox" Champion

Born a little before the death of Mencius, Xun-zi (*ca.* 298–238 B.C.E.) had greater immediate influence. This was in part due to his many-sidedness. He came to some extent under the influence of the Daoists on the one hand and of the Legalists on the other. Like the latter, he exalted the functions and prerogatives of the state and was brutally realistic about the weaknesses of human nature.

Xun-zi, whose personal name was Xun Qing, was a native of Zhao, but much of his life was spent in Qi, where he was one of the "great officers" of the court and an active member of a group of scholars and teachers at the capital. He taught Han Fei and Li Si, who became leaders in Legalist circles. On being the victim of slander, he went to Chu, where he spent his declining years as a magistrate at Lan-ling.

In developing his philosophy, Xun-zi rejected the two cardinal principles of Mencius: that human nature is innately good, and that Heaven watches over earth with something of a personal concern. He held that "man is by nature bad; his goodness is only acquired training."[S1] Though people are capable, under proper conditions, of indefinite improvement, left to themselves they grow crooked like saplings that must be tied into position before they will grow straight. The restraints that force improvement on their unruly nature are the rules of propriety and the laws compelling respect for property and the personal rights of others. Education of the right kind helps subdue the bad in human nature and develop the good.

These views led Xun-zi to emphasize, even more than Confucius did, the importance of li, the ceremonies and rules of proper conduct that are the legacy left by the great sage kings to aftertimes. The state should undertake to enforce education in li upon disorderly humanity.

> The nature of man is evil.... Therefore to give rein to man's original nature, to follow man's feelings, inevitably results in strife and rapacity.... Crooked wood needs to undergo steaming and bending to conform to the carpenter's rule; then only is it straight. Blunt metal needs to undergo grinding and whetting; then only is it sharp. The original nature of man is evil, so he needs to undergo the instruction of teachers and laws, then only will he be upright.[S2]

Against the Mencian view that the rules of proper conduct arise from human nature, Xun-zi argued,

> The relation of the Sage to the rules of proper conduct (Li) and justice (Yi) and accumulated acquired training is the same as that of the potter and the clay: he brings the pottery into being [by pounding and molding the clay].[S3]

The sage kings knew that human nature is evil, corrupt, rebellious, and disorderly. Hence they set forth clearly the rules for corrective education. They were aware that,

> If a man is without a teacher or precepts, then if he is intelligent, he will certainly become a robber; if he is brave, he will certainly become a murderer; if he has ability, he will certainly cause disorder; if he is a dialectician, he will certainly go far from the truth. [But] if he has a teacher and precepts, then if he is intelligent, he will quickly become learned; if he is brave, he will quickly become awe-inspiring; if he has ability, he will quickly become perfect; if he is a dialectician, he will quickly be able to determine the truth or falsity of things.[S4]

In his attitude toward Heaven (Tian), Xun-zi leaned far over in the direction of the Daoists' impersonal, naturalistic Way (Dao). Heaven is not to be anthropomorphically viewed, for it is just our name for the law of compensation operating within cosmic events, and one cannot ever expect it to respond to prayer.

One ought not to grumble at Heaven that things happen according to its Way [Dao]. . . . When stars fall or the sacred tree groans, the people of the whole state are afraid. They ask, "Why is it?" I answer: There is no reason. This is due to a modification of Heaven and Earth, to the mutation of *Yin* and *Yang.* . . . If people pray for rain and get rain, why is that? I answer: There is no reason for it. If people do not pray for rain, it will nevertheless rain.[55]

Heaven will not abolish winter just because mankind does not like cold weather. Nor will Earth shrink because we object to long distance. . . .

As long as we practice thriftiness and enrich the sources of our wealth, Heaven is powerless to make us poor. Likewise, Heaven can hardly make us sick if we nourish ourselves well, take proper care, and exercise regularly. . . .

The way to do things is neither the way of Heaven nor that of Earth but that of Man.[T1]

All natural events, then, come to pass according to natural law. There are no supernatural agencies anywhere. So sure was Xun-zi of this that he took the radical step of denying the existence of spirits: neither the popular deities nor the demons nor even the ancestral spirits exist. Divination may have some uncertain bearing on the future, but when the knowing decide an important affair after divination, this is not because they think in this way they will get what they seek, but only to "gloss over the matter"!

Xun-zi was obliged in the light of these naturalistic views to reevaluate the funeral and sacrificial ceremonies inherited from the great sage kings. He took a down-to-earth view of the matter. Rites and ceremonies are good for people. Nothing supernatural occurs during them, but they have a valuable subjective effect in allowing the expression and catharsis of human feeling, while also introducing beauty into human life and cultivating the sense of propriety.

Hence I say: Sacrifice is because of the emotions produced by memories, ideas, thoughts, and longings; it is the extreme of

loyalty, faithfulness, love and reverence. Among superior men it is considered to be a human practice; among the common people it is considered to be serving the spirits.[57]

The aesthetic value of ceremony especially appealed to Xun-zi.

All rites, if for the service of the living, are to beautify joy; or if to send off the dead, they are to beautify sorrow; or if for sacrifice, they are to beautify reverence; or if they are military, they are to beautify majesty.[58]

On the whole, Xun-zi was unwilling to go beyond what was required to guide the living. In funerals, for example, the living properly desire to "send off" the dead as though they were still living and to beautify their departure. Therefore, the living perform the traditional rituals with thoroughness and care. The carriages and all of the other articles traditionally sent along with the dead are duly burned or buried, but

the horses are sent away and informed that they are to be buried. . . . The metal rein-ends, the reins, the horse-collars do not go into the grave. . . . Things for the dead are showy, but not useful.[59]

This may be called a strictly rational propriety, expressing and yet reining in the emotions, lest they lead to extravagance, an unreasoning waste. The emotions have their place, but they are not to be allowed too much scope. There should be balance here as elsewhere. Each age should judge for itself what is useful in its traditions.

The rules of proper conduct (Li) cut off that which is too long and stretch out that which is too short; they diminish that which is too much and increase that which is insufficient; they attain to the beauty of love and reverence, and they strengthen the excellence of character and right moral feeling. . . . They provide for weeping and sorrow, but do not go

> "The people think it is supernatural. He who thinks it is glossing over the matter is fortunate; he who thinks it is supernatural is unfortunate."[S6]
>
> —Xun-zi

so far as an undue degree of distress and self-injury. This is the middle path of the rites (Li). . . . Anything beyond this is evil.[510]

Xun-zi was no narrow Confucian. He found such values in the Daoist point of view that he was led to equate li with the Dao, the latter being in his conception the cosmological principle "whereby Heaven and Earth unite, whereby the sun and moon are bright, whereby the four seasons are ordered, whereby the stars move in their courses," and "whereby joy and anger keep their proper place."[511] He also showed the extent of Daoist influence upon him in holding that meditative reflection confirms the faith that the universe at large tends steadily toward perfection and in its impersonal way is on the side of the righteous.

The Triumph of Confucianism as the State Orthodoxy

The Legalists scored their greatest victory in the reign of Shi Huang Di, but with the fall of his dynasty their school gradually disintegrated. Only those Legalist doctrines that were taken up by the Confucians ultimately entered the accepted body of Chinese political thought, for China had not taken kindly to the arbitrariness of the regime of Shi Huang Di and his attempted complete reordering of their lives and thinking. During the first years of the Early Han dynasty, the nation breathed a sigh of relief and relaxed into a Daoist-oriented quietude, as though worn out by the late disturbances. The Early Han emperors encouraged this psychological reaction. Daoism met with their approval. The people turned from fighting to dreaming. The Daoist geomancers were able to attract widespread attention to their alchemy and experimentation with the pill of immortality. But the Confucians also were busy. Gradually they were repossessing themselves of copies—in the new script—of the books that Shi Huang Di had taken from them and burned. They had not liked the regimentation of life under Shi Huang Di, but they liked anarchistic drifting and disorganization less, so they appealed to the Han emperors to reinstitute order and proper procedure in official life.

Not, however, until the reign of the great Han Emperor Wu Di, to whom we have already referred, were their pleas heeded. It was probably in 136 B.C.E., in the fourth year of that reign, that Dong Zhong-shu (Tung Chung-shu), the Confucian scholar (179?–104 B.C.E.), presented his famous memorandum to the emperor. Knowing the emperor to be desirous of greater national unity, he reminded the monarch that general unification would not come as long as the teachers and philosophic schools of the day had such diverse standards. The people did not know what to cling to, and the government statutes were in a state of confusion. The only way out, said Dong Zhong-shu, was a return to the Six Disciplines of Confucius. All other standards should be "cut short" and not allowed to progress further. Only then could the government statutes be made consistent and the people know what to follow. He accompanied this firm and unequivocal proposal with the suggestion that the emperor found an imperial academy or a college for the training of officials in the uniform procedures that the Confucians had worked out on the basis of the best experience of the past. The emperor was impressed. He adopted Dong Zhong-shu's suggestions. The Confucians were put in charge of a government-sponsored system of education designed to train officials.

Thereupon Confucianism began a two-thousand-year reign as the predominant intellectual discipline used in the training of the governing class. It was not the Confucianism of earlier times that triumphed, however, but a syncretism. It was Confucianism (1) modified by a tendency to magnify Confucius into a more-than-human being, (2) infused with Legalist ideas as to the nature of the enlarged bureaucracy that was needed to cope with the problems of an empire grown so vast as to lie on the borders of India, stretch into central Asia, and penetrate Korea, (3) tempered with Mo-zi's conviction that a government that was to win and hold the common people must have behind it the sanctions of religion—the approval of Heaven above and the spirits below, and (4) extended to include the recognition of yin-yang ups and downs in history and the rhythms in nature, as Daoism saw them.

Confucian Scholasticism and Rationalism

From the intellectual standpoint, Confucianism reached the end of its formative period when the Later

Han dynasty (23–220 C.E.) began. In fact, it would be correct to say, with Y. L. Fung, that this was true even earlier, for "with the putting into practice of Tung Chung-shu's suggestion, the Period of the Philosophers came to an end, and that of the Study of the Classics commenced."E10 The shift was from formative thinking to textual criticism, systematization, and syncretism.

This appears in the writings of Dong Zhong-shu himself. Self-consciously more a scholar than an imperial counselor, he followed Xun-zi rather than Mencius and sought to absorb into Confucianism the truth elements, as he saw them, in Daoist yin-yang interactionism and in the Five Forces theories. His pure scholasticism may be seen in a sentence or two from his treatises.

> Heaven has Five Forces, first Wood, second Fire, third Soil, fourth Metal, fifth Water. . . .
>
> These Five Forces correspond to the actions of filial sons and loyal ministers. . . . Thus, as a son welcomes the completion of his years (of nurture), so Fire delights in Wood; and, as (the time comes when) the son buries his father, so (the time comes when) Water conquers Metal. Also the service of one's sovereign is like the reverent service Soil renders to Heaven. Thus we may well say that there are Force men, and that there are both Five Forces, each keeping its right turn, and Five-Force officials, each doing his utmost.G10

And so forth. This sort of scholasticism was to absorb the Confucians for centuries.

But the systematizers were not to have it all their own way. Realizing, perhaps, that scholasticism already had or would become "a matter of intellectual sport, a game of puzzles, and finally a superstition,"R2 Wang Chong (Wang Ch'ung), a left-wing rationalist of the Confucian school (*ca.* 27–100 C.E.), strove for a less theoretical and more empirical viewpoint. He attacked the superstition and supernaturalism he found in religion. He was a thoroughgoing rationalist and humanist, armed with all of the vigor and clarity of style characteristic of so many of the Chinese writers we have quoted. It would be too bad not to quote him. The following passages speak for themselves:

> The Scholars at the present day have a passion for believing that what their teachers say is (genuinely) old, and they regard the words of worthies and sages as all of the very essence of truth. In expounding and learning these words off by heart, they do not realize that there are any difficulties requiring explanation.G11

> The common idea is that the dead become ghosts, have knowledge, and can injure people. . . . (I maintain that) the dead do not become ghosts, have no consciousness, and cannot injure people. How do I prove my position? By means of other beings. Man is a being and other creatures also are beings. When they die, they do not become ghosts: why then should man alone when he dies be able to become a ghost?G12

> At the height of summer, thunder and lightning come with tremendous force, splitting trees, demolishing houses, and from time to time killing people. The common idea is that this splitting of trees and demolishing of houses is Heaven setting a dragon to work. And when the thunder and lightning rush on people and kill them, this is described as due to hidden faults; for example, people eating unclean things, and so Heaven in its anger striking them and killing them. The roar of the thunder is the voice of Heaven's anger, like men gasping with rage. . . . This is all nonsense.G13

Wang Chong tried also to reverse the tendency to convert the fallible man Confucius into some kind of infallible authority touched with the qualities of divinity. In his treatment of the sayings in the *Analects,* he examined the teachings of Confucius as casually and critically as though he were looking into the opinions of a person who had to establish his authority like anyone else—by winning the assent of the reason.

Confucianism and Buddhism

The coming of Buddhism to China put Confucianism to a severe test. Daoism felt far less antipathy to the new religion when it first appeared and was aroused to resistance mostly by jealousy. But orthodox Confucians remained stiff in their opposition. Buddhism seemed to them too otherworldly and nihilistic. They did not like the Buddhist emphasis upon rebirth-redeath and the devaluing of the present world implicit in the samsara doctrine of impermanence. Above all, they condemned the Buddhists, as they already had the Daoists, for diverting people from the service of society to self-salvation. Yet two factors operated to make their protests without much effect: the novelty and freshness of Buddhism, and the formal and lifeless character of their own scholasticism and of the official ritualism and ceremony practiced in the court and at the Confucian temples, which by this time had appeared. Moreover, when the Later Han dynasty had collapsed in the turmoil in which the Three Kingdoms (220–280 C.E.) rose up to divide China, for 350 years China was to suffer inroads by "barbarians" from the north and to know disunion and misery. Many brilliant minds, distracted by the chaos, were unable to embrace Buddhism, yet were equally repelled by Confucian traditionalism, formalism, and "ineptitude."

Confucian Mythology

Caught between the scoffing Daoists on the one hand and the Buddhists on the other hand, who were riding high on the success of the spectacular and glamorous Mahayana, the Confucians weakened. Except for a few stern Old Text diehards who would not yield, they began to add semi-Buddhist touches to their Confucian temples and warmed up their beliefs about Confucius with stories of miracles and signs in heaven and on earth. Original Confucianism had been singularly free from legend and miracle, but now that even the Daoists attributed miracles to Confucius, the Confucians insensibly veered from their orthodox course toward meeting the Buddhist and Daoist challenges. They adopted stories of the appearance of a unicorn before Confucius' birth, saying his mother even tied a ribbon on its horn. On the night of his birth, two dragons appeared, and the five planets drew near in the shapes of interested old men. Heavenly harmonies sounded, and a voice said, "Divine harmony strikes the ear, because Heaven has caused a saint to be born. His doctrine will be the law of the world."[U] Other stories, circulated perhaps by the Daoists before the Confucianists themselves believed them, told how when Confucius was dying a meteor descended and turned into an inscribed jade tablet, and how when Shi Huang Di ordered his soldiers to open Confucius' tomb, they found within it a written prophecy of this very event

and a prediction of the death of the First Emperor, which was later exactly fulfilled.

One should not, probably, lay all of this entirely on the influence of Daoism and Buddhism; it might have happened anyway.

"Three Religions" Syncretism

What could not have occurred, however, without the presence of rival faiths was the rise of scholars who attempted a syncretism of the San Jiao (San Chiao), "the Three Religions." On the Daoist side was Tan Qiao (T'an C'hiao), who held that the Dao is the central or underlying principle of all three religions. The Buddhists on their part proved not averse to this type of thinking, for they quoted favorably Li Shi-qian (Li Shih-chien), who said (ca. 540 C.E.) Buddhism was the sun, Daoism the moon, and Confucianism the five planets. Later on, a Buddhist monk founded a cult that had official sanction for a long time, which placed the images of Confucius, Lao-zi, and Buddha side by side on the altar. Among the Confucians was Wang Tong (Wang T'ung), who held that the Doctrine of the Mean or Middle Way is the common ground between the three religions. We have already seen in chapter 7 how Buddhism combined with Chinese thought, Daoism in particular, to produce such varieties of Buddhism as the Chan (or Zen) sects.

But Confucianism was nevertheless able to maintain its distinctive character. It had a steadying factor to keep it on a straight course—the curriculum of its school. As long as the imperial academy and the lesser schools drilled their students in the Analects and the Five Classics—particularly the Li Ji and the Chun Qiu—Confucianism was safe from the temptation to stray too far from its historic basis. Indeed, its hard, resistant core finally gave rise to a Confucian revival.

IV. NEO-CONFUCIANISM

An early sign that such a revival would eventually come about was the famous protest made by the scholar Han Yu (Han Yü) to the thirteenth emperor of the Tang (T'ang) dynasty, Xian Zong (Hsien Tsung), concerning the bone of the Buddha. Han Yu (767–824

C.E.) was a valiant champion of the Mencian point of view in Confucianism. His protest was made in 820 C.E., when the emperor made a great pageant of receiving from the Buddhist priests, marching to him in public procession, a bone that was reputed to be a relic of the Buddha. Han Yu addressed a vigorous memorial to the emperor, reminding him that the founder of the Tang dynasty had contemplated exterminating Buddhism because its founder was a foreigner who could not speak Chinese, wore outlandish clothes such as a barbarian would wear, and had no conception of the sacred ties that bind ruler and subject or father and son. At that time, he went on, Gao Zu (Kao Tsu) had unfortunately been prevented from carrying out his intention by his foolish ministers. But now, Han Yu begged, let the present emperor give the noxious, putrid bone to the public executioner that he might throw it in the water or burn it in a fire—and, if the Buddha became angered at such action, let the blame be upon him, Han Yu, as alone responsible! For these spirited words the audacious scholar was banished to an official post in the far south, where he languished in virtual exile.

The Confucian revival foreshadowed by Han Yu came two centuries later during a period of distressing social change. The Song (Sung) dynasty (960–1279 C.E.), which, after an interval of civil wars, succeeded the brilliant Tang dynasty, was perhaps equally great in cultural matters but was dogged by disastrous military and political failures. Whereas the Tangs had come to grips with and mastered the "barbarian" tribes that surrounded China and had extended the domain of their empire from Korea in the northeast to Afghanistan in the west, the Songs, made inept and weak by internal corruption, failed to prevent the resurgence of the border tribes. First the Kitans, then the Jins (Chins), and finally the Mongols, fiercer yet, poured across the Yellow River and down to the Chang. The Mongols eventually were able, under Kublai Khan, to wipe out the dynasty altogether by conquering the regions south of the Chang and even rolling on into Indochina and Burma.

It was natural that the Chinese should from the very beginning of these events react to conquest by withdrawing into themselves until their conquerors should once more be absorbed and made over by Chinese culture. In particular, there was a return to the

older Confucianism. Han Yu had been an early voice presaging this, but the true Neo-Confucian revival did not begin until it was evident that the Song dynasty was to fall on evil days. The two figures within the movement whom we shall consider, Zhu Xi (Chu Hsi) and Wang Yang-ming, are only the most celebrated of a large group of scholars expressing the related views. What the Neo-Confucians professed to do was get back to pure Confucianism, before there had been any manifest borrowing from Daoist and Buddhist sources.

Zhu Xi (Chu Hsi), the New Orthodoxy

Zhu Xi (1130–1200) was a scholar of the first rank, whose commentaries on the Confucian Classics were immediately recognized as the final words on the subject. In his distress at the invasions of the Jin tribes, he said such bitter things about the official appeasement policy that he incurred imperial displeasure. But his lectures at the White Deer Grotto drew distinguished audiences of scholars. Of his austere personal habits we learn from a Chinese biographer,

> Rising at dawn, he clothed himself decently and paid homage to his ancestors and to Confucius. Then he went to his study and attended to his daily work. Sitting or sleeping he held himself erect; working or resting he behaved according to the model of behavior prescribed by Confucius in his Classics. Everything in his home was permanently in good order, and in this way he lived from youth to old age.[V]

To Zhu Xi fell the lot of determining finally the question of Xun-zi's orthodoxy. He pronounced the earlier thinker a heretic for departing from Confucius' belief in the original goodness of human nature. This proved enough to set up Mencius, Xun-zi's rival, as the orthodox interpreter of Confucius' thought. But it was only one of Zhu Xi's marks upon Confucianism that he thus distinguished between the "sound" and "unsound" interpretations. His chief contribution to the Confucian school lay in his clarification of the orthodox attitude toward the themes appearing in Daoism and Buddhism. In other words, he led the Neo-Confucians in their attempt to discuss the philosophical concepts of the rival religions and to adapt what was sound in them.

The way in which Zhu Xi went about his task was to take key passages from the Confucian texts and use them as touchstones of truth and error. To cite one (the chief) instance, he selected the passage from the *Great Learning* in which appears the sentence, "To extend their knowledge to the utmost they [the ancients] investigated things." Zhu Xi interpreted this to mean that the ancients examined the world about them objectively, in order to increase their grasp of general truth. He concluded, in short, that the ancients thought nature, quite apart from human nature, embodied laws or principles independent of the human mind.

The Great Ultimate (Tai Ji)

In his objective examination of the cosmos, Zhu Xi, speaking for his fellow Confucians as well as for himself, was, he said, led to the view that all things are brought into being by the following two elements mentioned by Confucius and Mencius: vital (or physical) force (qi), and law or rational principle (li). The latter, in its cosmic operations, where it may be called the *Tai Ji* (*T'ai Chi*) or Great Ultimate, impels the vital force to generate movement and change within matter, and thereby the two energy-modes (yang and yin) and the five elements (fire, water, wood, metal, and earth) are produced. Every object in nature exhibits some aspect of the rational principle (li), or Great Ultimate, that works within it.

This also is true of human beings. What we call the "soul" or "nature" is the supreme regulative principle of the universe working in a person as mind or spirit. This law of being works toward good, so one's nature is fundamentally good, whatever evil habits one may display.

The rational principle and the vital force interact in mutual dependence.

There is no Reason independent of the vital force, and there is no vital force independent of Reason. . . .

The Great Ultimate is Reason, whereas activity and tranquility are the vital force. The two are mutually dependent and never separated. The Great may be compared to a man, the activity and tranquility may be compared to a horse. The horse carries the man and the man rides on the horse. As the horse comes and goes, so does the man.[R4]

Though the description so far might suggest it, this was not conceived to be a purely nonphysical process, for it results in the creation of matter. The Great Ultimate or rational principle "rides on" the activating or physical principle, qi, and when the pace is swift, the yang energy mode is generated; when the pace slows down, the yin mode is produced. Once brought into being, the yang and yin, by their eternal interaction and alternation of dominance over each other, give rise to the energy structures that are the five elements or the physical constituents of the "myriad things" of the material world.

Zhu Xi found in the concept of the Great Ultimate what he felt to be the truth element in Daoism, for the law or reason of any entity was its "right way to go," or Dao. But he did not regard his Tai Ji, as the Daoists did their Dao, as something "still and silent," nor did he think it operated to reduce all things ultimately to equality and indistinguishability. By its cooperation with the energy in matter it exhibits itself as a differentiating principle that may at any moment produce something new. At this point also, Zhu Xi disagreed with Buddhism. He could not conceive of reality as a void (something devoid of any assignable attributes), nor did he expect the universe to return again to the void. There is a central harmony, but it is not a static harmony; it is a dynamic harmony. The Great Ultimate never ceases to act, and therefore it is not to be identified with the Buddhist Ultimate within which the universe forms, flowers, deteriorates, and is finally swallowed up again in eternal nothingness. To use an American phrase, "Whatever goes around comes around."

Heaven (Tian)

Though he had gone pretty far toward rendering the older terminology no longer usable, Zhu Xi tried to make some concessions to the

> "With reference to the entire universe, there is in it one Great Ultimate. With reference to the myriad things, there is a Great Ultimate in each of them."[R3]
>
> —Zhu Xi

ancient conception of Heaven. He refused to be anthropomorphic and, indeed, spoke of Heaven in such abstract language that he encouraged the agnostic tendency in Confucianism; but because his Great Ultimate is a rational principle, he sensed behind the cosmos something like an ordering will. In a passage in which he summed up the opinion of the Classics, he wrote,

> These passages indicate that there is a man, *as it were,* in the heavens ruling all.[W]

In other respects he gave religion in its traditional forms little place. Worship of spirits and offerings to images even excited his contempt, and although he granted to ancestor worship the slight basis that is found in biological and social immortality, he denied that the souls of ancestors exist; ancestor worship has the appropriateness and value that are derived from gratitude to forebears piously felt and expressed.

Meditation

In his personal practice Zhu Xi found his spiritual and moral development best served by devoting a certain portion of each day to solitary meditation, something he called "silent sitting." It resembled the Buddhist dhyana or meditation. He wrote,

> Introspection is most effective when employed quietly. One should with eternal vigilance constantly examine himself. If he finds himself too talkative, he should quiet down. If he is careless, he should learn to be prudent. If he is too fresh and shallow, he should balance this with dignity and dependability.[T2]

But he denied that this "self-correction through introspection"[T3] was actually the Buddhist dhyana, or *chan ding (ch'an-ting)*.

> Silent-sitting is not the Buddhist type of *ch'an-ting* which requires the cessation of all processes of thinking. Mine is to help aim our mind so that it will not be distracted by conflicting streams of thought. When our mind is calm and undisturbed, concentration is a matter of course.[T4]

As a matter of fact, for Zhu Xi, meditation, as was natural in a Confucian, had more of a moral than a metaphysical or mystical bearing. Feeling that "centrality is the order of the universe and harmony is its unalterable law,"[X1] he wished to get himself into the equable state that enabled him to apprehend this order and harmony and to feel at one with the reason in it. When he succeeded in doing so, he found that "all people are brothers and sisters, and all things are my companions."[X2]

Because of his combination of many-sidedness with practicality, Zhu Xi became, as we have little difficulty in understanding, the almost infallible interpreter of Confucianism from his time on. He has been called the Thomas Aquinas of Confucianism.

Wang Yang-ming: The Power of Mind

Zhu Xi did not dominate the scene so completely that no other interpretations were countenanced. He perhaps carried the majority with him, but there were many Neo-Confucians, more under the spell of Buddhism and Daoism, who thought that the clue to the reason or governing principle in things is to be found not so much in the investigation of nature as within the mind or consciousness of human beings. They therefore gave chief emphasis to an examination of the mental content disclosed in introspection. The greatest name of this group is that of Wang Yang-ming (1473–1529), a scholar appearing two and a half centuries after Zhu Xi, when both the Song and the Yuan (Yüan), or Mongol, dynasties had passed into history and the Ming dynasty (1368–1644) had for more than one hundred years demonstrated, in spite of licentiousness and corruption, its staying power. For offending a corrupt eunuch who had acquired great power in the imperial court, Wang Yang-ming was exiled for a time to a distant province, but he was able to summon up sufficient interior resources to spend the time developing his philosophy. His reflections led him to say that objects are not independent of the mind, for the mind shapes them. This emphasis on the part mind plays in constituting objects as they are known in experience may have been due to an experiment Wang Yang-ming performed when he was twenty-one. It seems he took seriously Ju Xi's suggestion that to know the reason in things one must investigate to the utmost all sorts of external objects. He chose his father's bamboo grove for a test of this method. For three days and nights, it is said, he sat among the bamboos to see what they would teach him, and caught a bad cold without arriving at any satisfactory results. He concluded that objects do not put reason into the mind, but the reverse. In a modern interpreter's words,

> In the case of bamboo, for instance, . . . if one views it as a plant which is humble enough to be hollow inside, hardy enough to stay green the year round, plain enough to adorn itself with slender leaves instead of luxurious blossoms, and dignified enough to stand straight and erect, then one perceives a number of reasons in its worth as a garden companion.[T5]

Our own minds, then, are the source of reasonableness in things.

All this had for Wang Yang-ming important moral bearings. The reason in us is a moral reason and is not only intelligent but good. It is an inner light, an innate goodness. Knowledge of the good is not imparted to us from without but is inborn, and if the inborn knowledge is clouded over, then all that is necessary is to have the reflective surface of the mind polished by teaching and experience.

> The mind may be compared to a mirror. . . . When, after effort has been made to polish the mirror, it is bright, the power of reflecting has not been lost.[R5]
>
> The mind has the native ability to know. If one follows his (pure) mind, he naturally is able to know (what is morally good). When he sees his parents, he naturally knows what filial piety is; . . . when he sees a child fall into a well, he naturally knows what commiseration is. This is inborn knowledge of the good, without any necessity of going beyond the mind itself.[R6]

In a further point that Wang Yang-ming makes, we perceive resemblances to a central belief of Socrates. Knowledge of the good leads immediately to practice of the good. ("Knowledge," said Socrates, as we know, "*is* virtue.")

It is important, then, to keep the mirror of one's mind clear by eliminating the selfish desires that cloud it. This may be done only by practicing a "tranquil repose" resembling the meditative self-discipline of Chan (Zen) Buddhism, by which one may be purged of such desires.

After Wang Yang-ming, during the slow collapse of the Ming dynasty and the ascendancy (1644–1911) of the Manchus, Neo-Confucianism entered a long period of self-criticism and reappraisal. During this time, distinguished scholars debated the strengths and weaknesses of Zhu Xi and Wang Yang-ming and either championed one or the other of them or in rejection led a return to a purer, less eclectic Confucianism, that of Han times, based on close study of the Five Classics. Together they exhibited Confucianism in its true light as a highly evolved philosophy of religion with a complexity and competence comparable to those we have already examined elsewhere in the world.

V. THE STATE CULT OF CONFUCIUS

All of this time a state cult honoring the spirit of Confucius had been in existence. It had developed slowly. The reason for this tardiness of growth is not far to seek. Confucius was in his own time unsuccessful as a public figure. Mencius, like his master, also was unable to make a great mark in public affairs. For several hundred years after the master's death, no Confucian anywhere came to power long enough to make permanent changes in the official outlook on problems of government. But then, suddenly, when the ways and works of Shi Huang Di, the First Emperor, had been swept away and the Confucian Classics had been recovered, the Emperor Wu Di of the Han dynasty (who reigned 141–87 B.C.E.) took up Confucianism and made its teaching the policy of the state. For officialdom, this was a momentous

> "There has been no one who really has knowledge and yet fails to practice it. . . . As soon as one perceives a bad odor, one already hates it."[R7]
>
> —Wang Yang-ming

decision, for from this time on, even when Daoist or Buddhist emperors sat on the throne, Confucius was honored by the state as a great sage and was periodically advanced in official status.

The progressive elevation of Confucius to higher and higher official rank makes an interesting story. At first only the Kong family and perhaps Confucius' immediate disciples rendered to his spirit a regular worship. Later on, sacrifices were made at the grave of Confucius by politically minded sovereigns, anxious to conciliate local feelings. The first of these to do so was the Early Han Emperor Gao Zu. Though himself inclined toward Daoism, he sacrificed three victims—an ox, a sheep, and a pig—when in 195 B.C.E. he passed through Lu on a tour of the empire and stopped at the grave of Confucius. Thereafter, other emperors with an eye toward political effect stopped off at the sage's grave to render tribute. In the year 1 C.E., the Han Emperor Ping (P'ing) ordered the repair of the nearby temple of Confucius and elevated the sage to the rank of duke. By this time readings, prayers, and gifts of money and silk were added to the sacrifices made at the grave. The habit of bestowing posthumous titles grew. At intervals during succeeding centuries, various emperors bestowed upon Confucius honorific titles such as "the Venerable, the Accomplished Sage," "the Sage of Former Times," and the like. He acquired a long string of these titles. His descendants also were elevated to nobility and were made recipients of state honors.

Another step in the development of the state cult came in 630 C.E., when the Tang Emperor Tai Zong (T'ai Tsung) issued a decree obliging every prefecture of China to erect a state temple to Confucius in which regular sacrifices to him were ordered. The same emperor converted these temples into national halls of fame by placing tablets to distinguished scholars and literary men alongside that of Confucius, thus honoring both him and them. In the eighth century, and under the influence of Buddhism, a Tang emperor adopted and carried out the suggestion that images of Confucius be placed in the great hall of the state temples and pictures of his chief followers be painted on the walls.

The sacrifices offered to the spirit of Confucius became progressively more elaborate. The Tang emperors came with great pomp, in spring and autumn, to the state temple at the capital to add the dignity of their presence to the celebrations. It was customary that a bull, a pig, and a sheep be offered to Confucius' image, while dances and pantomimes were performed to stately music and prayers were solemnly presented. By the time of the Mongol rulers the ritual of the sacrifices became still more impressive. Incense was freely used, and much formal kowtowing took place before the image of Confucius and the various altars. Hundreds of bronze, wood, and porcelain vessels were required for the ceremonies, two kinds of wine were offered, and an ox, five sheep, and five pigs, as well as much food, were presented. It was the opinion of the time that the music and rites used in this worship of Confucius were those of an emperor, though the actual title of "Emperor" (Di) was withheld because it was not deemed consistent with the practices of antiquity, and particularly not in accordance with Confucius' teaching condemning the bestowal of this title on men of less than imperial rank. However, there were those who said it would not have been too much if Confucius had been regarded as equal to Heaven.

In 1530, a remarkable reform in the cult of Confucius was effected, and proved permanent. The Ming Emperor Jia Jing (Chia Ching), on the advice of a learned Confucian scholar, revoked the lengthy and cumbrous titles borne by Confucius and called him simply "Master Kong, the Perfectly Holy Teacher of Antiquity." The temples to Confucius were ordered restored to their historic simplicity, the ceremonies were revised in accordance with the practices of antiquity, and the images of Confucius were replaced with tablets in the antique style or with plain wood panels with written characters inscribed on them.

At the beginning of the present century, when the Manchus were vainly seeking to recover the good opinion of the Chinese, an edict was issued abolishing the old classical examination system in favor of more modern educational training. To make good whatever disrespect to the memory of Confucius was involved in this significant change, another edict was issued in 1906 making the sacrifices to Confucius equal with those offered to Heaven and Earth, but this signal honor to the great sage came too late to save the Manchus from the revolution, led by Sun Zhongshan (Sun Yat-sen), that brought into being the Republic.

After 1911, the cult of reverence for Confucius languished. With no emperor to participate in the worship of Heaven at the altar in Peking, the famous marble terraces fell into such neglect that sometimes grass grew in their crevices. Only the nearby Temple of Heaven was kept in order. Elsewhere, except for the temple at Confucius' birthplace, the state temples either fell into disuse, many of them even becoming dilapidated in their utter abandonment, or were put to secular uses.

VI. RELIGION IN CHINA IN THE MODERN PERIOD

In intermittent attempts after the Revolution of 1911 to recover itself, Confucianism had some bad moments. After the Republic had written into its constitution a grant of religious liberty for all, the attempt of the scholars who formed the Confucian Society to have Confucianism made the state religion failed. But the situation was not without some hopeful signs from the Confucian point of view. Sun Zhongshan (Sun Yat-sen), the leader of the revolution, preserved echoes of Confucian values in his plans for the Republic. He spoke of the "world as an all-people community," a Confucian phrase, and his "five powers" of government plan made a place for civil service examinations and a Confucian censorate to admonish government leadership. Although semiannual ceremonies and compulsory study of the Classics ended in 1928, Confucius' birthday, November 28, was chosen as the annual Teachers' Day.

Although the Guomindang (Kuomintang), or Nationalist Party, in forming for political action, committed itself to no particular religious views, its motto was nevertheless a reassertion of the eight Confucian virtues: loyalty, filial piety, benevolence, human heartedness, fidelity, just attitudes, harmony, and peace. And when in 1934 Jiang Jie-shi (Chiang Kai-shek), head of the Guomindang, inaugurated the New Life movement, it proved to have a distinctly Confucian coloring. (Even after he was baptized a Christian, he still saw China's problems through Confucian eyes.) The movement was announced as having "four binding principles": *Li*, or courtesy and good manners, *Yi*, or justice and uprightness, *Lian* (*Lien*), or integrity, and *Chi* (*Ch'ih*), or modesty and self-respect.

However, the New Life movement was never officially affiliated with Confucianism. It was meant principally to be a movement of moral regeneration, and it found the traditional ethical concepts apt. More indicative of national goals was the temple that the government erected in 1937 at Nanjing. This imposing structure was intended as a national shrine. In the highest place was the tablet of Confucius and just below it a marble bust of Sun Zhongshan, "the father of modern China." On surrounding pillars were portraits of great Western "sages": Newton, Pasteur, Lavoisier, Galileo, James Watt, Lord Kelvin, John Dalton, and Benjamin Franklin. The meaning seemed to be that the China of the future would make a synthesis of the old and the new, combining the best of its philosophy and ethics with the best of the science and culture of the West.

But Jiang Jie-shi's regime failed to realize its cultural and political objectives. It did not achieve the political democracy that its constitution called for; instead, the landlord-tenant system established two millennia earlier, during the Early Han dynasty, and the local political bossism that had its rootage in the warlord period persisted. Although the Japanese invasion during World War II brought a degree of cooperation (in resistance) between all groups, including the Communists, then well-established in the northwest, real unity was not achieved. Much of the extensive military aid provided by the United States was diverted to the enrichment of corrupt officials and actually found its way into Communist hands. In 1949, the Communist revolution swept rapidly through China, and with the collapse of his regime, Jiang Jie-shi and his entourage fled to Taiwan.

Mao Zedong (Mao Tse-tung)

Mao Zedong's basic purposes excluded religion and any otherworldly ("philosophically idealistic") notions. His aims as a communist were, in his own terms, "materialistic" and "democratically socialistic." His goal was a diffusion of goods and services throughout China, in the countryside as well as in the towns, so that every Chinese could share in every benefit: food, clothing, shelter, education, cultural activities, and medical services. He attacked all concentrations of goods, services, or power—except his own, which he considered essential to overall socialist success. When any industry, educational institution, hospital, or medical school developed a dominant elite or gained self-importance, he decentralized it by relocating its parts, its personnel, or the whole institution in the remoter parts of China.

The effect of all of this on local tradition was not always immediately perceptible, but sometimes it amounted to a complete overturning of religious behavior. For while the peasants could teach the elite an ancient folk wisdom, the latter had something to offer also through clearing away superstition.

Maoist Revision of Confucian History

The entire history of Chinese philosophy and religion underwent revision. Communist periodization of history and emphasis upon the class position of scholars had the immediate effect of degrading figures like Confucius. In the sequence from primitive communism to slavery, to feudalism, to capitalism, Confucius was seen as a member of a slave-owning class. His innovations in private education were approved as "progressive," but his teaching of *ren* (humaneness) was usually interpreted as having reference only to the slave-owning class. Even if it was conceded to include the slaves, it defused the class antagonism necessary for the emergence of the proletariat, "the people" (*min*). At the height of the Cultural Revolution, other political factors came into play: verbal attacks on policies labelled "Confucian" were little more than veiled criticism of Prime Minister Chou En-lai for moderating Maoist extremism.

Nevertheless, Confucius was not eclipsed, and favorable evaluations appeared in some contexts. Broadly speaking, Confucius was attacked when radical social change was advocated and invoked when stabilization and national pride were in the foreground.

As Kam Louie describes the process, the pendulum swings went something like this:

> The early fifties as a transitional period paid little attention to Confucius. Then there was an extraordinary initiative, "Let One Hundred Flowers Bloom" (encouraging people to openly share their real aspirations). This revealed Confucius as a force to be reckoned with, especially among older intellectuals. Next came the Great Leap Forward (radically disrupting economic life). Its slogan, "More modern, less ancient," again put Confucius under a cloud. When the ten years of turmoil known as the Cultural Revolution came to an end, Dung Xiao-ping's moderate leadership allowed more varied and sympathetic views of Chinese tradition to flourish again.[Y]

The assessment of other ancient philosophers has undergone similar fluctuations. A government-sponsored text issued in 1959 under the title *A Short History of Chinese Philosophy* gives us the flavor of some typical evaluations. The chief issue in the development of Chinese thought, this text says, is one between "the feudal, bourgeois, reactionary culture and the democratic, socialist revolutionary culture"; ideologically, this is the issue between "the idealist, metaphysical theory and the dialectical materialist theory." Mo-zi, for example, represented the interests of the rising class of freemen and pitted his materialistic theory against the idealism of the Confucians. Lao-zi was on the whole an idealist and mystic who considered the Dao a transcendent absolute, but he was progressive in two respects: in discussing natural laws (*de*) he accepted some elements of materialism, and in seeing an opposition of yin and yang he developed the rudiments of dialectics. In rejecting political activism, he reflected the feeling of the peasants and their naive attitude of nonresistance. Zhuang-zi was so much of an idealist and a mystic that he settled for relativism, pessimism, and "philistinism" (i.e., opposition to the true trend of historical forces). As for Mencius, in turning for knowledge of right and wrong from objective reality to an innate power to distinguish them, he used an idealist logic that savored sophistry. Xun-zi, on the other hand, was materialistic and atheistic and said that man should conquer and exploit nature by using his mind to give him power over the objective world. He was a true progressive, as was Han Fei of the Legalist school. Han Fei represented the interests of free people in stressing that human nature is selfish and society is a battleground of calculating minds. At long last, from the sixteenth century onward, there came the beginnings of enlightenment and a brilliant development of materialism and atheism that prepared the way for a culmination of the wisdom of the Chinese people in the philosophy of Mao Zedong, so reads the government-sponsored text.

Mao Zedong's influence on the ideology of China is comparable to Lenin's on Russia's. It will endure. His death, however, was followed by a shift in internal policy from stress on constant revolution to stabilization and industrial and economic development.

By 1983, there were conspicuous moves toward the preservation of China's philosophical and religious heritage. The ancestral home of Confucius at Qufu, destroyed during the Cultural Revolution, was rebuilt and the damaged statues were replaced. Even though such projects are undertaken with an eye toward tourism and the improvement of China's image abroad, there are other signs of reappraisal. Confucius' emphasis on courtesy and ethics is perceived to be in accord with the "Four Beauties" (language, heart, behavior, and environment). One reads between the lines that anxiety about the moral education of the young is involved. Confucius taught respect for authority, which is useful in combatting "spiritual pollution."

"Confucianism" Today

Who speaks for Confucius today? On the present Asian scene the descriptor "Confucian" has been attached to a variety of competing value systems.

One school of thought proposes an economic theory: The Confucian ethic was to Asia as Max Weber's "Protestant ethic" had been to the West. In 1979, Hermann Kahn suggested that Confucianism furnished a driving force to the economics of the nations of the Pacific rim: Japan, Korea, Taiwan, Hong Kong, and Singapore. He summed up the ethic as the promotion of individual and family sobriety, a high value on education, a desire for accomplishment in various skills, and seriousness about tasks, job, family, and obligations. Kahn conceded that the skills were particularly academic and cultural and that there was a downplaying of individual (selfish) interests in deference to hierarchy and complementarity.[Z] In 1984, a Japanese economist, Michio Morishima, took a similar line in his book *Why Japan Succeeded,* and in 1987, an international gathering of Confucian scholars

weighed the Kahn thesis against the view that Confucianism fettered China's efforts to modernize. More recently, the Japanese Ministry of Education launched a major comparative study project to explore nineteenth-century Japanese and Chinese entrepreneurs in the context of their own Confucian traditions.

Critics who are against attributing Asian business success to Confucianism point out that Confucius was clearly an elitist who disdained manual labor and who ranked merchants at the very bottom of the social order. They find it hard to imagine entrepreneurial flair, risk taking, and experimentation flowering in persons trained to follow the rules of propriety (li).

Nevertheless, "Confucian" has become a popular (though imprecise) term to describe whatever makes up the "Chineseness" of places like Hong Kong and Singapore. Virtues promoting social harmony, rather than entrepreneurial energy, are the focus of a set of five "Shared Values" officially ratified in Singapore in 1991 and labelled "Confucian":

1. nation before community and society before self

2. family as the basic unit of society

3. respect and community support for the individual

4. consensus instead of conflict

5. racial and religious harmony[AA]

Members of ethnic and religious minorities in Singapore complain that the "Shared Values" are an expression of cultural chauvinism on the part of the Chinese majority in the ruling People's Action Party.

Professor Edward Chen of Hong Kong University notes the need for making a clear distinction between orthodox philosophical Confucianism and the everyday use of the term to characterize the family ethic/work ethic culture of Singapore and Hong Kong. The latter serves the early stages of an export-led economy very well, stages during which autocratic entrepreneurs and a docile labor force are suitable. He sees the attribution of early stage commercial successes to "Confucian" values as a generalized endorsement of Chineseness—a way of saying "We can modernize without becoming Westernized." But Chen wonders whether either orthodox Confucian values or the everyday popular version will, in fact, meet the challenges of a maturing world economy which will put more emphasis upon creativity and innovation.[BB]

Recent events point toward the development of a more complex and flexible "modern Confucianism." Urging that it deserves to be recognized as more than "a social discipline and a work ethic" W. T. deBary asserts that Confucianism "is a form of liberal learning (in the classic sense of liberal as broadening and liberating and not simply in the modern political sense)."[CC] With the assistance of the Confucius Foundation in Beijing, two conferences of international scholars were convened (1995 and 1998) on the topic, "Confucianism and Human Rights."

GLOSSARY*

Terms shown in color are pinyin forms; Wade-Giles forms are in *italics* to the right of parenthetical pronunciations.

Da Xue (dä shwä) *Ta Hsüeh the Great Learning*, 3rd c. B.C.E. treatise for educating gentlemen, a chapter of the *Li Ji*

Dong Zhong-shu (dōōng jōōng-shōō) *Tung Chung-shu* Han dynasty scholastic; through Emperor Wu Di initiated 2,000 years of state Confucianism

fa-jia (fä-jeǔ) *fa-chia*, the School of Laws or models (*fa*), Legalism

Han Fei (hän-fä) *Han Fei*, 3rd c. B.C.E. Legalist, author of the *Han Fei-zi* textbook of statecraft (*shu*) used by Qin emperors

Han Yu (hän yē) *Han Yu*, precursor of Neo-Confucianism, in 820 C.E., he protested official veneration of Buddhist relics

Jiang Jie-shi (jē-äng jēä-shǐ) *Chiang Kai-shek,* headed the Guomindang government 1928–1949, founded the syncretist New Life movement

jun-zi (jīn-dzǔ) *chün-tzu,* (morally) superior man; before Confucius, a gentleman by birth

li (lē) *li,* propriety, correct moral and ceremonial order in society

li (lē) *li,* principles, together with *qi,* material force, they give expression to the Great Ultimate

Li Ji (lē jē) *Li Chi,* Confucian Classic: the *Book of Rites*

Lun Yu (lwēn ü) *Lun Yu,* the *Analects,* a collection of the sayings of Confucius

Mao Zedong (mäō dzē-dǔng) *Mao Tse-tung,* founder of the People's Republic of China; his Marxist materialism excluded traditional religion

Mo-zi (mō-dzǔ) *Mo Tzu (ca.* 468–390 B.C.E.) proletarian advocate of universal love and a heaven-sanctioned utilitarian society

qi (chē) *ch'i,* material force, breath, flowing vital energy

ren (rǔn) *jen,* humaneness, the virtue of benevolence

ru jiao (rōō jǐ-äu) *ju chiao,* the way of the literati or scholar gentlemen

San Jiao (sän jǐ-äu) *San Chiao,* Tang period "Three Religions" school; sought to combine Daoism, Confucianism, and Buddhism

Shang Yang (shäng yäng) *Shang Yang,* minister of Qin, stressed totalitarian administration of law (*fa*)

shi (shǐr) *shih,* power as rank, position, or natural circumstance (as distinguished from law or talent)

Shi Jing (shǐr-jīng) Shih Ching, Confucian Classic: The *Book of Poetry*

shu (shōō) *shu,* mutuality, reciprocity, altruism

shu (shōō) *shu,* statecraft, the art of conducting affairs and managing subordinates

Shu Jing (shōō-jǐng) *Shu Ching,* Confucian Classic: the *Book of History*

Sun Zhongshan (sǔn jōōngshän) *Sun Yat-sen,* founder of the Republic of China (1912); sought a blend of socialist democracy and Confucian morality

Tai Ji (tī jē) *T'ai Chi,* the Great Ultimate, the supreme regulative principle of the cosmos; *li* acting through *qi*

Wang Chong (wäng chǔng) *Wang Chung,* 1st c. C.E. rationalist, opposed supernaturalism and excessive reverence for Confucius the man

Wang Yang-ming (wäng yäng-mǐng) *Wang Yang-ming,* 16th c. Neo-Confucian, brought together knowledge, morality, and action: knowing good by doing it

xiao (shǐ-ä-ō) *hsiao,* filial piety, in later Confucianism, "the source of all virtues"

xin (shǐn) *hsin,* good faith; one of the Five Virtues

Xun-zi (shün' dzǔ) *Hsün Tzu,* 3rd c. B.C.E. Confucian scholar, champion of the realist or naturalistic view of human nature

yi (ē) *i,* righteousness, justice; one of the Five Virtues

zheng-ming (jěng-mǐng) *cheng-ming,* rectification of names, making actuality conform to defined ideals

zhi (jǐr) *chih,* wisdom; one of the Five Virtues

Zhong Yong (jōōng yōōng) *Chung Yung,* the *Doctrine of the Mean,* essay on Confucian ideas of humanity and ethics, a chapter in the *Li Ji.*

Zhu Xi (jōōshē) *Chu Hsi,* 12th c. arbiter of Confucian orthodoxy; fixed the Neo-Confucian views of *qi, li,* and *Tai Ji.*

* For a guide to pronunciation, refer to page 99.

Shinto

The Native Contribution to Japanese Religion

CHAP**T**ER **11**

Shinto, the native religion of Japan, is not fundamentally a system of doctrines, although before World War II it did take on some doctrinal elements. It is basically a reverent alliance with supramundane realities encountered in Japanese life: in nature, society, and the home, for the Japanese love their land with great constancy. It is a love of the country as a whole, and of each part of it, existing less in abstract idea than in an aesthetic love of things and places. Every hill and lake, mountain and river, is dear to them, so dear that they can only with difficulty think of parting from them. Their cherry trees, their shrines, their scenic resorts seem indispensable to a full enjoyment of life. Among these scenes their ancestors lived and died. Here, with the ancestral spirits looking on, their families abide and have their complex being. Moreover, their country has always been their own. Until 1945, they believed their shores to be inviolable. Not only is it unthinkable that Japan should be peopled by others than themselves (this, of course, is true of other peoples in other lands), but to most resident Japanese, it is unthinkable that they should live anywhere but where they do. Chie Nakane observes that "there is no alienation, loneliness or irritability comparable to that of the Japanese whose work takes him to a foreign country."[A] This is emotional disposition bred in the bone. It is the sort of feeling that readily expresses itself in myth. And so it did express itself in Japan—in myth first, in nationalistic ideology afterward. The Japanese came early to the belief that their land was divine, but late to the nationalistic dogma that no other land was divine, that the divinity of Japan was so special and unique, so absent elsewhere, as to make Japan "the center of this phenomenal world."

WESTERN NAME: Shintoism

ADHERENTS IN 1997: 7 million

NAMES USED BY ADHERENTS: Shinto, Kami-no-michi

SACRED LITERATURE: Kojiki, 712 C.E., *Nihon Shoki,* 720 C.E., *Kogoshui,* 720 C.E., *Engi-shiki,* early tenth century C.E.

DEITIES (kami): "Upper beings," spirits—eight hundred myriads according to ancient myths—among them, Izanagi and Izanami, the primal pair; Amaterasu, the sun goddess; Susa-no-wo, the destructive storm god; Inari, the rain goddess; and many spirits attached to objects in nature and in household life

INSTITUTIONAL EXPRESSION:

1. State Shinto, officially set apart in 1882 and curtailed after 1945
2. Shrine Shinto, privately supported, mostly independent, but including
   a. Syncretistic (mixed) sects combining with Buddhist or Confucian elements: Ryobu, Shinbutsu Konko, and others
   b. Some "new religion" sects with Shintoist characteristics: Tenrikyo, Odoru Shinkyo, and others

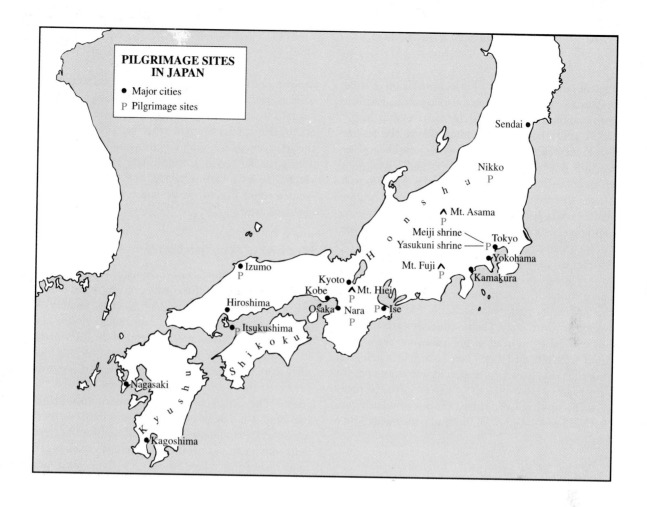

PILGRIMAGE SITES
IN JAPAN
● Major cities
P Pilgrimage sites

I. THE BACKGROUND OF SHINTO

The term *Shinto* is derived from the Chinese *shendao,* meaning "the way of the higher spirits or gods." Its equivalent in Japanese is *kami-no-michi,* or "the kami's way," kami meaning, in general, gods or deities, but, in a more inclusive sense, beings possessing sacred power or superior potency, filled with a numinous or charismatic force. It has been part of the myth of Shinto that Japan was once peopled exclusively with kami. The early Japanese regarded the whole of nature as imbued with kami powers, from the gods in the upper regions to spirits in mountains, lakes, and trees on earth, not to speak of powers in the sea and under the ground.

Shinto thus expresses a religious faith about Japan and its past. The customs of prehistoric Japan were the way followed by kami, the awe-inspiring beings from whom the Japanese people have descended. But this faith, as faiths often do, ignored or was unaware of certain historical facts about the true origins of the Japanese people.

Ethnic Origins

The Japanese are probably a mixed people, partly Korean, partly Mongolian, and partly Malayan. Their ancestors came at different times from the Asiatic mainland and South Pacific islands, and succeeded in uniting with or displacing and driving northward the aboriginal tribes. Apparently, the civil condition of ancient Japan was that of a loose conjunction of tribes and clans, each more or less independent and with its own traditions of nature and chieftain worship. Magic, taboo, and religion were commingled in the fashion that is characteristic of a primitive society. The fox was worshiped as a messenger of the gods. Bows and arrows were fetishes of so high an order that they were offered the reverence accorded to the gods. The constant warfare with the slowly yielding but still fierce aboriginal tribes gave a military color to all of life. Great warriors were treated with special respect, whether living or dead.

Though they were clothed in rough garments and primitively housed, the Japanese already showed the passion for personal cleanliness that is so characteristic of them today. Their attitude toward the dead was marked by a dread of pollution, so that when a death occurred, the funeral was immediately held, and after the ten-day mourning period was at an end, the whole family went into the water to wash. In many cases the survivors abandoned the primitive structure that had been the home of the dead person and built a new one.

Prehistoric Cultures

Archaeology yields only the sketchiest chronologies of prehistoric Japan. Surviving pottery dating possibly from as early as 6000 B.C.E. and still in use in 300 B.C.E. has a "cord pattern" that has given its name to the time in which it was in use, the *Jomon* period. This seems to have been a long Neolithic hunting and fishing period, when aboriginal tribes inhabited the land. Their relics imply ritual burials, with the dead interred in a flexed position along with stone implements and red ochre; there also seem to have been fertility rites in which phallic emblems (stone clubs) and clay figurines of an indeterminate sex were used. A district near Tokyo, where another and more advanced type of pottery has been found accounts for the name *Yayoi,* given to the period (250 B.C.E. to 250 C.E.). Apparently it was during this period that cultivation of rice in irrigated paddy fields was developed, an important advance over the gathering practices of earlier times. Historians have coined yet a third term, the *Kofun,* or Burial Mound period, to name the time from 250 C.E. to the historic breakthrough of Chinese influence in the fifth

century. During this period, tombs and earthen mausoleums were erected for the ruling classes, a fact that suggests to some scholars a large-scale invasion by Asiatic warriors, who brought with them the horse and the art of smelting bronze and iron and who drove the aborigines farther northward. The earliest Chinese records go back to this period, and they tell of able women ruling in south Japan and acting as influential shamans there.

Yamato Ascendancy

There were, it seems likely, three main centers of culture about the time of the first century B.C.E.: one in the southwest on the island of Kyushu, another at Izumo, on the western verge of the main island, and a third at Yamato, at the northern end of the Inland Sea. Far to the north were the light-skinned Ainu, originally from the subarctic areas of Siberia, who doggedly preserved their own cultural life down through the years. (They are now on the northernmost island, Hokkaido.) It may be an oversimplification, but there are indications that on the island of Kyushu the tribal cults were mainly concerned with gods of the sea, and upon the central island, the Izumo clans worshiped the storm god Susa-no-wo, while the Yamato clans adored the sun goddess, regarded as the ruler of the heavens and the ancestress of their chieftains. The Yamato clans, probably in the fourth century C.E., sealed their ascendancy over the other groups by placing their chieftain on a somewhat shaky imperial throne as a descendant of the sun. But perhaps they had to overcome the opposition of other groups who preferred as rulers women reigning in the matriarchal tradition and credited with special powers as diviners and shamanistic mediums.[B1]

The Effect of Chinese Culture

However arrived at, primitive Shinto was formless and without any particular sense of direction. It became a clearly worked-out pattern of national culture only when Chinese civilizing influences began to operate in Japan in the fifth century C.E. These influences were initially Sino-Korean, for the immediate teachers of the Japanese were Koreans. But because the Koreans had learned from the Chinese, the Japanese were not long in going directly to the Chinese for further advances in knowledge and skills. The transformation effected then in the national life and outlook is one of the most remarkable instances of its kind in history. The Japanese eagerly made their lives over by adapting Chinese ideas and procedures to their needs. They went about it very thoroughly.

Always adept in improving their methods and skills in the practical arts, once the way is shown, they quickly learned all that the Koreans, and beyond them, the Chinese, could teach them about metalworking, wood carving, farming, horticulture, gardening, silkworm culture, road and bridge building, and canal dredging. Almost at a bound the people passed from a primitive to a relatively advanced type of material culture. In the realm of writing and communication, they took over without change, except for cursive simplifications, the entire body of Chinese ideograms or characters, pronouncing them with the Japanese words that were the translations of the Chinese. Where there were no Japanese equivalents, they adopted the Chinese sounds with characteristic modifications. In the realm of social relations, Confucian ideas brought about permanent changes of emphasis in morals. There followed in particular a powerful reinforcement of the ideal of filial piety. Prehistoric Shinto had been mainly a haphazard cult of nature worship, loosely tied in with ancestor worship. It now took on the aspects of history's most comprehensive ancestor cult. Not only did the emperor's descent from the sun goddess receive stress, but the higher officials began to trace their own descent from the deities most closely related to the sun goddess, and the common people were supposed to be descendants of the more distantly related deities. In this way, the mythological basis was laid for the claim (so greatly emphasized during the last decades of the nineteenth century and the beginning of this) that the whole people were organically related to the emperor by a divine family relationship.

Early Sacred Literature

But an even greater impact was made upon the Japanese by Buddhism, coming first from Korea and then from China. When this religion came to Japan in the sixth century, it brought with it an exciting literature, a new, rich art, an emotionally satisfying ritual, and fresh insights into every field of human thought and action, including logic, medicine, and social service. Buddhism broke down Japanese provincialism by bringing the overseas world into the religious picture, for in the eyes of Buddhist priests, the seats of religious insight and authority lay not in Japan but in India and China. Buddhism had so much to contribute to Japan that the country's best, most progressive minds were irresistibly attracted to it.

One important result of the new ferment of ideas was the attempt, under imperial sanction, to use the Chinese characters and to put into writing the native myths and traditions still current among the local clans. In 712 C.E., the *Kojiki*, or Chronicle of Ancient Events, was completed, it being intended as a history of Japan from the creation of the world to the middle of the seventh century. Paralleling it, with variations and additions that gave it greater historical accuracy, was the *Nihongi* or *Nihon Shoki*, "Chronicles of Japan," issued in 720 C.E. Almost a century later (about 806 C.E.), during the first decade of the Heian era, appeared the *Kogoshui*, or Gleanings from Ancient Stories, a defense of the practices of ancient priestly families connected with Shinto. Still later, in the first quarter of the tenth century, came the *Engi-shiki*, an important compendium of Shinto traditions in fifty parts, the first ten of which contain lists of ritual prayers or litanies for various ceremonial occasions, called *norito*. The norito served then and for centuries afterward as the models, if not the actual words, of prayers in all Shinto shrines, whether in the country at large or in the court. All of these treatises showed the influence of Chinese and Buddhist ideas. Foreign modes of thought were evident, for example, in the opening paragraphs of the *Kojiki* and *Nihongi*, much as the influence of Greek philosophy on Christianity shows in the first chapter of the Fourth Gospel. The *Kojiki* and *Nihongi* were deeply indebted to overseas thought for their political orientation, which led them to endow the imperial line with a sovereignty reaching back to remote time and grounded in a divine order of things.

More undilutedly Japanese were two extraordinary works of the Heian period reflecting Japanese life, love, and religion. They came into being when Japanese minds were stirred to creativity by the exciting opportunity presented by the Chinese characters to put old and new thoughts into writing. One was the *Manyoshu,* a collection of old and new poems, four thousand in number, compiled toward the end of the eighth century. The other was a work of genius, Lady Murasaki's long novel *The Tale of Genji,* dealing with the sensuous, beauty-oriented court at Kyoto in its early years.

II. THE SHINTO MYTH

There can be no doubt of the interest the imperial court took in the formulation of an official version of the Shinto folk traditions. On the one hand, the court had displayed a desire to follow Chinese models in its official procedure and hierarchical structure, for it wished to be judged civilized or cultivated. But on the other hand, it had no wish to become un-Japanese, for inevitably and naturally it reflected in thousands of ways well-established Japanese folkways. The court therefore became the scene of elaborate rites and ceremonies, some in imitation of the procedures of the Chinese and Korean courts, but others based on quite ancient Shinto beliefs and practices. Among these were rituals for purification from pollution, ceremonies for every stage of the growing of rice, from planting to harvesting (important to all), sacred dances performed for their beauty as well as their magico-religious effects, taboos against moving in certain directions when the position of the moon and other objects was not favorable, and devout obeisance (kneeling with head lowered to the hands along the floor) toward spirits (kami) present in the surrounding world.

In another direction, it seemed required both by national pride and Chinese standards of rationality and order that the native myths concerning the early history of Japan and its people be woven into a more or less unified sequence. The result was what we may call the Shinto myth. Of the slightly variant forms of the officially approved versions of this myth, we have chosen that of the *Kojiki,* mentioned previously. The story runs as follows.[C1]

The Primal Progenitors

The Japanese islands are a special creation of the gods. After the primal chaos had in the course of events

separated into heaven and ocean, various gods appeared in the heavenly drift mist, only to disappear without event, until finally there came upon the scene the two deities who produced the Japanese islands and their inhabitants. These were the primal male and female, Izanagi, the Male-Who-Invites, and Izanami, the Female-Who-Invites. Their heavenly associates commanded them to "make, consolidate, and give birth to" the Japanese islands. These two beings descended the Floating Bridge of Heaven (a rainbow?), and when they reached its lower end, they pushed down Izanagi's jeweled spear into the muddy brine and stirred it about until the fluid below them became "thick and glutinous." Whereupon "the brine that dripped down from the end of the spear was piled up and became an island." Stepping down on the island, they came together, and Izanami bore from her womb the eight great islands of Japan. After that, they brought into being a populace of thirty-five deities, the last of whom, the fiery heat-god Kagu-Tsuchi, at his birth, fatally burned his mother. So enraged was Izanagi at Kagu-Tsuchi for causing Izanami's death that he hacked him up with rapid strokes of his sword, only to produce other deities out of the flying fragments.

Pollution and the Deities of Cleansing

The historically important part of this story is its sequel. When Izanami died and went to the underworld (the Land of Yomi), in due time the inconsolable Izanagi followed after her, hoping to get her to return to the upper world with him. But he had not come in time. She had begun to decompose and was unsightly. When he neared her in the darkness, she asked him not to look at her. But he lit the end tooth of the comb by which he kept his hair in place and saw her lying before him horribly swarming with maggots. "Thou has put me to shame," she screamed, and as he fled back, sent the Ugly Females of Yomi to pursue him. When by various stratagems he delayed this pursuit, she sent after him eight thunder deities, generated in the decay of her own body, and fifteen hundred warriors of Yomi. When he fought these off, she herself took up the chase. As he fled into the upper world, he picked up a rock that would have taken a thousand men to lift and blocked up the pass of the underworld with it. The two erstwhile loving deities, standing on opposite sides of the rock, exchanged angry farewells. Finally, Izanagi, who was now covered with pollution, went down to the ocean to bathe his august person. As he threw away his staff, his girdle, and the rest of his apparel, each item turned into a deity. But the major event was still to come. According to the *Kojiki*, when he stepped into the water and, in a typically Japanese act of purification, washed away the filth out of his left eye, he produced the most highly revered of the Japanese deities, Amaterasu, the goddess of the sun. This was an important creation. After that, he produced the moon-god, Tsuki-yomi, from the washing of his right eye, and the storm-god, Susa-no-wo, from his nostrils. The preoccupation of Shintoism with pollution and ablution is clearly foreshadowed in these myths.

Amaterasu and a Myriad of Other Kami

Years later, we find the sun goddess Amaterasu looking down from her seat in heaven and becoming concerned about the disorder in the islands below. The storm god's son was ruling there, but she was not satisfied. She finally commissioned her grandson Ni-ni-gi to descend to the islands and rule them for her. Her charge to him was in words that many a child in Japan once knew by heart: "This Luxuriant-Reed-Plain-Land-of-Fresh-Rice-Ears shall be the land which thou shalt rule." Ni-ni-gi obeyed. He first ruled from the southernmost island of Kyushu. In a later time, his great-grandson Jimmu Tenno, the first human emperor, embarked from Kyushu on a conquest of the province of Yamato, on the central Japanese island Honshu and set up his capital there, in the year set by tradition at 660 B.C.E. Meanwhile, the leading families of Japan and the whole Japanese people descended from the minor deities, or lesser kami, residing on the islands. Thus, we are to understand that the emperor of Japan is a descendant in an unbroken line from the sun goddess Amaterasu, and that the islands of Japan have a divine origin, and so also the Japanese people.

It will be observed that this account of things is concerned with Japan alone; no other countries are considered. Moreover, Japan is regarded as full of gods and goddesses. The polytheism is almost unlimited. It was characteristic of the earlier Japanese to deify

Izanagi Forms the First Island of Japan

Izanami watches as muddy brine dripping from the tip of the spear forms the Island of Onogoro upon which she will give birth to other islands, deities, and elements of the natural world. *(Courtesy of the William Sturgis Bigelow Collection, Museum of Fine Arts, Boston. Neg. # 11.7972.)*

everywhere; to see a god or godling in every kind of force or natural object. Hence it was that they called their country "the Land of the Gods," and in later times estimated that their deities must number some "eighty myriads" or even some "eight hundred myriads."

We may observe further that the chief place in the pantheon was given to sun goddess Amaterasu, whose temple at Isé is the holiest shrine in Japan, but she has never been regarded as more than the first among her peers. Associated with her were not only those born with her—Tsuki-yomi, the moon good, and Susa-no-wo, the amoral and capricious storm god—but also a vast company of deities, such as the wind deities, "Prince of the Long Wind" and "Lady of the Long Wind"; the god of lightning, "Terrible Swift Fire Deity"; the thunder god, "Fierce Thunder Male Deity"; the rain god, "Fierce Rain Chief"; the general mountain god, "Dark-Mountain Possessing Deity," under whose aegis many local mountain deities, like the goddess of Mt. Fuji, performed their functions; the fertility deities, such as "High August Producing God" and "Divine Producing Goddess"; the food deities—Inari, who is the grain goddess, and the still very popular Toyo-Uke-Hime, the food goddess, today widely worshiped by peasants and especially honored at the outer shrine of Isé; phallic deities; the gods of healing and purification; star gods and goddesses; the deities of the sea (those of the middle, the bottom, and the surface of the sea); not to mention river gods, harbor gods, mist gods, and deities of trees, leaves, rocks, earthquakes, volcanoes, and so on.

We need draw out the list no further. It is obvious that the Shinto myth pictured a pristine Japan thronging with deities.

The Composite Nature of the Myth

That this myth is a composite of various elements is obvious. To begin with, the opening sentences of the *Kojiki* reflect Chinese conceptions of the origin of the universe: it evolved out of an egglike chaotic mass. Probably the scholars of the imperial court were seeking an appropriate introduction to the native myths they were about to bring together.

That the myth also reflects an early response to nature, not far advanced above animism, is clear. It was proposed by D. C. Holtom, a leading authority, that

Izanagi and Izanami are Japanese forms of those familiar figures in the world's cosmogonic myths, "the Sky Father and the Earth Mother," and that the details of the myth fit into the general pattern of the worldwide descriptions of seasonal change in vegetation, typified by the Cybele-Attis myth of the Western world. He urged that the death of Izanami is caused by the earth-burning god of summer heat (which is his interpretation of the meaning of Kagu-Tsuchi), so when Izanagi hews up the fiery god with his sword, thus producing lightning, thunder, and rain deities, what is signified is the vengeful onslaught of the quenching rainstorm upon the drought child that has burned its earth mother. According to Holtom, the search of Izanagi for Izanami in the underworld is clearly in line with the chthonian myths of the West: the disappearance of the earth mother has brought about the death of vegetation, and the sky father endeavors to find her and return her to the world. His is a seeking that "re-echoes the search of the Egyptian Isis for the body of Osiris."[D1]

Much may be said for this interpretation of the Japanese myth, but it explains the myth only in part, for interwoven with this portion of the story, and cutting it short, are other parts dealing with the sun goddess and her struggles with her unruly brother, the storm god.

The story of these quarrels is susceptible of at least two different interpretations. The first interpretation sees in them the unending contest between sun and storm cloud, contrasting the cleansing, orderly sun with the pollutions of stormy disorder; the other reading finds in their geographical references an indication that Amaterasu represents the people of the southern district of Yamato, and Susa-no-wo the settlers in Izumo, two groups that in the early years of immigration from the continent of Asia struggled with each other for ascendancy. The total myth represents, therefore, the combination of several strands of tradition originating from different clans among the ancient population of Japan.

III. SHINTO IN MEDIEVAL AND MORE RECENT TIMES

By the middle of the seventh century, Buddhism had obtained a dominant influence in court circles. Years later, in thousands of villages, the common people were expanding their beliefs and practices (their "folk religion") by adopting congenial elements not only from Buddhism but also from other types of Chinese religion, particularly religious Daoism and yin-yang magic. The result was the so-called mixed Shinto.

An amplified Shinto was made possible and natural by two central orientations that have had a pronounced role in Japanese religious history: (1) the extension of the "family" concept and (2) hospitality to guests.

The Family Model

Japanese society has always retained a basic family or clan system, in and through which individuals have acquired their sense of selfhood or identity, religiously as well as socially. Although many young people in Japan are breaking away from it, this pattern of behavior has carried over into education, politics, and industry, particularly the last. It is common for employees of industrial plants to regard such plants as extensions of one's family and to feel attached to them.

Each family and clan has had its own shrine, where the *uji-gami* "family (tutelary) deity"—usually a long-honored ancestor, associated with later ancestral spirits and often with locally important gods—has been honored and asked for aid and protection.

Roadside stone pillars and images called *dosojin* (literally "road ancestor beings" or "ancestral way persons") blended protective and fertility themes. Sometimes they took the explicit forms of phallus and vulva in evocation of fertility; sometimes they depicted affectionate couples; sometimes they showed the three ideographs *do so jin* on a plain stone. The central part of the first character, "road," might be cut in a vulvar shape, and a part of the second "ancestor" character might take a phallic form.

Even after welcoming into its structure elements of Buddhism, Daoism, and Confucianism, rural Shinto retained this primary clan and family pattern and remained a vital and independent force. Members of families and clans continued to recognize deep ties with the kami who had done so much for them in the past. Aristocratic families residing in the capital continued to send subsidies to their home shrines.

The Guest Model

The villages and their clans were receptive to deities that may be called divine guests from the outside, who visited occasionally or came to stay, such as the emperor's ancestress Amaterasu, Inari the grain goddess, and overseas powers, like the Buddhist and Daoist deities. A leading Japanese scholar, Ichiro Hori, calls this the *hitogami* type of religion that joins an individual man (*hito*) with a power-bestowing *kami,* often a great god from over the seas. Professor Hori notes that the gods from the outside were usually introduced by religious specialists with a shamanistic reputation. Persons of shamanistic character did go from village to village, imparting Buddhist teachings concerning individual salvation by the Buddhas and introducing magical rites and incantations to cure illness and drive out evil spirits. Among them were "shamanesses (*miko*), Shinto priests (*onshi* or *oshi*), mountain ascetics (*yamabushi* or *gyōja*), yin-yang magicians (*onmyō-ji* and *shōmon-ji*), lower-class Nembutsu priests (*Nembutsu-hijiri*), semi-professional pilgrims (*kaikoku-hijiri*), migrating magicians and medicine men (*jussha* or *kitō-ja*), and magico-religious artisans and technicians such as blacksmiths (*imo-ji*), woodworkers (*kiji-ya*), or reciters named *sekkyō* (literally 'preacher') or *sai-mon* (literally, 'address to the deities'), or *utabikuni* (literally, 'singing nuns'), and so on."[E1]

Since at the village level much of the religious ritual was concerned with ingratiation of fertility spirits, mountain gods, and evilly disposed powers (*goryō*) that had to be conciliated or controlled, it was natural that yin-yang magic, Vajrayana Buddhism, Nembutsu formulas, and religious and magical Daoism were eagerly adapted to local Japanese needs. A farmer, for example, would be delighted to pin to his door or stable Chinese-style amulets and printed charms obtained from a shrine (or a Buddhist temple) to ward off harm. At the level of folk religion, then, Shinto has been an amalgam of many elements, native and borrowed.

Confucian and Buddhist Influence on the Elite

Meanwhile, at the favored level of the imperial court and the intellectually gifted, Buddhism and Confucianism supplied the norms of belief and behavior.

Confucianism came with the first Chinese immigrants and few Japanese questioned its ethics and philosophy; moreover, it gave scope and form to ancestor worship. As to Buddhism, we have previously seen (on p. 197) that in the sixth century the Empress Suiko and her nephew Shotoku, who became prince regent, strongly recommended Buddhism to the court and gave it official recognition. Immigrants from Korea and China, and Japanese scholars who went abroad to investigate and study the Buddhist sects, brought to Japan the skills and knowledge that transformed its political, economic, educational, and religious life. At first the beliefs and practices of China and Korea were adopted with little change. During the Nara period (710–794), the varieties of Buddhism were followed to the letter. This seemed to many Japanese too alien a point of view. But as we have seen in the chapter on the religious development of Buddhism (pp. 217–220), two Japanese scholars went to China and came back to found the Shingon and Tendai sects, which they shrewdly accommodated to Japanese needs. Later on, during the Kamakura period (1192–1336), the Zen, Shin, and Nichiren sects gave Buddhism even more explicitly Japanese expressions (see pp. 210–221).

Mixed (*Ryobu*) Shinto

Scholars have called the resultant "mixed" Shinto, with its architectural modifications and altered rituals, *Ryobu* (Two-Sided) *Shinto* or *Shinbutsu Konko* (Mixed Shinto and Buddhism). According to Ichiro Hori, when Buddhism appeared in the villages,

> the priests had to compromise with local people and their community gods. As a result of these compromises, a special Buddhist temple, called a *Jingu-ji*, was built within the precincts of almost every Shinto shrine and dedicated to the Shinto kami of that shrine. The *Jingu-ji* were built so that the Buddhist priests could serve the kami with Buddhist rituals by special permission of the kami. In reverse, the local or tutelary kami was enshrined in each Buddhist temple and served by Buddhist priests and Buddhist formulas.[E2]

When Shinto shrines began to give a place to Buddhist (and Daoist) rituals, there were certain doctrinal consequences. "At first the kami," says Joseph

Kitagawa, "were considered to be the 'protectors of Buddha's Law.' . . . Soon, however, this belief was reversed so that the kami were considered to be in need of salvation through the help of Buddha. . . . Some of the honored kami also received the Buddhist title of *bosatsu* (bodhisattva)."[B2] In the ninth century, Kōbō Daishi, founder of the Shingon school, taught that the Buddhas and bodhisattvas appeared as various gods in different countries and had so appeared in Japan (see p. 219). Dengyo Daishi, founder of the Tendai school, made a similar suggestion. Priests of various Buddhist sects reported having visions and intuitions that were accepted as proof that the gods of Japan were in reality Buddhas and bodhisattvas who "appeared" as gods of the Japanese islands. Amaterasu, the sun goddess, was identified as a manifestation of the Buddha Mahavairocana; Hachiman, the war god, was found to be the guise assumed on Japanese soil by the Bohisattva Kshitigarbha; and so on.

In this synthesis, the deities of the Buddhist pantheon were given the honored position of "the Originals," whereas the deities of the Shinto pantheon were thought to be their Japanese appearances or manifestations (*gongen*).

It is not surprising that Shinto almost succumbed completely. Certainly, Ryobu, or Two-Sided Shinto, had an immense influence on the people of Japan. It won the majority to its interpretations. In ensuing years, not only did most of the Shinto shrines make room for Buddhist worship and Buddhist priests, but the latter introduced into the old Shinto rites images, incense, sermons, and elaborate ceremonies. The simple primitive appearance of the Shinto shrines was greatly altered by the exterior application of the intricate ornament of Buddhist temples and by the addition to the shrine property of pagodas, drum towers, large bells, assembly halls for preaching services, and the like. Even the unadorned Shinto gateway, or *torii*, was supplied with curves and ornate decoration. So pervasive did the influence become that it is quite true to say with H. N. Wieman and W. M. Horton that "down to the Meiji era, Japan might fairly be described as a Buddhist nation," though one adds, as Wieman and Horton aptly did, the qualification that this only holds good "in the same sense in which certain western nations have been described as 'Christian.'"[F]

Japanese appropriation and adaptation of Buddhism continued to the fourteenth century, when public order dissolved in three hundred years of feudal strife, during which the emperor, his headship of the nation thoroughly obscured, was condemned to impotence, while dictators (*shoguns*) vainly strove to control the powerful nobles and the *samurai,* or military class. At the end of the sixteenth century, a shogun arose who brought an end to the centuries of feudal warfare. This marked the beginning of the period of the Tokugawa regime (1603–1867). It was a period of some importance to Shinto, for during it occurred its own revival or renaissance.

The Revival of Shinto as a Separate Religion

The revival of Shinto was a slow and gradual process. During the disorders that attended the end of the Kamakura period in the first half of the fourteenth century, those who supported the Emperor Go-Daigo in his unsuccessful effort to gain control of the nation could not have failed to raise the question whether the descendant of the sun goddess should have been rejected. That Shinto and its central themes should be so nearly submerged in Buddhism also worried many. As the fourteenth century wore on, several of the hereditary priests of the Watarai family who took care of the outer shrine at Isé sought without great success to free Shinto (their "Isé Shinto") from Buddhist and Chinese infusions, and a century later one of the Urabé priests at the Kasuga shrine at Nara wrote a treatise that tried to distinguish the ancient Shinto elements within the current Buddhized (Ryobu) Shinto. Then suggestions were made by the Watarai priests and others that the thesis of Ryobu Shinto should be reversed, that is, that the Japanese kami be declared the "originals" and the Buddhist deities their "appearances." But their voices were at first scarcely more than faint cries against the prevailing wind. Other Shintoists were not yet ready to give them a hearing. Moreover, they could not free even themselves from Buddhist and Confucian thinking when they set forth their own arguments.

But a purer Shinto had friends in other quarters. Support for its independence of Buddhism was unwittingly evoked by the Tokugawa shogunate. By the seventeenth century, Christianity was being suppressed, and the ports of Japan had been closed to all but a few Dutch and Chinese traders. (As the saying goes, Japan had become "a hermit nation.") After a desperate uprising of Christians during the period 1637–1638, the government attempted to smoke out all remaining Christians by ordering every Japanese to secure a certificate from a Buddhist temple (*tera-uke*) to prove that he or she was not an adherent of the proscribed religion. This greatly upset some Shinto priests, who, obliged to have recourse to Buddhist temples, asked recognition as representatives of an independent religion. They received immediate support from a number of Japanese Confucian scholars, who also desired the disengagement of Shinto from its Buddhist entanglements. Confucianism had been influential among the literary classes ever since the first introduction of Chinese learning into Japan in the fifth century. In medieval Japan, it took a new turn with the introduction of Neo-Confucianism and the philosophical views of Zhu Xi and Wang Yang-ming. The latter was generally frowned upon as being too theoretical and subjective, but Zhu Xi was widely received as a major guide to the nature of the world and its history. During the Tokugawa period, Japanese scholars from the seventeenth century on became his interpreters, and they took an anti-Buddhist "rationalist" position; this ultimately meant that they desired to see Shinto purged of its Buddhist accretions and restored to its "Ancient Way." There was even a proposal of a Confucian-Shinto amalgamation, to be called Suika Shinto, to displace Ryobu Shinto.[B3]

It was clear too that the Japanese masses still loved the "purer" Shinto rites, especially those performed at the grand shrine of the sun goddess Amaterasu at Isé, to which in times of plentiful harvests (and failing consumer prices) they flocked in great numbers to express their thanks for the sunshine that had favored the crops. Encouraged, the Isé priests toured the countryside promoting the practice of visiting Isé at least once in a lifetime.

Shinto Classical Scholars: Motoori

All of this heartened scholars of the Shinto classics in a nationalistic concentration on "native ancient learning." During the eighteenth and early nineteenth

Kasuga Shrine at Nara
Founded in 768 c.e., this is one of the oldest Shinto Shrines in Japan. Its tiled roof with upturned corners and vermilion painted woodwork reflect Chinese style, a contrast to the native Japanese thatch and natural wood of the Ise Shrine (p. 338). *(Courtesy Japan Airlines, JT-21.)*

centuries, three outstanding scholars, Kamo Mabuchi, Motoori Norinaga, and Hirata Atsutane, took advantage of the anti-foreign atmosphere to revive what came to be called "Pure Shinto," or the "True Ancient Way." The second of this group was perhaps the greatest scholar in Japanese history. His commentary on the *Kojiki* is still authoritative. But his conclusions were as subjective, as his scholarship in other respects was factual. Scorning to take the position of his contemporaries, who saw and unhesitatingly acknowledged the dependence of Japanese learning on Chinese sources, Motoori firmly upheld the superiority of the ancient way of Japan, citing the divine origin of the emperor (Mikado).

> From the central truth that the Mikado is the direct descendant of the gods, the tenet that Japan ranks far above other countries is a natural consequence. No other nation is entitled to equality with her, and all are bound to do homage to the Japanese sovereign and pay tribute to him.[D2]

He repudiated the suggestion that because the Japanese had no native system of ethics, they must borrow one from Confucianism. Only a depraved people need an ethics, he said; the Japanese, by reason of their divine motivation, were so naturally upright in their lives that they were in no need of a moral code, and consequently never had one. They should therefore give up forever all foreign modes of thought and action and walk in simplicity the ancient way of Shinto.

But these were scholarly opinions. Not until the nineteenth century did a political triumph of Shinto come to pass.

The Restoration of 1868

The vindication of the Shinto myth came in the second half of the nineteenth century, when the "second great transformation of Japan" took place (the first being the influx of Buddhism). The necessity for this transformation was borne in on the Japanese rather suddenly. Though they strove to remain a "hermit nation," they could not prevent American whaling ships from appearing off their coasts and from time to time suffering shipwreck. The sailors who reached shore were sometimes killed as "foreign devils," and it took many months for those who did not meet this fate to be repatriated through the Dutch traders who were the only foreigners allowed in Japanese waters. But this was not the sole problem of the whalers. Their vessels often ran out of water and provisions by the time they reached Japan, and they naturally desired to be able to put into port to stock up. President Millard Fillmore, aware of this need, and also anxious to open Japan to foreign trade, appealed by letter to the ruler of Japan to open up a few ports to American ships. Carrying this letter, Commodore Matthew Perry entered Tokyo Bay in 1853 with four gunboats and managed to deliver the president's message to the shogun. He sailed away to China, promising to return in the spring for an answer.

The shogun (military dictator, now the real power behind the throne in a centralized feudalism) circulated the president's letter among the Japanese feudal lords, who thereupon formed into three parties: the liberals, the compromisers, and the anti-foreign party, the last being much the largest and rejoicing in the adherence of the anti-foreign emperor, Komei. Commodore Perry returned in 1854 with ten ships and a force of two thousand men. The shogun yielded to this persuasion and concluded a treaty providing for kind treatment of shipwrecked sailors, permission for foreign vessels to obtain stores and water ashore, and the opening to trade of three unimportant ports. In concluding this treaty, the shogun did not obtain the sanction of the throne—an old habit of the shoguns. Although the emperor restrained the anti-shogunate forces of his court while he lived, after his death they entered into a determined struggle aimed at unseating the shogun. In the course of this struggle, the shogun was at last led to abolish his own office, retire to the background, and leave the way open for the restoration of the emperor to sovereignty over the nation, an event that occurred in 1868.

But the shogun had allowed a process of Westernization to begin that could not be stopped. The reactionary clan leaders tried to stop it, but after the startling experience of having some of their coastal defenses shattered by the guns of American, British, French, and Dutch ships, the anti-foreign leaders began to realize the military impotence of Japan and abruptly about-faced. They decided then and there to bring the military might of Japan up to par with that of the Western powers, and therefore entered, along with the liberals, upon the process of modernizing and industrializing Japan. It was a mighty task of transformation, and it was accomplished with amazing speed and thoroughness.

The Constitution of 1889 and the State Cult

The conservatives soon found that the adoption of Western economic and industrial methods, even when these were adapted to Japanese requirements, involved momentous changes in culture and outlook. But this made them even more resolved to preserve somehow the ancient military ideals and values in the modern setting. They saw to it that in the Constitution of 1899—an important step in the national reorganization—the army and navy were not placed under civilian control but were made responsible to the emperor alone. And, what is of chief interest to us here, they raised the old Shinto myth of the emperor's descent from the sun goddess to high place in the national life by incorporating it, by indirection, in the Constitution itself.

> Article I: The Empire of Japan shall be reigned over and governed by a line of Emperors unbroken for ages eternal.
> Article III: The Emperor is sacred and inviolable.

The proponents went about developing a state cult that could be expected to give it a continuing force in that nation's life. To this end they felt that the myth should be isolated from its Buddhist involvements and made to stand clear.

Accordingly, one of the first acts of the Emperor Meiji, after the restoration, was to disestablish Buddhism, make Shinto the state religion, and order the elimination of all Buddhist elements, including priests, from the Shinto shrines. A good deal of purging was done, some of it violent; even Buddhism as such was brought under attack. But so closely were Shinto and Buddhism intermingled that the national return to a "pure" Shinto proved impracticable. The common people continued to favor both religions. In 1877, Buddhism was given leave to exist by being granted autonomy. In the Constitution of 1889, the complete religious liberty of all citizens was guaranteed, though the government showed where its official heart lay by retaining a department, called the Bureau of Shrines, to express its attitude of special regard and care for the refurbished and redefined national faith. This department was subsequently divided into a Bureau of Shinto Shrines, under the Department of Home Affairs, and a Bureau of Religions, under the Department of Education. The division was made advisable by the official distinction drawn by the government between "State" Shinto and "Sectarian" Shinto, a matter that requires our further attention.

IV. STATE SHINTO TO 1945

State Shinto may be defined as the government-fostered program of patriotic rites that was conducted until 1945 in shrines removed from sectarian control and made national property. (The American occupation authority caused its compulsory features to be abolished in that year. Worship at the former state shrines is now theoretically voluntary—although for public officials it is virtually obligatory.) The purpose of the state cult was the systematic cultivation of patriotic feeling with the nation. Age-old traditions were stressed by it, because it rose initially out of the need to keep the Japanese people faithful to "the spirit of ancient Japan" through all the revolutionary changes wrought in the economic, educational, and political life of the nation by the adoption of the technology of the West.

Western Ideas and Agnosticism in Japan

The upheaval of Japanese life and culture that accompanied the wholesale importation of Western ideas in the post restoration era at first adversely affected the fortunes of Shinto. Thousands, in estrangement, turned away for a time from the officially sanctioned state shrines. The simultaneous resurgence of Buddhism, fighting for its life, and the reentrance of Christianity, raised as it were from the dead, helped produce a religious attitude among the people that portended

the end of the old native faith. But all religions suffered. Disbelief and agnosticism became widespread. The impact of Western science on the students in the newly founded universities hastened this tendency. Students began to laugh all religions out of court, and so far did this skepticism ultimately extend that a census of student opinion of the University of Tokyo in 1920 showed that "out of a total of 4,608, 2,989 listed themselves as agnostic, 1,511 as atheists, and only 118 as adhering to Christianity, Buddhism or Shinto"[G]—a truly extraordinary expression of religious disbelief and indifference. In the general population, half a century later, a similar trend was noted by Japanese sociologists. Following World War II and its subsequent disillusionments, the proportion of Japanese people willing to indicate a preference for some form of religion declined from 35 percent in 1958 to 31 percent in 1963, 30 percent in 1968, and 25 percent in 1973. A survey in 1987 found more than half of Japanese adults placed themselves in the "no religion" category.

Efforts to Revise the Myth

Shortly after its early contacts with Western science in the eighteenth century, the Japanese government began to take measures to shore up Shinto as a national faith. On the side of defense, it encouraged a reinterpretation of the Shinto myth that would make it acceptable to the critical intelligence of the nation. Semi-official sanction was given to the view that the deities of the national myth were originally human beings with superior gifts. The sun goddess was a noble woman ruler of a clan that had flourished in the Dawn Period of Japanese history, and she laid the foundations of Japanese culture and national organization. This view took advantage of the ambiguity of the Japanese term *kami*, which, we have said, means any being that has unusual power or is exceedingly awe inspiring or superior in potency. In the words of the famous scholar Motoori, uttered over two hundred years ago,

> Speaking in general, it may be said that *kami* signifies in the first place, the deities of heaven and earth that appear in the ancient records and also the spirits of the shrines where they are worshipped. It is hardly necessary to say that it

includes human beings; also such objects as birds, beasts, trees, plants, seas, mountains, and so forth. In ancient usage, anything whatsoever which was outside of the ordinary, which possessed superior virtues, or which was awe-inspiring was called *kami*.[D3]

Availing themselves of this interpretation of the meaning of the word for deity, Japanese scholars humanized and rationalized the whole of Japanese mythology, and thus tried to make their peace with historical science as is understood in the Western world. To cite a twentieth-century instance, a Japanese professor, writing in 1938, declared,

> Shinto, as the Chinese characters read, is the way of the Gods. What are gods? There are many things which go by the name "gods." In Greece, there is a god of stars; in India, Buddha is a god; in Occidental countries, they have one god, the ruler of Heaven. Thus, we find there are various gods in the world. Gods, in our country, are our forefathers. It is hardly necessary to mention that the Goddess Amaterasu is enshrined in Isé shrine; so are the Emperor Jimmu in Kashiwabara shrine, Emperor Ojin in Hachiman shrine, Emperor Kammu in Heian shrine and Emperor Godaigo in Yoshino shrine. To enshrine forefathers as gods is peculiar to our people. It is not seen in any other civilized countries of the world. It is true that in our country there also existed and exists even now to a certain extent the worship of animals, rocks, trees and mountains, but gods as taught by Shinto are our ancestors worshipped as gods. . . . In mystical groves, with sacred torii, the spirits of our forefathers are enshrined.[H]

This argument, besides being inaccurate in its references to other religions, has no sound historical basis as far as the major Shinto gods are concerned, because it flies in the face of the fact that in the Shinto myth Amaterasu, Susa-no-wo, Izanagi, and Izanami stand for aspects of nature—the radiant sun, the storm, ancient descendants from the sky country—and by no means

for apotheosized human beings of the past. The argument nevertheless has had an attraction for intelligent Japanese, anxious to be in harmony both with science and the national tradition.

Shinto as National Ethics

In another direction, the Japanese government endeavored to save Shinto by making it over into a positive force, a national institution of an ethical and a historical character. The official government view was that Shinto was not a religion, properly speaking, but a formulation of national ethics and a cult of loyalty to national institutions. To make this clear, the restoration (or Meiji) government in 1882 officially separated what is known as *Jinja-Shinto* or State Shinto, from *Kyoha-Shinto*, or Sectarian Shinto. The latter was declared ineligible for government financial support and was given the status of an independent religion on the same footing with Buddhism and Christianity. State Shinto was declared to be no more than a system of state ceremonials whose patriotic object it was to unify the popular mind in accordance with "the national morality." The official position was based on declarations made by the emperor Meiji from 1870 to 1890, when Japan was being reorganized to take its place in the modern world. Especial stress was laid on the famous Imperial Rescript on Education, issued in 1890 and regarded as the basis of the school system of Japan. The rescript reads

> Know Ye, Our Subjects:
>
> Our Imperial Ancestors have founded our Empire on a basis broad and everlasting, and have deeply and firmly implanted virtue; our subjects ever united in loyalty and filial piety have from generation to generation illustrated the beauty thereof. This is the glory of the fundamental character of Our Empire, and herein lies the source of Our education. Ye, Our subjects, be filial to your parents, affectionate to your brothers and sisters; as husbands and wives be harmonious, as friends true; bear yourselves in modesty and moderation; extend your benevolence to all;

> "The *kami* of the Divine Age were for the most part human beings of that time, and because the people of that age were all *kami*, it is called 'the Age of the Gods.'"[D3]
>
> —Motoori

pursue learning and cultivate arts and thereby develop intellectual faculties and perfect moral powers; furthermore, advance public good and promote common interests; always respect the Constitution and obey the laws; should emergency arise, offer yourselves courageously to the State; and thus guard and maintain the prosperity of Our Imperial Throne coeval with heaven and earth. So shall ye be not only Our good and faithful subjects but render illustrious the best traditions of your forefathers.

The Way here set forth is indeed the teaching bequeathed by Our Imperial Ancestors, to be observed alike by their descendants and the subjects, infallible for all ages and true for all places. It is Our wish to lay it to heart in all reverence, in common with you, Our subjects, that we may all attain the same virtue.[1]

It was generally accepted in Japan that this declaration not only laid down the best possible ethical principles—we may note these were Confucian in substance—but also called for the kind of complete loyalty to emperor and country upheld by State Shinto. For this reason, successive ministers of education issued orders such as the following to school officials:

Especially on the days of school ceremonies or on some date determined according to convenience, the pupils must be assembled and the Imperial Rescript on Education must be read before them. Furthermore, the meaning must be carefully explained to the pupils and they must be instructed to obey it at all times.[J1]

Another order, dated 1911, goes further

The sentiment of reverence is correlative with the feeling of respect for ancestors and is most important in establishing the foundations of national morality. Accordingly, on the occasion of the festivals of the local shrines of the districts where the schools are located, the teachers must conduct the children to the shrines and give expression to the true spirit of reverence.[D4]

These and subsequent orders, involving a daily bowing in school assemblies before the picture of the emperor, gave no end of trouble to some Christian groups. But leading Japanese nationalists, refusing to

see the ambiguity in the government's position, contended that Shinto shrines had no more than the significance of the memorial statues to be seen in London, Paris, or Berlin. "Foreigners," one spokesman said, "erect statues, we celebrate at shrines."[J2] Others compared shrines to national parks or such hallowed sites as the Tomb of the Unknown Soldier. So they saw no reason why all citizens might not, without inconsistency, present themselves on patriotic occasions at the shrines and participate in the ceremonies conducted there. And, by and large, this view was heartily endorsed by all Buddhists and with reservations by Christians.

State Shrines Before 1945

Before World War II, the shrines the government put under the control of the Home Ministry numbered about 110,000. Of these about 100 were maintained by the government. Others received partial government support. The rest were locally supported. Not included in the government count were many thousands of wayside shrines too small to mention in the records of the Home Ministry or too remote to be readily accessible. Many of these were memorial in character, being dedicated to legendary heroes or ancient clan figures. Others were small temples erected in honor of the fox, the messenger and symbol of the grain goddess Inari. Still others were placed in factory compounds, on the roofs of department stores, or in the small space between stores in a business district. The chief state shrines were served by some 16,000 priests who were appointed by the government and were officially instructed not to conduct unmistakably religious ceremonies, such as funerals, but only those officially prescribed rituals that were intended to establish the "national morality." (These ceremonies were said to be religious in form but not in intent.) In rural and out-of-the-way districts, one priest often served a large number of scattered shrines, but at the great shrines a staff of ten or more were in attendance.

The state shrines were, as tradition demanded, in appearance just what their name, *jinja,* implies— "god houses." In most cases they were unpainted Japanese houses of an ancient design and, in keeping with the characteristic Shinto abhorrence of decay and passion for cleanliness, it was common at some of the major shrines to tear down the shrine at regular intervals and rebuild it. (At Isé, this was done every twenty years, at other places at longer intervals.)

The Grand Imperial Shrine at Isé

The most honored of all state shrines was the Grand Imperial Shrine at Isé, sacred to the sun goddess Amaterasu. This shrine was of such importance to the government's Nationalist aims that citizens were for years bred in the notion that from ancient times the people of Japan made pilgrimages to this shrine once in a lifetime "without fail." Isé is situated some 200 miles southwest of Tokyo near the mouth of the beautiful bay that bears its name. There the shrine of the sun goddess still stands, linked with that of the food goddess Toyo-Uke-Hime, and between is a shrine-lined avenue four miles long, running through a forest of magnificent cryptomeria trees. Both shrines are made of unpainted cedar wood and are in the style of ancient Shinto. In each case, the superstructure rests on piles driven into the ground. The roofs are thatched and are secured at the top by three long planks, two fitted to form a ridge, and the third laid flat along the ridge to keep the rain from entering there. This third plank is weighted down by the ancient device of laying short sections of round logs at right angles to it along the whole interval between the end rafters. A narrow, railed veranda, also on piles, runs around the building.

From time immemorial, Amaterasu has had "the inner shrine." (Being less holy, the shrine of the food goddess stands in a smaller area than that of the sun goddess and is called "the outer shrine of Isé.") The shrine itself stands within two sacred fences, through which only authorized priests and officials of the government were in times past allowed to enter. The most treasured possessions of the shrine have been the "divine Imperial regalia," the three precious symbols of the sun goddess—a mirror, a sword, and a string of ancient "curved" stone jewels. The most highly valued of these, both in itself and for its symbolic meaning, has been the mirror, long declared to be the one with which the sun goddess was lured from the cave to which she once retreated in high dudgeon at the misdeeds of her brother Susa-no-wo. How the "divine Imperial regalia" reached earth is explained by the

story that the sun goddess gave them to Ni-ni-gi, her grandson, when she sent him down from heaven to rule the Japanese islands.

Although there are good grounds for believing that the three treasures were in fact gifts from the Chinese court, the *Kojiki* narrative (paraphrased) tells the story as follows:[C2]

> The sun-goddess locked herself in the rock-cave of heaven and left the world in darkness, save for the light of the moon and the stars. So the deities of the world (eighty myriads of them!) gathered outside the rock door and put on a seriocomic show to draw the offended deity out again into the open. They placed in front of the door a freshly dug-up sakaki tree, the most sacred of all trees, and hung on its branches a newly forged and very brightly polished metal mirror, a string of "curved" stone jewels, and blue and white offerings of cloth made from the inner bark of the sacred tree. Then Ame-no-uzume, the phallic goddess, danced so outrageously, to the rhythmic chanting of the other deities, that the sound of the laughter shook heaven and earth. Overcome with curiosity, the sun-goddess peeked out, saw her own face reflected in the mirror hanging from the branches of the sacred evergreen tree, the sakaki, and took a half-step to meet the beautiful rival she thus beheld. Immediately, Techikara-wo (Strength-of-Hand Deity) took her by the arm and drew her forth, while all the other deities shouted for joy. From this ancient myth of the reappearing of light in the world (after an eclipse?) Shintoists have derived the symbols of the mirror and the string of jewels and also their practice of using in their ceremonies and on altar-tables purification wands, called *nusa* and **gohei**, made to simulate branches of the sacred sakaki tree. The myth also provides the rationale for the two tall poles set up for formal ceremonies in front of the "worship sanctuary," on either side of the approach from the torii, the pole on the right bearing suspended, amid a flutter of silk streamers in five colors, a metal mirror and a string of stone jewels, and the pole on the left a small sword. In this latter case, the sword-symbol refers back to the exploit of the storm-god Susa-no-wo, in slaying a dragon, whose tail terminated in an imbedded sword blade, of a miraculous potency, which the storm-god extracted and presented to the sun-goddess.

The Inner Shrine at Isé

Dedicated to the worship of the sun goddess Ameterasu, its sacred precincts secluded behind one outer and two inner sacred fences, the shrine at Isé, and its accompanying buildings, conforms to the ancient architecture of Japan. It is rebuilt of unpainted wood every twenty years, and we see it here after it has been renewed. *(Courtesy of Japan National Tourist Organization.)*

The schoolbooks of Japan used to teach that from that time on the successive emperors, in a single dynasty unbroken through the ages, handed down the three sacred treasures as "symbols of the Imperial Throne."[D5]

Such was the sacredness of these treasures that so great a person as the emperor directly concerned himself with the conduct of the state ceremonies of the Grand Imperial Shrine of the Isé, though he was seldom present in person. An old school text explains the matter in the following way:

> The reverence accorded the Grand Imperial Shrine by the Imperial Family is of an extraordinary nature. . . . At the time of the Festival of Prayer for the Year's Crops (Kinen Sai), at the Festival of Presentation of First Fruits (Niiname Sai), he dispatches messengers and presents offerings. At the time of dispatching the Imperial messenger the Emperor personally views the offerings and delivers a ritualistic report to the messenger. Also, the Emperor does not withdraw prior to the departure of the Imperial messenger. Again, on the day of the Festival of the Presentation of First Fruits a solemn ceremony of distant worship (toward the Grand Imperial Shrine) is carried out. Each year at the Ceremony of Beginning State Affairs the first thing done is to receive a report relating to the Grand Imperial Shrine, and whenever there is an affair of great importance either to the Imperial Family or the nation it is reported to the Grand Imperial Shrine. Furthermore, at the time when the Emperor carries out the Ceremony of Accession to the Throne, he worships in person at the Grand Imperial Shrine.[D6]

On at least one other occasion of national importance the emperor customarily went to the Grand Imperial Shrine at Isé. It was when war was declared on some foreign power. He reported this solemn fact in person, as a matter of life-and-death import for the nation.

The *O-Harai* Ceremony

In the past, the emperor also played a part in the greatest of all Shinto ceremonies, the *O-Harai* or Great Purification. This was performed not only at Isé but at many other shrines throughout the country, twice each year, in June and December. It was in essence a national purgation by a purification ritual. Before the ceremony the priests sought for a month to attain inward as well as outward cleanliness by abstention (*imi*) from strong drink, sex, and food not purified by ritual fires. During the ceremony itself they waved slowly above the people a *nusa* or cleansing wand, read the ritual, and accepted purification offerings (*harai*). In olden times, the people rubbed their bodies with small straw or paper effigies representing themselves, thus transferring their guilt to their person substitutes. The priests collected and threw the effigies into some body of water—lake, river, or ocean as the case might be—and the guilt of the people was thus borne away. At the proper moment during the festival, the emperor, as a descendant of the forgiving sun goddess, pronounced from the imperial capital the absolution of the defiling impurities of the nation.

The waving of the purification wand during this and other ceremonies had been an important feature of Shinto ceremonies. The wand is said to originate from the ritual use of branches of the sacred sakaki tree by the deities of heaven. Priests wave a cleansing sakaki branch over children brought to shrines for a Shinto rite of passage. Other practices before and during Shinto ceremonies have a similar magical derivation. Instances are the hanging of a sacred rope (*shimenawa*) between the uprights of the torii and beneath the eaves of shrine buildings, the flying of streamers, banners, and flags from poles, the use of straw and paper objects twisted or cut into zigzag shapes (*gohei*) and set in the interior of the shrines or hung from the torii, and the wearing of grotesque masks by performers in festival processions.

Although in the past the emperor customarily took part in the great ceremonies of the year, the priests of Isé and elsewhere conducted by themselves the day-to-day ritual of the shrines. The services were of the utmost simplicity, consisting merely of a ceremonial approach to the inner shrine with offerings, the ritualistic presentation of the offerings, the reading of ritualistic prayers (*norito*), the removal of the offerings, and finally the quiet withdrawal of the worshipers and priests. The offerings have usually been of two kinds, food and cloth. The former have consisted typically of raw or cooked rice, rice brandy (*saké*), fish, fruit, vegetables, cakes, salt, and similar foodstuffs. The cloth offerings have sometimes included money, paper, jewels, or art objects, but normally consist of lengths of silk, cotton, and linen. These offerings are not only made to the gods but also are often proffered in the spirit of thanksgiving to the ever-glorious ancestress of the imperial family and the local clan leaders and heroes, whose spirits from remote times have guided the nation.

V. SHINTO AND THE WARRIOR

The way of the gods has from the beginning been easily reconcilable with the way of the warrior. In fact, the affinity of Shinto with the warrior's way was long ago made clear in the code practiced by the *samurai*, the military class of the feudal period of Japan. This code was called Bushido, literally "the warrior-knight-way." It was the Japanese equivalent of the code of chivalry of medieval Europe and had a comparable influence. Indeed, when its general provisions became known, the entire nation came under its spell, to the extent at least of applauding those who adhered to it.

Shimenawa

The Bushido Code

Bushido did not consist of finally fixed rules. It was a convention; more accurately, it was a system of propriety, preserved in unwritten law and expressing a spirit, an ideal of behavior. As such, it owed something to all the cultural and spiritual forces of the feudal era. Shinto supplied it the spirit of devotion to country and overlord, Confucianism provided its ethical substance, Zen Buddhism its method of private self-discipline, and the feudal habit of life contributed to it the spirit of unquestioning obedience to superiors and a sense of honor that was never to be compromised.

A missionary who knew the Japanese well has set forth the Bushido ethical code in the following eight attitudes:

> 1. Loyalty.
> This was due first of all to the Emperor and under him to the lord whom one more immediately serves. One of the most familiar proverbs says, "A loyal retainer does not serve two lords."
>
> 2. Gratitude.
> It may surprise some to hear that this is a Japanese characteristic, but the Christian doctrine that the spring of a right life is not duty, but gratitude, is one that is readily appreciated by the Japanese.
>
> 3. Courage.
> Life itself is to be surrendered gladly in the service of the lord. An American cannot fail to be touched by the noble words of a young warrior of ancient times to the effect that he wanted to die in battle for his lord and feared nothing so much as dying in bed before he had a chance to sacrifice his life for the object of his devotion.
>
> 4. Justice.
> This means not allowing any selfishness to stand in the way of one's duty.

5. Truthfulness.

A knight scorns to tell a lie in order to avoid harm or hurt to himself.

6. Politeness.

It is the mark of a strong man to be polite in all circumstances, even to an enemy.

7. Reserve.

No matter how deeply one is moved, feeling should not be shown.

8. Honor.

Death is preferable to disgrace. The knight always carried two swords, a long one to fight his foes, a short one to turn upon his own body in the case of blunder or defeat.[K]

The readiness to commit suicide, last mentioned, is perhaps the most startling feature of the Bushido code. Yet suicide was the accepted form of atonement for failure or misjudgment. The warrior knight was always preparing himself in thought and in mood for it. The kind of suicide he mentally rehearsed was *harakiri* (or *seppuku*, the more classical Chinese term), a ceremonial method of disembowelment, carried out coolly and deliberately according to rule, without any expression of emotion. (Women in a similar action cut their jugular veins by a method called *jigai*.)

The Example of "The Forty-Seven Ronin"

No story better illustrates the Bushido spirit than the famous tale of old Japan, known as "The Forty-Seven Ronin." A certain lord, we read, was repeatedly insulted by a superior, until, goaded beyond endurance, he aimed a dagger at his tormentor, and missed. A hastily summoned council of court officials condemned him to commit harakiri and ordered his castle and all of his goods to be confiscated by the state. After the noble lord had ceremonially killed himself, his samurai retainers became *ronin*, that is, men cast adrift by the death of their lord but in duty bound to avenge him. The court official who had brought on the tragedy and was the object of their vengeance thereafter kept to his castle, surrounded by a heavy guard. His spies reported that the leader of the ronin had embarked on a career of drunkenness and debauchery, evidently too craven to do his duty by his dead lord. They did not suspect

that this was a ruse adopted by the ronin leader to throw the enemy off guard. The ruse succeeded. A less strict watch began to be kept in the enemy castle, and finally half of the guard was sent away. Then the forty-seven ronin secretly came together, and on a snowy night stormed the castle and captured the enemy of their dead lord. The leader of the ronin respectfully addressed the captive noble, saying,

> My lord, we are the retainers of Asano Takumi no Kami. Last year your lordship and our master quarreled in the palace, and our master was sentenced to harakiri, and his family was ruined. We have come tonight to avenge him, as is the duty of faithful and loyal men. I pray your lordship to acknowledge the justice of our purpose. And now, my lord, we beseech you to perform harakiri. I myself shall have the honor to act as your second, and when, with all humility, I shall have received your lordship's head, it is my intention to lay it as an offering upon the grave of Asano Takumi no Kami.[L]

But the enemy lord sat speechless and trembling, unable to perform the act required of him, so the leader of the ronin leaped upon him and cut off his head with the same dagger with which his own lord had killed himself. All the ronin then went in a body to the grave of their dead lord and offered to his spirit the washed head of his enemy. After that they waited quietly for some days until the government sent word that they should atone for their crime by committing harakiri themselves, and this they all did, without exception. The whole of Japan rang with their praises, and ever since they have lived in Japanese imagination as peerless exemplars of the Bushido spirit.

Bushido and the Modern Warrior

That Bushido has greatly influenced the ideals cherished by modern Japanese is beyond doubt. When General Nogi, who became the military hero of the Russo-Japanese War, heard in 1894 that war with China had been declared, he left home for the front instantly, without stopping to say good-bye to his wife; when the Emperor Meiji died in 1912, the old general and his wife committed suicide (harakiri and jigai, respectively), believing that by this devoted act they had made possible their personal attendance on their sovereign in the next world. Many other instances of the Bushido or samurai spirit could be cited. One such instance has been supplied by a certain Lieutenant Sakurai, who was crippled in the siege of Port Arthur during the Russo-Japanese War and afterward wrote a book entitled *Human Bullets,* which was for many months a bestseller throughout Japan. The title of this book is an apt description of the soldiers who flung themselves at Port Arthur (in northeast China) with an unparalleled disregard of self-preservation, a swarm of men whom the machine guns of the Russians, which poured death into them at point-blank range, could not stop. Many of them exhibited an incredibly eager desire to make the supreme sacrifice in battle, for such a death was always thought of as patriotism's perfect gift. Lieutenant Sakurai himself, burning with devotion to emperor and country, gathered his men around him before one assault and passed among them a cup of water, saying, "This water you drink, please drink as if at your death-moment."[M] They resolved to be a "sure-death" band and went into battle with a firm determination to give their lives in the attack, or at any rate to fight with complete disregard of personal safety, until they should either conquer or die.

Sakurai's spirit was matched by the suicide missions of Japanese pilots in World War II: kamikaze volunteers flew explosive-laden aircraft into American naval vessels. And in 1970 the celebrated novelist Mishima took Bushido bravado to a further extreme: after exhorting his private rightist army to restore national purity and the military spirit, he sacrificed himself in a harakiri "protest suicide."

Most Japanese would say that such deeds are a distortion of the original spirit of the warrior way. Warriors were to be loyal to lord and country and filial to parents; they were to be brave and fearless in battle, incapable of flinching from danger or death, but they were not to throw their lives away in unthinking bravado. On the contrary, they were to make them count to the utmost in preserving the security of home and country, that is, they were to make their lives last as long as possible. However, this rule was subject to one exception: unbearable humiliation or disgrace justified honorable persons in committing harakiri. Thus, a warrior, especially one charged with responsibility, was expected to commit harakiri when captured in battle or unsuccessful in carrying out an important mission.

The high regard in which warriors have been held in Japan is kept before the public by special commemorative services dedicated to the soldiers who laid down their lives for their country. Throughout Japan, on the designated memorial day, Shinto priests say liturgies before special shrines called "soul-inviting altars," in which the spirits of the heroic dead are invited to reside during the ceremony to receive homage. The Japanese government maintains in Tokyo a Shinto shrine where an annual ritual of national importance is performed in honor of the army and navy dead. This shrine, the Yasukuni-jinja, is regularly used by military and naval leaders for ceremonies designed to instill in the armed forces the highest patriotism. The names of all of the war dead are preserved there.

Pre-World War II Ethnocentric Rationale

In the years before World War II, the military ardor of the warrior was fed from yet another source, the publications of professors in various departments of the imperial universities. The extreme to which a religious nationalism sometimes goes is well illustrated in the following interesting argument by a well-known professor. He declared that

> The center of this phenomenal world is the Mikado's land. From this center we must expand this Great Spirit throughout the world.... The expansion of Great Japan throughout the world and the elevation of the entire world into the land of the Gods is the urgent business of the present and, again, it is our eternal and unchanging object.[J3]

Shinto, the professor said, is the faith at the basis of all religions; it is the religion of all religions. The proof he offered for this broad assertion was that in the opening sentences of the *Kojiki* the first deity mentioned, Ame-no-mi-naka-nushi-no-kami ("the Deity Who Is the August Lord of the Center of Heaven"), is none other than the god who has been recognized in all other religions and philosophies as the unchanging foundation of all things, "the great Life of the Universe." Shinto thus has had from the beginning, he declared, a conception of a great all-inclusive spirit, manifested in the life of each individual human being, and this makes it so comprehensive a faith that it may be regarded as including all other religions. Buddha, Confucius, Laozi, and Jesus Christ were all missionaries of Shinto, unconscious of it though they may have been. (In seeking to show that Jesus was Shinto at heart, several books have in fact attempted to give plausibility to a story that he did not die on the cross; a younger brother was crucified in his stead, and Jesus then traversed Asia and died in northern Japan, his spiritual homeland, and a grave site is marked.)

From the military point of view, Shinto seemed a useful faith. Inspired by its hopes, the Japanese people were empowered to fight for what seemed to them to be their manifest destiny in Asia, and ultimately in the entire world. But the military point of view brought disaster. Shinto continues to nourish the Japanese consciousness of national identity in folklore and in many rituals of everyday life, but few modern Japanese make it the center of an ideational system or a worldview.

VI. SHRINE SHINTO TODAY

When in 1945 the 110,000 shrines formerly under the control of the Home Ministry were cut off from state supervision and subsidies, the first effect of this disestablishment and return of the shrines to local control was a measure of confusion and paralysis. Attendance at the shrines fell off sharply, and the priests, accustomed to the by-then obsolete rituals and prayers that had been supplied by the Home Ministry, were thrown on their own resources, although they were sometimes untrained and unprepared. But after a period of readjustment, a religious atmosphere more genuine than before was established, and the shrines began to regain their popularity. Although a number of shrines has fallen into disuse, others are kept in repair by local shrine associations, and some 86,000 are maintained by a nationwide Shrine Association supported by private funds and voluntary gifts. Most of the shrines are therefore back in business and enjoy genuine popular support.

The typical village shrine occupies a low knoll, where it reposes among cryptomerias and pines that give it a delightful woodland setting. Its rectangular space is hedged about by a sacred fence, pierced on one side by an exactly centered opening. Here stands the torii, the world-famous Shinto gateway. In its simplest and oldest form, a torii is constructed of three smooth tree trunks, two forming the uprights and one lying horizontally across their tops so as to project on either side, a cross-brace two or three feet from the top holding all in place. The torii, the fence, and perhaps a great tree or boulder nearby may be draped with a strand of special rope used to mark sacred sites and objects: *shimenawa*, a garland of twisted straw from which tassels and *gohei* shapes hang. Behind the torii a shaded path leads through other torii to the outer shrine, or *haiden*, which is the sanctuary for worship. This is a small building with a bell hung under its eaves.

As the worshiper draws near the haiden, he or she steps aside to wash both hands and cleanse out the mouth at the "water-purification place." First removing outer clothing such as a hat, coat, and scarf, he or she approaches the outer shrine, bows before it, claps both hands decorously (the distinctive Japanese way of obtaining the gods' attention), bows, rings the bell, bows again—or, having ascended the steps of the outer shrine, kneels on the top step and bows, head low to the floor—leaves an offering on a cloth or drops it in the treasury box provided for the purpose, prays, bows again in meditation and reverence, and then retires quietly, pausing to turn around and bow low.

A little beyond the outer shrine, and often connected with it by a covered passageway, stands the inner sanctuary, or *honden*. This the worshiper does not enter, but knows that the chief treasure of the shrine is housed within it, an object called the *shintai*, or "god body," a precious object that is never allowed to be seen, except in those rare instances where it is a large rock, a hill, or a tree. Usually it is small enough to go into a treasure chest. It often is an object of little value in itself, perhaps an old sword, a mirror, a crystal ball, or a bit of ancient parchment with writing on it. In all likelihood, it is an object that the ruling local clan in olden times prized as an intimate possession, or manufacture, of the powerful clan ancestors. In any case, it has become symbolic of the superhuman, and is therefore often called the "spirit substitute," that is, the outward representation of an invisible spiritual presence. Being precious, it usually is wrapped in finely woven cloths and enclosed in several sacred caskets, one inside the other, the whole covered over with another fine cloth. Seldom moved, it is carried once a year during the annual village festival in a shrine on wheels (the *mikoshi*), or in a palanquin, through the streets, while before and behind it, amidst banners and streamers, musicians in colorful masks play traditional music, actors on floats portray historical scenes drawn from local story, and singing girls posture to the sounds of drum and flute.

The meaning of the shintai has varied, of course, with the faith and sophistication of the worshiper. The more devout among the common people have clearly associated the sacred object with one of the old gods of the land or with a deified ancestor and have even offered prayers to it as though it had ears to hear. Perhaps, however, the majority no longer find in it a distinctly religious value; it signifies instead the locus of a magical power of some sort or the seat of a good luck agency to be coaxed into friendliness. The sophisticated regard it as an object symbolic solely of the ongoing virtue and spirit of deified ancestors and great men of the past.

The Festivals

Shrine Shinto has always enjoyed the indirect support of the Japanese love of festivals, *matsuri,* to which old and young rally at every season of the year with much gaiety. When the festival procession comes down the street, great crowds gather to look on. Five festivals are traditionally grouped as the *go-sekku.* At the beginning of the year comes the New Year Festival (or First Moon's Festival), beginning at midnight on December 31 and lasting three days. The government lists these as national holidays. They are the occasion for millions of people to worship at Buddhist temples and Shinto shrines (which are sometimes to be found in the same compound). Some shrines and temples record an attendance of more than one million each during these three days. On January 7, there is a Feast of the Seven Herbs (the *Nana-kusa*) in honor of the ancient custom of eating a rice gruel flavored with herbs. After this the people feel that the New Year has finally begun, and that they can resume their ordinary work. Odd-numbered days and months are propitious. On the third day of the third month (March), the Girls' (or Dolls') Festival (the *Hina Matsuri*) is celebrated, and on the fifth day of

the fifth month (May) the Boys' Festival (the *Tango-no-sekku*). (These two festivals will be further described in Section VII.) The seventh day of the seventh month (July) is devoted to the festival of the star Vega, a summer festival, and on the ninth day of the ninth month (September) comes the Chrysanthemum Festival.

More widely diffused and in some areas more or less in abeyance are the rites of the agricultural year. Every phase of the cultivation of rice is solemnized, beginning with the emperor's prayer in February that the farmers may have success when the rice is sown and while it is later transplanted to the well-watered paddy fields. In October occurs the *Kanname-sai,* when the first offering of the new rice is made to the gods, and in November the *Niiname-sai,* when the emperor and the people first taste the new rice.

It is customary to celebrate the Buddhist festivals as if they and the distinctively Shinto ones are of the same general interest and character. They are quite popular and stimulate community-wide participation. Among them are the celebration on April 8 of the Buddha's birthday (the *Kambutsu*) and from July 13 to 15 of the *Bon Festival.* This is observed in recognition of the return of the spirits of the dead, in whose honor joyful community dances are performed, and who are respectfully sent away with lanterns—or, where there is sufficient water, as at Matsushima on the east coast, with lanterns set adrift on rafts or miniature boats and then wafted away from the shore.

This is far from being a complete list of the festivals of the year, for there are many local and regional festivals, all arousing great interest and enthusiasm, to the number, by one count, of 450. In the great cities, these events of the ritual year are being infiltrated by such new festivals as Christmas, which is very popular in cities (especially among merchants and advertisers); but there is strong sentiment for continuing the old ceremonies as links with a meaningful and honorable past.

VII. DOMESTIC AND SECTARIAN SHINTO

The ambiguity that once enshrouded the government position has been absent in Domestic and Sectarian Shinto. Although among the sects there have been

The Torii of Itsukushima
The most famous gateway in Japan is partly submerged by the sea at high tide. It is off the shore of Miyajima Island and is dedicated to popular Itsukushima-Hima, daughter of the storm god Susa-no-wo. On sacred Miyajima, no one is allowed either to be born or to die, unless this is unpreventable. But the tame deer are under no such rule. *(Courtesy of Japan National Tourist Organization.)*

ethical culture groups committed to a disavowal of religious interests, the motives of the majority of those supporting the sects have been frankly and unreservedly religious.

Shinto in the Home

The heart and center of Domestic Shinto (the Shinto of the home) has been the *Kami-dana,* or god shelf. Most private homes possess one. On it are placed memorial tablets made of wood or paper, each inscribed with the name of an ancestor or of a patron deity of the household or locality. Sometimes Amaterasu, sometimes Inari, the goddess of rice, or both, are honored by the presence of their symbols. In most cases, a miniature shrine containing a sacred mirror, strips of paper with sacred texts written on them, or talismans obtained at Isé or elsewhere occupies the center of the god shelf. The god shelf itself in this case becomes a temple area in miniature. It may be the repository of any object surcharged with family history and significance. (One Japanese farmer, grateful for kindness rendered during illness in his family by a Christian missionary, rescued a pair of the latter's cast-off shoes from an ash pile and put them on his god shelf for veneration. One can scarcely conceive of a higher compliment.)

Unless in abeyance through neglect or discontinuance, the domestic rites are still performed daily. They may involve no more than the bringing of a small offering of food and the murmuring of a prayer. However, special occasions or crises in family life call forth more elaborate rites, such as the lighting of tapers and the offering of rice brandy, sprigs of the sakaki tree, and cloth as supplements to the usual food offerings, while the whole family, after prostration, head to floor, sits before the god shelf with bowed heads, while a prayer is said.

Usually, domestic religious life is not exclusively Shinto in character. Buddhist priests often are called in to perform rites connected with important aspects of family life. This is especially true after a death, the Buddhist priest being a "funeral specialist" whose services are nearly as indispensable in Japan as those of a funeral director in the West. The family also may maintain in addition to the kami-dana, but usually in another room, a Buddhist altar (or *butsu-dan,* the Buddha shrine), in which are placed wooden tablets bearing the "heavenly names" of the departed, which the Buddhist priest makes known. The priest may chant sutras here at stated intervals—another instance of how Buddhism interacts with Shinto in meeting the needs of a family. A 1981 newspaper poll showed 63 percent of households owning a *butsu-dan.*

Festivals for Girls and Boys

Family life is greatly enlivened by the two annual festivals, heretofore mentioned, for the boys and girls in the family. The Dolls' Festival (also called Girls' Day) takes place on the third day of the third month. (In ancient times, this day was the occasion for a purification rite in which pollution was transferred to paper effigies that were then tossed into streams.) It features within the home a display of beautiful dolls on ascending ceremonial shelves, with the highest shelf occupied by a brilliantly costumed emperor and empress. At a lower level are the dolls' furniture and utensils. The Boys' Festival, officially renamed Children's Day in 1948, is still observed in most families as the traditional occasion for the family to report to the community the number of boys belonging to it. On a special pole erected outside of the house, brightly colored paper carp, one for each boy, are suspended one below the other in order of age, and through their yawning mouths the breezes of early May enter to inflate and float them like banners. Inside the home, it has been traditional to set out an array of samurai dolls and their weapons, not simply to simulate war and martial exercises, but also to symbolize courage and patriotism. Some families nowadays omit such a display because it is no longer appropriate in an age of peace and industry.

Sectarian Shinto

During the years that the government sponsored the supposedly nonreligious ceremonies of State Shinto, a sphere for Sectarian, that is to say religious, Shinto was allowed. Under the provisions of the Constitution of 1889, which granted religious liberty to all citizens, Shinto sects were free to formulate their own beliefs and ceremonies, but obliged to find their own means of support, as were the various branches of Buddhism and Christianity. Of the thirteen sects recognized by the Bureau of Religions before World War II, about half came into existence after the restoration of 1868. Any attempt to classify these self-propagating religious orders reveals their generally eclectic character. In D. C. Holtom's classification, only three can be called pure Shinto sects. Of the others, two have sought amalgamation with Confucianism. Three have been called mountain sects, because they have specialized in the ascent of steep mountain slopes, the object being to experience on the summits ecstatic communion with the great spirits of Japan. Of these last-named sects, two have centered their faith on Mt. Fuji as the best symbol of the national life and the most sacred object in the world. The purification sects, so-called, of which there are two, have emphasized the regard for ceremonial purity that ran through primitive Shinto, but they also have adopted Hindu methods of cleansing the soul and mind, especially deep breathing and even fire walking. The most interesting and most influential of the sectarian orders have been the faith-healing sects. The oldest of them, Tenrikyo, is described later.

Since World War II, with the withdrawal of the government from the sphere of religion, hundreds of Shinto sects have formed, and some sixty or so have registered with the government as Sectarian Shinto denominations. Many other recently formed groups make no claim to be Shintoist, except in the most tenuous sense, and are commonly called new religions, for they include every variety of religious belief.

The New Religions

The more active sects adapt to their needs not only the doctrines of many foreign religions but also certain theories drawn from psychology and other sciences, in the hope of attaining ultimate truth and personal spiritual security. They search the world for helpful ideas, but it would be false to say that they are new in the sense of being complete breaks with the past. They are thoroughly Japanese, and all show the unmatched ability to adapt foreign ideas and practices to Japanese needs that we have seen in earlier Japan. In the second place, they are either reformulated "old" religions or splinter groups breaking away from the "new" religions themselves to express divergent liberal or conservative views.

Sects Founded by Women

There is good evidence that women played important roles as shamans (miko) before the seventh-century infusion of male-dominated Confucian and Buddhist influence. The early patterns survived in Okinawa, where the miko were equivalent to priestesses, and in the Ryukyu islands, where there was a full female religious hierarchy paralleling and supplementing the male ranks of priests. The realms of healing and necromancy (calling up the spirits of the dead and interpreting their messages) were their special preserve. After the infusions of Chinese models on the main islands, the role of the miko was reduced to that of a passive medium who transmitted the words of the dead, the interpreting of those messages being reserved for Buddhist monks or Shinto priests.

Yet from the mid-nineteenth century onward, a number of new religions received their impetus from the charismatic leadership of individual women. The founders shared typical shamanic characteristics: humble origin, physical hardship, possession by a divine spirit, and personal charisma. In many of the new sects, the deity was envisaged in feminine or androgynous terms.

Nakayama Miki received a revelation in 1838 and was hailed as a "living kami." Her message centered on the healing power of the Heavenly Parent, Tenri O no Mikoto (and a corollary rejection of medical interventions). Today, the Tenrikyo, "Heavenly Wisdom Teaching," claims over two and one-half million members.

In 1892, Deguchi Nao encountered a vision of the divine and revelations of a coming new age of peace. Her sect, Omoto, "Great Source," grew to over two million members in the 1920s, but, because of its antiwar, anticapitalist, and antilandlord emphases, it was subjected to severe repression by government authorities. Today there are only some 150,000 adherents, but the Omoto influenced the generation of larger offshoot religions, notably Seicho no Ie, "House of Growth," Sekai Kyusei Kyo, "Teaching of World Salvation," and PL Kyodan, "Perfect Liberty Teaching Society."

Kotani Kimi was a cofounder of the Reiyukai, "Friends of the Spirit Society," in 1925, essentially an offshoot from Nichiren Buddhism (p. 220), centering worship on the Lotus Sutra and the mantra "Namu myoho renge kyo." An offshoot of Reiyukai in turn was the even larger Rissho Koseikai, "Establishing Justice and Community Society," founded in 1938, partly through the inspiration of a rural housewife, Naganuma Myoko. The Rissho sect, featuring group counselling (hoza) sessions in its program, is thriving in the present, claiming some seven million members.

After World War II, Kitamura Sayo, a farm woman, declared that the male-female Shinto deity Tensho Kotai Jingu "took possession" of her. Regarded as a "living kami," she launched a society in the deity's name. It is popularly known as Odoru Shukyo, "The Dancing Religion," for its ecstatic rituals. Believers are called upon to confess sins (defined as the Buddhist Six Roots of Evil: regret, desire, hatred, fondness, love, and being loved), to shout out the Lotus Sutra mantra until "the throat bleeds," and to transcend their egos in the ecstasy of ego-annihilating dance. Odoru Shukyo is unlike many other new religions in declaring all other faiths to be false.

Continuing Growth of New Religions

The sects we have just mentioned, along with other newly formed societies, make up an array far beyond the scope of this chapter. When the Soka Gakkai (p. 221) are included, an estimated forty to fifty million adherents are involved. If a generalization can be made, it is that the new religions attract adherents who are "joiners" for whom doctrinal fine points are not important, the primary concern being the search of personal growth and supportive affiliations. PL (Perfect Liberty) Kyodan is a clear example. Its program includes self-realization and development groups, creative art activities, golf outings, "joy-bringing" fireworks displays, and many elaborate celebrations and festivals in accordance with its bland principles: "The individual is a manifestation of God," "Live radiantly as the sun," and "Live in perfect liberty."

On the other hand, some of the new religions have been keenly aware of their political potential and have been taking stands on social issues. When Prime Minister Nakasone made an official visit to Yasukuni shrine, which honors Japan's war dead, Soka Gakkai, Rissho Koseikai, Seicho no Ie, the New Pure Land sect, and most Christian denominations protested.

Many Japanese who continue in the old traditions confess, however, some puzzlement about all of this interest in religion. In their own lives Buddhism and Shinto command respect but not their personal involvement. They are satisfied to have the Shinto priests play an important role in Japanese festivals and, like the priests of ancient Rome, to conduct their ceremonies at important shrines, sometimes in groups numbering ten or more white-robed officiants, without the necessary presence of a congregation. In their own homes, a Buddhist priest comes at the appointed day of the month, finds the butsu-dan freshly decorated with flowers, reads sutras and offers prayers, then picks up the offering left for him, and quietly departs, with only occasional pastoral visits with members of the family who happen to be in the house.

And yet, when all is said and done, the materialistic culture now prevailing in Japan seems not to suffice for the total needs of such aspiring human beings as the Japanese are.

GLOSSARY

Ainu light-skinned, hairy, Caucasoid aboriginal inhabitants of northern Japan, driven ever further northward by Mongoloid immigrants, only a few thousand survive on Hokkaido reservations

Amaterasu the sun goddess, mythic ancestress of the imperial line of Japan

Bushido "way of the warrior," a code of ethics for samurai, a blend of Shinto national pride, Buddhist ideas on self-control, and Confucian moral teaching

dosojin "wayside guardian/progenitor," images of stone, wood, or straw, often explicitly sexual, intended to ensure protection and/or fertility

gohei an offertory wand with pendants of paper, wood, cloth, or metal folded in a zigzag pattern (perhaps to represent bolts of silk or other cloth)

Isé a sacred peninsula on the eastern shore of Japan, site of the principal shrine to Amaterasu

Izanagi and Izanami "He-who-invites" and "She-who-invites," mythic primal founders of the islands of Japan and progenitors of natural objects and humankind

Izumo north coastal site of an ancient shrine dedicated to kami, descended from Susa-no-wo

jinja "kami residence," a sacred area, usually with buildings, a site for worshiping kami; general term for Shinto shrines as distinguished from Buddhist tera or -dera

kami "upper being(s)," spirits, deities, or the sacred character of a place or person—anything inspiring awe (Chinese character also vocalized shen, shin, or jin)

Kojiki "Record of Ancient Matters," oldest (712 C.E.) Japanese text of sacred myth and history to the year 628

Kyoha Shinto "faith-group," sectarian, or shrine Shinto as distinguished from State Shinto (*Jinja Shinto*)

matsuri festival(s)

mikoshi portable shrines carried or pulled through the streets on *matsuri* occasions

Motoori Norinaga 18th c. scholar and intellectual leader of the revival and rationalization of Shinto

Nihongi, or *Nihon Shoki* "Chronicles of Japan," an extension (to 697 C.E.) and expansion of the materials of the *Kojiki;* written in Chinese

norito prayer(s) and liturgical formulas used in Shinto ceremonies

O-Harai "Great Purification," twice-a-year national cleansing ceremonies utilizing *haraigushi* wands and branches of the sacred sakaki tree

Ryobu Shinto "two aspect" Shinto, a syncretized Shinto in which Buddhist bodhisattvas and deities are attended by kami or equated with particular Shinto deities

shimenawa straw rope from which tassels and *gohei* shapes hang, used to make sacred sites and objects

Susa-no-wo "Valiant Male," brother of Amaterasu, in the *Kojiki* (assembled by priests of her cult), he appears as a mischief-, pollution-, and storm-causing adversary; his cult was associated with the Izumo shrine

Tenrikyo "heavenly wisdom sect," oldest of the Shinto "new" religions; a charismatic revelation in 1838 turned Nakayama Miki into a "living kami" who spread the healing power of the Heavenly Parent, Tenri O no Mikoto

torii a sacred gateway marking an entrance to a *jinja,* or a path toward it

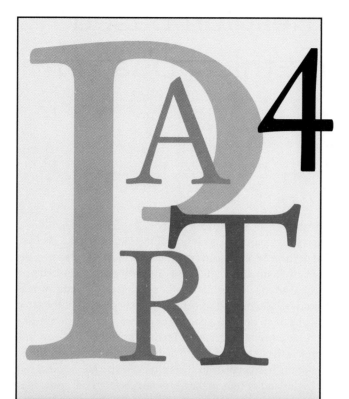

PART 4

THE RELIGIONS OF THE MIDDLE EAST

Zoroastrianism

A Religion Based on Ethical Dualism

In our study of the structure of religious experience around the world we have come to an interesting point. The evolution of the thought of the Zoroastrians, as compared to that of their Aryan cousins who entered India, shows more clearly than usual the effect of environment on the beliefs and attitudes of kindred peoples. The religion of Zoroaster had the same source as the religion of the Vedic Aryans. When the Indo-European wanderers who sometime at the beginning of the second millennium before Christ, or earlier, came to a parting of the ways somewhere near the Caspian Sea, one portion, perhaps the larger, went up the Oxus River Valley to India; the other penetrated into present-day Armenia, Azarbaijan, and the mountain valleys forming the northwest fringes of the Iranian plateau. This physical separation was paralleled by a cultural one.

In the land of Iran, as the historians prefer to call ancient Persia, the soil was for the most part arid, the climate dry and bracing. The inhabitants therefore tended to be aggressive and realistic, because it was necessary for them to be attentive farmers and herdsmen. In the somewhat enervating climate of India, on the other hand, human life tended to become recessive physically, yet rich in romantic and philosophical interests. There was more time for thought in India, perhaps because more time was taken for it. On the Iranian plateau, the situation was quite otherwise. Thought and life were concerned largely with this world and the exciting, if difficult, struggle for existence. Morality, while pursuing the business of life, became one of the chief concerns of religion, and the mood of asceticism was far removed from most minds.

Suppose that the Aryans of India and the Aryans of Iran had remained together, living side by side on the plains somewhere in southeastern Europe, as they once did. Would they have developed so great a difference as that between Zoroastrianism and Hinduism? It is fruitless to ask. They separated, and time and circumstance swung them poles apart.

The story of Zoroastrianism is not easy to tell. Our sources are not clear and authentic, as they were in our study of the religion of the Vedas. The sacred book of the Zoroastrian faith, the *Avesta,* was for centuries preserved orally; it was not put together before the third or fourth

WESTERN NAMES: Zoroastrianism, Zarathustrianism

ADHERENTS IN 1997: 190,000

NAMES USED BY ADHERENTS: Parsis (India) Zardushtis, Behdins (Iran)

SACRED LITERATURE: Avesta

   Subdivisions: Videvdat (spells and prescriptions); *Yasna* (liturgical material, including *Gathas,* hymns)

SUPREME PRINCIPLES (DEITIES): Ahura Mazda (Ormazd) and Angra-Mainyu (Ahriman)

OTHER SUPERHUMAN SPIRITS: Anahita, Druj, Mithra, Spenta-Mainyu, Vohu Manah, Zurvan, fravashis, daevas, and yazatas

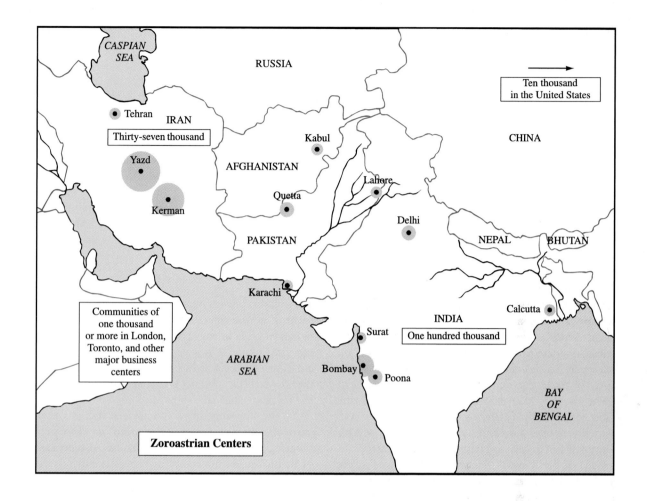

century C.E. during Sassanian times. It is more or less a miscellany, without cohesion; indeed, it is but the remnant of a far larger body of literature, a great part of which has perished. The portion of the *Avesta* most important for us is the *Yasna,* because it contains the *Gathas,* or Hymns of Zoroaster, written in an ancient dialect, Gathic, a dialect predating the Avestan language and closely related to the Vedic. These hymns give us our only really trustworthy information on Zoroaster's life and thought.

Our best course, in view of the difficulties that do not allow a complete historical reconstruction, is to begin with what can be recovered of Iranian religion before Zoroaster, then take up the life and teaching of Zoroaster himself, and finally set down the differences to be seen in the Zoroastrianism of later times.

I. IRANIAN RELIGION BEFORE ZOROASTER

Virtually all we know of Iranian religion before Zoroaster is derived from the openly hostile references to it in the *Gathas,* the hard-to-interpret references in the inscriptions of the Achaemenian kings, and the post-Gathic Avestan texts.

We know, however, that the popular religion of the Iranians was practically the same as that reflected in the Vedas.

The common people worshiped powers known as *daevas,* a name identical with the *devas,* or "shining ones," of the *Rig-Veda.* These were associated with the powers of nature—sun, moon, stars, earth, fire, water, and winds. The priests recognized also *asuras* ("lords") among the gods, who were considered to be high in the heavens and concerned with cosmic order. There was, therefore, some sort of hierarchical organization of the gods.

Among the gods was Intar, or Indara, a war god, best known by his epithet Verethragna, "he who struck down Verethra," an obstruction that held back the rain waters. (As in the Vedic analogue, Indra slew Vritra.) Intar, however, was not a paramount deity; he was overshadowed by Mithra (Vedic Mitra), a very popular god, who seems to have been widely known among Aryan folk everywhere. In a Hittite document of 1400–1300 B.C.E., found in Asia Minor, Mithra is mentioned under the name of Miidra, and he was, it appears, the chief god of the Mitanni, an Aryan group then controlling the mountain areas fringing the Mesopotamian plain on the north. The Iranians on their part gave him highest honors. He was to them the giver of cattle and sons; and he was the god of light (whence the Manichaeans, the Greeks, and the Romans drew the inference that he was a sun god, which may have been true). Particularly, he stood for the quality of loyalty and faith keeping. In a later Yasht (song) of the *Khordah Avesta,* he is portrayed as the god "to whom the princes pray when they go forth to battle," and in his function of supporter of the sanctity of treaties (Mithra seems to mean "treaty" or "pact") he sees to it that wherever bad faith exists

> the steeds of the deceivers refuse to bear their riders; though they run they do not advance, though they ride they make no progress, though they ride in their chariots they gain no advantage; backwards flies the lance hurled by the enemy of Mithra. Even if the enemy throw skillfully, even if his lance reach his enemy's body, the stroke does not hurt. The lance from the hand of Mithra's enemy is borne away by the wind.[A]

Along with Mithra, there appears a god called in the Hittite document Uruwana, who was known to the Greeks as Ouranos and is to be identified with the Vedic Varuna, the god of the domed sky and lord (ahura) of the moral order. He had a high ethical character. We shall have need to mention him again.

We also learn of a conception of an underlying order of the world, whether natural or moral, called Asha or Arta, whose attributes are truth, right, justice, and divine order (this is certainly the Vedic Rita); we hear, too, of the heavenly twins, the Nasatya or Asvins (in the Hittite document called the Nashaadtianna), who were reduced by the later Persians to one being; of Vayu, the wind, a companion of Indara, and appearing under the double aspect of good and bad winds, blowing from the beginning of time; of the ruler of the dead, the first man to die, Yima (the Vedic Yama); and of the Fravashi or Fathers, the beloved and protective ancestral spirits.

Fire Worship under Open Sky

These divine powers (and others whose names are lost to us, but were in every case probably akin to the names of gods in the *Rig-Veda*) were worshiped and sacrificed to under the open sky, beside altars, with the aid of priests, fire worship, and the sacramental use of the psychedelic potion prepared from the sacred *haoma* plant (the Vedic soma).

The fire worship of the ancient Iranians is of particular interest, not only because of its likeness to the fire ceremonies of ancient India, but also because of its historical importance in Zoroastrianism to the present day. The Vedic name "Agni" is not mentioned in the literature, but undoubtedly, under the Iranian name of Atar, it was he who was invoked and worshiped. Along with the ceremony by which the sacrificial fire was lit and reverenced, the grass around the altar was consecrated, sprinkled with haoma juice, and made the table upon which were laid portions of the sacrifice for the invisible divine guests, the gods. The sacrifice might be of a cereal, but it usually was that of an animal of some kind. In the latter case, the victim about to be sacrificed was touched with the *barsom,* a bundle of boughs that was worshiped as supernatural and held before the face during the adoration of the sacred fire. (In modern times, a metal replica is used in grace before meals.) The ceremony of the pressing of the haoma juice and the sacramental use of the sacred liquid were, one is led to conclude, so similar to the ceremonies of the kind in Vedic India that the reader is referred to chapter 3 on early Hinduism for the details.

In general, the ancient Iranians, for the most part settlers who cultivated gardens and put their livestock out to graze, followed a religion ill suited to their

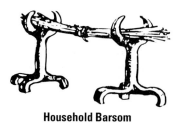

Household Barsom

mode of life and developing economy. Its animal sacrifices were becoming increasingly burdensome. What to nomads seemed natural and reasonable enough and involved no great economic sacrifice to settlers was far too costly. Reform was needed, and Zoroaster was at hand to effect it.

II. THE LIFE AND TEACHINGS OF ZOROASTER

Background

It is impossible to be certain about the details of Zoroaster's life. The date of his birth is uncertain. Persian tradition places the time at 660 B.C.E., which may be thirty or more years too early. This date, with misgivings, is accepted by most modern scholars, but others, with some plausibility, contend that Zoroaster must have lived at an earlier period, perhaps as early as 1000 B.C.E. or as late as the first half of the sixth century B.C.E.

Another elusive matter is the determination of his birthplace. It seems likely that was born somewhere in east central Iran but did his work farther to the east. One modern authority ventures to be quite specific: "The region in which he proclaimed his message was probably ancient Chorasmia—an area [south of the Aral Sea] comprising what is now Persian Khorasan, Western Afghanistan, and the Turkmen Republic of the [former] U.S.S.R."[B]

According to tradition, recorded at a time too far removed from his own to be reliable, Zoroaster received instruction in youth from a tutor, assumed the *kusti*, or sacred thread (note once more the parallelism with Indian custom), at the age of fifteen, and was known for his compassionate nature, expressed especially in solicitude toward the aged and toward cattle in time of famine. At twenty he left his father and mother and the wife they bad chosen for him to wander forth, seeking an answer to his deepest religious questionings.

Experience of Revelation

At the critical age of thirty (so often a time of crisis in the lives of religious geniuses), he received a revelation. Legend has magnified the original event into a series of miraculous visions. The traditional scene of the first and most startling vision is laid on the banks of the Daitya River near his home. A figure "nine times as large as a man" appeared before Zoroaster. It was the archangel Vohu Manah (Good Thought). Vohu Manah questioned Zoroaster and then bade him to lay aside the "vesture" of his material body and, as a disembodied soul, mount to the presence of Ahura Mazda, "the Wise Lord" and Supreme Being, holding court among his attendant angels.[C1] A curiously vivid detail of the account records the fact that as soon as Zoroaster appeared in the celestial assembly, he no longer beheld his own shadow upon the floor "on account of the great brilliance of the archangels" who encircled him.[C2] Ahura Mazda then instructed Zoroaster, called now to be a prophet, in the doctrines and duties of the true religion. The story goes on to say that during the next eight years he met in vision each of the six principal archangels, and each conference made more complete the original revelation. So runs the tradition.

But in the *Gathas,* where presumably we have Zoroaster's own words, the references to these revelations furnish us with more authentic, if fragmentary, details. Thus,

> As the holy one I recognized thee, Mazda Ahura, when Good Thought (Vohu Manah) came to me and asked me, "Who art thou? to whom dost thou belong? By what sign wilt thou appoint the days for questioning about thy possessions and thyself?"
>
> Then said I to him: "To the first (question), Zarathustra am I, a true foe to the Liar, to the utmost of my power, but a powerful support would I be to the Righteous, that I may attain the future things of the infinite Dominion, according as I praise and sing thee, Mazda."

As the holy one I recognized thee, Mazda Ahura, when Good Thought came to me. To his question, "For which wilt thou decide?" (I made reply), "At every offering of reverence to thy Fire, I will bethink me of Right [Asha] so long as I have power. Then show me Right, upon whom I call." . . .

And when thou saidst to me, "To Right shalt thou go for teaching," then thou didst not command what I did not obey: "Speed thee, ere my Obedience [Sraosha, the angel who judges the dead] come, followed by treasure-laden Destiny, who shall render to men severally the destinies of the two-fold award."[D1]

He began immediately to preach, the tradition says, but without success. Discouraged, he was visited by a severe temptation in which the Evil Spirit, Angra Mainyu, bade him to renounce worship of Mazda. "But Zarathustra answered him, 'No! I shall not renounce the good religion of the worshipers of Mazda, not though life, limb, and soul should part asunder.'"[C3]

Then he found himself somewhere in eastern Iran, it is said, in the court of an Aryan prince by the name of Vishtaspa or Hystaspes. (Some identify him as the father of Darius I of Persia, but the linguistic age of the *Gathas* suggests that this Hystaspes lived in an earlier time.) With renewed hope, he began a two-year effort to win this ruler to his faith. Vishtaspa, all but hidden from view in the mass of laudatory tradition gathered round him, gives the impression of being an honest-hearted man, simple and sincere in his habit of life. But he was dominated by the Karpans, so detested in the *Avesta*, a greedy throng of priests. With their numerous animal sacrifices and their magical procedures designed to make the crops grow, protect the cattle, keep the marauding nomads of the north (Turanians?) at a distance, and frustrate demonic influences of all sorts, they roused Zoroaster's most intense opposition. During the struggle with him they managed to have him cast into prison, but after two hard years he won the monarch over to his faith, aided, tradition tells us, by his wondrous cure of Vishtaspa's favorite black horse and helped by the sympathetic support of Vishtaspa's consort, Hutaosa.

The conversion was complete and unreserved. Vishtaspa put all of his power behind the propagation of the faith. The whole court followed the monarch into the new religion. The king's brother Zain and his gallant son Isfendir were of special importance as converts. Two brothers, both nobles who stood high in the councils of Vishtaspa, Frashaoshtra and Jamnaspa by name, became Zoroaster's kin by marriage; the former gave Zoroaster his daughter, Huovi, to wife, and the latter married Pourucista, Zoroaster's daughter by his first wife.

The next twenty years, as the late and not too trustworthy tradition records, were spent vigorously promulgating the faith among the Iranians and fighting two holy wars in its defense. The first of these saw the rise of Isfendir to great heights of heroism in routing the invading northern nomads. But, if tradition can be credited, the second invasion of the nomads, which took place when Zoroaster was seventy-seven years of age, was at first successful and led to Zoroaster's death. The later writers of the *Avesta* state, over one thousand years after the event, that when the nomads stormed Balkh, one of their number surprised and slew him before the fire altar at which he was officiating.

Whether or not this was the manner of it, Zoroaster's death did not mean the extinction of the faith. He had planted the roots of his new faith deeply in the rich soil of Iranian folk consciousness, where it was destined to flourish.

Teachings

The religion Zoroaster taught was a unique ethical monotheism; that is to say, he held that the moral law requiring human righteousness proceeded from one good God. In calling the supreme god Ahura Mazda ("Wise Lord"), he did not resort to invention. The name was already current. Nor was the god denoted by it hitherto unknown. Ahura Mazda was, there is little doubt, no other than the god of the moral and natural order whom the Aryans of India worshiped under the name of Varuna. It seems that Zoroaster's clan had long given their special allegiance to this highly ethical deity. Though the god was no longer called Varuna, many scholars, seeing in what aspects he was viewed (he is described in the *Gathas* as "clad with the massy heavens as with a garment"[D2]), have concluded that the honorific title had come to take the place of his ancient name, just as in India the title "Auspicious" (Shiva) dispossessed the ancient name Rudra. That Ahura Mazda was an honorific designation is quite apparent. Mazda means "the wise" or "the full of light." Ahura is the same word as the Vedic Asura, meaning "lord," and was an Indo-European name for outstanding figures among the devas, or gods.

Incidentally, it is interesting to follow the curious twist given by Zoroaster on the one hand and the Vedic Aryans on the other hand to the words for lord and god. The Indo-Aryans, like the Romans and Celts on the other side of the world, called their good spirits *devas* (Roman *deus,* Celtic *divin,* and English *deity,* or *divinity*), but their experience of the capricious natural forces of India somehow caused the name *asura* (lord) to be applied exclusively to evil spirits, the sublime and awful lords of mischief. (This shift in meaning may be seen taking place between the earlier and later hymns of the *Rig-Veda.*) In Iran, on the other hand, Zoroaster attached to these words quite the opposite meanings. In Mazda he saw the one true Ahura to whom his entire devotion should be paid, the sublime and awful "Lord" who was perfect wisdom and goodness. But he feared Mazda would not be recognized in the same way by the masses of the people. Under the leadership of the priests of the old religion, they worshiped along with the ahuras Mazda, Mithra, and Apam Napat (a designation for Agni, Fire), a host of *daevas,* gods called by many ancient Indo-European names, Indra and Vayu, for example. The "corrupt" priests made magic with the aid of these deities. The wild nomads to the north, who were the scourge of all good settlers, sacrificed to these deities before they made their raids on Iran to carry off the grain and cattle and gut the barns and homes with fire. There could be only one conclusion for Zoroaster: the daevas were malicious devils masquerading as good spirits, fathers of lies deceiving the very elect. Thus, for Zoroaster, ahura was vested with good and daevas with evil, whereas the Indo-Aryans saw evil in asuras and good in devas.

Opposing himself squarely and uncompromisingly, therefore, to the popular religion, Zoroaster set forth his religious system in a few clear-cut conceptions.

1. Final Revelation: One Supreme Deity

He took a firm stand, to begin with, on the revelation he had received. The *Gathas* again and again set forth his claim that he had been called to his prophetic mission by Ahura Mazda himself, and that the religion he taught was the final and true religion.

He gave all of his devotion to one god. Ahura Mazda was, to him, the supreme deity—that is to say, supreme in creation, supreme in value, and supreme by anticipation of the final apocalyptic event by which he would forever crush all evil and establish right and truth. In contradistinction to some of his later followers, Zoroaster believed that by the will of the one supreme Lord Mazda all things had come into being. As the following sentences from the *Gathas* declare, Mazda caused darkness as well as light:

> Who is by generation the Father of Right (Asha) at the first? Who determined the path of sun and stars? Who is it by whom the moon waxes and wanes again? . . . Who upheld the earth beneath and the firmament from falling? Who made the water and the plants? Who yoked swiftness to winds and clouds? . . . What artist made light and darkness? sleep and waking? Who made morning, noon, and night, that call the understanding man to his duty? . . . I strive to recognize by these things thee, O Mazda, creator of all things through the holy spirit.[D3]

2. Spenta Mainyu and Modes of Good Action

Zoroaster had a rich conception of Ahura Mazda's way of accomplishing results. Mazda expresses his will through a Holy Spirit (Spenta Mainyu) and various modes of divine action called the "Immortal Holy Ones," or Amesha Spentas (the Ameshaspands of later Persia). These modes of ethical activity bear such names as Vohu Manah (Good Thought or Sense), Asha (Right), Kshathra (Power or Dominion), Haurvatat (Prosperity), Armaiti (Piety), and Ameretat (Immortality). Asha (or Arta) is the Vedic Rita. Vohu Manah is the divine mode that conducted Zoroaster to Ahura Mazda for his first revelation (here the allegorical meaning that Zoroaster was led by inspiration to the true God seems to suggest itself). Armaiti, Kshathra, Haurvatat, and Ameretat are gifts of Ahura Mazda to man and also forces and facts in their own right. In name at least, they all are abstract qualities or states, and it is a little perplexing to know just what Zoroaster's conception of them was, whether he felt that they were good genii of Ahura Mazda, with their own being and individuality, or whether he meant to give them no more than the force of personalized abstractions. Jacques Duchesne-Guillemin finds that, in Zoroaster's belief, Ahura Mazda not only created all things but is "the father" of the Amesha Spentas, "which help him animate and govern the world," supplanting the other ahuras and the daevas. Zoroaster certainly did not invent the ahuras and daevas; most of them can be traced back to the Indo-Iranian period. But what engaged him most was a religious reorientation. The *Gathas* are "a meditation on the Amesha Spentas," for "the subject of his day-to-day mental life consisted in thinking them over" and applying to them "novel epithets" that reinforced his "monotheistic solution."[E]

Other modes of divine expression are named besides the Amesha Spentas—for example, Obedience (Sraosha), the Ox-Creator of Spirit that protects cows (Geus Urva), and still others. But none of these are very clearly visualized as divine beings with independent personalities. At all events, they are kept subordinate to Ahura Mazda as agents of his divine self-expression. In short, Zoroaster gives us a rich conception of deity without abandoning monotheism.

3. Angra Mainyu and Modes of Evil

Though Ahura Mazda is supreme, he is not unopposed. This is an important belief of Zoroaster. Against Asha (Right or Truth) is Druj (the Lie); Truth is confronted with Falsehood, Life with Death. The Good Spirit (Spenta Mainyu) is opposed by Angra Mainyu, literally, "the Bad Spirit." It is characteristic of the *Gathas* to lay continual emphasis on the fundamental cleavage in the world of nature and in human life between right and wrong, the true religion and the false. This cleavage began at the time Ahura Mazda created the world and established freedom of choice for his creatures.

> Now the two primal Spirits, who revealed themselves in vision as Twins, are the Better and the Bad in thought and word and action. And between these two the wise once chose aright, the foolish not so. And when these twain Spirits came together in the beginning, they established Life and Not-Life, and that at the last the Worst Existence (Hell) shall be to the followers of the Lie, but the Best Thought (Paradise) to him that follows Right. Of these twain Spirits he that followed the Lie *chose* doing the worst things; the holiest Spirit *chose* Right.[D4]

Again,

> I will speak of the Spirits twain at the first beginning of the world, of whom the holier thus spake to the enemy: "Neither thought nor teachings nor wills nor beliefs nor words nor deeds nor selves nor souls of us twain agree."[D5]

R. C. Zaehner recasts the data into this picture: In the beginning, Ahura Mazda had twin "sons," identical in potentialities; they and Ahura Mazda himself were faced by free choice, the constant condition of being a person; one by choice of Truth and Right became Spenta Mainyu, the Good or Holy Spirit; the other by misguided choice of the Lie became Angra Mainyu, the Evil Spirit.[F]

Thus, at the beginning of the world, the good spirit going forth from Ahura Mazda came to be opposed by an evil spirit—the spirit called in later times Shaitin or Satan.

4. The Soul as the Scene of Struggle

Although only a few words are needed to state it, it was perhaps Zoroaster's cardinal moral principle that each human soul is the seat of a war between good and evil. This war in the breast is of critical importance. In creating human beings, Ahura Mazda gave them freedom to determine their own actions and hence the power to choose between right and wrong. Though Ahura Mazda seeks always by the power of his Good Spirit (Spenta Mainyu) and through Vohu Manah to commend the right, he has not made humanity inaccessible to Angra Mainyu's evil suggestions. So it is required of each soul to decide the issue of the war in each bosom, and to choose either the good or the evil. The good soul chooses aright.

5. Honor and Husbandry versus Deceit and Plunder

Good and evil are not clearly defined, but we cannot rightly expect the *Gathas,* which are devotional hymns and not theological treatises, to be precise. The *Gathas,* however, give us an indication of the *practical difference* between right and wrong. The good people, for example, were to Zoroaster those who accepted the true religion, and the evil were those who rejected it, especially those who continued to practice the old popular religion with its worship of the daevas. The daevas, it seemed clear, had allied themselves with Angra Mainyu, the Evil Spirit, and so those who followed them were living in a condition fraught with evil. Such people were not merely to be shunned: "Resist them with the weapon!"[D6] If it is good always to speak the truth and to aid all those who follow Asha and Vohu Manah, it is evil to help the bad, to do them favors, or to give them gifts. The good—and here is an insight into Zoroaster's practical common sense—till the soil, raise grain, grow fruit, root out weeds, reclaim wasteland, irrigate the barren ground, and treat kindly the animals, especially the cow, that are of service to the farmers. In their personal relations, they are truth-speakers; they never lie. The evil have no agriculture. That is their condemnation.

> He that is no husbandman, O Mazda, however eager he be, has no part in the good message.[D7]

Angra Mainyu is always busy against husbandry.

> The Liar stays the supporters of Right from prospering the cattle in district and province, infamous that he is.[D8]

The meandering nomads represented evil at its worst. They prepared for their raids by worshiping the daevas, after wickedly slaying cattle as sacrifices for the altar. Then they fell upon the fields and destroyed their produce. Such is the evil one may expect from daeva worshipers!

The good soul would say, in the words of an old Zoroastrian pledge,

> I repudiate the Daevas. I confess myself a worshipper of Mazda, a Zarathustrian, as an enemy of the Daevas, a prophet of the Lord, praising and worshipping the Immortal Holy Ones (the Amesha Spentas). To the Wise Lord I promise all good; to him, the good, beneficent, righteous, glorious, venerable, I vow all the best; to him from whom is the cow, the law, the (celestial) luminaries, with whose luminaries (heavenly) blessedness is conjoined. I choose the holy, good Armaiti, she shall be mine. I abjure theft and cattle-stealing, plundering and devastating the villages of Mazda-worshippers.[G]

6. Ceremonies Purified

Of religious ceremonial, only the worshipful parts are left. The old Aryan ritual is purged (almost to the vanishing point) of magic and idolatry. Orgies attendant upon animal sacrifices are eliminated, and the ritual intoxication attendant upon drinking haoma juice is condemned.

Not only did Zoroaster disapprove of the hallucinogenic effects of haoma juice, he also condemned the practice (which is found also in Indo-Aryan and central Asian rites) of having laymen catch the urine of the soma-drinking priests and to drink it. Evidently "soma" passes through the body of those who drink it relatively unchanged, except for dilution, and those drinking the urine are psychedelically affected by it. In the *Avesta* (*Yasna* 48:10) occurs the indignant question of Zoroaster: "When wilt thou do away with the urine of drunkenness with which the priests delude the people?"—a question addressed to himself.

But there was one feature of the old ritual that Zoroaster fully retained. According to tradition, as we have seen, he was done to death while serving before the sacred fire. In a previous quotation from the *Gathas*, we have heard him say, "At every offering to thy Fire, I will bethink me of Right so long as I have power." Elsewhere he declares the sacred fire to be a gift of Ahura Mazda to mankind. But Zoroaster did not worship *the fire*, as his ancestors had done, or as some of his followers later did; it was to him a precious symbol of Ahura Mazda, and no more, through which he could realize the nature and essence of the Wise Lord. So, at least, his language and the logic of his whole position seem to have led him to believe.

7. The Final Victory of Ahura Mazda

What, finally, is to be the issue of the long struggle between good and evil? Will Ahura Mazda forever be opposed? Will Angra Mainyu, the Liar, always afflict human souls and lead them astray?

Whatever misgivings his later followers may have had on the subject, Zoroaster had no doubt that Ahura Mazda would, in the fullness of time, triumphantly overthrow all evil. He did not believe that the influence of evil is as eternal as good. He was thoroughly optimistic. Good would yet outlast and outwit evil.

How?

According to Zoroaster's teachings, a general resurrection will take place at the end of the present world order. The good and evil will then be subjected to an ordeal of fire and molten metal. By this fiery test, as a later amplification of the original teaching declares, the evil will be made known by their terrible burning, but the righteous will find the fire kindly and the molten metal harmless, as soft and healing as milk. In the *Gathas,* the picture is much less clearly defined, so it remains in doubt whether the forces of evil, including Angra Mainyu, will be entirely consumed by the fiery ordeal or will survive to be hurled into the abyss of the "Abode of Lies" (Hell).

8. The Judgment of Individual Souls

As long as the powers of evil persist, some consistency can be read into the rather confused imagery of individual judgment. Individual judgment follows shortly after death, and the state of the soul remains fixed thereafter until the general resurrection at the end of the world. The references to it—marked by excessive brevity—may, with a little interpretation, be made to yield a picture replete with picturesque detail. Each soul, good or bad, must face judgment at the Bridge of the Separator (the Chinvat Bridge), which spans the abyss of hell and at its farther end opens on paradise. At this bridge the record of the soul is read. The balance of merits and demerits is cast. If good deeds predominate over evil, the "pointing of the hand" (of Ahura Mazda?) will be toward paradise, but if evil overbalances good, the hand will point to the abyss below the bridge. The crossing of the bridge is most dramatically conceived. The righteous, guided by Zoroaster, will have no difficulty, but the evil, already condemned by the judges, will find themselves in no case able to go beyond its center. Why? Zoroaster held the profound doctrine that individuals fix their own destinies. He said of the evil,

> Their own Soul and their own Self [daena] shall torment them when they come to the Bridge of the Separator. To all time will they be guests for the House of the Lie.[H1]

The term *daena* refers to the moral center of personality, the higher nature—specifically, the seat of religion, the conscience. Evil persons, confronted and staggered

by their own guilty consciences, will of themselves topple to their doom.

They will dwell in "the House of the Lie," the *Gathas'* hell, a place called "the worst existence," the abode of "the worst thought," an ill-smelling region, most dreadful to the Iranian imagination because it is so foul. In its lightless depths, sad voices cry out, but each sufferer is forever "alone." On the other hand, the righteous will dwell beyond the great bridge in "the House of Song," the *Gathas'* paradise, described as "the best existence," the abode of "the best thought," where the sun shines forever, and the righteous enjoy spiritual bliss, happy in their ever-joyous companionship.

Zoroaster believed so earnestly that the good religion of Ahura Mazda would win enough adherents to bring about the eventual defeat of evil that he had the stout hope that some of these adherents would be, like him, "deliverers" [*saoshyants*]. He therefore had no doubt of Ahura Mazda's ultimate triumph—but, he also felt strongly, let no man who sees the nature of the struggle between truth and falsehood fail meanwhile to ally himself with truth!

Such was the militant note with which Zoroaster brought his moral challenge to the folk of his time. How far he was in advance of his age those who read further may judge.

III. THE RELIGION OF THE LATER AVESTA

So far, our story of Zoroaster's reform, while beset with difficulties, has had a solid anchor in the facts supplied by the *Gathas;* but now we are about to enter an area of the greatest uncertainty, where further research and additional data are much needed. Valuable records have disappeared in the tumults of one thousand years of history (300 B.C.E. to 700 C.E.), and the missing information is not likely to be recovered.

It is not clear whether Zoroaster's reform made its own way from eastern Iran to the main Mesopotamian basin or whether another parallel reform took place in the basin and Zoroaster's influence was later assimilated. In any case, we know that during the Achaemenid dynasty (559–330 B.C.E.), under such rulers as Cyrus the Great, Darius I, and

Xerxes, priests known as the Magi dominated the religious scene, and the Ahura Mazda in their rites was not the preeminent figure of the *Gathas.* He was venerated along with other deities: Zurvan of the Medes, and the Persian Mithra and Anahita, whom Zoroaster had rejected. With the conquests of Alexander the Great in 331 B.C.E., Greek cultural forces were added to the synthesis. A little later, the Arsacids, who were Parthians from eastern Iran speaking the language Pahlevi, came to power in Persia, ruling from 250 B.C.E. to 226 C.E. (The Romans came to grief trying to subdue them.) They were overthrown finally by the Sassanids from Fars (Old Persia), whose dynasty endured from 226 to 651 C.E., when the Muslims brought about their fall.

Changes Brought by the Sassanid Revival

During this long period, the name of Zoroaster (but not of Ahura Mazda) was sometimes lost in the shuffle of political, social, and religious forces; but when the Sassanian period opened, it came again into prominence. The *Avesta,* that is, the later Zoroastrian scriptures, were diligently assembled and given wide currency. Zoroastrianism, with all of its modifications of Zoroaster's original monotheism, became the state religion—to the dismay of Christians and Jews, who until this time had been tolerated and now began to suffer persecution.

The modifications that appeared in the revived Zoroastrianism of the Sassanid period might be considered typical of any religion founded on the views of a prophetic personality but propagated at a later time on alien soil by priests and kings.

1. Myths Elevating Zoroaster

To begin with, a highly worshipful attitude came to be taken toward Zoroaster himself. To the eyes of his later followers, that very human man, "the shepherd of the poor" of the *Gathas,* became a godlike personage whose whole existence was attended by supernatural manifestations. His coming was known and foretold three thousand years before by the mythical primeval bull, and King Yima, in the Golden Age, gave the demons warning that their defeat was impending. The demons, thus forewarned, strove to prevent the occur-

rence of what they feared. They noted with consternation the manner of Zoroaster's conception. The Glory of Ahura Mazda united itself with Zoroaster's future mother at her birth and rendered her fit thereby to bear the prophet. At the same time, a divinely protected stem of a haoma plant was infused with the *fravashi* (genius or ideal self) of the coming prophet, and at the proper time the parents of Zoroaster drank its juices mixed with a potent milk, which the demons vainly sought to destroy and which contained the material essence (elemental substance) of the child about to be conceived. After his birth, at which all nature rejoiced, and at the moment of which he himself laughed aloud, demons and hostile wizards surrounded him with every sort of hazard. His own father was rendered by magic arts indifferent to his fate. The baby was almost killed in his cradle, burnt in a huge fire, and trampled to death by a herd of cattle (whose leading ox, however, stood above him and saved him, exactly as did a leading horse, in a similar event where demons stampeded a herd of horses). He was placed in a cave with wolves whose young had been killed, but these savage creatures allowed a ewe to enter and suckle him!

According to the highly elaborated tradition, the same sort of miracle attended his adult life. The *Zartusht Namah* tells the famous story of the healing of Vishtaspa's horse. Zoroaster had been imprisoned as the result of a plot of the hostile nobles (Kavis) and priests of the daevas (Karpans). Thereupon King Vishtaspa's horse fell to the ground, unable to move, its four legs drawn up toward its belly. Zoroaster sent word from his cell that he could cure the animal. But he promised to act only on one condition—that the king would grant a boon for each leg he restored. Zoroaster was summoned to the king's presence. The first boon asked was that Vishtaspa accept the faith. When the king agreed, the right front leg was straightened. As readily the king granted the other three boons—that the king's son Isfendir should fight for the faith, that the queen should also become a convert, and that the names of those in the plot against Zoroaster should be revealed and the plotters punished—in consideration of which, one by one the quivering charger's other legs were restored to use and it leapt to its feet, full of strength and fire. In one stroke, Zoroaster had routed his enemies and multiplied his converts.

His miraculous powers should have afforded no one surprise, one observes, if his first appearance at Vishtaspa's court was, as some writers record, an entrance through the palace roof, which opened of itself to admit the prophet, holding in his hand "a cube of fire with which he played without its hurting him."[C4]

Zoroaster was highly venerated in antiquity. The Greeks and Romans were much impressed by what they heard of him and his religion. How greatly they were impressed is evidenced by the astonishingly numerous references to him in the extant literature and by the fact that Plato was reportedly prevented, shortly after the death of Socrates, from going to Persia to study Zoroastrianism firsthand only by the outbreak of the War of Sparta with Persia in 396 B.C.E.

2. Powers Shared with Other Divinities

A change came over the monotheism of Zoroaster. In theory—that is to say, according to the official creed of he later *Avesta*—Ahura Mazda (or Ohrmazd, as he came to be called) was always adored as a supreme deity, transcendent and without equal. He was held to be too great and spiritual to have images made of him, as though he could be contained in wood or stone. But he was no longer godhead undivided. The old Aryan nature gods whom Zoroaster condemned and fought crept back into the faith and provided powerful figures around him to share his powers.

The *Gathas* of earlier times had recognized the existence of Immortal Holy Ones, to be sure, but as "modes of divine action" such beings—perhaps because of a certain artificial quality about them—had attained only limited appeal in popular mythology. Their semi-mythological characterization was perfunctory, as when Vohu Manah (Good Thought), upon hearing in the lowing of the cattle a prayer to him to plead their cause, assumed certain agricultural functions and became the guardian divinity of the cattle; Asha (Right) became the guardian divinity of fire; and Kshathra (Dominion) the lord of metals. Because the other Amesha Spentas had feminine names, they became female archangels. Armaiti (Piety) became the goddess of the soil, Haurvatat (Prosperity) the goddess of waters, and Ameretat (Immortality) the goddess of vegetation.

YAZATAS.   The later *Avesta*, on the other hand, depicts *yazatas* (angels or subdeities) who have attained full mythological development and wide popular appeal. About forty are named, most of them Indo-Aryan in character, with many reminders of the *Rig-Veda*. We shall here mention only the more prominent among them.

(a) Greatest of them all was *Mithra*. Though Zoroaster apparently would have nothing to do with this radiant divinity, the people clung to him. In the later *Avesta*, he returns to his earlier prominence. His name is regularly mentioned, along with Ahura Mazda's in the inscriptions of the later Achaemenian kings, those of Artaxerxes, for instance. Theologically, he was, of course, subordinate to Ahura Mazda, but in the religion of the masses he attained a supreme stature as the god of light, the rewarder of those who spoke truth and kept faith, and the chief support of those who relied on him to aid them in the struggle with the powers of darkness in this life and the next. His associates were Rashnu (*perhaps an Iranian form of Vishnu*) and Sraosha (Obedience), who presided with him at the Bridge of the Separator.

Mithra also became the central figure in a separate cult called *Mithraism*, which in the second century C.E. spread to the west as far as Britain, especially among the Roman soldiery. He symbolized the "invincible sun," and in the legends told about him he was born in a cave, where shepherds adored him; in maturity he performed miracles; and finally he ascended to heaven. Because he was born in one, his worshipers pursued his worship in caves, natural or constructed, called *Mithraeums*.

Because his central exploit was the slaying of a sacred bull to fructify the earth with its blood, he was depicted in sculptured reliefs (many of which survive) as a handsome youth, wearing a Phrygian cap and flying cape, kneeling on a bull whose throat he is cutting. Part of the long initiation rites required that the initiate stand under a grating while the blood of a slain bull poured down on his naked body.

Mithraism was a rival of Christianity until it was suppressed in the fourth century after the latter became the official religion of the Roman Empire.

(b) Also brought back (albeit refined of the character of excess) was *Haoma*, the sacred intoxicant, "the enlivening, the healing, the beautiful, the lordly, with golden eyes." Animal sacrifices—this would have horrified Zoroaster—were made to him. He became again "the averter of Death," associated, as in the *Rig-Veda,* with long life and the immortality of the soul.

(c) The strongest and most aggressive of the gods, *Verethragna,* known to the Vedic Aryans as Indra, had at various times incarnated himself in ten strong creatures—a bull with golden horns, a white horse, a male camel, a wild boar, a wild ram, a falcon, a male antelope, a swift wind, a handsome youth, and a warrior. Vigor and sharp eyesight were said to be his gift to Zoroaster.

(d) Prominent also was the wind god *Vayu* (who appears under the same name in the Vedas). The Zoroastrians said he had a double nature, a good and an evil side, going back to the beginning of time. In his good manifestation, he protected the righteous and accompanied them as a fragrant wind over the Bridge of the Separator to Paradise; in his evil form, he harmed the soul and escorted it to a terrible fall to Hell.

One of the unique features of this later Zoroastrianism is the extraordinary claim that Ahura Mazda himself offers sacrifices to Mithra and Anahita (see below), and both Ahura Mazda and Mithra worship Vayu, the wind! (Yasht 10:123, 15:2–4.) No wonder one leading scholar says, "It must be allowed that monotheism is submitted to a severe strain when Ahura Mazda himself offers worship to angels like these."[H2]

(e) So far did the process of fitting out Ahura Mazda's realm with assistant deities go that the Persians availed themselves of opportunities provided outside of the Aryan scheme of things. In one of his inscriptions, Artaxerxes II (404–358 B.C.E.) for the first time mentions a female deity named *Anahita,* "the Spotless One." His high regard for her is evidenced by the fact that he erected images to her in Babylon, Susa, Ecbatana, Damascus, and Sardis. She had Indo-Iranian origins, if she may be identified with the Vedic Sarasvati, the goddess of the waters; but to the later Zoroastrians, she was, it appears, one of the many forms taken by the Babylonian goddess Ishtar; in this case, she assumed a purified form. In the Yasht, in which Anahita's praises are sung, she is called the goddess of the waters let down from heaven to fructify the earth in all of its seven regions. Trim of waist and ample of hips and bosom, with golden shoes on her feet, she brought fertility to vegetation and to flocks and herds, and she awakened in human beings, Ishtarlike, the

Anahita

powers of reproduction, her blessing resting especially on women, that they might have easy births and abundant milk.

FRAVASHIS.   There also were the *Fravashis.* These beings are hard to describe because of their rather mixed character. Originally, they seem to have been the ancestral spirits, guarding, and in return expecting worship from, the living. But later their significance broadened, until they stood for ideal selves, who also were guardian genii, both of gods and human beings. Each living person was finally thought to have a fravashi, or eternal element, and so also certain beings not yet born, namely, "the Saoshyants who are to restore the world." Much more, the Amesha Spentas, the Yazatas, and Ahura Mazda himself were each assumed to have a fravashi! Carefully narrowing down this meaning, we arrive at the conclusion that such fravashis are the spiritual or immortal parts of living personalities, which, like the human souls in Plato's philosophy, exist before birth and survive after death. Here they have the added function of subsisting as ideal or better selves separately from persons and pulling them heavenward away from danger. Prayers and sacrifices were owed to ancestral fravashis in return for their indispensable service in the work of salvation.

In all of this we see monotheism relapsing into polytheism, a not-uncommon occurrence in the history of religions.

3. The Doctrine of Evil Intensified

The doctrine of evil was developed further and approached an almost complete ethical dualism. Like the good angels, the spirits of evil were more sharply individualized than they were by Zoroaster. Angra Mainyu, of whom Zoroaster had spoken bitterly, although not in very concrete terms, as being from the beginning of creation in opposition to Ahura Mazda's Spirit of Good, now became the archfiend, and was set against Ahura Mazda in dualistic fashion. Portions of the later *Avesta* made Angra Mainyu coequal with as well as the contradiction of Ahura Mazda. For example, the world was regarded as their joint creation. In the first chapter of the *Videvdat*, Ahura Mazda is portrayed as telling Zoroaster the story of his struggle with Angra Mainyu at the creation of the world. He pictures himself creating the various Iranian districts and endowing them with every excellence; unfortunately, as he admits, Angra Mainyu was on hand too, busily creating an evil for every good—killing frost of winter, excessive heat of summer, snakes, locusts, ants, the wicked rich, evil sorcerers, non-Aryan lords of the land, human vices, lusts, witchcraft, doubt, disbelief, and so on, not to speak of such unpardonable offenses as burying the dead or cooking carrion, practices peculiarly abhorrent to the orthodox Zoroastrians of later days. Angra Mainyu's capacity for mischief was in fact boundless. The twenty-second chapter places the number of diseases created by him at 99,999, a stupendous number to the people of that time. But there was a final touch. He was the author of death.

The evil power Angra Mainyu possessed was many times multiplied by the demons he created to assist him, such as Aka Manah (Bad Thought), Andar (the Vedic Indra), Naonhaithya (the Vedic Nasatyas, "the heavenly twins," here reduced to one being), Sauru, Fauru, Zairi, and others. Besides these there also were "numberless myriads" of evil spirits, daevas (devils) all of them. In this connection we must not overlook Druj (the Lie), now appearing in the likeness of a female demon so destructive of righteousness among men that even Ahura Mazda, in one Yasht, exclaims, "Had not the awful Fravashis of the faithful given help unto me . . . dominion would belong to the Druj, the material world would belong to the Druj!"[1]

This is one way to solve the problem of evil, to say that all good comes from God, all evil from the Devil. But consistency demands that the Devil, if he is the true author of evil, be coeternal with God from the beginning of time; otherwise, God created evil in the beginning. Only later Zoroastrians embraced this logical corollary of their position.

4. Zurvan (Space-time) as Primordial

Another solution to this problem was offered in what is called *Zurvanism*. A powerful group among the Magi, attempting to avoid the unsatisfactory conclusion outlined earlier, proposed perhaps as early as the fourth century B.C.E. a doctrine that was rejected by the main body of Zoroastrians but that seems an interesting foreshadowing of a modern physical theory. They suggested that both Ahura Mazda and Angra Mainyu sprang as twins from a unitary world principle called Zurvan (boundless Time or Space, or was it Space-Time?). God and Devil were thus made coequal in length of years. But even in the working out of this doctrine, which in one form personalized Zurvan as the "father" of Ohrmazd and Ahriman, the ultimate victory of Ohrmazd was declared certain, and opposition to evil was still made the first duty of every right-thinking person.

5. Averting Defilement Emphasized

Though human conflict with the demons on the great battlefield of life is described as fundamentally moral, in the later *Avesta*, especially in the *Videvdat*, it increasingly becomes a struggle against the demonic attempt to fasten ceremonial impurity on the believers. In consequence of this shift of interest, ancient procedures designed to preserve life by aversive magic made their way back into the religion of Zoroaster. To counteract the power of demons over persons involved in ceremonial impurity, the *Videvdat* provided not ethical and moral instruction but directions for the use of powerful *manthras* (cf. the Vedic and Hindu *mantras*), passages taken from the *Gathas* of Zoroaster for use as spells and incantations. In fact, all of the *Gathas* became useful primarily as "spells of ineffable power, to be repeated without flaw, by men who may or may not understand them."[H3]

Besides the manthras, an effective means of daunting evil and avoiding its touch, defiling as pitch, was the offering of libations of haoma juice. To this day (see p. 368) the Parsis of India take the twigs of a sacred plant and mix the juice pressed from them with milk and holy water, the resulting fluid being in part offered as a libation and in part drunk by the officiating priests. This procedure is almost identical with that performed thousands of years ago by the Indo-Aryans on the banks of the Indus River.

But more directly effective were the methods of cleansing one's person of defilement and thus getting rid of a contaminating influence. According to the *Videvdat,* contact with the human dead is the source of greatest defilement. Anyone touching a corpse must immediately be purified by ablutions with water, or, in certain contingencies, with the urine of cattle. To modern as to ancient Parsis, corpses have always been so defiling that they are not allowed to enter the earth, lest they corrupt the ground, nor fall into the water, lest they render it unfit for any use, nor be burned on a funeral pyre, lest they defile the flame. In the early days of Zoroastrianism, the dead were laid on a bed of stones or a layer of lime or encased in stone to keep them isolated from earth and water. Today they are placed in stone "towers of silence" (dakhmas), open to the sky, so that birds of prey may feast on them. Any portion of a dead body, or, for that matter, any part severed from a living body—as, for example, nail parings or hair cut from the head or beard—is unclean. Spitting, especially in the presence of another person, is forbidden. Even the exhaled breath is defiling, so that, to the present day, priests wear cloths over their mouths while tending the sacred fire. Creatures that are known to feed on dead flesh—maggots, flies, and ants—are loathed. They are creations of Angra Mainyu, as are also snakes and frogs. In times past, the Magi have killed hundreds of thousands of them as an act of piety. Direct contact with any of them requires that the person involved must be cleansed and purified without delay.

This shift from moral regeneration to considerations of ceremonial purity marks much of the history of Zoroastrianism.

6. The Final Judgment Detailed

In one more direction Zoroastrianism grew ever more elaborate: the doctrine of the future life was worked out in graphic detail, highly stimulating to the imagination.

Much attention was paid to the drama of individual judgment. This was not supposed to take place until the fourth day after death. For three nights, it was thought, the soul of the dead person sits at the head of its former body and meditates on its past good or evil thoughts, words, and deeds. During this time, it is comforted, if it has been a righteous soul, by good angels, and tormented, if it has been wicked, by demons hovering about, ready to drag it off to punishment. On the fourth day, the soul makes its way to the Chinvat Bridge to stand before its judges, Mithra and his associates Sraosha and Rashnu, the last of whom holds the dread scales for the final weighing of merits and demerits. Judgment rendered and sentence passed, the soul then walks onto the Chinvat Bridge. Here, according to the Pahlevi text called the *Bundahishn,* in the middle part of the bridge

> there is a sharp edge which stands like a sword; . . . and Hell is below the Bridge. Then the soul is carried to where stands the sharp edge. Then, if it be righteous, the sharp edge presents its broad side. . . . If the soul be wicked, that sharp end continues to stand edgewise, and does not give a passage. . . . With three steps which it (the soul) takes forward— which are the evil thoughts, evil words, and evil deeds that it has performed—it is cut down from the head of the Bridge, and falls headlong to Hell.[J1]

A late text gives us a further account of the crossing: an attractive picture of how a righteous soul is guided over the bridge by its own *daena,* or conscience, in the form of a beautiful maiden, and how a wicked person is confronted by an ugly hag (a personification of one's own bad conscience).

> When (the righteous soul) takes a step over the Chinvat Bridge, there comes to it a fragrant wind from Paradise, which smells of musk and ambergris, and that fragrance is more pleasant to it than any other pleasure.
>
> When it reaches the middle of the Bridge, it beholds an apparition of such beauty that it hath never seen a figure of greater beauty. . . . And when the apparition appears to the soul, (the soul) speaks thus: "Who art thou with such beauty that a figure of greater beauty I have never seen?"
>
> The apparition speaks (thus): "I am thine own good actions. I myself was good, but thine actions have made me better."
>
> And she embraces him, and they both depart with complete joy and ease to Paradise.

But if the soul be that of a wicked man,

> when it takes a step over the Chinvat Bridge, there blows to him an exceedingly foul wind from Hell, so foul as is unheard of among all the stench in the world. There is no stench fouler than that; and that stench is the worst of all the punishments that are visited upon it.
>
> When it reaches the middle of the Chinvat Bridge, it sees an apparition of such extreme ugliness and frightfulness that it hath never seen one uglier and more unseemly.... And it is as much terrified on account of her as a sheep is of a wolf, and wants to flee away from her.
>
> And that apparition speaks thus: "Whither dost thou want to flee?"
>
> It (the soul) speaks thus: "Who art thou with such ugliness and terror that a figure worse than thou art, uglier and more frightful, I have never seen in the world?"
>
> She speaks (thus): "I am thine own bad actions. I myself was ugly, and thou madest me worse day after day, and now thou hast thrown me and thine own self into misery and damnation, and we shall suffer punishment till the day of the Resurrection."
>
> And she embraces it, and both fall headlong from the middle of the Chinvat Bridge and descend to Hell.[J2]

Thus did the later Zoroastrians elaborate the doctrine of their founder that the individual self—one's own moral consciousness—determines one's future destiny.

7. Final Rewards and Punishments

In these later accounts, it was held that those whose merits and demerits exactly balanced were sent to Hamestakan, a sort of limbo, located between earth and the stars. Hell, they believed, had several levels, the lowest being in the bowels of the earth, where the darkness could be grasped by the hand and where the stench was unbearable. Heaven, on the other hand, presented ascending levels, corresponding to good thoughts, good words, and good deeds, located, respectively, in the regions of the stars, the moon, and the sun. Through these ascending stations the good soul passed until it reached highest heaven, Garotman or Garodemana, "the House of Song," the realm where the Best Thought dwells, and where it would enjoy felicity beyond earth's highest joy until the day of resurrection and the final judgment of all souls.

In estimating when the final judgment would come, the later Zoroastrians developed a theory of world ages, each lasting three thousand years. They said Zoroaster had appeared at the beginning of the last of these aeons. He would be succeeded by three savior beings, each appearing at intervals of one thousand years: one, Aushetar, born one thousand years after Zoroaster; the second, Aushetarmah, two thousand years later; and the last, Soshyans (Saoshyant) at the end of the world; and Zoroaster would be their father! For it was said that Zoroaster's seed was being miraculously preserved in a lake in Persia, and at intervals of one thousand years, three pure virgins would bathe there and conceive the great deliverers.

With the appearance of Soshyans, the last Messiah, the "final days" would begin. All of the dead would be raised; heaven and hell would be emptied of their residents, in order to make up the great assembly where the final judgment would be passed on all souls. The righteous and the wicked would be separated, and a flood of molten metal would pour out upon the earth and roar through hell, purifying all regions with its scorching fires. Every living soul would have to walk through the flaming river, but to the righteous it would seem like warm milk, because there would be no evil in them to be burned away. To the wicked it would bring terrible agony, a purifying burning proportioned to their wickedness, which would sear all of the evil out of them and allow the survival only of their goodness.

As to the fate of Ahriman (Angra Mainyu), there are several versions. According to one, those who are resurrected will drive him into outer darkness, there to hide himself forever. According to another version, there will be a final conflict in which Ahura Mazda and his angels will hurl Ahriman and his demons into flames that will utterly consume them.

The survivors of fiery trials, whether formerly good or bad, would live together in the new heavens and the new earth, in utmost joy and felicity. Adults would remain forever at forty years of age and children at fifteen; friends and relatives would be reunited forever. Even hell, at last made pure, would be brought back "for the enlargement of the world," and the world in its totality would then be "immortal for ever and everlasting."[K]

IV. THE ZOROASTRIANS OF THE PRESENT DAY

The shifts in Zoroastrian doctrine that we have just reviewed began during the reigns of the Achaemenian kings and, after a prolonged period of disturbance occasioned by the invasion of Alexander the Great, were resumed during the time of the Sassanian dynasty (226–651 C.E.). The influence Zoroastrianism wielded on other Middle Eastern religions, including Judaism, Christianity, and the pre-Islamic Arabs, was considerable. During this period, a young camel driver, Muhammad, grew so obsessed by visions of the approaching last judgment foretold alike by Zoroastrians, Jews, and Christians that he became a warning prophet among his own incredulous townsmen, and then, in flight from his native place, began a career as a soldier prophet that in its effects not only transformed Arabia but shook the Jewish and Christian worlds to their foundations and almost extinguished Zoroastrianism.

The Effects of the Muslim Conquest

The successors of Muhammad conducted their conquests with astonishing swiftness and thoroughness. In 636, they took Syria from the Christians, and in 639, Egypt. During the decade following 637, the empire of the Sassanids was overrun, and in 651 (or 652) the last of the Sassanid rulers was surprised and slain, and Zoroastrianism suffered a nearly fatal blow. But for a century or more, the Arab conquerors attempted no wholesale pressure to bring about conversion, because the Qur'ān provided that peoples "to whom a Book (i.e., a scripture) has been given" were to be treated generously, and the Zoroastrians, like the Jews and Christians, had "a Book," in fact a whole library of sacred texts. It was some time after the Muslim conquest that pressure was exerted, and then the Arabs were not directly responsible.

Nevertheless, within one hundred years of the Arab conquest, a great number of Zoroastrians determined to leave Persia. From the eighth century onward, there was considerable emigration to India. Some made their way eastward overland; some moved to a town far down the coast, near the mouth of the Persian Gulf, then removed to an island off the coast of India, and finally to India itself. Other emigrant bands of Zoroastrians joined them, and among the tolerant Hindus, by whom they were called Parsis (i.e., Persians), all were allowed to pursue their religious rites and duties in freedom. We shall see shortly how well they fared.

Their coreligionists, who remained behind in Persia, were not so fortunate.

The Gabars, or Iranis

The Zoroastrians of Persia did not name themselves Gabars (a name that was fastened upon them by the Muslims and means, loosely, "infidels"). They are better called Iranis. They called themselves Zardushtians ("Zoroastrians") or Bahdinan ("those of the good religion"), but long persecution made them keep this name to themselves and hide away their light. To this day their clothes are rough and of a dull yellow, and their manners are subdued. But they have clung tenaciously to their faith. The priests are initiated according to the ancient rituals, keep the sacred fires fed in their unpretentious fire temples, and follow strict rules in performing all their offices. The layfolk are faithful to the old rites. They want no abbreviations of ceremony at the investiture of their boys with the sacred shirt (the *sudra*) and the sacred thread (the *kusti*, a three-ply cord symbolizing good thought, good words, and good deeds, and worn as a girdle), and they want the full rites at marriages and funerals, which end with placing the corpse for the vultures to eat in "towers of silence" (*dakhmas*, for a further description of which, see a later section). They are careful too to observe the ancient purification rites on the many occasions when they are polluted by contact with unclean things and persons. Like the Jews, they suffered for centuries from the old vicious circle into which religious persecution drew them: their sufferings made them secretive, and their secretiveness made them suspect. They number about thirty thousand now, found principally in Yazd, Kerman, and Tehran.

The Parsis in India

More fortunate have been the Parsis of India, who number today approximately one hundred thousand souls, most of them in Bombay and neighboring areas.

An outsider visiting Bombay soon recognizes them, not only by their relatively light complexion and Aryan features, but also by their dignified mixture of ancient and modern dress. The men commonly dress in European clothes, although they also wear snugly fitting white trousers. Until recently, all but the most Westernized of them did not appear with uncovered heads in or out of doors, the common headgear being a shiny hat of stiffened cloth, darkly colored, rimless, and sloping back from the forehead. The women drape their brightly colored Indian saris over dresses of European style and go about freely with unveiled faces. The priests with their white turbans, full beards, and immaculate white garments appear during their ceremonies in purely ancient garb.

As a class, the Parsis are wealthy and have the reputation of being the most highly educated and businesslike community in India. They are frequently described as India's best and most competent industrialists; they are said to control the best hotels, the biggest stores, the most cotton, jute, and steel mills, and the Indian air service. Many Parsis today have distinctive occupational surnames. When British administrators required all Indians to take surnames, Parsis proudly chose their callings. One reads in the Bombay newspapers of Narl Contractor and Faroukh Engineer (cricket stars) and of Geeta Doctor and Feroza Paymaster. The Parsis are noted, not only for their skill at money making, but also for their generosity as public benefactors. The Bombay Symphony, for example, was founded by a Parsi, Nelhi Mehta. (His son Zubin became a conductor of the New York Philharmonic Orchestra.) Yet in their dealings with non-Zoroastrians Parsis still preserve a certain self-protective dignity, a kind of ceremonial coldness, and, like the Gabars of Iran, they let no outsiders, however trusted, share their more sacred rites or look upon the holy fires burning in their fire temples.

Deities and Priests

To Zoroastrians everywhere, Ohrmazd is still the supreme Lord and Creator of all that is good in heaven and earth. Indeed, he is almost too exalted to be worshiped through small or humanly created things. He is best adored through the larger phenomena of the world, like mountains, the sun, and large bodies of water. Below him are the lesser deities, the *yazads,* or "worshipful ones," who serve as guardians and protectors of the chief divisions or aspects of the world, such as Mihr (Mithra), who defends people against the demons and protects the holy fires; Sarosh (Sraosha), his chief aide in guarding humankind from evil; Spendarmad (Armaiti), who prevents pollution of the soil; and Anahid (Anahita), who guards the waters (sea and rivers) and promotes fertility in womankind. Yet other deities have survived from Sassanian times. These lesser deities are sought by prayer and supplication for the special services they are assigned to render; they are all under Ohrmazd's general direction.

The ceremonial life of the Zoroastrians is regulated by the priesthood, which is hereditary and traces its descent to the ancient tribe of the Magi. Their high priests are called *dasturs,* and many of them today are highly educated. Yet the ceremonies in the fire temples are performed not by them but by a specially trained class of priests called *ervads* (in Iran, *mobeds*), whose ritual of initiation is very exacting and who keep themselves constantly purified by cleansing rites. The priests memorize fully half of the *Avesta,* without, as a rule, understanding a word of it because it is composed in what is now a dead language. In this they do not greatly differ from the ordinary worshipers who also memorize the more sacred passages of the *Avesta* and repeat them during ceremonial occasions.

Fire Temples

In both Iran and India, the fire temple is not always distinguishable from other buildings when viewed from the street. But the worshipers know the fire is kept there, and that it is better if the outsider is not made too curious by a distinctive exterior. In Iran, the fire temple may be merely a room in a quiet part of a dwelling; in India, the whole building usually is devoted to the fire keeping and ceremonies. Not all of the Indian temples are equally holy, however. Some, where the fire is more ancient or is purified to a greater degree, are holier. This matter of purifying the fire

Zoroastrian Priest
The hereditary Zoroastrian priestly orders trace their lineage to the ancient Mesopotamian tribe of the Magi. The highest orders train fire temple priests like the one shown here. Maintenance of the level of purity needed for tending sacred fires requires extensive training in ritual and repeated observance of cleansing rites. *(Courtesy of Magnum Photo.)*

is distinctive of Zoroastrians and is of more than ordinary interest. The more holy fire has to be compounded of sixteen different fires, all purified after a long and complicated ritual. One such fire is obtained in India from the cremation of a corpse.

A number of sandalwood logs are kindled from the cremation. Then above the flame, a little too high to touch it, a metal spoon is held, with small holes in it, containing chips of sandalwood. When these ignite, the flame is made to kindle a fresh fire. This process is repeated ninety-one times, to the accompaniment of recited prayers.[H4]

Other fires, purified to a greater or lesser degree by a similar use of spoons, are obtained from flames kindled by a bolt of lightning, from fire produced by flints, and from fires in idol temples, distilleries, and homes. Finally, the sixteen purified fires are brought together by priests (who hardly dare to breathe through the covering over their mouths) into one urn and placed in the fire chamber of the temple.

Typically, the fire occupies the center of an inner room, resting in its ash-filled urn on a four-legged stone pedestal. It is fed day in and day out by the attendant priests with pieces of sandalwood. During the performance of their duties in the fire chamber, the priests always wear a cloth over their mouths to prevent a single breath from coming directly upon and contaminating the pure flame, and they may not cough or sneeze, at any rate not near the fire.

Worship and Daily Observances

The worshipers come individually, at any time they wish. Inside the entrance each washes the uncovered parts of the body, recites the Kusti prayer in Avestan, and then, taking off shoes, proceeds barefooted through the inner hall to the threshold—no further—of the fire chamber, where a priest accepts an offering of sandalwood and money and gives in return a ladleful of ashes from the sacred urn, which the worshiper rubs on forehead and eyelids. Bowing toward the fire, the worshiper offers prayers (but not *to* the fire, for it is only a symbol), and then retreats slowly backward and with shoes replaced goes home.

Like the Muslims, the Zoroastrians (both Iranis and Parsis) divide each day into five periods for religious devotions. During each of these periods, worship in the fire temples is required of the priests and is meant to be observed (ideally) by laypersons there or elsewhere, morning and evening at least. Recitation of sacred texts and offering of traditional prayers provide the spoken substance of such worship. The priests at stated times recite from memory (in Avestan) whole books like the *Videvdat* (*Vendidad*) or the whole of the *Yasna* (seventy-two chapters); they perform other ceremonies lasting five hours or more. Their offices for the dead extend over the three days that the departing spirit is thought to remain on earth.

Special Rites

Since the earliest days of Zoroastrianism, perhaps the single most important ceremony has been the ritual of extracting the haoma (soma) juice. In India particularly this complicated ceremony centers around a pressing of the pith of plants of the genus *Ephedra,* thought to be haoma plants, which produces a juice that at the first pressing is mixed with purified water and the juice of crushed pomegranate twigs and at the second pressing with milk and water. In these rites, the drinking of the juice by the officiating priest and subsequently by the worshipers, after it is first offered to the fire, the symbol of Ahura Mazda, has been through the years the central act of the Zoroastrian ritual, in the faith that priests and worshipers may thus share in God's eternal life.

From ancient times, the New Year's observances have been a time of great celebration in both Persia (Iran) and India. Perhaps the most important visit to the fire temple is on New Year's Day. On that day the worshipers rise early, bathe, put on new clothes, go to the fire temple, worship, and, after giving alms to the poor, spend the rest of the day exchanging greetings and feasting.

In India, Parsi rites and practices are based on the later *Avesta* and not simply on the religion of Zoroaster himself. This is evident from the briefest study of the annual ceremonies. One festival honors Mithra, whose seat is the sun and who enjoins upon his devotees truth and friendship—faith keeping. A very solemn festival is that in honor of Farvadin, the deity who presides over the fravashis, or spirits, of the departed ancestors. During this festival, which lasts for ten days, the fravashis revisit the homes of their descendants. To give them welcome the worshipers attend special ceremonies for the dead on the hills before the towers of silence. Still another festival honors Vohu Manah, regarded as the guardian of cattle; during this period, the Parsis practice special kindness to animals. Other feasts commemorate the six phases of creation—heaven, water, earth, trees, animals, and human beings.

The Parsi Towers of Silence

The *dakhmas,* or towers of silence, provide the Parsis of India with an approved way of disposing of their

Tower of Silence
On a remote and barren hilltop the vultures gather to accomplish the desire of the Parsi mourners—the stripping of the corruptible flesh from the bones of the dead without contamination of the soil. The shallow pits in which the corpses are laid appear in the central enclosure. A minority of Zoroastrians now advocate cremation, with scattering of the ashes at sea.
(Drawing based on an old engraving.)

dead without contaminating soil and water with spoiling flesh. A dakhma is traditionally a stone floor with a circular brick or stone wall around it. The floor is built with a pit in the center and is in three sections—the highest section for men, the next for women, and the lowest for children. The corpse is brought to the dakhma by six bearers, followed by the mourners, all in white. After a final viewing of the remains by the funeral procession, the body is taken inside the tower, laid in a shallow pit on its proper level, and partially uncovered by a thorough slitting of its clothes with scissors. As to what follows,

> as soon as the corpse-bearers have left the Tower, the vultures swoop down from their post of observation round the wall, and in half an hour there is nothing left but the skeleton. Quickly the bones dry, and the corpse-bearers enter again after some days, and cast the bones into the central well, where they crumble away.[H5]

For obvious reasons, the towers of silence are situated on hilltops in vacant land. There are seven in the vicinity of Bombay, where deaths occur frequently enough to attract a constant attendance of vultures. Recently, a new high-rise building, found to offer a view into a dakhma, was closed for that reason. In other parts of India where the Parsis are not numerous, as in Calcutta, there is occasional difficulty in

attracting vultures at the right time. In communities too small to have a dakhma (and in all of Iran since the early 1970s), interment in lead coffins or in underground stone or cement chambers is common.

Modernization and Its Problems

The orthodox Bombay Parsis have recently shown concern about the decline in their numbers, estimated to be about one thousand per year. They reduced the childbearing span of their women by being among the first to abolish child marriages when European standards became known; also marriage has been put off by males and females alike to complete their higher education. Acute housing shortages also postpone marriages and contribute to a low birthrate. These factors, together with rules forbidding marriage outside of Parsi ranks and disallowing conversion to Zoroastrianism for the sake of marriage, have led to steadily shrinking numbers.

On the other hand, there are now liberal priests who accept converts from other faiths, officiate at such converts' marriage to born Zoroastrians, and preside when children of such marriages are invested with the *kusti,* or sacred thread. These and other liberals place chief stress on the ethical rather than the doctrinal teachings of Zoroastrianism and advocate the shortening of the lengthy temple rituals and their translation into everyday speech. Some supporters of modernization also advocate a "back to the *Gathas*" theological simplification that would bypass Avestan cosmology and ritual.

If one includes all of those who wish to count themselves Parsis (even if not accepted by the orthodox), the worldwide number of Parsis is increasing. In both Iran and India, the broader education now available, both at home and abroad, has led to the growing tendency of the sons of priests to adopt occupations other than the priesthood, with the result that the numbers now in the priesthood in both countries are shrinking. The issues of modernization and change are especially acute among Parsis resident in Western countries. There are significant communities in such cities as London and Toronto and an estimated ten thousand in the United States.

At this point we conclude our study of the Zoroastrian faith. More might have been discussed—for example, that the Parsis are divided over the question of the yearly calendar, or that there is a rising sentiment against the use of dakhmas. But enough has been told to present a picture of a religion, based on high moral standards, which has persisted through long periods of cultural change and has left an indelible mark on three other monotheisms—Judaism, Christianity, and Islam.

GLOSSARY*

Ahura Mazda (Ohrmazd) "wise lord," supreme deity of Good

Anahita "the spotless one," goddess of waters and fertility

Angra Mainyu (Ahriman) "the bad spirit," supreme principle of evil, darkness, and destruction

Asha (Arta) the divinity of truth, right, justice, and divine order

asuras (ū-shōōr′-ūz) or ahuras, "lords," divinities; in Zoroastrian usage, vested with good qualities

Avesta collection of the sacred literature of Zoroastrianism first assembled in writing *ca.* the 3rd or 4th century C.E.

Chinvat Bridge the "Bridge of the Separator" spanning the abyss of hell and reaching to paradise

daena one of the immortal parts of human beings, the moral center or personality, the higher religious self, the conscience

daevas (dä-ē-väz) gods, celestial beings; in Zoroastrian usage, demons given to malice and corruption

dakhmas "towers of silence," enclosures open to the sky within which corpses are left to be picked clean by vultures

dasturs hereditary order of Zoroastrian high priests

Druj divinity of falsehood, the Lie

ervads (mobeds) specially trained class of fire-tending priests

fravashi originally one of the immortal parts of human beings, the preexistent ancestral soul; later, a guardian genius associated with gods as well as humans

Gabars (Iranis) the continuing ritual community of Zoroastrians in present-day Iran

Gathas (gā-tūz) hymns of Zoroaster written in the ancient Gathic dialect; the oldest portion of the *Avesta*

haoma (hō-mū) or soma, a sacramental drink representing immortal sustenance; prepared in Iran today from a plant of the genus *Ephedra*

Magi an order of ancient Iranian priests versed in astrology and magic

Mithra (Mitra) essentially a deity of light, he appears as a *yazata* in Zoroastrianism as a judge of the dead and protector of cattle and pasturage, later, the deity of regeneration in the Roman mystery cult Mithraism

Spenta Mainyu the holy spirit of Good, supreme principle of truth and right

Videvdat (Vendidad) a portion of the *Avesta* devoted especially to spells against demons and prescriptions for purification

Vishtaspa (Hystaspes) a Chorasmian (Iranian) prince whom Zoroaster won over to his faith

* For a guide to pronunciation, refer to page 99.

Vohu Manah the mode of Good Thought or Sense; appeared to Zoroaster as an archangel and led him to the presence of Ahura Mazda

Yasht song of praise, a portion of the *Avesta*

Yasna liturgical scripture, written in Gathic (Old Persian); includes the *Gathas*

yazatas "ones worthy of worship," a broad category of angels and subdeities in later Avestan mythology

Zurvan boundless Time, or Space-Time, a unitary world principle; a cult of Zurvanism (condemned by the Magi) conceived of him as the "father" of both Ohrmazd and Ahriman

Judaism in its Early Phases

From Hebrew Origins to the Exile

It may be said that one great theme dominates the course of Jewish religion. This is the theme that a single, righteous God is at work in the social and natural order. This theme was not immediately arrived at, but somehow it seems implicit from the beginning. Only morally and socially sensitive minds could conceive of history in such terms or develop a group consciousness of such a god.

Being socially sensitive, the Hebrews were historical minded, and not in any casual or intermittent way, but steadily. This fact needs stressing. The Hebrew scriptures are as complete a record of the nation's history as the Hebrew historians could make them. That their work, from the eighth century B.C.E. onward, was fundamentally sound is more and more evident as modern archaeological research proceeds with the task of unearthing the vestiges of the early Palestinian cultures. At the same time, it should not be overlooked that the Hebrews wrote religious, not secular, history; the facts they cited and the traditions they invoked no longer have quite the values for us that they had for them. In fact, their narratives contain hidden meanings and significances to which they paid no heed because they took them for granted.

Known to the Christians as the Old Testament, the Hebrew scriptures have been regarded as "God's word"; for in the belief of the devout, these writings are a revelation of the will of God, not only to the Jews but to all humankind. Taken together, from Genesis to Malachi, they form a sacred canon; that is to say, they have been accepted as standard texts of the faith, having passed tests of their authenticity and having been pronounced inspired.

WESTERN NAMES: Early Judaism, Hebraism
ANCESTRAL FOUNDERS: Abraham, *ca.* 2000 B.C.E.; Moses, *ca.* 1300 B.C.E.
NAMES USED BY EARLY FOUNDING COMMUNITIES: The *Qahal*, "people of God" or tribal names: Israel, Judah
NAMES OF GOD: Yahweh, Elohim, El-Shaddai
EARLY SACRED LITERATURE: Substantial portions of the *Torah* (Law) and the *Nebi'im* (Prophets) materials in the Masoretic canon of later times were composed before the exile.

We shall see later how and when these sacred texts were written. Some centuries after the last of them was set down in writing, they were all gathered together into the present canon at a synod of rabbis held at Jabneh (Jamnia), in Palestine, about 90 C.E.; after this the canon became "fixed," that is, no longer subject to change and limited to these works only. Some books that were rejected as not fully meeting the standards for true revelation had nevertheless enough value to acquire the status of semisacred or semicanonical writings. Christians later gave them the Greek name the

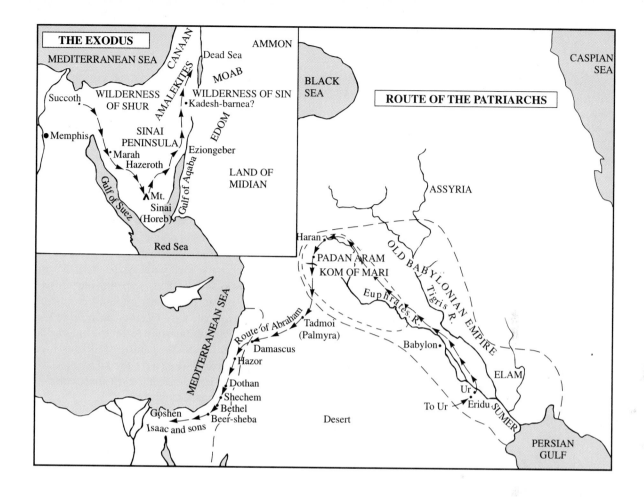

The map contains the following labels:

THE EXODUS

MEDITERRANEAN SEA

CANAAN
AMMON
Dead Sea
MOAB
AMALEKITES
WILDERNESS OF SHUR
WILDERNESS OF SIN
• Kadesh-barnea?
Succoth
EDOM
• Memphis
SINAI PENINSULA
Eziongeber
• Marah
Hazeroth
LAND OF MIDIAN
Gulf of Suez
Gulf of Aqaba
▲ Mt. Sinai (Horeb)
Red Sea

BLACK SEA

CASPIAN SEA

ROUTE OF THE PATRIARCHS

ASSYRIA

Haran
PADAN ARAM
KOM OF MARI
OLD BABYLONIAN EMPIRE
Euphrates R.
Tigris R.
MEDITERRANEAN SEA
Route of Abraham
Tadmoi (Palmyra)
Damascus
Babylon •
• Hazor
ELAM
Dothan
• Shechem
Ur
Goshen
• Bethel
To Ur ×
Eridu
Beer-sheba
SUMER
Isaac and sons
Desert
PERSIAN GULF

Apocrypha, and the Roman Catholic Church admitted all but two of them to its canon as a *deutero* (second or secondary) canonical collection, officially regarded to be just as authoritative as the other thirty-seven books.

The Jewish canon, like the New Testament, has been submitted to exhaustive textual, historical, and literary critical examination. In the process, each book has been taken apart and examined, tested against archaeological research, assigned to this or that tradition or authorship, and relegated, part by part, to this or that date or era. This testing has shattered some of the claims originally made for the canonical books, but historians are now confident that the Hebrew and Christian scriptures are better and more truly known and understood than ever before.

I. THE RELIGION OF THE PRE-MOSAIC HEBREWS

The origin of the biblical Hebrews, who belonged to the peoples speaking Semitic languages, can be traced to the Syro-Arabian desert, in which they wandered for centuries. As have other Semitic groups before and since, they camped on Arabia's northern steppes, beside oases or in areas of sparse vegetation, crossing and recrossing the desert's undulating wastes of flat stone, thinly covered with pebbles or shifting sand. At each encampment they erected straggling camel- or goat-skin tents, pitched close to the ground. Under such shelter their communal life ran its self-contained course. Each tribe lived to itself, and the day's routine was ordered by a single authoritative voice, that of the ruling elder or patriarch, to whom the Arab word *shaykh* is now applied. In those far-off times, the implements and weapons they possessed were of stone, and their beliefs were still in the formative stages. Suspicious of all strangers, and yet openhanded to a fault to any they received into their tents, they huddled together in the vast expanse of the desert, as if back to back against a hard and grudging world.

Early Semitic Animism and Polytheism

The biblical Hebrews (or Israelites) owed a great deal to their desert-bred forefathers, even though their monotheistic faith stood in sharp contrast to their desert heritage of polytheism, for elements of this heritage, reduced indeed to a minor role, remained in Israelite religion for a long time. As one reads the Bible, one finds vestiges (and also repudiations) of the beliefs and practices we are about to review.

Among the Semites of the desert of the period of about 2000 B.C.E., the veneration of stones and pillars was all but universal. Certain heaps of stones were particularly viewed with respect. A desert people will honor its landmarks. The Semitic name for a pillarlike rock that was sacred (*mazzebah*) was often on the lips of the earliest Hebrews, and the term *gilgal,* used later by the Hebrews as the name of a town in Palestine, meant a circular series of pillars. Stones and pillars provided convenient objects around which religious ceremonies and sacrifices might be conducted, but originally they had their own awesome significance, perhaps because of their odd shape, suggestively human appearance, or striking position on a mountaintop or athwart a much-traveled way. Often godlings and goddesses were thought to make their habitation there.

Sacred Springs, Groves, and Animals

It was natural among a desert people, unused to seeing enough of them, that wells, springs, and streams had a specially sacred character and usually were credited to the creative power of spirits or gods that had brought them into being and could readily, if angered, dry them up again.

Trees in general but evergreen trees in particular were, it was felt, full of spirit energy. Groves became holy places. But trees were sometimes as much dreaded as beheld with rejoicing, for a desert people must fear being entangled in a thicket—the lair of wild beasts and the ambush of demons—and, moreover, trees may draw down the lightning or even be animated demonic beings themselves. On the other hand, some trees whispered wisdom in the rustling of their leaves. They were protective spirits, giving relief and shelter, and under certain conditions they were capable of delivering oracles, should the rare individual who could understand their language be there to hear.

Of the "beasts of the field," serpents were universally feared (and as universally revered) for being demoniacally sly. Goats were regarded as incarnations of "hairy ones" (Hebrew *se'irim*). As for the untamable wild things of the desert—the panthers, leopards, hyenas, wolves, and foxes—they were the savage flock of demon gods of the wasteland. The swift-footed ostrich and birds of prey were demonic too.

Spirits in Human Shape

But the desert Semites believed in many spirits besides these. Some more or less fearsome spirits had a human shape but a nonhuman character, like the *jinn* of later Arabia. There were seductive female night demons, like the hairy Lilith who, according to later Hebrew tradition, led Adam astray. The raging desert wind that brought the sandstorm was a malevolent demon; he was connected with pestilence and ruin. There were others of a like evil disposition, but the beneficent spirits far outnumbered them.

And here we come upon a fact of some importance in the present study. Many spirits that possessed a high degree of power or dynamism were given a name universally current among Semitic peoples—it was *el* or *eloah* (sing.) or *elim* or *elohim* (pl.), a word with the general meaning of "superhuman being" or "divinity." This term was broad and inclusive; it was applicable to major and minor divinities alike, and although it usually designated the more beneficent powers, it was also applied to demons. As a rule, it referred to no specific supernatural individual, unless hyphenated with a descriptive adjective or with the name of a locality. This held good until among the

Aramaeans and the Hebrews it came to mean, whether in its singular or plural form, just one God.

Divinity and Plural Name Form

How the plural of *eloah* (*elohim*) could stand for one being may perhaps be explained thus: The many gods were eventually considered to be names of but one true God (as we have already seen happen elsewhere in the world), and then the plural term signified "the One who is All," "the All-god," or "the Totality of the Divine." This word has the distinct connotation of "the *real* god." In contrast, the word most used in the Hebrew scriptures for idols is *elilim,* which means the "null gods" or "non gods."

Other words used as appellations of the gods in the Semitic world were Adonis or Adoni (Hebrew, Adonai) meaning "Lord"; Malak or Moloch (Hebrew, Molech) meaning "King"; Bel or Baal meaning "Land-Lord" or "Possessor of the Land"; and 'Ab, meaning "Father," or "Head of the Family."

These names for the gods point to a significant fact. The relationship between gods and humankind was comparable to that of kings, landlords, and heads of families with their subjects and dependents. Of course, the higher in heaven the gods or the more extensively developed the polytheisms, with their proliferating mythologies and cults, the less close and personal the relationship. Among the desert tribes, on the other hand, the divine–human bond was warm, intimate, and personal. Perhaps the desert simplified the relationship of god and person by reducing nature to an empty waste. At any rate, the desert Semites adopted toward their gods an attitude that was not like that of frightened or wondering humans approaching the more or less impersonal and mysterious powers of nature, but rather like that of the people of a tribe in the presence of a chieftain or, more intimately, like that of children before a father.

By the time this point was reached, we note further, a distinctive choice had been made, either by the gods or by the people. Not all of the gods could be "father" or "personal lord" to the same people; intimacy cannot be general. What happened was this: one, or at most several, gods chose, or were chosen by, a larger or smaller group (a clan) for closer, more intimate connection than that of all the gods to all people.

The bond was "peculiar" and familiar and tended to be binding on both sides.

From the beginning, the Hebrews seem to have had this sense of being "chosen" and of making a choice. The Abraham sagas illustrate this.

Abraham and the Migration to Palestine

The ancestors of the Hebrew tribes migrated out of the edges of the desert into Mesopotamia in the same way other Semitic peoples had done—the groups that earlier became Babylonians, Arameans, Phoenicians, Amorites, and Canaanites. Abraham, an eponymous figure (i.e., one whose name represents a group of ancestors), is described as having dwelt at Ur for a time. Further migration northward and westward brought a pause at Haran. Despite the availability of a considerable mass of archaeological materials dealing with the region, evidence consistently supporting one or another date for the ancestral migration is difficult to marshal. Conjectures placing it in the Middle Bronze times or the earlier parts of the Late Bronze period stretch from 2100 to 1400 B.C.E.

Because the situation at Haran was disturbed, the people represented by Abraham's name moved further to the southwest in search of better conditions.

Briefly, in the nineteenth century B.C.E., the whole Middle East was in a state of flux and tension. The Kingdom of Mari, in whose northwestern region Haran was located, was in constant peril of being overrun by Akkadians to the east. Both in turn were threatened by hordes of Hurrians, poised for invasion from the Armenian mountains to the north. These "barbaric" hordes were themselves being pushed toward a movement southward. Behind them was the enormous pressure of a chariot-borne Indo-European (Indo-Iranian) irruption into the southlands. (Once more we are confronted by these extraordinary people, whom we have already followed into India and Iran, and whose fellow Indo-Europeans we found in Greece, Italy, and northern Europe.) Syria and Palestine were equally, if not more, disturbed. Eventually, the Hittites and Hurrians of eastern Asia Minor were driven, the former westward, the latter southward. The population of Palestine was swollen with refugees of many kinds: Hurrians (the biblical Horites), Amorites,

Aramaeans, and non-Semitic peoples from further north. And, apparently, the early nomadic tribe with which tradition has associated Abraham had already arrived and was about to be swept along in the general movement southward. A moving group of associated peoples, some of them Indo-Iranian, most of them Semitic, whom the Egyptians were to call Shashu, the Greeks Hyksos, were migrating toward the Nile.

Because the story of Abraham as told in Genesis is the interweaving of several strands of tradition, there is room for a variety of conjectural reconstructions. It is clear, though, that the Abraham saga is central and it is in connection with his name (Gen. 13:14) that the identification *Hebrew* is first introduced. (Possible relationships to the *habiru* of the Amarna tablets are discussed on p. 383.) We should observe, however, that the identifying ancestral reference preferred by later descendants came to be *children of Israel* or *Israelites* (derived from Abraham's grandson, Jacob/Israel).

The Story of Abraham in Genesis

The gist of the narrative in Genesis is this: Personal religious experience led Abraham to place all of his faith in a single protective deity, whom he chose, or who chose him, an *el* whom he called El-Shaddai (of uncertain meaning, perhaps "the El of the Rock or Mountain"), who far overshadowed the ancestral spirits or household gods represented by the *teraphim*— the wooden or stone images kept by his family for use in domestic magic and worship. When he longed to migrate to the safer and more favored grazing lands in the southwest, El-Shaddai encouraged him to go there. It is clear in the biblical account that Abraham gave his allegiance to this one being alone; that by a personal commitment he bound himself to follow the way of El-Shaddai, which was to do kindness and practice justice and righteousness; and that Abraham himself was generous, hospitable, and forgiving. (See the story of his intercession for the Sodomites in Genesis 18:23 f.) The tradition tells that when El-Shaddai demanded the human sacrifice of his son Isaac, he set out to obey, but his experience ended in his substituting a ram for his son (Gen. 22). (The story may reflect the ancient substitution of animal for human sacrifice.) Furthermore, El-Shaddai promised him and his descendants a permanent home in the Land of Canaan. So Abraham, trusting his divine patron (he is called "the friend of God"), took the long journey with the members of his small tribe. Once safely in the land where the Canaanites dwelt, he made his home on the limestone ridge that forms main contour of the land, and after his death his place was taken successively by his son Isaac and his grandson Jacob.

Abraham's Descendants Migrate to Egypt

When a terrible famine came, the descendants of Abraham migrated once more, this time to the borders of Egypt—here the story of Joseph explains the sequence of events—where lay the fertile Land of Goshen.

For generations, all went well. The Israelites in particular prospered and multiplied. Then the Egyptians arose and expelled the Hyksos (1580–1560 B.C.E.) and recovered control of the whole eastern Mediterranean coast. The Israelites were not included in this expulsion of the hated ruling caste. For a century and a half, no attempt was made to reduce them to a status below that of their Egyptian neighbors. But there came to the throne of Egypt a mad pharaoh, Ramses II (1304–1237 B.C.E.), whose passion was the building of great public works, including whole cities and monumental temples. Needing large forces of drafted or unpaid labor, he turned his eyes toward the northeastern border upon the Israelites, pounced on and made slaves of them. They were compelled, under the lash, to give their forced labor to the pharaoh's public works. Nothing appeared able to save them except either a catastrophe overwhelming Egypt or a leader arising in their own midst to rescue them from their plight. At least one, if not both, of these conditions for their escape was met.

II. MOSES AND THE COVENANT WITH YAHWEH (ABOUT 1250 B.C.E.)

The high place that Moses has held in Hebrew-Jewish devotion is deserved. Recent scholarship, though denying to him the authorship of the Pentateuch (the first five books of the Bible), has vindicated his place of highest honor in the early history of Israel. He was a creative personality of the first order. He revolutionized the religious orientation of his people by persuading them to adopt the basic idea of Israelite religion, namely, that for them there is but one God, supreme over their history and their lives. This God had chosen Israel to be his people and desired to make and abide by a covenant with them, a mutually binding pact. Thereafter, God would be active in their history, to bless or punish them according to their faithfulness to him. Elements of the ancient desert heritage—demonology, magic, and divination—remained in the new orientation, but they survived now as recognitions of realities present in the physical world *under God*. The contrast with Semitic polytheisms was sharp: the gods and myths of the polytheistic faiths were henceforth to be given no hearing; they were to be ignored. Israel had but one god.

The story of Moses has come down to us in the narratives known to scholars as "J" (a source using *Jahweh* as the name for God) and "E" (a source using *Elohim* as a name for God), intertwined in Exodus and Numbers. The written form of these traditions dates from four to six hundred years after his time.

The Story of Moses' Infancy

The Book of Exodus tells the story as follows:

> Then a new king arose over Egypt, who . . . said to his people, "See, the Israelite people have become too numerous and too strong for us; come, let us take precautions against them lest they become so numerous that in the case of a war they should join forces with our enemies and fight against us." . . .
>
> So Pharaoh commanded all his people, "Every boy that is born to the Hebrews, you must throw into the Nile, but you are to let all the girls live." Now a man belonging to the House of Levi went and married a daughter of Levi. The woman conceived and bore a son, and seeing he was robust, she hid him for three months. When she could no longer hide him, she procured an ark of papyrus reeds for him, and daubing it with bitumen and pitch, she put the child in it, and placed it among the reeds beside the bank of the Nile. His sister posted herself some distance away to see what would happen to him. Presently Pharaoh's daugh-

ter came down to bathe at the Nile, while her maids walked on the bank of the Nile. Then she saw the ark among the reeds and sent her maid to get it. On opening it, she saw the child, and it was a boy crying! She took pity on him, and said, "This is one of the Hebrews' children." Thereupon his sister said to Pharaoh's daughter, "Shall I go and summon a nurse for you from the Hebrew women, to nurse the child for you?" "Go," said Pharaoh's daughter to her. So the girl went and called the child's mother, to whom Pharaoh's daughter said, "Take this child away and nurse it for me, and I will pay the wages due you." So the woman took the child and nursed him; and when the child grew up, she brought him to Pharaoh's daughter, and he became her son. She called his name Moses (drawn out); "For," said she, "I drew him out of the water."[A1]

Moses Called from Refuge in Midian

The tradition continues that Moses, when grown to manhood, saw one day an Egyptian beating an Israelite, "one of his people." Moved by ungovernable rage, to which he allowed full scope because they were in a lonely place, he smote the Egyptian and killed him. The next day, finding that the deed was becoming known, he fled eastward beyond the Red Sea to the land of Midian, where, while in hiding, he joined the household of a Midianite priest by the name of Jethro (or Reuel). He married Jethro's daughter Zipporah and had two sons by her.

"In the course of this long time," continues the story, "the king of Egypt died," and far away in Midian the greatest single event in Hebrew history took place.

> While Moses was tending the flock of his father-in-law, Jethro, the priest of Midian, he led the flock to the western side of the desert, and came to the mountain of God, Horeb. Then the angel of the Lord appeared to him in a flame of fire, rising out of a bush. He looked, and there was the bush burning with fire without being consumed! . . . When the Lord saw that he turned aside to look at it, God called to him out of the bush. "Moses, Moses!" he said. "Here I am!" said he. "Do not come near here," he said; "take your sandals off your feet; for the place on which you are standing

is holy ground." . . . Then Moses hid his face; for he was afraid to look at God. "I have indeed seen the plight of my people who are in Egypt," the Lord said, "and I have heard their cry under their oppressors; for I know their sorrows, and I have come down to rescue them from the Egyptians and bring them up out of that land to a land, fine and large, to a land abounding in milk and honey, to the country of the Canaanites, Hittites, Amorites, Perizzites, Hivvites, and Jebusites. . . . So come now, let me send you to Pharaoh, that you may bring my people, the Israelites, out of Egypt." . . . "But," said Moses to God, "in case I go to the Israelites and say to them, 'The God of your fathers has sent me to you,' and they say to me, 'What is his name?' what am I to say to them?"

The reply of God to Moses' question is a very important one, no less to the modern historian than to the Moses of this tradition.

"I am who I am," God said to Moses. . . . God said further to Moses, "Thus you shall say to the Israelites: 'Yahweh . . . has sent me to you.'"A2

The New Name: Yahweh

That Yahweh was a new name for the Israelites to give to the God of Abraham, Isaac, and Jacob seems evident. Little doubt now exists that Moses introduced them for the first time to the worship of Yahweh (or Jehovah, as another vowel pointing reads). It is significant that in Exodus 6:3, Yahweh is seen admitting that though he appeared to Abraham, Isaac, and Jacob as El-Shaddai, he was not known to them as Yahweh. The word *Yahweh* can be variously translated as meaning, "I will be what I want to be" or "I am that (or who) I am," or yet again, "I am he that causes to be," that is, the Creator. Jews have long considered the word too holy to pronounce, and when they come to it in their reading, they say instead "Adonai," "Lord."

Behind the elaboration of later tradition embroidering the original historical incident, we may perceive the element of fact. Moses had had a direct, personal experience with a god of strong and determined character. It became evident that this vital being, Yahweh, was not just a nature god, although he

The Sacred Tetragram
YaHWeH "Adonai"

dwelt on the wild slopes of a wilderness mountain and descended upon it in fire and smoke. These elements of nature were his instrumentalities; he himself was distinct from them, a god behind the scenes, who could take into his keeping the destinies of a whole nation and swear a solemn compact with them, promising to give them in return for their loyalty and obedience: peace, prosperity, and plenty; rain and sun in their season; cattle on a thousand hills; victory in war; children; and a long life. He was a just god, but a god of strong feelings, happy in the loyalty of those who obeyed him, but disturbed if they were unfaithful.

The full character of Yahweh was, of course, not known to Moses at once. Moses' experience simply made him aware of a task, this task being the leading of the Israelites out of Egypt to Sinai, where the God who wanted a people could make a covenant with the people who needed a God.

The Exodus to Sinai

It is not necessary here to go into the well-known story of how Moses hurried to Egypt to win the Israelites over to his plan, how during their farewell Passover Yahweh, according to Exodus 12, "passed over" them but slew Egypt's firstborn, and how Moses finally led the Exodus by crossing the Red (or Reed) Sea with all of his people, just before the pursuing Egyptians drove up in their chariots in the attempt to turn them back. Apparently the Egyptians could not spare enough fighting men to prevent the Israelites' escape. There seems to be some historical warrant for saying that the Exodus came at a time when Egypt was threatened by barbaric enemies from Libya and pirates sailing up the mouth of the Nile. The distraction of Egypt by these dangers could have furnished the Israelites with their opportunity.

However, the leadership of Moses made its greatest contribution not in Egypt but at the foot of the sacred mountain, called in one strand of tradition Sinai and in another Horeb. The exact location of this mountain is still debatable. It has traditionally been located on what is known as the Sinai Peninsula, but many recent scholars place it nearer the head of the Gulf of Aqaba or in the region of Kadesh-Barnea, slightly to the southwest of the Dead Sea. The location matters little. What took place, in any event, is that Moses served as the intermediary between his followers and Yahweh, the God who had sent Moses to deliver them out of Egypt, had thus far saved them from all of their perils, and now desired to make a covenant with them. According to the tradition, the terms of the covenant were made known in the following manner: Leaving the people at the foot of the mountain, Moses went up the slope to commune with Yahweh, and after some days he returned with the knowledge of Yahweh's will for the people. This will, summarized in "commandments" inscribed on two tablets of stone, was subsequently amplified into the many provisions of the Torah or Law. (It should be noted that the term *Torah* has a variety of usages: often, as in this chapter, the reference is to the written law in the Pentateuch; in the Judaism of later times, Torah is used more broadly to mean God's teaching or guidance and thus to refer to all of Hebrew scripture and traditions or even to Jewish theology as a whole.)

Texts of the Commandments

Two lists of commandments are given in the records. One, the formulation of a high ethical code, is familiar to us as the Ten Commandments (Exodus 20). It is doubtful, however, that we have it in its original form. Evidently what we have is the full and elaborated form of later days, when it was finally the general conviction among Israelites that Yahweh was not just Israel's god but the creator of the entire physical world, the maker of sky and earth and sea and all that they contain. Furthermore, it is evident that these commandments, as do the parallels in Deuteronomy 6:4–22, assume that the Israelites live in homes, own livestock, and must deal with aliens in the community.

The other list of commandments, as found in Exodus 34, is largely ritualistic in character. Some scholars, seeing in this fact evidence of priority in time, prefer it as the earlier list. It is interestingly introduced in the records, thus,

> The Lord said to Moses,
> "Cut two stone tablets . . . and in the morning ascend Mount Sinai, and present yourself there to me on the top of the mountain. No one is to ascend with you, nor is anyone to be seen anywhere on the mountain, nor must the flocks and herds graze in front of that mountain."
> So Moses cut two stone tablets . . . and rising early next morning, he ascended Mount Sinai, as the Lord had commanded him, taking the two stone tablets in his hand. Then the Lord descended in a cloud, and took up a position with him there, while he called upon the name of the Lord. The Lord passed in front of him, proclaiming, "The Lord, the Lord, a God compassionate and gracious, slow to anger, abounding in kindness and fidelity, showing kindness to the thousandth generation, forgiving iniquity, transgression, and sin, without leaving it unpunished however, but avenging the iniquity of fathers upon their children and grandchildren down to the third or even the fourth generation."
> Then Moses quickly bowed his head to the ground, and made obeisance.[A3]

This passage is followed by Yahweh's announcement that he wishes to make a compact or covenant with the Israelites in the following specific terms:

> You must not make any molten gods for yourselves.
> You must keep the festival of unleavened cakes, eating unleavened cakes for seven days, as I commanded you. . . .
> Whatever first opens the womb belongs to me, in the case of all your livestock that are male, the firstlings of oxen and sheep; a firstling ass, however, you may redeem with a sheep, but if you do not redeem it, you must break its neck; any firstborn son of yours you may redeem.
> None may visit me empty-handed.
> Six days you are to labor, but on the seventh day you must rest, resting at ploughing-time and at harvest.

Traditional Mt. Sinai

According to long-standing tradition, it was on the top of this forbidding mountain that Moses met with Yahweh and received from him the tablets of the Ten Commandments. A Christian monastery huddles under the mountain to be near the place of God's descent. *(© Photograph by Erich Lessing/Art Resource.)*

You must observe the festival of weeks, that of the first-fruits of the wheat harvest, and also the festival of ingathering at the turn of the year; three times a year must all your males come to see the Lord God, the God of Israel. . . .

You must not offer the blood of a sacrifice to me with leavened bread.

The sacrifice of the Passover feast must not be left over night until morning.

The very first of the first-fruits of your land you must bring to the house of the Lord your God.

You must not boil a kid in its mother's milk.[A4]

Very clearly, however, this could not have been the original compact with Yahweh, because, like the Ten Commandments, it presupposes an agricultural, not a nomadic, community, and one, moreover, long established in its own land.

The most moving summary of the covenant law comes from Josiah's reform (see page 396) in Deuteronomy 6:4, "Hear, O Israel the Lord our God is one Lord"). (This is called the *Shema*, "Hear!" and is the core formula of Jewish devotion.) The next verse summarizes the rest of the law, "and you shall love the Lord your God with all your heart and with all your soul and with all your might."

Rituals Sealing the Covenant

The precise terms of the covenant are therefore irrecoverable. Later tradition has too thoroughly obscured the original situation. Nevertheless, the nature of the ceremony by which the pact was sealed between Yahweh and those who were thenceforth to be his people may be preserved in the following important passage:

Then Moses . . . recounted to the people all the regulations of the Lord and all the ordinances; and the people all answered with one voice,

"All the regulations that the Lord has given we will observe."

So Moses . . . built an attar at the foot of the mountain, along with twelve sacred pillars, one for each of the twelve tribes of Israel. Then he sent the young men of the Israelites to offer burnt-offerings and to sacrifice oxen as thank-offerings to the Lord, while Moses himself took half of the blood, and put it in basins, dashing the other half on the attar. He then took the book of the covenant, and read it in the hearing of the people who said, "All that the Lord has directed we will obediently do."

Then Moses took the blood and dashed it on the people saying, "Behold the blood of the covenant which the Lord has made with you on the basis of all these regulations."[A5]

Later times were well aware of the significance of such a ritual. The same blood was splashed on Yahweh's altar and on the people, and this made them "of one blood," that is, indissolubly joined. The people bound themselves to Yahweh by a solemn legal agreement, such as men might contract with each other and ratify in blood.

The Tabernacle: A Portable Sanctuary

When the Israelites prepared to journey on, they had the problem not so much of leaving Yahweh behind on his mountain (for they believed he could go with them in spirit and power) but of providing a medium of communication with him. At Sinai, Moses went up the mountain, and God talked to him. If they left the mountain behind, what then? The solution of the problem was the ancient one of providing a meeting place for God and his people, that is, a shrine or sanctuary. So they devised a portable "tent of meeting" (the "tabernacle of the Lord") and reserved it for purely sacred use. At each encampment it was set up by ritualistically proper persons (tradition says these were members of the tribe of Levi, from whom sprang the priests of later days), and in the silence of

its interior, Moses was able to listen as Yahweh spoke to him.

It is quite unlikely that the tabernacle had an unfurnished interior. The persistent and early tradition may be accepted that within it stood a box or chest in which were contained two stone tablets marked with the terms of the covenant. This was the famous Ark of the Covenant, which played such a vital part in later Hebrew history. In Moses' day, tradition insists, whenever the Israelites were on the march, they reverently bore the Ark in the van. Carried into battle, it gave strength to the warriors' arms. So holy a thing did it become that none but priests dared to touch it, for fear of being felled by the power it possessed.

Early Rituals: Passover, Sabbath

In a very natural way, a ritual of worship was developed that became more and more elaborate with the passing years. The oldest elements of this ritual were the annual celebration of the Passover and the weekly observance of the Sabbath. The Passover was an ancient Semitic festival appropriated to Israelite uses. Through it they celebrated the memory of their escape from Egyptian bondage. It was a spring festival, taking place during the night of the full moon nearest the spring equinox. Between twilight and dawn, each family made a meal of a sacrificial sheep (or goat) whose blood had been smeared on the doorposts of the tent or on the lintel and doorposts at the entrance to the house. The whole sheep was to be consumed, either by the eaters or in the fire; nothing was to be left over. The Sabbath day also appears to have an ancient date, originating long before the time of the Exodus, from the custom of taking one day of every "moon" for worship and recreation. Gradually, it became customary to set aside the seventh day of the week as a pious period of rest, sacred to the Lord.

Of an early origin also were the new moon festivals (more or less frowned upon and modified by the strict of later days), the feast of sheepshearing, circumcision (common to most Semites and to adjacent peoples), the taboo on food before battle, and the law of blood revenge.

Implicit Monotheism

In considering these adaptations of ancient rites to new purposes, it should be emphasized that through Moses' leadership Israelite religion successfully made the transition from polytheism to monotheism. And yet, despite his leadership, his people were not immune, in his own and in later times, to temporary relapse into polytheistic practices. This was partly due to the hold of older habits on their behavior and partly to the fact that the monotheism of Moses was initially one of *loyalty* and *practice* rather than one affirming explicitly and theologically that only one god exists. (Scholars are divided on whether or not Moses believed that the gods of other peoples were *fictions* and nonexistent. It would seem that such an assertion was implicit in his position but was not explicitly made until the time of the literary prophets.) That the people were not quite prepared in his own time for constancy in the practice of a strict ethical monotheism is implied in the story of the apostasy of Aaron at the foot of Mt. Sinai. A story—so much edited by later hands as to contain obviously self-contradictory elements—(Moses is told by the Lord that the people have made a golden calf; then he is surprised and angered to find them doing just that; then he returns to tell the Lord that the people have made gods of gold) proposes that when Moses went up the mountain for forty days and forty nights, the people became restive.

> When the people saw that Moses was long in coming down from the mountain, the people gathered about Aaron, and said to him "Come, make us a god to go ahead of us; for this is the way it is with Moses, the man who brought us up out of the land of Egypt—we do not know what has become of him."
>
> So Aaron said to them, "Tear off the gold rings which are in the ears of your wives, your sons, and your daughters, and bring them to me."
>
> So all the people tore off the gold rings which were in their ears, and brought them to Aaron, who took the material from them, and pouring it into a mold, made it into a molten bull, whereupon they said, "Here is your god, O Israel, who brought you up out of the land of Egypt!"
>
> On seeing this, Aaron built an altar in front of it, and Aaron made proclamation, "Tomorrow a feast shall be held to the Lord."

> So next day the people rose early, and offered burnt-offerings, and presented thank-offerings; the people sat down to eat and drink, after which they rose to make merry.
>
> Then the Lord said to Moses, "Go down at once; for your people whom you brought up out of the land of Egypt have acted perniciously. . . ."
>
> Moses then turned and descended from the mountain. . . .
>
> As soon as he came near the camp, he saw the bull and the dancing, whereupon Moses' anger blazed, and he flung the tablets [of the Commandments which he was carrying] from his hands, and broke them at the foot of the mountain; then he took the bull which they had made, and burned it up, and grinding it to powder, he scattered it on the surface of the water, and made the Israelites drink it. Then Moses said to Aaron, "What did this people do to you, that you have let them incur such great guilt?"
>
> Aaron said, "Let not my Lord's anger blaze; you know yourself how bad the people are. They said to me, 'Make us a god to go ahead of us!' . . . So I said to them, 'Whoever has any gold, let them tear it off; and when they gave it to me, I threw it into the fire, and out came this bull!'"[A6]

This sort of apostasy was to be not infrequent in the years to come.

III. YAHWEH AND THE BAALS

After wandering in the wilderness for a number of years (forty, according to tradition), the Exodus Hebrews or Israelites felt themselves strong enough to invade Canaan.

It is not easy to reconstruct the story of the "conquest" from the books of Joshua and Judges. According to those accounts, the main entry of the invaders was led by Ephraim and Manasseh—tribes descended from Joseph—which infiltrated across the Jordan under the generalship of Joshua, Moses' successor. (The narratives hold that Moses himself did not live to cross the Jordan into Canaan. The time was about 1200 B.C.E.) Joshua took Jericho, and from this base spread their conquest through central Palestine, in time capturing Shechem, Shiloh, and Samaria, to make good their control of the central territory. The tribes of Judah and Simeon, invading from the south, possessed themselves of the highlands in the vicinity of the walled city of the Jebusites (Jerusalem). In this they were assisted by the non-Hebraic Kenites on the south. Two tribes, Reuben and Gad, remained behind or turned back to their "portion" east of the Jordan. Others made their way among the northern Canaanites (with less fighting than immigrating), slowly penetrating and permeating the valley of Esdraelon and the north country. Dan, after an abortive settlement in the south, eventually occupied the extreme north, and Zebulun went north-westward toward the Phoenician coast and came to amicable terms with the Hittites. Still other tribes, like Issachar, Asher, and Naphtali, occupied the fertile lands around the Lake of Galilee. In the process of occupying the land, some of the tribes were either dissipated or absorbed, like the tribes of Simeon and Benjamin.

Infiltration over a Long Period

The tradition does not hide the fact that this was a long process. The Canaanites had strong walls around their principal cities and villages and possessed chariots and arms far superior to the crude weapons of the Israelite fighting men. On the heights where Jerusalem stood, a powerful tribe of Jebusites lived secure within the city's thick stone walls and repelled every attack made on them for two hundred years. Elsewhere as well, the Israelites had to content themselves with possession of the open country, because the Canaanites beat off their attacks on the towns from the top of their battlements. But in the end, by whatever means, whether by dispossession, annihilation, expulsion, or accommodation, they made the land theirs.

Their dominance of the land was not secure, however, until their external enemies were beaten off. Their Semitic enemies from the east, the Edomites, Moabites, and Ammonites, constantly harassed them by seeking to enter the land. In the struggle against them it is likely that many Canaanites made common cause with the Israelites. But the most formidable enemies were the Philistines, a non-Semitic people who had descended upon the southwestern coastal plain from the islands of the Mediterranean. Their original home, we learn from other sources, was Crete, and when driven out of it, they turned pirates. They may

actually have assisted the Israelites in their escape from Egypt by harrying the cities of the lower Nile. Unable to make a landing in Egypt, they sought a territory to colonize further north and found it on the south Palestinian shore. Gradually they spread inland and, with five fortified towns at their back, began to ascend the hills. The Israelites fought with them for generations and barely held them off.

The Exodus Hebrews and the *Habiru*

This story is now being amended and supplemented by historians, who do not question its substance as much as its narrowing of attention too exclusively to one group—the Israelites or Exodus Hebrews. New evidence has come to light of turmoil within Canaan caused by "outsiders" or "wanderers" known as *Habiru,* some of whom may be unhesitatingly identified as non-Exodus Hebrews, who had not gone down to Egypt but who joined forces with the Exodus Hebrews (the Israelites) when they entered Canaan. Others of the same or similar grouping had for years been appearing in Mesopotamia, Syria, and northern Egypt. They probably were Semites from the desert who had originally been engaged in conducting caravans along the desert trade routes but who, when these routes were closed, had no fixed location or occupation but wandered about, sometimes as shepherds, sometimes as musicians, smiths, and artisans, and sometimes as mercenaries for hire or free-roving guerrillas. (The Akkadians called them Khapiru and the Egyptians Apiru.) They often were very troublesome to local authorities and needed only organization into a group with common beliefs and purposes to be a menace. The famous Tell-el-Amarna Letters, found in Egypt by a peasant woman in 1887 and identified as dispatches sent by the Egyptian governors and minor officials in Canaan to the pharaohs from about 1400 to 1350 B.C.E., contain frantic appeals for help against groups of Habiru who were coming from the east and north-east and threatening to overrun the country.

> There are no lands left to the king, my lord. The Habiru plunder all the countries of the king!"
>
> The country of the king is fallen away to the Habiru. And now also a city of the country of

Jerusalem (its name is Beth-Shemesh), a city of the king, has gone over to the men of Keilah. May the king send mercenaries that the land may remain unto the king. If there are no mercenaries, lost is the land of the king to the Habiru!ᴮ

The alarm of the officials gradually subsided. The Habiru did not make a conquest. Their inflow was an infiltration process in the main, for the Canaanites were able to retain a string of fortresses and walled towns across the land, while the seminomadic "migrants" settled in the unoccupied hill country and made themselves at home.

Some time later, if our reconstruction—a precarious matter at best—is correct, the Exodus Hebrews, inspired by the Mosaic faith in Yahweh, entered the land, made common cause with the Habiru (whence their own later name of Hebrews?), and by vigorous assaults on important Canaanite towns put themselves in the position to become masters of the whole land eventually, and what is even more important for our story, so impressed their Habiru allies with their superior *élan* that Yahweh was adopted by the latter as their own Lord of Hosts. (The foregoing reconstruction is conjectural. There are other theories too complex to summarize here.)

Nomads Move Toward Nationhood

As the years passed, the Exodus Hebrews succeeded in imbuing their Canaanite neighbors as well as themselves and their allies with a sense of nationhood. The increasing menace of the Philistines (beginning in about 1150 B.C.E.) caused the feeling of difference to be forgotten, especially when, under the seer Samuel and the first king Saul, strong efforts were made to throw the Philistines back upon their coastal plain. These efforts began to bear fruit at last, for though in the generation before Saul the Philistines had captured the Ark of the Covenant in battle (and then in fear induced by bad luck had returned it in a cart drawn by cows turned loose across the frontier), they now began to taste repeated defeat. Saul took his own life when defeated at Mt. Gilboa, but his successor

David finally routed the Philistines and broke their fighting spirit.

David also captured at long last, about 1020 B.C.E., the city of the Jebusites (Jerusalem), made it his capital, and planned a temple in it to house the Ark of the Covenant properly, a project that was left for his son Solomon to carry out, as indeed he did.

Changes were necessarily involved in the passage from nomadic to agricultural and urban life. When the Israelites came in from the desert, they moved among a people with a well-developed culture and religion. They had much to learn from their new neighbors.

Nature Religion Implicit in Canaanite Agriculture

The Canaanites had developed a thoroughgoing nature religion, growing out of their agricultural life. Their gods were, in general character, farm gods. The class name by which they were known was *baal*, which, as we have seen, means "owner" or "possessor" (of the soil). Every stretch of fertile ground owed its fertility to the presence of some baal, who held sway, like a feudal lord, within his own boundaries, though, like a feudal lord, he himself was in turn subject to the two supreme lords of all lesser baals: (1) the elevated but inactive god El, who, if we can judge from recently recovered documents, resided in the "Source of the Two Deeps" in highest heaven, and (2) the subordinate but active storm god and chief of the lower gods, the great Baal of Heaven. El's consort was Ashirat, known to the Hebrews as Asherah, and the great Baal was associated with his sister Anath and the virgin but fertility-giving Astarte, who were aspects or even earthly forms of Ashirat. As to the males, one may conclude that these heavenly powers were represented on earth by local baals acting in the soil, and that each earthly baal in his sphere of operation at will imparted or withheld fertility power in the soil. The plant cycle was so closely associated with him that its various stages were considered his birth, life, and death and were ritually celebrated. At his death (the drying up of vegetation at the beginning of summer) those who owed most to him ceremonially wept at the remembrance of his past goodness. In a number of districts it was even the custom to tear out the hair in grief at his passing. At his birth (revival), it was common to hold festivals of rejoicing during which, in their gayest attire, the celebrants streamed together to the nearest shrine to dance and sing and give themselves up to orgiastic ceremonies, designed in part to assist him and in part to make recognition of his fertility power renewed in them.

The numerous baals whose presence was recognized on the hilltops, in the valleys, and at springs and wells all over the land each had their places of worship. On elevated ground, either within the walls or upon a nearby dominating height, each city built a sanctuary in honor of its patron baal, whose name was hyphenated with that of the city's. The priests in charge of these *bamoth* or high places conducted the worship in an open-air court facing the shrine of the god. An image of the god might occupy the shrine and be dimly seen by the worshipers, and near the altar outside stood a stone pillar, the mazzebah, a phallic symbol of the god. Perhaps also there would be a wooden column or pole, called the *asherah*, representing the goddess who was the god's consort (the *baalah*). Many sanctuaries boasted also bull images and bronze snakes, these being popular representations of the fertility power of the god.

Sacrifices were of two kinds: (1) gift sacrifices, either of the firstfruits of field or tree (a debt necessarily owing) or of animal flesh burnt upon the altar, and (2) communion sacrifices, through which the god and his people together partook of the sacrifice and thus strengthened the bond between them. There were three main festivals, in spring, early summer, and fall.

Goddess Worship: Anath/Astarte

By far the most important deity in the festivals was Anath/Astarte. It seems likely that Anath and Astarte were the same goddess, Anath being the proper name and Astarte the epithet. Anath was depicted in a variety of roles while the epithet Astarte, "she of the womb," drew attention to her fertility roles. While the baals had static landlord and seed-giver roles, Anath

exercised active creative/destructive powers. As with Kali/Durga of India, the underlying goddess power had a ferocious side: sometimes Anath took sword in hand, sprang naked upon a mount, and rode forth to bloody slaughter in defense of her devotees. As with her Sumerian (Ishtar) and Assyrian (Inanna) counterparts, there were strong associations with warfare. (I Samuel 31:10 says that the Philistines fastened Saul's body to the wall but put his armor in the "temple of Ashtaroth.")

As goddess of fertility among human beings as well as in animal husbandry and agriculture, Astarte took on all of the qualities of the Egyptian Isis, the Grecian Demeter, and the Roman Venus. The cypress, the myrtle, and the palm were sacred to her, as being evergreen, and her special symbol was a two-horned cow. In her own person she usually was represented naked, and the practice of honoring her through temple prostitution may have prompted her Hebrew wordplay name Ashtoreth (combining the consonants of Astarte with the vowels of *bosheth,* "shame"). The women attendants who ministered in her sanctuaries for this purpose were called Kedeshoth, meaning "consecrated women," a euphemistic term of respect. In the divine marriage between Astarte and Baal, which the Canaanites celebrated in the autumn, she was literally the soil become a wife, and he was the husband of the land who furnished seed.

Spirit Lore Absorbed with Farming Methods

Wavering Israelites found it natural to adopt some of these beliefs and practices. The strict monotheists considered these waverers apostate. Among those who remained true to the Mosaic faith were the herdsmen of the hills, still in a seminomadic condition, who felt no need of other help than that given by Yahweh, the god of mountain and storm, who had been their guide in the wilderness and was mighty still in war and in peace. But those who took up agriculture found themselves in a different case. Although some knowledge of agriculture may have existed, especially among the aged who remembered Egypt, the younger generation had to learn farming from their Canaanite neighbors.

Astarte Figurines

Terracotta pillar-style *Asherah* images from Judah in the Iron Age (*ca.* 1000–700 B.C.E.) depict Astarte in her role as fertility-granting mother goddess offering her breasts. The phallic pillar style also alludes to the role of the male consort, or *baal*. King Jehu's burning of a "pillar" (altar?) from the house of Baal *may* refer to such an image (II Kings 10:27). *(Courtesy of the Israel Museum, IDAM. © Photograph by Erich Lessing/Art Resource.)*

This involved more than ploughing, sowing, and reaping. It required a thorough grasp of the spirit lore of each locality, and this involved so much of magic and religion as to make it difficult for them to resist taking over the whole of the local religion. This is why, in the more fertile north, Israel (the ten northern tribes) was less true to the religion of Yahweh than were the people of rockbound Judah, with its large class of shepherds not dominated by Canaanite influences. Without abandoning their faith in Yahweh as the God who presided over the destiny of the whole people and guided them in war, many Israelite farmers went with the Canaanites to the village high places, gave of their firstfruits to the local baals and ashtoreths, brought gift and peace offerings, and learned how to make whole burnt offerings. They also observed the festivals of their Canaanite neighbors at the beginning and end of the wheat harvest and in the autumn.

Those who were faithful to Yahweh, on the other hand, had no doubt that Yahweh controlled the processes of agriculture as well as the events of the nation. This insight never left those on the highlands and in the border regions who remained true to the Mosaic tradition, but it also dawned as well on others who participated freely in baal worship, but who said to themselves, "Under these forms of baal-worship we worship Yahweh, for he is the Baal of Heaven and all the power behind the ashtoreths." Though in the period of the Book of Judges the Yahweh shrine at Shiloh held only the Ark of the Covenant, in later times the sanctuaries at Bethel and Dan contained bull images ("golden calves") that were regarded as symbols of Yahweh. This could have only one meaning, namely, that Yahweh had taken over in addition to his older functions those that the bull represented: the God who had led the Israelites through the desert was now proving his capacity to bring fertility to field and flock.

And yet it looked for a time as if Yahweh was not assimilating baalism to himself but was instead being absorbed by it, even submerged beneath it. Hence the prophet Hosea was moved vehemently to exclaim,

> My people ask a piece of wood to guide them,
> a pole gives them their oracles!
> For a harlot-spirit has led them astray,
> they have left their God for a faithless way;
> they sacrifice on mountain heights,
> and offer incense on the hills,
> below the oak, the terebinth, the poplar—
> so pleasant is their shade.
> So your daughters play the harlot,
> matrons commit adultery.
> But I will not punish your daughters for harlotry,
> nor your matrons for adultery,
> when the men themselves go off with harlots,
> and sacrifice with temple-prostitutes.
> This brings a senseless people to their ruin—
> liquor and lust deprive them of their wits.[C1]

At long last, inspired by a conception of Yahweh that made him greater than he ever was before, the prophets had risen to protest.

IV. PROPHETIC PROTEST AND REFORM

The danger that lay in the baalization of Yahweh has been well expressed by several modern scholars. It might be called the danger of naturization, that is, of absorption into the agricultural milieu. As Max Loehr puts it,

> Baalism saw the activity of the god in natural phenomena. In the annual cycle of the sprouting and decay of vegetation, in the fertilizing rain and the destructive heat of the sun, in the swelling and ripening of the fruits of garden and field, or in

their destruction by the forces of nature, the benignant or wrathful god made himself known, the god whom the Old Testament usually names Baal. It was a nature religion whose worship issued in the materializing of the godhead. Genuine Yahwehism, on the other hand, regarded history as the sphere of divine action. It separated nature and God.[D]

Rudolph Kittel says even more emphatically,

> Those who take a short-sighted view of the period succeeding the death of Moses always take it amiss when it is described as a retrograde period. This was the fact. . . . The nature-elements in Yahweh, instead of being overcome by the higher aspect of his being, were associated in Canaan with the nature-elements in Baal and threatened to submerge the moral and spiritual elements. . . . This was the situation in Israel against which the later prophets waged so fierce a war; for they saw that the exalted God of Moses was in danger of being degraded into a mere local nature-power. This then was the root cause of the appearance of the great prophets and of their frequent opposition to their nation.[E1]

The Origin of Hebrew Prophecy

The great prophets did not appear suddenly, without a background of preparation. Predecessors "made straight the way" for them. These early charismatic leaders came during the time of the Book of Judges, before 1000 B.C.E.

A person invested with charisma was often called a *nabi*. In Hebrew and Arabic this word basically seems to mean "one (divinely) called to speak out (for God)." In later times it was translated by the Greek term *prophet*, meaning "one who speaks for (God)." It was characteristic for a nabi to begin his message by saying, "Thus says the Lord."

Sometimes the title "prophet" or "prophetess" is assigned to persons who appear to have functioned as individual leaders. One of the earliest pieces of Hebrew literature in the Bible is the magnificent poem usually called "The Song of Deborah" (Judges 5:2–31). Together with the later prose narrative in Judges 4, it celebrates the role of the prophetess Deborah in rallying the isolated tribes to take heart, come together, and fight the forces of the Canaanite ruler Jabin, King of Hazor. It illustrates the central function of prophecy: to call forth faithfulness to the covenant of Yahweh with his people. Deborah proclaimed the power of Yahweh to keep his word, and she summoned the tribes in the name of their common allegiance to him.

But most prophets seem to have come to prophetic inspiration through participation in ecstatic groups. In I Samuel 10:5 f., Saul, who had just been anointed as the future military leader of the Israelites, is sent off by the aging Samuel with the following prediction: "As you approach the town [of Gibeah], you will meet a band of dervishes [nebi'im] coming down from the height with lutes, drums, flutes, and lyres playing in front of them, while they prophesy; the spirit of the Eternal [Yahweh] will then inspire you till you prophesy along with them and become a different man." But when this befalls Saul, he learns that he has not won favor with the people. They say scornfully, "Is Saul now numbered among the prophets?"

Court Prophets and Cultic Functions

The early, preliterary nebi'im, leaping in exaltation, were given to ecstatic utterance, unintelligible even to themselves, but alongside of and perhaps associated with them arose men of a cooler spirit, who were the real predecessors of the later prophets: such were Nathan in the time of David and Ahijah in the time of Solomon, prophets who appeared before kings and people to call for the faithfulness and justice demanded by the covenant with Yahweh. Their intelligent and inspired behavior may have in part resulted from a type of association that has only recently come to light. Analysis of the documentary finds of archaeologists during the last half century points to the strong probability that most, if not all, of the Hebrew nebi'im belonged to cult associations or guilds that contributed personnel to the working staff of the larger temples on "high places," or "heights." (Samuel, we have seen, told Saul the nebi'im would come down from the "height.") It is presumed now that the more accomplished nebi'im were given a place in the cultic rites and other activities of the temples as the "religious" ones who were in direct touch with God. In one sense or another,

they were "possessed" by Yahweh, often to the point of exaltation. Some found that music and group dancing led to possession, with ecstatic and generally unintelligible results. Others, apparently, chose solitary meditation as the means to being possessed by Yahweh; after experience of which, they were able to say what God wished to communicate through them.

But the "prophets" were by no means of one mind about Yahweh's message and will. They contradicted each other freely on many issues. It is usual to divide them into true and false prophets; and in this case, one or both of two criteria are applied: (1) the true prophet's message proved true, less in its particulars than in its general or universal sense, while the false prophet's proved mistaken; and (2) the true prophet spoke out boldly without considering his own popularity among his fellow prophets or among the "princes" and the people, since the source of his message was Yahweh alone, whereas the false prophets voiced the popular hopes and backed up official policies. The possibility of venality on the part of the false prophets must be recognized, but probably both kinds of prophets believed in the truth of their own pronouncements.

The messages of the prophets were made all the more trenchant by painful political developments. Ruling from the south (Judah) Solomon by his opulence and high taxes disaffected so many that a secession of the northern region under the name of Israel took place in about 887 B.C.E. At first economic success and military expansion toward Syria led to high hopes, but by 722 the might of the Assyrians overwhelmed and scattered the inhabitants of the Northern Kingdom (giving rise to legends of the "lost tribes"). The fall of Judah to the Babylonians and their exile would follow in 587 B.C.E.

The words of the true prophets were recorded for posterity, fragmentarily or fully. After the earlier period when no separate record was made (as in the cases of Elijah and Elisha), there arose the *literary prophets*, whose prophecies were written down either by themselves or by their followers.

Elijah and Elisha

With Elijah, the prophetic protest against degrading the ethical religion of Yahweh to a mere nature religion was begun in earnest. Appearing in the Northern Kingdom in the time of King Ahab, when that monarch was yielding to the strong pressure of his wife Jezebel to make the Tyrian Baal-Melkart dominant in Israel, Elijah made a truly noteworthy stand on behalf of the Mosaic tradition. The Hebrew historians say that when he began his reforming work there were only seven thousand men in Israel who had not bowed the knee to the Tyrian Baal, nor kissed him, but that before he was done he had reduced the worshipers of this Baal to so much less than that number that they could be crowded into one building. He was not a merciful man. Yahweh was to him a god of stern, unyielding righteousness and justice. When Jezebel contrived to have Naboth stoned so that Ahab could take his vineyard, Elijah dared to confront the king standing in the vineyard and uttered such terrible imprecations in the name of Yahweh that the king rent his garments, hastened away to put on sackcloth, and fasted in terror. In the story of the trial of the respective powers of Yahweh and the Tyrian Baal on Mt. Carmel, which, as it stands, is one of the most dramatic in religious literature, Elijah keeps to the stark issue—who is real, Yahweh or Baal-Melkart—and makes good his claim that Yahweh is real and Baal-Melkart is not.

But during Elijah's lifetime no substantial progress could be effected in permanently discrediting baalism. The opposition of the royal house was too strong, and the people as a whole were hard to change. When Elijah suddenly and, it was felt, supernaturally disappeared (he was said to have been taken to heaven in a whirlwind), his reforming work was continued by his disciple Elisha, who encouraged a certain Jehu to carry out a sweeping political and religious revolution. This was one of the most bloody in Hebrew history. Jehu, a violent man, whose headlong charioteering gave rise to the saying, "He drives like Jehu," annihilated the royal house and then destroyed every vestige of the cult of the Tyrian Baal. So great was the slaughter that a century later Hosea denounced it.

The sum of the matter is this: Baalism, in general, received a very telling blow from the activities of Elijah and Elisha, yet not a death blow; it recovered. One permanent and important result, however, was accomplished—the right of Yahweh to supremacy in Palestine was never afterward denied or even doubted. Baalism could be practiced only as a local cult, either because Yahweh's function was not conceived to be locally agricultural or because Yahweh was held to have made over the local baals into his ministrants. This was a great gain for the stricter followers of Yahweh, for it put them in a tactically good position. On the other hand, it was a gain that was not immediately apparent. Too large a loophole had been left for the continued practice of Canaanitish rites, and during the next century some of the common people, reluctant to part with the baals, availed themselves to the limit of their opportunity in this direction.

After Elisha a new era of prophecy dawned. In the eighth century B.C.E. we come upon individuals who reach us through works composed by themselves or records compiled by close contemporaries. Despite later editorial transformation, their witness comes through in articulate and poetic language heightened by clear-cut impressions of their personalities.

Literary Prophets: Amos

With a voice sturdily independent of king or guild, Amos, the first of the literary prophets and perhaps the greatest, came from the borderland of the south, where the debasement of Mosaic religion to the level of a nature cult had not progressed as far as elsewhere. He thus resembled in place of origin his great predecessor Elijah, who also sprang from the borders of Canaan, from the town of Tishbe, beyond Jordan. This fact suggests that prophetic reform was motivated by the more spiritual insights of the outlying districts that had remained true to the Mosaic tradition. Amos came from Tekoa, a small town about twelve miles south of Jerusalem, and was by occupation a herdsman and pruner of sycamore trees. In marketing sheep he drove them to the populous commercial centers of the Northern Kingdom (Israel), formed by the rebellion of the ten northern tribes against Rehoboam, the son of Solomon. This was about the year 760 B.C.E., during the reign of Uzziah in Judah and Jereboam II in Israel. What he saw set him to brooding. As a herdsman who enjoyed social equality among his fellows in Tekoa, he could not fail to note that under the more complex economic conditions of the north the independence of the farmers had been destroyed in the rise of great landlords, who had bought up farm after farm and who manipulated the grain markets to their own enrichment. The whole social structure had

Jehu Before Shalmaneser
One panel from the black obelisk of Shalmaneser III (9th c. B.C.E.) shows "the tribute of Jehu, son of Omri," the Israelite king, who kneels before "the mighty king of the universe, king without a rival, the autocrat, the powerful one of the four regions of the world." This political event is ignored in the biblical account. Jehu's murder of Ahaziah of Judah and his slaughter of baal worshipers had cut him off from support from the southern kingdom or from Phoenicia against an invasion by Syria. This must have prompted him to turn to Shalmaneser. *(Courtesy of the British Museum. © Photograph by Erich Lessing/Art Resource.)*

become abnormal. The wars of the past had nearly wiped out the middle class. Rich and poor alike were morally adrift. There was increasing laxity in religion and morals everywhere. Integrity was gone, and justice, mercy, and spiritual religion with it. While he reflected upon all this, suddenly he had visions foretelling the doom imminent over the north. Though he came from Judah, he did not hesitate. He hastened into the Northern Kingdom. Yahweh had called him to prophesy.

What he said in Bethel and elsewhere he (or some associate) set down in writing, casting his messages into poetic diction and rhythm to give them a high literary quality and a measure of permanency. His thundering words were a prophecy of doom grounded in deeply significant convictions.

Social Injustice as Covenant Violation

Amos saw social injustice and moral laxity as violations of the "covenant of brotherhood" that Yahweh would surely punish.

The Eternal [Yahweh] declares:
"After crime upon crime of Israel
I will not relent,
for they sell honest folk for money,
the needy for a pair of shoes,
they trample down the poor like dust,
and humble souls they harry;
father and son go in to the same girl
(a profanation of my sacred shrine!),
they loll on garments seized in pledge,
by every altar,
they drink the money taken in fines
in the temple of their God. . . .

"Woe to the careless citizens,
so confident in high Samaria,
leaders of this most ancient race
who are like gods in Israel!—
lolling on their ivory diwans,
sprawling on their couches,
dining off fresh lamb and fatted veal,
crooning to the music of the lute,

composing airs like David himself,
lapping wine by the bowlful,
and using for ointment the best of the oil!—
with never a single thought
for the bleeding wounds of the nation!"[C2]

To punish these social sins and injustices, Amos predicted, the dreaded foe from the north would overrun the land, laying its forts level, plundering the palaces, and carrying the citizens away into exile.

Religious Apostasy

But his indictment did not rest on charges of social iniquity alone. Amos declared that Yahweh was sick of the national apostasy in religion and despised the heathenish temple rites, even though they might be offered in his name.

No wonder Amaziah, the high priest at Bethel, feared the fiery prophet from Judah and charged him in the king's name: "Be off to Judah and earn your living there; play the prophet there, but never again at Bethel, for it is the royal shrine, the national temple." But Amos answered, "I am no prophet, no member of any prophet's guild; I am only a shepherd, and I tend sycamores. But the Eternal took me from the flock; the Eternal said to me, 'Go and prophesy to my people Israel.' Now then, listen to what the Eternal says. . . ."[C4] He had his say. He would not rest with less.

Amos opens a new epoch in creative religion. In the course of uttering his fearsome indictment, he revealed a conception of the nature and jurisdiction of Yahweh implicit in the Mosaic tradition but not clearly stated before. Yahweh was going to *send* the foe from the north, and was about to punish, along with Israel, the Philistines, the Ammonites, the Moabites, and the people of Damascus. Phoenicia and Edom were not beyond his chastisement. Unlimited power over the forces of nature was his; he had brought on a drought three months before the harvest, smitten the fields with blight and mildew, settled a cloud of locusts on the land, slain the soldiers of the army of Israel with an Egyptian plague, and sent a shattering earthquake, resembling the shaking of Sodom and Gomorrah. His might had been exhibited in a worldwide arena. Even more sweeping is the assertion made in Amos 5:8: It is the Lord (Yahweh) who made the Pleiades and Orion, and it is he who turns darkness into morning and day into night.

Monotheism was thus no longer a matter primarily of loyalty and practice; it also became a far-ranging theological conviction, a faith that Yahweh is the creator and sovereign lord of the universe.

Amos says, however, that only Israel knows this, not other nations, for Yahweh says, "Only you have I known out of all the nations of the earth" (Amos 3:2).

Hosea

If Amos was the prophet of the righteousness of God, then a younger contemporary of his, Hosea, must be called the prophet of God's love. Unlike Amos, Hosea was a native of the north and accustomed to the social conditions there. Because he thought disloyalty to God was the central issue, his deepest concern was religious. The state of the text of his prophecies leaves us in some doubt about the exact circumstances of his personal life. Our uncertainty is increased by the distinct possibility that there was an earlier and a later Hosea. Chapters 1 through 3 and 4 through 14 may be by different hands. If so, the first part of our present account is concerned with events from an earlier date than the second part.

It seems probable, on the basis of the first three chapters, that Hosea married a woman who was unfaithful to him and left him. He could not acknowledge her children as his own; yet, after years of apparent infidelity on her part, he was able to take her back into his home, reclaimed and regenerated.

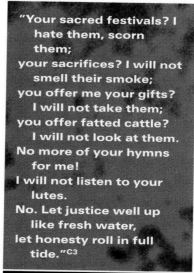

"Your sacred festivals? I hate them, scorn them;
your sacrifices? I will not smell their smoke;
you offer me your gifts? I will not take them;
you offer fatted cattle? I will not look at them.
No more of your hymns for me!
I will not listen to your lutes.
No. Let justice well up like fresh water,
let honesty roll in full tide."[C3]

—Amos 5:4–6

As Hosea contemplated his domestic trials, it would appear that he began to see a similarity between his inner history and the experience of Yahweh with Israel. Yahweh, too, suffered on account of the unfaithfulness of his people. Unfaithful they were in more than one way. Too blind to see that the political and social doom overhanging them was the inevitable result of abandoning the true God, they were seeking to forestall disaster by the political device of running after "foreign lovers," one party courting Damascus, another Egypt, a third climbing to the throne through alliance with Assyria. Religiously, they were wooing alien gods and futile native baals, their unholy religious paramours. Hosea put into Yahweh's mouth the following woeful words, ending on the note of inalienable love, anxious still to forgive:

> *"Bid her [Israel] clear her face of harlotry,*
> *and her breasts of adulterous charms;*
> *or I will strip her naked,*
> *bare as the day she was born;*
> *I will make her like a land forlorn. . . .*
> *On her children I will have no mercy,*
> *for they are born out of wedlock;*
> *their mother has played the harlot,*
> *she who conceived them has been shameless;*
> *she said, 'I will follow my lovers [the baals]*
> *who give me my bread and water,*
> *my wool, flax, oil, and wine.' . . .*
> *Little she knew it was I who had given her*
> *the grain and oil and wine. . . .*
>
> *"I will bring all her gaiety to an end,*
> *her festivals, new-moons, and sabbaths,*
> *to punish her for all the days*
> *when to the Baals she offered incense,*
> *decking herself with rings and jewels,*
> *running after her lovers,*
> *and forgetting me," says the Eternal.*
>
> *"Now then I will block up her path*
> *with a thorn-hedge,*
> *and bar the road against her,*
> *till she cannot find her way;*
> *she will pursue her lovers and miss them,*
> *seek them and never find them.*

> *Then at last she will say,*
> *'Let me go back to my first husband,*
> *I fared better with him than today.'*
>
> *"So I will allure her, . . .*
> *and speak to her heart; . . .*
> *then shall she answer me*
> *as in her youthful days,*
> *when she came up from Egypt's land. . . .*
>
> *"On that day," the Eternal declares, "she shall call me,*
> *'My husband,' no more 'My Baal';*
> *I will betroth her to me for ever,*
> *betroth her in a bond*
> *of goodness and of justice*
> *in kindness and in love."*[C5]

In the later sections of the prophecy (chapters 4–14), there is the same conviction: that Yahweh had been hurt by his people's disloyalty but would forgive them if they repented. However, if the nation remained corrupt and unrepentant, the national structures were doomed and would be swept away; kings, priests, and people would dwell in tents again (12:9) and become wanderers among the nations (9:17). Yet should this come to pass, there was still hope; for if disaster proved disciplinary rather than irreversible, and the people returned to their God in purity of heart and the old loyalty, he would reestablish the bonds that had once mutually held them.

It is doubtful whether Hosea received in his time the hearing that Amos did. He quotes his contemporaries as shouting angrily, "A prophet is a crazy fool, a man inspired is a man insane!"[C6] He discovered that within the very temple of God people were hostile to the prophet, God's watchman. Surely, if he lived to see the holocaust of the Assyrian conquest of the Northern Kingdom, he must have felt that the God of love had wooed Israel in vain, and that all he had predicted in that event had been fulfilled.

Isaiah

The Southern Kingdom, meanwhile, came in for its share of prophetic admonition. About 742 B.C.E., at the close of the reign of King Uzziah, a young man of good family appeared on the streets of Jerusalem in a prophetic role. His name was Isaiah. He had in youth an experience of the reality of Yahweh that had moved him deeply. He told of it in the following awestruck words:

> In the year that king Uzziah died, I saw the Lord seated on a high and lofty throne; his trailing robes spread over the temple-floor and seraphs hovered round him, each with six wings—two covering the face, two covering the body, and two to fly with. They kept calling to one another.
>
> *'Holy, holy, holy, is the Lord of hosts,*
> *his majesty splendour fills the whole earth!'*
>
> At the sound of the chant, the foundations of the threshold shook, and the temple began to fill with smoke. Then I said, 'Alas! I am undone! man of unclean lips that I am, living among a people of unclean lips! I am undone, for mine eyes have seen the King, the Lord of hosts!' But one of the seraphs flew towards me with a live coal in his hand, which he had lifted with tongs from the altar; he touched my mouth with it, saying,
>
> *'Now that this has touched your lips,*
> *your guilt is gone, your sin forgiven.'*
> *Then I heard the voice of the Lord saying,*
> *'Whom shall I send?*
> *Who will go for us?'*
> *I answered, 'Here am I; send me.'*[C7]

Security Linked to Covenant Faithfulness

Conscious of his divine commission, Isaiah remained active for nearly forty years as a prophet to the people at large and as a special advisor to the Judean kings. In a time of uncertainty, he stood unswervingly for trusting in the providence of God. He was the prophet of faith, of confidence in Yahweh beyond doubt or shaking, and he was forever warning the rulers of Jerusalem that the city's safety lay in ceasing to make leagues with the nations round about and relying upon the only trustworthy ally, Yahweh. "Your strength," he warned, "is quiet faith."[C8] In giving advice to Judah's kings, this was

his constant declaration. Thus, when the Northern Kingdom had been destroyed by the Assyrians (722 B.C.E.), and the Assyrians were camped before Jerusalem under their mighty general, Sennacherib, he sent panic-stricken King Hezekiah, who besought him to call upon Yahweh, assurances that the city would not be taken.[C9] His prophecy was wondrously fulfilled. The Assyrians suddenly raised the siege. (According to tradition, a plague struck them. But there is evidence that Sennacherib accepted a heavy ransom to withdraw his forces.)

But Isaiah was certain that the faithless and wicked would not survive to enjoy future security. They would perish by the sword or languish in miserable exile, far from the comfortable hills of home. As he looked about him, he saw many who were doomed to death or exile. In the manner of Amos, he saw nothing but woe in store for those who violated covenant justice: "soldier and warrior, governor and prophet, seer, sheikh, and official," for "the men who add house to house, who join one field to another, till there is room for none but them," for "those who get up early for a drinking bout, who sit far into the night, heated by their wine," or for "those who think themselves so wise, . . . who let off guilty men for a bribe, and deprive the innocent of his rights," "the unruly men," the rulers of the city, "hand in hand with thieves, every one fond of his bribe, keen upon fees, but careless of the orphan's rights, and of the widow's cause."[C10]

Impatience with Ritual

Like Amos, Isaiah records Yahweh's impatience with the elaborate ritual of the temple. Slaughtered rams, the fat from fatted beasts, the blood of bullocks and goats, offerings, the smoke of sacrifice, gatherings at the new moon and on the Sabbath, and fasts and festivals are "a weariness" to Yahweh. Though the worshipers stretch out their hands, he will never look at them, and though they offer many a prayer, he will not listen. Their hands are stained with blood! They are not really true to Yahweh!

It is not just blind fate that determines events. Yahweh is the moving force and contriver behind human history. He even considers Egypt "my people" and Assyria "my handiwork" (Isaiah 9:25). But he will punish and destroy the wicked everywhere, in Moab, in Edom, in Damascus, in Egypt, but no less in Judah. The wicked will destroy each other by Yahweh's contrivance. Assyria is doomed like all the rest, but meanwhile Yahweh has use for this exterminator of the nations, a use like that of a club swung in anger or a rod wielded in wrath. It will do its work well. Justice will be done even in the plundering and spoiling of the nations.

If Isaiah was as inflexible as Amos in the pronouncement of doom, he saw, however, like Hosea, that compassion and love are at the heart of Yahweh's divine plan. The purging of the nations is in the interest of spiritual betterment, a kindlier world.

After the day of doom, there will be a return of blessedness to the "remnant" who have lived through all the trouble and relied upon Yahweh for all good. Peace, prosperity, and health will be theirs. Upon them, Yahweh will have mercy; and he will abundantly pardon them.

Visions of a New Age

And here we come to the passages in Isaiah that have had great historic importance—the golden dreams of the new age that shall dawn after the terrible day of wrath and doom is past. Later generations lingered over them and relied on Isaiah's authority in indulging the eager hope of their fulfillment. Some scholars, it is true, and with good warrant, dispute the authenticity of these passages. In them Isaiah is seen, perhaps before the time was ripe for such prevision, painting a rosy picture of a warless world and of the benign rule of a great prince of peace, the Messiah, who should spring from the seed and lineage of David and bring in the new day. But these poems of hope and vision came out of the afflictions of his period in history, and so, for our interests in this study, it matters little whether they are from Isaiah's own hand or not. Isaiah was a grieving witness of the spoliation and dismemberment of

the Northern Kingdom, and he would quite naturally have dreamed these dreams and seen these visions, which forecast the gathering together from the four corners of the earth of the scattered, both of Judah and Israel too.

Of the prophecies attributed to Isaiah, consider the two notable passages that follow, both perhaps reworked or even written by later hands, although this is far from certain, the first dealing with the New Jerusalem, the second with the peaceful prince who is to sit on David's throne in the new age:

> *In after days it shall be*
> *that the Eternal's hill shall rise,*
> *towering over every hill,*
> *and higher than the heights.*
> *To it shall all the nations stream,*
> *and many a folk exclaim,*
> *"Come, let us go to the Eternal's hill,*
> *to the house of Jacob's God,*
> *that he may instruct us in his ways,*
> *to walk upon his paths."*
> *For instruction comes from Zion,*
> *and from Jerusalem the Eternal's word.*
> *He will decide the disputes of the nations,*
> *and settle many a people's case,*
> *till swords are beaten into ploughshares,*
> *spears into pruning hooks;*
> *no nation draws the sword against another,*
> *no longer shall men learn to fight.*
> *O household of Jacob, come,*
> *let us live by the light of the Eternal!*[C12]

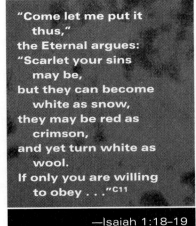

"Come let me put it thus," the Eternal argues: "Scarlet your sins may be, but they can become white as snow, they may be red as crimson, and yet turn white as wool. If only you are willing to obey . . ."[C11]

—Isaiah 1:18–19

> *From the stump of Jesse [the father of David] a shoot shall rise,*
> *and scion from his roots shall flourish;*
> *on him shall rest the spirit of the Eternal,*
> *and the spirit of wisdom and insight,*
> *the spirit of counsel and strength,*
> *the spirit that knows and reverences the Eternal. . . .*
> *Justice shall gird him up for action,*
> *he shall be belted with trustworthiness.*
> *The wolf shall couch then with the lamb,*
> *the leopard's lair shall be the kid's;*

the lion shall eat straw like any ox,
wolf and lion shall graze side by side,
herded by a little child;
the cow and the bear shall be friends,
and their young lie down together;
the infant shall play at the hole of an asp,
and the baby's feet at the nest of a viper.
None shall injure, none shall kill,
anywhere on my sacred hill;
for the land shall be as full of the knowledge of the
Eternal as the ocean-bed is full of water.
And the scion of Jesse who is to rally the peoples,
him shall the nations then consult,
and his seat shall be famous.[C13]

Micah

Inspired by Isaiah, a young man who came up from the country to Jerusalem, Micah by name, began to prophesy on the eve of the fall of the Northern Kingdom in 722 B.C.E. The prophecies attributed to him are remarkable for two utterances here quoted, one against the prophets who truckled to popular self-complacence about the supposed inviolability of Jerusalem, the other a notable definition of the essence of spiritual religion.

> *"And as for the prophets," the Eternal says,*
> *"who lead my folk astray,*
> *who cry 'All's well!' if they get food to eat,*
> *and open war on any who refuse them,*
> *it shall be night for you, devoid of vision,*
> *so dark you cannot divine;*
> *the sun shall set upon the prophets,*
> *daylight shall darken over them,*
> *till seers are shamed,*
> *and the diviners blush,*
> *in mourning, all of them,*
> *because no answer comes from God."*
> *. . . Listen to this, you. . . .*
> *priests pattering oracles for pay,*
> *prophets divining for money,*
> *. . . saying, "Surely the Eternal is among us;*
> *no evil can befall us!"*
> *Therefore on your account*
> *shall Zion be ploughed up like a field,*
> *Jerusalem shall become a heap of ruins,*
> *the temple-hill a mere wooded height.*[C14]

How shall I enter the Eternal's presence,
and bow before the God of Heaven?
Shall I come to him with sacrifices,
with yearling calves to offer?
Would the Eternal care for rams in thousands,
or for oil flowing in myriad streams?
Shall I offer my first-born son for my sin,
fruit of my body for guilt of my soul?
O man, he has told you what is good;
what does the Eternal ask from you
but to be just and kind
and live in quiet fellowship with your God?[C15]

The Deuteronomic Reform

After Micah, the prophets were silent for seventy years. Were they suppressed? It seems likely. For when the danger of an Assyrian siege of Jerusalem had passed and King Manasseh sat upon the throne, a serious relapse from ethical monotheism again set in. Two factors seem to have been in operation. One was a popular ebb-movement back to the Canaanitish form of Yahweh worship. The people were loath to give up the festive gaiety of the high places and altars. They feared the possible ill effects of relinquishing the magic arts, amulets, household spirits, and images on which they had depended for so long. Besides, the sternly ethical religion of the prophets appeared to them bare and cold compared to the festive practices that so pleased their senses and imaginations. Apostasy became widespread.

Assyrian Cults Officially Sponsored

The other factor in the relapse was an official sponsoring of Assyrian cults for reasons of state. Judah was, it must be remembered, a tribute-paying vassal of Assyria. In the very Temple itself, therefore, shrines were erected and offerings made to the gods and goddesses of Assyria. Something similar had happened before, but not to the same extent. In an earlier time, Solomon had sought to please his many wives by filling Jerusalem with shrines to foreign deities, but he had not erected them in the Temple area, and at best they had only a subrosa status. When King Ahaz, against the protests of the prophet Isaiah, tried to save

Judah by accepting vassalage to Assyria and paying tribute for the "protection" of the great king, the obsequious monarch set up an altar before the Temple that was a faithful copy of those used in the imperial Assyrian worship. The old Yahweh altar was put to one side; images of Assyrian sun-steeds were given a place in the Temple area, and an arbor for the worship of Tammuz (Adonis) was erected on the roof of a temple building. These profanations of Yahweh's holy shrine were suppressed in the puritanical reforms instituted under Isaiah's guidance by the next monarch, Hezekiah, but Assyrian pressure and popular religious laxity sufficed to restore them in the reign of King Manasseh, which followed. But Manasseh went far beyond the point reached by his grandfather, Ahaz. He built altars for the sun and star gods of Babylon and Nineveh in both the inner and outer courts of the Temple. He set up an asherah within the Temple area in honor of Ishtar, queen of heaven, to whom the people flocking there burned incense, poured libations, and offered cakes baked with her image on them. Not neglecting the nearer Semitic deities, Manasseh erected altars to various baals and sacrificed a son by giving him to the fires of the child-devouring Molech (or Moloch).

Between the state policy of fostering Assyrian forms of worship and the popular drift away from strict ethical conduct, the religion of Yahweh seemed about to suffer an entire eclipse.

But not so. Two things happened. Suddenly the prophets began to find their voices again—Zephaniah, Habakkuk, Nahum, and the greatest of all, Jeremiah. And as the Assyrian world empire began crumbling and falling, the grandson of Manasseh, King Josiah directed a great religious reform, commonly called the Deuteronomic Reform.

A Reform Document Discovered

King Josiah's reform came in this way. In 621 B.C.E., the king authorized the high priest to make a number of overdue repairs on the Temple, and the high priest subsequently reported a momentous "find." A previously unknown "book of the Law" had, he said, been discovered, laid away in a hiding place. This book, he declared, dated from the Mosaic era. (Now embodied in the Book of Deuteronomy (Chapters 12–26), this document is known to scholars as "D," or the Deutero-

nomic code. The identification of the "found" manuscript with the "D" code portion of the Book of Deuteronomy is based on the close correspondence between Josiah's reform as described in the Second Book of Kings and the covenant faithfulness called for in the code. It was undoubtedly a contemporary attempt to codify Hebrew ethical law; its "finding" may have been a stratagem intended to promote the public good.) When the king saw it and heard its provisions, he rent his garments and charged his councilors to find out from Yahweh if it was genuine, a true statement of divine law. The councilors consulted a prophetess called Huldah, who vouched for its authenticity. The king then summoned the people to a great assembly and led them in swearing a solemn covenant to keep with all earnestness and zeal the statutes written in the newly discovered code.

The reform thus determined upon began with a clean sweep of all of the religious practices condemned by the code. The Second Book of Kings gives, without being strictly chronological about it, a vivid account of this phase of the reform.

> Then the king commanded Hilkiah, the high priest, and the second priest and the keepers of the threshold to bring out of the temple of the Lord all the vessels that were made for the Baal and the Asherah and for all the host of the heavens; and he burned them outside Jerusalem in the limekilns by the Kidron, and carried their ashes to Bethel. He also removed the idolatrous priests . . . and those who offered sacrifices to the Baal, to the sun, the moon, and the constellations, and all the host of the heavens. . . . He tore down the houses of the devotees of the fertility cult which were in the house of the Lord, where the women wove tunics for the Asherah. . . . He tore down the high places of the Satyrs, which stood at the entrance of the gate of Joshua. . . . He also defiled Topheth, which is in the valley of the son of Hinnom, that no man might make his son or his daughter pass through the fire to Molech. He took away the horses which the kings of Judah had given to the sun, . . . and he burned the chariots of the sun with fire. Also the altars which were on the roof, and the altars which Manasseh had made in the two courts of the house of the Lord the king demolished and beat them down there, and cast the dust into the Brook Kidron. Moreover the high places that were east of

Jerusalem, which Solomon had built for Ashtart, the abomination of the Sidonians, and for Chemosh, the abomination of Moab, and for Milcom, the abomination of the Ammonites, the king defiled. He shattered the sacred pillars, and cut down the sacred poles, and filled their places with the bones of men.[A7]

The king did not stop with Jerusalem and its immediate environs. He ranged through the whole of Judah and as far as Bethel, demolishing and beating to dust the altars, pillars, and asherahs of the high places and sanctuaries.

Priestly Functions Centralized in Jerusalem

One very important feature of the reform followed upon this. The king fetched all of the priests from the sanctuaries of Yahweh, outside of Jerusalem, and centralized sacrifices, the priests' unique function, at Jerusalem. It was held that proper sacrifices could be offered only there.

Further phases of the reform were concerned with the ethical injunctions of the Deuteronomic code. A new social idealism spread throughout the land. The code called for greater humanitarianism toward slaves, more consideration for the needs of the poor. The old law of blood vengeance stood condemned in the light of the new law running, "Everyone is to be put to death for his own sin."[A8] Though savage and cruel elements still remained to mark the new code with reflections of a more primitive era, there was genuine ethical advance toward justice and righteousness.

But the reform that had begun with such thoroughness fell short of complete success, in large part due to its too-great severity in one respect—the centralizing of religion in Jerusalem. This had the effect of subtraction from the local community for the sake of addition to Jerusalem. The Jerusalem priesthood now had an absolute control over the Mosaic tradition and, moreover, a vested interest in it. The rural and village priesthoods were abolished, and the rural common people, expected now to go to Jerusalem "to find their chief joy," suffered a greatly diminished sense of the immediacy of the divine presence in their localities.

Yahweh, truly enough, had become ineffably holy and transcendent, and his stern will was clearly known from the pages of a sacred book, but he was a less intimate presence, not as near as before. Some of the common people, finding it hard to attain to so high and dedicated a faith, relapsed all too easily, but without abandoning Yahweh, into the more emotionally satisfying rites, outlawed now by the king's law and the Deuteronomic code as well as by the prophets.

Jeremiah (fl. 600 B.C.E.)

Jeremiah came from a priestly family which before the Deuteronomic reforms of Josiah ministered in the sanctuary at Anathoth, a small town four miles northeast of Jerusalem. Stirred by the disaster threatening his wayward nation, he felt called by Yahweh to prophecy.

> The word of the Lord came to me, saying
> "Before I formed you in the womb I knew you,
> And before you were born I set you apart,
> I appointed you a prophet to the nations."
> Then said I,
> "Ah, Lord God! I cannot speak;
> For I am only a youth."
> But the Lord said to me,
> "Do not say, 'I am only a youth';
> For to all to whom I send you shall you go,
> And all that I command you shall you speak . . ."
> Then the Lord stretched forth his hand, and touched
> my mouth. And the Lord said to me,
> "See! I put my words in your mouth."[A9]

Judah Caught Between Empires in Conflict

Jeremiah came at one of the most difficult and perplexing periods in Judah's entire history. He began his career when the Assyrian empire was in decline and a terrifying invasion of Scythian plunderers swept down through Syria and along the Palestinian coast toward Egypt. Judah was in a panic. Not long after the Scythian hordes withdrew into the north, a momentous change occurred in the east: Nineveh fell, and the Assyrian empire gave place to the Babylonian. Immediately there began a titanic contest between Egypt and

Babylon for supremacy in the east. Judah became the seat of international intrigue, Egypt hoping to win to its side the little hill country, with its almost impregnable fortress capital, and in good part succeeding. Yet during the tortuous contest, the good King Josiah, apparently siding with Babylonia, fell in battle against the very Egyptians who proposed to be his allies. Shortly afterward, Egypt met with a stunning defeat at the hands of the Babylonians at Carchemish. Judah, now bereft of its good king and its boastful ally from the Nile, came again under the control of an Oriental power. Heavy annual tribute was exacted of her by the Babylonians. Then Egypt resumed her intrigues, making fresh promises. In Jerusalem, king and people, hoping for relief from the paying of tribute, lent a ready ear.

But Jeremiah had the clear eye and good sense to see the folly of rebelling against the mighty Babylonian power. He aroused the fierce displeasure of his compatriots by denying that Yahweh would keep the city inviolable, should Judah rebel and the Babylonians attack. Rather the contrary; he declared on this and many other occasions that his ministry was to be mostly one of warning the nation—always in vain—of disasters that might be forestalled or averted with Yahweh's help. So difficult was his task that at times, in later days, his heart failed him, and he gave vent to very human outbursts at the thanklessness of it all.

> I have become a laughing-stock all day long,
> Everyone mocks me.
> As often as I speak, I must cry out,
> I must call, "Violence and spoil!"
> . . . If I say, "I will not think of it,
> Nor speak any more in his name,"
> It is in my heart like a burning fire,
> Shut up in my bones;
> I am worn out with holding it in . . .
> Cursed be the day on which I was born
> The day on which my mother bore me—
> Let it not be blessed!
> Cursed be the man who brought the good news to my
>   father,
> "A son is born to you"—
> Wishing him much joy!
> . . . Why came I out of the womb,
> To see trouble and sorrow,
> That my days might be spent in shame?[A10]

But although he became highly unpopular, Jeremiah never shrank from saying exactly what he felt the Lord meant him to say. When kings consulted him, he never broke the bad news gently. No threatening mob could make him speak softly. He was not an ingratiating person. Only one loyal friend stood by him through all the bitter days when he was reviled by kings, princes, common people, and fellow prophets. This was Baruch, his private secretary, the man who wrote down Jeremiah's prophecies at the prophet's dictation and afterward added valuable biographical notes to explain how the prophecies came to be uttered and what consequences then ensued.

Oracles Warning the Nation

Jeremiah appeared one day in the Temple to deliver a scathing arraignment of the apostate people, and shouted, "Thus says the Lord: 'I will make this house like [ruined] Shiloh, and will make this city a curse to all the nations of the earth.'" His life was immediately in danger, for we read,

> When Jeremiah had finished speaking all that the Lord had commanded him to speak to all the people, the priests and the prophets laid hold of him, saying, "You shall die! How dare you prophesy in the name of the Lord, saying, 'This house shall become like Shiloh, and this city shall become an uninhabited waste?'"
>
> Thereupon all the people crowded around Jeremiah in the house of the Lord.
>
> When the princes of Judah heard the news, they came up from the palace and took their seats at the entrance to the new gate of the house of the Lord. Then the priests and the prophets addressed the princes and all the people saying, "This man deserves to die; for he has prophesied against this city in the terms which you have heard."
>
> Then Jeremiah addressed the princes and all the people, saying, "The Lord sent me to prophesy against this house and this city all the words which you have heard. But now, if you amend your ways and your doings, and listen to the voice of the Lord your God, the Lord will repent of the evil which he has pronounced against you. As for myself, see! I am in your hands. Do to me as you think right and proper. Only be well assured of this, that, if you put me to death, you will be bringing innocent

blood upon yourselves, upon this city, and upon its people; for the Lord has truly sent me to you, to speak these words in your hearing."

This firm speech completely changed the situation. Jeremiah was saved.

Then the princes and all the people said to the priests and the prophets, "This man does not deserve to die; for he has spoken to us in the name of the Lord our God."[A11]

It required only that the elders of the land should remind the assembly how Micah (Micah 3:9–12) had prophesied in an earlier day that Jerusalem should become a ruin, and Jeremiah was released.

Opposition from Other Prophets

It will be noted that Jeremiah's fellow prophets united with the priests against him. Their constant opposition was a sore point. On one occasion he appeared in the streets with a wooden yoke upon his neck. This, he said, symbolized the yoke of the king of Babylon that would be laid upon the necks of the people. While he was walking through the Temple, a rival prophet named Hananiah stepped forward, bringing an opposite word from the Lord. He took the yoke from Jeremiah's neck and broke it, saying, "Thus says the Lord, 'So will I break the yoke of Nebuchadrezzar, king of Babylon, from the neck of all the nations within two years.'" Jeremiah retired to ponder this, and then came back to cry out that Hananiah, the false prophet, had made the people trust in a lie, and that the Lord would bind them with iron. He would put an unbreakable "yoke of iron on the neck of all the nations," that they might serve Nebuchadrezzar, the king of Babylon.[A12]

The other prophets in Jerusalem seemed to Jeremiah no better than Hananiah. He pronounced severe judgment on them.

Thus says the Lord of hosts:
"Listen not to the words of the prophets
who prophesy to you!
They fill you with vain hopes;
They speak a vision from their own minds,
Not from the mouth of the Lord. . . .

"Behold, I am against the prophets who deal in lying dreams," is the oracle of the Lord, "and tell them, and mislead my people by their lies and their bombast—when I neither sent them nor commissioned them."[A13]

Narrow Escapes

When Judah recklessly revolted against Babylon and the city was invested by the army of Nebuchadrezzar, Jeremiah exhausted the patience of the princes by openly telling the people that the city was doomed and that those who stayed in it would die by the sword, famine, and pestilence, but those who would go and surrender to the Babylonians would escape and have their lives given to them as a prize of war. The princes of Jerusalem naturally complained to the king that Jeremiah was disheartening the soldiers defending the city, and they urged that he be put out of the way. So Jeremiah was thrown into a dry cistern in the court of the royal guard, where he sank in the mud and was left to die. Had not an Ethiopian guard pricked the king's conscience with a description of Jeremiah's plight, he surely would have perished; as it happened, the king had the prophet secretly drawn up to terra firma. He was not set at liberty again until the city fell to the Babylonians.

This was not the first nor last time Jeremiah was in danger. Once he had been arrested and put in the stocks for twenty-four hours; at another time his fellow villagers at Anathoth had plotted to put him to death. He and Baruch had had to go into hiding during the reign of King Jehoiakim after that monarch became coldly enraged during a private palace reading of a scroll of Jeremiah's prophecies; the king cut up the scroll with his penknife piece by piece as it was being read to him and flung the pieces into the fire in the brazier before him, then ordered Jeremiah's arrest. The prophet went into hiding; the danger passed; but he was never to know peace thereafter. When Jerusalem was destroyed in 586 B.C.E., Nebuchadrezzar freed him as a friend and allowed him to remain in Judah along with the handful of citizens—the lower classes, really—who were not taken into exile. Jeremiah tried to reconcile those left behind with him to their lot, but Gedaliah, the governor appointed by Nebuchadrezzar, was assassinated, and the conspirators kidnapped Jeremiah and carried him to

Egypt, where he prophesied briefly before he came to his unknown, perhaps violent, end.

Doom Transcended by Hope

A reading of Jeremiah's oracles brings clearly before us a forthright, gloomy personality. The passages predicting doom burn with the prophet's own anguish. Yet Jeremiah was not an ultimate pessimist; he had grounds for hope. He predicted that after Yahweh had finished using Babylon as the means of accomplishing his just punishment of the nations, Babylon itself would be punished. Then the people of Judah, and those also of Israel, would "serve aliens no more" but would return to Judah to "serve the Lord their God, and David their king," whom Yahweh would raise up for them.

> *"For I am with you to save you,"*
> *is the oracle of the Lord;*
> *"And I will make a full end of all the nations*
> *among whom I scattered you;*
> *But of you will I not make a full end."*A14

Having corrected them "in just measure," Yahweh would make a "new covenant" with his people, Jeremiah said.

A Covenant with Individuals

At this point Jeremiah made a distinctive, if not original, contribution to the prophetic tradition. The new covenant that was to be made was to be between Yahweh and redeemed *individuals*. Former prophets had concentrated on the public, socially experienced relationship between Yahweh and the Hebrews—the basis of the old covenant. Jeremiah advanced the idea of a valid, subjective experience of relationship between Yahweh and the individual.

> "Behold, days are coming," is the oracle of the Lord, "when I will make a new covenant with the household of Israel and with the household of Judah, not like the covenant which I made with their fathers on the day that I took them by the hand to lead them out of the land of Egypt—that covenant of mine which they broke, so that I had to reject them—but this is the covenant which I

will make with the household of Israel. . . . I will put my law within them, and will write it on their hearts. . . . And they shall teach no more every one his neighbor, and every one his brother, saying, 'Know the Lord'; for all of them shall know me, from the least of them to the greatest of them."

Jeremiah accompanied this prediction with a succinct statement of individual responsibility:

> "In those days shall they say no more,
>
> *"The fathers have eaten sour grapes,*
> *And the children's teeth are set on edge';*
>
> but everyone shall die for his own guilt—everyone who eats the sour grapes shall have his own teeth set edge."A15

In other words, Jeremiah brought men face to face with God as individuals who were responsible directly to him for their conduct. They could no longer say that he dealt with men only through their group relationships; they were individually responsible.

This was a proposition of great importance, for its logical corollary was, if the human relationship to God is a direct and personal relationship, then the approach to God through temple sacrifice may not be all-important, and may even be no longer requisite to the highest spiritual living of the individual.

V. THE BABYLONIAN EXILE

As so often happens with fanatical Nationalist groups, the pro-Egyptian party in Jerusalem brought about the very disaster they most hoped to avert—the collapse of Hebrew national sovereignty. They persuaded the aging King Jehoiakim to withhold tribute from Nebuchadrezzar, king of Babylon, and to make a stand for national independence, relying on Egypt's military backing. When Nebuchadrezzar learned of this, he moved quickly, displaying in every decision an unyielding determination to crush Judean rebelliousness for good and all. In 597 B.C.E., he surrounded Jerusalem with his full forces. After a three-month siege during which Jehoiakim died, a new king, Jehoiachin, came to the throne and then surrendered the city in order to avoid its total destruction. Nebuchadrezzar looted the Temple and carried away captive to Babylon the king and ten thousand citizens, or, as the Second Book of Kings describes them, "all the nobles, and all the renowned warriors, and all the craftsmen, and all the smiths," as well as "all the strong men fit for war."[A16] At Babylon the king was thrown into prison and the people were settled as colonists on the river Chebar, a large canal running to the southeast out of Babylon. Those who were left behind in Judah were placed under the rule of the deported king's uncle, Zedekiah, the third son of Josiah. In 588, after nine years of wavering loyalty to Nebuchadrezzar, Zedekiah too rebelled.

The Destruction of Jerusalem

This time Jerusalem was not spared. In 586 B.C.E., after a siege lasting a year and a half, during which the Egyptians coming up to relieve the beleaguered city were decisively driven back by the besiegers, Jerusalem was taken. The Babylonians and their allies (the Edomites, Samaritans, Ammonites, and others) systematically looted, burned, and destroyed all of the buildings in the city, including the Temple, whose holy Ark was never again heard of, and they laboriously tore down the city walls. The city was so thoroughly laid in ruins that it was not completely rebuilt for over a century and a half. Before being carried away in chains to Babylon, King Zedekiah was forced to witness the execution of his sons and then had his own eyes put out. All of the inhabitants of Jerusalem, except Jeremiah and the poorest and lowliest citizens, were taken away. The towns around Jerusalem were drained of their upper classes. Meanwhile, many of those who could do so fled southward toward Egypt. The nation was disrupted. One part was in Babylonia; another portion reached Egypt and settled in scattered communities along the Nile and its delta; a third portion stayed on in the ruined homeland. So profound was the

change in national status that historians referring to the people who survived the fall of Jerusalem in 586 drop the name "Hebrew" and speak of them henceforward as "Judeans," or "Jews."

Initial Responses to Exile

Yet the Babylonian exile was not as disastrous to the Judean captives as the Assyrian deportation had been to the ten lost tribes. Nebuchadrezzar's hostility was of a political kind; it had been directed only against the continuance of Hebrew national sovereignty and not against the people as individuals. Once the Jews had been transported to the environs of Babylon, he allowed them comparative freedom. They could live together and follow their old ways of life and culture without disturbance. The region in which they were settled was part of a rich alluvial plain, intersected by irrigating canals, and therefore from an agricultural standpoint far superior to Palestine. Moreover, it lay between two of the greatest cities of the world—Babylon and Nippur—and hence provided economic advantages of an unusual kind, so that those who made themselves at home and developed their opportunities throve wonderfully.

At first, of course, it was hard to feel at home. Of this we have the clearest sort of evidence. The Old Testament contains no passage so full of mingled pathos and unhappy rage as the psalm that runs,

> *By the rivers of Babylon,*
> *There we sat down, and wept,*
> *When we remembered Zion.*
> *Upon the poplars, in the midst of her,*
> *We hung up our harps.*
> *For there our captors*
> *Demanded of us songs,*
> *And our tormentors, mirth:*
> *"Sing us some of the songs of Zion."*
>
> *How could we sing the songs of the Lord*
> *In a foreign land?*
> *If I forget you, O Jerusalem,*
> *May my right hand fail me!*
> *May my tongue cleave to my palate,*

> **"But this is the covenant which I will make with the household of Israel. . . . I will put my law within them and will write it on their hearts; and I will be their God, and they shall be my people."**
>
> —Jeremiah 31:33

If I do not remember you;
If I set not Jerusalem
Above my highest joy!

Remember, O Lord, against the Edomites,
The day of Jerusalem!
They who said, "Raze it, raze it,
To its very foundations!"
O daughter of Babylon, destructive one,
Blessed be he who requites to you
The treatment that you dealt out to us!
Blessed be he who seizes your little ones,
And dashes them to pieces upon a rock![A17]

But the mood of irreconcilability with their lot passed. Economically the situation became better than tolerable. Those who farmed the rich soil found themselves harvesting big crops. Stony Judah had never yielded such. Many Jews, freed from farming, entered government service as soldiers and officials. Others, turning their economic opportunities to advantage, became merchants and traders, following a direction that many of their ethnic brethren were even then pursuing in Egypt and Syria and were to pursue increasingly down the centuries. It would not be long before their great success would lead a Jewish writer (the author of Esther) to recognize the existence of anti-Semitism in Babylonia. He would make Haman say to King Xerxes in Susa: "There is a certain people scattered abroad and dispersed among the peoples throughout all the provinces of your kingdom, and their laws are different from every other people. . . . If it please the king, let it be prescribed that they be destroyed."[A18] The Book of Esther depicts Esther as a queen to Ahasueris (Xerxes), putting herself at risk to forestall the decree. The Jews had entered upon the long and troublous course of anti-Semitic persecution across the face of the earth.

The Origin of the Synagogue

The religion of the Torah and the prophets now had to pass a crucial test. Would the exiled people consider that their God had failed them and that the deities of foreign peoples were greater? Or would the viewpoint of the major prophets, that Yahweh was with his people everywhere and directed the destinies of other peoples besides the chosen race, prevail? Apparently, some gave up Yahweh to follow the gods that had prospered Babylon. An older apostasy recurred in Egypt. Among the refugees who kidnapped Jeremiah and dragged him off to Egypt were men and women who thus defied the old prophet.

> We will not listen to you, but will assuredly . . . [offer] sacrifices to the queen of the heavens [Asherah/Ishtar], and . . . [pour] libations to her, as we did, both we and our fathers, our kings and our princes, in the cities of Judah and in the streets of Jerusalem. For then we had plenty to eat, and were well, and met with no trouble; but since we gave up offering sacrifices to the queen of the heavens . . . we have been destitute of all things, and have been consumed by sword and famine.[A19]

These folk were lost to Jewish religion. But those with whom the future of Judaism lay were not shaken in their faith: it widened and deepened. Yahweh was in Egypt and Babylonia, with them; of this they were assured.

To the faithful in Babylonia there was only one place in the world where sacrifices could be offered to Yahweh, and that was on the altar in the Temple at Jerusalem. This means of approach to the High God was now denied to them. But they could draw near to him in other ways. They could, for example, gather together on the Sabbath day in their homes and read to each other the scrolls of the Torah and the writings of the prophets. Besides these, they could read aloud the early histories of their people, in various recensions, not yet finally combined into a canonical text. After reading from these texts, someone might lead in prayer. Assembling on every Sabbath (which may have already begun in Judah after the Deuteronomic reform as a way of promoting worship without animal sacrifice) became a regular practice among the exiles, and from such meetings came the synagogue, standardized by the Pharisees in later days. (The sermon so familiar to Christian churchgoers had its origin in the exposition and interpretation of selected portions of the sacred texts during the Sabbath meetings of the Jews in Babylonia.)

Along with the establishment of this form of worship came a marked increase in literary activity.

Esther and Ahasueris

After Ahasueris (that is, Xerxes I, 486–485 B.C.E.) deposed his queen Vashti for refusing to show off her beauty at a banquet, the lovely Jewish maiden Esther (or Hadassah by her Jewish name) easily triumphed over all other candidates in a beauty contest and captured the king's affections. She sits on the throne at the extreme right. Her rank as queen enabled her to avert a plot to liquidate her Jewish people. *(Courtesy of the Yale University Art Gallery, Dura-Europos Collection.)*

Copies of the older writings were prepared for use on the Sabbath day and during the festivals of the Jewish year, and those who feared that the new generation growing up in Babylon might forget the traditions that were still unrecorded made haste to write these traditions down and to revise and enlarge the older histories and codes by addition and expansion. Writings also appeared reflecting contemporary religious insights. Many psalms were composed. And two great prophets appeared to pour out their inspired thoughts in speech and writing.

Ezekiel

Little is known positively about the life of Ezekiel. It is possible that some of the book credited to him was written in his name at a later time. He apparently was a leader of what has been called the Deuteronomic circle among the exiles—those who leaned heavily on the Deuteronomic code and interpreted the whole of Hebrew history in its light, going so far as to rewrite much of Judges, and the books of Samuel and Kings in accordance with Deuteronomic value judgments. Ezekiel came from a priestly family of Jerusalem, was

carried captive to Babylonia in 597 B.C.E., and lived in the Jewish community by the river Chebar. For twenty-two years or more he was active as a prophet and self-styled "watchman to the household of Israel,"[A20] exercising pastoral oversight and care over his fellow exiles and dreaming always of the restoration and regeneration of his people.

In his earlier visions and allegories, written down in fervid and florid phrase, Ezekiel firmly prophesied the utter destruction of Jerusalem—a prophecy that was fulfilled in 586 B.C.E. Thereafter, a major concern emerged: When the exile ended, as it soon would, and the people returned to the homeland, what was to be the constitution under which they were to live, and especially, how were the services in the restored Temple to be conducted? Here Ezekiel showed himself to be what he has been called, "a priest in the prophet's mantle."[E2] Whereas Jeremiah realized in his day that the Temple and its divine services would soon come to an end, but that he could do without them, Ezekiel knew that "it was only a question of time before the temple and its divine services would be restored, and he could not do without them."[E3] So he concentrated on envisioning their restoration and did it in detail and with great enthusiasm. His descriptions of the temple-to-be and its ceremonies and his statement of the philosophy of worship that inspired him, while never accepted as a program that was to be exactly carried out, had a great influence on the attitudes and spirit of later Judaism.

The Holiness and Remoteness of Yahweh

Ezekiel's philosophy of worship combined the new emphasis on individual responsibility—new since Jeremiah and the issuance of the Deuteronomic code—with an exalted conception of Yahweh as a being sublimely transcendent and holy. The sinner needing pardon would not find Yahweh melting with love and foregiveness at the first sign of remorse. The holiness of Yahweh required the sacrificial approach of chastened individuals gathering in the Temple in a state of physical and ritual purity, under the guidance of expert priests. In his infinite sanctity, Yahweh had now withdrawn so far from the world of ordinary people that it was only through intermediaries, human and divine (priests and angels), that he could be reached.

Perhaps this emphasis on the remoteness and absoluteness of the Lord God was an effect of the expanding view of his movements in history that the exiles had. Did not the Lord God rule the nations with a rod of iron? Was he not using individual persons and single nations as a means to inscrutable but holy and righteous ends? Was he not bent on making his name known to all humankind? Questions such as these oppressed the minds of Ezekiel and his contemporaries and made them aware that God had other objects in view than just the showing of loving kindness and tender mercy to a chosen few. Ezekiel expressed their awareness in one saying of his.

> Thus says the Lord God: "It is not for your sake that I am about to act, O household of Israel, but for my holy name which you have caused to be profaned among the nations to which you came. . . . and when I restore my holiness in their sight, through my dealings with you, the nations shall know that I am the Lord."[A21]

Ezekiel thus alerted Israel to the fact that Yahweh would restore them to their homeland, whether or not they repented, but not for their sake, rather for his own, to sanctify his name in the eyes of the onlooking nations. The central facts of history were that God's purposes are just and holy, and that he acts out of strength—"with a strong hand and an outstretched arm"—for the sake of establishing his glory throughout the world.

Nevertheless, the Temple alone could offer the conditions of a proper approach to such a God—an approach of purified persons, in the beauty of holiness, seeking to add to the glory of God by fulfilling his will.

Deutero-Isaiah

To a great unknown prophet of the exile scholars have given a cumbrous name, Deutero-Isaiah, meaning Second Isaiah. His prophecies are preserved in the latter part of the Book of Isaiah, approximately from the fortieth chapter on. Nothing about his life or identity is known, but fortunately his mind and spirit do not thus elude us. In ethical and religious insight, his prophecies bring us to the culminating point of the Hebrew Scriptures.

The central problem with which Deutero-Isaiah was concerned loomed large in the minds of the exiled Jews. It was the problem of the evil that had befallen them. Why had Yahweh brought so much suffering upon them? The old answer that it was because of their sins was not wholly satisfactory, for it was evident that the people of Babylonia, who now prospered, were as bad as the Jews had ever been and even worse. Deutero-Isaiah did not reject the conventional explanation; he saw truth in it. But he did not think the sufferings of the Jews could be entirely explained on that basis. He set his people's trials against a world background. They were, he declared, a part of Yahweh's plan of eventual world redemption.

The conception here is magnificent in scope. The Lord becomes without any qualification the only God: "There is no other." His sphere of action is the whole world. Whatever he does must be seen against a cosmic background.

Have you not known? have you not heard?
The Lord is a God everlasting,
The Creator of the ends of the earth.[A22]

He is the first, and the last: "Before me was no God formed, and after me there shall be none."[A23] He alone created the heavens and the earth, and he gives breath to the peoples. He controls all history, forms the light and creates darkness, makes peace, and creates evil. This holy Lord of Hosts, who says from his seat of world power, "As the heavens are higher than the earth, so are my ways higher than your ways and my thoughts than your thoughts,"[A24] nevertheless dwells as an immanent savior and a redeemer in the hearts of the contrite and humble in spirit.

For thus says the high and exalted One,
Who dwells enthroned for ever, and whose name is
*   Holy:*
"I dwell enthroned on high, as the Holy One,
But with him also that is contrite and humble in
*   Spirit."*[A25]

Furthermore, God's redemptive purpose is not limited to one area or one people. It is universal; he means to save all humankind, Gentiles as well as Jews.

Israel as Servant Messenger

At this point, Deutero-Isaiah brought forward his most original conception, the finest fruit of his experience of living among the Gentiles. To bring the saving knowledge of himself and his holy will to all people, God needs a messenger, a servant. Israel is that servant and may say,

Listen, you coast lands, to me;
Hearken, you peoples afar!
The Lord called me from birth,
From my mother's womb he gave me my name. . . .
He said to me, "You are my servant,
Israel, through whom I will show forth my glory."[A26]

"I the Eternal have called you of set purpose,
And have taken you by the hand,

I have formed you for the rescuing of my people,
For a light to the nations."[C16]

The Jews were thus a chosen people, chosen not to be the recipients of unearned favors but to serve as bearers of light. It was not that they were to be active missionaries, it would seem, but that in their history the nations would see the presence of the Lord.

But, alas, they had been blind and deaf to their world mission and had had to be refined and purified "in the furnace of suffering." The Lord had to give up the chosen people to spoilers and plunderers because they had sinned and would not walk in his ways, nor listen to his instructions. "So he poured upon them the heat of his anger, and the fierceness of war."[A27] This punishment had to be. It was forced upon God by the chosen people's sins. But the prophet brought comforting word that the Lord God now declared that Jerusalem's guilt was paid in full, and her people would therefore not have to suffer any more afflictions; their suffering was over.

Redemption through Suffering

The suffering had not been in vain. It had purified the nation, and it had astonished and affected the onlooking Gentiles deeply. This conception is wrought out in one of the greatest religious odes ever written. The nations of the earth are heard saying of the Suffering Servant,

He was despised, and rejected of men;
A man of sorrow, and acquainted with grief:
And as one from whom men hide their face he was
*   despised,*
And we esteemed him not,

Surely he hath borne our griefs,
And carried our sorrows:
Yet we did esteem him stricken,
Smitten of God, and afflicted.

But he was wounded for our transgressions,
He was bruised for our iniquities:
The chastisement of our peace was upon him;
And with his stripes we are healed.

All we like sheep have gone astray;
We have turned every one to his own way:
And the Lord hath laid on him
The iniquity of us all.[F]

Deeply moved, the Gentile kings and their people understood at last that the sufferings of God's servant, Israel, were those of the innocent for the guilty. Before long, they would come with untold wealth from every direction to rebuild Jerusalem's walls and stand in the blazing light of the glory of God on Mt. Zion.

Restoration

Thus Deutero-Isaiah justified the ways of God to the Jews. But he not only looked into the past, he saw into the future. The next phase of God's redemptive plan, he declared, was a glorious restoration of the Jews to Jerusalem, where the work of redemption could proceed into all the world as from a center, amid the joy of all believers. This was to be effected through Cyrus, the Persian warlord, who by God's direction would tread down rulers as a potter tramples clay, overthrow Babylon, and release the Jews. (We shall see that Cyrus fulfilled these expectations.) Then, after their return to the homeland, the Jews would minister to the nations in the Lord's name. All the world would flock to Jerusalem to worship God, saying,

With you alone is God, and there is no other,
no God besides;
Truly with you God hides himself,
the God of Israel is a savior.[A28]

But not only would the world come to Jerusalem; Israel would find acclaim out in the world.

Thus says the Lord God:
"Behold! I will lift up my hands to the nations
And they shall bring your sons in their bosoms,
And your daughters shall be carried on their shoulders.
And kings shall be your foster fathers,
And their queens your nursing-mothers."[A29]

The God who saved Israel would reach out to all humankind through them.

Through the appeal of his high moral idealism, Deutero-Isaiah was to have a great influence on the best minds of later Judaism, and he was also to influence early Christianity. Some understood him; others did not. His prophecies were searched again and again by those who waited expectantly for the coming of a messiah. His descriptions of the suffering servant were so concrete and individualized that later generations readily concluded that he was speaking in them not of the exiles but of a messiah, and so they looked for a person who should some day redeem the world through his suffering. The early Christians found in Jesus of Nazareth one who, in their eyes, fit these descriptions perfectly.

GLOSSARY

Asherah a Canaanite goddess of fertility, or a sacred pillar dedicated to her

Ashtoreth (Gk. *Astarte*, Akkad. *Ishtar*), preeminent fertility goddess, especially associated with Sidon in the Bible; in plural, often a generic term for fertility goddesses, counterpart of the *baalim*, fertility gods

baal "lord" or "master," a nature deity common to the Western Semitic world; sometimes the title of a local deity: *Baal-hazor* or (fem.) *Baalat-beer*

Canaanites inhabitants of the land promised to the patriarchs (boundaries uncertain—in the Bible, usually west of the Jordan); not a homogeneous population, but mostly Semitic

Deutero-Isaiah "Second Isaiah," a name applied to Chapters 40–66 of the Book of Isaiah on the assumption that they represent a separate literary unit addressed to exiles in Babylonia

Deuteronomic Reform a cleansing of ritual and moral life under King Josiah in 621 B.C.E., based on a "second law" text brought to light during repair of the Temple

el common term for a superhuman being or a deity in Semitic languages

Elohim a name for God in Hebrew Scripture; although a plural form, it is taken to refer to the "One who is All" as distinguished from *elelim*, "nongods" or idols

El-Shaddai "deity of the mountains," a name for God, especially as the God of the covenant with Abraham

nabi one called to speak for God, a prophet

Shema Literally "Hear!"—the name given to the key commandment in all of Jewish law and devotional life "Hear, O Israel, the Lord our God is one Lord"—Deuteronomy 6:4

synagogue an assembly of Jews organized for worship and study (or the building in which they assemble)

Tammuz (Adonis) a Mesopotamian god of vegetation and fertility; cultic veneration of him by Hebrew women is mentioned in the Book of Ezekiel

Torah in narrow reference, the written law in the Pentateuch; broadly, God's teachings, all of scripture and tradition, or even Jewish theology as a whole

Yahweh the name of God, a vocalization of the sacred tetragram *YHWH* (*JHVH*); in ritual use, the vocalization *Adonai* is used where the tetragram appears

The Religious Development of Judaism

CHAPTER 14

In 538 B.C.E., Cyrus the Great took Babylon and made it the capital of a new empire, which was ultimately to stretch from the Persian Gulf to the Black Sea and from the Indus River to the Greek cities on the Ionian coast. When he looked about him, he found grouped together in the heart of Babylonia an unassimilated captive people, with ways different from the ways of other peoples, and upon inquiring about them, he heard their plaints. To win their friendship and at the same time have them go off to the border near Egypt to set up a buffer state, he gave them permission to return to Jerusalem. The return that was so longed for by the first generation of exiles was now possible.

I. THE RISE OF JUDAISM IN THE RESTORATION PERIOD

The Return of Judah and Jerusalem

An expedition of returning Jews was organized at once. According to later Jewish historians, Cyrus issued a decree giving them a privileged status; he not only restored to them the Temple vessels carried away by Nebuchadnezzar in 586 B.C.E., but even made funds available for the expedition and its goal, the rebuilding of the Temple. Apparently, the leaders of the return were two: Zerubbabel, a grandson of King Jehoiachin and hence as a lineal descendant of King David a person with messianic possibilities, and Joshua, a priest of the highly revered Zadokite branch of the Levite tribe. Though it was evident from the first that many Jews were not going to return, for Babylonia was their home now, thousands did. The latter were described by Ezra a century later as those "whose spirit God had aroused to go up to build the house of the Lord which is in Jerusalem."A30

Upon arrival in Jerusalem, the first act of the returning exiles was to erect an altar on the

ADHERENTS IN 1997: 14 million

SACRED LITERATURE: Torah, Mishnah, Gemara, Talmud

ETHNO-LINGUISTIC SUBDIVISIONS:

    Occidental Jews: Ashkenazi (North European, Yiddish)
    Sephardi (Early immigrants to Spain, later migrating to the Levant, England, and the Americas)
    Oriental Jews
    Black Jews: Falashas (Ethiopia) and Bene-Israel (India)

RELIGIOUS DENOMINATIONS IN THE WEST: Orthodox, Conservative, Reform

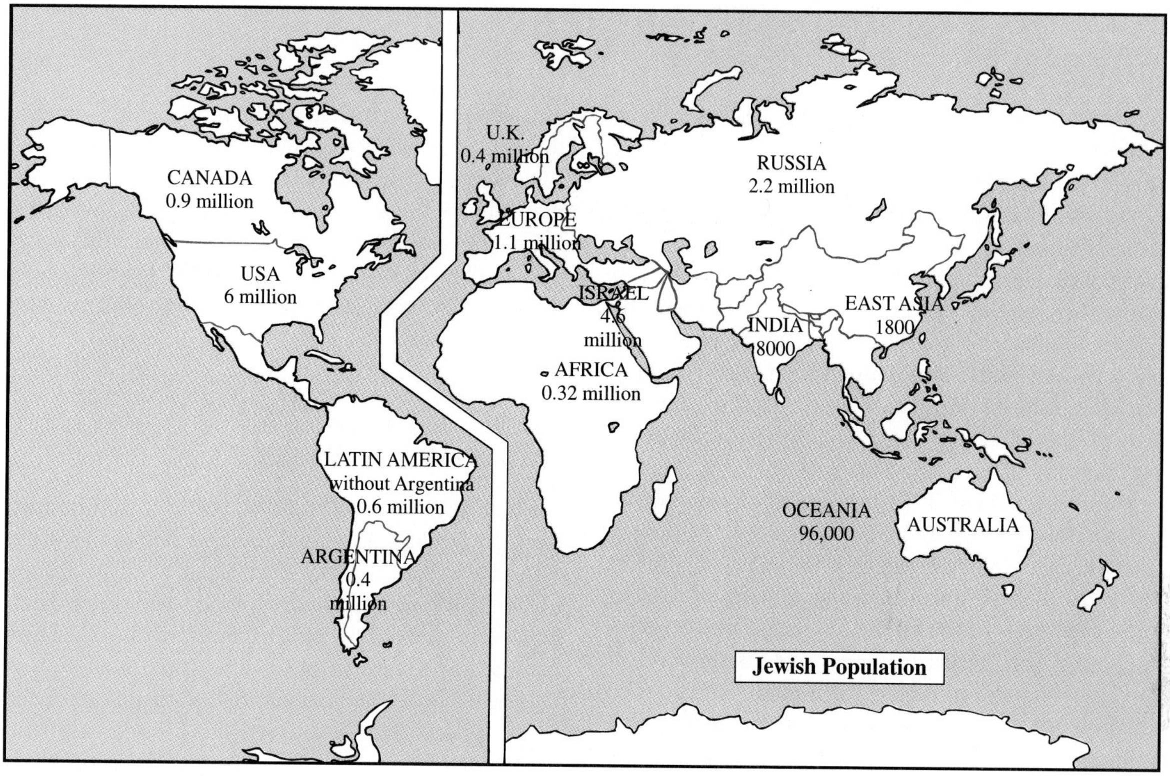
U.K.
0.4 million
CANADA
0.9 million
RUSSIA
2.2 million
EUROPE
1.1 million
USA
6 million
ISRAEL
4.6
million
EAST ASIA
1800
INDIA
8000
AFRICA
0.32 million
LATIN AMERICA
without Argentina
0.6 million
OCEANIA
96,000
AUSTRALIA
ARGENTINA
0.4
million
Jewish Population

site of the ruined Temple and to begin regular morning and evening sacrifices. The rebuilt altar was made the center of a communal life organized on lines like those suggested by the prophet Ezekiel. The Temple area was gradually cleared of debris, and amid shouts of joy and the weeping of the older folks, the foundation stone was laid for the reconstruction of the Temple.

Obstacles to Restoration

But the community soon proved unable to proceed with the task. Most of the people chose to live in the surrounding fields and villages, not in Jerusalem itself, where the heaps of burnt-over ruins discouraged the making of homes. But conditions outside of Jerusalem were scarcely better. Virtually no economic opportunities awaited the newcomers. Moreover, the "peoples of the land," that is, the nonexiles, had taken possession of the properties of the exiled upper classes and were undoubtedly annoyed to see so many returning claimants to old homesteads, for they themselves could claim sixty or seventy years of squatter's rights. But there were further factors of contention. The returning exiles had for decades idealized Jerusalem and the Law, and they looked with disdain on the nonexiles, because they had lapsed from the Deuteronomic standard and had, moreover, intermarried with Edomites, Ammonites, and Samaritans. So, on their part, the nonexiles, disgruntled at being treated as religious and social inferiors, withheld cooperation from the rebuilding of the Temple and other reconstruction projects. No wonder, then, that a stubborn depression, both spiritual and economic, overwhelmed the community, and for fifteen years the Temple lay untouched.

Further Impetus: Haggai and Zechariah

Then, at the urging of the prophets Haggai and Zechariah, the rebuilding was resumed. Haggai had indignantly scolded, how could the people expect prosperity as long as they left the Lord's house in ruins? Both prophets encouraged the community to resume the work quickly because of the great hope they held out: there would be a shaking up of the world powers and Judah would again become an independent kingdom, with Zerubbabel, the descendant of David, becoming their crowned head as Yahweh's Messianic "Chosen One." This hope animating them, the Jews made haste to complete the Temple. It was not like Solomon's, but it was strongly built and in the correct dimensions. Then they settled back to wait for signs of the Lord's favor. And no change in the situation came.

A century passed. The prophetic hopes concerning the restoration were plainly unrealized. Were they unrealizable? Some apparently thought so, for on every hand there were multiplying signs of ebbing faith. The writer of the Book of Malachi, who prophesied at this time, accused the people of slackening zeal, cynicism, and lack of respect for Yahweh. He said they did not pay their tithes properly, brought defective animals to the sacrifices, and were not reverent during the Temple ceremonies. How could they hope for the Lord's blessing?

Nehemiah and Ezra

Two figures, Nehemiah and Ezra, were prominent in reviving and completing the restoration of Jerusalem and its spiritual life. The chronology of their activities is uncertain. If we assume that they were active at about the same time, and that Nehemiah's work began first, the story would run like this: As a young man, Nehemiah was a cupbearer to King Artaxerxes (I or II?). On a day when he had received fresh reports of the woeful condition of Jerusalem and its inhabitants, he came before the king of Susa with a sad countenance. The king inquired about the reason for his melancholy and, learning the cause, generously sent Nehemiah on a special mission, with the powers of a governor, to Jerusalem to oversee the rebuilding of the city's walls and to reorganize the community. Nehemiah set out for Jerusalem, accompanied by army officers and horsemen and provided with enabling letters to the authorities, before or about the same time Ezra the Scribe and some seventeen hundred Babylonian Jews, many of them handpicked for the work of

reform, left for Jerusalem to push the spiritual renewal that was to parallel Nehemiah's rebuilding of the walls. The story of Nehemiah's successful leadership is dramatically told in the autobiography bearing his name. It was due entirely to his executive genius and energy that the breaches in the walls and the burnt gates of the city were repaired at last, after over 150 years of lying in ruin.

The Establishment of a Priestly State

Seeking the spiritual renewal of the community, Ezra the Scribe summoned the Jews before the Water Gate. Here the assembly heard read to them a book of the Law (presumably the holiness code from Leviticus xvii–xxvi) and bound themselves by a solemn covenant and oath to observe its provisions. A new theocratic state was inaugurated, with power vested in the priests. It reestablished the Mosaic covenant, but it might be called a new one at the same time. What occupied the center of attention—then and for the next 400 years—becomes clear in the following quotation from the pledge the assembly adopted under oath:

> "We make and sign a binding covenant . . . and take oath, under penalty of a curse, to walk in the law of God which was given by Moses, the servant of God, and to be careful to observe all the commands of the LORD our Lord, and his ordinances and his statutes; and that we will not give our daughters to the peoples of the land or take their daughters as wives for our sons; and that, if the peoples of the land bring wares or any grain on the Sabbath day to sell, we will not buy from them on the Sabbath or on a holy day; and that in the seventh year we will leave the land fallow and refrain from the exaction of any debt.
>
> "We also lay upon ourselves the charge to give the third part of a shekel yearly for the service of the house of our God, for the bread that is arranged in layers, and for the regular burnt-offering, for the sabbaths, the new moons, the fixed festivals, and the holy things, and for the sin-offerings to make atonement for Israel, and for all the work of the house of our God. Moreover,

we will cast lots, the priests, the Levites, and the people, concerning the wood-offering, to bring it into the house of our God, . . . to burn upon the altar of the LORD our God; . . . and to bring the first produce of our ground and the first of all fruit of every kind of tree year by year to the house of the LORD; also the firstborn of our sons and of our cattle, as it is written in the law, and the firstlings of our herds and our flocks, . . . and our first batch of baking, our contributions, the fruit of every kind of tree, the wine, and the oil, to the priests in the chambers of the house of our God; and the tithes of our ground to the Levites, since they, the Levites, take the tithes in all the cities dependent on our agriculture. Now the priest, the son of Aaron, shall be with the Levites, when the Levites tithe, and the Levites shall bring up the tithe of the tithes to the house of our God, to the chambers into the treasure house."[A31]

In thus laying primary stress on firstfruits, tithing, sacrifices, and fixed festivals, the Jews of Ezra's time established upon the foundation of the old pre-exilic faith—called, conveniently, the Religion of Israel—a religiously and morally demanding way of life. Its central concern was faithful adherence to the standards of the Mosaic Torah. It seems in that difficult time that this could best be brought about by obedience to the scriptural *mitzvoth* (precepts of the written Torah), the strict carrying out of the requirements of the newly sworn covenant before the Water Gate, and avoidance of all impurity before God. And when, after a struggle in which Ezra and Nehemiah had to exert utmost pressure, foreign wives were divorced and sent back to their fathers' homes with their children, the Jews adopted for that time the goal of becoming an ethnically as well as a religiously restricted group.

Resistance to the Priestly Code

Much future history, however, is anticipated in a revealing passage from Nehemiah, written of his second governorship, when presumably Ezra was dead and he himself had been away in Susa. There was a wide gulf between the rules of life for Jews as envisioned in a priestly code and the realities of everyday behavior.

In these days I saw in Judah men treading wine presses on the Sabbath and bringing heaps of grain loaded on asses, also wine, grapes, figs, and all kinds of burdens which they brought into Jerusalem on the Sabbath day; and I protested on the day when they sold provisions. Tyrians also dwelt therein, who brought in fish and all kinds of wares, and sold them on the Sabbath to the Judeans and in Jerusalem. Then I contended with the nobles of Judah and said to them, "What evil thing is this that you are doing, and thereby profaning the Sabbath day? Did not your fathers do this and did not our God bring all this misfortune upon us and upon this city? Yet you are bringing more wrath upon Israel by profaning the Sabbath."

Accordingly, when the gates of Jerusalem began to be in darkness, before the Sabbath, I commanded that the gates be shut; and I gave orders that they should not be opened until after the Sabbath. Also I put some of my servants in charge of the gates, that none should bring in a burden on the Sabbath day. Then the traders and sellers of all kinds of wares lodged outside Jerusalem once or twice. So I warned them and said to them, "Why do you lodge in front of the wall? If you repeat it, I shall arrest you."

From that time on they came no more on the Sabbath.[A32]

Nehemiah found to his horror that the portion of the Levites had not been given to them, so that the Levites and the singers at the services in the Temple were obliged to cultivate their own fields for a living. So he had to bring pressure upon the Judeans to pay their tithes. Also he found that some Jews had married foreign women, and that their children spoke foreign languages and "none of them could speak in the Jews' language." Here he felt he had to take direct action, reporting, "I contended with them and cursed them and beat some of them and pulled out their hair and made them swear by God,"[A33] after which they sent their foreign wives off. He even exiled a prominent priest married to a foreign woman.

These details have been given to show the situation. The common people continued to err, and yet the way of life established for them in law and in authority was laid inescapably upon their consciences and dominated all thought. As time went on, it would claim them more and more. In considering the postexilic period down to the end of the fourth century B.C.E., we cannot fail to see that however great their laxity at times, the people gave their increasing loyalty to the regular round of religious duties prescribed for them. The weekly Sabbath day observances drew them to the Temple at Jerusalem or to the gathering places in the outlying towns and villages that later acquired the Greek name for such places, "synagogues." The annual festivals and fasts became a matter of ingrained custom. These were the week-long Passover, including the Feast of Unleavened Bread, in the first month of the year (March or April); the Feast of Weeks (or First-fruits) occurring in the late spring; and the Feast of Trumpets (later called "Rosh Hashanah," or New Year), followed ten days later by the fast of the Day of Atonement, or Yom Kippur, and five days after by the Feast of Booths, or Tabernacles, all in the seventh month (September or October). The purely ethical religion of the prophets could not by itself firmly hold the common people, but these observances did.

Theocratic Leadership

Further, as the years passed, the self-preservative exclusiveness of the Jews threw them more and more upon their own religious authorities, both human and literary. Their supreme ecclesiastical personage was the high priest, who lived in the Temple at Jerusalem. He was a descendant of Zadok, a royally appointed priest of King David's time, said to be descended from Aaron, the brother of Moses. He was both the religious and civic ruler of Jerusalem. Under him were the ordained priests, who ministered in the Temple during religious ceremonies, and the Levites, who had the status of Temple servitors and were in charge of the musical services and Temple property. Authority also was vested in the learned profession of scribes, from which the rabbis sprang. The scribes had once been a more or less secular order, but they were now a religious class (the *Sopherim*) devoted to copying and interpreting the Torah and other sacred writings. Those of their number who developed a special talent for preaching came to be known as rabbis or "teachers." The rabbis performed a double service for the

common people, which gave them increasing importance as time went on.

In the first place, they met the growing need for a professional exposition of the sacred books, all the more necessary because Hebrew was being superseded as a spoken language by Aramaic, the vernacular that prevailed throughout Syria and Palestine, so that the common people could no longer fully understand their own Hebrew writings without the aid of an interpreter. Eventually a translation of important texts into Aramaic was finally made and called the "Targum." An earlier translation into Greek, begun in the third century B.C.E. in Alexandria, is known as the "Septuagint."

In the second place, the rabbis helped decentralize religious worship and make genuine group religious experience possible again in the villages—something that King Josiah's reformation in 621 B.C.E. had made difficult.

Compilation of Scripture

The priests and the scribes were not idle in providing authoritative religious literature for the people. Though the days of oral prophecy had virtually ended, testifying through the written word to the power of the holy and transcendent God of Israel in nature and history had become more and more common. In Babylonia and Jerusalem, the priests and scribes were diligently engaged in literary labors. They circulated copies of the writings of the more recent prophets—that is, Malachi, Obadiah, Ezekiel, Haggai, Zechariah, and Second Isaiah—and reedited the writing of the older prophets. This collection, reflecting the point of view of priests, is designated as "P." The five books of the Mosaic Torah were finally being completed: "J," "E," and "D" were dovetailed into one complete work, then recombined with "P," or the priestly code. This last document, newly written, furnished the strictly monotheistic first chapter of Genesis and many legal provisions interspersed through the five books, including "H," the holiness code used by Ezra and Nehemiah in their reforms. Joshua, Judges, I & II Samuel, and I & II Kings were further revised and expanded by the addition of new material. A group of priests, with a Deuteronomic slant, worked on I & II

ISRAEL'S TRADITIONS*

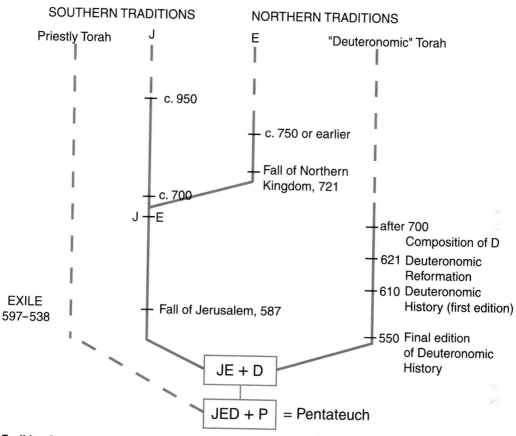

Israel's Traditions*

* In the above chart, the broken lines signify oral tradition, and solid lines signify the transmission of the tradition in written form. Notice that all the traditions are parallel developments out of the ancient period, although each was subject to a special development in the circle that preserved it. Like several streams flowing into one river, these traditions were joined and unified in a priestly edition, thus forming the Pentateuch.

Chronicles, Ezra, and Nehemiah. The singers in the Temple were using and composing the chants that were later to furnish much of the book of Psalms. Quite another type of poetry, originally erotic but interpreted as symbolizing the love relationship between God and Israel, is found in the *Song of Songs*. Fully two-thirds of the Hebrew canon as we know it today was in existence.

Culmination: The Age of the Torah

The significance of the new shift in interest has been well stated by Abram Sachar.

All through the fifth century there was a steady reaction against religious laxness, a reaction sponsored by the scribes, who were becoming ever more influential. The scribes, forerunners of the Pharisees, were the interpreters of the law, the leaders in the synagogues. . . . "Turn it and turn it again," the scribes admonished their people, "for everything is in it." And the Jews responded with unparalleled devotion. All existence was centered in the law. The Jews became a people of the book. The early Hebrews had created the Bible out of their lives; their descendants created their lives out of the Bible.[G1]

Or, as a group of Jewish scholars has pointed out in commenting on the effects of Ezra's reform,

> Henceforth, the distinguishing mark of a Jew would not be political identity but adherence to the Torah, even if he lived outside Palestine and did not participate in the Temple cult. After the Exile, Jewish nationality became identified with ethnic solidarity—common descent, destiny, religion, and culture—rather than territorial status.[H]

"Schools of expounders" arose to deduce new laws from the old, so that the ancient Torah might be made applicable to and practical in the life of later generations. These schools of the scribes were ultimately to become the solidly learned Pharisaic schools of the second and first centuries B.C.E. From the first they provided valuable insight into the problem of devising workable laws for conditions not dreamt of in the day of Moses. Improvements were made in civil law and Sabbath practices. But there were drawbacks, as evident in Abram Sachar's description of the development of rules concerning meat properly slaughtered (*kosher*).

> It was inevitable that the endless spinning of meanings from the old texts should go to extremes and become burdensome. The Biblical law which prohibited the eating of meat torn in the field was based upon the sensible hygienic principle that carrion was dangerous as food. In the hands of the dialecticians the law was elaborated into a complex dietary machinery. If meat torn in the field was prohibited, why not also meat torn in the city? But what was torn meat? If it were not properly slaughtered, it was surely torn. What was proper slaughter? A whole code, the basis for the practice of *Shehita* (ritual slaughter), grew up to meet these problems—rules governing the knife to be used and the manner of using it, rules governing the competency of the ritual slaughterer and his training, the prayers to be recited when the throat was cut and when the blood was covered with ashes. A simple Biblical precept grew into a labyrinth of observances.[G2]

II. NEW TRENDS OF THOUGHT IN THE GREEK AND MACCABEAN PERIODS

In 332 B.C.E., the Palestinian theocracy came under a new control—that of faraway Greece. Alexander the Great drove the Persian armies out of Asia Minor and Syria and then seized Palestine on his way to the conquest of Egypt. After founding on the Egyptian coast, and naming after himself, the new city of Alexandria, which he hoped would become the center of a culture that would revolutionize the civilization of the regions bordering on the southeastern Mediterranean, he turned his attention to what was left of the Persian empire and brought it tumbling down at his feet.

General Characteristics of the Hellenistic Influence

In Alexander's motivation, his personal ambition played the more considerable part without a doubt, but he also started out with an uncritical and altruistic passion for the spread of Greek civilization through the Middle East. Yet he had no notion of imparting Greek civilization by force. He believed in the self-evidencing power of truth and planned to convert the world to the Greek view of life by education and example. So, in Alexandria and at other strategic points, he ordered the establishment of new cities, which were to be laid out by Greek architects and provided with colonnaded municipal buildings, gymnasiums, open-air theaters, and libraries like those at Athens. Alexander encouraged Greek, Egyptian, Persian, and Jewish colonists to live in these model cities, under municipal governments that allowed each national group to live in its own quarter of the city, yet have a democratic share in certain processes of city government, such as rule by a council annually elected by the people.

Of course, no little pressure was brought to bear on each citizen to induce him—entirely of his own free will—to put on Greek dress, speak in Greek, build and furnish his home in the Hellenistic modes, and read and discuss Greek philosophical and political works, as far as his education allowed.

In his short reign—his death in Babylon was sudden—Alexander seemed to respect and favor the Jews. He wanted them in Alexandria, and in later days they filled two of the city's five sections. (They may have numbered one million souls there!) He hoped to make places for them elsewhere. The Jews, for their part, were more influenced by his cultural proposals than by those of any foreigner in their whole history. For one thing, the Hellenism for which he stood combined a new breadth of culture with unprecedented religious and racial tolerance. For another, it seemed to hold a great promise of vital world relationships overflowing into the economic and political back eddy that was Judah. The Jews wanted to be on good terms with the rest of the world. They may have been suspicious at first of the Hellenic colonists set up in model communities throughout Palestine, but these colonists proved after all to be persuasive exponents of Hellenism, because they were amusing, fraternal, and peaceful. In three generations, the higher-class Jews were freely admitting Greek words into their everyday speech and calling their children by Greek names. The cultured classes, and especially the Jerusalem priests, were, as might be expected, more profoundly influenced than the common people. Without giving up their religion, they welcomed the external features of Hellenistic civilization, so much so that in the heyday of the Greek influence the sacrifices were sometimes left half burnt on the altar at Jerusalem while the priests rushed off to some stadium to see the Greek athletes performing in the games. Yet there was a strong countercurrent. The Book of Daniel, written in this period, proudly depicts its young hero's resistance to Babylonianizing and clearly means him to be a model for resistance to Hellenizing pressure under the Seleucids.

The plain people were slow as always to adopt foreign ways. And the scribes and rabbis held back. With an unyielding loyalty to the Torah and the Jewish way of life, they kept resistance to Hellenism and all of its ways and works alive among the "quiet in the land," the conservatively Jewish "pious ones," or *hasidim,* as they were called then and later.

The process of Hellenization was retarded but not interrupted by the contention for the possession of Palestine that followed Alexander's early death in Babylon. For 100 years unhappy Palestine was overrun again and again by the armies of the Seleucids (of Syria) and the Ptolemies (of Egypt). The Ptolemies, whom the Jews preferred, were in ascendancy most of the time, but the Seleucids finally triumphed. There was peace after that for a while, and Palestinian Judaism might have gone over even more completely to Hellenism than had yet been the case, had not a head-strong Seleucid king caused his Jewish subjects to revolt against him and return to the ways of their fathers.

Oppression under Antiochus Epiphanes

It had now become a fact that as long as their religious life was not interfered with, the faithful Jews endured a good deal of oppression, but when their religion was endangered, they never hesitated to rebel. This was something that Antiochus Epiphanes, king of Syria, did not understand. Anxious to hasten the lagging process of welding all of the peoples of his kingdom into a Hellenistically minded whole, he determined to use force to make the Jews worship Zeus, of whom he claimed to be the earthly manifestation (hence his title of Epiphanes, "God-made-manifest"). He therefore forbade the Jews, on pain of death, to keep the Sabbath, own any copies of their sacred writings, or practice circumcision. He put his own candidates into the most sacred office—Hellenistic high priests with Greek names like Jason and Menelaus. He erected on the altar of burnt offerings in the Temple at Jerusalem an altar to Zeus of Olympus, and here sacrificed pigs (always an abomination to the Jews). Further, he commanded all Jews to join in similar sacrifices, not only at Jerusalem but in the villages. The horror and indignation of the faithful led to rebellion.

Rebellion and Independence under the Maccabees

When, then, an aged priest named Mattathias was ordered by a Syrian commissioner to participate in a sacrifice to Zeus at the village of Modin, he killed the commissioner and raised the standard of revolt. With his five sons, dubbed the Maccabees, or "hammer boys," at his side, and backed by many followers from among the Jews who rushed to him from every quarter, he took his stand in the wilderness. His able son, Judas Maccabeus, astounded the Syrian commanders by defeating four of their armies and forcing a fifth to retreat. In 165 B.C.E., Judas accomplished the surprising feat of recapturing all of Jerusalem except its garrisoned castle. The Temple was then purged of its "abominations," and the Jewish worship restored. Palestinian Judaism had been saved. In the subsequent phases of the campaign, the Syrians were obliged to quit Judea. Judas was killed in 161 B.C.E., and the leadership passed to his brother Jonathan, and after him to the last of the brothers, Simon, who was made high priest. Simon's son, John Hyrcanus, imperialistically added Idumea (Edom), Samaria, and Perea (the region beyond Jordan) to Judea, so that his kingdom approached King David's in size. Thirst for more power led to abuses, and we find John Hyrcanus forcing the Idumeans to accept Judaism at the point of the sword—a bad precedent. Though the Jews seemed here to be overreaching themselves, the period of Jewish independence lasted to 63 B.C.E., and might have lasted longer had it not been for the strife that broke out between divergent parties among the Jews themselves.

Before we tell that story and add the tragic aftermath, we need to examine the foreign ideas and modes of thought that now made an influx into Judaism and laid the basis for the rise of the postexilic Jewish parties.

Hellenistic Influence in the Wisdom Literature

In the theology and literature of these periods may be seen the influence of Greek and Persian ideas about nature and history. Written or being written were the books of Proverbs, Job, and Ecclesiastes, now in the Bible, and Ecclesiasticus and the Wisdom of Solomon, contained in the Apocrypha. Considered together, they are usually referred to as the Wisdom Books. Ruth, Esther, Jonah, and the Psalms made their appearance at this time, too. The last of the Jewish canonical scriptures to be completed was Daniel, and

along with it a host of extracanonical books in a like vein, giving expression to fervid Messianic hopes.

The Wisdom literature shows the influence of Greek ideas, although one cannot say that these ideas were the dominant ones. One may only say that Hellenism confirmed many thoughtful Jews in their disillusionment with the trend of their history. It developed skepticism and the rationalistic attitude of submitting every belief to the test of reason, and thus encouraged a taste for the more intellectual types of speculation. To take an example, the latest portions of Proverbs assimilate certain speculative concepts of Greek philosophy. Most of Proverbs is very old. Some of it may have had its origin in the days of Solomon as a translation and paraphrase of Egyptian collections of wise sayings about the nature and conduct of life. Solomon is said to have been attracted to these sayings and to have added some generalizations of his own. The collection grew slowly with the years by the accession to it of other independent collections, until by about 250 B.C.E., it assumed its present form. On the whole, it is pitched in a key of quite unecclesiastical lay wisdom. Morality is for the most part regarded not so much as the law of God (though that is not denied, certainly) but as the demand of reason and common sense. In its latest sections, however, Wisdom is personified as God's consultant at creation—a Greek notion, the word for *Wisdom* being *Sophia*, or *Logos*, and signifying in either case a combination of reason and sound judgment.

Another book that reflects Hellenism is Ecclesiastes. The writer seems to have had a knowledge of both Judaism and Hellenism, but to have been thrown into such mental confusion by the attempt to reconcile them that he could see no worth in human thought or effort. All that seemed to him good he summed up in such words as the following: "I know there is nothing good for man but to be glad and enjoy himself while he lives." Everything else involved futility, a vain striving to grasp the wind. Perhaps the writer had read the older book, Job, and had been unable to solve its fundamental problem: Why does God not make it the rule that the righteous prosper and the wicked suffer? But no, the righteous suffer and the wicked prosper. Ecclesiastes only vaguely catches Job's suggestion that the wise and pure in heart may transcend their suffering by rejoicing in the wisdom and majesty of God revealed in the awesome design of the world.

The Hellenistic influence on Judaism reached its height at Alexandria in Egypt rather than in Palestine. There near the time of Christ it made itself felt in the book called the Wisdom of Solomon and in the writings of the Jewish philosopher Philo, who consciously tried to synthesize Greek and Jewish thought by identifying the Wisdom of Jewish theology with the Logos of Greek philosophy. His teaching, that contact with the Supreme Being, in the fullest spiritual sense, was the work of the divine Logos as the mediator of the power or activity of God, was to have great influence on the thought forms to the early Christian Fathers.

Scripture in Greek: The Septuagint

Another effect of the pervasive Greek influence was the translation of the books of the Hebrew Bible into Greek by a group of scholarly translators, traditionally said to have numbered seventy (whence the name of the translation, the Septuagint. This translation was begun in the third century B.C.E. and was completed in the second. It is now apparent that the translators used only the most authentic manuscripts. The Septuagint proved to be the most reliable check scholars had on the accuracy of the Hebrew manuscripts that had survived up to 1947, none of which could be dated before the tenth century C.E. The discovery from 1947 on of the Dead Sea Scrolls has confirmed this earlier belief, for these oldest of Hebrew manuscripts (dated from the two centuries before Christ) are in accord at nearly every point with the Septuagint.

It may be added that the Dead Sea Scrolls have also confirmed the belief that the Latin translation (the Vulgate) made by St. Jerome in the fourth century C.E. was the result of his careful choices among variant readings in the Hebrew manuscripts he was able to gather.

But the influence of Hellenism on the religious conceptions of the main body of Jews was less enduring than that of Zoroastrianism, chiefly because the former was philosophical and secular in spirit, whereas the latter was religious and could offer supplementation to already existing beliefs.

Zoroastrian Influence

It is hazardous to draw conclusions concerning so elusive a thing as "influence," but the Jews came to know Zoroastrianism from observations near at hand in Babylonia, and certain Persian beliefs about Satan, the angels, the afterlife, and the messianic deliverer supplied what must have seemed missing elements in the old Jewish beliefs. Before they met the Satan of the Zoroastrians, the Jews had pondered the old stories about the serpent in the Garden of Eden and the fallen angels who had taken wives from among the daughters of men before the days of Noah. Then, too, there was the Adversary among the heavenly beings surrounding Yahweh who obtained permission to afflict Job and make him curse God. These stories antedated the exile, and in none of them is there the suggestion that the Spirit of Evil is a cosmic being, manifested from the beginning of time, and of a strength and creative power almost equal to that of the Spirit of Good. But after the exile, the Adversary among the heavenly beings became, for at least some of the Jews, an evil and infinitely malicious power, wholly in opposition to God, with attendant devils to match the angels who stood before God. In another direction, She'ol, the shadowy land of the dead, was replaced by a heaven and a hell, and some Jews also began to speak of a resurrection from the dead at the last day and of a last judgment, a final reward of the good and condemnation of the evil. Long before the exile, the prophets had foretold, of course, a day of doom and a purging of the nations, but now many Jews believed this with Persian amendments. Let us examine some of these specific changes.

Specific Areas of Change

1. The ancient Hebrew belief in demons, which scarcely rose above the animistic level and never implied strong resistance to Yahweh, much less a systematic or sustained opposition, now became the belief that the demons were *organized;* they had a

leader, a head. This head was variously named, but the most common name for him was Satan. One of his first appearances under this name is in a passage in the prophecies of Zechariah, where he is described as contending with an angel messenger of the Lord. As the Tempter, he also was read back by editors and revisers into the historical books, and the writers of "P" put him into the Garden of Eden. But he retained the character of a folklore figure.

2. The angels who, according to old belief, were Yahweh's divine messengers now were thought of as arranged in a hierarchy. In the Hellenistic and Maccabean periods this hierarchy consisted of seven archangels: Raphael, Uriel, Michael, Raguel, Saraqiel, Gabriel, and Remiel. The most prominent of these was Michael, with Gabriel coming next in importance.

3. The older Jewish belief that the dead descend to a colorless existence in the pit of She'ol, a land of forgetfulness not unlike the Greek Hades and the Babylonian Aralu, was in large part superseded by a belief in the resurrection of the body to an afterlife of full mental vigor and awareness.

4. The prediction of the older prophets that there would be a Day of Judgment in which the enemies of Israel would be carried down to doom, after which a new kingdom would be set up with a messianic king of Davidic lineage on the throne, underwent a radical change. This may have been a natural development and not a Zoroastrian suggestion; it probably was both. At any rate, the older hopes being unfulfilled and seemingly unfulfillable, the expectation now was that the coming of God's agent of deliverance would be from the clouds of heaven at the end of the world.

5. It looks as though the idea of a last judgment, a comparatively new concept, was taken over into Jewish apocalypticism with little basic change from Persian sources, although the locale was shifted.

This must suffice as a brief and somewhat speculative account of the influx of alien thought into Judaism. It raises a question for us. Was there, then, little opposition among the Jews to Gentile thought

pressures? Not so at all. Considerable opposition did arise, as we shall see in the next section. Yet, as one might suspect, attitudes were sharply divided. Some did not accept anything alien; some did. The books of Esther, Daniel, Ruth, and Jonah reflect these differences. Esther and Daniel were written by Jewish patriots, fired by wrath at the peoples who had anti-Semites among them. But the more tolerant and forgiving view toward aliens was given immortal expression in two stories, one concerning Ruth, the beautiful Moabite, who found acceptance among Jews, married one of them, and became an ancestor of King David, and the other concerning Jonah, the rebellious and anti-Gentile prophet, whom the Lord firmly bent to his more inclusive purposes.

The Rise of the Postexilic Jewish Parties: The Sadducees

Had Judea remained isolated from the rest of the world, there might perhaps have been among its people no divisions into parties. There might have been only the old clash between the popular majority and the prophetic minority that existed in the preexilic era.

In Judea, it was the priests, or at least the higher orders of the priesthood, who were the internationalists. This certainly seems a paradox, for priests are notoriously conservative and careful in their tolerances. But in this case the priests were the party in power. The high priest had become the civic as well as religious head of the country and raised taxes, collected tribute money, and grew wealthy along with the other members of the high priestly families. His actions were subject to some slight check by the Gerousia, the council of Jewish elders, later known as the Sanhedrin (significantly, both names derived from Greek), but in most respects he was archbishop, prime minister, and fiscal officer all in one. This meant that the higher orders of priests were constantly worried about stability in economic affairs and international relations. The psychological effect of this was a temptation to reduce the scope of religious requirements in order to minimize friction with Roman authorities. The ferment of new ideas and reform tended to complicate relationships and threatened public tranquility.

"Why rock the boat?" they reasoned, and the practical rule that they evolved was this: ideas in religion, local or foreign, not found in the written Torah were to be frowned upon, but cultural innovations promising to improve relations abroad and living standards at home were to be welcomed.

Out of this rose the important party of the *Sadducees* (a term derived from "Zadokites," designating the group of great families that formed the ruling clan of priests). The members of this wealthy, aristocratic, and somewhat worldly group dissociated themselves from the hopes of the masses and believed in the "reasonable" views of the ancient fathers as embodied in the written Torah, especially "the Books of Moses." They held that these last should be construed literally. In the realm of religion, therefore, they rejected the popular belief in angels, the new apocalyptic ideas, and particularly the conceptions of the resurrection of the body to full consciousness in afterlife. In matters of culture, however, they were so liberal to foreign points of view that they were called "Hellenizers," the implication being that they were active propagandists for the Greek way of life. But it was as patriots that they compromised with the Romans, seeing legal and economic stability as the means of saving their Jewish institutions from destruction.

The Pharisees

Compromise was religiously abhorrent to the Hasidim, the "pious ones" or "puritans" already mentioned, who were described as "the quiet in the land." They rallied quickly to fight beside Judas Maccabeus in the war for independence. They had no interest in politics as such, much less in internationalism or Greek culture. Their one major intellectual passion was the Jewish religion. From their ranks sprang the powerful party of the *Pharisees*, to which most of the scribes and rabbis and many of the lower orders of the priesthood belonged.

The Pharisees were as devoted to the written Torah as were the Sadducees, but they approached it as a living tradition whose application to current life had to be continuously worked out; it had to be interpreted and made applicable before it could be as scrupulously observed as they in fact tried to do. They therefore paid great attention to the oral tradition that accompanied the written Torah, that is, the expositions, interpretations, and commentaries of scribes and teachers (rabbis). Their attitude was not nearly as literalist as the Sadducees'; it was, in fact, quite liberal in accepting ideas that supplemented and expanded the written Torah. For them, the total Torah was a twofold body of precepts whose oral form was at times even more important than the written.

They believed that the world with which the Sadducees had so often compromised was under a sentence of doom; God meant to destroy it and bring in a new age. The Pharisees embraced messianic concepts involving the resurrection of the dead and the last judgment. Yet their dreams were harnessed to some very practical considerations. In the interim, before the end of the world, which would come only when God judged the time was ripe, they believed their prime duty was to be loyal to the Law, "written" and "unwritten." That meant not only the study of scriptures and "traditions," but also moral obedience, ceremonial purity (they had to keep themselves unspotted from unclean persons and things), and, above all, spiritual growth and development, the result of "living unto the Lord." It meant a life of continuous prayer, of remembrance of the dead, who, hopefully, had been righteous enough to deserve resurrection and reward at the last judgment; it meant also struggle here on earth for liberation from the worldly powers that restricted one's freedom to live a life of joyous obedience to God's will, and it meant a willingness to die rather than to compromise the holy faith.

When John Hyrcanus and his Maccabean successors became too enamored of their despotic power and oversympathetic with Saducean ideas, the Pharisees swung from support of the ruling family to fierce opposition. Sporadic open revolt was met with violent suppression and bloody massacre. When, in their turn, the Pharisees won an advantage, they took revenge in retaliatory bloodshed. The final result was civil war. But a stalemate resulted, and the Roman general Pompey, then resident in Syria, was called upon to arbitrate the issue. In 63 B.C.E., Pompey came down from Syria and promptly took over the country. It became a Roman province.

III. THE ROMAN PERIOD TO 70 C.E.

The Romans had been called in to umpire a dispute. That they seized the opportunity to make themselves masters of Palestine hardly pleased the Jews. The swift and bewildering succession of political changes that followed increased the sense of frustration and outrage. One source of deep resentment was the fact that a certain Antipater, an Idumean, who even though he professed Judaism was unacceptable to the Jews, had been active behind the scenes in winning Roman favor and gaining personal power. He won grudging approval from the Jews when he got the Romans to make Hyrcanus II, of the Maccabean family, the high priest. But when Pompey's successor, Julius Caesar, made Antipater the procurator of Judea, antagonism increased: Here was an Idumean as the civil ruler of Judea and the political superior of the high priest! In 40 B.C.E., Antipater's son Herod, whose favorite wife was a Maccabean princess, was chosen by Augustus Caesar to be king of Judea. It took three years of fighting, but Herod established himself as the absolute ruler of Palestine. In spite of the peace and prosperity that he brought and the special privileges he secured for Jews in the empire (including draft exemption) and his remodeling of the Temple into a thing of marble beauty, the Jews hated him because of his restoration of Greek and Roman temples and his cruelty and inhumanity. When he died horribly of a cancer in 4 B.C.E., they rejoiced.

Meanwhile, significant factors in the religious situation were operating.

Messianic Expectations Proliferate

From the coming of the Romans to the time of the destruction of Jerusalem in 70 C.E., the Messianic expectation increased its hold on thousands of suffering Jews. Deep in their hearts was the feeling that if God cared at all for his chosen people, he would act soon. The ardent hope of a supernatural deliverance from their unmerited suffering grew by what it fed on—an increasing flood of apocalyptic literature. Most of it followed the pattern of Daniel (written during the early years of the Maccabean revolt), which had set the fashion of rehearsing the history of the Jews, from the exile to the time of writing, in the cryptic terms of beasts with wings and images breaking under blows, to signify in symbols the end of the wicked world order and the resurrection of the righteous dead to join the righteous living in the enjoyment of a better world. There is not space here, nor necessity, to mention by name and assign to their decades the books that followed Daniel's pattern. Many of the books were lost, and the dates of those existing are hard to determine in any case. It will be enough to give a general picture of the messianic expectation when it reached its height.

Signs of the End and Messianic Titles

The central belief was that divine intervention would bring about a radical change in the world order. Through his messiah, God was going to gather together "his own," both living and dead, and live with them in blessedness forever. That necessitated first the "end of the age," as some held, or the end of the world, as others believed. The "end" would be foreshadowed by certain last evils—wars and rumors of wars, distress, fear, famine, plagues, the rise to power of even more wicked rulers on the earth, and the like. The discerning would recognize in them the "signs of the end." At the last moment, with the sounding of "the last trump," the Messiah would appear in the clouds, with all of the heavenly angels round him. He would be a supernatural personage, someone "like a man," and be called the Son of man, but bearing as well other titles, such as the Elect One, the Son of David, the Lord's Anointed, the Righteous Judge, the Prince of Peace, and the like. At his appearance the righteous on earth would be caught up to him in the air (many said), and the dead would rise from their graves.

Views of Final Judgment

The older views held that only the justified Jews would join the Messiah, but later expectations offered hope to the righteous Gentiles that they also would be among the redeemed. Finally, the Zoroastrian view was accepted that all human souls, good and bad, would be summoned to a last judgment. Before the Messiah's seat they would be separated into the redeemed and the lost. The bad would be sent away into everlasting hellfire, and the good would enter a state of blessedness with their Lord and King. This state of blessedness was variously conceived. Some writers thought it would be enjoyed on earth in a restored Garden of Eden, an earthly paradise; others placed it in one of the lower heavens. (There were thought to be seven heavens in all, God occupying the highest level along with his attendant angels.) Some combined the divergent conceptions, picturing an earthly paradise centered in a New Jerusalem to be inhabited by the Messiah and his chosen ones for a millennial period before the last judgment, and a heavenly paradise to be occupied by the redeemed after judgment was given. The heavenly paradise was most enthusiastically described as a place of green meadows, flowing streams, and fruit trees, where the righteous would banquet together with great joy and sing to the glory of God forever.

So great was the distress of many devout Jews in the period we are describing, and yet so high their faith, that the fulfillment of these dreams soon seemed completely reasonable. In fact, the world would not have seemed rational otherwise.

But not all of the Jews believed alike about these matters. Many subscribed to these views only in wistful half hope. Others considered them futile imaginings.

New Jewish Parties in the Roman Period

Throughout this period the old parties continued to function. The Sadducees were more concerned than ever with politics, and the Pharisees, with majority representation in the Sanhedrin, the deliberative body of organized Judean Judaism, regarded themselves as the true carriers of the Jewish religion. The schools that the latter maintained were the best in the Jewish world and boasted such great teachers as Hillel and Shammai. But two new parties with a distinct political orientation now sprang up.

Herodians

One, a minor group, went by the name of *Herodians*, because they supported the house of Herod. They came into existence as a party in 6 C.E., when Augustus Caesar, at the request of a Jewish deputation, deposed Herod's son Archelaus as ethnarch of Judea and appointed a Roman procurator in his stead. The Herodians were not inhospitable to Greco-Roman culture, but they wanted home rule at all costs.

Zealots

A far different and much larger group were the *Zealots*, passionate upholders of a policy of rebellion against Rome. The northern district of Galilee was their home base and stronghold. As an organized group, they made their first appearance in 6 C.E. under the leadership of a certain Judas the Gaulonite or Galilean, who led a revolt against the taking of a census by the Romans. The revolt was bloodily suppressed by the Roman general Varus, but this did not bring to an end the Zealot agitation. The Zealots all believed that meek submission to "Roman slavery" meant forsaking God, their only Lord and Master, and they were convinced that by taking the sword they could hasten the Messiah's coming or even be rewarded by finding the Messiah in their midst. (On occasion, they thought one of their own number was the Messiah.) The Romans called these "superpatriots," who hid out in the hills and fought in guerrilla fashion "bandits" and "robbers"—a not unfamiliar proceeding among conquerors.

Essenes

A third new group, which entirely dissociated itself from politics, bore the name of *Essenes*. They lived in various places throughout Palestine, some in the villages, others in the open country. In preparation for the Messiah's coming, they withdrew from the "corruption" of civilized society into monastic seclusion, where they fasted and prayed, ate together, washed themselves frequently in prescribed ceremonial ablutions, observed the Sabbath strictly, and engaged in daily chores of farming and handicraft. They practiced non-violence, meekly awaiting the world's end. As we learn from the famous Dead Sea Scrolls, the main group withdrew to a level hilltop near Qumran under the cliffs rimming the western shore of the Dead Sea. As early as the second century B.C.E., they sought this especially barren and isolated site in order to remain unmolested in their utter absorption in religious study and devotion. The founder of the community, as an expounder of the Law or Torah, bore the name "the Teacher of Righteousness." From his time on they held property in common, ate common meals, and worshiped and studied together, devoting themselves especially to copying scrolls for their library on a long table of solid plaster. Under the regimen described in the scroll, known as the *Manual of Discipline,* they formed a decidedly otherworldly covenant community. They practiced baptism as a rite of cleansing following on confession and repentance of sins, and it was repeated in individual cases whenever this seemed spiritually necessary. They called themselves, in a manner anticipating the early Christians, followers of "the way" and "sons of light," for they conceived themselves to be under the rule of "the Prince of Light" and opposed themselves therefore to the "sons of darkness" under the "Angel of Darkness"—a set of concepts with a Zoroastrian rather than Hebrew coloring. Leadership of the community—until its complete destruction in 68 C.E. during the Jewish War by a Roman legion—was exercised by a group of chosen priests and laymen. If we are to go by a rather obscure reference in the *Manual of Discipline,* twelve may have been the number, but this is conjectural.

IV. THE GREAT DISPERSION

The discontent of the Jews had been leading steadily to a gruesome climax. Bloodshed and turmoil, with only brief intervals of quiet, kept all Palestine seething for sixty years after the desperate revolt of Judas the Galilean in 6 C.E. The Romans were aware that the one indispensable condition of keeping the peace was to leave the Jewish religion alone, and they made it their policy to do so. In other directions, they used grim force. At the beginning of the first century, Palestine was divided into three districts—two ruled by sons of Herod, the third (comprising Judea, Idumea, and Samaria) governed by a Roman procurator residing at Caesarea on the coast below Jerusalem. In deference to Jewish feeling, the procurators did not bring the Roman imperial standards with their image of Caesar into Jerusalem, nor require that the statue of the emperor be erected in the Temple and made the object of worship.

They were satisfied with the Jewish agreement to offer a daily sacrifice *for* the emperor on the Temple altar. But the Jews were extremely sensitive when their Temple was interfered with. Pilate thought that he might meet with no objection if he brought the imperial standards into Jerusalem in the darkness of the night, but he found he had failed to reckon with Jewish alertness. When again he assumed that the Jews would take no offense at his seizing and applying Temple funds to the extension of an aqueduct into Jerusalem, he discovered they were offended to the point of revolt. A slight improvement of the condition of ill will came during the reigns of Caligula and Claudius, when Herod Agrippa I, a grandson of Herod the Great, ruled the whole of Palestine and the procurators were recalled. But when the well-liked Herod Agrippa died, the sending of procurators was resumed. As one succeeded another, disorder mounted; there were "bandits" everywhere, and rioting broke out in Jerusalem; a lax high priest was assassinated; there was conflict between Jew and Gentile, Jew and Samaritan, and Jew and Roman.

Rebellion: The Fall of Jerusalem

For a people in multiple jeopardy, the stage was now set for open rebellion. It came in 66 C.E., toward the close of Nero's reign. The war was begun with terrible determination on both sides. The Jews had been divided among themselves about having a war at all, but once the issue was joined, they entered the struggle together, still quarreling. The Romans on their part had lost all patience and would stand for no more "folly." Their forces were led by Vespasian, until Nero's death took him to Rome to be crowned emperor; he then appointed his son Titus to subdue the Jews. Titus did so. The struggle was unbelievably savage and bitter. After Titus finally invested Jerusalem, he more than once pleaded with the Jews to surrender, but they would not. The superhuman resistance of the city's defenders nearly baffled their besiegers, even though the Roman catapults threw huge stones a quarter of a mile into the defenses, and the battering rams, devastating in their weight and force, broke down wall after wall. Yet as soon as one wall was breached, another was found behind it. The defenders, starving and half maddened with horror, were driven back until they were at bay within the Temple area. The heroic resistance continued, even after a brand hurled through the air set the Temple on fire and the assaulting forces broke into the enclosure. Then the defenders retired to make a last stand in the upper city. At the end of another month, they could resist no more. Amid indescribable slaughter, the city was razed, and Titus, having executed great numbers of Jewish captives by crucifixion, went away to Rome, laden with plunder, to be borne in triumph under the beautiful arch that bears his name and stands proudly still in the ruins of the Forum, a mute testimony to Roman might and Jewish valor.

Disruption of Cultic Life

More than the city was destroyed. The priests and their sacrifices, and with them the Sadducean party, passed from the scene of history. The Zealots, Essenes, and Herodians were the next to follow them off the stage. Only the party of the rabbis—that is, the Pharisees—and a rising heretic sect, called the Christians, were destined to wield influence through the coming years. The Romans had succeeded, for the moment, in decentralizing the Jewish religion. The bonds joining each outlying synagogue with the Temple were sundered. Set adrift, the Jews had no reason to turn their faces in worship to Jerusalem, except in sorrow and mourning.

After 70 C.E., the Jewish dispersion reached the proportions of a national migration. Some of the inhabitants of Jerusalem fled east to Babylonia and southeast into the Arabian Desert, where they were beyond the power of Rome. Others went to join friends and relatives all over the Mediterranean world. Many who had no such ties emigrated to Jewish communities in Syria, Asia Minor, Rome, Egypt, North Africa, and far-off Spain.

But not all went away. Some retired to the rural parts of Palestine, hoping to be able to go back to Jerusalem some day and restore it. The Zealots, unwilling to believe their cause hopeless, continued active in the hills. Three years after the fall of Jerusalem, one grim band of insurgents on a mesa at Masada, far down the Dead Sea, fought heroically and then committed suicide.

The Final Rebellion: Bar Kochba

Then, sixty years after the fall of Jerusalem, a last, bloody revolt broke out in Palestine. On a visit to Judea,

The Rock Fortress of Masada
This was the site of major drama three years after the fall of Jerusalem, in 70 C.E., when the last remnants of Jewish troops and insurgents committed suicide rather than surrender to the Romans. (© Photograph by Erich Lessing/Art Resource, N.Y. S0132518. A0003405.)

the Emperor Hadrian had seen for himself that Jerusalem still lay in ruins after over half a century, and he had reissued his previous order, drawn up in Rome, that the city be rebuilt and that a temple to Jupiter Capitolinus be erected on the site of the razed Jewish sanctuary. As soon as Hadrian left Syria, Judea rose to arms. The most learned Jew of the day, Rabbi Akiba, had urged a messianic aspirant named Bar Kochba to be the military leader of a new war for liberation. In high anger, Hadrian banned Sabbath observance, circumcision, and study of the Torah, intensifying Jewish opposition. A brutal three-and-a-half-year campaign against the rebellion virtually eradicated the Jewish presence in Judea. Dio Cassius wrote that 580,000 perished. Recent discoveries show that a tiny remnant of Bar Kochba's followers survived in caves by the Dead Sea.

The Romans then proceeded to the rebuilding of Jerusalem as planned, but it was constituted a Roman colony in which only non-Jews were allowed to live, and its name was changed to Aelia Capitolina. With despairing eyes, the patriots who drew near the city beheld the new temple to Jupiter standing where the old sanctuary had been, but they were forbidden by imperial edict to set foot in the city or linger near it, on pain of death. Only on the anniversary of the destruction of the Temple—the ninth day of the month Ab— were they permitted to pay the sentries for the forlorn privilege of leaning against a remnant of the foundation wall of the old Temple to bewail the loss of their national home and complete dispersion of their nation. This lamentation at the Wailing Wall, begun then, continued, except when interrupted, until recent times. But now, as a result of the Israeli victory in the war of June 1967, the Western Wall is in Jewish control for the first time since 70 C.E.

V. THE MAKING OF THE TALMUD

The Jews would not give up. Although they lost their national independence, they remained faithful to the memory of life in the Holy Land. They held themselves together by a religious and cultural cohesion, a form of nonviolent resistance, under the direction of their intellectual and moral leaders, the rabbis; it was destined to survive every persecution of the future. The stages in a sustained effort to further define and preserve a portable body of tradition involved the founding of rabbinical schools, the defining of an official canon of scripture: the law, prophets, and writings, and the collecting of learned commentaries, the Talmud.

In the year 69 C.E., while Titus was before Jerusalem, a leading rabbi with the name of Johanan ben Zakkai escaped through the Roman army to the town of Jabneh (Jamnia) on the coastal plain, where he began teaching in a "house of learning," or "school," such as existed in connection with most synagogues throughout the Jewish world, another name being *academy*. Such schools were a farsighted endeavor to save Judaism from extinction by systematizing its laws and doctrines and adapting it to the changes now upon it. He was a follower of the great sage and teacher Hillel (died *ca.* 10 C.E.) and was himself a leader. Not only did he gather about him students and scholars who were to devote themselves earnestly to study and interpretation of the scriptures and the traditions, but

now that the Sanhedrin was defunct, he organized the leaders among them into a new council to fix the dates of the Jewish calendar—a task that had to be done each year—and to make such necessary regulations for Judaism as a whole as needed to be made. Gradually, this body became the one recognized authority throughout the Jewish world that could pronounce on the true meaning and right practice of Judaism. Its president, with the title of *Nasi* (prince or patriarch), was officially recognized by the Romans (until 425 C.E.) as the supreme head of all the Jews in the Roman empire.

The Final Selection and Delimitation of the Hebrew Canon

One of the urgent tasks of the Jabneh scholars was to submit to critical examination the writings honored and read in the synagogues as sources of teaching and inspiration, for it had become important and necessary to determine which were to be regarded as true scripture and which as failing to reach such quality. The central question was, which of them could be judged as revelation, that is, writings divinely inspired and not written from wholly human motivations.

We have already seen (p. 413) that fully two-thirds of the Hebrew canon existed in the period following the time of Ezra. Many books had been written since then, some of them in continuation of the Hebrew tradition, some sententious examples of wisdom literature, some wildly extravagant anticipations of the end of the world. Broadly, the scholars at Jabneh dealt with three groups of writings: (1) the *Torah,* or the basic literature centering in the Mosaic covenant, (2) the *Nebi'im,* or the literature stemming from the prophets, and (3) the *Kethubim* (or miscellaneous) writings, which had gained a sacred or semisacred status.

Five books, the Pentateuch, formed the "written" Torah (they came to be called "the Books of Moses")— Genesis, Exodus, Leviticus, Numbers, and Deuteronomy—whose scriptural status went back to the fifth century B.C.E.; the scholars of Jabneh included them in the canon as a matter of course. The books of the prophets had had canonical status since the third century B.C.E. They fell into three groups: (1) the historical books that told in part of the preliterary prophets—

Joshua, Judges, I & II Samuel, and I & II Kings; (2) the writings of the prophets leaving a major literary legacy—Isaiah, Jeremiah, and Ezekiel; and (3) the briefer ("minor") prophetic writings, Hosea, Joel, Amos, Obadiah, Jonah, Micah, Nahum, Habakkuk, Zephaniah, Haggai, Zechariah, and Malachi. There was no difficulty accepting all three groups as being divinely inspired. The Jabneh scholars had more difficulty finally determining the status of the books of the Kethubim, the writings that Jesus, son of Sirach, in the preface to the Ecclesiasticus (now in the Apocrypha and written about 180 B.C.E.) called "the other writings of our ancestors." The scholars, after scrutiny, accepted into the canon I & II Chronicles, Ezra, Nehemiah, Psalms, Proverbs, Job, Ruth, Lamentations, Daniel, Ecclesiastes, The Song of Songs, and Esther. The last three were somewhat hesitantly included, but accepted finally under the conviction that Ecclesiastes was by King Solomon, that The Song of Songs had a deeper meaning than its erotic contents at first sight indicated, and that Esther, with some chapters excluded, reported a series of events that were historically important. The Jabneh scholars set aside as useful and instructive but not of scriptural calibre I & II Esdras; Tobit; Judith; the excluded chapters of Esther; The Wisdom of Solomon; Ecclesiasticus; Baruch, coupled with A Letter of Jeremiah; The Song of the Three; Daniel and Susanna; Daniel, Bel, and the Snake; The Prayer of Manasseh; and I & II Maccabees, which last dealt with the liberation of Judea in the second century B.C.E.

This last group of books acquired the Greek name *Apocrypha* ("kept hidden," i.e., not given prominence). Later on, the Roman Catholic Church adopted them, with the exception of I & II Esdras, into its own canon. (There also was a New Testament Apocrypha, but the Roman Church never gave it canonical status.)

Taken together, the books admitted to the Jewish canon (in about 90 C.E.) were considered "the Word of God," and formed thenceforth a "fixed canon," that is, one not to be altered or added to. The Jews have ever since regarded the books of the canon as their distinctive scriptures. Among Christians it acquired the name *Old Testament,* or in a more accurate translation *Old Covenant,* in distinction from the New Testament or New Covenant, both being accepted by Christians as the word of God.

Akiba at Jabneh: Classifying Halakah and Midrash

During the sixty years of the Jabneh school's existence far more than the fixing of the Jewish canon was accomplished. In addition to making a detailed study of the written Law (the Torah), the school exactly recorded and defined the unwritten Law (the Halakah), conveyed through the traditions of the past and in the interpretations and opinions (the Midrash) of learned rabbis. This produced a vast accumulation of rules and judgments, which had at last to be sorted out. It was Rabbi Akiba (the same who backed up Bar Kochba in the disastrous rebellion during the reign of Hadrian) who determined how to group the material of the unwritten Law under six major heads, and thus simplified the task of classifying and codifying the whole body of tradition.

The repressive measures following in the train of the war under Hadrian brought a sudden end to the school at Jabneh. Akiba perished during the conflict, and other rabbis and scholars lost their lives. But those who survived carried the Jabneh records into Galilee, where work on them was presently resumed at Usha, in the interior, and then later at various other places, such as Sepphoris and Tiberias, further inland. Such repeated removals only increased the rabbi's sense of urgency.

The Schools of Galilee: The Mishnah

The schools in Galilee developed outstanding "masters," chief among them Rabbi Meir and Rabbi Judah. Their names are associated with the compilation of the *Mishnah* ("Repetition" or "Study"), a collection, under Akiba's six headings, of some four thousand precepts of rabbinic law, intended to "interpret" and adapt the original Torah to the conditions of the second century. The Mishnah was a large and detailed work that contained references to the legal decisions of the outstanding rabbis of past generations, pausing sometimes to give the varying points of view of noted rabbis on disputed points. After it left Rabbi Judah's hands, it acquired an authority almost as great as that of the Torah itself. Certainly it met a real need. With the Temple destroyed, it was no longer possible to carry out the traditional ritual sacrifices; even the Torah's civil law provisions, conceived for an earlier agricultural society, had to be adapted to the complex realities of the money economy of the Roman world. Completed by about 220 C.E. the Mishnah contained the decisions and judgments of almost 150 of the most revered teachers (Tannaim) of Israel and gathered its material from a period of several centuries. The range of its subjects was great, as may be seen by a glance at its contents as grouped into categories by Akiba.

One section was concerned with the seasonal festivals and fasts; another with prayers, agricultural laws, and the rights of the poor; a third with women and the laws relating to marriage and divorce; a fourth with civil and criminal law; a fifth with "consecrated things," particularly the ritual of offerings and sacrifices; a sixth with laws respecting what was clean and unclean in persons and things and prescriptions as to how Jews were to purify themselves when polluted.

One reads the Mishnah's pages with a sense of wonderment at its microscopic examination of every phase of Jewish life and cannot withhold sympathy, in spite of the overstrained interpretations and involved reasoning. It may even *seem,* as one modern Jew suggests, that some laws of the Mishnah were an overreaction on the rabbis' part. "But they were very sane, those rabbis. They saw how near their people were to death. Panic-stricken, they clutched at every imaginable regulation that might keep Israel alive."[11]

The schools in Galilee flourished for a century and then declined in importance. Their schools continued to exist for two centuries more and produced the *Palestinian Talmud,* an incomplete work. Intellectual leadership had long since passed to the scholars of Babylonia.

The Schools of Babylonia: The Gemara

The schools in Babylonia were of long standing. They were the expression, in fact, of an uninterrupted community life going back as far as 586 B.C.E., when Nebuchadrezzar carried away into exile the greater part of the upper classes of Jerusalem. It is estimated that after the destruction of Jerusalem in 70 C.E., the refugees who fled to Babylonia swelled its Jewish population to nearly one million persons. The importance of this group was increased during the Parthian dominance

of Babylonia by the fact that the government recognized a Jew of reputedly Davidic lineage, called the Resh Galuta or Chief of the Exile, as their civil head. But far greater importance for Judaism at large can be claimed for the deep learning and great ability of the rabbis in the Babylonian schools. Out of their labors came the voluminous work known as the *Gemara* (or Supplementary Learning).

The completion of the Mishnah did not bring an end to the process of exploring and defining the details of orthodox Jewish religion and life. Indeed, the Mishnah itself became the basis of further commentary, for in many parts it was so concise as to be very nearly cryptic, and therefore itself in need of elucidation. Moreover, it was devoted chiefly to the study of the unwritten Law (the Halakah) and contained a relatively small portion of the informal oral traditions that the Jews called the *Haggadah,* a name by which they meant the nonjuristic traditions. The Haggadah was more interesting by far than the Halakah, for its purpose was the instruction and entertainment of the lay person through discourse illustrating the meaning of moral and religious truths. It abounded in stories and anecdotes and pithy comments on Bible truths by the great rabbis and teachers of Israel. Therefore, when the basic Mishnah was completed, the Palestinian and Babylonian scholars busied themselves with recording the Haggadah and indeed every scrap of Jewish learning that was not in the Mishnah, so that nothing might be lost.

Then, in the second quarter of the third century, just after Jewish intellectual leadership had passed to the scholars of Babylonia, the tolerant Parthian rule was replaced by the severe reign of the Sassanian dynasty, dominated by the Magi—that is, the Zoroastrian priesthood. After centuries of security and prosperity, the Babylonian Jews began to experience persecution. They were forbidden to bury their dead in the ground, because in the Zoroastrian view that would pollute the soil, and they were ordered to send in a portion of all their table meat to be sacrificed on the Zoroastrian altars. Because the Magi of that period had a fanatically high regard for fire as a symbol of deity, they prohibited its religious use by all non-Zoroastrians. Immediate difficulties with the Jews arose as a result; for the Mishnah instructed them to light a Sabbath candle before dark on Friday and to kindle tapers when the holy day ended, observances practiced to this day.

Attempts to enforce the prohibition led to rioting and massacre. In the ensuing troubles, some of the schools and academies were raided and closed.

Completion of the Babylonian Talmud

The upshot of the new difficulties—which, however, never reached the proportions of an annihilating persecution—was a still greater zeal to preserve Jewish learning. The vast accumulations of rabbinic commentary were at last put in order. All unrecorded Halakah and Haggadah were brought together in the Gemara, the *magnum opus* of the Babylonian schools. When this was combined with the Mishnah, the *Talmud* was the result.

The Talmud was completed by the end of the fifth century. It marked an epoch in Jewish history. In all the years since its completion, it has never been superseded as an authoritative compendium or even an encyclopedia of descriptions and definitions in detail or every aspect of orthodox Jewish belief and practice. Its six major parts and sixty-three tractates have been like meat and drink to the persecuted Jews, who fled from east to west and back again during the long ordeal of the Middle Ages. Its physical bulk has had—and this constitutes a rather exceptional circumstance—no little relation to its spiritual inexhaustibility. It has served as a rampart of moral resistance that rose higher and stood firmer than the brick and stone of the ghetto walls that Europe raised to hem the Jew in. Though mistakenly adjudged magic and devil's lore, burned in the marketplaces by angry civil authorities or torn apart page by page and thrown on the waters, the Talmud always survived to feed the souls of a persecuted people determined to live by its regulations or have no further part in life. Others might laugh at what was contained in it, but to the Jew it was the wisdom that is of God.

VI. THE JEWS IN THE MIDDLE AGES

At the beginning of the Middle Ages, the situation of the Jewish people was profoundly affected by the impact upon them of two religions, Christianity and Islam. The first was inclined to be hostile; the second tolerant, if not friendly.

Jewish-Christian Mutual Antagonism

The relationship between Jews and Christians had never been good. Christian accounts of their origins persisted in picturing jealous Judaism rather than Roman repression as the cause of their savior's death. In the first two centuries, animosities were exacerbated by fear of Roman persecution. Each group perceived the other as jeopardizing their precarious status in the Empire. Jews naturally resented the fact that Christians (without conforming to Jewish laws) claimed the hard-won special consideration that Romans afforded Jews. Christians blamed Jewish repudiation for their difficulties with Roman authorities.

From the first century on, the attitude of Judaism had been clearly defined by rabbis who rejected the claim that Jesus was the Christ, that is, the Messiah. The Christians, however, tried with earnest persistence to win the Jews over to their faith, but their success was small in proportion to the efforts they expended. The Jews were for the most part not convinced by the Christian teaching, especially after St. Paul carried the Christian gospel into Europe. Greek converts placed the life of Jesus in the cosmological setting of Greek philosophy and developed a theology around the figure of Jesus that was daring in its speculative sweep. At the same time, St. Paul produced further alienation by claiming that Christians were not expected to observe all of the regulations of the Torah, as Jews were. It should be remembered that the rabbis, primarily concerned as they were with saving Judaism from dissolution, seldom strayed from the study of conduct of life. The Talmud is proof that they took off on no high flights of theological speculation. Consequently, they viewed "the Hellenizing of the Christian religion" with distaste. The antagonisms implicit in this situation became a political actuality after the conversion of the Emperor Constantine in 312 C.E. and the subsequent elevation of Christianity to the status of the state religion. The Christian bishops, who now became great powers in the world, were in no amiable mood when they found that the Jews only stiffened their resistance to Christian pressure with the state behind it. As the Middle Ages advanced, the hostility of Christians to Jews intensified and occasionally broke out into violence.

Mutual Respect Between Jews and Muslims

The Muslims treated the Jews better. In Palestine, Syria, and Babylonia, they displayed toward the Jews not only tolerance but kindness, partly because the Jews looked upon them as deliverers from the Christians and Zoroastrians and therefore lent them their service as spies and scouts, and partly for the reason that culturally, racially, and religiously there was a marked resemblance between them.

The Jews in Babylon did not have a council headed by a patriarch as the Jabneh community had had. They were subject to an exilarch, a "Prince of the Exile," who claimed descent from David via the King Jehoiachin, carried into exile by Nebuchadrezzar in 586 B.C.E. As a vassal of the Muslim ruler, the exilarch was a powerful figure in the court at Baghdad. The rabbinical schools in Babylonia therefore throve once more.

Jewish traders, following in the wake of Muslim conquerors, turned almost overnight into wealthy merchants who trafficked from one end of the Mediterranean world to the other. But it was too good to last. Economic conditions took a turn for the worse. The Turks came; the Jews again began to be oppressed. So, in the tenth and eleventh centuries, many Babylonian scholars set forth with their folk for Spain, at the other end of the world, where, since the eighth century, Jewish learning had been enjoying a heyday under the tolerant rule of the Moors. Here they joined forces with their Spanish brethren in creating the "golden age" of Jewish science, religious philosophy, and mysticism in the West.

New Thought in Babylonia and Spain

It took the combined resources of Eastern and Western Judaism to produce this notable Spanish interlude. Jewish scholarship in the West had at least these advantages: it was the beneficiary first of Arabic science, which excelled in mathematics and astronomy and had rediscovered Aristotle, and next of a renaissance of Jewish poetry and *belles-lettres,* then in progress (eleventh century). But the scholars from Babylonia were also ripe for creative advance. They were not narrow Talmudists; something had happened to them before they left Babylonia that freed them from too confined an adherence to the Talmud's text. This was the Karaite heresy and the corrective reaction, led by the great scholar Saadiah, which followed in its wake.

The Karaite Challenge in Babylonia

Acceptance of the Talmud as an infallible guide of life never was universal throughout the Jewish world. Occasionally, messianic aspirants would release their followers from obedience to its regulations and lead them "back to the Torah." But this was perhaps the least important reaction against the Talmud. There was greater disturbance when it was argued that the Talmud was a departure from the truths divinely revealed to ancient Israel. A significant protest of this kind was led by the scholar Anan ben David of Baghdad, a candidate for the title of exilarch, rejected (767 C.E.) for his heretical views, who declared that the supreme authority in Jewish life was the Hebrew canon, particularly the five books of the Torah, and not the Talmud. The new sect he founded was nicknamed "the Children of the Text" and more commonly bore the name of Karaites (Readers). Generally, among the Karaites the eating of almost any meat was forbidden, the Sabbath lights enjoined by the Mishnah were not kindled, recourse to physicians was regarded as lack of faith in the scriptural promise "I am the Lord that healeth thee," and many ancient practices that had fallen into disuse were revived in spite of the anachronisms involved. Because it stressed the validity of individual interpretations of the ancient scriptures, the Karaite movement splintered into many subsects and spread itself thinly through the Jewish world and up into Russia. Its chief historical importance lies in the fact that it awoke orthodox Jews from their complacency with strictly logical juristic deductions from divine Law and stimulated a reexamination of the Talmud's general suitability to the times. Just this was attempted by Saadiah ben Joseph (882–942 C.E.), head of the Sura Academy in Babylonia.

Massacre of Jews

An engraving from H. M. Gottfried's *Chronica,* 1642, depicts a riot against the Jews instigated by Vincent Fettmilch at Frankfurt-am-Main, August 22, 1614. The climates of hostility nurtured by greed, rumors of ritual child killing, and a perpetual excuse of "righteous wrath" against "Christ killers" account for the ease with which mob attacks could be stirred up on numerous occasions over hundreds of years in medieval Europe and up to the climactic Holocaust in modern times. *(Courtesy of the Bettmann Archive.)*

Arabic-Jewish Awakening: Saadiah

Saadiah realized that the Karaites, even though they reached the wrong conclusions, were obeying a sound impulse in returning to the original Hebrew Scriptures. He began the translation of these scriptures into Arabic, in order to make them available both to interested Muslims and to those Arabic-speaking Jews who had difficulty reading them in the original Hebrew. He also wished in his writings to demonstrate the reasonableness of the Talmud by references both to the Hebrew Scriptures and to the increasing number of Arabic translations of Greek philosophical and scientific works. Revelation and reason (scripture and philosophy) were, he said, complementary; both were needed. So he attempted a new systemization of Jewish thought,

harmonizing it with the best in world thought, and thus became the father of medieval Jewish philosophy.

When the Babylonian scholars migrated to Spain, they took Saadiah's mediating conceptions with them, and these ideas of his helped shape the course taken by enlightened Jewish opinion there.

In Spain, the fruitful meeting of Eastern and Western influences produced a mental quickening so marked that Spain quickly became the chief center of Jewish learning and culture. In the Jewish Academy of Cordoba, founded in the tenth century, a succession of distinguished scholars encouraged the fresh expression of Jewish learning and insight into literature. In the eleventh and twelfth centuries, Ibn Gabirol, Judah Halevi, and the two Ibn Ezras wrote books of verse and learned treatises with great clarity and power. So deeply devotional were many of their hymns and religious essays that portions of them have since found their way into the liturgy of the synagogues.

Moses Maimonides

Even more famous was the great twelfth-century scholar Moses ben Maimon (1135–1204), who is usually called Moses Maimonides. Born in Cordoba, he and his family fled during his youth from a persecution (this time at the hands of a group of conservative Muslims) that drove them from Spain across the Mediterranean to Cairo, where he became a trusted court physician to Saladin, the famous Muslim leader against the Crusaders. There he became known throughout the Jewish world for three great treatises.

The first treatise was a commentary on the Mishnah, in which he sought to summarize and clarify its complicated provisions, emphasizing its ethics and its basic reasonableness. He considered that the Mishnah, in seeking to define in practical and reasonable terms the Judaic way of life, adhered to the Greek principle supported by Aristotle, "Nothing in excess." Wishing to make his work as widely available as possible to Jews living in Muslim lands, he wrote the commentary in Arabic. He introduced at its close his famous statement of the thirteen cardinal principles of the Jewish faith, to which he also adhered.

> I believe with perfect faith that God is the creator of all things and he alone; that he is one with a unique unity; that he is without body or any form whatsoever; that he is eternal; that to him alone is it proper to pray; that all the words of the prophets are true; that Moses is the chief of the prophets; that the law given to Moses has been passed down without alteration: that this law will never be changed and no other will be given; that God knows all the thoughts and actions of men, that he rewards the obedient and punishes transgressors; that the Messiah will come; that there will be a resurrection of the dead.[J]

It is interesting that these articles appear in the Jewish Daily Prayer book (in a more amplified form and in rhyme) to serve as an introduction to the morning service, although they have never been completely accepted and are in no way binding.

Maimonides' second work was immediately accepted as authoritative, although it did not escape severe criticism. It was written for its Jewish readers in Mishnaic Hebrew and bore the name *Mishneh Torah* ("the Torah Reviewed"). Rational and liberal in treatment, it was a redaction of the written Torah and the Talmud, with great weight given to authorities (the Tannaim, Amoraim, and Geonim of Palestine and Babylonia), whose names, however, for the sake of simplicity were omitted. He did not hesitate to make decisions on his own authority, adding new laws that complemented or even contradicted the Talmud; but he succeeded in making the Torah, taken in its widest sense, comprehensible and easier to follow without puzzlement. The puzzled were much on his mind.

Maimonides' third and greatest work, written in Arabic to capture a wide readership, was called *Guide for the Perplexed,* a rational examination of the Jewish faith, conceived in a spirit more than cordial to Aristotle, even while it stood firm on the doctrine of the divine revelation of the Hebrew Torah. His purpose was to reconcile religion and science, faith and reason, and Judaism and philosophy. Revelation, certainly, is made to faith, he said; but reason also reaches truth. For reason can take one far, to the point in fact where revelation comes to supplement it. Such revelation, when it comes, cannot be contrary to reason but is rational in all of its parts. Miracles, being contrary to reason, should be explained rationally, and the anthropomorphisms of the scriptures so interpreted that they become figures of speech, charged with ethical meanings. The account of creation in Genesis must be interpreted allegorically. By such use of our understanding, we get to know the highest truth about God and his will for mankind.

The Kabbala: Speculative Mysticism

But the conviction that religion has hidden meanings was to receive another kind of statement—that of the Kabbala, a system of speculative theology and mystical number symbolism that gave new currency to old accumulations of secret wisdom and esoteric lore and that fascinated many by mysterious arrangements of words and numbers, purporting to reveal the "deeper meaning" in the Hebrew Scriptures. The fact that the letters of the Hebrew alphabet also stand for numbers enables interpreters to turn any word or sentence into a number series, and this seemed to the Kabbalists to yield significant results in the case of the various names and attributes of God. Even rabbis and scholars of note gave themselves up to acrostics, anagrams, and other forms of esoteric wordplay.

The Kabbala, whose most important book is the Zohar, said to have been written in the 1280s by Moses de Leon in Spain, is fundamentally an expression of a deep need not fully satisfied either by close adherence to the Talmud or by the cool rationalism of Maimonides. It has sought religious experience of hidden spiritual forces in the world—as is true of most religious mysticism.

But the Kabbala also addressed serious metaphysical problems, for example, how a perfect God could produce an imperfect or incomplete world, or, to put it in other terms, how the Infinite could bring forth the finite without being diminished. In one view God constricted himself, vacating enough space for a created world nourished by conduits of his divine splendor. When the conduits leaked, a disharmony of evil came about.

Gender-linked Emanations

Another typical line of speculation went back to Philo and Gnostic conceptions. From God as the Boundless (*Ein Sof*) there went forth, as light radiates from the sun, various spiritual entities called the ten *Sefirot* (literally ten "numbers," but understood as symbolizing "emanations" or "spheres"). Such was the Divine Will, which generated Wisdom (male) and Intelligence (female), these in turn generating Grace or Love (male) and Power (female), which later by their union produced Beauty; and from the last three sprang the natural world.

Along with the tendency in the Kabbala to accent the interaction of male and female principles operating in the order of the world, there was a further step of introducing the feminine principle into the concept of divinity (actually a reintroduction, since in biblical and Talmudic times there are peripheral traces of it). Sovereignty (*malkut*) included a feminine dimension, whether manifest as the Glory or Presence (*Shekina*) or the Community (*knesset*) of Israel, or personified as *Matrona*, the divine spouse.

The upshot of these speculations was the conviction that each human being is imbued with all of these

qualities and therefore is a kind of universe in miniature, a microcosm of magical forces, the direction of which can be controlled by efficacious formulas, names, and symbols. The Messiah himself will be identified at his coming by his mysterious name and symbol.

The exciting implications which flowed from these considerations produced in central Europe an abundant crop of false messiahs who only disappointed the faithful. Since the middle of the sixteenth century, Kabbalism has had its chief center in Safed (Zefat) in northern Israel.

The Crusades and Expulsions

The Jews had by this time long since spread out into France, England, and the Rhineland, where they settled in little clusters, followed similar occupations, and remained true to their faith. Because their religious ceremonies were carried out in virtual seclusion and never came under the direct observation of the general public, they excited curiosity and suspicion. Many on the outside took the attitude that the Jews were a secret order of conspirators against the public welfare. They were charged with every form of malevolent purpose. The launching of the Crusades at the end of the eleventh century produced such excitement against "infidels" that an open butchery of the Jews began, starting in Germany, where wholesale massacres took place, and spreading to the rest of Europe. After the butchery ran its course, orders of expulsion followed. In Germany, one town after another drove the Jews out, at least in law. They were expelled from England in 1290, and after two centuries of periodic expulsion and restoration, in 1394 they were denied residence in France. In Spain, persecution of the Jews accompanied the expulsion of the Moors, and in 1492 all unconverted Jews were ordered driven out.

The *Sephardim* and the *Ashkenazim*

Fleeing in the only direction open to them, eastward, the Jews of Spain and southern Europe found refuge in Turkey, Palestine, and Syria (where they spoke Ladino, basically a Spanish dialect interspersed with Hebrew). These Jews of the Middle East have acquired the name *Sephardim*. Their tendency has been to develop on the base of the Torah and Talmud an intense mysticism and speculation, Kabbalistic in form. The Jews of northern areas went in large numbers to Poland and neighboring areas, where they brought the welcome arts of trade and money lending to culturally backward villages. They spoke a dialect compounded of German and Hebrew, called Yiddish. They have come to be named *Ashkenazim,* and account for more than 70 percent of today's Jews. Their orientation, on the whole, has been provided by the Talmud and its highly regulated way of life, although there also have been mystics among them (see p. 435).

The Ghettos

As for those who remained in Italy and the towns of Austria and Germany that had not totally excluded them, they were forced to live in segregated quarters called ghettos, usually located in the worst part of town. Laws restricted their land holding and barred them from many occupations. To add to their distress, in most places where the Catholic Church was supreme, there was enforcement of the thirteenth-century law forbidding Jews on pain of death to appear on the streets without the Jew badge—a colored patch of cloth sewn onto their clothing. This badge became a mark of shame. In many towns, high walls were built around the ghettos, and the Jews were locked in at night. To be seen abroad after dark often meant death, and always a fine.

The Medieval Festivals and Fasts

Meanwhile, the calendar of Jewish festivals and fasts had undergone development and reinterpretation. The ancient Palestinian and Babylonian liturgies, somewhat divergent to begin with, were further but not radically modified to meet the particular needs or preferences of the Jews of Spain, Italy, North Africa, Turkey, Persia, and central and western Europe, or to admit Spanish, Kabbalistic, and other devotional materials. Of great importance was the fact that the agricultural interests expressed in the ancient Hebrew rites and ceremonies were no longer in the forefront, and therefore the inherited forms had to be charged with historical and ethical meanings that would call

out the continued loyalty and devotion of the Jews in every sort of occupation and environment.

The chief festivals and fasts of the year were assigned the procedures, meanings, and dates (determined according to the lunar calendar) that have been standard from Talmudic days to the present. Since Jews throughout the world have used practically the same prayer book (originally set up by Saadiah ben Joseph, 882–942 C.E.), uniformity of ritual has marked Jewish worship through the centuries. Differences arose at times, like those between Sephardic and Ashkenazic rituals, but they have been minor. They had by now taken approximately the following forms, which are in use today.

Passover (Pesach)

In late March or during April, Passover (Pesach), "the anniversary of Israel's liberation from Egypt," initially a spring festival of thanksgiving for the birth of lambs and the sprouting of grain, was ritually associated with the idea of individual and group liberation and renewal, in all periods, beginning with the Exodus and continuing through history. As in the ancient period, nothing leavened was eaten for a full week (whence its other name "the Feast of Unleavened Bread"). The biblically prescribed eating of the paschal lamb had from the time of the great dispersion been set aside, and the chief event of Passover had become the Seder Feast, observed on the eve of the first (or the first and second) day, when the whole family assembled. A brief booklet or liturgy containing the Haggadah or Narrative was read throughout the ceremony. After drinking the first cup of wine, the male head of the family washed his hands and assumed the function of family priest. Parsley dipped in salt water was eaten by each participant in remembrance of the trials of captivity. At other intervals, each partook of further cups of wine, bitter herbs, roots, and unleavened bread. Accompanying these symbolic acts was the running account of the Haggadah, designed to retell the story of the Exodus and explain the purpose of the Passover rite itself—that is, its challenge ever to seek freedom from any bondage. Psalms were sung, and finally the evening meal was served. Afterward a door was opened, amid a recitation of psalms and lamentations, and Elijah, the hoped-for precursor of the Messiah, was invited to come in and drink of the Elijah Cup,

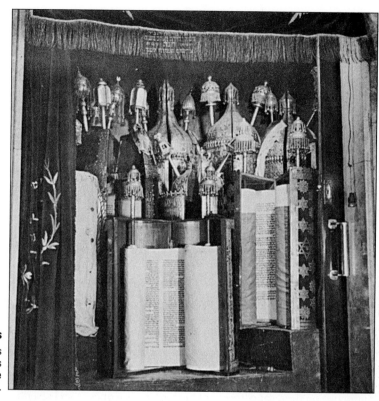

Torah Scrolls and Other Holy Objects
The opened Ark shows us the sacred scriptures that are read in the synagogue services. This photograph was taken in Tel Aviv, Israel, in the Ohel Mohed Sephardic Synagogue.

which had stood untouched on the table during the preceding rite. The service ended with a psalm of praise, a prayer, or the recitation of a grace. The solemnity then melted into general rejoicing in which the children present were encouraged to take a leading part.

For forty-nine days after the Seder Feast, except at the new moon or on the thirty-third day, no joyous occasions, including marriages, were allowed. Then on the fiftieth day came Shebhuoth—the Feast of Weeks (in the New Testament called Pentecost), a day of joy once set aside to commemorate the firstfruits of the spring wheat harvest, then modified to include thanksgiving for the giving of the Law at Sinai, which was held to have occurred at the same time of year.

Rosh Hashanah

The next great holiday came in September (or early October). It was Rosh Hashanah or New Year's Day.

This name took the place of the ancient biblical names, Day of Memorial and Day of Blowing the Trumpet (signalized by the sounding of the *shofar,* or ram's horn, a custom still solemnly observed as a means of summoning the Jew "to ponder over his deeds, remember his Creator, and go back to Him in penitence"). In recognition of the significance of the day, the Talmud called it the Day of Judgment. After it followed the Days of Repentance, and on the tenth day the solemn Day of Atonement (Yom Kippur), during which "repentance, prayer, and righteousness" were enjoined upon all the participants in the fast, who, as free agents, were urged to exert their wills to turn from wrongdoing and in true atonement for sin do God's will henceforth.

Succoth

Five days later came Succoth, the eight-day Feast of Booths or Tabernacles, basically a thanksgiving festival devoted to expression of gratitude for the autumnal fruits of vine and tree, and now associated with the thought of God's provident goodness in the days of Israel's wandering in the wilderness and during later times. In addition to the decoration of the synagogue with all sorts of fruits and flowers, a feature of the services was the ritualistic carrying in procession of four products of Palestine tied together, namely, a citron and a palm branch bound with branches of the myrtle and the willow. Those who could do so erected a booth or tabernacle in their courtyards or next to their homes and ate their meals there. (Some even slept there.)

The last day of the festival was the Simkhath Torah (Rejoicing Over the Torah), featuring the carrying of the scrolls from the Ark in procession around the synagogue.

Hanukkah and Purim

Two festivals not directly based on the ancient Mosaic tradition were Hanukkah in December and Purim in February or March. The former—the Feast of Lights—was celebrated for eight days, one light being lit in the synagogues and in every home on the first night, two on the second, three on the third, and so on, this being interpreted to commemorate the rededication of the Temple by Judas Maccabeus in 165 B.C.E. Purim, or the Feast of Lots, was associated with the Biblical Book of Esther and thus was made to celebrate the deliverance of the Jews from persecution through Esther's patriotic intervention. Gifts were exchanged within the family and sent to friends and to the poor, in the spirit of carnival. There was dancing and singing in the homes.

VII. JUDAISM IN THE MODERN WORLD

The Protestant Reformation was the product of many causes. Not least among the contributing factors was the return by the Reformers to the study of the Bible in the original Hebrew and Greek. So impressed was Martin Luther in his earlier years by his discovery of the close genetic relations of the Jewish and Christian faiths that he published in 1523 a pamphlet *Jesus Was Born a Jew,* in which he pleaded, "They (the Jews) are blood-relations of our Lord; and if it were proper to boast of flesh and blood, the Jews belong to Christ more than we.... Therefore it is my advice that we treat them kindly.... We must exercise not the law of the Pope, but that of Christian love, and show them a friendly spirit."[12] But Luther retraced in his own life the first three centuries of the Christian era. When he found the Jews solidly resistant to conversion, his anger slowly mounted, until in his later years he began to abuse them savagely. In a pamphlet *Concerning the Jews and Their Lies* (1542), he repeated in a passion of credulous rage all of the old rumors concerning the Jews—that they poisoned the wells of the Christians or murdered Christian children (presumably, as the current rumor had it, to get blood for the Passover). In his last sermons, he hinted that Jewish doctors knew and therefore practiced the art of poisoning their Christian patients. "If the Jews," he growled, "refuse to be converted, we ought not to suffer them or bear with them any longer!"[G3]

Luther was typical of his age in this. The Reformation brought no permanent improvement in the condition of the Jews of Europe. In fact, in the sixteenth and seventeenth centuries, their fortunes reached a very low point, as low as any in their history. Not only did they live in physical ghettos devised by their oppressors, but they themselves retired into mental ghettos of their own creation, which shut the world out—its science, art, and culture as well as its hostility and evil. Improvement in their lot came, but it came slowly.

Eastern Europe

In Eastern Europe, the Jews remained on the whole true to their heritage of ancient patterns of thought and life, until Soviet repression hampered their religious practices and Hitler's fanatic racism led to the killing of six million Jewish men, women, and children.

Not that the Jews of Eastern Europe ever had an easy time of it. In the seventeenth century, the Cossacks wreaked a terrible pogrom upon them, especially in Poland. These furious Russians rose in rebellion against their feudal lords and went on to slaughter five hundred thousand Jews. This and other pogroms have only confirmed eastern Jews in their unrelaxing grip upon every article of their inherited faith. But there were characteristic differences in the different areas. In Lithuania and White Russia, the emphasis has been on the intellectual study of the Talmud and the original Hebrew texts. In these regions, the Jews have been consistently antimystical; meticulous scholarship has been rated above emotional fervor. Their characteristic personality was the eighteenth-century scholar Elijah of Vilna, who became their ruling rabbi. He was an intellectual giant, at once a Hebrew grammarian, an astronomer, an author, and a critic of the mystical Hasidim (about to be described). In his honor, an academy rose to which students came from all over Europe during the nineteenth century to study the Talmud in the traditional manner of the Babylonian schools of over one thousand years earlier.

The Hasidim: Heirs of Kabbala Mysticism

South of the Pripet Marshes, in southern Poland and the Ukraine, eastern Talmudism took a warmly emotional and mystical turn that seemed to, but did not really, abandon the Talmudic point of view in its joyous espousal of the pantheistic slant of the Kabbala. Messianism ran riot for awhile, and more than one unstable soul, encouraged by the hopeful, ran a career among them as messiah, only to dash their hopes at last by some false step that brought ruin or disgrace. However, one notable religious personality emerged among them, Israel of Moldavia, affectionately renamed Baal Shem Tob, "the Master of the Good Name (of God)," a kindly itinerant faith healer of the eighteenth century, who scorned the Talmudists for studying the Law so narrowly that they had no time to think about God. Thinking about God meant to him realizing that God is everywhere—in nature, human life, and every human thought. Religion was feeling God in everything and praying joyously in the wholesome consciousness of God's indwelling. "All that I have achieved," he used to say, "I have achieved, not through study, but through prayer."G4 Reviving a name used in postexilic times two thousand years earlier, he called his followers, who were mostly common people, Hasidim, or "Pious Ones," hence, the movement initiated by him, Hasidism.

Central and Western Europe

In central and western Europe, the matter of chief import during the last two centuries has been the experience of slow but exhilarating liberation from civil disabilities, followed by what might be called "a return to the world." The justice of such a liberation was admitted by the leaders of the European Enlightenment during the eighteenth century and was made an actuality by the revolutionary movements in France and Germany in the eighteenth and nineteenth centuries.

The rationalism and skepticism of the eighteenth-century intellectuals in Europe, which tended to hold all religions up to mockery, led to a lowering of religious and class barriers in the centers of culture. It was thus that Moses Mendelssohn, one of the greatest of modern Jews, broke through the restrictions barring Jews in Berlin and reached the center of its intellectual life. While pursuing his studies there, he became the friend of Lessing, the literary lion of Berlin, and was accorded the signal honor of having the liberal drama, *Nathan the Wise,* Lessing's masterpiece, created around his personality. That the great Lessing should choose a humpbacked Jew as his intimate and enshrine him in a serious work of art was at first astounding, then thought provoking. Mendelssohn wrote German, not as the Jews spoke it, but as the Germans themselves desired to write it. A dialogue on immortality, which he composed on the Platonic model, was read throughout Europe. In the hope of doing a service to his fellow Jews, he translated the Pentateuch and other parts of the Hebrew canon into accomplished German prose (written out in Hebrew characters) and added a commentary of an advanced liberal character. But Mendelssohn's chief work was his earnest pleading on behalf of his people, that they might be freed from the ghettos to enter the stream of modern life on a basis approaching equality with other people. He did not live to see this happen, but in his own person he showed Europe how worthy the Jews were to be freed.

Climates of Liberalism and Reaction

The revolutionary changes wrought by the rise of democracy in America and Europe eventually gave the

Jews their full civil freedom. The American Revolution established the political principle that all persons are created free and equal. During the French Revolution, the Jews of France received the rights of full citizenship. Wherever Napoleon went, he abolished the ghettos and released the Jews into the world at large. After him reaction set in. All through Europe the Jews were faced with the choice: back to the ghettos or assimilation to European (nominally Christian) culture. Many, under the pressure, chose the latter alternative; others submitted to the reimposition of restrictions but entered avidly into all underground revolutionary movements looking toward the overthrow of reactionary governments, thereby providing conservatives and future reactionaries with the argument that Jews are by nature subversive. (Those Jews who had never tried to enter European life but clung to their ancient ways had, of course, no part in this.) Finally, the social upheavals of 1848 and after gave to Jews of western and central Europe some genuine equality with other people before the law. The universities opened their doors. From them Jewish doctors, politicians, dramatists, professors, and scientists poured forth into the communal life of Europe. In the vast processes of change accompanying the victory of political democracy, the Jews stood to benefit most.

Reform Judaism

Not least among the far-reaching consequences of the freeing of the Jews was the effect upon Judaism itself. The Jews found themselves in a world that was fast throwing aside the vestiges of the past that stood in the path of the liberal movement, and it was natural that they should consider doing the same among themselves. The educated Jew, engaged in the activities of the modern world, began to feel that Judaism should no longer stand aloof behind self-protective barriers but should resume its ancient progressive character. One result of this realization was the movement called Reform Judaism. It made a beginning in the German synagogues whose rabbis, imbued with the spirit of modernity, could persuade their congregations to go along with such innovations as simplifying and modernizing the synagogue worship. The Sabbath service was condensed, and most of it was translated into the vernacular. References to the coming of the Messiah, the resurrection of the dead on the last day, or to the

reestablishment of Jewish nationality and of the sacrificial rites of ancient Palestine were stricken out. Organ and choir were installed, and hymns in the vernacular were sung. The fundamental conviction of the movement was stated by Abraham Geiger, its leading exponent, in the words, "Judaism is not a finished tale; there is much in its present form that must be changed or abolished; it can assume a better and higher position in the world only if it will rejuvenate itself."[1] There were both moderates and radicals in the Reform movement. The latter shocked the Jewish world by declaring in 1843 that their principles were

> *First*, We recognize the possibility of unlimited development in the Mosaic religion. *Second*, The collection of controversies, dissertations, and prescriptions commonly designated by the name Talmud possesses for us no authority from either the doctrinal or practical standpoint. *Third*, A Messiah who is to lead back the Israelites to the land of Palestine is neither expected nor desired by us; we know no fatherland but that to which we belong by birth and citizenship.[2]

But after 1848 the conservatives fought the Reform movement to a halt, and even drove it into retreat. The movement then transferred itself largely to America. There it has moved away from such extreme pronouncements as the 1843 declaration toward positions, in regard to ritual, beliefs, and supportive attitudes toward Israel, resembling those of the modern Conservatives, whose principles are outlined below.

Orthodox Response

The Orthodox Jews earnestly fought Reform from its beginning because it denied the orthodox view that the divine revelation in the Torah is final and complete and awaits only its fulfillment. But the proposed changes in belief seemed less dangerous than the threatened changes in way of life. It is perhaps fair to say that the Orthodox Jew of today lays a heavier emphasis on practice than on belief. One need not believe exactly as the rabbis do, but one should adhere with absolute fidelity to the practical admonitions of the Torah, as they are interpreted and applied to daily life by the Talmud: the Sabbath lights should be lit and the Sabbath kept as of old; none of the ancient Jewish festivals should be skimped on or abbreviated; the dietary laws, with their prohibitions of certain foods and their regulations as to kosher meat and the nonmixing of milk and meat, requiring different sets of plates for serving meat and dairy products, should be observed.

It should be said, however, that most Orthodox Jews in America have moved away from extreme positions in these matters toward allowing more freedom in exceptional or difficult circumstances.

Zionism and the Establishment of the Nation of Israel

Neither Reform nor Orthodox Jews have had plain sailing, however. The racial theories of nineteenth-century extremists basing themselves on misinterpretations of Darwinian evolution, as well as the astonishing economic and professional successes of the Jews in the second half of the nineteenth century, stirred up a new wave of anti-Semitism in Europe, where pogroms in Russia, vindictive Jew baiting in Germany, and the famous Dreyfus case in France convinced many Jews that their only hope of permanent security lay in the reestablishment of a national home in Palestine. A landmark in the crystallization of this viewpoint was the book by Theodor Herzl, on *The Jewish State,* issued in 1896. Based on its premises, a Jewish movement called Zionism rose rapidly to international notice. From the start it gained wide support among Orthodox Jews and has by now won over most Reform Jews, who at first opposed it as being reactionary and impracticable. The Balfour Declaration during World War I, to the effect that the British government viewed with favor "the establishment in Palestine of a national home for the Jewish people" and would seek to "facilitate the achievement of this object," changed the political status of the movement overnight. Thousands of Jews went to Palestine during the next two decades, and under the protection of the British Mandate (the League of Nations' authorization of Great Britain to administer the territory of Palestine after World War I) laid the foundation of a Jewish national home.

The Holocaust

Savagery of dimensions unparalleled in human history marked the systematic extermination during World War II of six million Jews (one-third of all the Jews in the world). The Nazis spoke of their death camps as the Final Solution of the "Jewish Problem." Remembered today as the Holocaust, the campaign led to the coining of a new term, *genocide,* to refer to systematic efforts to annihilate a race.

Apart from the unspeakable trauma in the communal and personal lives of Jews, the Holocaust, together with all the other displacements of World War II, finally brought the United Nations Assembly to vote in 1947 for a partition of Palestine to make a Jewish state an internationally recognized actuality.

The new state called itself Israel. It maintained itself with vigor and success. But in establishing sovereignty over the territory assigned to it at the original partition, it frightened so many Arabs within its borders that they fled southward to the Gaza Strip, eastward into Jordan, northeast to Syria, and north to Lebanon, in which places they formed militant groups vowed to the reclamation of their "homeland" and consequently to the destruction of the state of Israel. Not all fled and became refugees; some remained in Israel and conformed with some uneasiness to Israeli law and practice, in moderate comfort. But the general intensity of Arab opposition did not abate.

Major Forms of Judaism as a Whole

Meanwhile, the need to find a median position between Orthodoxy and Reform resulted in the establishment of neo-Orthodoxy and Conservatism in Europe. These movements were founded in the nineteenth century and made some headway. In America, the Conservative movement experienced a rapid growth. With its own seminary in New York City, and its congregations organized into the United Synagogue of America, it has striven to find common ground between extreme Zionism and the position taken, say, by the Conference of Reform Jews meeting in Chicago in 1918 some six months after the Balfour Declaration, at which time (it reversed itself later) that body announced,

> We hold that Jewish people are and of right ought to be at home in all lands. Israel, like every other religious communion, has the right to live and assert its message in any part of the world. We are

opposed to the idea that Palestine should be considered *the homeland* of the Jews. Jews in America are part of the American nation. The ideal of the Jew is not the establishment of a Jewish state—not the reassertion of Jewish nationality which has long been outgrown. . . . The mission of the Jew is to witness to God all over the world.[J3]

The Conservatives see no inherent contradiction in witnessing to God all over the world and having a Jewish state in Palestine as a center from which Jewish culture may be disseminated among the nations. In effect, the Conservatives endorse the *religious* aspects of both right and left. In an essay surveying "Current Philosophies of Jewish Life," Milton Steinberg says,

> Conservative Judaism had its origin simultaneously in America and Western Europe among those Jews who either in theory or practice could no longer be orthodox, and who yet refused to accept what they regarded as the extreme nontraditionalism of Reform. . . . Two motifs dominate conservative Judaism. The first is the assertion of the centrality of religion in Jewish life. . . . The second theme, heavily underscored, is the sense of tradition, of history, of the continuity of Jewish life both through time and in space. It is this feeling of the organic unity of one Jewry with other Jewries which Professor Solomon Schechter, the leading figure in American Conservatism, caught in the phrase "Catholic Israel." This phrase is more than a description. It is intended to serve as a norm for the guidance of behavior. That shall be done by Jews, it implies, which is normal to Catholic Israel: . . . to hold on to the traditional, to sanction modifications slowly, reluctantly, and, if at all possible, within the framework of Jewish law.[K]

Meanwhile, a group a little left of center has arisen among the Conservatives, calling themselves the Reconstructionists. They advocate wide liberty in doctrine and "creative adjustment" to the conditions of modern life.

Recent Developments

There is some apprehensiveness among Jews of every persuasion that the increasing secularization of modern society is weakening the hold that religion has had in the past upon persons born into the Jewish tradition. (Catholics and Protestants have the same uneasiness.)

Concerned Jews point out that synagogue attendance has markedly declined in recent years and that intermarriage of Jews and Christians, once prohibited unless the Christian partner converted to Judaism, is now occurring with such frequency that observance of both the Jewish and Christian faiths in such instances is often abandoned. Estimates are that one-fifth to one-third of the marriages of Jews in America are to non-Jewish partners.

A small but significant countervailing trend has been the increase in conversions to Judaism among all three branches of American Judaism. Of approximately 6 million Americans who identify themselves as Jews, a 1996 report from the Council of Jewish Federations indicated 80 percent self-described as Reform or Conservative, 13 percent "just Jewish," and 7 percent Orthodox. In the same year Israel's 4.6 million Jews described themselves as two-thirds secular, one-third observant, and roughly 10 percent in ultraorthodox communities. (The latter make up 31 percent of the population of Jerusalem.)

Defining Jewish Identity

It is not surprising that in recent years the problem of defining Jewish identity has been the subject of intensified internal controversy. The debates have been worldwide, but they have been precipitated mainly by diversity of practice on the American scene. The related issues have to do with ordaining women as rabbis, the validity of procedures in regard to divorce and conversion, and redefining lineal descent.

Conservative and Reform congregations differ from Orthodox ones in giving full participation to women, including ordination. Most Conservative rabbis agree with the Orthodox that marriages can only be ended by a *get* (a bill of divorcement) from a rabbinic court. When a get is not obtained, the lineal legitimacy of the children of a subsequent marriage is in question. (To protect the legitimacy of children born to improperly

The Wannsee Conference
On January 20, 1942, Nazi leaders from all over Europe convened in Wannsee near Berlin to pool their information about the number of Jews in their territories and to set quotas for the exterminations that would be what they called the "Final Solution" to "the Jewish problem." (Source: Martin Gilbert, *The Holocaust: A Record of the Distinction of Jewish Life in Europe During the Dark Years of Nazi Rule,* Hill & Wang), Farrar, Straus, & Giroux, 1978, p. 159. © Martin Gilbert. Reprinted with permission.)

The number of Jews mentioned at the Wannsee Conference, country by country and area by area, for eventual deportation, and subsequent death. More than 14 million people were thus marked out for death.

One of the macabre features of the numerical list of the Jews submitted to the Wannsee Conference was the fact that no figure was given for the Jews of Estonia, merely a brief note that Estonia was 'Free of Jews'. This was true; the 1,000 Estonian Jews who had come under German rule in October 1941 had all been murdered during the three months before the Wannsee Conference.

NORWAY 1,300

ESTONIA "Free of Jews"

DENMARK 5,600

USSR 5 million

LATVIA 3,500

HOLLAND 160,800

BIALYSTOK DISTRICT 400,000

LITHUANIA 34,000

BELGIUM 43,000

WHITE RUSSIA 446,484

WANNSEE

CHELMNO

GERMANY 131,800 BERLIN

GENERAL GOVERNMENT 2,284,000

EASTERN TERRITORIES 420,000

FRANCE OCCUPIED ZONE 165,000

BOHEMIA AND MORAVIA 74,200

88,000

SLOVAKIA

UKRAINE 2,994,684

AUSTRIA

HUNGARY 742,800

FRANCE UNOCCUPIED ZONE 700,000

43,700

10,000

CROATIA 40,000

SERBIA

RUMANIA 342,000

ITALY 58,000

BULGARIA

ALBANIA 200

0 miles 200
0 km 300

48,000

GREECE 69,600

In December 1941, a month *before* the Wannsee Conference, the first Nazi extermination camp had already come into operation, at Chelmno, responsible for the mass-murder of Jews, Gypsies, and Soviet prisoners-of-war. After passing through corridors marked 'To the showers' and 'To the doctor', the victims were forced into a large truck which was in fact a gas-chamber, where they were killed within a few minutes. By the end of 1944 more than 360,000 Jews had been murdered in Chelmno alone.

The Wannsee Conference also specified the number of Jews in *unconquered* countries for eventual destruction, including 330,000 from Britain, 18,000 from Switzerland, 6,000 from Spain and 4,000 from Ireland.

German Official Plans for the "Final Solution," 20 January 1942

Praying at the Western Wall
Sometimes prayers are written on slips of paper and inserted into crevices in the wall. The area next to it is also a coveted site for Bar-Mitzvah coming-of-age ceremonies. It is a matter of concern to the non-orthodox that present rules exclude females from the area. (©Photograph by Erich Lessing/Art Resource.)

divorced women, rabbis sometimes find grounds to annul the previous marriage.)

Conservative and Reform rabbis are concerned that conversions, and some marriages, under their auspices, are not recognized by the Orthodox, but a 1991 decision by the Supreme Court of Israel held that the government must register such persons as Jews.

A sharp division concerns patrilineal descent. Concerned about growing numbers of interfaith marriages, the Union of American Hebrew Congregations (Reform Judaism) decided to recognize the children of Jewish fathers as Jews by lineal descent. Because of the long history of recognizing only the children of Jewish mothers, the decision widened the gulf between Reform and Orthodox Jews and increased some internal strains for Conservatives. Some Conservative congregations would like to rescind ordination of women rabbis; others would like to follow the Reform position on patrilineage.

A 1993 Guttman institute poll in Israel found that 64 to 79 percent (depending on wording) agreed that all denominations should have equal status. But conflict over religious issues escalated, and in 1996 the assassination of Prime Minister Rabin by a right-wing extremist further exacerbated feelings. The subsequent narrow election of Prime Minister Netanyahu was made possible only by the support of small ultraconservative minority parties. The Netanyahu era meant a drastic slowing of the peace process, but that in itself was less divisive for religion than the sheer fact that ultraconservative factions now had enormous leverage in the government. This development was the culmination of a process whereby Orthodox rabbis (who had remained aloof from the Jewish state in 1948) gradually switched to fervent participation with the aim of using the secular political process as a means of moving toward a religious state. Large families among the Orthodox and intensive community action produced advantages challenged only feebly by conversions to Judaism under non-Orthodox auspices. Yet the power of the ultraconservatives went further in legislation requiring all conversions and divorces to be approved by Orthodox authorities. Although it applied only to conversions within Israel, the law implied at the very least a loss of dignity for Reform and Conservative Jews in the rest of the world, and in Jerusalem putting up with public shouting that they were "not Jews at all."

Cohesive Forces

Major events in the recent past furnish the focus for renewed pride, loyalty, and awareness of the need for unity among Jews. There is common cause in keeping the Holocaust before the conscience of the world. The right to emigrate from segments of the former Soviet Union is a reality for more and more individuals, and there is symbolic significance in the movement of some eastern European states to rescind their 1975 votes for a United Nations resolution equating Zionism and racism.

The American Anti-Defamation League of B'nai' B'rith has reported that anti-Semitic incidents, which peaked in the early nineties, have declined since 1994 by percentages ranging from 10 percent to 20 percent in North America and in Europe. Nevertheless, the persistent recrudescence of anti-Semitism all around the globe has required constant vigilance and solidarity.

Generally speaking, continuing Arab-Israeli confrontations reinforce the sense of religious identity in the worldwide community, but the diverging political interests of Israelis and Jews elsewhere, especially in North America, hold a potential for escalating dissension and fragmentation.

GLOSSARY

Akiba ben Joseph (*ca.* 40–135 C.E.) founder of a rabbinic school and a specialist in oral law (Halakah), he perfected the midrash style for exposition of the implied meanings in Scripture

Ashkenazim West-, Central-, or East-European Jews as contrasted with Sephardim

Bar Kochba "son of the star"—a messianic appellation—leader of the "Second Rebellion," 132–135 C.E., against Hadrian

Essenes an ascetic Jewish sect, 2nd c. B.C.E. to 3rd c. C.E.

Gemara "completion," the secondary portion of the Talmud, consisting of Haggadah and some Halakah not included in the Mishnah

Haggadah (*'Aggadah*) "narrative," informal, nonjuristic oral tradition associated with Talmudic learning; sometimes a specific reference to the narrative of the Exodus used in the Seder

Halakah the formal, juridic portion of Talmudic tradition, or the written law together with oral commentary

Hasidim "pious ones," a sect founded in the 3rd c. B.C.E. to promote ritual purity and resist Hellenistic influences; also a sect of mystics founded in the 18th c. to resist rationalism

Kabbala a system of speculative theology, occult symbolism, and mystical practice prevalent in Europe and the Middle East from the 13th c. onward; less technically, all of Jewish and Christian esoteric doctrine

Karaites "readers," a reactionary "back-to-the-written-law" movement in 8th–9th c. Judaism, rejecting Talmudic rabbinism and oral tradition

Maccabees heroes of a successful rebellion against Hellenistic Seleucid rule in 165 B.C.E., their dynasty, the Hasmoneans, headed an independent Jewish state until the Romans came in 63 B.C.E.

Maimonides (Moses ben Maimon, 1135–1204) Spanish-born philosopher and physician in Cairo, a widely respected interpreter of Judaism for his day in rational terms

Midrash "commentary," an exposition of a passage of scripture, either halakic or haggadic

Mishnah the first section of the Talmud, oral interpretations collected up to about 200 C.E.

Passover (*Pesach*) an eight-day festival commemorating the deliverance of the Jews from captivity in Egypt

Pentateuch the first five books of the Bible

Pharisees a rabbinic party in Hellenistic and Roman times, adherents of comprehensive application of Jewish law. In contrast to the Sadducees, they accepted oral tradition and new ideas such as resurrection

Rosh Hashanah "beginning of the year," holy day on the first of Tishri, usually in September or October

Sadducees a party in Judaism active from the 2nd c. B.C.E. through the 1st c. C.E. They rejected recent oral tradition and reduced Judaism to matters specifically treated in written law

Seder a ritual meal commemorating the escape from captivity in Egypt, celebrated usually in the home on the first or second day of Passover

Sephardim Jews who emigrated from Spain, principally to Mediterranean and Middle Eastern areas—as distinguished from Ashkenazim

Septuagint a Greek version of the Hebrew Scriptures, dating from the 3rd c. B.C.E.

Succoth "booths," a harvest festival beginning on the eve of the 15th day of Tishri

Talmud the vast collection of ancient rabbinic oral tradition assembled as *Mishnah* and *Gemara*

Yom Kippur the Day of Atonement, observed from the eve of the 9th of Tishri to the eve of the 10th, a time for confession of sins, repentance, and reconciliation with God and fellow human beings

Zealots a sect dedicated to rebellion and the overthrow of Roman rule in 1st c. Palestine

Zionism a movement dedicated to the establishment of a Jewish national homeland—and subsequently to promoting the welfare of the state of Israel

CHAPTER 15

Christianity in Its Opening Phase

The Words and Work of Jesus in Apostolic Perspective

Christianity has sprung from the faith that in its founder God was made manifest in the flesh and dwelt among humankind. Other religions have developed a conception of incarnation, but none has given it such centrality. In the belief that Jesus is the clearest portrayal of the character of God, all the rest of Christian doctrine is implied.

Sources

It is not easy to tell the story briefly and clearly. The first Christian century has had more books written about it than any other comparable period of history. The chief sources bearing on its history are the Gospels and Epistles of the New Testament, and these—again we must make a comparative statement—have been more thoroughly searched by inquiring minds than any other books ever written. Historical criticism has been particularly busy with them during the last hundred years and has reached the verdict that in the New Testament the early Christian religion *about* Jesus has overlaid and modified the record of the religion *of* Jesus himself, that is, his own faith, but there is no unanimity about the degree of modification. It is known that Jesus himself did not write down his teachings but relied upon his disciples to go about preaching what he taught. It is generally assumed by historians that after his death some of them did write down his sayings, with occasional notes of the historical setting, before they should be forgotten, and thus that a document, or group of documents, came into being that scholars call "Q" (from the German word *Quelle,* or "source"). It is generally considered that "Q" was colored by the prepossessions of the early Christians and that they added amplifications that went beyond his own words. It is probable that such a collection of sayings became primary source material for the compilers of Matthew and Luke. These compilers used a great deal of other material also, both oral and written; for example they drew much of their material from Mark, already existent (65–70 C.E.), and they made use of sources unique to

WESTERN NAMES: Early Christianity
    New Testament Christianity

TIME: Origin to 150 C.E.

NAMES USED BY ADHERENTS: The Way, the People of God (*ekklesia tou theou*)

SACRED TRADITION: Scriptures of Judaism, letters, gospel materials and oral tradition from apostles

REFERENCES TO THE DEITY: God, the Father, the Father of the Lord Jesus

COMPONENT GROUPS: Palestinians, mostly Jewish in heritage, but of varying degrees of strictness in regard to the Law

    Gentiles and Jews of the *diaspora* strongly influenced by Greco-Roman (Hellenistic) culture

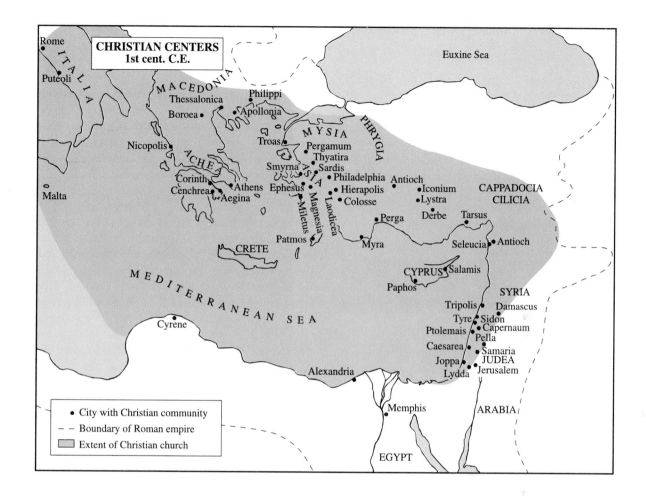

CHRISTIAN CENTERS 1st cent. C.E.

- City with Christian community
- - - Boundary of Roman empire
- Extent of Christian church

each of them: "M" in the case of Matthew, and "L" in the case of Luke. The Gospel of John was not written until the end of the century and then largely from concern with the theological implications of Jesus' life and death.

Through all of these records runs the often unseen division between what is from Jesus himself and what is from the Apostolic Age. But when scholars are asked to separate the material that authentically reveals the historical Jesus from the material that reflects the growing Christology of the early Christians, they vary widely in their interpretations. At certain points, each student is thrown back, after careful study, upon personal judgment, or even intuitive feeling in deciding what is from the historical Jesus and what is from the early church—or, indeed, whether it is impor-

tant, or even possible, to make such a distinction. Because there is no source material from "objective observers," every life of Jesus must be reconstructed from events as seen through a lens of faith, and, of course, modern interpreters look through lenses ground to their own value prescriptions.

Granting this, however, does not release conscientious scholars from the obligation to hold all views tentatively, as being open to change if a scholarly consensus concerning a particular saying or event calls for revision of previous opinions. One such consensus has emerged in this century following the appearance in 1910 of Albert Schweitzer's *The Quest of the Historical Jesus*. There has been increasingly wide agreement that Jesus' eschatological conviction of the imminent "end of the age" had central importance in impelling him

443

toward a prophetic mission. It is further held that when after his time these expectations were not fulfilled and his followers attempted to recall his life and teachings, they did this confusedly; the chronological structure of the Gospels and their assignment of events to particular geographical locations were to a large degree editorial and therefore not certain. But scholars continue to seek for a broader consensus regarding the most authentic interpretation of Jesus' faith, intentions, and teachings.

I. THE WORLD INTO WHICH JESUS CAME

That Jesus was born into a part of the world that had only recently been brought under Roman dominion is of some significance, to begin with. One of the last acquisitions of Roman arms was Palestine. The Jews, as we have seen in chapters 13 and 14, had been subjected over and over to a foreign yoke, yet the Roman rule came to seem more intolerable than any. This was due in large part to the fact that the Romans were an aloof, administrative group. They had in particular a purely regulatory feeling concerning local populations; there was no fellow feeling at all. It had been different with the Greeks, who were an imaginative and responsive people, able to enter into the spirit of a locality and weigh its ideas as though they deserved respect. But the Jews and the Romans were poles apart. There was so little of seeing eye to eye that they were enigmas to each other and gave up trying to arrive at an understanding.

The Political Divisions of Palestine in Jesus' Time

About the time of Jesus' birth, Herod the Great died. Three of Herod's sons had escaped the fatal consequences of exciting his suspicion, and so survived. In his will he divided Palestine among them. While that unhappy country trembled on the brink of insurrection, the three sons hurried to Rome to have their bequests confirmed. Augustus Caesar assigned Judea, Samaria, and Idumea to Archelaus, Galilee and Perea to Herod Antipas, and the region northeast of the Lake of Galilee to Philip. Archelaus was, however, not given outright control of his district, as the other two sons were. The caution of Augustus proved well founded, for after nine years of incompetence and brutality, Archelaus was accused before the emperor on a number of serious charges and banished to Gaul. His place was taken by a Roman official called a procurator, who was made responsible to the governor of Syria.

Procurator followed procurator in regular succession. They ruled Judea from Caesarea, on the coast northwest of Jerusalem. Few of them had any sense of the historic forces at work beneath the surface of the Jewish scene. Some of them were rapacious and unscrupulous men, anxious only to make enough money to retire in comfort to Rome. Though they allowed the Jews as much civil and religious liberty as political considerations (that is, Roman imperialism) permitted, they insisted on a kind of remote control over the Jewish religion. For example, they kept the robes of the high priest stored in the Tower of Antonia and released them only for the ceremonies in which they were worn. This meant that they could control the appointment of the high priest by signifying to whom they would be pleased to release the robes. They also from time to time tried to introduce into Jerusalem battle standards and shields displaying the image of Caesar as emperor-god, but the Jews angrily protested each time, and the procurators for the sake of preserving the peace did not insist.

Under these conditions, Judea was scarcely happy. Indeed, perplexed almost to despair by the difficulties besetting them, religious and political parties contended with each other—Pharisees with Sadducees, and Zealots and Herodians with the rest. (See again pp. 418–421.)

The Situation in Galilee

In Galilee, on the other hand, the irritation was less pervasive. There Herod Antipas ruled over a very mixed population. The Jews were barely in the majority. There were many Greek-speaking citizens, as well as Phoenicians from the coast and Syrians from interior regions to the north. In some districts the Jews were outnumbered by these Gentiles. Furthermore, across the Jordan and not under Herod's authority directly, though within the borders of Perea, there were ten self-governing towns (the Decapolis, the "tenfold city"), leagued together on the pattern of Hellenic city-states. These were the Palestinian expression of Alexander the Great's dream of a new international order. Their presence helps explain why Herod Antipas pursued a policy of internationalism. He hoped that a patient infusion of world culture into his area would unify his people under his rule. But the Galilean Jews were more than a little disturbed when he began to make their key towns over into Greco-Roman cities. One of these cultural ventures was the rebuilding of the largest city in Galilee, Sepphoris. This city was, however, outshone in magnificence, if not in size, by the new town of Tiberias on the western shore of the Lake of Galilee, a city provided with a colonnaded forum and named by Herod after the reigning Roman emperor. It is a mark of Antipas' eagerness to please the Romans that he named his new capital Tiberias after the reigning emperor, and it is a mark of his insensitivity that he built it over an old Jewish burial ground. Scrupulous Jews would not enter it.

Many of the Jews in Galilee might have reconciled themselves to all this, and even welcomed it, if they had not been obliged to foot the bill. It had formerly seemed onerous enough to have to pay the direct, personal tax for administrative expenses, for only part of it went to Herod Antipas, the rest to faraway Rome. Now they were obliged to pay additional taxes in the form of burdensome customs duties, not only on goods imported into or exported from the region, but also on those shipped from city to city and from farm to market. Tolls were collected, too, at bridges and harbors. And there was a salt tax—always irritating anywhere. The Jews thus found themselves contributing to the expenses of their own subjection. So, when in 6 C.E. Quirinius, the governor of Syria, ordered a census taken of the inhabitants of Palestine, in order that an even more thorough form of tax assessment might be worked out, there were immediate hostile repercussions among the people. Jesus may have been twelve or more years old at that time and must have been keenly aware of the general excitement of the Galilean Jews, which boiled up swiftly into insurrection.

A Zealot Rebellion: Judas the Galilean

A certain Judas the Galilean, assisted by a Pharisee named Zaddok, organized the Zealot party by calling around him the Galilean hotheads and forming a rebel army that stood ready to fight on the principle, "No God but Yahweh, no tax but to the Temple, no friend but the Zealot." Josephus, a historian of their time, writes of the Zealots as follows:

> These men agree in all other things with the Pharisaic notions; but they have an inviolable attachment to liberty, and say that *God* is to be their only Lord and Master. They also do not mind dying any death, nor indeed do they heed the deaths of their relations and friends, nor could the fear of death make them call any man their master. And . . . I fear that what I have said does not adequately express the determination that they show when they undergo pain.[A]

The fanaticism of the Zealots was due in some measure to the fact that many of them had a family history of death by violence for rebellion. Judas the Galilean's father was killed fifty-two years earlier while engaged in insurrection.

Judas and his followers surprised the city of Sepphoris, seized the armory, provided themselves with its store of weapons, and made the city their headquarters. So serious did the revolt become that the Roman general Varus had to bring up two Roman legions to suppress it. He burned and destroyed Sepphoris and crucified several thousand Zealots in a bloody attempt to stamp the movement out, but its secret spread continued. Jesus was faced with the realities created by it all his life, for one at least, if not two, of the Twelve Apostles (Simon the Zealot and possibly Judas Iscariot) had been affiliated with the Zealot party, and he himself was crucified finally, when the crowd in Pilate's courtyard reportedly shouted to have Barabbas, known to them as a Zealot, released to them instead of himself.

Celibate Communities: The Essenes

Not all of the Jews of Galilee supported the Zealot cause. The Essenes were opposed to violence on principle. They were even opposed to animal sacrifices—a radical departure for that day. Fairly numerous in Galilee, they paid little attention to the strife of the times but waited patiently for the Lord's Anointed One, the Messiah. Meanwhile, they lived by strict rules in celibate communities, holding their possessions in common, keeping the Sabbath day, laboring in their fields during the other days of the week, and devoting themselves to fasting, prayer, and frequent ceremonial ablutions, much as the Dead Sea community did. (See again p. 421.)

Prudent Organization: The Pharisees

The Pharisees, on their part, held themselves from violence largely out of considerations of prudence. They were by far the largest party in Galilee and were led by scribes and rabbis whose consciousness of mission was heightened by systematic training. The Jewish parties had all caught the concept of organization from the Greeks and Romans and knew their hopes of survival depended on unified leadership. Many attended schools the Pharisees maintained—academies, we might call them, for in attitude and method they resembled the academies of Greece. The largest of these schools was in Jerusalem and boasted great teachers like Shammai and Hillel. Caught, all of them, in a world of rapid and unpredictable change, the Pharisees made it their principle to live as nearly as conditions permitted according to their traditions. They felt that the only way to hasten the coming of the Messiah, and in the meantime save Judaism in their perverse and wicked generation from extinction, was to be scrupulous in religious practices that linked tradition with every detail of daily living. This meant that they endeavored to keep every one of the Sabbath laws, to fulfill to the letter the regulations for keeping the Jewish festivals, to tithe, to repeat the Shema constantly, to be very particular about ceremonial purity, correct treatment of "holy things," and dietary rules, to have no legal dealings with anyone in the civil courts (because Jews should have recourse only to the judicial proceedings set up by their own tribunal, the Sanhedrin), and so on. Though the time was not long distant when they would be obliged to alter many of their old rites and introduce others that would be new, they were at this time critical of all those who did not keep the Law as they interpreted it.

Conservatism: The Sadducees

The Sadducees, by comparison, were less influential in Galilee, but even more conservative. They were certain that the old cultus and Torah were unalterable, whereas the Pharisees, after much heart searching, were willing with changed circumstances to alter old customs, if that meant preserving Jewish communities against religious dissolution. But Sadducees and Pharisees alike opposed looseness, opportunism, and radicalism.

Some of the common people, perhaps most of them, were tolerant and easygoing in these things, readily influenced by "the world," and only loosely and vaguely religious. Many, on the other hand, considered themselves strict Jews, attended the services of the synagogues, revered the Law and the Prophets, kept the Jewish festivals and fasts, and went annually to the Temple in Jerusalem at Passover. This was not enough, the sterner Pharisees held. If they did not keep themselves free from ceremonial defilement, observe the strict dietary rules, tithe, wash their hands before meals, ceremonially cleanse their persons, clothes, cups, jugs, basins, and all the food bought in the markets, and do no work on the Sabbath day, they were impure and could not be considered pious. Many of the devout among the common people, however, were sure that one could be deeply devotional, truly religious, without being narrowly legalistic in obeying "the tradition of the elders." It was to this group that the parents of Jesus seem to have belonged.

II. THE LIFE OF JESUS: THE FIRST PHASE

Birth

The date of the birth of Jesus cannot be determined precisely. It was not until the middle of the sixth century C.E. that Christians began to reckon time as before and after the birth of Christ. Information available today shows that the monks who did the calculating did not set the year early enough. It should be added that we possess no scriptural data for fixing the month and day of the birth. Both the Roman date of December 25 and the Armenian date of January 6 are of later origin and reflect the needs and decisions of post–New Testament times. New Testament references relevant to the birth date follow.

Matthew says (2:1) that Jesus was born "in the days of Herod." Since Herod died in 4 B.C.E., this would suggest that Jesus' birth occurred earlier than the calendric year 1. Luke says (3:1–2, 23) that John the Baptist began preaching in the fifteenth year of the Emperor Tiberius (26 or 27 C.E.), and that Jesus was baptized by him shortly afterward and was "about thirty years old" when he began his own ministry. When we work back in time, we are obliged to date Jesus' birth four to six years B.C.E. In another place, Luke says (2:1–4) that Jesus was born during a census ordered by Augustus Caesar when Quirinius was governor of Syria (6–9 C.E.). This introduces a wide discrepancy. However, if we accept the evidence that Quirinius was in the service of the legate to Syria some time before his governorship, we can suppose, as some scholars do (but without clear evidence), that Luke was recalling a time when Quirinius was dispatched to Judea to conduct a census some ten or twelve years prior to his governorship.

Confidence in the fulfillment of Old Testament prophecies allowed early Christian writers to fill in gaps in their information. They had no doubt that events took place in accordance with the prophecies as they understood them. Matthew, for example, frequently asserts that things took place "in order that prophecy might be fulfilled." Other details of the birth narratives were no doubt inspired by a literalizing of the post–resurrection conviction that the messianic title "Son of God" applied to Jesus.

As to the place of Jesus' birth, we again face uncertainty. Matthew and Luke assert that Jesus was born in Bethlehem, "the city of David" (though their explanations of the circumstances are quite different). It is likely that they were confident of that conclusion on the basis of a messianic prophecy. Greater certainty attaches to an assertion in which all of the evangelists agree, that the home of the family was in Nazareth of Galilee. It was there that Joseph pursued the trade of carpenter, and as far as we know, up to his thirtieth year, all but a few weeks of Jesus' life were spent there.

Childhood and Youth

Of Jesus' childhood and youth we know little directly. The internal evidence of the Gospels leads us to assume—but it is an undocumented assumption—that his parents belonged to the common people, the 'Am ha'aretz, but were quietly religious, for Luke says that they took the time, "every year," to go to Jerusalem to observe Passover. Jesus came to know the Torah and the Prophets with enough familiarity to be able to quote them freely. It may be that he attended the local synagogue school. Somehow he came to know enough of the prophetic tradition to develop a distrust of whatever literalism and inelasticity the scribes and Pharisees were given to. As to his trade, he was apparently trained to be a carpenter. We know from the Gospels that he grew up in a large family. According to Mark (6:3), there were at least six other children: James, Joses, Jude, and Simon, as well as "sisters." (In support of the doctrine of the perpetual virginity of Mary, Roman Catholic tradition holds that the statement in Mark 6:3 should be understood as referring to cousins, possibly children of Mary's presumed sister, Mary Cleophas, or perhaps to children of Joseph by an earlier marriage.) Luke gives us one revealing glimpse into his religious experience as a child. The story of the boy Jesus in the Temple (Luke 2:41–52) is witness above all to the fact that he was capable of sustained interest in religious matters, an absorption so deep that he did not think of the effect his absence must be having upon his relatives and friends.

The next eighteen years of Jesus' life often are called the silent years, for we have no direct evidence about what took place during them. It has been traditionally assumed, from the fact that Joseph drops out of the story completely, that he died in this interval, and that Jesus, as the oldest son, took

> "And on the Sabbath he began to teach in the synagogue; and many who heard him were astonished, saying, 'Where did this man get all this? . . . Is not this the carpenter, the son of Mary and brother of James and Joses and Judas and Simon, and are not his sisters here with us?' And they took offense at him."
>
> —Mark 6:2–3

over the management of the carpenter business, his brothers helping him.

Baptism and Temptation

When he was about thirty years old, Jesus was drawn to John the Baptist, a desert prophet, and experienced a call to a prophetic mission of his own.

John the Baptist had appeared on the banks of the Jordan with an urgent message, "Repent! for the Kingdom of Heaven is coming!" He had emerged from the desert region beyond the Jordan, where he had been meditating on what appeared to him the crisis of the hour. We are told by the Gospels that he "wore clothing made of hair cloth, and had a leather belt around his waist and he lived on dried locusts and wild honey"[B1]— that is, he had assumed the life of a solitary ascetic. His periods of lonely brooding increased his feeling that the end of the present age was at hand; the Messiah who should judge the world was about to appear and bring in the day of wrath that the repentant alone would be able to face. So near did this day seem to him that he is reported to have used the vivid figure, "The axe is already lying at the roots of the trees." Another startling image of his was drawn from the threshing floor; he said the Messiah had already taken up the winnowing fork in his hand and would "clean up his threshing-floor, and store his wheat in his barn," but would "burn up the chaff with inextinguishable fire."[B2] He was not alone in so believing. The Essenes had a similar sense of the imminence of the end, but John did not join them. He had too much of the feeling of social responsibility to retire into watchful waiting. He therefore left the desert and began a career of fiery preaching, in order to warn the unwary. He succeeded in drawing people from all over Palestine to hear him. When these listeners confessed their sins and expressed repentance, immersion in the waters of the Jordan signified the washing away of their sins. He became known as the Baptist. He was more, however, than a ceremonialist. His instructions to his converts were on an ethical plane of highest urgency. In the interim before the coming of the Messiah, they were to practice the strictest individual and social right-eousness. The crowds would ask him, "What ought we to do?" He answered, "The man who has two shirts must share with the man who has none, and the man who has food must do the same."[B3] He told tax collec-tors not to collect more than they were authorized to, and soldiers not to extort money or make false charges against people, but to be satisfied with their pay. Though he roused the anger of Herod Antipas by con-demning his illegal marriage with Herodias, his brother's wife, and was arrested and finally executed while in prison, he had raised a loyal following that became self-propagating. St. Paul found a circle of his followers in Ephesus thirty years later.

It was natural that Jesus should be attracted. In the first chapter of Mark, the story is given barely and briefly.

> It was in those days that Jesus came from Nazareth in Galilee, and was baptized by John in the Jordan. And just as he was coming up out of the water he saw the heavens torn open and the Spirit coming down like a dove to enter into him, and out of the heavens came a voice:
> "You are my Son, my Beloved! You are my Chosen!"[B4]

This experience must have been profoundly mov-ing. For Mark (who makes no reference to Jesus' birth or to his life up to this point), the baptismal experience is the initial event of the revelation of God in Jesus.

It is significant that Jesus at once retired into the wilderness beyond Jordan to think through the course that he must now undertake. In the Christian tradi-tion, this time of meditation and decision is described as a period of forty days during which Satan tried to tempt him. As told by Matthew and Luke, the tempta-tion had three phases. Behind the imagery used we may see the elements of very real issues. Should he concentrate on meeting economic ("bread") needs? No, humanity needs more than that. Should he use spectacular methods that might attract attention but put him in jeopardy? No, he must not force God's hand, must not put God's choice of him to trial. Should he seek political power as a precondition of redeeming Israel? No, that would be indeed compro-mising with Satan.

The Beginning of the Galilean Ministry

About the time of John's arrest, Jesus crossed the Jor-dan and made his way to Galilee, "proclaiming," says

Mark, "the good news from God, saying, 'The time has come and the reign of God is near; repent, and believe this good news!'" His tone was urgent, and he produced such conviction about himself and is message that he was immediately followed by four disciples—Simon Peter and his brother Andrew, James and his brother John, both sons of Zebedee—all fishermen who dropped their nets and followed him. The Lake of Galilee was then surrounded by thriving towns—Tiberias, Capernaum, Chorazin, and Bethsaida. Jesus began his ministry among them, choosing Capernaum as his headquarters, perhaps because Simon Peter's home was there. At first he spoke in the synagogues, and when the crowds grew too large for that, he preached in the marketplaces and open fields.

The Events of One Day

The first chapter of Mark contains a full description of what happened on Jesus' first Sabbath day in Capernaum. It will serve our purpose well to analyze it at some length as a typical day in the early ministry of Jesus. First of all, "he went to the synagogue and taught." Probably there was more than one synagogue in Capernaum, and he went to the one to which he was invited. The synagogues were controlled, in matters of doctrine and polity, by the scribes and Pharisees, but the local administration was in the hands of a council of elders, one of whom was elected the "ruler of the synagogue" and had charge of the religious services. He would be in a position to invite Jesus to speak in the synagogue. Another officer, the *chazzan,* or attendant, was the synagogue's librarian, having in his care the rolls of the scriptures which were in the "Ark"; he was also the caretaker of the building, and if a person with scribal training, the teacher of the synagogue school.

In the synagogues scripture readings were recited, first in Hebrew, then in Aramaic. After that the ruler himself, or a person chosen by him, addressed the congregation through "teaching."

Such was the setting of Jesus' first important utterance in Capernaum. When he began speaking, we are told, his audience was amazed at his teaching, for he spoke "like one who had authority," that is, with the force and confidence of one called by God to an urgent mission and so with great freedom of interpretation

and from the fullness of his heart, not dryly "like the scribes." Whereupon a startling thing occurred. A man in the audience who believed he had a devil in him that had caused his abnormal physical and mental condition—the universally accepted explanation of certain ailments in that day—suddenly and hopefully interrupted the preacher.

> "What do you want of us, Jesus, you Nazarene? Have you come to destroy us? I know who you are, you are God's Holy One!"
>
> Jesus reproved him, and said, "Silence! Get out of him!"
>
> The foul spirit convulsed the man and gave a loud cry and went out of him.

It should be kept in mind in judging the situation that Jesus had no reason to question the diagnosis of puzzling ailments that was universal in his time, that is, that they were caused by an indwelling demonic power entering the person from elsewhere. His audience certainly had no doubt. We read further,

> And they were all so amazed that they discussed it with one another, and said,
>
> "What does this mean? It is a new teaching! He gives orders with authority even to the foul spirits, and they obey him!"
>
> And his fame immediately spread in all directions. . . .

After the synagogue service, the story continues, Jesus went with his disciples to the home of Simon Peter, where Simon's mother-in-law was in bed, sick with a fever. Jesus went up to her, and grasping her hand, made her rise. "And the fever left her, and she waited on them." Then followed one of the crucial episodes of Jesus' early ministry.

> In the evening, after sunset, they brought to him all who were sick or possessed by demons, and the whole town was gathered at the door. And he cured many. . . .

The first half of Mark's gospel pictures Jesus as resistant to open proclamation of a messianic role. When the demon possessed, sensing the extraordinary, hail him with lofty titles, he rebukes them. Healing is indeed

Synagogue at Capernaum
This third-century synagogue on the shore of the Lake of Galilee at Capernaum marks the site of an older synagogue in which Jesus preached. *(Courtesy of the Israel Government Tourist Office.)*

part of his message, but as the role rejections in the temptation accounts make clear, it is not central. The message is about faith and the character of the coming Reign of God. Healings are not intended to produce adulation of the healer.

There are in Matthew and Mark only two instances in which Jesus withdraws to pray. Both follow scenes with excited crowds and lead to withdrawals. So we surmise that the gathering of "the whole town" was unsettling, and that it prompted a withdrawal for prayer.

> Early in the morning, long before daylight, he got up and left the house and went off to a lonely spot, and prayed there. And Simon and his companions sought him out and found him, and said to him,
> "They are all looking for you!"
> He said to them,
> "Let us go somewhere else, to the neighboring country towns, so that I may preach in them, too, for that is why I came out here."[B5]

But his experience in the other towns was like that in Capernaum. For some days he could no longer go into a town openly but stayed in unfrequented places, and people came to him from every direction. People "ran" to him. They were hopeful of great things. When he came again into Capernaum, "such a crowd gathered that there was no room even around the door." On another occasion there were so many people in the house it was impossible to prepare a meal; on still another, so many people gathered along the lakeshore that for fear of being crushed, Jesus had his disciples keep a boat ready to remove him. Subsequently, he found the crowd so great "he got into a boat and sat in it, a little way from the shore, while all the people were on the land close to the water,"[B6] and from this vantage point, he taught them.

III. THE THEMES OF JESUS' TEACHING

What was it in Jesus' preaching that so attracted the crowds during the early part of his ministry? Several answers to this question must be given. In the first place, he brought an urgent message that was itself exciting; it had to do with the imminence of God's total rule. Further, he had a great deal to say about getting ready for the new age by doing God's will *now,* while there was still time. Finally, he spoke in simple and untechnical language about the central issues in religion, always with the use of homely illustrations drawn from nature and human life. Many of his most profound lessons were given through parables—brief stories drawn from everyday experience, stories that set the human experience in perspective or illustrated an aspect of Jesus' ministry. But it would not have been enough if the manner of his teaching had been its only attraction. What he really had achieved was a new synthesis of the religious insights of his people.

A. "The Kingdom of God Is Near"

It is apparent that Jesus shared with his people the expectation that the Messianic Reign long foretold was about to begin. The religious feeling of the Jewish people then centered in this expectation. From his youth on, Jesus was under the influence of the hopes raised by it, so he was responding normally to his environment when he entertained along with his people their general and passionate hope of a new order of things.

It was an electrifying expectation. The time was at hand when "the Son of man" would come as the judge and agent of judgment and redemption. It would not be a human event, a predictable political occurrence; it would be an unmistakably supernatural happening, caused, at a time unknown to humankind, by God alone.

In the Gospel of Mark there are passages (modified by the language of the Apostolic Age) that have a similar meaning.

> And he said to them, "I tell you, some of you who stand here will certainly live to see the reign of God come in its might."[B7]
>
> "I tell you, these things will all happen before the present age passes away. . . . But about that day or hour no one knows, not even the angels in heaven, nor the Son; only the Father. You must look out and be on the alert, for you do not know when it will be time."[B8]

Consider the following passages from Luke:

> And he said to his disciples, "The time will come when you will long to see one of the days of the Son of Man. . . . Men will say to you, 'Look! There he is!' or, 'Look! Here he is!' Do not go off in pursuit of him, for just as when lightning flashes, it shines from one end of the sky to the other, that will be the way with the Son of Man. . . . In the time of the Son of Man it will be just as in the time of Noah. People went on eating, drinking, marrying, and being married up to the very day that Noah got into the ark and the flood came and destroyed them all. . . . It will be like that on the day when the Son of Man appears."[B9]

The conviction clearly is that an apocalyptic "end of the age" was imminent. The thrill of expectancy produced by this conviction is hard for us to recreate, even in imagination. It was almost an obsession among the greater number of unhappy Jews of Palestine, and it was a large factor in the lives of the Jews who lived abroad. Not to believe it was unreasonable. In a world where the concept of social evolution and progress did not exist, and where faith in God's direct intervention in human affairs was unquestioned, no pious mind among the Jews doubted that God was soon to work his deliverance, just as he had in the past when his people were suffering beyond endurance.

As to the significance of this apocalypticism for contemporary Christianity, twentieth-century interpreters have taken differing stances. Albert Schweitzer, writing for a world still full of nineteenth-century confidence in social evolution and progress, declared that the Jesus who accepted thoroughgoing apocalypticism could be nothing other than a "stranger" to the modern spirit. Rudolf Bultmann, writing at mid century, could say, "It is possible that Biblical eschatology may rise again. It will not rise in its old mythological form, but from a terrifying vision that modern technology, especially atomic science, may bring about a destruction of our earth. . . ."[C]

Jesus also transformed some aspects of the apocalypticism of his day.

Apocalypticism Transformed

A careful examination of Jesus' use of the more or less fugitive thought forms of the eschatology (beliefs about the end of the world) of his time shows that though he shared the general apocalyptic hope, he transformed it. He took the narrowly conceived messianism of the less universalist Judaism of his day, which hoped principally for the restoration of the kingdom of David, and he replaced it with a new form of the old prophetic vision of a world where God's reign would be extended to all lands (see p. 405). As Jesus reconceived the old vision, the members of the Kingdom would *come* from everywhere. A passage presumably from "Q" puts it with the utmost directness.

> You must strain every nerve to get in through the narrow door, for I tell you many will try to get in, and will not succeed, when the master of the house gets up and shuts the door, and you begin to stand outside and knock on the door, and say, 'Open it for us, sir!' Then he will answer you and say, 'I do not know where you come from.... Get away from me, all you wrong-doers!' There you will weep and gnash your teeth when you see Abraham and Isaac and Jacob and all the prophets in the Kingdom of God, while you are put outside. People will come from the east and west and the north and south, and take their places in the Kingdom of God. There are those now last who will then be first, and there are those now first who will be last."[B10]

Matthew renders part of this passage still more clearly, thus,

> I tell you, many will come from the east and from the west and take their places at the feast with Abraham, Isaac, and Jacob, in the Kingdom of Heaven, while the heirs to the kingdom will be driven into darkness outside, there to weep and grind their teeth![B11]

As if this were not a drastic enough revision of the current Jewish hopes, Jesus predicted that the earthly center of the Davidic kingdom—Jerusalem and its Temple—would be destroyed because the inhabitants of the city had not repented. Only repentance would save them, or anyone. Since outcasts, publicans, harlots, and other sinners showed more signs of repentance than the scribes and Pharisees, they would enter the kingdom of Heaven before the so-called

servants of God who proudly justified themselves. God took more pleasure in one sinner who repented than in ninety-nine just persons who saw no need of repentance. Matthew's paraphrase of the Lukan Beatitudes is therefore not false to Jesus' conviction: it is the pure in heart who shall see God; it is the meek who shall inherit the earth.[B12]

B. "The Kingdom of God Is in Your Midst"

Jesus also deviated from the general thinking by teaching that while the Kingdom in its fullness was not present, it was in part already "realized" by events of which his own acts were the center. He told doubters that if "by the finger of God" he now cast out demons, then the Kingdom of God had already come upon them. He answered some Pharisees who asked when the Kingdom of God was coming, "The Kingdom of God is in your midst!"[B13]

Interpreted as "realized eschatology" (a term introduced by C. H. Dodd), sayings commonly taken to be references to a future apocalyptic event—such as Mark 9:1, "Some of you who stand here will not taste death until you see the Kingdom of God come in its power"—should be understood as referring, not to the chronological future, but to a *moment of realization* that the Kingdom had come.[D] As a reference to the future the saying looks no further than to the resurrection "in its power." According to the "realized" view, God's reign has already begun in time (*chronos*) as a historical plane, but the timing (*kairos*) or opportune situation of complete sovereignty is not to be sought in a chronological future. It is always a transcendent, vertical "now" intersecting the historical plane.

And this brings us to the very knotty problem of Jesus' conception of his own relationship with God. Did he consider himself the Son of man and Son of God in a special sense? Did he think of himself as the Messiah from the time of his baptism, or did he grow gradually into the conviction that he was the Lord's Anointed? Or did his followers endow him with Messiahship toward the end of his career and after his death, without any intimation from him that this was due him?

These questions are crucial and can perhaps never be answered finally. Nevertheless, some very definite things can be said about Jesus' sense of unique relationship with God.

C. Relationship to God

God was much more to Jesus than a transcendent being to whom one owes a morning and an evening prayer. The intimacy and rapport of his communion with God seemed to surpass anything he experienced in human relationships. In teaching his disciples to pray, he communicated something of this experience to them, but there was as well something incommunicable about it, so that they were reduced to wonder. Whatever his use of the terms *Son of man* and *the Christ* was, it is quite beyond doubt that he knew he was "sent." God had commissioned him to establish his Kingdom. As with Amos, so with Jesus: God "took" him and sent him to humankind.

Hence he could preach and teach and heal with authority. He could propound a law superseding that of Moses. And he could recite to the congregation in Nazareth the great passage from Isaiah and say, "This passage of scripture has been fulfilled here in your hearing today!"[B14]

> *The spirit of the Lord is upon me,*
> *For he has consecrated me to preach the good news to*
>   *the poor,*
> *He has sent me to announce to the prisoners their*
>   *release and to the blind the recovery of their sight.*
> *To set the down-trodden at liberty,*
> *To proclaim the year of the Lord's favor!*

D. Teaching about God

From the time of his baptism by John the Baptist the reality of God and of his own intimate relationship with God occupied the central place in Jesus' thinking. He was never moved to set in order his reasons for believing in the reality of God. In that age of universal faith in the divine existence, no one ever

asked him to. What people desired to know was what kind of a god was God, and what, in view of his character, he might be expected to do. On this point Jesus spoke with profound assurance. God was the sovereign moral personality ruling the universe, the moving spirit in the course and at the end of history, a transcendent being, sternly righteous, who never departed from perfect justice in determining the course of events or the destiny of an individual. This God drew near to one bowed down in prayer. He was forgiving and merciful, primarily occupied with human redemption, in character and action paternal. Jesus' favorite name for God was Father (or Father in Heaven). It is implied in his teaching that though God allows people to make their own decisions and, like the prodigal in the famous parable, take the means at their disposal and waste them in riotous living, he continues to love them throughout the redemptive process of retribution that inevitably follows and will forgive them when they return to him. God therefore is utterly good as well as holy. People should trust him and regularly seek spiritual enlightenment through prayer, especially private prayer in their rooms or in the solitude of the fields and hilltops.

E. Confidence in Nature

Jesus' attitude toward nature was conditioned by his conception of God. He was truly Jewish in thinking of nature as the stage setting of the sublime drama of human redemption. Nature was not the ultimate reality. God worked behind and through nature. (One might generalize and say that Jesus was like the Jews in looking through nature at God, and did not follow the Greek tendency to look through the gods at nature.) At the same time it is apparent in Jesus' teaching that he looked at nature directly with delight and trust. The lilies of the field, more beautifully arrayed than Solomon in all his glory, were of God's making and were, like the birds of the heavens—the ravens and sparrows— fully sustained by God's care. Surely,

> "On being asked by the Pharisees when the Reign of God was coming, he answered them, 'The Reign of God is not coming as you hope to catch sight of it; no one will say, "Here it is," or "There it is," for the Reign of God is now in your midst.'"[E1]
>
> —Luke 17:20 (Moffat)

if human beings would know how to live with each other in the righteousness of God's kingdom, they too would find in nature all they needed: in their anxiety, people seek food and clothing *first,* but if they would seek first the Kingdom, food and clothing would come in course; that was God's plan.

F. The Goodness of the Body

Jesus' attitude toward his body was similarly confident and trustful, and again typically Jewish. He apparently accepted the body as functionally integrated with the mind and spirit in a working unity. He was no ascetic. He enjoyed wedding feasts and banquets. He never suggested that the body is inherently corrupting and defiling, or that the soul is foully imprisoned in the flesh. The body may indeed become the dangerous instrument of an evil will, or it may be divided between good and evil because the will is so divided. In the latter case, Jesus used hyperbole to indicate that issues of personal integrity call for decisive action. "If your foot makes you fall, cut it off."[B15] Jesus, in short, did not distract his followers from the pursuit of personal and social goodness by suggesting that the body is the chief enemy of good and should first be subdued.

His attention was directed elsewhere. The will of God was that people should become fit for the coming Kingdom of Heaven by living together as persons religiously oriented toward him as children toward a parent and ethically oriented toward each other as family members. No person was natively unworthy either of God's grace or of dignity in the eyes of other persons. He invoked this principle particularly in the case of little children, but also in the case of the disinherited, sinful, and alien folk, with whom he was constantly in association. There were to be no exceptions to the law of love; it was to be interracial and international.

G. Morality above Legal and Ceremonial Practice

Jesus' teaching contained a constant challenge to do whatever might prepare the way for the coming of the Kingdom of God. Sayings in Luke underline the urgency of this challenge. A man invited to follow him says, "Let me first go and bury my father." Jesus said to him, "Leave the dead to bury their own dead; you must go and spread the news of the Kingdom of God!" Yet another man said to him, "Master, I am going to follow you, but let me first say goodbye to my people at home," to which Jesus replied, "No one who puts his to hand to the plough, and then looks back, is fitted for the Kingdom of God."[B16]

Besides calling for self-commitment, Jesus asked his followers to put their moral obligations above all social, legal, or ceremonial demands. Ceremony is subordinated to love in action but not summarily devalued: if one is about to make an offering and remembers an estrangement, one should *first* go and be reconciled and *then* make the offering. Jesus was especially critical of legalistic attitudes generally attributed to Pharisees who failed to heed the reforming spirit of their own party. They were guilty of certain obvious faults: complacency, the desire for honor and applause, spiritual pride, and hypocrisy. But, more profoundly, their gravest shortcoming lay in their neglect of the primary imperatives of the moral law. They had substituted legal and ceremonial practices for a creative and truly regenerating morality. They strained out the gnat, yet swallowed the camel; they cleaned the outside of the cup and the dish, but were themselves full inside of greed and self-indulgence; they were like whitewashed tombs, looking well on the outside but full inside of the bones of the dead and all that is unclean. Though they paid tithes on mint, dill, an cumin, they let the weightier matters of the Law go—justice, mercy, and integrity. It was indeed characteristic of Jesus, in all his ethical precepts, to transfer attention from the external features of moral behavior to its inward motivation, the spirit or attitude behind it. Good and evil have their origins in the heart.

H. Concern for Inner Integrity

Before we look at the application of this principle to morality, we should see clearly that Jesus linked it with a twofold demand: concern for one's own inner integrity and concern for the inner health of others. Woe, said Jesus, to anyone who hurts another at the center of his moral being! Anyone who causes a humble believer to fall might better have a millstone hung around his neck and be thrown into the sea. Harming the moral nature of another is the gravest of crimes.

With the same stress on the inward condition of the personality Jesus restated and then rephrased the old Hebrew laws. Matthew assembles a series of teachings in which Jesus looks behind a prohibited act to the motive that might cause it. Two examples may be cited. There was the law against murder that had been given to the men of old. "But I tell you that anyone who gets angry with his brother . . . and anyone who speaks contemptuously to his brother . . . and anyone who says to his brother 'You cursed fool!' will have to answer for it."[B17] There was the law against adultery. "But I tell you that anyone who looks at a woman with desire has already committed adultery with her in his heart."[B18]

But the stress on the spiritual and the inward in morality reached its most significant form in Jesus' teaching about love. This is a teaching that still requires the utmost effort of understanding, for although the command to use the method of love toward friend and foe alike is an absolute principle, its application to the details of conduct is always marked by such relativity that sincere Christians often differ in their judgments as to what that conduct should be.

The absolute principle is contained in the following words:

> You have heard that [the men of old] were told, "You must love your neighbor and hate your enemy." But I tell you, love your enemies and pray for your persecutors, so that you may show yourselves true sons of your Father in heaven, for he makes his sun rise on bad and good alike, and makes his rain fall on the upright and the wrongdoers. . . . You are to be perfect, as your heavenly Father is.
>
> You must always treat other people as you would like to have them treat you, for this sums up the Law and the Prophets.
>
> "You must love the Lord your God with your whole heart, your whole soul, and your whole mind." That is the great, first command. There is a second like it: "You must love your neighbor as

you do yourself." These two commands sum up the whole of the Law and the Prophets.[B19]

The application of this principle to the details of conduct must be left to the judgment of the moment. Just the central principle is stated, and the application is left to the conscience of the individual who espouses it.

I. Alternatives to Retaliation

In one direction, however, clear guidance is given. The hard rule is laid down that one should not resist with violence evil done to one's own self.

> You have heard that [the men of old] were told, "An eye for an eye and a tooth for a tooth." But I tell you not to resist injury, but if anyone strikes you on your right cheek, turn the other to him too; and if anyone wants to sue you for your shirt, let him have your coat too.[B20]

Retaliation is embittering and futile; it will only add to the moral confusion if one answers a personal injury with some similar one. One should respond to injury without vengefulness or hatred, but also without moral surrender or compromise. There can be the shock of an answering goodness immediately expressed by a gesture—the turning of a cheek, the giving of a coat, the second mile—symbolizing with shattering clearness the readiness of the wronged individual to live in fellowship with the wrongdoer.

A complementary teaching warns against rash or ill-considered criticism of another's conduct. For one thing, it is all too often true that the rash critic is himself in need of moral correction. For another, it is always best to be generous and thus call forth love from others.

> Pass no more judgments upon other people, so that you may not have judgment passed upon you. . . . Why do you keep looking at the speck in your brother's eye, and pay no attention to the beam that is in your own? How can you say to your brother, "Just let me get that speck out of

your eye," when all the time there is a beam in your own? You hypocrite! First get the beam out of your own eye, and then you can see to get the speck out of your brother's eye.[B21]

You must be merciful just as your Father is. Do not judge others. . . . Excuse others. . . . Give, and they will give to you; good measure, pressed down, shaken together, and running over, they will pour into your lap. For the measure you use with others they in turn will use with you.[B22]

In other words, goodness in any form has an all-conquering power to call forth a response of the same kind.

IV. THE CLIMACTIC EVENTS

The Growth of Opposition

The Gospels frame many sayings of Jesus in settings of verbal conflict. Pharisees and Sadducees are pictured as jealous guardians of orthodoxy. A typical encounter occurred when, in passing through the wheat fields on the Sabbath, Jesus' disciples began to pick the heads of the wheat as they made their way through. The Pharisees protested against this as a breaking of the Sabbath law forbidding the gathering of produce from the fields. Jesus retorted, "The Sabbath was made for man, not man for the Sabbath."[B23] The Pharisees would not have denied the truth of this assertion, but they disliked its radical tone. They were critical also of other elements in Jesus' teaching. Because physicians were prohibited from working on the Sabbath day, they attacked Jesus' healing on the Sabbath. On more than one occasion, they obliged Jesus to defend himself on this score. They noticed, too, that some of his disciples ate their food without first giving their hands a ceremonial washing to purify them, and accused Jesus of allowing the laxity. Jesus replied, "Listen to me all of you, and understand this. Nothing that goes into a man from outside can pollute him. It is what comes out of a man that pollutes him."[B24] Asked by his disciples to explain, he said, "It is from inside, from men's hearts, that designs of evil come; immorality, stealing, murder, adultery, greed, malice, deceit, indecency,

envy, abusiveness, arrogance, folly—all these evils come from inside, and they pollute a man."

What offended the Pharisees most, however, was the freedom with which Jesus interpreted the Law and the Prophets without respecting tradition. Too often the formula that Matthew uses in recording the Sermon on the Mount appeared in Jesus' discourse: "You have heard that the men of old were told . . . but I tell you. . . ." In short, Jesus had his authority from within.

The rumor that Jesus was "possessed" circulated among his opponents and among some of his townspeople, including his relatives. When he returned to his hometown of Nazareth and taught in the synagogue on the Sabbath day, he wondered at the lack of faith. "A prophet is treated with honor everywhere except in his native place and among his relatives and at his home," he is reported to have said.[B25] Mark records that on an earlier occasion his relatives had come to Capernaum to take him into their custody, believing him to be "beside himself." In the following instance Jesus makes it clear that his mission takes precedence over the wishes or claims of his lineal family:

His mother and his brothers came. And they stood outside the house and sent word in to him to come outside to them. There was a crowd sitting around him when they told him "Your mother and your brothers are outside asking for you."

He answered, "Who are my mother and my brothers?"

And looking around at the people sitting about said, "Here are my mother and my brothers! Whoever does the will of God is my brother and sister and my mother."[B26]

The answer Jesus made to the open accusations against him was, "How can Satan drive Satan out? . . . If Satan has rebelled against himself and become disunited, he cannot last."[B27] But the Pharisees brushed this aside.

A Messianic Banquet

As a controversial figure, Jesus is pictured as drawing large crowds. Some may have been merely curious; some may have hoped to see wonder working; but most significantly, some must have been attracted by the very fact that he was disapproved by the established authorities. This is the setting in which the Gospel narratives place the miraculous sharing of loaves and fish with the multitude (a symbol of a Messianic banquet, clearly foreshadowing the Christian eucharistic meal)—suggesting that the crowds were accepted into a kind of companionship but not into an army for rebellion. The Gospel of John says that on this occasion, Jesus became aware that the crowd wanted to make him their king, and so he withdrew. Soon after, he says that many who had followed Jesus turned away from him. Further on, the Gospel of John adds, "Even his brothers did not believe in him."

It was under these circumstances that Jesus made his way northwestward into the regions about Tyre and Sidon that were outside of Palestine, and then into southern Syria. This withdrawal to the north may have been a response to threats or to the fact that Jesus was now so conspicuously controversial as to make his normal mode of teaching impossible. It may have been a retreat to consider next steps and to train the disciples.

A Declaration at Caesarea Philippi

At a point near Caesarea Philippi, the capital city of the Tetrarch Philip, Jesus put a crucial question to the disciples: "Who do people say that I am?" They said to him, "John the Baptist; others say Elijah, and others that you are one of the prophets." (It was thus clear that the people had not thought he was the Messiah.) "But," he said, "who do you say I am?" Peter answered: "You are the Christ."[B28] The clear implication here is that this is the first time that any of the disciples had called Jesus specifically the Messiah. The account then goes on to say that Jesus warned the Twelve not to say this about him to anyone, and he went on to tell them that he must go to Jerusalem and face suffering and death for the consummation of his mission.

How did Jesus know of his impending arrest and death? Did he have miraculous foreknowledge? Was it imputed in after-the-fact (proleptic) narrative writing? Or should credence be given to a specific forty-day notice described in Talmudic literature? In any case, a frightened protest from the Twelve, voiced by Peter, met with a strong rebuke. The prospect would be hard enough to face without such fatuous optimism.

It is important to observe that this story—and indeed the whole account of the so-called retirement to the north—has been questioned by many scholars as a reading back of post–resurrection realizations (that, for instance, the message of Jesus was to the whole of humankind, or that Jesus was indeed the Messiah and had fulfilled all of the Old Testament prophecies) into Jesus' lifetime.

This reading back seems especially the case of Matthew 16:15 f., most scholars affirm. There we read: "He said to them, 'But who do you say I am?' Simon Peter answered, 'You are the Christ, the Son of the living God!' Jesus answered, 'Blessed are you, Simon, son of Jonah, for human nature has not disclosed this to you, but my Father in heaven! But I tell you, your name is Peter, a rock [petros], and on this rock [petra] I will build my church [ekklēsia], and the powers of death shall not subdue it. I will give you the keys of the kingdom of Heaven, and whatever you forbid on earth will be held in heaven to be forbidden, and whatever you permit on earth will be held in heaven to be permitted.'" In the next chapter (p. 479), we shall see how important this passage has been historically, but New Testament scholars accept it only with the greatest reserve, if at all, as a post–resurrection interpolation, because there exists no solid evidence elsewhere in the Gospels that Jesus foresaw the rise of the church after his death or used a term comparable to the Greek ekklēsia.

> "On the eve of Passover they hanged Yeshu. And an announcer went out, in front of him, for forty days (saying): 'He has enticed and led Israel astray. Anyone who knows anything in his favor, let him come and plead in his behalf.' But not having found anything in his favor, they hanged him on the eve of Passover."
>
> —The Talmud: Baraitha-B Sanhedrin 43a

Confrontations with Authorities

Jews from all over the world had come to Jerusalem to attend the great annual festival of the Passover. The Roman procurator Pilate had moved up to the city from the coastal town of Caesarea to be on hand to see order kept and to quell any attempted uprising. Herod Antipas had come down from Galilee to enjoy the festivities and to go through the motions of being a faithful Jew. There was no room in the inns. The Galileans came prepared to live in tents in the valley between the city and the Mount of Olives. Many of them knew Jesus and would welcome him if he put in an appearance. On a borrowed colt, he rode down the Mount of Olives, accompanied by his disciples, and into the city. The Galileans greeted him with shouts of joy and spread palm branches in the way, but the people of the city said, "Who is this?" and the people in the procession responded, "This is Jesus, the prophet of Nazareth in Galilee!"

In Jerusalem, Jesus went to an area in the Temple called the Court of the Gentiles. There he overturned the currency-exchange tables and the seats of those who sold sacrificial doves, and he forbade carrying anything through the courtyard. He cried out, "Does not the Scripture say, 'My house shall be called a house of prayer for all the nations'? But you have made it a robbers' cave.'" The fact that Mark includes the prohibition against carrying things refers to the fact that, because the Court of the Gentiles opened on more than one street, tradesmen sometimes disrespected it as nothing more than a shortcut. This also suggests that his objection was not necessarily to the sacrificial system as such or to the rule that only Temple currency could be offered in the Temple. The objection was to the *location* of the activity. Those whose main occupation was the care of the Temple had failed to keep sacred the area open to "all nations" for prayer and study.

This was, of course, a serious challenge, and it must have had popular support for we hear of no immediate reprisal. For several days Jesus taught in the courtyard and dealt with questions designed to discredit him. He was challenged on five issues: his authority, tax paying, the Resurrection, the greatest commandment, and the Messiah's ascendancy over David.

His opponents damaged him in the people's eyes, however, when he refused to make a declaration against paying the poll tax to the Roman emperor. Presented with the dilemma, "Is it right to pay taxes to Caesar or not?" he made the disappointing reply, "Give Caesar what belongs to Caesar, give God what belongs to God!"[E2] The sheer weight of the opposition to him must have impressed the people unfavorably; even the Herodians joined in the opposition. Seeing that this was so, Jesus began to tell the people, in pungent parables, that though the Jews had received the first invitation to sit at God's banquet table, now because they had refused the invitation, God was going to bring into the feast of the Kingdom outcasts and aliens. Matthew represents Jesus as saying pointedly to the Sadducees and Pharisees, "I tell you, the tax-collectors and prostitutes are going into the Kingdom of God ahead of you. . . . The Kingdom of God will be taken away from you, and given to a people that will produce its proper fruit."[B30]

The Last Supper and the Final Hours

All of the evangelists agree that Jesus knew the opposition would contrive his death and that he prepared himself for it. In their treatment of events, they clearly reflect the consuming interest of the early Christians in these final hours and especially in the Last Supper in an upper room in Jerusalem. As the early Christians told and retold the story, Jesus not only foresaw his death but knew who should betray him, and he performed a simple ceremony, during that last meal, to bring home to the Twelve the significance of his death.

> As they were eating, he took a loaf and blessed it, and he broke it in pieces and gave it to them saying, "Take this. It is my body."
> And he took the wine cup and gave thanks and gave it to them and they all drank from it. And he said to them, "This is my blood."[B31]

Later, in the Garden of Gethsemane, he was betrayed by Judas to a crowd of men with swords and clubs. Mark says they were from the high priests and elders. Had Pilate asked the Jewish authorities to arrest and question Jesus because he seemed to be clearly a disturber of the peace, at a time when insurrectionary riots were to be feared? Did he urge them to bring an indictment before him on which he could legally act? Whatever the reasons, Jesus was brought before the Sanhedrin and examined.

Hearings Before the Sanhedrin and Pilate

At the hearing before the Sanhedrin, "witnesses" testified. (Judas is not mentioned.) There must have been an advocate who cross-examined the witnesses, for they are reported as not agreeing (or agreeing on only one statement). In any case, the proceedings seem to conclude, not on the basis of testimony, but on Jesus' own affirmative answer to the question, "Are you the Christ?" He was declared guilty of blasphemy, a religious offense, and turned over to the Roman procurator. Pilate's first question, "Are you the King of the Jews?" suggests that Jesus had been remanded to him, not as a blasphemer, but as an insurrectionist challenging Roman authority. Pilate is pictured as first endeavoring to procure Jesus' release by offering him to the crowd in his courtyard as the prisoner to be released to them for that year. But the crowd cried for the release of Barabbas, known to them as a violent insurrectionist.

The accounts of hearings before authorities present many difficulties. A Sanhedrin meeting, presumed to have been held at night or at dawn, and during a sacred time, would have been against all custom, and its undue haste would have been against all regular procedure. Furthermore, a charge of blasphemy under Jewish religious law would not have been actionable under Roman law, which did not condemn people for religious differences. Execution by crucifixion fixes a Roman role. It might be accounted for as a routine decision of a minor official to rid himself of a potential troublemaker in an explosive time. The facts are obscured in swirling fogs of defensiveness and mutual recrimination.

Attributions of Responsibility

It must be remembered that the accounts of the hearings or "trials" of Jesus before authorities were written in an era of persecution when both Christians and Jews found themselves in jeopardy. Each party held the other responsible for Roman suspicions of their loyalty. Roman authorities had had long acquaintance with Jewish monotheism, tacitly accepted it, and even granted some exemptions from military duty to Jews. Christians sought shelter under the same umbrella. If an official were to ask, "Is your God the one worshiped by Jews?" a Christian would be likely to answer affirmatively. Jews, on their part, observing the diverse practices of Christians courting Gentile converts, perceived them as having rejected the Covenant. Thus the defensive tendency in Jewish accounts was to picture Jesus, not as a reformer within their tradition, but as a political rebel executed by the Romans. In their own defense, Christians depict a Pilate who found no fault in Jesus but who let himself be outmaneuvered. In their eyes, the real impetus for the Crucifixion was not secular; it was narrowness and jealousy on the part of Jewish religious leaders. Among the tragic outcomes of this effort were images that would later become foundation texts for anti-Semitism. One thinks especially of Matthew's picture of a Jerusalem crowd shouting "Let his blood be on us and on our children" (Matthew 27:25).

The Crucifixion

Pilate turned Jesus over to a guard of Roman soldiers to be crucified. At three o'clock in the afternoon, forsaken by all but the women who would not leave him, amidst a howling mob for whom he breathed out the prayer, "Father, forgive them, for they know not what they do," he cried out with a loud voice, "My God, my God, why have you forsaken me?" and resigning himself into God's care, expired.

No single death in the world's history has so affected Western imagination. To the Christians who have used the cross as a symbol of their faith, it has seemed that in his willingness to suffer death for the redemption of his fellow men and women, Jesus has given to them their clearest insight into the quality of the redemptive love of God himself.

To avoid having the body hanging on the cross over the Sabbath day, Joseph of Arimathea, a member of the Sanhedrin, offered the use of his empty tomb, and the body of Jesus was taken there.

V. THE APOSTOLIC AGE

To the Christians of the first century, the events that followed the death of Jesus were of greater importance than those that preceded it. It was true for them that the life and teachings of Jesus were of priceless value for their daily life and thought; yet his resurrection from the dead was of higher value still, for it was their proof of his *living* reality as a person, that is, as the unconquerable Lord of Life who was the assurance of their own resurrection.

According to the testimony of the Gospels, at the time of Jesus' arrest in the Garden of Gethsemane, the disciples scattered and fled. None of them, except John, dared draw near to the place of crucifixion. Peter had waited nearby while Jesus was being tried, but on being identified by a maidservant in the courtyard of the high priest as a follower of Jesus, he denied it. Sick with despair and fear, the disciples remained in hiding during the Sabbath day. On the morning of the third day, some of the women, before starting back to Galilee, sought out the tomb to which the body of Jesus had been taken. They found it empty.

The Resurrection

They reported extraordinary appearances of Jesus to them, as a result of which the despair of Jesus' followers gave way to a jubilant confidence and faith that were to spread a great new religion throughout the Mediterranean world.

The earliest extant account of the appearances of Jesus after the Resurrection is that of St. Paul. Around the year 52 C.E., he wrote to the church he had founded in Corinth,

> Now I want to remind you, brothers . . . [that] I passed on to you, as of first importance, the account I had received, that Christ died for our sins, as the Scriptures foretold, that he was buried, that on the third day he was raised from the dead, as the Scriptures foretold, and that he was seen by Cephas [Peter], and then by the Twelve. After that he was seen by more than five hundred brothers at one time, most of whom are still alive, although some of them have fallen asleep. Then he was seen by James, then by all the apostles, and finally he was seen by me also, as though I were born at the wrong time.[F1]

In Paul's case, "seen" can hardly mean merely a visual recognition, for he says elsewhere that he never knew Jesus in the flesh. In the Hebraic tradition, personal identity was always associated with some kind of body. Resurrection was not liberation of a soul from embodiment, but the taking on of a new body. Whatever the nature of the experience, it convinced Paul absolutely that God had raised Jesus from the dead. So he went on to write, "It is so with the resurrection of the dead. The body is sown in decay. . . . It is a physical body that is sown, it is a spiritual body that is raised."[F1]

The nature of the body of the risen Christ is ambiguous and/or irrelevant in all of the Gospel accounts. The locus of the Resurrection is in the heart of the witness, not in the chemistries of a reanimated cadaver. If the lives of the witnesses are not transformed, there is for them no resurrection. Even the account of "doubting" Thomas is ambiguous. A body that appears when all doors are shut is palpable to him. His demands are the epitome of what a believer should *not* demand, for "Blessed are they who have not seen and yet believe" (John 20:22).

Pentecost

The Resurrection appearances convinced the disciples that Jesus had been raised from the dead so that he might soon return on the clouds of heaven as the promised Son of man who should judge the nations at the great assize of the last day. His mission on earth, they now believed, had been to prepare the way for his second coming. So all the disciples who could do so, about 120 in number, left Galilee and went to live in Jerusalem, where they met in a large upper room for prayer and counsel. The Book of Acts (The Acts of the Apostles) says that among them were Jesus' mother Mary and his brothers. The Apostles were the official leaders of the group, but James, Jesus' brother, soon became a prominent figure.

The next great moment in their common experience is thus recorded.

> On the day of the Harvest Festival [the Jewish festival the Greek-speaking Christians called Pentecost], they were all meeting together, when suddenly there came from the sky a sound like a violent blast of wind, and it filled the whole house where they were sitting. And they saw tongues like flame separating and settling one on the head of each of them, and they were all filled with the holy Spirit and began to say in foreign languages whatever the Spirit prompted them to utter.[F2]

To the early Christians, the Resurrection was their proof of the truth of the Gospel, and the descent of the Holy Spirit at Pentecost was their guarantee that the power that was in Jesus Christ their Lord was in them too. The Apostles now took courage and began preaching boldly in the streets where but a few weeks earlier Jesus had encountered an opposition that had ended in his crucifixion. They met with startling success.

Confrontations: Gamaliel's Counsel

The Pharisees and Sadducees, in alarm, arrested Peter and John, brought them before the Sanhedrin, and ordered them to cease speaking as they did "in the name of Jesus." But upon their release, they continued their preaching undeterred. Once more they were arrested, with others of their number, and brought before the Sanhedrin. Reminded that they had been ordered to refrain from speaking in the name of Jesus, Peter, and the Apostles, we read, answered, "We must obey God rather than men."[F3] During the disturbance that followed, one of the leading Pharisees checked the rising anger of the other members of the Sanhedrin by suavely suggesting that fanatical messianic movements always destroy themselves in time; one may therefore safely leave them alone. This man was Gamaliel, a grandson of Hillel, and like his grandfather one of the great teachers of the rabbinical schools. He proceeded to draw upon history for his argument.

> Men of Israel, take care what you propose to do with these men. For some time ago Theudas appeared, claiming to be a person of importance, and a group of men numbering some four hundred joined him. But he was killed and all his followers were dispersed and disappeared. After him, at the time of the census, Judas of Galilee appeared, and raised a great following, but he too perished, and all his followers were scattered. So in the present case, I tell you, keep away from these men and let them alone, for if this idea or movement is of human origin, it will come to naught, but if it is from God, you will not be able to stop it.[F4]

This counsel prevailed; the authorities contented themselves with flogging the Apostles, in order to disgrace them in the eyes of the people, and let them go.

The Jerusalem Church

Two factors seem to have saved the Jerusalem church from annihilating persecution. First, the Apostles were followers of a dead leader and might be expected to lose their fervor with the passage of time. Second, the Apostles obviously kept all of the provisions of the Jewish Law. In fact, the Palestinian followers of Jesus went daily to the Temple and honored the Law of Moses as much as any Jew, requiring circumcision of every convert not already circumcised, as though they were a Jewish sect. But they had made some unorthodox additions to the accepted faith and practice. They believed Jesus was the Messiah foretold in the Jewish Scriptures and that he would shortly reappear on the clouds of heaven as the Son of Man. They met in private homes, such as the home of John Mark's mother in Jerusalem, for group gatherings, which were devoted to "the breaking of bread and prayers." The believers shared everything they had with one another, sold their property and belongings, and divided the proceeds according to their special needs. They all had a vigorous proselyting spirit and baptized their converts.

Greek-Speaking (Hellenist) Followers

But if it appeared true of the Palestinian followers of Jesus that they acted as though they were a Jewish sect, this was not true of all the converts. Some began to take the liberties Jesus had taken with the Law of Moses. There were synagogues in Jerusalem for the Jews who had returned from foreign lands and spoke Greek, and these Greek-speaking Jews, coming from various parts of the Hellenistic world, were notably less impressed by the Temple sacrifices than the Palestinian Jews and more given than the latter to stressing the passages in the prophetic writings condemning externalism in the practice of the Law. So, when any of the Greek-speaking or Hellenist Jews became Christians, they eagerly applied the more radical passages from the Prophets to the life and sayings of Jesus and stressed Jesus' criticism of the practices of the Sadducees and Pharisees.

Tension appeared not only between these Hellenist Christians and the Jewish authorities, but within the Christian group itself. On the one hand, the Apostles began to lose touch with the Greek-speaking radicals. On the other hand, the latter made complaints against the Palestinian Christians "that their [i.e., the Hellenist] widows were being neglected in the daily distribution of food."[F5] To allay this tension, the whole Christian group met and solved the problem by appointing from their number seven men who were not apostles (and all bearing Greek names) to take charge of the distribution of food and the keeping of accounts. One of these seven was a Greek-speaking man by the name of Stephen, who was a leader of the more libertarian wing of the Christian movement. All went well until the Jewish authorities brought him before the Sanhedrin, condemned him, and stoned him to death.

This violent action signalized the outbreak of a persecution of the church in Jerusalem. The Jewish authorities apparently directed it mainly against those who did not keep the Jewish Law, for the Book of Acts says, "They were all scattered over Judea and Samaria, except the apostles."[F6] However, King Herod Agrippa I, thinking to please Jewish leaders, beheaded a leading apostle, James, son of Zebedee and brother of John, and imprisoned Peter. Peter escaped and avoided rearrest, perhaps by leaving the area (Acts 12:2 f.)

Judaizers and Hellenists

Thenceforth, the Christian movement in Palestine was to have two parties within it, which never lost their sense of being bound together under the name of Christ, but which struggled with each other for the right to be the final interpreters of what Christianity meant. On one side stood the conservatives, often called Judaizers: James, the brother of Jesus, now the chief "pillar" of the Jerusalem church, and with him most of the Apostles. They held that, since they constituted the true Israel, Christians must not only follow Christ, but please God by also obeying the Law of Moses. One of the requirements for which they stood was circumcision, and they sent out their emissaries to the outlying churches to insist that this requirement be met before baptism. It also was considered necessary to observe the distinctions between clean and unclean and to refuse to sit down to a meal with the uncircumcised. Although some of the members of the Jerusalem church showed a willingness to compromise, the extremists carried their insistence to great lengths. In time, the remnant of the strictest Judaizers became an exclusive group of Jewish Christians called "Ebionites" or "Nazarenes."

Among the Jerusalem Christians who were disposed to make compromises was Peter. He saw that the Holy Spirit had descended freely upon the more liberal Christians. What was more, on visits to the coast towns he found the new faith spreading among uncircumcised foreigners, and the Holy Spirit had come upon them too. He approved of their being baptized and sat down to eat with them without being overly careful concerning the Jewish dietary restrictions. But when he visited Antioch, he was severely criticized by the Judaizers who were sent to keep an eye on him, and thereafter vacillated before his narrower brethren, without being able to take a bold stand. Subsequently, according to unconfirmed tradition, he went to Rome, where presumably he was able to follow a freer course, but suffered martyrdom.

Yet the more liberal elements in the Christian movement were to win the day and remake the heretical Jewish sect into a powerful independent religion that was to spread rapidly throughout the Gentile world. The leader of the liberals was their onetime fiercest persecutor, a man from Tarsus called Saul (or Paul).

The Conversion of Paul

Paul has frequently been called "the second founder of Christianity." Certain it is that he withstood and silenced the Judaizers, who thereafter steadily lost importance in the Christian movement, but more important, he developed certain basic theological concepts for stating the spiritual effects of Jesus on the lives of his followers, concepts that enabled Christianity to win the Gentile world. To that world he brought intact the religion *of* Jesus himself in one vehicle of a faith *about* Jesus as Lord.

All of this Paul accomplished only after an early career of fierce opposition to Christianity. He was a non-Palestinian Jew, born about the same time as Jesus in the town of Tarsus in Cilicia, then an important city and the seat of a university where the Stoic and Cynic philosophies were taught. Probably Paul here learned something of the Greek mystery cults and the desire of their adherents to achieve immortality by identification with dying and rising savior gods. His family was apparently well off, and presumably had purchased Roman citizenship; he therefore had the legal status of a free-born Roman. But he reacted adversely to the religious ideas of his Hellenistic environment and remained a strict Pharisee. Filled with an earnest desire for "the righteousness which is from the Law," he went to Jerusalem and "sat at the feet" of Gamaliel, the leading Pharisaic teacher. Of this period of his life he later wrote, "I surpassed many of my own age among my people in my devotion to Judaism, I was so fanatically devoted to what my forefathers had handed down."[F7] He joined furiously in the persecution of the early Church. He was present as an approving spectator at the stoning of Stephen.

When the Christian believers fled northward to Damascus and beyond, he went to the high priest and asked for letters to the synagogues in Damascus, where he probably lived, "so that if he found any men or women there who belonged to the Way, he might bring them in

chains to Jerusalem." "But," says the Book of Acts, "as he was approaching Damascus, a sudden light flashed around him from heaven, and he fell to the ground. Then he heard a voice saying to him, 'Saul! Saul! Why do you persecute me?'"[F8] Blinded by the bright vision, Paul was led by the hand into Damascus, where for three days he could not see and neither ate nor drank. He believed that the resurrected Jesus, in whom the Christians now centered their faith, had appeared also to him.

Paul's Missionary Activity

So vast a change in Paul's life was now made necessary that he went off into upper Arabia to think things through. Then he returned to Damascus. He became a Christian leader not only there but also far to the north at Antioch, the third largest city in the Roman Empire, where the new religion was making many converts among the Gentiles. Except for a two-week visit to Jerusalem after three years to become personally reacquainted with Peter and James, he confined himself to the districts of Syria and Cilicia. Then he set out on three famous missionary journeys.

Although he suffered from some physical malady, which he refers to as "a thorn in the flesh," in these journeys he displayed tremendous energy, zeal, and courage. His strength abounded, he said, because when he felt physically weak, he threw himself upon the strength of Christ, who dwelt within him. He wrote,

Five times I have been given one less than forty lashes, by the Jews. I have been beaten three times by the Romans, I have been stoned once, I have been shipwrecked three times, a night and a day I have been adrift at sea; with my frequent journeys, [I have been] in danger from rivers, danger from robbers, danger from my own people, danger from the

> "For I delivered to you as of first importance what I also received, that Christ died for our sins in accordance with the scriptures, that he was buried, that he was raised on the third day in accordance with the scriptures, and that he appeared to Cephas, then to the Twelve. Then he appeared to more than five hundred brethren at one time, most of whom are still alive, though some have fallen asleep. Then he appeared to James, then to all the apostles. Last of all, as to one untimely born, he appeared also to me."
>
> —I Cor. 15:3–8

heathen, danger in the city, danger in the desert, danger at sea, danger from false brothers, through toil and hardship, through many a sleepless night, through hunger and thirst, often without food, and exposed to cold.[F9]

Two great spiritual facts animated Paul and gave him his dynamic faith: the "freedom of the Spirit" and the "Lordship of Christ."

"Freedom of the Spirit"

He came to know the freedom of the Spirit during the early days of his conversion. The Christians of Syria and Cilicia were for the most part uncircumcised and without the knowledge of the Jewish Law. In his great hunger to know the secret of true righteousness, Paul had long held the Law (the Torah) to be the one and only condition of a good life enjoying the Lord's favor. But now he was surprised and delighted to discover that those who followed Christ were, quite apart from the Law, more profoundly good than those who obeyed the Law. The righteousness that was in Christ was greater than the righteousness that was from the Law. The reason was that Christ changed one's inward disposition and gave one the right relationship to all other people and to God, so that one did what is right from the heart, without having to refer constantly to outward legal requirements. Love was the fulfillment of the Law. Therefore, the weary bondage of the Law could be cast aside for the freedom of the Spirit. There was no further need, Paul declared, for circumcision, dietary restrictions, and distinctions between clean and unclean.

It was at this point that the "Judaizers" came into conflict with Paul. He had it out with Peter, James, and John at Jerusalem. In Galatians 2 he implies that obedience to Jewish law had become so critical an issue that, after fourteen years, he felt impelled to explain to the Jerusalem leaders the message he preached to the Gentiles. By God's power, he claimed, he had been made an apostle to the Gentiles, just as Peter was an apostle to the Jews. Peter, James, and John accepted his message and mission and shook hands, asking only that Christians in the Gentile world remember the needy in Jerusalem. Paul eagerly agreed.

"The Lordship of Christ"

The Lordship of Christ was another article of faith at the heart of Paul's conviction. To him it meant even more than the Messiahship of Jesus. He had joyously accepted Jesus as the Messianic savior who had inaugurated the Kingdom of God and would soon return on the clouds of heaven to judge the quick and the dead on the last day. But as a missionary to the Gentiles (to whom the Messiahship of Jesus, a purely Jewish concept, meant little), he was quick to see and herald the power of Christ to redeem individuals from sin and death by uniting them to himself by faith. Christ, he ardently declared, was a divine being who possessed the nature of God but who had humbled himself and come down from heaven and assumed human form, and, humbling himself still further, died on the cross, so that he might rise again, after his victory over death, to the right hand of God as the Lord of life and death. In setting forth this new and glorious mystery, Paul ascribed unqualified divinity to the pre-existent Christ: "He is a likeness of the unseen God, born before any creature, for it was through him that everything was created in heaven and earth, the seen and the unseen, angelic thrones, dominions, principalities, authorities—all things were created through and for him."[F10]

By this great conception—through which Paul expressed his intuition that Jesus was the expression in human history of God's redemptive spirit and love at work since the dawn of creation—Paul quite captivated the Gentiles. They had been brought up under the influence of the Greek mystery religions, which, as we have seen, satisfied the yearning for immortality by providing an experience of union with a resurrected savior god, thereby deifying and immortalizing the corrupt and perishable self.

To help Gentiles understand properly the significance of the redemption that Christ wrought in their lives, Paul put it thus: by the mystical experience of baptism, those who believe may identify themselves with Christ in his death and resurrection, for "through baptism we have been buried with him in death, so that just as he was raised from the dead through the Father's glory, we too may live a new life. . . . You must think of yourselves as dead to sin but alive to God, through union with Christ Jesus" (Roman 6:4, 11).

Paul's conception was more profound and regenerative than any of the alternatives most Gentiles had known. He not only offered assurance of immortality through union with Christ but provided a means of salvation from guilt and sin in this life. For Christ, the deified Lord of life and death had been the blameless Jesus of Nazareth of Galilee, who had proclaimed a high and noble ethics that led to individual and social remaking on the moral plane. Thus mysticism and ethics were in Paul's teaching one and inseparable. To follow Christ meant not only identifying oneself with him through baptism, the Lord's Supper, and the ecstasy of speaking in tongues, but even more, doing as Jesus did, living as he did.

> If I can speak the languages of men and even of angels, but have no love, I am only a noisy gong or a clashing cymbal.... I want you all to speak ecstatically.... But in public worship I would rather say five words with my understanding so as to instruct others also than ten thousand words in an ecstasy. (I Cor. 13:1; 14:5, 19)

This was important in the development of Christianity, for here Paul saved it from an extreme—that of nonethical mysticism—as dangerous to its balance and truth as the extreme of legalism from which he had earlier rescued it.

The letters Paul sent to the churches he established furnish abundant proof of the importance he attached to ethics. With an eagle's eye, he watched over his congregations and scolded them like a father for every infraction of the high Christian code of morality. He was far from believing that a capacity for religious ecstasy covers a multitude of sins.

His generosity toward his Christian brethren in Jerusalem brought to a sudden end his missionary career. He had taken upon himself the obligation to raise a collection for the poor in the Jerusalem church, and having done so, carried the funds to Jerusalem himself. Here he ran afoul of the Jews, who mobbed him and caused his arrest. As a Roman citizen, he appealed to Caesar, anxious as he was at any rate to get to Rome. He was taken under arrest to the Imperial City, but if he expected to be released after his trial, he was disappointed. The authorities continued to hold him in custody. He had time to write letters to churches and individuals, but presumably after a period of confinement whose length is not known, he was executed as a troublesome character, a disturber of the Roman peace.

But he had by this time fully demonstrated the power of the Christian religion to bring together Jew, Greek, and Roman, legalist, mystic, and rationalist, all under a common sense of their vital spiritual community in Christ. To such of the culturally divided and spiritually drifting people of the Roman Empire as heard them, words like these from the powerful Letter to the Ephesians—a letter that some scholars now attribute to a follower of Paul rather than to him, but that in any case is warmed and vitalized by his spirit—contained "good news."

> You also were dead because of the offenses and sins in the midst of which you once lived under the control of the present age of the world.... We lived among them once, indulging our physical cravings and obeying the impulses of our lower nature and its thoughts, and by nature we were doomed to God's wrath like other men. But God is so rich in mercy that because of the great love he had for us, he made us, dead as we were through our offenses, live again with the Christ. It is by his mercy that you have been saved.... It is not by your own action, it is the gift of God. It has not been earned, so that no one can boast of it....
>
> So remember that you were once physically heathen.... At that time you had no connection with Christ, you were aliens to the commonwealth of Israel; ... with no hope and no God in all the world. But now through your union with Christ Jesus you who were once far away have through the blood of Christ been brought near. For he is our peace. He has united the two divisions, and broken down the barrier that kept us apart; ... for it is through him that we both with one Spirit are now able to approach the Father. So you are no longer foreigners or strangers, but you are fellow-citizens of God's people and members of his family.[F11]

VI. THE EARLY CHURCH
(50–150 C.E.)

The Spread of the Early Christian Communities

But in calling Paul "the second founder of Christianity," we should not exaggerate his immediate influence. Before his time other leaders than he had successfully carried Christianity to Antioch, Alexandria, and Rome. Besides the Apostles, we hear of Barnabas, Symeon Niger, Lucius the Cyrenian, Manaen, "who had been brought up with Herod the governor," Apollos, and others, all actively engaged in organizing new Christian churches. So rapidly, in fact, were Christian converts springing up along the coasts of the eastern Mediterranean that it was Paul's ambition to proceed from Rome to Spain in order to carry Christianity to the farthest bounds of the known world.

The chief successes of early Christianity were in the commercial centers of the Roman Empire, largely because there were synagogues, or at least Jewish quarters, in them, and the Christian message could make its best appeal in places where the Jewish religion was already known. But when the orthodox Jewish communities rejected the new faith and refused to harbor it, independent Christian communities sprang up among the tradespeople and working people of the great cities and towns, first among the Greek-speaking citizens and then among those who spoke other languages. And not only did the new religion spread westward, it also was carried to the Tigris-Euphrates Valley and into Ethiopia.

Roman Suspicion, Perplexity, and Persecution

By the middle of the second century, the Christian religion had become a major problem the governors of the Roman provinces, especially in Syria and Asia Minor. For one thing, the Romans disliked mystery and secrecy. For another, the Christians considered themselves *in* the world but not *of* it. Though a few of them here and there joined the armed services of the Roman Empire and took office in the administrative branches of the government, the greater number dissociated themselves from all worldly power. In purely secular matters, they were obedient, but on the whole indifferent, to the civil authority. But they refused to take part in the official patriotic cult that required citizens to take an oath "by the genius" (the divine spirit) of the emperor and to offer incense and wine in honor of the emperor's godhead on the altar before his image. This refusal was a particularly sore point with the Roman administrative officials, less for religious reasons than because it signified disloyalty and rebellion. Moreover, the Christians met secretly, almost always at daybreak or at night, probably because so many of them were employed during the day. Distorted conceptions of their worship "orgies" were current. The Christians were accused of sexual perversions ("love feasts") and cannibalism. ("Take, eat; this is my body . . . this is my blood.") In addition, their staying away from theaters, gladiatorial combats, and popular festivals aroused rage.

A classic expression of official perplexity is contained in the letters of Pliny the Younger, governor of Bithynia (in Asia Minor), to the Roman Emperor Trajan. Wrote he (112 C.E.),

> It is my custom, my lord, to refer to you all questions about which I have doubts. . . . I have no little uncertainty whether pardon is granted on repentance, or whether when one has been a Christian there is no gain to him in that he has ceased to be such; whether the mere name, without crimes, or crimes connected with the name are punished. . . . Those who were accused before me as Christians . . . asserted that the amount of their fault or error was this: that they had been accustomed to assemble on a fixed day before daylight and sing by turns a hymn to Christ as a god; and that they bound themselves with an oath, not for any crime, but to commit neither theft, nor robbery, nor adultery, not to break their word and not to deny a deposit when demanded; after these things were done, it was their custom to depart and meet together again to take food, but ordinary and harmless food; and they said that even this had ceased after my edicts were issued, by which, according to your commands, I had forbidden the

Communal Meal

2nd c. catacomb art frequently shows a host distributing loaves and fishes, perhaps because the sequence of verbs: "he took, he blessed, he broke, and he gave," recalled the feeding of the multitudes as well as the Last Supper. *Fractio Panis* from the Catacomb of St. Callixtus, ca. 150 C.E. *(Photograph, British Museum, London)*

existence of clubs. On this account I believed it the more necessary to find out from two maid-servants, who were called deaconesses, and that by torture, what was the truth. I found nothing else than a perverse and excessive superstition. I there-fore adjourned the examination and hastened to consult you. The matter seemed to me to be worth deliberation.[G]

Pliny reported, however, that when he found Chris-tians who persisted three times over in saying they were Christians, he ordered them to be executed, "for," said he, "I did not doubt that, whatever it was they admitted, obstinacy and unbending perversity cer-tainly deserve to be punished." The Romans, on prin-ciple, expected obedience.

Christians were publicly done to death in Rome as early as 64 C.E. in the time of Nero. During the cen-tury that followed, Roman officials at times made examples of Christians who refused to worship Cae-sar's image by throwing them to the lions or burning them at the stake. The number of martyrs was not

large, perhaps, but the public commotion was some-times great and had far-reaching effects both on the Christians themselves and on the public at large, espe-cially in sharpening the feeling that the Christian reli-gion was to its adherents worth not only living by but dying for as well.

Developments in Worship

At the time of the apostle Paul, when the Christians were beginning to look upon themselves as a church called out of the world into a separate fellowship, their services were of two kinds: (1) meetings on the model of synagogue services, open to inquirers as well as believers, and consisting of readings from the Jewish scriptures (not until the second century were the Jew-ish scriptures supplemented with readings from the Gospels and Epistles), prayer, preaching, and the singing of psalms; and (2) the *agapé* or *"love feast,"* for the believers only, an evening meal in which all present shared and during which a brief ceremony, recalling the Last Supper, commemorated the sacrifice of Jesus' body and blood. Because this ceremony was couched in terms of thanksgiving, the Greek name for it was *Eucharist* ("the giving of thanks").

As the Christian communities grew larger, the common meal was gradually discontinued as impracticable, and the Lord's Supper was observed thereafter at the conclusion of the public portion of the Sunday services, when the unbaptized withdrew so that the baptized might celebrate together this inner mystery of the Christian faith.

About the year 150, Justin Martyr (who will be discussed in more detail later) described a typical Sunday observance, thus,

> On the day called Sunday there is a meeting in one place of those who live in cities or the country, and the memoirs of the apostles [the Gospels] or the writings of the prophets are read as long as time permits. When the reader has finished, the president urges and invites [us] to the imitation of these noble things. Then we all stand up together and offer prayers. [After this] bread is brought, and wine and water, and the president . . . sends up prayers and thanksgivings to the best of his ability, and the congregation assents, saying the Amen; the distribution and reception of the consecrated elements by each one takes place and they are sent to the absent by the deacons. Those who prosper, and who so wish, contribute [money], each one as much as he chooses to. What is collected is deposited with the president, and he takes care of orphans and widows, and those who are in want on account of sickness or any other cause, and those who are in bonds, and the strangers who are sojourners among [us].[H]

New Members and Church Organization

Entrance into the Christian community was formalized into definite steps. Candidates for church membership, of all ages, were first given a systematic course of instruction and testing (catechization), lasting for several months and ending in the rite of baptism, by immersion or sprinkling. (Commonly, the catechizing was given during Lent and the baptizing at Easter.) The believers appeared in white robes for their baptism,

and that rite was followed by confirmation, or the laying on of hands, that the Holy Spirit might descend upon each new member. After the laying on of hands came unction (anointing with oil), concluded with making the sign of the cross, while each new member vowed to give up the old gods and the old morality and to follow the law of Christ.

At first the churches were loosely organized, but by the end of the first century the congregations were directed by a board of elders, including one or more superintendents, or "bishops." These officers were assisted by deacons. Preaching and instruction were still, however, in the hands of prophets and teachers, who either belonged to the congregation or came from elsewhere, perhaps as traveling evangelists. Out of this type of government there naturally developed a more rigid and centralized form of organization. By the first quarter of the second century, we read of congregations being headed by a single bishop, assisted by elders and deacons, and, when this became general, this permanent head of the congregation included among his functions those of teaching and preaching, with the result that the Prophets and traveling evangelists of the early Church gradually disappeared from church life.

Christian Literature to the Year 150 C.E.

By the year 100 C.E., a Christian literature distinct from the Hebrew Scriptures (later called the Old Testament) and in some respects consciously designed to serve as a new scripture (it eventually became the New Testament) had come into being. Its appearance had become necessary with the gradual fading of the first generation's expectation of the imminent return of Jesus on the clouds of heaven—a faith that had once made the writing of a scripture seem superfluous. The eyewitnesses of Jesus' ministry were rapidly dying off by the time fifty years had passed, and the second-generation Christians, most of whom now lived far from Jerusalem, demanded a record of the master's life and teachings. The destruction of Jerusalem in 70 C.E. increased the urgency of this demand among those living outside of Palestine.

In the introduction to the preceding chapter, we reviewed the beginning of this literature. Something further needs to be said here about the nature and content of the completed literature that sprang from these beginnings, for each portion of it is significant of the greater and greater estimates placed on Jesus' teaching and person as time went on, and all combine to give us a sense of the factors, both Jewish and Greek, that operated in the first century of Christian history to give Christianity the richness and variety of thought and life handed down through the ages.

Of the earliest portions of the New Testament—the Epistles of Paul—we need say nothing more, for their doctrinal significance has already been discussed. So it is to the Gospels that we first turn, for each had a distinct Christological purpose in view.

Gospels

The Gospel of Mark, the earliest and briefest of the Gospels, was probably written in Antioch (or Rome?) during the years 65–70. According to Papias, a Christian writer of the early second century, it was based on the recollections of St. Peter as set down by John Mark, who had lived in Jerusalem before he came to Antioch. This Gospel shows no interest in Jesus' birth and youth, but begins with his baptism and gives a vivid account of his ministry, with pointed descriptions of his human feelings. But Jesus is much more than an average human being in Mark; he is the Son of God through the experience of divine election at his baptism, and the true Messiah, the "Holy One of God." No doctrine of divine incarnation nor any conception of preexistence such as Paul exhibits is found, however.

Matthew and Luke, going further, provide a basis for the doctrine of the incarnation. Both relate the stories of the virgin birth and of supernatural incidents occurring during Jesus' infancy. They concentrate throughout on the divine character of the Messiahship of Jesus and the manner in which, as one who came from heaven, he fulfilled Hebrew prophecy of the coming of the Son of man to redeem mankind.

But it is in the Fourth Gospel that we find the divine character of Jesus most clearly presented. The author sought to write a Gospel that would find the living, subjectively experienced Lord of Paul in the historic, objectively known Jesus of the first three Gospels. The fundamental thesis of this Gospel is, "So the Logos became flesh and tarried among us; we have seen his glory—glory such as only a son enjoys from his father."[E3] Though we are not allowed to forget the man Jesus, who was an objective personage in a world of real persons and things, the divinity of Jesus is the characteristic note of this Gospel. Jesus Christ is above all else "the Son of God." He is more than the Son of God in the Hebrew sense of being the Messiah, for though this simpler messianic significance is implicit, it is merged, even submerged, in the more comprehensive meanings found in the prologue of the Gospel. There Christ is represented as the visible bodying forth of the creative impulsion (the Logos) of the unseen and eternal Father and the mode or manifestation in a human person of the love of the Father for humankind. The Fourth Gospel therefore follows Paul in thinking of Christ as personally coming from God—that is, coming from a state of preexistence—and connecting him not only with the work of redemption on earth but with the creation of the world. In the body of the Gospel he is represented as remembering his preincarnate life, or at least that he had a preincarnate life. This preexistence, and not his human experience, accounts for his knowledge of God, to whom, therefore, he bears "true" witness. For, having come from heaven, "it is to what he has seen and heard that he gives testimony." What is more, not only are his words "the words of God," but he himself is the Word (the Logos); he himself is that to which he bears witness. To know him is to know the Father.

Later Epistles

The Epistle to the Hebrews, written in the decade before the Fourth Gospel, does not use the term logos (Word), but it is apparent that the writer had something like it in mind. In the first sentence he says that God, who spoke fragmentarily through the Prophets, has now spoken to us fully "in a Son, whom he had destined to possess everything, and through whom he had made the world." The Son while on earth resembled his fellow humans in every respect; he shared their flesh and blood and participated in their nature, even to suffering temptation and agonizing "with tears." But, because in his essential nature he was divine, his spiritual and psychological endowment was unique. The human Jesus and the divine Father were mutually accessible to each other at all times. In this Jesus differed from his fellow humans, who can have no such free access to the Father without his redemptive mediation as high priest.

A simpler and less doctrinal conception of the person and work of Christ appeared in the Epistles of James and Peter and in the noncanonical writings of the so-called Apostolic Fathers: Clement of Rome (writing *ca.* 93–97), Hermas of Rome (*ca.* 115–140), and the authors of such works as The Epistle of Barnabas (*ca.* 130), Second Clement (*ca.* 160), and The Teachings of the Twelve Apostles (*ca.* 130–160 or earlier). For the most part, these various writings gave expression to a straightforward adoration of Christ as the heaven-descended revealer of the true nature of God and the giver of a new law of life on the loftiest ethical plane.

Apologists

Addressed directly not to the religious needs of the growing Christian communities but rather to the world at large were individual works in the format of an *apologia* (defense) of the new faith. The Apologists were men educated in the best Greek and Roman schools and well versed in ancient philosophy, who sent their defenses of Christianity to the Roman emperors or to other non-Christians of high rank and reputation. Among their number were Aristides of Athens, Melito, bishop of Sardis, Minucius Felix, a cultivated gentleman of Rome, and most famous of all Justin, called the Martyr because of the nature of his death, who, like his disciple Tatian, had been successively a Stoic, an Aristotelian, a Pythagorean, and a Platonist. When he turned Christian, he found in his new faith the perfect philosophy. He was far from believing that all other thought systems were untrue. The divine Logos was at work in the world before the time of Christ, enlightening Socrates and Heraclitus and imparting truth to such "barbarians" (a truly Greek expression) as the patriarchs of the Old Testament, so that the Greek philosophers and the Hebrew prophets, insofar as the Logos enlightened them, were to this degree Christians before Christ. But Christianity was superior to all other thought systems, because the Logos not only spoke through Christ, the Logos *was* Christ. Christ perfectly revealed the truth of divine reason and was the peerless teacher whom all humanity should accept.

The significance of Justin Martyr and his fellow Apologists is that they successfully demonstrated how Christianity, when it chose to appear in Greek dress, could, at whatever sacrifice of its original Hebraic form, not only continue to make a powerful religious appeal but hold its own with any of the classic philosophies of the ancient world—Platonism and Stoicism especially. It became easier now for Christian writers to invade the field of general philosophy and to speak of the Christian religion as being truly universal in its scope and application. *Catholic* was the word they used.

GLOSSARY

agapé a love feast, a gathering of early Christians for a common meal, fellowship, and worship, from a Greek term for love as a spontaneous offering of care and esteem

'Am ha' aretz "people of the land," common folk, as distinguished from pious observers of religious practices

apocalypticism one type of eschatology: belief in an imminent, sudden ending of history and a disclosure of God's purpose through punishment of the wicked and vindication of the righteous

ekklesia (Latin *ecclesia*) an assembly of persons bound by common background or purpose; in Christian usage, "the people of God" gathered through Christ, that is, the church in either universal or local expression

eschatology "last things," generic term for ideas about the end of the world

Essenes an ascetic Jewish sect, 2nd c. B.C.E. to the 3rd c. C.E.

Eucharist the Lord's Supper, literally, "thanksgiving"

Hellenists in New Testament usage (Acts), Christian believers of Gentile background, or of Jewish origin but steeped in Greek culture and practice

Judaizers Christians of Jewish background who held that observance of the Law (circumcision, dietary laws, etc.) should be required of all converts

Logos "word" or "reason," in the Gospel of John the creative/redemptive intention or purpose of God that became manifest (incarnate) in Christ

Pentecost in Judaism a harvest festival (Shebhuoth) fifty days after Passover; in Christian calendars the seventh Sunday after Easter celebrating the coming of the Holy Spirit upon assembled believers (Acts 2:1 ff.)

Pharisees an influential Jewish sect of the Second Temple period advocating earnest and comprehensive application of Jewish law; they accepted oral tradition and new ideas such as resurrection

"Q" (Quelle) designation given to a hypothetical written collection of the sayings of Jesus presumed to have been shared by the compilers of the gospels of Matthew and Luke

Sadducees a party in Judaism active from the 2nd c. B.C.E. through the 1st c. C.E., they rejected recent oral tradition and reduced Judaism to matters specifically treated in written law

Sanhedrin the supreme political, religious, and judicial body of Judaism during the Roman period

Zealots a sect advocating armed resistance to Roman authority; also called sicarii ("dagger men") or lestai ("brigands") by their critics

CHAPTER 16

The Religious Development of Christianity

The word *catholic* was first applied to the Christian Church in its meaning of "universal." Descriptively, this was an apt designation for a religious faith that now reached into all provinces of the Empire and into every class of society. But it was too good an adjective to escape a more technical use. It became, in fact, part of the name of *the single* organized institution that expressed the Christian religion after the middle of the second century. With this name the Catholic Church could stand united in the resolve to maintain itself against its external foes and also to combat heresy and schism within.

I. THE ANCIENT CATHOLIC CHURCH (150–1054 B.C.E.)

In striving to keep both its outer and inner integrity, the ancient Catholic Church developed two things: (1) a system of doctrine, clarified and declared to be purged of error, and (2) an ecclesiastical organization characterized in its own eyes by apostolicity, catholicity, unity, and holiness. We shall now describe the several steps by which these developments were effected.

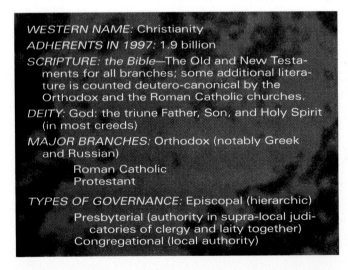

WESTERN NAME: Christianity

ADHERENTS IN 1997: 1.9 billion

SCRIPTURE: the Bible—The Old and New Testaments for all branches; some additional literature is counted deutero-canonical by the Orthodox and the Roman Catholic churches.

DEITY: God: the triune Father, Son, and Holy Spirit (in most creeds)

MAJOR BRANCHES: Orthodox (notably Greek and Russian)

  Roman Catholic
  Protestant

TYPES OF GOVERNANCE: Episcopal (hierarchic)

  Presbyterial (authority in supra-local judicatories of clergy and laity together)
  Congregational (local authority)

Heresies Rooted in Greek Thought

It was Jesus' fortune to appear not only at a time when the Jews were looking for a messiah but when the rest of the Mediterranean world was seeking an incarnation of godhead and had, at the same time, evolved the concept of the Logos, without realizing with what richness of meaning it might be endowed were it to be applied to a savior-god appearing in the flesh of a human personality. When Christian thinkers brought the Logos concept to bear upon Jesus, a whole theology sprang, almost without effort, into being, a theology that combined in the most satisfactory measure both religion and

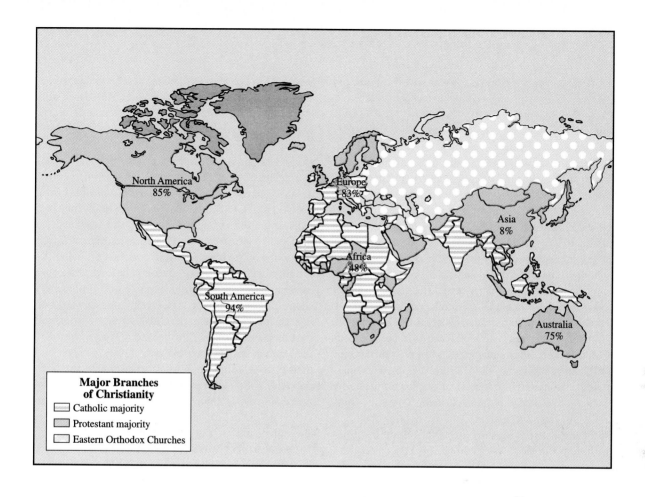

Major Branches
of Christianity

☐ Catholic majority
■ Protestant majority
☐ Eastern Orthodox Churches

North America 85%

South America 94%

Europe 83%

Africa 48%

Asia 8%

Australia 75%

philosophy. Yet there were dangers in the process. A just balance of elements had to be preserved, or the religious value of the new synthesis would be destroyed. It became the task of the Christian bishops and teachers of the second and third centuries to find that balance and to outlaw all deviations from the orthodox view.

Among the interpretations of the work and person of Christ during the second century that were later declared heretical were the Gnostic and Marcionite doctrines.

Gnosticism and Docetism

The view called Gnosticism (from *gnosis,* or esoteric knowledge) had a characteristic assumption running

through all of its varieties: the Gnostics (who were mainly in the East) started with a dualism that radically divided spirit from matter and regarded the material world as so vile and degrading that the impersonal and unknowable God—the ground of all being, dwelling ineffably in pure light—could have had nothing to do with making it. In its partially Christianized form, Gnosticism, instead of assimilating philosophy to the Christian religion, adopted the figure of Christ as the final ingredient in a Greco-Oriental synthesis. Surrounded by a society of male and female spiritual beings, called aeons, the preexistent Jesus among them, God dwelt far above the evil world. At a lower level lived and labored the artisan—maker of the earth, the son of a fallen aeon, Sophia, who in her fall nonetheless brought light down into

473

the darkness; this artisan is the deity of the book of Genesis, a spiritual vulgarian, who mechanically produced the evil mass that is the world of matter. The Old Testament and its way of life are hopelessly infected with this deity's inferior conception of things. To these Gnostics the serpent in the Garden of Eden, in bringing Adam and Eve to the Tree of Knowledge (that is, of Gnosis!), was a benefactor and not a vile tempter, and did his best to save the parents of the human race from Yahweh's misleading guidance! When Jesus, the compassionate divine aeon, saw how badly things were going on earth, he came down in the masquerade of a body. The flesh of this divine apparition only *seemed* (Greek *dokein*) real, for Spirit *actually* enfleshed (incarnate) would be defiled. This total rejection of the humanity of Jesus was called Docetism, a heresy not confined to Gnostics. If God can only be revealed through *gnosis*, not in any fleshly form or incarnation, then human souls struggling in their defiling envelopes of flesh should develop an ascetic discipline of the body and acquire esoteric saving wisdom for the mind. They could then free themselves from the defiling material world and escape from the prison of the flesh into pure spirituality of being.

Here were doctrines that the Church as a whole felt indeed it could not countenance without violence to its own historic foundations: that God does not control the entire universe, that the Yahweh of the Old Testament is an inferior being, that the Old Testament must be rejected as valueless, that Jesus was not really born and did not truly suffer and die, and that there can be no resurrection of the flesh.

Marcion's Proposed Canon

The suggestion that the Old Testament is valueless found, however, a tempestuous advocate in Marcion, an early Christian teacher from Sinope in Asia Minor who later settled in Rome. Without joining any of the Gnostic schools (which flourished chiefly in Egypt and Asia Minor), he nevertheless followed their lead in excoriating the God of the Old Testament as a just but cruelly legalistic and merciless deity, who, though he created the material world, was a demiurge of an inferior moral quality. The really good God, a god of love and mercy, who created the invisible, spiritual world, was not known to the prophets of the Old Testament; Christ was the first to reveal him. Human beings are in bondage to the bodies they have received from the God of the Old Testament, but their souls may find redemption through faith in the God of Jesus. Let them then follow Christ and St. Paul in asceticism, celibacy, and scorn of the physical world and strive to enter the Kingdom of the good God, here and hereafter. Marcion increased the alarm his views created by proposing a canon of scripture. The scripture he put forward—to *replace,* not supplement, the Old Testament—consisted of three parts: Gospel, Apostle, and a work of his own, the *Antitheses.* He accepted only Luke's Gospel, and then only as edited by himself to eliminate the birth narrative (because it suggested incarnation in a real earthly body). The only accepted apostle was Paul, ten Letters edited to emphasize the antithesis between Law and Spirit, and arranged in order of anti-Law content. To make matters worse, Marcion broke away from the church at Rome and began to organize Marcionite congregations.

The challenge of Marcionism was not a trivial thing. He was the first to edit and publish a new scripture, and by that action he shocked the leaders of the complacent main body of Christians into an awareness that, unless broader consensus on a canon could be found, the integrity of all their literature could be jeopardized by local teachers who might follow his example, editing received manuscripts to suit their own views.

Marcionite congregations survived at least into the fourth century. In fact, the oldest inscription from any Christian church is on a building in a village south of Damascus (*ca.* 319 C.E.): "gathering place (*synagogue*) of the Marcionites of Lebabon [sic] of the Lord and Savior Jesus Christ under the leadership of Paul the presbyter."

> "The prophet of the Creator-God, when the people were locked in battle, climbed to the top of the mountain and stretched forth his hands to God, that he might kill as many as possible in the battle; our Lord, the Good, stretched forth his hands not to kill men but to save them."
>
> —Marcion, *The Antithesis*

The Arian Controversy: Was Christ "Created"?

While all of these events were in progress, the theological formulation of the Catholic faith had gone steadily forward, Clement and Origen in Alexandria, and Tertullian and Cyprian, also in North Africa, began to clarify and define the still-inchoate doctrines concerning the relation of Father, Son, and Holy Spirit and to set forth the claims of the Church to power and authority. But lack of complete agreement among them gave scope to acrimonious disputes.

Constantine felt that the issues had to be settled by a world council of the churches. The circumstances were these: A learned presbyter of Alexandria, Arius, differed with his bishop on the question of whether Christ was a finite or an eternal being. Arius held that Christ, even as the Logos, was a created being. He was made like other creatures out of nothing, so he could not be eternal; neither could he be of the same substance as God. The Son, he argued, had a beginning, whereas God, who is eternally One, was without beginning. This view came to be called Arianism. Arius' bishop took issue with him, asserting that the Son was eternal, uncreated, and of like essence with God. Constantine, after failing in conciliatory efforts, called a council of the whole Church to settle the issue once and for all.

The Nicene Creed

In the summer of 325, some 300 delegate bishops, mostly from the East, met at Nicaea, across the Bosphorus from Constantinople, and produced the famous formula of the *Creed of Nicaea.* With its crucial phrases italicized, its text was the following:

> We believe in one God, Father Almighty, maker of all things, visible and invisible. And in one Lord Jesus Christ, the Son of God, begotten of [literally, "out of"] the Father, as His only Son, that is, from the substance of the Father, God from God, light from light, true God from true God, *begotten, not made, of the same substance [homo-ousios] with the Father,* through whom all things in heaven and earth were made; who for us men and our salvation came down and was made flesh, became man, suffered, and rose on the third day, ascended to heaven, and is coming to judge the living and the dead. And (we believe) in the Holy Spirit.

Attached to this creed was a rider declaring anathema those who say, "There was a time when he was not" or assert, "The Son of God is of a different subsistence or substance, or is created."

This creed, adopted under pressure from the emperor, who wanted peace, did not immediately solve the doctrinal difficulties or save the peace. The Council had turned to nonbiblical Greek philosophical terminology whereby an *active* unity, "God was in Christ reconciling..." was distilled into a *static* essence: "one substance." The phrases we have italicized were bitterly denounced by many and were actually revoked by later councils. Indeed, it was perhaps only the ardent, indefatigable, and patient defense of it by Athanasius, bishop of Alexandria, in tract after tract, that finally overbore opposition and led to its ultimate acceptance. And even then it was several generations before it became infallible in the eyes of the Church.

It should be noted that the Nicene Creed, as it is recited in many Christian churches today, is not the original creed adopted at Nicaea in 325 but an expanded form of it (often called the "Constantinopolitan Creed"), which came into use after the time of the General Council of 381. For completeness, we may add that the later formulation says firmly that the Godhead of Father, Son, and Holy Spirit is *one in essence* (or substance), though *in three hypostases* (subsistences or individualized manifestations). When this formulation was translated into Latin, the rather abstract Greek for *individualized manifestation* became the rather concrete word *persona,* and connotations of distinct and self-contained personality were suggested in a way not intended by the original Greek wording.

What Anthanasius successfully urged upon his at first unbelieving contemporaries in the East was that the issue at stake was no mere verbal matter, no question of words; it was the issue of whether Christ is truly a savior. For the East in general held to the Greek conception of salvation, that it consists in making divine and immortal the sinful mortality of the human being. Athanasius was eventually able to convince the East that only God can bring immortal life down into the realm of mortality, and so Jesus must

have been true God, truly so in substance or essence, not just a created being of lower quality, as Arius had urged.

Christological Issues: Two "Natures" or One?

The enterprise of transposing Hebraic Messianic concepts such as "Son of God" into the forms of Greek speculative thought, once begun, led to complications. The Creed of Nicaea said nothing about the mode of union of the divine Logos with the human Jesus. So the incarnation itself now became the center of heated theological argument.

Once the distinction was drawn between the divine and the human natures of Christ, it was possible to regard them as being so distinct as to make it difficult to account for Jesus' unified personality. On the other hand, it was equally easy to see such a dominance of the one nature over the other as to suggest the absorption of the one nature into the other.

The West had no great difficulty here, for among the definitive statements of Tertullian, made over a century earlier, was the generally accepted formula: "We see (in Christ) a twofold state, not confounded but conjoined in one person, Jesus, God and man."[B1] The practical-minded West puzzled over the matter no further.

Not so the East. It was soon fiercely, and deeply, divided. The great sees of Alexandria and Antioch became especially irreconcilable—until the Muslim conquests hammered them down in common disaster. Jesus was a man, the Antiochans declared; as the Jesus of history he was completely human, and was endowed with reason and free will like all other men; the Logos dwelt in him as in a temple, in perfect moral unity, such that the Logos and Jesus willed the same things. Nestorius, their chief spokesman, excited riots among the monks of Constantinople, where he became bishop, when he preached a sermon against calling the Virgin Mary "the mother of God," declaring she did not bear a deity, she bore "a man, the organ of deity."[C1] Cyril, bishop of Alexandria, now entered the fray on the other side. Christ's humanity, he said, indeed possessed body, rational soul, and spirit, but it was without personality; the Logos was its personality. What he meant was that the human nature of Jesus

was assimilated by the personality of the Logos, so that "from two natures [there arose] one," a wholly divine personality. Those who followed Nestorius (the Nestorians), however, felt that this denatured the humanity; the truth was that the humanity and divinity were "in conjunction" only; they were united in will without one absorbing the other.

Charges and countercharges flew thick and fast. A general council was called in 431 and found itself unwholesomely involved in political machinations and imperial pressures. Nestorius was deposed and banished. But the issues remained unsettled.

The Creed of Chalcedon

Finally, a general council met in 451 at Chalcedon in Asia Minor and formulated a definition of the relation of Christ's natures that became standard Catholic doctrine. It read:

> Following, therefore, the holy Fathers, we confess and all teach with one accord one and the same Son, our Lord Jesus Christ, at once complete in Godhead and complete in manhood, truly God and truly man, and, further, of a rational soul and body; of one essence with the Father as regards his Godhead, and at the same time of one essence with us as regards his manhood, in all respects like us, apart from sin; as regards his Godhead begotten of the Father before the ages, yet as regards his manhood—on account of us and our salvation—begotten in these last days of Mary the Virgin, bearer of God; one and the same Christ, Son, Lord, Only-begotten, proclaimed in two natures, without confusion, without change, without division, without separation; the difference of the natures being in no way destroyed on account of the union, but rather the peculiar property of each nature being preserved and concurring in one person and one hypostasis—not as though parted or divided into two persons, but one and the same Son and Only-begotten God the Logos, Lord, Jesus Christ, even as the prophets from of old and the Lord Jesus Christ taught us concerning him, and the Creed of the Fathers has handed down to us.

This creed, like the Nicene, was a triumph for the West, and of course the West accepted it without demur. But the East did not find it so satisfactory. Those who

followed the Alexandrian lead dissented as "partisans of the *one* nature" and were called, accordingly, Monophysites. From them sprang the Coptic Church of Egypt and Abyssinia and the "Jacobite" churches of Syria and Armenia, which dissent to this day.

The Nestorians persisted as a sect in Syria, however, and they found the peoples to the east of them receptive. So they took their doctrines into Persia, and from thence to India and China, which they reached in the seventh century. In Syria, Nestorianism has survived the Muslim conquest. Nestorian churches also still exist in southern India and northwestern Iran.

The Growth of the Papacy

It was the good fortune of the church of Rome to be on the victorious side in the great doctrinal controversies of the second and fourth centuries. During the Gnostic crisis it was the church of Rome that framed the Apostles' Creed, and it was the same church that led in the formation of the New Testament canon. The superior dignity of the church of Rome was acknowledged by eminent authorities of the West. Irenaeus, from his place in Gaul (France), urged the Western churches to agree with Rome in all matters involving the apostolic tradition. Cyprian, from his place in North Africa, thought of Rome as "the chief church whence priestly unity takes its source."[B2]

Aware of all these things, and sure that if civil authority rested at Constantinople in the person of the emperor, spiritual authority rested at Rome in his own person, Pope Leo I (440–461) declared that because St. Peter was the first among the Apostles, St. Peter's church should be accorded primacy among the churches. He based his claim on transmittable powers held to have been granted to Peter in Matthew 16:18–19: "I tell you, your name is Peter, a rock, and on this rock I will build my church, and the powers of death will not subdue it. I will give you the keys of the Kingdom of Heaven, and whatever you forbid on earth will be held in heaven to be forbidden, and whatever you permit on earth will be held in heaven to be permitted." Critics in opposition to the use of this passage to support papal authority question its authenticity and say further that the feminine gender of "this rock" in Greek suggests that it has an impersonal

rather than a personal reference, perhaps not to Peter as an individual, but to what he had just said: "Thou art the Christ."

Leo thus made a special application, we note, of the doctrine of "apostolic succession," a doctrine that had early been formulated, for example, by Clement of Rome at the close of the first century, and that was generally understood to apply to *all* bishops as the successors, through the laying on of hands at ordination, of *all* the apostles. But Leo held that St. Peter was the first in rank among the apostles, and hence the successors of Peter were the first among bishops.

He and his successors took steps to make good this claim, but their success was in suspense while the Roman Empire fell. Well was it for the pope, indeed, that most of the Empire's invaders—Visigoths, Ostrogoths, Vandals, Burgundians, and Lombards—had already been converted to Christianity by missionaries of the heretical Arian sects. They were heretics, but they were Christians, so when Alaric the Visigoth captured Rome, he treated the pope with favor and spared the churches, while rapine and ruin overwhelmed all else around.

As the inroads of the barbarians swelled to a disastrous flood tide and civilization faltered, the popes drew some consolation from the fact that the Arian invaders were after a while persuaded to become Catholics.

Early Monasticism in the East

Monasticism grew rapidly in the Catholic Church after Christianity was made the imperial state religion. Early tendencies in its direction appeared in the individuals who followed St. Paul's suggestion that men and women believers might well practice sexual abstinence and live as "virgins." But as a movement involving a definite break with society, it did not begin until toward the end of the third century. Its first great representative was St. Anthony of Korma in Egypt. After trying to practice asceticism in his own village, an attempt that failed, he went away into the solitude of the desert. There he was beset by his famous temptations, at peace only when asleep, when awake fasting and praying ceaselessly, but haunted by demons, in male and female form, enticing him to every sin. Egypt was full of lonely exiles and friendless persons; its climate was favorable for austerity and its people were

respectful toward asceticism. The belief was prevalent (in accordance with the Gnostic and Alexandrian theologies) that the world and the body were defiling, so Anthony attracted many followers. It was soon apparent, however, that those who strove to live entirely alone often went mad and just as often failed through lack of guidance, so a communal type of hermit life (cenobitism) was developed by Pachomius, a convert to Coptic Christianity in southern Egypt, who organized monasteries (and one nunnery) under a rule of balanced work and meditation, directed by an abbot.

Both the solitary and communal types of monasticism quickly spread to Syria and Asia Minor. Many solitary hermits drew great attention to themselves. Though a few retired to caves and desert places; others, like Simeon the Stylite, lived on the tops of pillars in ruined cities and had their food lifted up to them on poles; others (the Dendrites) resided in trees; still others, in the same manner as Buddhist monks in China and Tibet, walled themselves up in narrow enclosures and had food tossed in to them or pushed through slits in the wall. But this form of asceticism was never more than the rage of the moment. By far the greater number of hermits gathered together in monasteries (that is, became monks) and maintained themselves by their own husbandry. They early won the favor of Basil, bishop of Caesarea, one of the three great Cappadocians still honored by the Eastern Orthodox churches, and he laid down for them a rule that is universal in the East to this day. By it the monasteries submitted themselves to the bishops of their localities and, in addition to the monastic practices shared with the West, prohibited strong drink and outside or noncanonical reading. Social service among the poor and orphaned was prescribed.

Monasticism in the West: St. Benedict

In the West the monastic movement was slow in getting started, but when the Germanic invasions turned society upside down, it became popular and developed many independent orders. For some time each monastery had its own rule, and some were shockingly lax. In the sixth century, therefore, appeared the order of St. Benedict, whose founder prescribed for those who joined his order a full life of manual labor in the monastery's fields or shops, serious directed reading, and above all, worship throughout the day and part of the night. The severity of the *Benedictine Rule* is suggested by the following passage from it:

> Idleness is the great enemy of the soul, therefore the monks should always be occupied, either in manual labor or in holy reading. The hours for these occupations should be arranged according to the seasons, as follows: From Easter to the first of October, the monks shall go to work at the first hour [6 A.M.], and the time from the fourth to the sixth hour shall be spent in reading. After dinner, which comes at the sixth hour [noon], they shall lie down and rest in silence; but anyone who wishes may read, if he does it so as not to disturb anyone else. Nones [a service designed for 3 P.M.] shall be observed a little earlier, about the middle of the eighth hour, and the monks shall go back to work, laboring until vespers. . . . From the first of October to the beginning of Lent, the monks shall have until the full second hour for reading, at which hour the service of terce [a service for 9 A.M.] shall be held. After terce, they shall work at their respective tasks until the ninth hour [3 P.M.]. When the ninth hour sounds, they shall cease from labor and be ready for the service at the second bell. After dinner they shall spend the time in reading the lessons and the psalms. During Lent, the time from daybreak to the third hour shall be devoted to reading, and then they shall work at their appointed tasks until the tenth hour. At the beginning of Lent each of the monks shall be given a book from the library of the monastery which he shall read entirely through. One or two of the older monks shall be appointed to go about through the monastery during the hours set apart for reading, to see that none of the monks are idling away the time, instead of reading, and so not only wasting their own time but perhaps disturbing others as well. . . . And if any brother is negligent or lazy, refusing or being unable to read or meditate at the time, let him be made to work, so that he shall at any rate not be idle.[D]

That the Benedictine monasteries, which eventually spread through western Europe, had libraries was in itself a fact of great consequence for the future. Books were thereby saved that might otherwise have been lost.

St. Jerome, St. Chrysostom, and Gregory I

Just how consistent monasticism was, at least in the case of some individuals, with an active purpose of serving society at large was apparent in the life, first, of St. Jerome, who while in monastic seclusion in Palestine completed the *Vulgate,* the translation of the Old and New Testaments into Latin; and in the career also of St. Chrysostom, the "golden-mouthed," who emerged from hermit life to attract great congregations in Antioch by his sermons and was therefore called to the bishopric of Constantinople (and the jealousies that plunged him into the obscurity of ill-deserved exile).

Another influential representative of the hermit life was Gregory the Great, the first monk to be chosen to the papal office (590–604). An administrator with great personal gifts, he so managed the financial resources of the papacy (the church in Rome now had great landholdings in Italy) that he virtually ruled Italy like a monarch. He laid the foundations of later papal authority in England, in whose conversion to Christianity he took great interest. (England was converted from the north by way of Ireland and Scotland, from the south by missionaries sent out from Rome directly. Ireland had been converted earlier by St. Patrick. His converts crossed to Scotland; after they won it, missionaries entered England from Scotland.)

Gregory increased his ecclesiastical power in France and Spain. His emphasis on penance and his stress on purification of the soul after death (purgatory) brought these aspects of belief and practice for the first-time to the forefront in Catholicism. He anticipated later practice by advising penitents to seek the aid of the saints. He took it to be a fact that as the apostolic successor to St. Peter, who was "the prince of all the Apostles" to whom "by the Lord's voice the care of the whole church was committed," he should be acknowledged to be the head of the whole Church. He thus was the forerunner and model of the powerful medieval popes.

Augustine of Hippo: His Life

But the greatest personality of the ancient Catholic Church was Augustine (354–430), bishop of Hippo, in North Africa. He was a person in whose temperament almost every human quality was present in great intensity, yet such was the clarity and strength of his mind that he was able to master his unruly passions and harness them to a Christian purpose. His autobiographical *Confessions* is a literary landmark, not only as a sustained effort in self-analysis, but also as one of the world's first autobiographies to deal seriously with the thoughts and feelings of childhood.

Born of a pagan father and Christian mother, he attended the schools of his native North Africa, and at seventeen, while pursuing the study of rhetoric, he followed the promptings of his ardently sensuous nature and took a concubine. He rejected the New Testament at first as being "unworthy to be compared with the dignity of Cicero,"[E1] whose works he was studying. But Cicero was not enough, so he became an adherent of Manichaeism. He derived only small comfort from this doctrine, however, for he never became one of the "perfect"; he could only be a "hearer," because he was unable to give up the lusts of the flesh, as Manichaeism demanded. His prayer at that time, he says in his famous *Confessions,* was, "Grant me chastity and continence, but not yet."[E2]

At twenty-nine he went to Italy. There, in Milan, he heard the powerful sermons of Ambrose, another of the great personalities of the ancient Catholic Church. His conscience was touched. When his mother, upon joining him, urged him to enter upon betrothal to someone of his own class, he sorrowfully sent away his faithful concubine, who had borne him a son, and agreed to do as his mother asked; though on account of the tender years of the girl to whom he contracted himself, he put his marriage off. Then, finding himself still a prey to desire, he took another concubine. He almost despaired of himself now, for it seemed indeed true to him, as the Manichaeans taught, that the flesh is incurably evil.

Radical changes in his point of view followed from an awakened interest in Neo-Platonism. He began to consider it true that the temptations of the flesh follow from a falling away from God rather than from the presence of any positive and inherent element of badness in the flesh. In fact, he came to believe that God is the source of all things, and that matter and evil are to be defined in terms of an absence of the creative energy of God, due to spiritual remoteness from the one eternal good Being.

His conversion to Christianity occurred with apparent suddenness. Learning of a Neo-Platonist who had turned Christian, and then of some Egyptian monks who overcame their temptations by simple faithfulness to their monastic discipline, he ran distractedly from his friend Alypius into the farther reaches of a garden and heard a child's voice from across the wall saying, "Take up and read." Returning to his friend, he seized a copy of the Epistles of the New Testament lying on the bench, and opening it, read, "Not in rioting; and drunkenness, not in chambering and wantonness ... but put ye on the Lord Jesus Christ, and make not provision for the flesh to fulfil the lusts thereof." These words brought him to a decision.[E3] Thenceforth, he lived in strict continence. Baptized by Ambrose, he left for North Africa, resolved to found a monastery. There he became the bishop of Hippo, wrote voluminously for the next thirty years, and died while the Vandals were besieging his city.

Augustine was so many-sided that his theology is a synthesis of various trends. One sees in it a Neo-Platonist strain that modifies his basic reliance on Hebraic insights. But he yielded to no one tendency exclusively. So germinal was his thinking that we should not take leave of him without briefly summarizing his doctrines of God, human nature, and the Church, and his philosophy of history.

Augustine on God

Augustine's mystical personal experience of God kept him from thinking of God as a pure abstraction. God is near and very real, and both in the person of Jesus and through the activity of the Holy Spirit has broken into history and is continuously at work in human hearts. And yet, Augustine's conception had a Neo-Platonist tinge. God is the one eternal Being, alone absolutely real and absolutely good. He is the source of all other things, and they depend on him at every moment for their continued existence. The physical universe especially has only a derived reality and is scarcely worthy of study in itself.

How he could invoke God as being at every moment literally at hand and yet experience him as not identifiable with physical reality is evident in the famous vision he shared with his beloved mother at Ostia a few days before her death.

The day now approaching whereon she was to depart this life (which day Thou well knewest, we knew not), it came to pass ... that she and I stood alone, leaning in a certain window, which looked into the garden of the house where we now lay, at Ostia.... We were discoursing then together, alone, very sweetly ... enquiring between ourselves in the presence of the Truth, which Thou art, of what sort the eternal life of the saints was to be.... And when our discourse was brought to that point, that the very delight of the earthly senses was ... in respect of the sweetness of [Eternity], not only not worthy of comparison, but not even of mention; we, raising up ourselves with a more glowing affection towards the "Self-same," did by degrees pass through all things bodily, even the very heaven whence sun and moon and stars shine upon the earth; yea, we were soaring higher yet, by inward musing, and discourse, and admiring of Thy works; and we came to our own minds, and went beyond them, that we might arrive at that region of never-failing plenty, where *Thou feedest Israel* forever with the food of truths....

We were saying then: If to any the tumult of the flesh were hushed, hushed the images of earth, and waters, and air, hushed also the poles of heaven, yea, the very soul be hushed to herself, and by not thinking on self surmount self, hushed all dreams and imaginary revelations, every tongue and every sign, ... and He alone speak, ... that we might hear His Word, not through any tongue of flesh, nor angel's voice, nor sound of thunder, nor in the dark riddle of a similitude, but might hear His Very Self ... were not this [to] *Enter into thy Master's Joy?* ...

Lord, Thou knowest that in that day when we were speaking these things, and this world with all its delights became, as we speak, contemptible to us, my mother said, "Son, for mine own part I have no further delight in any thing in this life.... One thing there was for which I desired to linger for a while in this life, that I might see thee a Catholic Christian before I died. My God hath done this for me more abundantly, that I should now see thee withal, despising earthly happiness, become His servant: what do I here?"[F]

Augustine adapted his conception of God to his Christian conviction that God is "one in three." In the Trinity he saw no subordination of one member to another, as earlier theologians did. "There is so great an equality in that Trinity," he wrote, "that not only the Father is not greater than the Son, as regards divinity, but neither are the Father and the Son together greater than the Holy Spirit."[E4] Going further, he suggested that the Holy Spirit, though equal with the Father and the Son regarding divinity, "proceeds not only from the Father but also from the Son (*filioque*)."[E5] Yet again, the Trinity is as united as lover, loved, and love, or as memory, understanding, and will, of which he said, "Since, then, these three, memory, understanding, will, are not three lives, but one life; nor three minds, but one mind; it follows certainly that neither are they three substances, but one substance."[E6]

Augustine on Human Nature

In forming his doctrine of human nature—which had enormous influence not only on Catholic theologians but also on the Protestant Reformers—Augustine drew upon his bitter experiences of his own moral weakness in youth. Human beings in and of themselves are depraved, "the entire mass of [their] nature ruined,"[E7] "bound by original sin."[E8] This is the inheritance we all have from Adam. Adam was created good and with a fine intelligence. But he was endowed with free will, and though he could have chosen not to sin, he, along with Eve, ate of the forbidden fruit in willfulness and pride. After that he and all his descendants have been in a state of original sin, from which no one can now escape by his own efforts. It is as though the whole human race were morally diseased.

But God is merciful. Those whom he chooses, he saves by divine grace. Not that they deserve such mercy; it is entirely a free gift. This is the love of God, on which no human claims can be made. And when the divine grace comes, no one can resist it. Uplifted to effort and perseverance— "the perseverance of the saints"[E9]— the sinner is changed, justified, sanctified. To others the grace never comes, for they are doomed to damnation.

This hard doctrine involved Augustine in fierce controversy with a British monk called Pelagius, and with others. These men contended that there is no such thing as original sin, all men having an aptitude for goodness. Adam may have left to his descendants a bad example, but no inherited and inescapable moral weakness. Anyone who has faith is justified. But Augustine fought stoutly for his view. He knew from experience how inescapable are pride and lust in a life spent apart from God and how irresistible is God's sudden grace.

Augustine on the Church and History

The Church, according to Augustine, is the divinely appointed institution to perform the sacraments that are the means of grace. There is only one Church, and none who are outside of it, whether heathen or heretic, can be saved. In opposition to a purist group in North Africa called the Donatists, who maintained that the sacraments performed by unworthy priests were ineffectual, Augustine held that the sacraments are instituted by God, not by human beings, and therefore they communicate grace regardless of the unworthy character of any person who performs them.

Augustine expressed his philosophy of history in his treatise *The City of God*. When he wrote it, Rome, "the mistress of the world," had been sacked by barbaric conquerors, and the pagan writers of the time were loudly lamenting what they conceived to be a fact, that the city had declined and fallen because the grand old deities that had brought greatness to it had been abandoned for the enfeebling god of the Christians. In defending Christianity against this charge, Augustine boldly contrasted the Earthly City, which in history reached its clearest forms in Babylon and Rome, with the City of God, to which God's elect in every generation have belonged. In his own day, he said, not all those who were in the visible Church were members of the invisible City of God. They,

> "We conclude that a man is not justified by the precepts of a holy life but by faith in Jesus Christ. That is to say, not by the law of works, but by that of faith; not by the letter, but by the spirit; not by the merits of deeds, but by gratuitous grace."
>
> —Augustine[E10]

the non-elect, together with all of those outside the Church, belonged to the Earthly City, which must decline and pass away. But the City of God will survive even the death of "civilization" and ultimately inherit the earth, so wrote Augustine, even while the barbarians hammered at the gates of the cities of his Africa.

It cannot be said that the Roman Catholic Church adopted all of the Augustinian theology. Other influences, as we shall see, intervened. But in its emphasis on justification by faith, the Protestant Reformation was a return to Augustine just as much as it was a return to Paul and Jesus.

The Division of the Church into East and West

Not only was the Roman Empire brought low by invasions from the north, in the seventh century other invaders appeared in the southeast and rapidly overran Palestine, Syria, Asia Minor, North Africa, and Spain. The staunch defense of Constantinople checked them for a time in the East, and a Frankish chieftain named Charles Martel turned them back in France in 732. Otherwise, perhaps, the Muslims would have taken Europe.

The effect of the Muslim conquests on what was left of the Roman Empire was to divide it more seriously than ever. The Emperor Leo III at Constantinople incurred the displeasure of Pope Gregory II by his efforts to obtain reform in the face of the onrushing Muslim peril. Recoiling sharply from the criticisms coming from Arab (and Christian) quarters concerning the "idolatrous" veneration of images and pictures in the Christian churches, the emperor forbade, in 726, their further use—thus fathering the first iconoclastic (image-destroying) movement in Christian history. There was immediate remonstrance both in the East and West. In the East, Leo used his army to enforce his decree. But Rome was far enough away to make good its disobedience. What was more, the pope called a Roman synod and obtained an action excommunicating those who opposed the use of pictures, namely, the emperor and those who sided with him. The emperor then retaliated by removing Sicily and southern Italy from the pope's spiritual jurisdiction. This left the pope in a precarious situation, for north-

ern Italy was occupied by Lombards, and they had their hearts set on the conquest of Rome. So the pope called for help from Charles Martel, whose prowess against the Muslims made his aid worth seeking. Both Gregory and Charles were to die before that help was forthcoming, but Charles's son, Pippin the Short, invaded Italy, brought the Lombard king to terms, and made a present of the province of Ravenna to the pope. He thus caused the pope to fix the orientation of the papacy toward the northern European or transalpine lands rather than toward the East and, without knowing it, laid the foundations of a huge, unstable, Western empire.

The pope gained much. He was now not only the largest landholder in Italy, with an immense annual income, but a temporal sovereign, the ruler of "the states of the Church," as they came to be called, and these were very important to him. (From 740 to 1870, the popes held firmly to their States of the Church, and, when bereft of them by King Victor Emmanuel, were outraged. In 1929, Mussolini restored the pope's temporal sovereignty over the Vatican and the grounds immediately around it.) Pippin's son, Charlemagne, gained much too. He built up an empire that included almost all of western Europe—in modern terms, France, northeastern Spain, Belgium, Holland, most of Germany, Austria, Hungary, and northern Italy. Cordial to the Church, Charlemagne came to Rome, and on Christmas Day, 800, was formally crowned Holy Roman Emperor by Leo III. This act signalized the fact that West and East were at the parting of the ways, a fact accepted some years later by Emperor Leo V in Constantinople when he officially recognized the title of Charlemagne, and thus acknowledged that the Empire had fallen in two.

The Doctrinal Rift

Meanwhile, a serious doctrinal split between East and West had been preparing. We have already seen that Augustine thought the Holy Spirit proceeds from the Father *and* the Son. In 589, a Western council, meeting in Spain, added to the Nicene Creed (the creed of 381 C.E.) the word *filioque* ("and from the Son") immediately after the words saying that the Holy Spirit proceeds from the Father. The theologians of the East protested the change strongly, believing that to make it meant denying that God is the source of all things. The West held out generally for the *filioque.* The rift of opinion hung fire for several centuries. Finally, in 876, a synod at Constantinople condemned the pope both for his political activities and because he did not correct the heresy of the *filioque* clause. This action was part of the East's entire rejection of the pope's claim of universal jurisdiction over the Church. A bitter break came in 1054, when the long-smoldering schism led a papal legate, without authorization, to excommunicate the patriarch of Constantinople and the patriarch to hurl back anathemas in return. Since then, the two branches of the Catholic Church have gone their separate ways.

However, as individuals brought the final break, its decisiveness was in doubt for a time, but after Good Friday in 1204, when Crusaders from northwestern Europe, on their way to delivering Jerusalem from the Muslims, inexcusably sacked and pillaged Constantinople, the break became final and complete.

II. THE EASTERN ORTHODOX CHURCHES

Although until recently the patriarch of Constantinople claimed spiritual supremacy over them, the various bodies of the Eastern Orthodox Church have been virtually independent of each other, divided as they are into units corresponding more or less to the national states in which they have existed. Yet none of them has departed to any great degree from the Orthodox tradition accepted in the East. Inasmuch as the ancient sees of Alexandria, Jerusalem, and Antioch early fell into Muslim hands, theological development in those areas virtually ceased after the eighth century. It ceased elsewhere as well. The only real changes have been in liturgy and religious practice. Here leadership was for a long time held by the patriarch of Constantinople, and when Constantinople fell to the Turks in 1453, it passed to the Slavic Orthodox churches, and particularly to the largest of them all, the Russian Orthodox Church, whose patriarch once said that even as Constantinople had been the second Rome, so Moscow should be the third.

The unity of the Orthodox churches has never been really broken. Although, as a consequence of international changes and conflicts, the various nationalized churches have sometimes had such violent disputes concerning jurisdiction that more than once one branch of the Church has excommunicated another, they have all learned to fall back finally on a doctrine of expediency, called "economy," whereby acts of excommunicated Church leaders have been first tolerated, and then validated, on the grounds of keeping the churches operating without loss of power and authority. Basically, this reaction to occasional divergence rests on a sense of "wholeness" or essential indivisibility (the Orthodox interpretation of catholicity) of the Church, which preserves its unity even in the diversifications that arise from the exercise of freedom.

Eastern Orthodox Doctrine

In spite of differences of administration, the various branches of the Eastern Orthodox Church have remained more or less united in matters of doctrine. The ancient creeds are accepted as infallible definitions of orthodox apostolic teaching. There have been local divergences in faith and practice, but in general the churches have not departed from the doctrinal position reached by the last of their acknowledged ancient fathers, John of Damascus, who one century after the Muslims seized Syria made a last effort on the basis of the completed creeds and the writings of preceding fathers to systematize the Eastern faith.

The position taken by John of Damascus fairly well characterizes the general attitude of the Orthodox churches—a mystical emphasis on the life-giving incarnation of God in Christ conveyed down to the present time through the seven sacraments and the other rites and devotional practices of the churches. The Western interest in the practical, juridical (analytical and individualistic) aspects of the relation between God and humankind had no great place in the concern of John of Damascus, or, for that matter, of the Eastern Church before or after him.

There are some interesting aspects in this position. John of Damascus appeared at a time when the Byzantine type of church architecture had been highly developed. The chief external mark of the Eastern churches had become a dome resting on a rectangular or an octagonal substructure, supported by half domes and buttresses. In the interior, the nave led to a chancel within which was the altar and to the rear of it a semicircle of seats for the bishops and presbyters. The pulpit stood outside of the chancel, closer to the congregation. The floor, walls, ceiling, and screens were richly decorated with pictures and mosaics, representing in the formal manner of symbolical and devotional art the Holy Trinity, the Virgin Mary, Christ, the apostles, and many saints and martyrs. Icons, with images shown in low relief against a plaque (such as Christ on the cross and Mary as the Mother of God), were colored in red, gold, and blue, and these, together with multicolored mosaics of the same subjects, were venerated by the worshipers, prayers being addressed in their direction and kisses and strokings bestowed on them. In due time, some of these images and pictures were credited with miraculous powers and became objects of special pilgrimage. When the Emperor Leo III was moved to order the suppression of such veneration, and there ensued the uproar in the East and West that we have described, John of Damascus came to the defense of images. He declared that the question of icons "is a question for Synods and not for Emperors." He went on to argue that the synods would see in images an incarnation of God in Christ. Again, icons were analogous to the sacraments in that they conveyed divine grace to the believer. Yet again, they were analogous to books, for "what a book is to the literate, that an image is to the illiterate." Indeed, the reverend father went so far as to put all of the rites, creeds, and institutions of the Church in the same position: all alike convey divine life and grace to the believer.

It was in accordance with this reasoning that in 787 the Seventh General Council—the last in which the Greek and Roman churches concurred—declared that pictures and images, the cross, and the Gospels "should be given due salutation and honorable reverence, (though) not indeed that true worship which pertains to the divine nature. . . . For the honor which is paid to the image passes on to that which the image represents, and he who shows reverence to the image shows reverence to the subject represented in it."[C2] (So far, the East and West could agree.)

Differences: Images "Catholic," and "Orthodox"

But even in the attitude toward images the Eastern and Roman churches have differed. In the East, icons are not humanized, and the figures remain symbols, simplified representations of "essential" meanings. As such they are rendered in formalized bas-relief rather than in the round as in the Roman Church. In other words, the East regards icons as signifying divine nature and spirit, whereas the Roman Church on the whole uses images to bring the Virgin and the saints within human range. Hence the attitude to Jesus' mother differs fundamentally in the two churches: the Roman Catholics venerate the Blessed Virgin as one who loves her child and is compassionate and humane to her suppliants; the Eastern churches worship her as the holy Mother of God, the exalted being in whom the human and the divine met in the Incarnation.

These differences in attitude are considered by representatives of the Eastern churches as being not contradictory but complementary. As one puts it,

> The Western mind, being more analytical, approaches spirit and matter as distinct and even opposite entities, whereas Orthodoxy conceives matter and spirit as two interdependent manifestations of the same ultimate reality. These attitudes are not contradictory but complementary to each other; yet in their own way they color every aspect of Church life, and, as a result, the same terms are differently understood by the Christian East and West. . . . An example of this is the word "Catholic," which in the West has acquired the meaning of universal in the sense of the geographical extension of the Church throughout the world. . . . In the East "Catholic" means "integral" or "whole"; the word signifies the inner quality of the true Church as opposed to heresies or sects. . . . The same difference in interpretation applies to the word "Orthodoxy." In the West this word stands for "correct doctrine"; in the East it is also interpreted as "right praise," for the Eastern mind links teaching with worship, and considers that only those Christians who pray to God in the spirit of love and humility have proper access to Orthodox belief and profess it in the right way.[G]

Differences: Sacraments and Christology

Other points of difference persisting down to the Second Vatican Council (1962–1965) may be briefly mentioned. The East has sacraments differing from those

Orthodox Iconic Style
Iconic symbols of the King and Queen of Heaven flank the Virgin Mother and Son. As in most icons the Son is not a realistic "child" but a representation of the Son as a member of the Godhead. *(Courtesy of the Greek National Tourism Organization.)*

of the Roman Catholic Church in certain respects: baptism in infancy by triple immersion, chrismation (annointing after baptism with oil consecrated by a bishop), the Eucharist or sacrament of communion in both kinds (bread and wine), confession only after reconciliation with those wronged or estranged, the taking of holy orders only after the congregation has given its unanimous approval, marriage with the bride and groom wearing crowns of glory, and extreme unction, which is given not, as in the West before Vatican II only before death, but in serious illness to encourage recovery. In describing the sacramental miracle of the "real presence" in the Mass, Eastern Orthodoxy stops short of the explicitness of the Roman doctrine of *transubstantiation* (the doctrine that by the priest's words of institution in the Mass the substance of the bread and of the wine is converted into the actual or real body and blood of Christ). The Orthodox prefer to speak in more general terms of the "real presence" occurring as a response to the *epiklesis* (invocation) of the Holy Spirit.

The Liturgy of the Eucharist has been developed into an elaborate work of devotional art, enriched by antiphonal choral chants, sung in different voices, without instrumental accompaniment, by priests in gorgeous vestments. Long recitatives at a high level of devotional poetry and beauty precede and follow the

central act of elevating the sanctified bread and wine before the altar. The sign of the cross is made by the priest with candles, of which two in the left hand, with lighted tips meeting, symbolize the union of the divine and human natures in Christ, and three in the right hand, similarly joined, symbolize the Trinity of Father, Son, and Holy Spirit.

The list of differences could be extended. It must suffice to mention one or two more. In addition to refusing to add *filioque* to the Nicene Creed, the East repudiates the belief in purgatory taught in the Roman West. The Orthodox churches do not demand celibacy of all the clergy, allowing to marry those who are content to remain among the "lower" clergy. Of course, the Eastern churches firmly "renounce" as "erroneous" the belief "that a man, to wit, the Bishop of Rome, can be the head of Christ's Body, that is to say, of the whole church." With equal firmness they reject "the erroneous belief that the Holy Apostles did not receive from our Lord equal spiritual power, but that the holy Apostle Peter was their Prince: and that the Bishop of Rome alone is his successor: and that the Bishops of Jerusalem, Alexandria, Antioch, and others are not, equally with the bishops of Rome, successors of the Apostles."[H] They contend that the pope of Rome cannot be infallible in matters of faith and morals, because several of the popes have been condemned as heretics by the Church councils; and certainly, they say, the Pope cannot claim to be superior to the Church councils.

III. THE ROMAN CATHOLIC CHURCH IN THE MIDDLE AGES

The Great Period of the Papacy

The Roman Catholic Church entered the Middle Ages with a head who was a temporal sovereign quite equal in political and financial position to some of the secular sovereigns of the West. The pope's territorial ambitions were bolstered by an extraordinary forgery that was circulated at this time and won widespread acceptance as genuine. Known as the *Donation of Constantine,* this forgery represented Constantine as granting to the popes not only spiritual supremacy over the whole Church but also temporal dominion over Rome, Italy, and the "provinces, places, and cities of the western regions." Not until the middle of the fifteenth century was the forgery successfully discredited.

In any case, the kings and chieftains of the West, on their part, were willing to concede the spiritual supremacy of the Roman pontiff, but they were equally sure that the pope should not intrude in their purely temporal affairs.

Hence arose vexing conflicts between the popes and secular powers. Such churchmen as were elevated to high office at the behest or by the appointment of kings and princes were often easygoing and worldly minded. Some had even bought and paid for their appointment—a practice called "simony." They were prone to take their churchly honors as a personal prerogative, to do with as they liked, and the farther they were from Rome the more this was the case. In northern areas, especially in Germany, bishops even married and passed their bishoprics on to their sons, in complete disregard of the rule laid down long before by Pope Leo I that all the clergy, even to the subdeacons, should be celibate. Again, northern bishops were frequently complaisant toward, and sanctioned, easy divorce among kings and princes when political marriages proved unsatisfactory. In another direction, conflicts arose between canon law (the law of the Church

drawn from the decrees of councils, synods, and popes) and the civil law of the various states, and where the state was strong, the canon law was often violated in the administration of parishes and monasteries.

Gregory VII (Hildebrand), versus Henry IV

A head-on contest between pope and emperor could not long be avoided. Its outbreak simply awaited the appearance of personalities sufficiently strong to enter upon it. This occurred when Hildebrand became pope in 1073, under the name of Gregory VII. He wasted no time. A new emperor, Henry IV, had ascended the throne in Germany. The pope ordered Henry to conform to the decree that bishops receive their staff of office from the pope and not from the emperor, and he charged the married bishops of Germany to give up their wives. But Henry IV was to prove a formidable opponent. He defiantly appointed a cleric of his own choice to the bishopric of Milan, then under his control. Hildebrand called him to task. Henry held a council with his nobles and bishops and led them in rejecting Hildebrand's authority as pope. Hildebrand replied with a decree falling like a thunderbolt upon Henry, excommunicating him and releasing his subjects in Germany and Italy from their oaths of allegiance to him. Though Henry sent the pope a fierce letter calling him "now no pope, but a false monk," and telling him to "come down, to be damned through all eternity," he was merely blustering. In reality, he was hard hit. His nobles told him that if he were not released from his excommunication within a year and a day, they would depose him.

In great trouble, Henry crossed the Alps. It was midwinter. He followed the pope to a castle at Canossa, and for three days stood in the snow of the courtyard, a white-clad, barefooted penitent, while Gregory considered what to do about him. Finally, the Pope, utterly avenged, admitted Henry to an audience and released him from his excommunication.

The Pope's great triumph—one of the most dramatic in history—was short lived. Three years later he made the mistake of again excommunicating Henry. Henry's answer was a march on Rome that enabled him to drive the pope out of it and to set up a rival pontiff. But the contest had reached an inconclusive stage. Soon

Gregory and Henry were both dead, and their successors, Henry V and Pope Calixtus II, came to a compromise. Bishops everywhere and in all cases were to be chosen by the Church in accordance with canon law, yet before their consecration the German bishops were to appear before the emperor to be invested by the touch of the royal scepter with the temporal possession of their sees. In other words, all new German bishops were to be acceptable to the emperor. Furthermore, it was agreed that bishops should be celibate. Hildebrand's reforms in great part had been achieved.

The Zenith of Papal Power: Innocent III

More powerful even than Hildebrand was Pope Innocent III (1193–1216) one hundred years later. Innocent entered his office when papal prestige had reached a new height, largely due to his predecessor's effective discipline of Henry II of England.

From the security of his island kingdom, Henry II had challenged the Roman pontiff by passing laws limiting the application of canon law in ecclesiastical cases and putting the election of bishops into the hands of the king, to whom these prelates were required to do homage. The archbishop of Canterbury, Thomas à Becket, an old friend of Henry's, had sternly opposed him at this juncture, and Henry's expression of anger caused four knights to ride to Canterbury and murder the archbishop before the cathedral's very altar. The pope, capitalizing on Becket's popularity, canonized him; streams of pilgrims (precisely like those pictured in *The Canterbury Tales*) poured through the cathedral's doors and wore down the stone floor by kneeling before the new saint's tomb. The king, full of dismay and remorse, withdrew the offending laws, and as a penitent submitted himself to being scourged before Becket's tomb!

Although Innocent III was conceded, on his accession, to be without qualification the spiritual superior of every terrestrial sovereign, he acted on the principle that he was the first among his peers in the temporal sphere also. When Germany was torn between rival claimants to the throne, he crowned one of them, Otto III, Holy Roman Emperor—after wringing large promises from him. When the new emperor forgot his promises, the pope put a rival in the field and

with the help of the king of France established him on the imperial throne. He thus proved that he could make and unmake kings. The king of France, too, felt the pope's whip hand. Resolved to rid himself of his unloved queen, the Swedish princess Ingeborg, the French monarch divorced her. The pope then put all France under an interdict (i.e., a ban on all religious services), and the king, yielding to popular clamor, took back his queen. In Spain, the pope first assumed control of Aragon and then granted it back as a fief to its king, Peter. He imposed a similar status on the rebellious English. Richard the Lion-Hearted's unpopular brother, King John, tried to force his candidate for archbishop on the see of Canterbury, and the pope placed England under an interdict, to last until Stephen Langton, his choice, should be made archbishop. When King John resisted, the pope excommunicated him, declared his throne vacant, and proclaimed a crusade against him. John capitulated but was not restored to grace until he acknowledged his kingdom to be a fief of the papacy from which a thousand marks were due annually to the pope as a feudal tax!

Within the Church itself, Innocent III became the undisputed head of the whole ecclesiastical domain. All disagreements of the higher clergy were ordered to be referred to him, and his decisions were final. He reserved the right to move bishops about among their sees. He forced through the Fourth Lateran Council (in 1215) the acceptance of the dogma of transubstantiation and the rule that the good standing of a Catholic was conditioned upon periodic confession, absolution, and communion.

The papacy had reached its all-time height of spiritual and temporal power.

Meanwhile, the medieval world, unified as never before under the Church, turned its creative energies toward these attainments: the medieval cathedrals, refinement of the mass, monastic orders oriented toward social mission (in a medieval version of the Hindu way of works), scholasticism (a medieval way of knowledge), and profound ventures into mysticism (a medieval way of devotion).

The Medieval Cathedrals

Cathedrals were the principal or mother churches of a diocese, and took their name from the fact that they were the locus, or seat, of a *cathedra* (throne) of a bishop. They usually were in large towns. Because the dignity of the cathedra called for equal dignity in the sanctuary, the architecture of a cathedral was usually impressive, especially from the twelfth century on, through the next 300 years.

Cathedrals were of three chief types: Byzantine, Romanesque, and Gothic, and this ordering of adjectives roughly corresponds to their chronological development. The first was characterized by domes supported on pendentives and columns (or piers), the second by semicircular arches and vaults, as in Roman architecture, and the third by pointed arches and ribbed construction. The Byzantine and Romanesque cathedrals required thick walls to hold up the heavy roofs and domes, hence their windows were relatively small; but since the basic structure of the Gothic cathedrals consisted of ribs of stone springing from the columns lining the nave and transepts and reaching up in high pointed arches far above the floor—a skeletal structure that was capable of standing by itself if properly buttressed from the outside—the roofs and side walls could be, and were, reduced to a mere skin of stone, and the side walls were pierced by large windows of colored glass, in beautiful designs. Almost everywhere, both inside and outside, there was room for statues and bas-reliefs of Jesus, Mary, the apostles, and the saints of the church, as well as for numerous figures and symbols of the faith, while at the roof edges the waterspouts were often shaped into such grotesqueries as gargoyles. The stained glass windows gave scope for vividly colored symbols and portrayals of the life of Christ and of the history and significance of the Church.

In its totality, a great cathedral was a complex symbol, and summary, of the faith. In fact, before the invention of the printing press, a cathedral was, as were the icons and mosaics of the Byzantine churches, a "Bible for the poor," and indeed an essential element in every person's religious education.

Because of its importance, in central and western Europe the building of a cathedral became in the favored towns a true community enterprise in which bishops, priests, artisans, guilds, and common people joined together in an act of faith; it often required, in fact, centuries of effort to bring to completion the huge structure that was to dominate both the landscape and the spiritual life of its town and countryside.

Mass in the Cathedral

The basic reason for the erection of cathedrals, as well as other Catholic churches, was of course the celebration of the Mass; but they also were the scene of coronations, investitures, ordinations, funerals, weddings, and other events in the life of the community that needed religious or ecclesiastical sanction. There often was high pageantry.

The Mass had evolved through the centuries into a colorful event, marked by a liturgy so enriched by symbol and gesture that the common person could grasp its significance and multiple meanings without understanding all of the Latin that was its spoken medium. The vestments of those officiating—priests, deacons, subdeacons, clerks, sometimes cardinals and archbishops, as well as others—made all ceremonies and processions occasions of color and drama. The ritual of the Mass varied from region to region, but its central act remained the same. To illustrate, consider the following partial description of the Mass as it was celebrated at York Minster, one of the great cathedrals of England, during the late medieval period:

> The elements—wine in a chalice and the host (a wheaten wafer) on a paten or plate—are on the altar upon linen cloths. The priest and his attendants are kneeling at and below the altar. With his hands held together, the priest says in Latin:
> *Thee therefore most Merciful Father, through Jesus Christ, thy Son, our Lord, we humbly pray and beseech:* (Here the priest rises from his knees, kisses the altar, and makes the sign of the cross over the chalice) *that thou wouldest hold accepted and bless these gifts, these offerings, these holy undefiled sacrifices . . . which oblation do thou, we beseech thee, O God Almighty, vouchsafe to render altogether blessed, counted, reckoned reasonable and acceptable, that it may be made unto us the Body and Blood of thy most beloved, our Lord Jesus Christ.*
> The priest now bows his head over the linen cloths preparatory to taking up the host, and continues: *Who on the day before he suffered took bread into his holy and most honored hands* (Here the priest raises his eyes) *and with his eyes raised*

toward heaven unto thee, O God, his Father Almighty, giving thanks to thee, blessed (Here the priest touches or elevates the host, enabling the host's transubstantiation to occur) *and brake and gave to his disciples, saying, Take and eat ye all of this, for this is my Body. In like manner, after supper, taking this most excellent cup into his holy and most honored hands,* (Here, if he follows the Continental practice, the priest elevates the chalice, and the miracle of transubstantiation again takes place) *and likewise giving thanks unto thee, he blessed and gave to his disciples, saying, Take and drink ye all of this, for this is the cup of my Blood, of the new and everlasting covenant, a mystery of faith, which shall be shed for you and for many for the remission of sins.* (Here the priest covers the chalice with linen cloths because it has been transubstantiated into the real Blood of Christ and is most holy.) *As often as ye do these things, ye shall do them in memory of me.*

As the mass proceeds the priest spreads his arms to make of himself a semblance of the cross, and prays for himself and others. During the prayer he draws back his arms and makes the sign of the cross. Next he breaks the wafer into three pieces and puts one portion into the Blood and says: *May this all-holy mingling of the Body and Blood of our Lord Jesus Christ be unto us and to all who receive them health of mind and body, and a healthful preparation for the laying hold on eternal life, through the same Jesus Christ our Lord. Amen.*

The priest now kisses the chalice and its linens, blesses those before him, prays for them, and then prays for himself that he may partake worthily of the sacrament. He communes first himself. At taking the Body, he says:

The Body of our Lord Jesus Christ be unto me an everlasting medicine unto eternal life. Amen.

At receiving the Blood, he says:

The Blood of our Lord Jesus Christ preserve me unto everlasting life. Amen.

At receiving the Body and Blood commingled, he says:

The Body and Blood of our Lord Jesus Christ preserve my body and my soul unto everlasting life. Amen.[1]

Chartres Cathedral
The facade of this most praised of Gothic cathedrals is interestingly asymmetrical, its two spires being in different styles. Its doorways are decorated with spirited sculpture of great refinement. In the interior the stained glass windows, seen from between columns and arches faultlessly executed, are the finest in the world. It is seven hundred years old. *(French Government Tourist Office.)*

In the events that followed, the laity partook of the wafer but not of the wine, for as the doctrine of the Mass developed through the years into the full theory of transubstantiation, the laity, especially of England, shrank more and more from communing in the Blood of Christ; and until the Second Vatican Council the Church forbade it.

Throughout Europe there was a place in most masses for prayers of intercession; generally, those for the living were offered just before the words of institution that converted the bread and wine into the body and blood of Christ; those for the dead followed after them, and became the basis for "masses for the dead," which were a prominent feature of the activities of the Church.

Scholasticism

Since the time of Charlemagne the cathedrals and monasteries had devoted more and more attention to the schools they had founded for boys and young men. Some of the teachers, pursuing truth for its own sake, began to develop an interest in every kind of subject matter. They not only taught what was in the old books—the Vulgate, the creeds, collections of canon law, fragments of Aristotle, Plato, the Stoics, the chief writings of the Neo-Platonists, the works of St. Augustine, and so on—but they began to compose new treatises, which were circulated among the various monasteries and aroused debate, controversy, and dialectical discussion. As the fame of individual teachers increased, students came from far and near, and the conditions were created for the founding of universities, the first of which were established late in the twelfth century. Soon Bologna became famous for canon and civil law, Salerno for medicine, and Paris and Oxford for theology.

Scholasticism was the brainchild of these medieval schools. It quite naturally concerned itself with the logic of the faith. After its first tentative emergence in the time of Charlemagne, it became with time more responsible, philosophically more weighty. Its dialectical method was applied at last to the really great problem of theology: how to reconcile reason and revelation—a problem that becomes in one direction the problem of the reconciliation of science and religion and, in another, that of the reconciliation of philosophy (reason) and theology (faith).

Augustine had laid a basis for Scholasticism by saying, "Faith seeks the support of reason" (*fides quaerit intellectum*), meaning that the intellect explores and corroborates the divinely revealed dogmas of the Church. A basis of Scholasticism was also suggested by Anselm (1033–1109) in one of his works, *credo ut intelligam*, "I believe (or have faith) in order that I may understand (or gain reasons)." On the one hand, then, the Scholastics proceeded on faith: the revelation was to be accepted as true, and then understanding of God, man, and world would follow. On the other hand, revelation was supported and defended by reason, as Augustine had suggested.

Realism and Nominalism

The early schoolmen started out with high hopes, drawing heavily upon the opinions of the church fathers and the great pagan philosophers. But they soon hit upon serious snags, which no amount of discussion seemed entirely to remove. Among them, as Anselm had pointed out, was the problem of the status to be assigned to unchanging ideas or universals. Were universals real (the position of medieval realism) or names merely (the position of nominalism)? Take the Church, for example. "Church" is a universal. Did the Church exist as an ideal form in the mind of God prior to all individual churches, which must then have come into existence to exemplify its nature, or is "Church" a name given to individual institutions with certain marked resemblances and thus bestowed after they came into existence? If the answer was in terms of the first alternative, then the Church was indeed a divine institution; if the answer was in terms of the second alternative, then it was a much more human institution than it claimed to be.

The Church was actively behind the realists, yet nominalism had sown such doubts, left such problems, and won so many followers that the effort of the Scholastic theologians to bring philosophy wholly into the service of theology (which they called "the queen of the sciences") proved at last a failure. By the fourteenth century Catholic theology had to let philosophy go on its own way of free intellectual inquiry, untrammeled by tradition and authority.

Late in the twelfth century the recovery of the Aristotelian writings helped win for philosophy this freedom from theology. Up to the twelfth century, only fragments of Aristotle's writings had survived the wreck of Roman civilization, but then from Spain came translations of his works from the Arabic texts studied in the University of Cordoba. These translations were later checked against recovered Greek texts. For the first time in 700 years the West had before it a systematic treatment of natural science. The final result of its study was a "new theology," ably presented by Thomas Aquinas, the greatest of the Scholastics. His synthesis of faith and philosophy, which reconciled without discrediting either, proved to be the most influential Scholastic achievement.

Thomas Aquinas: Reason and Revelation

Born in 1227, Thomas Aquinas was a native of Italy, a member of a noble family of part Roman and part German blood. He became a Dominican friar, of such promise that he was sent to Paris and Cologne to study under Albertus Magnus, another Dominican friar and one of the encyclopedic minds of his time. Afterward he taught first at Cologne and then at Paris, and finally in Italy, where he wrote his great books—now the standard theological treatises of the Roman Catholic Church—the *Summa Contra Gentiles* and the *Summa Theologiae*.

In his endeavor to reconcile reason and revelation, philosophy and theology, Aristotle and Christ, Aquinas tried to show that natural reason and faith are lower and higher forms of apprehension that are complementary to each other. By itself human or natural reason, that is, such reason as Aristotle used, can go very far, not only in exploring the natural world but also in proving the existence of God. It is possible for human reason by its own efforts to establish God's existence, using at least five cogent arguments: an argument from motion to an unmoved mover, an argument based on the necessity of a first efficient cause, an argument from possibility to necessity, an argument accounting for the gradation to be found in things, and a teleological argument drawn from consideration of design in the structure of the world. Nor is this all that reason can do. It can discover without divine help the nature of God; that is, it can by itself establish that God is pure actuality, one and unchanging, perfect and therefore good, infinite and therefore possessed of infinite intelligence, knowledge, goodness, freedom, and power.

But reason is unable to establish more than general propositions. It cannot know what God hath wrought historically unless it receives divine supplementation of its knowledge. Therefore, it needs to have added to its conclusions what revelation alone can supply, namely, knowledge of the tragic nature of the fall of Adam, by which humankind has been infected with original sin, the facts of the Incarnation and the Atonement, the doctrine of the Trinity, the fact of saving grace through the sacraments, assurance of the resurrection of the body, and knowledge of hell, purgatory, and paradise. Thus a faith based on revelation knows things that are *above* reason, that is, that are beyond reason's unaided power to establish.

Yet faith needs reason nonetheless. Nothing should be accepted by faith that is contrary to reason. There is no risk in this. Candid examination of the Christian revelation shows it to be in no part contrary to reason, but in all of its parts according to reason.

Similar reasoning enabled Thomas Aquinas to reconcile philosophy and theology. Philosophy begins with the world of sense experience and by the exercise of scientific reflection (reason) ascends to God. Theology begins with the revealed truths that are from God and descend to humankind and the world. Both supplement and need each other.

Aquinas on Humankind and Sacraments

In his doctrine of humankind, Aquinas reshaped the received Hebrew-Christian tradition to make it systematically consistent with Aristotle's dualism. (Hebraic elements had seen the human person as a unity.) Aquinas followed Aristotle in seeing body and soul as always separate but functionally necessary to each other. The body without the soul cannot live, and the soul, though immortal, can neither develop nor maintain the characteristics of an individual self without the body.

On the one hand, this was a great comfort as an assurance of the resurrection of the body. But Aquinas was uncertain about the beginning of personhood. He was not sure about the point in gestation at which the ensoulment of a fetus took place, hazarding guesses that forty days was enough to prepare for male ensoulment but that female ensoulment might require twice as much fetal development.

Aquinas clarified the Catholic conception of the sacraments by a similar Aristotelian distinction of lower and higher elements. Every sacrament has two elements in it, a material element (water, bread, wine, oil) and a formal element (the liturgical formulas). Together they make an organic union and supply a means of grace. Present during the performance of each sacrament are the human or affected and the divine or causal elements. When the conditions are duly present, supernatural grace is conveyed through the sacraments to the human recipients as regenerating power. In each case a miracle takes place. This is especially so in the celebration of the Mass. There, at the words of consecration by the priest, the unleavened bread and the wine are transubstantiated, so that without changing in shape or taste they are the very body and blood of Christ. The miracle of the Incarnation is thus repeated at each celebration of the Mass.

Penance, though a sacrament, is not as meticulously defined. It is more prolonged and requires greater human participation. It involves contrition, confession (to a priest), satisfaction, and absolution (by a priest). Here, as in all human regeneration, there is a lower and a higher side. In their life on earth individuals find themselves able to attain a certain degree of natural virtue. Without God's aid they may exemplify wisdom, justice, courage, and temperance. But these will not redeem them; these are but the virtues of the natural human being. To attain to eternal life, one must attain the theological virtues, which have God for their source and their object and are nourished by God's grace alone. These virtues, which people cannot achieve by themselves but must receive from God, are faith, hope, and love.

To go no further with the summary of Aquinas' synthesis, we may see how orthodox and yet how flexible it is. The whole system is dogmatic from beginning to end, yet science is granted competence in the discovery of truth. Theology is in highest place, but humanism and naturalism also are given roles to play.

Medieval Monasticism: The Dominicans

Monastic reform was in the air before the Crusades. (In fact, the Crusades were first projected by popes schooled in the reforms initiated by the Cluny movement of the tenth century.) Significantly, the whole monastic scene in Europe during the Crusades was dominated by the reforming Cistercian order—French and Benedictine, like the Cluny group—its greatest exponent, as organizer and preacher, being the saintly Bernard of Clairvaux. But the most notable expressions of medieval monastic piety were achieved a little later by the Dominican and Franciscan orders.

The Dominican order was in origin a missionary movement, whose first objective was the conversion of the heretical Cathari of southern France. But Dominic (1170–1221), its Spanish founder, had the inspiration to send his "preachers," as imitators of the apostle Paul, to many other parts of Europe, especially to the university towns, and their success caused his order to grow swiftly. The friars, as his monks were called, were devoted to learning because they were primarily preachers and teachers sent to the uninstructed and the unconvinced. They dressed plainly in black (whence their name of Black Friars) and were vowed to a mendicant poverty, begging their daily food in the spirit of Matthew 10:7–14. The order was headed by a "master-general" who supervised the work of the "provincial priors" in the Dominican "provinces." At the head of each monastery or nunnery was a "prior" or "prioress," chosen for a term of four years by the monks or nuns themselves, something of a democratic innovation. It was the misfortune of the Dominicans that the popes chose them as inquisitors; they had no original leaning in that direction. When they followed their own natural path, they had wide success among the higher classes and produced great writers and teachers, like theologians Albertus Magnus and Thomas Aquinas; the reformer of Florence, Savonarola; and mystics Eckhart and Tauler.

Medieval Monasticism: The Franciscans

The Franciscans had their great success among the common people. The founder of their order, St. Francis of Assisi (1182–1226), was one of the world's great personalities—as an individual the most winsome of saints, as a world figure Christ in a medieval incarnation. After a gay and frivolous youth, during which his father, a businessman, disinherited him for showing no interest in accumulating riches, he underwent after an illness a religious experience that led him back to the "rule of Christ" as described in the New Testament. Thereafter he said he was "married to Lady Poverty," ate the plainest food, wore unadorned grey garments, possessed no other property other than his immediate personal belongings, worked when he could, not for money, which he would not take, but just for the needs of the hour, or begged for his food when work failed. He preached to the poor or, when afield, to birds and beasts, in a love of nature that was a revelation to his hardheaded and practical age. He ministered to the unfortunate, the lepers, and the outcast with a compassion drawn both from his own nature and from his imitation of Christ. His way of life immediately attracted others, and he prescribed for them no more than the New Testament "rule of Christ." When twelve men had joined him, he went with them to Pope Innocent III for recognition of their order, and it was at once granted. Francis attempted no organization beyond sending his grey-clad friars out two by two on preaching missions. Even so, his movement spread like wildfire. It became necessary for others to step in and organize it, putting at its head a "minister-general" who directed the "provincial ministers" of the "provinces," which were composed in turn of local groups under a "custos." A second order, for nuns, was formed under Clara, daughter of Favorino Sciffi of Assisi (Sisters of Clare), and later a third order was created for lay people who wished, while pursuing a livelihood, to fast, pray, and practice benevolence in association with the order. St. Francis did not oppose the organizers who came to help him, but he regretted the necessity of putting a spiritual movement in leading strings. Today the order consists of three branches of varying degrees of strictness: the Friars Minor (dressed in dark brown tunics), the more rigorous Capuchins (clad in grey), and the less rigorous, property-accumulating Conventuals (in black tunics).

Both the Dominican and Franciscan orders had enormous influence in suggesting that the Christian religion transcends all organization and reaches into every department of life with an elemental appeal directly addressed to every person's reason and conscience.

Medieval Mysticism

While under the leadership of men like Thomas Aquinas the schoolmen were pursuing what the Hindus would call "the way of knowledge," and while at the same time the common man was following "the way of works," there were others who cultivated a mystic "way of devotion" that was deeply rooted in the Church's past. Monasticism had always had its mystic aspect. When the monk retired to solitary meditation, he sought to purge himself of evil and to lift his soul to ecstatic union with God and the saints. The mystics were those who refused to believe that the direct vision of God himself, Christ, or the saints had to await the passage from this world to the next; the mystic vision was possible here on earth.

Medieval mysticism had both an individual and a cultic form. In the twelfth century the Cistercian leader, Bernard of Clairvaux, tried to bring new vigor into the religious life of his time by preaching and writing of the blessing that came from the mystic's love of the Virgin and of Christ. In his *Homilies on the Song of Songs* he provided later mystics with valuable concepts for the description of their feelings. He saw in Christ the bridegroom of the soul and so vividly defined this relationship of the Redeemer and his adorers that he made it possible for mystics to interpret their raptures as ideal and heavenly love. It seemed to Bernard that such a relationship would transcend earthly feeling. Love for Jesus can be so warm and personal that the entire being of the enraptured mystic becomes flooded with a sense of tenderness, fervor, and sweetness.

Hugo of St. Victor and Bonaventura in the twelfth and thirteenth centuries carried mysticism into the schools. The Dominican preachers Meister Eckhart and Johann Tauler, in the late thirteenth and early fourteenth centuries in Germany, succeeded in developing an influential mystic cult in central Europe. Both were impatient with the externalism of the then-current Catholicism. To Eckhart, even "individuality" was something to be laid aside; it was "nothing." Only the divine spark in the soul is real; it alone matters. Following the same path, the Dominican ascetic Henry Suso illustrated in his own life the privations that more extreme mystics determinedly underwent. As long as he felt within himself any element of self-love and fleshly desire, he submitted his body to the extremes of self-torture, carrying on his back a heavy cross studded with nails and needles and sometimes lying down upon it in stern self-chastisement, until at last God did "gladden the heart of the sufferer in return for all his suffering with inward peace of heart, so that he praised God with all his heart for his past suffering."[J]

Around these German mystics a cult calling itself the "Friends of God" arose and spread through southwestern Germany, Switzerland, and Holland. In Holland the movement led to the founding of a group called the "Brethren of the Common Life," whose members, renouncing sex, lived in separate houses of brethren and sisters, practicing the mystic discipline in semimonastic seclusion. The finest literary product of this group was a book of simple and earnest piety called the *Imitation of Christ,* by Thomas à Kempis. No book produced during the Middle Ages has reached so many readers as this one, for it commended itself long after as much to Protestants as to Catholics.

The Decline of the Papacy in the Fourteenth Century

The papacy was unable to maintain itself on the height of authority and power reached during the thirteenth century. The factors that led to its decline were many. The unremitting papal pressure at the top only accentuated the divisive effect of a new sense of nationalism rising among the different European peoples from below. France and England, particularly, were able to move toward independence. Indeed, the Holy Roman Empire (now "neither holy, nor Roman, nor an empire") broke up into a collection of loosely united petty kingdoms. When this happened, France began to wield a more powerful influence than Italy. There was an immediate clash of interests. The French clergy, forced to take sides, began to distinguish between the spiritual and temporal authority of the pope and often sided with the king of France in disputes involving temporal matters. When Pope Boniface VIII (1294–1303) and Philip the Fair fell out, the latter did an epochal thing, a demonstration both of the force of rising nationalism and of the stirring of democracy in western Europe. He called together a parliament such as the English already had; it was the first French States-General and had representation from clergy, nobility, and commoners. This body gave him full support. The Pope thereupon issued the famous bull *Unam Sanctam,* containing the unqualified words, "We declare, we say, we define and pronounce that to every creature it is absolutely necessary to salvation to be subject to the Roman pontiff." This attempt to bring him to heel only led Philip to call another ses-

sion of the States-General, during which the Holy Father was defiantly arraigned as a criminal, a heretic, and immoral, and an appeal was issued for a general council of the churches to put him on trial. Because neither side would yield, the Pope, a spiritual authority without military power, suffered at length the indignity of imprisonment by some of Philip's armed supporters. He was soon released, but the harm was done: in the name of nationalism, rough men had seized the Pope's person and put him under duress.

A succession of "French" popes followed (1305–1377). Fearing violence in Italy, they retired to "Babylonish Captivity" at Avignon, where the power of the king of France over them was so unlimited that rival popes were elsewhere put in the field (1378–1417), thus to the great damage of papal prestige producing what is known as the "Great Schism." Thenceforth, France and England became increasingly independent. The papal power waned. In the great chorus of liberated voices that was rising, the popes were no longer able to command a hushed silence when they spoke.

Female Mystics

The fourteenth century produced a number of women whose leadership was nourished by mystical experience. Julian (Juliana) of Norwich (1342–1416+), a woman without formal education, found herself healed of a serious illness after experiencing a series of "shewings" (visions or revelations) of God's love. She took up the life of a recluse at St. Julian's Church in Norwich and produced accounts of her visions and her reflections upon their meaning. The accounts are models of clarity and precision in English prose as well as powerful expressions of theological insight and devotional earnestness. Reflecting on her separation from God by sin she wrote, "I wondered why sin was not hindered by the great foreseeing wisdom of God." The Jesus of her vision responded by first showing her the "utter naughting" that he bore in his passion and then offering the serene assurance: "Sin is behovely [something that must be] . . . but all shall be well and all manner of thing shall be well."[K] (These phrases were to become the comforting refrain in T. S. Eliot's *Little Gidding* almost six centuries later.)

Catherine of Siena (1347–1380), energized by a mystic experience of "marriage" with Christ, the heavenly bridegroom, worked among the victims of the Black Plague and, being distressed by the "Babylonish Captivity" of the popes at Avignon, personally persuaded Gregory XI to move the seat of the papacy back to Rome.

Almost two centuries later, Teresa of Avila in Spain (1515–1582), after similar experiences, reformed the Carmelite order. She found guidance and help from a fellow mystic, the ascetic John of the Cross.

The Movement Toward Individualism, Freedom and Reform

During the Crusades and especially after the fall of Constantinople in the fifteenth century—an event that brought many scholars fleeing to Italy with the literary masterpieces of the ancient Greeks in the original tongue—there began that revival of classical learning known as the Renaissance. Poets and tale tellers like Petrarch and Boccaccio were the literary masters who joined the great Renaissance painters and sculptors in popularizing the "humanist" outlook, with its ever-fresh delight in human beings and nature. Even the popes became zealous patrons of art and learning and all but forgot the duties they owed to the Christian world as Holy Fathers.

This was not lost on the common people. With the world rapidly expanding and enlarging their view—as stories first of the Crusades, then of the discoveries of Marco Polo, of Columbus, and later of Magellan and others were conveyed to them—and with their own lives vastly altered by the rise of commercial towns independent of lords and princes, the common people began, in guildhall and marketplace, to question the manners and morals of the clergy, from the pope down, and to criticize many recently established practices of the Church, especially those involving fund-raising. The sale of indulgences, for example, was based on the claim that the pope had access to a treasury of merits accumulated by the saints and that he had unlimited dispensation of these credits. Indulgences were sold in the form of documents transferring credits to the purchaser's spiritual account. Other practices that drew criticism were obligatory confession and papal taxation in the form of money fees for baptisms, weddings, funerals, and all appointments to office in the Church, and for hundreds of other transactions. Moreover, the common people began to want learning for themselves. They knew they could not master the classics of antiquity known to the learned, but they became curious about the Bible. They reveled in the mystery plays that dramatized episodes from the biblical story and moral dilemmas from everyday life. These whetted the appetite for direct acquaintance with the literary sources of these productions.

The common people's criticism of the Church and their hunger for scripture reached more intense forms in northern Europe than anywhere else and there aroused the English priest John Wyclif to condemn papal taxation as greed and the doctrine of transubstantiation as unscriptural and to send his Lollard priests among the people of England to teach them the leveling doctrines of the Bible directly from translations out of the Vulgate into the English tongue. Wyclif influenced John Huss in Bohemia to lead a popular religious revolt of such proportions that the Council of Constance in 1415 condemned Huss to be burned at the stake. A quite unrelated reform later in the fifteenth century was led by the Dominican monk Savonarola in the city of Florence, which, after a brief triumph over the lives and spirits of the entire citizenry, procured for Savonarola finally only his own death by hanging.

In vain, the Church at large attempted, through the cooperation of bishops, kings, emperors, and by the councils called at Constance and at Basel in the first half of the fifteenth century, to introduce needed reforms in Church life and administration. The only reform they seemed able to effect was the healing of the scandalous papal schism, an accomplishment brought about by forcing the rival popes from office and then restoring a single pontiff to the see of Rome. Otherwise, the situation remained fundamentally unaltered and provocative of greater upheavals to come.

IV. THE PROTESTANT REFORMATION

The sixteenth century witnessed a seeking of thorough-going religious reforms. At their onset in Germany, the initial intent was to obtain reforms within the Church by pointing out faults and making a vigorous protest;

but the "protestants" soon found themselves outside of the Church. Thereafter the pattern became more and more common of first breaking away and then obtaining reform, until Protestants began breaking away from Protestants. The only general reform of a church from within occurred through reappraisal, redefinition, and renewal; this was the Catholic Reformation undertaken at the Council of Trent beginning in 1545.

Let us examine these developments in the pages that follow.

Some Precipitating Factors

The Protestant Reformation split Western Christianity into two apparently irreconcilable groups. It was long in preparation as any study of medieval thought, even one as brief as ours, shows. It remained only for certain new developments, which chief among was the rise of the middle class to economic and cultural self-sufficiency, to bring it to pass. When the people of Europe gathered into towns along the rivers and coasts, as a consequence of the increase of commerce and trade, wealth was no longer immobilized in land or in produce offered for near-at-hand barter. It became fluid in the form of money, and modern capitalism was born. Gradually the lords and princes were forced to relax their hold on the growing middle class, and thousands of townspeople began to be true individuals. With no immediate overlords, save only burgomasters and town councilors, they increased rapidly in self-confidence and ability to meet life's problems on their own initiative. Politically they began to evolve a point of view that was later to issue in democracy. John Ball, the so-called mad priest of Kent, cried out in England as early as the fourteenth century,

> My good friends, matters cannot go on well in England until all things shall be in common; when there shall be neither vassals nor lords; when the lords shall be no more masters than ourselves. . . . Are we not all descended from the same parents, Adam and Eve? So what reason can they give why they should be more masters than ourselves? They are clothed in velvet and rich stuffs, ornamented with ermine and other furs, while we are forced to wear coarse linen. They have wine, spices, and good bread, while we have only rye bread and the refuse of the straw; and when we drink it must be water. They have handsome seats and manors, while we have the trouble and the work, and must brave the rain and the wind in the fields. And it is by our labor they have wherewith to support their pomp.[L]

In such words lay the seeds of the peasant revolts of the fourteenth and fifteenth centuries in England and central Europe.

It is not surprising that the common citizens of Europe began to want their religious competence recognized too, whether through reason or exercise of conscience. Martin Luther well expressed the feeling of laypeople when he passionately asserted,

> I say, then, neither pope, nor bishop, nor any man whatever has the right of making one syllable binding on a Christian man, unless it be done with his own consent. Whatever is done otherwise is done in the spirit of tyranny. . . . I cry aloud on behalf of liberty and conscience, and I proclaim with confidence that no kind of law can with any justice be imposed on Christians, except so far as they themselves will; for we are free from all.[M1]

The spiritual fact was that at the very time when the laity began to feel their own competence most, the Church seemed to them most corrupt. The Church had become identified in their minds with a vast system of financial exactions, rapaciously draining gold from every corner of Europe to Rome, where luxury, materialism, irreverence, and even harlotry seemed to reign unchecked among the clergy. Not only was the Church in lay eyes corrupt, it also seemed to be left behind in the onward sweep of progress. In a changing world it represented cramping institutionalism, conservatism, conformity from age to age to one inflexible law, one worship, one order of life for every individual. Worse still, a yawning gulf had opened between religion and life, and the disparity between the Church and human need increased more and more, until the pious layperson, just a little appalled anyway by the secularizing effects of capitalism and nationalism, began to wish for changes in the Church that would make it better serve the needs of people.

All that was lacking was a leader who would precipitate the needed reforms.

Martin Luther's Spiritual Quest

In Germany such a man appeared. He was Martin Luther (1483–1546), an honest, impetuous, heavyset German, a man who habitually linked convictions with decisive action. Born in Saxony of peasant stock, he absorbed from his environment no particular respect for priests, but a great fear of the wrath of God. His father wanted him to become a lawyer, but midway through his study of the law he responded to his intense religious need and entered a monastery of the Augustinian order, bent on winning God's favor by a pure and arduous conformity to monastic discipline. He punctiliously obeyed all of the rules of his order; he swept the floor, fasted, bent over his books, almost froze. But though he wept and prayed and became mere skin and bone, he failed to find God gracious. Indeed, he was not sure of his salvation. In 1507, he was ordained to the priesthood and later was appointed a professor in the new university established at Wittenberg by Frederick the Wise, elector of Saxony. There he came to despise Aristotle as an "accursed, proud, knavish heathen" who had led many of the best Christians astray by his emptiness and "false words."[M2] The reason for this animus seems to have been the lack in Aristotle of any profound religious conviction. Luther obtained what he most needed directly from the Bible, and on its books, especially the Book of Psalms and the Epistles of Paul, he lectured with growing enthusiasm and comfort to himself.

A journey to Rome in the meantime, even while it deepened his love of the Holy City, confirmed in him the conviction that the papacy had fallen into unworthy hands. He saw in the lives of the priests at Rome not the poverty and humility of Christ but pomp, worldliness and pride. He later was to say,

> It is of a piece with this revolting pride that the Pope is not satisfied with riding on horseback or in a carriage, but though he be hale and strong, is carried by men like an idol in unheard-of pomp. My friend, how does this Lucifer-like pride agree with the example of Christ, who went on foot, as did also all the Apostles?[M3]

His own inner life was illuminated suddenly by a sentence from St. Paul; its words were determinative in clearing up his own uncertainty: "The just shall live by faith" (Romans 1:17). Faith! It alone was sufficient! God cannot be *made* gracious by good works; God, like a father, *is* gracious toward his own. All who live in this love and trust know that they are justified *sola fide* (by faith alone) and will gratefully live a life of good works, without any urging, like a child who knows a parent's love. Gratitude, not fear, is the spring of Christian life.

The Ninety-five Theses

While Luther was forming these convictions, he was disturbed by the arrival of Tetzel, a papal agent, to sell indulgences in a nearby town. When members of his Wittenberg congregation (he preached in the castle church besides teaching in the university) went to buy these indulgences, he spoke out against their doing so. Urged by friends, tradition says, on October 31, 1517, he posted on the door of the castle church the famous Ninety-five Theses, a detailed attack on the selling of indulgences, drawn up in the form of propositions for public discussion. In accordance with the prevailing academic etiquette, he politely invited debate on each point he made, but he hardly anticipated the effect of his action. So great was the demand both for copies of the Latin original of his Theses and for its German translation that the university press could not issue copies fast enough to meet the demand from every part of Germany.

The fat was in the fire now. All north Germany began to buzz with talk. There was no thought then on anyone's part of leaving the Church; there was only a demand for reform. Yet there was present a deeper desire—scarcely conscious—for greater freedom from Rome. It was natural that Luther should be immediately attacked by Tetzel and others. His own bishop sent a copy of the Theses to the pope, who promptly ordered Luther to appear at Rome for trial and discipline. The elector of Saxony, who was proud of Luther, intervened, however, and the pope modified his demand to the order that Luther appear before the papal legate at Augsburg, which he did.

Authority from Scripture

All of this pressure had the effect, in itself a basic reaction of the entire Protestant Reformation, of making

Luther Posts His Theses

Luther search the scriptures to verify his position and justify his actions. His examination of the Bible convinced him that the Catholic Church had departed so far from its scriptural basis that many of its practices were actually anti-Christian. He was driven to question not only the sale through indulgences of the infinite merits of Christ and the merits of the saints, but also the whole medieval attitude toward penance and good works conceived as transactions made with God for his favor through the necessary mediation of priest, bishop, and pope. True repentance is an inward matter and puts a person into direct touch with the forgiving Father. Therefore, in the words of the thirty-sixth Thesis: "Every Christian who feels true compunction has of right plenary remission of pain and guilt, even without letters of pardon."[M4] Forgiveness of sins comes through the change wrought in one's soul by direct personal relationship with Christ and through Christ with God. Gradually, Luther reached the position that the true Church is not any particular ecclesiastical organization but simply the community of the faithful whose head is Christ. The only final religious authority is the Bible made understandable to believers by the Holy Spirit through their faith. So competent is every person of faith that each is potentially a priest. The Church should therefore proclaim "the universal priesthood of all believers." Said he,

> To put the matter plainly, if a little company of pious Christian laymen were taken prisoners and carried away to a desert, and had not among them a priest consecrated by a bishop, and were there to agree to elect one of them, born in wedlock or not, and were to order him to baptise, to celebrate the mass, to absolve, and to preach, this man would as truly be a priest, as if all the bishops and all the popes had consecrated him. That is why in cases of necessity every man can baptise and absolve, which would not be possible if we were not all priests.[M5]

Further, because believers should be enabled to participate in religious exercises to the full, services should be in German rather than Latin, and they should be simplified and given a clearer intent.

The Diet at Worms

Luther's appearance before the papal legate proved inconclusive. Ordered to recant, he refused and made good his escape back to Wittenberg. A lull in the papal agitation against him followed, produced by political developments in the Empire, but it ended abruptly when Luther was led into a debate with the Catholic theologian John of Eck and forced to admit that he thought the Council of Constance had erred in condemning John Huss. Was Luther now repudiating the authority of the Catholic Church wherever it ran counter to his own judgment of what the Bible meant? It appeared so, and the pope issued a bull of condemnation against him. The Emperor Charles V being called upon to act, Luther was summoned in 1521 to appear before the imperial Diet, meeting at Worms. The elector of Saxony consented to this only if Luther were promised safe conduct, which being assured, Luther appeared. He readily acknowledged that the writings issued under his name were his, but he would not retract, he said, unless he should be convinced *sola scriptura* (from Scripture alone) that he was in error. While some of his admirers among the German princes looked on, he boldly told the emperor and assembled delegates of the Church that

> unless I am convinced by the testimony of Scripture or by evident reason—for I confide neither in the pope nor in a Council alone, since it is certain they have often erred and contradicted themselves—I am held fast by the Scriptures adduced

by me, and my conscience is taken captive by God's Word, and I neither can nor will revoke anything, seeing that it is not safe or right to act against conscience. God help me. Amen.[N]

Because he was under safe conduct, Luther left Worms unharmed, but it was understood that as soon as he returned home, he could be apprehended for punishment. The Diet therefore put him under a ban, ordered him to surrender, and forbade anyone to shelter him or to read his books. But Luther could not be found. His prince, the elector Frederick, had had him seized on the way home, and he was hidden away in Wartburg Castle.

Luther used his enforced leisure to good purpose. He set to work on a translation of the New Testament into German. (Some years later, in 1534, he issued a complete translation of the Bible, an epochal achievement in more than one sense. Not only did it carry out the Reformation principle that the Bible must be put into the hands of the common people, it also gave the Germans for the first time a uniform language through which they could achieve national cultural unity.)

Princes Join the Lutheran Cause

The Edict of Worms was never enforced. When Luther emerged from hiding, the emperor was busy with wars and quarrels elsewhere, and, moreover, it was apparent that the German people were largely on Luther's side. Whole provinces became Protestant at one stroke when their princes renounced allegiance to the pope and turned Lutheran. By the time of Luther's death in 1546, his reforms had spread from central Germany into much of southern Germany, all of northern Germany, and beyond into Denmark, Norway, Sweden, and the Baltic states.

Luther did not leave to his followers a fixed system of theology and polity. He himself showed many inconsistencies, due in no small degree to his caution and growing conservatism. He was not a radical. He had repudiated Thomas Aquinas and Aristotle, yet, as though he were appealing from medieval Catholicism back to the ancient Catholic Church, he found in St. Augustine a man after his own heart, and back of Augustine he rested, of course, on St. Paul. So vehemently did

he cling to what he conceived to be Augustine's doctrine of determinism and predestination that he alienated the humanist Erasmus. Others found him too conservative in matters of worship, inasmuch as he retained the use of candles, the crucifix, the organ, and certain elements of the Roman Mass. He did, however, delete the priestly sacrificial aspects of the sacrament and may be said to have moved back toward the Lord's Supper, as described in the New Testament.

When an attempt was made to bring Luther and the Swiss Reformer Zwingli together, the conference between them broke down because Luther insisted that although there is no transubstantiation in the Lord's Supper, the "Real Presence" is to be found in, with, and under the elements of bread and wine "like the red glow in a heated bar of iron" (consubstantiation). His conservatism appeared, too, in his social and political views. He turned to virulent anti-Semitism in later life, and in the peasant revolt of 1524 he disappointed many by siding with the princes. In fact, he laid the basis of German statism by commanding submissive obedience to state authorities on the part of all Lutherans.

The Unraveling of Monastic Tradition

Wherever the Lutheran Reformation spread, the Catholic monks and nuns either left the district or abandoned their former way of life and dress and joined the Lutheran community as parish priests, teachers, and layfolk, free to marry and raise families. Luther himself married a former nun and enjoyed a happy family life with the five children he had by her. In organizing the new Lutheran communities, he concerned himself most with three functions: the pastorate, charity, and training and educating of the children. The monasteries that were appropriated by the town councilors or by princes were often turned, on his advice, into schools and universities.

Luther did not live to see the religious war that brought Germany during the mid-century years to the brink of chaos and resulted in the compromise Peace of Augsburg (September 1555), by which equal rights were guaranteed to Catholics and Lutherans, but which left the religion of each province to the determination of its prince, on the principle *cujus regio, ejus religio* ("whose the rule, his the religion"). The Lutheran Reformation had really put the ruling prince where the bishop had formerly been, that is, in a position to exercise general jurisdiction over the churches.

The Swiss Reformation: Ulrich Zwingli

A more radical Reformation came in Switzerland, when Ulrich Zwingli (1484–1531), a highly educated parish priest whose sympathies lay from youth with the humanists, especially in their war on superstition and irrationalism, advocated a return to the New Testament as the basic source of Christian truth. In Zurich, therefore, he began a systematic public exposition of the books of the Bible, beginning with the Gospels. By 1522, he reached the conviction that Christians are bound by and should practice only what is commanded in the Bible—a far more radical position than that of Luther, who held that Christians need not give up the elements in Catholic practice that are helpful and not forbidden in the Bible. In accordance with his convictions, Zwingli persuaded the people of Zurich to remove all images and crosses from the churches and to sing without organ accompaniment.

In putting a stop to the celebration of the Catholic Mass, he took the view that when Jesus said "This is my body," he meant "This *signifies* my body." It was irrational to suppose, he contended, that Christ's body and blood could be at once in heaven and with equal reality on ten thousand altars on earth all at the same time, as Luther argued. The bread and wine must be regarded as symbolic in character; they were blessed memorials of Jesus' sacrifice of himself upon the cross. The proper way to celebrate the Lord's Supper was to reproduce as nearly as possible the atmosphere and situation of the early Christian eucharist. Ritual should be at a minimum. And as to the regular church services, the sermon should be the central element in worship. It was the chief means by which the will of God could be made known. Local church government was to be reposed in the hands of the elders of each congregation, called collectively the spiritual council, for this seemed a close approximation to early Christian church organization.

The Zwinglian Reformation spread in his lifetime to Basel, Bern, Glarus, Mulhausen, and Strassburg. Ultimately it produced civil war between Catholic and Reformed forces, and Zwingli fell in one of the battles (1531).

John Calvin

In the southwestern part of Switzerland, in Geneva, a young French scholar named John Calvin (1509–1564) came to stay. He was at the time (1536) in flight from France, where he had just published, at twenty-six years of age, the Reformation classic *The Institutes of the Christian Religion,* a crystal-clear definition of the Protestant position, which was destined to lay the foundations of Presbyterianism.

Because the public policies of Calvin flowed logically from his religious convictions, it would be well to list at once the chief affirmations of the *Institutes.*

1. The central fact of religion is the sovereignty of God. God wills whatever happens in the physical world and in human history and thereby assures his own glory. His will is inscrutable, and from the human point of view he may seem to follow merely his good pleasure, but his character is holy and righteous, and all his decisions are just.

2. Human beings are possessed of a certain natural knowledge of God as the moving spirit in nature and history, but their understanding

> "I believe that in the holy Eucharist, that is, the supper of thanksgiving, the true body of Christ is present by the contemplation of faith. . . . The ancients always spoke figuratively when they attributed so much to the eating of the body of Christ in the supper; meaning, not that sacramental eating could cleanse the soul, but faith in God through Jesus Christ, which is spiritual eating, whereof this external eating is but symbol and shadow."°
>
> —Ulrich Zwingli

is dimmed by innate depravity, inherited from Adam, and so this knowledge must be supplemented by the revelation of holy writ.

3. This human depravity vitiates not only one's understanding but one's whole nature. With a conviction going straight back to St. Augustine, Calvin wrote,

> Original sin may be defined as an hereditary corruption and depravity of our nature, extending to all parts of the soul, which makes us obnoxious to the wrath of God, and then produces in us those works which the Scripture calls "works of the flesh." . . . We are, on account of this corruption, justly condemned in the sight of God. And this liableness to punishment arises not from the delinquency of another; for when it is said that the sin of Adam has made us obnoxious to the justice of God, the meaning is not that we, in ourselves innocent and blameless, are bearing his guilt. The Apostle himself expressly declares, that "death has passed upon all men, for that all have sinned" (Rom. 5:12), that is, have been involved in original sin, and defiled.[P1]

4. But not all individuals are lost. There is a justification by faith that saves some, and these go on to sanctification. Justification comes through the work of Christ in the believer's behalf and is "the acceptance with which God receives us into His favor, as if we were righteous."[P2] But God justifies only those believers in Christ whom he *elects* to receive into favor.

5. This idea of election leads into the Calvinistic doctrine of predestination. "By predestination we mean," wrote Calvin, "the eternal decree of God, by which he determined with himself whatever he wished to happen with regard to every man. All are not created on equal terms, but some are preordained to eternal life, others to eternal damnation."[P3]

This reasoning led Calvin to regard life with more than usual gravity and seriousness. Duty and self-discipline were to him uppermost. One must live as under God's eye. Frivolous people lower themselves to the level of brutes when they succumb to drunkenness or spend excessive hours in card playing, dancing, and masquerades. Yet Calvin was by no means the teetotaler, ascetic, or sabbatarian imagined in later caricatures. He wrote that only an "inhuman philosophy"

would make no use of the creator's gifts except for necessity. Customers at village taverns were to be fined only for buying drinks "during the sermon" or for encouraging others to drink by buying for them. John Knox is said to have been a little shocked to find Calvin bowling on a Sunday. It probably was a quiet game. There was no room in Geneva for Luther's playfulness and laughter, his roaring, lusty voice raised in song around the organ, nor for his glad sense of the passing of God's wrath and the outpouring of his gracious love. Calvin found pleasure in more measured and temperate enjoyment of the gifts of God's Providence.

In Geneva arose a new kind of community. Working with the Small and General Town Councils, over which he gained increasing if sometimes stormy ascendancy, Calvin instituted both a church life and an educational system that gave Geneva a trained ministry and a people sufficiently informed regarding their faith to be able to give a clear account of it. Refugee scholars and exiles from all over Europe flocked to Geneva as to an asylum, so that the city increased its original thirteen thousand population by six thousand. Among the brilliant men who came there was the Scottish refugee John Knox.

The Protestant Reformation in Other Lands

France

The Reformation had begun rather quietly in France, yet with every prospect of soon sweeping the country. Then all at once it was very nearly drowned in blood. The forces on either side were brought into such violent conflict that civil war engulfed the country. Much more completely than in Geneva, the French Protestants, or Huguenots, adopted John Calvin's conception of church organization. The local congregation "called" its own ministers through the elders and deacons. The Catholic clergy and nobility, particularly the zealously Catholic House of Guise, took alarm. As a consequence there ensued a series of civil wars; but these proved inconclusive, the Huguenots having acquired local control of a number of fortified towns and being served by very competent military leaders, notably Admiral Gaspard de Coligny and the Prince of Condé. The Huguenots fought on through five wars and at last by the Edict of Nantes (1598) won complete liberty of conscience, full civil rights, and the control of two hundred towns. Protestantism in France had not grown strong, but it had won the protection of the state. However, Louis XIV revoked the Edict of Nantes in 1685, and caused the Huguenots to emigrate in large numbers (some two hundred thousand of them) to Switzerland, England, Holland, South Africa, Prussia, and North America. Not until the time of Napoleon were Protestant rights restored.

The Netherlands

Bitter too was the struggle in the Low Countries. The Spaniards were in control there, and Philip II of Spain was determined to stamp out the Reformed faith wherever it showed itself. The people of the Low Countries were in some sense prepared for the Reformation by the Brethren of the Common Life, already described, who had expressed what really was a people's movement toward personal piety, accompanied by a strong love of biblical learning. Luther's writings were eagerly circulated when they appeared; later Zwingli won devoted adherents; and still later Calvin's conception of church organization was to prevail. Some Netherlanders were attracted to the Anabaptists. Open rebellion against Spain came when Philip II sent the cruel Duke of Alva to suppress every form of heresy at any necessary cost of blood. The struggle was long and drawn out, but at last William the Silent was able to form a group of northern states that won independence as the nation of Holland. Holland became a Calvinist land, sturdy and self-reliant, with its churches (the Dutch Reformed) organized on the democratic principles already established among the French Protestants.

England

The English Reformation was one of those more or less inevitable outcomes that thrive upon accidents. A king's private whim opened the way for the religious revolution that the nation basically wanted. With the moderation so characteristic of them, the English leaders nourished a desire to enjoy at least the degree of religious self-determination the Reformation had brought to the continental Protestants, and yet they bowed to the forms of legality in their national life and patiently waited. Eventually, they made their will felt, which was as soon as the opportunity presented itself.

The uninhibited Henry VIII, in the grip of a personal desire for a change in his marital status, vowed that if the Roman Curia would not annul his marriage to Catherine of Aragon so that he might marry Anne Boleyn, he would break with the pope. The Roman Curia turned him down, and Henry did not hesitate to act. Though much that he did and said shocked all shades of opinion in the nation, he had powerful elements among his people with him when he got Parliament to declare that "the bishop of Rome" had no more jurisdiction in England than any other foreign ecclesiastic, that the only true head of the Church of England was the king of England, that bishops in England were thenceforth to be nominated by the king and were to give their oath of obedience to him instead of to the pope, and that denial of the king's supremacy in the Church was an act of high treason. Henry quickly won the support of many of his nobles by first suppressing the monasteries in his realm and then distributing generous grants of land to them from among the great possessions thereby confiscated. Besides winning these powerful supporters, he cut off the flow of papal taxes to Rome and satisfied the growing desire of the English people for national self-determination in all things.

But Henry VIII was theologically conservative. He did not intend that there should be a doctrinal break with the past to match his jurisdictional break with the pope. In 1539 he had Parliament pass what is known as the "Bloody Statute," which declared the doctrine of transubsantiation to be the faith of the Church of England and the denial of it to be punishable by burning at the stake and confiscation of goods. It forbade the marriage of priests and disallowed communion in both bread and wine. The only considerable concession he made to liberal views, aside from his break with Rome, was in having a copy of the Bible in English placed in all of the churches. (The so-called Great Bible was drawn largely from the translation of Tyndale, but with some parts taken from Coverdale's version.) Many English followers of Luther and the Swiss Reformers were put to death under the Bloody Statute. More fled to the Continent, where they found their chief asylum in Switzerland.

These exiles returned when Henry was succeeded by his nine-year-old son Edward VI, for then it became apparent that under the protectorate established for the immature king the national policy would shift religiously to the left. The young king's advisors strongly favored doctrinal as well as political changes. The Bloody Statute was repealed, communion in both kinds was allowed, private masses were brought to an end by the confiscation of the chapels where they were said, priests were permitted to marry, and images were removed from the churches as instances of papist idolatry. But Edward died when he was only fifteen and was succeeded by his sister Mary, an ardent Catholic, who loved and married the Spanish heir apparent (Charles V's son, soon to become the intolerant Philip II). She led the return to Rome by restoring the Pope's jurisdiction over the English churches, and herself earned the name of "Bloody Mary" because of the ruthlessness with which leading Protestants were at her behest apprehended and burned at the stake. When she died after a reign as brief as Edward's, her sister Elizabeth, the daughter of Anne Boleyn, finally brought the nation to the Protestant fold. "Good Queen Bess," as her subjects affectionately called her, completed the unfinished work of her young brother's reign. The Prayer Book of Edward VI was revised so as to be made palatable to Catholics and Protestants alike, and under the name of *The Book of Common Prayer* was, by the Act of Uniformity of 1559, prescribed for use in all churches without alteration or deviation. The beliefs of the Church were stated clearly in the famous creedal statement, "The Thirty-nine Articles of the Church of England," which is to this day the formally authoritative summary of its doctrines. England remained Protestant henceforth, even when Catholic monarchs were on the throne.

Scotland

In a sense, the case of Scotland was critical for the whole Protestant Reformation. To many at the time it seemed quite possible that Mary Queen of Scots, both by her marriage to Francis II of France (through which she became an adherent of the French Catholic party in European politics) and by making good her claim to the English throne as a Stuart (which she never was able to do), might bring both Scotland and England back to the Catholic fold.

But Mary's marriage to the French king actually gave the Protestants of Scotland a chance they were not slow to seize. She was long absent in France, and during that time John Knox led his Protestant colleagues in the rapid development of a Calvinistic church. Knox did not introduce the Protestant Reformation to Scotland; he himself was a product of it. Captured in youth by a French force sent to Scotland to apprehend a group of Protestant rebels there, he was carried to France and compelled to row in the galleys for nineteen bitter months. Upon his release he went to England, then under the Protestant government of Edward VI, and served in various towns as a royal chaplain. On the accession of Mary Tudor, he escaped to the Continent and made his way to Geneva, where he became an enthusiastic disciple of Calvin. Ultimately he returned to Scotland, and in 1560, not long after his return, he had the great triumph of having the Scottish Parliament ratify the "Confession of Faith Professed and Believed by the Protestants within the Realm of Scotland," which he and five others prepared and which remained the creedal formula of the Church of Scotland until it was replaced by the Westminster Confession in 1647. A week later the Parliament decreed that "the bishops of Rome have no jurisdiction nor authority in this realm," and forbade the saying, hearing, or being present at Mass. Eventually the Roman Catholic bishops and priests were expelled from the Church lands, which then came largely into the possession of the Scottish nobles.

In subsequent developments, the so-called Presbyterian system of church government was worked out on a national scale. In its complete form, it established a representative democracy. The congregation elected and called the minister, who thereafter was alone responsible for the conduct of public worship. But this was his only unlimited prerogative. All local matters affecting the discipline and administration of the parish were entrusted to the kirk session, composed of the minister, who presided, and the elders, chosen by election. Above the kirk session was the presbytery, which consisted of the ministers of the parishes of a designated area and an equal number of elders representing each parish. Above the presbyteries was the Synod, with jurisdiction over certain groups of presbyteries, and over all was the General Assembly, the supreme judicatory of the national Church, consisting of delegate ministers and an equal number of elders. The center of gravity of this system was the presbytery, which was small enough to be vitally representative of its locality and large enough to have plenty of fight in it when its survival was threatened.

It was a bad moment for the Scottish Reformers when the fascinating and calculating Mary Queen of Scots came back from France a widow. They knew that she was a devout Catholic and that she meant to overthrow Protestantism in Scotland if she could. When she first arrived, she pursued a moderate course, insisting only on having Mass for her own household but promising to maintain elsewhere the laws that made it illegal in Scotland. She summoned Knox to five interviews, in which she used all of her skill to win him over, but he remained firm in opposition to any concession to the papacy. In other quarters, Mary had more success and might have won all had she not fallen into disgrace through her intrigue with Bothwell and been deposed in favor of her year-old son, who later became James I of England. With her fall the Protestant forces recovered their strength, and Scotland was made secure for the Scottish Reformation.

Other Early Protestants: The Anabaptists

While the national Reformation movements just described were coming to terms in one way or another with the civil powers, quiet searchers of the scriptures all over Europe were finding their own way to a much more radical break with constituted authority.

Prominent among them were the Anabaptists (literally "rebaptizers"), groups largely recruited from the common people—peasants and artisans—and led in the first instance by immediate associates of Luther and Zwingli. Most took the New Testament literally and with great seriousness, determined to depart in no way from the manner of life they saw depicted in it. Others felt themselves not bound thus by the "letter" of scripture, because the "Word" is a "living spirit" expressed in but not confined to scripture nor present equally in all parts of it. The living Word of God speaks through prophetic personalities and in the inner consciousness of all who are justified by faith.

It seemed to all of the Anabaptists that the first requisite of being a Christian is that one should grasp clearly in one's own mind the meaning of each aspect of the Christian life and practice and then act upon that understanding no matter what the cost. Cere-monies and rituals must, they thought, have a clear meaning to the participants or cease being real and vital. Accordingly, they rejected infant baptism; plainly, the baby could not know what was being done, so the rite could mean nothing. Those who had been baptized in infancy therefore baptized each other all over again (hence the name they bore).

In the wider realm of conduct, a clear understanding and sincerity, they held, are just as imperatively needed. The New Testament teaches the principle of overcoming evil with good instead of resisting one injury with another. Most Anabaptists concluded that they should not join the armed forces of the state, contribute to warfare in any way at all, or even take part in the civil administration during peacetime, because of the policy of force all states adopt. They found New Testament warrant for never taking oaths; so, when taken to court, they insisted that their simple word be taken for truth: their yea was yea and their nay nay. Because they felt priests and ministers were prone to please worldly powers and make compromises in vital areas, the Anabaptists were anticlerical and met outside of the regular church circles in their own houses; churches were to them idolatrous "steeple-houses." They did not agree on all matters, but they made it a principle to exercise tolerance where differences as to the literal meaning of scripture appeared. Some, for instance, took with greater literalness than others the apocalyptic or millenarian passages of the New Testament, expressing the expectation that Christ would return on the clouds of heaven to be the judge on the last day. Others practiced the communism of the early Christian fellowship in Jerusalem. Occasionally, some Anabaptist would proclaim himself a prophet, as did the noted Hans Hut, who won many of the working people of Austria and adjacent parts of Germany to the view that a Turkish invasion would be followed by the appearance of Christ to inaugurate the millennium.

The finality with which the Anabaptists separated themselves from the established churches and the state (whence the name Separatists that they also bore) and the radical views that many of them espoused led to intense persecution. Luther parted company with them, or, rather, they with him. Zwingli engaged them in bitter public debates, which were usually followed by the decision of the Swiss cantonal authorities that his views alone were to be recognized as lawful.

Later on, the bad name the Anabaptists earned was partially redeemed by the gentle and reasonable Anabaptist leader Menno Simons (1492–1547), whose followers in the Netherlands and in United States were called, after him, Mennonites. They were pacifists, and practiced a person-to-person tolerance that enabled individual Mennonites to house, with simple Christian charity, such exiles as the ostracized Jew Spinoza and certain refugee English Separatists.

V. THE CATHOLIC REFORMATION

The Protestant Reformation resulted in intensifying latent Catholic self-criticism and stirred up a Church wide call for overdue reform. The popes, however, were not among the motivating forces; they were too much on the defensive. It was the Holy Roman Emperor Charles V, anxious like Constantine in the fourth century to reduce disunity, who earnestly sought for reforms in the Church and a redefinition of Catholic doctrine in order to offset the effectiveness of Protestant critical propaganda. He came to this position only after his prolonged efforts to bring about a reconciliation of Catholics and Protestants on the basis of projected reforms had failed. It was he who brought pressure on Pope Paul III to call the Council of Trent.

This pressure was decisive, because it had behind it all of the accumulated power generated by the cries for reform, both clerical and lay, which had been heard in Europe for centuries. John Wyclif, John Huss, Savonarola, and Erasmus, not to mention Luther and Zwingli before they left the mother church, were simply the more recent figures among those who advocated reform. But the Catholic Reformation (by Protestants, labeled the Counter-Reformation) did not get underway until momentum was imparted to it by determined and militant forces for reform and enlightenment in Spain, where the expulsion of the Moors in the fifteenth century had been followed by the reform of the clergy under Ximenes, the great archbishop of Toledo and confessor to Queen Isabella. The Spanish Church had been purified of unworthy

monks and priests; universities for the training of the clergy had been founded; the union of church and state under Ferdinand and Isabella had been made very close; and the means of keeping church and state purified had been found in the reorganization of the Inquisition on a national basis, with inquisitors appointed by the Spanish monarchs. The result had been a revitalization of the Spanish Church to match the rapid rise of Spain itself to the position of the first power in Europe. When, therefore, the Spanish king became the Holy Roman Emperor, in the person of Charles V, the drive for reform, all the more urgent because of the Protestant surge, had secured powerful support.

The Council of Trent

When Charles V got Pope Paul III to call the Council of Trent in 1545, he hoped first to get needed reforms and afterward a redefinition of the Catholic position. He pressed for Protestant participation. It was thus that he planned to conciliate the Protestant leadership and follow up his military victories over the German Protestant princes with a psychological master stroke that would bring the recalcitrants back into the Catholic fold. But the Catholic leaders insisted that doctrine be discussed alternately with reform and soon made reconciliation with the Protestants impossible by firmly redefining the medieval Catholic doctrines. The Council met over a period of eighteen years (1545–1563) and during its course declared the following:

1. Catholic tradition is coequal with scripture as a source of truth and in authority over Christian life [a rejection of Protestant *sola scriptura*].

2. The Latin Vulgate is the sacred canon.

3. The Catholic Church has sole right of scriptural interpretation.

4. The sacraments are defined as seven: baptism, the Eucharist, confirmation, matrimony, holy orders, penance, and extreme unction, all believed to have been, at least implicitly, instituted by Christ. (Protestants had introduced a distinction between sacraments and other rites, reserving the term *sacrament* for those rites that were explicitly instituted by Christ himself and necessary for *all* believers.)

5. Justification rests on faith, but not *sola fide* (on faith alone) as the Protestants assert. Good works also procure God's grace.

In the sphere of discipline and church management, the Council turned to the broad task of preserving morals and furthering education. It ordered stricter regulation of the issuance of indulgences and the veneration of saints, limited the number of holy days observed during the year (in deference in part to demands of economic interests), and ordered bishops and priests in the larger towns to offer public expositions and interpretations of scripture, and in general to preach and teach what is necessary for salvation. Of far-reaching effect was the council's instruction to the pope to prepare an index of prohibited books, a step that helped limit the reading of Protestant literature by Catholics.

An administrative step taken three years prior to the Council of Trent provided the means for effective enforcement of its actions. This was the expansion of the Inquisition into a Churchwide operation. In 1542, Pope Paul III was persuaded by his advisors to reorganize the Inquisition on a scale that made its immediate use possible in any part of Europe where the civil authorities asked for it or were willing to support it. The Catholic Reformation thus acquired the instrumentality by which Catholic areas could quickly be purged of Protestants. The first country to be thus cleared was Italy.

New Religious Orders: The Jesuits

Of greatest importance for the revival of Catholic spirit and zeal was the rise of new religious orders, the most famous of which has been the Jesuit order founded by Ignatius Loyola.

Loyola (1491–1556) was a Spanish nobleman, who, after being a page at the court of Ferdinand and Isabella, became a soldier and was seriously wounded in a battle with the French. During convalescence, he read the lives of Christ, St. Dominic, and St. Francis and resolved to become a "knight of the Virgin." He accordingly hung his weapons on the Virgin's altar at Montserrat and at a Dominican monastery began the self-directed visualizations of the life and work of

Christ and of Christian warfare against evil that he later systematized as the Jesuit spiritual "exercises." While on a pilgrimage to Jerusalem, he came to feel the need for more education, so he hurried home to study in Spain and at the University of Paris. He gathered around him student associates with whom he practiced his spiritual exercises. It was thus that he attracted to himself Francis Xavier, who became the famous missionary to India and Japan, and men like Diegoez Lain and Simon Rodriguez. In Paris, in 1534, he organized these friends into a military "company of Jesus." They vowed to go to Jerusalem, if possible, as missionaries to the infidel Muslims, or, failing that, to offer their services to the pope. When war with the Turks barred the way to Jerusalem, they went to Rome and in 1540 obtained the authorization of the pope, Paul III, to establish the Society of Jesus, with Loyola as the first general.

Known as the Jesuits, they dedicated themselves to study and to translating into their own everyday activities the life and spirit of Christ himself. To this end, as "good soldiers of the cross," they bound themselves to a life of strict militialike discipline, spiritual exercises, and absolute obedience to their superiors short of sin, never ceasing to train their wills to serve Christ absolutely, unreservedly, and unselfishly. Yet "sin" was so defined that it was seldom confronted in the course of carrying out the instructions of their superiors, for they held that there could be no sin in a doubtful course of action if "probable" grounds for it existed or if it had been accepted by people of greater experience or who had authority for it. Moreover, so sure were they that a good end justifies secrecy about means that they sanctioned "mental reservation" on being required to tell the whole truth: one was not bound to give the whole truth even under oath. The main thing was absolute self-commitment to the aims of the Jesuit order and unreserved and complete surrender of self in doing what one's superiors considered to be in the interests of Christ. This sacrificial devotion was intensively cultivated in each Jesuit during his novitiate, a regimen that included a unique and very effective four weeks of spiritual exercises under the point-to-point direction of a spiritual drillmaster. On the basis of the capacities revealed during this period, each Jesuit was assigned by his superiors to the tasks he was judged best suited to, and when sent to some post, no matter how far away, he was under an obligation to send back a continuous stream of reports to his superiors who had sent him.

The Jesuit order had spectacular success in the field of missions. Not only did Francis Xavier and his associates carry Catholicism to India, Japan, and China, but others during the sixteenth and seventeenth centuries won their way into South America, the St. Lawrence and Mississippi valleys, Mexico, and California.

Here it is important to observe that the natives sensed that the priests had come not to exploit and rob them, as the conquistadors often did, but to save them. In Europe itself, Jesuits diligently and intelligently sought and occupied important commercial and governmental posts, which took them into far-flung places abroad as well as into the council chambers of kings and princes at home. Their political influence in France, Portugal, Spain, and Austria during the sixteenth and seventeenth centuries was great. They led in checking the spread of Lutheranism into south Germany and were powerful factors behind the scenes when the Huguenots in France were fought and massacred. But they aroused the enmity eventually not only of all Protestant but also of many Catholic groups. In the eighteenth century, they found Portugal, France, and Spain successively closed to them. At last they lost their temporal power, but they have continued to this day to promote the supremacy of the pope implied in the decrees of the Council of Trent.

Other Orders

The Jesuit was not the only new organization to witness the forces of Catholic renewal. The sixteenth and seventeenth centuries saw the rise of the Oratorians, Theatines, Ursulines, Visitandines, and Lazaristes. The first two sought, respectively, the reform of the breviary and the improvement of preaching; the last three were orders for women that laid emphasis on education for women and remedial social work.

These movements were both effects and causes. They sprang from the heightened Catholic sense of the seriousness of the Church's mission in the world, and they caused the older organizations in the Church to look into their ways and replace their former laxity with greater earnestness. The Franciscan and Domini-

can orders were thus revitalized. Even the papal office was affected. The popes from this time forward were uniformly men of more austere character and earnestly Catholic aims.

VI. CROSSCURRENTS IN THE SEVENTEENTH AND EIGHTEENTH CENTURIES

In the first half of the seventeenth century, wars of religion broke out on the continent of Europe. The emperor and the Pope, alike subscribing to the decisions of the Council of Trent, sought Catholic recovery of lost ground, while the Protestants fought for freedom from suppression and for dominance in central Europe. The Thirty Years' War, which decimated central Europe, changed little territorially. However, the Catholics regained some ground, and the Protestants established their right to exist independently of a pope or an emperor. An exhausted Europe breathed a sigh of relief when the Treaty of Westphalia (1648) drew lines that granted Calvinists and Lutherans the right to certain territories without further interference by an emperor or a pope, and recognized Catholic dominance in other, largely southern, areas of central Europe.

England was comparatively uninvolved in the Thirty Years' War, and so there, although persecution and suppression were not uncommon, sufficient tolerance existed to allow the rise of nonconformists and dissidents who broke away from the Church of England and survived as independent religious bodies destined to spread their views to the New World. The independents were alike in demanding self-determination in matters of belief and polity (church administration) as their Protestant right.

We have to go back a little in time to consider the first of these groups.

The Puritans

The Puritans got their name in the time of Queen Elizabeth. Her accession in 1558 brought back to England, as we have seen, many exiles who had fled from

"Bloody Mary." Their residence abroad in Calvinistic areas had inclined them toward presbyterial forms of church government and simplicity of worship and life, but they had no wish to be separatists. Rather, they desired only to purify the worship of the Church of England of what they called its "Romish" elements, such as kneeling to receive the bread and wine at communion services, the sign of the cross at baptism and confirmation, the use of the ring at weddings, and special clerical garb for ministers. The Puritan aim was to give emphasis to preaching the Word rather than to ritual and sacraments. Most of them resigned themselves, at least for the time being, to episcopacy—bishops, archbishops, archdeacons, and the like—provided that locally they could be served by sympathetic parish ministers, but a few openly advocated a presbyterial system such as existed in Scotland. When these presbyterial Puritans increased in numbers, the Puritans became divided. Those who wished to reform the Church of England from within retained their membership in it in patience and hope; those who could not wait broke away from time to time as separatists and found the government so determined to crush them that they emigrated to Holland. They were the first Congregationalists and Baptists, and we shall return to them shortly.

The Puritans still within the Church of England found the government hardening against them when James I became king. Charles I after him was even more resolved than his father not only to make the English Puritans conform in full to the practices of the Established Church but to carry further his father's attempt to force episcopacy on the Scots. It was a literally fatal attempt on his part. To his astonishment, he provoked the Scots (thousands of them as "Covenanters" sworn to a life-and-death struggle against him) to rebellion, and their success in arms brought him to such a pass that he had to summon Parliament, only to find that the Puritans were now in the majority in that body! The Puritans had not for some time been faring so well. They had fared so ill while Archbishop Laud was in power, that twenty thousand of them from 1628 to 1640 followed the Pilgrims over the sea, and in Massachusetts and Connecticut they became New England Congregationalists. But now, in 1640, they were in such majority in Parliament that they could cast Laud into prison. When the angered king opposed them,

they as angrily rose to arms as representatives of the people driven by their sovereign's stubbornness to make a six-year war upon him. So came about Charles I's beheading and the Puritan Revolution under Oliver Cromwell. For twelve years England was a Puritan land, and all of the people were bound by a stern religion's purifying restraints.

Not only the Puritan way of life but also Presbyterianism seemed about to triumph in England, for in 1646 the Westminster Assembly, called to advise Parliament and composed of English ministers and laymen, with Scottish commissioners sitting in an advisory capacity, presented to Parliament the *Westminster Confession,* the last of the great confessional standards of the Reformation and still treasured (along with more recent confessional statements) by Presbyterians throughout the world. The Parliament rather hesitantly adopted it, as well as the *Larger and Shorter Catechisms* prepared to accompany it. But as it happened, little came of the Parliament's action, for the return of Charles II to England in 1660 brought with it the Restoration, and reaction was thereafter so triumphant that by the Act of Uniformity of 1662 the Puritans were forced out of the Church of England into the ranks of the Dissenters, ultimately to become Congregationalists, Baptists, Quakers, Presbyterians, and Unitarians.

The Baptists

Meanwhile, the separatists who had left England prior to the Puritan Revolution had had an interesting and important history abroad. One group that settled at Amsterdam in about 1607 was led by John Smyth, formerly a Church of England minister, who, upon learning from Mennonite neighbors their views on adult baptism and being convinced by study of the New Testament that it was not the early Christian practice to baptize infants, rebaptized himself and his whole flock. Members of his congregation returned to London and established there in about 1612 the first Baptist Church of England that endured. This was the beginning of the Baptist denomination, soon to spread throughout the British Isles. They found unity in one distinctive position: baptism of believers only, and that by total immersion. In 1639, a group of Baptists, to whose number Roger Williams belonged, founded a church in Rhode Island. Baptists subsequently appeared in all of the American colonies, especially in the South.

The Congregationalists

Other emigrants in Holland passed their first years of exile there quietly enough. At Middleburg, in 1582, Robert Browne, a Cambridge man, published the clearest definition of Congregationalism ever to be penned. His logic was firm. Said he, the Church of Christ, in the view of true Christians, is not an ecclesiastical organization but a local group of believers who have experienced union with Christ, the only real and permanent head of the Church, and by a voluntary covenant with each other have consented to be ruled by officers—pastor, elders, deacons, teachers—chosen by themselves as moved by the spirit of Christ. Each church is absolutely self-governing, none has authority over any other, but all are under the Christian obligation to extend each other brotherly help and good will.

But if all of this was quietly done and said, a notable course in history was run by one group among them. In 1609, a Congregationalist group that had come over from Scrooby, England—under the leadership of John Robinson and William Brewster, with William Bradford in their number—settled in Leyden. Not content there, they made a momentous decision: to return to England in order to send their more adventurous and able-bodied members to America. On the *Mayflower*, then, in 1620, the Pilgrims crossed the Atlantic, and, in the spirit of their solemn covenant made at sea, founded the colony of Plymouth. Other immigrants, mostly Puritans from England, followed them over the waters, until all of New England, except Rhode Island, was won to Congregationalism. There it enjoyed the status virtually of a state religion for two centuries.

The Unitarians

The Unitarians can trace their history back to the early days of the Protestant Reformation. At that time Michael Servetus, a Spaniard by birth, was struck, on a close reading of the New Testament while traveling in the retinue of a Catholic prelate, by the fact that the Nicene doctrine of the Trinity, in whose name so many of his own country's citizens were being burned at the stake or exiled, was not to be found in it, and that, moreover, his reason found fault with the doctrine itself. So he wrote down his ideas secretly and audaciously and in 1531 published his heretical treatise *Concerning the Errors of the Trinity.* The doctrine of the Trinity he felt to be a Catholic perversion and himself to be a good New Testament Christian in combatting it. Twenty-two years later, when he came to Geneva, he fell afoul of Calvin and his supporters, was tried, condemned, and burned at the stake. But his writings stirred groups of already existent anti-Trinitarians, who, when made the object of persecution both by the Inquisition and by Protestants, took refuge in the only areas that would at that time harbor them, Poland and Transylvania (now part of Romania). But after the Thirty Years' War, when the Catholics returned to power in Poland and south-central Europe, the Unitarians were driven into exile and fled to eastern Germany, Holland, and England. When the English passed a law in 1648 making the denial of the divinity of Christ a crime punishable by death, some of the more liberal Unitarians were obliged to flee again to Holland. During the eighteenth century, many of them quietly appeared in New England, and in the early nineteenth century, under the preaching of William Ellery Channing and Theodore Parker, they grew in strength, formed the American Unitarian Association (1825), and received many Congregational ministers and churches into their organized fellowship. In 1961, they united with the Universalist Church, a denomination formed in the eighteenth century to proclaim that a God of love, truth, and right can have no less a purpose than to save every member of the human race.

The Quakers

One more English nonconformist group of this period, the Quakers, requires our attention. They were in many respects the most radical of all. Founded during the civil war that resulted in the Puritan Revolution, the Quaker movement was in essence a revolt against formalism and sham. The Quakers were nicknamed so, but preferred to call themselves the Society of Friends. Their founder was George Fox (1624–1691), a religious genius who may be reckoned one of the world's great mystics. In a profound experience of conversion, which occurred in 1646, he came to a belief much like that of some of the early Anabaptists. True Christianity was to him not a matter of conforming to a set of doctrines or of believing in scripture without having "a concern" as the result of so doing, nor was it a going to a "steeple-house" to listen to a sermon or prayers read by a professional priest. It was a being illuminated by an inner light. The Word of God is a living thing not confined to the scriptures, though it is there. It comes directly into the consciousness of the believer whom God chooses for the purpose of speaking through him.

Fox would not hear of training a professional clergy. God speaks through whom he will when he will. Every man or woman is potentially God's spokesperson. Fellow human beings are to be treated as friends, with infinite reverence for the divine possibilities in any personality. War and any violence are therefore thoroughly wicked. Slavery is abhorrent. The requirement to take an oath should not be imposed upon Christians, for they always speak soberly and truthfully.

At a religious meeting of Friends there were no sacraments (sacraments by their material symbolism are the occasion of leading the mind out of its subjective state of contemplation into the idolatry of fixation on an object) and no prepared discourses (God will stir up thought in someone present, at need). It was admitted that prayer is appropriate to begin with, but let it be followed by silent meditation, until the inner light illumines someone's understanding.

Fox and his followers promptly obeyed every prophetic impulse to action. Fox, for instance, would march boldly into a "steeple-house," if inspired to do so, interrupt the "priest" in the middle of his sermon, and denounce the proceedings, to the accompaniment of outcries and tumult. Consequently, the authorities vigorously opposed Quakers as being disturbers of the peace. Thousands were imprisoned or heavily fined. Fox himself was often jailed. But no persecution could quench his ardor.

During the intensely repressive persecutions of the Restoration period, William Penn (1644–1718) became a Quaker, and after obtaining in 1681 the grant of Pennsylvania from Charles II, he threw it open to colonization by all who might desire freedom of religion, the Quakers being especially invited to Philadelphia.

In England it was not until the "Glorious Revolution" that accompanied the accession of William and Mary (1689) that full religious tolerance for the Quakers and all other dissenting groups was made into law.

VII. EASTERN ORTHODOXY IN THE MODERN WORLD

Under antireligious Marxist regimes in the former Soviet Union and its eastern European allies, the Orthodox churches struggled to maintain as much autonomy as they could. The Russian Church, impelled by its deep-rooted commitment to *sobernost* (a conciliatory spirit, or Christian unity in love), aspired to ecumenical contacts through membership in the World Council of Churches. Permission to join was obtained in 1961, but the price was a compromisingly cooperative relationship with the Soviet regime. The dissolution of the Soviet Union removed some restraints and invigorated the Russian churches, not only to new growth in numbers, but also to some new boldness. A December 1996 manifesto supported democratic reforms and human rights and also called for real assistance to those "caught between life and death" because of poverty. On the other hand, a 1996 Russian law restricting the right to conversion to Orthodox Christians encountered no criticism from among them.

Relationships with the Roman Catholic Church also improved. Patriarch Athenagoras I of Constantinople met with Pope Paul, and in 1965 the mutual excommunications that were pronounced in 1054 were annulled simultaneously in Rome and Constantinople. Succeeding Athenagoras in 1972, Patriarch Dimitrios joined with Pope John Paul II in 1979 to create a Joint International Orthodox-Catholic Commission for Theological Dialogue. The commission issued a statement after sessions at Bari, Italy, in 1987, affirming large areas of agreement based upon the creed of Nicaea and Constantinople (without the once-controversial *filioque* clause). But the Bari report also took note of Orthodox uneasiness with several Roman practices: baptism by infusion (rather than immersion), the administering of baptism by deacons, and permitting the sacrament of First Communion to be administered to children before their reception into the Church by Confirmation.

Elevated to be "first among equals" in 1991, Patriarch Bartholomew of Constantinople assiduously pursued the delicate task of promoting unity among the Orthodox churches while at the same time improving relationships with the Roman Catholic Church.

The new Patriarch made a number of trips to Rome, and at a symbolic event in 1995, he and Pope John Paul II led worship in St. Peter's Square (omitting only the institution of the Mass). But courting loyalty from fifteen different national jurisdictions—always difficult for a Turkish prelate dealing with a largely Greek constituency—proved even more perilous in light of unstable relationships between Serbia, Macedonia, and Greece—to say nothing of the rivalry of Turkey and Greece in many arenas. There also were differences with the Russian Patriarch Aleksai, occasioned by the defection of the Ukranian and Estonian churches and by disagreement over efforts to rekindle dialogue with the Roman Catholic Church.

The American Scene

In the Americas, the assimilation process has gradually softened the hard ethnic edges of the some twenty jurisdictions. Over half of the seminarians in some seminaries are converts. As one priest put it, "Orthodox 'Serbs' with the name Petrocelli and blond 'Greeks' with the name Olson" are to be found.

Nevertheless, the pursuit of unity and the further healing of ethnic differences remained in the foreground as the Orthodox Synod in Istanbul in 1996 reconfigured a jurisdiction that formerly included both North and South America to create a diocese comprising only the United States. To head the new diocese, it elected Archbishop Spyridon, an American whose career took him to study and service in Turkey, Switzerland, Germany, and Italy, and equipped him with fluency in English, Greek, French, Italian, and German. There was for the first time an American primate presiding over a constituency within the borders of the United States.

Tensions with Protestantism, according to one American Orthodox spokesperson, come from two sources: (1) resentment at the influx into eastern Europe of naive but well-funded American evangelicals who "shower candy on those from whom bread has been stolen." (The 1996 restrictions on conversions in Russia is a case in point.) (2) a new firmness in regard to Orthodox theological positions that rule out intercommunion, recognition of homosexuality as an acceptable lifestyle, inclusive language with respect to God and the Trinity, and the ordination of women to the priesthood.[Q] (Orthodox theology speaks of the *iconic* nature of priest as *alter Christus* in the fatherhood and husbandship of God and Christ.) Sensitivities in regard to these points have led the Orthodox churches to a partial suspension of their participation in the National Council of Churches in the United States.

VIII. CATHOLICISM IN THE MODERN WORLD

The Erosion of Papal Power

The eighteenth century saw much of the force of the Catholic Reformation wane. In France, Louis XIV had already stemmed the power of the papacy by appropriating the income of vacant bishoprics and by encouraging the French clergy to assert openly their right to certain "Gallic liberties," which included the view that the Pope was not infallible because general councils are superior to him. The rise of the rationalistic spirit among great numbers of French citizens during the eighteenth century reached a climax in the French Revolution, when anticlericalism developed to the point of violence and Christianity itself was for a time "abolished." Although religious freedom for all was later proclaimed, Napoleon, in coming to terms with the Catholic Church, was determined to constrain it within government control. In Germany, the Catholics painfully recovered from the effects of the Thirty Years' War, which had reduced the population of the German states by 65 percent without effecting any real changes in the lines separating Catholics and Protestants. Not until after the Napoleonic wars, when romanticism led the reaction against the rationalistic spirit of the eighteenth century, did the Catholic Church revive some of its old power.

In Europe, generally, during the nineteenth century, the assertion of papal supremacy in the name of worldwide Catholic unity reappeared in Ultramontanism—the movement among Catholics north of the Alps in favor of the view that final authority lay "beyond the mountains," that is, in the Vatican and the regularized channels of the papal government (the Roman Congregation). The popes for obvious reasons encouraged this opinion.

Doctrinal Declarations: The Immaculate Conception, Infallibility

Some major doctrinal developments mark the nineteenth century. Medieval theologians, starting from a long-held premise that original sin was a "substance" transmitted in the act of procreation, saw that a virgin birth alone would not have insulated Jesus from the stain of original sin transmitted in the maternal line. They had concluded that there must have been a miracle whereby the conception of his mother was immaculate (free of the staining substance). In 1854, Pius IX proclaimed the Immaculate Conception of the Virgin to be a dogma of the Catholic Church. This meant that the faithful could no longer question or debate the teaching that Mary was, in anticipation of the merits of Christ, miraculously kept free from the stain of original sin ordinarily transmitted at conception.

By the mid-nineteenth century, accelerating developments in science, social theory, and the democratization of society and of governments so menaced the authority of the papacy that Pope Pius issued in 1864 a blunt *Syllabus of Errors,* in which he condemned socialism, communism, rationalism, naturalism, the separation of church and state, and freedom of the press and of religion. "The Roman pontiff," he said, "cannot and should not be reconciled and come to terms with progress, liberalism, and modern civilization." This pronouncement stunned and inhibited the Catholic liberals without totally silencing them. (Since then they have accommodated themselves to the pope's declaration by reading it in context, that is, by maintaining that he was inveighing against particular contemporary errors and not against all liberal movements.)

The same embattled pope, still seeking to stem the erosion of papal authority, received judiciously limited support from the First Vatican Council in 1870, which set out the conditions under which infallibility might apply.

> The Roman pontiff, when he speaks *ex cathedra*, that is, when in discharge of the office of pastor and doctor of all Christians, by virtue of his supreme apostolic authority, he defines a doctrine regarding faith or morals to be held by the universal church, by the divine assistance promised to him in blessed Peter, is possessed of that infallibility with which the divine Redeemer willed that His church should be endowed.

This doctrine elevated the pope to a supreme height in the field of faith and morals. But it did not save him from the consequences of the rise of Italian nationalism in the wake of the agitations of Mazzini and Garibaldi. For no sooner had the Vatican Council made its declaration than King Victor Emmanuel came along to capture Rome, and after a plebiscite of the inhabitants overwhelmingly directed him to do so, took from the pope the States of the Church, leaving only the Vatican, the Lateran, and Castel Gondolfo as the area where papal secular sovereignty could be exercised.

Catholic Modernism

Toward the end of the nineteenth century, modernism showed further development, when many thoughtful Catholics, both clerical and lay, began to see the need of taking into account theories based on modern historical and biblical criticism and the discoveries of modern science. There thus came into being the short-lived movement called Catholic Modernism, which sought the reconciliation of Catholicism with modern scientific knowledge and critical methods. A group of Catholic scholars tried to come to terms with the theories of biological and geophysical evolution, while others adopted the methods of biblical criticism current among Protestant scholars, and among other things went so far as to question the historicity of the Virgin Birth, although they were willing to accept its truth as an enlightening myth. Modernist voices were heard suddenly in all parts of Europe. Notable were those of George Tyrrell in England, Alfred Loisy in France, and Hermann Schell in Germany. But Pope Pius X found their thought dangerous and firmly condemned it in an encyclical in 1907, which, together with a number of excommunications in 1910, silenced the movement for awhile, or as some would say, drove it underground.

More successful as an attempt to put Catholic doctrine into current thought forms is recent Neo-Thomism—so-called because its representatives, Jacques Maritain and others, have sought to state the philosophy of Thomas Aquinas in modern terms and to apply it to modern issues.

In 1950, Pope Pius XII pleased conservatives when he proclaimed as a dogma of the Church the assumption of the uncorrupted body of the Virgin Mary to heaven after her death. This completed a cycle of declarations in Mariology, which brought the body of the Virgin into parallel status with that of the Christ: immaculate conception, perpetual virginity, and bodily ascension.

Pope John XXIII and Vatican II

In 1959, Pope John XXIII issued a summons embracing the entire Catholic world. He asked that delegates be sent to an ecumenical council, to be known as Vatican II. It met for its first session in 1962 in Rome and was attended by 2,500 bishops of the Catholic Church. It met in three further sessions, in 1963, 1964, and 1965, at the call of Pope Paul VI, the successor of Pope John, who died in 1963. Official observers from Protestant and Orthodox churches (including the Russian but not the Greek) and selected laymen and women "auditors" were present. The Council, during its four sessions, sought adjustment to the twentieth-century world and the promotion of Christian unity. Its decisions included the following: authorization of a more extensive use of vernaculars in the celebration of the sacraments and in public worship (with the effect of worldwide liturgical change and increased congregational participation in ritual responses and singing); endorsement of "collegiality," or the principle that all bishops as successors of the apostles share with the pope in the government of the Church; provision for greater lay participation in church administration by creation of a permanent separate order of deacons, to include mature married men and not merely celibate youths preparing for the priesthood as heretofore; approval of a declaration that no person should be forced to act against his or her conscience and that nations should neither impose religion nor prohibit freedom of religious belief and association; authorization of worship by Catholics with non-Catholics in special circumstances; and definitive recognition of the possibility of salvation outside of the Catholic Church.

Vatican II on Non-Christian Religions

The Council's declaration on the relation of the Church to non-Christian religions contains the following highly significant passages:

> From ancient times to the present, there is found among various peoples a certain perception of that mysterious power abiding in the course of nature and in the happenings of human life; at times some indeed have come to the recognition of a Supreme Being, or even of a Father. This perception and recognition penetrates their lives with a profound religious sense.
>
> Religions, however, that are bound up with an advanced culture have struggled to answer the same questions by means of more refined concepts and a more developed language. [Here follow paragraphs enumerating the "good things" found in other religions: Hinduism, Buddhism, Islam, and Judaism.]

The treatment of Judaism, however, included some special acknowledgments.

> True, the Jewish authorities and those who followed their lead pressed for the death of Christ; still, what happened in his passion cannot be charged against all the Jews, without distinction, then alive, nor against the Jews of today. . . . In her rejection of every persecution against any man, the Church, mindful of the patrimony she shares with the Jews and led not by political reasons but by the Gospel's spiritual love, decries hatred, persecutions, manifestations of anti-Semitism, directed against Jews at any time and by anyone. . . .[R]

The decrying of anti-Semitism was welcomed throughout the world, but critics noted that the phrase "at any time and by anyone" fell far short of explicit

St. Peter's Cathedral, Rome
A notable example of the Renaissance style, St. Peter's is a basilica rebuilt in the form of a Roman cross. Its dome and cupola were designed by Michelangelo, its splendid plaza and colonnade by Bernini. The Vatican Palace, the residence of the pope, adjoins it. The whole is known as Vatican City, the ecclesiastical center of the Roman Catholic Church. *(Courtesy of the Italian Government Travel Office.)*

repentance for the Church's own past actions against Jews over many centuries.

A Vatican document, "We Remember: A Reflection on the Shoah [holocaust]" published March 16, 1998, went much further and was characterized as being more than an apology—"an act of repentance." Yet it disappointed many on two points: its gratuitous defense of the silence of Pope Pius XII, and its failure to accept for the Church even the "co-responsibility" for the tragedy as previously acknowledged by some German bishops and by Protestants generally. It sought to separate a mistaken anti-Judaism "of which Christians [not the Church] have been guilty," and Nazi anti-Semitism, which it pictured as rooted elsewhere: "The Shoah was the work of a thoroughly modern neo-pagan regime. Its anti-Semitism had its roots outside Christianity."

The writings of widely respected theologians, however, probably were more representative of the new openness in Roman Catholicism. Karl Rahner (1904–1984), for example, defined even dogma as a living, growing thing, "a *form* of the abiding vitality" of the deposit of faith. In speaking of revelation, he ranked communication to human beings "as personal spirit" above the "secondary" authority of scripture and creeds. Among other religions, he said, many "anonymous Christians" were to be found. He defended the

right to teach for other theologians more radical than he, notably Edward Shillebeeckx and Han Küng. Although the latter, according to a declaration by the Vatican in 1979, could "no longer be considered as a Catholic theologian," both have had strong followings among Catholic theologians.

Pope Paul VI: *Humanae vitae*

In accordance with the principle of collegiality and at the request of the Council, Pope Paul organized in 1967 a Synod of Bishops, representing national hierarchies from all over the world, to advise him in doctrinal matters and administrative decisions. it convenes upon call in Rome.

But discontent within the Church has developed, not only over liturgical changes, but also over the issues of birth control and optional marriage of the clergy. Pope Paul's encyclical on birth control (*Humanae vitae*, 1968) reiterated the Church's previous stand against all forms of artificial birth control. It met with considerable resistance throughout the Catholic world, not only among laity but also among priests and nuns. Some hierarchies, while upholding the encyclical officially, have left to the conscience of the individual its application.

In 1978, Pope Paul died and was succeeded by Pope John Paul I, who at once affirmed that he would follow his two predecessors in conforming to the decisions of Vatican II. He in turn died and was succeeded by a surprise choice, a non-Italian (Polish) cardinal, John Paul II, similarly committed to Vatican II.

John Paul II: World Tensions, and Ecumenism

Desiring to bring theological insights to the conflicts between capitalism and socialism and between the rich and the poor, John Paul II launched an energetic program of worldwide visitation and prolific publishing. Of the seven encyclicals issued in the 1980s, the most notable for addressing worldwide tensions was *Sollicitudo Rei Socialis* (1988), typical of his efforts to mediate evenhandedly the East–West and North–South conflicts. On the one hand, the encyclical spoke positively of "the right of economic initiative," but counterbalancing comments on social planning led the *Wall Street Journal* to call it "warmed over Marxism." In any case, the document went beyond advocacy of improved moral attitudes toward the poor and called for changes in institutions.

Among encyclicals issued in the 1990s *Ut Unum Sint* "That They May Be One" was ecumenically significant. It put forward personal conversion, fidelity to scripture, and service to humanity as the basis for ecumenism. The tone throughout was cordial, but, as the Anglican Archbishop of Canterbury put it, there was a "rub" harking back to *Lumen Gentium* "Light of the People" produced in 1963 during Vatican II. It had presented the Church as being analogous to the person of Christ in being "a complex reality which comes together from a human and divine element," a reality which "subsists in the Catholic Church, which is governed by the successor to Peter. . . ." In other words, its governance is not historically determined but is part of the faith itself. "No matter how charitably it is reiterated," said the Archbishop, that definition "remains a significant problem," for dialogue could not start from the premise that "the Catholic Church is 'more church' than the rest of us."

Attrition within religious orders, a worldwide shortage of priests, and general dissatisfaction with the slowness of the implementation of Vatican II prompted the convening of the world Synod of Bishops in 1987 to consider "proper and specific tasks" for laypeople. The bishops disagreed about how to respond to proliferating independent lay movements. The Synod ended without accepting a proposal from American bishops that all ministries (short of the priesthood itself) be open to women, but the impetus for finding new patterns of ministry was shown to be growing.

In January 1989, a gathering of 163 German-speaking Catholic theologians put together the Cologne Declaration, criticizing the pope for (1) unilaterally filling vacant sees, (2) too frequently denying theologians ecclesiastical permission to teach, and (3) asserting doctrinal and jurisdictional authority in exaggerated form, especially through "intense fixation" on birth control, a "highly particular teaching which can be grounded neither in Holy Scripture nor in the Tradition of the Church." The main points of the declaration were subsequently supported by responses from French, Flemish, Spanish, and Brazilian theologians.

IX. PROTESTANTISM IN THE MODERN WORLD

With perhaps one exception, the basic diversifications within the Protestant world all occurred before the eighteenth century. The exception might be Methodism. Methodism, however, was not really a Reformation movement, but essentially an awakening in response to new conditions created by the development of science and the rapid rise of industrial capitalism, and it therefore should be considered a phenomenon not immediately related to the Reformation.

Deism in the Eighteenth Century

It was not until the eighteenth century that Western science in its modern sense became generally diffused among thinking persons. When it did, the eighteenth-century Enlightenment came. Religion was for the first time in the Western world compelled to justify its case inductively. The empirically minded people of the eighteenth century were so little content with the dogmas of the Church that they asked themselves curiously what made primitives religious, or what "natural religion" was. The whole structure of revealed religion was abandoned, and in the estimation of many wide-eyed men of reason, it came tumbling down. In their awe before the iron laws of the beautifully running mechanical universe, viewed through the eyes of a Galileo or a Newton in mathematical terms, they ruled out all miracles and special divine providences. God was no longer invoked to explain immediate causes; he was not any longer necessarily *inside* the physical frame of nature. He seemed distant in both space and time. The Deists, who adopted these views, "ushered God to the frontiers of the universe." To them he was the Ancient of Days, who was to be revered as the creator who made all, but they virtually "bowed Him out over the threshold of the world," courteously but firmly.

The Deists were representative of their age in avoiding a clash between religion and science by thus separating God from his creation and conceiving that the latter ran by itself and could therefore be a separate object of study.

A great many clergymen of the English churches, and many also on the Continent, highly educated as a class, held views similar to those of the Deists. Indeed, so lukewarm were their devotions, so utterly nonmystical their public utterances, that it was inevitable that something like Methodism should appear to bring heart and soul back into English Christianity. When this renewal of religious warmth among the clergy came to pass, the people responded eagerly.

Methodism: The Wesleys

The industrial revolution was in the making. Drawn from the land to the towns, the people had lost anchorage. Drunkenness was so widespread among them as to menace the national well-being. The spiritual hunger of the common people was not satisfied by the skeptical intellectualism of the sermons they heard in the established Church—mere discourses, virtually essays, prepared as an accompaniment to the formal reading of the Book of Common Prayer. John Wesley was enhungered too. He and his associates kindled the emotional fire and hearty conviction that was most needed.

The name *Methodist* was applied at first in ridicule by Wesley's fellow students at Oxford to the little group—also derisively called the "Holy Club"—

of which he was a leader, and which met regularly for *methodical* study and prayer in their rooms, endeavoring to bring God down to them out of the skies to which he had been relegated by their Deist teachers. At the start, in seeking to "revive" their fellow Christians of the churches, they had no intention of leaving the Church of England; they hoped only to reform that Church from within. But when the Wesley brothers and George Whitefield began to preach up and down the British Isles, and the people flocking to them in all of the towns were converted in astonishing numbers, it was natural to form a new denomination and to call it the Methodist Church.

John Wesley had been born in an Anglican manse in 1703, the fifteenth child of Samuel and Susannah Wesley. His brother Charles was the eighteenth. After their years at Oxford, during which the most important accession to their young Methodist Club was George Whitefield, the talented son of an innkeeper, John and Charles Wesley went as missionaries to the new colony of Georgia. Neither met with much success there, though John Wesley made fruitful friendships with Moravians. On their return to England, both brothers resorted to a Moravian, Peter Böhler, in London, who convinced them that they would not be true Christians until they had experienced genuine conversion. That experience subsequently came to both. Together with Whitefield, also changed, they were soon preaching in the open fields to tens of thousands of deeply stirred miners and workers in England, Scotland, and Ireland. It was common for their hearers to exhibit their emotion in ecstasies, bodily excitement, cries and groans, and lapses of consciousness. Methodist "chapels" were soon erected for more orderly worship, and as circumstances showed the need for them, characteristically Methodist innovations appeared: "classes," "bands," "circuits," "stewards," "superintendents," and the like. On the devotional side, Charles Wesley contributed to the cause the highly emotional hymns that were to have the usefulness to evangelistic Christianity that the hymns of Isaac Watts and of the Lutherans and Moravians had to the older Churches.

Whitefield's visits to America began in 1739. He frequently preached to immense throngs in the open air. Benjamin Franklin, in his autobiography, recounts in his dryly objective manner how, after having experienced

Whitefield's persuasiveness indoors (and emptied his pocket into the collection plate), he responded to him out of doors in downtown Philadelphia.

> He had a loud and clear voice, and articulated his words and sentences so perfectly, that he might be heard and understood at a great distance.... He preach'd one evening from the top of the Court-house steps, which are in the middle of Market-street, and on the west side of Second-street.... Being among the hindmost in Market-street, I had the curiosity to learn how far he could be heard by retiring backwards down the street towards the river; and I found his voice distinct till I came near Front-street, when some noise in that street obscur'd it. Imagining then a semi-circle, of which my distance should be the radius, and that it were fill'd with auditors, to each of whom I allow'd two square feet, I computed that he might well be heard by more than thirty thousand. This reconcil'd me to the newspaper accounts of his having preach'd to twenty-five thousand people in the fields, and to the ancient histories of generals haranguing whole armies, of which I had sometimes doubted.[S]

Systematic organizational work on behalf of Methodism was begun in New York by 1766, and the epic labors of Francis Asbury (1745–1816), the great "circuit rider," secured the spread of Methodism across the Alleghenies into the vast spaces of the Middle West. Since then, the Methodist Church has become one of the great denominations in the United States.

Jonathan Edwards and the "Great Awakening" in America

In Jonathan Edwards (1703–1758) New England Congregationalism had a powerful theologian—not always rigidly orthodox, as his proposal of a "Quaternity" as an alternative to a Trinity would indicate. But it was for the terrifying message in his preaching that he came to be best remembered. His sermon, "Sinners in the Hands of an Angry God," delivered at Enfield, Connecticut, in 1741, became the emblem of a movement called "the Great Awakening."

> The congregation sat under him at first with but mild interest, little expecting the fury that was to be let loose on them. He read his sermon from a manuscript, but it frightened the people almost to death. Swept into panic, they began to sob out their distress, weeping, crying out, and fainting.... The preacher at length could scarcely be heard, and paused to bid them be quiet. Speaking on the topic "Sinners in the Hands of an Angry God," Edwards pointed out the precarious position of the wicked, of whom his text declared, "Their foot shall slide in due time." Only the restraining grace of God, he said, kept the wicked from sliding on the slippery ground into the pit, where the flames raged and the devils were waiting like lions greedy for their prey....

Perhaps in all sermonic literature there is no climax as intense and breathtaking as one of his last paragraphs.

> If we knew that there was one person and but one, in the whole congregation, that was to be the subject of this misery, what an awful thing it would be to think of! If we knew who it was, what an awful sight would it be to see such a person! How might all the rest of the congregation lift up a lamentable and bitter cry over him! But, alas! instead of one, how many it is likely will remember this discourse in hell! And it would be a wonder if some that are now present should not be in hell in a very short time, before this year is out. And it would be no wonder if some persons that now sit here in some seats of this meeting-house, in health and quiet and secure, *should not be there before tomorrow morning.*[T]

The Missionary Movement

The nineteenth century may be reckoned a great one by Protestants. It opened with a second "great awakening" in the United States, a series of revivals that much increased the number of Baptists and Methodists in the midwestern states. In Great Britain, the Church of England was powerfully moved by a pietistic Evangelical movement, which in later decades issued in the Oxford or Tractarian Movement, the formation of the Young Men's Christian Association (in London in 1844), and the organization of the Salvation Army (by William Booth in 1865). In Germany, theologians Schleiermacher (1768–1834) and Ritschl (1822–1889) gave a new and liberal turn to Protestant religious thought. But perhaps the two most significant developments of the century were the organization of worldwide Protestant missions and the rapid expansion of Christian presence into developing countries around the globe.

In missionary activity, the Catholics had long shown the way. They had made South America and Mexico Catholic and had had huge success in Japan and the Philippines. The Protestants gathered momentum more slowly. When the Dutch established trading stations in the East Indies in the seventeenth century, they encouraged missionaries to follow behind them. In the same century, the Church of England felt a responsibility to the American Indians and organized the Society for the Propagation of the Gospel in New England, a group that at the beginning of the eighteenth century was largely superseded by the Society for the Propagation of the Gospel in Foreign Parts. The Quakers, from the start, sent missionaries to the West Indies, Palestine, and various parts of Europe. The Moravians fostered missions vigorously during the eighteenth century.

A new phase of missionary effort began with the publication of the journals of Captain Cook, whose vivid descriptions of the condition of the natives of the many South Pacific islands he visited from 1768 to 1779 stirred up William Carey to go to India as the first missionary of the Baptist Society for Propagating the Gospel among the Heathen, which he helped organize in 1792. In 1795, an interdenominational group formed the London Missionary Society, which sent its first appointees to Tahiti. (This society has since been Congregationalist.) There followed the formation of the Edinburgh Missionary Society, the Glasgow Missionary Society, the Church Missionary Society (of the Church of England), and the Wesleyan Methodist Missionary Society.

To match these British efforts with like devotion to the expansion of the Christian world, Congregationalists in Massachusetts joined in discussions that led in 1810 to the birth of the famous missionary arm of American Congregationalism, the American Board of Commissioners for Foreign Missions. Subsequently, like organizations were formed in the other American churches. In 1888, the Student Volunteer Movement for Foreign Missions was organized for the study of missions and recruitment of new missionaries in colleges.

Some nine thousand volunteers were placed in the first three decades of its work.

While missionary efforts flourished, traditional Christian conceptions were being challenged on the American scene from two directions. On the one hand, there were claims of an entirely fresh revelation: the Book of Mormon. On the other hand, scientific developments challenged literalist biblical revelation.

The Mormons

Stirred by the revivalist excitement of the Great Awakening in upstate New York, Joseph Smith (1805–1844) experienced visitations from an angel who warned him away from existing churches and promised a restoration of the true Church of Jesus Christ. At Fayette, New York, in 1830, he founded that church (the name amended in 1838 to the Church of Jesus Christ of the Latter Day Saints). The new body was guided by direct revelations that Smith received from an angel he called Moroni, and by written revelation engraved on golden plates he unearthed (and later returned to the angel). Smith said that through the "gift and power of God" he was able to translate the "reformed Egyptian" language of *The Book of Mormon.* The book described how three groups of ancient people migrated to the Americas in the pre-Columbian period, among them the ancestors of the American Indians, and how Christ visited these migrants after his crucifixion and instituted his church among them. Although the *Book of Mormon* is sometimes called the Mormon Bible, Smith regarded it as a supplement to biblical scripture. Other revelations to Smith became sacred books, notably *Doctrine and Covenants* and *Pearl of Great Price.* At the time of his death, Smith had been working on a revision of the New Testament that would include prophecies of his own coming.

Smith and his converts established colonies in Kirtland, Ohio, and in Jackson County, Missouri. Driven out of Missouri in 1838, they established a political domain at Nauvoo, Illinois. Smith aroused the fears of his neighbors by organizing a Mormon militia and announcing his candidacy for the presidency of the United States. By this time, he and some close associates had secretly been taking numerous wives and had put forward controversial new doctrines such as the preexistence of humankind and a plurality of gods. Internal disaffection, combined with external hostility, erupted in a mob attack in which Smith was killed.

Brigham Young succeeded Smith, leading those who accepted the Nauvoo innovations and eventually establishing a new Zion in Utah. Some of those who remained behind established the Reorganized Church of Jesus Christ of the Latter Day Saints, with headquarters in Independence, Missouri. The Utah group wanted to establish a Mormon State of Deseret, but compromised with the federal authorities in the creation of Utah Territory, with Brigham Young as governor. By 1890, pressure from Congress forced Mormon President Wilford Woodruff to sign a manifesto renouncing multiple marriages. This symbolized the passing of an era of communal sharing and aspirations to a political kingdom, and the settling in to a role as part of a pluralistic American scene.

For regulation of their internal life, Mormons rejected professional clergy, creating instead a system in which all mature males (including blacks, since 1978) have offices in an elaborate hierarchy of priesthoods. All households are regulated in a structure of stakes (dioceses) and wards (parishes). Abstention from alcohol, tobacco, tea, and coffee is expected of everyone, and the contribution of a tithe (tenth) of one's income to the church is mandatory. Young men are assigned to two years of missionary service, and the results in numbers have been impressive. In 1996, the Church of Jesus Christ of the Latter-day Saints estimated its membership around the world to be just under ten million.

The Conflict of Science and Faith

The nineteenth century dawned with little inkling of the hazards that science was to place in the way of faith, but long before the century was out, a momentous struggle began between orthodox religion and a naturalism bred by science.

One of the earliest controversies was precipitated by the development of historical criticism and the rewriting of history. David Strauss and Ernest Renan, in epoch-making German and French works, radically rewrote the life of Jesus. Lower (or textual) and higher (or historico-literary) criticism of the Bible demonstrated that its books were the work of many different authors at many different times. The Pentateuch was shown to have had a composite authorship, stretching over at least five centuries. The New Testament Gospels were dissected into "Q," "M," "L," and other strata of tradition. Fierce controversy over these findings, as they were made, divided Protestantism into two camps, later to be called Fundamentalists (who rejected biblical criticism as gross unbelief) and Modernists (who accepted it as sound).

But though bitter and long drawn out, this controversy was all but overshadowed during the latter half of the nineteenth century by the chorus of angry protest that followed the publication of Darwin's *Origin of Species*. For Darwin, and his predecessor in formulating the evolutionary theory, Lamarck, were interpreted not only to deny the story of creation in the first chapters of Genesis but to rule out any theory of creation whatever. Philosophers like Thomas Huxley and Herbert Spencer increased the sense of outrage among the conservatives by rejecting the doctrine of an impassable gulf between human beings and the beasts, arguing instead for the theory that humankind has emerged by slow evolution from the anthropoid apes and is not a separate, special creation of God.

Many devout believers felt they were faced by an inflexible choice between irreconcilable positions: one that science is true and religion is false, and the other that science is preposterous guesswork and the biblical revelation God's own infallible word, true from beginning to end exactly as it is contained in the Bible. Advocacy groups demanded that "creation science" be added to public school curricula on the grounds that evolution is only a *theory*. Most school boards resisted such efforts because they viewed arguments that the universe is less than ten thousand years old as being based on religious belief rather than scientific evidence.

Acceptance of Science: Liberalism and Neo-Orthodoxy

Liberal Christians remained sure that no such irreconcilability between science and religion existed. Men like Henry Drummond in Scotland (in his *Natural Law in the Spiritual World*) and John Fiske in New England (in *Outlines of Cosmic Philosophy* and *The Idea of God as Affected by Modern Knowledge*) endeavored to show that on the theory that evolution is God's method of creation, religion and science can indeed be reconciled. The biblical story of creation has to be taken as devout, prescientific theorizing, poetically if not literally true, its essence not disproved, though its form requires reinterpretation. With this beginning, liberal theology proceeded confidently to a task of reconstruction, assured that the essentials of the Christian faith were never shaken by the findings of a careful, non-metaphysical (or "pure") science. In fact, liberals often spoke as if the humanitarian values of the Christian faith, coupled with the creative objectivity of science, made for continual progress in the state of humankind.

This liberal view, so confident and optimistic in its faith in God and humankind, was itself severely shaken by the catastrophe of World War I. Thereafter emerged a neo-Orthodoxy, which accepted the findings of science and historical criticism but insisted that God is not in nature and history in the way in which the liberals say, but is transcendent, existing quite apart from nature and humankind, indeed is the Wholly Other, the Absolute, who must break through the wall of human error and self-contradiction that separates him from humans in order to appear in human history. Without such breaking through, humankind is lost. The champions—Karl Barth and his followers—of this dualism of God and the world for awhile swept the field; but the champions of divine immanence in one sense or another returned to deny that the God of neo-Orthodoxy has any contemporary relevance, some going so far in locating God in the world that they have been called "religious secularists."

Fundamentalism

Fundamentalism is the conservative movement that first appeared as a reaction to the applications of science; it found a name and a continuing sense of identity (in opposition to modernism) through the appearance of a series of pamphlets, *The Fundamentals: A Testimony of Truth* (1910). Fundamentalism came to be associated with the following five points, emphasized in these pamphlets:

1. the verbal inspiration of the Bible
2. the virgin birth of Christ
3. the substitutionary atonement of Christ
4. the bodily resurrection of Christ
5. the second coming of Christ

The movement was most commonly known as "fundamentalism" until the formation of the National Association of Evangelicals in 1942. Sharing much of the Fundamentalist outlook, Evangelicals have taken somewhat less rigid literal views of biblical interpretation and have been more articulate in offering an alternative to liberalism in theological discussion. Other conservatives, preferring to put more emphasis on the personal experience of conversion, prefer to be known as "charismatics" or "born-again" Christians.

Movements Toward Church Union

The fissions and separations within Protestantism have diminished since the trauma of World War II. Union among the Protestant churches has been urged for over a century, and the recent turn to active ecumenism by the Roman Catholic Church has broadened the purview to include the prospect of the reunion of all Christians.

In Europe, the first great achievements in unity were in the area of foreign missions. The problems of interdenominational comity on the mission fields led to the calling of the great Edinburgh Missionary Conference of 1910, which resulted in the formation of the International Missionary Council (1921), a body that has now merged with the World Council of Churches. The World Council itself emerged from the Church of England's (or Episcopal's) hopes of serving as a mediator between the Protestant and Catholic worlds; these hopes finally led to the first assembly of the World Council of Churches, held in Amsterdam, Holland, in 1948. The Council has since met in such countries as the United States, India, Sweden, and Kenya. It has admitted to its membership all of the Eastern Orthodox churches; it also has always invited observers from the Roman Catholic Church, who have attended each session in increasing numbers.

Organic Unions

Ecumenism has expressed itself not only in federations like the World Council of Churches, which leave the member denominations intact, but also in organic unions through merger. Of the latter kind was the organic union in Canada of Presbyterians, Methodists, and Congregationalists in the United Church of Canada (1925). Along denominational lines, separate branches of the Lutheran and also the Presbyterian churches in the United States have united. Ecumenically more significant because it crossed "family" lines was the organic union in 1957 of the Congregational–Christian Churches and the Evangelical and Reformed Church under the name of the United Church of Christ. Similarly significant was the formation of the Church of South India in 1947 because it was also an organic union to cross denominational family lines; it united Anglican dioceses with churches of non-Episcopal heritage.

The "Electronic Church"

Access to large audiences (and funding) through computerized mailings, radio, and television ("televangelism" or the "electronic church") has associated Protestant conservatism with broader, quasi-religious movements, described in political terms as the "religious right." Reverend Jerry Falwell's Moral Majority, for example, united many white Protestant conservatives, Mormons, Zionist Jews, and politically conservative Catholics in a coalition opposing abortion, busing, homosexuality, pornography, sex education in public schools, easy divorce, and the proposed Equal Rights Amendment. The coalition advocated prayer in public schools, the teaching of creationism, community censorship of textbooks, capital punishment, a traditional family, a buildup of military power, and increased U.S. support for Israel.

Though the movement was conspicuous in the conservative tide of the 1980 election, its political effectiveness is a matter of debate because political analysts found the swing to the right more pronounced among non-Evangelicals than among Evangelicals of the same socioeconomic level. On the other hand, Reverend Pat Robertson was able to make effective use of his network followers in an unsuccessful bid for nomination in the Republican primaries of 1987–1988. During the same period, revelations of sexual misconduct on the part of two prominent broadcasters, Jim Bakker and Jimmy Swaggart, seriously damaged the public standing of televangelism, and in the fall of 1989, the Moral Majority organization was disbanded. In 1992, new criticism of Pat Robertson came from ethicists questioning conversion of funds for himself and his son, totalling some forty-seven million dollars.

On the political scene the activism of the Moral Majority was replaced by the Christian Coalition, a tax-exempt lobbying organization whose principle outreach to individuals was the distribution through local churches of "Voters' Guides," showing how candidates had voted on issues important to conservative Christians—abortion, homosexuality, and pornography in particular. The coalition was effective in getting voters to the polls, but singularly ineffective on the issues most important to them. Talk of "taking over" the Republican Party was tempered by questions about who was using whom. The most conspicuous effort by a single denomination to apply moral censure was the resolution in the Southern Baptist convention in 1997 calling upon all of its members to boycott the Disney corporation for employment policies and productions deemed to be supportive of homosexuality as an acceptable lifestyle. In 1998 the same traditionally non-creedal church adopted a "Baptist Faith and Message" document including a declaration that "A wife is to submit graciously to the servant leadership of her husband even as the church willingly submits to the headship of Christ."

States of Mind: Anxiety and Eclecticism

The mainstream of Christian expression in the nineties has been flanked by diverging countercurrents not clearly enough defined to be described as anything other than states of mind: on the one hand, an extreme distrust of conventional authority, religious or secular; on the other hand, an easygoing acceptance of "spirituality" in any form as a life-enhancing alternative to "organized religion"—"spirituality" in this case being virtually undefinable.

The condition of anxiety and distrust crystallizes in cults too diverse in doctrine to be detailed here. The state of mind is usually marked by a kind of bunker mentality, coupled with specific apocalyptic hopes—all under the tight control of a charismatic leader. Examples might be the Branch Davidians of

Waco, the Applewhite Heaven's Gate group, and the Jim Jones cult. These, of course, came to international renown for resorting to mass suicide, but a similar mind-set characterizes less extreme collective and individualized religious expression. Its more secular expression is found in some militia groups.

On the opposite fringe is a state of mind that may be a uniquely American response to multicultural exposure and religious pluralism: a disposition to regard openness to *all* religions as *a* religion, an alternative to hard-edged moral judgments and personal commitment. Ignoring differences between world religions in their cognitive and ethical dimensions makes it possible to see all of them as equivalent expressions of "spirituality." This makes any choice between them unnecessary and encourages personal blends to suit individual tastes. A leaning toward meditation and an acceptance of the idea of multiple rebirths is reminiscent of Hindu–Buddhist modes, but rebirths are viewed in Western style, not as returning to a scene of suffering, but as rewards. An encyclopedia of New Age religious options begins with Madam Blavatsky's theosophy and runs through channeling and fruitarianism (an offshoot of vegetarianism) to Americanized versions of Yoga and Zen.

X. RECENT THEOLOGICAL TRENDS

It is a central Christian conviction that God continually reveals himself in history, and recent trends in theology are quite naturally responses to recent historical events and to social upheavals over racism, sexism, and the widening gulf between the rich and poor.

On the American scene, the widespread experience of alienation in the countercultural rebellion against traditional values evoked sympathetic theological responses. Harvey Cox, William Hamilton, and others found reason to celebrate the liberation of individuals in a secular and pluralistic society. In times like these, they were saying, it is only honest to confess one's alienation from complacent talk about a loving and powerful God. "Death of God" theology as represented by Paul Van Buren had to do with the meaninglessness of all God talk, and for Thomas Altizer it

meant the death of transcendence. Christianity for him was about people, not about God; after the cross, God was born again as here-and-now immanence.

In Europe, theologians like Jurgen Moltmann and Wolfhart Pannenberg responded to secularism and the collapse of traditional values by reinterpreting the eschatological dimensions of the Gospels: the Coming One, who is also present, offers the power and hope of the future. Aspects of the theology of hope anticipated and paralleled some new developments in the Americas where particular facets of oppression (and attendant forms of hope for redress) came to be the focal points of black, liberation, and feminist theology.

Black Theology

"The white Jesus is dead. He was slain somewhere between Hiroshima or Nagasaki and the road to Selma, Alabama."[U] [Selma was the scene of police violence against civil rights advocates.] Statements like this link black theology to the death and rebirth themes of the 1960s. In May 1969, white churches were presented with a "Black Manifesto," drawn up by a Detroit conference on black economic development. Its demand for five hundred million dollars in "reparations" provoked widespread turmoil, but its rationale reached only a limited audience of theologians. Books and articles by Albert Cleage, James Cone, Deotis Roberts, and others gave currency to black theology as a separate genre. In that arena, the continuing painful battles over separation and integration were renewed in theological terms. Can one *care* about whites and seek reconciliation while calling for the destruction of everything white? Searing indictments were compromised by ambiguities. Cone could write, "To be black means that your heart, your soul, your mind, and your body are where the dispossessed are,"[V] but other, more strident passages sounded like appeals for black racist separatism. It seems likely that black theology will continue to serve as a forum of theological debate, but it is not clear to what extent it will relate its concerns to other liberation theologies.

Liberation Theology

Stimulated by the social messages of Vatican II translated into an agenda for Latin America by a conference of Catholic bishops at Medellin, Colombia, in 1968, a variety of alliances between churches and socialist revolutionary movements emerged in the late 1960s and 1970s. The liberation theology of these movements first reached worldwide attention in 1971 through a book, *A Theology of Liberation,* by Gustavo Gutierrez of Peru. The dehumanizing forces of poverty and exclusion challenge the Church, Gutierrez said, to set a course of practical liberating action, or *praxis:* "How do you say to the poor that God loves you?" He and his associates, some Protestants as well as Catholics, agreed that what was needed was not irrelevant (European) orthodoxy (correct doctrine) but *orthopraxis* (right doing), obedience to a liberating God.

Torn between historic connections with wealth and power and their present awareness of the desperate social needs of their constituency, the Latin American bishops meeting at Puebla, Mexico, in 1979 found the issues of liberation theology at the center of their debates. Right-wing forces controlled the preliminary papers and the conference procedures (the prominent liberation theologians were excluded from direct participation). Pope John Paul II opened the conference and took a cautious, mediating position, but the liberation theologians felt that their indirect input through friendly bishops had succeeded in reintroducing some activist themes into the very conservative preliminary document.

The encyclical *Dominum et Vivificantem,* "The Lord and Giver of Life (1986)," focused on issues of great concern to advocates of liberation theology but proved on the whole to be a disappointment to them. While it called upon Christians to work to aid the poor, it was critical of political involvement and Marxist materialism. The Church should not be distracted from striving for the "conversion of hearts." Many found it ironic that when John Paul II visited Third World countries where population growth was outstripping food production, he chose to emphasize the Church's position against birth control.

Feminist Theology

Also largely a product of the social movements of the late 1960s and the 1970s, feminist theology has had two preeminent spokespersons, both Catholic in back-

Bishop Barbara Harris

A 2,000-year barrier for women was broken in February 1989 when the Rt. Rev. Barbara Clementine Harris was consecrated suffragan (assistant) bishop in the Episcopal Church. Coming from a background of social activism at the Church of the Advocate in Philadelphia, Bishop Harris had been ordained to the priesthood in 1980. From her pulpit she had supported gay rights and criticized the Episcopal Church as being "male dominated" and "racist." *(Courtesy of AP Worldwide Photos.)*

ground. Identifying the Church as the leading instrument in the oppression of women, Mary Daly held out hope in 1968 when she called for its radical transformation; in her subsequent writing, however, she has moved to a post–Christian feminist position from which wanting equality in the Church would be "comparable to a black person's demanding equality in the Ku Klux Klan."[W] In positive terms, she has called for celebration of feminine "Be-ing."

Be-ing is the verb that says the dimensions of depth in all verbs, such as intuiting, loving, imaging, making, acting, as well as the couraging, hoping, and playing that are always there when one is really living."[W2]

While Mary Daly's views have not had a wide following, more and more women find themselves angered by paternalistic behaviors and attitudes that exist today. Some modern-day evangelists have equated equal rights advocacy with child killing, witchcraft, and socialism. Their extreme statements, coupled with increased attention to sexual harassment and misconduct charges, not only against celebrities like Supreme Court Justice Clarence Thomas and Archbishop Eugene Marino of Atlanta, but also to thousands of harassment complaints on college campuses and in workplaces, has created an atmosphere receptive to such newly coined terms as "Womanspirit"—a reference to spiritual sensibilities and teachings born out of feminist rejection of the male religious imagery and male authority found in most traditional religions. In short, minds shaped in the paternalistic worldview "simply don't get it."

Rosemary Radford Ruether has remained in the mainstream of theological discourse, finding links between feminist and other liberation theologies and contributing her own critical assessments. She warns, for example, against the oversimplification of oppressor-oppressed analyses.

> To the extent that they [oppressed groups] are not at all concerned about maintaining an authentic prophetic address to the oppressors, to the extent that they repudiate them as persons . . . they both abort their possibilities as a liberating force for the oppressors, and, ultimately derail their own power to liberate themselves.[X]

Our space is limited. Much is unsaid, and there will be more to say daily about a faith community which, along with Judaism, makes the revelation of God in history its constant focus.

GLOSSARY

Anabaptists "rebaptizers," Protestant sects in the 16th c. holding that the call to Christian faith is experiential and that baptism is valid only as a voluntary commitment of a person mature enough to be a believer.

Arianism the views promoted by Arius of Alexandria in the 4th c. that Christ was a created being, "made" at a point in time and not coeternal with God—a heresy ruled out in the Creed of Nicaea by the phrases "begotten not made" and "of one substance with the Father"

Docetism "seemingism," a heretical view of the person of Christ derived from applying Gnostic dualism: any real humanity being excluded because divinity incarnated would be contaminated; thus, the saving truth (*gnosis*) could only be delivered by a divine apparition, a "seeming" human being

electronic church delivery of religious messages by computerized mailings, radio, and television ("televangelism"), a method especially associated with Protestant conservatism and the "religious right" in politics

filioque "and from the Son," a clause emphasizing the equality of the Persons of the Trinity (the Spirit "proceeds from the Father and from the Son"); St. Augustine urged it, and it found its way into Latin versions of the Creed of Chalcedon, much to the distress of the Greek Orthodox Church

fundamentalism conservative doctrine, as opposed to modernist-liberal theology and evolutionary science. Often defined in terms of five points: verbal inspiration of Scripture, literal Virgin Birth, substitutionary atonement, bodily resurrection, and the Second Coming of Christ

Gnosticism a dualistic view completely separating God, goodness, and Spirit from the contaminated material world; salvation comes from esoteric knowledge (*gnosis*) alone, not by embodied (matter-contaminated) human beings or historical events

Immaculate Conception the doctrine, proclaimed an official dogma of the Roman Catholic Church in 1854, that Mary at her conception was insulated from inheriting original sin—a logically necessary view if sin is defined in Aristotelian terms as a *substance*

liberal theology a movement in the 19th and early 20th centuries accepting the findings of evolutionary science and historical-critical study of the Bible and stressing the immanence of God, the Atonement as moral example, the potential for good in human nature, and a social gospel for the constructive reform of society

Marcionism views attributed to Marcion of Sinope (2nd c. C.E.), who accepted Gnostic-Docetic ideas and urged that Christians should repudiate the Old Testament and its matter-contaminated deity; he proposed a canon of edited Gospels and ten Letters of Paul

neo-Orthodoxy born during the existential crises presented by totalitarianism in Europe, this movement shared with liberalism acceptance of science, historically conditioned revelation, and a social gospel, but stressed a sinful (pridefully arrogant) human nature, the transcendence of God, and a dialectic relationship between theology and culture

Nestorianism the doctrine of Nestorius of Constantinople (5th c.), still held in some Eastern Churches, that Christ had two distinct "natures," human and divine, and that the Virgin Mary should not be called Mother of God (*theotokos*)

Scholasticism a form of medieval Christian thought that built upon religious dogma a system to keep separate and yet reconcile the spheres of religion and philosophy, faith and reason

"sola fide/sola scriptura" Luther's view that salvation is based on "faith alone," rather than works, and that authority in the Church is based on "Scripture alone," rather than ecclesiastically controlled "tradition"; the availability of these two sources to individuals led to the Reformation view of the priesthood of all believers

transubstantiation the Roman Catholic doctrine that the eucharistic wine and bread are changed in *substance* to Christ's body and blood (though not in *accidental* properties such as odor, texture, etc.); Eastern Orthodox and Protestant churches (not committed to a *substance* philosophy) use more mystical and metaphoric language to describe the real presence of Christ in the Eucharist

Islam: The Religion of Submission to God

Beginnings

The heart of Islam is well hidden from most Westerners, and the outer images of Islamic countries present bewildering contrasts: stern ayatollahs ordering the lash for prostitutes, camel drivers putting down prayer mats in the desert, sophisticated royal princes discussing international investments, and fiery national liberators proclaiming equality and denouncing Western values. It is not easy to look beyond these images into the heart of Islam.

A "Muslim" is "one who submits" or "one who commits himself to Islam." The word *Islam* is a noun formed from the infinitive of a verb meaning "to accept," "to submit," "to commit oneself," and means "submission" or "surrender." Of this word, Charles J. Adams says, "By its very form [as a verbal noun] it conveys a feeling of action and ongoingness, not of something that is static and finished, once and for all, but of an inward state which is always repeated and renewed. . . . One who thoughtfully declares 'I am a Muslim' has done much more than affirm his membership in a community. . . . [He is saying] 'I am one who commits himself to God [Allāh].'"[A]

Although the challenge of Islam daunted its opponents, its force and clarity appealed to those who accepted it. Over 950 million people, by a conservative estimate, are now numbered among its adherents, and their number is increasing. They accept it as the absolute and final faith, and they are proud to be able to follow it. Over the years, Islam has kept to one basic scripture, preserved from the first in a state of textual purity such that comparatively few variant readings have arisen to confuse the commentators. The Qur'ān (or Koran, in traditional spelling), not the Prophet, is the revelation.

Muslims revere Muḥammad for transmitting the revelation and for translating it into action, but they do not perceive him as an innovative founder or an author. Thus a Muslim's account of his or her faith does not dwell on the Prophet's biography or ponder the contribution of his personality to the faith. When we begin our investigation in such a way we need to be aware that we are asking un-Islamic questions and encountering "difficulties" that Muslims may find irrelevant.

An initial difficulty is the scarcity of information about the Prophet in the Qur'ān itself. This information comes to us first through the Ḥadīth, the body of tradition originating from the first generation of Muslims and handed down both orally and in writing, and second, through Muslim biographies of the Prophet that appeared during the first centuries of

WESTERN NAME: Islam
LANGUAGE: Arabic
DEITY: Allāh
MEANS OF REVELATION: His prophets (Muḥammad the Last)
    His books (the Qur'ān the Last)
    His angels
FOUNDING EVENT: The Hegira (*Hijira*), 622 C.E.
SUPPLEMENTARY LITERATURE: Hadiths (traditions)
PRINCIPAL BRANCHES: Sunni
    Shī'ah (Shī'ites)

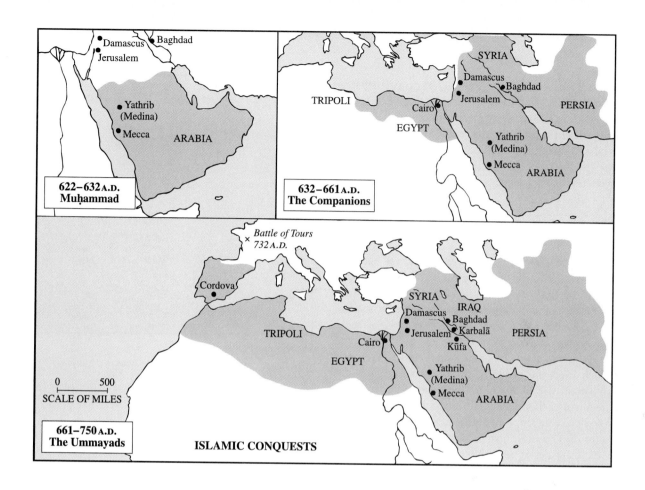

ISLAMIC CONQUESTS

Muslim history. Such sources contain unreliable material, but as early reports of what Muḥammad said and did, or was believed to have said and done, they are extremely valuable.

I. ARABIAN BELIEFS AND PRACTICES BEFORE MUḤAMMAD

Racial and Geo-Economic Factors

The Arabians, like any other people who might be mentioned, were not culturally homogeneous. Those who spoke Semitic languages outnumbered other groups; but in the south, non-Semitic Ethiopians crossed the Red Sea to establish settlements along the coastal plain; in the northeast, conquests dating as far back as the second millennium B.C.E. somewhat altered the groupings there by infusion of Sumerian, Babylonian, and Persian elements. From Egypt, a Hamitic element entered the population.

Divisive modes of thought produced further variations. Cultural differences that often proved irreconcilable were introduced when Semites who left the desert returned again after the passage of centuries. During periods of international convulsion, many refugees from lands to the north and west retreated into the desert wastes that their fathers had put behind them. In the time of Muḥammad, the western portions of Arabia contained considerable numbers of Jews who had fled from their enemies—Assyrian,

Babylonian, Greek, and Roman. They participated with the Arabs in the intensive cultivation of the oases in western Arabia. They were numerous in Medina (the ancient Yathrib) and its neighborhood as "clients" of the Arabian tribes; that is, they were welcomed into the area and adopted as accepted outsiders who would thenceforth enjoy tribal protection.

The Vacant Quarter and the North

There were some rather marked differences between northern and southern Arabs. The huge Arabian peninsula (natively and aptly called Jazīrat al-'Arab, "the Island of the Arabs," because it is virtually isolated by its surrounding waters and its own sands) is geographically marked by a clamshell-shaped tract of sand dunes, a third of a million square miles in extent, which even the bedouins avoid (it being generally known as Al-Rub 'al-Khalī, "the Vacant Quarter"). To the north of this badland are stretches of more habitable desert steppe, containing oases and arable valley bottoms. This more hospitable territory is bounded by a band of desert resembling a crescent moon and reaching from Al-Rub 'al-Khalī for five hundred miles to another desert, the Great Nafud, lying in the northwest. The Nafud's shifting dunes of red and white sand stretch midway between Medina and Damascus. On the steppe land, coarse soil supports a sparse, hardy verdure that springs up when the infrequent winter rains fall and provides grazing for the camels, sheep, goats, and horses of the bedouin tribes.

South Arabia

South of the "Vacant Quarter" is the rain-bathed area of Yemen, or South Arabia—the classical Arabia Felix—bounded on the southeast by the Gulf of Aden and on the southwest by the lower end of the Red Sea. This was the region so famed among the Greeks and Romans for its frankincense and spices. The geographical separation of north and south Arabia was paralleled by ethnic differences among the people. The north Arabians of Muḥammad's day were longheaded, wiry nomads who spoke a pure Arabic and were by nature liberty loving and imaginative. Thousands of years of hungry struggle had schooled them

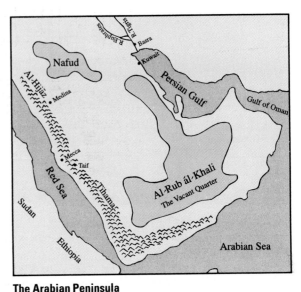

The Arabian Peninsula
The birth and spreading of Islam was influenced by the physical features of Arabia.

in both predatory and cooperative habits. They were quite different in speech and customs from their comfortable brethren below the "Vacant Quarter," the round-headed, hook-nosed southerners who were farmers and horticulturists and spoke a Semitic dialect, with Ethiopic loanwords that sounded strange in northern ears. Before the time of Muḥammad, the north Arabians, although they had many outside contacts, never knew a conqueror, but the south Arabians, blessed with fertilizing rain and sun, grew prosperous through trade, built cities and towns surrounded by green fields and gardens, and brought down upon themselves in consequence raids from the desert, wars from abroad, the expense of fortifications, heavy taxes, economic rivalries, commercial anxieties, and recurrent depressions coming close on the heels of boom times. And when the Ptolemies (and the Romans after them) learned how to sail past them to India, they went into permanent decline.

The Coastal Mountains (Al-Hijāz)

A third section of Arabia happens to be more important to us. It consists of the mountain range running parallel with the Red Sea from the Gulf of 'Aqaba to Yemen. Rising at some points over ten thousand feet above sea level, this range falls swiftly to the Red Sea, but its eastern slope declines gradually through bare, volcanic lavatracts, scoured with deep wadis, or watercourses, toward the red sands of the central desert and the flat coastal plains bordering the faraway Persian Gulf. Although at places like Ṭā'if or Medina subterranean waters rising to the surface moisten an arable soil, this mountain range is for the most part dry and barren. Violent rainstorms sometimes visit it, but then the water rushes off in floods that wash out more deeply the gullies or wadis. Yet it figures historically as the most vital part of the peninsula, for it once furnished a connecting link between the southern spicelands and the markets of the Mediterranean world. On the cool, hard surface of its uplands, caravans long before the time of Christ plodded their way through the trading posts of Ṭā'if, Mecca, and Yathrib (Medina), and at Petra forked off west or north to Egypt or Syria. The pre-Islamic prosperity of the communities of Al-Hijāz, this mountain home of Islam, was primarily due to the passage through them of the spice-laden caravans of the south.

Although the interrelations of the three sections of Arabia were at times strife riven, the existence of commerce and trade indicates that these interrelations were generally cooperative, if not warm.

Religious Conceptions

The religion of pre-Islamic Arabia was a development out of the primitive Semitic desert faith already sketched in the chapter on Judaism. In some parts of Arabia that development had gone quite far in one or another direction. In south Arabia, for example, a rather advanced astral cult prevailed, centered in the moon god and reflecting Babylonian and Zoroastrian influences. In other regions where Jews and Christians had secured a foothold (which was in most of the commercial centers of Arabia), the native converts to these faiths abandoned their primitive beliefs and espoused monotheism. But the great majority of Arabs, both in the towns and on the steppes, worshiped local gods and goddesses. Some of these deities were strictly tribal; others presided over certain geographical areas and obliged all who entered their domains to reverence them. There was also widespread veneration of certain astral deities. Some had Babylonian names and were readily identified by Greek and Roman visitors as local forms of Jupiter, Venus, Mercury, Uranus, and other deities. In Mecca, three almost indistinguishable goddesses were adored: al-Lāt, a mother goddess (perhaps the sun), al-Manāt, the goddess of fate, and al-'Uzzā, the morning star, a pale sort of Venus, their idols being the center of a worship much like that accorded across the frontiers in olden times to Ishtar and Isis. They were reckoned to be "the daughters of Allāh." Allāh (meaning God or "the deity," like the Hebrew *El* and the Babylonian *Bel*; Arabic accent falls on the second syllable) was vaguely conceived as the creator, a far-off high god, venerated by Muḥammad's tribe, the Quraysh.

In addition to these beings of the rank of high divinity, there were lesser spirits, scarcely less honored—namely, angels and various sorts of jinn, some friendly, some hostile and demonic. It is interesting to mark the differences in character that seem to have existed between these lesser spirits. The angels were, of course, morally irreproachable and of a uniformly beneficent nature. The jinn were, according to fable, created from fire two thousand years before Adam and could at will appear to human eyes or remain invisible. They could assume animal or human forms and have sexual relations and progeny. The friendly jinn were beautiful in form and kind in disposition. In contrast, the desert-ranging jinn, a predominantly demonic group, struck terror into Arab hearts as active agents of evil. Yet some of them could be bent to good use, for anyone who could control their movements might convert them into helpful agents to the attainment of beneficial ends, like finding treasure, building palaces, or whirling young men away on the wings of the wind to far places and new fortunes. Among the demonic beings who were always evil were the ghouls, who lay in wait where people were destined to perish, that they might satisfy their appetite for corrupt human flesh, or who robbed graves of their bodies to furnish the main dish for their midnight orgies. The ever-active imagination of the Arabs and their Persian coreligionists, which came to such colorful expression in aftertimes in the tales of *The Thousand and One Nights,* whiled away the hours weaving innumerable stories out of these concepts.

Particularly among the bedouin, but in every part of Arabia, animism existed. Pillarlike stones and noteworthy rocks, caves, springs, and wells were held in great respect. In some districts there were sacred palm trees on which offerings of weapons and cloth were hung. Totemism may or may not have been involved in the reverence paid to the gazelle, eagle, vulture, and camel.

Mecca: The Ka'ba

Mecca offered the most conspicuous instance of veneration given to a stone—that given to the meteorite built into the corner of the holiest shrine in Arabia, the Ka'ba ("cube"), a structure with no exterior ornament. It was later covered with a tissue of black cloth. The earliest reference to it comes from the Roman historian Diodorus Siculus (*ca.* 60 B.C.E.). In some far past the people of that part of Arabia had been startled by the rush of a meteor, which quenched its heaven fire in Mecca's sandy glen. Afterward the awed inhabitants worshiped it, calling it "the black stone that fell from heaven in the days of Adam." From far and near across the desert, the tribes of Arabia, year after year, came on a *hajj* (pilgrimage) to offer near it sacrifices of sheep and camels and to run the circuit of the stone seven times and kiss it, in the hope of heaven's blessing on them. In the course of years, the cube-shaped Ka'ba was erected and the holy stone placed in the southeast corner at a height that permitted it to be kissed by those who made the sevenfold circuit. Images of local and distant deities were placed in the dark interior. The Meccans declared that the great patriarch Abraham, while on a visit to his outcast son Ishmael, had built the Ka'ba and imbedded the Black Stone in it. (Tradition was not content with this legend, however; it asserted that the first Ka'ba was built by Adam from a celestial prototype, and was rebuilt by Abraham and Ishmael.)

Even in the present day, the Ka'ba defines sacred space physically: the column air above it is held to be inviolate (no bird or aircraft passes through it); all praying is oriented to it; and no unclean activity should take place facing toward it. (The floor plans of mosques and restrooms are carefully oriented.)

Zamzam, Hagar, and Pilgrimage Tradition

Only a few steps away from the Ka'ba was the holy well Zamzam, whose water was sacred to the pilgrims who ran the circuit of the shrine. Meccan tradition endowed it with a curious history. In the third century C.E., when the men of the Bani-Jurhum tribe were driven from Mecca by the Bani-Khuza'a, their shaykh, so it was said, before giving up the town, threw down into the well some suits of armor, several swords, and two gazelles of gold, and then covered up all with tamped-down earth and sand, so that when the captors of the city entered it, the location of the well was not known to them. After the Quraysh came into control of Mecca, Muḥammad's grandfather, 'Abd-al-Muṭṭalib, the leading chief, found the well and restored it. The Meccans were grateful, for they had an old tradition that after Hagar was expelled from Abraham's tent, she came with her little son Ishmael to the future site of their city, at the time a barren valley, and because her child was dying of thirst, she left him lying on the hot earth while she searched despairingly for water; behind her the child, in a tantrum, kicked his heels into the ground, and the waters of Zamzam welled up into the depression. (The Arabs learned the Hagar story from the Hebrews. See Genesis 21:9–21.) In recognition of this fabled event, it was considered meritorious for pilgrims to add to the circling of the Ka'ba an exercise called the Lesser Pilgrimage, which involved a rapid pacing back and forth seven times between two hills and the Ka'ba in imitation of Hagar's anguished search. And because Ishmael was declared the founder of the city, it was thought well to extend this exercise into something more arduous, called the Greater Pilgrimage. This was performed during the holy month, Dhū-al-Ḥijja, and required, besides the exercises of the Lesser Pilgrimage, a tour of the hills east of Mecca taking several days and including in its scope visits to places celebrated for great events in Arabian history.

Within the Ka'ba itself were murals on the walls, and a number of idols ranged around Hubal, the chief male deity. Next in importance to him were the three goddesses, al-Lāt, al-Manāt, and al-'Uzzā. Together with their associates, including the far-off Allāh, who was imageless, these deities constituted a sort of pantheon for Arabia, designed to draw to Mecca the people of every region. So holy did Mecca become, in fact, that the city and its immediate environs were declared sacred territory, and pilgrims were obliged to disarm when entering it.

By agreement throughout Arabia, four months were reserved out of each year for pilgrimage and trade. During these months no violence or warfare was permitted, and Mecca, along with many other places, profited by the fairs and markets that then sprang up.

Mecca as a Center of Commerce

However, in spite of its preeminent station as the chief pilgrim center and one of the chief crossroads towns of Arabia, Mecca had to depend on commerce to keep going. There were three reasons for this, all rooted in long-standing conditions, the first geographical, the second economic, the third civic. The trouble with Mecca physically was that it lay in a barren mountain pass. Neither the city nor the sacred territory around it could sustain gardens and date palms, hence, the city's chief reliance was on its commerce. This was extensive enough to keep the inhabitants fairly prosperous, for Mecca was not only the central town on the Caravan route between Yemen and Syria but the focus of caravan routes all over Arabia. Its fortunes, however, declined considerably after the Arab monopoly in the spice trade was broken by the reopening of the old Egyptian maritime route through the Red Sea. This was a serious blow not only to the Al-Hijāz transport towns but to south Arabia as well, for it forced down prices by bringing India and Somaliland into play as trade rivals. In the subsequent decline of Arab commerce, some hill towns had to fall back on agriculture for survival, but barren Mecca could have recourse to no such expedient. Fortunately, Mecca's position athwart the trade routes of Arabia remained secure, and its power to attract pilgrims to its Black Stone was undiminished. The margin of security was none too large. Should the city be overrun, a crisis of real magnitude would threaten. Tradition had it that such a crisis actually developed in the very year in which Muḥammad was born. This was the year known in Arabia as "the year of the elephant," because the Abyssinian (and Christian) governor of south Arabia marched on Mecca in force, with a battle elephant, professing a vengeful desire to destroy the heathen shrine, but he had to retreat, just when Mecca lay defenseless before him, because of an outbreak of smallpox among his troops.

Internal Rivalries

What endangered Mecca more was the civic tension between her rival factions. Civic peace was dependent on the precarious balance maintained by the law of vendetta. Exactly like the free-roaming bedouin tribes, the rival clans that lived together within the city's limits subscribed to the ancient principle that the murder of any member of one's own clan called for the answering death of a member of the murderer's clan. If the murder was done within a clan, the murderer would be without defense; if he was caught he was put to death, and if he escaped he became an outlaw, a member of no clan, with every man's hand against him. But when a member of a clan was murdered by an outsider, his whole clan rose up to avenge him. A principal deterrent to violent crime in Arabia and also the guarantee of civic order was, it seems, the fear of blood vengeance.

Before the time of Muḥammad, the two chief tribes that contended for mastery in Mecca were the Quraysh and Khuzaʿa, the former having risen to dominance around the middle of the fifth century and driven the latter out. But the Quraysh tribe was itself inwardly at tension among its twelve clans, the Hāshimite clan to which Muḥammad belonged being one of those most influential and disinclined to civic struggle.

II. THE PROPHET MUḤAMMAD

Muḥammad belongs to the charismatic company of the prophets who by a display of complex personal traits and qualities—particularly vitality, intelligence, articulateness, and dedication—effected momentous changes in the lives of other persons. These traits and qualities did not lie dormant or merely latent but were stirred to vigorous expression. Even with the supposition of divine inspiration, it is always something of a mystery how this comes about in the development of any great individual. In Muḥammad's case, his genius is not any more susceptible of easy explanation than in other instances of prophetic power.

Birth and Early Influences

The date of Muḥammad's birth is uncertain; it was perhaps in 571 C.E. According to tradition, his father, a

Quraysh of the Hashimite clan, died before his birth and his mother died when he was six years old. He then became a ward first of his paternal grandfather, ʿAbd-al-Muṭṭalib, and then of his uncle, Abū Ṭālib. It would seem that the Hashimite clan, although sharing with the rest of the Quraysh the office of trustee of the Kaʿba, its idols, its Black Stone, and the nearby sacred well, was at that time in straitened circumstances. The Qurʾān attests that Muḥammad grew up in poverty (Sura 93, v, 6 f.). He began by sharing the religious beliefs of his community—their worship of Hubal and al-ʿUzzā, their belief in jinn, Satan, good and evil omens, and the like—but as he came to maturity he more and more looked upon the Meccan religion with a critical appraisal born of questioning and distaste. He was disturbed by incessant quarreling in the avowed interests of religion and honor among the Quraysh chiefs. Stronger still was his dissatisfaction with the primitive survivals in Arabian religion, the idolatrous polytheism and animism, the immorality at religious convocations and fairs, the drinking, gambling, and dancing that were fashionable, and the burial alive of unwanted infant daughters practiced not only in Mecca but throughout Arabia. He must have been puzzled by the senseless bloodshed and intertribal anarchy that accompanied the so-called "sacrilegious wars" that occurred during his youth. There was little to commend these conflicts, called sacrilegious, because they broke out during the sacred month Dhū-āl-Qaʿda, at the time of the fair annually held at ʿUkāz, three days east of Mecca. The Quraysh were involved, and Muḥammad is said to have attended his uncles during one of the skirmishes, but without enthusiasm.

Why were his views changing? And particularly, how did he become receptive to ideas of God, the last judgment, and the religious life paralleling those of the Jewish and Christian religions? Our information is so scanty that we are driven largely to conjecture. There is no evidence that he had direct knowledge of the Old and New Testaments, although he always expressed a high regard for written scriptures and the people who used them ("the peoples of the Book"). The venerable tradition he learned about Judaism and Christianity during caravan trips to Syria, the first when he was twelve in the company of Abū Ṭālib, and the second when he was twenty-five and in the employ of Khadīja, whom he subsequently married, must be set aside as untrustworthy. Greater importance should be given to the possible influence of Christians and Jews in caravans passing through Mecca, foreign merchants trading in Mecca, and Jews and Christians at the commercial fairs, where representatives of these faiths used to address the crowds. As a matter of fact, the Qurʾān contains references that indicate his curiosity was aroused by the exposition of these faiths that he so heard. Traditions that may be given some weight say that some of his acquaintances in Mecca were versed in the traditions of the Jews and Christians, in particular a cousin of Khadīja, Waraqa by name, and the poet Umaiya (born Abiʾl-Salt). What he learned he acquired gradually, and from a variety of sources. As far as Christianity is concerned, he was most influenced by Nestorian conceptions and popular traditions that reflected apocryphal as well as canonical Christian literature.

Muslim Views of "Influences"

Two things need to be said here in deference to Muslim conviction. The first is that when listing the "influences" that possibly helped the future Prophet form his opinions, we should at the same time stress the interior force that led him ultimately to transcend both his environment and what he learned from persons in it. Muslims have good grounds for contending that he was not molded and set in motion by his environment, but reacted to and upon it. The second observation is that Muslims reject any implication that Muḥammad took the information he received from other persons and incorporated it later in the Qurʾān. The Qurʾān, they believe, was not the work of Muḥammad; it was revealed to him in its entirety either directly or by an angelic messenger sent down from God, and therefore could not have been his work. The most they can acknowledge is that in the days before the revelations, he received from others a "foreknowledge," that is, truths and moral laws made known through prophets such as Abraham, Moses, and Jesus, and by its means was enabled to understand and interpret what was later revealed to him. As one Muslim writer put it, "If Muḥammad had not known 'historically' (as distinguished from 'through revelation') the *materials* of the Prophets' stories, he would himself have been at a complete loss to understand what the Revelation was saying to him"[B]

Muḥammad's need to resolve his religious perplexities became more urgent during the leisure that his marriage to Khadīja, a rich Qurayshite widow, brought him. Muslim traditions describe how Khadīja, fifteen years his senior, mothered as well as loved him and encouraged his religious interests. The two sons, possibly three, she bore him died in infancy, to Muḥammad's lasting grief. Their four daughters lived long enough to marry associates of Muḥammad. Zainab married Aub-al-ʿĀs; Ruqayya, ʿUthmān, who became the third caliph; Fāṭima, ʿAlī, the fourth caliph; and Umm-Qulthūm, Utayba. Of their four daughters, only Fāṭima survived him.

Religious Awakening

Muḥammad now seemed to have entered a period of spiritual stress. He had apparently been struck by the belief common to both Jews and Christians, that there would be a last judgment and punishment of idolaters by everlasting fire. The one true God, they said, could not be represented by any image but only by prophetic spokespersons. Such spokespersons had in times past appeared in Palestine and Persia. Would no one come to Arabia to give warning? Surely God would send a prophet there.

His private thought during this period was quickened by persons brought close to him by marriage. Khadīja's cousin, the blind Waraqa, a venerable old man who had some influence in her household, may have been a Christian; in any case, Muḥammad found him a useful source of knowledge concerning matters of faith and conduct. Less information was perhaps provided by a Christian slave boy called Zaid, whom Muḥammad liberated and adopted as a son, just as he had already adopted his cousin ʿAlī, the child of his uncle Abū Ṭālib. The thought that the last day and the last judgment might be near began to agitate him. He wandered off to the hills around Mecca to brood privately. He was now about forty years old.

Prophetic Call

According to Muslim tradition, he visited a cave near the base of Mt. Hirā, a few miles north of Mecca, for days at a time. Suddenly one night ("the Night of Power and Excellence," Muslims call it) there rose in a vision before him the angel Gabriel, the messenger of Allāh, at about "two bows'-length," crying "Recite!"

> Recite: In the Name of thy Lord who created,
>   created Man of a blood-clot.
> Recite: And thy Lord is the Most Generous,
>   who taught by the Pen,
> taught Man that [which] he knew not. . . .[C1]

When the vision ended, Muḥammad was able to reproduce the whole revelation (Sūra 96 of the Qur'ān, of which only the first lines are here given). He rushed home in great excitement, half doubting, half believing. The Qur'ān defends the authenticity of his experience in the following words (Sūra 53):

> By the Star when it plunges,
> your comrade is not astray, neither errs,
> nor speaks he out of caprice.
> This is naught but a revelation revealed,
> taught him by one terrible in power,
> very strong; he stood poised,
> being on the higher horizon,
> then drew near and suspended hung,
> two bows'-length away, or nearer,
> then revealed to his servant that he revealed.
> His heart lies not of what he saw;
> what, will you dispute with him what he sees?[C2]

Yet at first Muḥammad's heart did nearly dispute what he saw. He had fears for his sanity. According to an early tradition (recorded by al-Tabirī as having come first from ʿĀ'isha, daughter of Abū Bakr and one of Muḥammad's favorite wives), after meeting with Gabriel he hurried home to his wife Khadīja.

> I said, "I am worried about myself." Then I told her the whole story. She said, "Rejoice, for by Allah, Allah will never put thee to shame. By Allah, thou art mindful of thy kinsfolk, speakest truthfully, renderest what is given thee in trust, bearest burdens, art ever hospitable to the guest, and dost always uphold the right against any wrong." Then she took me to Waraqa (to whom) she said, "Give ear to [him]." So he questioned me, and I told him (the whole) story. He said, "This is the *namus* [the Greek word *nomos*, Law] which was sent down upon Moses."[D1]

But Muḥammad was not at once comforted. In popular belief, poets and soothsayers were inspired by a familiar spirit among the jinn. Muḥammad seems to have been in doubt about whether the voice he heard really came from a heavenly messenger or from a mere jinn. In the latter case, he would be "possessed," even "mad."

Another early tradition has him say

> now it so happened that no creature of Allah was more loathsome to me than a poet or a man possessed by jinn, the sight of neither of whom could I bear. So I said, "That one [meaning himself] has become either a poet or a man jinn-possessed. The Quraish will never say this about me. I shall go to some high mountain cliff and cast myself down therefrom so that I may kill myself and be at rest." I went off with this in mind, but when I was in the midst of the mountains I heard a voice from heaven saying, "O Muḥammad, thou art (indeed) Allah's Apostle, and I am Gabriel." At that I raised my head to the skies, and there was Gabriel in clear human form, with his feet on the edges of the skies. . . . I began to turn my face to the whole expanse of the skies but no matter in what direction I looked there I saw him.[D2]

In connection with the Night of Power and Excellence some Ḥadīth traditions envision a magical journey upon the winged mare Buraq enabling the Prophet to visit the heavens and appear before Allah.

Without attempting to straighten out the tangle of fact and tradition, we may conclude that Muḥammad, after a period of self-questioning, lasting perhaps many months, finally came to look upon himself as being, miraculously enough, a true prophet (nabī) and apostle (rasūl) of Allah, that is to say, a messenger of the one and only God already known to the Jews and Christians. When it began to appear that the strange experiences, in which rhapsodies in Arabic flowed across his lips, would continue to occur spontaneously, without his willing them, he came to believe that Allah was using him as a mouthpiece; the verses he uttered, half in trance, were real revelations. His first doubts about them disappeared. He now saw that what his wife and friends asserted was true, that they made sense. At last Arabia was being provided with a

Night Journey
Muhammad on Buraq

scripture—of later date and greater authority than the scriptures of the Jews and Christians.

The Meccan Ministry: The Message

After privately expounding his message to relatives and friends, he appeared in the streets and in the courtyard of the Kaʿba to recite "in the name of the Lord" the verses of the revelations. The listening Meccans gaped, and then, hearing strange doctrine, broke into ridicule. The incredible substance of his preaching seemed to be a warning of a divine judgment day, along with predictions of the resurrection of the body and of a consuming fire. They gave him a poor reception, but in spite of that he kept coming back day after day to recite the rhythmically composed verses that had come to him.

> When the sun shall be darkened,
> when the stars shall be thrown down,
> when the mountains shall be set moving,
> when the pregnant camels shall be neglected,
> when the savage beasts shall be mustered,
> when the seas shall be set boiling,
> when the souls shall be coupled [reunited?]
> when the buried infant shall be asked for what sin she
> was slain,

when the scrolls shall be unrolled,
when heaven shall be stripped off
when Hell shall be set blazing,
when Paradise shall be brought nigh,
then shall a soul know what it has produced.[C3]

Could much credence be accorded such an utterance his critics cried, or to what follows?

And when the Blast shall sound,
upon the day when a man shall flee from his brother,
his mother, his father,
his consort, his sons,
every man that day shall have business to suffice him.
Some faces on that day shall shine laughing, joyous;
Some faces on that day shall be dusty,
O'erspread with darkness—
those—they are the unbelievers, the libertines.[C4]

The Qur'ān identifies his critics as "criers of lies."

Woe that day unto those who cry it lies,
who cry lies to the Day of Doom;
and none cries lies to it but every guilty aggressor.
When our signs are recited to him, he says,
"Fairy-tales of the ancients!"
No indeed; but that they were earning has rusted upon their hearts.
No indeed; but upon that day they shall be veiled from their Lord,
then they shall roast in Hell.
Then it shall be said to them, "This is that you cried lies to."[C5]

There was in the early revelations not so much said of the unity of God (which was taken for granted) but a great deal of the power and final judgment of God. The verses quoted God as speaking in the first person plural.

Behold, We shall cast upon thee a weighty word. . . .
Surely We have sent unto you a Messenger as a witness over you even as We sent to Pharaoh a Messenger.[C6]

Opposition in Mecca

Unimpressed though they were at first, his hearers, especially those of the Quraysh tribe, at last became seriously disturbed. They did not object so much to Muḥammad's insistence that there is but one God, but they stiffened with opposition at his claim to be a prophet, for this seemed to them to be a claim to leadership, as if he intended to assert his dominance over the whole community. He could talk all he liked about his belief in the resurrection of the dead and a last judgment, but he was not entitled to authority over the city. Moreover, his prophecies emphasized social justice and duties to the poor; by their moral judgments, they threatened the wealthier families that controlled the economic and social vested interests of Mecca.

It would not serve our purpose to go into the chronology of the ensuing trials and tribulations of Muḥammad during a whole decade of disheartening community opposition. His following seemed doomed to be small. Khadīja was apparently the first to accept his mission, believing in it even before he himself did. Her faith was quickly echoed by his adopted sons, Zaid, the liberated slave boy, and ʿAlī, the son of Abū Ṭālib. A very important convert, one of the first and destined to be Muḥammad's first successor ("caliph"), was Abū Bakr, a kinsman from the Quraysh tribe, a merchant and therefore a person of some prestige. Abū Bakr's proselyting for the new faith secured five other early converts, among whom ʿUthmān, an Ummayyad and later the third caliph, was outstanding. They formed the habit of meeting together in the house of a young convert named al-Arqan. But conversions came slowly. In the first four years, they numbered only about forty, including wives of male believers and liberated slaves.

Muḥammad's revelations were meanwhile continuing. When he appeared to recite them, the hostile members of the Quraysh did all they could to break up his gatherings. Tradition has it that they scattered thorns about, threw filth and dirt on him and his hearers, and stirred up the rowdies to hurl insults and threats. They longed to be able to use violence, but from this they were deterred by the stout protection of his uncle, Abū Ṭālib. In an attempt to prevent his public appearances, the Ummayyads and other hostile elements of the Quraysh issued a solemn ban (boycott) against the Hāshimites, the branch of the tribe to which Muḥammad belonged, and tried to restrict them to the quarter of the town where Abū Ṭālib lived—a narrow defile among the hills—for over two years. But the rest of the community brought pressure to have the ban removed. For a time many of his followers took refuge in Abyssinia. Then greater blows were to fall on Muḥammad personally. Khadīja, his greatest support, died, and five weeks later his protector, faithful Abū Ṭālib, still unconverted but nonetheless always loyal. This severe double bereavement weakened the position of Muḥammad in the eyes of his enemies, and though the vendetta law still shielded him, it was apparent that some of the Hāshimites were becoming disaffected and might be persuaded to consent to his imprisonment or execution.

The Hijra (Latin: Hegira), 622 C.E.

Muḥammad began to look afield. An attempt to establish himself in Ṭā'if, some sixty miles to the southeast, proved abortive. His cause seemed almost hopeless. Then, suddenly, hope revived. During the truce period of 620 C.E., he held a lengthy conference at the ʿUkāz fair with six men from Yathrib (Medina), who thought he might be their man. Their native city, three hundred miles to the north, had not recovered from the effects of open dissension caused by blood feuds between two Arab tribes, the Aws and the Khazraj, and stood to benefit if someone could be brought to impose a firm check on them. They agreed to prepare their town for the Prophet's coming. By the next pilgrimage season they reported progress, and in the following year the preparations for Muḥammad's emigration were complete.

Secrecy had been well maintained, but at the last moment the Meccans got wind of the matter, and the hostile Quraysh (chiefly Ummayyads under the leadership of Abū Sufyān) determined to strike and strike quickly. But Muḥammad and Abū Bakr escaped on swift camels and successfully made the Hijra (the Migration) to Yathrib, ordinarily eleven days off, in the short period of eight days. Muslims regard this migration as the birth of Islam—the year one of their calendar.

Establishment of the Theocracy at Medina

How Muḥammad succeeded in so short a time, both in subduing the long-standing feuds among the Arabs of Medina and in establishing a brotherly unity between his Meccan fellow immigrants and the native Medinese Arabs, has been a marvel to historians. Much of the secret of his success lay in the visible proofs his followers had of the genuineness of his prophetic experience, especially when revelations came to him. Many were witnesses to the exhausting physical accompaniments of the "coming down" of revelations. We are told that he would suddenly become silent in their midst, bowing his head and groaning as he experienced being "seized" and even "squeezed." According to an early tradition, ʿĀ'isha, his favorite wife after Khadīja, recalled, "I saw revelation coming down on him in the severest cold, and when that condition was over, perspiration ran down his forehead."[E1] He himself, according to a tradition from Hārith, son of Hishām, said that revelation sometimes came upon him "like the ringing of a bell," and this was hardest on him; at other times, the angel came to him in the shape of a man and talked to him, although none around him heard or saw the heavenly visitant. It can hardly be doubted that witnesses of his revelatory process, if the reports are genuine, spread word of it through the community, and that doubters and those who resisted Muḥammad's authority were struck with awe and inclined to listen to the revelations, when they were recited, with acceptance, especially since these were in themselves "words of power" and formed a consistent whole.

After several years of establishing himself as an unquestioned prophet, Muḥammad was given astonishingly unrestricted power over the town, whose name was changed in his honor to Medina (*Madīnat an nabī,* the City of the Prophet). He set about the erection of a house that was both his home (with subsequent additions for his later wives) and a place of worship, the first mosque. Rapidly and simply, he evolved a new cultus. Weekly services on Friday, prostration during prayer (at first in the direction, or *qibla,* of Jerusalem, but after the Jews in Medina conspired against him, toward Mecca), a call to prayer from the mosque's roof (at first only for the Friday services, and then every day at the times for private prayer), the taking up of alms for the poor and for the support of the cause—these and other practices soon were established.

Warfare with Mecca: Final Ascendancy

Perhaps to supply his followers with arms and treasure, or perhaps to strike at Mecca's source of power, he led out a small force to waylay a Meccan caravan. War with Mecca was the result. In the first engagement, Muḥammad had the better of it, in the next the Meccans, but neither won a decisive victory, and then the Meccans prepared for a grand assault. With ten thousand men they invested Medina in 627, but Muḥammad, probably on the advice of a Persian follower, had an encircling trench dug to halt the Meccan cavalry. The "Battle of the Ditch" that followed persuaded the Meccans that Muḥammad was beyond their taking. Three years later, in January 630, Muḥammad in his turn marched to Mecca with ten thousand men. Mecca, whose trade routes had been severed by Muḥammad, surrendered. The Prophet of Allāh, at a bound, reached the stature of the greatest chief in Arabia. As such, he acted with great magnanimity toward his former fellow townspeople, excluding only a handful of them from the general amnesty he proclaimed.

One of his first acts was to go reverently to the Ka'ba, yet he showed no signs of yielding to the ancient Meccan polytheism. After honoring the Black Stone and riding seven times around the shrine, he ordered the destruction of the idols within it and the scraping of the paintings of Abraham and the angels from the walls. He sanctioned the use of the well Zamzam and restored the boundary pillars defining the sacred territory around Mecca. Thenceforth, no Muslim would have cause to hesitate about going on a pilgrimage to the ancient holy city.

Muḥammad now made sure of his political and prophetic ascendancy in Arabia. Active opponents near at hand were conquered by the sword, and tribes far away were invited to send delegations offering their allegiance. Before his sudden death in 632, he knew he was well on the way to unifying the Arab tribes under a theocracy governed by the will of God. Because he was no longer so conscious of imminent divine judgment on the world, an immediate task absorbed him—the

moral elevation and unification of the Arab tribes. On his last visit to Mecca, just before his death, tradition pictures him as preaching a memorable sermon in which he proclaimed a central fact of the Muslim movement in these words: "O ye men! harken unto my words and take ye them to heart! Know ye that every Muslim is a brother unto every other Muslim, and that ye are now one brotherhood."[F1]

Muḥammad's death was unexpected, and the problem of choosing a new leader almost split up his followers, but in a desperate move to forestall such a disaster Abū Bakr, whom Muḥammad had often designated to lead the prayers when he had to be absent, was chosen to be his successor (or caliph). Thus Muḥammad's death only momentarily checked the rapid spread of Islam.

III. THE FAITH AND PRACTICE OF ISLAM

The words Muḥammad spoke and the examples he set became after his death the basis of the faith (īmān) and practice or duty (dīn) of Islam. Many elements were, as far as their final fomulation is concerned, the product of later times, for the process by which Muḥammad's utterances were put into permanent form and distilled into a creed and way of life did not take place overnight. Divergent groups appealed to Muḥammad's remembered talk and conduct; faithfulness to his instruction and example was from the first required. The differences in interpretation were in no case marked by consciousness of departure from the example set by Muḥammad.

Because the faith and practice of Muslims after Muḥammad's time were so closely related to his teaching and personal example, it seems well to consider them now, even before we follow the story of the spread of Islam, for in essence what the Qur'ān said and what Muḥammad did, although still not finally condensed into fixed articles of faith and prescribed practices, inspired, motivated, and guided the history of Islam.

Ultimately, Muslim authorities subsumed most of Islam under three heads: īmān, or articles of faith, ihsān, or right conduct, and 'ibādāt, or religious duty.

Because faith (īmān) and good conduct (ihsān) were set forth in the Qur'ān, and religious duty ('ibādāt) was defined later, we shall consider the former two first.

A. Articles of Faith: Īmān

In the famous Muslim creedal formula the first part reads: *lā ilāha illa Allāh*, "(There is) no god but God." This is the most important declaration in the Muslim īmān (articles of faith). No statement about God seemed to Muḥammad more fundamental than the declaration that God is one, and no sin seemed to him so unpardonable as associating another being with God on terms of equality. (The Arabian idolaters who worshiped many gods and goddesses were obviously guilty of this sin of sins, but so also were any Christians who said, "God is the third of three.") God stands alone and supreme. He existed before any other being or thing, is self-subsistent, omniscient, and omnipotent ("all-seeing, all-hearing, all-willing"). He is the creator, and in the awful day of judgment, he is the sole arbiter who shall save the believer out of the dissolution of the world and place him in paradise.

In one respect, however, in its numerous references to God's "guidance," the Qur'ān is varied and loose enough in statement (as is not unusual in the world's Scriptures) to be open to differing interpretations. Does God "guide" humankind by challenging them to choose aright in freedom, or by determining their choices in advance (predestination)? Some passages imply free will, but more suggest predestination. (This variance should occasion no surprise. Muḥammad was a prophet who over a period of twenty years or more spoke out of ecstatic states. He was inspired, not to produce a systematic theology, but rather to bring a message to the people that would tell them what they needed to hear.) Atlthough Sunni Muslims have, as we shall see later (p. 557), generally come to the conclusion that the Qur'ān comes down on the side of predestination, it is possible to reconcile the variant passages, if one keeps in mind the conditions of desert life, as Muḥammad must have done.

Sūras Implying Freedom

Typical of the apparently variant passages are the following. Freedom of choice is implied in, "Say: 'The truth is from your Lord; so let whosoever will believe, and let whosoever will disbelieve.'"[C7] A Meccan passage says, "If you do good, it is your own souls you do good to."[C8] This is matched by a Medinian passage, "Whatever evil visits thee is of thyself."[C9] Freedom of action is implied also in passages dealing with the forgiveness of God, as for instance in, "Whoever does evil, or wrongs himself, and then prays God's forgiveness, he shall find God All-forgiving, All-compassionate";[C10] or, "God shall turn [in forgiveness] only towards those who do evil in ignorance, then shortly repent."[C11]

Sūras on Foreknowledge and Control

But many other passages say God not only has perfect foreknowledge of everyone's actions but controls their choices as well. As to foreknowledge: "Very well he knows you, when He produced you from the earth, and when you were yet unborn in your mothers' wombs."[C12] More to the point: "Whomsoever God will, He leads astray, and whomsoever He will, He sets him on a straight path."[C13] God declares indeed: "We elected them, and We guided them to a straight path."[C14] Furthermore, God rules men's inner lives. "Whomsoever God desires to guide, He expands his breast to Islam; whomsoever He desires to lead astray, He makes his breast narrow, tight."[C15] An early sūra is even more explicit: "But will you shall not, unless God wills."[C16] And yet there are still other passages that seem to fall between the two extremes. In Sūra 6:78, we hear Abraham saying, "If my Lord does not guide me I shall surely be of the people gone astray."[C17] Freedom and divine determinism seemingly appear side by side in a Medinan passage, "Whomsoever God leads astray, no guide he has; He leaves them in their insolence blindly wandering."[C18] This last suggests the view that reconciles the variant passages, as we are about to see.

Reconciling Freedom and Foreknowledge

To follow I. Goldziher's illuminating comments,

> If, in many passages of the Koran it is said: "Allah guides whom he will, and lets whom he will go astray," such passages do not imply that God

The Dome of the Rock, Jerusalem
Above the pinnacle rock of Mt. Moriah, the temple hill, this gorgeous shrine, dating from 691 C.E., marks the spot where tradition says that Abraham prepared to sacrifice Isaac, where the Temple of Solomon stood, and where Muhammad upon Buraq began his Night Journey to heaven. *(Photo by Scala, courtesy Art Resource, N.Y., S0058434.)*

directly brings the latter class into the evil path. The decisive word *adalla* is not to be taken in such a connection as meaning to "lead astray," but to allow to go astray, not to trouble about a person, not to show him the way out. . . . Let us conjure up the picture of a lonely wanderer in the desert—it is from this idea that the language of the Koran concerning leading and wandering has sprung. The wanderer errs in the boundless expanse, gazing about for the right direction to his goal. So is man in his wanderings through life. He who, through faith and good works, has deserved the good will of God, him he rewards with his guidance. He lets the evil-doer go astray. He leaves him to his fate, and takes his protection from him. He does not offer him the guiding hand, but he does not bring him directly to the evil path. . . . Guidance is the reward of the good. "Allah does not guide the wicked." (Sūra 9, v. 110)[GI]

Allāh reveals his will and guides men in three distinct ways; through Muḥammad, his messenger; through the Qur'ān, his revelation; and through the angels. (Considered another way, the three are part of one process: revelation came to Muḥammad by agency of an angel. Revelation is the thing.)

Guidance through the Prophet: Ḥadīths

The second half of the Muslim creedal formula declares: *Muḥammad rasūl Allāh*, "Muḥammad is the messenger (or prophet) of Allāh." It seems self-evident to Muslims that God must reveal himself through prophets, else people could not know him. God would not leave himself without witness, and so there has been a long line of such prophets, including Abraham, Moses, and Jesus. But Muḥammad is the last and greatest of them all, the "seal" of those who appeared before him. None is his equal, either in knowledge or in authority; none has received or handed down so perfect a revelation. But though his authority is supreme, he was not a divine being appearing in the flesh. He was human like the rest of men and women. Nor did he pretend to supernatural powers; he performed no miracles, instituted no mystical, deifying sacraments, ordained no holy priesthood, set apart none to a sacred office by ordination or a mystical laying on of hands. He was simply humankind at its best, and God was still the wholly Other, with whom he was united in will but not in substance. The most celebrated suggestion in Muslim tradition that Muḥammad had a special relationship with heaven is to be found in the traditions (*ḥadīths*) concerning the Mir'āj, or Night Journey of the Prophet to paradise. These traditions are based on a passage in Sūra XVII.т, which says, "Glory be to Him Who carried His servant by night from the Holy Mosque [at Mecca] to the Further Mosque [at Jerusalem], the precincts of which We have blessed, that We might show him some of Our signs."C19 The traditions vary with those who tell or attest to them, but they add up to something like this story: On a certain night while the Prophet still lived in Mecca (a night whose anniversary is celebrated each year throughout the Muslim world), Gabriel came, cleansed him within, and took him through the air (on the back of the winged steed Burāq) first to Jerusalem and then up through the seven heavens, where as he passed through he spoke successively with Adam, John the Baptist and Jesus, Joseph, Enoch, Aaron, Moses, and (in the seventh heaven) Abraham. Finally, without Gabriel, who could go no further perhaps, he was lifted on a flying carpet (a *rafraf*) high into the presence, without a clear sight, of Allāh, who spoke with him about many unutterable matters and told him: "O Muḥammad, I take you as a friend just as I took Abraham as a friend. I am speaking to you just as I spoke face to face with Moses."D3 Thus Muḥammad is demonstrated to have a status in God's sight at least equal to that of any of his prophetic predecessors. But even with such a story to give it encouragement, no claim is made by Muslims that Muḥammad was other than human, even though Allāh viewed him with special favor.

Guidance through the Qur'ān

The second way Allāh guides humankind is through the Qur'ān. The Qur'ān, revealed to Muḥammad, is the undistorted and final word of Allāh to humankind. The traditional Muslim position is that the Qur'ān is identical with words transmitted, without change, from "the well-preserved tablet," "the mother of the Book," an eternal and uncreated archetype; they are the very words of God himself. Previous authoritative revelations, such as the Jewish and Christian scriptures, are also genuine transmissions from the Umm-al-Kitāb, the uncreated heavenly archetype, but they have been changed and corrupted by men and are therefore not absolutely true like the Qur'ān.

This conviction concerning the infallibility of the Qur'ān as the word of God is, of course, of highest importance to Muslims. Its corollary that the present text has not been corrupted by faulty transmission is of almost equal importance. Many, if not all, of the revelations to Muḥammad were either written down or memorized during his lifetime. There is some indication that he may even have assigned some of them to groups or collections that fitted together logically and that turned out later to be sūras or chapters of the Qur'ān. This is not certain. According to tradition, in the year that followed Muḥammad's death, Abū Bakr, on the advice of 'Umar, who feared that the Companions, who were the "reciters" of the revelations that they had memorized, might die off or perish in battle, ordered Muḥammad's secretary, Zaid ibn Thābit, to make a collection of the revelations. The collection was composed from "ribs of palm-leaves and tablets of white stone and from the breasts of men," we read. There is strong evidence that other collections were made that varied in containing more or less materials and to a certain extent in wording. A second and variant tradition says that the final canonical text resulted from the work of a committee appointed by the Caliph 'Uthmān and headed again by Muḥammad's secretary. Four identical copies were made, and all previous texts were pronounced defective. The 'Uthmānic text met some resistance, but finally prevailed.

Guidance through the Angels

The third means by which Allāh makes known his will is through the angels. Of these the chief is Gabriel, the agent of revelation, who is described in terms reminiscent of Zoroastrian angelology as "the faithful spirit" and "the spirit of holiness." Allāh sits in the seventh heaven on a high throne, surrounded by angels who serve him as kings are served by their ministers and attendants.

The Devil (called either *Iblīs*, a contraction of Diabolos, or *Shayṭān*, in Hebrew Satan) is an angel who fell through pride (his vanity caused him to disobey Allāh's command that all of the angels should prostrate themselves before the newly created Adam) and became an accursed tempter. He and his assistants busy themselves on earth to obstruct the plans of Allāh and to tempt people to go astray. This sounds worse than things really are, for—at least in the light of the later Medina sūras—the scope of the Devil's operations is in fact restricted to Allāh's calculated permission and noninterferences.

As to the last judgment, Muḥammad's revelations contain phrases resembling those of Zoroastrian, Jewish, and Christian apocalypticism. There will be "signs" of its imminence: portents, ominous rumblings, strange occurrences in nature, and finally the last trumpet, at whose sound the dead will rise and all souls will assemble before Allāh's judgment throne. During the judgment itself, the books in which each person's deeds have been recorded will be read, and eternal judgment will be passed accordingly.

Heaven and hell are concretely described.

> *God has cursed the unbelievers, and prepared*
> *for them a Blaze,*
> *therein to dwell for ever; they shall find*
> *neither protector nor helper.*
> *Upon the day when their faces are turned about in the*
> *Fire they shall say, 'Ah, would we had obeyed God and*
> *the Messenger!'*[C20]

> *The Companions of the Left (O Companions*
> *of the Left!)*
> *mid burning winds and boiling waters*
> *and the shadow of a smoking blaze*
> *neither cool, neither goodly; . . .*
> *Then you erring ones, you that cried lies,*
> *you shall eat of a tree called Zakkoum. . . .*[C21]

> *It is a tree that comes forth in*
> *the root of Hell;*
> *its spathes are as the heads of Satans,*
> *and they eat of it, and of it fill*
> *their bellies,*
> *then on top of it they have a brew*
> *of boiling water. . . .*[C22]

> *Lo the Tree of Ez-Zakkoum*
> *is the food of the guilty,*
> *like molten copper, bubbling in the belly*
> *as boiling water bubbles.*
> *"Take him, and thrust him into the midst of Hell,*
> *then pour over his head the chastisement of*
> *boiling water!"*
> *"Taste! Surely thou art the mighty, the noble.*
> *This is that concerning which you were doubting."*[C23]

Page from the Qur`ān

The Arabic text appears here in the Kufic script, originating from the town of Kūfa on the Euphrates River and using primitive Arabic characters. It comes from the thirteenth century but aims to be a worthy resemblance to the eternal Umm-al-Kitāb, the uncreated heavenly archetype that is the source of the whole Qur'ān, transmitted without error or change to Muḥammad. *(Courtesy of the Museum of Fine Arts, Boston, George Bruce Upton Fund. Neg. # 20.588.)*

On the other hand, the Companions of the Right, especially those who "outstrip" their fellows in faithfulness, enter gardens of delight.

> *Surely the godfearing shall be in a station secure*
> *among gardens and fountains,*
> *robed in silk and brocade, set face to face.*[C24]

> *Upon close-wrought couches*
> *reclining upon them, set face to face,*
> *immortal youths going round about them*
> *with goblets, and ewers, and a cup from a spring*
> *(no brows throbbing, no intoxication)*
> *and such fruits as they shall choose,*
> *and such flesh of fowl as they desire,*

and wide-eyed houris
as the likeness for that they laboured. . . .
a recompense for that they laboured. . . .
and We made them spotless virgins,
chastely amorous, like of age
for the Companions of the Right.[C25]

These promises of houris or hūr'īn in paradise date from Muḥammad's Meccan days. Later on, to correct false conclusions, the Qur'ān more than once suggests that the faithful take their *wives* with them to paradise. Sūra 13:23 says, "Gardens of Eden . . . they shall enter, and also those who were righteous of their fathers, and their wives, and their descendants."[C26] These predictions can be reconciled as follows:

> Although the Koran hardly provides a basis for such a view, the earliest traditon of Islam supports the definite conception that the virgins of Paradise were once earthly wives. The Prophet himself is supposed to have said: "They are devout wives, and those who with grey hair and watery eyes died in old age. After death Allah re-makes them into virgins." (Tabarī, Tasfir xxvii)[H]

B. Right Conduct

The Qur'ān has through the centuries supplied Muslims with such comprehensive guidance for everyday life that their schools of the law have been able to prescribe a wide range of acts for Muslims, of either sex, from birth to death. The following selections from the Qur'ān show how comprehensive these regulations are and, incidentally, how reformatory. The laws prohibiting wine and gambling, as well as the regulations covering the relations of the sexes and granting a higher status to women, must have meant to Muḥammad's early followers a considerable change in their moral life.

It is not piety, that you turn your faces
to the East and to the West.
    True piety is this:
to believe in God, and the Last Day,
the angels, the Book, and the Prophets.
to give of one's substance, however cherished,
    to kinsmen, and orphans,
the needy, the traveller, beggars,
    and to ransom the slave,

to perform the prayer, to pay the alms.
And they who fulfil their covenant
when they have engaged in a covenant,
    and endure with fortitude
    misfortune, hardship and peril,
these are they who are true in their faith,
    these are the truly godfearing.[C27]

. . . and to be good to parents,
    whether one or both of them
    attains old age with thee;
        say not to them "Fie"
        neither chide them, but
    speak unto them words
        respectful,
    and lower to them the
    wing of humbleness
    out of mercy and say,
        "My Lord,
    have mercy upon them,
    as they raised me up
    when I was little."[C28]

And slay not your children for fear of poverty;
    We will provide for you and them;
surely the slaying of them is a grievous sin.
    And approach not fornication;
surely it is an indecency, and evil as a way.[C29]

Give the orphans their property, and do not
exchange the corrupt for the good; and devour
not their property with your property; surely
    that is a great crime.
If you fear that you will not act justly
towards the orphans, marry such women
as seem good to you, two, three, four;
but if you fear you will not be equitable,
then only one, or what your right hands own;
so it is likelier you will not be partial.
And give the women their dowries as a gift
spontaneous; but if they are pleased
to offer you any of it, consume it
    with wholesome appetite. . . .
Test well the orphans, until they reach
the age of marrying; then, if you perceive
in them right judgment, deliver to them
their property; consume it not wastefully
    and hastily

ere they are grown. . . .
Those who devour the property of orphans
unjustly, devour Fire in their bellies,
and shall assuredly roast in a Blaze.[C30]

Marry the spouseless among you, and your
slaves and handmaidens that are righteous;
if they are poor, God will enrich them
of His bounty; God is All-embracing,
    All-knowing.
And let those who find not the means to
marry be abstinent till God enriches them
    of His bounty.[C31]

When you divorce women, and they have reached
their term [three months], then retain them honourably
or set them free honourably; do not retain them
by force, to transgress.[C32]

And fight in the way of God with those
who fight with you, but aggress not: God loves
    not the aggressors. . . .
Fight them, till there is no persecution
and the religion is God's; then if they
give over, there shall be no enmity
    save for the evildoers.[C33]

Permitted to you is the beast of the flocks,
except that which is now recited to you. . . .
    Forbidden to you are
carrion, blood, the flesh of swine,
what has been hallowed to other than God,
the beast strangled, the beast beaten down,
the beast fallen to death, the beast gored,
and that devoured by beasts of prey—
excepting that you have sacrificed duly—
as also things sacrificed to idols.[C34]

O believers, wine and arrow-shuffling [gambling],
idols and divining-arrows are an abomination,
some of Satan's work; so avoid it; haply
    so you will prosper.
Satan only desires to precipitate enmity
and hatred between you in regard to wine
and arrow-shuffling, and to bar you from
the remembrance of God, and from prayer.
Will you then desist? And obey God
and obey the Messenger, and beware.[C35]

C. Religious Duty: The "Five Pillars"

We come now to that part of Muslim religious practice that except for the fast of the month of Ramadān, which is prescribed in the Qur'ān, took some time to fix in tradition. It is summed up as the "Five Pillars" (*al-Arkan*). For many centuries now, all Muslims have felt obligated to engage in the following.

1. The Creed (*Shahāda*)

The central utterance of Islam is *lā ilāha illa Allāh; Muḥammad rasūl Allāh*: "There is no god but Allāh, and Muḥammad is the prophet of Allāh." Acceptance of this confession of faith, Shahāda, and its faithful repetition constitute the first step in being a Muslim. These simple words are heard everywhere in the Muslim world and come down as if out of the sky from the minaret in the muezzin's calls to prayer.

2. Prayer (*Salāt*)

The good Muslim reserves time each day for five acts of devotion and prayer. The first comes at dawn, the second at midday, the others at midafternoon, sunset, and after the fall of darkness or at bedtime. In town or country or on the desert, the devotee typically goes through a ritual of ablution, rolls out a prayer rug, stands reverentially, and offers certain prayers; bows down toward Mecca with hands on knees, to offer to Allāh less a petition than ascriptions of praise and declarations of submission to His holy will; then straightens up again, still praising Allāh; then falls prostrate, kneeling with head to the ground, glorifying God the while; then sits up reverentially and offers a petition; and finally bows down once more. Throughout, the sacred sentence *Allāh akbar* ("God is the greatest") is repeated again and again. It is common, at the beginning especially, simply to repeat the *Fatiha*, the Muslim Lord's Prayer (Sūra I).

> *Praise belongs to God, the Lord of all Being,*
> *the All-merciful, the All-compassionate,*
>   *the Master of the Day of Doom.*
> *Thee only we serve; to Thee alone we pray for succour.*
>   *Guide us in the straight path,*
> *the path of those whom Thou hast blessed,*
> *not of those against whom Thou art wrathful,*
>   *nor of those who are astray.*[C36]

In towns and villages it is possible to observe the five times of prayer in the mosque congregationally, and then it is common to make two prostrations (*rak'as*) at morning prayer, four at the noontime and late afternoon prayers, three at sundown, and four after dark.

Friday is the special day of public prayer for all Muslims, when the faithful assemble in the mosque, under the leadership of the *imām,* usually at noon, or perhaps at sunset. The service is in the mosque's paved courtyard, or where the worship area has been covered over, under the dome or vault. The people have assembled at the call from the minaret, left their shoes at the entrance, gone to the pool or fountain to perform their ablutions (of hands, mouth, nostrils, face, forearms, neck, and feet), sat for a few minutes to hear a "reader" (*qari*) recite from the Qur'ān, and then on the appearance of the imām have taken their places without any discrimination of race, nationality, or social status (except that women, if they attend, customarily stay behind screens and are "not seen"). Worshipers are seated in long rows, facing Mecca and spaced so as to allow their throwing themselves forward in "prostration" on their prayer mats. Before the prayer service is held, the imām preaches a sermon having for its primary purpose the exposition of Muslim doctrine. During the ritual of prayer (or salāt) that follows, the imām recites all of the necessary words, and the worshipers silently and as one follow him in his motions, standing erect when he does so, or inclining the head and body, or dropping on their knees to place their hands upon the ground a little in front of them and press their foreheads to the pavement in prostration, at the exact moment they see him do so.

3. Almsgiving (*Zakāt*)

Zakāt is a free-will offering consisting of gifts to the poor, the needy, debtors, slaves, wayfarers, beggars, and charities of various kinds. In the early days of Islam, it was a "loan to Allāh," exacted from Muslims in money or in kind. It was gathered by religious officials into a common treasury and distributed in part as charity to the poor and in part to mosques and imāms for repairs and administrative expenses. It was a fund quite apart from the tribute (the *jizyat*) exacted of non-Muslims for political and military expenses. The zakāt was once universally obligatory in Muslim lands. It is now common under Muslim governments for the zakāt to be calculated at the rate of 2½ percent of the accumulated wealth of a man or his family at the end of each year and to be levied by the government. In such situations, it is more like a tax than a free-will offering. In non-Muslim countries, the collection and distribution of the zakāt must be undertaken by the Muslim community itself. In this latter case, the zakāt is neither alms nor a tax, but a little of both, with stress laid on the individual to respect Muslim social, moral, and spiritual values, or face community disapproval.

4. Fasting During the Month of *Ramaḍān*

Except for the sick and ailing or those on a journey, this fast is laid upon all as an obligation. Ideally it is carried out in this manner: As soon as it becomes possible at dawn to distinguish a white thread from a black one, no food or drink may be taken until sundown; then enough food or drink should be consumed to enable one to fast the next day without physical weakness. In practice, there are great differences in observance according to local custom and the degree of piety of believers. For some Muslims, the nights of Ramaḍān are occasions for feasting and merriment. Since the month is determined by a lunar calendar, it comes earlier by about ten days in each solar year.

5. Pilgrimage (*Hajj*)

Once in a lifetime every Muslim, man or woman, is expected, unless it is impossible, to make a pilgrimage (a *hajj*) to Mecca. The pilgrim should be there during the sacred month, Dhū-al-Ḥijja, so as to enter with thousands of others into the annual mass observance of the circumambulation of the Ka'ba, the Lesser and Greater pilgrimages, and the Great Feast.

When war or other untoward conditions do not interfere, a great number of the pilgrims nowadays go by rail, ship, or air to points near Mecca. In ancient times they joined far-traveling overland caravans, which in the last stages of the journey crossed the desert from Baṣra in Iraq, or followed the trade routes from Yemen, Cairo, or Damascus. Each such caravan had as an indispensable part of its insignia (at least since the thirteenth century) a camel bearing on its back an unoccupied *maḥmal,* or richly ornamented

Muslims Worshipping Ka'ba

The Ka'ba is viewed in Muslim tradition as the site of the first "house of God" built by Abraham and his son Ishmael at God's command. It is held to have fallen later into idolatrous use until Muhammad's victory over the Meccans and his cleansing of the holy cubical structure (ka'ba means cube). The Ka'ba is the geographical point toward which all Muslims face when performing ritual prayer. It and the plain of Arafat outside Mecca are the two foci of the pilgrimage of Hajj that each Muslim aspires to make at least once in a lifetime. *(Photo by Mehmet Biber, courtesy Photo Researchers, Inc., 2A 5826.)*

litter, the resplendent symbol of the piety and sacrificial spirit of the pilgrims.

Since Muḥammad's day, all male pilgrims have been required, whether rich or poor, to enter the sacred precincts of Mecca wearing the same kind of seamless white garments and practicing the proper abstinences: no food or drink by day, continence, and no harm to living things, animal or vegetable. This is the first of a long series of leveling practices by which people of all countries and languages are made to mingle in one unifying mass observance without distinction of race or class.

The principal ceremonies in Mecca begin with circumambulation of the Ka'ba. The pilgrims start at the Black Stone and run three times fast and four times slowly around the building, stopping each time at the southeast corner to kiss the Black Stone, or, if the crowd is too great, to touch it with hand or stick, or perhaps just look keenly at it. The next observance is the Lesser Pilgrimage, which consists of trotting, with shoulders shaking, seven times between Safā and Marwa, two low hills across the valley from each other—this in imitation of frantic Hagar seeking in despair for water for wailing little Ishmael.

On the eighth day of Dhū-al-Hijja, the Greater Pilgrimage begins. The pilgrims, in a dense mass, move off toward 'Arafāt, nine miles to the east. They pass the night at Minā, halfway, which they reach by noon. The next day, all arrive at the ʿArafāt plain, the pilgrims engage in a prayer service conducted by an imām, listen to his sermon, and, of utmost importance, stand or move slowly about, absorbed in pious meditation. After sunset, they begin running en masse, and with the greatest possible joyous commotion, to Muzdalifa, a fourth of the way back to Mecca, where they pass the night in the open. At sunrise, they continue to Minā, where each pilgrim casts seven pebbles at three places down the slope below the mountain road, crying out at each throw, "In the name of God! Allāh is almighty!" Those who are able to do so then make the Great Feast possible by offering as a sacrifice a camel, sheep, or horned animal, keeping in mind the injunction in the pilgrimage sūra of the Qurʾān (Sūra XX.37).

> *Mention God's Name over them, standing in ranks;*
> *then, when their flanks collapse, eat of them*
> *and feed the beggar and the suppliant.*[C37]

That is to say, the sacrificer eats part of the meat and gives the rest of it to the poorer pilgrims who stand by, whoever they may be.

The three days following are spent in eating, talking, and merrymaking, in the strictest continence, and then as a final act of the pilgrimage all return to Mecca and make the circuit of the Kaʿba once more.

IV. THE SPREAD OF ISLAM

It may be doubted whether the spread of Islam, at least in its early stages, was the result of studied calculation. Neither the devout Muslim view that it was a purely religious movement engaged in a farsighted effort to save the world from error and corruption, nor the medieval Christian view that it was the outgrowth first of pure imposture and then of rapacity, will bear scrutiny. Both religion and rapacity may be granted to have played their part as motivating impulses, but it is far closer to the mark to say that Muḥammad unified the bedouins for the first time in their history and thus made it possible for them, as a potentially powerful military group, to yoke together their economic need and their religious faith in an overwhelming drive out of the desert into lands where destiny beckoned and

God's will could be fulfilled. Furthermore, the weakness of the Byzantine and Persian empires, exhausted by years of strife with each other, made a permanent conquest of the Middle East possible. Only then did calculated efforts to extend the spread of Muslim conquests represent one more of the long succession of Semitic migrations from the Arabian desert—the last and the greatest.

Abū Bakr and the Unification of Arabia

When Muḥammad died so suddenly, he had designated no successor (caliph). His followers had to decide who should exercise that function. Should the principle of succession be that of heredity, or should the caliphs be elected by (and from) some properly qualified group? The answer to these questions was supplied differently at different times by the three major political parties of early Muslim history. The Companions (so-called because they were composed of Muḥammad's closest associates, the Muhājirīn, or Emigrants, and the Anṣār, or Supporters) assumed that the caliph should be elected from their number. A later group, the Legitimists, following the hereditary principle of succession, thought the caliphs should be Muḥammad's descendants through Fāṭima and her husband, ʿAlī, Muḥammad's son-in-law and cousin. Later still, the Ummayyads, as the leaders of Muḥammad's tribe, sought to be the sole determinants of the question of who should occupy the caliphate.

The Companions were the first to act and gained the initial decision. Abū Bakr was their choice for caliph, the first of four thus chosen. His caliphate lasted only a year, for he soon followed the Prophet in death, but his administration was notable for two things: great firmness in bringing to heel not only those tribes that took the opportunity provided by Muḥammad's death to break away from control but also those that had not yet "submitted" (which was accomplished by the so-called Riddah wars), and the fusing of these forces in the first organized assault on the outside world. Three armies, totaling ten thousand men, whose ranks were soon swollen to twice that number, took separate routes into Syria, in accordance, it was said, with Muḥammad's own well-laid plans. Abū Bakr did not live to see their startling triumphs.

from India to Spain. But in 750, the 'Abbāssids (deriving their name from Muḥammad's uncle, al-'Abbās, thus blood relations of the descendants of 'Alī) overthrew them everywhere except in Spain and moved the capital to Baghdad, which they built up into a great city, on the "crossroads of the world," famous both in the Orient and in the Occident for its wealth, culture, and gaiety, qualities all exemplified in the person of their most celebrated representative, the Caliph Hārūn al-Rashīd (736–809). Then came slow political decadence; the Muslim empire fell apart into separate autonomous states. In two regions anticaliphates declared themselves. In Spain, survivors of the Ummayyad caliphate established an independent rule, and in Egypt and neighboring areas, including Palestine, a Shī'ite anticaliphate, the Fāṭimid, claiming for their imāms (or caliphs) descent from Muḥammad's daughter Fāṭima, ruled from 909 to 1171, with such success for a while that the 'Alīd or Shī'ite cause (see chapter 18) seemed about to attain ascendancy in the Muslim world. But the Seljuk Turks, moving down from the steppes of central Asia, seized power in Persia, Iraq, and Syria in the eleventh century and reached the borders of Egypt and Byzantium.

It was at this point that the Crusaders came, their first expedition resulting in the capture of Jerusalem in 1099 C.E. Then followed the Muslim counterattacks and the emergence of the great leader Saladin, a Sunnite who put an end to the Fāṭimid caliphate in Egypt. Saladin prepared the way carefully for his successes against the Crusaders by slowly contracting the area they held; he finally recaptured Jerusalem (1187). He and his successors came to terms with the Crusaders left clinging to the coast for a time before being ousted. Suddenly, seventy years later, came the Mongols, burning and pillaging as they went, with incredible massacres, advancing and receding in two separate waves of conquest. Repelled by the Mamelūkes of Egypt, who managed to hold on to Syria and Arabia, the Mongols fell back into Iraq and Persia, where they held on for a century longer and were converted to Islam, largely through Ṣūfism (see p. 558).

With the receding of the Mongol tide, four new Islamic empires arose: the Uzbek in the Oxus-Jaxartes basin, the Safawi in Persia (or western Iran), the Mughal in India, and the Ottoman in Asia Minor. The Ottoman Turks rose to power in Asia Minor in the thirteenth century, crossed the Bosphorus, took Byzantium (Constantinople) in 1453, and fought their way into the Balkans and along the Danube as far as Vienna before they were forced back into areas that they could hold (sixteenth century). The Ottoman empire also stretched southward through Palestine into Egypt. It endured to World War I.

But now we must return to earlier centuries.

V. THE FIRST FIVE CENTURIES OF MUSLIM THOUGHT

That the relative homogeneity of the Arabs of the period of the first four caliphs did not long persist should afford no surprise. The Caliph 'Umar's laws, designed to keep the Arabs permanently Arabian as a culturally distinct military unit, were soon and inevitably modified. Multitudes of Arabs migrated out of their barren homeland to enjoy the possession of richer holdings elsewhere—and were changed in the process. For some centuries the Arabs normally functioned within the conquered territories according to the tribal relations to which they were accustomed. They granted the status of then "clients" to some of the conquered peoples; that is, they treated them as adopted members of the Arab tribes. In this case clientship was a way of assimilating some of the conquered peoples; but culturally the process worked both ways. But if they were won over culturally by the subject peoples (the Mawālī or "client peoples") among whom they settled, they successfully won over most of the Mawālīs to their religion, and this resulted in a new culture of a distinctive kind.

The Formation of the Ḥadīth Canons

Lines of divergence appeared early in the Muslim "Traditions." We have already referred, in the opening paragraphs of this chapter, to the Ḥadīth or Tradition. It consisted to a large extent of recollections of Muḥammad's sayings and doings traced back through "attestors" or "authorities" to Muḥammad himself or to a Companion in Medina. There were many of these, but they were not the only authenticated traditions.

Many others dealt with the way things had been done in Medina during Muḥammad's lifetime with his "silent approval" (taqrir)—in short, they described the customs, usages, or precedents established in Muḥammad's days. They soon swelled to formidable bulk, and some of them were contradictory. Some lines of tradition were suspiciously favorable either to the partisans of 'Alī (the Shī'ites), or to the Ummayyads, or, later on, to the 'Abbāssids.

As traditional Islamic scholarship itself points out, there was some invention or fabrication. Ibn-Abī-al-'Awja confessed before his execution 150 years after the Hijra that he had profited financially by fabricating four thousand ḥadīths. But this was undoubtedly, if true, an exceptional case. There can be no doubt that the drive to preserve the memory of Muḥammad's daily habits, oral judgments, and even his offhand comments, was pursued with great earnestness, even though there were some indications at times of bias among those who bore all the marks of trustworthiness. 'Ā'isha's prejudice against 'Alī, for instance, appears in her 2,210 traditions. Some of Muḥammad's Companions seemed almost too voluble. But although there seems to be a very ready remembrance indeed on the part of Abū-Huraira, one of the Companions, with his 5,300 traditions, his integrity and general reliability are beyond question. As such things go, and quite naturally, there were those who had it from someone, who had it from someone else, that still another person had heard a Companion say, "Muḥammad used to do so and so." It became a major concern of the Muslim scholars and theologians to sift and weigh this evidence.

But not until over two centuries had passed after Muḥammad's death were critical attempts made to select the more trustworthy traditions and bring them into a collection, and then the criterion used was an "external" one: the trustworthiness of the contributors of each ḥadīth was the measure of its authenticity. The traditions had to have, as it were, a good pedigree. The authenticity and value of a tradition were judged by its isnād, or chain of attestors, each of whom had to stand up under examination for veracity. The traditions were then declared either "genuine" or "fair" or "weak." At last six separate (and overlapping) collections made their appearance and won general acceptance. Of these, the most highly regarded is the book of al-Bukhārī (d. 870),

a Persian Muslim who diligently visited all through Arabia, Syria, Egypt, and Iraq gathering a vast number of ḥadīths (reportedly numbering six hundred thousand, but undoubtedly containing many duplications and overlappings) and then sifted them down to the 7,275 that he found "genuine." In influence this collection ranks next to the Qur'ān itself. Another highly regarded collection, usually ranked second, is that of Muslim ibn al-Hajjaj (d. 875).

But the six canonical books were not the only collections of ḥadīths in common use among Muslims. Such collections as the *Muwaṭṭā* of Mālik ibn Anas or the *Musnad* of Aḥmad ibn Ḥanbal, founders of two schools of the law, have been given as much authority as some of the six canonical books. Their authority derives from that of their compilers. (For Mālik and Ibn Ḥanbal, see p. 554.)

The interpretation and reconciliation of the "genuine" traditions, being as they are the basis of the *Sunna*, or Custom, of traditionalist Islam, became a preoccupation of Muslim minds, and they allowed some room for divergence of thought.

The First Controversies

Does a Muslim remain a Muslim after committing a sin? Can a conflict between one's faith and one's acts be permitted? Can there be true faith without good works? Should expediency or political considerations have any weight in the choices a Muslim makes? Must a Muslim, to be such, hew straight to the line of what are known to be true Islamic principles without compromise or delay, or may one let events take their course and leave the ultimate decision or action to Allāh? These were some of the issues underlying the first Muslim controversies. For there was then no fixed standard or orthodoxy for all Muslims, and never would be.

When 'Alī was chosen caliph, he was supported by fiercely anti-Ummayyad elements who watched him narrowly to see if he would be as firm and decisive as Muḥammad had been. But midway in the struggle with Mu'āwiya, he had, as we have seen, agreed to arbitrate the issues, whereupon twelve thousand disgusted warriors marched out of his camp, so disillusioned with him that some of them later assassinated him.

The Khārijites

Those who withdrew became the Khārijites (Arabian *Khawrij*), "separatists" or "secessionists." Viewing with hostile eyes the political developments occurring behind the scenes among the Muslim leaders, this group of Muslims concluded bitterly that the only sure way of getting the right caliph was to select the best qualified person, not necessarily a person from just the Prophet's family or just his tribe. The caliph need not come from either group, they said. Not enough of them were true Muslims! The Ummayyads, for instance, had joined the Muslim movement at the last minute, just before it would be too late, obviously less from conviction than from expediency. No, the true caliph could be the choice only of true Muslims, men of proven good works acting solely on the religious principle of doing the will of Allāh in complete self-surrender. All of those who had become Muslims for political or economic reasons, or who went through the practices of Islam as a mere outward form, were not true Muslims at all and must be destroyed in a great purge. This was imperative to save the cause of Allāh and Muḥammad. It was natural that these fierce puritans should find the full force of the Ummayyads arrayed against them. The more radical and uncompromising were wiped out in bloody slaughter as heretics. Yet, their beliefs spread in time to the utmost fringes of the Muslim empire and still persist in a more moderate form in Zanzibar and Algeria.

The Murjites

Opposed to them were the Murjites (Arabian *Murji'ah*), the advocates of "delayed judgment." Their position was that only God can judge who is a true Muslim and who is not. One who sees a believer sinning cannot call that person forthwith an infidel or without faith. Therefore, believers should treat all practicing Muslims, tentatively at least, as real Muslims,

leaving to the last judgment, that is, to Allāh, the fixing of their final status. Hence, even the Ummayyads were to be tolerated—not to mention the converted Christians and Jews who appeared to be merely halfhearted in their "submission."

When it appeared that the weight of Muslim opinion agreed more with the Murjites than the Khārijites, the outlines of a coming traditionalist position began to emerge.

The Sunnīs and the Sharī`a (or Law)

The rapid expansion of Islam confronted Muslims with other crucial, and even more complex, decisions concerning Muslim behavior. Situations early appeared in areas outside of Arabia where the injunctions of the Qur'ān proved either insufficient or inapplicable. The natural first step in these cases was to appeal to the *sunna* (the behavior or practice) of Muḥammad in Medina or to the ḥadīth that reported his spoken decisions or judgments. In the event that this proved inconclusive, the next step was to ask what the sunna and/or consensus of opinion (*ijmā`*) of the Medina community was, in or shortly after the time of Muḥammad. If no light was yet obtainable, the only recourse was either to draw an analogy (*qiyās*) from the principles embodied in the Qur'ān or in Medinan precedents and then apply it, or to follow the consensus of opinion of the local Muslim community as crystallized and expressed by its Qur'ānic authorities.

Such a process might involve *ijtihād*, or the exercise of reason in the forming of a judgment, something that came to be regarded with great reserve in later times. Muslim liberals hold that *ijtihād* was freely resorted to when necessary, but others disagree and regard the ḥadīth cited as questionable.

The Muslims who followed such procedures for solving their

> On being appointed governor of Yaman, Mu'ādh was asked by the Holy Prophet as to the rule by which he would abide. He replied, "By the law of the Qur'ān." "But if you do not find any direction therein," asked the Prophet. "Then I will act according to the Sunna of the Prophet," was the reply. "But if you do not find any direction in the Sunna," he was asked again. "Then I will exercise my judgment (*ajtahidu*) and act on that," came the reply.
>
> —A Ḥadīth[E2]

behavioral problems were, and are to this day, called *Sunnīs* (or Sunnites).

In considering their general position, it is obvious that the Sunnīs (and Muslims in general) do not distinguish sharply between law and religion, inasmuch as the former is based on the ordinances of God revealed to Muḥammad in the Qur'ān. For this reason, the word finally chosen and now used for the law of Islam—*Sharī'a*—means the Way, that is, the true path of religion. The word in earlier use, *fiqh,* or "understanding," was at first applied equally to law and theology, although in common usage it has usually referred to the former. It is well said that "Muslims conceive of their religion as a community that says 'Yes' to God and His world, and the joyful performance of the Law, in most areas of the Islamic world, is looked on as a positive religious value."[1] Accordingly, the recognized scholars of religion (the *'ulamā'*, "the learned," that is, trained Islamic teachers, theologians, and jurists) have ceaselessly watched over the observance of the law in human life, especially the *muftīs*, the jurists appointed to be consultants to the religious courts, who have framed with care each legal opinion (*fatwā*) followed on the bench by the *qāḍīs* (judges).

A distinction is drawn between the religious courts and those established by civil governments. Sometimes civil courts have proceeded separately from the Sharī'a, which in such a case serves as the ideal law according to Islam as opposed to the actual working law of the civil courts. A more practical difference exists in jurisdiction. The religious courts have usually passed judgment in private and family affairs of Muslims, such as marriage, divorce, inheritance, and individual moral and religious conduct, whereas the civil courts have administered the statute laws laid down for a particular country by sovereigns and officials to regulate the actions of the citizenry of whatever faith.

In cases where religious courts have found it difficult to arrive at a legal opinion clearly compatible with the Qur'ān, *ijtihād* (reason and common sense) has been called upon, but used with the greatest caution. For, especially in conservative circles, the resort to reason and common sense may smack too much of speculation, and this is likely to bring one into conflict with Revelation. The safest procedure is to examine Revelation and Tradition reverently and arrange them

into order and system. When this is done, then some use of reasoning, preferably no more than a resort to analogy (*qiyās*), may be cautiously attempted to fill in gaps or to meet new contingencies.

Roughly, this is the path followed by the four "schools of the law," which arose during the first two centuries of Islam and are still recognized as being authoritative.

The Four Schools of the Law

1. The Ḥanīfite

Of the four schools, the first in time, the *Ḥanīfite,* was the most liberal in its use of speculation, by which, of course, is meant juridical, not theological, speculation. It was founded in Iraq by Abū Ḥanīfa (d. 767), a Persian whose followers put down his teachings in Arabic. His general practice was to begin with the Qur'ān (taking little notice of the Ḥadīth) and to ask himself how its precepts could be applied by analogy (*qiyās*) to the somewhat different situation in Iraq. If a particular situation for which Muhammad legislated was closely analogous to a situation existing in Iraq, he applied the Qur'ān as it stood. If, however, the two situations differed widely, he developed by deduction an analogy applicable to Iraq, and if the analogy thus obtained was not acceptable because it ran counter to the public good or the general principles of justice, he consulted *ra'y,* "considered personal opinion" or "reasoned justice," derived from *istihsan* or careful judgment of what is for the public good; and made a ruling. The ruling might in this last case even supersede the Qur'ān. (For example, the Qur'ān prescribes cutting off the hand for theft, but that was meant for a situation not analogous to the one obtaining in more diversified Iraq; so it was not meant for Iraq. By analogical deduction from other parts of the Qur'ān we derive for Iraq other, more effective punishment, namely, imprisonment.) It was natural for the 'Abbāssids and the Ottoman Turks after them to follow the Ḥanīfite rulings on laws and religious rites. They have been followed in Iraq, Iran, Pakistan, and by Muslims in India and central Asia.

2. The Mālikite

The second school, the *Mālikite,* founded in Medina by Mālik ibn Anas (*ca.* 715–795), interpreted laws and rites in the light of the Qur'ān and the Ḥadīth together, and when in difficulty leaned heavily on the "consensus of opinion" (*ijmā'*) that prevailed in Medina. It was he who put together the ḥadīths of the Medina-centered *Muwaṭṭa,* which has been mentioned earlier. For especially perplexing situations he used analogy, and when analogy conflicted with the consensus of scholarly opinion, he fell back on "public advantage." This school is still generally followed in North Africa, upper Egypt, and eastern Arabia.

3. The Shāfi'ite

The *Shāfi'ite,* the third school in time, is important because it can be said to have scrutinized the other two schools and arrived at a science of the law based on what had been previously determined. It was founded by al-Shāfi'i, an Arab born in Persia but descended from the Quraysh tribe. He clearly distinguished four roots or sources of the law: the words of God (the Qur'ān), the words and deeds of the Prophet (his sunna or practice discerned in the Ḥadīth), the consensus of the Muslim community (*ijmā'*), especially as voiced by the jurists, and analogy (*qiyās*) elicited by reasoning. This formulation has been accepted by all schools of the law as the classical theory of the sources of the law, but each school reserves the right to stress these sources differently. The Shāfi'ite school gives equal weight to the Qur'ān and the ḥadīths that authentically reflect the words and deeds of the Prophet, but sometimes, where one of these ḥadīths may be more specific and clear, prefers it even to the Qur'ān. At times the traditions, it is held, represent the Muslim world in expansion and therefore the more developed situation, but although liberal in this respect, the Shāfi'ites reject *ra'y* (opinion) in any form as using speculation in an unwarranted manner. The Shāfi'ite school still prevails in the East Indies, and influences lower Egypt (Cairo), eastern Africa, southern Arabia, and southern India.

4. The Ḥanbalite

The most conservative of the four schools is the *Ḥanbalite.* It was founded at Baghdad in the loose and merry days of Hārūn al-Rashīd by the shocked Ibn-Ḥanbal, a student of al-Shāfi'i who was even more uncompromising than his master toward "opinion." He seems to have been in special opposition to the Mu'tazilites (see next topic) and adhered primarily to the letter of the Qur'ān, with secondary reliance on the

Ḥadīth. For refusal to deny the eternity of the Qur'ān, he was shackled in chains by the 'Abbāssid Caliph al-Ma'mūn, and by a succeeding caliph scourged and imprisoned. The Ḥanbalite laws and ritual are followed today in the Hijāz and in Sa'ūdi Arabia as a whole.

While these conclusions were being reached in the area of law, controversy was being aroused in the area of philosophy of religion.

The Mu'tazilites: Theology and Reason

The vigorous defenders of the faith called Mu'tazilites (Mu'tazilah) appeared first in Syria and Iraq during the Ummayyad caliphate among the converts to Islam who were familiar with Greek, Jewish, Christian, and Zoroastrian thought. Initially, they may have been politically motivated, but in large part they were moved by a desire to convince the unpersuaded non-Muslims of the soundness of the Muslim position. They thus provide a Muslim analogue to the Christian apologists (p. 470). In any case, they were among the first Muslims to engage in what came to be called *kalām,* or reasoned argument in defense of the faith.

In an attempt to find neutral ground between the Khārijites and the Murjites, they laid emphasis on the free response of individuals to the moral demands of Allāh, as seen in the Qur'ān, particularly when confronted by the "promise and threat" of Allāh contained there. But they were also sure, and believed that they were acting in the spirit of Muḥammad in affirming, that not only does Allāh challenge the consciences of individuals, he also seeks their rational assent. Hence, the Mu'tazilites took it for granted that the theological doctrines that might be erected on the foundation supplied by the Qur'ān, whose truth they never questioned, were subject to rational testing. Their reading of translations of works of Greek philosophy, which may not have been extensive, made it seem to them a foregone conclusion that no doctrine could be true that did not survive such a test. How could a true doctrine be contrary to reason?

Justice Requires Some Freedom

Reason, for example, the Mu'tazilites argued, insists on both the justice and unity of God. Doctrines that throw doubt on either cannot be accepted. In defense of the justice of God, the Mu'tazilites made an all-out attack on the doctrine that *all* human deeds are decreed by the inscrutable will of Allāh, and that therefore people are not the authors of any of their acts. Because the inconclusiveness of the Qur'ān on this point allowed some room for further clarification, the Mu'tazilites insisted that no final position should be taken that would put to the question the justice of Allāh: Allāh *must* be just; it would be monstrous to think him moved by arbitrariness alone or by mere good pleasure. How could it be just for God to predestine a person to commit mortal sin or to maintain an attitude of heresy or unbelief, and then punish that person for being guilty of either? It would not be fair or right. Hence, Allāh must allow every person enough freedom to choose between right and wrong, truth and falsehood. Only then could humans be held responsible for their acts.

That Allāh *had* to do anything whatever, as of necessity, was a doctrine that many Muslims viewed with distaste and horror. But the Mu'tazilites nevertheless insisted further that because Allāh most certainly was the Merciful, the Compassionate, and desired the good of all creatures, he *had* to send down revelations to the Prophet to indicate the way of salvation—an act that showed both graciousness and an inner necessity to be just and merciful. Hence, a "necessary grace" is to be seen in the delivery to humankind of the Qur'ān.

The Qur'ān as "Created"

And this brought the Mu'tazilites to the declaration that stirred up the greatest dissension. They denied that the revelation—that is, the Qur'ān—is eternal and uncreated. Allāh created it when the need arose and sent it down. To suppose that it was uncreated and eternal would destroy the unity of God by setting up beside him something else coeternal with him and this would be polytheism, which the Qur'ān itself condemned.

So persuasive did this point seem, perhaps more on political than intellectual grounds, to one of the 'Abbāssid caliphs (al-Ma'mūn), that in 827 C.E. he proclaimed it a heresy to assert the eternity of the Qur'ān and went so far as to set up an inquisition to purge all government departments of those who held such a view. But twenty years later another caliph thought the reverse view the true one, called the Mu'tazilites heretical, and began a purge of them in turn.

Before their final overthrow in the tenth century, the Mu'tazilites turned their rationalistic method on the habit of conceiving God in human form, that is, upon the anthropomorphism inherent in the literal interpretation of the Qur'ān. Some sects spoke of God as a being made of flesh and blood. Mu'tazilites refused to take literally the descriptions of Allāh as sitting on a throne in heaven among the angels and as having hands and feet, eyes and ears. Allāh is infinite and eternal and nowhere particular in space. It endangered the unity of God, they said, to be too literal about his agents or about his attributes or qualities, as though these last could be his "members," as some of the orthodox maintained. It would be consistent with the unity of God only to speak of his attributes as being of his essence or as being his modes or states, not as being separable parts. God is one as to his essence, without division or qualifications. This reasoning was applied as well to the language of the Qur'ān about heaven and hell. The imagery was to be taken figuratively, or at any rate modified by the consideration that those who are intellectual or spiritual will not, in paradise, for example, go in for sensual delights.

But though the Mu'tazilites did manage to teach the Muslim thinkers who came after them the value of using a rational method of exposition, the weight of opinion turned against them, and the tenth century saw their school as such come to an end. But their ideas survived among the Shī'ites (see chapter 18), and many modernists have revived them.

Muslim Philosophers and Classical Learning

The Mu'tazilites used the rationalistic methods and tools of philosophy to argue from within Islam about its meaning and message; there were others who, without giving up their Muslim faith, moved amid the concepts and issues of Greek philosophy. They were known as the *falāsifa* (philosophers). It appeared to these thinkers that the Muslim faith, as the final truth in religion, should be stated in philosophical terms to gain the full assent of reason. In doing this they were ready to reject whatever reason rejected. But their tradition-nurtured fellow Muslims were distrustful, and after seeing where their reasoning led them, agreed with al-Ghazālī, whom we shall meet on a later page, when he condemned the falāsifa for self-contradiction in espousing such Greek doctrines as the eternity of the world, the impossibility of resurrection from the dead, and God's having no knowledge of particulars. Nevertheless, during the first five centuries of Muslim thought, powerful intellects, displaying an encyclopedic learning, appeared among the philosophers. Perhaps the greatest was ibn-Sīnā (Avicenna), who lived in Persia from 980 to 1037. His predecessors, the Arab al-Kindi of Basra and Baghdad (d. 873) and the Turk al-Fārābi (870–950), were scarcely less able. In Spain, ibn-Rushed (Averroës, 1126–1198) was to follow in Avicenna's steps, seeking like him to forge a syncretism of Islam, Plato, Aristotle, and Plotinus. These men all gained the respect of Jewish and Christian thinkers of their times, because their grounding in Greek philosophy was sounder than was then possible in the West, with its large loss of classical learning. But Muslims came to think that they had stepped outside of Islam onto alien ground.

The Orthodox Champion: Al-Ash`arī

The downfall of the Mu'tazilites came about when the more conservative defenders of the Surma adopted the methods of rationalism (the construction of logical systems) in order to confute them. It was a man trained in a Mu'tazilite school, named al-Ash'arī, who thus turned the tables on them.

Abu'l al-Ḥasan al-Ash'arī was born about 250 years after the Hijra, made his final home in Baghdad, and died there in his early sixties (935 C.E.). He became one of the two great thinkers most honored by conservative Muslims, the other being al-Ghazālī. After studying and publicly advocating the Mu'tazilites' teachings, he found himself at the age of forty suddenly and violently disagreeing, and went on to develop a differing exposition of the Islamic revelation. He now swung all the way over to the ultraconservative Ḥanbalite school of law. His new interpretation made God not only one but all in all. All life, all knowledge, power, will, hearing, sight, and speech—the seven divine attributes—no matter where or when experienced, are Allāh in action, for Allāh has created humankind and

all of their acts. People cannot see, hear, know, or will anything of themselves; it is Allāh who causes what happens in and through them. This position enabled al-Ash'arī to supply logical grounds for traditionalist doctrines, whether drawn from the Qur'ān or the Hadīth. For example, because it is Allāh who immediately causes all events, internal and external, it is he who determined us to think of him as he is described in the Qur'ān. Allāh, then, can be spoken of as sitting on a throne and as having hands and feet, eyes and ears; the Qur'ān says so; but the Qur'ān also says that he is "not like anything" in the universe; therefore, the nature of God's sitting and seeing is not known to humankind, and they must believe what they are told bi-lā kayf, "without conceiving how" it may be so. Similarly, the concrete imagery of heaven and hell supplied by the Qur'ān is to be taken as descriptive of reality; the believers in paradise will really have a vision of Allāh sitting on his throne; but it must not be supposed that their seeing or sitting is to be compared with this world's seeing or sitting. As for the Qur'ān, al-Ash'arī said its words are, as ideas in the mind of Allāh, eternal, but the letters on sheets of paper forming the words and read and recited on earth are produced by human effort and are of temporal origin—a solution of the old puzzle as to the uncreated nature of the Qur'ān that was immediately satisfactory to most Muslims. Finally, that the conception of Allāh as being the immediate cause of every act made him responsible for evil as well as good did not daunt al-Ash'arī: it was just a fact that Allāh, in accordance with his inscrutable good pleasure, decreed the unbelief of the infidel and damned him for it. Allāh has his own reasons, which are not like human reasons and which men cannot know and should not have the temerity to seek to know. But al-Ash'arī modified this hard teaching by saying that even though actions are predestined, individuals "acquire" guilt or righteousness by acting as though they were free, under the consciousness of making their own decisions, thus involving themselves in their predestined acts, good or bad.

Al-Māturīdī

Al-Ash'arī influence spread far and wide. He was read and studied in places as far away as Samarkand, in central Asia, north of the Hindu Kush Mountains. There al-Māturīdī, a contemporary and a Ḥanīfite, both agreed and disagreed with him. Standing on the same basically Sunnite position as al-Ash'arī's in affirming that all acts are willed by God, al-Māturīdi made the qualification, generally accepted in the Muslim world, that the sins of men occur by God's will but not with his good pleasure; God created disbelief and willed it "in a general way" but "did not order men to it; rather he ordered the infidel to believe, but did not will it for him"[1] (i.e., he left it to the individual to believe or disbelieve). The act of the unbeliever is willful and not pleasing to God, since he finds it hateful and punishes him for it.

The Mystics: Forerunners of Sūfism

But what concerned the majority of Muslims more than the kalām of al-Ash'arī' and al-Māturīdī were such immediate and present things as (1) the practice of the Five Pillars and the ceremonies of the ritual year, (2) the vaguely mystical experience of the presence of God in worship and daily life, with both its "promise and threat," and (3) assurance of the vitality and reality of Islam in the lives and persons of true people of God.

Islam had no priests, then or now, ordained and set apart for a life dedicated to the worship of God and the pursuit of holiness (the imāms, who lead the prayers in the mosques, have always been laymen who serve full or part time to the glory of God).

It was the popular yearning for the presence among them of unworldly men dedicated to God, asceticism, and holiness that encouraged the eventual emergence of Islamic mysticism.

The forerunners of the mystics appeared almost as soon as Islam reached Syria. Early in the Ummayyad caliphate, Syrian Muslims, yearning to know Allāh in this strange context and influenced by, among other things, passages from the New Testament, wandered about, neither begging or yet working for a living, but endlessly reciting a litany of the "beautiful names" and titles of Allāh and resigning themselves to his care, in trustful dependence on such a promise as that contained in the saying of Jesus, "Take therefore no thought for the morrow: for the morrow shall take thought for the things of itself." Ascetics rather than mystics, they practiced an utter indifference toward hunger and illness or the abuse they received from others, saying that they must be under the hand of Allāh "as passive as a corpse under the hand of him who washes it."[11] In Iraq there was al-Ḥasan of Basra (d. 728), an ascetic who was at the same time a religious scholar. His holy life caused him to be revered as a saint in his own lifetime. He rejected this world (dunyā) as a "lower" place full of wretchedness and grief and called upon his hearers to seek heavenly "mansions which long ages will not decay nor alter."

The First Ṣūfīs

The first Ṣūfīs to bear the name (meaning "wool wearers," i.e., wearers of the ascetics' coarse, undyed woolen robe) appeared in the eighth century, but they soon went beyond their forerunners in the development of intellectual and mystical interests that took them into directed contemplation. Eventually, although they based themselves on the Qur'ān, they sought philosophical aid from Neo-Platonism and Gnosticism, while Christian monasticism supplied them with hints toward organization. They adopted a monkish rule of life, practiced long vigils and stated periods of meditation, and finally gathered into fraternities (this by the twelfth century) with communal religious services, marked by Muslim rituals and music much like that of the Christian churches. Their consuming interest was union with God now rather than after death. Because there were no distinctively Muslim lines of thought to guide them, they strained at the leash of Muslim orthodoxy toward mysticism and pantheism.

The Ṣūfīs claimed Muḥammad as their example (witness his use of caves on Mt. Hirā), but they had to overlook the ḥadīth quoting Muḥammad as being critical of "monkery" (e.g., in the saying attributed to him, "Either you propose to be a Christian monk; in that case, join them openly! Or you belong to our people; then you must follow our custom [sunna]. Our custom is married life.").[12] The Qur'ān itself says of the followers of Jesus: "And monasticism they invented—We did not prescribe it for them—only seeking the good pleasure of God; but they observed it now as it should be observed."[C38]

Some early Ṣūfīs, like the poetess Rābi'ah of Basra (d. 801 C.E.), sought communion with God but were wary of ulterior motives in monastic regimens: ambition or fear. Quoting the Qur'ānic verse, "He loves them and they love him," (Sura 5:59), Rābi'ah celebrated love of God as pure and uncomplicated. In one legend she is pictured with a torch in one hand and a pitcher of water in the other—to burn Paradise and to quench hell so that God could be loved solely for his beauty. Asked if she herself did not hope for Paradise, she said, "First the neighbor, then the house."

When the Ṣūfīs were establishing themselves, they were influenced by what they heard of the mystical speculations of an Egyptian Muslim, Dhu'l-Nūn al-Miṣrī (d. 859 C.E.), who perhaps received the name "the Man of the Fish from Egypt," that is, the Jonah of Egypt, because he said that individuality is a deadly sin and the soul must be "swallowed up" in God by complete mystic union. But neither he nor the Ṣūfīs in general thought that the swallowing up of the soul could be achieved at once without the soul being prepared for it. There were stages to pass through. To follow the figure of Ḥārith al-Muḥāsibī of Basra (d. 857), the Ṣūfī was a pilgrim on the road that leads to "the truth," and there were way stations he must pass, under the guidance of a Muslim director, such as repentance, abstinence, renunciation, poverty, patience, trust in God, and satisfaction (the "seven stages" most commonly prescribed). Final entrance into the transcendent realm of knowledge and truth would crown the various "states" of longing, fear, hope, love, intimacy, and trust that Allāh had bestowed. The climactic state would be experienced as an intoxicating and ineffable flash of divine illumination, bringing with it the certainty of divine love—the goal of the mystical theist in all lands.

Ṣūfīs Accused of Heresy: Al-Ḥallāj

But a few mystics were not theists. They defined Allāh as the realm of true being, and when certain Buddhist influences penetrated Iraq, the Ṣūfīs there moved perilously close to atheism (as did some *zindiq* or free-thinking Muslims of Zoroastrian background) and emphasized self-annihilation, conceived as complete absorption into True Being, as the entire goal.

These and others among the more extreme Ṣūfīs (the "ecstatics") were recognized by conservative Mus-

lims as heretics. There was more than one martyrdom. A Persian Ṣūfī called al-Ḥallāj was in 922 scourged, mutilated, nailed to a gibbet, and then beheaded for crying out publicly, "I am the True (*al-Ḥaqq*)," by which his hearers, accustomed to hearing Allāh named "the True," judged he was committing the ultimate in blasphemy. They were right in understanding that he felt he and his creator were one, but he meant no blasphemy. He felt much the same way the Persian mystic Abū Yazīd al-Bisṭāmī (d. 875) did, to whom the saying was attributed, "Thirty years the transcendent God was my mirror, now I am my own mirror—that is, that which I was I am no more, for 'I' and 'God' is a denial of the Unity of God. Since I am no more, the transcendent God is His own mirror. I say that I am my own mirror, for 'tis God that speaks with my tongue, and I have vanished."[K1]

To al-Ḥallāj, the hope of mystic union with God is that of the lover who suffers with separation from his beloved, and in his famous verses he bewails any absence of perfect harmony with the Great Beloved. When he can, he celebrates its presence with intimacy and tenderness.

> Betwixt me and Thee there lingers an "it is I" that
> torments me.
> Ah, of Thy grace, take away this "I" from between us![K2]

> I am He whom I love, and He whom I love is I,
> We are two spirits dwelling in one body.
> If thou seest me, thou seest Him,
> And if thou seest Him, thou seest us both.[K3]

Later Moderate Ṣūfīsm

Alarmed by the execution of al-Ḥallāj, and quite aware of the extravagance of language that had provoked it, more moderate Ṣūfīs appeared who made an earnest effort during the next two centuries to show their Sunnī critics that they were not in contradiction to the Qur'ān, and the Ḥadīth. They sought to prove, in chastened language, that Ṣūfīsm could be and was truly Muslim. In volume after volume, Abū Naṣr al-Sarrāj, Abū Ṭālib al-Makkī, Abū Bakr al-Kālābadhī, and especially Abū'l-Qāsim al-Qushayrī, along with others, attempted to rehabilitate Ṣūfī mysticism in Sunnī eyes, claiming that it sought a revival of Islam from within.

In the next section we shall see how al-Ghazālī produced the great synthesis of the themes of both Sunnī and Ṣūfī Muslims, a feat that prevented the Sunnīs from driving the Ṣūfīs from the Muslim fold and convinced the Ṣūfīs that their future lay with Islam.

After the time of al-Ghazālī (whom we shall meet later), the Ṣūfīs gained more confidence; in a sense, he had given them license to exist and to continue their quest for personal experience of Allāh's living presence. They conceded the legitimacy of Sharī'a and kalām insofar as they rested on the revelation to Muḥammad, but they claimed for their mysticism the validity of intuitive insight that cannot be expressed in rational, historical, or practical terms but has to be clothed in the language of poetry and symbolism. Moreover, they found that this resort to poetic and intuitional language made it difficult for the logicians of the Sunnī to attack them successfully, and this further freed them in their literary self-expression.

Ṣūfī Poetry: Rūmī

When the later Ṣūfī poets let themselves go, they approximated the language of al-Ḥallāj, it being now safe, short of claiming divinity, to do so. Consider the words of the poet Jālal al-Dīn Rūmī (he is the author of the famous *Mathnavī*, "the Qur'ān of the Persian language," and on the foundations he laid the Maulawī order of dervishes (see p. 572) was based) written nearly three hundred years after al-Ḥallāj's execution.

> When God appears to His ardent lover the lover is absorbed in Him, and not so much as a hair of the lover remains. True lovers are as shadows, and when the sun shines in glory the shadows vanish away. He is a true lover of God to whom God says, "I am thine, and thou art mine."[L1]

> Let me then become nonexistent,
>   for nonexistence
> Sings to me in organ tones, "To
>   him shall we return."
> Behold water in a pitcher, pour
>   it out;

> "If the picture of our Beloved is found in a heathen temple, it is an error to encircle the Ka'bah: if the Ka'bah is deprived of its sweet smell, it is a synagogue: and if in the synagogue we feel the sweet smell of union with him, it is our Ka'bah."[G2]
>
> —Rumi

> Will that water run away from the stream?
> When that water joins the water of the stream
> It is lost therein, and becomes itself the stream.
> Its individuality is lost, but its essence remains,
> And thereby it becomes not less nor inferior.[L2]

> In the world of Divine Unity is no room for Number,
> But Number necessarily exists in the world of Five and
>   Four.
> You may count a hundred thousand sweet apples in
>   your hand:
> If you wish to make One, crush them all together.[L3]

> In the house of water and clay this heart is desolate
>   without thee;
> O Beloved, enter the house, or I will leave it.[L4]

For his disciples, Rūmī wrote the famous "Song of the Reed Flute," celebrating the love of God that the flute symbolized.

A central passage cries out in celebration of the ecstasy of the love of God.

> Hail to thee, then, O LOVE, sweet madness!
> Thou who healest all our infirmities!
> Who art the physician of our pride and self-conceit!
> Who art our Plato and our Galen!
> Love exalts our earthly bodies to heaven,
> And makes the very hills to dance with joy!
> O lover, 'twas love that gave life to Mount Sinai,
> When "it quaked, and Moses fell down in a swoon."

> Did my Beloved only touch me with his lips,
>   I too, like the flute, would burst out in
>   melody.[L5]

The references here to the Greeks point to the fact that the Ṣūfīs, especially in their manifestation as dervishes, were hospitable to any point of view that lent aid to their quest. They felt the essential oneness of all seekers of union with God, no matter what their name or sign. A hundred years earlier, the Spanish philosopher-poet Ibn al-'Arabī, had said,

There was a time, when I blamed my companion if his
religion did not resemble mine;
    Now, however, my heart accepts every form: it is a
    pasture
ground for gazelles, a cloister for monks,
    A temple for idols and a Ka'bah for the pilgrim, the
    tables
of the Torah and the sacred books of the Koran.
    Love alone is my religion.[G3]

Rūmī on Religious Experience

The conviction of the Ṣūfīs that the essential thing in religion—any religion—is religious experience ("the inward spirit and the state of feeling") rather than its fixed forms, shines clear in the following famous passage from Rūmī's *Mathnavī*:

Moses saw a shepherd on the way, who was saying, "O God who choosest whom Thou wilt, where art Thou, that I may become Thy servant and sew Thy shoes and comb Thy head? That I may wash Thy clothes and kill Thy lice and bring milk to Thee, O worshipful One; that I may kiss Thy little hand and rub Thy little foot, and when bedtime comes I may sweep Thy little room, O Thou to whom all my goats be a sacrifice, O Thou in remembrance of whom are my cries of ay and ah!"

The shepherd was speaking foolish words in this wise. Moses said, "Man, to whom is this addressed?"

He answered, "To that One who created us; by whom this earth and sky were brought to sight."

"Hark!" said Moses, "you have become very backsliding; indeed you have not become a Moslem, you have become an infidel. What babble is this? What blasphemy and raving? Stuff some cotton into your mouth! The stench of your blasphemy has made the whole world stinking: your blasphemy has turned the silk robe of religion into rags. Shoes and socks are fitting for you, but how are such things right for One who is a Sun?"

The shepherd said, "O Moses, thou hast closed my mouth and thou hast burned my soul with repentance." He rent his garment and heaved a sigh, and hastily turned his head towards the desert and went his way.

A revelation came to Moses from God—"Thou hast parted My servant from Me. Didst thou come

as a prophet to unite, or didst thou come to sever? So far as thou canst, do not set foot in separation: of all things the most hateful to Me is divorce. I have bestowed on every one a special way of acting. . . . In the Hindoos the idiom of India is praiseworthy; in the Sindians the idiom of Sind is praiseworthy. I am not sanctified by their glorification of Me; 'tis they that become sanctified. . . . I look not at the tongue and the speech; I look at the inward spirit and the state of feeling. I gaze into the heart to see whether it be lowly, though the words uttered be not lowly, because the heart is the substance. . . . In substance is the real object. How much more of these phrases and conceptions and metaphors? I want burning, burning: become friendly with that burning! Light up a fire of love in thy soul, burn thought and expression entirely away! O Moses, they that know the conventions are of one sort, they whose souls and spirits burn are of another sort."[M]

But the accent by the mystics on the immanence and omnipresence of God was so at odds with the Sunnī emphasis on the transcendence and omnipotence of God that there was great need of a reconciliation of these themes, and this need was met by al-Ghazālī, the great synthesizer of Muslim thought.

The Synthesis of al-Ghazālī

After the tension between the traditionalists and the Khārijites and Mu'talizites, and the straining in different directions of the jurists and the mystics, the kalām of al-Ghazālī, when it was understood, "came like a deliverance."[N] In recognition of the fact that he pulled diverging trends together and rescued the schools from the barren legalisms into which they had fallen after al-Ash'arī, Muslims have called him Muḥyī al-Dīn, "the Restorer (or Renewer) of Religion."

And yet his value was not immediately recognized. It was only after his synthesis had been before them awhile that the Muslim schoolmen began to appreciate its balance and wisdom.

Born in a Persian village in 1058 C.E., Abū Ḥāmid al-Ghazālī attained his fame elsewhere but returned home before he died in 1111. After an education in jurisprudence in a Shāfi'ite school and in theology under a famous Ash'arite imām, he was invited to

Baghdad as a lecturer in the Niẓāmiyah, a newly founded university where the Ashʿārite doctrine predominated. During his four years of teaching, he reached a spiritual crisis. Not satisfied with Scholasticism, he veered to skepticism, then to Ṣūfīsm. His intellectual appetite led him across the broad sweep of human learning. Near the end of his life, he wrote,

> Ever since I was under twenty (now I am over fifty) . . . I have not ceased to investigate every dogma and belief. No Batinite did I come across without desiring to investigate his esotericism; no Zaharite, without wishing to acquire the gist of his literalism; no philosopher (Neo-Platonist), without wanting to learn the essence of his philosophy; no dialectical theologian, without striving to ascertain the object of his dialectics and theology; no Sufi, without coveting to probe the secret of his Sufism; no ascetic, without trying to delve into the origin of his asceticism; no atheistic *zindiq*, without groping for the causes of his bold atheism and *zindiqism*. Such was the unquenchable thirst of my soul for research and investigation from the early days of my youth, an instinct and a temperament implanted in me by God through no choice of mine.[F5]

The swing to Ṣūfīsm proved decisive. He left the university, went to Syria to find out for himself, under the Ṣūfīs there, whether their way was the right path to religious certainty, and after two years of meditation and prayer made a holy pilgrimage to Mecca before returning to his wife and children. He had renewed his faith in the Sunnī ideal, but he felt that Ṣūfī mysticism, moderately practiced, could help him reach it. He began writing. Though at the command of the sultan he returned to teaching for a short time, he soon resumed his meditation and writing in his native village until his death at age fifty-three.

The Revival of the Religious Sciences

Al-Ghazālī's greatest book was *The Revival of the Religious Sciences*. As a fundamentally religious person, he was not satisfied with the legalism and intellectualism of the Sunnīs. Theology was unreal without religious experience. In fact, all human thinking and life itself were flat and unprofitable without God. He took the time to analyze in detail the philosophies of certain Muslim followers of Aristotle, only to condemn them as being self-contradictory and essentially irreligious rational systems. To him the universe was not eternal but was created out of nothing by the creative will of Allāh.

The relation between persons and the great being who has produced them and the world about them should be fundamentally moral and experimental. It is not enough to observe the laws and rites of Islam or to have a kalām that one is ready to defend against all comers. A humble soul may be profoundly religious, even while being ignorant of the details of Qurʾānic interpretation or theology. The core of religion—which may be practiced even by a non-Muslim—is to repent of one's sins, purge the heart of all but God, and by the exercises of religion attain a virtuous character. And here, he said, the Ṣūfī methods of self-discipline and meditation, if practiced with common sense and wisdom, are of great value. Of priceless value, too, are the Five Pillars of the faith, accepted as obligatory for all Muslims; yet they do not yield their full profit unless they are performed from the heart and with the right attitude of mind. Only thus can the Muslim hope to escape punishment on the last day.

The vigor with which Al-Ghazālī censured the teachers of law, theology, and philosophy for their lack of religious fire and for encouraging sectarian tendencies caused his works to be bitterly assailed when they were first published. But it was clear that the same man who censured error where he found it also reached out humbly and sensitively in his personal search for God. On second thought, all but the extreme sects in areas dominated by formalistic jurisprudence, like far-off Spain, acknowledged the sanity and general truth of his position. Ultimately, he was given the rank of the greatest of Muslim thinkers and was at last revered as a saint. Muslim thinkers have remained in the main with Al-Ghazālī's formulations, his word being taken as all but final.

GLOSSARY

Allāh (äl-läh') God, a contraction of *al-ilāh,* "the deity"; the form "Allāh" has no plural and is used by all Arabic-speaking monotheists to refer to "the one God"

dīn practice, custom, or usage (as distinguished from *imān,* "faith")

Ḥadīth the body of tradition concerning the actions and sayings of the Prophet

hajj pilgrimage to Mecca, fifth of the "Five Pillars" of Islam

Hijra (Latin Hegira), "withdrawal," the migration of the Prophet and his followers from Mecca to Medina in 622 C.E., the founding event of the Islamic faith community and the first year of its calendar

ijtihād exercise of reason or judgment on a case in theology or law (an expert in this exercise is a *mujtahid,* "judge")

īmān faith, commitment, manifesting one's trust in Allāh

jinn (pl.) spirits; though essentially made of "smokeless flame," they are capable of assuming human and animal shapes to aid or frustrate human efforts (sing. *jinni,* cp. the "genie" in Aladdin's bottle)

Kaʿba "the cube," a grey stone structure at Mecca; reshrouded annually in black brocade, it marks the geoaxial center of the Islamic world, the focal point of prayer orientation and pilgrimage

kalām Islamic theology, reasoned argument in defense of the faith

Muslim "one who submits" (to Allāh), a member of the community of "submission": *Islām*—a term from the same Arabic root

Shahāda "witness," the Muslim profession of faith: "There is no god but Allāh; Muḥammad is the Prophet of Allāh."

Sharīʿa "clear path," the right way of life set forth for humankind in the Qurʾān

Ṣūfīs "wool-clad ones," members of mystical sects of Islam, the earliest dating from the 8th c. in Persia

ʿulamā "the learned," Islamic custodians of tradition, theologians; sometimes directly involved in governing, sometimes the Islamic counterforce to de facto governments

zakāt the alms-tax charitable obligation, third of the "Five Pillars" of Islamic duty—in general terms, one-fortieth of accumulated wealth, though rules are often complex

CHAPTER 18

The Shī`ah Alternative and Regional Developments

It must be obvious by now that Islam is not and never has been a monolithic faith. Divergences in doctrine, divisions of a political nature, and variations in law and the development of the spiritual life have frequently occurred. Even the conservative position was long in emerging and then proved unable to achieve a fixed and final form. But we have not seen, so far, any major deviation. There was one that focused on issues of spiritual perfection and political succession. It had its own selections of ḥadīths for interpreting the early stages of Islamic history. It occurred before there existed any Islamic standard or norm to block it effectively, and perhaps it could not have been blocked anyway, for it was motivated by a very powerful desire: to have Islam directed by Muḥammad's own descendants, the *Ahl al-Bayt,* "the people of the house,"—specifically the descendants of his daughter Fāṭima, his cousin and son-in-law ʿAlī, and his grandsons al-Ḥasan and al-Ḥusayn. The Shī`ah declaration of faith is "There is no God but God; Muḥammad is the Prophet of God, and ʿAlī is the Saint of God."

I. THE PARTY (SHĪ`AH) OF `ALĪ

The tragedy that befell the House of ʿAlī, beginning with the murder of ʿAlī himself and including the deaths of his two sons, grandsons of Muḥammad, has haunted the lives of the Shī`ah, "the party of ʿAlī." They have brooded upon these dark happenings down the years as Christians do upon the death of Jesus. As a separated community, they have drawn the censure and yet also have had sympathy of the Sunnīs and Ṣūfīs. They were among the sects whose radical elements al-Ghazālī attacked as guilty of resting their claims on false grounds and sinfully dividing Islam. And yet, although agreeing with this indictment, the Muslim world at large has suppressed its annoyance at them, because their movement goes back to the very beginnings of Islam

WESTERN NAME: Shīʿites

TOTAL MUSLIM POPULATION IN 1997: 1.15 billion (16 percent Shīʿite)

NAME USED BY ADHERENTS: The Shīʿa (party) of ʿAlī

MAIN LANGUAGES: Arabic
   Farsi

SHAPING EVENT: The martyrdom of al-Husayn and Karbalā

MAJOR SECTS: Zaidites (Zaydis)
   Twelvers (IthnāʿAshari)
   Seveners (Ismāʿīlites)

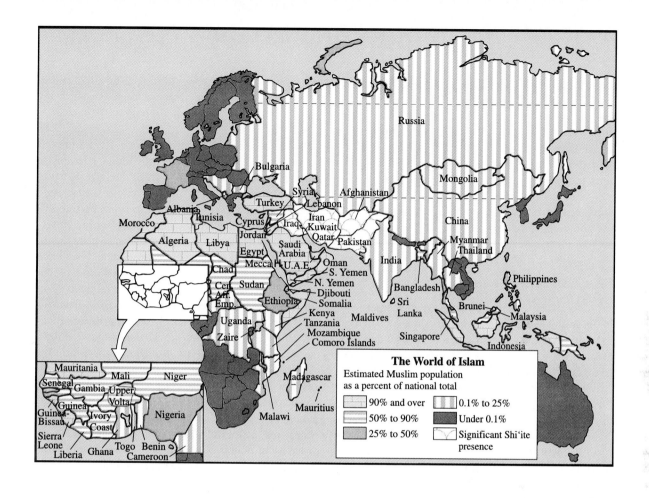

The World of Islam
Estimated Muslim population
as a percent of national total

90% and over	0.1% to 25%
50% to 90%	Under 0.1%
25% to 50%	Significant Shīʿite presence

and has a kind of perverse justification, even in orthodox eyes.

The partisans of ʿAlī only gradually worked out the final claims made by the various Shīʿite sects. In the beginning there was simply the assertion—which as events unfolded became more and more heated—that only Muḥammad's direct descendants, no others, could be legitimate caliphs; only they should have been given first place in the leadership of Islam. This "legitimism" could be called their political and dynastic claim, and at first this seems to have been all that they were interested in claiming. But this was not enough for adherents of their cause in Iraq, who over the years developed the religious theory that every legitimate leader of the ʿAlīds, beginning with ʿAlī, was an *imām Mahdī*, a divinely appointed and supernaturally guided spiritual leader, endowed by Allāh with special knowledge and insight—an assertion that the main body of Muslims, significantly enough, called *ghuluw*, "exaggeration," rather than heresy.

In assessing Shīʿite claims one needs to keep in mind that the word *imām* (literally "exemplar") is used in a variety of senses. In common usage, it refers to any leader of congregational prayers. Many Sunnī Muslims also use it figuratively to mean the leader of the Islamic community. Among Shīʿites, it may refer to that particular descendant of ʿAlī who is Allāh's designated holder of the spiritual authority inherent in the line. (The term *caliph* is considered too secular.) Along with the title "Mahdī," it may refer to a messianic figure.

The political claim of the earlier days was, then, gradually supplemented by such sincere convictions as these: that Allāh was determinedly behind ʿAlī and his descendants, that he would not be frustrated by death, and that he would surely conduct the Shīʿite cause to a final triumph, even if this might mean bringing a descendant of ʿAlī back from death or "withdrawal" to be a messianic figure capable of accomplishing the aims that Muḥammad and ʿAlī had espoused when they were leaders of the Muslim world. Such expectations were at first scarcely more than hopes born of frustration and faith, but gradually the hope and faith became a firm conviction.

The Shīʿite Version of Succession

In the eyes of the Shīʿites, Muḥammad was the divinely chosen Prophet of Islam, and ʿAlī, his cousin and son-in-law, the Imām, the divinely designated "leader" and commander-in-chief of the faithful, and also their "pattern," for they came to believe that before his death Muḥammad, the revealer of the truth in Arabia, under the guidance of Allāh, chose ʿAlī as the successor (caliph) who should establish this truth throughout the earth. Muḥammad's designation of ʿAlī as his successor therefore conferred on ʿAlī the same kind of supernatural status as Catholics claim Jesus bestowed on Peter at Caesarea Philippi. Hence, the appointment of Abū Bakr, ʿUmar, and ʿUthmān as caliphs was a usurpation—a usurpation with disastrous consequences, for when ʿAlī at last was elected caliph, the opposition had developed so much power that it was able to bring his caliphate to a tragic conclusion. So bitter are all but one of the Shīʿite sects about this great "betrayal" that to this day they curse Abū Bakr, ʿUmar, and ʿUthmān as usurpers in their Friday prayers.

The Shīʿites found the same kind of tragedy overwhelming ʿAlī's sons, who by heritage were endowed with his unique spiritual quality. Al-Ḥasan, the older of the two sons ʿAlī had by Fāṭima, was led by the opposition to resign his imāmship for a mere pension and shortly thereafter died. Believing that he had been poisoned, later Shīʿites gave him the title "Lord of All Martyrs." The younger son, al-Ḥusayn, the third imām according to this reading of history, fell a martyr (680 C.E.), along with his little son, in a battle at Karbalā during a futile attempt to establish himself as the rightful caliph over the Ummayyad incumbent, Yazīd.

While this interpretation of history was still in its formative stage, the Shīʿites struggled against the Ummayyads and gave their support to the rebellions that led to the triumph of the ʿAbbāssids. (The ʿAbbāssids, who derived their name from Muḥammad's uncle, al-ʿAbbās, were thus blood relations of the descendants of ʿAlī.) But the Shīʿites were no better treated by the ʿAbbāssids than by the Ummayyads, and in seeking attainment of their aims broke up into different sects (which we shall examine shortly). Nevertheless, they continued to regard the descendants of al-Ḥasan and al-Ḥusayn as "nobles" and "lords" and among their number distinguished, according to their various sectarian principles, certain individuals as divinely ordained imams, who had inherited from ʿAlī and the intermediate imams two extraordinary qualities: infallibility in interpreting the law, and sinlessness. Historically, it was not until about the time of the sixth imām after ʿAlī (Jaʿfar al-Ṣādiq) that these claims assumed a clear-cut form. Supporting them were two principles: that of the *nass* (designation of the next imām by the preceding one), a principle that was read back into history all the way to Muḥammad, as we have seen; and that of the *ʿilm* (special knowledge, such as would give an imām the warrant to exercise authority, impose discipline, and make decisions of a binding character in cases at issue).

Eventually another belief was to be added. It came later and concerned the expected return of some one of the imams as a "divinely guided" messianic personage, the *Imām Mahdī*. Where their line of imams ended, various sects were to believe that the last of these divine leaders had just "withdrawn" from sight and would return again as the Mahdī before the last day, to gather his own about him once more.

Theology of Saintliness: Ethics for Special Conditions

Concurrent with the explicit political implications of the claim of authority for the household (*Ahl al-Bayt*) of the Prophet, there developed a theology emphasizing roles of saintliness and perfection. Believers emphasized the sanctity of the Prophet's clan, the Banū Hāshim, as caretakers of the Kaʿba—almost a hereditary priesthood. ʿAlī and al-Ḥusayn came to be perceived as having been martyred because they put spiritual purity before political expediency. Al-Ḥusayn, for example, took his whole household to Karbalā, trusting in the holiness of the *Ahl al-Bayt*. He would not have brought his family, Shī`ah historians reason, if he had had worldly battle in mind.

Thus Shī`ites follow in the footsteps of saints. Especially on Iranian soil, where stark Zoroastrian contrasts of good and evil were in customary language, there was the urge to make unambiguous perfection possible. Accordingly, Shī`ites came to accept two significant "allowances" in ethical practice: *taqīya* (dissimulation) and *mut`a* (temporary marriage).

Dissimulation

Suffering under intense Sunnī compulsion and persecution for their loyalty to the imāms, Shī`ites found in *taqīya* the possibility of conforming outwardly to the requirements laid upon them by the persecuting authorities while keeping secret mental reservations. By this means they were able to survive as an underground movement in the areas where their views were proscribed. Modern Shī`ism considers dissimulation to be permissible under certain other extreme conditions—where failure to employ it might compromise a female relative or put a relative into an absolutely destitute condition.

Temporary Marriage

Accommodation to practical necessity lay behind Shī`ite acceptance of temporary marriage. *Mut`a* (marriage with a fixed termination contract, subject to renewal) legalizes sexual liaisons that might otherwise fall outside of the law and legitimizes any offspring. It differs from marriage in that it requires no formal divorce. Agreements require no witnesses and may be as brief as one night or as long as a lifetime. Conceived especially for periods of war, foreign travel, and social upheaval, *mut`a* had precedents in the earliest day of the Muslim community of Medina, but it was banned by `Umar, the second caliph. It is unacceptable to Sunnīs, and in recent times proscribed or looked down upon by Shī`ites. Yet in November 1990 Iranian President Hashimi Rafsanjani stunned a huge audience at Friday prayers by suggesting temporary marriage as a remedy for the sexual deprivation of widows and young persons not yet ready for longer-term marriages. In the ensuing storm of controversy, most women decried the proposal as a regression to prostitution. Defenders cited the "unhealthiness" of prolonged abstinence, approved the recognition of female sexuality, and appreciated a "solution" within the realm of Islamic discourse.

Subjected to constant opposition from the Sunnī Muslims, Shī`ites found themselves in sympathy with some heterodox theological positions. Like the Mu`tazilites, they did not believe the Qur'ān to be eternal, nor humans to be without any freedom of will. Refusing to accept their centuries of hardship and frustration as the ultimate will of Allāh, they reasoned that Allāh is bound by justice (`adl) and holds humans responsible for their acts. Thus, he *must* one day vindicate the righteous.

The Shī`ite Sects

The repressions suffered by the Shī`ites have had a result that might well have been expected. Underground sects and terrorist groups, often outlawed by the main body of the Shī`ites themselves, have continued to form. Some have preyed on whole communities or built states within states; some have seized large areas and ruled them as outlaw kingdoms; others have conspired secretly to annihilate their enemies by poison and dagger. These have, of course, been the violent minority.

Let us begin with the less extreme sects. In order to do so without too much confusion, the reader is invited to consider the chart or tree (Figure 18.2) on p. 568, which shows the family relationship of the successors of `Alī, who figure so largely in the thoughts of the Shī`ite world.

Following down the extreme left side of this chart, we find the three general groups that form the Shī`ite sects. A discussion of each follows.

A. The Zaidites (Zaydis)

The Zaidites are the Shī`ites who approximate most closely the traditionalist (Sunnite) position. They differ with the other sects in considering Zaid (see chart) as the fifth imām instead of Muḥammad al-Bāqir, the fifth imām of the other sects. The Zaidites did not realize that they were a separate sect until the time of Ja`far al-Sādiq and have quite generally shied away from the

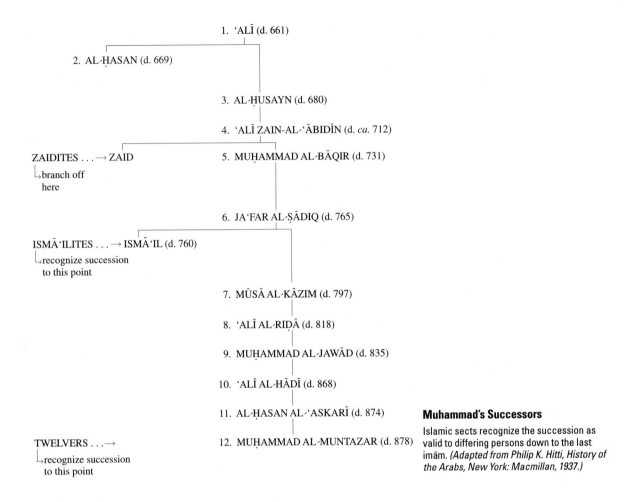

1. 'ALĪ (d. 661)

2. AL-ḤASAN (d. 669)

3. AL-ḤUSAYN (d. 680)

4. 'ALĪ ZAIN-AL-'ĀBIDĪN (d. *ca.* 712)

ZAIDITES . . . → ZAID

↳branch off
  here

5. MUḤAMMAD AL-BĀQIR (d. 731)

6. JA'FAR AL-ṢĀDIQ (d. 765)

ISMĀ'ILITES . . . → ISMĀ'IL (d. 760)

↳recognize succession
  to this point

7. MŪSĀ AL-KĀZIM (d. 797)

8. 'ALĪ AL-RIDĀ (d. 818)

9. MUḤAMMAD AL-JAWĀD (d. 835)

10. 'ALĪ AL-HĀDĪ (d. 868)

11. AL-ḤASAN AL-'ASKARĪ (d. 874)

TWELVERS . . . →

↳recognize succession
  to this point

12. MUḤAMMAD AL-MUNTAZAR (d. 878)

Muhammad's Successors

Islamic sects recognize the succession as valid to differing persons down to the last imām. *(Adapted from Philip K. Hitti, History of the Arabs, New York: Macmillan, 1937.)*

principle of the *nass,* especially if it is interpreted as having a supernatural significance. It is typical for them to assert that 'Alī, not having been designated as the first caliph by Muḥammad, freely gave Abū Bakr and 'Umar his allegiance when they were chosen, and therefore these two caliphs are not cursed in the Friday prayers. Some of them execrate 'Uthmān for being an Ummayyad who displaced 'Alī as the third caliph, but not all of the Zaidites feel the same resentment, though all agree that the Ummayyads who succeeded 'Alī were usurpers of the lowest kind: they were and are accursed. As a force in history, the Zaidites have maintained a dynasty (now on the point of extinction) since the ninth century in Yemen (south Arabia), and in the past have had dynasties for periods varying from

sixty to two hundred years in Tabaristan, Dailan, Gilan, and Morocco.

B. The Twelvers (Ithnā`Ashari)

The sect of the Twelvers claims the great majority of the Shī'ites as members. They get their name from reckoning from the twelfth imām, Muḥammad al-Muntazar. This imām is of great importance to them. They say that in 878 C.E., he "disappeared" or "withdrew" into the cave of the great mosque at Samarra, up the river from Baghdad. Being only five years of age, he left no issue, but the Twelvers refused to believe that Allāh could have let the divinely instituted line of imāms come to an end. The twelfth imām therefore had simply gone into concealment; he had withdrawn from human sight until the fullness of the time when he would return as the Mahdī, "the divinely guided one," who will usher in a period of righteousness and peace before the end of the world and the last judgment.

A widely accepted ḥadīth declares that Muḥammad prophesied there would come in the last days a man of his own family who would do this. He would be known as the Mahdī. The Shī'ites seized upon the phrase "of his own family" and made the prophecy apply to the 'Alīds, which meant the Imāms. But another ḥadīth contradicts all this with the saying, "There is no Mahdī but Jesus the Son of Mary!"[3]

Shī'ites maintain that the "concealed imām," while remaining in his hidden state where death cannot touch him, never leaves his waiting followers without guidance. He has selected representatives on earth to lead them for him. In Persia (now Iran), where almost the whole population of about forty million is Shī'ite (and Twelver) and where Islam has been since the beginning of the sixteenth century the religion of the state, the shāhs were once regarded as such representatives and possessed therefore of special inspired insight. During the last two centuries, however, this claim has not been made officially, much to their disadvantage politically; in fact, the most recent shah lost support so completely that a revolution deposed him. We shall see later that Islamic opponents considered his pressing for a Western-styled modernization of Iran, not only unacceptable but cruel and oppressive.

C. The Ismāʻīlites (Seveners) and Their Offshoots

After the Twelvers of Iran and the Zaidites of Yemen, the next largest body of Shī'ites are the Ismā'īlites (*Ismā'īlis*), found chiefly in India, Pakistan, and East Africa; smaller groups are in Syria, Lebanon, and Yemen. The Ismā'īlites are so called because they have remained loyal to Ismā'īl, the first son of the sixth imām. After being designated by his father as the next imām (by the *nass*), Ismā'īl was set aside for his younger brother when his father was told of his drunkenness. But the Ismā'īlites refused to believe the accusation against their favorite. They considered that the father must have yielded to a slanderous attack that was false, for Ismā'īl, as imām-designate, and

therefore already infallible and sinless, simply could not have been guilty of the charge against him. The fact that Ismā'īl was reported to have died (760 C.E.) five years before his father excited the Ismā'īlites even more. They concluded that he was not dead, but hidden: he would come again as the Mahdī. (Some admitted that he did die, but left a son, Muḥammad ibn-Ismā'īl, who "disappeared" in India and would return as the Mahdī.) In their fervid belief, Ismā'īl was the very incarnation of God himself and would soon return. To find support for these views in the Qur'ān, they began to interpret it allegorically and arrived at a kind of hidden Gnostic doctrine so esoteric that they spread it only through secret missionary activity directed to other Gnostic adepts. (For example, the universe was seen in cycles of sevens: seven "speaking" Messengers bringing scriptures [Muḥammad being the last] and then seven "silent" Imāms, who in a sense ranked even higher because their revelations came directly from God rather than through angels.) When apprehended and questioned about such esoteric doctrines, some Ismā'īlites resorted to concealment of their faith by *taqīya*, or momentary denial of their actual convictions.

This aspect of Ismā'īlite activity attracted groups disposed to rebellion, especially refractory Mawālī with Persian, Christian, and Jewish backgrounds, disinclined to accept the prevailing Sunnī line or to respect the authority of the caliphate. Some startling political effects resulted. Sporadic sectional revolts broke the general calm. The forces of the central government had to be called upon to suppress these insurrections, and were occasionally held at bay.

Qarmatians, Assassins, and Druzes

A few examples of movements having long-term effects may be cited. A secret Ismā'īlite society organized along communistic lines, whose members were called *Qarmatians*, was formed near the head of the Persian Gulf and spread into Arabia. (Some settled in Syria independently.) They were founded toward the close of the ninth century, presumably by a certain Hamdān Qarmaṭ, from whom they took their name. After fighting off the government forces, they set up a rebel state encompassing all of eastern Arabia from the borders of Iraq to the Yemen, where they maintained themselves successfully against the caliphs at Baghdad, and in one remarkable and hair-raising sortie dared to capture and loot Mecca during the pilgrimage season! In this astonishing assault on the holy city, they carried off the Black Stone and returned it after twenty years only because the Fāṭimid (fellow-Ismāʻīlite) caliph, the powerful al-Manṣūr of Egypt, requested it. The Qarmatians cut the roads from Iraq to Mecca, and pilgrims over these routes either paid heavily for the privilege or were turned back. Before they finally fell, the Qarmatians set a record of a century of revolutionary violence and bloodshed.

Actually less dangerous but even more dreaded were the mysterious *Assassins,* who, as exponents of what they called "the new propaganda," developed to a high point the terrorist art of worming one's way in disguise into the presence of Muslim rulers and officials and striking them down with a poisoned dagger. It did not matter how public the occasion was—the Friday prayers at the mosque, the holding of court by a prince or king—the more people present, the better. The terrorist aimed and struck and was himself struck down, or else seized and put to death after torture, but he endured all in the confident expectation of going directly to paradise, the promised reward he was seeking.

The founder and first grand master of this order was Ḥasan Ṣabbāh (d. 1124 C.E.), probably a Persian, though he claimed descent from a line of kings in south Arabia. It was he who had the inspiration to seize the mountain stronghold of Alamūt, in Persia, perched on a high narrow ledge of rock three-quarters of a mile long and several hundred feet wide, which he and his men fortified so expertly that it remained impregnable for two centuries. Here they supported themselves by their own farming and gardening of the land beneath the heights of their fortress. By sorties in force from their mountain fortress, the Assassins captured other strongholds in northern Persia, and by sending missionaries into northern Syria, they also were able to start a vigorous movement there, which eventually led to the establishment of a powerful mountain kingdom with ten or more fortresses in the order's hands. It was here that the Crusaders came to know and fear them, and to be in awe of their leader Rashīd al-Sinān, whose title "shaykh al-jabal" was translated for them into "the Old Man of the Mountain."

Another aberrant Ismāʻili movement, that of the *Druzes* of the Lebanon Mountains, was the result of the missionary efforts of al-Darazi (from whom the Druzes take their name) in the eleventh century. He persuaded these mountain dwellers that the Fāṭimid (Egyptian) Caliph al-Ḥākim, who mysteriously disappeared, was the last and most perfect of ten successive incarnations of God and would return as Mahdī. It is said that the Druzes, who have formed a closed society for centuries, and blend Jewish and Christian elements with their faith, number today some one hundred thousand in several separate locations.

Among sects that have blended Islamic and Christian elements, the ʻAlawites, or Nusayrīs, of northwest Syria should be mentioned. Sunnī sources sometimes classify them with the Ismāʻili-rooted Assassins and Druzes on the grounds of sharing "exaggeration" (*ghuluw*) in doctrine, but their views were actually grounded in the Twelver "concealed imam" concept. In Muḥammad ibn Nusayr, a contemporary of the Tenth Imam, they find a "gateway" (*bab*) to the Mahdī. The crusades, eastern Orthodoxy, and French influences contributed to an outlook deifying ʻAlī in a trinitarian mode. Today they number somewhat less than one million adherents. President Hafiz Assad of Syria and President Saddam Hussein of Iraq have their roots in areas of ʻAlawite strength.

Modern Moderates: Mustaʻlīs, Nizārīs

The majority of Ismāʻilites today, perhaps between one and two million, are moderates who have drawn closer to the mainstream of Islam. Offshoots of the Assassins, most of them came from Persia into India and Pakistan, and some resettled from there into East Africa. Of their two sects, *Mustaʻlīs* and *Nizārīs,* (named for two sons of the eleventh-century Caliph al-Mustansir), the Nizārīs are better known in the West as followers of the Aga Khan. The hereditary title "Aga Khan" (Chief Commander) was first bestowed on the forty-sixth Ismāʻili Imam, Hasan ʻAlī Shāh, by the Shāh of Persia in 1818. Later he revolted against the Shāh and joined with the British in the conquest of Sind, settling finally in Bombay on a British pension. His grandson, the Aga Khan III (Aga Sultan Sir Mohammed Shah), was a distinguished diplomat who

The Royal Badshadi Mosque in Lahore, Pakistan
This handsome Mosque was built for the Mughal ruler Aurangzeb in the seventeenth century. To save the pavement from soiling, Pilgrims proceed to the mosque on marked walkways. *(Courtesy of the United Nations.)*

served as president of the All-India Muslim League and later became India's representative to the League of Nations. In 1937, he was elected president of the League. Some Westerners knew him only by the facts that his followers supported him by contributing his weight in gold, diamonds, and platinum; that his thoroughbreds won the English Derby five times; and that his playboy son Aly Khan excited international society pages with marriages to the daughter of the third Baron Churston and to Hollywood actress Rita Hayworth.

The Aga Khan III encouraged his followers to cooperate with each other in such enterprises as banks, insurance companies, and organizations for social welfare. At his wish, the Imāmate bypassed his son Aly and went to his Harvard-educated grandson, installed as the Aga Khan IV in 1957. The present incumbent has continued his grandfather's interests in business and philanthropy and has urged his followers to take citizenship in the countries where they reside and to enter the mainstreams of community life. In India, many Ismā'īlis, known as *Bhojas,* had long ago accommodated to local caste custom, but they still have no mosques and follow worship practices quite different from those of other Muslims in their *jamā'at khānahs* ("gathering houses").

The greatest achievement of the Ismā'īlis was their establishment of dominance over a major country for two centuries. We have previously mentioned the *Fāṭimid Caliphate* of Egypt (see p. 551). This regime, claiming for its caliphs descent from the Prophet's daughter Fāṭima, came to power in North Africa, conquered Egypt, founded and built Cairo, including its great mosque, al-Azhar, and at its peak controlled, from its power base in Egypt, North Africa, Sicily, Palestine, Syria, and both shores of the Red Sea, including Mecca and Medina. The Fāṭimids claimed that they were by descent and by the *nass* infallible imāms and the only legitimate caliphs in Islam; therefore, the Sunnī ʿAbbāssids were usurpers who should be driven from power, hence, their interest in and long-attempted control of Syria. But it was in Syria that they met their most serious reverses and were never able to get to Baghdad. When the tide had irreversibly turned against them, the last of the Fāṭimids was unseated by Saladin, himself a Kurd and a Sunnite, who as nominal *wazir* of Egypt commanded the army of Egypt that encircled the Crusaders by sealing off Syria and retaking Jerusalem. (Egypt is prevailingly Sunnite to this day.)

II. FURTHER DEVELOPMENTS

Ṣūfī Dervish Orders

As we have seen, the Ṣūfī movement, after observing in Syria the advantage of certain types of Christian organization, gave rise to the nearest approach in Islam to church worship and ecclesiastical organization. Under masters or guides, the devotees of Ṣūfī mystical experiences drew apart into retreats or monastic houses, to live fraternally in something like communal societies and to enjoy social fellowship along with their mystical raptures. Those who began a wandering life, dependent on charity, came to be called "dervishes" (from the Persian *darwīsh,* "poor"). Because of their distinctive dress, their begging baskets (though not all dervishes beg), and their known addiction to ecstatic experiences, they excited great interest.

The poets celebrated them, some in fun, others to pay them grave respect. The "nightingale of Shīrāz," the poet Saʿdī, believed in the dervishes, and himself practiced meditation with them, but he warned them that a dervish is not made such by his clothes.

> The dervish's course of life is spent in commemorating, and thanking, and serving, and obeying God; and in beneficence and contentment; and in the acknowledgement of one God and reliance on Him; and in resignation and patience. Everyone

who is endued with these qualities is, in fact, a dervish, though dressed in a tunic. But a babbler, who neglects prayer, and is given to sensuality, and the gratification of his appetite; who spends his days till nightfall in the pursuit of licentiousness, and passes his night till day returns in careless slumber; eats whatever is set before him, and says whatever comes uppermost; is a profligate, though he wear the habit of a dervish.[16]

Since the twelfth century, a large and far-flung number of dervish orders or brotherhoods have been founded, each with its own monastic retreats or houses, special rites, and methods of inducing ecstasy. The Qādariya is the first of these orders. Founded in Baghdad by ʿAbd-al-Qādir al-Jīlānī (1077–1166), it has spread, thinly to be sure, to Java in the East and Algeria in the West. The so-called Howling Dervishes (the Rifāʿiya) came next, being founded in the second half of the twelfth century by Aḥmad al-Rifāʿī. The widely known Whirling Dervishes (the Maulawīya) are members of an order founded by disciples of the Persian poet Jalāl al-Dīn Rūmī, whom we have quoted on a previous page (p. 560), and who bequeathed to his followers not his verses only but also, to accompany them, a method of using music as an important and a stimulating element in their rites, whereby they were made to whirl about in ecstasy.

The more extreme of the dervishes have turned out to be little more than shamans. They astonish the pious, in the manner of their Hindu prototypes, by swallowing live coals and snakes and by passing needles, hooks, and knives through their flesh. Many wear special badges, use rosaries, and venerate the founders of their orders as saints.

The dervish orders parallel the Franciscans of Europe in admitting lay members, who live and work in the world but have stated times, usually in the evening, when they come to the monasteries to take part in religious exercises directed by a leader.

It should be added that though the sort of dervishes who have whirled, howled, or lashed themselves into frenzy by using whips or knives have given dervishes as a group much notoriety, the majority are content to practice their quiet devotional life in the fellowship of their houses and do not show themselves often in public. Their popular following has been

Dervish

often quite large, for in medieval times, for most people, the Ṣūfī orders *were* religion in its most sincere form.

Veneration of Saints

The earlier mention of the practice by dervish orders of the veneration of their founders as saints brings before us another variation on the standard Muslim themes, the veneration of saints. In early Muslim literature, the name *walī* (pl. *awliyā*) is given to persons who are "near or close in feeling." In a religious context, the term comes to mean "friend of God," or "one who is near to God," as in Qur'ān X.64. But the Ṣūfīs made *walī* mean "saint," that is, a person possessed by God. R. A. Nicholson, in *The Mystics of Islam,* shows how human and natural this was: the walī conversing with a small circle of friends became first a teacher and spiritual guide gathering disciples around him during his lifetime, and finally the sainted head of a religious order bearing his name. But saints are not exclusively Ṣūfī. The Muslim world has produced them everywhere, as the long list of saints in Baghdad ("the city of saints"), Turkey (where each province had a saint), Arabia, Egypt, North Africa, and India attests. These saints have usually been placed in a hierarchical order differing slightly with the area. Those who are on earth are not always apparent or known even to themselves (hundreds live "hidden" in the world),

whereas those who know one another and act together are arranged in an ascending order of merit, with decreasing numbers on the higher levels, until at the top or pole of the hierarchy stands the figure of the greatest saint of his age or time. Saints are sometimes distinguished from prophets, the holy proclaimers of the word of God; their special merit is to experience the ecstasy of union with God and afterward to exhibit God in their own persons. In doing so, particularly those associated with the Ṣūfīs and the dervish orders are often credited with performing miracles (*karāmāt,* "favors" that God bestows), such as flying through the air, walking on water, being in several places at once, resurrecting the dead, turning earth into gold or jewels, and the like.

Although the practice is not Qur'ānic, the Ṣūfīs and the common people, fairly generally throughout the Muslim world, visit the tombs of Muslim saints to leave votive offerings, pray for the intercession of the saints, and ask their blessing (*baraka*) upon them personally. Many of these tombs are found in the vicinity of mosques and may quite often be surrounded by the graves of those whose last wish it was to be buried nearby. Of course, to worship the sainted dead is in direct conflict with the spirit, if not the letter, of the Qur'ān, but most of the 'ulamā' have tolerated and even joined in it, because the consensus of the community (ijmā') has almost everywhere overridden the objections of the critics.

The Feasts and Festivals of the Muslim Year

Although the Sunnīs, Ṣūfīs, and Shī'ites have tended at certain points to differ to the extent of irreconcilability, it must be said that powerful unitive forces have always been at work. Chief is the Qur'ān itself, and running a close second are the Five Pillars, especially the observance of the five daily times of prayer and the pilgrimage to Mecca. Not far behind in bringing a sense of overall unity to the Muslim world are the recurring feasts and festivals of the Muslim year. They were gradually developed through the centuries to a total of five. (Five plays a role in Islam comparable to three in Christianity.) These feasts and festivals are observed differently in the various Muslim lands, but they have a common intention.

The feasts are two:

1. The so-called "little feast" at the end of the fast of Ramaḍān, called *'Id al-Fiṭr*. It is the occasion of great merriment and occurs on the first day of the month Shawwāl.

2. The Feast of Sacrifice (*Id al-Aḍḥā*), or the "great feast." It falls on the day (the tenth of the month Dhū-al-Ḥijja) when the pilgrims outside of Mecca have returned halfway from the Great Pilgrimage and are making a feast of sacrifice by ritually offering the allowed animals and joining in a joyous sharing of their flesh (p. 546f.).

The festivals are three:

1. The New Year Festival (*Muḥarram*), observed during the first days of the first month. The Shī'ites take this occasion to commemorate the death of al-Ḥusayn and his little son in the night battle of Karbalā; they do so by dedicating the first ten days to lamentation, at the end of which a passion play (*ta'ziya*) is performed with much attention to the suffering and death of the son and grandson of 'Alī.

It could be said that whereas the celebration of the New Year throughout the Muslim world is unitive, this particular observance is divisive, for the "passion play" of the Shī'ites magnifies the tragedy of Karbalā' and perpetuates its memory. The story of the assault which caused the death of Ḥusayn's son by a flying arrow, the slaying of a nephew by mutilation by the sword, and Ḥusayn's own death and mutilation under the hooves of horses is dramatically reenacted, its effects heightened by amplifications bringing in angels, prophets, and kings. Also stressed are such peculiarly Shī'ite assertions as the preexistence of Muḥammad (who is said to have designated 'Alī as his rightful successor some days before he "went back to heaven"), the divine powers and attributes of 'Alī, and the savior roles of Ḥasan and Ḥusayn, the latter portrayed, like Christ, as vicariously atoning by his death for the sins of mankind. Little wonder that Shī'ites, particularly in Iran (see p. 585), have at times been so aroused that they have rioted in vengeful fury, not without the sympathy of non-Shī'ite witnesses of the dramatic episodes.

2. The Festival of the Prophet's Birthday (*Mawlid an-Nabī*), held traditionally on the twelfth day of the month Rabī'al-awwal. (In point of time, this is the last of the festivals to be evolved.)

3. The Festival of the Prophet's Night Journey (*Lailat al-Mir'āj*), during which he passed through the heavens, observed as a rule on the night preceding the twenty-seventh day of the month Rajab. Mosques and minarets are lighted in honor of the famous "night journey," and the ḥadīths concerning the event are reverentially read.

III. ISLAM AND CULTURE

Of necessity, all of the world's religions, whether formative or reformative, emerged from a preexistent culture, and depending on their relative success in winning assent, have partially or totally affected the cultural milieu from which they emerged or to which they spread. They have had stimulating effects not only on religious thought and literature but also on secular prose and poetry, architecture, music, painting, sculpture, social patterns, and politics. In the case of Islam, these developments need to be pointed out to the Western reader, because the cultural effects Islam has had on the many lands to which it has spread have, in Western minds, been overshadowed by the literary ascendancy of the Qur'ān; consequently, the former have not been given their rightful place in histories of universal culture. We shall look briefly at both aspects of Islam's cultural impact.

But first it is interesting to mark the suddenness with which Islam's cultural history began. A rapidly expanding religion, it did not remain in its own land, as Hinduism, Daoism, and Confucianism remained for centuries in theirs; nor did it spread beyond the place of its origin by a long process of converting others to its faith, as did Buddhism, or by its adherents being dispersed, as were the Jews. Like European Christianity, it made its way both by conversion and by the military and political successes of its adherents; but unlike its European rival, which took centuries to reach its high watermark, it came with a rush out of Arabia and in a very short time overspread a vast domain, where it radically affected a variety of cultures.

The Literary Effects of the Qur'ān and Its Language

The Qur'ān has not only been the religious and moral standard by which Muslims have lived; its language, Arabic, has had the place in Islam that Latin has had in Roman Catholicism. As a result, Arabic is the liturgical language of Islam; and to the degree that it is used in mosques all over the world, it aids in the Arabization that unites Muslims of many different tongues.

In the early days of Islam, naturally enough the ḥadīths, commentaries on the Qur'ān, biographies of the Prophet, and other religious works were written in Arabic. Secular poetry and prose, when they were allowed a public role, followed suit. Furthermore, Plato, Aristotle, Hippocrates, Galen and other non-Muslim writers were translated into Arabic (and were incidentally thus preserved for retranslation).

It thus became the general rule in the western half of Islam, from Baghdad to Cordoba, for all serious writings to appear in Arabic, the international language of Muslim scholars. It was the accepted language for the "religious sciences" that set out to explain and interpret the basic Arabic works; and it was as well the language for the "instrumental sciences": *falāsifa* (philosophy), astronomy, medicine, mathematics, chemistry, and so on.

The Christian West came to be grateful for these Arabic writings. When the Muslim conquests had ended and the Mediterranean basin ceased to be in turmoil (from "barbarian" or northern as well as from Muslim or eastern invasions and raids), the Christian West found itself far less informed than were the Muslim lands about Plato, Aristotle, medicine, mathematics, astronomy, and science generally. The West was alerted to the riches of Muslim science, philosophy, and culture during the Crusades and through contact with Muslims in southern Italy and Sicily; but from the eleventh to thirteenth centuries, the chief sources of knowledge of "the wisdom of the ancients and the East" (knowledge of which initiated the Italian Renaissance) were the schools and scholars of Muslim Spain. Jews were to a great degree the intermediaries

A Page from the Qur'ān in North African Script

This page is from a manuscript dated about 1300 C.E. and written in decorative script on parchment. It is more typical of Arabic characters in general than the Kufic script seen on p. 543. *(Courtesy of the Metropolitan Museum of Art, Rogers Fund, 1942. 42.63.)*

when the old Greek philosophic and scientific texts were retranslated from Arabic into Latin and thus "recovered." But beyond this the considerable contributions of Muslim science and philosophy also were discovered. By rendering this service, the Muslim world greatly stimulated the development of Western thought.

Arabic, in its classical, or written, as distinguished from its dialect, forms, has continued to the present as the preferred language of Muslim scholarship. Although, as we shall see, Persian, Turkish, and other literatures developed within the overall Islamic framework, they never became independent and autonomous as did works in the Romance languages that evolved out of Latin into independence, because Arabic has retained its character as a sacred language, the language by which God revealed himself to Muḥammad. Nor is this all: Arabic has been not only a liturgical and sacred language but also one in which Muslims have done much of their thinking.

Architecture, Painting, and Other Art Forms

Any visitor to Islamic lands is immediately aware of an outstanding architectural feature clearly indicative of the presence of Islam—the mosque. In general plan it still resembles Muḥammad's mosque in Medina, long since gone. After his time, highly trained builders and artisans of the conquered territories provided the structural and decorative skills that have added domes, minarets, columns, arcades, porticoes, wall tiles, mosaics, and other adaptations from Byzantine, Persian, Coptic, and central Asian structures. Three surviving mosques from the earlier centuries are world famous: the Dome of the Rock in Jerusalem, the Ummayyad mosque in Damascus, and the al-Azhar in Cairo. Magnificent palaces, forts, and mausoleums are other representative achievements of Muslim architecture, the best-known palace being the Alhambra in Granada, Spain, and the supreme example of a mausoleum being the Taj Mahal at Agra, India, commonly regarded as fully comparable with the Parthenon at Athens.

One form of Muslim art has provided the English language with the term *arabesque;* it refers to an architectural detail carved in wood or stone, usually an ornament or design of leaves, fruits, or flowers intertwined. Typical of Muslim interior decoration, it vies for favor with flat designs inlaid with colored stones or with metals such as silver, copper, and gold; painted lusterware and colorful enameled masterpieces of the potter's art; wall tiles; and carpets woven in exquisite designs (the famous "Persian rugs"). All of these were produced in abundance from central Asia to Spain and are prized possessions of many Western museums.

Muslim calligraphy and painting have attained a similar classic rank. Manuscripts with illuminated lettering and paintings in red, yellow, and blue provide brilliant examples of this art form. In Persia, the art of painting reached a peak in the fifteenth century, when Bihzād, the most imitated painter in Islamic art, pursued his career in Herat and Tabrīz, Persia. He and his followers set a high example for the Mughal and Rajput (Hindu) artists of India in later centuries. Subjects in Islamic painting range from luxuriant landscapes with human and animal figures to battle scenes with horses and elephants.

Perso-Muslim Literature

In due time, poetry and prose of a secular and often highly romantic and erotic character appeared in Persian (in the Arabic script). The reasons for their appearance were complex. It was natural, for one thing, to use the vernacular in conveying ideas to Persians not in a *mawālī* (client) relationship with Arab tribes but belonging to the *shuʿūbiyya* ("confederates" of the Arabs as a whole). They were in a sense still foreigners, even though they had embraced Islam, and they constantly used and were proud of their own language and of their past. They could communicate freely in Persian and were even a little defiant in doing so. Some Muslim writers refer here to the "quarrel (or revolt) of the Shuʿūbiyya." But "quarrel" does not account for all of the facts. In addition to the prompting of propriety that led to the use of Persian rather than Arabic for the earthy love lyrics that were composed, sheer creativity had a part to play. A talented line of court poets appeared from the tenth to the fourteenth centuries to delight and entertain the Persian-speaking princes who had asserted their autonomy when the ʿAbāssid caliphate weakened and self-governing states appeared (see p. 551). The blind poet Rūdakī, "the father of Persian poetry," came at the turn of the tenth century. It was natural for Firdawsī after him to compose in Persian his powerful national epic, the *Shāhnāma*, glorifying the exploits of Rustam, the doughty warrior-hero who unknowingly killed his heroic son Suhrab, in a tragic tale known to every school child of Iran. Nizami followed in his steps when he wrote the long epic about the star-crossed lovers Layla and Majnun and four other long poems.

Shīʿism had an Arabic origin, and many of its great writers preferred Arabic, but when the Shīʿite masses in Iran were addressed in their *rowza* assemblies with poems, hymns, and *taʿziya* dramas dealing with the martyrdoms of ʿAlī and Ḥusayn, the language was almost necessarily Persian.

As to the Ṣūfīs, from the tenth century onward they expressed their mysticism and their earthly and

The Taj Mahal, Agra, India
Erected by Shah Jahan in memory of his wife, this marble mausoleum is considered by many the most perfect building in the world. Only the Greek Parthenon is compared with it. The Shah had planned to build an exact duplicate in black marble as his own mausoleum. There is poignancy in the fact that he was overthrown by his son and spent his last nine years imprisoned in quarters from which the only view was of the vacant site. *(Courtesy of the Government of India Tourist Office. Information Service of India.)*

heavenly love in the kind of poetry to which the Persian language has been so suited. Although they poured their Persian into Arabic molds, they altered the borrowed verse forms in composing their odes (*qaṣīdas*), lyrics (*ghazals*), and quatrains (*rubā'is*), the last being employed in the *Rubāiyat* by Umar Khayyam. The master poets Sa'dī, Ḥāfiz, and Rūmī, whose mystic lyrics and "Qur'ān of Persia" we have quoted elsewhere, and Jāmī after them, made Persian poetry famous from the Euphrates to the Ganges. (In India, it became a mark of culture to be able to read and write in Persian.)

As for Persian prose, although it was used for scholarly writing, it also took the form of a brilliant fictional and anecdotal literature, which culminated in Sa'dī's *Gulistān* generally considered the masterpiece of Persian prose—witty, humorous, full of anecdotes and moral maxims extolling the religious life.

If space permitted, we could consider the rich Turko-Muslim culture and look into the considerable literatures in Albanian, Berber, Swahili, Somali, Urdu, Panjabi, Bengali, Tamil, Malay, Javanese, and other languages—a literary field prolific in insights into the diversity of the Muslim world and its cultures.

IV. ISSUES IN THE MODERN PERIOD

That Islam has continued in the more recent past to give rise to powerful new movements within itself—movements even of a disruptive kind—is plain in the history of the last two centuries. These movements may generally be said, on analysis, to emphasize in various degrees purification, secularism, conservatism, reformulation, nationalism, and in at least one heretical development, syncretism (the mingling of elements from different religions).

Conservatism and Purification

The prime instance of the first form of Islamic self-searching is the *purification* begun in inner Arabia in the eighteenth century—the Wahhābī movement, a stern puritan reform that grew to great strength through the support of the emirs of the house of Saʿud. It represented a return to earlier Ḥanbalite theories of conduct and was greatly influenced by the anti-Ṣūfism of the fourteenth-century writer Ibn Taymīya. The movement took its name from its originator Muhammad ibn ʿAbd al-Wahhāb, whose aim was to lead Muslims in a return to Muḥammad and the Qurʾān. To this end he rejected all modifications of Muslim belief and practice traced to "the consensus of community opinion" (ijmāʿ), except for those that went back authentically to the Medina community immediately after the death of Muḥammad. "Ṣūfī innovations" were especially frowned upon. Accordingly, the Wahhābīs condemned all blood feuds and tribal distinctions and urged the utmost purity and simplicity of life, without wine or tobacco. Through the years they have firmly emphasized Muslim unitarianism, and so fierce has been their rejection of Ṣūfī-inspired intercessory prayers at the tombs and shrines of holy men and women (which they denounce as saint worship, and therefore polytheism) that when they temporarily captured Mecca in 1806, they destroyed the tombs before which pilgrims did reverence. Again, in the period 1924–1925, when Mecca and Medina were ceded to Saʿūdi Arabia, they turned the birthplace of Muḥammad himself into a camel's resting place and demolished the markers on the graves of Muḥammad's family and of his companions. To accept as true any belief not confirmed by the Qurʾān, the authentic ḥadīths, or strict (conservative) reasoning, was an act of infidelity. Houses and clothes were to be plain; joking, music, and gold ornaments were forbidden. Such games as chess were to be given up, because they might make the players forget the hours of prayer.

The Ṣūfīs, however, have had too great a measure of support among the common people to worry over much because the Wahhābīs assailed them. In the name of long-corroborated religious experience, they have continued to uphold the validity of personal religious response, intuition, and practices of their religious orders, and reverence for sainted leaders. This has been true especially in the non-Arab areas and particularly among the Berbers, Iranians, and Turks. But the Ṣūfīs have been chastened by Wah-

hābī puritanism and orthodoxy; in fact, they have abandoned many a practice to which they were once devoted.

Western Cultural Influence

When most of Africa and much of Asia came under the rule of the European powers, it was inevitable that Western books and periodicals, Western-sponsored schools and academies, and still more the colonial administrations themselves, with all of the political and economic changes that accompanied them, should introduce new concepts of law and political organization, new forms of commercial and industrial enterprise, new modes of transport by land, sea, and air, improvements in agriculture, scientific medicine, and never-before-dreamed-of wealth through the exploitation of newly discovered natural resources, particularly oil.

Secularism

The most startling changes toward secularization occurred in Turkey. There secularism reached an open form. The Young Turks, led by Muṣṭaphā Kemāl, overthrew the Ottoman caliphate in 1924 and went on to revolutionary changes that were openly designed to Westernize and secularize Turkey. The separation of "church" and state was inaugurated by the abolition of the Sharīʿa-oriented religious courts and the establishment of civil courts to preside over the application of new laws affecting marriage, divorce, the rights of women, education, and public conduct in general. The wearing of the *fez* by men and the veil by women was prohibited, and European dress was encouraged. Laws were passed to replace Arabic with Turkish in religious ceremonies and the Arabic script with the Latin alphabet in the public prints. The effect was to remove Turkey from close interrelationships with the rest of the Muslim world and turn it toward the West.

But after World War II a "revaluation of Islam" took place in Turkey. The state introduced state-regulated religious instruction into the educational system (with no intention of reuniting church and state); and villagers and their imāms were allowed to persist in rejecting translations of the Qurʾān into Turkish and continuing the use of Arabic in recitations of the Qur'ān and in ritual prayers, both in the mosque and in private homes.

Between 1987 and 1995, the Islamic Welfare Party in Turkey tripled its percentage at the polls from 7 percent to 21 percent under the leadership of Necmettin Erbakan. It was unclear how much of the vote represented core support for the Islamist program and how much was simply protest against corruption in the previous government. With the cooperation of the preceding Prime Minister Tansu Ciller and her secular True Path Party, Erbakan was able to put together a coalition government, but his efforts to inch toward an Islamist agenda provoked constitutional challenges from the National Security Council, leading to a bloodless coup and a new government under the secularist Yesut Yilmaz in July 1997. The Islamic Welfare Party was banned, constitutional rules against head scarves were reinstated, required time in secular state schools was extended from five to eight years, and external financial support for religious schools was outlawed.

Modernism and Reformulation

During the last hundred years, Egypt has been the scene of religious and political developments that have had great importance in Muslim eyes. The revival of Egyptian influence began with the untiring efforts of Jamāl al-Dīn al-Afghānī (1839–1897), the founder of the pan-Islamic movement, to unite the Muslims against European domination and to incite them to rid themselves of religious and social departures from a pure Islam and thus enable them to meet the challenge of the European world. But a certain ambiguity attended his total stance. On the one hand, he called upon Muslims to oppose the West politically and to go back to early Islam religiously; on the other hand, he urged them to democratize the Muslim states and prove a match for the West by cultivating modern science and philosophy. Concentrating on the latter objective, his disciple, Muhammad 'Abduh (1849–1905), a teacher and later a member of the administrative committee of the old University of Cairo (al-Azhar), urged not only the necessity of renewed study of the classical Arabic theological works but also the introduction into the university curriculum of courses in modern science, geography, and European history

and religion. He was resolved to take seriously the orthodox position that reason cannot contradict revelation but can only confirm it. Reason is, moreover, of decisive importance not only in moral conduct and the quest of happiness, to which all men and women are entitled, but also in the understanding of the principles of the Qur'ān.

One of the consequences of his teaching has been the strengthening of tendencies toward a "modernism" that advocates a reformulation of Muslim doctrines and laws using modern as opposed to traditional language. But, on the other hand, his return, in the spirit of Wahhābism, to Muhammad and the traditions of the early Medina community resulted in the formation of a back-to-the-Qur'ān religious group called the Salafīya, led by his Syrian disciple Rashīd Ridā, the editor of a periodical that was read from one end of the Muslim world to the other.

Reformulation in India

Turning now to India before its independence, that is, to a time when British influence was still strong, we find a type of reformulation by a number of the Muslim liberal leaders that recalls that of the Hindu founders of the Brahmo Samaj. The readiness of intellectuals in India through the centuries to consider open-mindedly every variety of thought is reflected in the broad-mindedness of Sir Sayyid Ahmad Khān (1817–1898). He was aided rather than hindered, curiously enough, by the spread of the Wahhābī movement among Indian Muslims, for, as we have seen, its rejection of Sūfī emotionalism and its insistence on a return to Muhammad and the early Medina community gave new importance to reason as a guide in religion. He took his stand on the supreme authority of Muhammad, the Qur'ān, and the early traditions, asserting that both nature and reason confirm any open-minded person in such a stand. Because Allāh has created and supports nature as well as revelation, reason can find no real contradiction between them. Hence, science or the study of nature, when properly pursued, cannot conflict with the Qur'ān but only confirm it. Accordingly, in 1875, Sir Sayyid founded a Muslim Anglo-Oriental College at 'Aligarh (now 'Aligarh University) with a curriculum that accompanied the study of Muslim religion with courses in Western natural and social sciences.

Among the Indian intellectual leaders who were encouraged to take liberal positions influenced by Western thought was Sayyid Amīr Alī, a Shī'ite, whose book *The Spirit of Islam* (first published in 1891 with the title *The Life and Teachings of Mohammad*) defends Islam as a progressive religion based on the perfect moral personality of Muḥammad and the liberalizing teaching of the Qur'ān. He felt that the medieval interpreters of Islam lost this vision of the true character of their faith and hardened its beliefs into too great rigidity. Even so, Islam has been more humane and fundamentally more liberal than Christianity has been. Islam, he said, was "founded on divine love" and has proceeded on the basis of the equality of people in God's sight. This book is a classic among Muslim liberals and is widely used also by conservatives who wish to know what a modernist might believe.

Even more liberal were the lectures delivered in English in 1928 by Sir Muḥammad Iqbāl and published under the title *The Reconstruction of Religious Thought in Islam.* A poet at once cautious of and yet inspired by Ṣūfī mysticism, Iqbāl proposed a reconstruction of Muslim thought in quite nontraditional terms; he stressed the validity of personal religious experience, the immanence of God, human creativity, and the to-be-expected emergence of the superman. He implied that the Western thinkers he cited, such as Bergson, Nietzsche, and Whitehead, were indebted to, if not descendants of, the giants of Muslim philosophy and science, and were therefore fulfilling a promise inherent in Islām itself. He further hoped that the dynamism that marked the spirit of Islām would break through the rigid patterns to which Muslims traditionally clung. Iqbāl also published poetry in Urdu and Persian to express his lyrical views of the freedom of the self and its duty of selflessness toward society.

We should not exaggerate the influence of such intellectuals as these, for we need to be reminded of the words of H. A. R. Gibb, that "the illiterate Muslim, the villager, is in no danger yet of losing his faith, and, even if he were, the educated town-bred modernist would have no word to meet his needs. His spiritual life is cared for by the Ṣūfī brotherhoods, regular or irregular, by the imām of the local mosque, or by the itinerant revivalist preacher."[O]

Multinational Unity: Pan-Islamic Aspirations

Jamāl al-Dīn al-Afghānī, to whom we have already referred as having, whether intentionally or not, encouraged the rise of Muslim modernism, was more directly interested in two political aims that often seemed contradictory: (1) Muslim unity (or Pan-Islamism) and (2) regional reform of governments to ensure the carrying out of the popular will to have autonomy in Muslim-dominated areas. The former aim was universalistic, the latter nationalistic, both being held in an uneasy tension, a tension, however, that corresponded to political realities.

The Muslim historian Fazlur Rahman has put the political realities thus,

> A Turkish, an Egyptian or a Pakistani peasant is a "nationalist" [in the sense of having "a sentiment for a certain community of mores, including language," that gives a sense of regional cohesiveness] and has always been so. But a Turkish, an Egyptian and a Pakistani peasant are also bound by a strong Islamic sentiment. [Their "nationalism"] is not averse to a wider loyalty and, in face of a non-Muslim aggressor (as we have often witnessed during this and the preceding century) the two sentiments make an extraordinary powerful liaison.[P]

Multinational Unity: Pan-Arab Aspirations

The full story of the nominally secular Pan-Arab movement falls beyond the scope of a history of religions, but the intertwining of its interests with those of multinational Islamic movements is obvious, as the 1991 Gulf War demonstrated. The Ba'ath Party (Arab Renaissance Party), strongest in Syria and Iraq, was founded in 1943 by Michel 'Aflaq of Damascus, the son of a Greek Orthodox merchant and two associates, one a Sunnī Muslim and the other an 'Alawite (see p. 570). Their goal was the creation of "One Arab Nation" to be founded upon freedom and socialism and governed by one National Command. Arabs were defined by language and by common "culture," but the latter did *not* include religion. Much was made of the fact that not all Arabs are Muslims and that attempting to include religion as a basis of unity would only lead to disruptions.

By 1966, rivalries between Syrian and Iraqi leadership produced two competing National Commands. In 1982, President Saddam Hussein of Iraq repudiated the One Nation concept: "Iraqis are now of the opinion that Arab unity can only take place after a clear demarcation of borders between all countries." In the 1980s, during his war against Iran (a non-Arab country), Saddam Hussein courted Western support by emphasizing the secular democratic heritage of the Ba'ath movement: his Christian foreign minister, the civil rights enjoyed by Iraqi women, the contrast with the Pan-Islamic ambitions of Iranian Shī'ism, and so on. At the outset of the war with Iran, a bomb thrown at his foreign minister was blamed on the Shī'ite al-Da'wa, and Muḥammad Baqir al-Sadr, "the Khomeini of Iraq," was executed (see pp. 587–588 on Iran).

Ten years later, Saddam Hussein annexed and occupied Kuwait. In the heat of the ensuing Gulf War, he ignored the secular basis of the Ba'ath Party and claimed the role of defender of Islam in a holy war against Zionism and Western interference. Although the governments of a number of predominantly Islamic countries condemned the seizure of Kuwait, it was evident that in many cases the majority of the citizenry applauded Saddam Hussein in such a role even though they were aware of the secular origins of the Ba'ath movement.

We turn now to the development of these national and multinational aspirations in selected regional arenas: North Coastal Africa, Iran, Indonesia, and Pakistan.

V. REGIONAL DEVELOPMENTS

North Coastal Africa

Egypt

Numbering close to 60 million, the Muslims of Egypt are the largest national community of believers in the Arab world. In the nineteenth century, the University of Cairo (al-Azhar) was the intellectual capital of Islam. It was there that Jamāl al-Dīn al-Afghānī and Muḥammad 'Abduh laid the foundations of Islamic modernism and a Pan-Islamic movement. It was also in Egypt that in 1928 an Islamic fundamentalist countermovement, the Muslim Brotherhood, was founded by Hassan al-Banna. The Brotherhood rejected Islamic socialism and other modernizing programs and stood for the full implementation of Islamic law in a unitary religious state. Al-Azhar sheltered militant Muslim Brothers as well as leaders of reform, but the larger part of its influential leadership remained conservative and traditional.

During the period 1900 to 1952, competing efforts to define the role of Islam in an independent Egyptian state produced no theological consensus, but the momentum of common desire to rid the country of British rule carried events forward to results not sought for by any of the Muslim groups. In 1952, a revolution overthrew King Farouk of Egypt and established a military regime. Two years later, Jamāl 'Abd al-Nasir (Nasser) assumed power as president. The Suez Canal was nationalized in 1956, and within a few years the United Arab Republic came into being with Syria and Yemen as partners. Egypt had been freed from the last vestiges of colonial rule, and it appeared that Pan-Arab unity was under way.

What did this mean for Muslim movements? The modernists had succeeded in giving impetus to educational reform, but their specific religious objectives were swamped in the tide of nationalism. They were to see a nominally Islamic socialist state emerge, but it was under a military leadership with which they had little influence. The Muslim Brotherhood, although it had penetrated the military forces at the lower levels and had abetted the harassment of the British, found itself not only unable to control Nasser and his colleagues but actively suppressed. After an unsuccessful assassin named the Brotherhood as his inspiration, it was officially banned in 1954.

The conservative Islamic 'Ulamā' fared little better. Compliant shaykhs at al-Azhar were treated with respect, but the real sources of traditionalist power eroded rapidly. The university came under direct government control, and its traditional curriculum was overwhelmed by expansion into new secular disciplines. Islamic law (Sharī'a) courts were abolished, private religious endowments (awqāf), and all mosques not deemed private were taken over by the government. In the 1960s, grand muftīs (religious advisors) from the university issued pronouncements to smooth the way for government policy: activities as diverse as birth control and lunar exploration were declared to be in accordance with the Qur'ān.

Wars with Israel   Meanwhile, the determined presence of Israel stimulated both cohesive and divisive forces among Muslims. The high hopes generated by the recovery of Suez, the United Nations intervention after the inconclusive 1956 skirmishes, and the creation of the United Arab Republic were soon dashed: the federation fell apart; Israel won a decisive victory in the 1967 war; the Sinai was occupied; and the Suez Canal was blocked. There was widespread soul-searching. If *this* was the will of Allāh, might it not mean that his people had not been good enough Muslims, not totally submitted to his will? This climate, and the coming to power of Anwar Sadat at the death of Nasser in 1970, led to some significant changes.

The new 1971 constitution proclaimed Islam the official state religion, and Sharī'a law was named as "a major source" of legislation. Traditionalists were unsatisfied, however, preferring that it should be *the* source. But in setting a centrist course and gradually diminishing the power of Nasser's Arab Socialist Union Party, Sadat opened the way for more direct Muslim activity in politics.

Proposals made in 1972 for the unification of Egypt and Libya triggered an eager response from Libya's Muammar al-Qaddafi, who intensified propaganda in Egypt for his own egalitarian interpretation of Islam. Rioting and other internal pressures pushed Sadat into crossing the Nile in the brief "1973 War." (The names given to this engagement suggest the religious emotion connected with it. Israelis refer to the "Yom Kippur War," and some Muslims call it the "Ramaḍān War." Egyptian official papers sometimes refer to it simply as "The Crossing.") Creditable Egyptian military performance gave Sadat fresh prestige and helped restore some of the Muslim pride that had been lost in 1967. This new strength made it possible for him to turn away decisively from Libya and enter into a special relationship with more moderate Sa'ūdi Arabia. This brought financial help, but it also increased the influence of conservatives in the 'Ulamā'. The banned Muslim Brotherhood was tacitly allowed to function again, their journal *al-Dawah* resumed publication, and aspects of such causes as the emancipation of women came under renewed criticism.

After a conciliatory trip to Jerusalem in 1977, Sadat joined Menachem Begin of Israel in the historic Camp David agreements during the following year. By this initiative Sadat forfeited leadership in the Arab League and faced intensified criticism at home. In September 1981, he reacted with massive arrests of Muslim, Christian, and secular critics, and a month later he fell fatally wounded in an assassination by members of the conservative Takfir wal Hijra (Repentance and Holy Withdrawal). His successor, Hosni Mubarak, who pledged himself to continue the Camp David peace process, has been perceived as a moderate, open to working with the Palestinian Liberation Organization as well.

Despite the fact that extremist activism continued (there were three assassination attempts in 1987 and a large number of retaliatory arrests), the recent trend has been toward increased participation of Sunnī fundamentalist Muslims in the mainstream of Egyptian life. The Muslim Brotherhood (*al-Ikwan al-Muslimun*), still officially outlawed as a political party, has been "allowed" to support candidates since the 1987 elections under the cover of secular parties, and it now comprises the largest faction in the opposition's third of the People's Assembly. The government's National Democratic Party (NDP) holds a two-thirds majority. Recent low turnouts at the polls indicate despair of effecting change at the ballot box.

Since 1992, a loosely organized al-Gamaa al Islamiyya, or "Islamic Group," favoring government by the Sharia (Islamic law) has been strong in upper Egypt. It has made terrorist attacks on tourists to embarrass and weaken the Mubarak government. Thousands of arrests and eighty death sentences have resulted in little more than a continuing stalemate. The government contends that its laws are already based on the Sharia, but bars are allowed to operate, and women are not required to be veiled.

Much is at stake in Egypt. The world watches to see whether a policy of sharing power with moderate Fundamentalists while dealing harshly with extremists will eventually bring about a consensus concerning the application of Islam to a modernizing state.

Libya: Egalitarian Islamic Reform   Libya, having been occupied at one time or another by Turkey, Italy, and Great Britain, developed anticolonialist and nationalist feelings long before it first gained independence in 1951. It began as a monarchy under Idris, the leader of a Ṣūfī-originated sect called the Sanūsīyah. At that time, Libya was the poorest country in the world. Oil was struck in 1959, and within a decade per capita income rose from $50 per year to $1,500.

In 1969, Muammar al-Qaddafī, a young army captain, seized power in a coup. He held political views derived from Nasser's Arab socialism and pan-Arab antiimperialism. His religious outlook had been shaped by Sanūsī and Wahhābist ideas of an Islam of simple purity. His first steps were the expropriation of foreign oil interests, redistribution of income, and extension of education. Within ten years, literacy rose above 75 percent, and university enrollments went from 3,000 to 20,000. During that time, Colonel Qaddafī had developed his own brand of egalitarian Islamic thought and published it in two volumes of *The Green Book*. He called it the Third International Theory (to distinguish it from both capitalism and communism). He held that the participation of the people in government and the economy should be direct (not through layers of representatives); there were to be no wages or rents, only profit participation in a worker-managed economy.

In 1977, the name of the nation became the Socialist People's Libyan Arab Jamahiriyah (a coined term meaning something like "peopledom"), and Colonel Qaddafī gave up all of his political titles to become "philosopher of the revolution." (Twenty years later, his title would be reduced even further to "first brother" of the revolution, though no discernable shred of his power would be gone.

By the early 1980s, the path for Qaddafī's reforms became more difficult. Libya's annual income amounted to about $9,000 per capita, and Qaddafī's ambivalence about wealth began to produce what one writer called "a domestic policy which oscillated between wasteful spending and artificial austerity and arbitrary traditionalism."Q Erratic enforcement of austerities eroded his popular support. His expropriation of *waqf* (religious endowment) lands brought opposition from the 'Ulamā', and Qaddafī retaliated with verbal attacks on them and insistence on a religious calendar ten years out of step with the rest of the Islamic world. International interventions prompted by his anti-Israeli fervor and Pan-Arab ambitions naturally brought mixed responses, but his invasion of Chad in 1981 seriously damaged his stature in the Organization for African Unity.

In 1992, the United Nations imposed sanctions on Libya for refusing to extradite two suspects in the bombing of a Pan-American jet over Lockerbie, Scotland. Qaddafī won some praise from other Organization for African Unity (OAU) members for his refusal, and in 1997 President Mandela of South Africa made a cordial visit. On the other hand, his credibility probably suffered some damage shortly after the deaths of Princess Diana and Dodi Fayed in an automobile accident when he said that Britain "committed a crime by executing an Arab citizen who wanted to marry an English princess. And it prepared the accident with the French intelligence service." In short, the Libyan brand of Islamic egalitarianism has challenged Muslims everywhere and won the admiration of some, but so far it has not been successfully exported.

Algeria

Islam is the official religion of Algeria and virtually all of its native populace are at least nominally Muslims. The 'Ulamā and Ṣūfī-style Berber holy men (*marabouts*) were politically ineffective until the 1970s, when a younger generation were stirred to activism by events in Libya and Iran. In June 1990, Islamic fundamentalist (FIS Party) victories in local elections so alarmed the government that it postponed national elections and imposed restrictions on political activities by religious groups. Elections were cancelled again in 1993. Six years later, the fighting between government forces and armed Islamic militants was estimated to have cost more than sixty thousand lives. An estimated 3,700 women were among the victims. The fragmentation of the militant groups and indications that some of the night murderings were by government forces has compounded the difficulty of reaching any accord. The government refused to permit a United Nations fact-finding group to enter the country in the spring of 1998.

Central Africa

Sub-Saharan African cultures never absorbed as much of Muslim culture as their northern neighbors did. Islam permeated the cultures of Egypt and the north coastal Maghrib quite thoroughly: theology and literature in the Arabic language travelled with the core of Islamic law. In contrast, Muslim influence on the diverse tribes of central Africa has been limited to selected spheres, leaving large portions of the indigenous cultures relatively untouched. In the west-to-east Sahel belt—from Senegal, through northern Nigeria, Chad, and the Sudan to Somalia—Islam furnished common external norms: systematizing legal codes, providing a common lunar calendar, modifying birth, marriage, and funerary customs, and imposing taboos against nakedness and pork eating. But this Islamicization left in place the deep structures, the native mythologies and perceptions of the world held by ordinary people not literate in Arabic. Local names for the high god were often interchanged with the name Allāh. Animism continued to play a large part in everyday life but with a new tendency to identify spirits as allied either with angels or demons. Magic and divination continued, but the intermediaries were often Islamic clerics, some of them in clans of *maraboutiques,* or hereditary orders.

In the towns and in the male worlds of commerce, Islam furnishes an intertribal law and value system, but among nomads and hunters and among women everywhere, Islam is marginal, and traditional culture continues to hold its place. Exceptions occur where theocratic states emerged, as among the Hausa and later the Fulani in northern Nigeria. The Sultan of Sokoto claims the allegiance of some sixty million Muslims in West Africa.

The incumbent from 1988 to 1996 was Ibrahim Dasuki, an Oxford-trained investment banker, a modernist, yet able to get along with the miltary government. But in 1996, the military dictator General Sani Abacha abruptly deposed him on the pretext of having violated a "constitutional" rule and put in his place his cousin Ibrahim Muhammad Maccido, a less wealthy and influential personage. This may have been a preparatory move for General Abacha's intention to legitimize his rule by running for president of Nigeria in the fall of 1998. Whatever the circumstances, the influence of the Sultan over half of the population of Nigeria seemed to be undiminished.

Iran: Islamic Dimensions of Revolution

The Iranian Revolution deserves special attention, not only because of its international impact, but because it demonstrated a major branch of Shiʿah theology (the Twelver, or *Ithna'Ashari*) in undiluted form.

In 1979, a number of deeply embedded forces in Shiʿah Islam came to the surface in the overthrow of Shah Moḥammad Reza. Many Iranians regarded the Shah as a puppet of Anglo-American interests credited with installing him in 1953 after ousting the duty elected Leftist government of Premier Mohammed Mossadegh. Criticism from clerics mounted, and in 1978 Ayatollah Khomeini, the most respected critic, sought asylum in France. In November 1979, Islamist student rebels seized the U.S. embassy and took most of its foreign personnel hostage. Within months, Khomeini returned, and by March 1980, a national referendum approved the creation of a new Islamic state.

The causes of the revolution were, of course, complex, involving international intervention into Iran's economy and political life. Yet, Shiʿah Islam profoundly affected three aspects of the revolution: its rationale, its emotional fervor, and its institutional mechanism. The rationale of the revolution drew upon long-standing Shiʿite reservations about civil authority. Its emotional energy boiled up from uniquely Shiʿite mixtures of grievance and hope carried along nerves that reached back as far as the martyrdom of al-Hoseyn* at Karbalā in the seventh century. The institutional strength of the revolution was furnished by the authority vested in the *mojtaheds* (scholar/judges) and the widespread network of mosques and *mollahs*.

Rationale

The rationale of Islamic revolution flows from confidence in the all-sufficiency of the revelation in the Qur'ān. As a complete system of faith and practice, Islam, whether Sunnī or Shiʿah, has always subsumed law and government; it has never been at home with Western conceptions of secular states within which religious communities conduct their lives. In Iran, the situation is even more complex. At the heart of Shiʿism is the millenarian expectation of the return of the Mahdī, the only rightful ruler. In the interim, all governments, even quasi-Islamic ones, are illegitimate. Temporary arrangements are tolerable to the degree that they are endorsed by Shiʿite theologians.

---

* Arabic: al-Ḥusayn. In this section, Irani transliteration approximating Persian pronunciation is used.

The Shah was required to profess and propagate 'Ashari (Twelver) Shi'ism as the state religion. The parliament (*Majles*) could not pass laws contradicting the Qur'ān, and a committee of five ayatollahs selected by the Majles was created to oversee all legislation and to keep it in accordance with Islamic law (Sharī'a). Even this did not go far enough for some conservatives, and the ayatollahs of today state flatly that the shahs of the Pahlavi dynasty ignored the requirement from its inception. Shah Moḥammad Reza, on his part, sought to legitimate his rule in Islamic terms, pointing out in his autobiography that his father had named him the eighth Shi'ah Imām Reza. He wrote of dreams of Allāh's call and of Allāh's protection and deliverance from assassins. He referred to his program of economic reforms (the White Revolution) as being for the "redemption of Iran." In official literature, the Imperial Majesty Shahbanou Farah Pahlavi was described as a descendent of "Her Holiness Fatemah Zahra" (daughter of the Prophet). The title "the Great" was annexed to his father's name and his body was brought to a new tomb in the complex of traditional Shi'ah shrines near the capital.

Emotional Fervor

The passionate fervor of public demonstrations during the revolution awed many Western observers. The frustrations, economic and political, were understandable, but the idioms were unfamiliar because they referred to a special Shi'ite reading of history. To comprehend the extravagant language, the "Great Satans," the "death to . . ." cries, and the constant references to blood, one can hardly overemphasize the connection with the annual theatrical rehearsing of the passion of al-Hoseyn at Karbalā'. Just as Yazid, the usurper, had persecuted Hoseyn in 680 C.E., the Shah was persecuting Ayatollah Khomeini and his followers. When the Ayatollah Khomeini urged his demonstrating followers to "wear white robes the better to display the blood" from their wounds, the allusion was directly to blood-stained garments in the passion plays (*ta'ziya*). One needs to remember, too, that months after the slaughter of al-Hoseyn and his family, a movement known as the Tawwabun (penitents) joined him in martyrdom in a campaign of reckless loyalty. More than half of a force of some 3,000 are said to have sacrificed themselves at Ayn al-Warda, engaging a force of 30,000 Syrians. Thus, during the month of Muḥarram, one sees solemn processions of men wearing black, often beating themselves with chains, affirming their solidarity in grief and penitence with those of former ages who failed to effectually aid the martyrs.

On the ninth and tenth of Muḥarram special preaching (*rowza*) assemblies for intensification of grief and fresh resolve are held in mosques and private homes. Gatherings, often separate ones for men and for women, hear sermons, recitations from the Qur'ān, and religious poems, the emphasis being on the tragedy of Karbalā. The lines that follow are samples from the strophes of the sixteenth-century poet Mohtasham:

> *Many a blow whereby the heart of Mustafa*
> *[Mohammad]*
> *was rent did they inflict on the thirsty throat of*
> *Mortaza 'Ali's successor [al-Hoseyn],*
> *While his women, with collars torn and hair unloosed,*
> *raised their laments to the Sanctuary of the Divine*
> *Majesty,*
> *And the Trusted Spirit [Gabriel] laid his head in shame*
> *on*
> *his knees, and the eye of the sun was darkened at the*
> *sight,*
> *When the blood of his thirsty throat fell on the ground,*
> *turmoil arose from the earth to the summit of God's*
> *high Throne.*

> . . . . .

> *When the People of the House shall lay hands on the*
> *People of Tyranny, the hand of God's reproach shall*
> *come forth from its sleeve.*
> *Alas for the moment when the House of 'Ali, with blood*
> *dripping from their winding sheets, shall raise their*
> *standards from the dust like a flame of fire!*[R]

During the days of the ta'ziya, passion plays climaxing on 'ashura, the tenth day of the month of Muḥarram, villagers physically rehearse the stabbing, beheading, and trampling of Hoseyn. These are uniquely Shi'ite rites of intensification, the emotional roots of modern revolutionary fervor.

Institutional Mechanisms

The institutional mechanisms of Islamic power in Iran include the authority of mojtaheds, the network of governing authority during the interim when the Twelfth Imām is in "concealment." The exercise of this power is supervisory rather than direct. In Iran, it is perceived as having been continuous, although showdown confrontations have been relatively infrequent.

Yet the power of the ayatollahs and the mollahs demonstrated in the overthrow of the Shah in 1979 had historical antecedents. In 1890 and 1906, there were significant victories over secular authority. In 1890, when Nasr al-Din Shah sought to increase his income by the creation of a tobacco monopoly controlling prices to growers and raising prices to consumers, the leading mojtahed of the time forbade smoking. His order, undergirded by the mollahs, was obeyed throughout the land (even in the palace) and the concession had to be canceled.

The mojtaheds and the mollahs also played an important role in the constitutional crisis of 1906. The extravagances of Mozaffaru-Din Shah had led to the granting of unpopular concessions to foreign powers. Popular discontent was mobilized and channeled by mollah leadership into a dramatic sit-in occupation (*bast*) of the British Legation compound. The first Majles (National Assembly) was convened and a parliamentary constitution was forced upon the Shah.

Mojtaheds organize and administer educational institutions. Village elementary schools and centers of higher learning (*madrasas*) are supported by religious endowments and by a portion of the religious tax (*khoms*, "one-fifth") contributed by the faithful. Shah Moḥammad Reza's creation of counterorganizations indicates his perception of the power of these traditional institutions. A central Religious Endowments office preempted and redistributed income from endowments formerly under local control. A Faculty of Islamic Theology at the University of Teheran began to train experts in theology and jurisprudence; a Religious Corps, something like the Peace Corps, was created; and government schools drew more and more pupils away from the religious schools.

Although enrollments and income fell, the madrasas continued to serve as centers for criticism of the regime, and when the Ayatollah Khomeini began to send tape-recorded messages from exile in France, the schools and the pulpits in the mosques gave him continuing access to the Islamic public. When he returned from exile, the mollahs, like precinct captains, were

Iranian Revolutionary Poster (1979)

Ayatollah Khomeini is portrayed as Moses victorious over pharaoh Shah Moḥammad Reza, who hangs on to the coattails of an Uncle Sam with added British and Israeli insignia. The verses at the upper right say, "We said: Fear not! Lo, thou art the higher" (Qur'ān 20:68); "Go thou unto Pharaoh! Lo, he hath transgressed" (20:24), "He [God] said: Cast it down, O Moses! So he cast it down, and, lo, it was a serpent, gliding" (20:19–20). The single line below reads, "There is a Moses for every Pharaoh" (not a Qur'ānic line). To the left the verses read, "In that day their excuses will not profit those who did injustice" (Qur'ān 30:57); "Theirs is the curse and theirs the ill abode" (13:25). A hell of tortures is portrayed in the upper left. *(Picture courtesy of Franz Brunner. Caption details courtesy of Michael M. J. Fischer.)*

mosques and training schools, and the day-to-day instruction and alms distribution by lower-level clerics (*akhunds* or *mollahs*).

We have seen that in the Twelver reading of history it is the mojtaheds (some meriting the special honorific ayatollah) who are granted the supreme ready to coordinate the demonstrations. Thus the verdict of the revolution in 1979 was to put supreme power in the hands of an ayatollah from a Qom madrasa and to entrust administration of such vital necessities as ration cards to the mollahs at the mosques.

Iran as an Islamic State

We have seen that in the days of rising revolutionary fervor (and continuing frustration) *rowza* preaching used the paradigm of Karbala'—identifying the Shah with the usurper Yazid, who ordered the death of Hoseyn, and identifying Khomeini with the martyred Imām. After the victory a new pattern was needed: a model of social justice as 'Alī would have had it. It soon became clear who would be defining the intentions of 'Alī.

Michael M. J. Fischer traces the application of these paradigms in detail, concluding, "The Karbala' paradigm helped unite disparate interest groups into a mass movement against an entrenched tyranny. But once the tyranny was removed, a new rhetorical discourse was required. For that, as Bazargan and Khomeini both pointed out, one had to shift to the principles of social justice associated with the name 'Alī."[5]

In 1979, the consolidation of power into conservative clerical hands was swift. Ayatollah Khomeini agreed only reluctantly to a national referendum. When it came, it was on his terms: the choice was *"for"* an undefined Islamic republic with a green (the color of Islam) ballot, or *"against"* with a red (the color of Yazid) ballot. Instead of holding a constitutional convention—as advocated by Ayatollah Shariatmadari, other moderate mojtaheds, the National Front, and the Leftists—the Khomeini forces released their own draft of a constitution and scheduled the election of an Assembly of Experts to approve or amend it. Criteria for candidates were so restrictive (383 of 417 candidates were mollahs) that Shariatmadari and the National

Front parties boycotted the election. Outmaneuvered, these less theocratic groups had to stand by as the electorate overwhelmingly endorsed a constitution modeled on Khomeini's views.

The constitution created a unicameral republic with a president and a prime minister and a special new post of Guiding Legal Expert (*Vali Faq'eh*). Holding this office, Khomeini had power to intervene in any affair of state; his confirmation was required for any candidate for the office of president. He nominated the six clerics who formed the majority on an eleven-member Council of Guardians.

These provisions were consonant with the views expressed in Khomeini's book, *Islamic Government* (1971). The central principle is "rule exercised by the legal scholar" (*velayat-e faqih*). The key sentence in the Qur'ān is Sūra Nisa' 62, "O you who have faith, obey God, obey the prophet of God and obey the issuer of orders" (*uli'l-amr*). What is meant by the "issuer of orders"? The Sunnī reading is that it means the caliph or sultan (as long as he does not violate the principles of Islam). Purists might say that the Qur'ān itself is meant. Iranian Shī'ites hold that 'Alī and then the Twelve Imāms are meant, and after that the *velayat-e faqih*, the guidance of the legal scholar.

From Khomeini's viewpoint, an absolutely fresh page of history was being written. Islamic government had never been tried before. *Nothing* that had happened since the Twelve Imāms could be cited as illustrative of true Islam.

In the Iranian constitution there is an obvious lack of clarity about the division of function between the Guiding Legal Expert and the other branches of government. Sometimes Khomeini was active, sometimes passive. In his view, sovereignty belonged to God; all necessary law had already been revealed. A parliament's role is best described as "agenda setting" (*barnamah-rizi*) rather than lawmaking, and a parliament should do no more than

> "God has arranged that the actual government [on earth] has that same power, authority and rule that the prophet and the *imāms* possessed in terms of provisioning and mobilizing troops, appointing governors, collecting revenues, and expending them in the interests of the Muslims. But [the only difference is that] there *is* no specific person [who has such power, authority and rule]; instead [these are wielded by] "a just clergyman" (*'alem-e 'adel*).[T]
>
> —Khomeini

implement the preexistent law as interpreted for them by Islamic experts.

The initial economic moves were in the direction of nationalization of resources and larger industries and the imposition of Fundamentalist austerity. Ration cards and access to upper-level education must be obtained at the mosques. Bans upon alcohol, coeducation, and frivolous entertainment have been strict. Merchants have been forbidden by law to wait on women whose heads are not covered.

In February 1989, Khomeini celebrated the tenth anniversary of his success and moved to consolidate his standing with militants by calling on "all zealous Muslims" to murder Salman Rushdie, the author of *The Satanic Verses,* a novel deemed slanderous to the memory of the Prophet. Khomeini's designated successor, Ayatollah Hussein Ali Montazeri, called for moderation and the avoidance of "slogans that might set us off from the rest of the world." Shortly afterward, Montazeri withdrew as designated successor. Khomeini died in 1989 and was succeeded by Ayatollah Sayed Khameni, who tacitly cooperated with President Rafsanjani in moderating the influence of fiercely Fundamentalist clerics.

The election in May 1997, put a moderate religious scholar, Mohammed Khatami, into the office of president. Early indications of the direction of his leadership were his support for relaxing controls on the press, book publishing, and films, his nomination of several politicians who had lived in the West, and his promise to appoint as a vice president a woman educated in the United States.

Indonesia: Islam in Asian Compromise

Numbering some 174 million, the Muslims of Indonesia are the largest national grouping within Islam, and they make up approximately 87 percent of the world's fifth most populous nation. Although they have been inconspicuous on the world scene and thus far politically hobbled within their own nation, Indonesian Muslims make up a unique pattern in the mosaic of Islamic civilization.

Historical Factors

In the thirteenth century, Islam gained its first foothold in the archipelago through Gujarati traders from the Indian subcontinent. The westernmost island of Sumatra, lying opposite the Malay Peninsula, was most directly exposed to trade routes and received the earliest Muslim influence and settlements. By the fifteenth century, the Sultanate of Malacca became a center for the spread of Islam, rivaling the declining power of Madjapahit, the last of the Hindu-Javanese empires.

The circumstances of the introduction of Islam account for the unique character of Indonesian Islam today. In the first place, much of Islam had been filtered through a pantheistic, mystical Indian culture before its arrival. Second, it was superimposed on previous layers of well-developed religious and social tradition: a deep layer of indigenous culture and a fairly well assimilated layer of Hindu and/or Buddhist culture. As a third circumstance, Islam was introduced partly because of its usefulness in the struggles of outlying regions to free themselves from the Hindu-Javanese empire. It offered an alternative ideology and served as a symbol of resistance.

Islam made its earliest converts in trading centers. As a religion without a hierarchy, it fit the commercial world well. Its emphasis on equality and individualism matched the freedom of the marketplace, and its simplicity appealed to traders impatient with the rituals and formalities of stratified Hindu-Javanese society.

But the commercial world was probably not the only early point of entry. Malay and Javanese mythologies connect Islamization with supernatural conversions of rulers and visitations by renowned foreign shaykhs to the courts of the elite. These myths reflect a perception that the Islamic message was brought by sages possessing mystical insight and miraculous powers. It seems unlikely that the ruling elite took Islam directly from traders in port cities. It is

> "For Hinduism's attempt to sacralize a political community built around inequalities in military power, Islam substituted an attempt to sacralize a commercial community, built around commonalities in economic motivation."[U]
>
> —Clifford Geertz

more probable that Ṣūfī sages were invited to courts by rulers curious about the spiritual lore of distant lands.

In rural areas and in cities away from the coastal trade routes, the acceptance of Islamic teaching and practice came more slowly, and everywhere it was qualified by continuing adherence to customary law (adat), elements of the Hindu worldview, and indigenous animistic beliefs. The characteristic Javanese impulse was to accept the Islamic label while clinging to cultural ideals and artistic conventions formed over centuries of blending Hindu and Javanese views of the world. Such qualified acceptance was, of course, inimical to the spirit of the mainstream of Islam, but it became one of the realities of the Indonesian scene. To this day, astonishing combinations of ideas surface in casual ways. The puppet theatre, for example, with its themes derived from Indian epics, has served for centuries as the medium for discourse about values. And so one hears a village-level interpretation that has the five Pandava heroes representing the Five Pillars of Islam!

Continuing Diversification

As a result of many historical and social forces, the adherence to Islam by some 87 percent of Indonesians today is marked by diverse geographical and social gradations. There are wide variations in the perception of Islam and in commitment to its claims. Atjeh (in the northwest) is staunchly Islamic, while Bali (to the east of Java) is still essentially Hindu-Buddhist.

In towns and villages in Java, a distinction is commonly made between the devout Muslims (santri) and the ordinary adherents (abangan) who count selves as Muslims but give more place to pre-Islamic religious practices and adat customary law. Santri Muslims put a higher priority on purity of doctrine and move toward displacing older custom with Islamic law. Abangan Muslims may take some aspects of the faith quite seriously: the sovereignty of Allāh, the prohibition of pork, and the Ramaḍān fast. But they resist santri efforts to promote radical displacement of local custom.

Whatever the diversities in the perception of Islam, there is no question that most Indonesians have seen in it a basis of protest against foreign oppression: it is not English, not Dutch, not Japanese. Muslims can be spoken of as bumiputra (sons of the soil, native). Native Christians are not likely to be so described.

Islam and Nationhood

Many leaders, attracted to Western democratic ideals as well as to Islam, began to look to Islamic modernism. They looked beyond Meccan piety to the University of Cairo (al-Azhar) for inspiration. A reformist Muḥammadiyah (Way of Muḥammad) society was organized in 1912. After World War II, the Muḥammadiyah became the main source of the Masjumi political party, rivaling the Nahdatul Ulama party of conservative Muslims.

Japanese occupation during World War II opened up opportunities for Muslims as well as for Indonesian Nationalists. Leaders like Sukarno were put forward to consolidate national anti-Western feeling, and they survived to lead the independence movement against the returning Dutch. It was the Japanese who insisted upon the creation of an all-inclusive Muslim organization out of the Muḥammadiyah and the Nahdatul Ulama party and thus laid the foundation for united Islamic political activity.

The Independent Republic of Indonesia came into being in 1945, but the struggle against Dutch efforts to regain control led to three more years of turmoil. One interesting product of the maneuvering was the brief flowering of an independent Islamic government in West Java. Popularly called Darul Islam, it was founded by the charismatic leader Kartosuwirjo, who proclaimed himself its imām in 1948. Darul Islam produced a detailed Islamic constitution and survived as a regional guerilla rebellion until Kartosuwirjo's death in 1962. It is significant in the picture of Islam in Indonesia for two special reasons: (1) holy warfare (jihād) was directed, not against an external nation of unbelievers, but against a nominally Islamic Javanese majority perceived to be munafiq (obstructors of the observance of Islam under the guise of Islam); and (2) decisions to join this Islamic state (as researched by Karl D. Jackson) seem to have been made on the basis of traditional authority rather than religious zeal.[V] This authority runs along chains of dyadic relations: the "father" (bapak) advising the "child" (anak huah). In village society, where alternative options are not available, the dependent person is accustomed to getting advice from one person on a whole range of personal, financial, and social decisions. The leader, accustomed to the power of traditional authority (with physical force as its sanction), dispenses judgment rather than information about alternatives. The leader rather than the cause is the primary motivating force.

The Guiding Leader

The preeminent national leader of Indonesia during its first twenty years was Sukarno, the son of a school teacher in an abangan Javanese community. His mother came from Hinduized Bali. His education took him through a European higher middle school and a technical college. The synthesis of native Indonesian, Hindu, Islamic, and European elements in his own background became his model for the nation. The Five Principles (*Pancasila*), the official basis of the Indonesian constitution, were first proposed by Sukarno in 1945: belief in God, nationalism, humanitarianism, social justice, and democracy. There were Muslim objections to the fact that Islam was given no special place, and a compromise known as the Jakarta Charter added an ambiguous modification to the first principle, "belief in God with the obligation for adherents of Islam to carry out Islamic law." This phrasing was destined to provoke years of bitter and frustrating disputes between ardent Muslims and advocates of a religiously neutral government. It epitomizes the muddled compromise of Islam in Indonesia.

Up to the present, the secular Nationalists have had their way. Building on a Javanese and military power base, Sukarno's Guided Democracy banned the reformist Muslim Party, dissolved genuine representative government, and leaned more and more upon Leftist support outside of Java. On September 30, 1965, with economic and political structures near collapse, Leftist military elements attempted a coup and were thwarted by General Suharto and conservative army forces. Years of frustration for non-Javanese and for Muslims then erupted into a backlash of violence as Communists and their suspected sympathizers were slaughtered. An estimated 500,000 died, and twelve years later some 100,000 political prisoners were being held.

The crushing of the Leftists has not meant success for Muslims. At the polls, Suharto's New Order rests on an army- and government-controlled "functional groups" (Golkar) party that swept elections from 1971 to 1998. Economic woes brought about President Suharto's resignation in May, 1998, leaving Vice President Habibie in power until promised new elections in December 1999. The prospect of increased influence for moderate Muslims appeared to rest with prospects for a coalition between the parties of Sukarno's daughter Megawati and the Nahdatul Ulama headed by her friend Abdurrahman Wahid.

Islamic Agenda

Many Islamic leaders no longer strive for an official Islamic state, and many do not speak of "Islamic Law" in general, but only of a partial realization of certain "elements" (*unsur-unsur*) of Islam in accordance with the Jakarta Charter: family law, marriage, divorce by repudiation, and inheritance. Later, perhaps, the alms tax (*zakāt*), recognition of Islamic courts for family law, and pious foundations (*awqaf*) might be legally undergirded.

Only Atjeh in the extreme northwest has gone so far as to create an official Assembly of Islamic Scholars (*Madjlis Ulama*). Proud of its nickname "Verandah of Mecca," Atjeh enjoys "special territory" status. Its regional assembly adopted a regulation concerning "The Realization of Elements of the Religious Law" outlining the obligations of Muslims to believe, oppose unbelief, worship, observe Islamic ethics in business and family life, combat immorality in dress as well as in the media and in public amusements, and contribute to charity.

At the national level, there is one significant institutional product of the Indonesian compromise in regard to Islam. This is the Ministry of Religion, an agency first created by the Japanese as an instrument of control. Indonesians now see it as one way to make an operative principle of Article One in the *Pancasila*: belief in God (expanded in the description of the ministry to "Belief in the One and Only God"). For Muslims, the furtherance of this principle obviously means the furtherance of Islam, and the most conspicuous functions are those of the Islamic Section: financial aid for the building of mosques, facilitating pilgrimages to Mecca, the promotion and regulation of Ramaḍān fasting and special feasts, promoting the contribution of *zakāt,* and the production of a large number of Islamic publications. There are smaller Christian and Hindu-Buddhist sections of the Ministry of Religion, but no recognition of tribal religions.

The handling of the *zakāt* (almsgiving) issue typifies the ways by which the national father figures adroitly avoid confrontation with Islamic purists. The purists see no reason why *zakāt* should not be a regularly levied, systematically collected tax. This desire is deflected by having a Ministry of Religion "to promote and assist" in the collection, leaving *zakāt* at the level of an obligation rather than a regular tax. The goodwill of the government is demonstrated in the capital where a relatively high number (30 percent) of Muslims contribute. (Civil servants find evasion difficult!) During the fall of 1968, when fresh initiatives toward Islamic legislation were in the air, President Suharto came forward with a special plea for Muslims to make more generous contributions when paying *zakāt*. He took the lead personally by contributing 100,000 rupiahs, and many large sums came in. There was no new legislation.

On the other hand, the *Pancasila* emphases on tolerance and harmony have also been invoked to restrain Muslim activism: in 1987, the government barred the Muslim United Development Party (PPP) from further use of the Ka'ba as its ballot symbol on the ground that it was sectarian (making campaigning among illiterate villagers more difficult), and Muslim intellectuals use the *Pancasila* as grounds for urging that "all religions" be taught in local schools (*pesantrèn*).

It is not clear what direction Islamic aspirations may take in the future. Indonesian Muslims do not have the tradition and institutional structures to produce a Khomeini-style theocratic experiment. On the other hand, there is little indication that Atjeh-style Muslim leadership will openly accept a cultural (as distinguished from a political) role.

E. Pakistan: A New State Facing an Old Dilemma

Muḥammad Iqbāl (see p. 580), while decrying regionalism as divisive, nevertheless concluded that in view of the impracticability of a caliphate who could draw the Muslim world into one, the best chance of preserving unity lay in establishing national states that would subscribe to the principle of multinational unity. Hence he proposed a regional Muslim state for northwest India, provided this would not mean "a displacement of the Islamic principle of solidarity," for that would be "unthinkable." This opinion had a great deal to do with the founding of Pakistan as an independent state. In 1947, a Muslim state, composed of West and East Pakistan, was born. In India, fifty million Muslims became a religious minority, with the political right to be represented in the Indian Parliament. As to Pakistan, Wilfred Cantwell Smith has said,

> Before August 14, 1947, the Muslims of India had their art, their theology, their mysticism; but they had no state. When Jinnāh proposed to them that they should work to get themselves one, they responded with a surging enthusiasm. Their attainment, on that date, of a state of their own was greeted with an elation that was religious as well as personal. It was considered a triumph not only for Muslims but for Islam.[W]

But what is an Islamic state? The framers of the constitution decided against making Pakistan a theocracy, for they did not wish the final decisions to be the prerogative of the 'Ulamā'; it was decided to make the whole people the final political authority.

The framers of the constitution envisioned a homeland where Muslims could implement their values through modified (but essentially secular) democratic institutions. But the 'Ulamā' and the uneducated masses saw those institutions as standing in the way of truly Islamic reform. The 1956 constitution papered over this difference by proposing an essentially secular republic with Islamic trimmings: a preamble (sovereignty belongs to Allāh), a name (Islamic Republic), a Muslim president, and advisory bodies to see that no laws repugnant to Islam would be passed.

There was clearly no ideological consensus. Even the question "Who is a Muslim?" was answered only negatively in the form of anti-Aḥmadiya (see p. 592) disturbances and rulings. Strong leaders coming to power by military coup filled the void left by the lack of ideological consensus: Ayub Khan (1958–1969), Zulfikar Ali Bhutto (1971–1977), and Muhammad Zia-ul-Haq (1977–1988). Modernist and secular in background, the first two sought *ad hoc* solutions to pressing economic and social problems, found themselves accused of giving only lip service to Islamic agenda, and were pushed into piecemeal concessions such as outlawing drinking and gambling and replacing the Sunday sabbath with a Muslim Friday holiday.

The secession of East Pakistan/Bangladesh in 1971 had been a blow to national pride, but Zia-ul-Haq came to power vowing that his martial-law administration would be a bridge to a truly Islamic system, *Nizām-i-Islam*. Immediate proposals included instituting harsh Qur'ānic penalties for crimes, enforcing *zakāt* taxation for social welfare, and abolishing usury. A 288-member federal council (*Majlis-e-shūrā*), which he appointed in 1982, was charged with the task of Islamization. It has only advisory power, but it may wield significant influence because it includes representatives from most of the wealthy families and institutions in Pakistan. On the other side are ranged zealous mullahs and their followings, the Shī'ah Muslim minority, and a relatively small Jamat-e-Islami Fundamentalist party. Their real power stems from government fears of huge street protests.

After the death of Zia-ul-Haq, an election put Benazir Bhutto, daughter of Zulfikar Ali Bhutto, into power. The fragility of her coalition inhibited steps toward secular democratic reform. In fact, the prime minister's gender and Western education as well as accusations of corruption made her extremely unpopular with Islamists and the military. Her tenure was short.

In 1990, Nawaz Sharif became prime minister, and more years of near stalemate and wrangling followed: between the Sharif and Bhutto coalitions, between branches of government, and between secularists and Islamists. In 1993, the president of Pakistan, Ishaq Khan, dismissed Sharif. Sharif challenged the president's authority and the Supreme Court. New elections brought back Benazir Bhutto, who in turn lost out again to Sharif in 1996. The jousting coalitions differed little in regard to religion. Both gave lip service to Islamic goals while cultivating moneyed interests content with the essentially secularist status quo. Election turnouts shrank from 60 percent in the seventies to 26 percent in 1996. In the same year, a private poll reported that 81 percent of respondents said religious leaders should stay out of politics. The radical Islamic party (*Jamat-e Ulema Islam*) won only two seats in the Majlis. Clerics, however, still wielded power by their ability to turn out crowds in public protests.

In 1998, the fiftieth anniversary of its separation from India, Pakistan, a nation of 130 million, had yet to agree upon a consensus definition of its Islamic identity and establish a stable separation of powers in its government.

Afghanistan

No Muslim country has suffered as much wrenching conflict in the two decades since 1978 as sparsely populated Afghanistan, where some twenty million remain after some eight million were displaced and perhaps more than one million were killed in fierce guerrilla fighting. Through Soviet occupation until 1989 and frequent incursions from Pakistan (with U.S. assistance), tribal rivalries intensified, pitting Muslims against Muslims in struggles for power. Most were Sunni of the Hanifite school, a plurality being Pushtun (Pathan) in language and culture. In 1996, an army led by ultraconservative theological students trained in Pakistan took control of most of the country. They called themselves the Taliban ("seekers of knowledge") and governed through an interim ruling council of six clerics. They imposed extremely rigid regulations to shut out frivolous un-Islamic activity and Western influences. Men were required to grow beards; general prohibitions included not only movies and T.V., but even kite flying, chess, and marbles. But it was women who took the brunt of restrictions. All were ordered to wear the full-length black *burka,* and to stay at home except for necessary food shopping. (Allowing even an ankle to show was punished by the lash.) No women could be employed or go to school.

Visitations by U.N. and private human rights groups had not prompted much change up to the spring of 1998, but there were widespread expectations that some relaxation of rules would be bound to come, at least to permit the return of women to the workforce, especially in health care and education.

VI. MOVEMENTS TOWARD INNOVATION AND SYNCRETISM

Beneath the surface of every religion one discovers a consuming desire on the part of many earnest souls to recover its vitality or the dynamism inherent in its beginnings. This often leads them to a revivalist return to earlier periods and sometimes in the opposite direction to radical thrusts toward the future.

The history of Islam is full of examples. The modernism we have reviewed is one. Prophetic movements proclaiming new light on the religious situation are another.

The Aḥmadiya

One such developed in India into an organized religious movement that has distinctly heretical aspects in the eyes of the orthodox. Its leader, Mīrzā Ghulām Aḥmad of Qādiyān (d. 1908), accepted homage as a Mahdī in the closing decades of the nineteenth century. A reading of the Bible convinced him that he was also the Messiah (Jesus in a second coming), and in 1904 he proclaimed himself an avatar of Krishna. But he remained a Muslim in the sense that he said he was not a prophet in himself but only in and through Muḥammad, whose reappearance (burūz) he claimed to be. In his teaching he made it clear that holy war (jihād) is not to be carried out by the use of force but only through preaching. His followers, the Aḥmadiya, are therefore at once pacifists and ardent missionaries. The Aḥmadiya have split into several branches. The original or Qādiyānī branch is consciously syncretist and all but outside of the Muslim community. The Lahore branch is devotedly Muslim in character and has rejected the extreme claims that Aḥmad made for himself, although they consider him a genuine "renewer of religion." Aḥmadiya missionaries of both these branches are active in England, America, Africa, and the East Indies, where they make considerable use of the printed page and regard Christian leaders as their chief adversaries. They often maintain, as for example on the outskirts of London, their own mosques, to which they cordially welcome all comers, including conservative Muslims.

Bahā'i

Persia (or Iran) has unwillingly given rise to another syncretistic movement, one that has, like Sikhism, become a separate and distinct faith. This is Bahā'i. Its background is Shī'ite. Influenced by the teachings of a heretical Shī'ite to the effect that the imāms of the Twelver sect were "gates" by which the believers gained access to the true faith, and that the hidden imām seeks further "gates" to conduct men to himself, a certain Mīrzā Alī Muḥammad in 1844 added his name to the list and called himself Bāb-ud-Dīn ("Gate of the Faith"). His followers were called after him Bābis. He proclaimed that his mission was to prepare the way for one greater than himself who should come after him and complete the work of reform and righteousness that he had begun. When he said his writings were scripture equaling, if not superseding, the Qur'ān, and on their basis advocated sweeping religious and social

reforms, he was executed in 1850 as a heretic and disturber of the peace. Among his followers was a well-born youth who, following Bābi custom, took the name of Bahā'u'llāh ("Glory of God"). He was accused of complicity in an attempt by a fanatical Bābi to assassinate the shāh in 1852 and was exiled to Baghdad. After some ten years there, when he and his followers were on the point of departure, he announced that he was the one-who-should-come of whom the Bāb had spoken. Moving with his followers, who now called themselves after him Bahā'is, he sought asylum in the Muslim areas to the west and was finally imprisoned by the Turks in Acre, Palestine, for the balance of his life. His writings reached the outside world. They advocated a broad religious view upholding the unity of God and the essential harmony of all prophecy when rightly understood. He called upon all religions to unite, for every religion contains some truth, because all prophets are witnesses to the one Truth that Bahāism supremely represents. The human race is one under God and will be united through his spirit when the Bahā'i cause is known and joined. Outlawed in Iran, Bahā'i, with its headquarters in Haifa in Israel, is active in many countries, and especially in the United States.

The Black Muslims of the United States

"Black Muslims" is an unofficial name that gained currency after its use in a book by C. Eric Lincoln, *The Black Muslims in America* (Beacon Press, 1963). The movement was founded for the purpose of redeeming American "so-called Negroes" by giving them pride and self-knowledge through Islam (as reinterpreted for Americans). The Lost-Found Nation of Islam was established in Detroit in 1930 by W. D. Fard (Master Wali Farrad Muhammad), referred to as Allāh incarnate, and his successor Elijah Poole (Elijah Muhammad), the Messenger of Allāh. In 1934, shortly after Elijah had established a headquarters Temple (later Mosque) in Chicago, Fard withdrew and disappeared (like a Mahdī).

The liberating mythology of the movement held that "so-called Negroes" were descendants of a black Original Man and had been Muslims from the ancient tribe of Shabazz. Yakub, a mad scientist, rebelled against Allāh and created the weak and hybrid white race of devils, who are responsible for the temporary

Haifa, Israel
The Bahā'i Shrine on the slopes of Mt. Carmel is sacred to the members of this unique faith. The faith originated in Persia and has spread throughout the world. *(Courtesy of the Israel Government Tourist Office.)*

degradation of blacks, but in a final Armageddon, Allāh will overthrow Evil.

Elijah's appeal was chiefly to poor blacks in large cities. He insisted that his followers stay out of politics, carry no weapons, and initiate no aggression (but take an eye for an eye if attacked). His emphasis was on building self-esteem through cooperative efforts in education and business ventures. A strong work ethic and an abstemious lifestyle were required. Disciplined guardian groups of young people were formed: the Fruit of Islam, trained in *karate,* for young men, and for young women, the counterpart M.G.T. (Muslim Girl Training).

Malcolm Little, known as Malcolm X (Malik Shabazz), a gifted leader and fiery speaker, attracted many middle-class blacks in the 1960s. He broke with Elijah in 1963 and founded his own Muslim Mosque, Inc., in the following year. Before his assassination in 1965, he made a pilgrimage to Mecca, embraced orthodox Islam, and acknowledged the possibility of a nonracist world brotherhood.

As the movement prospered, denunciation of whites declined, and when Elijah was succeeded by his son Wallace (Warith) in 1975, steps in the direction of Sunnī orthodoxy were accelerated: racial restrictions and requirements in dress and diet were relaxed; members could enter the political process and serve in the armed forces; the Fruit of Islam and the M.G.T. were dismantled. The name of the organization was changed from Nation of Islam to World Community of Islam in 1976, and then to the American Muslim Mission in 1980. "Bilalians" (after Bilal, an Ethiopian and the first *muezzin* of ancient Islam) became the preferred designation for members.

Such changes were attractive to a middle-class following and to some immigrants from Islamic countries, but the original constituency of the poorest and most alienated urban blacks began to drift away. In the late 1980s, the organization was estimated to have over 150 mosques and a membership of over 125,000.

In 1955, a Bermuda-born calypso singer named Louis Eugene Wolcott joined the Nation of Islam, first taking the name Louis X. He studied the ideas of Elijah Muhammad, worked his way up in the organization, took the name Minister Louis Farrakhan, and headed the Harlem Mosque from 1965 to 1975, the year in which Elijah Muhammad died. Two years later, he organized his own sect, and by 1978 began to challenge Wallace, calling for the resurrection of the Nation of Islam and its original teaching. He came to national attention when his reorganized Fruit of Islam troops served as bodyguards for the Reverend Jesse Jackson in the 1984 election campaign. The Nation of Islam won respect through programs of rehabilitation for prisoners, drug addicts, and gang members, and for job training in their bakeries, markets, and bookstores.

Minister Farrakhan was the conspicuous figure among the organizers of a "Million Man March" to Washington, D.C., in October 1995, which was designed to enhance dignity, brotherhood , and commitment to service among black males. His two-and-one-half-hour address was, on the one hand, admired as a call to service, but, on the other hand, it was a national exposure of the fierce antiwhite, anti-integrationist and anti-Semitic elements in his outlook. There were mixed assessments of the outcomes: criticisms of poorly organized follow-up training, but also anecdotal reports of increased volunteering to the Urban League and to local programs like Detroit's Man to Man. Perhaps the most unassailable statistic was a marked increase in black male voting in the 1996 presidential election, while most race or gender groups decreased or remained the same.

During the period 1997–1998, Minister Farrakhan stayed in the headlines by launching a series of visits to foreign countries: Libya, Iraq, Iran, South Africa (where President Mandela made it clear that he "often met with people with whom he disagreed"). Many more were on the itinerary, including Muslim states where scholars had found nothing authentically Islamic in his organization.

Finally, what is Islam? We have come far enough to see that it cannot be treated simply as a set of more or less narrowly defined "religious" beliefs, for it also is a way of life and an entire cultural complex, including art, philosophical, and literary works. In this study we have become aware of these various aspects of Islam as we have pondered what constitutes the Islamic tradition, a tradition no more immune to inner movements of change, growth, and diversification than the other religious traditions of the world.

GLOSSARY

awqāf (pl.) religious endowments for "work pleasing to Allāh," usually for aid to the poor or for support of schools

imām "exemplar," a leader of prayers and religious life; among Sunnīs, the leader of the Islamic community; among Shī`ites, the descendant of `Alī whom Allāh designates as holder of the authority inherent in the line

Imām Mahdī "guided exemplar," in Shī`ism an imām divinely appointed to a special messianic role

jihād holy war, the duty to spread Islam by arms, recently modified to "holy struggle" by persuasion (Aḥmadiya) and sometimes extended to include war against other Muslims deemed too Westernized (extremist fundamentalism).

mojtahed (Irani) "judge," an expert scholar in the application of reasoning (ijtihād) to interpret Islamic law. (Arabic: mujtahid)

mollah (Irani) a Muslim local cleric: tutor and administrator of communal activity centered at a mosque. (Arabic: mawlā)

mut`a temporary marriage requiring at least an oral contract for compensation and a fixed, but renewable, termination

Pancasila the Five Principles of the Indonesian constitution: belief in God, nationalism, humanitarianism, social justice, and democracy

rowza (Irani) a special assembly at a mosque for reading and preaching to intensify grief over Hoseyn's martyrdom and fresh resolve

Shī`ah "party" or faction, usually "the party of `Alī," the branch of Islam holding that the proper succession of authority must be through that cousin and son-in-law of the Prophet

taqīya "caution," "dissimulation," dispensation from the requirements of religion under compulsion or threat of injury

ta`ziya "lamentation," a Shī`ite passion play reenacting events centered upon the martyrdom of al-Hoseyn (Arabic: al-Ḥusayn) at Karbalā

REFERENCES FOR QUOTATIONS

References are arranged in the order in which they are first quoted in the body of the text. They are preceded in the left-hand margin by the capital letters that are their identifying symbols. The page numbers of the books from which quotations are taken are immediately preceded, in small type, by the number that is affixed to the end of the quotation in the body of the text. Where a book has been more than once quoted, as often happens when original sources are drawn upon, page numbers are arranged in the order of quotation in the text.

Chapter 1.
Religion in Prehistoric and Primal Cultures

A. G. Rachel Levy, *Religious Conceptions of the Stone Age,* Harper Torchbooks, 1963, p. 20.

B. William H. McNeill, *The Rise of the West,* a Mentor Book, first published in 1963 by University of Chicago Press, p. 28.

C. Marija Gimbutas, *The Language of the Goddess,* Harper & Row, 1989, p. xix.

D. Marija Gimbutas, *The Goddesses and Gods of Old Europe: 6500–3500 B.C.,* University of California Press, 1982, pp. 237–38.

E. Rudolph Otto, *The Idea of the Holy,* Oxford University Press, 1923, p. 6.

F. Bronislaw Malinowski, article "Culture," in *An Encyclopaedia of the Social Sciences,* the Macmillan Company, New York, 1931, p. 630.

G. Ralph Linton, *The Study of Man,* Appleton Century, 1936, p. 89.

H. E. B. Tylor, *Primitive Culture,* 2 vols., G. P. Putnam's Sons, New York, 1871. [1]Vol. II, p. 185, [2]Vol. I, p. 427.

I. E. W. Hopkins, *The Origin and Evolution of Religion,* Yale University Press, 1923, p. 13.

J. Mabel Cooke Cole, *Savage Gentlemen,* D. Van Nostrand Company, New York, 1929, p. 15.

K. Vergilias Ferm, ed., *Forgotten Religions,* Philosophical Library, New York, 1950, p. 275.

L. A. W. Howitt, *The Native Tribes of South-East Australia,* Macmillan and Company, London, 1904. [1]p. 395; [2]p. 798; [3]p. 650; [4]p. 661.

M. Hugh Stayt, *The BaVenda,* Oxford University Press, publishing for the International African Institute, London, 1928. [1]p. 262; [2]p. 276; [3]p. 276; [4]p. 162; [5]p. 230. Reprinted with permission of the publishers.

N. William Bartram, "Observations on the Creek and Cherokee Indians," *American Ethnological Society Transactions,* Washington, D.C., 1853, 3:1–81. [1]p. 28; [2]p. 65.

O. James Mooney, "Myths of the Cherokee," *Nineteenth Annual Report of the Bureau of American Ethnology,* Washington, 1900 (Reprinted, Johnson Reprint Co., New York, 1970). [1]p. 239; [2]p. 240; [3]p. 328; [4]p. 329; [5]pp. 256–57; [6]p. 242; [7]p. 244; [8]p. 245.

P. Charles Hudson, *The Southeastern Indians,* University of Tennessee Press, 1977. [1]p. 147; [2]p. 348; [3]p. 359; [4]p. 32; [5]p. 201; [6]p. 239.

Q. James Mooney, "The Sacred Formulas of the Cherokees," *Seventh Annual Report of the Bureau of Ethnology, 1885–1886,* Washington, D.C., 1891, pp. 301–97. [1]p. 347; [2]pp. 378–79.

R. Clemens de Baillou, "A Contribution to the Mythology and Conceptual World of the Cherokee Indian." *Ethnohistory,* 8:92–102.

S. John Witthoft, "Green Corn Ceremonialism in the Eastern Woodlands," *Occasional Contributions from the Museum of Anthropology of the University of Michigan,* No. 13, Ann Arbor, 1949, p. 68.

Chapter 2.
Bygone Religions That Have Left Their Mark on the West

A. Samuel N. Kramer, *Sumerian Mythology,* Harper Torchbooks, 1961, p. 73 f.

B. James B. Pritchard, ed., *Ancient Near Eastern Texts Relating to the Old Testament.* 3rd ed., Princeton University Press, 1969. [1]p. 61; [2]p. 62 f.; [3]p. 107; [4]p.

108; [5]pp. 384–385. Reprinted with permission of Princeton University Press.

C. R. W. Rogers, *The Religion of Babylonia and Assyria,* Easton and Mains, New York, 1908. [1]pp. 124–126; [2]p. 201; [3]pp. 202–4.

D. Morris Jastrow, *Aspects of Religious Belief and Practice in Babylonia and Assyria,* G. P. Putnam's Sons, New York, 1991. [1]p. 374; [2]p. 303. Reprinted with permission of the publishers.

E. Marija Gimbutas, *The Goddesses and Gods of Old Europe: 6500–3500 B.C.,* University of California Press, 1982, p. 237.

F. H. J. Rose, *Religion in Greece and Rome,* Harper Torchbooks, 1959, p. 12.

G. Jane E. Harrison, *Mythology,* Marshall Jones, Boston, 1924, p. 94.

H. *The Iliad of Homer,* translated by Edward, Earl of Derby, Everyman's Library, J. M. Dent and Sons, London, 1910. [1]p. 2 (Bk. I); [2]p. 94 (Bk. V), substituting Hera for Juno in the translation; [3]p. 212 (Bk. XIII); [4]p. 239 (Bk. XIV).

I. Jane E. Harrison, *Prolegomena to the Study of Greek Religion,* Cambridge University Press, London, 1903, p. 321.

J. Martin P. Nilsson, *Greek Piety,* Oxford University Press, 1948, p. 10.

K. *Greek Religious Thought from Homer to the Age of Alexander,* edited by F. M. Cornford, J. M. Dent and Sons, London, and E. P. Dutton and Company, New York, 1923. [1]p. 94; [2]p. 50, arranging lines in verse form; [3]p. 51, arranged as verse; [4]p. 51; [5]p. 87; [6]p. 85. Reprinted with permission of the publishers.

L. *The House of Atreus, Being the Agamemnon, Libation-bearers, and Furies of Aeschylus,* translated by E. D. A. Morshead, the Macmillan Company, London, 1901, pp. 18, 22 ("Agamemnon," 380–385, 467–76).

M. *The Plays of Euripides,* translated into rhyming verse by Gilbert Murray. George Allen & Unwin, London, 1914. [1]"Hippolytus," 1347 ff.; [2]Ibid., 1144f.; [3]Ibid., 1102f.; [4]"The Trojan Women," 884–88. Reprinted with permission of the publishers.

N. *The Dialogues of Plato,* translated and edited by Benjamin Jowett, Oxford University Press, London, 1893. [1]Bk. II, 378; [2]Bk. II, 364–65.

O. Carl Clemen, ed., *Religions of the World: Their Nature and History,* George G. Harrap and Company, London, and Harcourt, Brace and Company, New York, 1931. [1]p. 204; [2]p. 220. Quoted with permission of the publishers.

P. George Foot Moore, *History of Religions,* 2 vols., Charles Scribner's Sons, New York, and T. & T. Clark, Ltd., Edinburgh, 1913, 1919. [1]Vol. I, p. 544; [2]Vol. I, p. 541. Reprinted with permission of the publishers.

Q. Cyril Bailey, *The Religion of Ancient Rome,* Constable and Company, London, 1907, pp. 18–19. Reprinted with permission.

R. C. J. Bleeker and G. Widengren, eds., *Historia Religiounum,* Vol. I, *The Religions of the Past,* E. J. Brill, Leiden, 1969, p. 470.

S. Cyril Bailey, *Phases of the Religion of Ancient Rome,* University of California Press, 1932, p. 74.

T. J. Eric S. Thompson, *The Rise and Fall of Maya Civilization,* 2nd ed., University of Oklahoma Press, 1966. [1]p. 47; [2]p. 277; [3]p. 278; [4]p. 164; [5]p. 164; [6]p. 271; [7]p. 180.

U. Sylvanus Griswold Morley, *The Ancient Maya,* 3rd ed., revised by G. W. Brainerd. Stanford University Press, 1956, [1]p. 140; [2]p. 156.

V. Linda Schele and David Friedel, *A Forest of Kings: The Untold Story of the Ancient Maya,* William Morrow and Company, 1990: [1]pp. 255, 266; [2]p. 19.

W. J. Eric S. Thompson, *Maya History and Religion,* University of Oklahoma Press, 1970. [1]p. 172; [2]p. 171; [3]p. 180.

Chapter 3.
Early Hinduism

A. *The Hymns of the Rig Veda,* translated by Ralph T. H. Griffith, E. J. Lazarus and Company, Benares, 1896. [1]VI. 23.6, 7; [2]X. 90.10–13; [3]I. 50.2; [4]X. 139.1, I. 35.11; [5]V. 85.7, 8; [6]VII. 98.7, 8; [7]X. 129; [8]I. 164.46. Reprinted by arrangement with the publishers.

B. *The Satapatha Brahmana in Sacred Books of the East,* Oxford, Clarendon Press, 1879–1910. [1]X. 6.4.1 (Vol. XLIII, p. 40); [2]XIII. 3.1.1 (Vol. XLIV, p. 328); [3]II. 4.2.8–24 (Vol. XII, pp. 363–69).

C. *Vedic Hymns,* translated by Edward J. Thomas, *Wisdom of the East* series, John Murray, London, 1923.

[1]p. 45 (Bk. I. 32.2, 3); [2]pp. 48–51 (II. 12.7–9, 15); [3]p. 70 (I. 114.7–9); [4]p. 31 (I. 113.7); [5]pp. 65–66 (V. 57.4–5). Reprinted with permission of the publisher.

D. *Sources of Indian Tradition,* Compiled by W. T. deBary et al. Columbia University Press, New York, 1958, p. 13.

E. Franklin Edgerton, *The Beginnings of Indian Philosophy,* George Allen & Unwin, London, 1963, p. 18 f.

F. *Hymns from the Rig Veda,* metrically translated by A. A. Macdonell, Association Press, Calcutta; printed by the Wesleyan Mission Press, Mysore, without date, p. 80 (Bk. VIII. 48.3).

G. H. Zimmer, *Philosophies of India,* Pantheon Books, Inc. 1951, p. 411.

H. *Sacred Books of the East,* Vol. XLII, *The Hymns of the Atharva Veda,* translated by Maurice Bloomfield. Oxford, Clarendon Press, 1897. [1]p. 163 (Bk. VI. 26); [2]p. 31 (VI. 136). Reprinted with permission of the publishers.

I. *The Thirteen Principal Upanishads,* translated by R. E. Hume, 2nd ed., Oxford University Press, London, 1934. [1]Svet. 6.17, p. 410; [2]Mait. 6.17, p. 435; [3]Chand. 3.14.1, p. 209; [4]Mait. 6.3, 7, p. 425; [5]Brih. 2.1–20, pp. 92–95; [6]Kath. 5.2, p. 356; [7]Mund. 2.2.11, p. 373; [8]Brih. 3.7.1–23, pp. 115–117; [9]Chand. 6.8.6, p. 246 f.; [10]Brih. 1.4.7, p. 82; [11]Chand. 3.14.3, p. 210; [12]Chand. 6.12, p. 247; [13]Tait, 2.4, p. 285; [14]Chand. 5.10.7, p. 233; [15]Mait. 1.4, p. 413. Reprinted with permission.

J. S. Radhakrishnan, *The Philosophy of the Upanishads,* George Allen & Unwin, London, 1924. [1]p. 36; [2]pp. 36–37. Reprinted with permission of the publishers.

K. Sir Charles Eliot, *Hinduism and Buddhism,* 3 vols., Edward Arnold and Company, London, 1921, Vol. I, p. lix. Reprinted with permission of the publishers.

L. George Foot Moore, *The Birth and Growth of Religion,* Charles Scribner's Sons, New York, and T. & T. Clark, Ltd., Edinburgh, 1923, p. 118. Quoted with permission of the publishers.

M. *Sacred Books of the East,* Vol. XXV, *The Laws of Manu,* translated by G. Bühler, Oxford, Clarendon Press, 1886, pp. 484, 496–98 (XII. 9.54–67). Reprinted with permission of the publishers.

Chapter 4. Later Hinduism

A. *Sacred Books of the East,* Vol. XII, *Satapatha-Brahmana,* translated by Julius Eggeling. Oxford, Clarendon Press, 1882, pp. 190–91 (I.7.2.5). Reprinted with permission of the publishers.

B. W. Crooke, article "Ancestor-Worship (Indian)," in *Encyclopaedia of Religion and Ethics,* T. & T. Clark, Edinburgh, and Charles Scribner's Sons, New York, 1959, Vol. I, p. 453. Reprinted with permission of the publishers.

C. *Sacred Books of the East,* Vol. XXV, *The Laws of Manu,* translated by G. Bühler. Oxford, Clarendon Press, 1886. [1]p. 195 (V. 148); [2]p. 196 (V. 154); [3]p. 196 (V. 157, 158); [4]p. 197 (V. 161, 164); [5]pp. 87–88 (III. 68–70); [6]p. 198 (VI. 2); [7]pp. 199–205 (VI. 3–6, 8, 16, 29, 33); [8]p. 213 (VI. 82); [9]p. 200–13 (VI. 42, 43, 55, 56, 44, 45, 65, 81, 79); [10]p. 25 (I. 93, 98); [11]p. 398 (IX. 317–319). Reprinted with permission of the publishers.

D. This quotation is from a newspaper clipping, which does not identify the passage except to say it is from the *Padmapurana.* The authors have been unsuccessful in tracing it. It is an amplification of the *Laws of Manu,* V. 154. (See above.)

E. *The Thirteen Principal Upanishads,* translated by R. E. Hume, 2nd ed., Oxford University Press, London, 1934. [1]Svet. I.6, p. 395; [2]Mun. 3.2.8, p. 376; [3]Mun. 2.2.8, p. 373; [4]Mait. 6.18, p. 435; [5]Svet. 4.9, p. 404. Reprinted with permission of the publisher.

F. Mircea Eliade, *Yoga: Immortality and Freedom,* Pantheon Books, published for and copyrighted by Bollingen Foundation, New York, 1958. [1]p. 13; [2]p. 16 (quoting Sankhya-Karika, 19).

G. Sir Edwin Arnold, *The Bhagavad Gita: The Song Celestial,* in any edition. [1]I.13–23; [2]I.24–26; [3]I.28–47; [4]2.11–20; [5]2.47–51; 319, 30; [6]6.10–15, 25–31; [7]9.16–19; [8]11.12; [9]12.8–12; [10]18.64–66; [11]12.13–20; [12]9.28–30.

H. Sarvapelli Radhakrishnan, *The Bhagavadgita,* Harper & Brothers, New York, p. 147.

I. A. L. Basham, *The Wonder That Was India,* Sidgwick and Jackson, London, 1954. [1]p. 330, (quoting "Guide to the Lord Murugan"); [2]p. 331 (quoting Manikka Vassagar translated in Kingsbury and

Philips, *Hymns of the Tamil Shaivite Saints,* Calcutta, 1921).

J. Thomas Hopkins, "The Social Teaching of the Bhagavata Purana," in *Krishna: Myths, Rites and Attitudes,* edited by Milton Singer. University of Chicago Press, 1968, p. 13.

K. Romain Rolland, *Prophets of the New India,* translated by E. F. Malcolm-Smith. Albert and Charles Boni, New York, 1930. [1]pp. 42–43; [2]p. 43 n.

L. Mohandas Gandhi, *Young India, 1919–1922,* Huebsch, New York, 1923, p. 804.

M. Gertrude Emerson, *Voiceless India,* Doubleday, Doran and Company, New York, 1931, p. 110. Reprinted with permission.

N. *The Gospel of Ramakrishna,* Vedanta Society, New York, 1907. [1]pp. 158–60; [2]pp. 207–14.

O. Ramakrishna, *Teachings of Ramakrishna,* Amora, Advaita Ashrama, 1934, p. 31.

P. Shri Goparaju Ramchandra Roy, *A Note on Atheism,* 1974, p. 1.

Q. Paul D. Devanandan, "The Contemporary Attitude to Conversion," in *Religion in Life,* Vol. XXVII (1958), pp. 381–92.

Chapter 5. Jainism

A. *Sacred Books of the East,* Vol. XXII, *The Gaina Sutras,* translated by Hermann Jacobi. Oxford, Clarendon Press, 1884. [1]pp. 192–93; [2]p. 250; [3]p. 194; [4]p. 194; [5]p. 200; [6]pp. 80, 79, 82, 79, 87; [7]pp. 82, 83, 86, 82, 86; [8]pp. 80, 84, 85; [9]p. 201; [10]p. 264; [11]p. 52; [12]p. 152; [13]p. 33; [14]pp. 202–10; [15]p. 21; [16]p. 81; [17]p. 264. Reprinted with permission of the publishers.

B. James Bissett Pratt, *India and Its Faiths,* Houghton Mifflin Company, Boston, 1915, p. 255.

Chapter 6. Buddhism in Its First Phase

A. Kenneth J. Saunders, *Gotama Buddha: A Biography Based on the Canonical Books of the Theravadin,* Association Press, New York, 1920. [1]p. 9 (quoting Anguttara Nikaya 1.45); [2]p. 21 (quoting Jataka 1.71); [3]p. 112 (Samyutta IV). Quoted with permission of the publisher.

B. *Asvaghosa's Life of Buddha* (Buddha Carita), translated from the Chinese version by Samuel Beal, *The World's Great Classics,* Colonial Press, New York, 1900. [1]p. 306; [2]condensation of a lengthy passage from Bk. XII (following L. Adams Beck, *The Story of Oriental Philosophy,* p. 133).

C. Henry Clarke Warren, *Buddhism in Translation,* Harvard University Press, 1992. [1]p. 55 (Jataka I.58.7); [2]p. 122 (Majjhima Nikaya 63); [3]p. 129 (Milindapanha 25.1); [4]p. 234 (Ibid. 71.16); [5]p. 239 (Vissudhi Magga 17); [6]p. 136 (Maha-Nidana-Sutta of the Digha-Nikaya, 256.21); [7]p. 436 (Vissudhi Magga 3). Reprinted with permission of the publisher.

D. Sir Charles Eliot, *Hinduism and Buddhism,* 3 vols., Edward Arnold and Company, London, 1921. [1]Vol. I, p. 135 (Anguttara Nikaya 3.35); [2]Vol. I, p. 139 (Majjhima Nikaya 1.22); [3]Vol. I, p. 160 (Maha-Parinibbana 5.25). Reprinted with permission of the publishers.

E. *Further Dialogues of the Buddha,* translated from the *Majjhima Nikaya* by Lord Chalmers for the Pali Text Society, Oxford University Press, London, 1926. [1]I, p. 115 (1.163); [2]I, pp. 115–117 (1.163–166); [3]I, p. 117 (1.166); [4]I, p. 173 (1.240–241); [5]I, p. 174 (1.242); [6]I, p. 56 (1.80); [7]I, p. 176 (1.246); [8]I, p. 15 (1.22); [9]I, p. 17 (1.24); [10]I, p. 118 (1.167). Reprinted with permission of the publishers.

F. For various accounts, see C above, p. 71 f. (*Jataka* 1.68), which provides the more elaborated version condensed in the text; and Clarence H. Hamilton, ed., *Buddhism, A Religion of Infinite Compassion,* p. 18 f., the *Sutta-Nipata's* version, which makes Mara little more than the personification of Gautama's own doubts.

G. *Sacred Books of the East,* Vol. XIII, *Vinaya Texts,* translated by T. W. Rhys Davids and Hermann Oldenberg. Oxford, Clarendon Press, 1883. [1]p. 94; [2]p. 75 f.; [3]p. 150. Reprinted with permission of the publishers.

H. *Buddhist Scriptures,* translated by Edward J. Thomas, *Wisdom of the East* series, John Murray, London, 1913. p. 52 (Khuddaka Patha 2). Quoted with permission of the publisher.

I. T. W. Rhys Davids, *Buddhism,* Society for Promoting Christian Knowledge, London, 1890, pp. 81–83.

J. George Foot Moore, *History of Religions,* 2 vols., Charles Scribner's Sons, New York, and T. & T. Clark, Ltd., Edinburgh, 1913–1919. Vol. I, p. 296. Quoted with permission of the publishers.

K. *Sacred Books of the East,* Vol. XI, *Buddhist Suttas,* translated by T. W. Rhys Davids, Oxford, Clarendon Press, 1881, pp. 148–150. Quoted with permission of the publishers.

L. *Sacred Books of the East,* Vol. X, *The Dhammapada,* translated by F. Max Müller. Oxford, Clarendon Press, 1881. [1]XVI.211; [2]1:2–5. Quoted with permission of the publishers.

M. James Bissett Pratt, *The Pilgrimage of Buddhism,* the Macmillan Company, New York, 1928. [1]p. 30 (Udana VIII.8, following the German of Seiden-stucken); [2]p. 30 (Samyutta 21, following Mrs. Rhys Davids); [3]p. 54 (Majjhima Nikaya, XXXI.). Reprinted with permission of the publisher.

N. Mrs. T. W. Rhys Davids, *Psalms of the Brethren,* Published for the Pali Text Society by Henry Frowde, London, 1913, p. 362 (CCLXI).

O. Bikshu Sangharakshita, *A Survey of Buddhism,* Indian Institute of World Culture, Bangalore, 1957, p. 175 (Samyutta-Nikaya, III.235).

P. Edward Conze, ed., *Buddhist Texts Through the Ages,* Harper Torchbooks, 1964, p. 94 (changing *perception* to *ideation*).

Q. Melford E. Spiro, *Buddhism and Society,* Harper & Row Paperbacks, 1970, p. 58f.

R. *Sacred Books of the East,* Vol. X, Part 2, *The Sutta Nipata,* translated by V. Fausböll. Oxford, Clarendon Press, 1881. [1]p. 6 f. (Khaggavissana Sutta 1–13); [2]p. 25. Quoted with permission of the publishers.

Chapter 7.
The Religious Development of Buddhism

A. Carl Clemen, ed., *Religions of the World: Their Nature and History,* George G. Harrap and Company, London, and Harcourt, Brace and Company, New York, 1931, pp. 308–9. Quoted with permission of the publishers.

B. Melford E. Spiro, *Buddhism and Society,* Harper & Row, New York, 1970, p. 74.

C. Vincent A. Smith, *Asoka, the Buddhist Emperor of India,* Oxford, Clarendon Press, 1920. [1]p. 186;

[2]pp. 150, 178. Reprinted with permission of the publishers.

D. T. W. Rhys Davids, *Buddhism,* Society for Promoting Christian Knowledge, London, 1890, pp. 170–71.

E. Arvind Sharma, "How and Why Did Women in Ancient India Become Buddhist Nuns?" *Sociological Analysis,* Vol. 38, fall 1977, p. 248.

F. Caroline Augusta Davids, *Psalms of the Sisters,* Pali Text Society, London, 1909, *passim.*

G. John Lagerweg, "The Taoist Religious Community," in *The Encyclopedia of Religion,* edited by Mircea Eliade, Macmillan Publishing Co., New York, 1987. Vol. 14, [1]pp. 311–12; [2]p. 312.

H. *All Men are Brothers [Shui Hu Zhuan],* translated from the Chinese by Pearl S. Buck. A John Day Book. Grosset & Dunlap, New York, 1933, 1937, p. 119.

I. Edward Conze, *Buddhism, Its Essence and Development,* Philosophical Library, 1954, p. 38.

J. Sir Charles Eliot, *Hinduism and Buddhism,* 3 vols., Edward Arnold and Company, London, 1921. [1]Vol. II, p. 30 (quoting the Lesser Sukhavati-vyuha); [2]Vol. II, p. 43 (quoting Nagarjuna); [3]Vol. III, p. 404; [4]Vol. II, p. 284 n. 2. Reprinted with permission of the publishers.

K. *Sacred Books of the East,* Vol. XXI, 1884, *Saddharma-Pundarika or the Lotus of the True Law,* translated by H. Kern, New York, Dover Publications, Inc. 1963, p. 253.

L. Bhikshu Sangharakshita, *A Survey of Buddhism,* Indian Institute of World Culture, Bangalore, 1957. [1]p. 371 f.; [2]pp. 64, 66.

M. *Sacred Books of the East,* Vol. XLIX, *Buddhist Mahayana Texts,* translated by E. B. Cowell, Max Müller, and I. Takakusu. Oxford, Clarendon Press, 1893, pp. 153–54. Reprinted with permission of the publishers.

N. Richard H. Robinson, *The Buddhist Religion,* Dickensen Publishing Company, Belmont, Calif., 1970, p. 74.

O. Heinrich Zimmer, *Philosophies of India,* edited by Joseph Campbell, Bollingen Foundation, 1951; reference here is to Meridian edition, 1956. [1]pp. 447–48, quoting *Majjhima Nikaya* 3.2.22.135; [2]p. 485, quoting *Astasahasrika Prajnaparamita,* I.

P. James Bissett Pratt, *The Pilgrimage of Buddhism,* the Macmillan Company, 1928, p. 480 (quoting Coates and Ishizuka, *Honen, the Buddhist Saint,* pp. 185–87). Quoted with permission of the publishers.

Q. Dwight Goddard, ed., *A Buddhist Bible,* Dwight Goddard, Thetford, Vermont, 1938, pp. 497–98 (Sutra Spoken by the Sixth Patriarch). Quoted with permission of the Dwight Goddard estate.

R. Zenkei Shibayama, *Zen Comments on the Mumonkan,* translated by Sumiko Kudo, Harper & Row, 1984 (c. 1974), p. 293.

S. Masaharu Anesaki, *Nichiren the Buddhist Prophet,* Harvard University Press, 1916, p. 29.

T. Erik Haarh, "Contributions to the Study of Mandala and Mudra," in *Acta Orientalia,* Vol. XXIII, Nos. 1–2 (1958), pp. 57–91.

U. Holmes Welch, *The Practices of Chinese Buddhism,* Harvard University Press, 1967, p. 414.

V. Jane Bunnag, *Buddhist Monk, Buddhist Layman: A Study of Urban Monastic Organization in Central Thailand,* Cambridge University Press, England, pp. 200–1.

Chapter 8.
Sikhism

A. M. A. MacAuliffe, *The Sikh Religion: Its Gurus, Sacred Writings and Anthems,* 6 vols; Oxford, Clarendon Press, 1909. Vol I: [1]pp. 33–34; [2]p. 35; [3]p. 37; [4]p. 58; [5]p. 175; [6]pp. 190–191; [7]p. 219; [8]p. 377; [9]p. 328; [10]p. 40; [11]p. 60. Vol. II; [12]p. 238. Vol. IV; [13]p. 2. Reprinted with permission of the publishers.

B. *The Sacred Writing of the Sikhs,* translated by Trilochan Singh, Bhai Jodh Singh, Kapur Singh, Bawa Harkishen Singh, and Khushwant Singh, under the auspices of the National Academy of Letters, India, George Allen & Unwin, London, 1960. [1]p. 82; [2]p. 105; [3]p. 46; [4]p. 77; [5]p. 84; [6]p. 268; [7]p. 270. Reprinted with permission of the publishers.

C. Dorothy Field, *The Religion of the Sikhs,* in *Wisdom of the East* series, John Murray, London, 1914. [1]p. 54; [2]p. 19; [3]p. 106. Quoted with permission of the publisher.

D. Duncan Greenlees, *The Gospel of the Guru Granth Sahib,* the Theosophical Publishing House, Adyar, Madras, 1960, p. lxiv.

E. Fauja Singh, *Sikhism,* Punjabi University, Patiala, 1969, p. 30.

F. Sir Monier Williams, *Brahmanism and Hinduism,* the Macmillan Company, London, 1891, p. 177. With permission of the publisher.

Chapter 9.
Native Chinese Religion and Daoism

A. Tsui Chi, *A Short History of Chinese Civilization,* G. P. Putnam's Sons, New York, 1943, p. 3. Reprinted with permission of the publisher.

B. S. Wells Williams, *The Middle Kingdom,* Charles Scribner's Sons, New York, 1899. II, p. 139 (slightly condensed). Reprinted with permission of the publisher.

C. H. G. Creel, *Sinism: A Study of the Evolution of the Chinese World-View,* Open Court Publishing Company, Chicago, 1928, p. 21.

D. *The Shi-King,* metrically translated by James Legge, the World's Great Classics, Colonial Press, New York, 1900, pp. 195–99.

E. E. R. Hughes, ed., *Chinese Philosophy in Classical Times,* Everyman's Library No. 973, J. M. Dent and Sons, London, and E. P. Dutton, and Co., Inc., New York, 1941. [1]p. 308; [2]p. 163; [3]p. 154. Reprinted with permission of the publishers.

F. *Sacred Books of the East,* Vol. III, *The Texts of Confucianism,* Part I, Translated by James Legge, Oxford, Clarendon Press, 1879, p. 443 f., arranged in verse. Reprinted with permission of the publishers.

G. L. A. Lyall, *China,* Ernest Benn, London, and Charles Scribner's Sons, New York, 1934, pp. 28–33 (translating G. E. Simon, *La Cité Chinoise*). Reprinted with permission of the publishers.

H. *The Analects of Confucius,* etc. A translation by Charles A. Wong, published in China without imprint of publisher or date. (A partial American reprint is to be found in Robert O. Ballou, *The Bible of the World.* Viking Press, New York, 1939, p. 398 f.) Analects, Bk. XIII. 18.

I. *A Reader's Guide to the Great Religions,* edited by Charles J. Adams, The Free Press, Collier-Macmillan, Ltd., London, 1965, p. 39.

J. Y. L. Fung, *A History of Chinese Philosophy (From the Beginnings to Circa 100 B.C.),* translated by Derk Bodde, Henri Vetc, Peiping, 1937. [1]pp. 133–134 (quoting Mencius and Huai-nan-tzu); [2]p. 156

(quoting Chaung-tzu); [3]p. 153 (Chuang-tzu); [4]p. 237. Reprinted with permission of the publishers.

K. *The Sayings of Lao Tzu,* translated by Lionel Giles, *Wisdom of the East* series. John Murray, London, 1905. [1]p. 20 (XXI); [2]p. 43 (V); [3]p. 23 (XXX); [4]p. 25 (XXIV); [5]p. 32 (LXIII); [6]p. 46 (LXXVIII); [7]p. 50 (L); [8]p. 30 (XXXVII); [9]p. 38 (LVII); [10]p. 41 (XXXI); [11]p. 34 (LXI). Reprinted with permission of the publisher.

L. Ch'u Ta-kao, *The Tao Te Ching,* a translation published by the Buddhist Society, London, [1]LI; [2]XXXVII; [3]XVI; [4]XL; [5]XXII; [6]XXII; [7]II; [8]XLVII; [9]VIII; [10]LV; [11]XVI. Reprinted with permission of the publishers.

M. Lin Yutang, ed., *The Wisdom of China and India,* Random House, New York, 1942, from the *Tao Te Ching:* [1]p. 586 (VI); [2]p. 594 (XXII); From *Chuang-tzu:* [3]p. 686; [4]p. 685; [5]p. 686; [6]p. 647; [7]p. 664; [8]p. 672; [9]p. 660; [10]pp. 660–61. Reprinted with permission of the publishers.

N. Arthur Waley, *The Way and Its Power,* Houghton Mifflin Company, Boston, and George Allen & Unwin, London, 1934. [1]p. 195 (XLII); [2]p. 152 (IX); [3]p. 159 (XIV); [4]p. 164 (XVII). Reprinted with permission of the publishers.

O. Witter Bynner, *The Way of Life,* John Day Company, New York, 1944, p. 38 (XXIII). Reprinted with permission of the publishers.

P. *Sacred Books of the East,* Vol. XXXIX, *The Texts of Taoism,* translated by James Legge. Oxford, Clarendon Press, 1891, p. 91. Reprinted with permission of the publishers.

Q. H. A. Giles, *Chuang Tzu: Mystic, Moralist and Social Reformer,* Kelly and Walsh, Shanghai, 1889. [1]II.4; [2]XII.2; [3]II.5; [4]XII.3; [5]XII.3; [6]VIII.2; [7]II.6. Reprinted with permission of the publishers.

R. Edward J. Jurji, ed., *The Great Religions of the Modern World,* Princeton University Press, 1946, p. 27. Quoted by permission of the publisher.

S. Leon Wieger, *A History of the Religious Beliefs and Philosophical Opinions in China,* translated by E. C. Werner. Hsien-hsien Press, China, 1927. [1]p. 187; [2]pp. 395–401 passim; [3]pp. 203–5; [4]p. 603.

T. Chan Wing-tsit, "The Story of Chinese Philosophy," in *Philosophy–East and West,* edited by Charles A. Moore. Princeton University Press, 1944, p. 45. Quoted with permission of the publisher.

U. Holmes Welch, *Taoism: The Parting of the Way,* Beacon Press, Boston, 1966, p. 108.

V. Ch'u Chai, *The Story of Chinese Philosophy,* Washington Square Press, New York, 1961, p. 117 f.

W. John Lagerweg, "The Taoist Religious Community," in *The Encyclopedia of Religion,* edited by Mircea Eliade, Macmillan Publishing Co., New York, 1987, Vol. 14, p. 312.

Chapter 10.
Confucius and Confucianism

A. James Legge, *The Analects of Confucius,* Vol. I of *The Chinese Classics,* 2nd ed. Oxford, Clarendon Press, 1893–1895. [1]XIV.11; [2]VII.26; [3]III.7; [4]IX.2; [5]X.1–17 (changing *king* to *duke* in the translation); [6]XIV.13. Reprinted with permission of the publishers.

B. Lin Yutang, ed., *The Wisdom of China and India,* Random House, New York, 1942. [1]p. 817 (An VII. 17); [2]p. 816 (An. VII. 19); [3]p. 828 (An. XIV. 36); [4]p. 838 (Mencius); [5]p. 833 (An. III. 3); [6]p. 835 (An. XIII. 21); [7]p. 819 (An. III. 13); [8]p. 817 (An. IX. 5); [9]p. 604 (Tao-Te-Ching, XXXVIII); [10]p. 592 (Tao-Te-Ching, XVIII); [11]p. 677 (Chuang-tzu); [12]p. 665 (Chuang-tzu). Reprinted with permission of the publisher.

C. Arthur Waley, *The Analects of Confucius,* Houghton Mifflin Company, Boston, and George Allen & Unwin, London, 1938, p. 127 (VIII. 22). Reprinted with permission of the publishers.

D. Lin Yutang, *The Wisdom of Confucius,* The Modern Library, Random House, 1938. [1]p. 83; [2]p. 13; [3]p. 216 (LiKi XXVII); [4]pp. 228–29 (LiKi IX); [5]p. 238; [6]p. 14; [7]p. 280 (Mencius VI.I). Reprinted with permission of the publisher.

E. Y. L. Fung, *A History of Chinese Philosophy (From the Beginnings to Circa 100 B.C.),* translated by Derk Bodde, Henri Vetch, Peiping, 1937. [1]p. 108 (quoting Sse-ma Ch'ien); [2]p. 15; [3]p. 59 (An. XIII. 30); [4]p. 72; [5]p. 58 (An. VI. 20); [6]p. 106; [7]p. 318; [8]p. 327; [9]p. 113; [10]p. 17. Reprinted with permission of the publisher.

F. Brian Brown, *The Story of Confucius,* David Mackay Company, Philadelphia, 1927. [1]p. 94 (An. VII. 1); [2]p. 137 (An. IV. 5); [3]p. 94 (An. VII. 1); [4]p. 100 (An. VII. 34). Reprinted with permission of the publisher.

G. E. R. Hughes, ed., *Chinese Philosophy in Classical Times,* Everyman's Library No. 973, J. M. Dent and

Sons, London, and E. P. Dutton and Co., Inc., New York, 1941. [1]p. 12; [2]p. 87; [3]pp. 265–66; [4]p. 261; [5]pp. 259–60; [6]p. 101; [7]p. 100–1; [8]p. 102; [9]p. 102; [10]pp. 294–95; [11]p. 317; [12]pp. 335–36; [13]pp. 324–25. Reprinted with permission of the publishers.

H. The Chinese characters are translatable into a variety of terms suggesting the many facets of each word. This is the translation (and assignment of analogies from a tree) of Y. C. Yang, in *China's Religious Heritage.* Abingdon-Cokesbury Press, New York and Nashville, 1943, p. 81.

I. Charles A. Wong, *The Analects of Confucius, The Great Learning, The Doctrine of the Mean, and the Works of Mencius.* Translation published in China without the imprint of a publisher or date. A partial American reprint is to be found in Robert O. Ballou, *The Bible of the World,* Viking Press, New York, 1939. Because of the great rarity of the original work, the following references are made, for reader convenience, to this American reprint. [1]p. 413 (An. XV. 23); [2]p. 420 (Gr. Learn.); [3]p. 399 (An. II.4); [4]p. 400 (An.III.17); [5]p. 451 (Men.); [6]p. 444 (Men.); [7]p. 455 (Men.); [8]p. 452 (Men.); [9]pp. 431, 433, 434 (Men.); [10]p. 458 (Men.); [11]p. 459 (Men.); [12]p. 460 (Men.)

J. Ku Hung Ming, *The Conduct of Life: A Translation of the Doctrine of the Mean,* in *Wisdom of the East* series, John Murray, London, 1906. [1]p. 26 (XIII); [2]p. 28 (XV); [3]p. 42 (XIX); [4]p. 29 (XVI); [5]p. 39 (XVII); [6]p. 53 (XXIX). Reprinted with permission of the publisher.

K. L. A. Lyall, *The Sayings of Confucius,* 3rd ed., Longmans, Green and Company, London, New York, 1935. [1]p. 2 (I. 11); [2]p. 4 (II. 6); [3]p. 5 (II.7); [4]p. 15 (IV. 19); [5]p. 4 (II. 3, slightly modified); [6]p. 10 (III. 12). Reprinted with permission of the publisher.

L. Ivan Chen, *The Book of Filial Duty,* in *Wisdom of the East* series, John Murray, London, 1920, p. 22. Quoted with permission of the publisher.

M. Lional Giles, *The Sayings of Confucius,* in *Wisdom of the East* series, John Murray, London, 1917. [1]p. 41 (XII. 17); [2]p. 42 (XII. 19); [3]p. 45 (XII. 11); [4]p. 46 (XIII. 15); [5]p. 69 (XVII. 6); [6]p. 108 (XVII. 13); [7]p. 57 (IV. 10); [8]p. 64 (XII. 20); [9]p. 68 (XV. 17); [10]p. 60 (VI. 27); [11]p. 87 (VII. 33); [12]p. 86 (VII. 27); [13]p. 94 (II. 16); [14]p. 102 (XI. 11); [15]p. 95 (III. 11). Reprinted with permission of the publisher.

N. Hu Shih, *The Development of the Logical Method in Ancient China,* The New China Book Company, Shanghai, 1917, p. 26.

O. Ku Hung Ming, *The Discourses and Sayings of Confucius,* Kelly and Walsh, Shanghai, 1898, p. 46 (An. IV. 27).

P. James Legge, *Mencius,* Vol. II of *The Chinese Classics,* 2nd ed., Oxford, Clarendon Press, 1893–1895, III. 1. iv, 13. Reprinted with permission of the publishers.

Q. Yi-apo Mei, *Motse, the Neglected Rival of Confucius,* Probsthain, London, 1929. [1]p. 80 f.; [2]p. 89; [3]p. 83; [4]p. 87; [5]p. 145; [6]p. 142; [7]p. 83. Reprinted with permission of the publisher.

R. Wing-tsit Chan, "The Story of Chinese Philosophy," in *Philosophy–East and West,* edited by Charles A. Moore, Princeton University Press, 1944. [1]p. 30; [2]p. 50; [3]p. 57; [4]p. 58; [5]p. 63; [6]pp. 63–64; [7]p. 64. Reprinted with permission of the publisher.

S. H. H. Dubs, *The Works of Hsüntse Translated from the Chinese,* Probsthain, London, 1928. [1]p. 301; [2]pp. 301, 302; [3]p. 310; [4]pp. 113–14; [5]pp. 179, 181; [6]p. 182; [7]pp. 244–45; [8]p. 327; [9]pp. 236–37; [10]pp. 232–33; [11]p. 223. Reprinted with permission of the publisher.

T. Gung-hsing Wang, *The Chinese Mind,* John Day Company, New York, 1946. [1]p. 46; [2]p. 138; [3]p. 139; [4]p. 139; [5]p. 145. Reprinted with permission of the publisher.

U. John K. Shryock, *The Origin and Development of the State Cult of Confucius,* The Century Company, New York, 1932, p. 123. Reprinted with permission of Appleton-Century Company.

V. Tsui Chi, *A Short History of Chinese Civilization,* G. P. Putnam's Sons, New York, 1943, pp. 168–169. Reprinted with permission of the publishers.

W. P. J. MacClagan, *Chinese Religious Ideas,* Student Christian Movement Press, London, 1926, p. 112.

X. Dagobert D. Runes, ed., *The Dictionary of Philosophy,* Philosophical Library, New York, 1942. [1]p. 52 (article, "Chinese Philosophy," by Wing-tsit Chan); [2]p. 53 (Ibid.).

Y. Kam Louie, *Critiques of Confucius in Contemporary China,* St. Martin's Press, New York, 1980, p. 148.

Z. Hermann Kahn, *World Economic Development: 1979 and Beyond,* Westview Press, Boulder, Colo., 1979, p. 121.

AA. N. Balakrishnan, "Singapore: Ideological Thrust," in *Far Eastern Economic Review,* February 7, 1991, pp. 27–28.

BB. Lynn Pan, "Playing Fast and Loose with Confucian Values," in *Far Eastern Economic Review,* May 19, 1988, p. 47.

CC. W. T. deBary and Tu Weiming, *Confucianism and Human Rights,* Columbia University Press, New York, 1998, p. xvi.

Chapter 11.
Shinto

A. Chie Nakane, *Japanese Society,* University of California Press, 1970, p. 390.

B. Joseph M. Kitagawa, *Religion in Japanese History,* Columbia University Press, 1966. [1]p. 3 f.; [2]p. 68; [3]p. 167 f.

C. *The Ko-ji-ki,* translated by Basil H. Chamberlain, 2nd ed. J. L. Thompson and Company, Kobe, 1932. [1]pp. 17–51, 127–29; [2]pp. 62–70.

D. D. C. Holtom, *The National Faith of Japan,* Kegan, Paul, Trench, Trubner and Company, London, 1938. [1]p. 113; [2]p. 49; [3]p. 23; [4]p. 73; [5]pp. 81–82; [6]pp. 133–34. Reprinted with permission.

E. Ichiro Hori, *Folk Religion in Japan: Continuity and Change,* University of Chicago Press, 1968. [1]p. 40; [2]p. 37 f.

F. H. N. Wieman and W. M. Horton, *The Growth of Religion,* Willett, Clark and Company, Chicago, 1938, p. 88. Quoted with permission of the publisher.

G. Charles S. Braden, *Modern Tendencies in World Religions,* The Macmillan Company, New York, 1933, p. 169. Quoted with permission of the publishers.

H. Yoshito Tanaka, "The True Import of Shinto," in *The University Review,* issued by the National League of Japanese University Professors, 1938, Vol. I, No. 2, p. 4.

I. N. Hozumi, *Ancestor-Worship and Japanese Law,* 6th ed., Hokuseido Press, Tokyo, 1940, pp. 107–8.

J. D. C. Holtom, *The Political Philosophy of Modern Shinto,* Vol. XLIX, Part II, of Transactions of the Asiatic Society of Japan, Tokyo, 1922. [1]p. 73; [2]p. 88; [3]pp. 107–8.

K. Christopher Noss, *Tohoku, the Scotland of Japan,* Board of Foreign Missions of the Reformed Church in the United States, Philadelphia, 1918, pp. 87–88.

L. A. B. Mitford (Lord Redesdale), *Tales of Old Japan,* reprint of 1928, The Macmillan Company, London, p. 13.

M. Tadayoshi Sakurai, *Human Bullets: A Soldier's Story of Port Arthur,* 9th ed., translated by Masujiro Honda and Alice M. Bacon, Teibo Publishing Company, Tokyo, 1911, p. 221.

Chapter 12.
Zoroastrianism

A. Carl Clemen, ed., *The Religions of the World: Their Nature and History,* George G. Harrap and Company, London, and Harcourt, Brace and Company, New York, 1931, p. 142. Quoted with permission of the publishers.

B. R. C. Zaehner, "Zoroastrianism," in *Concise Encyclopedia of Living Faiths,* edited by R. C. Zaehner, Hawthorn Books, New York, 1959, p. 209.

C. A. V. Williams Jackson, *Zoroaster, the Prophet of Ancient Iran,* Columbia University Press, New York, 1898. [1]p. 41; [2]p. 41; [3]p. 52; [4]p. 60. Reprinted with permission of the publisher.

D. James Hope Moulton, *Early Zoroastrianism,* Constable and Company (for Hibbert Trust), London, 1913. [1]pp. 365–66 (Yasna 43.7 f.); [2]p. 350 (Ys. 30.5); [3]p. 367 (Ys. 44.3–7); [4]p. 349 (Ys. 30.3–5); [5]p. 370 (Ys. 45.2); [6]p. 354 (Ys. 31.18); [7]p. 53 (Ys. 31.10); [8]p. 373 (Ys. 45.4). Reprinted with permission of the publisher.

E. Jacques Duchesne-Guillemin, "The Religion of Ancient Iran," in *Historia Religionum,* Vol. I, edited by C. J. Bleeker and G. Widengren, E. J. Brill, Leiden, 1969, *passim.*

F. R. C. Zaehner, *The Dawn and Twilight of Zoroastrianism,* G. P. Putnam's Sons, New York, 1961, p. 146.

G. George Foot Moore, *History of Religions,* 2 vols., Charles Scribner's Sons, New York, and T. & T. Clark, Ltd., Edinburgh, 1913–1919. Vol. I, p. 366 (Ys. 12). Quoted with permission of the publishers.

H. James Hope Moulton, *The Treasure of the Magi,* Oxford University Press, London, 1917. [1]p. 37

(Yasna 46.11); [2]p. 87; [3]p. 89; [4]p. 142; [5]p. 149. Quoted with permission.

I. *Sacred Books of the East,* Vol. XXIII, *The Zend Avesta,* translated by J. Darmesteter, Oxford, Clarendon Press, 1883, p. 183 (Ys. 13.12). Reprinted with permission of the publishers.

J. Jal Dastur Cursetji Pavry, *The Zoroastrian Doctrine of a Future Life,* Columbia University Press, New York, 1926. [1]pp. 92–93; [2]pp. 44–45 (from Sar Dar Bundahish 99.5–20). Reprinted with permission of the publisher.

K. *Sacred Books of the East,* Vol. V, Part I, *The Pahlavi Texts,* translated by E. W. West, Oxford, Clarendon Press, 1880, p. 248 (Bundahishn 30). Reprinted with permission of the publisher.

Chapters 13 and 14.
Judaism

A. Smith and Goodspeed, *The Bible: An American Translation,* University of Chicago Press, 1935. [1]Ex. 1:8–10, 22; 2:1–10; [2]Ex. 3:1–15; [3]Ex. 34:1–8; [4]Ex. 34:17–26; [5]Ex. 24:3–8; [6]Ex. 32:1–24; [7]II Kings 23:4–14; [8]Deut. 24:16; [9]Jer. 1:4–9; [10]Jer. 20:7–18; [11]Jer. 26:5–24; [12]Jer. 28:10–14; [13]Jer. 23:16, 31–32; [14]Jer. 30:11; [15]Jer. 31:27–34; [16]II Kings 24:14–16; [17]Ps. 137; [18]Esther 3:8–9; [19]Jer. 44:17–18; [20]Ezek. 3:17; [21]Ezek. 36:22–23; [22]Is. 40:28; [23]Is. 43:10; [24]Is. 55:9; [25]Is. 57:15; [26]Is. 49:1–3; [27]Is. 42:25; [28]Is. 45:14–15; [29]Is. 49:22–23; [30]Ezra 1:5; [31]Neh. 9:38–10:39; [32]Neh. 13:15–21; [33]Neh. 13:25. Reprinted with permission of the publishers.

B. George A. Barton, *Archaeology and the Bible,* 6th ed., rev. American Sunday School Union, 1933, p. 442, 444 (substituting *Habiru* for *Habiri*).

C. James Moffatt, *The Holy Bible: A New Translation,* Hodder and Stoughton Ltd., London, and George H. Doran Company, New York, 1922, 1924, 1926. [1]Hosea 4:11–14; [2]Amos 2:6–8; 5:7–11; 6:1–6; [3]Amos 5:4–6, 21–24; [4]Amos 7:1–17; [5]Hosea 2:2–19; [6]Hosea 10:7, [7]Is. 6:1–9; [8]Is. 30:15; [9]Is. 7:1–9; [10]Is. 3:2, 5:8, 11; 6:21–23; 1:23; [11]Is. 1:18–19; [12]Is. 2:1–5; [13]Is. 11:1–10; [14]Micah 3:5–12; [15]Micah 6:6–8; [16]Is. 42:6. Reprinted with permission.

D. Max Loehr, *A History of Religion in the Old Testament,* Ivor Nicholson & Watson, Ltd., London, and

Charles Scribner's Sons, New York, 1936, pp. 51–52. Quoted with permission of the publishers.

E. Rudolph Kittel, *The Religion of the People of Israel,* The Macmillan Company, New York, 1925. [1]p. 71; [2]p. 162; [3]p. 162. Reprinted with permission of the publisher.

F. R. G. Moulton, *The Modern Reader's Bible,* The Macmillan Company, New York, 1907. Is. 53:3–6. Reprinted with permission of the publisher.

G. Abram Leon Sachar, *A History of the Jews,* Alfred Knopf, New York, 1930. [1]p. 88; [2]p. 89; [3]p. 229; [4]p. 265.

H. Gaalyahu Cornfeld, ed., *Adam to Daniel,* The Macmillan Company, New York, 1961, p. 381.

I. Lewis Browne, *Stranger than Fiction: A Short History of the Jews,* The Macmillan Company, New York, 1931. [1]p. 171, [2]p. 249. Reprinted with permission of the publishers.

J. David Philipson, *The Reform Movement in Judaism,* rev. ed. The Macmillan Company, New York, 1931. [1]p. 54; [2]p. 122; [3]p. 363. Reprinted with permission of the publishers.

K. Oscar I. Janowsky, ed., *The American Jew: A Composite Portrait,* 2nd ed., Harper and Brothers, New York, 1932, pp. 214–15. Quoted with permission of the publisher.

Chapter 15.
Christianity in Its Opening Phase

A. Josephus, *Antiquities,* XVIII, 1, 6.

B. J. M. Powis Smith and E. J. Goodspeed, *The Bible: An American Translation,* University of Chicago Press, 1935. [1]Matt. 3:4; [2]Matt. 3:12; [3]Lk. 3:11; [4]Mk. 1:9–11; [5]Mk. 1:24–38 *passim;* [6]Mk. 4:1; [7]Mk. 9:1; [8]Mk. 13:30–33; [9]Lk. 17:22–24, 26–27, 30; [10]Lk. 13:24–30; [11]Matt. 8:11–12; [12]Matt. 5:3–12; Lk. 6:20–26; [13]Matt. 12:28; Lk. 17:20 f.; [14]Lk. 4:18–21; [15]Mk. 9:45; [16]Lk. 9:59–62; [17]Matt. 5:22; [18]Matt. 5:28; [19]Matt. 5:43–48, 7:12, 22:37–40; [20]Matt. 5:38–40; [21]Matt. 7:1–5; [22]Lk. 6:36–38; [23]Mk. 2:27–28; [24]Mk. 7:14–15; [25]Mk. 6:4; [26]Mk. 3:31–35; [27]Mk. 3:24–26; [28]Mk. 8:27–29; [29]Mk. 11:17; [30]Matt. 21:31, 43; [31]Mk. 14:22–24. Reprinted with permission of the publisher.

C. Rudolf Bultmann, *Jesus Christ and Mythology,* Scribner's Sons, New York, 1951, p. 25.

D. C. H. Dodd, *The Parables of the Kingdom,* Nisbet & Co., Ltd., London, 1946, p. 54.

E. James Moffatt, *The Holy Bible: A New Translation,* Hodder and Stoughton, Ltd., London, and George H. Doran Company, New York, 1922, 1924, 1926, [1]Lk. 17:20; [2]Mk. 12:14–17; [3]John 1:14. Quoted with permission.

F. J. M. Powis Smith and E. J. Goodspeed, *The Bible: An American Translation,* University of Chicago Press, 1935. [1]Cor. 15:1–8, 42–44, 50; [2]Acts 2:1–4; [3]Acts 5:29; [4]Acts 5:35–39; [5]Acts 6:1; [6]Acts 8:1; [7]Gal. 1:14; [8]Acts 9:2–19; [9]II Cor. 11:24–27; [10]Cor. 1:15–16; [11]Eph. 2:1–19. Reprinted with permission of the publisher.

G. Joseph Cullen Ayer Jr., *A Source Book for Ancient Church History,* Charles Scribner's Sons, New York, 1913, pp. 20–21. Reprinted with permission of the publishers.

H. C. C. Richardson et al., *Early Christian Fathers,* Library of Christian Classics, Westminster Press, Philadelphia, 1953, p. 287 f.

Chapter 16.
The Religious Development of Christianity

A. Williston Walker, *A History of the Christian Church,* Charles Scribner's Sons, New York, 1918, p. 61. Reprinted with permission of the publisher.

B. *The Ante-Nicene Fathers,* 10 vols., edited by Alexander Roberts and James Donaldson. American reprint of the Edinburgh edition, revised and rearranged. The Christian Literature Publishing Company, Buffalo, 1885–1887. [1]Praxes 27 (Vol. III, 624); [2]Letter 54.14 (Vol. V, p. 344).

C. Joseph Cullen Ayer Jr., *A Source Book for Ancient Church History,* Charles Scribner's Sons, New York, 1913. [1]p. 501; [2]pp. 696–97. Reprinted with permission of the publishers.

D. O. J. Thatcher and E. H. McNeals, *A Source Book for Medieval History,* New York, 1905, p. 445.

E. *A Select Library of Nicene and Post-Nicene Fathers,* 1st ser., 14 vols., The Christian Literature Company, New York, 1886–1890. [1]Confession 2.5 (Vol. I, p. 62); [2]Ibid. 8.7 (Vol. I, p. 124); [3]Ibid. 8.12 (Vol. I, p. 127); [4]On Trinity, Bk. 8, pref. (Vol. III, p. 115); [5]Ibid. Bk. 4.20 (Vol. III, p. 84); [6]Ibid. Bk. 10.11 (Vol. III, p. 142); [7]On Original Sin, 2.34 (Vol. V, p. 249); [8]Marriage and Concp., 1.27 (Vol. V, p. 275); [9]Gift of Perseverance, 1 Vol. V, p. 526 f.); [10]*De Spiritu,* Vol. V, xiii, 22.

F. *The Confessions of St. Augustine,* ninth book, translated by Edward B. Pusey. (Available in *Harvard Classics.*)

G. Nicolas Zernov, "Christianity: The Eastern Schism and the Eastern Orthodox Church," in *The Concise Encyclopedia of Living Faiths,* edited by R. C. Zaehner, Hawthorn Books, Inc., New York, 1959, p. 98.

H. Isabel Florence Hapgood, ed., *Service Book of the Holy Orthodox Catholic Apostolic (Greco-Russian) Church,* Cambridge, Mass., 1922, pp. 455–56.

I. T. F. Simmons, ed., *The Lay Folks Mass Book,* Early English Text Society, No. 71, pp. 104–15.

J. D. C. Somervell, *A Short History of Our Religion,* G. Bell and Sons, London, 1922, p. 190. Reprinted with permission of the publisher.

K. Julian of Norwich, *A Shewing of God's Love,* edited by Anna Maria Reynolds, Longmans, Green and Co., London, 1958, pp. 39–40.

L. Froissart, Vol. I of rev. ed. *Chronicles,* translated from the French by Thomas Johnes, *The World's Great Classics,* Colonial Press, New York, 1901, pp. 212–13 (Chap. IX).

M. Henry Wace and C. A. Bucheim, *Luther's Primary Works,* Lutheran Publication Society, Philadelphia, 1885. [1]pp. 194–96; [2]p. 78; [3]p. 53; [4]p. 9; [5]p. 21.

N. J. MacKinnon, *Luther and the Reformation,* 4 vols. Longmans, Green and Company, London, 1925–1930, Vol. II, pp. 301–2. Reprinted with permission of the publishers.

O. *The Latin Works of Huldreich Zwingli,* 3 vols. Tr. by S. M. Jackson, The Heidelberg Press, 1929. Vol. III, p. 229.

P. John Calvin, *Institutes of the Christian Religion,* 3 vols., translated by Henry Beveridge. Calvin Tract Society, Edinburgh, 1845. [1]Bk. II, chap. 1.8 (Vol. I, pp. 292–93); [2]Bk. III, chap. 11.2 (Vol. II, p. 303); [3]Bk. III, chap. 21–25 (Vol. II, p. 534).

Q. Anthony Ugolnik, "An Ecumenical Estrangement: Orthodoxy in America," in *The Christian Century,* 109, June 17–24, 1992, pp. 610–16.

R. Augustin Cardinal Bea, *The Church and the Jewish People,* Harper and Row, 1966, pp. 148–52.

S. *Benjamin Franklin, His Autobiography,* third section.

T. From an unpublished paper by John B. Noss.

U. Columbus Salley and Roland Behm, *Your God Is Too White,* Intervarsity Press, 1971, p. 7.

V. James Cone, *Black Theology and Black Power,* The Seabury Press, 1969, p. 151.

W. Mary Daly, *The Church and the Second Sex,* Rev. ed., Harper & Row, 1975. [1]p. 6; [2]p. 49.

X. Rosemary Ruether, ed., *Liberation Theology,* Paulist Press, 1972. p. 13.

Chapters 17 and 18.
Islam

A. Charles J. Adams, ed., *A Reader's Guide to the Great Religions,* the Free Press, New York, 1965, p. 287 f.

B. Fazlur Rahman, *Islam,* Anchor Books, 1968, p. 7.

C. A. J. Arberry, *The Koran Interpreted,* 2 vols., George Allen & Unwin Ltd., London, 1955. (A one-vol. paperback edition has been issued in New York by The Macmillan Company.) Reprinted with permission. [1]XCVI.1–5 (Vol. II, p. 344); [2]LIII.1–13 (II, 244); [3]LXXXI.2–14 (II, 326); [4]LXXX.33 f. (II, 325); [5]LXXXIII.6–18 (II, 329); [6]LXXIII.5–15 (II, 308); [7]XVIII.28 (I, 319); [8]XVII.7 (I, 302); [9]IV.82 (I, 112); [10]IV.110 f. (I, 117); [11]IV.21 (I, 103); [12]LIII.34 (II, 245); [13]VI.39 (I, 153); [14]VI.84 (I, 159); [15]VI.125 (I, 164); [16]LXXXI.27 (II, 327); [17]VI.77 (I, 158); [18]VII.185 (I, 194); [19]XVII.1 (I, 302); [20]XXXIII.64 f. (II, 129); [21]LVI.40, 50 (II, 255); [22]XXXVII.63 f. (II, 152); [23]XLIV.44–50 (I, 209); [24]XLIV.51 (II, 209); [25]LVI.15–23, 34 f. (II, 254 f.); [26]XIII.23 (I, 270); [27]II.173 f. (I, 50 f.); [28]XVII.24 f. (I, 304 f.); [29]XVII.34 (I, 305); [30]IV.2–5, 10 (I, 100 f.); [31]XXIV.33 (II, 50); [32]II.231 (I, 60); [33]II.187, 189 (I, 51 f.); [34]V.1–4 (I, 127); [35]V.93 (I, 142); [36]I (I, 29); [37]XXII.37 (II, 31); [38]LVII.27.

D. Arthur Jeffery, ed., *Islam: Muhammad and His Religion,* Liberal Arts Press, New York, 1958. [1]p. 16; [2]p. 19; [3]p. 45.

E. Maulana Muhammad Ali, *The Religion of Islam,* S. Chand, Lahore, 1970. [1]p. 23f., [2]p. 98.

F. Philip K. Hitti, *History of the Arabs,* The Macmillan Company, New York, 1937. [1]p. 120; [2]p. 150; [3]p. 153; [4]p. 153; [5]p. 431. Reprinted with permission.

G. I. Goldziher, *Mohammed and Islam,* translated by K. C. Seelye, Yale University Press, 1917. [1]pp. 97–98; [2]p. 183; [3]p. 183. Reprinted with permission of the publishers.

H. Tor Andrae, *Mohammed: The Man and His Faith,* translated by Theophil Menzel, George Allen & Unwin, London, 1936, p. 77. (Available as Harper Torchbook.)

I. John A. Williams, ed., *Islam, A Book of Readings,* George Braziller, New York, 1961, p. 79.

J. George Foot Moore, *History of Religions,* 2 vols., Charles Scribner's Sons, New York, and T. & T. Clark, Ltd., Edinburgh, 1913–1919. [1]II, p. 442; [2]II, p. 441; [3]II, p. 435. Reprinted with permission of the publishers.

K. *The Legacy of Islam,* edited by Sir Thomas Arnold and Alfred Guillaume, Oxford, Clarendon Press, 1931. [1]pp. 215–16; [2]p. 218; [3]p. 218. Reprinted with permission of the publishers.

L. *The Persian Poets,* edited by N. H. Dole and Belle M. Walker, Thomas Y. Crowell, 1901. [1]p. 216; [2]p. 219; [3]p. 241; [4]p. 242; [5]pp. 207–9; [6]p. 289.

M. John D. Yohannan, ed., *A Treasury of Asian Literature,* Mentor Books, 1958, p. 31 f.

N. Carl Clemen, ed., *The Religions of the World,* George C. Harrap & Co., Ltd., London, and Harcourt, Brace and Company, New York, 1931, p. 454.

O. H. A. R. Gibb, *Modern Trends in Islam,* University of Chicago Press, 1947, p. 69.

P. Fazlur Rahman, *Islam,* Anchor Books, 1968, p. 280.

Q. Lisa Anderson, "Libya and American Foreign Policy," in *The Middle East Journal,* autumn 1982, p. 519.

R. Edward G. Browne, *A Literary History of Persia,* 4 vols., Cambridge University Press, Cambridge, England 1953. Vol. IV, p. 176.

S. Michael M. J. Fischer, *Iran: From Religious Dispute to Revolution,* Harvard University Press, 1980, p. 183.

T. Ayatallah R. Khumayni, *Islamic Government,* 1971, in S. Akhavi, *Religion and Politics in Contemporary Islam,* State University of New York Press, 1980, p. 212.

U. Clifford Geertz, *The Development of the Javanese Economy,* Massachusetts Institute of Technology Center for International Studies, Cambridge, 1956, p. 91.

V. Karl D. Jackson, *Traditional Authority, Islam and Rebellion,* University of California Press, 1980, p. 277.

W. Wilfred Cantwell Smith, *Islam in Modern History,* Princeton University Press, 1957, p. 213.

Chapter 1.
Religion in Prehistoric and Primal Cultures

BERNDT, RONALD M., AND CATHERINE H. BERNDT. *The World of the First Australians.* University of Chicago Press, 1965.

CHARLESWORTH, M., et al. *Religion in Aboriginal Australia: An Anthology.* University of Queensland Press, St. Lucia, 1984.

DURKHEIM, ÉMILE. *Elementary Forms of Religious Life.* George Allen & Unwin, Ltd., 1915, 1965.

ELIADE, MIRCEA. *Birth and Rebirth.* Harper & Brothers, Inc., 1958 (A study of initiation rites).

GENNEP, G. VAN. *Rites of Passage.* Translated by Vizedom and Caffee. University of Chicago Press, 1960.

GIMBUTAS, MARIJA. *The Goddesses and Gods of Old Europe: 6500–3500 B.C.* University of California Press, 1982.

———. *The Language of the Goddess: Unearthing the Hidden Symbols of Western Civilization.* Harper & Row, 1989.

HAYS, H. R. *In the Beginnings: Early Man and His Gods.* G. P. Putnam's Sons, 1963.

HOPPAL, M. *Shamanism in Eurasia.* Herodot, Goettingen, 1984.

HUDSON, CHARLES. *The Southeastern Indians.* University of Tennessee Press, 1977.

HULTKRANTZ, A. *The Religions of American Indians.* University of California Press, Berkeley, 1979.

LESSA, W. A., AND E. Z. VOGT, EDS. *Reader in Comparative Religion: An Anthropological Approach.* Row, Peterson and Co., 1958.

LEVY, G. RACHEL. *Religious Conceptions of the Stone Age.* Harper Torchbooks, 1963.

LOWIE, ROBERT H. *Primitive Religion.* Enl. ed. Liveright, 1948.

MALINOWSKI, BRONISLAW. *Magic, Science, and Religion.* Beacon Press, 1948.

MOONEY, JAMES. *Myths of the Cherokee* and *Sacred Formulas of the Cherokees* (c. 1900 and 1891). Reprint, C. Elder, Nashville, Tenn., 1982.

RAY, B. C. *African Religions: Symbol, Ritual, and Community.* Heinemann Educational, London, 1972.

SWANSON, GUY E. *The Birth of the Gods: The Origin of Primitive Beliefs.* University of Michigan Press, 1960, 1966.

TWOHIG, ELIZABETH SHEE. *The Megalithic Art of Western Europe,* Oxford, 1981.

TYLOR, E. B. *Primitive Culture.* London 1871, Harper Torchbooks, 1958.

WAAL MALEFIJT, ANNEMARIE DE. *Religion and Culture: An Introduction to Anthropology of Religion.* The Macmillan Company, 1968.

Chapter 2. Bygone Religions That Have Left Their Mark on the West

General

Historia Religionum, Vol. I: Religions of the Past. E. J. BRILL, Leiden, 1969.

Mythologies of the Ancient World. Edited by S. N. KRAMER. Anchor Books, pb, 1961.

Mesopotamia

FRANKFORT, HENRI. *Kingship and the Gods.* University of Chicago Press, 1948. (Deals also with Egypt.)

HEIDEL, A. *The Gilgamesh Epic and Old Testament Parallels.* 2nd ed. University of Chicago Press, 1949.

JACOBSON, THORKILD. *The Treasures of Darkness: A History of Mesopotamian Religion.* Yale University Press, 1976.

MENDELSOHN, ISAAC, ED. *The Religions of the Ancient Near East: Sumero-Akkadian Religious Texts and Ugaritic Epics.* Liberal Arts Press, pb, 1955.

Greece

GARLAND, ROBERT. *The Greek Way of Life: From Conception to Old Age.* Cornell University Press, Ithaca, N.Y., 1990.

———. *Introducing New Gods: The Politics of Athenian Religion.* Cornell University Press, Ithaca, N.Y., 1992.

GRANT, F. C., ED. *Hellenistic Religions.* Liberal Arts Press, pb, 1954.

GUTHRIE, W. K. C. *The Greeks and Their Gods.* Beacon, 1950. (Available as Beacon pb.)

KERENYI, KAROLY. *Dyonysus: Archetypal Image of Indestructible Life.* Translated by R. Mannheim, Princeton, 1976.

LLOYD-JONES, HUGH. *The Justice of Zeus.* University of California Press, 1971.

OTTO, WALTER F. *The Homeric Gods.* Thames and Hudson, London, (c. 1954), 1979.

Rome

BAILEY, CYRIL. *Phases of the Religion of Ancient Rome.* University of California Press, 1932.

DUMEZIL, GEORGES. *Archaic Roman Religion.* 2 vols. Translated Philip Krapp. University of Chicago Press, 1970. (First published in 1966.)

FERGUSON, JOHN. *The Religions of the Roman Empire.* Cornell University Press, 1970.

LUTHER, H. MARTIN. *Hellenistic Religions.* Oxford University Press, 1987.

PRESTON, JAMES J. ED. *Mother Worship: Theme and Variations.* University of North Carolina Press, Chapel Hill, 1982.

WAGENVOORT, H. *Roman Dynamism.* Blackwell, 1947.

Beyond the Alps

BRANSTON, BRIAN. *Gods of the North.* Vanguard Press, 1955.

DAVIDSON, HILDA R. ELLIS. *Gods and Myths of Northern Europe.* Hammondsworth, Penguin Books, 1964.

KOLEHMAINEN, JOHN I. *Epic of the North.* The Northwestern Publishing Co., New York Mills, Minn., 1973.

MACCULLOCH, J. A. *The Celtic and Scandinavian Religions.* Hutchinson & Co., Ltd., 1948.

PIGGOTT, STUART. *The Druids.* Frederick A. Praeger, 1968.

The Maya

MORLEY, SYLVANUS GRISWOLD. *The Ancient Maya.* 3rd ed., revised by G. W. Brainerd. Stanford University Press, 1956.

SCHELE, LINDA, AND DAVID FRIEDEL. *A Forest of Kings: The Untold Story of the Ancient Maya.* William Morrow and Company, 1990.

THOMPSON, J. ERIC S. *The Rise and Fall of Maya Civilization.* 2nd ed. University of California Press, 1966.

Chapter 3.
Early Hinduism

BASHAM, A. L. *The Origins and Development of Classical Hinduism.* Beacon Press, 1989.

EDGERTON, FRANKLIN. *The Beginnings of Indian Philosophy.* Harvard University Press, 1965.

EMBREE, AINSLIE T., ED. *The Hindu Tradition.* The Modern Library, 1966.

HOPKINS, THOMAS J. *The Hindu Religious Tradition.* Dickensen Publishing Company, Inc., 1971.

KEITH, A. B. *The Religion and Philosophy of the Veda and the Upanishads.* Harvard University Press, 1920.

PIGGOTT, S. *Prehistoric India.* Penguin, pb, 1950.

RENOU, L. *Religions of Ancient India.* Oxford University Press, 1953.

WHEELER, SIR MORTIMER. *Civilizations of the Indus Valley and Beyond.* McGraw-Hill, 1966.

Chapter 4.
Later Hinduism

BROCKINGTON, J. L. *The Sacred Thread: Hinduism in Its Continuity and Diversity.* Columbia University Press, 1981.

BUITENEN, J. A. B. VON. "Hindu Mythology" and "Hindu Sacred Literature," in *The New Encyclopaedia Britannica.* 15th ed. Macropaedia, Vol. 8.

COURTRIGHT, PAUL B. *Ganesa, Lord of Obstacles, Lord of Beginnings.* Oxford University Press, 1985.

EDGERTON, FRANKLIN, TR. *The Bhagavad Gita.* Harvard Oriental Series, 1944. (Harper Torchbook, pb, 1964.)

GONDA, JAN. *Visnuism and Sivaism.* International Publications Service, 1970, 1976.

GROWSE, F. S., TR. *The Ramayana of Tulsi Das.* 7th ed. Ram Narain Lal, Allahabad, 1937.

HAZRA, R. C. *Studies in the Puranic Records on Hindu Rites and Customs.* University of Dacca, Calcutta, 1940.

HILTEBEITEL, ALF. "Hinduism," in *The Encyclopedia of Religion.* Edited by Mircea Eliade. Macmillan Publishing Company, 1987.

KINSLEY, DAVID, *The Goddesses' Mirror: Visions of the Divine from East and West.* State University of New York Press, Albany, 1989.

KRAMRISCH, STELLA. *The Presence of Siva.* Princeton University Press, 1981.

LESLIE, JULIA, ED. *Roles and Rituals for Hindu Women.* Farleigh-Dickinson (Dist. Associated University Press, 1991).

MARGLIN, FREDERIQUE APFFEL. *Wives of the God-King: The Rituals of the Devadasis of Puri.* Oxford University Press, 1985.

MILLER, DAVID, AND DOROTHY C. WERTZ. *Hindu Monastic Life: The Monks and Monasteries of Bhubaneswar.* McGill-Queens University Press, 1976.

MITCHELL, GEORGE. *Hindu Temple.* Harper & Row, 1978.

NIKHILANANDA, SWAMI, TR. *The Gospel of Sri Ramakrishna.* Ramakrishna-Vivekananda Center, New York, 1952.

O'FLAHERTY, WENDY DONIGER, TR. *Hindu Myths.* Penguin, 1975.

————. *Shiva: The Erotic Ascetic.* Oxford University Press, 1973, 1981.

————. *Women, Androgynes, and Other Mythical Beasts.* University of Chicago Press, 1980.

RADHAKRISHNAN, S., AND CHARLES MOORE, EDS. *Source Book in Indian Philosophy.* Princeton University Press, 1957.

SHARMA, ARVIND. *A Hindu Perspective on the Philosophy of Religion.* St. Martin's Press, 1991.

STUTLEY, MARGARET, AND JAMES STUTLEY. *Harper's Dictionary of Hinduism.* Harper & Row, 1977.

VALMIKI. *The Ramayana of Valmiki.* Translated by Hari Prasad Shastri, 3rd ed. Shanti Sadan, London, 1976.

ZAEHNER, RICHARD C. *Hinduism.* Oxford University Press, 1962.

ZIMMER, H. *Myth and Symbol in Indian Art and Civilization.* Pantheon Books, Inc., 1946. (Harper Torchbook, pb, 1962.)

————. *Philosophies of India.* Pantheon Books, Inc., 1951. (Meridian Books, pb, 1956.)

Chapter 5.
Jainism

CAILLAT, COLETTE. *The Jain Cosmology.* Translated by K. R. Norman. Basel, 1981.

JAINI, PADMANABH S. *The Jaina Path of Purification.* Berkeley, 1979.

MEHTA, M. L. *Outlines of Jaina Philosophy.* Bangalore, 1954.

————. *Jaina Culture.* P. V. Research Institute, Varanasi, 1962.

SAMGAVE, VILAS A. *Jaina Community.* 2nd rev. ed. Bombay, 1980.

STEVENSON, MRS. SINCLAIR. *The Heart of Jainism.* Oxford University Press, 1915.

WILLIAMS, R. H. B. *Jaina Yoga.* Oxford University Press, 1963.

ZIMMER, HEINRICH. *Philosophies of India.* Part III, Chap. 1. Meridian Books, pb, 1956.

Chapter 6.
Buddhism in Its First Phase

Sources in Translation

CONZE, EDWARD, TR. *Buddhist Scriptures.* Penguin, pb, 1959.

————, ED. AND TR. *Buddhist Meditation.* George Allen & Unwin, Ltd., 1956.

DAVIDS, T. W. RHYS, TR. *Dialogues of the Buddha.* Oxford University Press, 1899–1921.

DAVIDS, MRS. T. W. RHYS. *Psalms of the Brethren.* Oxford University Press, 1909.

————. *Psalms of the Sisters.* Oxford University Press, 1913.

HURWITZ, LEON, TR. *Sutra of the Lotus Blossom of the Fine Dharma,* Columbia University Press, 1976.

Sacred Books of the East, especially *Sutta Nipata* in vol. 10 and the *Vinaya* texts in vols. 13, 17, and 20.

Modern Works

RAHULA, WALPOLA. "Buddha," in the *New Encyclopaedia Brittanica.* 15th ed. Macropaedia, vol. 3.

————. *What the Buddha Taught.* Grove Press, 1962.

REYNOLDS, FRANK E. "The Many Lives of the Buddha: A Study of Sacred Biography and Theravada Tradition," in Frank E. Reynolds and Donald Capps, eds., *The Biographical Process.* Mouton DeGruyter, 1976.

ROBINSON, RICHARD H., AND WILLARD L. JOHNSON. *The Buddhist Religion: A Historical Introduction.* 3rd ed. Wadsworth, 1982.

THOMAS, E. J. *History of Buddhist Thought.* 2nd ed. Alfred A. Knopf, Inc., 1951.

————. *The Life of Buddha as Legend and History.* 3rd ed., rev. Kegan Paul, Trench, Trubner & Co., 1949; reprinted 1969.

Chapter 7.
The Religious Development of Buddhism

On the Buddhist World as a Whole

CONZE, EDWARD. *Buddhism, Its Essence and Development.* Philosophical Library, 1954. (Available as Harper Torchbooks, pb.)

————. *A Short History of Buddhism.* Chetana, Bombay, 1960.

REYNOLDS, FRANK E., AND CHARLES HALLISEY. "Buddha" and "Buddhism, an Overview," in *The Encyclopedia of Reli-*

gion. Edited by Mircea Eliade. Macmillan Publishing Co., 1987.

On Indian Buddhism

AMBEDKAR, B. R. *The Buddha and His Dhamma.* People's Education Society, Bombay, 1957.

CONZE, EDWARD. *Buddhist Thought in India.* George Allen & Unwin, Ltd., 1962. (Also Harper Torchbook, pb.)

GOMEZ, LUIS O. "Buddhism in India," in *The Encyclopedia of Religion.* Edited by Mircea Eliade. Macmillan Publishing Co., 1987.

ROBINSON, RICHARD H. *Classical Indian Philosophy.* Madison, Wis., 1968.

———. *Early Madyamika in India and China.* University of Wisconsin Press, 1967.

On Buddhism in Burma, Thailand, and Southeast Asia

AUNG, MAUNG HTIN. *Folk Elements in Burmese Buddhism.* Oxford University Press, 1962.

BUNNAG, JANE. *Buddhist Monk, Buddhist Layman.* Cambridge University Press, 1973.

DHANNINIVAT, PRINCE K. B. *A History of Buddhism in Siam.* The Siam Society, Bangkok, 1960.

KING, WINSTON L. *A Thousand Lives Away.* Harvard University Press, 1964. (Deals with Burma.)

———. *In the Hope of Nibbana: Theravada Buddhist Ethics.* Open Court Publishing Co., 1964.

LESTER, ROBERT C. *Theravada Buddhism in Southeast Asia.* University of Michigan Press, 1973.

SPIRO, MELFORD E. *Buddhism and Society: A Great Tradition and Its Burmese Vicissitudes.* Harper & Row Paperbacks, N.Y., 1970.

SWEARER, DONALD K. *Buddhism and Society in Southeast Asia.* Anima Books, 1981.

———. "Buddhism in Southeast Asia," in *The Encyclopedia of Religion.* Edited by Mircea Eliade. Macmillan Publishing Co., 1987.

On Buddhism in Sri Lanka

BUDDHIST COUNCIL OF CEYLON, ED. *The Path of Buddhism.* Lanka Bauddha Mandalaya, Colombo, 1956.

LOUNSBURY, G. CONSTANT. *Buddhist Meditation in the Southern School.* Kegan Paul, Trench, Trubner & Co., 1950.

MALALASEKERA, G. P. *The Buddha and His Teachings.* Lanka Bauddha Mandalaya, Colombo, 1957.

RAHULA, WALPOLA. *History of Buddhism in Ceylon.* Gunasena, Colombo, 1956.

On Chinese Buddhism

CHANG, WING-TSIT. *Religious Trends in Modern China.* Columbia University Press, 1953.

———. ED. *A Source Book in Chinese Philosophy.* Princeton University Press, 1963.

MACINNES, DONALD E. *Religion in China Today: Policy and Practice.* Orbis Books, 1989.

———. ED. *Religious Policy and Practices in Communist China.* Macmillan Publishing Co., 1972.

OVERMYER, DANIEL L. *Folk Buddhist Religion: Dissenting Sects in Late Traditional China.* Harvard University Press, 1976.

PRIP-MOLLER, J. *Chinese Buddhist Monasteries: Their Plan and Its Function as a Setting for Buddhist Monastic Life.* Oxford University Press, 1937. (Reprinted 1967).

TSUKAMOTO, ZENRYU. *A History of Early Chinese Buddhism: From Its Introduction to the Death of Hui-yüan.* Translated by Leon Hurvitz. Tokyo, 1985.

WELCH, HOLMES. *The Buddhist Revival in China.* Harvard University Press, 1968.

———. *Buddhism Under Mao.* Harvard University Press, 1972.

———. *The Chinese Transformation of Buddhism.* Princeton University Press, 1973.

———. *The Practice of Chinese Buddhism, 1900–1950.* Harvard University Press, 1967.

WRIGHT, ARTHUR F. *Buddhism in Chinese History.* Stanford University Press, 1959.

On Japanese Buddhism

BLOOM, ALFRED. *Shinran's Gospel of Pure Grace.* University of Arizona Press, 1965.

DUMOULIN, HEINRICH. *A History of Zen Buddhism.* Translated by Paul Peachey. Pantheon Books, 1963. (Available in pb).

EARHART, H. BYRON. *Japanese Religion: Unity and Diversity.* Dickenson Publishing Co., Belmont, Calif., 1969.

HARDACRE, HELEN. *Lay Buddhism in Contemporary Japan: Reiyukai Kyodan.* Princeton University Press, 1984.

KITAGAWA, JOSEPH M. *Religion in Japanese History.* Columbia University Press, 1966.

———. *On Understanding Japanese Religion.* Princeton University Press, 1987.

NARIYOSHI, TAMARU. "Buddhism in Japan," in *The Encyclopedia of Religion.* Edited by Mircea Eliade. Macmillan Publishing Co., 1987.

SUZUKI, D. T. *Essays in Zen Buddhism.* Luzac & Co., 1928–1934.

———. *The Training of the Zen Buddhist Monk.* Eastern Buddhist Society, Kyoto, 1934.

———. *Zen Buddhism.* Selected writings. Edited by William Barrett. Anchor, pb, 1956.

TSUNODA, RYUSAKU, ET AL. *Sources of the Japanese Tradition.* Columbia University Press, 1958. (Available in pb)

On Tibetan Buddhism

EVANS-WENTZ, W. Y. *Tibetan Yoga and Secret Doctrines.* 2nd enl. Edited by H. Milford, 1958.

———, ED. *The Tibetan Book of the Dead.* Oxford University Press, Galaxy Book, pb, 1960.

———, ED. *The Tibetan Book of the Great Liberation, or The Method of Realizing Nirvana Through Knowing the Mind,* Oxford University Press, 1954.

GUENTHER, HERBERT. "Buddhism in Tibet," in *The Encyclopedia of Religion.* Edited by Mircea Eliade. Macmillan Publishing Co., 1987.

HOFFMAN, HELMUT. *The Religions of Tibet.* George Allen & Unwin, Ltd., 1961.

NORBU, THUBTEN JIGME, AND C. M. TURNBULL. *Tibet.* Simon and Schuster, 1968.

SNELLGROVE, DAVID, AND HUGH RICHARDSON. *A Cultural History of Tibet.* Praeger Publishers, Inc., 1968.

SNELLGROVE, D. L. *Indo-Tibetan Buddhism, Indian Buddhists and Their Tibetan Successors.* Shambala Publications, Boston, 1987.

TUCCI, G. *The Religions of Tibet.* Routledge & Kegan Paul, London, 1980.

Chapter 8.
Sikhism

COLE, W. O. AND PIARA SINGH SAMBHI. *The Sikhs, Their Religious Beliefs and Practices.* Routledge and Kegan Paul, London, 1978.

KHUSHWANT SINGH. *A History of the Sikhs.* 2 vols. Princeton University Press, 1963–66.

———. *Hymns of Guru Nanak.* Orient Longman, Ltd., New Delhi, 1969.

———. "Sikhism," in *The New Encyclopaedia Britannica.* 15th ed. Macropaedia, vol. 16.

MACAULIFFE, M. A. *The Sikh Religion: Its Gurus, Sacred Writings, and Anthems.* 6 vols. Oxford University Press, 1909.

McLEOD, W. H. *Guru Nanak and the Sikh Religion.* Oxford University Press, 1969.

The Sacred Writings of the Sikhs. Translated by Trilochan Singh, Jodh Singh, Kapur Singh, Bawa Harkishen Singh, and Khushwant Singh. George Allen & Unwin, Ltd., 1960.

SINGH, HARBANS. *The Heritage of the Sikhs.* 2nd ed. New Delhi, 1983.

Chapter 9.
Native Chinese Religion and Daoism

General Works

CHANG, WING-TSIT. *A Sourcebook in Chinese Philosophy.* Princeton University Press, 1963.

CREEL, H. G. *The Birth of China.* The John Day Company, Inc., 1937.

———. *Chinese Thought from Confucius to Mao Tse-tung.* University of Chicago Press, 1953. (Mentor, pb, 1960)

GIRARDOT, N. J. *Myth and Meaning in Early Taoism.* University of California Press, 1983.

HENDERSON, JOHN B. *Development and Decline of Chinese Cosmology.* Columbia University Press, 1984.

SIVIN, NATHAN. *Chinese Alchemy: Preliminary Studies.* Harvard University Press, 1968.

THOMPSON, LAURENCE G. *Chinese Religion: An Introduction.* Dickenson Publishing Co., 1969. (pb).

WELCH, HOLMES. *The Parting of the Way: Lao Tzu and the Taoist Movement.* Beacon, 1957. (Beacon, pb, 1966).

———, AND SEIDEL, ANNA, EDS. *Facets of Taoism: Essays in Chinese Religion* (1972). Yale University Press, 1979.

YANG, C. K. *Religion in Chinese Society.* University of California Press, 1961. (also pb).

Daoist Texts

BLAKNEY, R. B. *The Way of Life Lao Tzu.* Mentor, pb, 1955.

CARUS, PAUL. *The Canon of Reason and Virtue.* Open Court, 1913. (available in pb).

CHAN, WING-TSIT. *The Way of Lao Tzu.* Bobbs-Merrill, Indianapolis, 1978 (c. 1963).

WALEY, ARTHUR. *The Way and Its Power, a Study of the Tao Te Ching.* George Allen & Unwin, Ltd., 1934.

WATSON, BURTON, TR. *Chaung-tzu: Basic Writings.* Columbia University Press, 1964.

Later Daoism and Folk Religion

EBERHARD, W. *Chinese Festivals.* Henry Schuman, New York, 1952.

ELLIOTT, ALAN. *Chinese Spirit Medium Cults in Singapore.* (1955) Oriental Bookstore, Pasadena, 1981.

Hsü, Francis L. K. *Under the Ancestors' Shadow: Chinese Culture and Personality* (1948). Stanford University Press, 1967.

Jordan, David K. *Gods, Ghosts, and Ancestors: The Folk Religion of a Taiwanese Village.* University of California Press, 1972.

———, and Daniel L. Overmyer. *The Flying Phoenix: Aspects of Sectarianism in Taiwan.* Princeton University Press, 1986.

Loewe, Michael. *Ways to Paradise: The Chinese Quest for Immortality.* Allen Unwin, 1979.

Maspero, Henri. *Taoism and Chinese Religion.* (1971). Translated by Frank A. Kierman Jr. University of Massachusetts Press, 1981.

Wolf, Arthur P., ed. *Religion and Ritual in Chinese Society.* Stanford University Press, 1974.

Chapter 10.
Confucius and Confucianism

General Works

Chang, Wing-tsit. *A Sourcebook in Chinese Philosophy.* Princeton University Press, 1970.

Chiang, Yee. *A Chinese Childhood.* W. W. Norton & Company, Inc., 1963.

Ching, Julia. *Confucianism and Christianity: A Comparative Study.* Kodansha International, 1977.

de Bary, William Theodore and Tu Weiming, eds. *Confucianism and Human Rights.* Columbia University Press, 1998.

de Bary, William Theodore, ed. *Sources of the Chinese Tradition.* Columbia University Press, 1960.

Fung, Y. L. *A History of Chinese Philosophy.* 2 vols. Translated by Derk Bodde. Princeton University Press, 1952.

———. *A Short History of Chinese Philosophy.* Edited by Derk Bodde. The Macmillan Company, 1948. (Macmillan pb ed., 1960).

Nivison, David S., and Arthur Wright, eds. *Confucianism in Action.* Stanford University Press, 1959.

Wright, Arthur F., ed. *The Confucian Persuasion.* Stanford University Press, 1960.

Confucius

Creel, H. G. *Confucius and the Chinese Way.* Harper, 1960.

Fingarette, Herbert. *Confucius—The Secular as Sacred.* Ungar, New York, 1937.

Liu, Wu-Chi. *Confucius: His Life and Time.* Philosophical Library, 1955.

Louie, Kam. *Critiques of Confucius in Contemporary China.* St. Martin's Press, 1980.

Waley, Arthur. *The Analects of Confucius.* George Allen & Unwin, Ltd., 1938.

Mo Zi (Motzu)

Mei Yi Pao. *The Ethical and Political Works of Motse.* Probsthain, 1930.

———. *Motse, the Neglected Rival of Confucius.* Probsthain, 1934.

Han Fei

Han Fei Tzu. *The Complete Works of Han Fei Tzu.* 2 vols. Translated by W. K. Liao. Probsthain 1939, 1959.

Watson, B. *Han Fei Tsu: Basic Writings.* Columbia University Press, 1964.

Mencius

Dobson, W. A. C. H. *Mencius.* University of Toronto Press, 1963.

Lyall, L. A., tr. *Mencius.* Longmans, Green & Company, 1932.

Xun-zi (Hsün Tzu)

Dubs, H. H. *Hsüntze, the Moulder of Ancient Confucianism.* Probsthain, 1927.

———. *The Works of Hsüntze.* Probsthain, 1928.

Watson, B. *Hsin Tsu: Basic Writings.* Columbia University Press, 1963.

Neo-Confucianism (General)

Chang, Carsun. *The Development of Neo-Confucian Thought.* Twayne Publishers, New York, 1957.

de Bary, William Theodore, ed. *The Liberal Tradition in China.* Columbia University Press, 1983.

———. *The Unfolding of Neo-Confucianism.* Columbia University Press, 1975.

———, and Irene Bloom, eds. *Principle and Practicality: Essays in Neo-Confucianism and Practical Learning.* Columbia University Press, 1979.

Zhu-xi (Chu Hsi)

Bruce, J. P. *Chu Hsi and His Masters.* Probsthain, 1923.

Chu Hsi. *Reflections on Things at Hand.* Translated by Wing-tsit Chan. Columbia University Press, 1967.

Wang Yang-ming

Ching, Julia. *To Acquire Wisdom: The Way of Wang Yang-ming (1492–1529).* Columbia University Press, 1976.

WANG, SHOU-JEN. *The Philosophical Letters of Wang Yang-ming.* Translated by Julia Ching. University of South Carolina Press, 1973.

VAN STRAELEN, HENRY. *The Religion of Divine Wisdom: Japan's Most Powerful Movement.* Tenrikyo Kyoto, Veritas Shoin, 1957.

Chapter 11.
Shinto

ASTON, W. G., TR. *Nihongi.* George Allen & Unwin, Ltd., 1956.

———. *Shinto: The Way of the Gods.* Longmans, Green & Co. 1905.

BELLAH, ROBERT N. *Tokugawa Religion.* The Free Press, 1957, 1969.

BLACKER, CARMEN. *The Catalpa Bow: A Study of Shamanistic Practices in Japan.* George Allen & Unwin, 1975.

BROWN, D. M. *Nationalism in Japan: An Introductory Historical Analysis.* University of California Press, 1955.

CASAL, U. A. *The Five Sacred Festivals of Ancient Japan.* Chas. E. Tuttle, Rutland, Vt., 1967.

CREEMERS, WILHELMUS H. *Shrine Shinto after World War II.* E. J. Brill, 1968.

CZAJA, MICHAEL. *Gods of Myth and Stone.* John Weatherhill, Inc., 1974.

EARHART, H. BYRON. *Japanese Religion: Unity and Diversity.* 3rd ed. Wadsworth Publishing Co., 1982.

———. *Religion in the Japanese Experience.* Wadsworth Publishing Co., 1974.

HORI, ICHIRO. *Folk Religion in Japan, Continuity and Change.* University of Chicago Press, 1968.

KITAGAWA, JOSEPH M. *Religion in Japanese History.* Columbia University Press, 1966.

McFARLAND, H. NEILL. *The Rush Hour of the Gods: A Study of the New Religious Movements in Japan.* Macmillan, 1967.

MURANO, SENCHU. "Shinto," in *The Encyclopedia of Religion.* Edited by Mircea Eliade. Macmillan Publishing Co., 1987.

MURAOKA, TSUNETSUGU. *Studies in Shinto Thought.* Translated by D. Brown and J. Araki. Tokyo, Ministry of Education, 1964.

PHILIPPI, DONALD L. TR. *Kojiki.* Tokyo University Press, 1968.

———. *Norito. A New Translation of the Ancient Japanese Ritual Prayers.* The Institute for Japanese Culture and Classics, Kokugakuin University, 1959.

PICKEN, STUART D. B. *Shinto, Japan's Spiritual Roots.* Kodansha International, Ltd., 1980.

TSUNODO, RYUSAKU, ET AL. *Sources of the Japanese Tradition.* Columbia University Press, 1958. (Issued in pb, with different pagination).

Chapter 12.
Zoroastrianism

BOYCE, MARY. *A History of Zoroastrianism.* 2 vols. E. J. Brill, Leiden, 1975, 1982.

———. *Zoroastrians.* Edited by John Hinnells. Methuen Inc., London, 1986.

DARMESTETER, J., TR. *The Zend Avesta.* Vols. IV, XXXI, and XXXIII in the *Sacred Books of the East* series. Oxford University Press, 1883.

DUCHESNE-GUILLEMIN, JACQUES. *The Hymns of Zoroaster.* London, 1952.

———. "Zoroastrianism and Parsiism," in *The New Encyclopaedia Britannica,* 15th ed. Macropaedia, vol. 19, pp. 1171–76.

GNOLI, GERARDO. "Zoroastrianism," in *The Encyclopedia of Religion.* Edited by Mircea Eliade. Macmillan Publishing Co., 1987.

HENNING, M., TR. *Avesta: The Hymns of Zarathustra.* Hyperion Press, 1980. (Reprint of 1952 edition).

HERZFELD, ERNEST. *Zoroaster and His World.* 2 vols. Princeton University Press, 1947.

MODI, J. J. *Religious Ceremonies and Customs of the Parsis.* 2nd ed. Luzac & Co., 1954.

OXTOBY, WILLARD G. "Parsis," in *The Encyclopedia of Religion.* Edited by Mircea Eliade. Macmillan Publishing Co., 1987.

ZAEHNER, R. C. *The Dawn and Twilight of Zoroastrianism.* G. P. Putnam's Sons, 1961.

———. *The Teachings of the Magi.* George Allen & Unwin, Ltd., 1956.

———. *Zurvan: A Zoroastrian Dilemma.* Oxford University Press, 1955.

Chapters 13 and 14.
Judaism

BARON, S. W. *A Social and Religious History of the Jews,* 3 vols. Columbia University Press, 1952.

———, AND JOSEPH L. BLAU, EDS. *Judaism, Postbiblical and Talmudic Period.* Liberal Arts Press, 1954. (an anthology in pb).

BAUER, YEHUDA. *A History of the Holocaust.* Franklin Watts, 1982.

BOROWITZ, EUGENE B., ET AL. "Judaism," in *The Encyclopedia of Religion.* Edited by Mircea Eliade. Macmillan Publishing Co., 1987.

BRIGHT, JOHN. *History of Israel.* Westminster Press, 1981.

BUBER, MARTIN. *Prophetic Faith.* The Macmillan Company, 1949.

———. *Tales of the Hasidim.* 2 vols. Schocken Books, Inc. 1947–1948. (Schocken pb).

CHRIST, CAROL P., AND JUDITH PLASKOW, EDS. *Womanspirit Rising.* Harper & Row, 1979.

COHON, SAMUEL S. *Jewish Theology.* Royal Van Gurcum, Assen, Holland; Beaverton, Ore., 1971.

FINKELSTEIN, L., ED. *The Jews: Their History, Culture and Religion.* Harper & Brothers, Inc., 1960.

———. *The Pharisees.* 2 vols. 3rd ed. Jewish Publication Society, 1962.

GROBMAN, ALEX, AND DANIEL LANDES, EDS. *Genocide: Critical Issues of the Holocaust.* Simon Wiesenthal Center, Los Angeles, 1983.

HILLERS, DELBERT R. *Covenant: The History of a Biblical Idea.* Johns Hopkins University Press, 1969.

KATZ, JACOB. *Exclusiveness and Tolerance: Jewish–Gentile Relations in Medieval and Modern Times.* Oxford University Press, 1961. (Schocken pb)

KAUFMANN, YEHEZKEL. *The Religion of Israel: From Its Beginnings to the Babylonian Exile.* Tr. and abr. Moshe Greenberg. University of Chicago Press, 1966.

KNIGHT, DOUGLAS A., AND GENE M. TUCKER, EDS. *The Hebrew Bible and Its Modern Interpreters.* Fortress Press, 1985.

MARCUS, JACOB R., ED. *The Jews and the Medieval World: A Source Book: the Years 351–1791.* Harper and Row, 1965.

MONTEFIORE, C. G., AND H. LOEWE, EDS. *A Rabbinic Anthology.* Jewish Publication Society, 1960. (Harper Torchbook pb)

NEUSNER, JACOB. *The Way of Torah: An Introduction to Judaism.* Dickenson, Belmont, Calif., 1970.

OTWELL, JOHN H. *And Sarah Laughed: The Status of Women in the Old Testament.* Westminster Press, 1977.

PLASKOW, JUDITH, AND CAROL P. CHRIST, EDS. *Weaving the Visions: New Patterns in Feminist Spirituality.* Harper & Row, San Francisco, 1989.

SCHOLEN, G. G. *Major Trends in Jewish Mysticism.* 3rd rev. ed. Schocken Books, Inc., 1964.

SCHÜRER, EMIL. *A History of the Jewish People in the Time of Jesus.* Abr. and tr. by N. N. Glatzer. Schocken Books pb, 1961.

TCHERIKOVER, V. HELLENISTIC CIVILIZATION AND THE JEWS. Translated by S. Appelbaum. Jewish Publication Society of America, 1959.

VON RAD, GERHARD. *Old Testament Theology.* 2 vols. Harper & Row, 1962, 1965.

WIESEL, ELIE. *Souls on Fire: Portraits and Legends of Hasidic Masters.* Random House, 1972.

Chapter 15.
Christianity in Its Opening Phase

BARRETT, C. K. *The New Testament Background: Selected Documents.* Harper and Row, 1961.

BULTMANN, R. *Jesus Christ and Mythology.* Charles Scribner's Sons, 1958.

CULLMANN, OSCAR. *The Early Church.* Westminster Press, 1956.

DIBELIUS, M. *Jesus.* Translated by Hedrick and Grant. Westminster Press, 1949.

DODD, C. H. *According to the Scriptures: The Substructure of New Testament Theology.* Charles Scribner's Sons, 1953.

GOGUEL, M. *The Life of Jesus.* Translation by Olive Wyon. The Macmillan Company, 1945. (Available in 2 vols. as Harper Torchbooks pb)

HARNER, PHILIP B. *Everlasting Life in Biblical Thought.* Carlton Press, 1981.

HIERS, RICHARD H. *Jesus and the Future.* John Knox Press, 1981.

JEREMIAS, J. *The Eucharistic Words of Jesus.* Blackwell, London, 1955.

———. *The Parables of Jesus.* Translated by S. H. Hooke. Charles Scribner's Sons, 1955.

KLAUSNER, JOSEPH. *From Jesus to Paul.* The Macmillan Company, 1943. (Available as Beacon pb., a Jewish view)

———. *Jesus of Nazareth.* The Macmillan Company, 1925. (a classic Jewish interpretation).

KNOX, JOHN. *Chapters in a Life of Paul.* Abingdon Press, 1950.

KOESTER, HELMUT. *Introduction to the New Testament:* Vol. II, *History and Literature of Early Christianity.* Fortress Press, 1982.

KUMMEL, WERNER GEORG. *The Theology of the New Testament.* Abingdon, 1973.

LEON-DUFOUR, XAVIER. *The Gospels and the Jews of History.* Doubleday & Company, Inc., Image books pb, 1970. (a Catholic view using the methods of historical criticism)

McArthur, H. K., ed. *In Search of the Historical Jesus.* Charles Scribner's Sons, pb, 1969. (an anthology of selections from twenty-two authors)

Ruether, Rosemary Radford, and Eleanor McLaughlin. *Women of the Spirit: Female Leadership in the Jewish and Christian Traditions.* Simon & Schuster, 1979.

Schweitzer, Albert. *The Quest of the Historical Jesus.* A. & C. Black, London, 1910. (reissue with new Introduction by James M. Robinson, the Macmillan Company, 1968).

Streeter, B. H. *The Four Gospels. A Study of Origins.* Macmillan, 1924.

Weiss, Johannes. *Earliest Christianity.* 2 vols. Harper, 1959.

Chapter 16.
The Religious Development of Christianity

Augustine, St. *City of God.* 8th ed. T. & T. Clark, Edinburgh, 1934.

———. *Confessions.* Any edition.

Baer, Hans A., and Marriel Singer. *Afro-American Religion in the Twentieth Century: Varieties of Protest and Accommodation.* University of Tennessee, 1992.

Bainton, R. *Here I Stand, a Life of Martin Luther.* Abingdon-Cokesbury, 1950. (available as Mentor pb)

Battenhouse, R. W., ed. *A Companion to the Study of Saint Augustine.* Oxford University Press, 1955.

Ferm, Deane William. *Contemporary American Theologies.* The Seabury Press, 1981.

Frazier, E. Franklin. *The Negro Church in America.* Schocken Books, New York, 1963.

French, R. M. *The Eastern Orthodox Church.* Hutchinson & Co., Ltd., 1951.

Gasper, Louis. *The Fundamentalist Movement.* Mouton & Co., 1963.

Gilby, Thomas. *St. Thomas Aquinas' Philosophical Texts.* Oxford University Press, 1952.

Gilson, E. *History of Christian Philosophy in the Middle Ages.* Random House, Inc., 1954.

Grant, R. M. *Gnosticism and Early Christianity.* New York, 1966.

Gutierrez, Gustavo. *A Theology of Liberation.* Orbis Books, 1971.

Hopkins, C. H. *The Rise of the Social Gospel in American Protestantism 1865–1915.* Yale University Press, 1940.

Latourette, K. S. *A History of Christianity.* 7 vols. Harper & Brothers, Inc., 1937–1945.

———. *History of the Expansion of Christianity.* 7 vols. Harper & Brothers, Inc., 1937–1945.

Lossky, V. *The Mystical Theology of the Eastern Church.* James Clarke, 1957.

Manschreck, C. L., ed. *A History of Christianity.* Vol. II: *Readings in the History of the Church from the Reformation to the Present.* Prentice-Hall, Inc., 1964.

Marty, Martin, and R. S. Appleby, eds. *Fundamentalisms Observed.* University of Chicago Press, 1992. (includes fundamentalisms in a number of religions)

Nuth, Joan M. *Wisdom's Daughter: The Theology of Julian of Norwich.* Crossroad, New York, 1991.

Petry, R. C., ed. *A History of Christianity.* Vol. I: *Readings in the History of the Early and Medieval Church.* Prentice-Hall, Inc., 1962.

Rilliet, Jean. *Zwingli, Third Man of the Reformation,* The Westminster Press, 1959.

Ruether, Rosemary Radford. *Religion and Sexism.* Simon & Schuster, 1974.

———. *Womanguides: Readings Toward a Feminist Theology.* Beacon Press, 1985.

Walker, Williston. *A History of the Christian Church.* Rev. by Richardson, Pauck, and Handy. Charles Scribner's Sons, 1959.

Chapters 17 and 18.
Islam

'Abduh, Muhammad. *The Theology of Unity.* Translated by Ishāq Masa'ad and Kenneth Cragg. George Allen & Unwin, Ltd., 1966.

Ahmad, Aziz. *Islamic Modernism in India and Pakistan, 1957–1964.* Oxford University Press, 1967.

Akhavi, Sharough. *Religion and Politics in Contemporary Iran.* State University of New York Press, 1980.

Arberry, A. J. *The Koran Interpreted.* George Allen & Unwin, Ltd., 1955. (a translation of the Qur'ān in 2 vols. Combined in a one-vol. pb by Macmillan).

———, ed. *Religion in the Middle East.* Vol. 2: *Islam.* Cambridge University Press, 1969.

———. *Sufism.* George Allen & Unwin, Ltd., 1950.

Armstrong, Karen. *Muhammad: An Introduction.* State University of New York Press, Albany, 1992.

Ash'ārī, Al-, *al-Ibanah 'an Usul ad-Diyanah.* Translated by Walter Klein. American Oriental Society, New Haven, 1940. (Ash'arī's principal work)

BERGER, MORROE. *Islam in Egypt Today.* Cambridge University Press, 1970.

BOLAND, B. J. *The Struggle of Islam in Modern Indonesia.* The Hague–Martinus Nijhoff, 1971.

DESSOUKI, ALI E. HILLAL. *Islamic Resurgence in the Arab World.* Praeger Publishers, 1982.

ESPOSITO, JOHN L., ED. *Islam and Development.* Syracuse University Press, 1980.

FISCHER, MICHAEL M. J. *Iran: From Religious Dispute to Revolution.* Harvard University Press, 1980.

GEERTZ, CLIFFORD. *The Religion of Java.* The Free Press, 1960.

HITTI, PHILIP K. *The History of the Arabs.* 8th ed. The Macmillan Company, 1964.

HOLT, LAMBTON, AND LEWIS, EDS. *The Cambridge History of Islam,* 2 vols. Cambridge University Press, 1970.

IBN ISHAQ, MUHAMMAD IBN YASAR. *The Life of Muhammad.* Translated by A. Guillaume. Oxford University Press, 1955.

JACKSON, KARL D. *Traditional Authority, Islam and Rebellion.* University of California, 1980. (Indonesia)

LEVTZION, N., ED. *Conversion to Islam.* Holmes & Meier, 1979.

LINCOLN C. ERIC. *The Black Muslims in America.* Beacon Press, 1963.

MOMEN, MUJAN. *An Introduction to Shi'i Islam: The History and Doctrines of Twelver Shi'ism.* Yale University Press, 1985.

PELLY, LEWIS. *The Miracle Play of Hasan and Husain.* 2 vols. Wm. H. Allen and Co., 1879. Republished in 1970 by Gregg International Publishers, Ltd.

RAHMAN, FAZLUR. *Islam.* Doubleday Anchor Book pb, 1968

———. "Islam: An Overview" (followed by articles by others on Islam in regional areas) in *The Encyclopedia of Religion.* Edited by Mircea Eliade. Macmillan Publishing Co., 1987

SCHIMMEL, ANNEMARIE. *Islam: an Introduction.* State University of New York Press, Albany, 1992.

———. *Mystical Dimensions of Islam.* University of North Carolina Press, Chapel Hill, 1975.

SMITH, JANE I., *Women in Contemporary Muslim Countries.* Bucknell University Press, Lewisburg, PA.

SMITH, W. C. *Islam in Modern History.* Princeton University Press, 1957 (Available as Mentor pb, 1959).

WATT, W. M. *Free Will and Predestination in Early Islam.* Luzac & Co., 1948.

———. *Islam and the Integration of Society.* Routledge & Kegan Paul, 1961

———. *Islamic Philosophy and Theology.* Edinburgh University Press, 1962

———. *Muhammed: Prophet and Statesman.* Oxford University Press, 1961

———. *What is Islam?* Praeger Publishers, 1968

WAUGH, EARLE H. ET AL., EDS. *The Muslim Community in North America.* University of Alberta Press, 1983

Selected Readings on Gender Issues

CABEZON, JOSE IGNACIO, ED. *Buddhism, Sexuality, and Gender.* State University of New York Press, Albany, 1992.

CARMODY, DENISE LARDNER. *Women and World Religions.* Abingdon Press, Nashville, 1979.

CONDREN, MARY. *The Serpent and the Goddess: Women, Religion, and Power in Celtic Ireland.* Harper & Row, 1989.

DAVIDS, MRS. T. W. RHYS. *Psalms of the Brethren.* Oxford University Press, 1909.

———. *Psalms of the Sisters.* Oxford University Press, 1913.

ELIADE, MIRCEA. *Birth and Rebirth.* Harper & Brothers, Inc., 1958 (A study of initiation rites).

GENNEP, G. VAN. *Rites of Passage.* Translated by Vizedom and Caffee. University of Chicago Press, 1960.

GIMBUTAS, MARIJA. *The Goddesses and Gods of Old Europe: 6500–3500 B.C.* University of California Press, 1982.

———. *The Language of the Goddess: Unearthing the Hidden Symbols of Western Civilization.* Harper & Row, 1989.

GROSS, RITA, ED. *Beyond Androcentrism.* Scholars Press. Missoula, Mont., 1979.

HARLAN, LINDSEY, AND PAUL B. COURTRIGHT. *From the Margins of Hindu Marriage: Essays on Gender, Religion, and Culture.* Oxford University Press, 1995.

HAWLEY, JOHN STRATTON. *Sati, the Blessing and the Curse: The Burning of Wives in India.* Oxford University Press, 1994.

HAWLEY, JOHN STRATTON AND DONNA MARIE WULF. *Devi, Goddess of India.* University of California Press, 1996.

HOPKO, THOMAS, ED. *Women and the Priesthood.* St. Vladimir's Seminary Press, 1983.

HORNER, I. B. *Women Under Primitive Buddhism.* Routledge, 1930.

KINSLEY, DAVID, *The Goddesses' Mirror: Visions of the Divine from East and West.* State University of New York Press, Albany, 1989.

Leslie, Julia, ed. *Roles and Rituals for Hindu Women.* Farleigh-Dickinson (Dist. Associated University Press, 1991).

MARGLIN, FREDERIQUE APFFEL. *Wives of the God-King: The Rituals of the Devadasis of Puri.* Oxford University Press, 1985.

NUTH, JOAN M. *Wisdom's Daughter: The Theology of Julian of Norwich.* Crossroad, New York, 1991.

O'FLAHERTY, WENDY DONIGER, TR. *Hindu Myths.* Penguin, 1975.

———. *Shiva: The Erotic Ascetic.* Oxford University Press, 1973, 1981.

———. *Women, Androgynes, and Other Mythical Beasts.* University of Chicago Press, 1980.

PAUL, DIANA. *Women in Buddhism.* Asian Humanities Press, 1980.

PLASKOW, JUDITH, AND CAROL P. CHRIST, EDS. *Weaving the Visions: New Patterns in Feminist Spirituality.* Harper & Row, San Francisco, 1989.

PRESTON, JAMES J. ED. *Mother Worship: Theme and Variations.* University of North Carolina Press, Chapel Hill, 1982.

RUETHER, ROSEMARY RADFORD. *Religion and Sexism.* Simon & Schuster, 1974.

———. *Womanguides: Readings Toward a Feminist Theology.* Beacon Press, 1985.

RUETHER, ROSEMARY RADFORD AND ROSEMARY SKINNER KELLER, EDS. *Women and Religion in America, Vol. 3: 1900–1968.* Harper & Row, 1986.

SHARMA, ARVIND. *A Hindu Perspective on the Philosophy of Religion.* St. Martin's Press, 1991.

SHARMA, ARVIND, ED. *Women in World Religions.* State University of New York Press, Albany, 1987.

SMITH, JANE I., *Women in Contemporary Muslim Countries.* Bucknell University Press, Lewisburg, Penn.

STOWASSER, BARBARA F. *Women in the Qur'an, Traditions, and Interpretation.* Oxford University Press, 1994.

ACKNOWLEDGMENTS

Ancient Near Eastern Texts Relating to the Old Testament, third edition, edited by James B. Pritchard. Copyright © 1950, 1955, 1969, renewed 1978 by Princeton University Press. Reprinted by permission of Princeton University Press.

The Way and Its Power, edited and translated by Arthur Waley. Copyright © 1934 by George Allen & Unwin, Ltd., London. Reprinted with permission of Unwin Hyman (formerly George Allen & Unwin, Ltd.), an imprint of HarperCollins Publishers Ltd., London, England.

Six lines of verse from *The Way of Life,* by Witter Bynner. Copyright 1944 by Witter Bynner. Copyright renewed 1972 by Dorothy Chauvenet and Paul Horgan. Reprinted with permission of HarperCollins Publishers, Inc., New York.

From *The Wisdom of China and India,* edited by Lin Yutang. Copyright 1942 and renewed 1970 by Random House, Inc. Reprinted with permission of Random House, Inc.

The Zoroastrian Doctrine of a Future Life, by Jai D. C. Parvry. Copyright 1926, 1929 © Columbia University Press, New York. Reprinted with the permission of the publisher.

Excerpts from *The Bible: An American Translation,* edited by J. M. Powis Smith and E. J. Goodspeed. Copyright 1935 by the University of Chicago. Reprinted with permission of the University of Chicago Press.

Excerpts from *The Holy Bible: A New Translation,* by James Moffat. Copyright 1922, 1924, 1926 by George H. Doran Company, New York. Reprinted with permission of Hodder & Stoughton, Sevenoaks, Kent, England.

Excerpts from *The Koran Interpreted,* by A. J. Arberry. Copyright 1955 by George Allen & Unwin Ltd., London. Reprinted with permission of Unwin Hyman (formerly George Allen & Unwin, Ltd.), an imprint of HarperCollins Publishers Ltd., London, England.

INDEX

"G" Prefixes: The letter **"G"** prefixed to a page number indicates that the reference is to a glossary page including a definition.

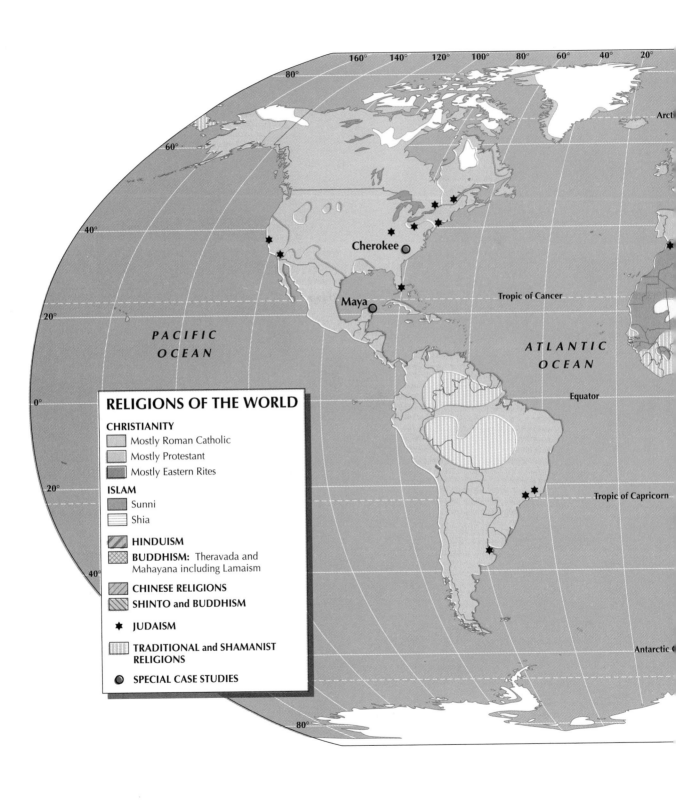

RELIGIONS OF THE WORLD

CHRISTIANITY
Mostly Roman Catholic
Mostly Protestant
Mostly Eastern Rites

ISLAM
Sunni
Shia

HINDUISM
BUDDHISM: Theravada and Mahayana including Lamaism

CHINESE RELIGIONS
SHINTO and BUDDHISM

★ JUDAISM

TRADITIONAL and SHAMANIST RELIGIONS

◉ **SPECIAL CASE STUDIES**

Cherokee ◉

Maya ◉

PACIFIC OCEAN

ATLANTIC OCEAN

Tropic of Cancer

Equator

Tropic of Capricorn

Arcti

Antarctic